Boswell's Edinburgh Journals

Boswell's Edinburgh Journals
1767–1786

edited by

Hugh M Milne

MERCAT PRESS
EDINBURGH
www.mercatpress.com

First published in 2001 by Mercat Press
This revised edition published 2003
Mercat Press, 10 Coates Crescent, Edinburgh EH3 7AL
www.mercatpress.com

© Yale University, 2001
Introduction and notes © Hugh M Milne, 2003

ISBN 184183 0208

The publisher acknowledges subsidy from the Scottish Arts Council
towards the publication of this volume.

This volume is dedicated by the editor to
Odell, Natasha and Alexandra

Set in Caslon at Mercat Press
Printed and bound in Great Britain by
Antony Rowe Ltd, Chippenham, Wiltshire

CONTENTS

Preface

This volume has been prepared as a reading edition of the journals kept by Boswell while practising in Edinburgh as an advocate from 1767 to 1786. The text of the selected journal entries is taken from the following volumes of the Yale Editions of the Private Papers of James Boswell: *Boswell in Search of a Wife, 1766-1769*; *Boswell for the Defence, 1769-1774*; *Boswell's Journal of a Tour to the Hebrides with Samuel Johnson, LL.D., 1773*; *Boswell: The Ominous Years, 1774-1776*; *Boswell in Extremes, 1776-1778*; *Boswell, Laird of Auchinleck, 1778-1782*; *Boswell: The Applause of the Jury, 1782-1785*; and *Boswell: The English Experiment, 1785-1789*. The extracts from Boswell's correspondence which are to be found amongst the journal entries are likewise taken from those volumes. Parts of the Introduction, Epilogue and annotations (including bridging passages between journal entries) are based on, or contain quotations from, the text of journal entries as set out in those and other volumes of the Yale Editions. To avoid an excessive number of footnotes, dates of journal entries from which extracts are quoted in bridging passages between journal entries are not normally supplied unless the dates cannot be ascertained from the context. All quotations from Boswell's correspondence in the Introduction, Epilogue and annotations, unless otherwise indicated, are from the Yale Editions and, except where the contrary is shown, are from volumes containing the journals rather than volumes relating primarily to correspondence.

For full bibliographical details of the various volumes of the Yale Editions from which material has been used, reference should be made to the list of sources (pp. 565-70), where the volumes in question are marked with an asterisk.

The text is exactly as it appears in the Yale Editions apart from changes to the spelling of some names, minor stylistic alterations, the omission of certain passages and the occasional insertion of words (in square brackets) either to make a passage grammatically correct following the removal of words or to make the meaning of a passage clearer (being a device also used by the editors of the Yale Editions). I have made alterations to the spelling of the names of places in only a few instances: "Livingston" instead of "Livingstone", "Blair Drummond" instead of "Blair-Drummond" (the former being the spelling adopted by the editors of *Boswell, Laird of Auchinleck* while the latter was chosen by the editors of *Boswell: The Applause of the Jury*), and "Advocate's Close" instead of "Advocates' Close". The only alteration I have made to the name of a person in the text has been the insertion where it does not already appear of a hyphen in the name "James Hunter-Blair" (being the spelling given in G E Cokayne's *Complete Baronetage*). No distinction is made between square brackets already inserted in the text by the editors of the Yale Editions and square brackets inserted by me. Differences in editorial practices adopted by the editors of the various volumes of the Yale Editions have resulted in some minor inconsistencies in the text of this volume, such as "memorial" in certain passages and "Memorial" in others, but I trust that such discrepancies will be seen as immaterial.

Although this volume is not a complete version of the journals kept by Boswell while living and working in Edinburgh, the book contains the bulk of those journals, and, it is hoped, conveys a fair representation of every aspect of Boswell's life during the relevant period. Omissions from the text have been made with reluctance and have primarily been made in order to remove those passages—or in some instances complete entries—which are uninteresting or obscure, or which would result in needless repetition. Omissions are not marked except to the extent that where they require the restructuring of a sentence the necessary alteration is shown in square brackets.

In a few instances, my annotations have supplemented the text by quoting from passages in the journals which are not included in the Yale Editions but which feature in the privately published *Private Papers of James Boswell from Malahide Castle, in the Collection of Lt-Colonel Ralph Heyward Isham.*

In the Introduction, Epilogue and annotations I have drawn extensively on the editorial material in the relevant volumes of the Yale Editions, including the indexes to those volumes and the Genealogical Tables in Appendix C to *Boswell: The Ominous Years* (pp. 374-9). The editorial material in the Yale Editions has been invaluable in many respects, particularly with regard to identifying some of the more obscure characters who appear in the text, naming the authors of plays, supplying translations of Latin passages, providing details of military ranks, identifying biblical passages and quotations from literary works, supplying quotations from eighteenth-century newspapers and magazines, providing details of Boswell's law cases, and specifying the newspapers and magazines in which Boswell's articles and essays appeared.

Although the influence of the Yale editors can be felt at every turn, the text of the journal entries in my work, spanning as it does the period covered by no less than eight volumes of the Yale Editions, has required a complete re-editing of the journal entries in question. Furthermore, I have tried, where possible, to provide more biographical detail of the lawyers and public figures who appear in the journals than is to be found in the Yale Editions. The Introduction and annotations also contain additional information about eighteenth-century Edinburgh, including, where available, particulars of the addresses of the numerous inhabitants whom Boswell visited (the latter information being derived, for the most part, from a study of the various volumes of Williamson's *Edinburgh Directory* from 1773/74 onwards and articles in the *Book of the Old Edinburgh Club*). Insofar as Boswell's law cases are concerned, I have in many instances adopted (in a fully attributed manner) the information supplied by the editors of the Yale Editions (especially the information in the later volumes in the series), but I have also included some significant additional material obtained as a result of my study of a number of Boswell's manuscript legal papers, and other legal documents, held in Edinburgh. Further supplementary material in respect of Boswell's law cases has been derived from the very detailed catalogues in the National Library of Scotland relating to Boswell's session papers held in the Advocates' Library and the Signet Library, namely, *The Session Papers by Boswell in the Advocates' Library* (volume (a): catalogue of the Arniston and Campbell Collections), searched by Dr C J M MacLachlan (1975), and G H Ballantyne's *The Session Papers of James Boswell in the Signet Library, Edinburgh* (1969/71). I have supplied information and quotations gained from my study of certain of those papers, some of which were not available to the editors of the Yale Editions. Moreover, I have referred wherever possible to the information to be found concerning those of Boswell's cases which featured in the law reports of the day and I have provided notes of the relevant citations so as to enable the interested reader to refer to those reports.

Basic biographical details supplied in the annotations in respect of Scottish lawyers are principally derived from Sir F J Grant's *The Faculty of Advocates in Scotland 1532-1943* (1944), Brunton and Haig's *An Historical Account of the Senators of the College of Justice* (1836) and the *Register of the Society of Writers to Her Majesty's Signet* (1983). Other basic biographical details are largely taken from standard reference works such as the *Dictionary of National Biography*, G E Cokayne's *Complete Baronetage*, John and Julia Keay's edition of the *Collins Encyclopaedia of Scotland*, Sir Lewis Namier and John Brooke's *The House of Commons, 1754-1790* and Sir James Balfour Paul's *The Scots Peerage*.

With regard to Boswell's life up to 1769, my indebtedness to Frederick A Pottle's *James Boswell, The Earlier Years, 1740-1769* (1966) cannot be over-estimated. I have also derived much help from David Daiches' *James Boswell and His World* (1976), Frank Brady's *James Boswell: The Later Years, 1769-1795* (1984), Sheriff Roger Craik's *James Boswell (1740-1795), The Scottish Perspective* (1994), Stuart Harris's *The Place Names of Edinburgh* (1996), and *The Minute Book of the Faculty of Advocates*, Vol. 3, 1751-1783, edited by Angus Stewart, Q.C. (1999).

ACKNOWLEDGEMENTS

I am immensely indebted to a number of individuals and institutions for assistance given to me during the preparation of this book. First, I must express my heartfelt gratitude to the Editorial Committee of the Yale Editions of the Private Papers of James Boswell, and in particular to the General Editor, Dr Gordon Turnbull, for generously giving me permission to use vast amounts of material from their volumes. It has been an enormous privilege to be allowed to use this material. I wish also to express my thanks for all the advice and encouragement given to me by Dr Turnbull, who, in addition to reading the Introduction and making valuable suggestions for improvements, has been a fount of wisdom on many matters.

I am likewise most grateful to Edinburgh University Press for kindly giving their consent to the reproduction of material from *Boswell's London Journal, 1762-1763* and *Boswell, Laird of Auchinleck, 1778-1782.*

I have to thank the Faculty of Advocates for their financial support for the publication. Without the Faculty's generosity, publication would not have been possible. I wish also to acknowledge with the utmost gratitude the assistance given to me by the Hon. G N H Emslie, Q.C., the Dean of Faculty; S Neil Brailsford, Q.C., the Treasurer of Faculty; and Angus Stewart, Q.C., the Keeper of the Library. Mr Stewart kindly read the Introduction and gave me permission to consult and quote from material in the Faculty's collection lodged for safe keeping in the National Library of Scotland, together with permission to consult and transcribe material from certain of Boswell's session papers held in the Arniston Collection in the Advocates' Library. In addition, Mr Stewart gave me permission to quote from his invaluable edition of *The Minute Book of the Faculty of Advocates,* Vol. 3, 1751-1783, and to use material from his unpublished transcript of the minute of the Faculty meeting of 20 December 1783.

Most grateful thanks also go to the Scottish Arts Council for its financial support for the publication.

I acknowledge with gratitude the permission given to me by Dr John W Cairns of the Edinburgh Law School in his capacity as Chairman of the Council of the Stair Society to refer to, and quote from, *The Minute Book of the Faculty of Advocates,* Vol. 3, 1751-1783. He has also kindly allowed me to refer to, and quote from, his helpful and learned article on *Alfenus Varus and the Faculty of Advocates.*

I am much indebted to Jane Brown, Head of the Historical Search Section, H M General Register House, Edinburgh, for permission to quote from papers held in the National Archives of Scotland, including many of Boswell's manuscript legal papers; to the Trustees of the National Library of Scotland for permission to use material from the manuscript minutes of the Select Society of Edinburgh; and to the Society of Writers to Her Majesty's Signet for permission to consult, and transcribe material from, certain of Boswell's session papers held in their collection and to refer to and quote from the *Register of the Society of Writers to Her Majesty's Signet* and G H Ballantyne's catalogue, *Session Papers of James Boswell in the Signet Library, Edinburgh.*

Librarians and archivists throughout Edinburgh have given me much invaluable assistance. Those to whom I particularly owe my thanks are: Iain F Maciver, Head of the Manuscripts Division, National Library of Scotland; Dr Brian Hillyard, Head of Rare Books, National Library of Scotland; all the staff at the National Library of Scotland, in particular those in the North Reading Room; Mrs Catherine Smith, Senior Librarian, Advocates' Library; Audrey Walker, Librarian, and Kate Corbett, Assistant Librarian, Signet Library; all the staff at the Central Library, George IV Bridge, Edinburgh, particularly in the Scottish Library, the Reference Library, and, above all, the Edinburgh Room, where the librarians obligingly produced large numbers of volumes on seemingly innumerable occasions; the staff at Edinburgh University Library; the staff at Edinburgh City Archives, City Chambers, and in particular Stefanie Davidson, Archivist; and all the staff in the Historical Search Room at H M General Register House, Edinburgh. I am particularly grateful to the staff at West Register House, Edinburgh, who had to locate countless obscure manuscripts and did so most willingly and with unfailing courtesy. Special thanks go to Alison Lindsay at West Register House who patiently and carefully explained to me the various methods which have to be used to trace eighteenth-century legal papers held there.

Seán Costello at the Mercat Press has been unfailingly supportive and I am most grateful to him and his colleagues, in particular Tom Johnstone and Camilla James, for seeing the possible merit in producing a work of this nature and for doing everything possible to ensure publication, including assisting with the proof-reading.

My interest in Boswell was first stimulated by my former colleague Tom Scott, to whom I am much indebted. I am also grateful to my colleague Ian K Laing for helping me to find some of the rarer volumes of the Yale Editions and other publications relating to Boswell.

Other persons to whom I owe my thanks for assistance, encouragement and other acts of kindness are: Nicola Carr and Carol Duncan of Edinburgh University Press; N Croumbie Macpherson, C.B.E.; Philip Ridd, Solicitor of Inland Revenue; John A Clare, Secretary, Scottish Historic Buildings Trust; Mrs Chrissie Wilson, Auchinleck; Johnny Stariski, Auchinleck; Dr Andrew G Fraser, BSc, MD, FSA Scot, editor of the *Book of the Old Edinburgh Club*; and my father-in-law Charles J Leven, without whose computer skills (and, in particular, his knowledge of optical character recognition) this work would have taken much longer to produce.

Although this work reflects in various ways the help I have received from others, I alone am responsible for its errors and shortcomings.

Finally, I wish to convey very special thanks to my wife, who, throughout the four years it has taken to bring this project to fruition, has carried out with great ability and cheerfulness the seemingly impossible task of being simultaneously severe critic and loyal supporter and has selflessly dedicated endless hours to checking drafts, assisting with typing and discussing points of concern. My gratitude to her is more than can be expressed.

H.M.M., Edinburgh, June 2001

NOTE TO THE REVISED EDITION

I have taken the opportunity afforded by this new edition to make amendments to the Introduction and other editorial material, primarily to clarify certain matters, correct some factual errors and supply additional information. Several amendments have been made in the light of helpful comments from perceptive readers, to whom I am much obliged.

H.M.M., Edinburgh, January 2003

ABBREVIATIONS

For full bibliographical details, see Sources, pp. 565-70.

Applause	Boswell: *The Applause of the Jury, 1782-1785* (ed. Lustig and Pottle)
Arniston	Omond, *The Arniston Memoirs*
Arnot	Arnot, *The History of Edinburgh* (1779 edition, reprinted 1998)
Ballantyne	Ballantyne, *The Session Papers of James Boswell in the Signet Library, Edinburgh*
B.O.E.C.	*Book of the Old Edinburgh Club*
Brady	Brady, *James Boswell: The Later Years, 1769-1795*
Brunton and Haig	Brunton and Haig, *An Historical Account of the Senators of the College of Justice*
Carlyle	*The Autobiography of Dr Alexander Carlyle of Inveresk 1722-1805*
Chambers	Chambers, *Traditions of Edinburgh*
Cloyd	Cloyd, *James Burnett, Lord Monboddo*
Cockburn	Cockburn, *Memorials of His Time*
Consultation Book	Boswell's *Consultation Book*, 1766-1772
CSD	*Concise Scots Dictionary*
Defence	*Boswell for the Defence, 1769-1774* (ed. Wimsatt and Pottle)
DNB	*Dictionary of National Biography*
Experiment	Boswell: *The English Experiment, 1785-1789* (ed. Lustig and Pottle)
Extremes	*Boswell in Extremes, 1776-1778* (ed. Weis and Pottle)
Faculty Decisions	*Faculty Decisions*, Old Series, 14 volumes, 1752-1808
Forbes	Forbes, *A Journal of the Session*
Fry	Fry, *The Dundas Despotism*
Graham	Graham, *Scottish Men of Letters in the Eighteenth Century*
Grand Tour I	*Boswell on the Grand Tour: Germany and Switzerland, 1764* (ed. Pottle)
Grand Tour II	*Boswell on the Grand Tour: Italy, Corsica, and France, 1765-1766* (ed. Brady and Pottle)
Grant	Grant, *Old and New Edinburgh*, 3 volumes
Great Biographer	Boswell: *The Great Biographer, 1789-1795* (ed. Danziger and Brady)
Harris	Harris, *The Place Names of Edinburgh*
Hebrides	*Boswell's Journal of a Tour to the Hebrides with Samuel Johnson, LL.D., 1773* (ed. Pottle and Bennett)
Holland	*Boswell in Holland, 1763-1764* (ed. Pottle)
Jeffrey	Cockburn, *Life of Lord Jeffrey*
Journal	Boswell's journals as published in the Yale Editions of the Private Papers of James Boswell
Kay	Paterson and Maidment, *Kay's Edinburgh Portraits*, 2 volumes
Keay and Keay	*Collins Encyclopaedia of Scotland* (ed. Keay and Keay)
Laird	*Boswell, Laird of Auchinleck, 1778-1782* (ed. Reed and Pottle)
Life	Boswell, *The Life of Samuel Johnson* (ed. Ingpen), 2 volumes

London	*Boswell's London Journal, 1762-1763* (ed. Pottle)
Namier and Brooke	Namier and Brooke, *The House of Commons, 1754-1790*, 3 volumes
N.A.S.	National Archives of Scotland
Ominous Years	*Boswell: The Ominous Years, 1774-1776* (ed. Ryskamp and Pottle)
Omond	Omond, *The Lord Advocates of Scotland*, 2 volumes
Paton	*Paton's Reports of Cases decided in the House of Lords, upon Appeal from Scotland*, Vols II and III.
Pottle	Pottle, *James Boswell, The Earlier Years, 1740-1769*
Pride and Negligence	Pottle, *Pride and Negligence: The History of the Boswell Papers*
Private Papers	*Private Papers of James Boswell from Malahide Castle, in the Collection of Lt-Colonel Ralph Heyward Isham* (ed. Scott and Pottle), 18 volumes
Ramsay	Ramsay, *Scotland and Scotsmen in the Eighteenth Century*, Vol. I
Reminiscences	Ramsay, *Reminiscences of Scottish Life and Character*
Scots Peerage	Paul, *The Scots Peerage*, 9 volumes
Scott	*The Journal of Sir Walter Scott* (ed. Anderson)
Session Papers	*The Session Papers by Boswell in the Advocates' Library* (volume (a): catalogue of the Arniston and Campbell Collections)
Somerville	Somerville, *My Own Life and Times, 1741-1814*
SPAL	*Session Papers*, Advocates' Library (Arniston Collection)
SPSL	*Session Papers*, Signet Library
Stewart	*The Minute Book of the Faculty of Advocates*, Vol. 3, 1751-1783 (ed. Stewart)
Stuart	Stuart, *Old Edinburgh Taverns*
Tinker	*Letters of James Boswell* (ed. Tinker), 2 volumes
Topham	Topham, *Letters from Edinburgh 1774-1775*
Walker	*The Correspondence of James Boswell and John Johnston of Grange* (ed. Walker)
Wife	*Boswell in Search of a Wife, 1766-1769* (ed. Brady and Pottle)
Wilson	Wilson, *Memorials of Edinburgh in the Olden Time*
W.S.	Writer to the Signet

INTRODUCTION

James Boswell is famous as the author of *The Life of Samuel Johnson*, which was first published in 1791 and is still regarded by many as being perhaps the finest biography ever written in the English language. He is also well known for having travelled with Johnson through Scotland in 1773 and subsequently publishing an account of their travels under the title of *The Journal of a Tour to the Hebrides with Samuel Johnson, LL.D*. Furthermore, following the recovery of Boswell's private papers, and particularly since the publication in 1950 of his *London Journal* of 1762-1763, Boswell has become renowned as a great diarist.

What is perhaps not so widely appreciated, however, is that for nearly twenty years, while residing in Edinburgh from 1766 to 1786, Boswell was a busy advocate at the Scottish bar and for significant periods during that era kept detailed journals in Edinburgh narrating the course of much of his life there. In these journals we find a quite unparalleled account of the Edinburgh legal circles of the day and, in particular, a unique insight into the day-to-day life of a Scottish advocate. Boswell was on intimate terms with many of the leading counsel and was familiar with several members of the judiciary, two of whom—namely, Lord Kames and Lord Monboddo—were prominent figures in the movement which was to become known as the Scottish Enlightenment; and his journals contain innumerable examples of conversations—and sometimes confrontations—with such characters. There are also many references to Boswell's law cases, including criminal trials; and we read about both his triumphs and his failures. We even find mention of a wild scheme to recover the body of one of Boswell's executed clients and resuscitate him. And we are told about a number of occasions when Boswell came close to engaging in duels as a result of disagreements with legal colleagues.

In addition to this, the journals not only contain an intimate account of Boswell's domestic life with his wife and children but also convey a wonderfully vivid impression of Edinburgh social life—both high and low—during the second half of the eighteenth century. We hear about riotous scenes in taverns; all-night gambling sessions at whist and brag; fashionable dinners and suppers at the elegant houses of prominent lawyers or other men of distinction; and attendance at dancing assemblies, concerts and plays. Furthermore, Boswell entertains us by recording his innermost reflections on many matters, ranging from purely personal concerns such as his hopes and aspirations to wider issues such as difficult religious points and philosophical perplexities. He narrates several fascinating conversations on these and similar issues which he had with that great luminary and pillar of the Scottish Enlightenment, David Hume; and he gives us valuable first-hand accounts of several significant moments in the history of Edinburgh.

The journals at times reveal a dissatisfied, restless spirit tormented with self-doubts. Boswell had a tendency to suffer from periodic bouts of depression, the attacks of which were often brought on for no apparent reason. On the whole, the busier his life, and the more varied his existence, the happier he was; it was when he was comparatively idle that the dark fits of melancholy were more likely to descend on him. During these gloomy periods his depression manifested itself in self-flagellating feelings of failure as a result of thwarted ambitions, and he became discontented with what he perceived as being the "narrow sphere" of the law in Scotland, thinking that he would be happier in London where he felt that his literary and social abilities were more widely appreciated; but when his mind was focused on a difficult and challenging legal case or some other demanding, novel or distracting matter, his spirits would rise and the vapours would disperse. This may have been an inherited characteristic, for Boswell's paternal grandfather evidently suffered from similar tendencies to a marked degree.

It is sometimes suggested that Boswell was mentally unbalanced: Macaulay, for example, in his famous essay on Samuel Johnson, wrote of Boswell's "weak and diseased mind";[1] and, indeed, Boswell's contemporary, David Hume, said of him in 1766 that he was "very good-humoured, very agreeable—and very mad".[2] However, it is clear that Hume did not intend his remark to be taken literally, or even seriously; he was probably merely adverting either to Boswell's frolicsome sense of fun—which he possessed in large measure as a young man—or to his occasional lapses of judgment (one example of this latter weakness being his fondness for publishing ill-advised newspaper articles, pamphlets and letters which cannot but have been injurious to his reputation). On the other hand, there was undoubtedly a serious streak of insanity in Boswell's family: his younger brother John, in particular, was subject to severe psychological problems. But in Boswell's case it seems that the most he ever suffered from was what he termed "hypochondria", or fits of low spirits, which would perhaps today be analysed as bouts of mild clinical depression. Admittedly, there were for a time occasional uncontrolled domestic outbursts induced by excessive drinking, but these paroxysms passed without injury to anyone and with no lasting harm having been done.

On the whole, Boswell was a sympathetic and sensitive character, being a popular and pleasant companion with easy manners and a ready wit, a devoted husband, a doting father, and a loyal (albeit somewhat wayward) son.

His character, however, was full of contradictions and inconsistencies: he would be happy in the law court one day, thinking it a suitable sphere for his talents, and the next day would consider it a dull and insignificant place; he would complain that it was unfortunate that his native city of Edinburgh should affect him "with such wretchedness",[3] but would later write of experiencing "an impression of Edinburgh being a very good place";[4] he would express profound Jacobite sympathies and emotional attachment to the Stewart family, yet would court the favours of George III and his government and would ultimately come to revere the Hanoverian king; he would regret that Scotland had thrown away its independence by the Treaty of Union with England in 1707, taking the view that Scots had "lost all principle and spirit of patriotism",[5] but would express support for public appointments in Scotland being available to English "gentlemen of distinction" on the basis that this would "make a beneficial mixture of manners, and render our union more complete",[6] and he would consistently emulate English manners and modes of speech, spending much of his time in London and eventually even settling there; he would be appalled at his excessive drinking and gambling and would repeatedly vow to curb these activities, but would forget his resolutions with tedious regularity; he would likewise be horrified by his marital infidelities—or "dalliances"— and would solemnly promise to reform himself, but would succumb to temptation again and again; he would plead passionately with his father to leave his estate to a line of male heirs, thus effectively disinheriting Boswell's own daughters by excluding them from the main order of succession, all merely to satisfy Boswell's feudal notions, but then after a fit of remorse would beg his father to include the daughters after all, only to be secretly pleased when his father refused his request; and he would be overawed by his father's dominating, scathing, scornful and sarcastic manner, yet had great affection for him, and during his father's latter years would treasure the rare moments when he could get him to himself.

The great value of the Edinburgh journals lies not only in the fact that Boswell always had the strictest regard for the truth but also in their immense breadth, touching as they do on so many aspects of Boswell's life, including moments of deep psychological self-awareness. Indeed, the journals do not merely give us an insight into the man: they also give us an invaluable chronicle of his times. It is to be hoped that the selected entries included in this volume will serve to illustrate the wealth of material which the journals contain.

§II

Boswell was born at Edinburgh on 29 October 1740, probably in his parents' residence, which was on the fourth floor of a tenement known as Blair's Land on the east side of Parliament Close (now known as Parliament Square), situated behind the great Church of St Giles.* There was no difficulty in choosing a name for the

---

* Unfortunately, the tenement no longer exists, having been destroyed in a great fire in 1824.

3

young boy, for he was the first son to be born in the family and it was then the custom for the first son to be given the name of his father's father, which in this case was James.

Boswell entered life in comfortable circumstances. His father, Alexander Boswell, who was then thirty-three years old, was the heir to the Boswell family estate in Auchinleck (in those days pronounced *Affléck*) in Ayrshire and had been an advocate for almost eleven years; and although his practice was evidently not particularly extensive, he was held in high regard.

Boswell's paternal grandfather, James Boswell, who was likewise an advocate and had been in practice for almost forty-two years, was the seventh Laird of Auchinleck. The first laird was Thomas Boswell, who was given the castle and barony in 1504 by James IV as a reward for his devoted service and was later to die fighting with his king at Flodden in 1513.

Little is known of the early life of Alexander Boswell, who was born on 1 March 1707, except that he was apparently regarded as being something of a classical scholar. Like his father before him, he decided to become an advocate, and, again like his father, he went to study Roman law at Leyden (now known as Leiden) in Holland. Scots law being to a large extent influenced by Roman law, and the Dutch being regarded at that time as the great masters of Roman law, it was customary in those days for an aspiring advocate to study Roman law in Holland before applying for admission to the Faculty of Advocates. He was called to the bar in December 1729 and evidently soon made himself popular with his fellow advocates with his dry and ironical sense of humour. We also know that he consistently spoke in colloquial Scots, was a staunch Presbyterian, had a fondness for money and was very reluctant to part with it.

James Boswell's mother was Alexander Boswell's first wife, Euphemia Erskine, his first cousin once removed. She was the youngest daughter of Lieutenant-Colonel John Erskine of Alva, Deputy Governor of Stirling Castle (who died in 1737). Proud though Boswell was of his ancestry on his father's side, he had cause to be even prouder of his ancestry on his mother's side, for her father's paternal grandfather was John Erskine, the second Earl of Mar (died 1634), and her father's grandmother (the Earl's second wife) was a daughter of Esmé Stewart, Duke of Lennox (a first cousin of Lord Darnley, the father of James VI). Boswell wrote of his mother (who had a secluded childhood at Culross Palace in Fife) that "she had been brought up quite out of the world, and her notions were pious, visionary, and scrupulous. When she was once made to go to the theatre, she cried, and would never go again."[7] However, she was a doting mother and the young Boswell was somewhat spoilt and over-protected by her.

When Boswell was born, he had an elder sister, Euphemia, but she died when he was only three months old. When he was nearly three, he acquired a younger brother, John; followed, when he was nearly eight, by another brother, David. Boswell was thus brought up in a family in which he was the eldest of three sons.

§III

The Edinburgh in which Boswell was born retained many of the features of a medieval town and was still enclosed within its ancient city wall. It has rightly been claimed that from a distance the city had a truly romantic appearance: to the east, beyond the city wall, lay the royal Palace of Holyroodhouse, overshadowed by the brooding mass of Arthur's Seat; while to the west was the magnificent Castle perched on its mighty rock; and in between the Castle and the palace were many high buildings, towers and spires, all climbing skywards.

However, the palace was neglected and deteriorating and had not been occupied by royalty since 1682; and the city was not the same as it had been prior to the Union of 1707 when the meetings of the Scottish Parliament had conferred on it a dignity and even a certain brilliance. The pace of progress in Edinburgh during the first few decades after 1707 was slow, the economic advantages of the Union not beginning to be felt to any appreciable extent by society at large until the middle of the century.

From an early age, Boswell acquired a great attachment to the Palace of Holyroodhouse and its environs; and no doubt as a young boy he was often taken for walks in that area. Indeed, many years later he was to recall seeing large numbers of moustached Hessian troops there in February 1746 while Arthur's Seat resounded with their drums. These soldiers, who were under the command of the Prince of Hesse, had been brought over to help crush the Jacobite Rebellion of 1745. All his life, Boswell had a fascination for military matters, and he was always especially thrilled at the sight of a regiment marching.

If after any of his boyhood visits to Holyrood Boswell had visited the Castle, he would have commenced his journey there by proceeding up the long, gradually-ascending street known as the Canongate towards the city wall. On reaching the wall he would have come to the Nether Bow Port, which was a large fortified gate with round towers and battlements, all surmounted by a high central spire. Having passed through this gate, which led to the High Street, Boswell would have been back in the bustling, congested, over-crowded city with which he was familiar. All the way up the High Street were rows of high tenements—built, for the most part, with stone—with dark entrances leading to innumerable narrow wynds and closes sloping steeply down from either side of the street. Many of the buildings had been built in the medieval tradition with timber galleries abutting the street, sometimes one above another, each overhanging the one below. Other distinctive features of some of the houses were high chimneys, crow-stepped gables, and outside stairs. The breadth and length of the High Street and the great height of the houses never failed to make a deep impression on visitors to the city; but the outward appearance of the buildings was often somewhat marred by the sight of washed clothes, drying in the wind, suspended from poles projecting over the street.

As the young Boswell proceeded up the street towards the Castle, he would have passed numerous taverns and ale-houses and a great variety of shops. On his left, he would have passed the old Tron Kirk, opposite which, on the other side of the street, he would quite likely have seen a row of hackney-carriages wait-ing for fares.[8] A little further up the street, on his left, he would very probably have seen a row of sedan chairs, attended by the chair-carriers (or "chairmen" as they were called) ready to carry passengers to any part of the city.[9] The usual attire of the chairmen was a long blue coat, knee-breeches and a three-cornered hat.[10]

A little further on, in the middle of the street, was the old City Guard-house, described by Scott in *The Heart of Midlothian* as "a long, low, ugly building... which to a fanciful imagination might have suggested the idea of a long black snail crawling up the middle of the High Street, and deforming its beautiful espla-nade".[11] Not far from this ungainly construction was the ancient city cross, known as the "Mercat Cross".

The Cross was an attractive octagonal structure, about sixteen feet in diam-eter and fifteen feet high, surmounted by a stone column about twenty feet high with a Gothic capital, on top of which was a unicorn. This was the city's principal meeting place for business and gossip. And although the Cross was to be demolished in 1756 to make more room in the street for traffic, the spot where the Cross had stood continued to be the central meeting place of the city and, indeed, was still known as "the Cross".

In addition to being frequented by merchants, lawyers, town councillors, men of letters and clergymen, the Cross was "the peculiar citadel and rallying-point of a species of lazzaroni [Neapolitan street-loungers] called *Caddies* or *Cawdies*..., employing themselves chiefly as street-messengers and valets-de-place. A ragged, half-blackguard-looking set they were, but allowed to be amazingly acute and intelligent, and also faithful to any duty intrusted to them."[12] The shabby appearance of the caddies belied their social usefulness; indeed, the remarkably low crime rate in Edinburgh in those days was largely attributed to them, while the official protectors of the people, the City Guard, were regarded as objects of ridicule.

A very short distance up the street from the Cross was the medieval Church of St Giles, dominating the centre of the city with its great central tower surmounted by an "open crown", which formed a particularly distinctive feature of the sky-line of the city in those days. The interior of St Giles' was somewhat odd in that it was sub-divided into four separate churches: the East or New Kirk, the Mid or Old Kirk, the Tolbooth Kirk, and West St Giles' or Haddo's Hole Kirk.

Immediately to the north of St Giles' were the "Luckenbooths", a row of quaint buildings up to five or six storeys high, mostly timber-fronted, standing in the middle of the street, parallel to St Giles', from which they were separated by a dark and narrow lane through which only pedestrians could pass. These build-ings contained a number of enclosed shops, hence the name "Luckenbooths" (which literally means booths capable of being locked up). The narrow passage between the Luckenbooths and the church contained a large number of tiny shops (called "the Krames") which typically sold hats, gloves, hosiery, drapery and haberdashery.

Immediately beyond the Luckenbooths was the "grim and massive" Tolbooth prison, situated at the north-west corner of the Church of St Giles and encroaching so far upon the High Street as to leave the thoroughfare only fourteen feet wide at that point. "Antique in form, gloomy and haggard in aspect, its black stanchioned windows opening through its dingy walls like the apertures of a hearse, it was calculated to impress all beholders with a due and deep sense of what was meant in Scottish law by the *squalor carceris*.* At the west end was a projecting ground-floor... The building itself was composed of two parts, one more solid and antique than the other, and much resembling, with its turret staircase, one of those tall narrow fortalices [fortified houses] which are so numerous in the Border counties."[13] The conditions inside this intimidating building were notoriously bad, the foul stench being particularly intolerable.

Having passed the grim old Tolbooth, Boswell, on his way up to the Castle, would have proceeded up the High Street through the area known as the Lawnmarket (being a corruption of "Land Market" or "Inland Market"). On his left, at the end of the Lawnmarket, he would have passed the head of the West Bow, a narrow, zig-zagging street sloping steeply down from the High Street to the Grassmarket. "No part of Edinburgh was so rich in quaint old houses as... the Bow—singular edifices, many of them of vast and unknown antiquity, and all more or less irregular, with stone gables and dovecot gablets, timber-galleries, outshots, and strange projections, the dormer windows, patches and additions made in the succession of centuries, overhanging the narrow and tortuous street... Its antique tenements, covered with heraldic carvings and quaint dates, half hidden by sign-boards or sordid rags drying on poles, its nooks, crooks, trap-doors, and gloomy chambers, abounded with old memories, with heroic stories of ancient martial families, and with grim legends and grandmother's tales of ghosts and diablerie."[14]

The Grassmarket, which was where the corn and livestock markets were held, was the principal place where public executions were carried out. The very thought of that area must have made the impressionable young Boswell shudder. In *The Heart of Midlothian*, Scott observed that the Grassmarket, being "a large open street, or rather oblong square, surrounded by high houses... was not ill chosen for such a scene, being of considerable extent, and therefore fit to accommodate a great number of spectators, such as are usually assembled by this melancholy spectacle", and "the place is not without some features of grandeur, being overhung by the southern side of the huge rock on which the castle stands, and by the moss-grown battlements and turreted walls of that ancient fortress."[15] Scott went on to describe how it was the custom for the condemned man to walk from the place of detention, which was normally the old Tolbooth, down the West Bow to the place of execution, during which procession he could be seen stalking between the attendant clergymen, dressed in his grave-clothes, "looking like a moving and walking corpse, while yet an inhabitant of this world".[16] The dreadful impact of such a scene on the spectators does not need to be described. However,

* The right of a creditor to have his debtor imprisoned for failure to pay the debt.

there were actually very few executions in Edinburgh, or anywhere else in Scotland, at this time. It was reckoned that there were on average only three executions a year in the whole of Scotland.

After passing the head of the West Bow, Boswell would finally have made his way up the Castle Hill towards the Castle. From this high vantage-point, he would have had a panoramic view and would have been able to discern the general shape of the city, the boundaries of which were defined by the ancient city wall, which was of great height. However, the wall did not entirely surround the city, for the only protection ever given to the northern part of the city was the North Loch, or the "Nor' Loch" as it was commonly called, which was artificially created in the fourteenth or early fifteenth century. Although originally regarded as an attractive feature of the city, by the 1740s the loch had become unwholesome and was considered to be a nuisance.

§IV

The way of life of the populace of Edinburgh when Boswell was growing up was in some respects undeniably crude, one of the main problems being the lack of hygiene. Although water was passed to wells in the High Street from a large reservoir on the Castle Hill, which was supplied with water piped from a large cistern at the Comiston Springs (situated to the south of the city towards the Pentland Hills), there was no running water in the high tenements and so occupiers or their servants either had to collect water from the wells themselves and carry it upstairs or had to employ men or women, known as "water caddies", to do so.

As if the problems with transporting water to the tenements were not bad enough, what happened to the filth and waste accumulated in the houses during the day was even worse, and, indeed, is a well known aspect of eighteenth-century Edinburgh social life: "[At or after] ten o'clock each night the filth collected in each household was poured from the high windows, and fell in malodorous plash upon the pavement, and not seldom on unwary passers-by. At the warning call of 'Gardy loo' (*Gardez l'eau*) from the servants preparing to outpour the contents of stoups, pots, and cans, the passengers beneath would agonisingly cry out 'Haud yer hand'; but too often the shout was unheard or too late, and a drenched periwig and besmirched three-cornered hat were borne dripping and ill-scented home. At the dreaded hour when the domestic abominations were flung out, when the smells (known as the 'flowers of Edinburgh') filled the air, the citizens burnt their sheets of brown paper to neutralise the odours of the outside, which penetrated their room within. On the ground all night the dirt and ordure lay awaiting the few and leisurely scavengers, who came nominally at seven o'clock next morning with wheel-barrows to remove it. But ere that morning hour the streets were becoming thronged, for people rose and business began early, and the shopkeepers, treading cautiously amid the filth and over the teeming gutters, had set forth to open their booths. Worst of all was the Sunday, when strict piety forbade all work, deeming that street-cleaning was neither an act of necessity nor one of mercy, and required the dirt to remain till Monday morning."[17]

The Town Council, by a series of Acts under which fines and other punishments of a severer nature could be imposed,[18] took steps to try to discourage the obnoxious habit of throwing foul waste from the windows, but met initially with little success. Indeed, even in the latter part of the eighteenth century, when filth was no longer thrown into the open street, the old practice of throwing filth from windows still continued with impunity in the dark, narrow wynds and closes.

In spite of the unhygienic conditions, however, Edinburgh was in other respects a pleasant place to live, for these were remarkably sociable times. Meals, including breakfast, were social occasions and it was common to have large numbers of guests at dinner (which was at two or three o'clock, the latter being the hour favoured by fashionable society) and at supper (which was normally at seven or eight o'clock), and it was not unusual for people to have a standing invitation to drop in when they wished. And in spite of the prevalent inclination in favour of strict religious observance, many people, including judges, and even sometimes church ministers, spent their evenings in taverns over bottles of wine with convivial company.

For members of the nobility or gentry who preferred a more cultural form of entertainment than that offered in taverns, there were the weekly performances of the aristocratic Musical Society of Edinburgh at St Mary's Chapel in Niddry's Wynd, off the south side of the High Street near the Tron Kirk. The Society's concerts were performed there from 1726 until 1762, when the Society moved to the St Cecilia Hall which was built for it further down the Wynd.

A form of entertainment very popular with members of fashionable society were the dancing sessions at the Assembly Hall (or Assembly Room), which from 1736 was to be found in a close off the south side of the High Street which came to be known as New Assembly Close.[19] The assemblies were visually glittering occasions, with ladies and gentlemen all dressed in the height of fashion; but beneath the superficial brilliance it seems that the reality was that the assemblies were rather rigid, dull affairs. Couples were only allowed to take part in one or two dances and were assigned tickets dictating which sets and couples they belonged to; moreover, strict segregation of the sexes was observed during the intervals between the dances. Nevertheless, at the end of the evening there was always an imposing sight, for, as the gaily-dressed company departed, the entrance to the Assembly Hall was surrounded by footmen and chairmen, all carrying flambeaux.

Dancing was, of course, much frowned on by staunch Presbyterians, who thoroughly disapproved of any form of "promiscuous" entertainment. Another form of entertainment which incurred the displeasure of the Presbyterians was the theatre. However, a theatre known as the Canongate Concert Hall, situated at the foot of a close on the south side of the Canongate, was opened in 1747. In order to get round the terms of the Licensing Act of 1737,[20] it was customary to advertise the theatre's productions as concerts of music followed by gratuitous theatrical performances. Given the ferocious opposition of the Church, the irony was that one of the greatest successes which the theatre was to have—the tragedy of *Douglas* (first performed during the winter session of 1756-57)—was written by a Presbyterian minister, the Reverend John Home, Minister of Athelstaneford in East Lothian.

§V

The Court of Session (the supreme civil court in Scotland), where Boswell's father and grandfather practised, sat in the Parliament House, situated at the south-west corner of Parliament Close to the south of the Church of St Giles. The Parliament House consisted of a hall (which before the Treaty of Union of 1707 was used for the sessions of the Scottish Parliament) and a wing to the east. The outward appearance of this building was very different from the way it looks today. The front of the Parliament House facing Parliament Close was built of ashlar, while the remainder of the building was constructed largely of rubble, and at the corners all round were large ashlar pilasters with rectangular turrets on top. Sun-dials with copper gnomons were fixed on the two turrets at the south end of the building. In the angle between the hall and the east wing was a large circular turret containing a spiral staircase.

In those days as now, the Court of Session consisted of an Inner House and an Outer House. In the Inner House there were fifteen judges, known as Lords of Session, who sat together at a large semi-circular bench, presided over by one of their number, known as the Lord President, and their courtroom occupied the ground floor of the east wing. The Outer House judges, on the other hand, were individual judges from the Inner House sitting on their own in the hall. The principal feature of the Court of Session in those days was that it was a unitary court whose judges (in theory, at least) always sat and decided causes together as one body; and the judges who sat in the Outer House did not do so as fully independent judges, but rather as representatives of the Court as a whole. When all the judges were sitting together, which was quite often, they were commonly referred to as "the haill fifteen". The judges when sitting in the Inner House or Outer House all wore dark blue robes with burgundy red facings, decorated with red bows designed for fastening the robes.

The floor above the Inner House was where the Court of Exchequer sat. The Court of Exchequer had jurisdiction in all revenue matters in Scotland; but although it sat in Scotland it was governed by English procedures, and both Scottish and English counsel were entitled to appear before it. This anomalous court consisted of a Lord Chief Baron and four other Barons. Some of the Barons were appointed from the English bar.

The most imposing feature of the spacious hall where the Outer House sat was, and still is, the high roof, formed of dark oak tie-and-hammer beams with cross braces. In the hall as it was in Boswell's day there was a high bench at the south end for the "Lord Ordinary" of the week to sit at (the judges took turns to sit there for a week at a time) and in front of this was a bar, up a few steps, called the "Fore-Bar", at which advocates had to stand when pleading. At the east side of the hall were two "Side-Bars" for other judges to sit at and be addressed by counsel. One purpose of the Side-Bars was to enable judges to finish causes which had begun during their respective weeks as Lord Ordinary. It was said of these Side-Bars that they were "of a very singular construction, being merely an Arm Chair in a small recess, with a narrow shelf in front, which brought the Judge, Counsel and Agents in such close connection that they almost touched each other".[21]

The remainder of the Outer House was a large open area where advocates waiting to address the court attended until called by the macer. While waiting, they frequently walked up and down the hall discussing causes, or other matters, with other counsel or agents. Consequently, the Outer House tended to be noisy and one wonders how the Outer House judges were able to cope with the distractions. At the northern end of that part of the hall occupied by the Outer House was a slight timber partition, about half the height of the wall, which divided the hall into two main parts. Beyond this partition was a section of the building containing numerous little booths (known as "krames"), all made of the flimsiest materials, which were occupied as taverns, booksellers' shops and toy shops. Here also was to be found the Bailie Court, which sat every Monday to hear small causes.

The High Court of Justiciary (Scotland's highest criminal court) sat in a hall on one of the upper floors of a building known as the "New Tolbooth" (also referred to as the "Council House"), which was connected to the south-west corner of the Church of St Giles by a covered passage. This court consisted of the Lord Justice-General, the Lord Justice-Clerk and five judges of the Court of Session holding office as Lords Commissioners of Justiciary. In addition to sitting in Edinburgh, the judges also held "circuit courts" at various towns around Scotland. The nominal President of the Court was the Lord Justice-General, but throughout the eighteenth century the Lord Justice-General was always a layman and in practice the presidency was held by the Lord Justice-Clerk. When sitting as Lords Commissioners of Justiciary, the judges wore red robes with white satin facings, decorated with red rosettes and ribbons, which were used for tying the robes; and, to distinguish the Lord Justice-Clerk from the others, there were rows of small square holes in the white facings on his robe which were designed to give the appearance of ermine. Trials in Edinburgh were normally heard by five judges sitting together, and all trials took place before a jury consisting of fifteen members. A simple majority was sufficient for a verdict; and the verdict could normally be any one of "guilty", "not guilty" or "not proven", the last resulting in as full an acquittal as a verdict of "not guilty". Responsibility for the prosecution of trials in the Court of Justiciary lay with the Lord Advocate, the principal law officer of the Crown in Scotland. In the performance of his criminal duties, the Lord Advocate had the assistance of the Solicitor-General for Scotland and a few specially appointed "Advocates-Depute". Other advocates were also called on from time to time to assist if required.

The whole of that part of Parliament Close to the south of St Giles' was enclosed by buildings, principally the Treasury Chambers, the Royal Exchange (which was rarely used by businessmen, the Cross being the preferred rendezvous) and the Post Office. On the east side of Parliament Close was the Custom House and a number of tenements of considerable height, some of which contained shops at the ground level; and under the arcade or "piazza" at the north-east corner of the Close was John's Coffee House—a popular meeting place for lawyers and their clients, where, in addition to coffee, alcohol was served. One of the tall tenements was "Blair's Land", where the Boswell family home was situated. Although the Boswell residence was for many years on the fourth floor of this building, the family were to move to another floor of the same building in or about 1762.

Partly obscuring the south wall of St Giles' Church, was a row of small, two- or three-storey shops occupied by booksellers, watchmakers, jewellers and goldsmiths, they being the only tradesmen permitted by the Town Council to set up shop there. Between the north side of the Parliament House and the church stood the Goldsmiths' Hall.

A rather delightful feature of Parliament Close and its environs was the sound of the "music bells" which were heard playing a wide variety of popular tunes from the great central tower of St Giles' for an hour each day at midday, except on Sundays and holidays. The bells were played by a musician on keys (said to have been like those on a harpsichord) which had to be struck with some force; and the larger bells were controlled with treadles.

St Giles' Church was the meeting place of the Scottish supreme ecclesiastical tribunal, the General Assembly of the Church of Scotland, which met for about twelve days a year and consisted of about 200 clergymen and 150 lay elders, presided over by the elected "Moderator". This body—"the only established popular assembly then in Scotland"—met in one of the aisles of the church, and advocates were often instructed to appear in cases there. "That plain, square, galleried, apartment was admirably suited for the purpose; the more so that it was not too large; and it was more interesting, from the men who had acted in it, and the scenes it had witnessed, than any other existing room in Scotland. It had beheld the best exertions of the best men in the kingdom, ever since the year 1640... Its bar... needed no legal learning, and no labour beyond attendance; but always required judgment and management; [and] it presented excellent opportunities for speaking, especially as the two inconvenient checks of relevancy and pertinency were seldom in rigid observance."[22]

§VI

Boswell's formal education started at the age of six when he was sent to the private academy of James Mundell in the West Bow. He detested the school and did his best to avoid attendance by virtue of real or imagined ailments which his mother was all too ready to treat as good reasons for absence. Mundell's school (which admitted girls as well as boys) taught Latin, English, writing and arithmetic, and was highly regarded. Many of the pupils later became lawyers, including at least four Lords of Session. The school was probably situated on the right-hand side of the West Bow half-way up from the Grassmarket, and Boswell may well have seen from the school windows men being led to execution at the gallows erected at the east end of the Grassmarket.

The servants of the Boswell household told the young boy frightening stories about robbers, murderers, witches, and ghosts, with the consequence that his imagination was "continually in a state of terror".[23] The servants are bound to have mentioned one particularly appalling character, the infamous Major Weir, who had lived in a house in the West Bow in the seventeenth century and was reputed to have been a terrible wizard. He and his sister Jean were arrested in 1670 and after a trial in which they were found guilty of their heinous offences (incest, adultery and bestiality on his part, and incest and sorcery on his sister's part[24]) he was strangled and burned at a spot between Edinburgh and Leith, and his sister was hanged in the Grassmarket. For many years afterwards the West Bow was said to be haunted by Weir's ghost.

For reasons which are not entirely clear, Boswell was removed from Mundell's school when he was eight and was then educated at home by governors who, Boswell later complained, were "without manners" and "of the meanest sort of education". But the first governor was at least "not without sentiment and sensibility" and it is clear that it was from him that the young Boswell first acquired a taste for the Roman poets. The second governor, on the other hand, was "harsh and without knowledge of the human mind" and was a dogmatist who "felt and acted according to system".[25]

In 1748, in the first round of shrieval appointments following the abolition of heritable jurisdictions in 1747, Boswell's father was appointed Sheriff-Depute* of Wigtownshire, which post he held until 1750 when he resigned. He was evidently very proud of the post and had a reputation for being one of the best of the new sheriffs.

When Boswell's paternal grandfather died in 1749, Alexander Boswell became Laird of Auchinleck and the family began to spend a substantial part of every year at the ancestral estate. The family residence was an old baronial tower-house built of red sandstone with barrel-vaults and thick walls, which had probably been constructed in the early seventeenth century. Some time later, Boswell's father started to build a new house about half a mile up the hill to the east of the old house, but this new house was not completed until the early 1760s. The estate has been described in appropriately evocative terms: "[T]he grounds... deserve Boswell's often-repeated epithet of 'romantic'. The Dippol burn winds through a narrow gorge one hundred and fifty feet deep, its precipitous sides covered with trees that even then were large; the bridges

---

* The "Sheriff-Depute" in each sheriffdom, notwithstanding the contrary impression conveyed by the title, was the principal sheriff there and had power to appoint Sheriffs-Substitute to act for him.

across it have been placed so as to make the most of the sheer drop to the stream. [Near the] old manor house…, at the junction of the Dippol and the Lugar, stood the dwindling ruin of the old keep perched on its sandstone rock, the streams a hundred feet below—a ruin which the eye of fancy could reconstruct with towering walls, drawbridge, and portcullis."[26]

In his twelfth year, Boswell came down with an illness which he described as scorbutic (i.e., scurvy), but which was diagnosed by the doctors as being fundamentally of nervous origin. With a view to remedying this condition, Boswell was sent to Moffat, which was then a popular health resort on account of the famous sulphur water of the spring there. Boswell makes no mention of being expected to drink the waters during his visit on this occasion—the only treatment he describes is that of bathing in "a horrible tub"[27]—but at all events he gradually recovered his health.

At about the time of his thirteenth birthday, in the academic year 1753-1754, Boswell enrolled as a student at the University of Edinburgh, where he attended for six years, first studying Arts and then Law. Although it seems nowadays that admission to university at the age of only thirteen would be abnormally young, that was by no means unusual in those days; indeed, the usual age for admission was then fourteen. At that time, the University was situated in a quadrangle of dilapidated buildings on the southern edge of the city in the area now occupied by the building known as the "Old College". The Arts courses which Boswell is believed to have attended were Latin, Greek, Logic, Natural Philosophy, Moral Philosophy, Mathematics and French.

During Boswell's first year at the University, his father's career progressed further, for on 15 February 1754 he was appointed a Lord of Session and took his place on the bench with the judicial title of Lord Auchinleck. It was said that "for more than twenty years he was looked upon as one of the most useful and upright judges on the bench".[28] And on 22 July 1755 Lord Auchinleck was also appointed a Lord Commissioner of Justiciary. "As a criminal judge", we are told, "his character stood very high. His mind and body were, for a number of years, so strong, that he seemed to take delight in a very long trial, which some of his brethren considered as an intolerable burden. In delivering his sentiments from the bench, the goodness of the matter more than compensated for the homeliness of his phrase. In conducting trials on the circuit he avoided indecent keenness no less than ill-judged lenity to culprits. So great was Lord Auchinleck's candour, discernment, and knowledge of business, that a man standing trial for his life could not wish for a more impartial, dispassionate judge."[29]

While Lord Auchinleck was busy presiding over proofs and trials, young Boswell was continuing with his studies at the University and was starting to make long-standing friendships. Two particularly close friends were an Englishman named William Johnson Temple (1739-96), whom Boswell considered to be "of the most worthy and amiable character", and a Scot named John Johnston (c. 1729-86), whose character was described by Boswell as "masculine and hearty".[30]

John Johnston was laird of Grange, a small property in Annandale, Dumfriesshire. Boswell's measure of respect for him can be gauged from the fact that he frequently refers to him in his journals as "worthy Grange". Johnston was probably in his mid-twenties when they met (and, if so, was Boswell's senior by at least ten years) and was planning to become a lawyer, but as a "writer" or solicitor rather than as an advocate. In Johnston, Boswell found a fellow "hypochondriac", for Johnston, like Boswell, had a tendency to suffer from fits of depression. They were also drawn to each other for other reasons in that they shared an enthusiasm for Scottish history and they both had an emotional attachment to the royal house of Stewart. Boswell was to have a great deal of contact with Johnston over the years and always recognised in him a kindred spirit.

Boswell's friendship with Temple, who was from Berwick-upon-Tweed, was entirely different. Although they regularly corresponded with each other throughout Boswell's life, Boswell came more and more to regard Temple as a sort of distant father confessor. And when they met later in life their relationship was sometimes strained as a result of their having totally different interests and preoccupations. But when they first met, Temple and Boswell were attracted to each other because they had mutual interests in literature, the classics and religion. Temple was an Anglican and shortly after they became friends he took Boswell to St Paul's Chapel, a "qualified" Church of England chapel at the foot of Carrubber's Close off the north side of the High Street. Boswell cherished the memory of this experience and continued to recall it many years later. He was enchanted by the Anglican form of service, which, he said, always raised his mind "to exalted devotion and meditation on the joys of heaven",[31] whereas the Presbyterian form of service made him think of hell. Boswell was particularly miserable when attending services at the Tolbooth Kirk in St Giles', the very thought of which brought into his mind "dreary... ideas" and "gloomy feelings".[32]

Long hours of study at college gave Boswell a huge appetite. He later wrote in a letter to Johnston how with "rapacious haste", after hearing the two o'clock bell which announced the customary dinner time, he used to rush home "down the Horse Wynd, up Borthwick's Close,... by the crowded Cross, regardless of Advocates, Writers, Scotch Hunters, Cloth-merchants, Presbyterian ministers, country lairds, captains both by land and sea, porters, Chairmen, and caddies. With what rapid steps or rather jumps did I ascend the Custom House stairs and with what a tremendous noise did I burst open the door of the house of my father making it shake to its very foundations, while lock and key sent forth a horrid clank... With what amazing velocity did I scamper about, traversing the house, like a lion in search of his prey... But when at last the dear dinner was upon the table..., then did I mightily fall on, and make a meal most prodigious."[33]

During his first three years at the University when he was studying languages, Boswell was evidently happy and progressed very well. However, in the autumn of 1756, when he started to study metaphysics, he fell victim to what he later described as "a terrible hypochondria".[34] The main problem was that with metaphysics Boswell encountered determinism, which he perceived as being an alien and deeply disturbing concept, for he instinctively believed in man's free will. Furthermore, he saw determinism as being a threat to his religious beliefs. For the rest of his life Boswell attempted to cling tenaciously to those beliefs, which undoubtedly appealed to him on an emotional level; but on an intellectual level, Boswell, although clearly reluctant to do so, sometimes felt it difficult not to accept a deterministic view of life, and this caused him endless anguish.

By the summer of 1757, Boswell's "hypochondria" had become sufficiently serious that he was sent back to Moffat to recover. Once again, he duly regained his health; and, in fact, it seems that it was about this time that he acquired those extrovert characteristics which were to remain with him, apart from fits of depression, for the rest of his life. It has been observed that at this stage "the timid, priggish, prematurely grave youngster was replaced outwardly by a vain, noisy, bouncing, odd, comical, good-humoured youth of manly features and masculine bearing whom many men and most women found immediately attractive".[35] And although he continued to suffer periodically from depression, it is a remarkable feature of Boswell's character that he never allowed the gloomy despondency to which he was prey to have an adverse effect on his relations with others.

In the spring of 1758, Boswell was given a rare taste of freedom, for both of his parents went to stay at Auchinleck, leaving Boswell in lodgings (probably in the same building as the family home at Blair's Land) for over two months. He evidently took the opportunity to attend as many plays as possible and to socialise with the actors, and he no doubt spent a great deal of time in the company of his friend Johnston, who seems to have introduced him to some of the forbidden delights of Edinburgh.

In addition to his passion for the theatre, Boswell acquired a fondness for writing poetry. In May 1758 he composed a poem entitled *An Evening Walk in the Abbey Church of Holyroodhouse*, which appeared in *The Scots Magazine* in August of that year and is believed to be the first of his works to be published. The poem contains strong hints of a tendency towards Jacobitism, and reveals Boswell's romantic fondness for Scottish history and his disapproval of the neglect of the Abbey Church following the damage inflicted on it by the Edinburgh mob during the 1688 Revolution. Holyrood ideas and associations were recurring themes in Boswell's life at this time and were subjects on which he particularly enjoyed conversing with his friend John Johnston. Holyrood was also forever associated with his first patron, James Somerville, the twelfth Lord Somerville, who had apartments there, and who befriended Boswell at about this time, if not earlier.

In a letter to Temple dated 29 July 1758,[36] Boswell reported having met David Hume, the famous Scottish philosopher and historian and one of the foremost geniuses of the Scottish Enlightenment. The meeting was at Hume's residence, which at that time was at "Jack's Land" in the Canongate. Hume was wide-faced, thick-lipped and very portly; always had a kindly, good-humoured expression; and was renowned for his amiability. Boswell formed the usual favourable impression of him and told Temple that Hume "is a most discreet, affable man as ever I met with". As to Hume's intellectual abilities, Boswell wrote: "Mr Hume, I think, is a very proper person for a young man to cultivate an acquaintance with; though he has not, perhaps, the most delicate taste, yet he has applied himself with great attention to the study of the ancients, and is likeways a great historian, so that you are not only entertained in his company, but may reap a great deal of useful instruction." It is significant that there is no mention in this letter of Hume's famous scepticism with regard to religion, which earned him the soubriquet of "The Great Infidel". Boswell must have been aware of Hume's views and must have found them most disquieting; and he certainly later complained vehemently about David Hume and "other infidels" who "destroyed our principles and put nothing firm in their place".[37]

Later that year, Boswell went on the Northern Circuit with his father and, to his great content, travelled the whole way in the same chaise as Sir David Dalrymple, the Advocate-Depute appointed to appear at the circuit. In his letter to Temple of 29 July 1758 Boswell had said: "You must know I am vastly happy with the thoughts of the North Circuit; my worthy Maecenas,* Sir David Dalrymple, goes as Advocate Depute; there I will enjoy the happiness of his agreeable and improving conversation, and see the country with a double relish in such refined company."

Dalrymple was born at Edinburgh on 28 October 1726 and was the eldest of the sixteen children of Sir James Dalrymple, Baronet, of Hailes, Auditor-Genaral of the Exchequer in Scotland, whose estate was at New Hailes (or Newhailes), near Inveresk and Musselburgh, overlooking the Firth of Forth. Very unusually for a Scotsman in those days, Dalrymple was educated at Eton, where he acquired "that predilection for English modes and manners which marked his conduct and conversation in the after-part of life".[38] He was admitted advocate on 24 February 1748, but although regarded as honest and diligent and having a "concise, elegant, perspicuous style of speaking", he did not make a very great reputation for himself at the bar, for his "weak ill-tuned voice and ungraceful elocution" prevented him from excelling as an orator; and it was alleged that he "did not sufficiently concentrate his ideas or direct his arguments to the essential points at issue".[39] His written pleadings, on the other hand, were highly praised.

Dalrymple's father died in 1751 and Dalrymple then succeeded to the ancestral estate and the baronetcy. At New Hailes he fitted up a magnificent library, and having no fondness for the boisterous tavern company so much enjoyed by most of his legal brethren, he liked nothing more than to lead a quiet, studious life

---

* This is a reference to Gaius Maecenas (d. 8 B.C.), right-hand man of the Emperor Augustus and great patron of men of letters such as Virgil and Horace.

at his estate. He soon acquired a reputation as a serious and learned antiquarian scholar, and even at the time Boswell came to know him he had become a man of letters. Boswell was captivated by Dalrymple, who represented so much that he aspired to himself: refined English manners, wide-ranging intellect, and sincere religious beliefs. It is of particular significance that Dalrymple encouraged Boswell in his high opinion of Samuel Johnson well before Boswell and Johnson were to meet.

In a letter to Temple dated 16 December 1758, Boswell said that he had kept an exact journal of the trip on the Northern Circuit for his friend James Love (1722-1774), the actor. This seems to be the first record of any journal kept by Boswell. Unfortunately, however, no trace of the journal has been found. But it should not pass unremarked that it is to Love, who was regarded by Boswell at that time as being his "second-best friend", and who had given Boswell lessons in pronunciation, that one must give the credit for being the person who first encouraged Boswell to keep a journal.

In the autumn of 1758, Boswell started studying Civil Law (that is, Roman Law). This, he complained to Temple, was "a most laborious task". The law class was taught by Robert Dick, who was evidently regarded as somewhat incompetent. "From 9 to 10," Boswell told Temple, "I attend the law class; from 10 to 11, the Astronomy; from 11 to 1, study at home; and from 1 to 2, attend a college upon Roman Antiquities. The afternoon and evening I likeways spend in study. I never walk except on Saturdays." [40]

During the spring of 1759, as in the previous year, Boswell's parents went to stay at Auchinleck and left Boswell on his own in Edinburgh. He took full advantage of this second period of freedom to resume his fraternisation with actors. Later that year, on 14 August, he was admitted as a Freemason in the Canongate Kilwinning (or St John's) Lodge, which met on the west side of St John's Street off the south side of the Canongate. He became an active member and was to be appointed Junior Warden of the Lodge in 1761, Depute Master from 1767 to 1768, and Master from 1773 to 1775. And in November 1776 he would become Deputy Grand Master of the Freemasons in Scotland.

In September 1759, Boswell joined his parents at Auchinleck, fully anticipating returning to Edinburgh at the beginning of the autumn term. However, Lord Auchinleck, who was evidently alarmed at his son's renowned conviviality with actors and actresses, announced that Boswell was no longer to attend Edinburgh University but was, instead, to attend the University of Glasgow. This was no doubt an attempt by Lord Auchinleck to lead his aberrant son from his wicked ways, for there were no theatres in Glasgow. At that time, Glasgow, unlike Edinburgh, which was very much a city of professionals—in particular, lawyers—was primarily associated with business and commerce.

In those days, the buildings of the University of Glasgow were situated in the High Street and were some of the most notable examples of seventeenth-century Scottish architecture. During the period when Boswell studied there the whole city had a reputation for righteousness and sobriety, and crime was very rare. The students at the university—which had a collegiate atmosphere—wore red gowns and some of them lodged and ate at the college. It seems that Boswell probably lodged in the house of James Clow, the Professor of Logic.

The Professor of Civil Law, Dr Hercules Lindsay, published nothing and is now unknown; but, in a letter to John Johnston, Boswell described Dr Lindsay as "one of the best teachers I ever saw".[41] Dr Lindsay was evidently the first Professor to deliver lectures on Roman law in English rather than Latin.

The Professor of Moral Philosophy was none other than Adam Smith, the future author of *An Inquiry into the Nature and Causes of the Wealth of Nations* (published in 1776), whose lectures on Moral Philosophy, and also Rhetoric and Belles-Lettres, were highly regarded. Smith took a great personal interest in his students and he made a very favourable impression on Boswell.

However, the serious, sober, academic way of life cannot have been entirely to Boswell's liking; and the lack of theatrical entertainment must have been a considerable blow for him. Indeed, it seems that his mind was still very much on theatrical matters, for in February 1760 a pamphlet was published in London entitled *A View of the Edinburgh Theatre during the Summer Season, 1759, containing an Exact List of the Several Pieces represented, and Impartial Observations on Each Performance* and although this publication was ostensibly written by "a Society of Gentlemen" it is believed that it was in fact written by Boswell.

In any event, matters finally got out of hand. Although he had made a determined effort to study hard and to conform to a well-regimented existence, Boswell made a desperate bid for freedom on 1 March 1760 by fleeing to London. There is a certain amount of mystery about the whole affair, but it appears that the position was as follows.[42] Boswell had fallen in love with an actress in Edinburgh who was a devout Roman Catholic and Boswell had made it known to her that he was attracted to her religion. She referred him to her priest in Edinburgh, who gave Boswell some Roman Catholic literature which he studied at Auchinleck, no doubt much to his father's discomfiture, for not only did Lord Auchinleck hold bigoted prejudices against Catholicism, he was also well aware that conversion to that religion would, among other things, have barred Boswell from entry into the legal profession and would have prevented him from legally succeeding to the family estate at Auchinleck. These considerations, indeed, may have been additional factors in prompting Lord Auchinleck to decide to take Boswell away from the University at Edinburgh and send him to Glasgow, for there were no resident priests in Glasgow at that time. However, in spite of his father's solicitations, it seems that Boswell wrote to his father at the end of February 1760 to advise him that he found Roman Catholicism so persuasive that he was intending to adopt that faith and was even considering becoming a monk or a priest. When his father responded—perhaps by ordering him to come to Edinburgh—Boswell resolved to make a dash for London.

§VII

Boswell travelled most, if not all, of the journey to London on horseback and certainly did so from Carlisle, which he claimed to have done in only two and a half days. On arrival in London, he took up cheap lodgings and got himself introduced to a priest at the Bavarian chapel, where "with a wonderful enthusiasm"[43] he observed for the first time the celebration of mass and was received into the Roman Catholic Church. He continued to contemplate entering a monastery with a view to becoming a monk, but this scheme came to an end when he made the acquaintance of Samuel Derrick, "a dingy fifth-rate man of letters",[44] who showed him London "in all its variety of departments, both literary and sportive".[45] The "sportive" departments included experiencing for the first time what Boswell later referred to as "the melting and transporting rites of Love".[46] This was with a prostitute by the name of Sally Forrester at the Blue Periwig, Southampton Street, The Strand. Boswell was nineteen at the time.

As soon as he had arrived in London, Boswell informed his father of his whereabouts, and Lord Auchinleck got in touch with Alexander Montgomerie (1723-69), tenth Earl of Eglinton, the owner of a neighbouring estate in Ayrshire who was staying at his London residence at that time. Eglinton had Boswell traced, gave him money to enable him to take decent lodgings, and subsequently allowed Boswell to stay in an apartment in Eglington's own house (which was in Queen Street, Mayfair). Boswell, who was introduced by Eglington "into the circles of the great, the gay, and the ingenious",[47] later recalled that Eglinton "made me a deist. I gave myself up to pleasure without limit. I was in a delirium of joy."[48] The consequence was that Boswell ended up suffering an attack of a venereal disease, probably gonorrhea, which he later described as "that distemper with which Venus, when cross, takes it into her head to plague her votaries".[49]

Eglinton suggested to Boswell that he consider endeavouring to become an officer of the Guards. This idea pleased Boswell so much that he wrote to his father asking that he purchase a commission for him. However, he did not relish the notion of active service in campaigns; indeed, although he was certainly attracted to the idea of wearing military uniform, his main objective was simply to obtain a post which would enable him to stay in London. Lord Auchinleck responded by coming to London to try to persuade his wayward son to give up such ideas. Although Lord Auchinleck was not totally opposed to the idea of a military career for his sons—he had very recently allowed his second son, John, to adopt precisely such a career by joining a regiment—he obviously had other ideas for his elder son and clearly had hopes that Boswell would follow the family tradition by becoming an advocate. He prevailed on Boswell to return home with him to consider the matter there with care; and they travelled together at the end of May, taking a detour to Cambridge to visit Temple.

On their return to Edinburgh, Boswell and his father duly discussed the position and it was agreed that Boswell should continue with his legal studies; but, rather than returning to either Edinburgh or Glasgow University, it was decided that he would study at home under his father's guidance. This arrangement evidently lasted about two years, although it was not at all to Boswell's liking. He described his miserable fate in a letter to Temple: "[C]onsider my particular situation. A young fellow whose happiness was always centred in London, who had at last got there and had begun to taste its delights, who had got his mind filled with the most gay ideas: getting into the Guards, being about Court, enjoying the happiness of the *beau monde* and the company of men of genius—in short, everything that he could wish—consider this poor fellow hauled away to the town of Edinburgh, obliged to conform to every Scotch custom or be laughed at..., his flighty imagination quite cramped, and be obliged to study *Corpus Juris Civilis*** and live in his father's strict family—is there any wonder, Sir, that the unlucky dog should be somewhat fretful."[50]

In an effort to make up for the loss of London society, Boswell, soon after his return to Edinburgh, formed what he termed a "jovial society", emulating the notorious men's societies then so popular in London. This society was known as the Soaping Club, the expression "Every man soap his own beard" being, according to Boswell, the reigning phrase for "Every man in his humour". The club met every Tuesday evening at Thom's Tavern at the lower end of the West Bow.

It is easy to imagine Boswell, after a night of revelry, staggering homewards along the ill-lit streets, doing his best to avoid the inevitable abominations deposited on the ground for the street cleaners the following morning. It seems, however, that he did not always return home direct, for he confessed to Temple that he had been to a "house of recreation", probably in the Canongate, and had "catch'd a Tartar, too, with a vengeance". His affliction on this occasion took as much as four months to be cured, if indeed it was cured at all, and so distressed him that he informed Temple: "This season, I never have been, nor do intend again to be a guest in the mansions of gross sensuality."[51]

Notwithstanding his nocturnal revelries, it was Boswell's invariable practice in the morning to attend the public baths, where, even in the depths of winter, he always had a cold bath rather than a warm one, taking the view that "a young man should guard against effeminacy" and should "avoid warm baths and accustom himself rather to the cold bath, which will give him vigour and liveliness".[52] The bath house was situated in the west wing of the Royal Infirmary building, near the University, on a site which is now on the south side of Infirmary Street. (This building, which was designed by William Adam and completed in about 1748, was demolished in the latter part of the nineteenth century.)

By the summer of 1761, Boswell had acquired two new friends, Andrew Erskine (1740-93) and George Dempster (1732-1818). Erskine, who was a fellow "hypochondriac" of about the same age as Boswell, was an Army officer and was a son of the fifth Earl of Kellie. He had theatrical ambitions and had contributed several poems to a miscellany published in Edinburgh in 1760

---

* The codification of Roman law instructed by the Emperor Justinian in the 6th century A.D.

under the title *A Collection of Original Poems by the Rev. Mr Blacklock and Other Scotch Gentlemen*; and both he and Boswell were to contribute poems to a subsequent volume published in 1762. Boswell gives us this description of him: "Captain Erskine is a tall black [dark] man with a great sagaciousness of countenance. He has an awkward bashfulness amongst strangers, but with his friends is easy and excellent company. He has a richness of imagination, a wildness of fancy, a strength of feeling, and a fluency of expression which render him a very fine poet. He has a great deal of humour and simplicity of manners. He has a turn for speculation and has none of the common notions of mankind."[53] In spite of his aristocratic background, however, Erskine was never well-off.

Dempster, on the other hand, was born into a wealthy trading family in Dundee in 1732. He was admitted advocate in 1755 and the following year set off on the Grand Tour. On his return he is believed to have practised for a brief period at the bar, but he soon abandoned the law and decided to apply himself to politics. In 1761 he got himself elected, at ruinous expense, independent Member of Parliament for the Perth Burghs. It was at about this time that Boswell became acquainted with him, and they were to remain on good terms for the rest of Boswell's life. Boswell had a high regard for him, referring to him as "a most agreeable well-bred man, sensible and clever, gentle and amiable, quite a gentleman".[54] Throughout his career in Parliament, Dempster had a high reputation for honesty, altruism and incorruptibility.

Together with his two new-found friends, Boswell attended a series of lectures on elocution given by Thomas Sheridan (the father of Richard Sheridan) in June and July 1761 at St Paul's Chapel at the foot of Carrubber's Close, where Temple had taken Boswell for his first Church of England service. These lectures were designed for persons wishing to acquire the ability to speak English with a correct pronunciation and it was said that the lectures were attended by "more than 300 gentlemen, the most eminent in this country for their rank and abilities".[55] It has to be recalled that in those days many people, even among the professional classes, still spoke colloquial Scots, or at any rate spoke English with a strong native dialect, and it was thus generally perceived as being desirable, given the closer connection between England and Scotland following the Union, to acquire the ability to converse with equal ease in "the King's English". Although it is often remarked that Sheridan was an Irish actor from Dublin and thus not self-evidently well qualified to give lectures on correct English pronunciation, Boswell was much impressed with his lectures and later said of him: "He is a man of great genius and understands propriety of speech better than anybody."[56]

In the latter part of 1761, Boswell became a member of the Select Society of Edinburgh, which had enthusiastically supported Sheridan's lectures in St Paul's Chapel. The initial objects of the Society, which was founded in 1754, were literary discussion, philosophical inquiry and improvement in the art of public speaking, and its membership (which included David Hume and Adam Smith) was originally restricted to a maximum of fifty, consisting primarily of prominent lawyers, university professors and church ministers. Boswell was very proud of his election as member of the Society, but by that time it had come to be regarded as being no longer truly "select", for its membership had swollen and the Society had taken up much wider interests, including the encouragement of arts, science and manufactures in Scotland.*

During this period Boswell was kept busy with several amorous adventures involving in some instances real or imaginary prospects of matrimony. The most significant of these intrigues seems to have been the illicit affair which Boswell is believed to have had in the latter part of 1761 and during 1762 with Jean Heron, the only daughter of one of Lord Auchinleck's judicial colleagues, Henry Home, Lord Kames. At the start of the relationship, Jean, who was about sixteen at the time, had only recently married. Her husband was a wealthy landowner, Patrick Heron, of Kirroughtrie, near Newton Stewart.

Boswell was a frequent visitor at Lord Kames' Edinburgh residence and regularly enjoyed Lord Kames' renowned hospitality at supper. Kames, who was a tall, long-nosed man with a slightly supercilious expression, was appointed a Lord of Session on 6 February 1752 and was about sixty-five years old when he struck up his friendship with Boswell. He derived his judicial title from his estate of Kames, in Eccles parish, Berwickshire. His character as a judge was in marked contrast to his character in his social hours, for when sitting on the bench he had a pronounced tendency to be intolerant, impatient, irritable, and downright rude. Indeed, he was renowned for addressing colleagues and litigants alike as "bitches". The truth was that Lord Kames had no great fondness for the practice of the law, his real interests being more inclined towards philosophy, history and literature, in all of which areas he was an author of some note. He repeatedly said that "had he been assured of £50 Sterling a-year, no consideration should have made him submit to the drudgery of mind and body which he underwent for years before and after coming to the bar".[57] As to the nature of his relationship with Boswell, it is well known that Kames was fond of encouraging protégés and it seems that Boswell was one of the chosen few; two others of note who had had that distinction were Adam Smith and David Hume, but they had eventually fallen out with him.

In January 1762, while Boswell was on the one hand carrying on erudite and witty conversations with Lord Kames, he was also, and somewhat less to his credit, not only carrying on his illicit affair with Lord Kames' daughter, but was also carrying on affairs with two actresses (one being Mrs Love, the wife of his friend James Love, the actor) and an intrigue with a "curious young little pretty"[58] named Peggy Doig, who later that year was to bear him a son. This latter misdemeanour naturally incurred the displeasure of the Kirk, but Boswell was only required to pay a fine.

In the spring, Lord Auchinleck, alarmed at the activities of his aberrant son, got Boswell to sign a deed purporting to allow Lord Auchinleck, if he wished, to convey the estate of Auchinleck on his death to trustees, leaving Boswell with a right to occupy the house and to receive certain rents but with no rights with

* The Society collapsed in or about 1763.

23

regard to the administration of the estate. However, sugar was provided with the pill, for less than a month later Lord Auchinleck signed a deed granting Boswell an irrevocable allowance of £100 a year (which by today's standards represents an annual allowance of about £6,000). This sum was a sizeable proportion of Lord Auchinleck's salary, which was £900 a year (£700 as a Lord of Session and an additional £200 as a Lord Commissioner of Justiciary). By today's standards, that represents about £54,000 free of tax (income tax not being introduced until 1799). An income of £900 a year in 1762 was a considerable sum, bearing in mind that the wages paid to, say, a maid-servant were generally from £3 to £4 a year, while the most a man servant could expect to earn was from £6 to £10 a year. It is therefore small wonder that judges in those days were able to employ large numbers of domestics.

At about the same time as Boswell had his allowance conferred on him, he revived his idea of attempting to join the Guards; and his father, no doubt worn out with the whole business, finally agreed to a proposal to the effect that, if Boswell were to study law at Auchinleck until June and then sit the private trials in the Civil Law, Boswell would be allowed to take a commission in the Guards. Lord Auchinleck even went so far as to undertake to do what he could to assist Boswell in realising his ambition.

This satisfactory agreement having been reached, Boswell duly set off for Auchinleck. Here he indulged in "the most agreeable reveries imaginable" with regard to the prospect of a glorious career commencing with appointment as an officer of the Guards followed in due course by election as a Member of Parliament.[59] He also continued to indulge his passion for Jean Heron by arranging assignations with her which took place at Dumfries, where Lord Auchinleck was the judge at the Circuit Court. He also no doubt spent the requisite amount of time on his legal studies, as had been agreed, for he sat and passed the Civil Law examination on 30 July.*

The next hurdle to be overcome in gaining admission to the Faculty of Advocates was to pass an examination in Scots law. But Boswell had no intention of seeking admission to the Faculty at this stage. Having fulfilled his side of his bargain with his father by passing the Civil Law examination, Boswell was now entitled to pursue his aim of becoming an officer of the Guards, and to that end he persuaded Lord Auchinleck to allow him to go once more to London. However, it was decided that, before setting off, he would spend the autumn in the company of Lord and Lady Kames on a jaunt round southern Scotland and northern England, with visits to Jean and Patrick Heron at Kirroughtrie and also to Kames itself. In the meantime, Boswell went with his parents to Auchinleck in the middle of August when the Court of Session rose for the vacation.

The new house at Auchinleck had now become habitable and Boswell reported to his friend Johnston that he was staying there and had "a neat elegant

---

* Prior to sitting this examination the sum of £60—equivalent to about £3,600 by today's standards—was payable to the Faculty of Advocates by way of entry money.

apartment".[60] This house, situated at the top of a brae up a rugged road from the old house, is in the "Adam style" and has a commanding view over open fields at the front.

Boswell's jaunt started on 14 September and he kept a full journal of the noteworthy sights and events. It is with this journal—entitled *Journal of My Jaunt, Harvest 1762*—that "we emerge from the twilight of speculation into the full sunlight of Boswellian self-revelation".[61] At the end of his trip with Lord Kames, Boswell was entertained as a guest of his lordship at Kames, where Boswell soon fell prey to an attack of low spirits. After returning briefly to Edinburgh in October, he set off for Fife, where he was due to visit Kellie Castle at the invitation of his friend, Andrew Erskine. On arrival at Kellie, he was enthusiastically greeted by Erskine and his three sisters—Lady Betty, Lady Anne and Lady Jenny. Boswell felt at this time a strong passion for Lady Betty, but it seems that he did not declare it. In any event, his feelings towards her were not to last long, although he and she remained on the best of terms and he came very much to value her company.

Boswell, together with Erskine, returned to Edinburgh on 3 November and the following morning they visited David Hume. "We found him", says Boswell, "in his house in James's Court, in a good room newly fitted up, hung round with Strange's prints. He was sitting at his ease reading Homer."[62] A few days later, Boswell and Erskine went to the opening night of the 1762-63 season at the Canongate Theatre, where the performance was *The Beggar's Opera* by John Gay, a work for which Boswell had a lifelong fondness. "Erskine and I", says Boswell, "sat snug in the pit. Digges played Macheath as well as ever. I glowed with fancy and was convinced that life is to be altogether despised."[63]

Boswell had by now resolved to leave for London the following Monday, 15 November. Much of his remaining time in Edinburgh was spent in getting his affairs in order and saying his farewells to friends and family. Of crucial importance were his financial arrangements, and these had been entrusted to his great-uncle, Basil Cochrane (1701-88), who was a Commissioner of Excise in Scotland (and later became a Commissioner of Customs). Boswell visited Commissioner Cochrane at the Excise Office on the morning of 11 November where he was told that Lord Auchinleck had agreed to pay off Boswell's debts and to allow him £200 a year. With this arrangement Boswell was perfectly content, and no wonder, for he was now to receive a generous allowance, roughly equivalent in today's terms to about £12,000 a year, with which to indulge himself, at least for a time, in his beloved London; and moreover he was to be freed of his debts and was thus to be able to set off with a clean slate and a clear conscience.

On the day set for his departure for London, Boswell rose elated with the thought of his journey. After a long and serious conversation with his parents he got into his chaise, and away he went.

> As I passed the Cross, the caddies and the chairmen bowed and seemed to say, 'GOD prosper long our noble Boswell.' I rattled down the High Street in high

elevation of spirits, bowed and smiled to acquaintances, and took up my partner at Boyd's Close... I made the chaise stop at the foot of the Canongate;... walked to the Abbey of Holyroodhouse, went round the Piazzas, bowed thrice: once to the Palace itself, once to the crown of Scotland above the gate in front, and once to the venerable old Chapel. I next stood in the court before the Palace, and bowed thrice to Arthur Seat, that lofty romantic mountain on which I have so often strayed in my days of youth, indulged meditation and felt the raptures of a soul filled with ideas of the magnificence of GOD and his creation. Having thus gratified my agreeable whim and superstitious humour, I felt a warm glow of satisfaction... We then pursued our journey.[64]

Boswell was never to see his mother again, and he was not to see Scotland again for three and a half years.

§VIII

After a not uneventful journey of four days (from 15-19 November 1762) in which the chaise was overturned and had one of its windows broken, resulting in Boswell and his companion having to endure cold and draughty conditions, the chaise finally reached London; whereupon, says Boswell, "I gave three huzzas, and we went briskly in."[65] A few days later Boswell obtained accommodation in Downing Street at the house of a Scotsman, Thomas Terrie, who was chamber-keeper to the Office for Trade and Plantations in Whitehall. Boswell was to stay at Terrie's house for over seven months.

A major change in London had occurred since Boswell's last visit. George II had died suddenly on 25 October 1760 and was succeeded by his grandson, George III, who was to remain on the throne for the rest of Boswell's life (and was to do so for a long time thereafter as well, for he did not die until 1820). George III's accession saw the rise of his favourite, John Stuart, third Earl of Bute, who became Prime Minister (as First Lord of the Treasury) in May 1762. Bute, a Scotsman, was much disliked by the English, not only for being a Scot but also for allegedly giving undue preferment to his countrymen. This animosity had the unfortunate effect of causing Scots in general to be unpopular in London, a fact which Boswell was soon to discover for himself when he attended a comic opera at Covent Garden:

> Just before the overture began to be played, two Highland officers came in. The mob in the upper gallery roared out, 'No Scots! No Scots! Out with them!', hissed and pelted them with apples. My heart warmed to my countrymen, my Scotch blood boiled with indignation. I jumped up on the benches, roared out, 'Damn you, you rascals!', hissed and was in the greatest rage. I am very sure at that time I should have been the most distinguished of heroes. I hated the English; I wished from my soul that the Union was broke and that we might give them another battle of Bannockburn. I went close to the officers and asked them of what regiment they were of. They told me Lord John Murray's, and that they were just come from Havana. 'And this', said they, 'is the thanks that we get—to be hissed when we come home. If it was French, what could they do worse?' 'But', said one, 'if I had a *grup o yin or twa o the tamd rascals I sud let them ken what they're about.*' The rudeness of the English vulgar is terrible. This indeed is the liberty which they have: the liberty of bullying and being abusive with their blackguard tongues.[66]

Boswell's reaction to this incident reveals his patriotism and strong sense of national identity; but the anti-English sentiments expressed in that passage are totally untypical of him and were no doubt merely the result of righteous indignation on being sorely provoked. Indeed, Boswell almost invariably held the highest regard for the English, notwithstanding the fact that he sometimes expressed strong views against the Union.*

On his arrival in London, Boswell's chief objective was to call on his countryman, the sixty-four-year-old Charles Douglas, third Duke of Queensberry (1698-1778), whose influence with the King and Bute he thought might help to secure him a commission in the Guards. The Duke received Boswell on 2 December and did so "with the greatest politeness",[67] but he told Boswell that although he would try to get him a commission he would find it very difficult to accomplish. After two weeks of anxious waiting Boswell received a disappointing letter in which Queensberry informed him that he was convinced that Boswell's aim of getting into the Guards was "a fruitless pursuit".[68]

Boswell records that on receipt of this letter he was "quite stupefied and enraged"[69] and he imagined that his father was at the bottom of it. However, he entertained hopes that a commission might be obtained through the influence of his friend Lady Northumberland, who was connected to the Marquis of Granby, the Commander-in-Chief of the British forces in Germany. Lady Northumberland promised to apply to the Marquis on his return to Britain, but nothing came of this. Some time later, Boswell's friend Lord Eglinton undertook to plead Boswell's case with Bute personally, but although he did as he promised his mission proved unsuccessful. Indeed, it seems that Boswell's ambition was doomed to failure, for he was not prepared to accept a commission in a marching regiment, which could have been easily obtained, but would only settle for a commission in the Guards, which could only be obtained by being purchased or by patronage.

Not long after coming to London, Boswell was surprised by the arrival of his friend Andrew Erskine together with Erskine's sisters, Lady Betty and Lady Anne. Boswell, however, was not altogether pleased to see them. "To tell the plain truth," he confessed in his journal, "I was vexed at their coming. For to see just the plain *hamely* Fife family hurt my grand ideas of London. Besides, I was now upon a plan of studying polite reserved behaviour, which is the only way to keep up dignity of character. And as I have a good share of pride, which I think is very proper and even noble, I am hurt with the taunts of ridicule and am unsatisfied if I do not feel myself something of a superior animal."[70] One evening, says Boswell, there was an altercation about standards of taste and the Erskine sisters "grew hot and showed a strong example of the Edinburgh women's roughness of manners, which disgusted me. They have all a too-great violence in dispute, and are sometimes put quite out of humour by it."[71] However, in spite of the banter and raillery of the Erskines, Boswell in due course came more to appreciate their company.

---

* For Boswell's inconsistent views with regard to the Union, see page 3. In 1774 he contemplated writing a work extolling the benefits which Scotland had derived from the Union (Journal, 28 October 1774); but he once described the Union as "shameful" (Journal, 6 October 1764), and even as late as 15 February 1790 we find him recording in his journal that in conversation that day he had "attacked the Union and said the nation was gone".

Another Scottish friend in town was George Dempster, who was attending Parliament as the member for the Perth Burghs. Much of Boswell's time in London was spent in Dempster's company, or in the company of Erskine, or with both of them together; and this in spite of his disapproval of their "Scotch tones and rough and roaring freedom of manners".[72] Another Scotsman with whom Boswell socialised during this stay in London was James Macpherson, the poet, who at the end of 1761 had published his *Fingal*, purportedly being translations by him of original ancient Gaelic poetry by Ossian, son of Fingal. This work had been received with enormous popular acclaim, but it ultimately transpired that the poems were largely compositions of Macpherson's own making.

While awaiting the outcome of his efforts to achieve his ambition of obtaining a commission in the Guards, Boswell had a brief but exciting affair with an actress by the name of Mrs Lewis, which, after an initial period of several weeks when he was kept by her in a state of considerable suspense, finally culminated in a night of unbridled passion at an inn, the room at which had been booked in the name of Mr and Mrs Digges, Boswell purporting to be the cousin of his actor friend and hero, West Digges, whose performances as Macheath at the Edinburgh Theatre he had much admired. "A more voluptuous night I never enjoyed", says Boswell. "Five times", he boasts, "was I fairly lost in supreme rapture."[73] However, the outcome of this torrid affair was the unfortunate reappearance—"too, too plain"—of "Signor Gonorrhoea".[74] Boswell consulted a surgeon friend who prescribed medication. Thereafter, Boswell laid by his hat and sword and confined himself to his room for five weeks, apart from a jaunt to the theatre with Dempster and Erskine. During this period he consoled himself by reading Hume's *History of England*, which, he wrote, "elevates my mind and excites noble feelings of every kind".[75] And he also had plenty of time to consider his future.

After several days of anxious deliberation he came close to accepting the inevitable: that his destiny was to become a Scottish advocate. However, the following day he had further thoughts on the matter and considered that if he embarked on a legal career he would spend his whole life "in a labyrinth of care" and that his mind would be "harassed with vexation", whereas if he were in the Guards he would be able to stay in London and lead a life of pleasure. "I would find it very irksome", he reflected, "to sit for hours hearing a heavy agent explain a heavy cause, and then to be obliged to remember and repeat distinctly the dull story, probably of some very trivial affair."[76]

One consolation at this difficult time was that Boswell's old friend Temple arrived in town. They had not seen each other for five years, apart from the day when Boswell visited Temple at Cambridge when returning to Edinburgh from London with his father in 1760. Boswell was initially concerned that the two of them might not get on so well as formerly, but he soon found that they were still very much soul-mates.

Another person who came to town was the Reverend Dr Hugh Blair (1718-1800), the well-known Scottish preacher, who, since 1758, had been minister at the New Church in St Giles' and, since 1762, Professor of Rhetoric and Belles Lettres at Edinburgh University. Boswell considered Blair to be "a very amiable man" and had a high regard for him. "He is learned and ingenious, and has a degree of simplicity about him that is extremely engaging."[77] One day, while they were walking the streets of London together, Boswell was diverted with a sudden notion. "I marched him down Southampton Street in the Strand, from the whimsical idea of passing under the windows of my first London lady of the town with an Edinburgh minister whom I had so often heard preach in the New Church."[78]

In April 1763 Boswell and Erskine published a book of their letters by the title of *Letters between the Honourable Andrew Erskine and James Boswell, Esq.* These letters, several of which contained poems, were written in a high-flown style, but were largely of unremarkable content apart from extravagant expressions such as Boswell's reference to "We great geniuses".[79] The work attracted some favourable reviews, but Temple had reservations, Blair was vexed and Eglinton was not impressed: "Upon my soul, Jamie," he said, "I would not take the direction of you upon any account, for as much as I like you, except you would agree to give over that damned publishing... By the Lord, it's a thing Dean Swift would not do—to publish a collection of letters upon nothing."[80] Boswell himself was later to say that, on re-reading the *Letters*, he could not bear his own except one or two. He felt that in general they contained "mere forced extravagance and no real humour". Erskine's contributions, however, he conceded "will please still, though not so greatly as once".[81]

During this stay in London, Boswell widened his social circle by becoming familiar with, or at least acquainted with, persons as varied as Oliver Goldsmith, David Garrick, John Wilkes, Charles Churchill and—in Boswell's eyes, the greatest prize of all—Samuel Johnson, whose acquaintance he made on that celebrated occasion on 16 May 1763 at Thomas Davies' bookshop. But Boswell was also on occasions to be found in the company of prostitutes, and it can thus justly be said that his social life during this period ranged from the height of intellectualism, on the one hand, to unrestrained sensuality on the other.

It was during this state of affairs that Boswell, on 8 June 1763, received from his father a letter dated 30 May 1763 which was to have a profound effect on his plans for the future. Lord Auchinleck was not at all amused by what he had learned of his son's antics, including the publication of the *Letters between the Honourable Andrew Erskine and James Boswell, Esq.* In his letter, Lord Auchinleck, after fulminating against these follies, came round to answering his son's request for paternal advice as to the best schemes to pursue.

> As for your manner of life, I never declared positively against any kind of life except that of dissipation and vice, and as a consequence against your going into the Guards... [When] you fell to the study of the law... I can say with truth, [you] showed as much genius for it when you applied as any ever I knew. Be assured that your following the study of the law, whether as a lawyer or as a gentleman, to fit you to be useful in the world, is what to me is most agreeable and what I verily think is the only thing will make you go through life agreeably; for as you well observe,

without some pursuit that is rational, one of your turn can never be happy. In the plan I propose you have for your objects being respected, being useful with your advice, getting into Parliament, and having the power of conferring places, instead of going about begging one. And to these I may add, you have the satisfaction of making your parents happy and adding more lustre to the family you have the honour to be come of. And if you were truly fixed on this plan, I would make no difficulty, when you were a little settled from your reelings, to let you go abroad for a while.[82]

In spite of the criticisms of Boswell's behaviour contained in this letter, he regarded the letter as being "very kind" and "most sensible and indulgent". "It made me think seriously," he records, "and I considered that I had now experienced how little I could depend on the favour of the great, which, when only founded on personal liking, is very slight. I considered too that I could have no prospect of rising in the army. That my being in that way contrary to my parents' advice was uphill work, and that I could not long be fond of it. I considered that by getting into the plan of civil life, I should have all things smooth and easy, be on a respectful footing and of consequence in my own country, and please my worthy father, who, though somewhat narrow in his notions, is one of the best men in the world."[83] However, says Boswell, "I... determined to insist on first going abroad, as I am resolved to maintain a grave and respectful character."[84]

Lord Auchinleck's response to Boswell's request to be allowed to go abroad was that if Boswell would pass the winter studying Civil Law at a university in Holland, and would undertake to become an advocate after getting back to Scotland, he would be permitted to spend some time travelling in Europe. Boswell duly promised to do as his father wished, but a letter which he sent to Temple on 15 July 1763 makes it clear that Boswell had still not fully reconciled himself to the idea of a career as a practising advocate, for he indicated that whilst he was prepared to have himself admitted as a member of the Faculty of Advocates, he would not necessarily endeavour to build up a practice; he might merely adopt the status of an advocate as a means of furthering his ambition of becoming a Member of Parliament.

Although Leyden was the Dutch university chosen by both Boswell's father and paternal grandfather when they studied law at Holland, it was decided in Boswell's case that he should study at Utrecht. This was on the recommendation of Sir David Dalrymple, who had studied there himself and imagined that Boswell would find it more congenial as it was reputed to have a livelier social life.

These important decisions as to Boswell's future having been made, he still had a few weeks in which to enjoy himself in London. One evening, he brought together his friends Samuel Johnson and George Dempster. However, Johnson and Dempster did not get on at all well together, for Dempster, who had republican sympathies and was much influenced by David Hume's religious scepticism, was naturally anathema to Johnson. And Dempster, for his part, like many Scotsmen of that time, had no great regard for Johnson.

At about this same time, Boswell discovered that an old flame from Edinburgh was in town—Peggy Doig, the mother of his young son, Charles, who had been born in November 1762 shortly after Boswell had set off for London, and had been named, at Boswell's request, after "the Royal Martyr" (that is, Charles I). When Boswell saw Peggy Doig he advised her "not to fall into such a scrape again"; but, he confessed to himself, "I really don't know how to talk on such a subject, when I consider that I led her into the scrape. However, it was not the first time, and she has been well taken care of."[85] Young Charles was not with her, for he had been placed with a foster-mother in Edinburgh, and Boswell was never to see him. However, John Johnston, at Boswell's behest, was watching over the progress of the boy and was sending reports, which were eagerly awaited by Boswell. Before departing for Holland, one of Boswell's main concerns was to ensure that during his absence abroad young Charles's needs would be adequately met. He therefore wrote to Johnston saying, "I leave you in the first place a strict charge to look diligently after my little boy. See him from time to time, and see that he have every thing that is proper for him."[86] Boswell went on to explain that he had made arrangements for funds to be made available on which Johnston could draw for this purpose.

To Boswell's delight, Samuel Johnson undertook to accompany him on his journey from London to Harwich on 5 August 1763. "This prodigious mark of his affection", says Boswell, "filled me with gratitude and vanity."[87]

§IX

Boswell was at first extremely unhappy in Utrecht. However, after a few weeks he settled down, took rooms in a large inn situated in the Cathedral Square and started to attend seriously to his studies. He devised a regular plan as follows: "Seven to eight, Ovid; eight to nine, French version; ten to eleven, Tacitus; three to four, French; four to five, Greek; six to seven, Civil Law; seven to eight, Scots [Law]; eight to ten, Voltaire. Then journal, letters, and other books."[88]

In a letter dated 20 January 1764 to John Johnston, Boswell brought his friend up to date with developments:

> I have found Utrecht to be a most excellent place. I have here excellent opportunity to study, and at the same time to see foreign company. There are a number of noble families who reside here in the winter. I have been received into their assemblies, where I pass two or three evenings a week improving in French and in politeness. At Christmas we had a month of vacation. I then went to The Hague, where I passed three weeks in the most brilliant gaiety. The style of living there is much in the manner of Paris. I found my relations there to be people of the first rank, and was treated by them with the utmost civility.* I had recommendations to a variety of people. I was presented to the Prince of Orange and the other princes there, to all the foreign ambassadors—in short, to everybody. I passed a couple of days at Leyden, where I supped twice with the young Prince of Strelitz, our Queen's brother, once at his own house, once at the house of Mr Gordon, Lord Aberdeen's brother; and now I am returned to this seat of the Dutch muses and have resumed my studious regularity with much satisfaction... [89]

But a few weeks later Boswell received a letter from Johnston containing tragic news: Boswell's young son, Charles, whom he had never seen, had died.

---

* Boswell was related through both his father and mother to the Dutch noble Sommelsdyck family.

This plunged Boswell into a fit of deep depression lasting several days. Never-theless, he managed to persevere with his studies and he even started to put into execution a plan to compile a Scots dictionary, but in the event he did not make much progress with the work.

Boswell's course of studies came to an end in June 1764 and it was arranged by Lord Auchinleck that Boswell would then start his Grand Tour by going to Berlin in the company of George Keith, tenth Earl Marischal of Scotland, one of Frederick the Great's most respected advisers. Prior to his departure, Boswell made a point of calling several times on the Dutch intellectual, Belle de Zuylen (otherwise known as "Zélide"), with whom he had struck up a serious, but platonic, relationship, and with whom he was to enter into a diverting correspondence containing, at one and the same time, mutual recriminations and hints of a possible marriage.

On 18 June 1764, Boswell, in a "glow of spirits",[90] set off on his journeys in a coach and four with Lord Marischal. Thus began what was to become Boswell's grand tour of Germany, Switzerland, Italy, Corsica and France. In Germany Boswell visited various principalities, where he was generally entertained and accommo-dated graciously at the courts. While staying in Berlin, he saw Frederick the Great and endeavoured, but failed, to be introduced to him. But Boswell was at least introduced to Andrew Mitchell (1708-1771), the British envoy to Prussia and close personal friend of Frederick. Mitchell (who was knighted in 1765) was a Scottish advocate (admitted on 24 November 1736) and was on friendly terms with Lord Auchinleck.

It was in Berlin that Boswell unexpectedly lost his chastity which he had somehow managed to maintain for a whole year. He describes the incident in his journal: "To punish my extravagant rodomontading [he had displayed exces-sive pride the previous evening], and to bring up my affairs and compose my spirit, I had sitten up all night. Grievous was it to the flesh till seven in the morning, when my blood took a fine flow. I was quite drunk with brisk spirits, and about eight, in came a woman with a basket of chocolate to sell. I toyed with her and found she was with child. Oho! a safe piece. Into my closet. 'Habs er ein Man?' 'Ja, in den Gards bei Potsdam.'* To bed directly. In a minute— over. I rose cool and astonished, half angry, half laughing. I sent her off. Bless me, have I now committed adultery?"[91]

On 24 November Boswell entered Switzerland where he was able to realise his ambition of meeting Rousseau and Voltaire, for after sending an imploring letter to Rousseau he succeeded in obtaining several interviews with the "wild philosopher" at his temporary retreat in the small mountain village of Môtiers, and, although calling unexpectedly, was received by Voltaire at his château at Ferney and subsequently also managed to get himself invited there. His con-versations with these eminent and highly influential men were wide-ranging and fascinating and are fortunately recorded in some detail in his journal of that period and in other writings.

After visiting Switzerland, Boswell moved on to Italy. Here he was determined

---

* "Have you a husband?" "Yes, in the Guards at Potsdam."

to act out the role of a gallant and to have at least one amorous intrigue. However, in the first city in which he stayed, Turin, he found that although the ladies were very beautiful he had no success, for he was "too modest a gallant to succeed with ladies who scorned the detours of delicacy, and who thought anyone a peasant or an imbecile who did not head straight for the main chance". To compensate himself for this loss, he resorted to "willing girls". And during his stay in Naples he was by his own admission "truly libertine" and "ran after girls without restraint". Similarly, in Rome, while on the one hand enjoying the study of antiquities, he "indulged in sensual relaxations". "I sallied forth", he wrote, "of an evening like an imperious lion." But, as he tells us, it was not long before he was "brought to a halt by an unpleasant occurrence which all libertines have to reckon with".[92]

While in Rome Boswell was delighted to renew his acquaintance with the notorious John Wilkes, who was temporarily residing there after having been declared an outlaw by Parliament on the ground that he had published the famous No. 45 of *The North Briton* containing what was construed as a seditious libel against the King. Another man who was potentially dangerous to know and with whom Boswell became friendly in Rome was Andrew Lumisden (1720-1801), the secretary to the Old Pretender, who resided at the Palazzo Muti-Papazzurri. Boswell was afraid that his contact with Lumisden—whom he described as a "true worthy Scotsman" and a "genteel man"[93]—could be construed as treasonable on account of his connection with the Jacobite cause, but as Lumisden never introduced him to the Pretender and they did not discuss politics together, their relationship was above reproach.

Another Scotsman with whom Boswell formed a close connection in Rome was John Stuart, Lord Mountstuart (1744-1814), eldest son of Lord Bute. The self-indulgent, rakish Mountstuart, who was travelling around Italy with two companions, persuaded Boswell to accompany him on the remainder of his tour. However, the party tended to be very quarrelsome and argumentative, and tempers rose on several occasions. Nevertheless, they made their way together to a number of places of interest, including Padua, Venice and Milan.* After parting from his temporary travelling companions in Milan, Boswell proceeded through Parma, Florence and Siena. It was in Siena that Boswell finally realised his ambition of having an amorous intrigue with an Italian lady. This lady was Girolama ("Moma") Piccolomini, who took the affair very seriously and over a number of years sent Boswell a series of touching letters in which, whilst upbraiding him for his neglect, she professed her eternal love for him.

Boswell left Siena at the end of September and after visiting Lucca and Pisa he arrived at Leghorn from whence he sailed to Corsica. The notion of travelling to

---

* While in Padua, Boswell wrote a letter to John Johnston of Grange noting certain differences in lifestyle between the Scots and the Italians. "My good Edinburgh old friend," he wrote, "you have no notion of the coffee houses of this country, in which you see crowds of ladies and gentlemen in full dress, some walking about, some set down to card tables, and some making love in convenient corners. Johnston, it will be long before you see such doings in the Forrest's Coffee House to which your letters are addressed" (letter dated 26 June 1765, reproduced in Walker, p. 170).

Corsica had first come to his mind as a consequence of one of his conversations with Rousseau at Môtiers. Rousseau had informed Boswell that the Corsicans, who were struggling by way of armed revolt for independence against the Republic of Genoa, had invited Rousseau to draft their constitution. The idea of the heroic struggle of the insurgents stirred Boswell's imagination and he resolved to go to Corsica to see what was happening there with his own eyes. Once on the island Boswell established a rapport with the rebel leader, General Pasquale de Paoli, and the two of them in due course formed a close connection. Boswell's adventures in Corsica were to bring him great fame—and, indeed, were to earn him the soubriquet of "Corsica Boswell"—for he was later to publish a detailed account of his experiences there (*An Account of Corsica, The Journal of a Tour to That Island; and Memoirs of Pascal Paoli*).

From Corsica Boswell sailed for Genoa, where he arrived on 30 November. Here a number of letters were waiting for him from his father, who, in the first of these letters, was complaining with evident impatience about the mounting expense of Boswell's travels and was demanding that he return home as soon as possible. In another of these letters, Lord Auchinleck reported that after a criminal trial he had been taken seriously ill with a total suppression of urine. This is believed to have been caused by an enlargement of his prostate gland, induced, it is thought, by his sitting listening to the evidence of the principal witness for the prosecution for nine hours without rising from his seat. Lord Auchinleck was to suffer from this painful and distressing ailment for the rest of his life.

In Paris, Boswell was due to receive a nasty shock, for on 27 January 1766, while browsing through a newspaper, he suddenly saw a notice that his mother had died. He was, he says, "quite stunned".[94] Nevertheless, later that same day we find him attending a brothel "as in fever". The next day he received a letter from his father, written by Boswell's brother David, confirming the tragic news. "[I] was quite stupefied", records Boswell, "[and] wept in bursts".[95]

While Boswell was in Paris, he heard that Rousseau's mistress, Thérèse Le Vasseur, had arrived in town on her way to join Rousseau, who was staying in England at the invitation of David Hume. She made it clear that she would be grateful if Boswell would accompany her to London, which he duly offered to do, and they set off together on 30 January. During the journey, Boswell, notwithstanding his hitherto high regard for the "wild philosopher", saw fit to have an amorous affair with the forty-five-year-old Thérèse.

The day after arriving in London, Boswell rushed to see Samuel Johnson, who received him "with open arms"[96] and Boswell knelt down and asked for his blessing. Another person on whom Boswell called was the Earl of Eglinton. "He talked of your father," says Boswell, "and bid you *affect* gravity. You told him you now *was* grave."[97] Boswell also spent a few days in the company of his old friend Temple, who happened to be in London at the time; and he called on George Dempster, who, writes Boswell, "had a real ministerial look. Our conversation was not at all so free as formerly, and I was not ill pleased at this."[98] On 17 February, Lord Eglinton took Boswell to Court to be presented to the King, whose only utterance addressed to Boswell was, "Lately come over?" The occasion was not overawing, and Boswell was "quite easy and not a bit struck, but liked it".[99]

Boswell was anxious while in London to have an audience with William Pitt (who, although not a member of the government at that time, was the most influential politician outside the government) to apprise him of what he had learned of the circumstances in Corsica in the hope of persuading Pitt to lend his support to General de Paoli's cause. Boswell gained an audience on 22 February, but the meeting was largely unproductive, for, as Pitt explained, he was a Privy Councillor and had taken an oath to hear nothing from any foreign power that might concern Great Britain without declaring it to the King and Council.

It was now high time, considering his father's entreaties, for Boswell to return home and so he duly set off a few days later. He arrived in Edinburgh on or about 7 March; here, in addition to consoling his father, he no doubt rushed excitedly to see John Johnston to give him all his news. Boswell must also be assumed to have called on Sir David Dalrymple, with whom he had corresponded regularly while abroad and who had just been elevated to the bench as a Lord of Session, taking the title of Lord Hailes. It is likely that Boswell also visited his old mentor, Lord Kames; if so, one wonders to what extent Boswell displayed that acquisition of *gravitas* and the abandonment of his former "extravagant love of ridicule" which in his last letter to Kames he had indicated would be in evidence.[100]

After a few days, Boswell and his father travelled to Auchinleck, where Boswell was to begin the serious business of studying Scots law under his father's guidance in preparation for his examination for admittance to the Faculty of Advocates. At this time, Lord Auchinleck was still in vigorous health in spite of his prostate problems and he continued to spend as much time as possible during court vacations at Auchinleck. Here his chief pleasure was now the planting of forest trees on his estate, and one of his favourite pastimes was personally to prune the trees that he himself had planted.

Inevitably, after the excitements of his foreign travels Boswell found the close confinement and strict attention to studies to be somewhat irksome at first. However, his spirits rose after his cousin, Claud Boswell of Balmuto (1742-1824), also came to study law under Lord Auchinleck. Claud was to have a steady and respectable career at the bar, eventually being elevated to the bench as a Lord of Session in 1799 with the judicial title of Lord Balmuto. One circumstance, however, was disturbing Boswell's peace of mind, namely, his sudden, but undeclared, infatuation for Euphemia Bruce, the eldest daughter of James Bruce, the gardener (and later overseer) at the estate.

On or about 10 May, Boswell paid another visit to Moffat, the scene of his youthful convalescences. His purpose in going there, he says, was "to wash off a few scurvy spots which the warmer climates of Europe had brought out on my skin".[101] After only a week there he was able to inform Temple that "my love for the handsome chambermaid is already like a dream that is past".[102] The reason for this, as he goes on to explain, was not mere absence; for what had happened was that soon after arriving in Moffat he had started an amorous liaison with a Mrs Dodds, a Scottish lady, who, according to Boswell, had been deserted by her husband.

Boswell returned to Edinburgh in the middle of June to make final preparations for his examination in Scots law, which was to take place on 11 July. Mrs Dodds followed him there and obtained lodgings so that they could continue their relationship. However, as it was not possible to carry on their intrigue at these lodgings, Boswell had to look for other premises suitable for this purpose, and such accommodation was found in the house of "a sober widow".[103] Boswell, meanwhile, continued to live at his father's house, which was somewhat stressful for Boswell as his father was low in spirits as a result of losing his wife. Moreover, as Boswell observed in a letter to Temple: "His character is such that he must have his son in a great degree of subjection to him."[104]

The examination in Scots law duly proceeded on 11 July and Boswell was declared to have passed. He then had to submit a printed thesis, in Latin, containing a dissertation on an aspect of the Civil Law, after which he was required to undergo a public examination on the thesis. The subject which Boswell chose was "Legacies of Household Furniture". The thesis consisted of seven pages and was printed at Boswell's expense. The public examination took place on 26 July and Boswell was found sufficiently qualified.

Boswell, having thus "passed advocate", was now ready to be formally admitted as an advocate and to commence his career at the bar.

§X

When Boswell passed advocate, the Lord President of the Court of Session was Robert Dundas of Arniston, who was sometimes referred to as "the second Lord President Dundas" to distinguish him from his father, who bore the same name and was a former Lord President. The Lord Justice-Clerk was Thomas Miller of Barskimming, who had only very recently been elevated to the bench. The other judges, in order of seniority on the bench, were Lords Milton, Strichen, Kames, Auchinleck, Coalston, Alemoor, Elliock, Barjarg (later Lord Alva), Stonefield, Pitfour, Gardenstone, Kennet, and Hailes. The seventy-four-year-old Lord Milton, however, was to die only a few months later and was replaced by the eccentric fifty-two-year-old James Burnett, who took his seat on 12 February 1767 with the judicial title of Lord Monboddo. Of these judges, the ones to whom there were to be the most frequent references in Boswell's Edinburgh journals were (apart from Lord Auchinleck, who, naturally enough, appears the most regularly) the Lord President, the Lord Justice-Clerk, Lord Kames, Lord Monboddo, Lord Hailes and Lord Gardenstone. Further details of these judges may be found in the Appendix, together with an account of some of the leading advocates at the bar at the time when Boswell was admitted advocate, namely, Alexander Lockhart, James Montgomery, Robert Macqueen, David Rae, John Maclaurin, Ilay Campbell, Andrew Crosbie, Alexander Murray and Henry Dundas. In those days the bar consisted of over 200 members.

Boswell "put on the Gown"[105] and commenced practice as an advocate on 29 July 1766 following an admission ceremony that day. At the ceremony, in conformity with the Faculty of Advocates' regulations, he would have delivered a speech before the assembled Lords on a text of the Civil Law assigned to him beforehand and then taken the usual oaths of allegiance and fidelity. We are to imagine him later that day, like many other advocates, pacing up and down the busy Parliament Hall, dressed in black gown and white wig, eagerly hoping for instructions from any solicitors in need of the services of counsel. He did not have to wait long, for that very day he received instructions from William Wilson, Writer to the Signet (or "W.S." for short)*, to draft a memorial for a hosiery manufacturing company in Glasgow which alleged that one of its stocking frames in the possession of one of the company's weavers had been wrongly seized by the weaver's former landlord on the strength of a claim for outstanding house rent.[106] The purpose of memorials was to enable parties to state what they saw as being the relevant facts and to give a summary of their legal submissions. Boswell's presentation of his legal submissions was closely argued and ran to over eight pages of manuscript. His main arguments contained flashes of genuine insight and also a certain degree of humour. He would later appear at several hearings in this case, but it is not known what the final outcome was, although it may well be that the parties came to some agreement between themselves whereby the matter was settled amicably. Boswell's fee for drafting the memorial in this case was one guinea, which was a standard fee charged by him for this kind of work. His fees were normally either one or two, but occasionally three, guineas; and in a few exceptional cases his fees were higher.

We are fortunately able to follow the first few years of Boswell's practice at the bar with some ease in that he kept during the years 1766 to 1772 a note of each case in which he was involved (including details of the nature of the work carried out and the fee paid) in a volume which he called his "Consultation Book". We therefore know that the next case in which Boswell was involved was an action in which he was instructed by John Chalmer, W.S., to appear at a hearing before Lord Auchinleck on 30 July. As this was only one day after Boswell had commenced practice it seems almost certain that this was his first appearance in court, and it was no doubt considered appropriate that his début should be before his father. It is likely that the hearing took the form of a legal debate and that Lord Auchinleck sat at the high bench at the south end of the hall. We are therefore to imagine Boswell climbing, perhaps with some trepidation, the steps up to the Fore-Bar from which he would be expected to address his father on the intricacies of the case.

It is often remarked, with truth, that Boswell was frequently instructed in cases which came before his father and that, in fact, he appeared before his father on more occasions than before any other judge. The implication seems

---

* Writers to the Signet were (and still are) solicitors admitted to membership of the ancient legal society known as The Society of Writers to the Signet.

to be that Boswell was not necessarily highly regarded as an advocate and that a large part of his business may simply have arisen as a consequence of canny solicitors taking the view that in actions coming before Lord Auchinleck an outcome favourable to their clients might be more likely if the counsel representing them was Lord Auchinleck's son. However, while there was no doubt an element of opportunism on the part of certain solicitors, who were, after all, simply endeavouring to do the best for their clients, the fact is that Boswell appeared in front of many judges and was evidently highly thought of by at least some of them. For example, Lord Monboddo was to have sufficient faith in Boswell as to entrust Boswell (along with other counsel) to represent him before the Inner House in his case against the unfortunate farrier in whose custody Monboddo's horse had died.*

During these early days at the bar, it must be assumed that after labouring hard all day on weighty legal matters, Boswell would have been eager to sally forth whenever possible to his favourite nocturnal haunts. He was, for example, no doubt regularly to be seen with his friends John Johnston and Andrew Erskine at Thom's Tavern, which had moved from the West Bow to new premises down Fishmarket Close, off the south side of the High Street near the site of the old Mercat Cross. These premises were all too conveniently situated for Boswell, his father's house being just round the corner. It must also be the case that Boswell frequented other popular establishments, such as Fortune's Tavern in what came to be called Old Stamp Office Close, off the north side of the High Street opposite the City Guard-house. Another popular rendezvous in those days was the "Star and Garter" in Writers' Court, off the north side of the High Street opposite the Luckenbooths, which was kept by John Clerihue and was hence often referred to as "Clerihue's". In addition to attending such places of public amusement, Boswell also had entertainment of a more private kind, namely, the desirable company of his mistress, Mrs Dodds. Boswell describes her in a letter to Temple as being kind and generous. On the other hand, he says she is "ill-bred", "quite a rompish girl" and lacking in refinement. "But", he adds significantly, "she is very handsome, very lively, and admirably formed for amorous dalliance."[107] Furthermore, he says in a later letter, "she is like a girl of eighteen" and "has the finest black hair [and] is paradisial in bed".[108] Whatever nocturnal revelry Boswell indulged in, however, he had to be up bright and early the following morning to pursue his career at the bar. The Court of Session sat every week during session time from Tuesday to Saturday, and each day started at nine o'clock.

In a letter which Boswell sent to Temple after he had been at the bar for several months, Boswell gave a brief account of his daily existence as an advocate and the court procedures which he commonly encountered:

> I am at present leading the strangest life. You know one half of the business before the Court of Session is carried on by writing. In the first instance, a cause is pleaded before the Lord Ordinary, that is to say one of the fifteen judges who

---

* See Appendix, pp. 557-8.

sits in his turn for a week in the Outer House. But no sooner does he give judgment than we give him in representations and answers and replies and duplies and triplies, and he will sometimes order memorials to give him a full view of the cause. Then we reclaim to the Inner House by petition, and there again we give in variety of printed papers, from which the Lords determine the cause. For it is only in causes of great consequence that the Court orders a hearing in presence. This method of procedure is admirable, for it gives the judges a complete state of every question, and by binding up the session papers a man may lay up a treasure of law reasoning and a collection of extraordinary facts.[109]

After he had been at the bar for a few days, Boswell became involved in the case of *Sir Alexander Dick v The Earl of Abercorn*,[110] in which he was instructed on behalf of the pursuer, who was to become (if he was not so already) a close friend of Boswell's. Sir Alexander Dick (1703-1785) was a retired physician who resided at the mansion of Prestonfield, then near (but not in) Edinburgh, to the south of Arthur's Seat. In 1756 he was elected president of the Royal College of Physicians in Edinburgh, which office he held until he relinquished it in 1763. Thereafter he continued to promote the interests of the college, and for many years he was a manager of the Royal Infirmary of Edinburgh, where he helped forward the foundation of a medical school. He was renowned for "a kind and amiable character",[111] and his friendship was greatly appreciated by Boswell, who was to spend much time as a guest at Prestonfield.

The case in which Boswell acted for Sir Alexander was concerned with a dispute as to the ownership of the soil of Duddingston Loch adjacent to Sir Alexander's land at Prestonfield. Sir Alexander had title to the loch, while the defender, the Earl of Abercorn, owned the land at Duddingston and had the right of watering his cattle at the loch. The Earl of Abercorn maintained that he had title to the soil of the loch and that Sir Alexander's right was solely in respect of the water. Consequently, Sir Alexander commenced proceedings for declarator that he had "the sole property of the loch and of the whole ground, soil, and bounds thereof". In a memorial which Boswell was to draft for Sir Alexander in February 1767, Boswell explained the background to the matter and the nature of the arguments advanced for each party. The memorial was written in a characteristically robust manner and is a good example of Boswell's colourful style of advocacy, although it has to be said that some of his contentions were clearly somewhat fanciful and may have been inserted simply for the amusement of the judge. The outcome of Boswell's memorial (and that lodged on behalf of the Earl of Abercorn) was that Lord Gardenstone pronounced an interlocutor finding in favour of Sir Alexander.

Boswell had been at the bar for less than two weeks when the court, on 9 August 1766, rose for the usual three-month autumn vacation, during which period Boswell spent at least part of the time at Auchinleck. From here he attended the Western and Southern Circuits of the Court of Justiciary in the hope of picking up some criminal work with a view to making a name for himself. He met with success, for on 13 September, at Glasgow, he obtained his first criminal client. This was John Reid, who was accused of being by "habit and repute" a common thief and of having stolen one hundred and twenty sheep from a farm in

Peeblesshire. This offence, if proved, was a capital offence. Reid did not deny that the sheep were stolen, but maintained that they constituted a flock of sheep which he had been employed to drive to Glasgow to be sold. Boswell, together with another advocate, persuaded the court to postpone the trial to allow further time for the appointment of an agent and the preparation of the defence. The case was then transferred to Edinburgh, away from what the defence suspected was a prejudiced jury in Glasgow. At Ayr, Boswell represented a James Haddow, who was convicted, after trial on 11 October, on two charges of housebreaking and was sentenced to be hanged, but subsequently obtained a reprieve.[112]

The winter term of the Court of Session commenced on 12 November and Boswell soon started to receive further instructions, including a case on behalf of the one-year-old Countess of Sutherland. During the last week of November he appeared at hearings in three separate cases before his father. And on or about 4 December 1766 Boswell made his first appearance before the whole court in the Inner House. This was the case of *Hugh Cairncross v William Heatly*, which was referred to by Boswell in a letter to Sir Alexander Dick as "the great Cause of Cairncross". "I am", he explained, "for the Descendant of an ancient family who after an obscurity of several generations lays claim to the estate of his Forefathers. You know my old feudal soul and how much a Cause of this kind must interest me."[113] Sir Alexander later reported to Boswell that many of Boswell's brethren dining at Clerihue's had spoken with full approval of Boswell's long speech before the Lords. That same month, in addition to appearing at four separate hearings before his father, he appeared at a hearing before Lord Barjarg, three hearings before Lord Elliock (in one of which he represented his friend and publisher, Alexander Donaldson,[114] and in another of which he represented the Earl of Eglinton[115]), and a hearing before Lord Coalston, followed by the criminal trial of John Reid.

John Reid's trial[116] took place on 15 December before the Court of Justiciary sitting in the New Tolbooth. An additional counsel had been brought in to represent Reid, namely, Andrew Crosbie, who had a high reputation in cases of this nature. The defence led no witnesses, but Boswell made a speech to the jury arguing that the evidence against his client was purely circumstantial. The verdict was one of "not proven", which result met with the severe disapproval of the judges (including the Lord Justice-Clerk, Thomas Miller of Barskimming) who each stated that the verdict was contrary to clear evidence.

Boswell's style in his written pleadings was greatly more entertaining and readable than that of many of his colleagues. He consistently made effective use of colourful and emotive language in order to get his point across and there were frequent flashes of diverting wit to prevent the reader from tiring too quickly and losing interest in what was no doubt all too often a dry and trying case. Consequently, Boswell's written pleadings, compared with the normal run, were a relative pleasure to read and were perhaps almost as effective as oral pleadings. It would be wrong, however, to suggest that Boswell ever attained to any great eminence as a remarkably profound lawyer; his merit lay more in his presentational ability and his skilful use of the art of persuasion.

It seems that the last appearance which Boswell made in a case in 1766 was in a criminal trial before the Court of Justiciary on 22 December in which he and Andrew Crosbie represented the accused, Joseph Taylor, who was charged with stealing three mares near Carlisle. Boswell argued that this offence, if committed at all, had occurred in England and was therefore outwith the court's jurisdiction. The court ordered that written submissions be lodged and there was a delay of about three months, but the outcome was that the court held that the indictment was relevant, whereupon Taylor pleaded to be deported to the plantations and the court acceded to his request.[117]

Boswell's practice was to continue much as it started, but in time he was also to take on ecclesiastical cases before the General Assembly of the Church of Scotland, and was additionally to be instructed in a number of Scottish appeals before the House of Lords.

Early in 1767, when Boswell had only been at the bar for a few months, he was already feeling that he was making a success of his career. Writing to Temple on 1 February 1767 he declared, "I am now advancing fast in the law. I am coming into great employment. I have this winter made sixty-four guineas, which is a considerable sum for a young man. I expect that this first year I shall clear, in all, above a hundred pieces."[118] In a later letter to Temple, Boswell wrote: "I am surprised at myself. I already speak with so much ease and boldness, and have already the language of the bar so much at command. I have now cleared eighty guineas. I am kept very throng. My clerk comes to me every morning at six, and I have dictated to him forty folio pages in one day. It is impossible to give you an idea of my present life... I am doing nobly. But I have not leisure for learning. I can hardly even answer the letters of my friends... It is very odd that I can labour so hard at law when I am so indolent in other things."[119]

A major action going through the courts when Boswell commenced practice, but in which he did not play any active part as counsel, although he took a very great interest in it, was the *cause célèbre* of eighteenth-century Scottish legal history, that of *The Duke of Hamilton v Archibald Douglas*, commonly known simply as the Douglas Cause. The background to this action was that the young Archibald Douglas had been served heir to the huge estates of the deceased Duke of Douglas on the basis of being his nephew. This prompted the young Duke of Hamilton to start an action to have the service set aside, contending that the boy calling himself Archibald Douglas, who was born in Paris, was not related to the Duke of Douglas but was actually a suppositious child. The parties employed the greatest counsel at the bar and went to immense lengths collecting evidence in France. Boswell became a fervent supporter of Douglas and was to become an active campaigner on his behalf

Although Boswell did not keep a journal during the first few months of his practice at the bar, his busy and colourful life as an advocate is vividly described in the journals which he kept, off and on, from January 1767 to January 1786, and it is to those journals that the reader is now invited to turn.

§NOTES

1 Lord Macaulay, *Samuel Johnson*, in *The Works of Lord Macaulay*, Vol. I, p. 278.

2 Burton, *Life and Correspondence of David Hume*, Vol. II, p. 307.

3 Letter to Temple dated 20 July 1784, reproduced in *Applause*, pp. 261-2, at p. 261.

4 Journal, 12 January 1786.

5 Journal, 26 December 1765.

6 Journal, 15 August 1773.

7 Quoted in Pottle, p. 12.

8 By an Act of the Town Council dated 10 September 1740 regulating the use of hackney coaches, the Council ordered that "all the Coaches, while they are attending for a Fare, shall stand below the lower End of *Miln's* Squair, with their Horses unbridled".

9 By an Act of the Town Council dated 1 March 1738 regulating the use of "Hackney-Chairs", the Council ordered that "all Chairs attending for a Fare, shall stand on the South-side of the Street, from the lower End of the Guard to *Blackfriar* Wynd, and no where else on the High-Streets".

10 See James H Jamieson, "The Sedan Chair in Edinburgh", *B.O.E.C.*, Vol. 9, p. 183.

11 Sir Walter Scott, *The Heart of Midlothian*, p. 60.

12 Chambers, p. 193.

13 *Ibid.*, pp. 95-6.

14 Grant, Vol. I, p. 309.

15 Sir Walter Scott, *The Heart of Midlothian*, p. 27.

16 *Ibid.*, p.28.

17 Graham, *The Social Life of Scotland in the Eighteenth Century*, pp. 83-4.

18 Acts of the Town Council dated 19 December 1701, 6 January 1714 and 14 August 1745.

19 See James H Jamieson, "Social Assemblies of the Eighteenth Century", *B.O.E.C.*, Vol. 19, pp. 45-6.

20 10 Geo. 2, c. 28.

21 Alexander Young, Writer to the Signet, *Memoir of Robert McQueen of Braxfield*, Edinburgh University Library, Laing MSS Div. Ii 113, quoted in Osborne, *Braxfield the Hanging Judge?*, p. 68.

22 *Jeffrey*, Vol. I, pp. 179-183.

23 From the *Sketch of My Life* prepared by Boswell for Rousseau, reproduced in Pottle, pp. 1-6.

24 N.A.S. JC7/38.

25 From the *Sketch of My Life* (*supra*) and Pottle, p. 18, quoting from a discarded portion of the *Sketch*.

26 Pottle, p. 19.

27 From French Theme 12-14 October 1763, reproduced in *Holland*, p. 44.

28 Ramsay, p. 163.

29 *Ibid.*, p. 164.

30 Pottle, p. 28, quoting from a discarded part of the *Sketch of My Life* (*supra*).

31 From Boswell's *Inviolable Plan*, reproduced in *Holland*, pp. 375-8, at p. 376.

32 Journal, 22 December 1762.

33 Letter from Boswell to John Johnston of Grange dated 15 February 1763, reproduced in Walker, pp. 45-6. In the passage quoted the spelling and punctuation have been corrected where necessary.

34 From the *Sketch of My Life* (*supra*).

35 Pottle, p. 35.

36 Reproduced in Tinker, Vol. I, pp 1-4.

37 Journal, 14 November 1764.

38 Ramsay, p. 394.

39 *Ibid.*, pp. 395 and 397.

40 Letter from Boswell to Temple dated 16 December 1758, reproduced in Tinker, Vol. I, pp. 4-7.

41 Letter from Boswell to John Johnston of Grange dated 11 January 1760, reproduced in Walker, pp. 6-9.

42 This account is based on Pottle, pp. 45-6, 569-574.

43 Journal, 2 April 1775.

44 Pottle, p. 47.

45 *Life*, Vol. I, p. 276 (28 July 1763).

46 Journal, 13 March 1763.

47 *Memoirs of James Boswell, Esq.*, reproduced in Pottle, *The Literary Career of James Boswell*, pp. xxix-xliv, at p. xxxi.

48 From the *Sketch of My Life* (*supra*).

49 Journal, 18 January 1763.

50 Letter from Boswell to Temple dated 1 May 1761, reproduced in Tinker, Vol. I, pp. 7-8. The spelling has been corrected where necessary.

51 From *ibid*.

52 From French Theme 12-14 October 1763, reproduced in *Holland*, pp. 44-5.

53 Journal, 30 October 1762.

54 Journal, 3 November 1762.

55 *The Scots Magazine*, 23, 1761, pp. 389-90.

56 Journal, 28 November 1762.

57 Ramsay, pp. 182-3.

58 Boswell's Journal Notes, 3 January and 14 February 1762, quoted in Pottle, pp. 79, 479.

59 Letter from Boswell to Andrew Erskine dated 9 May 1762, quoted in Pottle, p. 83.

60 Letter from Boswell to John Johnston of Grange dated 17 August 1762, reproduced in Walker, pp. 13-14.

61 Pottle, p. 92.

62 Journal, 4 November 1762.

63 Journal, 10 November 1762.

64 Journal, 15 November 1762.

65 Journal, 19 November 1762.

66 Journal, 8 December 1762.

67 Journal, 2 December 1762.

68 *London*, p. 107, n. 6.

69 Journal, 26 December 1762.

70 Journal, 1 December 1762.

71 Journal, 11 December 1762.

72 Journal, 3 June 1763.

73 Journal, 12 January 1763.

74 Journal, 19 January 1763.

75 Journal, 29 January 1763.

76 Journal, 25 February 1763.

77 Journal, 6 April 1763.

78 Journal, 9 April 1763.

79 *Letters between the Honourable Andrew Erskine and James Boswell, Esq.*, p. 18.

80 *London*, p. 241, n. 1.

81 Journal, 17 February 1766.

82 Letter from Lord Auchinleck to Boswell dated 30 May 1763, reproduced in *London*, pp. 337-342.

83 Journal, 8 June 1763.

84 Journal, 9 June 1763.

85 Journal, 28 July 1763.

86 Letter from Boswell to John Johnston of Grange dated 4 August 1763, reproduced in Walker, p. 106.

87 Journal, 30 July 1763.

88 Journal, 5 October 1763.

89 Letter from Boswell to John Johnston of Grange dated 20 January 1764, reproduced in *Holland*, pp. 117-121, at p. 118.

90 Journal, 18 June 1764.

91 Journal, 11 September 1764.

92 Letter from Boswell to Rousseau dated 3 October 1765, reproduced in *Grand Tour II*, pp. 3-21, at pp. 3-7.

93 *Grand Tour II*, p. 64, n. 2.

94 Journal, 27 January 1766.

95 Journal, 28 January 1766.

96 Journal, 13 February 1766.

97 Journal, 15 February 1766.

98 Journal, 17 February 1766.

99 Journal, 18 February 1766.

100 Journal, 27 September 1764.

101 Letter from Boswell to Temple dated 17 May 1766, reproduced in *Wife*, pp. 6-12, at p. 9.

102 *Ibid*., at p. 6.

103 Letter from Boswell to Temple dated 1 February 1767, reproduced in *Wife*, pp. 22-26, at p. 26.

104 *Ibid*., at p. 24.

105 From the title page of Boswell's Consultation Book.

106 *James Johnston & Company v Quintin Hamilton and John McAulay*, N.A.S. CS 228/I&J/1/83.

107 Letter from Boswell to Temple dated 4 March 1767, reproduced in *Wife*, pp. 35-8, at p. 36.

108 Letter from Boswell to Temple dated 8 March 1767, reproduced in *Wife*, pp. 38-41, at p. 41.

109 Letter from Boswell to Temple dated 28 February 1767, reproduced in *Wife*, p. 34.

110 N.A.S. CS 226/2729; reported in *Faculty Decisions*, Vol. V, 1769-1772, p. 1.

111 Chambers's *Scottish Biographical Dictionary*.

112 The information contained in this paragraph is based on Pottle, pp. 299-300.

113 Letter from Boswell to Sir Alexander Dick dated 9 December 1766, reproduced in Cole (ed.), *The General Correspondence of James Boswell 1766-1769*, Vol. I, p. 93.

114 *Alexander Donaldson v John Reid*, N.A.S. CS 238/D2/15.

115 *Alexander Lockhart v The Earl of Eglinton*, N.A.S. CS 235/L/2/10; reported in *Faculty Decisions*, Vol. IV, 1765-69, p. 295.

116 N.A.S. JC3/34, p. 489 ff.

117 The information contained in this paragraph is based on Pottle, p. 310.

118 Letter from Boswell to Temple dated 1 February 1767, reproduced in *Wife*, p. 26.

119 Letter from Boswell to Temple dated 4 March 1767, reproduced in *Wife*, p. 35.

1767

Boswell has been spending some time as a guest of Lord President Dundas[1] at the Lord President's estate at Arniston, near Temple, Midlothian, and is about to return to Edinburgh, where he is awaited by Mrs Dodds[2] (who is referred to by Boswell as "Miss ——" or "Miss", except in the entry for 3 March 1767, where she is named).

MONDAY 12 JANUARY. Breakfasted early. President walked you about in room, and told you with fire how Justiciary Court[3] brought itself down sending one judge by himself to circuit[4] [and by] not sending impertinent counsel to prison. Complained of putting improper people into that office; talked of political connections with masterly force. You came all in [to town] in coach. Miss Dundas, fine girl. Liked her very well; was *retenu*[5] for fear of appearing lover. Quite proper; was really sorry to think of her and her sister, who might perhaps become maiden aunts.[6] Safe journey through monstrous deep snow to town. Sorry to part. Afternoon, Miss —— ; very well.

The following day, at four o'clock in the afternoon, Boswell attended his first meeting of the Faculty of Advocates, which was something he had "long wished to see". He found his preconceived ideas of Faculty meetings to be "just" and he was pleased to have his "fancy realised". The Faculty afterwards adjourned to Clerihue's tavern,[7] where they had an "excellent entertainment" with "mirth and jollity" and Boswell "drank freely".[8] At the meeting, Boswell was elected one of the fifteen "Publick Examinators",[9] that is, one of the body of examiners appointed annually to try applicants to the Faculty at that stage of the examination process at which each candidate was required to defend publicly his Latin thesis.[10]

In the evening, Boswell called on Mrs Dodds:

TUESDAY 13 JANUARY. Before nine, Miss —— , quite fond. She reproved you for drinking so much. Home,[11] and had clerk, and corrected Caithness memorial till twelve.[12]

1 For Lord President Dundas, see Introduction, p. 36, and Appendix, p. 554.
2 For Mrs Dodds, see Introduction, pp. 36 and 38.
3 The High Court of Justiciary (as to which, see Introduction, pp. 11-12).
4 Prior to 1746 two judges were required for each circuit, but the Heritable Jurisdictions (Scotland) Act 1746 (20 Geo. 2, c. 43) provided that it was competent for one judge to dispatch the business of a circuit court in the necessary absence of a colleague.
5 Reserved; restrained. As a young man, Boswell often exhorted himself to be *retenu* with a view to appearing to possess a degree of gravity.
6 "Miss Dundas" and her sister were two of the four daughters of Lord President Dundas by his first wife. At this time, the eldest unmarried daughter was Dundas's second daughter, Henrietta (born in or about 1749). She eventually found a husband, but not until 1777. Dundas's third daughter, Margaret, married in 1773.
7 The "Star and Garter" (as to which, see Introduction, p. 38).
8 *Private Papers*, Vol. 7, p. 101.
9 Stewart, p. 170.
10 For that stage of the examination process, see Introduction, p. 36.
11 "Blair's Land" in Parliament Close. For Blair's Land, see Introduction, pp. 3 and 12.
12 For memorials, see Introduction, p. 37.   This memorial was in connection with the case of *Margaret, Countess of Caithness v The Countess Fife and Earl Fife and another*, in which Boswell was instructed on behalf of Margaret, Countess of Caithness (SPSL, 137:11). The case was concerned with "a dispute between mother on one hand and daughter and son-in-law on the other regarding aliment [maintenance] from the father's estate" (Ballantyne, 67 01 16).

THURSDAY 15 JANUARY. Evening, called Miss —— ; gentleman with her. Came away jealous. Erskine[13] came; very happy together.

FRIDAY 16 JANUARY. At six, after torment with jealousy, went to Miss. She was gay. She declared [that she had] no fear [of you]. You was torn with passion. You was quite serious; said you was much obliged to her. She must not think you ungrateful; but really you could not be miserable together, therefore you'd try to cease. You'd be her friend, &c., &c. But you again grew fond. Note came; 'twas open. Said she: "We can understand one another, though [our letters are] open", and laughed. You said nothing, but like Spaniard mused on the fire. Murmuring between you. She [said she] would not make you uneasy. YOU. "Then show me card." She did so freely. 'Twas from a poor woman you had got into Infirmary.[14] Bless me! She just tried my jealousy. You asked pardon for weakness. She smiled, as well she might.

On 27 January Boswell wrote to John Johnston of Grange[15] *as follows: "I am to give a very curious pleading this morning. A woman whose husband is absent in England has been defamed as a whore by a tide-waiter [customs officer]. I am for her in a process of defamation. Pray come. I shall speak a little after ten. I have sent for Erskine."* [16]

WEDNESDAY 4 FEBRUARY. Was hurt to find soul ravaged by passion; determined to be firm, [as you] saw it hurt ideas of family. Had been looking at houses for Miss —— ; at last fell on one in Borthwick's Close,[17] quite neat and light.

THURSDAY 5 FEBRUARY. In morning went to Mrs Leith and took house. Mind at ease; determined to be generous and let Miss —— do as she pleased. Very busy all day. Tea, Lord Hailes.[18] [Was] going to write noble letter to Miss ——; sent for by her; went. She tender as ever, quite affectionate. Saw all was easy. You felt too much like married man, but 'twas gay. Then at nine, Clerihue's and Mr William Wilson[19] and Bryce, [a] client. Saw [that

---

13 Andrew Erskine (as to whom, see Introduction, pp. 21-2, 25 and 27-9).
14 The Royal Infirmary (for which, see Introduction, p. 21).
15 For John Johnston of Grange, see Introduction, pp. 14-16 and 31. Johnston is now in practice as a "writer" (that is, a solicitor or law agent); but in a letter dated 30 March 1767 to William Johnson Temple (as to whom, see Introduction, pp. 14-15 and 28) Boswell says that Johnston is "too much of an indolent philosopher to have great business".
16 This was a reference to the case of *Jean Robertson v James Storrie* in which Boswell appeared for the pursuer at a hearing before Lord Kennet on 27 January. However, the case was simply continued for a week for discussions between the parties. Boswell appeared again on 3 February, when, the other party being absent, judgment was pronounced in favour of Boswell's client (N.A.S. CS21/1767/2/7). Boswell's letter of 27 January is reproduced in Walker, pp. 220-1. For Robert Bruce, Lord Kennet, see the entry for 5 February 1768 and relevant footnote.
17 A short distance down the High Street from the Parliament Close.
18 Sir David Dalrymple, Lord Hailes (as to whom, see Introduction, pp. 17-18, 30 and 35-6, and Appendix, p. 558). Perhaps by this time, and certainly by 1773, Lord Hailes's Edinburgh residence was a mansion at 23 New Street, off the north side of the Canongate, on the west side of the street.
19 The same William Wilson (1710-87) who gave Boswell his first case (see Introduction, p. 37). He was admitted W.S. on 15 January 1739. Wilson is sometimes referred to by Boswell as "William Wilson, S." The "S" stands either for "Senior" or "Writer to the Signet". When Wilson was sixty years old Boswell said of him that there was "nothing of an old man about him except experience, being healthy and cheerful though most laborious in his profession" (Journal, 14 March 1772).

law was a] form of fleecing poor lieges. Hurt *tant soit peu*,[20] [soon] firm again.

SATURDAY 7 FEBRUARY. With honest Doctor [Boswell][21] and a Doctor Livingston walked out to Sir Alexander [Dick]'s.[22] Fine day. Was powerful like Johnson; very much satisfied. Evening with Miss ——. She had taken other house, so resolved to give up yours. A little gloom still, a little fever.

MONDAY 9 FEBRUARY. Robert Hay's trial.[23] You opened and strongly protested his innocence; quite calm. Lasted till eight. Jaded a little.

TUESDAY 10 FEBRUARY. Very busy. Poor Hay condemned. Dined Mr John Gordon's:[24] George Wallace[25] and James Stevenson[26] — new scene, or rather old one revived. Quite comfortable and plain; saw how various happiness is. Very good conversation. Busy all the evening.

WEDNESDAY 11 FEBRUARY. Visited Robert Hay. Why it is, I know not, but we compassionate less a genteel man [in affliction than a poor man]. He was very quiet. You had a kind of sentiment as if he was utterly insensible to good. But he said if he had got time, he would have been a new man as from his mother's breast, and wept. Had Bible. Spoke to him seriously and calmly; bid him free innocent people, but not impeach a companion if [he held information] in trust. At eight, Miss —— a little.

SATURDAY 14 FEBRUARY. Had composed song on [the memorial for the]

20 "Ever so little."
21 Boswell's uncle, Dr John Boswell (1710-1780), younger brother of Boswell's father, Lord Auchinleck (as to whom, see Introduction, pp. 4, 13, 14, 18-21, 23-5, 29, 30 and 34-8). Dr Boswell, of whom his nephew was very fond, was a doctor of medicine in Edinburgh and was President of the Royal College of Physicians from 1770 to 1772. Although somewhat eccentric, he was evidently a most agreeable character. The close now called Boswell's Court, off the south side of the Castle Hill, was so named on account of the fact that he resided there.
22 For Sir Alexander Dick, see Introduction, p. 39.
23 The trial took place before the High Court of Justiciary sitting in the New Tolbooth (as to which, see Introduction, p. 11). Robert Hay, a soldier in his early twenties, was accused of having robbed a sailor of 40 shillings and a silver watch. He was apprehended the day after the robbery while trying to sell the watch. At the opening of the trial, Boswell, having informed the five judges hearing the case that he had been told that his client had a very fair character and had behaved remarkably well as a soldier in several German campaigns, advised the court that at the time when the robbery was said to have been committed his client was, for the first time in his life, so much intoxicated as to be unable to give a proper account of his conduct. Boswell argued that, in these circumstances, if his client was in any way accessory to the offence, the punishment sought should not be capital punishment, but should be restricted to an "arbitrary punishment". However, the court ruled that the trial should proceed with the indictment as it stood. The sailor's evidence was to the effect that he had been pursued by two men in soldiers' clothes and that one of them had robbed him in a close off the Cowgate while the other stood guard. The sailor was not able to identify Hay as being one of the men as it was dark at the time of the offence. Nevertheless, the jury unanimously found Hay art and part guilty of the crime libelled. Hay was then duly sentenced to be hanged, the execution to take place on 25 March (N.A.S. JC7/34, p. 292ff). Eleven days later, Hay confessed to Boswell that, although he had not taken an active part in the robbery, he was an accomplice of the principal attacker, having kept a look-out for him, and that he had been given the watch so as not to reveal that person's identity. Boswell then petitioned to the King for clemency, but the petition was refused.
24 John Gordon of Balmoor (d.1789), W.S. (admitted 8 July 1763).
25 George Wallace (1727-1805), advocate (admitted 19 February 1754).
26 Unidentified.

Hamilton cause.[27] Lord Hailes [said], "Very witty, but put it in the fire; you'll make yourself enemies." He had frightened you, such is still your weakness. Showed it to Sir Adam [Fergusson],[28] David Hume,[29] &c. All liked it; no venom. "No," said David Hume, "'tis not in you." Sung it in Parliament House[29a] with circle round you; had the *vivida vis*[30] of Wilkes.[31] Resolved to follow your own plan. Walked down with Sir Adam and Nairne[32] to Lord Alemoor's;[33] viewed my Lord calmly. Felt the sentiment of awe for others gone. Afternoon very busy. Mr William Wilson, S., at tea with you. At six, Miss —— at Philippi.[34] Had been indifferent for this week. You and she this night first cold and upbraiding, then kind as ever. Home, and labour again.

SUNDAY 15 FEBRUARY. Morning, Erskine called; told you what applause you got. You was quite firm and gay. Church, forenoon.[35] Home between sermons, then to prison.[36] Such an audience! Young divine preached: "Be not slothful in business" &c.[37]— not at all applicable to his hearers. Great genius required for a jail preacher. You sat in the closet, like an aisle. You did not like to hear the divine in his prayer talk of a *disgraceful death*. 'Twas too shocking to his unhappy hearers. He should have preached on patience, on the necessity of punishment, on the corruption of man's nature, on the mercy of God. [They sang] psalms, with precentor reading [them] line [by line] with a doleful tone. Your mind now so strong [that such a scene produces] no impression.

Went and saw poor Hay. He was bad and all heaving—could not speak. His aged mother there, and his wife (a soldier's wife), very well looked. Then David Hume's, who was next day to set out for London; tea with him. He agreed to

27 This was a song ridiculing the memorial for the Duke of Hamilton in the great Douglas Cause (as to which, see Introduction, p. 41). The song appeared in *The Scots Magazine*, Vol. 29 (March 1767), p. 119.
28 Sir Adam Fergusson of Kilkerran (1733-1813), Bt, advocate (admitted 23 December 1755), M.P. Ayrshire 1774-84 and 1790-96, Edinburgh 1784-90, died unmarried. Fergusson was one of the counsel employed for the Duke of Hamilton and had written the memorial (which extended to over 800 pages). He would therefore have had grounds for taking offence at Boswell's song.
29 The famous philosopher. For Boswell's association with Hume, see Introduction, pp. 16-17 and 25.
29a For the Parliament House, see Introduction, pp. 10-11.
30 "Lively force."
31 John Wilkes (as to whom, see Introduction, pp. 29 and 33).
32 William Nairne, advocate (admitted 11 March 1755), later Lord Dunsinnan (appointed Lord of Session 9 March 1786 and Lord Commissioner of Justiciary 24 December 1792), died 20 March 1811. Boswell was a close friend of Nairne and described him as "an honest upright fellow; somewhat stiff in his manner, but not without parts in a moderate degree" (Journal, 4 November 1762).
33 Andrew Pringle, Lord Alemoor. Admitted advocate 3 February 1736; appointed Sheriff-Depute of Wigtownshire in 1750; Sheriff-Depute of Selkirkshire in 1751; Solicitor-General on 5 July 1755; Lord of Session and Lord Commissioner of Justiciary on 14 June 1759; died 14 January 1776. Lord Alemoor had a reputation for strict impartiality in court proceedings, mild and courteous manners both on and off the bench, and great eloquence in delivering opinions. By 1766 he suffered much from gout, being very partial to good food and wines. His Edinburgh residence was in Niddry's Wynd, off the south side of the High Street.
34 The editors of *Wife* (at p. 29, n. 4) suggest that the use of "Philippi" to signify a place of assignation was probably derived from *Julius Caesar*, IV. iii. 284: "To tell thee thou shalt see me at Philippi".
35 The New Church in St Giles' (as to which, see Introduction, p. 6).
36 The Tolbooth (as to which, see Introduction, p. 7).
37 Romans 12. 10-11.

manage your Account of Corsica with Millar. You very pleasantly maintained your happiness in being a Christian. Then Miss ——'s, where you met La Cara[38] in black. Your love returned gay and fine. Supped Lord Kames;[39] rather too high. What a variety you have made of Edinburgh!

TUESDAY 17 FEBRUARY. Evening with Miss ——, dressed in the very black she had charmed you with on Sunday. You was delighted with her.

SATURDAY 21 FEBRUARY. You was quite overpowered with papers to draw. Had been accustomed too much to make the law easy, and write papers like essays for a newspaper, without reading much. Saw labour and poring necessary, and reading long papers. Dined Samuel Mitchelson's[40] with Sir Alexander Dick and family. Evening with Miss ——, again in black. Allowed you full sight; enchanted with her. She said, "Next night I'll wear black and let candles burn to keep you longer."

SUNDAY 22 FEBRUARY. You stayed in the afternoon and wrote letters. Evening was with Miss ——, who came instantly on your sending [for her, and was] very kind.

WEDNESDAY 25 FEBRUARY. At five Miss —— with you; pretty well. At eight, at Mrs Dunbar's in Gosford's Close,[41] low house but comfortable, with William Taylor[42] and John Stobie[43] consulting on cause of old Barclay, [the] Quaker [of] London. Four bottles [of] good claret drunk, quite style of old consultations.[44] Home and finished paper. Was with Father;[45] was hearty. Asked him, "Am I not doing as well as you would wish?" HE. "Yes." Took his hand.

SATURDAY 28 FEBRUARY. At six with Miss ——, in varying humour. She upbraided you; almost would give up *concert*. Talked of expense offending you, [and] parted angry with you. [As you came out] met ——,[46] [and showed] alarm. You supped Lady Betty's[47] with Grange,[48] Dr Gregory,[49] Arbuthnot and his ladies. Pleasant, but you was a little drowsy.

SUNDAY 1 MARCH. Miss Blair of Adamton[50] in [our] seat [at church], handsome,

---

38 The dear one; beloved (Italian).
39 Henry Home, Lord Kames (as to whom, see Introduction, pp. 23-5, 35 and 36, and Appendix, pp. 555-6).
40 Samuel Mitchelson, senior, W.S. (admitted 12 March 1736), died 1788.
41 Off the south side of the Lawnmarket.
42 A "writer" (admitted by the Court of Session in 1755).
43 John Stobie was a "writer" (admitted by the Court of Session in 1755) and was clerk to Lord Auchinleck.
44 It had formerly been the custom for almost all business, including consultations with counsel, to be carried out at taverns.
45 Alexander Boswell, Lord Auchinleck (as to whom, see Introduction, pp. 4, 13, 14, 18-21, 23-5, 29, 30 and 34-8).
46 The editors of *Wife* (at p. 33, n. 3) surmise that this was Lord Auchinleck.
47 Andrew Erskine's sister, Lady Elizabeth ("Betty") Macfarlane (as to whom, see Introduction, pp. 25 and 27). She is now married to the aged antiquary, Walter Macfarlane of Macfarlane.
48 John Johnston of Grange.
49 John Gregory (1724-73), M.D., Professor of Medicine at the University of Edinburgh.
50 Catherine Blair of Adamton in Ayrshire, who is frequently referred to by Boswell as "the Heiress" (on account of being heiress to the estate of Adamton) or "the Princess".

stately woman; good countenance. Dined Duchess of Douglas,[51] very hearty. Before dinner had been with Miss ——, and settled plan how to explain last night's alarm. You and she were as fine as ever. At six she met you. By having lived luxuriously so much last week, you was confused and debilitate, [and] performed only one—a kind of ludicrous distress.

TUESDAY 3 MARCH. Tea, Grange; Erskine there. Read part of your London Journal; delighted [them]. Talked of your fever for Mrs Dodds. They showed you weakness; you saw 'twas only sudden resolution to be free. Sat till near three—extraordinary night.

WEDNESDAY 4 MARCH. Was so much hurt to hear scandal of Miss —— would not visit her.[52] Was on rack.

THURSDAY 5 MARCH. Had message from Miss ——; went to her. Could not conceal [you] was black and dreary. She was much affected. You begged of her to have patience. You was unhappy, but you would not tell why. Supped Lord Coalston's.[53] Some young lawyers there, and Miss Nisbet of Dirleton, a most charming creature, did not she speak too broad. Her mother, a genteel, amiable woman. You was much in spirits. You consented to sing your Hamilton song. You was asked about the prison, &c. You was well understood.

[Extracts from letter from Boswell to Temple[54] dated 8 March 1767.] "[Miss ——] took [my distress] very seriously, and was so much affected that she went [in the] morning [of 6 March] and gave up our house. I went in the afternoon and secured the house, and then drank tea with her. She was much agitated. She said she was determined to go and board herself in the north of England, and that I used her very ill. I expostulated with her. I was sometimes resolved to let her go, and sometimes my heart was like to burst within me. I held her dear hand. Her eyes were full of passion. I took her in my arms. I told her what made me miserable. She was pleased to find it was nothing worse. She had imagined that I was suspicious of her fidelity, and she thought that very ungenerous in me, considering her behaviour. She said I should not mind her faults before I knew

51 Margaret, or "Peggy", Duchess of Douglas, widow of Archibald, third Marquess of Douglas and first Duke of Douglas (the uncle of Archibald Douglas, the defender in the great Douglas Cause). She was outspoken and forceful, but warm-hearted and witty, and was regarded as being "quite a character". Her nephew's success in retaining his estate was to a large extent attributed to her strenuous efforts on his behalf. It was said of her that "she was the last of the nobility to be attended by halberdiers when going about the country. When she visited, she left her dress behind her as a present" (*Scots Peerage*, Vol. IX, p. 13). When Boswell made arrangements to visit Bothwell Castle (the principal Douglas residence) in October 1767 he asked the Duchess to let him have a "warm, orthodox room", to which the Duchess responded that the warmest bed in the house was her own and that Boswell would be welcome to it.
52 In a letter to Temple dated 4 March 1767 Boswell explained that he had had "more intelligence of her former intrigues" and that he was "hurt to think of them" and was "jealous".
53 George Brown, Lord Coalston. Admitted advocate 31 January 1734; Sheriff-Depute of Forfarshire 1748-53; appointed Lord of Session 18 December 1756; appointed Lord Commissioner of Justiciary 18 January 1765; died 6 November 1776. Lord Coalston's Edinburgh residence was a mansion on the Castle Hill.
54 William Johnson Temple (as to whom, see Introduction, pp. 14-15 and 28).

her, since her conduct was now most circumspect. We renewed our fondness. She owned she loved me more than she had ever done her husband. All was again well. She said she did not reproach me with my former follies, and we should be on an equal footing. My mind all at once felt a spring. I agreed with her. I embraced her with transport.

[In the] evening I gave a supper to two or three of my acquaintance, having before I left Scotland laid a guinea that I should not catch the venereal disorder for three years, which bet I had most certainly lost and now was paying. We drank a great deal, till I was so much intoxicated that instead of going home I went to a low house in one of the alleys in Edinburgh where I knew a common girl lodged, and like a brute as I was I lay all night with her. I had still so much reason left as not to "dive into the bottom of the deep", but I gratified my coarse desires by tumbling about on the brink of destruction.

Next morning I was like a man ordered for ignominious execution. But by noon I was worse, for I discovered that some infection had reached me. I had an assignation in the evening with my charmer. How lucky was it that I knew my misfortune in time. I might have polluted her sweet body. Bless me! what a risk! But how could I tell her my shocking story? I took courage. I told how drunk I had been. I told the consequences. I lay down and kissed her feet. I said I was unworthy of any other favour. But I took[55] myself. I gloried that I had ever been firmly constant to her while I was myself. I hoped she would consider my being drunk as a fatal accident which I should never again fall into. I called her my friend in whom I had confidence, and entreated she would comfort me. She bid me rise; she took me by the hand. She said she forgave me. She kissed me. She gently upbraided me for entertaining any unfavourable ideas of her. She bid me take great care of myself and in time coming never drink upon any account. [A]ll the time her beauty enchanted me more than ever. May I not then be hers? In the meantime I must be shut up, and honest Thomas[56] must be my guardian. He does excellently well.

My present misfortune is occasioned by drinking. Since my return to Scotland I have given a great deal too much in to that habit, which still prevails in Scotland.[57] Perhaps the coldness of the Scots requires it. But my fiery blood is turned to madness by it. This will be a warning to me, and from henceforth I shall be a perfect man. At least I hope so."

WEDNESDAY 11 MARCH. [Felt] a kind of gloom to think this was the last day of

55 That is, checked.
56 Boswell's servant, Thomas Edmondson (*Wife*, p. 401).
57 Notwithstanding Boswell's reputation as being something of a drunkard, it was indeed the case that until he commenced practice at the bar he was relatively abstemious. Admittedly, a drinking song which he wrote describing the dissipations of the Soaping Club in 1761 (as to which, see Introduction, p. 21) stated of himself that "hock is the liquor he drinks" (*B —, a Song*, published as one of Boswell's contributions to *A Collection of Original Poems by Scotch Gentlemen*), but at that time of his life he evidently preferred tea to strong alcohol. In his journal entry for 13 February 1763 he wrote: "I am so fond of tea that I could write a whole dissertation on its virtues. It comforts and enlivens without the risks attendant on spiritous liquors. Gentle herb! Let the florid grape yield to thee. Thy soft influence is a more safe inspirer of social joy."

the session. You drank tea at Mr Alexander Tait's.[58] He was not in. You had for company Mrs Tait [and] Mrs and Miss Blair. You was quite easy. You liked Miss Blair more and more without any fever. Saw Miss —— a little.

FRIDAY 13 MARCH. Had a kind card from Miss ——; went to her and stayed from twelve to two.

SATURDAY 14 MARCH. Tea, Miss ——; provoked her with old stories. Grange had been with you in the forenoon, and insisted you had no morals. You was shocked. You saw Miss —— had no sentiment. You had sore conflict. But you resolved to try one winter, to enjoy fully so strong a passion. You then fancied you could inspire her with finer feelings. You grew fond. Her eyes looked like precious stones. Some delirium seized you. She seemed an angel.

SUNDAY 15 MARCH. Had message from Miss ——; she was to set out next day. Was in, quiet all this day. Captain Erskine[59] and Houston Stewart[60] drank tea with you. Houston was dissipated as ever. You felt calm superiority, but not to shock him you assumed dissipation a little. You had wrote earnestly to Miss ——. She came at eight, and sat a while with you. It was vastly kind.

MONDAY 16 MARCH. You called on Miss —— and passed a great part of the forenoon, as she was not to go till Tuesday. You again spoke of old stories. She was fretted. You were both very uneasy. You saw her temper such that no eloquence could touch her. But you was her slave. Returned at five to tea. She was young and vivacious. What a temperament! You gave word in honour you'd never again allow her to be ill spoken of by Grange in your presence. You were like man and wife. Went to Lady Betty's. She had been ill; you was so. [She still] appeared invalid. Was restless, having promised to Miss —— to return. You talked much of Miss ——, and Lady Betty and the Captain rated you about her. At eleven you went to her. You was let softly in. She was quite kind. But the recollection of her former tricks galled you, for your heart was affected. You had been with Lord Monboddo[61] and talked of your flame. He quoted Ulysses and Circe: "Sub domina meretrice vixisset turpis et excors."[62] You saw how lightly passions appear to those not immediately affected by them, for even to yourself will this afterwards seem light. You was all resigned to sweet Miss ——. You chased away all reflection. You drank in instant delight. You sat till one, and parted with great fondness in hopes of meeting. Home, Father still up. Lady Betty bore the blame of late hours.

TUESDAY 17 MARCH. [Was] feverish [and felt like] Mark Antony, quite given up to violent love. Then Miss G——[63] and gave money for [your] house, &c.

58 One of the Principal Clerks of Session.
59 Andrew Erskine.
60 A son of Sir Michael Stewart of Blackhall, Bt, advocate (1712-96).
61 James Burnett, Lord Monboddo (as to whom, see Introduction, pp. 36 and 38, and Appendix, pp. 556-8).
62 "'He would have lived filthy and stupid ruled by a whore' (Horace, *Epistles*, I. ii. 25, 'vixisset' for 'fuisset')" (*Wife*, p. 44, n. 2). Circe was the enchantress of Greek and Roman legend who detained Ulysses on the island of Aeaea, took him as her lover and turned his men into swine.
63 An unidentified landlady in Edinburgh.

Had laboured hard all winter, but now passion made you at once give up the fruits of your labour, which you had carefully collected.

WEDNESDAY 18 MARCH. Found a listlessness creeping on you. Reviewed winter; wondered at the variety of business you had gone through, having made fourscore and four guineas.[64] Went to Lord Hailes to have him examined by Lord Elliock[65] in Cairncross cause.[66] The other party could not attend. You was hurt to find reverence for Lords ceasing. You feared that *caelum ipsum*[67] might lose its dignity if you got to it. Wild idea! Can finite beings be at all compared to infinity? You had a tête-à-tête with Lord Hailes. He commended you in some causes, said you had fought a good battle; but in Warnock's cause[68] you had drawn a paper with as unfair a state of the facts as Lockhart[69] could have done. You told him of feverish passion. He bid you break off, but he seemed not rigid.

Then Dr Blair's.[70] Had not seen him of a long time. He was comfortable. Talked of Corsica.[71] He was roused with it. Complained of sickly love. He talked of it calmly as a bad thing. Talked of marriage, how agreeable, and how suited to you. Talked of action as quite necessary. You said yes, but [only] as a remedy to distempered minds. The sound and perfect human being can sit under a spreading tree like the Spaniard, playing on his guitar, his mistress by him, and glowing with gratitude to his God. Music, love, adoration! there is a soul. The Doctor was struck and pleased with this warm effusion. Commissioner [Cochrane][72] dined with you.

At five, Lady Betty's, comfortable tea. You was still in fever about Miss ——. She and the Captain showed you what a weakness [this was], what want of firmness, and how in all such cases a man of imagination supposed his mistress to have virtues. Lady Betty talked to me as a Christian. In short, everything was said, and the Captain recalled all the scandalous stories, [her living with the] waiter and all, which revolted you. You resolved to be self, to break free from slavery. What strength of mind you have had this winter, to go through so much business and at the same time have so violent a passion! You held Lady Betty's

---

64 The pound in those days was very approximately equivalent to sixty pounds by today's standards (see Introduction, p. 24).

65 James Veitch, Lord Elliock (1712-1793), was admitted advocate on 15 February 1738 and was appointed Sheriff-Depute of Peeblesshire on 13 July 1747. In 1755 he was elected M.P. for Dumfriesshire, and on 6 March 1761 he was appointed a Lord of Session as Lord Elliock. It was said of him that he was "endowed with mental abilities of the first order, and was generally allowed to be one of the most accomplished scholars of his time" (Brunton and Haig, pp. 525-6). Boswell remarked that Lord Elliock always had "a kind of smile or grin" (Journal, 17 September 1769).

66 *Hugh Cairncross v William Heatly* (as to which, see Introduction, p. 40). Lord Hailes had formerly been counsel for Hugh Cairncross.

67 "Heaven itself."

68 *Warnock v Maxwell*, in which Boswell drafted a reclaiming petition on 2 February 1767 (Consultation Book). For reclaiming petitions, see Introduction, p. 39.

69 Alexander Lockhart, Dean of the Faculty of Advocates (as to whom, see Appendix, p. 559).

70 The Rev. Hugh Blair (as to whom, see Introduction, pp. 28-9).

71 For Boswell's interest in Corsica, see Introduction, pp. 33-4.

72 For Commissioner Cochrane, see Introduction, p. 25. He was a Commissioner of Excise from 1761 to 1764 and was appointed a Commissioner of Customs in May 1764. He died unmarried in 1788.

hand. Owned error; said, "Have hope of me"; and gave honour you'd never again allow yourself to fall into such a scrape.

Home. David[73] sat long with you. Told him fairly your situation (all but paradisial completion). He, like a man, advised you to get free; you'd ruin yourself. You would fain have indulged for one year. "No," said he, "you might acquire habit of slavery, and, besides, it would then be ungenerous to quit." You wavered and knew not how to determine. You saw yourself gone. You wondered how you would feel if a notorious villain; for, from your violent passions, you dreaded its possibility. Was stunned; resolved firm. To bed quite agitated.

THURSDAY 19 MARCH. Waked in tender anguish: "What, shall I give her up?" Your melting moments rushed on your mind: her generosity—ah! For some seconds a real fit of delirium [seized you], tossing in your distempered mind [the thought of] instant self-destruction. Bless me! is this possible? It was literally true. Got up, roused, grew better. Bad weather had kept you still in town yesterday. However set out today [for Auchinleck],[73a] the same family form. John Bruce,[74] Mr Stobie, Matthew Dickie,[75] [and] Bob Boswell[76] all down with you to the Back Stairs.[77] This composed your mind. It was, as it were, quilted with good, comfortable, family ideas. Jogged on. Good conversation on law. Dined Livingston; night, Bedlay's new house.[78] Father gave you account of the Hamilton memorial after supper, [but] left it off. In your room begun letter to Miss ———. Was gloomy but resolved; considered she had not feeling [enough] to be much affected.

Boswell sent his letter to Mrs Dodds on 20 March and arrived at Auchinleck on 21 March, where he reflected on his "emancipation from Circe" and thought, with astonishment, "Is it really true that a man of such variety of genius, who has seen so much, who is in constant friendship with General Paoli,[79] is it possible that he was all last winter the slave of a woman without one elegant quality?" However, on 27 April he received a letter from Mrs Dodds intimating that she was pregnant. Somewhat surprisingly, Boswell was not unpleased at this news. "I was", he wrote, "very composed; half delighted to obtain what I had wished, and half vexed to think of the expense, &c.—a curious example of the vanity of human wishes."

Boswell and his father (who, of course, was not made aware of the position with regard to Mrs Dodds) were at this time on good terms. "We are now friends", Boswell remarked, "as much as my father's singular grave and steady temper will allow; for he has not that quick sensibility which animates me. Since the beginning of last winter he has ceased to treat me like a boy."

---

73 Boswell's brother (for whom, see Introduction, p. 4).
73a Boswell's father's Ayrshire estate (for which, see Introduction, pp. 4, 13-14 and 24-25).
74 Lord Auchinleck's major-domo.
75 A "writer" in Edinburgh who later became Boswell's clerk.
76 Robert Boswell (1746-1804), son of Dr John Boswell. Robert Boswell was a "writer", and on 25 February 1773 he was to be admitted a Writer to the Signet.
77 The reference to the "Back Stairs" is a reference to the long flight of stone steps (also known as the "Parliament Stairs") which descended from the south side of the Parliament Close to the Cowgate.
78 Archibald Roberton of Bedlay (d. 1798), advocate (admitted 29 June 1748).
79 As to whom, see Introduction, p. 34.

On 16 April there was an auction of the neighbouring estate of Dalblair, an extensive farm consisting mainly of peaty marshland, and Boswell decided to bid for it with a view to being seen to be extending the influence of the family of Auchinleck. Having obtained Lord Auchinleck's prior agreement to stand surety to the extent of £900, Boswell put in a successful bid of £2,410, thus becoming a proud landed proprietor and "Laird of Dalblair". But the financial problems occasioned by the purchase were to have adverse repercussions for many years to come.

In May Lord Auchinleck presided at the circuit courts at Dumfries and Ayr. Boswell accompanied his father on both occasions, and at Ayr he successfully defended a number of poor and hungry "meal rioters" who had stolen stocks of flour destined for export abroad. For this he received the very handsome fee of six guineas. He also represented a lady referred to as the "Kilmarnock necromancing Irishwoman", for whom he secured a new trial.[80] Another case in which Boswell was involved was that of two prisoners (Hay and McClure) charged with ambushing three persons from Ayr. One of the alleged victims was unavailable and so Boswell obtained letters of liberation for the prisoners, but at the same time received a little lecture from the Lord Advocate, James Montgomery,[81] who wrote to him in these terms: "It is your duty to defend your clients, and I observe your zeal in doing so upon every occasion with great pleasure and satisfaction, but it is both your duty and mine to wish a detection of the persons guilty of so foul a crime."[82]

While staying at Auchinleck, Boswell began his Account of Corsica, *most of which was completed by the end of April. It was also at this time that he wrote a fifty-page pamphlet entitled* Dorando, *which was a biased account of the history of the Douglas Cause[83] dressed up as a Spanish tale (with the principal characters given names such as "Don Carlos", "Don Spirito", "Princess Maria" and "Don Ferdinand"). This pamphlet, which was to be published on 15 June, was to be so much in demand that a third edition was required. In November Boswell was to publish two further works on the Douglas Cause, one being the* Letters of Lady Jane Douglas *and the other being* The Essence of the Douglas Cause, *the latter of which was a serious and carefully laid out exposition of the case for Archibald Douglas. The reason for the great interest in* Dorando *was that its publication occurred just as the Court of Session proceedings in the Douglas Cause were coming to a head. There was mounting public excitement, partly fuelled by a series of bogus (and sometimes very amusing) newspaper articles written by Boswell. These articles were to lead to the publishers of the four newspapers in question being cited for contempt of court, and Boswell (whose identity as the author was not disclosed) was to be instructed to act for John Donaldson, one of the publishers of* The Edinburgh Advertiser, *for whom, with some audacity, he produced a memorial containing suitable apologies and excuses for the newspaper's actions. The outcome of these representations, and those submitted by counsel on behalf of the other newspapers, was that the publishers were merely reprimanded.[84]*

80 Pottle, p. 328; *Private Papers,* Vol. 7, pp. 132-3.
81 As to whom, see Appendix, pp. 559-60.
82 Letter from James Montgomerie dated 4 June 1767, quoted in Pottle, p. 329.
83 For the Douglas Cause, see Introduction, p. 41.
84 Pottle, pp. 330-4 and 540.

At the end of May, Boswell's "Princess", the eighteen-year-old Catherine Blair, came for a four-days' visit to Auchinleck with her mother. Miss Blair's charms completely captivated Boswell, and his father made it known that he was very keen to see the couple married.

Boswell and his father returned to Edinburgh on or about 7 June for the summer session.

[Extract from letter from Boswell to Temple dated 26 June 1767.] "On Tuesday [23 June], drinking Miss Blair's health, I got myself quite intoxicated, went to a bawdy-house, and passed a whole night in the arms of a whore. She indeed was a fine, strong, spirited girl, a whore worthy of Boswell if Boswell must have a whore, and I apprehend no bad consequences. But I am abashed, and determined to keep the strictest watch over my passions."

From 29 June to 4 July Lord Auchinleck took his turn as Lord Ordinary in the Outer House[85] *and as a consequence Boswell expected to receive "a load of business". As he explained in a letter to Temple dated 26 June, "The absurdity of mankind makes nineteen out of twenty employ the son of the judge before whom their cause is heard. And you must take it along with you that I am as yet but a very raw counsellor, so that a moderate share of business is really a load to me." In fact, however, Boswell had no hearings before Lord Auchinleck during the week in question, but had no fewer than six hearings before him between 8 and 16 July.*[86]

The opinions of the judges in the Douglas Cause were given in the Inner House[87] *between 7 and 14 July. The Lord Justice-Clerk, Thomas Miller of Barskimming,*[88] *in giving his judgment, referred ominously to Boswell's defence in the criminal trial of John Reid in 1766.*[89] *Clearly still indignant over the acquittal of Reid, the Lord Justice-Clerk made the following comments: "We have indeed seen cases where there was a moral impossibility of the prisoner's innocence, and yet we have seen juries acquit such a one. Such a case was that of Reid, who was lately tried before the criminal Court, for the crime of sheep-stealing. This Reid was a poor man of a very suspicious character. He was found with the exact number of sheep in his possession upon the road leading from the very farm from off which they were stole, and he pretended not to bring any proof whatever, that he had attained the property of them in any lawful way. A counsel at that bar, who likes to distinguish himself upon such occasions, patronized the prisoner's defence, and notwithstanding the clearest and most positive evidence of all the facts which I have mentioned, 'The jury acquitted the prisoner'."*[90]

On 14 July it was ascertained that seven judges had voted in favour of Hamilton and seven in favour of Douglas. The Lord President thereupon gave his casting vote for Hamilton. This outcome provoked a great public outcry and the Lord President received threatening letters. The Douglas camp appealed to the House of Lords. Meanwhile, Boswell

---

85 For the Outer House, see Introduction, pp. 10-11.
86 Consultation Book.
87 For the Inner House, see Introduction, p. 10.
88 As to whom, see Introduction, pp. 36 and 40, and Appendix, p. 555.
89 For details of John Reid's trial in 1766, see Introduction, pp. 39-40.
90 Steuart (ed.), *The Douglas Cause*, p. 115.

discovered that, contrary to his expectations, he had not survived the incident on 23 June completely unscathed.

[Extract from letter from Boswell to Temple dated 29 July 1767.] "I am an unhappy man. The consequences of my debauch are now fatal, for I have got a disease from which I suffer severely. It has been long of appearing and is a heavy one. I shall stay a month here after the Session rises, and be cured. I am patient under it, as a just retribution for my licentiousness. But I greatly fear that Mrs —— is infected, for I have been with her several times since my debauch, and once within less than a week of the full appearance of mischief. In her present situation the consequences will be dreadful; for, besides the pain that she must endure, an innocent being cannot fail to be injured. I am not, however, certain that Mrs —— will be ill. I would fain hope that she may have escaped. I have told her the risk she runs. Her good temper is astonishing. She does not upbraid me in the least degree."

[Extract from letter from Boswell to Temple dated 11 August 1767.] "[M]y present unhappy distemper joined with a cold brought on a most terrible fever, and I was for several days in a very alarming situation. I am not yet got up, though I am in a fair way of recovery from every evil. I am in great hopes that my black friend[91] is safe. No symptoms have yet appeared."

Boswell's fees for the summer session (from mid-June to mid-August) amounted to sixty-four guineas and would no doubt have been somewhat higher if it had not been for his fever, which confined him to his bed for several days. He earned no fees during the period from 30 July to 10 August. However, during the course of August he started to recover.

[Extract from letter from Boswell to Temple dated 29 August 1767.] "I am so well that I hope to be abroad in a few days. My health must be restored in the first place. Then I have Mrs —— to take care of. [S]he is a good girl. She [has] a contented, cheerful temper, and is perfectly generous. It is my duty to be kind to her while she bears *Edward, the Black Prince.*[92] I am indeed fond of her. But some tender feelings must be forgotten. She comes and drinks tea with me once or twice a week. This connection keeps me reasonable in my attachment to the Princess. Next month will probably fix our alliance, which may be completed next year."

[Extract from letter from Boswell to John Johnston of Grange dated 9 October 1767.] "[T]his unhappy distemper has been very obstinate, and as I have done so well hitherto I have determined to finish my course of medicines in the most complete [manner]. I am now, I may say, perfectly recovered."

On or about 13 October Boswell and his brother David[93] *(who was shortly to leave Scotland to become a merchant in Spain) set off for Auchinleck. In early November Boswell spent a few days with his "Princess" at Adamton, where, he told Temple in a letter dated 8 November 1767, he found*

---

91 Mrs Dodds, who had black hair.
92 Boswell, like Mrs Dodds, had a dark complexion and black hair. He of course did not yet know that the child which Mrs Dodds was bearing was in fact a girl.
93 For David Boswell, see Introduction, p. 4.

her "*more engaging than you can conceive… and yet, Temple, with what a cold reserve does she behave. Let her go.*" Part of the problem was that Boswell had mentioned to her a former quarrel which they had had and which, he thought, "*should have taught her that she had a lover of an anxious temper*", but she "*did not appear in the least inclined to own herself in the wrong.*" However, in a letter written the following day Boswell told his friend: "*I love her, Temple, with my whole heart. I am entirely in her power.*"

Boswell returned to Edinburgh on 9 November to be in time for the opening of the winter session on 12 November.

[Extract from letter from Boswell to Temple dated 18 December 1767.] "At last [the Princess has come] to town, and I have had a long conversation with her. She assured me she did not believe me serious or that I was uneasy, and that it was my own fault if ever she and I quarrelled. I in short adored her, and was convinced she was not to blame. I told her that henceforth she should entertain no doubt that I sincerely loved her—and I ventured to seize her hand. She is really the finest woman to me I ever saw."

[Extracts from letter from Boswell to Temple dated 24 December 1767.] "[On Friday 18 December] I was at the concert[94] with [the Princess and her most intimate friend, the beautiful young Duchess of Gordon[95]] and afterwards supped at Lord Kames's. The Princess appeared distant and reserved. I could hardly believe that it was the same woman with whom I had been quite easy the day before. I was then uneasy.

Next evening I was at the play with them.[96] It was *Othello*. I sat close behind the Princess, and at the most affecting scenes I pressed my hand upon her waist. She was in tears, and rather leaned to me. The jealous Moor described my very soul. I often spoke to her of the torment which she saw before her. Still I thought her distant, and still I was uneasy.

On Sunday [20 December] the Duchess of Gordon went away. I met the Princess at church. She was distant as before. I passed the evening at her aunt's, where I met a cousin of my Princess, a young lady of Glasgow who had been with us at Adamton. She told me she had something to communicate, and she then said that my behaviour to the Princess was such that Mrs Blair and her daughter did not know how to behave to me. That it was not honourable to engage a young lady's affections while I kept myself free. In short, the good cousin persuaded me that the Princess had formed an attachment for me, and she assured me the Nabob had been refused.[97]

94 At the St Cecilia Hall (as to which, see Introduction, p. 9).
95 Jane, Duchess of Gordon, a daughter of Lady Maxwell of Monreith. As children, Lady Maxwell's daughters were said to have been "the wildest romps imaginable" and Jane was regularly seen riding on a sow in the High Street (Chambers, p. 298).
96 The play was at Edinburgh's first Theatre Royal, which occupied the premises formerly occupied by the old Edinburgh Theatre at the Canongate Concert Hall, which premises had recently been granted a royal patent. The theatre was thus for the first time operating wholly legally. At the opening of the new theatre, on 9 December 1767, the prologue was a composition of Boswell's consisting of a set of verses. For the old Edinburgh Theatre, see Introduction, pp. 9-10.
97 The "Nabob" was William Fullarton of Rosemount, an Ayrshire surgeon who had acquired considerable wealth in India and had evinced an interest in Miss Blair ("the Princess").

On Monday forenoon I waited on Miss Blair; I found her alone, and she did not seem distant. I told her that I was most sincerely in love with her, and that I only dreaded those faults which I had acknowledged to her. I asked her seriously if she now believed me in earnest. She said she did. I then asked her to be candid and fair as I had been with her, and to tell me if she had any particular liking for me. 'I really', said she, 'have no particular liking for you. I like many people as well as you.'

BOSWELL. 'Do you indeed? Well, I cannot help it. I am obliged to you for telling me so in time. I am sorry for it.' PRINCESS. 'I like Jeanie Maxwell (Duchess of Gordon) better than you.' BOSWELL. 'Very well. But do you like no man better than me?' PRINCESS. 'No.' BOSWELL. 'Is it possible that you may like me better than other men?' PRINCESS. 'I don't know what is possible.' (By this time I had risen and placed myself by her, and was in real agitation.) BOSWELL. 'I'll tell you what, my dear Miss Blair, I love you so much that I am very unhappy. If you cannot love me, I must if possible endeavour to forget you. What would you have me do?' PRINCESS. 'I really don't know what you should do.' BOSWELL. 'It is certainly possible that you *may* love me, and if you shall ever do so I shall be the happiest man in the world. Will you make a fair bargain with me? If you should happen to love me, will you own it?' PRINCESS. 'Yes.' BOSWELL. 'And if you should happen to love another, will you tell me immediately, and help me to make myself easy?' PRINCESS. 'Yes, I will.' BOSWELL. 'Well, you are very good' (often squeezing and kissing her fine hand, while she looked at me with those beautiful black eyes).

PRINCESS. 'I may tell you as a cousin what I would not tell to another man.' BOSWELL. 'You may indeed. You are very fond of Auchinleck; that is one good circumstance.' PRINCESS. 'I confess I am. I wish I liked you as well as I do Auchinleck.' BOSWELL. 'I have told you how fond I am of you. But unless you like me sincerely, I have too much spirit to ask you to live with me, as I know that you do not like me. If I could have you this moment for my wife I would not.' PRINCESS. 'I should not like to put myself in your offer, though.' BOSWELL. 'Remember, you are both my cousin and my mistress. You must make me suffer as little as possible. As it may happen that I may engage your affections, I should think myself a most dishonourable man if I were not now in earnest, and remember I depend upon your sincerity; and whatever happens you and I shall never again have any quarrel.' PRINCESS. 'Never.' BOSWELL. 'And I may come and see you as much as I please?' PRINCESS. 'Yes.'

[W]hat sort of a scene was this? It was most curious. She said she would submit to her husband in most things. She said that to see one loving her would go far to make her love that person; but she could not talk anyhow positively, for she never had felt the uneasy anxiety of love. We were an hour and a half together, and seemed pleased all the time. I think she behaved with spirit and propriety. I admired her more than ever. She intended to go to her aunt's twelve miles from town next day. Her jaunt was put off for some days. [On Wednesday] I saw her again. I was easy and cheerful, and just endeavoured to make myself agreeable.

[On Thursday] forenoon I was again with her. I told her how uneasy I was that she should be three weeks absent. She said I might amuse myself well enough. She seemed quite indifferent. I was growing angry again. But I recollected how she had candidly told me that she had no particular liking for me. I drank tea with her [in the] afternoon and sat near four hours with her mother and her. Our conversation turned all on the manner in which two people might live. She has the justest ideas. She said she knew me now. She could laugh me out of my ill humour. She could give Lord Auchinleck a lesson how to manage me.

Amidst all this love I have been wild as ever. I have catched another memorandum of vice, but a very slight one.

My black friend has brought me the finest little girl I ever saw. I have named it Sally. It is healthy and strong. I take the greatest care of the mother, but shall have her no more in keeping."

1768

FRIDAY 1 JANUARY. Busy all day drawing replies in the Forfar elections.[1]

SATURDAY 2 JANUARY. Went with my father to Arniston. By the way talked of the antiquities and constitution of the election law in Scotland. Found it difficult to fix my attention. But by degrees wrought my mind into a knowledge of the subject. Was amazed at my father's memory and patience. Well at Arniston. All old ideas had no longer any force, but the traces of them diversified and amused my thoughts. At night played whist. Still had gloom, because I have never played at it when well so as to get free of former prejudices.

About nine my father was taken ill with his old complaint.[2] Thomas went express to Edinburgh. The President showed a friendly concern which will ever make him be regarded by me. For some hours my father was in agony. In the view of death he gave me the best and most affectionate advices. He spoke of Miss Blair as the woman whom he wished I would marry. How strong was this. I was in terrible concern. He said if business did not succeed with me after his death I should retire to the country. He charged me to take care of my brothers, to be a worthy man, and keep up the character of the family. I firmly resolved to be as he wished, though in somewhat a different taste of life. I looked my watch a hundred times. A quarter before one Thomas arrived with the catheter. In five minutes my father was easy. What a happy change! Went calmly to bed. It was an intense frost and the ground was covered with snow.

SUNDAY 3 JANUARY. My father was quite easy. I went out for an hour with the President in his chariot. Talked freely on the Douglas cause. Heard how it struck him in its various points. Saw how foolish the suspicions against him were. Resolved to take men as I find them. Was assured by the President that I should do well as a lawyer. Saw no difficulties in life. Saw that all depends on our frame of mind. Lord and Lady Hyndford were there.[3] The day passed well. In the evening I adored my God; I had now no doubt of the Christian revelation. I was quite satisfied with my being. I hoped to be happy with Miss Blair.

1 It was known that there would have to be a General Election in 1768 and campaigning had started in earnest. The reference to Forfar suggests that Boswell was involved in this particular case because of his friendship with George Dempster who was M.P. for the Perth Burghs, of which Forfar was one. The case was presumably concerned with a dispute over the election of the Forfar town councillors at the burgh election held on 8 October 1767. It was the town councillors who would determine for whom the burgh voted at the General Election. Dempster was opposed by Robert Mackintosh (as to whom, and the outcome of the election, see the entry for 26 February 1783 and relevant footnote) and the campaigning gave rise to much litigation. It was said that the campaigning and litigation cost Dempster over £10,000, an enormous sum in those days. For Dempster, see Introduction, pp. 21-2, 28, 30 and 34.
2 Lord Auchinleck's prostate problem (as to which, see Introduction, p. 34).
3 John Carmichael (1710-1787), 4th Earl of Hyndford, advocate (admitted 25 January 1737), and Janet Grant, Countess of Hyndford (d. 1818), the eldest daughter of William Grant, Lord Prestongrange (Lord of Session and Lord Commissioner of Justiciary 1754-1764). They lived in a mansion in Hyndford's Close, off the south side of the High Street.

MONDAY 4 JANUARY. After breakfast, set off. My father remarked how fool-ish and wicked evil-speaking was. The President afforded a good instance, as so many false reports had been raised against him as to the Douglas cause. We dined at Newbattle. I experienced that calm tranquillity in presence of great people for which I have often wished and have now acquired. Much attention was paid me. Returned to town. Supped Sir George Preston's.[4]

TUESDAY 5 JANUARY. I was at home all day except calling half an hour for Sally's mother. Felt all inclination gone and that I now acted from principle alone.

WEDNESDAY 6 JANUARY. In all day. Matthew Dickie dined with us. The terrible cold weather made me consider keeping warm as almost business enough.

THURSDAY 7 JANUARY. Breakfast Mr Webster's.[5] Old ideas revived in an agreeable manner. When my mind was weak, ideas were too powerful for me. I am now strong; I can discern all their qualities but am master of them.

FRIDAY 8 JANUARY. In all day. Felt myself now quite free of fancies. Was amazed to find how much happiness and misery is ideal. Passed the evening at Mr Moncrieffe's[6] with the Chief Baron,[7] Miss Ords, &c. Felt myself now quite in-different about making a figure in company. Am I grown dull? Or is it a calm confidence in a fixed reputation?

SATURDAY 9 JANUARY. Busy with election law. John Chalmer[8] showed me an old opinion of Duncan Forbes,[9] and reflected how curious it was that the opin-ion remained while the man was no more. A hint such as this brings to my mind

---

4 Sir George Preston of Valleyfield, Bt. Sir George's wife, Lady Anne Preston (née Cochrane), was aunt to Boswell's mother and helped to bring her up when she lived as a child at Culross in Fife. His Edinburgh house was on the Castle Hill.

5 The Rev. Alexander Webster, D.D. His wife was Boswell's aunt, Mary Erskine (sister of Lord Auchinleck's first wife), with whom he had a "runaway marriage", which initially caused great resent-ment on the part of her family, but soon resulted in general content. He was minister at the Tolbooth Kirk, one of the churches in St Giles', being "the peculiar resort of a set of rigid Calvinists... who loved nothing but *extempore* evangelical sermons" (Chambers, p. 127). As a young man, Boswell was particu-larly miserable when attending services at the Tolbooth Kirk, "than which", he wrote, "nothing has given me more gloomy feelings" (Journal, 22 December 1762). Webster was a leader of the "high-flying" or "Evangelical" (or "Popular") party in the Church of Scotland and was revered by his congre-gation. He was very sociable and particularly fond of a convivial drink, so much so that he was known as a "five-bottle man" and acquired the soubriquet of "Dr Bonum Magnum". However, he was never observed to be grossly intoxicated and his conduct was always becoming a man of the cloth. He lived in Webster's Close, off the south side of the Castle Hill.

6 David Stewart Moncrieffe (1710-1790), advocate (admitted 22 June 1736), Joint Deputy King's Remembrancer 1743, sole Deputy 1752, Baron of Exchequer 1781, died unmarried. Each Friday during the court session a sociable group of fellow advocates met at Moncrieffe's house at Horse Wynd (one of the alleys connecting the College, on the south side of the city, with the Cowgate), where he ran a club for cards and supper.

7 The Right Hon. Robert Ord, Lord Chief Baron of the Court of Exchequer, who with a handsome salary of £2,000 per annum was a respectable, elegant and "splendidly hospitable" Englishman (see the entry for 15 August 1773 and relevant footnote). He died on 4 February 1778. For the Court of Exchequer, see Introduction, p. 10.

8 John Muir Chalmer (1726-1774), W.S. (admitted 7 January 1756).

9 Duncan Forbes of Culloden (1685-1747), Lord President of the Court of Session.

all that passed, though it would be barren to anybody but myself. At home all day consulting and writing law papers till six.[10] Went and saw *The Suspicious Husband* and *Citizen*[11]; had my London ideas revived. Went home with Mr Ross[12] and supped and drank a cheerful glass. He gave me all the history of his marriage. He put me into my old romantic frame. I wished again for adventures, for proofs of my own address and of the generosity of charming women. I was for breaking loose from Scots marriage. But my elegant heiress and the old family of Auchinleck brought me back again.

SUNDAY 10 JANUARY. In forenoon, writing to Zélide,[13] &c. Church afternoon. Heard Heiress was to have a knight.[14] Was not so much shocked as before. I did not indeed fully believe it. Visited Sally's mother. Was tired of her.

MONDAY 11 JANUARY. Busy with law. Lord Chief Baron, Mr Moncrieffe, Lord Strichen,[15] &c., dined.

TUESDAY 12 JANUARY. Went in coach with my father, visited Mr James Ker.[16] Felt myself quite established. Dined Lady Alva's[17] with Lord Chief Baron, Miss Ords, and Mr John Mackenzie.[18] Was well, but found I was ignorant and had no turn for the common affairs of life.

WEDNESDAY 13 JANUARY. Dined Mrs Boswell's of Balmuto.[19] Found I had formed a habit there of constant jocularity, insomuch that I never said one serious word. This must be corrected; they are good people. Relations should be regarded. In the immense multiplicity of human beings, the more attachments we can form, the better. Do as we please, they are all few enough. Saw Martin's portraits.[20] Drank tea at Mr Kincaid's.[21] Mrs Kincaid not in; just the father and son and his governor. I appeared a formed man of learning.

THURSDAY 14 JANUARY. Was entertained to find myself again in the Parliament House in all the hurry of business. Mr Kincaid and his family dined with us.

10 The practice of holding consultations at an advocate's house rather than at a tavern was only just developing. According to Somerville, James Ferguson of Pitfour (prior to being elevated to the bench as Lord Pitfour on 14 June 1764) was "the first Scottish lawyer who made a point of being consulted in his own private lodgings" (Somerville, p. 374).
11 Plays by Benjamin Hoadly and Arthur Murphy respectively.
12 David Ross, actor, who was patentee and manager of the newly opened Theatre Royal.
13 For Zélide, see Introduction, p. 32.
14 Sir Alexander Gilmour of Craigmillar, Bt, M.P. for Edinburghshire (Midlothian) 1761-1774.
15 Alexander Fraser, Lord Strichen (died 15 February 1775). Admitted advocate 23 June 1722, appointed Lord of Session 5 June 1730, Lord Commissioner of Justiciary 11 June 1735 (but resigned seat as Justiciary judge on appointment as General of the Mint in 1764).
16 James Ker, Deputy Keeper of the Records (from 1746 to 1777).
17 Elizabeth Erskine (née Hairstanes), *styled* Lady Alva, widow of Charles Erskine, Lord Justice-Clerk Tinwald (1680-1763), mother of James Erskine, Lord Barjarg (*later* Lord Alva).
18 John Mackenzie of Dolphinton (1748-88), who was to be admitted advocate on 25 June 1771 and appointed a judge in the Commissary Court in 1776. In 1773 he married Lord Chief Baron Ord's daughter Alice.
19 Lord Auchinleck's aunt and Claud Boswell's mother (*Wife*, p. 124, n. 2).
20 David Martin (1737-1798), painter and engraver, who studied under, and painted in the style of, Allan Ramsay.
21 Alexander Kincaid, bookseller and publisher, King's Printer and Stationer for Edinburgh, elected to Town Council in 1734, Lord Provost 1776-7.

FRIDAY 15 JANUARY. Breakfasted with Mr William Alexander—genteel people.[22] I thought myself among strangers and not in Edinburgh. Was busy with election causes; found the law fatigue me greatly, and from my indolent and anxious temper I was really harassed with it.

SATURDAY 16 JANUARY. This morning I was amazed when I thought of Mr Lockhart, who is all the forenoon in the Parliament House and is never hurried or fretted, and yet goes through such multitudes of causes. I told him he was just a *brownie* in business. In a few hours the work of a dozen of men is performed by him. He never talks of himself, or complains anyhow. He said he wondered how the story of *brownies* came ever to be believed. I never before saw him aim at philosophy. It is indeed odd how the existence of a being who actually performed work, as a *brownie* was said to do, came to be believed; for it is not like imagining one sees a vision or hears a noise. Miss Montgomerie[23] and Doctor Boswell and I were carried out by worthy Sir Alexander Dick in his coach to Prestonfield. We were very happy. I don't believe there ever existed a man more continually amiable than Sir Alexander. Came home in his coach.

Had a consultation on the Forfar politics. In the forenoon, as we went along in the coach, the Earl of Eglinton[24] was at the Cross.[25] I jumped out, and he and I embraced most cordially. I had a strange pleasure in showing my intimacy with his Lordship before the citizens of Edinburgh. It is fine to be sensible of all one's various sentiments and to analyse them. After my consultation, I went to Fortune's[26] and supped with Lord Eglinton, Lord Galloway,[27] Matthew Henderson,[28] and several more. I saw a genteel, profligate society who live like a distinct nation in Edinburgh, having constant recruits going and coming. I was ill of a venereal disorder, but resolved to make myself easy and eat and drink, though not to excess, yet freely.

About one, Lord Eglinton and I went upstairs and had a friendly conference. I told him I loved Miss Blair much and wished to marry her if she liked me, and I gave him all our history. He said I was right to be honest with her; that her answers were very clever, and that it was probable she liked me. But he said I did not show her attention enough; that a woman had a right to be courted as much as a husband after marriage had a right to command. That if I insisted on a woman showing much love for me, I was certain of being taken in by any artful girl who wanted to have a man with a good estate. That I should tell Miss Blair,

---

22 William Alexander was a merchant.

23 Margaret Montgomerie, Boswell's future wife.

24 Alexander Montgomerie, 10th Earl of Eglinton (as to whom, see Introduction, pp. 20, 27, 29 and 34).

25 For the Cross, see Introduction, p. 6.

26 Fortune's tavern (as to which, see Introduction, p. 38).

27 Alexander Stewart (born c. 1694; died 1773), 6th Earl of Galloway, who lived in a mansion in the Horse Wynd. His wife was the beautiful Catherine Cochrane, the third and youngest daughter of John Cochrane, 4th Earl of Dundonald.

28 Captain Matthew Henderson (1737-88), a very popular antiquary who "dined constantly at Fortune's tavern" (Grant, Vol. I, p. 239) and was immortalised by Robert Burns's elegy on him in 1790.

"If I have any chance, I'll do all in my power to be agreeable. If not, I'll make myself easy as soon as possible." He said my Yorkshire beauty[29] would not do so well, that she would be miserable in this country; and he quoted a blunt saying of the Highlanders that "a cow fed in fine Lowland parks was unco bonny, but turned lean and scabbed when she was turned out to the wild hills". Up came Matthew Henderson and swore he believed Sir Alexander Gilmour was to have the Heiress. My Lord advised me to write to her and know as to this. Such admirable advice did I get from a man of great genius who knows the world perfectly. He talked to me of my neutrality in the Ayrshire elections. I felt I was wrong. I was now quite free of hypochondria. Walking home after convoying my Lord to the Bow,[30] I met a girl. Like a madman I would try the experiment of cooling myself when ill. What more mischief may it not bring!

SUNDAY 17 JANUARY. In all forenoon. At dinner my father was out of humour because I had been so late abroad. I bore with him quite calmly. At five met at Mr Macqueen's[31] with Messieurs Rae,[32] Alexander Murray,[33] and Armstrong,[34] as counsel for Raybould, the forger,[35] as I allow myself to consult on criminal business on Sundays. Went to bed at nine that I might be up early next morning.

MONDAY 18 JANUARY. Rose at three. Wrote a reply in the Forfar politics, and prepared a charge to the jury for Raybould. Went to the Justiciary Court at nine. Dull reading of the decreet of the Court of Session for many hours. At two I went home, dined and drank a glass or two of malaga, and wrote another reply. Returned to the court. The Solicitor[36] charged the jury for the Crown. I was very

---

29 Miss Elizabeth Diana Bosville, *later* Lady Macdonald, wife of Sir Alexander Macdonald of Sleat. Boswell first met her in London on 16 February 1766.
30 The West Bow (as to which, see Introduction, p. 7).
31 Robert Macqueen, advocate (as to whom, see Appendix, p. 560).
32 David Rae, advocate (as to whom, see Appendix, pp. 560-1).
33 Alexander Murray, advocate (as to whom, see Appendix, p. 562).
34 David Armstrong, advocate (admitted 13 December 1763), Sheriff-Depute of Dumfriesshire 1777-88.
35 John Raybould was indicted on the capital charge of counterfeiting banknotes. The Court of Session had found the allegations proved in civil proceedings. At the criminal trial, which commenced on 18 January, Raybould was defended by Alexander Murray, David Armstrong and Boswell. In a preliminary plea, Murray unsuccessfully argued that the indictment was irrelevant on the basis that the offence with which Raybould was charged did not amount to forgery and that, in any event, forgery was not punishable as a capital offence but only by way of "arbitrary punishment". The five judges held that the charge was "relevant to infer the pains of death" and ordered that the trial proceed. Henry Dundas (the Solicitor General), for the prosecution, produced the Decreet of Reduction which had been obtained in the Court of Session and the Decreet was read out in court. Another counsel for the prosecution, Andrew Crosbie (for whom, see the following entry and relevant footnote), then stated to the court that, although he considered that the Decreet was full evidence in the case and could not be challenged by any other evidence whatever and did not require to be corroborated, the prosecution consented to exhibit all the documents which had been produced in the Court of Session proceedings "in order that the Jury might have an opportunity of informing their consciences of every particular relative to this affair in so far as the nature of the thing will permit". The documents were then duly exhibited, after which Dundas, on behalf of the prosecution, and Boswell, on behalf of the accused, respectively charged the jury. The following day the jury returned a unanimous verdict that the accused was art and part guilty of the offences charged. Raybould was then sentenced to be hanged, the execution to take place on 24 February in the Grassmarket (N.A.S. JC7/35).
36 The Solicitor-General, Henry Dundas (as to whom, see Appendix, pp. 562-3).

uneasy and frightened. I however began, and was soon warm and in spirits, and recollected all my arguments. I really spoke well for above half an hour. I saw my imperfections, and hoped in time to make a real good speaker. I felt sound ambition and clear faculties. At eight went to Crosbie's[37] and had tea and a consultation with Mr James Hay, Writer to the Signet.[38] He revived in my mind worthy Scots family ideas. What a variety do I enjoy by observation! I went to bed in good time.

TUESDAY 19 JANUARY. Was at the anniversary meeting of the Faculty of Advocates.[39] Had the true old sensations, and felt myself *Mr James Boswell*, comfortable and secure. Recollected how formerly I should have been wretched with a life so void of vivid enjoyment, but now had force of mind enough to be content. At Clerihue's we were very merry. The Dean[40] after many ladies had been drank called out, "Here is a toast: a young lady just in her teens—Miss Corsica. Give her a gentleman!" All called out, "Paoli!" I drank too much. I went to a close in the Luckenbooths[41] to seek a girl whom I had once seen in the street. I found a natural daughter of the late Lord Kinnaird, a fine lass. I stayed an hour and a half with her and drank malaga and was most amorous, being so well that no infection remained. I felt now that the indifference of the Heiress had cured me, and I was indifferent as to her. I was so happy with Jeanie Kinnaird that I very philosophically reasoned that there was to me so much virtue mixed with licentious love that perhaps I might be privileged. For it made me humane, polite, generous. But then lawful love with a woman I really like would make me still better. I forgot the risk I run with this girl. She looked so healthy and so honest I had no fears.

THURSDAY 21 JANUARY. Lords Stonefield[42] and Barjarg,[43] Walter Campbell,[44]

---

37 Andrew Crosbie, advocate (as to whom, see Appendix, p. 562). Crosbie's house at this time was in the West Bow and it is said that "he was probably the last lawyer that lived in the heart of the coppersmiths of the Bow" (Ramsay, p. 456, n. 1).
38 At this time there were two Writers to the Signet by the name of James Hay, but this was probably James Hay of Cocklaw (admitted W.S. 9 December 1728, died 20 June 1771), the father of Charles Hay, who was to be admitted advocate on 24 December 1768 and would become a very close friend of Boswell's.
39 At this meeting, Boswell was appointed to a committee to find a suitable new site for the Advocates' Library and he was re-elected one of the fifteen "Publick Examiners". On 16 January 1770 and again on 17 January 1775 Boswell was to be appointed to serve for one year as one of the nine private examinators for the examination of intrants on the Civil Law; and on 14 January 1772, 18 December 1779 and 21 December 1782 respectively he was to be appointed to serve for one year as one of the seven private examinators on Scots law (Stewart, pp. 179-181, 198, 221, 257, 308 and 337).
40 Alexander Lockhart, Dean of the Faculty of Advocates (as to whom, see Appendix, p. 559).
41 For the Luckenbooths, see Introduction, p. 6.
42 John Campbell, Lord Stonefield (died 19 June 1801), admitted advocate 9 January 1748, appointed Sheriff-Depute of Forfarshire 5 June 1753, appointed Lord of Session 16 June 1762.
43 James Erskine, Lord Barjarg (*later* Lord Alva), son of Lord Tinwald (Charles Erskine, Lord Justice-Clerk (1680-1763)), and second cousin to Boswell. Erskine, who was born in 1723 and was of exceedingly small stature, was admitted advocate 6 December 1743, appointed Sheriff-Depute of Perthshire 1748, Baron of Exchequer 1754, Knight-Marshall of Scotland 1758, and Lord of Session 18 June 1761. In 1772 he was to change his title to Lord Alva on becoming owner of the estate of the Erskines of Alva, near Tillicoutry in Clackmannanshire. He died on 13 May 1796.
44 Walter Campbell of Shawfield (1741-1816), advocate (admitted 27 July 1763), Sheriff-Depute of Kincardineshire 1767-77.

George Cockburn,[45] &c., dined. I drank tea with Johnston.[46] Supped with Dempster[47] at Peter Ramsay's.[48] Had a most pleasant evening.

FRIDAY 22 JANUARY. My father and I dined at Lord Coalston's. I had written to Miss Blair to tell me if she was going to be married to Sir Alexander Gilmour, and if she was disengaged and did not write me so I should *upon honour* consider it to be the same thing as if she was engaged. No answer had come yet, so I began to exert all my spirit to be free. I drank tea at Mrs Hamilton of Bangour's, and made my peace for not having visited her since I came home.

SATURDAY 23 JANUARY. My father and I dined at Lord Galloway's. Old ideas of true people of quality revived. I then went to the play, to Mrs Hamilton's box. It was *Venice Preserved*:[49] Jaffier, Ross; Pierre, Sowdon; I relished it much. The Heiress began to lose her dominion over me. I supped at Ross's after the play. Sowdon was there and Cullen,[50] &c. Felt myself now calm and improved, as I used to wish.

MONDAY 25 JANUARY. In all day. M. Dupont[51] drank tea with me; had two consultations. Supped Mrs Hamilton of Bangour's, an Edinburgh evening. Found I was fit for any company. Before my Account of Corsica came out, I was desirous to have all my visits paid, as I thenceforward intended if possible to maintain a propriety and strictness of manners.

WEDNESDAY 27 JANUARY. My father and Claud[52] and I dined at Lord Barjarg's. It was just a family dinner. I felt myself palled with insipidity, so high is my taste of society grown. [H]ad a consultation at the Hon. Alexander

45 George Cockburn of Gleneagles (1729-1799), advocate (admitted 10 July 1751), *later* George Cockburn Haldane, Sheriff-Depute of Banffshire 1756-1763, Sheriff-Depute of Stirlingshire and Clackmannanshire 1764-1770.

46 John Johnston's house at this time was in Roxburgh's Close (off the north side of the High Street opposite the Luckenbooths) and he was to remain there until at least June 1772.

47 George Dempster, M.P. (as to whom, see Introduction, pp. 21-2, 28, 30 and 34).

48 Peter Ramsay was the landlord of the "Red Lion" inn, a stabler's hostelry at the foot of St Mary's Wynd, where were "commodious premises, stables, hay-lofts, coach-sheds and pump all enclosed within a courtyard" (Stuart, p. 114).

49 By Thomas Otway, a very popular play in the eighteenth century. Boswell saw it on several occasions and in a letter to John Johnston dated 13 July 1763 remarked that the play "has often roused our souls in the good Theatre of Edinburgh" (Walker, p. 170).

50 Robert Cullen (1742-1810), advocate (admitted December 1764), son of the celebrated physician and chemist William Cullen, M.D. (1710-90). Cullen, who was renowned as an accomplished mimic, was to be appointed a Lord of Session (as Lord Cullen) on 17 November 1796.

51 The Rev. Pierre Loumeau Dupont, minister of the Huguenot congregation in Edinburgh (*Wife*, p. 131, n. 1).

52 Boswell's first cousin once removed, Claud Boswell of Balmuto, advocate (as to whom, see Introduction, p. 35). Boswell was not on particularly close terms with his cousin. Indeed, he considered him to be somewhat unimaginative and narrow-minded. "Balmuto saw nothing but what was solid, and substantially his own", wrote Boswell, "[and] he had thick, high stone walls built round that extent, and had that only in his view, except when I surprised him by sometimes taking a hammer and beating a hole in his walls so as to give him a peep of the fields of fancy, which made him caper; but his mother and sisters took care to build all up again directly" (Journal, 29 April 1769). He is said to have been "a robust and athletic man" who "spoke with a strong Scotch accent" and "was fond of his joke" (Kay, Vol. II, p. 190). His eldest sister, Elizabeth, was to become Lord Auchinleck's second wife.

Gordon's.[53] Then supped Mrs Cockburn's.[54] A great company there. Felt myself quite easy, but still subject to fall in love with the woman next me at table. I have from nature a feverish constitution which time has moderated and will at last cure. Mrs Cockburn said a man much versant in love was not so valuable. I maintained he was, for a hack, if not lamed or too much worn down, is the cleverest horse when put on good pasture.

THURSDAY 28 JANUARY. My father was confined with a severe cold. I saw his great worth and value to me, when I was reminded of the danger of losing him. I resolved to act towards him in such a way as to make his life comfortable, and give me the consolation after he is gone that I have done my duty, and may hope for the same attention from my son. I was not abroad but at the Parliament House and dining at Lord President's.[55]

FRIDAY 29 JANUARY. Had Hallglenmuir[56] and Knockroon[57] to dine. Went after supper to Bailie Hunter's,[58] and sat a while with Lady Crawford and a good many more company. Sat too late. I resolved to be more regular, as I really had a constant fever and sweating every morning.

SUNDAY 31 JANUARY. Forenoon at church. At night went to Sally's mother and renewed gallantry.

MONDAY 1 FEBRUARY. Was busy all day with law till five, when I drank tea at Miss Montgomerie's. At seven consulted at Solicitor's.

53 The Hon. Alexander Gordon (1739-1792), advocate (admitted 7 August 1759), was the third son of William Gordon, second Earl of Aberdeen, by Lady Anne Gordon, daughter of Alexander, second Duke of Gordon. He was appointed Sheriff-Depute of Kirkcudbrightshire in 1764, which post he was to hold until appointed Lord of Session (as Lord Rockville) on 1 July 1784. It was said of him as a judge that he adorned the bench "by the dignified manliness of his appearance and polished urbanity of his manners" (Douglas, *The Peerage of Scotland*, Vol. I, p. 22). Boswell and Alexander Gordon were to become very close friends.

54 Alison (or Alice or Alicia) Cockburn (née Rutherford) (c.1712-1794), authoress and tireless correspondent. She was the widow of Patrick Cockburn of Ormiston, advocate, who died in 1753, leaving her with an inconsiderable income. "She never, however, lost her liveliness, her insatiable love of mischief, mockery, and match-making... At the gatherings at her little parlour, Mrs Cockburn was to be seen attired in her striped silk saque, with her auburn hair turned back and covered with cap or lace hood, bound beneath her chin" (Graham, p. 331). In or about 1764 was published her famous song "The Flowers of the Forest" (possibly written more than thirty years earlier), which was set to an existing air. "Nimble with her pen, clever in her verses, it is on [this] one song Mrs Cockburn's reputation lasts" (*ibid.*, p. 332). "This woman had the kindliest of souls... There were merry dancings in the tiny sitting-room of her flat in [what came to be called Blair's Close] near the Castle... On these nights the furniture was piled up high in the lobby, and the fiddler in the cupboard played and panted over strathspeys, or Lord Kellie's last minuet" (*ibid.*, pp. 332-3).

55 The Lord President's house was in Adam's Court, to the south of the Cowgate and immediately to the north of Adam Square. His address was later given as being Adam Square, which suggests that his house was situated at the southern end of the Court adjoining the Square. The Court and the Square were displaced by the construction of Chambers Street and the buildings on the west side of the South Bridge.

56 Alexander Mitchell of Hallglenmuir, an Ayrshire neighbour and distant relative (*Wife*, p. 47, n. 4).

57 John Boswell of Knockroon (1741-1805), a distant relative of Boswell's who became a "writer" practising in Ayr.

58 This is almost certainly James Hunter, the future Sir James Hunter-Blair (for whom, see the entry for 4 March 1776 and relevant footnote). He served on the Town Council from 1763 to 1768 and for part of that time was a bailie. He was re-elected to the Council in 1777.

TUESDAY 2 FEBRUARY. At seven met Mr Alexander Orme[59] and Holmains, George Frazer,[60] William Hay,[61] and Jamie Baillie[62] at Clerihue's at a treat given by the heritors of Lochmaben.[63] Mr Ross had come up to me and asked me to sup with him; so I went and found Sir Johns Cathcart and Whitefoord. We were very merry and pleasant. I drank a great deal, though I was not well yet. Between two and three I went to Sally's mother's and renewed again. What a life do I lead!

WEDNESDAY 3 FEBRUARY. I awaked so ill I could hardly rise, and all forenoon I was quite out of order and feverish after my debauchery. I felt myself a very rake as I pleaded a cause before Lord Monboddo.

FRIDAY 5 FEBRUARY. I supped at Lord Monboddo's with Lords Coalston and Kennet,[64] &c. I was quite easy. I saw lords of session in a quite different light from what I have done by looking only at awful judges. Claret fevered me, and I again went to Sally's mother and renewed.

SATURDAY 6 FEBRUARY. Breakfasted at the President's. Was too late for a cause before Lord Monboddo. Determined to confine myself to the Parliament House all the forenoon. Considered the law is my profession, my occupation in life. Saw it not to be such a mystery as I apprehended.

SUNDAY 7 FEBRUARY. Church forenoon. Heard Mr Butter in St Paul's Chapel,[65] afternoon. Drank tea with Mrs Montgomerie-Cuninghame.[66] Then visited Lady Maxwell. Was quite cheerful and well. Mr Fullarton (the Nabob) came in. Miss Blair was now arrived. He proposed we should go and visit her. We went. She was reserved and distant. I saw plainly all was over. Yet I could not be quite certain. Fullarton and I came away together. I liked the man. I asked him freely how he was. We owned candidly to each other that we were both for Miss Blair. I insisted that he and I should not part that night. I carried him to sup at Mrs Montgomerie-Cuninghame's and then we adjourned to Clerihue's. I opened the Nabob's mind, and he and I gave each other a fair recital of all that we hoped from the Heiress. It was agreed I had her heart once, and perhaps still, if she was not engaged to Sir Alexander Gilmour. "Come," said I, "we shall be at our wits' end. If you'll ask her tomorrow, upon honour I'll ask her." We shook hands and wished all happiness to him who should succeed. Never was there a more curious scene. At two in the

59 Alexander Orme of Mugdrum, W.S. (admitted 3 February 1755), died 8 January 1789.
60 Excise officer.
61 William Hay, W.S. (admitted 13 January 1755), died 1776.
62 A "writer".
63 At this time, Boswell was counsel for the heritors of Lochmaben in an action against them by the minister of Lochmaben.
64 Robert Bruce, Lord Kennet (died 8 April 1785), admitted advocate 15 January 1743, appointed Professor of the Law of Nature and Nations at the University of Edinburgh in 1759, Sheriff-Depute of Stirlingshire and Clackmannanshire in 1760, Lord of Session 4 July 1764. After his elevation to the bench he and his family moved from cramped and dark accommodation in Forrester's Wynd (where the maid had to sleep under the kitchen-dresser) to a genteel house consisting of two flats in Horse Wynd.
65 For St Paul's Chapel, see Introduction, pp. 15 and 22.
66 Mrs Elizabeth Montgomerie-Cuninghame (née Montgomerie) of Lainshaw, wife of Capt. Alexander Montgomerie-Cuninghame and younger sister of Boswell's future wife, Margaret Montgomerie.

morning I went to Sally's mother, and, being flushed with claret, renewed my love.

MONDAY 8 FEBRUARY. Between nine and ten went to Miss Blair. "Come, before they come in, are you engaged or no?" She seemed reserved. I said, "You know I am much in love with you, and, if you are not engaged, I would take a good deal of trouble to make myself agreeable to you." She said, "You need not take the trouble. Now you must not be angry with me." "Indeed no", said I. "But is it really so? Say upon your word, upon honour." She did so. I therefore was satisfied. My spirit was such that, though I felt some regret, I appeared quite easy and gay. I made her give me breakfast, and with true philosophy I put my mind in a proper frame. It was agreed that we were not to ask her if she was engaged. She gave me a lecture on my conduct towards her, in talking without reserve. At twelve the Nabob was with her, and she treated him with the greatest coldness. He and I met at the Cross at two and joked and laughed with all our acquaintance. I did the Nabob much good, for I relieved him from serious love by my vivacity. I have one of the most singular minds ever was formed.

TUESDAY 9 FEBRUARY. Mr Claud[67] and I visited the Heiress. She seemed very ordinary today. My Lord President and his lady,[68] Mrs Montgomerie-Cuninghame, Professor Stevenson,[69] &c., dined. Mrs Dundas and I danced at a private ball at Fortune's, a very good company. The Nabob was there, and I made him talk easily and be quite cheerful. After supper I gave for my toast, "May we bear our misfortunes with spirit", and sung, "The mind of a woman." Lord Monboddo was there and highly pleased. All my prejudices against Edinburgh were worn off. I saw the company quite agreeable and elegant enough, with a great deal of virtuous manners.

WEDNESDAY 10 FEBRUARY. I breakfasted at Lord President's.

FRIDAY 12 FEBRUARY. Lord Justice-Clerk, Mr David Kennedy,[70] Ilay Campbell,[71] Mr Alexander Tait, John Davidson,[72] &c., dined.

SATURDAY 13 FEBRUARY. I dined at Lord Justice-Clerk's with my father.

---

67 Claud Boswell of Balmuto.

68 This was Lord President Dundas's second wife, Jean Grant (third daughter of William Grant, Lord Prestongrange), by whom he had four sons and two daughters.

69 Professor John Stevenson, Professor of Logic at Edinburgh University. Boswell had studied under Stevenson during his university education. Stevenson's lectures on logic were delivered in Latin and were said to have been "dry and barren"; but he also taught his pupils *Belles Lettres*, and these classes, which were given in English, were considered to be highly "inviting and profitable" (Somerville, pp. 12-14).

70 David Kennedy, advocate (admitted 25 February 1752), M.P. Ayrshire 1768-74, tenth Earl of Cassillis 1775, died 1792, unmarried. Boswell was to refer to him as being a "joker... and nothing more" and "a good, honest, merry fellow indeed, but... devoid of the talents which distinguish a man in public life" (Journal, 5 April 1773).

71 For Ilay Campbell, see Appendix, p. 562.

72 John Davidson, W.S. (admitted 3 April 1749), author, Crown Agent, Deputy Keeper of the Signet 1778-97, died 29 November 1797.

Lords Kinnoul, Coalston, Kames, Baron Winn,[73] &c., were there. I drank pretty freely, and after five went to Sally's mother and renewed. She told me she was again, she believed, as before. I was a little embarrassed, but just submitted my mind to it. I then went to Crosbie and had some tea. Then he and I went to Mr James Hay's and had a consultation with Mrs Smith of Forret. It was quite in old style, and when it was over honest Mr Hay gave us a couple of bottles of claret. This inflamed me again and I went back to Sally's mother. She really looked pretty.

MONDAY 15 FEBRUARY. This day I heard from Mr Dilly that my Account of Corsica was ready for publication, so I ordered Mr Neill to give out copies in Scotland.[74]

THURSDAY 18 FEBRUARY. I breakfasted with Lord Hailes and gave him my book. I dined with my father, Lord Coalston, &c., at the Solicitor's with the ladies of Cromartie. Lady Augusta, the famed beauty, did not strike me. I then went to an Ayrshire ball at Fortune's. My book was published this day, and felt my own importance. I danced with the Countess of Crawford, so opened the ball. I was quite as I wished to be; only I am positive I had not so high an opinion of myself as other people had. I look back with wonder on the mysterious and respectful notions I used to have of authors. I felt that I was still subject to attacks of feverish love, but I also knew that my mind is now firm enough soon to recover its tone.

SATURDAY 20 FEBRUARY. I dined at Lord Dundonald's. There had been a coldness between that family and me, and I had not seen them of a long time.[75] All was well again, and old ideas of Major Cochrane, my dear mother,[76] &c., &c., &c. revived.

SUNDAY 21 FEBRUARY. In all forenoon. I had dreamt of Raybould under sentence of death. I was gloomy. Afternoon, church. Tea home, then visited Raybould, that my gloomy imagination might be cured by seeing the reality. I was shown up to him by Archibald, the soldier who was to be tried for murder.[77] The clanking of the iron-room door was terrible.[78] I found him very composed. I sat by him an hour and a half by the light of a dim farthing candle. He spoke very properly on

73 George Winn (1725-1798), called to the English bar in 1755, Baron of Exchequer in Scotland 1761-1776, created Lord Headley in 1797.
74 The London publishing firm of Edward and Charles Dilly had purchased the copyright of the work (which included Boswell's *Journal of a Tour to Corsica*, generally considered to be by far the superior part of the book) for 100 guineas. Adam Neill was a printer in Edinburgh. The first edition of the book was out of print within six weeks and a third edition was required the following year. "By the publication of *An Account of Corsica* Boswell became at twenty-seven a literary figure of international reputation. His book could be read in five languages and was the concern of statesmen... For many years he was to be known as Corsica Boswell, and though he was to publish two greater books, he was never again to be so admired, never again to take such unalloyed satisfaction in his fame" (Pottle, pp. 367-8).
75 Thomas Cochrane, eighth Earl of Dundonald (formerly known as Major Cochrane), was Boswell's maternal great-uncle. The editors of *Wife* (at p. 139, n. 1) suggest that "the 'coldness' may have been occasioned by the Douglas cause, Lord Dundonald being a violent partisan of the Hamilton interest".
76 For Boswell's mother, see Introduction, pp. 4 and 34.
77 James Archibald was to be defended at his trial by Boswell, who secured a verdict of "not guilty" (N.A.S. JC7/35).
78 The iron room was the room in which prisoners awaiting execution were incarcerated.

religion. I read him the 4 Chapter of the I Epistle of John and lectured upon it. On verse 18 I discoursed on *fear* very appositely,[79] by an illustration taken from Robert Hay, the soldier who was hanged last year. "There, John," said I, "did he lie quite sunk, quite desperate, and neither would eat nor drink, and all for *fear*, just terror for dying. But the comfortable doctrine of Christianity prevents this." I was quite firm, and I was astonished to compare myself now with myself when a boy, remarkably timorous. Raybould seemed wonderfully easy. I therefore talked quite freely to him. "But, John, have you no fear for the immediate pain of dying?" "No," said he, "I have had none as yet. I know not how it may be at the very moment. But I do think I shall be quite composed." I looked steadfastly at him during this and saw he was speaking truly. One certain sign of his being much at ease was the readiness with which his attention was diverted to any other subject than his own melancholy situation; for when a man is much distressed he is still fixed in brooding over his calamity. But Raybould talked of his wife's journey down in all its particulars, just as if he had been an indifferent, ordinary man.

He told me when he came first to Scotland he did not know the difference between an agent and an advocate. I saw him beginning to smile at his own ignorance. I considered how amazing it would be if a man under sentence of death should really laugh, and, with the nicest care of a diligent student of human nature, I as decently as possible first smiled as he did, and gradually cherished the risible exertion, till he and I together fairly laughed. How strange! He very calmly examined whether a man dying of sickness or one in his situation was worst. He said one in his situation. I argued that one dying of sickness was worst, because he is weakened and unable to support the fear of death, whereas one in his situation was quite well but for the prospect before him. Raybould, however, maintained his proposition, because, he said, the man weakened by sickness was brought to a state of indifference. I bid him farewell. It was truly a curious scene. I went and sat a while at the worthy Doctor's.

WEDNESDAY 24 FEBRUARY. I went to see Raybould's execution. I was invited up to the window of one——, a merchant, by——, who knew me. I tried to be quite firm and philosophical, and imagined Raybould in some future period telling what he felt at his execution. The most dreadful event seems light when past, and I made it past by imagination. I felt very little; but when he stood long on the ladder I grew impatient, and was beginning to have uneasy sensations. I came home. Mr William Wilson, S., Mr Walter Scott,[80] &c. dined. At night I was with Lady Crawford at *The Beggar's Opera*, which quite relieved any gloom. The songs revived London ideas, and my old intrigues with actresses who used to play in this opera. I was happy in being free of Miss Blair. The farce was *The Vintner Tricked*.[81] It was curious that after seeing a real hanging I should meet with two mock ones on the stage. I went with Houston Stewart and renewed our old

79 "There is no fear in love; but perfect love casteth out fear."
80 Sir Walter Scott's father (1729-99), who was a W.S. (admitted 13 January 1755).
81 A play by Henry Ward.

acquaintance at Caddie[82] Miller's with oysters and claret. We sat till two, very agreeably. When I came home I was a little dreary, but it went off and I slept well.

SATURDAY 27 FEBRUARY. Sir Alexander Dick carried me out in his coach to Prestonfield. No other person was there. We were quite happy.

The winter session of the court ended in mid-March and Boswell's total fees for the session (which had started in mid-November 1767) amounted to 131 guineas. Boswell now made preparations for a jaunt to London.

WEDNESDAY 16 MARCH. It is very odd that it is hardly possible to set out upon a journey without being in confusion. I was so not a little this morning. My worthy friend Johnston came and stayed by me while I packed my trunk, the sign of a real friend. He who can stand by a man while he packs his trunk would attend him to the place of execution were he going to be hanged; for really one packing his trunk and one going to be hanged are pretty much the same company to a friend. My travelling companion was Mr Robertson near Alloway, one of the contractors for paving the streets of London, but who was going thither for the first time. Mr John Small, one of the macers of the Court of Session,[83] was to ride by us all the way. He could not get a horse this morning, so we took him into the chaise to Haddington, where we had a beefsteak, having set out at two o'clock. We seemed hearty and easy. Only I, whose combustible, or rather inflammable, soul is always taking fire, was uneasy at having left *Mary*, a pretty, lively little girl whom accident had thrown in my way a few days before. She was one of those females who either from wickedness or misfortune are the slaves of profligate men. She was very young, and I resolved to try if there was virtue in her; so I left her as many guineas as she said she could live upon till my return. I got two of my friends to promise to go to her and offer her a high bribe to break her engagement to me, and to write me what she did. I find I am still somewhat of a Don Quixote, for now am I in love with perhaps an abandoned, worthless being; but we shall see.[84] We went to Dunbar at night, where we drank the finest small beer I ever tasted in my life, and had a good supper and warm punch.

Boswell and his companions had a comfortable and enjoyable journey to London. On his arrival on 22 March, Boswell noted that the "streets and squares of the metropolis with all the hurry and variety struck me to a certain degree, but by no means as they had once done, and I contentedly felt myself an Edinburgh advocate". However, he was clearly soon taking full advantage of the opportunities available, for he records that that same evening "I sallied

---

82 For the caddies, see Introduction, p. 6.

83 There were four macers in the Court of Session. They carried silver maces and ushered the Lords to their seats. They also called causes and executed the immediate orders of the Lords "as to cite and apprehend Persons Summarily complained of; imprison Advocates' Servants for unduly keeping up Processes, and to see good Order observed in the session-house by inferior servants and the common people" (Forbes, pp. ix-x.).

84 John Johnston wrote to Boswell about the girl in May 1768. His letter is missing, but its content can be deduced from the relevant part of Boswell's response dated 10 June 1768: "I am sorry to find that there is not a spark of virtue in Mary. This instance will be some cure to me of my disposition to be made a dupe" (Walker, p. 238).

forth like a roaring lion after girls, blending philosophy and raking. I had a neat little lass in armour,[85] *at a tavern in the Strand." Having ascertained that Samuel Johnson, whom he was very anxious to see, had gone to Oxford, Boswell travelled there on 26 March. On his arrival, records Boswell, Johnson "took me all in his arms and kissed me on both sides of the head, and was as cordial as ever I saw him...I told him how I was settled as a lawyer and how I had made two hundred pounds by the law this year. He grumbled and laughed and was wonderfully pleased. 'What, Bozzy? Two hundred pounds! A great deal.'" Boswell then took the opportunity of asking Johnson for advice on a matter that was perplexing him and which he had been longing to discuss: was it not morally wrong for a lawyer to plead a cause which he knew to be bad? "Sir," said Johnson, "you don't know it to be bad till the judge determines it." It was on this same occasion that Johnson renewed a promise he had made to Boswell to come to Scotland and to visit with Boswell some of the Western Isles. Two days later, writes Boswell, "I...talked of law and of our courts of justice in Scotland, of which I gave...a very good account. I found that having been two years a lawyer in real business had given me great force. I could not be sensible of it, while living always with the same people. But I felt it when I was with Mr Johnson."*

On his return to London, Boswell had a bad attack of a venereal disease and was confined to his room. While in this state, "the great men of the literary and political world came to pay their respects to the author of Corsica, the book of the hour".[86] Among his many visitors was David Hume, who remarked that it required "great goodness of disposition to withstand [the] baleful effects of Christianity".

One of the highlights of Boswell's visit to London was a lengthy private interview with the Lord Chief Justice, Lord Mansfield (who, although an English lawyer, was a Scotsman, by the name of William Murray). The main topic of conversation was the great Douglas Cause, which was due to be considered by the House of Lords, where Mansfield was one of the Law Lords. Boswell was delighted to find that Mansfield was keen to hear all that he had to say on the matter. Warming to his subject, Boswell told Mansfield that "what made the judges on the Hamilton side so obnoxious was their maintaining that there was no law in the cause... My Lord, when you thus deny a man the great privilege of filiation, you are taking the very pavement from under his feet. You are depriving him of half his cause." To this Mansfield expressed his agreement.

On 9 June Boswell left London to return to Edinburgh for the summer session. He was soon very busy again with much work and his fees for the session (which ran for two months, from mid-June to mid-August) amounted to fifty-eight guineas.[87] As usual, Boswell went to Auchinleck for the court vacation. Here he had a recurrence of a former rage for gaming, but, as he told Temple in a letter dated 24 August, he recovered himself sufficiently to resolve "never to play at a game of chance, and never at whist but for a trifle to make up a party". He also announced that he had now found a new object of his affections — "the finest creature that ever was formed: la belle Irlandaise". This was Mary Ann Boyd, the sixteen-year-old daughter of a wealthy counsellor-at-law in Ireland. Boswell met this

---

85 That is, with a prophylactic.
86 *Wife*, p. 174.
87 Consultation Book.

"*Grecian nymph*" *when the Boyds made a brief visit to Ayrshire, and on their departure he was given an invitation to come and see them in Dublin. Boswell promised to be there in March when the court rose at the end of the winter session.*

In September Boswell attended the circuit courts at Dumfries and Ayr and received instructions in two causes. He later reported to John Johnston that these circuits had been "riotous". "I must henceforth", he told his friend, "resolve to observe the strictest sobriety; for my inclination towards drinking is twice as strong as your honour's; and that is saying not a little." [88]

---

88 Letter from Boswell to John Johnston of Grange dated 21 September 1768, reproduced in Walker, pp. 242-4, at p. 243.

1769

On 27 February 1769, the House of Lords delivered its judgment in the Douglas Cause. The court found in favour of Douglas and overturned the decree of the Court of Session. What happened next was sheer drama. Ilay Campbell, who was one of the counsel for Douglas, set off straight away on horseback to announce the outcome to the citizens of Edinburgh, who were eagerly awaiting news. On the evening of 2 March he arrived in Edinburgh and went to the Cross, where he waved his hat in the air and cried, "Douglas for ever!" The entire town then erupted in joyful celebration. Householders in favour of the outcome illuminated their windows, many toasts were made to the health of Douglas and his supporters, and bonfires were lit in various places. Boswell, after calling on his father to tell him the "glorious news" (to which Lord Auchinleck reacted "very cooly"), went to the Cross to find out what was happening. Matters then became rather more serious, for the mob, after marching up and down the streets, decided to break the windows of those who had failed to illuminate, paying particular attention to the windows of the Lord President and the Lord Justice-Clerk. It seems that Boswell took a leading part in these activities, and it is thought that he was the witty gentleman who is said to have remarked as stones were thrown at the Lord President's windows that the members of the mob were giving their casting votes. Several of the judges (such as Lord Auchinleck) who had voted for Douglas but, in support of the Lord President, refused to illuminate, had their windows broken too. The mob even tried to break down the Lord President's door, much to the alarm of his family; and the following morning he was jostled when carried to the Parliament House in his chair and was put in considerable fear of physical harm. However, order was finally restored when two troops of dragoons were summoned to guard the streets.[1]

According to Lord Auchinleck's friend, John Ramsay of Ochtertyre, Lord Auchinleck was so outraged by his son's wild and irresponsible behaviour that he "entreated the President, with tears in his eyes, to put his son in the Tolbooth".[2] Boswell was examined on the matter by Sheriff Cockburn[3] to whom Boswell said that, when he went to the Cross to see what was going on, one of the group there asked what sort of a man the sheriff was and whether he was not to be dreaded. The answer of another member of the group, according to Boswell, was "No, no, he is a puppy of the President's making." Ramsay tells us that "on hearing this exordium, Mr Cockburn went off, leaving the culprit to himself."[4]

During the winter session from mid-November 1768 to mid-March 1769 Boswell's fees amounted to one hundred and twenty-three guineas, and, in addition to all his other work, he appeared at no less than fifteen hearings before his father.[5] At the end of the session, Boswell and his father went to Auchinleck and on their way there spent six days visiting Boswell's impoverished cousins, the Montgomeries of Lainshaw, in Ayrshire. It seems that

1 Ramsay, p. 173, n. 1; Omond, Vol. II, pp. 65-6; *The London Chronicle*, 11-14 March, 18-20 April 1769; Pottle, pp. 398-9.
2 Ramsay, p. 173, n. 1. For the Tolbooth, see Introduction, p. 7.
3 Archibald Cockburn of Cockpen (1738-1820), advocate (admitted 10 August 1762), Sheriff-Depute of Edinburghshire 1765, Judge of Admiralty 1782, Baron of Exchequer 1790-1809.
4 Ramsay, *loc.cit.*
5 Consultation Book.

it was there decided that during Boswell's forthcoming jaunt to Ireland to see la belle Irlandaise *he would be accompanied by his unmarried first cousin, Margaret Montgomerie, the thirty-one-year-old daughter of David Montgomerie of Lainshaw and of Lord Auchinleck's sister, Veronica Boswell. The two of them set off together from Auchinleck on 25 April, calling at first for a couple of days at Lainshaw. During the trip to Ireland Boswell started to feel that he was falling in love with Margaret. They sailed from Portpatrick on the night between 1 and 2 May, and on 3 May Boswell wrote to Temple declaring his passion for Margaret: "She and I have always been in the greatest intimacy. I have proved her on a thousand occasions, and found her sensible, agreeable, and generous... [H]er person is to me the most desirable that I ever saw... I [have] found her both by sea and land the best companion I ever saw. I am exceedingly in love with her. I highly value her. If ever a man had his full choice of a wife, I would have it in her. But the objections are she is two years older than I. She has only a thousand pounds.[6] My father would be violent against my marrying her, as she would bring neither money nor interest." Boswell showed this letter to Margaret who begged him not to send it. (He did, however, send it eventually—see the entry for 16 June.) By the time Boswell reached Dublin, he was becoming increasingly certain that Margaret was the woman for him and he evidently treated* la belle Irlandaise *(whom he now found childish) with great reserve, to such an extent as to cause offence.*

Boswell returned to Scotland with Margaret on or about 7 June, and on 12 June he set off for Edinburgh to be in time for the opening of the summer session the following day.

MONDAY 12 JUNE. I arrived at Edinburgh about nine [in the evening]. Captain Erskine was at the Cross, and followed the chaise. He welcomed me to town, and asked me if I had not carried Miss Montgomerie to Ireland to compare her with Miss Boyd and take the one I liked best. Found my father and John quite well.[7] Conversation slow and rather dry. In my own room thought of *my lady.*

TUESDAY 13 JUNE. Went to Parliament House; found it just as usual. Had many questions put to me as to my Irish jaunt, and where was my heiress? I was prepared, and laughed them off with "My time's not come", or, "Aha, I'm just as I was." Mr Claud and Miss Betty[8] dined with us. Claud and I drank tea at the Doctor's and saw Bob[9] and his wife. It was humbling and yet agreeable to see them all so happy. Came and sat a while with Mrs Betty. Called for Lord Mountstuart.[10]

WEDNESDAY 14 JUNE. Lord Mountstuart begged to see me in the morning. I went to him and found him as agreeable as ever. But I was in a different style from

6 Invested in an annuity.
7 Boswell's younger brother, John (as to whom, see Introduction, pp. 2, 4 and 20).
8 Claud Boswell's eldest sister, Elizabeth (Lord Auchinleck's cousin and future second wife). She is also the Mrs Betty mentioned later in this entry.
9 Dr Boswell's son, Robert.
10 For Mountstuart (*styled* Lord Mountstuart), see Introduction, p. 33. In 1766 Mountstuart had been elected M.P. for Bossiney, which seat he was to hold until 1776. He succeeded his father, the 3rd Earl of Bute, in 1792.

the gay, thoughtless way in which he and I used to be. Baron Mure[11] and many more of the Bute train[12] were with him. I dined at home quietly, and supped at Fortune's with Lord Mountstuart, &c.

THURSDAY 15 JUNE. Mrs Fullarton and her son, Sandy Tait, Drs Gregory and Austin, and Willy Wallace[13] dined with us. I was not well, and in very bad spirits. At such times all the varnish of life is off, and I see it as it really is. Or why not may it be that there is a shade thrown over it which is merely ideal darkness? All my comfort was piety, my friends, and *my lady*.

FRIDAY 16 JUNE. I dined along with Lord Mountstuart at Fortune's. There was a great crowd there. I had little joy. Among others, Andrew Stuart was there.[14] I was very angry. "Why?" said Dr Blair. "Because", said I, "there is no telling what he may do. He may bring a process to show my leg is not my own. In vain have I acknowledged it all my life long. He would insist it belonged to another person and should be cut off, and he would get a majority of the Court of Session for this, Doctor." My ludicrous indignation silenced the Doctor. "Ay," said Erskine, "it would be in proof that you had let the nail grow into your great toe, which no man would do were the leg his own!" I drank tea in comfortable quietness with Grange, whom I saw today for the first time this session. He and I had much conversation. He argued me quite out of my mercenary views for marriage, and was clear for *my lady* if I thought myself sure of happiness. But he wished to see Temple's answer to my letter, which I sent off. I supped at Mr Moncrieffe's. The Club was merry.[14a] Sandy Maxwell[15] had some jokes on me. I said he was hard on me. He kept a close fire: *grape-shot* from a *wine-merchant*. This set me up. But I had only forced spirits.

SATURDAY 17 JUNE. The reports concerning the Corsicans were various. I was uneasy.[16] Grange brought me Mr Macdonald, an obliging and clever surgeon, to take care of me. I passed part of the forenoon at Lord Mountstuart's, but was both ill and low-spirited. So sent an apology to Mr David Ross, where I was engaged to dine, and stayed quietly at home. Was very gloomy. Wrote to *my lady*.

SUNDAY 18 JUNE. Lay quiet abed all day. Was calm. Sir George Preston, Dr Webster, and Grange visited me.

MONDAY 19 JUNE. The Commissioner[17] dined. I had mentioned *my lady* by

11 William Mure of Caldwell (1718-1776), admitted advocate 18 December 1739, M.P. Renfrewshire 1742-61, appointed Baron of Exchequer 1761.
12 That is, adherents of Lord Mountstuart's father, the 3rd Earl of Bute (as to whom, see Introduction, p. 26).
13 Not positively identified, but perhaps a "writer".
14 Andrew Stuart, W.S. (admitted 10 August 1759), Commissioner for Trade and Plantations 1779, M.P. for Lanarkshire 1777-84, M.P. for Weymouth 1790-1801, Keeper of the Register of Sasines 1781-99 (and thereafter joint Keeper), died 1801. Stuart was agent for the Duke of Hamilton in the Douglas Cause, hence Boswell's animosity towards him.
14a For this club, see p. 62, n. 6.
15 Alexander Maxwell, wine merchant.
16 Paoli had been beaten by the French at the battle of Ponte Nuovo on 8 May 1769.
17 Basil Cochrane.

the by to many as a supposable case, if I had spirit to overcome my mercenary views. All approved. Even the Commissioner and Mr Stobie were not against it. The Lieutenant[18] indeed was. I stayed at home all day and was rather better. Sir Alexander Dick drank tea, and ——.

TUESDAY 20 JUNE. The Dean of Faculty[19] showed me a letter from Colonel Lockhart of Carnwath, from Florence, confirming the defeat and destruction of the Corsicans. I was quite sunk. I thought of retiring to the country. I felt myself unable for the law. I saw I had parts to make a figure at times. But could not stand a constant trial. I received a most comforting letter from M.[20] I just worshipped her. I was at home all day, except paying a short visit to Lord Mountstuart, and being at the Parliament House. The Doctor was with me a while. He commended M. highly as a sensible woman, a fine woman. But seemed to have some extravagant idea of a wife for me.

WEDNESDAY 21 JUNE. I breakfasted at Sandy Gordon's tête-à-tête. He was for M. He and Claud and Miss Betty dined with us.

THURSDAY 22 JUNE. Dupont and George Webster[21] drank tea with us. I was quite fixed to a comfortable, quiet life. I paid a visit to Lord Barjarg.

FRIDAY 23 JUNE. I breakfasted at Sir George Preston's. My father dined abroad. I had Grange to dine with John and me. Grange and Dr Cairnie[22] drank tea with me, and consulted as to my managing with economy that unlucky affair of Mrs ——.[23] Dr Cairnie's friendly activity pleased me.

SATURDAY 24 JUNE. I was obtuse at night. My father talked to me of marriage. I avoided the subject. M. had my heart.

SUNDAY 25 JUNE. I lay quietly abed all day. At night I rose and read a good deal of the Bible. I was a Christian, but regretted my not being more devout, more regularly pious. This would make me happier.

MONDAY 26 JUNE. Lady Preston[24] visited me this morning. I received a letter from M. which made me value her more and more, and one from Dempster in a gay, pleasant style which made me for a little lay marriage out of my mind, and so relieved me. Miss Betty Boswell, Professor Hunter,[25] and M. Cauvin dined

---

18 Boswell's brother John.

19 Alexander Lockhart (as to whom, see Appendix, p. 559).

20 Margaret Montgomerie.

21 Son of Dr Alexander Webster.

22 John Cairnie, M.D., who had been an active Jacobite and was the doctor to whom Boswell entrusted his former dallying companion, Peggy Doig, when she gave birth to Boswell's short-lived son Charles in December 1762.

23 There are no further references by Boswell to Mrs Dodds or her child Sally. It is assumed that Sally died young.

24 Anne Preston (née Cochrane), wife of Sir George Preston.

25 Robert Hunter, Professor of Greek at the University of Edinburgh. Boswell studied under Hunter during his university education and in letters to Temple later recalled with horror Hunter's broad Scots and parochial mannerisms: "'*Will you hae some jeel?* O fie! O fie!'"... "Would it not *torture* you to be back again at Professor Hunter's eating jeel?" (letters to Temple dated 1 May 1761 and 2 April 1791, respectively reproduced in Tinker, Vol. I, p. 8, and Vol. II, p. 432).

with us. I was quiet, but dispirited on account of Corsica. My views of life sunk very low. I wished merely for comfort. I drank tea at Crosbie's at a consultation, my fourth only for this session. There seems to be little business. I must study law.

TUESDAY 27 JUNE. The Reverend Mr Foord, our housekeeper's brother, and Matthew Dickie dined with us. At seven I went to the Goldsmiths' Hall to the first night of a new society for speaking on different subjects.[26] I was quite flat and had no ambition, yet I spoke with force and spirit on Britain's right to tax her colonies.

THURSDAY 29 JUNE. I was called out of the Parliament House by Mr Capper, who had been in Corsica. He sat some time with me, and gave me much interesting news of Paoli, and made me have better hopes. I dined at Lord Monboddo's. We were alone before dinner a while, and I talked to him of my marrying. He was first for the child, as a man may form such a one as he pleases. But when I assured him I had a bad temper, and he observed that it requires great patience to breed a wife, as it does to breed a horse, he was clear for one already formed, and for Margaret, saying, "How it will tell is nothing." We were interrupted. I was quiet at dinner. I drank tea at home. Dupont and George Webster were with us. My father and I supped at Balmuto's.[27]

FRIDAY 30 JUNE. Captain Lyon, an old schoolfellow who was just come from Berlin, Captain Charles Cochrane,[28] David Stewart,[29] Nairne, Balbarton,[30] and Mr Stevenson, Under-clerk of Session, dined with us; and the two Captains and Stevenson drank tea with me. I was just resigned to my fate, and had no farther views. I had a most interesting letter from Margaret. I was much affected by it, and wrote a long letter to her. At night I was at Mr Moncrieffe's, but finding brag run high, I calmly gave it up and looked on. I was quite dull, thinking that I had given up all gay and brilliant schemes of marriage. At supper they talked of the Duke of Kingston marrying Miss Chudleigh from principles of honour and gratitude. I thought if he acted so towards a woman of her character, what ought I to do for a woman of real worth? I was resolved; and, what is really curious, as I considered that I was to make up for the want of £10,000 by frugality, my mind took the strongest bend that way, and I looked with aversion on a fine table and every piece of elegance then around me, wishing just for absolute plainness. I had, however, some suspicions that my father intended to

---

26 There were several debating societies in Edinburgh in the latter half of the eighteenth century. "The excitement of debate was the passion of the hour... The debating societies... were not exclusive. The actual membership was often very limited in number, but the outside public were admitted to the debates on payment of a small charge, and were invited to join in the controversies" (John A Fairley, "The Pantheon: An Old Edinburgh Debating Society", *B.O.E.C.*, Vol. 1, pp. 47-8). For the Goldsmiths' Hall, see Introduction, p. 12.

27 Balmuto is Boswell's cousin, Claud Boswell of Balmuto.

28 Son of the eighth Earl of Dundonald.

29 David Stewart of Stewarthall (1744-1823), W.S. (admitted 6 July 1768), served apprenticeship with Samuel Mitchelson.

30 James Boswell of Balbarton, an elderly distant cousin of Boswell's (*Wife*, p. 230, n. 1).

prendre encore une femme,[31] and that soured me totally. But I had no certainty for this.

SATURDAY 1 JULY. I walked out early and met the Sixth Regiment of Foot and marched with my cousin, Captain Maxwell of Dalswinton, a captain in it, from about half a mile west from town, through the city, and till the Regiment was fairly out at the *Water Get* (gate).[32] I have always had a great fondness for the army, at least for the show and parade of it, though I am fixed to the law. I am like a man who has married one woman while he is in love with another. Perhaps, indeed, if I had enjoyed my military mistress, I should have been heartily tired of her. Captain Maxwell returned to town, and he and his brother Hugh and Grange dined with us. The two former and I drank tea with Miss Webster.[33] At night my father hinted to me something of what I had suspected. I was amazed and hurt. It threw me quite into wild melancholy. It is many years since I, as it were, pulled myself up by the roots from the place where nature placed me; and though I have allowed myself to be brought back I have never taken firm root, but am like a tree sunk in a flowerpot that may be lifted at any time very easily. I must now endeavour to get matters settled so as to determine either on remaining where I am, or going somewhere else.

SUNDAY 2 JULY. I was at church all day decently. Between sermons I called on Grange and told him my uneasiness and wild schemes. He conjured me to lay aside such thoughts as would ruin me, and bid me consider how much it would please my enemies. I answered readily, "There is one comfort: it would not please them so much as it would me." So wild yet is my imagination. But my honest friend's advice weighed with me. Sir George, Lady Preston, and Miss Preston[34] dined with us. I drank tea at Mrs Scott's[35] and spoke French, but was observed to look ill. I then called on Lady Crawford, who was not able to see company. But I sat a long time with Miss Macredie and had a very agreeable conversation with her, much indeed in praise of M. But she hurt me by saying she thought M. would do very well with the Irish doctor, and that she had a *hankering kindness* for Mr C.[36] Strange that I, whose heart has been tossed about by all the winds, cannot bear to think that my friend has ever had a kindness for anybody, though I am sure she never thought of anyone as she does of me. I supped quietly with my father, and resolved to be prudent.

MONDAY 3 JULY. My father and I dined at Mr Kincaid's, where I drank tea. I then went to Mr Charles Brown's[37] and saw DOUGLAS, who was just come to town. I had not seen him since the great decision. He was dressing and without

31 "Take a wife again."
32 The Water Gate, at the foot of the Canongate, was so named on account of its proximity to a large horse-pond.
33 Anne Webster, daughter of Dr Alexander Webster.
34 Agnes Preston, daughter of Sir George Preston.
35 Housekeeper for the Rev. M. Dupont (*Wife*, p. 419).
36 The Irish doctor and Mr C have not been identified.
37 Charles Brown of Coalston, advocate (admitted 6 August 1765), son of George Brown, Lord Coalston. Died 1804.

coat or waistcoat when I came in. He expressed much joy on seeing me, and invited me to celebrate his birthday at Bothwell Castle. I was truly happy and easy. But wished I could feel the same joy I did on the glorious news.

TUESDAY 4 JULY. Whenever I do not mention my breakfasting, dining, drinking tea, or supping somewhere abroad, it is to be understood that I was at home. Business now began to look better. I walked in the Meadow with Lord Monboddo and talked of M. He said there was no question she was the woman for me, thought her being a little older nothing, and said she'd bring me children worth rearing, which is seldom the case nowadays. I mentioned to him my apprehensions concerning my father. He said it would be very foolish at his time of life—a terrible thing—a burthen on a family, &c. Bid me not delay getting a settlement made, which my marriage only would do. I saw Lord Monboddo's regard for me, and I was really happy with the scheme of *my lady*. I wrote to her at night and was in fine spirits. I drank tea at Mr Thomas Boswall's.[38]

WEDNESDAY 5 JULY. I was quite enamoured in the forenoon, and impatient to have M. for certain. I drank tea at Balmuto's. Mrs Betty and I had much conversation about M. I was hurt by talking too much of her faults. It made me miserable. But I went home, wrote to her, and recovered all my fondness and really admiration.

THURSDAY 6 JULY. I heard a pleading in the case of the creditors of Auchinbreck, and really shuddered to think of the consequences of debt. I then waited on the Duke of Queensberry,[39] who was just come to town, and was well received. I dined at Mr Charles Brown's with [Patrick Home of] Billy, young Pitfour,[40] Sir John Whitefoord, and Mr Stewart of Blantyre. After dinner Mr Charles read us a genuine copy of the Chancellor's speech on the Douglas cause.[41] I drank tea at home with my father and M. Dupont, and my father and I and John and Mr Claud and Mrs Betty all supped at Mr Thomas Boswall's. I liked to see a good, open Scots wife, and a sensible, understanding man of business.

FRIDAY 7 JULY. Messieurs Baillie,[42] Colquhoun,[43] George Fergusson,[44] Blair,[45] and

---

38 Thomas Boswall, an accountant, was a very distant cousin of Boswell's.

39 Charles Douglas, 3rd Duke of Queensberry (as to whom, see Introduction, p. 27). Under George III he was made a Privy Councillor, Keeper of the Great Seal of Scotland (1761) and Lord Justice-General of Scotland (15 April 1763). He was married to the beautiful and eccentric Catherine Hyde, second daughter of Henry, 4th Earl of Clarendon. The Duke and Duchess were famous as patrons of John Gay.

40 James Ferguson of Pitfour (1735-1820), advocate (admitted 2 August 1757), son of James Ferguson, Lord Pitfour. M.P. Banffshire 1789-90, M.P. Aberdeenshire 1790-1820. Died unmarried.

41 The Lord Chancellor was Lord Camden.

42 William Baillie of Polkemmet, advocate (admitted 14 December 1758), Sheriff-Depute of Linlithgowshire 1772-93, appointed Lord of Session as Lord Polkemmet on 14 November 1793. Died 14 March 1816.

43 James Colquhoun (1741-1805), *later* Sir James Colquhoun of Luss, advocate (admitted 3 December 1765), Sheriff-Depute of Dumbartonshire 1775-1805.

44 George Fergusson of Hermand (1743-1827), advocate (admitted 17 December 1765). Appointed Lord of Session as Lord Hermand on 11 July 1799.

45 Robert Blair of Avonton (1741-1811), advocate (admitted 7 August 1764), Advocate-Depute 1789, Solicitor-General 1789-1806, Dean of the Faculty of Advocates 1801, appointed Lord President of the Court of Session on 16 November 1808.

Law,[46] advocates, and William Macdonald[47] and James Frazer,[48] writers, dined with us. I was dull enough, but contented to be so. I had this day an answer from Temple, finely written, but preferring interest and ambition to the heart. I hoped easily to bring him into my opinion. Yet I considered what I owed to my family. But then again, insuring health, sense, and genius to my successor would be better than great riches. A man too rich is like a man too fat. Besides, I could save more than £10,000 portion by the manner in which I would live with M. So I continued firm, but was uneasy at not hearing from her for some days. At seven I was at Clerihue's at a consultation for Douglas against Duke Hamilton and Lord Selkirk. I felt myself weak and without much memory or application. I was humble and modest. I consoled myself that M. thought so highly of me, and I hoped in time to acquire law and application. I rejoiced at being a regular counsel for the great Douglas, for whom I had done so much as a volunteer. Indeed, I received a handsome retaining fee, ten guineas. The news of Duke Hamilton's death struck us.[49] We all supped together.

SATURDAY 8 JULY. About noon Mr Maconochie[50] and I set out in a post-chaise for Bothwell Castle, to be present at the celebration of Douglas's birthday on Monday the 10 of July. We had a great deal of conversation. I wavered somewhat as to my plan of life still: whether to remain here, or go to the English bar. Maconochie showed himself a little man of admirable common sense, observation, activity, and really a good share of neat taste from having seen so much of the world. We dined at Whitburn, and got to Bothwell Castle to tea.

TUESDAY 11 JULY. I got to town just in time to throw off my laced coat and waistcoat, get on black clothes, and be ready at nine o'clock to attend some causes in the Parliament House. A thousand questions were put to me. I was sleepy all day, but stood it very well.

WEDNESDAY 12 JULY. I had received a letter from Sir John Dick[51] informing me that Paoli was safe at Leghorn. This was great comfort to me. I was anxious and uneasy at having no letter from M. this week. I was apprehensive she was offended with me. Dempster was now in town. He came and saw me, and heard my anxious, irresolute situation with patience and complacency. He bid me treat it lightly. He said I was yet far from matrimony, and could easier return than advance. That supposing Glasgow to be marriage and Edinburgh the state of a bachelor, I was no farther on my road than Fountainbridge.[52] But, upon the whole, he was for M. Said she must have a noble mind, and that I would be happy. He put me in spirits. I told him of my reception in Ireland. "You know", said I, "how finely I can show away to

---

46 William Law of Elvingston (1715-1806), advocate (admitted 6 December 1737), Sheriff-Substitute of Haddingtonshire 1755, Sheriff- Depute 1762-1803.
47 William Macdonald of St Martins (1732-1814), W.S. (admitted 11 January 1762).
48 James Frazer of Gortulleg (1729-1805), W.S. (admitted 29 July 1762).
49 The Duke was only fourteen years old at the time of his death.
50 Alexander Maconochie of Meadowbank, "writer" (father of Allan Maconochie, *later* Lord Meadowbank (for whom, see p. 254, n. 63)).
51 British Consul at Leghorn.
52 Fountainbridge was then a suburb of Edinburgh.

strangers who see me for a little only. I can run the gauntlet very well, but cannot bear being tied up to the halberts"—a curious representation of my small degree of merit, or rather knowledge, that passes very well on a cursory view, but is found out to be very superficial if deliberately examined. I drank tea with worthy Johnston calmly and cordially.

THURSDAY 13 JULY. I received a letter from M. in a style that made me think she was angry and had given up all love for me. She appeared to me so cool and indifferent that I was absolutely shocked. I thought with a kind of distraction of the world in which one whom I thought I knew so intimately could be so changeable. My head turned giddy, and I am positive no man was ever more severely tortured by love. Worthy Grange represented to me that it was all my own fault, for I had acknowledged to him that I had written to her with such censure that no woman of spirit could bear; and that I ought rather to be grateful to her for writing at all, and should make an apology for what I had written. He pacified me a little. But I have a wretched satisfaction in being surly. I, however, was much affected, and could for gleams of thought have almost cried; and, had she been near me, would have fallen at her feet. Yet my obstinate, unreasonable pride still rose again. I determined not to write till I was more moderate. Dempster was gone home, which I regretted.

After the House I had a walk with Lord Monboddo. He said I might be sure my father had thoughts *de se remarier*, and pushed me to think of marrying directly. He was clear and irresistible for M. I thought, "How curious is this compared with her last letter and its effects on me." Mr Claud, Miss Betty, and Grange dined with us. I was quite thoughtful and vexed on a complication of accounts: my father, Margaret, and a very bad symptom of illness. I drank tea at Grange's along with Mr Macdonald, the surgeon. But was really low. My heart was softened. I was all gratitude to M. But alas! what could I do for her? I was ready to give her myself, but was persuaded it would make her miserable.

At night I had a serious conversation with my father. He talked of my not minding affairs at home. That gave me a good opportunity to say that I really had no encouragement as I was in so incertain a way, and that he even talked *de se remarier*. He in a manner acknowledged his having such views. I spoke in the strongest terms, and fairly told him he should be no more troubled with me. I was really calm and determined. It is wonderful to think how he and I have differed to such a degree for so many years. I was somewhat hurt to find myself again thrown loose on the world. But my love of adventure and hope made me surprisingly easy. My great unhappiness was thinking of M. And yet in any way she could not but suffer, for I could not think of marriage when he exposed himself at his years and forgot my valuable mother. O unfeeling world! I declare I am not, nor ever could be, so much so. And yet, honest man! he talked of his affection for me and what he had suffered on my account with a tone that moved me, though I was quite irritated against him now. I am truly a composition of many opposite qualities.

FRIDAY 14 JULY. I continued most unhappy. Having sat up till four in the morning, I was very feverish. I love M. from my soul, but saw myself to be incapable of any lasting connection. Grange and I walked down to Leith Links and saw a review of [General George] Cary's, the Forty-third Regiment. It entertained me somewhat. One of the Scots Greys, who stood as a sentinel to keep off the mob, did his duty so faithfully and yet with so much good nature that I gave him a shilling to drink. A little after this, I wanted to buy a bit of gingerbread. So, to make a trial of human nature, I came to my Grey and asked if he would give me some halfpence to buy some gingerbread. This was a pretty severe trial, for many fellows would have damned me and denied they had ever seen me. But my honest Grey said, "O yes, Sir", and immediately pulled out a leathern purse. He had indeed but one halfpenny, but he gave me it very cheerfully; and, instead of buying gingerbread with it, I keep it with a piece of paper wrapped round it, on which I have written the anecdote.

I came home for a little. My father came into my room and spoke to me a little on indifferent subjects. But I shunned him. Grange and I dined comfortably at Purves's.[53] He advised me strongly against any desperate scheme. But I was quite determined. Mr Macdonald blooded me today to begin the cure of a severe symptom. It is hard for one night of Irish extravagance to suffer so much.[54] I wrote a law paper this afternoon. But could hardly fix my attention. I then went to Mr Moncrieffe's and played three rubbers at whist with him and Lord Galloway and David Kennedy, and then supped. I was observed to be very dull. It passed all to be on account of the fate of Corsica.

SATURDAY 15 JULY. I took a walk on the Castle Hill[55] with Mr Maconochie, and told him my dilemma. He was vexed, but advised me to be prudent. I became quite outrageous, and was mad enough to ask him if it would not be allowable to cut off——, before he ruined his family. But this I certainly did not seriously mean for a moment. I went in the stage to Pinkie, to have talked with Commissioner Cochrane.[56] But he was from home. My father and Miss Betty drove past in a chaise. I was quite chagrined. I hired a chaise and went to Sir Alexander Dick's. Amidst all my gloom the sweet place and amiable people soothed me. I told him my dilemma. He was vexed, and bid me do anything to prevent it. I was at home all the evening. My father sent for me to him. But I would not sit down. I just spoke a few sullen words. I was quite gone.

SUNDAY 16 JULY. After a wretched, feverish night I awaked in a dreadful state.

---

53 Thomas Purves's tavern at the President's Stairs, off the south side of the Parliament Close. The President's Stairs were named after Sir Hew Dalrymple of North Berwick, Lord President of the Court of Session from 1698 to 1737 (Harris, p. 504).

54 During his visit to Dublin, Boswell had spent an evening at a brothel.

55 Between the buildings of the city and the row of palisades in front of the drawbridge of the Castle there was "a space about 350 feet in length, and 300 broad on the summit, called the Castle-hill, where the inhabitants frequently resort[ed] for the benefit of the free air" (Kinnaird, *The History of Edinburgh from the Earliest Accounts to the Present Time*, p. 136). From this site on the hill (now occupied by the Esplanade) there was a commanding view of Fife and the Firth of Forth on the north, Calton Hill on the east, Salisbury Crags and Arthur's Seat on the south-east and the Pentland Hills on the south.

56 Commissioner Cochrane resided at this time at Pinkie, near Musselburgh.

I have no doubt that evil spirits, enemies to mankind, are permitted to tempt and torment them. "Damn him. Curse him", sounded somehow involuntarily in my ears perpetually. I was absolutely mad. I sent for worthy Grange, and was so furious and black-minded and uttered such horrid ideas that he could not help shedding tears, and even went so far as to say that if I talked so he would never see me again. I looked on my father's marrying again as the most ungrateful return to me for my having submitted so much to please him. I thought it an insult on the memory of my valuable mother. I thought it would totally estrange him from his children by her. In short, my wild imagination made it appear as terrible as can be conceived. I rose and took a little broth, and, in order to try if what I liked most could have any effect on me when in such a frame, I went to the chapel in Carrubber's Close,[57] which has always made me fancy myself in heaven. I was really relieved. I thought of M., and loved her fervently. But I was still obstinate. A clergyman from Leith preached on these words, "I have learned, in whatever state I am, therewith to be content."[58] He said many good things on contentment, and that the text informed us it was to be *learnt*. I was averse to learn any good.

I then went and drank tea at the Miss Mackenzies'. M. again here in fancy. I am really constant. I wanted to be gloomy and like a man of such resolutions as I then had. But the agreeable company around me and my own gaiety insensibly made me otherwise. I then sat a while with Lady Crawford, with whom I have always a great deal of sentimental conversation. She made me love M. still more. I should have mentioned that in the forenoon my father wanted to speak to me, and I absolutely refused it by running away from him. I was very gloomy at night.

MONDAY 17 JULY. A kind letter from M., without taking any notice of our late quarrel, warmed my heart. I went and breakfasted with my uncle, the Doctor, who agreed with me in thinking my father would marry again, and said he had heard it. The family madness was kept up to a great pitch by the Doctor and me. I was determined to throw myself on the wide world. I went and sat a while with Lady Crawford, and told her both my uneasiness and my love. She was anxious to have me prevent the one, and clearly of opinion for the other. I took my clerk, Mr Brown, to dine with me at Purves's. I had been with the Duchess and Douglas in the morning. At night I laboured at the law, but could hardly fix my attention at all. I wrote to Mrs Montgomerie-Cuninghame to beg she would interpose in the unlucky affair. I also wrote to Margaret and to Temple.

TUESDAY 18 JULY. I continued as bad as ever. I appeared before my father in some causes, and had a strange satisfaction in pleading calmly to a man with whom I could not have any intercourse in private. I felt a kind of regret to leave the Parliament House, to which I have a kind of family attachment. But I considered all attachments to be now at an end. I was really in a terrible state. Lord

57 St Paul's Chapel (as to which, see Introduction, pp. 15 and 22).
58 Philippians 4. 11.

Monboddo desired to speak with me after the House. I accordingly took a walk with him, when he told me that he had just had a long and serious conversation with my father, who had complained to him of my behaviour, told him that it was my choosing to live in the irregular state of a bachelor which made him think of marrying again, and my Lord said if I would not alter my plan he was right. "But", said he, "will you let me negotiate between you? Yours is an estate and a family worth preserving." I said I could marry no other woman but Margaret. "Well," said he, "be serious and firm, and I hope to settle matters." This gave me quite a new set of thoughts.

I had told Douglas my uneasiness, and he promised to be my firm friend in all events. I went in the coach with the Duchess to Lord Chief Baron's, where we dined along with the Duke of Queensberry and Douglas. I was in perfect good spirits. The sight of grandeur made me for a second or two consider if I was not wrong to give up all schemes of marrying for ambition and wealth. But M. soon brought me back. I soon saw that my real happiness is not in such objects. That I only love sometimes to contemplate them, and that I would do it with double satisfaction when I have Margaret for my companion. Every different attempt to make me waver makes my love steadier. The Duchess and I paid a visit to Lady Alva and the young Countess of Sutherland,[59] and then returned to town, the mob huzzaing and crying, "Douglas for ever!" I supped with my father. But Mr Brown was with us, as I wished to avoid particular conversation. We were, however, tolerably well.

WEDNESDAY 19 JULY. Mr Walter Campbell and his wife, Mrs Ritchie, Lord Monboddo, and Tilquhilly[60] dined with us. I was persuaded to go to the assembly. There was a very fine company, and I felt myself wonderfully calm and constant.[61] I renewed my acquaintance with my old friend, Lady Colville.[62] I was mad enough to dance one country dance. Mrs Walter Campbell was my partner, which made me dance with violence. It did me much ill. I supped at Queensberry House[63] with the Duke and the three Douglases. We were gay and easy. I thought all the time how perhaps I should by and by be in a company.

59 Elizabeth, Countess of Sutherland, was born on 24 May 1765 and was therefore only four years old at the time of this visit. Lady Alva, who had the care of the young Countess, was her maternal grandmother.

60 John Douglas of Tilquhilly (1737-1773), advocate (admitted 18 December 1759).

61 The "assembly" was the regular dancing session at the Assembly Hall. For details of the assemblies, see Introduction, p. 9. Assemblies were under the direction of the Honourable Miss Nicky Murray (Helen Nicolas Murray, 1707-77, a sister of Lord Mansfield), who sat at a high chair resembling a throne at one end of the room. "Much good sense, firmness, knowledge of the world and of the histories of individuals, as well as a due share of patience and benevolence, were required for this office of unrecognised though real power; and it was generally admitted that Miss Murray possessed the needful qualifications in a remarkable degree, though rather more marked by good-manners than good-nature" (Chambers, p. 288).

62 Andrew Erskine's sister, Elizabeth, whose first husband, Walter Macfarlane, had died in June 1767. In 1768 she married Alexander, seventh Lord Colville of Culross. Her house stood to the west of the city in a hamlet which formed part of the area then known as Drumsheugh.

63 A large mansion on the south side of the Canongate. Long a hospital for the elderly, Queensberry House is now part of the complex of buildings on the site of the new Scottish Parliament.

Talking of the Hamilton Lords, the Duke said, "Why, the devil entered into them." "Yes," said I, "just as he did into the swine."

THURSDAY 20 JULY. I was hurt by having danced. David Armstrong, Grange, and I took a chaise and saw a race at Leith. At night I resolved to put M.'s affection to the strictest trial. I wrote to her, taking no notice of any hopes of a compromise, but told her plainly that if she would go off with me and live on my £100 a year, with the interest of her £1,000, I was ready to marry her. I bid her think fully, and give me no reasoning but a direct answer. I wrote to Temple of this, while I told him of the prospect of a compromise. This was truly romantic, and perhaps too severe a trial of a woman of so much good sense and so high a character.

SATURDAY 22 JULY. I breakfasted at Queensberry House with all the excellent friends there. Then Douglas carried me in his phaeton to the race at Leith. It was a handsome carriage with pretty mares, and he drove with great spirit among the crowd of company, always coming to pay his attentive duty to the worthy Duke. I was exceedingly happy. I exulted in reflecting that the author of the *Essence* had his charge so prosperous. As we drove home, I tried to make Douglas talk of immortality. He seemed to believe, and be animated with the idea of seeing the great who have appeared in the world. After the race, the Duke, Lord Monboddo, &c., and I went with Douglas to Willison's, and I made him fairly sit once to his picture, in order to begin it. I dined quietly at home with my brother. Grange drank tea with me. At night my father, having dined abroad and drank, cheerfully spoke to me of Lord Monboddo's telling him of my scheme as to M. I endeavoured to be as reserved as possible, but insensibly he and I fell into our usual bad humour. It is hard.

SUNDAY 23 JULY. I breakfasted with Professor Wallace,[64] who showed me a genealogy of the family of Fullarton vouched by papers for above five hundred years. It is curious how pleasing variety is. Mr Wallace's style of conversation amused me much, and when I saw his law papers neatly bound up, with accurate indexes, and amongst them some of my own writing, the business of a Scotch lawyer acquired value in my mind, and I thought of continuing at it even in the worst event. But while I was in church, I thought that if M. gave me a prudent, cold, evasive answer, I would set sail for America and become a wild Indian. I had great thoughts of my acquiring strength and fortitude, and could not regret much leaving all I had known, as I should adore God and be happy hereafter.

MONDAY 24 JULY. The Commissioner called on me a little. I told him my dilemma. He could not believe it. But when I raged, he stopped me and said, "No. You must make the best of it." His cool sense for a moment communicated itself to me. But I soon regained my usual warmth.

---

64 William Wallace, advocate (admitted 15 February 1752), appointed Professor of History at Edinburgh University 1755, Keeper of the Advocates' Library 1758, Professor of Scots Law 1765, Sheriff-Depute of Ayrshire 1775-86, died 1786.

TUESDAY 25 JULY. The important answer from M. was brought to me in the Parliament House: "I accept of your terms." For a minute or two my habits of terror for marriage returned. I found myself at last fixed for ever; my heart beat and my head was giddy. But I soon recovered and felt the highest admiration and gratitude on a conduct so generous. Her letter was finely written, and did me more real honour than anything I have ever met with in life. I determined to make it my study to do all in my power to show my sense of her goodness. And I became calm and easy, thinking that as I was now fixed in the most important concern, everything else was but secondary. The Commissioner dined with us. At night I was at the Society,[65] and spoke against repealing the Marriage Act.[66]

WEDNESDAY 26 JULY. I was in great uneasiness on account of my illness, but Macdonald and Dr Cairnie, whom I also consulted, made me give over terrible apprehensions. I was this afternoon at a meeting of the late Mr Adie's trustees. At night I wrote to M. She had proposed to meet me on Saturday at Glasgow. But I could not get so far, as the Duke was to dine with us. I begged to know if she could come to Whitburn. I was very desirous to see her.

FRIDAY 28 JULY. I was chancellor to the Jury who served Horatius Cannan of Barlay heir to his father and grandfather. I liked a ceremony of this kind, and was pleased to think of my standing upon record in it. We all dined with the heir at Small's. It was quite a comfortable Edinburgh dinner, and I was neither better nor worse than my neighbours, but just plain and content. I supped at Mr Moncrieffe's. It was a jovial meeting over a capercailzie.

SATURDAY 29 JULY. This has been a good week for me in the way of business. I have cleared twenty guineas, and have really been able to do very well. I am ready for whatever may happen. My dearest Margaret is my great object. The Duke of Queensberry, Douglas, Lords Pitfour[67] and Monboddo, Mr Stewart of Blantyre, Mr Solicitor, Captain Douglas, Mr Douglas of Fechil, and Lord Chief Baron dined with us. Things went on admirably. I then went with the Duke,

---

65 Probably the same debating society as was mentioned in the entry for 27 June 1769.

66 This is either a reference to an Act of the Parliament of Scotland of 1695 (c. 15) which was discriminatory in that it prohibited the solemnization of marriages by ministers not of the established church (but was subsequently relaxed by an Act of 1711 which allowed marriages to be celebrated by certain Episcopalian ministers), or to the (English) Marriage Act of 1753 (26 Geo. 2, c. 33) "which made null and void any marriage in England not preceded by banns or official licence and not carried out publicly in a church or chapel by a regular clergyman within prescribed daylight hours" (Walker, *A Legal History of Scotland, The Eighteenth Century*, p. 657). The latter Act "successfully curtailed the operations of rogue parsons but led to an increasing traffic northwards, to Gretna Green and other border towns, by English couples seeking to take advantage of the more flexible Scottish marriage laws" (Clive, *Husband and Wife*, 4th edn, para. 01.013).

67 James Ferguson, Lord Pitfour (1700-1777), was admitted advocate on 17 February 1722 and elected Dean of the Faculty of Advocates on 24 June 1760. He was a popular advocate, and in spite of a weak, high-pitched voice and an awkwardness of demeanour he impressed his colleagues with his knowledge of the law and his mastery of the art of persuasion. He was appointed Lord of Session on 14 June 1764, having been at the bar for no less than forty-two years. The following year, on 9 July, he was appointed a Lord Commissioner of Justiciary. The delay in Pitfour's elevation to the bench was attributed to his being an Episcopalian. He had a reputation in the Justiciary Court for showing too much favour for the accused, a rare characteristic in those days.

Douglas, &c., to Lord Advocate's,[68] from whence Mrs Montgomery, Lady Mary Hay, and her aunt, Miss Lockhart, were attended by us to Comely Garden.[69] Lady Mary was a fine, good-humoured young lady of a noble carriage, stately person, and the daughter of the Lord High Constable of Scotland. I was truly desirous to have a match between her and Douglas. We walked some time in the garden, then went in and drank tea, I in excellent spirits observing Douglas and Lady Mary taking to one another. They danced a country dance, and I stood with my black clothes and my cane, looking on as grave and anxious as if I had been their parent. There was a good company. I was quite constant to Margaret. I had once been with her here, and I had some conversation about her tonight with her correspondent, Miss Kitty Mackenzie, which pleased me more than I can tell. I was all affection and admiration. The Duke and Douglas and the Captain and I supped at the Duchess's, where we met my father, and my uncle the Doctor, and David Moncrieffe and Maconochie. We were all friends and very good company.

I find it is impossible to put upon paper an exact journal of the life of man. External circumstances may be marked. But the variations within, the workings of reason and passion, and, what perhaps influence happiness most, the colourings of fancy, are too fleeting to be recorded. In short, so it is that I defy any man to write down anything like a perfect account of what he has been conscious during one day of his life, if in any degree of spirits. However, what I put down has so far an effect that I can, by reading my Journal, recall a good deal of my life.

SUNDAY 30 JULY. I was at church all day. I fancied M. sitting beside me as she used to do. Sir George [Preston] and George Webster dined with us. It was curious to observe how my father's manner awed and checked the freedom of conversation. This is really hard to bear. I was in very good humour today. I recollected my former follies; I saw that my father had indulged and forgiven me more than I could a son of mine if I had one. I therefore would have no resentment against him, let him do as he pleased. I would just consider his marrying again as a fatality by which he was killed and his estate overwhelmed, and, without farther connection either with the one or the other, I would go and live as easily and agreeably as possible with my dearest M. I wished to tell him something like this at night. But I found myself kept back as usual.

MONDAY 31 JULY. The Commissioner carried me out in his chaise to Pinkie, where I dined with him most comfortably along with my brother John. The Commissioner did not seem very fond of my scheme with M. However, that will be got over. He spoke to me very seriously against being outrageous on my

---

68 The Lord Advocate was James Montgomery of Stanhope (as to whom, see Appendix, pp. 559-60).
69 Comely Gardens, in the Abbey Hill area of Edinburgh, were said to have been "a species of lively Tivoli Gardens for the lower classes in Edinburgh" (Grant, Vol. III, p. 128), but the company on this occasion suggests that, at this time at least, the Gardens were popular with the upper ranks of society. It was also said that Comely Gardens were "a wretched attempt to imitate Vauxhall for which neither the climate nor the gardens are adapted" (Arnot, p. 224).

father's marrying again, and really his notions were rational. I came to town in the fly.

TUESDAY 1 AUGUST. Mr John Chalmer, Mr James Neill from Ayr, and Grange dined with us. At five I drank tea along with Maclaurin[70] at Mr John Swinton's,[71] at a consultation. I really, for the most part, like the business of the law. There is a kind of entertainment in observing the progression of causes, and a great variety of ideas are made to work.

WEDNESDAY 2 AUGUST. Dempster was in town in his way to London. I had written him a letter while he was sick, which I said just came on its tiptoes to enquire how he was. I went now and found him at Peter Ramsay's, and observing him thin, "Dempster," said I, "your belly has been imitating the India stock of late—falling"; a very proper similitude for a director of the East India Company. I told him I was fixed to M. He said he was much pleased; that his only surprise was how I could do so rational a thing. He said it was just as if either he or I could be transformed into a female, and the one marry the other. He was quite against my outrage, supposing my father to marry again. He said I had a title to remonstrate, and try to prevent it; but if my father insisted for it, it was my duty to submit. He said it was not an insult to the memory of a first wife to marry a second. I was sorry to part with him. I dined at Lord Monboddo's with the Duke of Queensberry and Douglas, and we were so well and cheerful that it was agreed we should all meet again at supper too. I was in admirable spirits, with perfect sobriety.

FRIDAY 4 AUGUST. My father came into my room this morning and told me that although he thought my scheme of marriage improper and that Margaret and I would part in half a year, yet as I insisted for it he would agree. I was really very grateful to him, and hoped to be able to behave to his satisfaction.

SATURDAY 5 AUGUST. I had agreed to go to Lainshaw to see Margaret. I accordingly set out this morning in the fly. There was a very good company, and I was calm and just as I could wish.

Boswell arrived at Lainshaw that evening. "When I saw my valuable Margaret," he wrote, "I was in more agitation than I could have believed. Mrs Cunninghame and I had a serious conversation, and all was now certainly fixed. It is impossible to write down all that M. and I said." The next day, records Boswell, "I felt myself serene and happy, and I had infinite satisfaction in seeing my dear M. as happy as I was." The day after this (i.e., on 7 August), having spent the night worrying that he might perhaps not have Margaret after all, he insisted that they take each other's hands and solemnly engage themselves, which they did, thus making him easy. Boswell returned to Edinburgh that evening.

---

70 John Maclaurin, advocate (as to whom, see Appendix, p. 561).
71 John Swinton of Swinton, advocate (admitted 20 December 1743), Sheriff-Depute of Perthshire 1754, appointed Lord of Session as Lord Swinton 21 December 1782, appointed Lord Commissioner of Justiciary 1788, died 1799. His house was in Teviot Row.

MONDAY 7 AUGUST. When I got to town, I went to the opera of *Artaxerxes*.[72] Archie Stewart, my old Rotterdam friend, and Captain Erskine sat with me in a dark corner. I told them I was now fixed, and they rejoiced at my happiness, though they could not help hinting that they had apprehensions of my inconstancy. I was not afraid. My father was pretty kind when I came home.

TUESDAY 8 AUGUST. [After dinner] I went to Fortune's, where Mr Moncrieffe's guests were entertaining him, and there I became outrageously jovial and intoxicated myself terribly, and was absurd and played at brag and was quarrelsome. How unhappy is this!

WEDNESDAY 9 AUGUST. I was quite gloomy and dejected. I wrote a long letter to Margaret. That valuable woman will make me the man I wish to be. William Macdonald and I supped at Mr Surgeon Macdonald's and drank bottles apiece of the finest old claret that I ever tasted. I consulted Dr Gregory this afternoon. He thought me in no bad way and was of opinion I might be cured very well here, but as it would make my mind easy advised me to go to London and drink some of Kennedy's decoction.

THURSDAY 10 AUGUST. Mr Riddel gave a dinner at Leith to Sir Thomas Wentworth and a number of others, amongst whom I was one. My spirits sparkled in an extraordinary degree. Lord Kellie[73] was in high glee. "Upon my soul," said he, "we are merry. We have said a devilish number of good things." "Why," said I, "my Lord, it is very natural for puns and rebuses, &c., to keep company with Riddels." I drank immensely and was so joyous that I was clearly of opinion that intoxication is a noble thing. Such is the effect of wine. And perhaps a good quantity of it may at times do well for many people. But I, who have so much extravagance and vice to subdue, must observe the strictest sobriety. Sir Thomas and William Macdonald and I walked up, and I was fit for business and wrote a law paper. I must mention that during all our excess of merriment I was continually wafting my fervent vows to M., and rejoicing that I was at last so happily fixed.

FRIDAY 11 AUGUST. Lord Galloway carried Sir Thomas Wentworth and me in his coach out to St Catherine's, Lord Gardenstone's country place.[74] Mr Lockhart and Mr and Mrs Macqueen were with us at dinner. I drank too much

72 By Thomas Arne.
73 Thomas Alexander Erskine (1732-81), sixth Earl of Kellie, elder brother of Boswell's friend Andrew Erskine. Although known in his earlier years as "fiddler Tam" (Keay and Keay, p. 359), he became one of the most notable British musicians of his era. When his father, the fifth Earl of Kellie, was imprisoned in Edinburgh Castle for participating in the Jacobite rebellion of 1745, he went to Germany and studied music at Mannheim under Johann Stamitz the elder. He returned to Scotland in 1756 as a talented violinist and composer. That same year he succeeded to his father, thus becoming the sixth Earl of Kellie. For many years he was Deputy Governor of the Musical Society of Edinburgh and he composed a large number of minuets which were very popular at the dancing assemblies in Edinburgh. At one and the same time he was Grand Master of the Freemasons in both England and Scotland (*ibid.*, p. 360), and he was well known as a dedicated imbiber and *bon viveur*. Samuel Foote, the actor, said of him, famously, that his face was so red it would ripen cucumbers.
74 In Newington. For Francis Garden, Lord Gardenstone, see Introduction, p. 36, and Appendix, pp. 558-9.

burgundy. I came to town in Mrs Macqueen's chaise, with her and Sir Thomas. I supped at Charles Small's with Captain Erskine. I was in liquor, but good company. We drank bottles of claret apiece. Erskine would not let me call for any more.

SATURDAY 12 AUGUST. The session rose today.[75] Lord Monboddo took leave of me, hoping to meet me next as a married man. My father was to have set out for Auchinleck today. But some business detained him. John went, and my father and I were easy and well. After dinner he talked of Margaret and me. Said we had both very good sense, but were thoughtless, and must become just different beings. I told him I was under a necessity to go to London for a little to clear my constitution. He acquiesced. The evening passed well.

SUNDAY 13 AUGUST. My illness was visibly decreasing, so I resolved to stay in and take care of it for a week or a fortnight, and be pretty well before I set out for London. My father and I had a warm dispute at night on male and female succession. I argued that a male alone could support a family, could represent his forefathers. That females, in a feudal light, were only vehicles for carrying down men to posterity, and that a man might as well entail his estate on his post-chaise, and put one into it who should bear his name, as entail it upon his daughter and make her husband take his name.[76] I told him that the principle of family, of supporting the race of Thomas Boswell of Auchinleck,[76a] was what supported my mind, and that, were it not for that, I would not submit to the burthen of life here, but would go and pass my days in a warm climate, easy and gay. I bid him consider that he held the estate of Auchinleck, at least the old stamen of it,[77] in prejudice of no less than four females. That excluding females might at a time hurt a fond father who had daughters and no sons. "But what", said I, "is a sorry individual to the preservation of a family? Is there any comparison? Besides, in that view, why will you make the son whom you see miserable on account of some woman who may appear nobody knows when?" I saw he was quite positive in the strange, delusive notion of *heirs whatsoever*,[78] and I had the mortification to be sensible that my dissipated and profligate conduct had made him at all think of an entail, and made any arguments from me of little force. I, however, hoped to get him prevented from ruining his family. I was quite in a fever, for I declare that the family of Auchinleck is my only constant object in this world. I should say, *has been* so. For my dearest M. is now as firmly established. I determined to leave the country if he made the settlement which shocked me.

75 Boswell's fees for the session (13 June to 12 August) amounted to fifty-nine guineas. During this period he attended seven hearings in separate cases before Lord Auchinleck (Consultation Book).

76 "An entail is a disposition of feudal heritable property, particularly land, under which the property is conveyed to a series of heirs other than those to whom it would otherwise pass, under prohibitions which are designed to keep the subjects intact in the hands of the successive heirs of entail" (Gordon, *Scottish Land Law*, p. 500). The question of Lord Auchinleck's entail is to feature prominently in these journals (see from 9 January 1775 onwards).

76a The first Laird of Auchinleck (for whom, see Introduction, p. 4).

77 In this and the following paragraph, Boswell uses the word "stamen" in the sense of the fundamental or essential element of something but at the same time is obviously conscious of the *double entendre* implied by the word in its botanical sense.

78 That is, without restriction to heirs through the male line.

I told him so, and I knew M. would not complain. Indeed I was too hot for a son to a father. But I could not help it. I was like an old Roman when his country was at stake.

I fell upon a most curious argument which diverted my own fancy so much that it was with difficulty I could preserve my gravity when uttering it. "If", said I, "you believe the Bible, you must allow male succession. Turn to the first chapter of Matthew: 'Abraham begat Isaac, Isaac begat Jacob', &c. If you are not an infidel, if you do not renounce Christianity, you must be for males." Worthy man! he had patience with me. I am quite firm in my opinion on this point. It will not do to say a grandson by a daughter is as near as a grandson by a son. It leads into a nice disquisition in natural philosophy. I say the *stamen* is derived from the *man*. The woman is only like the ground where a tree is planted. A grandson by a daughter has no connection with my original stock. A new race is begun by a father of another name. It is true a child partakes of the constitution of his mother, gets some of his mother's blood in his veins. But so does he as to his nurse, so does he as to the ox whose beef he eats. The most of the particles of the human frame are changed in a few years' rotation. The stamen only continues the same. Let females be well portioned. Let them enjoy liberally what is naturally intended for them: dowries as virgins, a share of what their husbands have while wives, jointures when widows. But for goodness' sake let us not make feudal lords, let us not make barons, of them. As well might we equip them with breeches, swords, and gold-laced hats.

MONDAY 14 AUGUST. The Commissioner and I had a serious conversation in which he gave me hopes that by patience, calmness, attention, and good behaviour I would get all matters made easy with my father. This cheered me. My father was quite in good humour again, and took a kind leave of me as he set out for Auchinleck. I was now left quiet, and hoped to get away soon to London.

THURSDAY 24 AUGUST. Having from [Tuesday 15 August] till [this day] omitted to mark what passed every day, it is enough to say that I have been close keeping the house, that Dr Cairnie has attended me now and then, and Mr Macdonald constantly. That my distemper has been gradually melting away. That I have written a great many pages of law papers, and been employed several hours for several evenings in sorting a large mass of session papers belonging to my father and selecting such as are worth binding; and, to show the force of custom, I have been very fond of this business. I have been visited by Sir George Preston very frequently, by M. Dupont every Thursday, by worthy Grange often. One day Mr David Hume came and sat a while with me.[79]

FRIDAY 25 AUGUST. The day passed on with a variety of business. Dr Boswell was a while with me. I told him he and I had frequent flows of high spirits: we had bottles of champagne in our heads which were every now and then poured

79 In a letter from Boswell to Margaret Montgomerie dated 21 August 1769 Boswell said that on this occasion Hume "gave a philosophical opinion that our marriage must be a happy one". "Were it not for his infidel writings," added Boswell, "everybody would love him. He is a plain, obliging, kind-hearted man."

out. It will do better in French: "Nous avons des bouteilles du vin de champagne à la tête qui se versant de temps à autre", or "de temps en temps". M.
Dupont says of me, "Vous êtes né pour le francais." I must make my dear Margaret
a good French scholar.

SATURDAY 26 AUGUST. I took a chaise and carried George Webster with me
to dine at the Commissioner's. We were very comfortable. I relished much being again in life after a fortnight's confinement and starving. The Commissioner
gave me some more good advice. George and I went and saw a singular curiosity, a playhouse in Musselburgh. Fisher's strolling company were there; the
play was *The Provoked Husband*.[80] We just saw the beginning of it. We supped at
Sir George Preston's.

SUNDAY 27 AUGUST. [At Dr Webster's house] Miss Webster said of my marriage, "It's in every drawing-room in town." "Ay," said George, "but it is not in a
bedroom yet." A real *bon mot*, upon honour—by an Edinburgh cloth merchant.

*Boswell set off for London on the morning of 28 August having sat up till five in the morning
writing letters. His companion in the chaise was a London merchant from whom Boswell
obtained much information of relevance to some mercantile causes in which he was involved.
They arrived in London on 1 September and two days later Boswell dined with his friend
Sir John Pringle, the celebrated Scottish physician.[81] "He spoke", wrote Boswell, "of the
inconveniency of the old town of Edinburgh. I told him I would never leave it, for I preferred
our good old house in the Parliament Close to all the elegance of the new buildings. I
made him almost angry by maintaining this."[82] Later, says Boswell, "Pringle observed
that the manners of Edinburgh are very bad. That the people there have a familiarity, an inquisitiveness, a way of looking through one, that is extremely disagreeable.
He is very right. But how can a man do who is to live amongst them? He must be
exceedingly reserved, for, if he allows his vivacity to play, the sarcastic rogues willl
attack him; and should he, with the politeness well known abroad, show his displeasure,
they would raise a hoarse laugh and never mind him. So that nothing less than a downright quarrel can make them understand that they have hurt him."*

*While in London, Boswell decided to attend the Shakespeare Jubilee at Stratford-on-Avon,
which event took place from 6 to 8 September and was organised by David Garrick. At the
masquerade Boswell made his famous appearance as an armed Corsican chief with a black cap
bearing the words* Viva la Libertà.

*After his return to London on 10 September, Boswell at last started to implement the
plan which had been the ostensible reason for his visit to London, namely to endeavour to
cure his venereal disease by taking Dr Kennedy's decoction, the "Lisbon Diet Drink".*

80 By Sir John Vanbrugh and Colley Cibber.
81 Pringle (1707-1782) was a great reformer of military medicine and sanitation and it has been
said of him that "he may fairly be regarded as the founder of modern military medicine" and "few
physicians have rendered more definite and brilliant services to science and humanity" (DNB).
In 1774 he was to be appointed physician to George III.
82 James Craig's plan for the New Town of Edinburgh was adopted by the Town Council in July 1767
and work on the erection of buildings started shortly afterwards. Boswell never moved to the
New Town but seriously considered moving there in 1782 for the sake of the health of his wife
and children (see the entry for 19 February 1782).

However, Boswell's illness seemed to take a long time to be cured (and even required a surgical incision); and so, while waiting for the supposed curative qualities of the nostrum to take effect, Boswell took lodgings in various houses and passed his time indulging in the activity which was the real objective of his visit—socialising with his wide circle of London friends and acquaintances. This circle included, in particular, Johnson, Thomas Sheridan,[83] George Dempster, James Love,[84] Goldsmith, Paoli (who had escaped from Corsica in a British ship and had had a Crown pension conferred on him) and, for the first time, Sir Joshua Reynolds.

At the end of October, Boswell received a letter from Margaret Montgomerie containing dismal news of his friend the Earl of Eglinton, who had been the first to introduce the young Boswell to "the pleasures of elegant society".[85] The Earl had found an excise officer by the name of Mungo Campbell on his land whom he had suspected of poaching. Campbell, on being challenged, had shot the earl fatally.[86]

From 3 to 5 November, Boswell stayed with his friend Temple and his wife at their little thatched parsonage in Mamhead, Devonshire, where Temple was rector of the small parish. This was a most enjoyable and successful visit.

Boswell returned briefly to London and on 10 November finally set off for Scotland where he was eagerly awaited by his fiancée. Boswell had by now resolved that after their marriage they should not live under the same roof as his father. "It would be mixing gall with my honey", he told Margaret. He arrived in Edinburgh just in time for the opening of the winter session on 14 November and shortly afterwards travelled to Lainshaw where the marriage took place on 25 November, the same day as Lord Auchinleck married his new wife, his cousin Elizabeth Boswell of Balmuto, at Edinburgh. The timing of Boswell's marriage was obviously intended not only as a gesture of defiance and disapproval of his father's wedding, but also as an expression of awakening independence. The Marriage Contract which Boswell and Margaret signed (and which Boswell wrote) declared that they solemnly engaged "to be faithful spouses, to bear with one another's faults, and to contribute as much as possible to each other's happiness in this world; hoping through the merits of their blessed Saviour, Jesus Christ, for eternal happiness in the world which is to come."

After the wedding ceremony, Boswell stayed away from the Court of Session for a week while he and Margaret had a honeymoon, part of which seems to have been spent at Auchinleck. At the end of the honeymoon, they travelled to Edinburgh, arriving there on 1 December. They lodged briefly in the house above Lord Auchinleck's, but on 5 December moved to a house in the Cowgate (a long, low-lying street running parallel with, and to the south of, the High Street through what had once been a fashionable quarter of the city).

---

83 As to whom, see Introduction, p. 22.
84 As to whom, see Introduction, p. 18.
85 Journal, 9 November 1778.
86 Campbell was subsequently found guilty of murder and condemned to death, but committed suicide in prison by hanging himself.

1770~1772

Boswell did not resume his journal until the spring of 1772 and so our information about the first two years of the 1770s is inevitably somewhat sketchy. But he evidently settled down straight away as a faithful husband and a diligent, sober advocate with a steady practice.

At the end of May 1770 Boswell and his wife moved to newer and more spacious premises in a large tenement block known as Chessel's Buildings (or Chessel's Court), off the south side of the Canongate.[1] It was at this same time that there occurred a potentially lucrative development in Boswell's career, for he was then admitted to practise at the bar of the General Assembly of the Church of Scotland.[2] His first two General Assembly cases were given to him by Walter Scott, W.S., and earned him an extra seven guineas.[3] This line of work was to become a regular source of income for Boswell each year when the Assembly met in May.

In August 1770 Mrs Boswell delivered a son, but he died within two hours, much to Boswell's distress.

In May 1771 the Boswells moved once again, this time to the flat in James's Court in the Lawnmarket which was owned, and formerly occupied, by David Hume. In a letter to John Johnston of Grange dated 22 May 1771, Boswell said of this new house that "we find [it] large enough for us, very convenient, and exceedingly healthful and pleasant. My wife is very fond of it."[4] The building was of vast height on its northern elevation, rising to no fewer than eight storeys, and had a spectacular view over the New Town and across the Firth of Forth to Fife. It was erected in or about 1725 by James Brownhill, from whom it took its name, and for many years was regarded as being one of the most fashionable quarters in the city. "The inhabitants, who were all persons of consequence in society, although each had but a single floor of four or five rooms and a kitchen, kept a clerk to record their names and proceedings, had a scavenger of their own, clubbed in many public measures, and had balls and parties among themselves exclusively. In those days it must have been quite a step in life when a man was able to fix his family in one of the flats of James's Court."[5] It was at Boswell's new house that he entertained Paoli during Paoli's famous visit to Scotland in the autumn of 1771.

During these years, Boswell made several visits to Auchinleck and attended circuits with his father. He also took the opportunity of receiving lessons from Lord Auchinleck on the pruning of trees and on estate husbandry generally. During a visit in October 1770 Boswell was accompanied by his wife, but when he went to Auchinleck in May 1771 she stayed away. It seems that she found the atmosphere there oppressive.

---

1 Part of the original tenement still stands, albeit in an extensively refurbished form.
2 For the General Assembly of the Church of Scotland, see Introduction, p. 12.
3 Consultation Book.
4 Reproduced in Walker, pp. 264-7, at p. 265.
5 Chambers, p. 68. Unfortunately, the western half of James's Court, where Boswell's house was situated, was destroyed by a fire in 1857.

Boswell did not visit London again until the spring of 1772, when he was due to appear with Andrew Crosbie in an appeal from the Court of Session to the House of Lords. This was the case of John Hastie v Campbell and Others.[6] *Hastie had been employed as rector and head-master of the grammar school of Campbeltown, but after the magistrates discovered evidence that he had neglected the school and had frequently inflicted severe corporal punishment on the boys he was dismissed. He then brought an action of reduction in the Court of Session to set aside his dismissal. The court found in his favour, taking the view (as explained by Boswell in a letter to Johnson dated 3 March 1772) that it is "a very delicate matter to interfere between a master and his boys, and rather dangerous to the interests of learning and education in general to lessen the dignity of teachers and make them afraid of the resentment of too indulgent parents, instigated by the complaints of their children". Boswell does not appear to have received a fee for his efforts in this case, but he willingly took the case with a view to enhancing his reputation as an advocate. Indeed, one of the reasons recorded by him for coming to London was to "see how the land might lie for me at the English bar". Another reason was "to try if I could get something for myself… by means of the Duke of Queensberry, Lord Mountstuart, or Douglas, all of whom had given me reason to expect their assistance".*

While waiting in London for the appeal to be heard, Boswell socialised with the usual wide circle of friends and acquaintances and he discussed the forthcoming appeal with Johnson, who gave him helpful hints on the presentation of the case. One morning Boswell called on Andrew Crosbie to get him to assist in the drawing of the case, but, says Boswell, he "was so miserably dissipated that I could not get him to fix to it for any time". The evening before the hearing Boswell was suffering from nerves. "I could not help being under considerable anxiety, partly for fear of my client, whom I had saved in the Court of Session, partly on account of myself, as I considered my first appearance at the bar of the House of Lords to be an important era in my life, on which my reputation as a speaker in this part of the island might depend." On the morning of the appeal (14 April), Boswell went to Crosbie's lodgings, where he was assured he had nothing to fear and that they would prevail. "But", records Boswell, "I was anxious and uneasy, and took an advice which Sir John Pringle gave me last night, which was to drink some wine. I drank a couple of large bumpers[7] of white wine. It did me no good. It confused me without inspiriting me.[But] when we got to Westminster Hall, I grew better." Boswell's principal opponents at the appeal were none other than the Lord Advocate (James Montgomery) and the Solicitor-General (Henry Dundas). The line of argument chosen by Boswell was that, while school masters should not be barbarians, no school could possibly exist without corporal punishment and that as Hastie had not exceeded the proper bounds of chastisement he should be re-instated in his post. Boswell was "in a flutter" until it was his turn to speak, and he relates that "when Lord Mansfield called out, 'Mr Boswell', and I mounted the little elevation on which the counsel who speaks is placed, I felt much palpitation. But I knew I was master of my cause, and had my speech in writing. I had seen that Lord Mansfield was against us, which was discouraging. My client was now no longer at stake. I had only my own reputation to mind. I begun with a very low voice and rose gradually; but restrained myself

6 Reported in Paton, Vol. II, pp. 277-283.
7 A bumper is a brim-full glass.

from appearing anyhow bold or even easy. I spoke slowly and distinctly, and, as I was told afterwards, very well. I indulged only one sally of wit... 'My Lords,' said I, 'I speak with warmth for this schoolmaster who is accused of too much severity. I speak from gratitude, for [I] am sensible that if I had not been very severely beat by my master, I should not have been able to make even the weak defence which I now make for this schoolmaster.' Lord Mansfield smiled. Lord Gower and some other Lords called out, 'Bravo!'" However, all was to no avail, for their Lordships found in favour of the magistrates and overturned the decree of the Court of Session.

The summer session from mid-June to mid-August 1772 is the last session for which Boswell recorded his cases in his Consultation Book.[8] His fees earned in that session amounted to seventy-six guineas, the highest sum recorded in the Consultation Book for a summer session. But although Boswell was now coming into much business, he was showing signs of relapsing with regard to drinking, gaming and whoring, the latter activity coinciding with Mrs Boswell being pregnant again.

---

8 For Boswell's Consultation Book, see Introduction, p. 37.

1773

On 15 March 1773 Mrs Boswell gave birth to a daughter, Veronica—"a fine, healthy, lively child", as Boswell reported in a letter to Goldsmith dated 29 March. This happy event occurred while Boswell was strenuously engaged as counsel for the defence in two consecutive trials arising out of "meal riots" which had taken place in Perth and Dundee.

On 30 March, before Mrs Boswell was fully recovered from her child-birth, Boswell set off for another jaunt to London. He describes how, having been woken early by his clerk, Mr Lawrie, he "walked down the High Street of Edinburgh, which has a grand appearance in the silence and dusky light of three in the morning". One of his companions in the coach was his brother John, who was going to Newcastle. During the journey John was silent and sullen. "It is difficult", wrote Boswell, "to describe how very heavy his disagreeable behaviour is to those with whom he lives. He is incapable of being pleased by them. Never was there a greater difference between human beings than between him and my brother David and me."

On arrival in London, Boswell immersed himself in the usual whirl of social activity. While he was away, Mrs Boswell sublet David Hume's flat in James's Court and moved to the flat below, which was more spacious. This flat, which was level with the ground on the south side facing the Lawnmarket, but four floors up on the north elevation, was said to have been "an extraordinary house in its day; for it consisted of two floors connected by an internal stair".[1]

Boswell returned to Edinburgh on 15 May. During the summer session he was part of a team of advocates who won an extremely important case in the Court of Session—John Hinton v Alexander Donaldson and Others[2]—in which Boswell, together with Ilay Campbell and John Maclaurin, acted for the defenders, of whom the first-named defender was the well-known Edinburgh bookseller (and Boswell's friend and publisher). The action was concerned with the question of copyright and became a leading case on the subject. Donaldson, much to the annoyance of certain London booksellers, who had taken the view that copyright was perpetual at common law, had published many cheap editions of popular works in which the statutory copyright conferred by the Copyright Act 1709 (8 Anne, c. 19) had expired. The court hearing lasted from 20 to 24 July. Boswell opened for the defenders on 21 July and Ilay Campbell followed. The judges, several of whom praised the quality of the speeches given for both sides, found by a majority (Lord Monboddo dissenting) in favour of the defenders, holding that a perpetual copyright was not recognised in the common law of Scotland.

In August, Samuel Johnson finally made his long-awaited journey to Scotland. It had been agreed that he and Boswell would make a tour of Scotland together after the summer session ended in mid-August, when Boswell would be free from the pressures of work; and

1 Chambers, p. 73.
2 Reported briefly at (1773) Morison's *Dictionary of Decisions*, 8307. Further details are to be found in Murray, *Some Civil Cases of James Boswell, 1772-74*, (1940) 52 Juridical Review, at pp. 234-249.

Boswell looked forward to his eminent friend's arrival with eagerness. Johnson, who was very much prejudiced against Scotland, was sixty-three years old, very large and corpulent, clumsy in his movements, hard of hearing, short-sighted, and prone to bodily convulsions. He had received an LL.D. from Trinity College, Dublin, in 1765 and so Boswell sometimes refers to him as "the Doctor". Johnson arrived in Edinburgh in the company of William Scott (1745-1836), then of University College, Oxford, who was later a distinguished judge in the English High Court of Admiralty and was raised to the peerage as Baron Stowell in 1821.

SATURDAY 14 AUGUST. Late in the evening, I received a note from [Mr Johnson] that he was arrived at Boyd's Inn, at the head of the Canongate.[3] I went to him directly. He embraced me cordially, and I exulted in the thought that I now had him actually in Caledonia. Mr Scott's amiable manners and attachment to our Socrates at once united me to him. He told me that before I came in the Doctor had unluckily had a bad specimen of Scottish cleanliness. He then drank no fermented liquor. He asked to have his lemonade made sweeter, upon which the waiter with his greasy fingers lifted a lump of sugar and put it into it. The Doctor in indignation threw it out of the window. Scott said he was afraid he would have knocked the waiter down. Mr Johnson told me that such another trick was played him at the house of a lady in Paris. He was to do me the honour to lodge under my roof. I regretted sincerely that I had not also a room for Mr Scott. Mr Johnson and I walked arm-in-arm up the High Street to my house in James's Court; it was a dusky night; I could not prevent his being assailed by the evening effluvia of Edinburgh. I heard a baronet[4] of some distinction in the political world in the beginning of the present reign observe that "walking the streets of Edinburgh at night was pretty perilous and a good deal odoriferous." The peril is much abated by the care which the magistrates have taken to enforce the city laws against throwing foul water from the windows; but, from the structure of the houses in the old town, which consist of many storeys in each of which a different family lives, and there being no covered sewers, the odour still continues.[5] A zealous Scotsman would have wished Mr Johnson to be without one of his five senses upon this occasion. As we marched slowly along, he grumbled in my ear, "I smell you in the dark!" But he acknowledged that the breadth of the street and the loftiness of the buildings on each side made a noble appearance.

My wife had tea ready for him, which it is well known he delighted to drink at all hours, particularly when sitting up late. He showed much complacency upon finding that the mistress of the house was so attentive to his singular habit; and as no man could be more polite when he chose to be so, his address to her was most

---

3 This was the "White Horse", an extensive but "crowded and confused" stabler's inn owned by James Boyd, and hence often referred to as "Boyd's Inn" (Stuart, p. 112).

4 In this passage the baronet is referred to by Boswell (writing in 1785) as "a late baronet". The editors of *Hebrides* (at p. 11, n. 17) suggest that this may have been Sir Gilbert Elliot, Bt, of Minto (as to whom, see the entry for 17 January 1777 and relevant footnote). Since he did not die until 1777, the word "late" has been removed from the text.

5 For the unhygienic conditions of the city in those days, see Introduction, pp. 8-9.

courteous and engaging, and his conversation soon charmed her into a forget-fulness of his external appearance.

We had, a little before this, had a trial for murder, in which the judges had allowed the lapse of twenty years since its commission as a plea in bar, in con-formity with the doctrine of prescription in the civil law, which Scotland and several other countries in Europe have adopted.[6] He at first disapproved of this, but then he thought there was something in it if there had been for twenty years a neglect to prosecute a crime which was *known*. He would not allow that a murder, by not being *discovered* for twenty years, should escape punishment.

We sat till near two in the morning, having chatted a good while after my wife left us. She had insisted that, to show all respect to the sage, she would give up her own bedchamber to him and take a worse. This I cannot but grate-fully mention, as one of a thousand obligations which I owe her, since the great obligation of her being pleased to accept of me as her husband.

SUNDAY 15 AUGUST. Mr Scott came to breakfast, at which I introduced to Dr Johnson and him my friend Sir William Forbes, a man of whom too much good cannot be said; who, with distinguished abilities and application in his profession of a banker, is at once a good companion and a good Christian.[7]

Mr Johnson was pleased with my daughter Veronica, then a child of about four months old. She had the appearance of listening to him. His motions seemed to her to be intended for her amusement, and when he stopped, she fluttered and made a little infantine noise and a kind of signal for him to begin again. She would be held close to him, which was a proof from simple nature that his figure was not horrid. Her fondness for him endeared her still more to me, and I declared she should have five hundred pounds of additional fortune.[8]

We talked of the practice of the Law. Sir William Forbes said he thought an honest lawyer should never undertake a cause which he was satisfied was not a just one. "Sir," said Mr Johnson, "a lawyer has no business with the justice or

6 This was the case of Callum McGregor in which, earlier that month, "it was solemnly decided, after great consideration, that the lapse of twenty years is a complete bar to any ulterior criminal proceedings" (Alison, *Practice of the Criminal Law in Scotland*, p. 97).
7 Sir William Forbes of Monymusk, Bt (1739-1806), *later* of Pitsligo, banker and author. After serving his apprenticeship with the Edinburgh banking firm of John Coutts and Company, he was assumed as a partner in the firm in 1761. In 1773 he became senior partner and the firm changed its name to Sir William Forbes, James Hunter & Co. "The house speedily became one of the most trusted in Scotland, and proved its claim to public credit by the excellence of the stand it made during the financial crises and panics of 1772, 1788, and 1793. In 1783 the firm, after difficult preliminaries, began to issue notes, and the success of the experiment was immediate, decided, and continuous. Forbes had now come to be regarded as an authority on finance, and in the same year he took a leading part in preparing the revised Bankruptcy Act" (DNB). His bank was situated at the south side of the Parliament Close. He was actively involved in the management of several charitable institutions in Edinburgh, including the Charity Workhouse and the Royal Infirmary, and he wrote an *Account of the Life and Writings of James Beattie, LL.D.*, which was published in 1806. It was said of him that he was "a gentleman of the most polished and dignified manners" (Kay, Vol. I, p. 131) and that he was "one of the most benevolent and public-spirited citizens of whom Edinburgh ever had to boast" (Wilson, Vol. I, p. 273). Boswell respected him immensely and appointed him one of his executors.
8 Boswell kept his word: in 1795 he signed a deed giving Veronica an additional £500. Unfortu-nately, however, she died before the bequest could be paid to her (*Hebrides*, pp. 407-8).

injustice of the cause which he undertakes, unless his client asks his opinion, and then he is bound to give it honestly. The justice or injustice of the cause is to be decided by the judge. Consider, sir; what is the purpose of courts of justice? It is that every man may have his cause fairly tried by men appointed to try causes. A lawyer is not to tell what he knows to be a lie: he is not to produce what he knows to be a false deed; but he is not to usurp the province of the jury and of the judge and determine what shall be the effect of evidence, what shall be the result of legal argument. As it rarely happens that a man is fit to plead his own cause, lawyers are a class of the community, who, by study and experience, have acquired the art and power of arranging evidence and of applying to the points at issue what the law has settled. A lawyer is to do for his client all that his client might fairly do for himself if he could. If, by a superiority of attention, of knowledge, of skill, and a better method of communication, he has the advantage of his adversary, it is an advantage to which he is entitled. There must always be some advantage on one side or other, and it is better that advantage should be had by talents than by chance. If lawyers were to undertake no causes till they were sure they were just, a man might be precluded altogether from a trial of his claim, though, were it judicially examined, it might be found a very just claim." This was sound practical doctrine, and rationally repressed a too-refined scrupulosity of conscience.

Sir William Forbes, Mr Scott, and I accompanied Mr Johnson to the chapel founded by Lord Chief Baron Smith for the service of the Church of England.[9] The Reverend Mr Carr, the senior clergyman, preached from these words: "Because the Lord reigneth, let the earth be glad." I was sorry to think Mr Johnson did not attend to the sermon, Mr Carr's low voice not being strong enough to reach his hearing.

Here I obtained a promise from Lord Chief Baron Ord that he would dine at my house next day. I presented Mr Johnson to his lordship, who politely said to him, "I have not the honour of knowing you, but I hope for it and to see you at my house. I am to wait on you tomorrow."[10]

When we got home, Dr Johnson desired to see my books. He took down Ogden's *Sermons on Prayer*, on which I set a very high value, having been much edified by them, and he retired with them to his room. He did not stay long, but soon joined us in the drawing room.

Of Dr Beattie[11] Mr Johnson said, "Sir, he has written like a man conscious of the truth and feeling his own strength. Treating your adversary with respect is giving him an advantage to which he is not entitled. The greatest part of men

9 This chapel (known as "Baron Smith's Chapel") was founded in 1722 by John Smith, Lord Chief Baron of Exchequer, and was situated in Blackfriars Wynd (off the south side of the High Street). "The Baron's chapel existed for exactly a century; it was demolished in 1822, after serving as a place of worship for all loyal and devout Episcopal High Churchmen at a time when Episcopacy and Jacobitism were nearly synonymous terms in Scotland. It was the most fashionable church in the city" (Grant, Vol. I, p. 262).
10 At this point, Boswell (writing in 1785) adds: "This respectable English judge [who died in 1778] will be long remembered in Scotland, where he built an elegant house and lived in it magnificently. His own ample fortune, with the addition of his salary, enabled him to be splendidly hospitable."
11 James Beattie (1735-1803), LL.D., poet and Professor of Moral Philosophy and Logic at Marischal College, Aberdeen. In 1770 Beattie published his *Essay on the Nature and Immutablity of Truth* in which he violently attacked the philosophy of David Hume.

cannot judge of reasoning, and are impressed by character; so that if you allow your adversary a respectable character, they will think that though you differ from him, you may be in the wrong. Sir, treating your adversary with respect is striking soft in a battle. And as to Hume—a man who has so much conceit as to tell all mankind that they have been bubbled for ages and he is the wise man who sees better than they, a man who has so little scrupulosity as to venture to oppose those principles which have been thought necessary to human happiness—is he to be surprised if another man comes and laughs at him? If he is the great man he thinks himself, all this cannot hurt him; it is like throwing peas against a rock."

While we were talking, there came a note to me from Dr William Robertson:[12]

Sunday

DEAR SIR,—I have been expecting every day to hear from you of Dr Johnson's arrival. Pray what do you know about his motions? I long to take him by the hand. I write this from the college, where I have only this scrap of paper. Ever yours,

W.R.

It pleased me to find Dr Robertson thus eager to meet Dr Johnson. I was glad that I could answer that he was come; and I begged Dr Robertson might be with us as soon as he could.

Sir William Forbes, Mr Scott, Mr Arbuthnot, and another gentleman [Charles Hay][13] dined with us. "Come, Dr Johnson," said I, "it is commonly thought that

12 Dr William Robertson (1721-93), historian. He was appointed Principal of Edinburgh University in 1762 and is accordingly sometimes referred to by Boswell as "Principal Robertson". Described as "the foremost historian in eighteenth-century Scotland" with a "lucid and elegant" style, it has been said that his *History of Scotland during the Reigns of Queen Mary and James VI* (1759) "was a remarkable book for its time and probably the best 'national' history then in existence" (Ferguson, *Scotland: 1689 to the Present*, p. 215). His later major works, the three-volume *History of the Reign of Charles V* (1769) and the two-volume *History of America* (1777), added to his renown, the latter work being referred to as his *tour de force* and "the standard authority in English until the middle of the nineteenth century" (Lynch, *Scotland: A New History*, p. 349). He was the leader of the "Moderate" party in the Church of Scotland and was appointed Moderator of the General Assembly in 1763. "His works, translated into all the main European languages, brought him fame throughout Europe and considerable income, but his lasting achievement was the growth under his principalship of the University of Edinburgh. In the late seventeenth century, it had some 400 students; by 1789, its numbers were almost 1,100" (*ibid., loc. cit.*).
13 Charles Hay of Newton (1747-1811), advocate (admitted 24 December 1768), son of James Hay of Cocklaw, Writer to the Signet. Hay, who never married, was to be appointed a Lord of Session as Lord Newton on 7 March 1806. Cockburn, writing after Hay's elevation to the bench, said of him: "He was a bulky man with short legs, twinkling eyes, and a large purple visage; no speaker, but an excellent legal writer and adviser; deep and accurate in his law, in which he had had extensive employment. Honest, warm-hearted, and considerate, he was always true to his principles and his friends." He was particularly renowned for his love of joining in convivial drinking sessions, when "his delight was to sit smiling, quiet, and listening; saying little, but that little always sensible" (Cockburn, pp. 209-10). Boswell and Hay became great friends and remained so for several years. However, the explanation for Boswell's omitting to name Hay in this entry is that Boswell was writing in 1785 from rough notes and by that time he had somewhat fallen out with Hay, the reasons for this being surmisable from the entries dated 25 January and 12 July 1777.

our veal in Scotland is not good. But here is some which I believe you will like." There was no catching him. JOHNSON. "Why, sir, what is commonly thought I should take to be true. *Your* veal may be good, but that will only be an exception to the general opinion, not a proof against it."

We had not the pleasure of [Dr Robertson's] company till dinner was over, when he came and drank wine with us. And then began some animated dialogue.

In the evening I introduced to Mr Johnson two good friends of mine, Mr William Nairne, advocate, and Mr Hamilton of Sundrum, my neighbour in the country, both of whom supped with us.

MONDAY 16 AUGUST. Dr William Robertson came to breakfast. [Dr Johnson] had last night looked into Lord Hailes's *Remarks on the History of Scotland*.[14] Dr Robertson and I said it was a pity Lord Hailes did not write greater things.

We walked out, that Dr Johnson might see some of the things which we have to show at Edinburgh. We went to the Parliament House, where the Parliament of Scotland sat and where the Ordinary Lords of Session hold their courts; and to the New Session House adjoining to it, where our Court of Fifteen (the fourteen Ordinaries with the Lord President at their head) sit as a court of review.[15] We went to the Advocates' Library, of which Dr Johnson took a cursory view, and then to what is called the *Laigh* (or under) Parliament House, where the records of Scotland (which has an universal security by register) are deposited.[15a] I was pleased to behold Dr Samuel Johnson rolling about in this old magazine of antiquities. There was by this time a pretty numerous circle of us attending upon him. Somebody talked of happy moments for composition, and how a man can write at one time and not at another. "Nay," said Dr Johnson, "a man may write at any time if he will set himself *doggedly* to it."

I here began to indulge old Scottish sentiments and to express a warm regret that by our Union with England, we were no more—our independent kingdom was lost.[15b] JOHNSON. "Sir, never talk of your independency, who could let your Queen remain twenty years in captivity and then be put to death without even a pretence of justice, without your ever attempting to rescue her; and such a Queen, too!—as every man of any gallantry of spirit would have sacrificed his life for." Worthy MR JAMES KER, Keeper of the Records: "Half our nation was bribed by English money." JOHNSON. "Sir, that is no defence; that makes you worse." Good MR BROWN, Keeper of the Advocates' Library: "We had better say nothing about it." BOSWELL. "You would have been glad, however, to have

14 Published earlier that year.
15 Boswell's reference to the New Session House as adjoining the hall in the Parliament House where the Outer House judges sat is somewhat confusing in that the New Session House was generally regarded as including the whole of the Parliament House (Miller, *The Municipal Buildings of Edinburgh*, p. 55), and, indeed, also the New Tolbooth adjacent to it. The Justiciary records invariably state that trials or hearings before the Court of Justiciary, which sat in the New Tolbooth, took place in the New Session House. For the New Tolbooth and the room in which the judges of the Inner House sat, see Introduction, pp. 10 and 11.
15a The Advocates' Library was in the Laigh Hall below the Parliament House. The records of Scotland were kept in the rooms below the Inner House.
15b For Boswell's inconsistent feelings with regard to the Union, see Introduction, pp. 3, 26, 27 and note.

had us last war, sir, to fight your battles!" JOHNSON. "We should have had you for the same price, though there had been no Union, as we might have had Swiss, or other troops. No, no, I shall agree to a separation. You have only to *go home*." Just as he had said this, I, to divert the subject, showed him the signed assurances of the three successive Kings of the Hanover family to maintain the Presbyterian establishment in Scotland. "We'll give you that", said he, "into the bargain."

We next went to the great church of St Giles, which has lost its original magnificence in the inside by being divided into four places of Presbyterian worship.[16] "Come," said Dr Johnson jocularly to Principal Robertson, "let me see what was once a church!" We entered that division called the New Church,[17] so well known by the eloquence of Dr Hugh Blair. It was shamefully dirty. Dr Johnson said nothing at the time, but when we came to the great door of the Royal Infirmary,[18] where, upon a board, was this inscription, "*Clean your feet!*", he turned about slyly and said, "There is no occasion for putting this at the doors of your churches!"

We then conducted him down the Post House stairs, Parliament Close, and made him look up from the Cowgate to the highest building in Edinburgh (from which he had just descended), being thirteen floors or storeys from the ground upon the back elevation, the front wall being built upon the edge of the hill and the back wall rising from the bottom of the hill several storeys before it comes to a level with the front wall. We proceeded to the College[19] with the Principal at our head. Dr Adam Ferguson, whose *Essay on the History of Civil Society* gives him a respectable place in the ranks of literature, was with us.[20] As the College buildings are indeed very mean, the Principal said to Dr Johnson that he must give them the same epithet that a Jesuit did when showing a poor college abroad: "*Hae miseriae nostrae.*"[21] Dr Johnson was, however, much pleased with the library, and with the conversation of Dr James Robertson, Professor of Oriental Languages, the Librarian. We talked of Kennicott's edition of the Hebrew Bible and hoped it would be quite faithful. JOHNSON. "Sir, I know not any crime so great that a man could contrive to commit as poisoning the sources of eternal truth."

We showed him the Royal Infirmary, for which, and for every other exertion of generous public spirit in his power, that noble-minded citizen of Edinburgh, George Drummond, will be ever held in honourable remembrance.[22] And we were too proud not to carry him to the Abbey of Holyroodhouse, that beautiful piece of

16 As to which, see Introduction, p. 6.
17 In the text, Boswell adds here "and of late the High Church", but that was because he was writing in 1785. At the time of Johnson's visit the church was still known as the New Church.
18 For the Royal Infirmary, see Introduction, p. 21.
19 For the College (i.e., the University), see Introduction, p. 14.
20 Adam Ferguson (1723-1816), philosopher and historian, credited with being the originator of modern sociology.
21 "These are our miseries."
22 George Drummond (1687-1766), six times Lord Provost of Edinburgh, was an active proponent of improvements to the city, including the conception and development of the New Town.

architecture, but, alas! that deserted mansion of royalty, which Hamilton of Bangour[23] in one of his elegant poems calls

A virtuous palace, where no monarch dwells.

I was much entertained while Principal Robertson fluently harangued to Dr Johnson upon the spot concerning scenes of his celebrated *History of Scotland.*[24] We surveyed that part of the palace appropriated to the Duke of Hamilton, as Keeper, in which our beautiful Queen Mary lived, and in which David Rizzio was murdered, and also the State Rooms.

We returned to my house, where there met him at dinner the Duchess of Douglas, Sir Adolphus Oughton,[25] Lord Chief Baron, Sir William Forbes, Principal Robertson, Mr Cullen, advocate.

We gave him as good a dinner as we could. Our Scotch moorfowl or grouse were then abundant and quite in season; and so far as wisdom and wit can be aided by administering agreeable sensations to the palate, my wife took care that our great guest should not be deficient.

Sir Adolphus Oughton, then our Deputy Commander-in-Chief, who was not only an excellent officer but one of the most universal scholars I ever knew, had learned the Erse language, and expressed his belief in the authenticity of Ossian's poetry.[26] Dr Johnson took the opposite side of that perplexed question, and I was afraid the dispute would have run high between them. But Sir Adolphus, who had a very sweet temper, changed the discourse, grew playful, laughed at Lord Monboddo's notion of men having tails,[27] and called him "a judge *a posteriori*", which amused Dr Johnson, and thus hostilities were prevented.

At supper we had Dr Cullen, his son the advocate, Dr Adam Ferguson, and Mr Crosbie, advocate. We talked of the orang-outang, and of Lord Monboddo's thinking that he might be taught to speak. Dr Johnson treated this with ridicule. Mr Crosbie said that Lord Monboddo believed the existence of everything possible; in short that all which is in *posse* might be found in *esse*. JOHNSON. "But, sir, it is as possible that the orang-outang does not speak as that he speaks. However, I shall not contest the point. I should have thought it not possible to find a Monboddo, yet *he* exists."

TUESDAY 17 AUGUST. At dinner this day we had Sir Alexander Dick, whose amiable character and ingenious and cultivated mind are so generally known; Sir David Dalrymple (Lord Hailes); Mr Maclaurin, advocate; Dr Gregory; and my uncle, Dr Boswell. This was one of Dr Johnson's best days. He was quite in his element. All was literature and taste, without any interruption. Lord Hailes, who is one of the best philologists in Great Britain, who has written papers in the *World*, and a variety of other works in prose and in verse, both Latin and

23 William Hamilton of Bangour (1704-54), poet and supporter of the Jacobite cause.
24 *The History of Scotland during the Reigns of Queen Mary and James VI*, published in 1759 (as to which, see p. 104, n. 12).
25 Lieutenant-General Sir James Adolphus Oughton.
26 James Macpherson's *Fingal* (as to which, see Introduction, p. 28).
27 For Lord Monboddo's belief in men with tails, and for his views with regard to the orang-outang (touched on in the next paragraph), see Appendix, p. 558.

English, pleased him highly. He told him he had discovered the *Life of Cheynell*, in the *Student*, to be his. JOHNSON. "No one else knows it." Dr Johnson had before this dictated to me a law paper, upon a question purely in the law of Scotland, concerning *vicious intromission*,[28] that is to say, intermeddling with the effects of a deceased person without a regular title, which formerly was understood to subject the intermeddler to payment of all the defunct's debts. The principle has of late been relaxed. Dr Johnson's argument was for a renewal of its strictness. The paper was printed, with additions by me, and given into the Court of Session.[29] Lord Hailes knew Dr Johnson's part not to be mine, and pointed out exactly where it began and where it ended.[30] Dr Johnson said, "It is much, now, that his lordship can distinguish so."

Mr Maclaurin's learning and talents enabled him to do his part very well in Dr Johnson's company. He produced two epitaphs upon his father, the celebrated mathematician. One was in English, of which Dr Johnson did not change one word. In the other, which was in Latin, he made several alterations.

Mr [Alexander] Murray, advocate, who married a niece of Lord Mansfield's,[31] sat with us a part of the evening, but did not venture to say anything that I remember, though he is certainly possessed of talents which would have enabled him to have shown himself to advantage if too great anxiety had not prevented him.

At supper we had Dr Alexander Webster, who, though not learned, had such a knowledge of mankind, such a fund of information and entertainment, so clear a head and such accommodating manners, that Dr Johnson found him a very agreeable companion.

When Dr Johnson and I were left by ourselves, I read to him my notes of the opinions of our judges upon the question of literary property.[32] He did not like them, and said, "They make me think of your judges not with that respect which I should wish to do."

Boswell and Johnson set off for their tour of Scotland the following day. This tour, which was to take them to St Andrews, Aberdeen, Inverness, Fort Augustus, the Hebrides, Inveraray, Loch Lomond, Dumbarton, Glasgow, Hamilton and Auchinleck, was fully narrated by Boswell in his Journal of a Tour to the Hebrides with Samuel Johnson, LL.D. *After visiting St Andrews, the two travellers called on Lord Monboddo at his country estate of Monboddo in Kincardineshire. "Monboddo", wrote Boswell, "is a wretched*

---

28 This is how the phrase appears in *Hebrides*, at p. 30, but the usual spelling of the first word is "vitious" (which, indeed, was the spelling used by Boswell in the petition mentioned in the following note).
29 This was the case of *James Wilson v Janet Smith and Robert Armour*, reported in *Faculty Decisions*, Vol. VI, 1772-1774, p. 41. Boswell, who consulted Johnson about this case during his visit to London during the spring of 1772, submitted a 22-page reclaiming petition on 1 July 1772 (Ballantyne, 72 07 01) and this appears to be the paper to which Boswell refers. A copy of the petition is in the Signet Library (SPSL, Kennet Collection 1769-73, M4: 26). The court rejected Boswell's argument, holding that the ancient principle should not apply where the intromission was inconsiderable.
30 It seems clear that Dr Johnson's argument started on page 17 of the petition and continued to near the end.
31 Murray married Katherine, second daughter of Sir Alexander Lindsay of Evelick, on 15 April 1773.
32 That is, in the case of *Hinton v Alexander Donaldson and Others* (as to which, see p. 100).

place, wild and naked, with a poor old house; though, if I recollect right, there are two turrets which mark an old baron's residence. Lord Monboddo received us at his gate most courteously; pointed to the Douglas arms upon his house, and told us that his great-grand-mother was of that family. 'In such houses', said he, 'our ancestors lived, who were better men than we.' 'No, no, my lord', said Dr Johnson. 'We are as strong as they, and a great deal wiser.' This was an assault upon one of Lord Monboddo's capital dogmas, and I was afraid there would have been a violent altercation in the very close, before we got into the house. But his lordship is distinguished not only for 'ancient metaphysics', but for ancient politesse—'le vieille cour'—and made no reply. His lordship was dressed in a rustic suit and wore a little round hat. He told us we now saw him as Farmer Burnett, and we should have his family dinner, a farmer's dinner." To Boswell's great pleasure and relief, Johnson and Monboddo, having entered the house, discoursed pleasantly on the classics and on the state of learning in Scotland. "My lord was extremely hospitable," wrote Boswell, "and I saw both Dr Johnson and him liking each other better every hour…I had a particular satisfaction in being under the roof of Monboddo, my lord being my father's old friend, and having been always very good to me. We were cordial together." After their visit, Johnson said that he had been much pleased with Monboddo that day.

At Inveraray, where Boswell and Johnson arrived on 23 October as the guests of the hospitable John Campbell, fifth Duke of Argyll (1723-1806), there was tension between Boswell and the beautiful Duchess of Argyll (Elizabeth Gunning), formerly the Duchess of Hamilton. Because of Boswell's strenuous efforts for the Douglas camp (and hence against the Duke of Hamilton) in the Douglas Cause, the Duchess of Argyll hated Boswell and did her utmost to ignore his presence. When she asked Johnson why he made his journey so late in the year, he replied, "Why, madam, you know Mr Boswell must attend the Court of Session, and it does not rise till the twelfth of August." To this she responded, spitefully, "I know nothing of Mr Boswell." Boswell heard this and "despised it". "It was", he wrote, "weak as well as impertinent." And when Boswell said something of his belief in the second sight, the Duchess said, "I fancy (or "I suppose") you will be a Methodist." "This", says Boswell, "was the only sentence she ever deigned to utter to me; and I take if for granted she thought it a good hit on my credulity in the Douglas Cause."

Boswell and Johnson arrived at Auchinleck on 2 November. The meeting between Lord Auchinleck and Johnson was potentially hazardous, for Lord Auchinleck, as Boswell observes, "was as sanguine a Whig and Presbyterian as Dr Johnson was a Tory and Church of England man; and as he had not much leisure to be informed of Dr Johnson's great merits by reading his works, he had a partial and unfavourable notion of him, founded on his supposed political tenets, which were so discordant to his own that, instead of speaking of him with that respect to which he was entitled, he used to call him 'a Jacobite fellow'. Knowing all this, I should not have ventured to bring them together, had not my father, out of kindness to me, desired me to invite Dr Johnson to his house." Having got Johnson to promise not to mention Whiggism and Presbyterianism, Boswell hoped that these areas of potential conflict would be avoided, but after they had been at Auchinleck for a few days Johnson and Lord Auchinleck "came in collision", as Boswell put it. "If I recollect right, the contest began while my father was showing him his collection of medals; and Oliver Cromwell's coin unfortunately introduced Charles the First, and Toryism.

They became exceedingly warm and violent, and I was very much distressed by being present at such an altercation between two men, both of whom I reverenced; yet I durst not inter-fere." A year later, according to Lord Auchinleck's friend John Ramsay of Ochtertyre, Lord Auchinleck said that "the great Dr Johnson, of whom he had heard wonders, was just a dominie,[33] and the worst-bred dominie he had ever seen".[34]

The two travellers returned to Edinburgh on 9 November. The winter session was about to begin and Boswell had to attend to court cases almost immediately. Meanwhile, Johnson stayed in Edinburgh for a further ten days, during which time he was fêted by the Edinburgh literati. "On the mornings when he breakfasted at my house," wrote Boswell, "he had, from ten o'clock till one or two, a constant levee of various persons, of very different characters and descriptions. I could not attend him, being obliged to be in the Court of Session; but my wife was so good as to devote the greater part of the morning to the endless task of pouring out tea for my friend and his visitors."

Many years later Boswell recorded in his Life of Samuel Johnson that his wife had paid Johnson "the most assiduous and respectful attention while he was our guest", but he added that "the truth is, that his irregular hours and uncouth habits, such as turning the candles with their heads downwards when they did not burn bright enough, and letting the wax drop upon the carpet, could not but be disagreeable to a lady...; and what was very natural to a female mind, she thought he had too much influence over her husband."[35]

33 A schoolmaster.
34 Ramsay, p. 176, n. 1.
35 *Life*, Vol. I, p. 464, note.

1774

Boswell tells us that "from the confusion of credit and scarcity of money, there was less business done in the Court of Session, Winter Session 1773-1774, than almost ever was known. I had not near so much practice as in former winters, which happened well for my indolent and listless state. I wrote few papers, and never was up any one morning before eight. Yet there was no great deficiency in the amount of my fees. I got one hundred and fifty guineas [and] I was engaged in several criminal trials... I charged the jury in three [of those] trials."

On 20 May Boswell's second daughter, Euphemia, was born.

The summer session started on 14 June and on that day Boswell started once again to keep a full journal.

TUESDAY 14 JUNE. I began to rise at seven. This day I got home another servant, James Dalrymple, a young man from Dumfriesshire who had been with Dr Hunter at Moffat. He had a wife and two children in Edinburgh. Seemed to be clever and obliging. Between nine and ten called on my father, who had come from Auchinleck in one day and arrived late the night before. The Court of Session seemed to be crowded. I said, "There must be carrion in the wind when there's so many of us." The President was ill. Cosmo Gordon[1] affected much concern, and perhaps felt some. I neither felt nor affected any. "Cosmo," said I, "upon this subject you and I are Heraclitus and Democritus, the weeping and laughing philosophers." "And", said Maclaurin, "I am the Stoic between you." I was in good sound hearty spirits, and found many of my brethren at the bar in the same humour. The Outer House is a scene of unbounded conversation and merriment. Everything is thrown out, and amongst such a quantity of stuff some good things cast up. I dined quietly at home. Nobody with us but Mrs Montgomerie.[2] My father, Lady Auchinleck, and Dr Young[3] drank tea. My father was pleased with Veronica, who applied to him for raisins which he had for her.

WEDNESDAY 15 JUNE. We dined at my father's. George Frazer, George Webster, and Claud were there. At five I was at the Solicitor's for my first consultation this session.[4] I have at the beginning of several sessions felt a peculiar cast of ideas by which I could distinguish, in my own mind, one session from the rest. This came on quite simple. It was just the Summer Session 1774 without any other perceptible mark. I began to receive my fees this session, as I begin to eat my two eggs on any night, with a pure sameness. I called on

1 Cosmo Gordon (c. 1736-1800), advocate (admitted 1 August 1758), M.P. Nairnshire 1774-77, Baron of Exchequer 27 March 1777.
2 Mrs Boswell's widowed sister-in-law, Jean Montgomerie (née Maxwell) of Lainshaw, who had come to stay for a few weeks.
3 Thomas Young, M.D., Physician and Professor of Midwifery at Edinburgh University, Mrs Boswell's obstetrician.
4 Henry Dundas's house was at 5 George Square (*B.O.E.C.*, Vol. 26, p. 139). George Square, then a suburb to the south of the city, was the most fashionable, healthy and elegant area of the city and suburbs until overtaken by the New Town.

Maclaurin as I returned and drank tea with him. I should have observed that as I was walking out to the Solicitor's with Taylor, Sandy Mackenzie's clerk—the consultation being on the cause, Ross of Auchnacloich against Mackenzie of Ardross[5]—Taylor said we would not be the worse of the President's being present; that both he and Gardenstone were good friends to Ardross. I said there was now very little to be expected on the Bench from private regard. It is true. For in the first place, the nation is more civilised and judges have better notions of justice. But, secondly, there is actually not such strong friendships or family attachments as were long ago. I do not blame our judges of the last age so much as many people do, because at that time there were many of them plain country gentlemen, not lawyers at all, and because the warmth of their hearts gave them a considerable imperceptible bias to one side. And it must be owned that of the many causes that come before the Court of Session there is a good proportion such as the judges will differ upon merely in cool opinion. No wonder then that regard casts the balance without their knowing it. Maclaurin and I sat an hour very socially. I had a consultation on Earl Fife's politics at eight,[6] and the session opened well.

THURSDAY 16 JUNE. After the House rose, I walked half round the Meadow with Lord Monboddo. He talked to me of the severe stroke of his son's death.[7] But I saw he bore it with philosophical composure. His conversation was manly; and, while he discussed his favourite subject of language, I felt my own inferiority to him in knowledge and precision of ideas. But we are so formed that almost every man is superior, or thinks himself superior, to any other man in something; and, fixing his view upon that, he is in good temper with himself. I was busy with session papers till near nine o'clock, when the Hon. Sandy Gordon called on me to go and walk. I was sitting with my escritoire open. He saw the word *Milton*, which began a copy of verses, and his curiosity was attracted. I indulged his curiosity and my own vanity by reading a good deal to him both of my *Boswelliana*[8] and my "Ten Lines".[9] Nairne called, and Gordon and he and I walked round the Meadow. We met Macqueen walking, which I said was an emblem of idleness, as grass growing at the Cross of Edinburgh was an emblem of desolation. Gordon came home with me and took a little supper and some port negus.

FRIDAY 17 JUNE. In the evening I went to Mr Stewart Moncrieffe's. I played at sixpenny brag, and found I was as keen as ever. Luckily I lost only eight shillings. I was in excellent spirits for that kind of club.

SATURDAY 18 JUNE. I walked out to Prestonfield, and was in the same social

5 Boswell acted for Murdoch Mackenzie of Ardross. For further details, see the entry for 31 January 1776.

6 "James Duff, Earl Fife, was struggling with the Duke of Gordon for control of the counties of Banff and Elgin. Both sides were 'making' as many votes as they could, while contesting those of the other" (*Defence*, p. 220, n. 4).

7 Arthur Burnett, Lord Monboddo's only son, had died on 27 April of this year at the age of eleven (*Defence*, p. 221, n. 1).

8 Boswell's miscellaneous collection of *bons mots* and other interesting items.

9 While in Holland and on his grand tour Boswell had disciplined himself to compose ten lines of verse a day. He had now resumed the practice, but he was to discontinue it after 14 July (*Defence*, p. 221, n. 3).

pleasant humour that I always am there. There was nobody there but the eldest Miss Keith and Mr Andrew Bennet, nephew to the minister. After dinner Sir Alexander and he and I and Mr Sharp, the tutor, had a stout match at the bowls.

SUNDAY 19 JUNE. I was at the New Church both forenoon and afternoon. Dr Blair and Mr Walker[10] preached. I dined at my father's between sermons.

MONDAY 20 JUNE. It was wet. I was at home all day writing law papers, except being at a consultation from four to six at Mr Rae's[11] on Earl Fife's politics, where we had a tedious reading of papers, which is really an irksome operation. I observed Rae pretty sound asleep at one time; and I myself was once or twice in that drowsy nodding state which is very disagreeable. How much attention a lawyer ought to give to the causes in which he is employed is not easy to say. But it is certain that when there are many lawyers employed in the same cause not one of them gives as much attention as he would do were he single. In the evening I received a long letter from General Oglethorpe.[12] It stirred my mind, revived my idea of my own consequence in London, and made me impatient to be there and not lost in this provincial corner where I find nothing to engage me warmly.

TUESDAY 21 JUNE. Still wet. Mrs Montgomerie and I went in a chaise to Bob Chalmers's[13] country-house on the seaside, near Musselburgh, to eat a fish dinner. My wife would not venture out, the day was so bad and she was but a month and a day brought to bed. I know not how it has happened that we have had no intercourse since our marriage with Bob Chalmers's family; though, before that, both of us used to visit and be well entertained there. We had refused several invitations from them and never asked them again. These cessations of acquaintance will happen unaccountably. Mrs Montgomerie's being with us renewed the intercourse, and it was this day renewed as to me very effectually; for I eat of nine kinds of fish and drank various drams and a great deal of port, and was really much intoxicated. Mr Baron Mure, his lady, and Miss Annie were there. With them, too, I have had no intercourse, though invited, and though he is so much connected with Lord Mountstuart, my *carus Maecenas*,[14] and is a friendly, sensible, agreeable man. However, things are put to rights at once by some happy occasion. I engaged him, his lady, and daughter to dine with us on Friday, and at the same time Mr and Mrs Chalmers; and I engaged that we should dine at the Baron's the week after. I was talkative and vociferous from the liquor which I had drank.

I supped at Sir George Preston's with my wife and Mrs Montgomerie. Dr Webster was there with his son Jamie, now Colonel Webster, just arrived from Ireland. I was by this time outrageously intoxicated and *would* drink a great deal of strong port negus, which made me worse. After I got home, I was very ill; not sick,

---

10 The Rev. Robert Walker (1716-1783), Hugh Blair's fellow minister at the New Church in St Giles' (from 1754 to 1783). Walker was an eloquent and popular Calvinistic preacher, appealing mainly to the poorer members of society. He strongly disapproved of many public amusements (Kay, Vol. I, pp. 234-5).
11 David Rae resided in Old Assembly Close, off the south side of the High Street.
12 Gen. James Edward Oglethorpe, a friend of Samuel Johnson.
13 Robert Chalmers, "writer".
14 "My dear Maecenas". For Maecenas, see Introduction, p. 17 and note.

but like to suffocate—a dangerous state—and my valuable spouse was much alarmed.

WEDNESDAY 22 JUNE. I had a miserable headache and in pleading a short cause before Lord Elliock I felt myself incapable of any distinctness. I was vexed at my conduct.

FRIDAY 24 JUNE. Baron Mure, his lady and daughter, and Bob Chalmers dined with us. Sandy Gordon, who was engaged also to come but had sent an apology, came to us after dinner. We were cheerful and easy. Mrs Chalmers was not well, so could not come. We did not drink much. The Baron and Mr Chalmers and I drank tea calmly. I then went to St John's Lodge, it being St John the Baptist's Day, on which the election of officers is made. I was chosen Master for the second year.[15] Dr Cairnie was there for the first time for, I believe, some years. I was but moderately in Mason humour; though I have associated ideas of solemnity and spirit and foreign parts and my brother David with St John's Lodge, which makes it always pleasing to me. Such agreeable associations are formed, we know not how, by a kind of chance, as the foam of the horse was by the dashing down the painter's brush on the canvas. I suppose the picture might be easily washed off. But it would be losing a satisfaction which perhaps we cannot equal by design.

SATURDAY 25 JUNE. Mr Samuel Johnson has often recommended to me to keep a journal, of which he is so sensible of the utility that he has several times tried it, but never could persist. I have at different periods of my life persisted a good time, and I am now hopeful that I may continue longer than ever. I shall only put down hints of what I have thought, seen, or heard every day, that I may not have too much labour; and I shall from these, at certain periods, make up masses or larger views of my existence. Mr Johnson said that the great thing was to register the state of my mind.

I went out today to Lady Colville's,[16] and had a most agreeable walk with her Ladyship and Lady Anne and Captain Andrew before dinner. My mind has of late years been so sound that I can assure myself of being suitably affected by certain objects. At Lady Colville's I am always soothed, comforted, and cheered. The cares of life are taken off with a velvet brush. I observed to Captain Andrew that we never have a long continuation of agreeable life. It is frequently interrupted. A company who have been very happy together must have the pain of parting. After every enjoyment comes weariness or disgust. We never have a large lawn of agreeable life. It is cut to pieces with sunk fences, ha-has, even where it is smoothest. Captain Erskine always revives notions of family and antiquity and Toryism in my mind. There was nobody there today but one young lady who was quiet and inoffensive. So we were quite in our own style. I drank hardly any; so was undisturbed. After tea Captain Andrew walked into town with me.

I found a letter from Mr Samuel Johnson, informing me that the first sheets of his *Journey to the Hebrides* were sent to the press. This gave me a lively joy; and

15 For Boswell's Masonic activities, see Introduction, p. 18.
16 Lady Colville was now once more a widow, Lord Colville having died on 21 May 1770.

I was much elated by his writing, "I have endeavoured to do you some justice in the first paragraph." One must pause and think, to have a full feeling of the value of any praise from Mr Johnson. His works and his majesty of mind must be kept in view. I had the same sensation tonight as on hearing from General Oglethorpe: that it was hard that I should not be in London. It is true Hume, Robertson, and other greater geniuses than I am prefer Scotland. But they have neither that peculiar and permanent love of London and all its circumstances which I have; nor are they so much in unison with the English as I am, which I have clearly perceived, and of which Mr Johnson has assured me. I supped at Sir George Preston's with my wife and Mrs Montgomerie.

MONDAY 27 JUNE. I went to see the foundation-stone of the Register Office laid.[17] I was very angry that there was no procession, no show or solemnity of any kind upon such an occasion.[18] There was a fine sight both of well-dressed people and mob, so that there was spirit enough in the country to relish a show; and such things do good. It should have been laid either privately in the morning, or with some dignity. But cards were sent to all the judges as private men, and they accordingly dropped in, one by one, without their gowns and several of them with bob-wigs. The Lord Provost[19] too was there as a private man. To appear so at noon before a crowd of spectators was very poor. I was for satirising the Lord Register, who tripped about *delicately*.[20] I would not just have hewn him like King Agag,[20a] but would have lashed him smartly—"Lord Freddie with a foolish face."

TUESDAY 28 JUNE. The President was in the chair. His animal spirits made the court seem more alive. It was like ringing the glasses at a drinking bout, or striking a shuttlecock with a sounding battledore.

WEDNESDAY 29 JUNE. We dined at Baron Mure's,[21] where was a kind of second-rate grandeur but much cheerfulness. I sat by Miss Campbell of Carrick. Sandy Gordon was there, and Bob Adam the architect,[22] who was lively enough, though vain, for which I forgave him. I drank rather too much. I drank tea there too.

FRIDAY 1 JULY. I dined at Lord Monboddo's, where we had Miss Fletcher, Baron Winn, Crosbie, Maclaurin, Sandy Gordon, etc., and Bob Adam. We were sufficiently jovial. To go home to business seemed dull. However, after drinking tea (the only man except my Lord himself), I did go home and had a short consultation; and was pleased that Mr Lawrie[23] was out of the way, so that it was not my fault that I was idle. I supped at the Horse Wynd Tavern and drank my

17 The Register Office (now called Register House) is a handsome neo-classical building designed by Robert Adam. The building, which stands at the east end of Princes Street, was erected to house the national archives, which until then had been stored in the Laigh Parliament House (see the entry for 16 August 1773).
18 Arnot says that "the ceremony was performed under a discharge of artillery" (Arnot, p. 186).
19 Gilbert Laurie, merchant in Edinburgh, Lord Provost 1766-8, 1772-4.
20 Lord Frederick Campbell, the Lord Clerk Register (from 1768 to 1816), who was accompanied by the Lord Advocate (James Montgomery) and the Lord Justice-Clerk (Thomas Miller of Barskimming). The Lord Clerk Register was responsible for the custody of the national archives.
20a See I Samuel 15: 32-33.
21 Baron Mure's house was at the Abbey Hill, which was then a fashionable suburb to the east of the city.
22 Robert Adam (1728-92).
23 John Lawrie, Boswell's clerk.

bottle of old hock, which did me no harm. There was but eight of us. Lord Monboddo was one.

SATURDAY 2 JULY. Dined at Craighouse,[24] and had a party at bowls both before and after dinner. It was wonderful to see Mr Lockhart, who has now stood fifty-two years at the bar, playing with all the keenness of a young man. Maclaurin and I led one another on to bet and I lost thirteen shillings. To play for a crown, as we did, is incongruous with the healthful field-sport of the bowls. It poisons it with a certain degree of avaricious anxiety. I resolved never to play for more than a shilling.

SUNDAY 3 JULY. Was at New Church in the forenoon. The Reverend Dr Ewing of Philadelphia preached admirably on "My ways are not as your ways," etc. At my father's between sermons. Afternoon, Tolbooth Church;[25] heard Dr Webster, as well as ever. We all again took our Sunday's supper with him. We were comfortable and more quiet than last Sunday. I was for setting up a hogshead of wine as a Lord of Session in place of a drunken judge. Dr Webster said it was a good thought; and let the parties or their agents take glass about, and he who happened to get the last glass win the cause. This he said would be cheaper than giving a salary to a judge and feeing lawyers. It is curious how a thought once started may be pursued. A reclaiming petition would come in against an interlocutor of Vintage 1754, Ordinary. Parties might agree before the hogshead was drank out.

MONDAY 4 JULY. Was busy all day. I had a consultation at seven in the morning to draw a bill of suspension,[26] which was done by eleven. I finished a long memorial before night.

WEDNESDAY 6 JULY. My wife, Mrs Montgomerie, and I dined at Sandy Gordon's.[27] Lord Monboddo, Crosbie, Stewart Moncrieffe, Cosmo Gordon, etc., etc., were there. Crosbie was obliged to go to the Commissary Court immediately after dinner to attend a process of divorce. I said it was a severe divorce to him to dissever him from us. It was a separation *a mensa*.[28] Monboddo was in excellent spirits and did not seem inclined to rise. Cosmo Gordon and I sat to cherish his festivity, and we were really joyous. I repeated my ballad, *The Boston Bill*.[29] Lord Monboddo said it would do well in America. It was better than *Lilliburlero*, which brought about the Revolution; and Cosmo Gordon said it was equal to anything of Sir Charles Hanbury Williams. I had drank rather too much and was a good deal heated, and at the same time had several papers to write which hung heavy upon my mind. One representation was to be done this very night. I did it, however; though to be sure not very sufficiently. Social dinners and the practice of the law are really incompatible. I must restrain myself from them; and yet there is not company here to make them

24 Alexander Lockhart's residence was the ancient mansion of Craighouse on the slopes of Easter Craiglockhart Hill to the south of the city. The building is now known as Old Craig and is to be found on the Craighouse Campus of Napier University.
25 The Tolbooth Church in St Giles' (as to which, see Introduction, p. 6, and p. 62, n. 5).
26 An application to the Court of Session seeking an order suspending the enforceability of a decree.
27 The Hon. A Gordon's house was a "stately old mansion" on the south side of the Castle Hill (Grant, Vol. I, p.90).
28 This is an allusion to the legal expression *divortium a mensa et thoro*, which means "separation from bed and table". For the Commissary Court, see p. 502, n. 33.
29 The Boston Tea Party had occurred on 16 December 1773 and Boswell's ballad (published in *The London Chronicle* for 21-23 July 1774) was in support of the Americans.

but in session time, and life must be enjoyed. I was this night firmly resolved to go to the English bar if ever I should be quite my own master; or at any rate to pass half my time in London, where my talents have their full value.

THURSDAY 7 JULY. Many of my brethren in the House asked to hear *The Boston Bill*, which I repeated with excellent applause. I lost two causes in the Inner House, I thought unjustly; and I spoke in both with a manly ease. I was at a consultation at Mr Ilay Campbell's;[30] then at St John's Lodge, where were but six present. But my spirits made a choice meeting.

FRIDAY 8 JULY. Lord and Lady Dundonald[31] and Lady Betty Cochrane,[32] Mr Heron of Heron,[33] and Dr and Mrs Hunter dined with us. It was a substantial creditable dinner, without my being obliged to drink any. It was curious to see Lord Dundonald, at the age of eighty-three, stout and fresh, with a flow of spirits. The tide, to be sure, appeared to be out. But there was a high sea. In the evening, after a long consultation on two causes of Colonel Rickson's widow,[34] I felt myself in a pleasing indolence. I yielded to it and went early to bed.

SATURDAY 9 JULY. The state of my mind must be gathered from the little circumstances inserted in my journal. The life of every man, take it day by day, is pretty much a series of uniformity; at least a series of repeated alternations. It is like a journal of the weather: rainy—fair—fair—rainy, etc. It is seldom that a great storm or an abundant harvest occurs in the life of man or in the progress of years. Of this week I can observe that my mind has been more lively than usual, more fertile in images, more agreeably sensible of enjoying existence.

An important part of my life should be my practice as a lawyer. I must record an anecdote. The Reverend Mr William Macqueen had a legacy of two thousand merks Scots[35] left to him by a testament subscribed in the Isle of Skye by one notary and two witnesses. He consulted me to know if it was good. I gave him my advice as a friend, and was of the opinion that it was not good, as the Act of Parliament, ——, requires the subscriptions of two notaries and four witnesses to all deeds concerning heritage, and to all deeds of importance, i.e., which convey £100 Scots.[36] At the same time, I said I had some faint idea that there was an exception as to a testament; and I should *think* of the subject. I talked with some of my brethren. *Sandy Murray* said it would not do; and that there was no hardship upon people in remote countries where it was difficult to get

30 Ilay Campbell's house was in Brown Square, a small, fashionable quadrangle lying to the east of Candlemaker Row. The houses, which were erected in 1763-4, "were deemed fine mansions, and found favour with the upper classes, before a stone of the New Town was laid" (Grant, Vol. II, p. 269).
31 Jean (née Stuart), Countess of Dundonald, married Lord Dundonald in 1744. She was thirty years younger than her husband, and was considered to be very beautiful when she married him (*Applause*, p. 33, n. 2).
32 Lady Elizabeth Cochrane, eldest daughter of Lord and Lady Dundonald.
33 Patrick Heron, who had divorced his first wife, Jean Home (Boswell's erstwhile lover, the daughter of Lord Kames), for adultery. He married Lady Betty Cochrane at the end of 1775 (*Defence*, p. 232, n. 6).
34 For details of one of these cases, see the entry for 16 November 1775 and relevant footnote.
35 A merk was a silver coin worth 13s. 4d. Scots.
36 Act of 1579, c. 18, "anent the inserting of witnesses in obligationis and writtis of importance" (*The Acts of the Parliaments of Scotland*, Vol. III (1567-1592), p. 145). Notaries' subscriptions were only required if the grantor could not write.

two notaries, as clergymen were held as notaries in the case of testaments. *Crosbie* was clear it would not do. He said the Act was express; and how absurd would it be to allow one to make a settlement with less formality and fewer checks against imposition when he was ill than when in good health. I then told honest Mr Macqueen that I was sorry to find that he would make nothing of his legacy, as some of my brethren agreed with me; but that I should also ask his namesake, Mr *Macqueen*. I did so; and Macqueen, with that excellent candour which he always has, told me that he really could not tell how the matter stood; that he thought it would not do. But like myself he said he had some kind of idea of a testament being privileged. I asked him if he actually did not know so plain a thing one way or other. He declared he did not. "Well," said I, "that flatters me very much, for I'm like to hang myself when I cannot answer a question, and here are *you* at a loss." He desired me to look into the law books, and had I at first *read*, instead of *thinking* and *asking*, I might at once have been made certain. Upon looking into Erskine,[37] I found it to be clear that testaments to any extent were good with one notary and two witnesses. This is a curious practical anecdote. I must observe that *Nairne* seemed to think it would do, and *Charles Hay* was certain it would do. A man picks up his firmest particles of knowledge occasionally. Charles told me that he knew this of the testament well, because he happened to call on Michael Nasmith[38] when he was examining a notary, and heard that point mentioned. I made honest Mr Macqueen very happy by telling him that his legacy was good.

This day I had fixed for paying a bet of five guineas to the Hon. Andrew Erskine, Grange, James Currie, Sandy Abercrombie[39] and James Loch,[40] writers, which I had lost six years ago. It was agreed at the time of the bet that it should be a supper at *Thom's*, in whose house I had paid two former bets. But Thom having now given up his tavern, and the sum being handsome, we resolved to have a dinner at Fortune's. Dr Webster was with us as chaplain; and we had an excellent dinner at No. 9 and abundance of drinking. While Webster sat, we had several good stories and songs. He left us between seven and eight, and then we grew very noisy and drunk, but very cordial as old friends. In short we had a complete riot, which lasted until near twelve at night. We had eleven Scotch pints of claret,[40a] two bottles of old hock, and two of port, and drams of brandy and gin; and the bill was 6. 18. 5. So my five-guinea bet turned to a seven-guinea one; for I gave the waiter the balance of that sum over the bill. In our great warmth we signed an agreement to meet annually on the second Saturday of July, as we had "now

37 John Erskine, *An Institute of the Law of Scotland*, Edinburgh, 1773. The passage to which Boswell refers is in Book III, Tit. II, 23.
38 Michael Nasmith, W.S. (admitted 19 December 1767), apprentice to James Hay of Cocklaw, died 1777.
39 Alexander Abercromby, W.S. (admitted 10 July 1770), died 1804.
40 James Loch, W.S. (admitted 4 July 1769), appointed H.M. Remembrancer to the Court of Exchequer in 1786, died 1793.
40a A Scots pint was equal to about three imperial pints (*CSD*, p. 818).

met, after an interval of six years, in the same good humour and with the same cordial regard for each other that we then did, and considering that such things were rare and valuable in human life". I sat after the rest were gone and took a large bowl of admirable soup, which did me much good, for I was not sick; though after I was in bed my dear wife was apprehensive that I might die, I breathed so ill.

SUNDAY 10 JULY. Though I was neither sick nor had hardly any headache, I was, as it were, half boiled with last night's debauch, and I was vexed to think of having given my valuable spouse so much uneasiness; for she had scarcely slept any the whole night watching me. The reflection, too, of my having this summer so frequently been intoxicated, galled me. A circumstance occurred this morning which I hope will have a lasting impression upon me. There had come a letter to me from Mr Samuel Johnson last night. My wife improved it well. She said she would not give me it, as I did not deserve it, since I had put myself into a state of incapacity to receive it when it came, and that it would not have been written to me had the writer of it known how I was to be. She would therefore send it back. She thus made me think how shocking it was that a letter from Mr Samuel Johnson should find me drunk. She then delivered it, and it was a more than ordinary good one. It put me in the best frame, and I determined vigorously to resist temptation for the future.

I was soberly at the New Church in the forenoon. Mr Logan, minister at Leith, preached.

MONDAY 11 JULY. My Saturday's debauch had relaxed me so as that business seemed irksome; and yet I had a number of papers which I was absolutely obliged to write in a short time, and some of the agents were complaining of delay. In the forenoon Captain Erskine called and gave me a special invitation from Lady Colville to dine with her. To accept of it seemed incompatible with my present state of business. Yet I could not resist. I considered that it would only throw me an hour or two more behind, and that I should be so refreshed with the agreeable interview with quality friends in the country air that I should be able to labour twice as well. I accordingly went. We had only the two Captains,[41] Lady Dalrymple, and her grandchild, Lady Anne Lindsay.[42] I was gently happy and did not heat myself at all with wine. My wife came and drank tea. Captain Erskine walked with me as far as the New Town. I came home in admirable spirits and dictated papers with ease and alacrity.

THURSDAY 14 JULY. My father and Lady Auchinleck, Commissioner Cochrane, the Laird of Fullarton and his mother, Mr Nairne, Dr Boswell, and Messieurs Alexander Mackenzie[43] and Andrew Stewart, Junior,[44] dined with us.

41 Captain Andrew Erskine and his brother, Captain Archibald Erskine (1736-1797). Archibald Erskine was later promoted to Major and then to Lieutenant-Colonel. He became 7th Earl of Kellie in 1781 and died unmarried.
42 Lady Anne Lindsay (1750-1825), the authoress of the popular ballad "Auld Robin Gray", *later* Lady Anne Barnard.
43 Alexander Mackenzie (1735-1805), W.S. (admitted 15 July 1763).
44 Andrew Stewart (or Steuart), W.S. (admitted 15 July 1763), died 10 October 1798.

The company went away gradually till I was left with Fullarton, who drank nothing at all hardly, and the two writers, who were both very social. In such circumstances my strong attraction from within requires little aid from any external impulse and easily makes me think that it is a kind of duty or necessity for me to drink. I took rather too much and was to a certain degree feverish with it. I must steadily keep in mind that no man is more easily hurt with wine than I am, and that there is no real advantage gained by being a good bottle-companion, and whenever I am set with company after dinner or after supper I must beware of thinking of Duncan Forbes, whose hard drinking often misleads me. It was unpleasing today to see my father not at all frank or cordial with me or my wife. At seven Lady Dundonald came herself and consulted me about a lawsuit which she had with a weaver whom she had employed to make some rich table linen. I was vexed to find myself confused while her Ladyship talked with me. However, I was prudent and plausible. In the evening I wrote a very good representation in a cause concerning a bill, which consoled me so far. I had been much pressed to sup at Walter Campbell's with Maclaurin and Sandy Gordon. But I resisted and kept at home.

FRIDAY 15 JULY. This was a day of complete sobriety and diligence; and I extricated myself from a very difficult cause by persevering till I was master of it. I went in the afternoon to the prison and conferred with my old client John Reid.[45]

SATURDAY 16 JULY. Mrs Montgomerie, my wife, and I dined at Mr Mitchelson's[46] at Corstorphine. He sent his chaise, which carried us out. I was unusually delighted with the prospect of the country. Mr Aytoun, Writer to the Signet,[47] and Mr Claud Boswell were there. We were perfectly sober. At six I had a hackney-coach which carried Mrs Montgomerie, Claud, my wife, and me to the play. There was just forty people in the boxes and pit. The play was *The Man of Business*, and the farce, *Cross Purposes*.[48] It was wonderful to see with what spirit the players performed. In one view it was more agreeable tonight than being at a crowded play. One could attend fully to what passed on the stage, whereas in a great audience the attention is distracted and one has a great deal to do in behaving properly. The difference was the same as viewing a country when upon a calm horse at a slow walk or viewing it upon a fiery horse at a gallop, when you must attend to the reins and to your seat. But the laughable passages did not go off so well as in a crowd, for laughter is augmented by sympathetic power. Supped quietly at home.

SUNDAY 17 JULY. Was in a calm, reflecting frame. Considered how very little I read during the course of a week except mere matter of business. I thought of lying

45 Reid (as to whom, see Introduction, pp. 39-40) had been charged once again with sheep-stealing.
46 Samuel Mitchelson, Senior.
47 William Aytoun, W.S. (admitted 16 December 1760), died May 1780.
48 By George Colman and William O'Brien, respectively. The plays were at the new Edinburgh Theatre Royal in Shakespeare Square, at the east end of Princes Street opposite the Register Office. The new theatre had opened on 9 January 1769.

in bed all forenoon and indulging the humour in which I then was. I had a slight conflict between what I really thought would do me most good and the desire of being externally decent and going to church. I rose and breakfasted; but being too late for church, I read a part of my Bible and began the Life of Bishop Sanderson by Walton, which I have heard Mr Samuel Johnson commend much and which I had borrowed from the Advocates' Library. I read [it] today, all but some leaves which were a-wanting in the copy which I had. I shall get the defect supplied. The simplicity and pious spirit of Walton was, as it were, transfused into my soul. I resolved that amidst business and every other worldly pursuit I should still keep in mind religious duty. I had stripped and gone to bed again in my nightgown after breakfast, which favoured my tranquillity. A man who *knows himself* should use means to do him good which to others may seem trifling or ridiculous.

My wife and I dined at my father's, where were Sir George Preston and George Webster. There was the usual constraint joined with the usual small conversation. In the afternoon I was at the New Church and heard Dr Blair preach. My wife and I drank tea at home by ourselves. We all supped at Dr Webster's.

MONDAY 18 JULY. Mrs Montgomerie, my wife, and I dined at Lady Colville's, where we had Sir George Preston, his lady, and daughter. Captain Andrew was not there. I was in a disagreeable humour, domineering and ill-bred, insisting to have Sir George's punch made stronger, and in short being really rude. A fit of impatience and coarse violence of temper had come upon me. I was angry at myself and yet so proud that when I saw it was observed with dissatisfaction, I persisted. We drank tea, and I grew calmer. Lady Anne walked in with my wife and me.

TUESDAY 19 JULY. Lord Alemoor and his sister, Lord Monboddo, Mr Walter Campbell and wife, and Miss Douglas Ker, Crosbie, and Charles Hay dined with us. It was a very creditable and agreeable meeting, for we were all in good humour. After the ladies went to the drawing-room, there was too much drinking. Lord Alemoor sat by till about seven and was very pleasant. I gave them my *Boston Bill* and read some of Goldsmith's *Retaliation*, which dashed some finer genius in our jovial cup. Crosbie spoke more than usual. He had consultations both at six and seven. But he did not stir. He told me afterwards, "I could not tear myself away from you." Monboddo was excellent company. It pleased me to have my good professor, Charles Hay, in a party which satisfied him to the full.[49] The future Shawfield[50] was steadily merry. I had a consultation at Mr Rae's on Earl Fife's politics at seven. But I thought there were enough there without me—that I could read the papers by myself—and that I should come in long before their tedious conference was over. In the situation I then was, I could not get away. At eight my company insisted to break up. I went to Mr Rae's and got as much of the consultation as was necessary. I was a good deal intoxicated, but had as much command of myself as to be decent.

49 Boswell refers to Hay as his "good professor" as he and Hay had been studying law together during the court vacation.
50 Walter Campbell of Shawfield.

THURSDAY 21 JULY. Mr Alexander Donaldson and his son,[51] Mr Charles Hay, Mr Michael Nasmith, and Grange supped with me. I told Mr Alexander Donaldson that, as Alexander the Great sat down and wept that he had no more worlds to conquer, he might now, after his victory on Literary Property, sit down and weep that he had no more booksellers to conquer. We were jovial and merry. My wife and Mrs Montgomerie were at the play, and sent to us not to wait supper for them. They came to us about eleven, and enlivened us. We sat till one in the morning.

FRIDAY 22 JULY. I dined at Lord Dundonald's[52] with my wife and Mrs Montgomerie. Old General Colville,[53] Captain Blair, Mr Nairne, and George Webster were there. The Earl was in great spirits; but it was not quite agreeable to hear a man of eighty-three swearing and talking bawdy. One regretted that such admirable vivacity had taken such habits. He, however, showed a sense of piety; for he said he "never rose in the morning nor lay down at night without thanking GOD for his goodness" to him. I, in my way, rattled too much, and being grand-nephew to the Earl, who did not drink himself, I willingly thought it incumbent on me to be landlord, and pushed about the bottle pretty briskly. We drank tea. I felt myself somewhat flustered with wine; was at a consultation at the Solicitor's at seven. Then being unquiet after I got home, so that I could not work, went to Mr Stewart Moncrieffe's, betted at the whist table, and lost a crown, which I grudged. We were ten at supper. I indulged in old hock and became very drunk. Drinking never fails to make me ill-bred. I insisted to know Moncrieffe's age. He parried me well. How I appeared this night to others, I know not. But I recollect having felt much warmth of heart, fertility of fancy, and joyous complacency mingled in a sort of delirium. Such a state is at least equal to a pleasing dream. I drank near three bottles of hock, and then staggered away. I got home about three in the morning. Mr Nairne had supped at my house, expecting me home. Mrs Montgomerie had sat up till two waiting to see me, as she was to set out next morning. I was incapable of knowing anything; and my wife was waiting all the time, drowsy and anxious. What a price does such an evening's, or rather night's, riot cost me!

SATURDAY 23 JULY. I had been sick without being sensible of it. But I was so ill at seven that I could not bid adieu to Mrs Montgomerie. I however grew so well as to be able to get up and go to the Parliament House at nine. I was still quite giddy with liquor, and, squeamishness having gone off, I was in a good, vigorous, sparkling frame, and did what was necessary to be done in several causes, and was most entertaining amongst my brother lawyers. I dined at Crosbie's,[54] where were the Lords Alemoor, Elliock, and Monboddo, a very good fifth of the Bench. I was in prodigious spirits, dined with a great appetite, and

51 Alexander Donaldson's son was James Donaldson, who, like his father, was a printer and bookseller.
52 Lord Dundonald's town house was at Belleville, between the Palace of Holyroodhouse and the Abbey Hill (*Ominous Years*, p. 11, n. 3).
53 Lieutenant-General Charles Colville (1691-1775).
54 Andrew Crosbie's house was a magnificent newly-constructed house at 35 St Andrew Square in the New Town (see p. 491, n. 4).

drank beer copiously to allay the thirst of last night's drinking. We had a deal of merriment; and I drank old hock, which just cooled my fever and really sobered me. The judges sat well. I talked of the long time that the same Bench had sat. "As long as Duncan Forbes drove the same horses" (as I expressed his being at the head of the same Lords). "I am glad", said Lord Alemoor, "you give us so good an epithet as *horses*." As the wine went freely about, he said, "You'll make a vacancy tonight." Said I: "Maclaurin has Lord Kennet dining with him today, to try what he can make of *him*. We are fighting the Bench in parties." I afterwards (not this day) observed that Kennet's insipidity and Maclaurin's peevishness would make poor work. It would be like skate and vinegar. It was pleasant to have the Bench and the bar so easy together as we were today, but in my opinion the ease was too much. The character of a judge should not only have dignity but reverence. Between eleven and twelve, Crosbie, who had drank very faithfully, seemed much overcome. He pressed us to sit, but none of us were drunk and we all came off. I walked home with great composure.

SUNDAY 24 JULY. I was very well, and was at the New Church all day and at my father's between sermons. Dr Blair preached well in the forenoon on, "Who art thou that judgest another man's servant?" He recommended calmness in judging of others to man, who has so much need of indulgence from his Maker. The sermon was very applicable to me. I took it home and resolved to check violence of temper and make allowance even for the President.[55]

I called this evening on Sir William Forbes[56] and had a long comfortable tête-à-tête with him upon literary subjects and religious principles, and on the conduct of life. He told me that he kept an accurate account of his expenses, which he was resolved to do to the day of his death; that from his being so much used to figures, it was quite easy to him; that it served as a kind of Journal of his life; that perhaps once a quarter he classed his expenses under different articles, and so saw where to retrench, where to extend. I determined to have myself put in a way by him of doing the same. I value him highly and regret that we are not more together, for, as I told him tonight, I am always the better of being with him.

MONDAY 25 JULY. Passed the day principally in writing law papers. I received a letter from Mr Gentleman[57] that he was in distress and begging the loan of five guineas. My wife very genteelly was for my complying.

THURSDAY 28 JULY. Mr Wood the surgeon[58] having called on us a little before

---

55 Boswell had been enraged by the Lord President's interference in Ayrshire politics during the General Election that year. Boswell had lent his support to the sitting M.P., his fellow advocate David Kennedy (later tenth Earl of Cassillis), who was opposed by Sir Adam Fergusson. Dundas prevailed on Lord Auchinleck to use his interest on behalf of Fergusson and even to create some "fictitious votes" (a practice which Lord Auchinleck had hitherto held to be reprehensible). The consequence was that Sir Adam was elected.
56 Sir William's house was at 39 George Street in the New Town (*B.O.E.C.*, New Series, Vol. 1, p. 74).
57 Francis Gentleman, actor and dramatist.
58 Alexander ("Sandy") Wood (1725-1807), eminent fellow of the Royal College of Surgeons, renowned for his "perfect simplicity and openness of character" and "universally beloved" for his remarkably benevolent and convivial nature (Kay, Vol. I, pp. 115-6).

three, we persuaded him to stay and dine. He very earnestly spoke to me to agree to make such a settlement of the estate of Auchinleck as my father chose, that my wife and children might have provisions secured to them in case of my death; and he said it was his opinion my father's chance of life was better than mine. This struck me much. But I felt a firmness in my old male feudal principles, though honest Wood could not see them but as wild romantic fancies. I have a strong conflict in my mind between my concern for my valuable wife, who in case of my death would be left in a miserable state of dependence, and those principles which are interwoven with my very heart, and which I hold myself bound in honour to maintain, as my great-great-grand-uncle gave the estate to his nephew, my grandfather,[59] in prejudice of his own four daughters; so that all who receive it as a male fief should faithfully transmit it as such. Mr Johnson confirmed me in that principle and inculcated upon me that the chance of my wife and children being in a bad situation was nothing in the general calculation of things. I shall therefore be steady, conscious of my sincere affection for my wife and children, and trusting that I may have it in my power to make them all easy.

FRIDAY 29 JULY. Between one and two in the forenoon Mr William Wilson and I went to a consultation at Mr Lockhart's[60] on a perplexed question between Fairholm's trustee—Johnston—and Mitchell and Buchanan of Mountvernon. It vexed me that I could not understand it upon reading the papers. It was astonishing to see Mr Lockhart, who had only read them over as I had done, much master of the cause. He is certainly a prodigy in his profession. My wife and I dined at Lord Alemoor's.[61] Lord Gardenstone, Macqueen, Crosbie, and Cullen were there. I was in very good spirits, but rather too much in the rough style of joking.

We had an elegant dinner, but I do not recollect much conversation that passed. Lord Alemoor observed that story-telling was the fashion of the last age, but that our wits now entertained with their own sayings. He asked me if I ever studied beforehand the good things which I said in company. I told him I did not. Crosbie agreed that it was so, but said I spoke enough about them *afterwards*; a very just remark. My wife and I stayed to tea. I was well warmed with wine here, and as Lord Gardenstone and Macqueen spoke jovially of supping at Moncrieffe's, this being the last night of meeting for the season and a neck of venison being promised, I determined to go. I did so, and flashed away. I was really excellent company. I never saw any man more pleased with another than Seton seemed to be with me. There was very hard drinking. I however did not exceed a

59 This was in fact Boswell's great-grandfather (*Life*, Vol. I, p.560 (January 1776)).
60 Alexander Lockhart's town house was in Adam's Court.
61 It was said of Lord Alemoor that his manner was "cold and unanimated, and he seldom raised his eyes from the ground" (Ramsay, p. 323). He suffered badly from gout, which ailment was evidently to some extent self-induced in that he is said to have been "too much addicted to the pleasures of the table, being fond of dressed dishes and generous wines" (*ibid.*, p. 327). Boswell regarded Lord Alemoor as being a rare example of a "respectable character", and cited as an example of this the fact that he "made his jokes float between you and him like bubbles blown from soap into the air, so that he himself was kept distinct from the jocularity" (Journal, 25 April 1777).

bottle and a half of old hock. But, with what I had taken at dinner, I was far gone.

SATURDAY 30 JULY. My head was inflamed and confused considerably. However, I went to the Parliament House a little after nine. I found the Solicitor, who had been with us last night and drank heartily, standing in the outer hall looking very ill. He told me he was not able to stay, so he went home. He had struggled to attend his business, but it would not do. Peter Murray[62] told me he had seen him this morning come out of a dram-shop in the Back Stairs, in all his formalities of large wig and cravat. He had been trying to settle his stomach. In some countries such an officer of the Crown as Solicitor-General being seen in such a state would be thought shocking. Such are our manners in Scotland that it is nothing at all. I kept up well all forenoon, and after the court rose attended a Faculty meeting, made two motions, and presented some antiquities sent as a present to the Faculty by the Reverend Mr Donald Macqueen in Skye.[63]

John Reid's trial was to come on next Monday. Michael Nasmith, who at my desire was agent for him, seemed anxious. I promised to him what I had resolved in my own mind: that I should taste no wine till the trial was over. In the afternoon I went with my wife and Veronica to Heriot's Gardens,[64] which soothed and refreshed me. Veronica walked briskly, with a little help, pulled flowers, and I held her up till she pulled a cherry for the first time. I played a party at bowls with Adam Bell[65] and so many more, drank tea at home calmly, as I had dined, and made up for yesterday's excess. In the evening when it was dusky I visited John Reid. I felt a sort of dreary tremor as he and I walked together in the dark in the iron room. He would own nothing to me. I sent for a pot of lenitive electuary[66] at night, that I might open and cool my body, and took a part of it. I had not taken physic before for two years. I wished to do a kindness to poor Gentleman, who had always paid me much attention, but my debts far exceeded my funds. I sent him an order on Messrs Dilly for three guineas.

SUNDAY 31 JULY. The physic had a benign effect. I took the rest of the pot this morning, and lay in bed all forenoon except when a motion made me rise. I

62 Patrick ("Peter") Murray (1727-1780), advocate (admitted 17 December 1751), Sheriff-Depute of Roxburghshire 1769.

63 The first motion which Boswell made was that the Faculty should recommend that the Dean give in a Memorial to the Lords seeking orders to remedy the inconvenience which had arisen as a result of the macers of court being very negligent in calling causes to be determined in the Inner House with the consequence that counsel sometimes arrived too late to make representations. The second motion was to the effect that the Dean's Memorial to the Lords should also suggest having further seating at the bar in the Inner House so as to make sufficient space for counsel on occasions when large numbers of advocates were required to appear. Both motions were passed. The antiquities which Boswell mentions were an ancient stone sacrificial knife used by Druids, a Druidical spade and a sling stone (Stewart, p. 255).

64 The gardens at George Heriot's Hospital (*later* George Heriot's School) were open to the public and were a popular place of recreation. The gardens included a green (called Heriot's Green) where games of bowls took place. The Hospital—described as a "great Renaissance palace" (Keay and Keay, p. 306)—was constructed with funds bequeathed by James VI's jeweller and moneylender, George Heriot ("Jingling Geordie"), who died in 1624. The bequest was for the maintenance, relief, bringing up and education of destitute and fatherless children of freemen of Edinburgh.

65 A "writer".

66 A gentle laxative.

read the Lives of Dr Donne, Sir Henry Wotton, Mr Hooker, and Mr George Herbert, by Izaak Walton. I read them, all but a part of the last, in the forenoon, and was in the most placid and pious frame.

I was in a fine state of preparation for John Reid's trial, which was to come on next day. Michael Nasmith, who at my desire had agreed to be agent, called on me between one and two, when I got up and talked with him. Crosbie positively refused to appear for John Reid, as he had warned him after his last trial, but he was willing to give his aid privately. I went in a chair to his house at two, and consulted with him as to my plan of conducting the trial. He instructed me as to the subject of a charge of being habit and repute a thief. He asked me to dine with him, but as he had a company who I knew would drink, I declined his invitation, being resolved to keep myself perfectly cool. I went to the New Church in the afternoon and heard Dr Blair preach. Sir George and Lady Preston and Miss Preston drank tea with us. In the evening I finished what remained of Walton from the morning. Looked into Sir George Mackenzie's *Criminals*, meditated on the various circumstances of John Reid's trial, and examined separately two exculpatory witnesses as to his getting the sheep (with the theft of which he was charged) from one Gardner. One of them seemed so positive, notwithstanding my earnest request to tell me nothing but truth, that I began to give some credit to John's tale; but it afterwards appeared that great endeavours had been used to procure false evidence. Notwithstanding all my care to be cool, anxiety made me restless and hot after I went to bed.

MONDAY 1 AUGUST. Having passed an uneasy night from anxiety as to the defence of John Reid, who was my first client in criminal business, I rose between six and seven and dictated to Mr Lawrie my pleading on the indictment. My dear wife, who always takes good care of me, had a bowl of soup ready for my breakfast, which was an excellent morning cordial.

The trial commenced in the Court of Justiciary at eight o'clock in the morning.[67] *The bench initially consisted of four judges: The Lord Justice-Clerk (Thomas Miller of Barskimming), Lord Auchinleck, Lord Kames and Lord Coalston. At a later stage they were joined by Lords Pitfour and Kennet. The charge set out in the indictment was that Reid, either on his own, or art and part, had stolen nineteen or so sheep on or about 6 October 1773 from a farm in the county of Peebles, or, alternatively, that he was guilty of the crime of "reset of theft" (that is, receiving stolen goods knowing them to have been stolen). It was also alleged in the indictment that Reid was "a person of bad fame, habit and repute a sheep-stealer". There were four counsel for the prosecution: the Lord Advocate (James Montgomery), the Solicitor-General (Henry Dundas), William Nairne and Robert Sinclair.*[68] *Against this impressive group of counsel Reid was represented by Boswell on his own. At the outset of the trial, Boswell put forward a plea to the relevancy of the "libel",*[69] *in the*

---

67 The details of this case which follow are taken from *Defence*, pp. 249-264.

68 Robert Sinclair (d. 1802), advocate (admitted 7 December 1762), Advocate-Depute March 1773, Sheriff-Depute of Lanarkshire 1775-86, died unmarried.

69 That is, he argued that the libel (being that part of the indictment specifying the grounds on which the charge was based) was irrelevant as a matter of law.

course of which he stated that if Reid had sheep in his possession which were stolen, he did not know them to be so, and "as to the charge of his being a person of bad fame, habit and repute as sheep-stealer…he was tried for that very charge in December 1766, and a verdict of his country was returned finding it not proved, and nothing is better established than that a man cannot be again tried for the same charge of which he has been acquitted; and supposing this charge to be restricted to the time since his former trial, it is well known that when a man has had the misfortune to be tried for any crime, a prejudice is thereby created against his character which is seldom entirely removed from vulgar minds, though he obtains a verdict in his favour."

On the question of habit and repute, the judges all agreed with Lord Auchinleck that "habit and repute…is not a crime in our law. It is a misfortunate thing when a man has it, but a man cannot be punished for having a bad character. It is pretty fair if we get them punished when there is both habit and repute and a proof of the crime. Then habit and repute [is] not only an aggravation but a strong circumstance of guilt."

The court, having found the indictment to be relevant, remitted the case to be heard by an "assize" or jury. Once the members of the jury were assembled, the prosecution called their witnesses, of whom there were eight. Thereafter, Boswell adduced his one and only witness (all other potential witnesses having proved to be unsatisfactory). This witness gave evidence to the effect that he had been told by a William Gardner (who was at the time of the trial a prisoner in the Tolbooth of Stirling) that there had been a bargain between Reid and Gardner more than a year earlier with regard to some sheep. This evidence was intended to support the declaration which Reid had made when brought before Sheriff Cockburn on 23 March 1774. In that declaration Reid had stated that he acquired the sheep from Gardner, who had said that he had got the sheep from some horse-dealers in Carnwath.

At this point, Boswell returned to the subject of Reid's being alleged to be a common thief by habit and repute and submitted that "it was of great importance to [Reid] to show cause for such bad report having prevailed",[70] and he offered to prove by two of the jury who had sat at Reid's last trial that, after he had been acquitted by the jury, "the five judges present strongly expressed their disapprobation of the verdict and in such terms as to convey to the minds of a numerous audience that notwithstanding that verdict he was still a guilty man". However, it was not necessary to lead this evidence, for the Lord Advocate stated to the court that, to save the court's time, he had no objection to admitting the fact.

In his charge to the jury, the Lord Advocate argued that the evidence clearly demonstrated theft rather than the lesser offence of reset of theft. "My learned friend," he told the jury, "who always does great justice to his clients, especially in this court, but is sometimes righteous overmuch (it is excusable when pleading for a panel), set out with a distinction between theft and reset. But he must have greater abilities than he really has (and he has great abilities) if he can persuade you that there was here not a theft but a reset."

---

70 The reason for Boswell's particular concern on this matter was that if the allegation that Reid was by "habit and repute" a sheep-stealer was found proved, there was little or no prospect of persuading the jury that Reid had acquired the sheep innocently. A further consideration was that although the offence of theft of a flock of sheep, if proved, was a capital offence whether or not there was a finding that Reid was by "habit and repute" a sheepstealer, such a finding would (as Lord Auchinleck indicated) result in the offence being regarded as an aggravated form of theft, thus considerably reducing the chance of having the sentence reversed, or reduced to one of transportation, by way of petition to the King.

After Boswell's charge to the jury (of which Michael Nasmith wrote that "Boswell was great" and "there never was a charge made with greater dignity and judgment"[71]), the jury retired to consider their verdict. They reached a verdict that evening and word got out that the verdict was one of guilty of theft as libelled.

MONDAY 1 AUGUST [continued]. Michael Nasmith came home with me between five and six, when we dined, drank some porter and port and a bottle of claret. I was in a kind of agitation, which is not without something agreeable, in an odd way of feeling. Having heard that a verdict was found against John Reid, I went at eight to Walker's Tavern,[72] where the jury were met (I having first visited my client and intimated his fate to him), and being elated with the admirable appearance which I had made in the court, I was in such a frame as to think myself an Edmund Burke—and a man who united pleasantry in conversation with abilities in business and powers as an orator. I enjoyed the applause which several individuals of the jury now gave me and the general attention with which I was treated. The Crown entertains the jury on an occasion of this kind, and the bill is authenticated by the initials of the chancellor. We drank a great deal, and by imposing a fine of a pint of claret on any man who mentioned the trial, bets, etc., we had six pints of claret secured for a future meeting; and we appointed to dine together in the same place that day sennight. There was a strange mixture of characters. I was not much pleased at being fixed for another meeting. However, I considered it as unavoidable, and as the buck in one of our farces says, 'twas *life*. We parted about twelve. I was much in liquor, and strolled in the streets a good while—a very bad habit which I have when intoxicated. I got home before one. My dear wife had been very anxious.

TUESDAY 2 AUGUST. My bad rest during the night between Sunday and yesterday, the anxiety of the trial, and the debauch of last night made me in a woeful plight and very unwilling to rise. Worthy Sir John Hall called between seven and eight. I got up, and though hurt by the comparison between his decent sobriety and my riotous conduct, I was comforted to find myself entrusted by him, and the friendship of the family of Stichell continued to one of our family by his connexion.[73]

In the court in the forenoon I received great applause for my spirited behaviour yesterday; and I could also see Scottish envy showing itself. John Reid received his sentence at two o'clock, or rather a little before three.[74] My wife and I dined at Lord Alva's.[75] The only company were a Mrs Bradshaw, wife to an

---

71 Letter from Michael Nasmith to John Wilson, Jr, reproduced in *Defence*, pp. 315-7, at p. 316.
72 In Writers' Court, off the north side of the High Street opposite the Luckenbooths.
73 "Sir John's mother was a daughter of Sir John Pringle, second Baronet of Stichell; he was therefore a nephew of Sir John Pringle the physician" (*Defence*, p. 265, n. 1).
74 Immediately prior to sentence being pronounced, Boswell rather desperately moved for a delay in sentence to enable him to try to persuade the court that a capital punishment was not appropriate. However, the court refused this motion, holding, in accordance with well-established case law, that the offence was clearly capital. "It would hurt my mind", observed the Lord Justice-Clerk, "to think that a *grex* [a flock] should not be capital". The sentence of death fixed the execution to take place on 7 September between the hours of two and four in the afternoon.
75 James Erskine, Lord Alva (formerly Lord Barjarg). His house was in Argyle Square, which was all removed to make way for the present Chambers Street. The square was "an open area of 150 feet long, by the same in breadth, including the front gardens of the houses on the north side. The houses were all massive, convenient, and not inelegant, and in some instances, three storeys in height" (Grant, Vol. II, p. 271).

officer of the 66 regiment lying in the Castle, and Mr Cosmo Gordon. We were kindly, easily, and luxuriously entertained. My Lord's son *only* was at home. At four I went to a consultation at Mr Rae's on Earl Fife's politics. It lasted a very little while. I then returned and drank a few glasses of wine.

WEDNESDAY 3 AUGUST. Adam Bell, who consulted me, drank tea. My uncle the Doctor came and took a dish. He applied to me for the loan of £20. My heart was moved to think he needed it; and I promised to send him it next morning. I was at Macqueen's[76] at seven, consulting with him and the Solicitor on Sir Allan Maclean's plea for recovering a part of the estate of his ancestors from the family of Argyll.[77] My blood stirred at this consultation.

THURSDAY 4 AUGUST. Sir John Dalrymple[78] told me, either yesterday or today, that my behaviour in John Reid's trial would have made my fortune in England. This increased my desire to go; and, either yesterday or today while I walked in the Meadow with Maclaurin, he seemed to think I would do well to try. I was tonight at St John's Lodge. Rather a dull meeting. I was then at Signora Marcoucci's[79] ball.

SATURDAY 6 AUGUST. In the morning my father asked me to dine with him today, as he had the President with him. I told him I would do anything to oblige him, but that I really wished not to be with the President. He said it was on my account, to have me with people of respect. "Then", said I, "I'll be obliged to you if you will not ask me today." It gave me concern to have different views from my father. But as I cannot help having a bad opinion of the President—as he behaved in a most ungentlemanly manner to me, in privately persuading my father to make votes in Ayrshire against the nobility whose cause I had warmly espoused, and [had] done a most unfriendly thing to my father in leading him to do the very thing which he had for a course of years condemned[80]—I think it more honest and more spirited to show him that I will have no connexion with him; and notwithstanding his pride of office and the gross flattery which he receives, he must be sensible that he is not what he ought to be.

Sandy Gordon begged as a particular favour that I would dine with him as a friend and be present at the baptism of a son which was born to him last night. I accepted. Dr Webster was there. We drank cheerfully, but I had resolution not to take too much, being engaged to sup at Captain Schaw's with Lord Pembroke.[81] I came home between seven and eight somewhat heated, but wrote a

---

76 Robert Macqueen's house was at 13 George Square (*B.O.E.C.*, Vol. 26, p. 142).

77 "Sir Allan, landless chief of the Macleans of Duart, was attempting to recover from the Argyll family the estate which his forbears had lost through debt and overt Jacobitism. He was partially successful, recovering the lands of Brolass in 1783" (*Extremes*, p. 70, n. 1).

78 Sir John Dalrymple of Cousland and Cranstoun (1726-1810), advocate (admitted 20 December 1748), succeeded to the baronetcy in 1771, Baron of Exchequer 1776-1807.

79 A dancing mistress who ran a dancing school in Edinburgh and was a neighbour of Boswell's, being a resident at James's Court.

80 That is, creating fictitious votes (see p. 123, n. 55).

81 Henry Herbert (1734-1794), 10th Earl of Pembroke, Lord of the Bedchamber to George III.

paper well enough. My wife was at the play with Mrs Schaw. About eleven we assembled.[82] Lord Pembroke, to whom I had been introduced some years ago in London, was very affable to me. We had a very genteel company, and the most brilliant table that ever I saw in a private house in Edinburgh: a row of crystal lustres down the middle of the table; fruits and flowers interspersed in gay profusion. There was as little good conversation as at any genteel supper.

SUNDAY 7 AUGUST. Was at New Church in the forenoon and heard Dr Blair. My wife and I dined at my father's between sermons. Dr Boswell, Sir George Preston, and Mr Webster were there. Veronica always visits there at that time and gets raisins from her grandfather. In the afternoon I went and walked in St Anne's Yards[83] and the Abbey of Holyrood House.

MONDAY 8 AUGUST. Breakfasted at Lady Colville's and engaged her and Lady Anne and Captain Erskine to dine on Thursday with Lord Pembroke. Walked in the garden and was much refreshed. Lady Betty Cochrane, Lord Advocate, Sandy Gordon, Sandy Murray, Maclaurin, and Mr Henderson (Sir Robert's son) supped with us. This was a good genteel company. We spoke against drinking, but drank four pint bottles of claret.

TUESDAY 9 AUGUST. Mr Bruce of Kinnaird, who was just returned from his most curious travels, was in the Court of Session, a tall stout bluff man in green and gold.[84] I was very desirous to be with him. I was quite impatient to hear him talk. I consulted with Monboddo and Maclaurin, and set out to try what I could do to get an appointment made to dine or sup in a tavern. He had now gone out of the Court. I went home, changed my wig, and then went and called for him at his lodgings in Mrs Reynolds's in Miln's Square.[85] Luckily he was just come in, and I found him alone; and a most curious scene I had with him. I at first felt myself feeble and awkward with him, owing in part to my consciousness how very ignorant I was of the very rudiments of the knowledge respecting the countries which he had been seeing. My curiosity and vanity united, were, however, sufficient to impel me, and as he grew more rough I grew more forward; so that I forced in a manner a good deal from him, while he looked big and stamped and took me short and held his head high and talked with a forcible loudness as if he had been trying whether the room had an echo.

WEDNESDAY 10 AUGUST. This last week of the session was not a very busy

---

82 Captain Schaw resided in the flat below Boswell's flat in James's Court (Journal, 27 June 1774).

83 An enclosed garden at the Palace of Holyroodhouse.

84 James Bruce of Kinnaird (1730-94), explorer. "Six foot four inches tall, red-haired and arrogant... In 1768 he set out on his famous journey in search of the source of the Nile... After a year at Gondar [in Abyssinia],... he travelled on to Lake Tana which he mistakenly took to be the Nile's source... So extraordinary were the tales he had to tell about his adventures, and in particular about the habits and customs of the peoples of Abyssinia, that he was dismissed by many, including Dr Johnson, as a fraud" (Keay and Keay, p. 106).

85 A "lofty and gloomy court" (Grant, Vol. I, p. 236) off the north side of the High Street. "In 1899 the Square [which had by then been long known as Milne's Square] was cleared to become part of the *Scotsman Building*, completed in 1902" (Harris, p. 435).

one to me. But I had several little petitions to draw today. I called on Mr William Wilson about one of them in the afternoon. He was drinking a glass with Dr Young and Mr Speirs of Glasgow.[86] He insisted on my joining them; and, though I was not fond of being at all fevered with liquor in the end of a session when I might have sudden calls to write, yet, as Mr Wilson gave me my first guinea and has always been my very good friend as a man of business, I complied and was solidly social. I really can adapt myself to any company wonderfully well.

In the forenoon I had visited John Reid, whom I found very composed. He persisted in averring that he got the sheep from Gardner. I really believed him after I had adjured him, as he should answer to GOD, to tell me the truth. I told him that I was of opinion that a petition to the King would have no effect, but that his wife had applied to me, and I should draw one which he should sign; but that he must not expect anything but death. He very calmly assured me he would expect nothing else. I wondered at my own firmness of mind while I talked with a man under sentence of death, without much emotion, but with solemnity and humanity. I desired John to write his life very fully, which he promised to do. I bid him say nothing as to the *facts* with which he was formerly charged. He had been acquitted by his country. That was enough. His acknowledging that he had been guilty might hurt some unhappy panel who was innocent by making a jury condemn on imperfect circumstantial evidence. It will be a curious thing if he gives a narrative of his life.

THURSDAY 11 AUGUST. The confusion and hurry of the last day of the session were much the same as usual. I philosophised, thinking that in all probability all the members of Court would not be alive against another session, though indeed it is remarkable that the members of our College of Justice[87] live long. Death makes as little impression upon the minds of those who are occupied in the profession of the law as it does in an army. The survivors are busy, and share the employment of the deceased. Archibald McHarg, writer, died this session, and though he had a great deal of business, he was never missed. His death was only occasionally mentioned as an apology for delay in giving in a paper. The succession in business is so quick that there is not time to perceive a blank.

Lord Pembroke had hurt his leg and been confined to the house for two days. I was afraid that he would not dine with me today. I called on him in the morning about ten. He was not up; but his servant said he was much better. I had good hopes of seeing him, but still was uncertain. I had a good company besides his Lordship invited; but he being the capital person, I should have been much disappointed if he did not come. My vanity made me very anxious; and I paid the tax of suffering a very disagreeable suspense till he arrived. The company was: Lord Pembroke (whom I contemplated as the *Herbert*, the master of

---

86 "Alexander Speirs was a founder of the Glasgow Arms Bank in 1750 and was a great importer of tobacco" (*Defence*, p. 276, n. 2).
87 The College of Justice, founded by James V in 1532, comprised (as it still does) the judges of the Court of Session (designated Senators of the College), advocates, Writers to the Signet, clerks of session, and certain others.

Wilton, etc., and was happy that one of the family of Auchinleck entertained an English nobleman of such rank), Lady Colville, Lady Anne and Captain Erskine, General Lockhart of Carnwath, who had also been in Corsica, Colonel Stopford (Lieutenant-Colonel of the 66 regiment and brother to Lord Courtown, an Irish earl), and Colonel Webster.[88] Everything went on with as much ease and as genteelly as I could wish. This was not my own idea only, for I was told so by Lady Colville and Lady Anne, who were attentive as friends. My wife was just as I should have been satisfied to see her in London. Lord Pembroke was lively and pleasant; General Lockhart was more affable than usual. Veronica was brought in after dinner, and Lord Pembroke shook hands with her. I was really the man of fashion. We drank only two bottles of wine after dinner, and then drank tea and coffee with the ladies. So agreeable a day I have not seen in Edinburgh. I went to the Assembly in the evening, not having been at one since I was married. I felt no awkwardness, but saw a very fine company with cheerful satisfaction. Lady Anne Erskine and my wife and Captain Erskine and I met there. I had a full crop from my entertainment of Lord Pembroke, it was so well known. Keith Stewart[89] came up: "Boswell, what have you done with your guest Pembroke?" LORD HADDINGTON.[89a] "Mr B-B-Boswell, what have you done with Lord P-embroke?" He and Colonel Stopford had gone to the play and came in to the Assembly after it. Douglas and I met tonight. His coldness to his best supporters makes him appear to great disadvantage.

FRIDAY 12 AUGUST. I shall take a short review of this summer session. I never was so busy, having written fifty law papers, nor made so much money, having got 120 guineas. I had been up almost every morning at seven, and sometimes earlier. I had been in the Court of Session almost every morning precisely at nine, Charles Hay and I having agreed that whichever of us was later of coming than the other, after the nine o'clock bell was rung out, should lose a shilling; and I think I was a few mornings a little late, and he a few, so that upon the whole we were equal. I had advanced in practice and kept clear of the President, I had distinguished myself nobly in a capital trial. I had been a good deal in company, and in the best company of the place, both in my own house and in their houses. I had therefore great reason to be satisfied, having enjoyed, withal, good health and spirits. BUT I had been much intoxicated—I may say *drunk*—six times, and still oftener heated with liquor to feverishness. I had read hardly anything but mere law; I had paid very little attention to the duties of piety, though I had almost every day, morning and evening, addressed a short prayer to GOD. Old Izaak Walton had done me good; and frequently in the course of the day I had meditated on death and a future state. Let me endeavour every session and every year to improve.

SUNDAY 14 AUGUST. Captain Erskine's company that I had engaged on Friday, Lady Betty Cochrane, Captain and Mrs Schaw, and Colonel Stopford and Lieutenant Vowel of the same regiment, supped. I was in the same easy genteel style as on

88 Col. James Webster, son of Dr Alexander Webster.
89 "Naval officer, ultimately vice-admiral, son of the sixth Earl of Galloway" (*Defence*, p. 279, n. 1).
89a Thomas Hamilton, 7th Earl of Haddington (1721-1794).

Lord Pembroke's day, and so was my dear wife. I never saw a supper go on more agreeably. We drank socially in the time of supper; and after it just one bottle of claret and a little out of a second. Ladies and gentlemen rose from table together. It was quite as I could wish.

MONDAY 15 AUGUST. This day I paid a visit to the worthy Lord Chief Baron,[90] whom I had not waited on for a long time, which was very wrong, as he had all along treated me with great kindness. I found him much better than I expected, as he had been ill a good while and was said to be much failed. He revived ideas of the dignity of the English law. His son was now with him, but was not in. I afterwards met him, and he and I went with Mr David Hume to the philosopher's own house[91] and sat awhile, and from both of them I got many particulars of Mr Bruce's travels, which I gathered with much attention. I then called on Crosbie and consulted with him about the mode of applying for a transportation pardon for John Reid.

Mr Longlands,[92] Mr William Macdonald, young Mr Robert Syme,[93] and Mr Cummyng, the curious *Herald*[94] (for that is his chief designation), dined with me. We were well enough, and drank only three bottles of claret, which may be considered as a moderate quantity for a company of five Scotsmen. Mr Syme indeed and Mr Lawrie, my clerk, drank about a bottle of port. In the evening I dictated part of a paper for Lady Dundonald in her linen cause.

TUESDAY 16 AUGUST. Finished Lady Dundonald's paper before breakfast. Was busy all day dictating some account of Bruce's travels for *The London Magazine*. I made out, I think, twenty-four folio pages.[95] I was glad to find myself an useful partner, as I had received notice of my having a dividend of £15 odds of profit. Lady Dundonald and Lady Betty, Miss Roebuck, Captain and Mrs Schaw drank tea. It was a very wet day.

WEDNESDAY 17 AUGUST. The weather continued to be very wet, which made me very lazy. In the morning Captain Schaw called and consulted me about the consequences of his wounding a horse in the Canongate, which had run off with a loaded cart and was running directly upon him at the head of the battalion. I went down to his house and examined a sergeant and two corporals as to the particulars. I made the Captain easy by assuring him that he would not be liable in damages; though I found in one of our old Acts of Parliament of Ro. 2 that where a beast was killed unintentionally the damage should be divided equally between the owner and the killer. There is an appearance of equity

90 Lord Chief Baron Ord's house was at 8 Queen Street.
91 Hume was now residing in his new house at the south-west corner of St Andrew Square. The house was entered from the side street, which came to be known as St David Street.
92 A solicitor practising in England.
93 Robert Syme (1752-1845), who was apprentice to Robert Syme, W.S., his uncle (for whom, see the entry for 8 December 1775 and relevant footnote), and was to be admitted a W.S. on 30 November 1775.
94 James Cummyng, herald-painter and Lyon Clerk Depute, later Keeper of the Lyon Records.
95 "His account appeared in two numbers of the magazine: August and September 1774" (*Defence*, p. 284, n. 2).

in this. But it is contrary to the maxim that everything perishes to its proper owner.

Mr Lawrie was to go home to his father's for the autumn tomorrow. I therefore dictated all day papers which were to be finished immediately: a memorial for the Lyon Fiscal,[96] part of which was left unfinished, as I told Mr Lawrie that I would be clerk myself; and a decreet arbitral[97] (a matter of form) between the trustees for the fund for ministers' widows and the town of Kirkcaldy. After dinner I drank several glasses of old hock, just indulging in the gloomy rainy weather. After tea Steuart Hall[98] called and sat awhile. As I had never seen him but in the country, he brought strong upon my mind the dreary ideas of wet weather and weary nights which I have endured in Ayrshire, when all things appeared dismal. I have not had such a cloud of hypochondria this long time. I wish it may not press upon me in my old age.

THURSDAY 18 AUGUST. Mr Lawrie set off in the fly at eight o'clock. I shall miss him much, as he goes errands, copies letters, and is very serviceable; but it is good for him to be at his father's in the vacation. As I began this summer to allow him the whole dues both of my first and second clerk—Matthew Dickie,[99] who does nothing for me, being allowed to keep the full clerk's dues of all the consultations which he gives me—I am hopeful that Mr Lawrie may by degrees make a competency in my service. He made about £24 this session, of which I put £5 for his behoof into Sir W. Forbes & Co.'s hands at £4 per cent interest, among the money lodged in my name. This was a fair beginning of Mr Lawrie's fortune. I shall be happy if he is one day as rich as Stobie.

I called on Michael Nasmith and he engaged to get my petition for John Reid well copied. I settled my account with the Bank of Scotland; sat awhile with Ilay Campbell about Bedlay.[100] Went to Heriot's Garden with my wife and Veronica, who is really a charming child. She began to walk by herself on Friday the 12th current. She could now cry "Papa" very distinctly.

FRIDAY 19 AUGUST. Mr Charles Hay and I this day resumed our study of Erskine's *Institute* where we left off last vacation. I went to his house then.[101] He agreed to come to mine now. After we had read a portion, we fell to some of my Justiciary records, which took us up an hour, they were so interesting.

SATURDAY 20 AUGUST. This morning I drew a petition to His Majesty for John Reid. I could think of nothing else; so Mr Charles Hay and I read no law,

---

96 William Black, Procurator-Fiscal of the Lyon Court, representing the interest of the Lord Lyon King of Arms. The Lord Lyon was insisting that he had the exclusive right to deal with all armorial matters in Scotland and that the Court of Session had no jurisdiction over him. On 16 November 1773, the Lyon Court had ordered William Murray of Touchadam to pay a penalty for failing to register his arms in the Lyon register. Murray had then taken the case to the Court of Session by way of bill of advocation and Lord Hailes had called for memorials to be lodged (SPSL, 593:1). It is now clear that judicial decisions of the Lord Lyon may be reviewed by the Court of Session and House of Lords.
97 The decision of an arbiter in respect of a dispute referred to him for arbitration.
98 Archibald Steuart of Steuart Hall.
99 Matthew Dickie had by now become a "writer".
100 Boswell was involved in an action for his fellow advocate, Archibald Roberton of Bedlay (*Defence*, p. 285, n. 4).
101 Charles Hay's house was in Nicolson Street.

but went with it to Michael Nasmith's,[102] who was very much pleased with it, and undertook to have two fair copies on large paper ready to go by the post at night. Charles went with me to see John. His wife was with him. I adjured him not to say that he was innocent of the theft found proved against him if he was not so; that I had put into the petition what he said, but he would have as good, if not a better, chance by fairly confessing to His Majesty. Charles very properly said to him, "Take care and do not fill up the measure of your iniquity by telling a lie to your Sovereign." I in the strongest manner assured him that I thought the petition would have no effect—that I wrote it only because I had promised to do it; but that I really thought it would be better not to send it, as it might make him entertain vain hopes and prevent him from thinking seriously of death. John professed his conviction that the chance was hardly anything, but was for using the means. I could not therefore refuse him. Charles again addressed him as to his telling a lie, and said, "I may say, you are putting your salvation against one to ten thousand; nay, against nothing." John expressed his willingness to submit to what was *foreordained* for him. "John," said I, "this would not have been *foreordained* for you if you had not stolen sheep, and that was not *foreordained*. GOD does not foreordain wickedness. Your Bible tells you that." I then took it up and read from the Epistle of James, Chap. I, v. 13 and 14: "Let no man say when he is tempted, I am tempted of GOD; for GOD cannot be tempted with evil, neither tempteth he any man. But every man is tempted, when he is drawn away of his own lust, and enticed." This seemed to satisfy him. But people in his situation are very apt to become predestinarians. Dr Daniel Macqueen, one of the ministers of Edinburgh, told me that when he was minister at Stirling, there was a man under sentence of death there whom some Cameronian or seceding minister had tutored deeply upon predestination till the man was positive that the crime which he had committed was decreed by his Maker; nor could Mr Macqueen argue him out of this notion. When he came to the place of execution, the man was beginning to harangue the people upon this subject. Upon which, Mr Macqueen, with his forcible and hurried manner, insisted with the magistrate to order the executioner to do his duty directly; and accordingly the man was thrown off, which prevented his mystical discourse. "He might have put more nonsense into their heads", said Macqueen, "than I could have driven out again in half a year." There was good sense in Mr Macqueen's conduct; though his acquaintances do not fail in keeping up as a joke upon him his mode of opposing an argument.

Between five and six Mr Nasmith and George Webster accompanied me to the prison, when I read over the petition to John Reid, and he signed two copies of it. I again adjured him not to sign it if he was not innocent, and again pressed home upon him my conviction that his chance for life was hardly anything. I was wonderfully firm. I told him that I really thought it was happy for him that he was to die by a sentence of the law, as he had so much time to think seriously and

102 In the Luckenbooths in the High Steet.

prepare for death; whereas, if he was not stopped in that manner, his unhappy disposition to steal was such that it was to be feared he would have been cut off in the midst of his wickedness. I enclosed one copy of the petition to Lord Suffolk, Secretary of State for the Northern Department, and one to Lord Pembroke, and wrote a letter with each copy. I could not help entertaining some faint hope. John Reid's petition was business enough to me for one day.

TUESDAY 23 AUGUST. The Law College went on,[103] and must be understood to do so when I do not mention a cessation, Sundays excepted.

WEDNESDAY 24 AUGUST. Mr Hay and I played a stout match at bowls. He gave me one, and I beat him three games. I dined at Nairne's,[104] who had ten guests assembled without any kind of assortment, so that drinking only made the cement of the company. A great deal of wine was drank today. I swallowed about a bottle of port, which inflamed me much, the weather being hot. I called at home; then sauntered in the streets; and then supped with my wife at Sir George Preston's, where I had sent four moor-fowl which I had in presents from Ayrshire, agreeable marks of kind remembrance from James Johnston in Cumnock and John Herbert in Auchencross. Dr Webster and the Colonel and Mr Wood, the surgeon, were at Sir George's. I devoured moor-fowl, and poured more port down my throat. I was sadly intoxicated. *Perdidi diem.*[105]

THURSDAY 25 AUGUST. I was very sick and had a severe headache, and lay till between ten and eleven, when I grew better. There was no Law College today. Crosbie called on me in the forenoon, in great indignation at the Bailies of Edinburgh for having sentenced Henry McGraugh, an Irishman, to be imprisoned, whipped, and banished because he had called for victuals and drink in public houses and then told that he had not money to pay for them. Crosbie begged that I would inquire into the affair.

I communicated to Crosbie a scheme which I had of making an experiment on John Reid, in case he was hanged, to try to recover him. I had mentioned it in secrecy to Charles Hay and Mr Wood the surgeon, who promised me assistance. Crosbie told me that he had lately had a long conversation on the subject with Dr Cullen,[106] who thought it practicable. It was lucky that I spoke of it to Crosbie, for he was clear for trying it, and threw out many good hints as to what should be done. I resolved to wait on Dr Cullen and get his instructions. I was this forenoon at the burial of a daughter of the late Mr Sands, bookseller here. There is something usefully solemn in such a scene, and I make it a rule to attend every burial to which I am invited unless I have a sufficient excuse; as I expect that those who are invited to mine will pay their piece of decent attention.

I afterwards called at the prison, where I found Mr Todd, Lady Maxwell's

103 That is, Boswell's studies with Charles Hay.
104 William Nairne's house was on the Back Stairs (to the south of Parliament Close).
105 "I have lost a day."
106 William Cullen (1710-90), M.D., Professor of Chemistry and the Practice of Medicine at Edinburgh University, father of Robert Cullen, the advocate.

chaplain, with John Reid. He seemed to be a weak, well-meaning young man. I again told John in his presence that there was hardly the least chance of a pardon and therefore that he ought to consider himself as a dying man. Yet I did now entertain a small additional glimpse of hope, because I saw in the newspapers that, a few days before, one Madan got a reprieve after he was at Tyburn, ready to be turned off, the man who really committed the robbery for which he was condemned having voluntarily appeared and owned it. I thought this incident might make the Ministry more ready to listen to John Reid's story that Gardner was the real thief. John was looking gloomy today. He told me he had some bad dreams which made him believe he was now to die.

I then called for McGraugh, who was put into the cage, he was so violent a prisoner. He was a true Teague. I asked him why he was confined. He could give but a very confused account; but he assured me that he had neither stolen victuals and drink nor taken them by force, but only called for them. I asked him if he had stolen anything. "Only a paice (piece) of wood", said he; "but then, an't *plaise* your Honour, it was in the dark." "That will not make it better", said I. Afterwards, however, I saw that this odd saying of his, like all the Irish sayings at which we laugh as bulls or absurdities, had a meaning. For he meant that as he had taken the wood in the dark, it could not be known he had done it; so that it could be no part of the charge against him and consequently was no justification of the sentence of the magistrates. I promised to do what I could for him. I also saw one Macpherson, a young goldsmith confined for debt, from whom I had a letter telling me that a young woman had come into prison and lent him her clothes, in which he made his escape but was taken again; and that the *innocent* girl was imprisoned. I told him that breaking prison was a crime; that the girl had been aiding in the escape of a prisoner and therefore was not innocent; but that she would not be long confined.

My wife and I drank tea at Dr Grant's.[107] He was clear that a man who has hung ten minutes cannot be recovered; and he had dissected two. I was, however, resolved that the experiment should be tried. Dr Grant carried me up to a very good library which he has and showed me a number of anatomical preparations. The survey of skulls and other parts of the human body, and the reflection upon all of us being so frail and liable to so many painful diseases, made me dreary.

FRIDAY 26 AUGUST. Sir George and Lady Preston and Miss Preston, Colonel, George, and Sandy Websters,[108] Mr Wood the surgeon, and Mr Bennet the Minister of Duddingston dined with us. I gave only port, being resolved to give claret seldom while I am not able to afford it commonly. We were comfortable. I drank port and water, and did not discompose myself. I went to the

---

107 Gregory Grant, M.D., an eminent physician who resided at James's Court, where part of his flat (which was "the top flat of the left hand turnpike") was fitted up for chemistry experiments. He was well known for his convivial "musical suppers" and he had a particular fondness for drama; but he dressed austerely in old-fashioned dark clothes and was a strict Presbyterian, regularly attending the Tolbooth Church. He died in 1803, at an advanced age (Kay, Vol. II, pp. 112-4).
108 Alexander Webster, son of Dr Alexander Webster.

Justiciary Office[109] and wrote a bill of suspension with my own hand for McGraugh.[110]

SATURDAY 27 AUGUST. After our law, Charles Hay and I set out to dine at Leith, at Yeats the trumpeter's,[111] where we had dined before very well. I fixed it as a good Saturday's dining-place during our course of study, and fancied our tête-à-tête there to be like that of my grandfather and Lord Cullen on the Saturdays. As we walked down the street we met Crosbie and tried to prevail with him to go with us. But he was obstinate in a resolution to labour at law papers all this day. A heavy shower came on, and we went with him into John Balfour the bookseller's shop,[112] where we chatted a good while. We then walked with him as far as his house, where we left him; and there we were joined by Ilay Campbell, who walked on with us. He insisted that we should go and dine with him at a little country-house which he had near Leith. We did so, and shared his family dinner with Mrs Campbell and his children. It was a scene worth taking: a family country dinner with the first writing lawyer at our bar. He told us that when Macqueen married, which was only about eighteen years ago, his practice did not exceed —— a year, though he had since realised many thousands. Macqueen told him that one year he had made £1900. Ilay told us that he himself had made £1600 in a year in the ordinary course of business; and that a lawyer's labour is not increased in proportion with his gains, for that he now wrote less than he had done. This kind of conversation excited the solid coarse ambition of making money in the Court of Session. We drank a bottle of claret apiece and a fourth among us. We then drank tea, and Mr Campbell walked with us a good [way] up as a convoy. I was not a bit intoxicated with what I had drank. Mr Hay was engaged at home.

MONDAY 29 AUGUST. A very curious whim had come into my head: that I would have a portrait of John Reid as my first client in criminal business and as a very remarkable person in the annals of the Court of Justiciary. Keith Ralph, a young painter who had studied under Runciman,[113] had drawn Mr Lawrie's picture very like. I had him with me this forenoon, and he agreed to paint John. He desired to see him today, to have an idea of his face, to see what kind of light was in the room where he lay, and to judge what should be the size of the picture. Accordingly I went with him. I had before this given a hint of my design to Richard Lock, the inner turnkey, a very sensible, good kind of man; and he had no objection. Accordingly we went up. Mr Ritchie, a kind of lay teacher who humanely attends all the people under sentence of death, was with John. After standing a little and speaking a few words in a serious

---

109 Presumably in the New Tolbooth.

110 "The Lord of Justiciary whom Boswell petitioned suspended the sentence of whipping. The Procurator-Fiscal reclaimed, and McGraugh was detained in prison... On 4 February 1775 he was set at liberty on the order of the Court of Justiciary, the Procurator-Fiscal having waived the whipping in view of his long confinement" (*Defence*, p. 294, n. 3).

111 The inn of John Yeats at the shore of Leith. Yeats was called "trumpeter Yeats" because he was one of the trumpeters who rode in front of the Lords of Justiciary during processions when they were on circuit (*Universal Scots Almanack*, 1776, p. 104).

112 At the head of Anchor Close, off the north side of the High Street.

113 Alexander Runciman (1736-85), a Scots painter.

strain, I addressed myself to Ritchie in a kind of soft voice and mentioned my desire to have a remembrance of John Reid, by having a picture of him; that Mr Ritchie and I could sit by and talk to him, and that I imagined John would have no objection, as it would not disturb him. Ritchie said he supposed John would have none; that he was so much obliged to me, he would do much more at my request; and he would come and be present. Next morning between nine and ten was fixed. Mr Charles Hay, who waited in the street, went with me to Ralph's and saw some of his performances.

At four this afternoon Adam Bell was with me, along with Nimmo his landlord, consulting me to draw answers to a petition. I found myself much as in session time. Steuart Hall and Mr Wood the surgeon drank tea. Wood dispelled the dreary country ideas which Steuart Hall would have raised. I took a walk with him to Drumsheugh and round by the New Town, and talked of the scheme of recovering John Reid. He said he did not think it practicable. But that he should give all the assistance in his power to have the experiment fairly tried.

TUESDAY 30 AUGUST. At ten o'clock I was with John Reid. Before I got there, Ralph was begun with his chalk and honest Ritchie was exhorting him quietly. I was happy to see that this whim of mine gave no trouble to John. One of his legs was fixed to a large iron goad, but he could rise very easily; and he at any rate used to sit upon a form, so that he just kept his ordinary posture, and Ritchie and I conversed with him. He seemed to be quite composed, and said he had no hopes of life on account of the dreams which he had. That he dreamt he was riding on one white horse and leading another. "That", said he, "was too good a dream, and dreams are contrary." He said he also dreamt a great deal of being on the seashore and of passing deep waters. "However," said he, "I allwaye (always) get through them." "Well," said I, "John, I hope that shall not be contrary; but that you shall get through the great deep of death." I called for a dram of whisky. I had not thought how I should drink to John till I had the glass in my hand, and I felt some embarrassment. I could not say, "Your good health"; and "Here's to you" was too much in the style of hearty fellowship. I said, "John, I wish you well", or words pretty much the same, as "Wishing you well"—or some such phrase. The painter and Mr Ritchie tasted the spirits. Richard the gaoler makes it a rule never to taste them within the walls of the prison.

John seemed to be the better of a dram. He told me that the Reids of Muiravonside[114] had been there, he believed, for three hundred years; that they had been butchers for many generations. He could trace himself, his father, and grandfather in that business; that he never was worth £10 and never in much debt, so that he was always evens with the world; that since his trial in 1766 he had led an honest, industrious life; that he received the sheep for which he was condemned from Gardner, and did not suspect them to be stolen. That his wife and children would be present at his death. I dissuaded him from this. He said his wife and he had lived comfortably fifteen years, and she said she would see

114 Reid's house was at Hillend in the parish of Muiravonside, Stirlingshire.

him to the last and would *kep* him (i.e., receive his body when cut down); that his son, who was a boy of ten years of age, might forget it (meaning his execution) if he only heard of it, but that he would not readily forget it if he saw it. To hear a man talk of his own execution gave me a strange kind of feeling. He said he would be carried to his own burial-place at Muiravonside; that it was the second best in the kirkyard. There were symptoms of vanity in the long line of the Reids and the good burial-place; a proof that ideas of these kinds are natural and universal.

Ritchie and I sat awhile with him after the painter was gone, the first sitting being over. John said, "Death is no terror to me at present. I know not what it may be." Said Ritchie, "You must either be infatuated, or you have, by grace, a reliance on the merits of Jesus Christ." John said he trusted to the mercy of GOD in Christ; that he had been an unfortunate man, and insinuated that his fate was foreordained. Ritchie quoted the passage in James which I had quoted; but he seemed to be much hampered with Calvinistical notions about decrees, while he struggled to controvert John's wickedness being foreordained. Indeed the system of predestination includes all actions, bad as well as good. Ritchie pressed John much to make an authentic last speech. I told him that if he was guilty of the crime for which he was condemned, it was his duty to his country and the only reparation he could make, to acknowledge it, that his example might have a proper effect. He persisted in his denial, and did not seem willing to have any speech published. Ritchie said to me in his hearing that it was a perquisite for Richard, who had a great deal of trouble. I said we should get John to make a speech.

John complained much of Peter Reid for deceiving him by promising to swear as to the bargain between him and Gardner, and then drawing back. "For", said he, "if I had not trusted to him, I would not have told you that I could bring such proof, and then you could have done what you thought proper." He told me that he said to Peter in this very room: "Peter, mony (many) a lee (lie) I have telt (told)[115] for you for which I repent"; and Peter said he would help him to the utmost on this occasion; and he did not think there was much harm in it, as it was to save a man's life; "though it was very wrang (wrong) to swear awa (away) a man's life." This was a kind of casuistical explanation of the ninth commandment: Thou shalt not bear false witness *against* thy neighbour. But—thou mayst do so *for* him. John cried a good deal when he told me this story of Peter Reid. He did not seem to be affected on any other occasion. I argued with him that it was happy that Peter Reid's conscience had checked him and prevented him from being guilty of perjury; that, to be sure, it was wrong in him to say that he would swear in John's support, but that it was better that he stopped than if he had gone on. John's system upon this subject was so crooked that he did not appear at all convinced.

It was a very wet day. I grew dreary and wanted either Charles Hay or Grange to dine with me, but neither of them could come. I took a little bowl of warm punch by myself, except a glass which Veronica drank. Her sweet

---

115 As the editors of *Defence* observe, at p. 301, n. 3, "Boswell's glosses upon quite easily interpreted Scots forms... suggest that he has in mind some other audience than himself—an English-speaking audience."

little society was a gentle relief, but I was too dismal to enjoy it much. I had a letter from my brother David which was a cordial. I drank tea with Grange, but was gloomy. I had by sympathy sucked the dismal ideas of John Reid's situation, and as spirits or strong substance of any kind, when transferred to another body of a more delicate nature, will have much more influence than on the body from which it is transferred, so I suffered much more than John did. Grange very sensibly observed that we should keep at a distance from dreary objects; that we should shun what hurts the mind as we shun what disagrees with the stomach and hurts the body—a very good maxim for preserving a *mens sana*. At night Mr Nairne called in and supped with us. He did me some good by his conversation.

WEDNESDAY 31 AUGUST. This was the second day of John Reid's sitting for his picture. Ralph the painter went through his part with perfect composure, hardly ever opening his mouth. I spoke to [John] of his execution, thinking it humane to familiarise his mind to it. I asked him if he was here when Murdison died.[116] He said no, and on my saying, "So you did not see him die", told me that he had never seen an execution. "No?" said I. "I wonder you never had the curiosity." He said he never had. That once, as he and some other drivers of cattle were coming from Yorkshire, they stopped at Penrith in Cumberland, where there was a man to be executed for murder next day; that some of his companions stayed to see it, but he and the rest did not. I then spoke of the way in England of having a cart and ours of having a ladder, and that it was said ours was the easiest way. "I take it, John," said I, "I shall die a severer death than you." "I dinna (do not) think", said he, "they can feel much; or that it can last ony (any) time; but there's nane (none) of them to tell how it is." I mentioned Maggy Dickson, who had been hanged less than the usual time and was recovered, and said she felt no pain.[117] He told me he saw a Highlandman at Glasgow, a big strong man, who had escaped twice; first, the rope broke. "And", said John, "at that time it was thought they coudna (could not) hang them up again; and the second time, the gallows fell." He said his wife was resolved that he should die in white; that it was the custom in his part of the country to dress the dead body in linen, and she thought it would cost no more to do it when he was alive. He this day again averred the truth of his story that he got the sheep from Gardner. He said to me that there was something he had done a great many years ago, before any of his trials, that had followed him all this time. That it was not a great thing either, nor yet a small thing, and he would let me know it. This was somehow curious and awful. Honest Ritchie, from time to time, threw out serious reflections, as thus: "If any man sin, we have an advocate with the Father, even Christ the righteous. Christ is an advocate, indeed. Other advocates only plead for panels. But he takes upon him the offences of the panels and suffers in their stead."

I mentioned that it was remarkable that there was always fine weather on execution days, and I asked Ritchie what was the meaning of pigeons flying when people were executed. He said that he thought the notions which some

116 Alexander Murdison, a convicted sheep-stealer, had been hanged on 24 March. Boswell attended the execution.
117 This was Margaret Dickson, who had been hanged for child-murder in 1724 (*Defence*, p. 301, n. 4).

people entertained of that signifying good to the persons executed were *fablish*. John then told of a woman who was executed, who told that morning to a minister after awaking from a sound sleep, "If ye see some clear draps o' (drops of) rain faw (fall) on me after I'm custen owr (thrown over), I'm happy." And John said the clear drops did fall. All this was most suitable conversation for John. I asked him if he had ever seen the hangman. He said no. I said I had seen him this forenoon going into the office of the prison. "Ay," said John, "he'll be going about thinking there's something for him." He seemed to think of him with much aversion and declared he would have no intercourse with him, one way or other; but he seemed somewhat reconciled when I told him that the hangman was a humane creature, and shed tears for unhappy people when they were to be executed. I inculcated upon John that he was now to have no hopes, since no answer had come to his application. He asked if there would not come an answer of some kind. I said not unless they were to grant something favourable, and that must have come before now had it been to come. He said he was thrown into a panic by hearing a horn blow in the street. I was desirous to have his picture done *while under sentence of death* and was therefore rather desirous that, in case a respite was to come, it should not arrive till he had sat his full time. It was finished today and was a striking likeness, a gloomy head. He asked if it would not be better to have had on his bonnet, and said he should have had on a better waistcoat. He asked too if his name would be upon it. I said it would be on the back of it. Said he: "I thought it would have been on the fore (front) side of it." There was vanity again. As the painter advanced in doing it, I felt as if he had been raising a spectre. It was a strange thought. Here is a man sitting for his picture who is to be hanged this day eight days. John himself seemed to wonder somewhat at the operation, and said, "I'm sure you maun hae an unco (must have a strange) concern about this", or words to that purpose. When it was finished and hung upon a nail to dry, it swung, which looked ominous, and made an impression on my fancy. I gave John a dram of whisky today again. When I got home I found several vermin upon me which I had attracted while in the gaol. It was shocking. I changed all my clothes.

Lady Colville and Lady Anne Erskine drank tea with us, very agreeably. Mr Hay and I had read no law today. When I came from the prison, we had gone to Heriot's Garden and played at bowls. Maclaurin was in town today, and played with us.

THURSDAY 1 SEPTEMBER. I breakfasted at Mr David Steuart's, Writer to the Signet,[118] where was his father, Steuart Hall. At ten I called on Dr Cullen[119] to talk with him of recovering John Reid. He was gone abroad. I found his son,[120] my brother lawyer, and trusted him with the secret, and he engaged to get me a meeting with his father. It came on a heavy rain; so I sat a good while with Cullen in his study, and had very good ideas presented to my mind about books and criminal

118 David Stewart of Stewarthall. Stewart's house was at the foot of Mint Close (also known as Gray's Close), off the south side of the High Street.
119 Dr Cullen's house was the old Scottish Mint in Mint Close.
120 Robert Cullen, like his father, resided in Mint Close.

law, etc. Every man has some peculiar views which seem new to another. After taking a tolerable dose of law, Mr Hay and I went for a walk to Heriot's Garden, and then I dined with him. He had Dr Monro[121] and several more company with him, and it was concerted that we should get information from the Anatomical Professor as to recovering a hanged person, which would be useful to Reid. Harry Erskine[122] was there, and talked so much that it was long before we could get Dr Monro set upon the subject. He said in his opinion a man who is hanged suffers a great deal; that he is not at once stupefied by the shock, suffocation being a thing which must be gradual and cannot be forced on instantaneously; so that a man is suffocated by hanging in a rope just as by having his respiration stopped by having a pillow pressed on the face, in Othello's way, or by stopping the mouth and nostrils, which one may try; and he said that for some time after a man is thrown over he is sensible and is conscious that he is *hanging*; but that in three minutes or so he is stupefied. He said that it was more difficult to recover a hanged person than a drowned, because hanging forces the blood up to the brain with more violence, there being a local compression at the neck; but that he thought the thing might be done by heat and rubbing to put the blood in motion, and by blowing air into the lungs; and he said the best way was to cut a hole in the throat, in the trachea, and introduce a pipe. I laid up all this for service in case it should be necessary. He told me that ten or twelve of his students had, unknown to him, tried to recover my clients Brown and Wilson,[123] but had only blown with their own breaths into the mouths of the *subjects*, which was not sufficient. He said some people had applied to him for leave to put on fires and make preparations for recovering Lieutenant Ogilvy[124] in his class. That he

121 Dr Alexander Monro (1733-1817), Professor of Anatomy and Surgery at Edinburgh University. Arnot wrote that in Monro's lectures and demonstrations "he illustrates his doctrines not only by dissection, but also by a great variety of anatomical preparations, and by parts of morbid bodies preserved, which he and his father have been collecting at great pains and expense, for more than half a century" (Arnot, pp. 235-6).
122 The Hon. Henry Erskine (1746-1817), advocate (admitted 23 February 1768), M.P. Haddington Burghs 1806, Dumfries Burghs 1806-7, Lord Advocate 1783-4, 1806-7, Dean of the Faculty of Advocates February 1785. "Erskine, with his tall lithe figure, handsome face, and graceful bearing, adorned the Parliament House for more than forty years" and he was much admired for "his clear full voice, his fascinating manner, his polished language, his close reasoning, and his sound judgment". Moreover, "he was a wit, he made good jokes, and he told good stories" (Omond, Vol. II, p. 163).
123 Two tinkers who were hanged on 15 September 1773 having been convicted of fatally injuring a defenceless rag-gatherer at his lonely hut on the Carnwath moorland (*Defence*, p. 201).
124 Lieutenant Patrick Ogilvie (otherwise Ogilvy) and Katharine Nairn were the accused at a celebrated trial in 1765. They were lovers, and were charged with incest and with the murder of Ogilvie's brother, who was Katharine Nairn's husband. At the close of the trial, Lord Kames (who was one of the seven judges hearing the case) made what was then considered the astonishing and reprehensible innovation of addressing the jury on the evidence after the counsel for the defence had concluded their speeches. This, however, soon became standard practice and, indeed, a statutory requirement (Justiciary and Circuit Courts (Scotland) Act 1783 (23 Geo. 3, c. 45)). It was immediately after this trial that Lord Auchinleck first suffered from his prostate problem, which, it is thought, was induced by his having to listen to the evidence of a principal witness for nine hours without rising from his seat. Ogilvie and Nairn were both convicted, and Ogilvie was hanged on 13 November 1765. Nairn, however, satisfied the court that she was pregnant, whereupon the court deferred sentence against her until the following March; but on 15 March she escaped from the Tolbooth and managed to get to France. It was widely suspected that her uncle, Boswell's friend William Nairne, advocate (later Lord Dunsinnan), had a hand in her escape.

thought it would be very wrong in him to allow it, and told them he should have no objection if Lord Justice-Clerk gave his consent.[125] That he spoke to Lord Justice-Clerk, who said that if such a thing was allowed, the College of Edinburgh should never again get a body from the Court of Justiciary. Indeed it would have been counteracting their sentence. He said he dissected Ogilvy publicly, and that there was no hurt on his head by the fall from the gibbet.

I sat here today, thinking myself well employed in listening to Dr Monro, whom I seldom met. He asked me to sup with him next day with the Laird of MacLeod. I drank rather more than a bottle of Madeira. It was about ten when we parted. I made a good deal of impression on the company in favour of John Reid's innocence. As I considered him as now a gone man, I resolved to know the truth by being with him to the very last moment of his life, even to walk a step or two up the ladder and ask him *then*, just before his going off, what was the real matter of fact; for if he should deny *then*, I could not resist the conviction.

FRIDAY 2 SEPTEMBER. I lay till near ten. A little after I rose and was at breakfast and Mr Hay was come, while the tea-things were standing, I was called out to a man—and who was this but Richard Lock, who informed me that John Reid had got a respite for fourteen days; that Captain Fraser had been up with him and read it to him, and that he teared more now than he had ever seen him. I was put into great agitation. All my nerves started. I instantly dressed, and Mr Hay and I walked out, met Michael Nasmith, who had seen the respite in the Council Chamber,[126] and he went thither with us, when Bailie Brown showed us it. Wright, the stationer, cried out with a kind of unfeeling sneer, "It will be lang (long) life and ill health"; and all the people in the Chamber seemed against poor John. We then went up to John, whom we found in a dreadful state. He was quite unhinged. His knees knocked against each other, he trembled so; and he cried bitterly. I spoke to him in most earnest manner and told him, since the respite was only for fourteen days, the judges would be consulted and they would report against him. He must therefore consider that he had just fourteen days more allowed him to prepare for his awful change. He moaned and spoke of his being "cut off after all, with a hale (whole) heart". I said he must compose himself. He said he hoped he should, if it pleased GOD to continue him in his senses, as he had hitherto done. I said, "You *would* make this application, though I told you I thought it would have no effect. If you suffer from it, it is owing to yourself." It was striking to see a man who had been quite composed when he thought his execution certain become so weak and so much agitated by a respite. My wife put a construction on his conduct which seemed probable. She said it was plain he had all along been

---

125 Given that Lieutenant Ogilvie was hanged on 13 November 1765, this is either a reference to Sir Gilbert Elliot of Minto (c. 1693-1766), Bt, who as Lord Minto was Lord Justice-Clerk from 3 May 1763 to 16 April 1766, or to Thomas Miller of Barskimming, who, although not appointed as Lord Justice-Clerk until 14 June 1766, may have been consulted in his capacity as Lord Advocate.
126 In the New Tolbooth (as to which, see Introduction, p. 11).

expecting a pardon and therefore was composed, but that now when he found that only a respite for fourteen days had come and that inquiry was to be made at the judges, he for the first time had the view of death. But if I can judge of human nature by close observation, I think he was before this time reconciled to his fate, and that the respite affected him by throwing him into a wretched state of incertainty. I gave him a shilling to get some spirits as a cordial. [John's] wife had been with me since the respite came. I gave her no hopes, but bid her have a cart to carry away his body. "Ay," said she, "there shall be a cart if there's occasion for it"; so I saw that all I could say did not prevent her from imagining that he had a pretty good chance for life.[127] Messrs Hay and Nasmith went with me to the Justiciary Office, but we could learn nothing there but that John Davidson, the Crown Agent, had applied for an extract of the trial on Monday. The respite therefore must have been kept up some days.

I was quite agitated, partly by feeling for Reid, whom I had seen in so miserable a condition, partly by keenness for my own consequence, that I should not fail in what I had undertaken, but get a transportation pardon for my client, since a respite had come. I resolved to walk a little in the fresh air in the Meadow. Hay and Nasmith accompanied me and helped me to calm myself. I thought of applying to Lord Advocate. They were for my taking a chaise and going directly to his country-house at the Whim, which was but fourteen miles off. I thought it would be better to send an express to him with a letter, as I could write in stronger terms than I could speak; and I would ask a transportation pardon from him as a favour which I should consider as a serious obligation for life. I determined that we should call on worthy Nairne and take his advice. He humanely said that since I had obtained a respite, he wished I might save Reid from execution; and he gave it as his opinion that I had better go to Lord Advocate in person. Honest Charles Hay would not leave me in my distress, but accompanied me, as honest Kent did Lear.

We got a chaise at Peter Ramsay's directly, and set off. Charles agreed to wait at an inn not far from the Advocate's, as he was ill-dressed, and it would be better I should wait on the Advocate alone. We talked or rather raved of all the possibilities as to John Reid's affair as we drove along, and Mr Hay was by this time grown almost as eager to save him as I was. He stopped at an inn at Howgate three miles from the Whim. I was uneasy when by myself, restless and impatient. When I arrived at the house, I was told my Lord was gone to Sir James Clerk's at Penicuik. I drove back to Howgate, where Hay had dined. I took a glass of port and a bit of bread, and then we got into the chaise again and drove to Penicuik. We put up our horses at the inn. He walked with me half way to Sir James's and promised to wait at the village. It was now between five and six. As I approached the house, I saw Sir James and Lord Advocate and some other gentlemen taking a walk after dinner. I had dined here before with Sir

127 This and the preceding two sentences (from "[John's] wife") are taken from the journal entry for 7 September.

James. After making my bow to him, I said, "My Lord Advocate, I am in quest of your Lordship. I have been at the Whim. May I beg to speak with you?" We went aside. He immediately started the subject, answering, "About your friend John Reid". I spoke to him very earnestly. He told me he had seen the respite and my letter to Lord Suffolk and the petition for John. He expressed his unwillingness to have an execution after a respite, but said that the respite here had been compelled by the application coming so late. That the King's business required that an example should be made of this man, and if it were to be asked at him, he could not say that Reid was a proper object of mercy. But that he was to give no opinion one way or other. He made for a little a kind of secret of what was doing. But upon my urging him, he said it lay with the judges, and I must apply to them. I said I did not like to apply to them, and I told him with great sincerity that he was the only man employed by the Crown in the Justiciary Court who had not a strong bias against the panels. I said the Justice-Clerk stood in a very delicate situation here, as he had attacked Reid after being acquitted by his country, and would be supposed to be much preju-diced against him. If I were in his place, I would not wish to make a severe report in such circumstances. The Advocate smiled. He gave me full time and never seemed inclined to go in, but walked on the lawn with a complacent easy behaviour. I showed him that I was really very much concerned here and begged he would assist me; that I should never forget the obligation. He said it would be improper for him to interfere.

Sir James sent and invited me to tea. I went in with Lord Advocate and drank some coffee and eat a crumb of biscuit. Sir James was extremely polite to me. Lord Advocate carried me in his coach to the village, but as he had a gentle-man and lady with him I could get but little said. I however resumed my solicitation and said, "Well, my Lord, you'll think of it." He with a pleasing tone said something to this purpose: "Then as King William said, 'You must not think no more of it.'" Though I did not distinctly hear what he said, it appeared to me that he had an intention to do something for me. He pressed me much to go home with him, but I told him I was engaged in town. Mr Hay and I drank a pint of white wine and eat a bit of biscuit and then took our chaise again. I observed how curious it was that two beings who were not sure of their own lives a day should be driving about in this manner to preserve the life of a wretch a little longer. Said Charles: "Can we be better employed?" On my coming home, and Mr Hay with me, my wife, who never favoured John Reid and who was sorry to see me so much interested about him, told me that she had heard some decent-looking men talking tonight on the street against him. One of them said, "I think no laws will get leave to stand now. I wish the law of Moses may get leave to stand." She delivered me a letter from Lord Pembroke in most polite terms, mentioning that he had written to Lord Rochford and urged the affair strongly. This revived my hopes. I went to Dr Monro's.[128] Colonel Campbell of Finab and his family and the Laird of MacLeod and some other

128 Monro's house was in Nicolson Street.

company were there. I played awhile at loo and lost only 18d. We supped very genteelly. I was in a very good frame, had taken a liking to claret and drank a bottle of it. I was pleased at this acquisition to the number of my convivial acquaintances.

SATURDAY 3 SEPTEMBER. I had an opportunity of doing a great kindness to a friend by lending him £50.[129] My wife very handsomely was clear for my doing it, and the gratitude which he expressed in a line which he wrote to me was valuable.

SUNDAY 4 SEPTEMBER. I was at the New Church all day; Dr Blair in the forenoon, Mr Walker in the afternoon. Nothing remarkable was impressed upon me.

WEDNESDAY 7 SEPTEMBER. Mr Nasmith called with a letter from Brown, the messenger who had taken up John Reid, addressed to John, and mentioning that, as they were upon the road, John asked him if he could apprehend anyone else and mentioned Gardner, who was accordingly apprehended. From this letter it appeared to me and Messrs Hay and Nasmith that John had been lying; for if he had got the sheep from Gardner without suspicion, would not he, when accused of stealing them, have instantly accused Gardner, loudly and keenly? No law was read today, we talked so long of John Reid. I determined to try again to know the truth.

I went up to John a little before two, with the messenger's letter in my hand. Seeing me have a paper, he gave an earnest look, I suppose in expectation that it was his pardon. But I at once accosted him as a dying man, upbraided him with having imposed on me, and said to him what I and Mr Nasmith had concluded from perusal of the letter. He calmly explained his conduct. "Sir," said he, "Gardner had before this time come to my house and owned to me that he had stolen the sheep, and promised me great rewards if I would not discover him. Therefore, when I was taken up, I would not speak out against him, but wanted him to be apprehended, that he and I might concert what was to be done to keep ourselves safe. But he was but a very little time with me, and then was carried to Stirling." I was not much convinced by this account of the matter. I had wrought myself into a passion against John for deceiving me, and spoke violently to him, not feeling for him at the time. I had chosen my time so as to be with him when two o'clock struck. "John," said I, "you hear that clock strike. You hear that bell. If this does not move you, nothing will. That you are to consider as your last bell. You remember your sentence. On Wednesday the 7 of September. This is the day. Between the hours of two and four in the afternoon; this is that very time. After this day you are to look upon yourself as a dead man; as a man in a middle state between the two worlds. You are not in eternity, because you are still in the body; but you are not properly alive, because this is the day appointed for your death. You are to look on this fortnight as so much time allowed to you to repent of all your wickedness, and particularly of your lying

129 Probably Andrew Erskine (*Defence*, p. 311, n. 2).

to me in such a way as you have done. Think that this day fortnight by four o'clock you will be rendering an account to your Maker. I am afraid that you are encouraged by your wife to persist in obstinacy, not to disgrace her and your children. But that is a small consideration to a man going into eternity. I think it your duty to own your being guilty on this occasion if you be really so, which I cannot but think is the case. By doing so you will make all the atonement in your power to society. But at any rate I beseech you not to deny your guilt contrary to truth." This was as vehement and solemn a harangue as could be made upon any occasion. The circumstance of the clock striking and the two o'clock bell ringing were finely adapted to touch the imagination. But John seemed to be very unfeeling today. He persisted in his tale. There was something approaching to the ludicrous when, in the middle of my speech to him about his not being properly alive, he said very gravely, "Ay; I'm dead in law." I was too violent with him. I said, "With what face can you go into the other world?" And: "If your ghost should come and tell me this, I would not believe it." This last sentence made me frightened, as I have faith in apparitions, and had a kind of idea that perhaps his ghost might come to me and tell me that I had been unjust to him. I concluded with saying, "You have paper, pen, and ink there. Let me have a real account of everything." He said he would. Richard Lock had come into the room before I was done speaking. I desired him to advise John to be candid.

Mr Nasmith met me when I came out of prison and was very impatient to hear about John. In telling him John's explanation of his behaviour when taken up, I became impressed that it might be true, and enlarged on the uncertainty of circumstantial evidence. Nasmith was convinced too, and said, "We are as much in the dark as ever." I took him home with me to dinner; and, after drinking a bottle of port between us, a curious thought struck me that I would write the case of John Reid as if dictated by himself on this the day fixed for his execution. I accordingly did it, and hit off very well the thoughts and style of what such a case would have been. Nasmith suggested the idea of Gardner confessing in America. He took it home to get it copied, and undertook to send it to Galbraith, a printer, that it might be hawked about the streets this very night; which would have a striking effect, as it called on his readers to think that it was his *ghost* speaking to them.[130]

THURSDAY 8 SEPTEMBER. Mr Donaldson and his son, Mr Mylne the architect,[131] Balbarton,[132] Sir George and Lady Preston and Miss Preston dined with us. My servant James had a child ill of the smallpox. He would not agree to stay away from it; and as I was afraid that my little Effie might be infected, I would not allow him to come into my house; so I was now without a manservant. I saw that a married servant would not do in a family where only one is kept, and

---

130 The work did not appear that night, but was brought out a few days later (by a different publisher) as a broadside entitled "The Mournful Case of Poor Misfortunate and Unhappy John Reid".
131 Robert Mylne (1733-1811), the designer of St Cecilia's Hall, built in 1762 as the new home for the Musical Society (for which, see Introduction, p. 9).
132 James Boswell of Balbarton.

therefore I gave him warning to provide himself against the term. It gave me some uneasiness to think that a poor man should be dismissed because he had strong natural affection; but I considered that a man in his station of life is bound to submit to many disadvantages, and if he cannot do so, he is at least unfit for being the sole manservant in a family; and I hoped that he would get a good place somewhere else. Sir George's ladies went home early. He and the rest of the company drank tea. I had taken too much claret. I strolled in the streets a long time. I supped at Sir George's with my wife. I drank too much strong port negus. After I came home I was monstrously passionate.

FRIDAY 9 SEPTEMBER. After our law Mr Hay and I had a game at bowls. He dined with me and drank tea. I was now become a man of high estimation in the prison, in so much that prisoners applied to me by petition: "Unto the Honourable James Boswell, Esq., Advocate, The Petition of —— Humbly Showeth." I did them what service I could. Henry McGraugh's case was now become an object of great attention, the newspapers having many letters about it. Some of them I wrote myself. Dr Young drank tea with us. He thought hanging a quick death, there being violence besides suffocation.

SATURDAY 10 SEPTEMBER. After breakfast Mr Nasmith called, which interrupted the Law College. Mr Hay and he agreed with me that as I was to transmit a memorial on the evidence against John Reid, showing its insufficiency, it would be proper to send along with it a declaration by his wife that he was in his own house the night when the theft was committed, and for several nights before. This the woman all along affirmed, and her testimony was the only proof that in the circumstances of the case could be had. I drew a short petition to the Magistrates which Mr Nasmith got John to sign, and then presented it. Bailie Torry, who then officiated, was timorous, and some clerk advised that it should be intimated to the King's Advocate, Solicitor, or Crown Agent. The Bailie gave judgement accordingly. They were all out of town; and at any rate would have opposed it, though in reality they had no concern with it. The trial was over. The declaration was only a piece of evidence, perhaps not strictly legal, but which might have weight with His Majesty, after a respite had been granted. Bailie Macqueen, to whom Mr Nasmith spoke first, very gravely said that taking the declaration would be to destroy a trial by jury. We were now in a dilemma. We thought of trying a Justice of Peace, but we could not bear being refused again. Mr —— suggested that the declaration might be taken before two notaries public. We sallied forth into the street to look for another notary to join Mr Nasmith. We met Andrew Dick, Writer to the Signet.[133] He would not be concerned in the matter; and said with a dull sort of sneer, "He may prepare himself for Wednesday come eight days." I was angry at the animal, and told him before Messieurs Hay and Nasmith that John told me that Mr Andrew Dick and he were fourth cousins. This the creature could not deny; and to have it known mortified him not a little. It occurred that perhaps a commissary might take the declaration.

133 Andrew Dick, W.S. (admitted 11 January 1762), died 1778.

We walked out to George's Square, and I called on Commissary Smollett[133a] and laid the matter before him. He said that, as a commissary was not *virtute officii*[134] a Justice of Peace all over the country like the Lords of Session and Barons of Exchequer, and had no criminal jurisdiction, he could not take the declaration. I then suggested that a protest might be taken against the Bailie for delaying it. He thought this right, and said that along with the protest a petition from the poor woman might be sent, setting forth what she would have declared had she not been prevented; which would probably not have been the case in our neighbouring country, affidavits being readily taken by magistrates in England.

Messieurs Hay and Nasmith waited for me in the Square, and we went and dined together at Baptie's in Bruntsfield Links, very soberly, and came to the resolution of taking no protest, as that would occasion a noise, but just having the declaration certified by two notaries public. We came in to town, sauntered at the Cross, anxious for another notary to join Mr Nasmith. One Tyrie appeared but declined to give his assistance. We were in a great dilemma. At last I found Matthew Dickie. We went into Hutchinson's[135] and had a bottle of claret for ourselves and a bottle of porter for Mrs Reid and Richard Lock, who brought her. I then exhorted her to tell nothing but truth; said I was not a judge, so could not administer an oath to her; but that solemnly to declare what was not true would be a great sin. She said, "I am in the presence of GOD." Her declaration then was taken, and she really seemed to speak what was genuine truth. Mr Dickie went home. I and my two zealous coadjutors drank tea, and I wrote two letters to Lord Rochford: one as to the Secretary of State and another as to the private nobleman; and I put them, with a memorial and the declaration, into the post-office[136] with my own hand, as I have done every letter concerning John Reid. Messieurs Hay and Nasmith came home and supped with me. This was a day of much agitation. I was quite exhausted. We drank little.

TUESDAY 13 SEPTEMBER. The Laird of Dundas[137] had asked me to eat turtle with him this day at Fortune's. After a good match at bowls with Mr Hay, I went to Fortune's, but found the feast was put off till next day; but as it had not been notified to me, I resolved not to attend next day. Charles Hay had told me that he had excellent mutton to dinner today; so I hastened to his house, but found dinner over and him eating some of the mutton by himself. I joined him and dined heartily, and saw I was made very welcome. He and I and his brother drank a bottle of Madeira and a bottle of claret. I then, for the first time for many months, played at whist, Maclaurin and I having freed each other from a bet of five guineas who should first play again. I won, and also drank tea.

133a James Smollett of Bonhill, admitted advocate 17 January 1733, appointed a judge in the Commissary Court 1744 and Sheriff-Depute of Dunbartonshire 1749, died 12 November 1775. He was a cousin of the novelist Tobias Smollett.
134 By virtue of his office.
135 Although the editors of *Defence* (at p. 392) indicate that Hutchinson's tavern was in the High Street in the vicinity of the Town Guard, this may actually have been the tavern of James Hutchison in Advocate's Close (off the north side of the High Street opposite the Luckenbooths).
136 The Post Office was in Parliament Close (see Introduction, p. 12).
137 James Dundas, a distant cousin of the Lord President and the Solicitor-General (*Defence*, p. 329, n. 2).

On 13 September Boswell sent a letter to The London Chronicle, *signed "A ROYALIST",* *containing the following comments on Reid's trial: "We have at present in this city a* *remarkable man lying under sentence of death, being convicted of the theft of a few* *sheep. His name is John Reid. He is remarkable because he was formerly tried and* *acquitted by a very worthy jury, notwithstanding which some persons in high office publicly* *represented him as guilty. In particular one great man of the law exclaimed against him* *in his speech in the great Douglas Cause. This is a striking specimen of what goes on in* *this narrow country. A strong prejudice was raised against him, and now he was con-* *demned upon circumstantial evidence which several impartial gentlemen of very good* *skill were of opinion was inconclusive… A respite for fourteen days was sent to Reid* *from the office of Lord Rochford… But, according to my information, an opinion from* *Scotland was desired upon the case: an opinion from that very man who exclaimed in* *the Civil Court against a man acquitted by a jury in the Criminal Court, when his life* *was staked upon the issue."*

WEDNESDAY 14 SEPTEMBER. Having gone out to the Justiciary Office in the morning, Mr Hay had called and missed me; so we had no law. I called at the bank for Maclaurin, and he and I took a walk in the Meadow. After dinner Ritchie called on me and said he was very desirous that John Reid should de-clare what he had committed long ago, which he thought had followed him. I promised to come to the prison, and accordingly went.

John was very sedate. He told Mr Ritchie and me that, before his first trial, one night he drank hard and lay all night at the side of a sheep-fold; that when he awaked the devil put it into his head (or some such expression) and he drove off all the sheep in the fold (the "*hail hirsle*"); that before he was off the farm to which they belonged, he came to a water, and there he separated four of them, which he took home, killed, and sold; and he said it was alleged that he had taken five, but it never came to any trial. This was but a small matter. John said he would have it published. His owning this theft made me give more credit to his denial of that for which he was condemned, for why should he deny the one and confess the other? I told him that now I believed him, and I acknowledged that I had been too violent with him this day eight days. He seemed to be grateful to me; and said that few would have done so much for a brother, though a twin, as I had done for him. He said that he had always had something heavy about his mind since his last trial and never could be merry as formerly. He said that last night he had strange dreams. He saw a wonderful moon with many streamers.

I asked John if he ever saw anything in the iron room where he lay. He said no; but that he heard yesterday at nine in the morning a noise upon the form, as if something had fallen upon it with a *clash*. Ritchie and he seemed to consider this as some sort of warning. He said he had heard such a noise in the corner of the room a little before his respite came. And he said that the night before James Brown's pardon came, Brown was asleep, and he was awake, and heard like swine running from the door, round a part of the room, and *grumphling*.[138] He

138 Boswell represented James Brown at his trial for horse-stealing in February 1774. Brown was found guilty, but was subsequently pardoned on condition that he transported himself (*Defence*, pp. 208-9).

seemed to be in a very composed frame. I said it was an awful thought that this day sennight at this time he would be in eternity. I said I hoped his repentance was sincere and his faith in Christ sincere, and that he would be saved through the merits of the Saviour, and perhaps he might this day eight days be looking down with pity on Mr Ritchie and me. I found that he had hardly written anything.

FRIDAY 16 SEPTEMBER. Charles Hay and I this day completed our course of Erskine's *Institute*. I dined with him, with Maclaurin, who was in good spirits but offended me by a kind of profaneness in quoting Scripture. He was of opinion that it was wrong to apply for John Reid; and when I asserted that he was innocent, Maclaurin had a pretty good simile. He said I had worked up my mind upon the subject. That the mind of man might be worked up from little or nothing like soap suds, till the basin is overflowed. We drank moderately, and then played at whist. I went home at night, and was in a strange wearied humour; so went directly to bed.

SATURDAY 17 SEPTEMBER. Mr Robert Boswell and I breakfasted at my uncle the Doctor's. Richard Lock came in the morning, after my return from the Doctor's, and told me, "It is all over with John Reid. He dies on Wednesday. There's a letter come that no farther respite is to be granted." I was struck with concern. Mr Hay came, and he and I walked a little on the Castle Hill and then called on Mr Nasmith. We agreed to dine together at Leith to relieve our vexation at the bad news. I first went up a little to John Reid. His wife was with him. He was not much affected with the bad news, as he had not been indulging hopes. I again exhorted him to tell nothing but truth.

Messieurs Hay, Nasmith, and I walked down to Leith, and dined at Trumpeter Yeats's. We were fain to fly to wine to get rid of the uneasiness which we felt that, after all that had been done, poor John Reid should fall a victim. I thought myself like Duncan Forbes. We drank two bottles of port each. I was not satisfied with this, but stopped at a shop in Leith and insisted that we should drink some gin. Mr Nasmith and one Ronald, the master of the shop, and I drank each a gill. Nasmith was very drunk, Mr Hay and I quite in our senses. We all walked up some way or other. Mr Hay came home with me. I found a letter from Lord Pembroke which gave me still hopes, for he said he would go to town and see the King himself; and I flattered myself that his Lordship might procure an alteration of the doom. Mr Hay left me. I grew monstrously drunk, and was in a state of mingled frenzy and stupefaction. I do not recollect what passed.

SUNDAY 18 SEPTEMBER. It gave me much concern to be informed by my dear wife that I had been quite outrageous in my drunkenness the night before; that I had cursed her in a shocking manner and even thrown a candlestick with a lighted candle at her. It made me shudder to hear such an account of my behaviour to one whom I have so much reason to love and regard; and I considered that, since drinking has so violent an effect on me, there is no knowing

what dreadful crime I may commit. I therefore most firmly resolved to be sober. I was very ill today. Both Mr Hay and Mr Nasmith called on me. About
twelve I called on Grange, and he and I walked out by the West Kirk[139] and
round by Watson's Hospital,[140] which did me much good. I found my uncle the
Doctor when I got home. He dined with us. I stayed at home in the afternoon as
I had done in the forenoon. Mr Hay came after church, and he and I walked in
Heriot's Garden. Lady Dundonald and Lady Betty Cochrane drank tea with us.

MONDAY 19 SEPTEMBER. Between seven and eight I was with the Doctor
by appointment, and he and I walked out to Sir James Foulis's[141] at Colinton,
where we breakfasted. It was melancholy to see an ancient respectable family
in decay. Sir James has much curious knowledge, but his whim and want of
dignity displeased me. We saw his lady and youngest daughter. He walked with
us to Dreghorn (Mr Maclaurin's), where I was engaged to dine and play at
bowls.[142] Charles Hay and his sister came. It was a wet day, but we had a stout
bowling match. Sir James went home. We dined very well and drank little. Then
Maclaurin, Hay, and I took a rubber, Hay playing the dead man. Maclaurin told
me that I had the character of speaking ill of my companions, but that he did
not believe it. Hay justified me, owning at the same time that I would have my
joke on them when it could not really hurt them. I said I certainly did speak
freely of those of whom I had not a good opinion, but I did not live with them as
companions. Maclaurin said I carried that too far. It gave me some sort of uneasiness to hear that I was misrepresented; but then my full consciousness of
my real goodness made me easy. We drank tea; and then the Doctor and I came
off in a hackney-coach which my wife sent for us. By the road he disputed warmly
for his particular tenets as to the Christian religion: salvation by faith alone,
etc. I felt some pain when I found how ill I could argue on the most important of
all subjects, and cold clouds of doubt went athwart my mind.

When I got home I found letters for me from Lord Rochford, Lord Pembroke,
Mr Eden, Under-Secretary in Lord Suffolk's office, and the Duke of Queensberry,
and was finally assured that John Reid would be executed. I was hurt, and also
felt an indignation at the Justice-Clerk, whose violent report had prevented my

139 The West Church, which stood at the site now occupied by St Cuthbert's Church, was said to have been "one of
the most hideous churches in Edinburgh", resembling (apart from its steeple) "a huge stone box" (Grant, Vol. II, pp.
131, 134). Work on the construction of the building started in or about 1772 and was not completed until 1775. The
steeple, which was added in 1789, still stands (as part of St Cuthbert's Church).
140 George Watson's Hospital, an impressive building designed by William Adam and standing on a
site to the south of the city wall in the district of Lauriston (being part of the grounds now occupied
by the Royal Infirmary). Work on the construction of the building started in 1738 and was financed
by funds bequeathed by George Watson, latterly accountant with the Bank of Scotland, to build a
"hospital" for the maintenance and instruction of the male children and grandchildren of "decayed"
merchants in Edinburgh. The "hospital" later became George Watson's College, which since 1932 has
been situated at Colinton Road and is now the largest co-educational school in Scotland.
141 Sir James Foulis, Bt, who was "a Celtic scholar, engaged in research on the place names of
Scotland and the origin of the Scots" (*Defence*, p. 335, n. 1).
142 John Maclaurin was the owner of Dreghorn Castle, Colinton. The Castle, which was
demolished in 1955, was "one of Colinton's grandest houses" and "lay amid extensive wooded
policies entirely hidden from view" (Cant, *Villages of Edinburgh*, Vol. 2, p. 46).

obtaining for John Reid the royal mercy; but I resolved not to write against him till time had cooled me. Mr Hay called, and was much concerned. He and I went to Mr Nasmith, who was very impatient. We all agreed that it was a shocking affair. The last resort now was the scheme of recovering John. Mr Hay promised to call at my house next morning to talk of it. Mr Nasmith and I went to see Mr Wood. He was not at home. We found him at Mrs Alison's in New Street, Canongate, at supper, got him into a room, and spoke with him. He said that a house must be found as near the place of execution as possible, for that the rumbling of a cart would destroy John altogether. He said a stable or any place would do. He would attend and have the proper apparatus, and get Mr Innes, Dr Monro's dissector, to attend. I was much agitated tonight. It rained very heavily. I wished it might do so on Wednesday, that the execution might perhaps be hastened.

TUESDAY 20 SEPTEMBER. Before breakfast I received a very good letter from Mr Nasmith dissuading me from the scheme of recovering John Reid, but he did not persuade me. Mr Hay came and he and I called on Mr Nasmith and took him with us to look for a place where the corpse might be deposited. We walked about the Grassmarket[143] and Portsburgh,[144] and saw some small houses to let. Mr Nasmith proposed that we might take one till Martinmas; but then it occurred that the landlord would make a noise if a hanged man was put into it. In short, we were in a dilemma. I thought of the Canongate Kilwinning Lodge, of which I was Master and could excuse myself to the brethren for taking liberty with it; but it was too far off. I did not think it right to trust a caddie, or any low man, with the secret. I asked John Robertson the chairman[145] if he could find a house that would take in the corpse till the mob dispersed. He thought none would do it. Mr Nasmith went out of town. Mr Hay, after a short party at bowls, went with me and called for Mr Innes, Dr Monro's dissector.[146] Mr Wood had not yet spoken to him; but he very readily agreed to give his help. He however could not help us to get a house. I called on Wood. Neither could he help us as to that article; and he began to doubt of the propriety of the scheme. I however remained firm to it, and Mr Hay stood by me. Mr Innes suggested one George Macfarlane, a stabler, where a puppet-show had been kept. Mr Hay and I went to the Grassmarket, where he lived. But first it occurred to me that there was one Andrew Bennet, a stabler, whom I had lately got out of prison. We went to him. He had no family but his wife, and they were both fools. They were prodigiously grateful to me, called me *his Grace*, Andrew having reproved his wife for calling me only *his Honour*. I told them that the friends of the poor man who was to be executed next day were anxious to lodge his body in some place till the mob should disperse, and, as he was a client of mine, I was desirous to assist them; so I hoped Andrew would let them

143 For the Grassmarket, see Introduction, p. 7.
144 Portsburgh was a suburb lying to the west of the Grassmarket and consisted chiefly of "a narrow street, formed by mean houses, and dirty miserable alleys running from it" (Arnot, p. 191).
145 That is, a sedan-carrier. For the chairmen, see Introduction, p. 6.
146 The address of John Innes, surgeon, was the College.

have his stable for that purpose. He agreed to it, though his wife made some objection, and though he said he would rather let his *craig* (throat) be cut than allow it, unless to oblige me. I sounded them as to letting the body into their house; but Mrs Bennet screamed, and Andrew said very justly that nobody would come to it any more if that was done. It is amazing what difficulty I found in such a place as Edinburgh to get a place for my purpose. The stable here entered by a close next entry to the door of the house, and had no communication with the house; so that the operators must be obliged to take their stations in the stable some time before the execution was over. It was a small stable, and there was a smith's shop just at the door of it; so that we could not be private enough. However, I was glad to have secured any place.

Mr Hay and I then went to George Macfarlane's. He was not in. We had not dined, as we did not choose to see my wife while we were about such a project, which I had communicated to her and which shocked her. We called for punch and bread and cheese, all of which proved wretched. We sat about an hour, waiting for the landlord's coming in, that we might have tried if he would let us have a better place, but he did not come. I observed that we were reduced to do the meanest and most disagreeable things for this strange scheme, as much so as candidates in a borough election.

I called at home at five, Hay having gone to a coffee-house and engaged to meet me at the Cross at six. I found my wife so shocked that I left her immediately and went down to the prison. I was now more firmly impressed with a belief of John Reid's innocence, the Reverend Dr Dick having come to the bowling-green in the forenoon and told me that, as he was to attend him to his execution, he had talked with him very seriously, and (the Doctor used a very good expression) had got behind all the subterfuges of such a mind as his, such as his thinking it right to deny, to leave a better character for the sake of his wife and children, and had found him firm and consistent in his declaration that he was not guilty. The Doctor said this affair gave him great uneasiness; and he told me that the Reverend Dr Macqueen was to go along with him to attend at the execution; that he also had been with John, and was of the same opinion. I begged that he and Dr Macqueen would be particularly attentive to investigate the truth as much as possible, as I really believed he was condemned on insufficient evidence, and, from his solemn averments of his innocence, thought him not guilty of the crime for which he was condemned; such averments being in my opinion an overbalance not for positive, or even strong circumstantial, evidence, but for such evidence as was brought against him, which I thought could produce no more than suspicion.

When I came to the prison I found that John Reid's wife and children were with him. The door of the iron room was now left open and they were allowed to go and come as they pleased. He was very composed. His daughter Janet was a girl about fifteen, his eldest son Benjamin about ten, his youngest son Daniel between two and three. It was a striking scene to see John on the last night of his life surrounded by his family. His wife and two eldest children behaved very quietly. It was really curious to see the young child Daniel, who knew nothing of the melancholy situation of his father, jumping upon him with great fondness, laughing and calling to him with vivacity. The contrast was remarkable between the father in chains and in gloom and the child quite free and frolicsome. John took him on his knee with affection. He said to me that his daughter Jenny was the only one of his children whom he had named after any relation; and he went over all the names of the rest. They had almost all Old Testament names. They were seven in all. I again exhorted him to truth. One Miln in Leith Wynd, a kind of lay teacher, and Mr Ritchie were with him; and he was to have some good Christians to sit up with him all night.

Mr Hay went with me again to Mr Innes, who was satisfied with Bennet's stable and desired that there should be a blanket and a good quantity of warm salt prepared. We went again to Bennet's, and took a dram of whisky of his own distilling; and he and his wife promised to have the blanket and the salt in readiness, I having said that some surgeon had advised his friends to rub the body with warm salt to preserve it, as it was to be carried to the country. Bennet, though a fool, had smoked what was intended; for he said, "Could they not cut him down living?" I said that would be wrong. I should have observed, when I was with John this evening, it gave me some uneasiness to think that he was solemnly preparing for an awful eternity while at the same time I was to try to keep him back. He spoke himself very calmly of *the corpse*, by which he meant his own dead body; for I spoke to his wife before him about it: that I had secured a place for it, but I wished she could get a better place for it to be laid in till the mob dispersed. She said she would try Mrs Walker at the sign of the Bishop in the Grassmarket, who was very friendly to her. It was a comfort to me that neither John nor his wife had the least idea of any attempt to recover him.

Mr Hay and I met my worthy friend Grange in the Grassmarket tonight. He was much against the attempt. After supper Mr Wood called and told me that he had the proper apparatus ready; that he had also engaged Mr Aitkin, another surgeon, to attend, and that, if I insisted on it, he was willing to make the experiment, but that as a friend he could not but advise me against it; that it would be impossible to conceal it; the mob would press upon us, and continue looking in at the door. A great clamour would be made against me as defying the laws and as doing a ridiculous thing, and that a man in business must pay attention in prudence to the voice of mankind; that the chance of success was hardly anything, and this was to be put in the scale against a certainty of so many disagreeable consequences. But he suggested another thought which had great weight with me. "This man", said he, "has got over the bitterness of death; he is resigned to his fate. He will have got over the pain of death. He may curse you for bringing him back. He may tell you that you kept him from heaven." I determined to give up the scheme. Wood got into a disagreeable kind of sceptical conversation about the soul being material, from all that we could observe. It is hard that our most valuable articles of belief are rather the effects of sentiment than of demonstration. I disliked Wood because he revived doubts in my mind which I could not at once dispel. Yet he had no bad meaning, but was honestly and in confidence expressing his own uneasiness. He said that the fear of death sometimes distressed him in the night. He seemed to have formed no principles upon the subject, but just had ideas, sometimes of one kind, sometimes of another, floating in his mind. He had a notion, which I have heard the Reverend Mr Wyvill support, that only some souls were designed for immortality. What a blessing it is to have steady religious sentiments.

WEDNESDAY 21 SEPTEMBER. John Reid's wife called on me before breakfast and told me that Mrs Walker said she was welcome to the best room in her house for the corpse; but that afterwards her landlord had sent to her that she must quit his house if she allowed such a thing. I said that there would be no occasion for any place. The mob would not trouble the corpse; and it might be put directly on the cart that she expected was to come for it. After breakfast Mr Nasmith came, and was pleased to find that the scheme of recovery was given up. He and I went to Bennet's and told him there was no use for his stable. We walked backwards and forwards in the Grassmarket, looking at the gallows and talking of John Reid. Mr Nasmith said he imagined he would yet confess; for his wife had said this morning that he had something to tell me which he had as yet told to no mortal. We went to the prison about half an hour after twelve. He was now released from the iron about his leg. The Reverend Dr Webster and Mr Ritchie were with him. We waited in the hall along with his wife, who had white linen clothes with black ribbons in a bundle, ready to put on him before he should go out to execution. There was a deep settled grief in her countenance. She was resolved to attend him to the last; but Richard whispered me that the Magistrates had given orders that she should be detained in the prison till the execution was over. I dissuaded her from going and she agreed to take my advice; and then Richard told her the orders of the Magistrates. I said aloud I was glad to hear of it. The Reverend Dr Macqueen, who afterwards came in, told her it would be a tempting of Providence to go; that it might affect her so as to render her incapable to take care of her fatherless children; and Mr Ritchie said that the best thing she could do was to remain in the prison and pray for her husband. Dr Macqueen said to me he was so much impressed with the poor man's innocence that he had some difficulty whether he ought to attend the execution and authorise it by his presence. I said he certainly should attend, for it was *legal*; and, besides, supposing it ever so unjust, it was humane to attend an unhappy man in his last moments. "But", said Dr Macqueen, "I will not pray for him as a guilty man." "You would be very much in the wrong to do so", said I, "if you think him not guilty." Dr Webster and I had no conversation as he passed through the hall except inquiring at each other how we did.

John's wife then went up to him for a little, having been told both by me and Mr Nasmith that she could not hope for the blessing of Providence on her and her children if by her advice John went out of the world with a lie in his mouth. I followed in a little, and found him in his usual dress, standing at the window. I told him I understood he had something to mention to me. He said he *would* mention it. He had since his trial in 1766 stolen a few sheep (I think five), of which he never was suspected. "John," said I, "it gives me concern to find that even such a warning as you got then did not prevent you from stealing. I really imagine that if you had now got off you might again have been guilty, such influence has Satan over you." He said he did not know but he might. Then I observed that his untimely death might be a mercy to him, as he had time for repentance. He seemed to admit that it might be so. He said that what he had now told me he had not mentioned even to his wife; and I might let it rest. I called up Mr Nasmith, with whom came Mr Ritchie. I said he might acknowledge this fact to them, which he did. I asked him, if I saw it proper to mention it as making his denial of the theft for which he was condemned more probable, I might be at liberty to do so? He said I might dispose of it as I thought proper. But he persisted in denying the theft for which he was condemned. He now began to put on his white dress, and we left him. Some time after, his wife came down and begged that we would go up to him, that he might not be alone. Dress has a wonderful impression on the fancy. I was not much affected when I saw him this morning in his usual dress. But now he was all in white, with a high nightcap on, and he appeared much taller, and upon the whole struck me with a kind of tremor. He was praying; but stopped when we came in. I bid him not be disturbed, but go on with his devotions. He did so, and prayed with decent fervency, while his wife, Mr Nasmith, and I stood close around him. He prayed in particular, "Grant, O Lord, through the merits of my Saviour, that this the day of my death may be the day of my birth unto life eternal." Poor man, I felt now a kind of regard for him. He said calmly, "I think I'll be in eternity in about an hour." His wife said something from which he saw that she was not to attend him to his execution; and he said, "So you're no (not) to be wi' me." I satisfied him that it was right she should not go. I said, "I suppose, John, you know that the executioner is down in the hall." He said no. I told him that he was there and would tie his arms before he went out. "Ay," said his wife, "to keep him from catching at the *tow* (rope)." "Yes," said I, "that it may be easier for him." John said he would submit to everything.

I once more conjured him to tell the truth. "John," said I, "you must excuse me for still entertaining some doubt, as you know you have formerly deceived me in some particulars. I have done more for you in this world than ever was done for any man in your circumstances. I beseech you let me be of some use to you for the next world. Consider what a shocking thing it is to go out of the world with a lie in your mouth. How can you expect mercy, if you are in rebellion against the GOD of truth?" I thus pressed him; and while he stood in his dead clothes, on the very brink of the grave, with his knees knocking together, partly from the cold occasioned by his linen clothes, partly from an awful apprehension of death, he most solemnly averred that what he had told concerning the present alleged crime was the truth. Before this, I had at Mr Ritchie's desire read over his last speech to him, which was rather an irksome task as it was very long; and he said it was all right except some immaterial circumstance about his meeting Wilson with the six score of sheep. Vulgar minds, and indeed all minds, will be more struck with some unusual thought than with the most awful consideration which they have often heard. I tried John thus: "We are all mortal. Our life is uncertain. I may perhaps die in a week hence. Now, John, consider how terrible it would be if I should come into the other world and find" (looking him steadfastly in the face) "that you have been imposing on me." He was roused by this, but still persisted. "Then," said I, "John, I shall trouble you no more upon this head. I believe you. GOD forbid that I should not believe the word of a fellow man in your awful situation, when there is no strong evidence against it, as I should hope to be believed myself in the same situation. But remember, John, it is trusting to you that I believe. It is between GOD and your own conscience if you have told the truth; and you should not allow me to believe if it is not true." He adhered. I asked him if he had anything more to tell. He said he had been guilty of one other act of sheep-stealing. I think he said of seven sheep; but I think he did not mention precisely when. As he shivered, his wife took off her green cloth cloak and threw it about his shoulders. It was curious to see such care taken to keep from a little cold one who was so soon to be violently put to death. He desired she might think no more of him, and let his children push their way in the world. "The eldest boy", said he, "is reading very well. Take care that he reads the word of GOD." He desired her to keep a New Testament and a psalm-book which he had got in a present from Mr Ritchie and which he was to take with him to the scaffold. He was quite sensible and judicious. He had written a kind of circular letter to all his friends on whom he could depend, begging them to be kind to his family.

Two o'clock struck. I said, with a solemn tone, "There's two o'clock." In a little Richard came up. The sound of his feet on the stair struck me. He said calmly, "Will you come awa now?" This was a striking period. John said yes, and readily prepared to go down. Mr Nasmith and I went down a little before him. A pretty, well-dressed young woman and her maid were in a small closet off the hall; and a number of prisoners formed a kind of audience, being placed as spectators in a sort of loft looking down to the hall. There was a dead silence, all waiting to see the dying man appear. The sound of his steps coming down the stair affected me like what one fancies to be the impression of a supernatural grave noise before any solemn event. When he stepped into the hall, it was quite the appearance of a ghost. The hangman, who was in a small room off the hall, then came forth. He took off his hat and made a low bow to the prisoner. John bowed his head towards him. They stood looking at each other with an awkward uneasy attention. I interfered, and said, "John, you are to have no resentment against this poor man. He only does his duty." "I only do my duty", repeated the hangman. "I have no resentment against him", said John. "I desire to forgive all mankind." "Well, John," said I, "you are leaving the world with a very proper disposition: forgiving as you hope to be forgiven." I forgot to mention that before he left the iron room Mr Ritchie said to him, "Our merciful King was hindered from pardoning you by a representation against you; but you are going before the King of Heaven, who knows all things and whose mercy cannot be prevented by any representation." The hangman advanced and *pinioned* him, as the phrase is; that is, tied his arms with a small cord. John stood quiet and undisturbed. I said, "Richard, give him another glass of wine." Captain Fraser, the gaoler, had sent him the night before a bottle of claret, part of which Richard had given him, warmed with sugar, early in the morning, two glasses of it in the forenoon, and now he gave him another. John drank to us. He then paused a little, then kissed his wife with a sad adieu, then Mr Ritchie kissed him. I then took him by the hand with both mine, saying, "John, it is not yet too late. If you have anything to acknowledge, do it at the last to the reverend gentlemen, Dr Macqueen and Dr Dick, to whom you are much obliged. Farewell, and I pray GOD may be merciful to you." He seemed faint and deep in thought. The prison door then opened and he stepped away with the hangman behind him, and the door was instantly shut. His wife then cried, "O Richard, let me up", and got to the window and looked earnestly out till he was out of sight. Mr Nasmith and I went to a window more to the west, and saw him stalking forward in the gloomy procession. I then desired his wife to retire and pray that he might be supported in this his hour of trial. Captain Fraser gave her four shillings. It was very agreeable to see such humanity in the gaoler, and indeed the tenderness with which the last hours of a convict were soothed pleased me much.

The mob were gone from the prison door in a moment. Mr Nasmith and I walked through the Parliament Close, down the Back Stairs and up the Cowgate, both of us satisfied of John Reid's innocence, and Mr Nasmith observing the littleness of human justice, that could not reach a man for the crimes which he committed but punished him for what he did not commit.

We got to the place of execution about the time that the procession did. We would not go upon the scaffold nor be seen by John, lest it should be thought that we prevented him from confessing. It was a fine day. The sun shone bright. We stood close to the scaffold on the south side between two of the Town Guard. There were fewer people present than upon any such occasion that I ever saw. He behaved with great calmness and piety. Just as he was going to mount the ladder, he desired to see his wife and children; but was told they were taken care of. There was his sister and his daughter near to the gibbet, but they were removed. Dr Dick asked him if what he had said was the truth. He said it was. Just as he was going off, he made an attempt to speak. Somebody on the scaffold called, "Pull up his cap." The executioner did so. He then said, "Take warning. Mine is an unjust sentence." Then his cap was pulled down and he went off. He catched the ladder; but soon quitted his hold. To me it sounded as if he said, "just sentence"; and the people were divided, some crying, "He says his sentence is *just*." Some: "No. He says *unjust*." Mr Laing, clerk to Mr Tait, one of the town clerks, put me out of doubt, by telling me he had asked the executioner, who said it was *unjust*. I was not at all shocked with this execution at the time.

John died seemingly without much pain. He was effectually hanged, the rope having fixed upon his neck very firmly, and he was allowed to hang near three quarters of an hour; so that any attempt to recover him would have been in vain. I comforted myself in thinking that by giving up the scheme I had avoided much anxiety and uneasiness.[147]

We waited till he was cut down; and then walked to the Greyfriars Churchyard, in the office of which his corpse was deposited by porters whom Mr Nasmith and I paid, no cart having come for his body. A considerable mob gathered about the office. Mr Nasmith went to Hutchinson's to bespeak some dinner and write a note to *The Courant* that there would be a paragraph tonight giving an account of the execution; for we agreed that a recent account would make a strong impression. I walked seriously backwards and forwards a considerable time in the churchyard waiting for John Reid's wife coming, that I might resign the corpse to her charge. I at last wearied, and then went to the office of the prison. There I asked the executioner myself what had passed. He told me that John first spoke to him on the ladder and said he suffered wrongfully; and then called to the people that his sentence was unjust. John's sister came here, and returned me many thanks for what I had done for her brother. She was for burying him in the Greyfriars Churchyard, since no cart had come. "No," said I, "the will of the dead shall be fulfilled. He was anxious to be laid in his own burying-place, and it shall be done." I then desired Richard to see if he could get a cart to hire, and bid him bring John's wife to Hutchinson's. Mr Nasmith and I eat some cold beef and cold fowl and drank some port, and then I wrote a paragraph to be inserted in the newspapers. Mr Nasmith threw in a few words. I made two

---

147 The execution was witnessed by Edward Topham, who gave the following vivid account of the scene in a letter which he wrote in Edinburgh on 9 December 1774: "The town of Edinburgh, from the amazing height of its buildings, seems peculiarly formed to make a spectacle of this kind solemn and affecting. The houses, from the bottom up to the top, were lined with people, every window crowded with spectators to see the unfortunate man pass by. At one o'clock the City Guard went to the door of the Tolbooth, the common gaol here, to receive and conduct their prisoner to the place of execution, which is always in the Grass Market, at a very great distance from the prison. All the remaining length of the High Street was filled with people, not only from the town itself, but the country around, whom the novelty of the sight had brought together. On the Guard knocking at the door of the Tolbooth, the unhappy criminal made his appearance. He was dressed in a white waistcoat and breeches, usual on these occasions, bound with black ribands, and a night-cap tied with the same. His white hairs, which were spread over his face, made his appearance still more pitiable. Two clergymen walked on each side of him, and were discoursing with him on subjects of religion. The executioner, who seemed ashamed of the meanness of his office, followed muffled up in a great coat, and the City Guards, with their arms ready, marched around him. The criminal, whose hands were tied behind him, and the rope about his neck, walked up the remaining part of the street. It is the custom in this country for the criminal to walk to the gallows, which has something much more decent in it than being thrown into a cart, as in England, and carried, like a beast, to slaughter. The slow, pensive, melancholy step of a man in these circumstances, has something in it that seems to accord with affliction, and affects the mind forcibly with its distress... When the criminal had descended three parts of the hill which leads to the Grass Market, he beheld the crowd waiting for his coming, and the instrument of execution at the end of it. He made a short stop here, naturally shocked at such a site, and the people seemed to sympathize with his affliction. When he reached the end, he recalled his resolution; and, after passing some time in prayer with the clergymen, and once addressing himself to the people, he was turned off, and expired" (Topham, pp. 59-61).

copies of it, and, both to the printer of *The Courant* and *Mercury*,[148] subjoined my name to be kept as the authority. Richard brought John's wife and daughter. "Well," said I, "Mrs Reid, I have the satisfaction to tell you that your husband behaved as well as we could wish." "And that is a great satisfaction", said she. We made her eat a little and take a glass, but she was, though not violently or very tenderly affected, in a kind of dull grief. The girl did not seem moved. She eat heartily. I told Mrs Reid that I insisted that John should be buried at home; and as I found that as yet no carter would undertake to go but at an extravagant price, the corpse might lie till tomorrow night, and then perhaps a reasonable carter might be had. Mr Nasmith went to *The Courant* with the paragraph, and I to *The Mercury*. I sat till it was printed. It was liberal in Robertson,[149] who was himself one of the jury, to admit it; and he corrected the press.

It was now about eight in the evening, and gloom came upon me. I went home and found my wife no comforter, as she thought I had carried my zeal for John too far, might hurt my own character and interest by it, and as she thought him guilty. I was so affrighted that I started every now and then and durst hardly rise from my chair at the fireside. I sent for Grange, but he was not at home. I however got Dr Webster, who came and supped, and he and I drank a bottle of claret. But still I was quite dismal.

THURSDAY 22 SEPTEMBER. I had passed the night much better than I expected and was easier in the morning. Charles Hay called and after I had given him a detail of all my conduct towards poor John, he said emphatically, "Well, GOD has blessed you with one of the best hearts that ever man had." Luckily for me, Bedlay had come to town anxious to get a bill of suspension drawn by me instantly. This diverted the gloom, for I kept him by me, and I wrote while both he and I dictated, and had it finished by dinner time. He drank tea with me. To touch a fee again was pleasant. Ritchie had secured a cart, and John's wife took leave of me at night when she set out with the corpse.

FRIDAY 23 SEPTEMBER. Yesterday morning I had a visit from Mr George McQueen, one of the bailies of Edinburgh. As I had attacked his sentence about Henry McGraugh, I imagined that he was come to find fault with my conduct in some strange manner, as I was not acquainted with him. But I was agreeably surprised when he asked me to dine with him on Wednesday next with Dr Macqueen and Dr Dick. I then saw that our connexion was on account of John Reid, the Bailie having been one of the former jury who voted to acquit him, and being convinced of his innocence on the last occasion. I told him I was sorry that my defending McGraugh was interpreted as disrespectful to the Magistrates. I thought the sentence too severe and did what in my opinion was right, as the Bailie had done in pronouncing the sentence. We were at once on an easy footing. He told me that he had been quite unmanned at John Reid's

148 Both *The Edinburgh Evening Courant* and *The Caledonian Mercury* were papers which were published three times a week.
149 John Robertson, the publisher of *The Caledonian Mercury*.

execution, as he really believed him to be an innocent man; and he was even under some difficulty how to act. To be sure, the case was nice—to be authorising as a magistrate what a man believed to be unjust. But private judgement must submit in public administration. He said the Justice-Clerk had behaved as he always does: cruelly. And he said he had great peace in his mind when he reflected on the verdict of which he had a share. This evening the Reverend Dr Ewing, who was returned, and on his way to London, Dr Webster, Miss Webster, Sandy Webster, and Mr Nasmith supped with us. I was now pretty easy. My wife made a very good application of a passage in *Douglas, a Tragedy*, saying that John Reid was now gone, but that his jury, fifteen men upon oath, were alive. By my speaking strongly of the injustice of the sentence, I did John no good and in some measure attacked them.

SATURDAY 24 SEPTEMBER. Mr Ritchie called and informed me that when John Reid's wife came to Muiravonside churchyard, she could not get the key. Therefore she and some women and the carter laid the coffin on the dyke (wall), and, some of them being on one side, some on the other, they lifted it over. They then had to send two miles for a spade, and then the carter dug a grave and buried the corpse. I got afterwards a circumstantial account of the burial in a letter from the schoolmaster of the parish, Mr Ritchie having written to him that I was informed that the corpse was to be lifted, and that they who did it should be prosecuted. It would have been a curious question on the right of sepulture. John had, no doubt, a piece of burying-ground, but the voice of the country is that a malefactor cannot be laid in an usual burying-place, though in a churchyard. Yet there is no law as to that.

FRIDAY 30 SEPTEMBER. Lord Gardenstone had applied to me in behalf of a Mr Smith who had been deprived of the office of Surveyor of the Customs at Aberdeen. I went to Commissioner Cochrane, who seemed to be very unfavourable to him. I wrote to Lord Gardenstone that the Boards of Customs and Excise were secret and severe as the Inquisition, and obstinate as the Medes and Persians. The Commissioner told me he heard that I drank hard pretty often. That I should take care, or it would put me wrong in the head.

SATURDAY 1 OCTOBER. Sir Alexander and Lady Dick and Miss Dick sent in a friendly manner that they would come and take pot luck with us today. I got Grange to be of the party. After playing at bowls, I was in excellent humour, and we had a very agreeable day of it. I had not seen Sir Alexander for a long time. After tea Grange and I walked awhile on the Castle Hill.

MONDAY 3 OCTOBER. Bailie Macqueen and Bailie John Grieve, who had been the principal means of acquitting John Reid on his former trial, and Drs Macqueen and Dick dined with us. Lady Betty Cochrane was so obliging as to come and grace this curious dinner. Matters went on very well. But we drank too much; and I was too open in my disapprobation of the Justice-Clerk.

THURSDAY 6 OCTOBER. We dined at Lord Dundonald's with the Valleyfield family.[150] Commissioner Cochrane was there. I drank moderately. We supped at Mr Wellwood's,[151] along with Captain Preston[152] and his friends. I drank little.

When I came home, I found my wife in great distress. She had been home about an hour before me; and a letter had come for me, without any postmark. She imagined that it contained some merchant's account, and opened it. But it proved to be a letter from the Justice-Clerk's son,[153] demanding to know if I wrote a paper signed "A Royalist" in *The London Chronicle*, which he set forth as an injurious charge against his father; and, if I did write it, to know if I would avow in the public papers that the insinuations contained in that attack against his father were false and scandalous, and ask forgiveness of the injury offered him; and that I knew the consequences of answering in the negative. My wife was gone to bed in a miserable alarm. She said she hoped I had not written a paper signed "A Royalist". I said I had. "Then", said she, "you will be called to account by the Justice-Clerk's son." "Nonsense", said I. "Oh," said she, "it is done already. There is his letter lying." I was confounded at reading such a peremptory address from a boy. My wife said he was nineteen or twenty. I said I would either give him no answer, or write to him that he had no title to question me; and I would give him no satisfaction. My wife cried bitterly, and said that would not do. The lad would insist to fight. "Well," said I, "let him do so." "What!" said she. "And make me and your poor children quite miserable?" She was really like a person almost frantic, and earnestly begged I would give her my word of honour that I would deny having written the letter. I did so, being quite shaken by her distress. And, indeed, it is a kind of principle or resolution which I have long held, though with some dubiety, that a man is as well entitled to deny an anonymous publication as to say that he is engaged when asked to a house where he does not choose to be, or to make his servant say that he is not at home when he does not choose to be seen. The difference, however, is that a man who thinks himself hurt by an anonymous publication has perhaps a right to ask a man suspected of it if the suspicion be true; and, though one may make his servant say he is not at home to an ordinary visitor, it would not be well to do so to a gentleman who calls upon him for satisfaction. Yet, if a man is obliged to confess

150 That is, the family of Sir George and Lady Preston.

151 Robert Wellwood of Garvock (1720-1791), advocate (admitted 15 November 1743). He had recently become Sir George Preston's son-in-law having married Sir George's daughter Mary on 16 August of that year.

152 Captain Robert Preston (1740-1834), fifth son of Sir George and Lady Preston. He was in the sea service of the East India Company and was to acquire a considerable fortune. He was M.P. for Dover 1784-90 and Cirencester 1792-1806.

153 William Miller (1755-1846), who was at this time nineteen years old. He was to be admitted advocate on 9 August 1777. From 1780 to 1781 he was M.P. for Edinburgh, and in 1783 he was appointed Principal Clerk of Justiciary. On 23 May 1795 he was appointed a Lord of Session as Lord Glenlee. Cockburn, writing after Miller's elevation to the bench, said of him: "[T]hough deep in legal knowledge, and most ingenious in its application, law was not the highest of his spheres. His favourite and most successful pursuit was mathematics... His appearance was striking, and very expressive of his intellect and habits. The figure was slender; the countenance pale, but with a full dark eye;... his air and manner polite. Everything indicated the philosophical and abstracted gentleman. And another thing which added to his peculiarity, was, that he never used an English word when a Scotch one could be got" (*Jeffrey*, Vol. I, pp. 122-4).

or deny to a person hurt by an anonymous publication, it would be a great check on a due censure of men in public office; as a man must be zealous indeed for propriety and the general good who would expose himself to a duel for it. It occurred that perhaps the Justice-Clerk's friends had obtained from the printer my original manuscript, and, if I should deny it, then they would have a hold of me. My wife was for my setting out for London immediately, quite privately, to get the manuscript, if the printer still had it, and to determine whether to deny or not according as I found that matter to stand. I liked the proposal at first, as in a matter of such deep consequence I would have the advice of Mr Samuel Johnson, with whom I would hold secret and solemn interviews. But then I considered that my going out of the way would have a strange appearance, that it would be an idle expense, and that my wife and I would suffer terrible anxiety during our separation. She was for doing anything for safety, even flying to a foreign country. I was very ill of a cold, which added to my uneasiness. We lay awake in a sort of burning fever all night, suggesting various schemes.

FRIDAY 7 OCTOBER. After five we got a little broken sleep. At seven I rose, and went to worthy Grange, whom we considered as a real comfortable friend. He rose, and we walked on the Castle Hill. He was much perplexed with the affair, and knew not well what to advise. Sometimes he thought I should write to the lad that he had no title to question me. Sometimes that I should write to him that I would answer the Justice-Clerk himself if he called upon me. Sometimes that I should go west to my father, let him know the affair, and his prudence would settle it properly. He considered it as most disagreeable to be thus engaged with a boy, so that I could gain nothing in any way. But then he was anxious that the world should not have it in their power to represent me as without the proper resolution of a man. He came home with me. My wife was up, and appeared pale as a spectre. She was quite wretched, and looked most melancholy when poor little Veronica came into the room. For myself, as I had heard Mr Johnson demonstrate that it is lawful for a Christian to fight a duel, as it is lawful for him to engage in war, I had no scruple; and notwithstanding the vivacity of my imagination, which figured dreary pictures, while my wife's misery softened and tormented my mind, I felt that if it really should be necessary to fight, I could do it. I considered how many duels had been fought without any hurt, or without much hurt; and that, if I should even be killed, it was not a worse kind of death than what might happen to me in the ordinary course of things; and that my father and friends would certainly take care of my wife and children. But it vexed me to think that I had a boy for my antagonist.

My wife grew rather better and said she was anxious that my honour should be preserved. I resolved that we should take a chaise and go out to Commissioner Cochrane, who, being my uncle and an old soldier, could give a most proper advice. Charles Hay had been told by me of the "Royalist"; and therefore it was absolutely necessary to talk with him in case I should deny it. I sent for him, and he was very uneasy at the incident. Grange thought it best that Hay should not know that he was told of it. Hay said it would be very unlucky if a man so well known in the world, and so well esteemed as I was, should be thought deficient in courage. At the same [time], he thought that as my wife knew of this affair, and as it was a boy who had written to me, there was great difficulty in determining what to do. He consulted with a most friendly attention. He was once for denying it; but, then, as I had been so long of receiving the boy's letter, it occurred to him that it was probable evidence was already procured that I had written the "Royalist". I myself hit upon this plan: to write to the boy, telling him that the letter was written by me; but assuring him, as I truly could, that he was in a mistake in supposing that I attacked either his father's honour or honesty. That I meant no injury, and, if I had used any expressions which had been misunderstood, I was sorry for it. That if after this candid explanation any disagreeable consequences should ensue, I should have the comfort to think I was not to blame. Hay was quite pleased with this. I sat down directly and wrote a scroll, and put it in my pocket to show to Commissioner Cochrane.

My wife and I drove out in an anxious state. She said she envied every passenger we met, as unconscious of future evil. I left her at the gate of the avenue, and found the Commissioner walking. I told him the story, and read to him the passages in the "Royalist" relative to the Justice-Clerk. He thought there was little in them, but they might have been spared. I then read him the boy's letter, and my answer. He approved entirely of it. Said that I had not said too much. That I had said I meant no injury, and was sorry that one was supposed. That was enough; and there would be no more of it. He said it would have been quite wrong to have denied it; and he was of opinion that a son might call upon a man for satisfaction if he thought his father's character attacked. He said I should never write in newspapers. It was below me. He talked with such coolness, indifference and ease, like a man who knew the world, and looked on the boy's letter as a youthful flash, that I was much relieved. We went for my wife, and he told her there would be no more of it. We walked a little, then went in and took a glass of wine and a biscuit, and then returned to Edinburgh.

Worthy Grange was waiting for us. My wife relapsed and had almost fainted. Never did I see so affecting a scene. She viewed herself as on the brink of the deepest affliction. I wavered in my resolution while I beheld her, but she bid me arm myself with fortitude. Hay called again too, and thought that the letter which I was to write could not fail to settle the affair. We had been engaged to dine at Mr Webster's with Sir George Preston's family. My wife was so ill that she insisted to be excused. I went by myself. I found the company so comfortable and friendly-like that I thought she would be soothed if there, and kept from brooding over her woe by herself. They were all for her coming still, saying that her complaint was only low spirits. George[154] and I went for her; and with much entreaty I got her to take a chair and come. She had a faintness in her countenance that was very interesting, and her anxiety about me endeared her

154 Captain George Preston, son of Sir George.

to me. The kind attention which everybody showed her, particularly Lady Preston's motherly kindness, did her good, and she grew easier. I was for a while like a man with some mortification or gnawing distemper at his heart, and envied worthy Sir George and every man whose heart was at ease. It was so vexatious to be entangled with a boy, and to run the risks of a serious duel with one that would make it really ludicrous, being not only young, but a little, effeminate-looking creature. I however resolved to take the comforts of life heartily in the mean time. I eat a good dinner, and drank freely of excellent claret, and by degrees I felt myself firm.

My wife called me into another room, and begged I would allow her to mention the affair to Lady Preston. I thought it would relieve her much to have a female friend to whom she could unbosom herself; and therefore, since she had unhappily come to the knowledge of it, I allowed her to mention it in the utmost confidence. When the company went to tea, I spoke of the affair to Dr Webster, as to a sagacious man. He said, if my letter did not give satisfaction, the boy's father should confine him as a Bedlamite. My wife had desired that I would speak of it to Captain Preston, who was a younger man than Commissioner Cochrane, for she was anxious that there should not be the least imputation on my spirit. I did so; and he was of opinion with the Commissioner. I engaged him to be my second in case matters should come to an extremity; and I begged of him that, as I was so much concerned on my wife's account, and might therefore lean to a too gentle conduct, he would as a true friend take care that I should do nothing but what was perfectly becoming a gentleman. He said he would. He made me read both the letter and the answer twice over, and was satisfied that I was doing quite properly. After tea I went home and wrote out my answer, with a very little variation. My wife and Grange sat by me. Then Grange went with me, and saw me put it into the post-house.

My wife and I supped at Sir George's, and were pretty easy. At night she told me that Captain Preston said to her she might make herself quite easy. Let the boy give what answer he pleased, he would not leave Scotland till he saw the affair ended without any harm being done. Wearied both in body and mind, we slept tolerably.

SATURDAY 8 OCTOBER. Mr Hay and I took a walk in the King's Park and piazza of the Abbey of Holyroodhouse. He was clear that my letter was enough; and that if the boy should return an impertinent answer, I should treat him as a boy, and despise it. Mr William Wilson had sent me some papers to consider. It was an irksome task in my present state. I however did it, and called on him for a little this forenoon. I had a serious conversation with Grange, walking backwards and forwards in the court of the Royal Bank.[155] He said he was really puzzled. He did not imagine the boy would be satisfied by my letter, otherwise he would make a foolish figure after writing to me with so much keenness. He

155 The Royal Bank was situated in what had come to be known as New Bank Close on account of the Bank having moved there in about 1750 (Harris, p. 548, s.v. "St Monan's Wynd"). The close was off the south side of the High Street to the east of Parliament Close.

was for acquainting his father or uncle of the affair, before fighting, lest they might have reflections against me as going to extremities with a minor without their knowledge. Yet he had some suspicion that they already knew of it.

The smallpox being frequent, and little Effie unfit for inoculation, her nurse and she went this day to Prestonfield, where they were kindly received.

SUNDAY 9 OCTOBER. I got up tolerably well, and called on Grange, who now thought there would be no more of the quarrel. I was at the New Church and heard Mr Walker and Mr Stuart of Cramond,[156] who preached on a gloomy subject: death being without any order. The text, I think, was in Job.[157]

TUESDAY 11 OCTOBER. No answer had come to my letter; so I concluded that it was satisfactory. At breakfast my wife suggested very well that I was not bound to answer the young man. That if an injury had been done to his sister or any female relation, or to an old superannuated father, he might step forth. But that in this case the father was my proper antagonist. This view of the case seemed quite just. Hay called, and was of that opinion; Grange also agreed. My wife had written to my cousin Claud, begging that he would come to town, as she had something that made her very uneasy to communicate. He came with a most friendly readiness, and she told him the story. He agreed with her; and then he came and called on me. I showed him all that had passed. He thought there was nothing in the "Royalist" that could be made the subject of a serious question, and that I had written a proper and spirited answer to the young man. He said to fight with a boy would be like fighting with a footman, as no honour could be had by it, in any event; and he was clear that I should hold the Justice-Clerk as the only person to whom I was bound to answer. It gave me much satisfaction to find Claud, who is both very sensible and abundantly resolute, agreeing with me. He and Charles Hay dined with us. Then my wife and I accompanied him in a coach to Leith, and saw him sail for Kinghorn. Grange drank tea with us when we came home. Sir George's family were all abroad this day. We supped by ourselves.

MONDAY 17 OCTOBER. Captain Preston gave out that he was not to leave Edinburgh till next morning, that he might shun a farewell parting with his parents, whom he had little chance of finding alive on his return from India; but he let me and his brother, etc., know that he was to go this afternoon. We rose soon after dinner, and went out before tea, as it were to return. We met at Mrs Brown's in the Exchange,[158] where was Dr Webster; and there we drank a

---

156 The Rev. Charles Stuart, whose eldest son, James Stuart of Dunearn, W.S., was to kill Boswell's eldest son, Sir Alexander, in a duel in 1822 (an account of which is to be found in Cockburn, pp. 367-374; and see Epilogue, p. 551).

157 "A land... of the shadow of death, without any order" (Job 10. 22).

158 The "Exchange" was the Royal Exchange on the north side of the High Street close to the eastern end of the Luckenbooths. This handsome building, work on the construction of which started in 1753 and which was one of the most obvious of the early material manifestations of the improvement in the economy of Scotland after the union with England in 1707, was designed by John Adam and was funded to a large extent by private subscriptions. Lord Auchinleck was one of the thirty-three Commissioners appointed to supervise the scheme. The building is now occupied as the main part of the City Chambers.

couple of magnum bonums of claret to the Captain's health and success. Webster sat still, and the rest of us saw the Captain to his chaise. He assured me that there would be no more of the disagreeable affair as to which he had engaged to stand by me. But I understood that he had mentioned it to his brother, Mr Preston,[159] who would willingly take his place. I spoke to Mr Preston, and he assured me that he would conduct the affair with prudence and honour, if anything more was necessary. Webster had whispered to him that he and I should return to Mrs Brown's. We did so, and we three drank two more pints very cordially.

We supped at Sir George's. I was called into another room after supper, and found my wife in a most miserable state, as she had notice that the Justice-Clerk's son was come to Paxton's,[160] and wanted to see me there. This appeared to be a determined purpose of a duel, and she was quite overcome with fear. Mr Preston was called out and bid her be easy; advised that no notice should be taken of the thing tonight; and that, when the young man's letter came in the morning, we should send for Mr Preston, and he would settle matters properly. We went home and gave orders not to open the door, though there should be a knock. After we were in bed, somebody knocked several times, but no answer was made. I felt myself somewhat uneasy, but sufficiently determined. No doubt the claret which I had taken was of use to me.

TUESDAY 18 OCTOBER. I slept pretty well till near six. My wife never shut her eye the whole night. At six she rose and called for Grange, that he might come down to me immediately; and also for Mr Preston, that he might be in the house when the message came. Grange was with me before I got up, and spoke calmly to me as a true friend, but was very anxious. Mr Preston came between seven and eight. Grange went away and was to return between nine and ten. A note from the young man came before eight, insisting to see me before nine, either at Paxton's or my own house; and mentioning that it would be proper I should have a friend with me. My wife was like one in a kind of delirium. Mr Preston made her give us some tea, and told her that he would go and talk with the young man. I sent a card by him with my compliments, and that my friend Mr Preston would communicate my sentiments. As he went away I took him by the hand, and told him I trusted that he would say nothing inconsistent with my honour. He promised he would not. That he would say he thought my letter was a sufficient satisfaction; but, if anything farther was necessary, I was ready to answer my Lord Justice-Clerk. That, if he could not convince the young man himself, he would endeavour to get him to agree that the advice of his uncle, Mr Peter Miller, Mr Preston's very good friend, should be taken. After Mr Preston was gone, Grange came; and he and I walked backwards and forwards in my dining-room.

A long time passed without any appearance. At last between ten and eleven a

---

159 Major Patrick Preston (died 1776), Captain Preston's eldest brother (*Ominous Years*, Chart V, p. 378). He was now retired from the army and was no longer addressed by his military title (*ibid.*, p. 4).
160 James Paxton's "New Inn" in the Grassmarket.

servant of the Justice-Clerk's came running into the court, and went to the house of Mr Peter Miller, who lived in the same stair with me; and in a little he went back, followed by Mr Peter Miller. This made me think all was well. Grange followed, and saw them go to the Grassmarket. He was obliged to go as far as Linlithgow this day, but from kind anxiety kept his chaise waiting till he should know what was done. By and by Mr Preston and Mr Peter Miller came down the court arm in arm. Mr Preston told me when he came in that he had gone to the bottom of the matter, and it was now as we could wish. I informed Grange, who waited in the next room; and he went to his chaise in peace. My wife was, as she herself said, like one who had been upon the rack, so that she felt a most pleasing relief. Mr Preston told me that he was much pleased with the young man, and with his friend whom he had with him, Principal Robertson's son.[161] That he had some difficulty to convince young Miller, or to get him to agree to send for his uncle; but when his uncle came and was of the same opinion with Mr Preston, things went smoothly. That the young man expressed great concern on being told that his letter had fallen into my wife's hands. Mr Preston then went down and brought up Mr Peter Miller, and we three talked over the matter. Mr Peter Miller acquitted himself with great good sense, proper spirit, and an uncommon ease and propriety of expression. He said that I was in a disagreeable situation; for in whatever way this matter might end, his nephew would have the world on his side. That had his advice been taken by either party, he would have been against the writing of his nephew's letter, and my answer. But as matters stood it was of consequence to me to avoid an affair with this young man. That he thought I had said what was sufficient; and that at any rate to be sure the Justice-Clerk was the only person whom I was bound to answer. "At the same time," said he, "my nephew, though not yet known in the world, is, I assure you, an uncommon young man. He is a thinking, metaphysical fellow, and he will argue himself into a persuasion that he is in the right; and though upon this occasion he has nothing to say, he may keep a resentment in his mind, and some years after this easily contrive to make a quarrel with you, in which he shall be a principal. It were therefore to be wished that this affair were effectually settled, that no bad blood may remain." He told me that so far from there being any reason for blaming the Justice-Clerk for being severe against John Reid, the fact was that Lord Rochford sent the respite to him with a power to deliver it or put it in the fire as he should judge proper. That the Justice-Clerk would not take upon him such an exercise of the royal prerogative, but delivered the respite; and though he sent up his own opinion, sent also up a full copy of the trial that it might be judged of by the King in Council. Mr Peter Miller said he imagined that when I knew this, I would wish to tell Lord Justice-Clerk that I was sorry any paper of mine had been understood to be injurious to his character. I said I would tell him so.

It was then agreed that Mr Peter Miller with his nephew should meet Mr

161 Probably Principal Robertson's eldest son, William Robertson, who was to be admitted advocate on 21 January 1775 and would be appointed a Lord of Session as Lord Robertson on 14 November 1805.

Preston and me in half an hour at Mrs Brown's in the Exchange. Mr Preston and I called at the Custom House[162] and told Commissioner Cochrane what had passed, and he was quite satisfied. We then went to Mrs Brown's; and in a little appeared the two Millers. The young man and I met and took each other by the hand as easily as at any meeting. He seemed to be quite calm and mild and genteel, with spirited ideas of honour and the regard he owed to his father's character, but not clearly knowing how he should proceed. I told him that I had given him more satisfaction than I should have done in a common case, because I was pleased with the feelings which he showed; that he could not expect, and I was sure would not wish, that I should make any improper concessions. I had assured him he was mistaken. He declared that he was satisfied. I said I hoped this was not merely a ceremonious adjusting of the affair, but that he was quite satisfied and that nothing would lurk behind. He said nothing should. I told him that his father was certainly the person whom I was bound to answer. That I would wait on him and assure him of my regret that anything I had written had been misunderstood to mean an attack upon him, and I was sure he would be satisfied. I asked the young man as a favour that this affair might not be mentioned; for, though I had owned to him as a gentleman that I had written the "Royalist", I did not choose it should be known. He said he would not speak of it. We parted in perfect good terms. Thus did my friend Preston relieve me from a very disagreeable dilemma. He dined with my wife and me comfortably; and he and I just drank a pint bottle of claret. We all drank tea and supped at Sir George's.

WEDNESDAY 19 OCTOBER. Mr Preston went home to Valleyfield. I dined at home with my wife. After so many days of warm living and agitation I felt a sort of depression. This forenoon I called on Charles Hay, and told him how the disagreeable affair was happily settled. We supped at Sir George's.

FRIDAY 28 OCTOBER. My wife and I dined at Prestonfield and saw Effie, who was a fine thriving child.

I had called in the forenoon on David Hume to pay him half an year's rent of his house.[162a] He told me he thought I should write the history of the Union, which might be a neat popular piece of history. That when Wedderburn was a young man, and wished to be known, he asked Mr Hume to suggest a subject of history for him to write; and he suggested the Union. That Wedderburn made himself known in another line and so did not pursue the plan.[163] He said I would

---

162 The new Custom House, which from 1761 was situated on the upper floors of the northern part of the Royal Exchange (for which, see p. 168, n. 158).

162a Although Boswell no longer occupied Hume's old flat in James's Court and had sub-let it, he was still Hume's tenant and therefore remained obliged to pay the rent.

163 Alexander Wedderburn (1733-1805), who was admitted advocate in 1754. He resigned from the Scottish bar in 1757 and is said to have done so in dramatic fashion on account of an incident in a case in which he was opposed to Alexander Lockhart. "Stung by a depreciatory remark made by Lockhart, the young advocate replied so intemperately that he was rebuked by the presiding judge, Lord President Craigie [d. 10 March 1760]. The other judges were of opinion that Wedderburn should retract and apologise; but instead of doing so, he took off his advocate's gown, laid it on the bar, and, declaring that he would wear it no more, he left the court, never again to enter it. That night he set out for London, determined to make his way at the English bar" (DNB). He had great success in England, rising, as Lord Loughborough, to Lord Chief Justice of the Court of Common Pleas in 1780 and Lord Chancellor in 1793. He was later created first Earl of Rosslyn.

find materials in the Advocates' Library. That I might with great justice to my countrymen please the English by my account of our advantages by the Union. That we had made many attempts. But when the English inclined to it, then our Jacobites opposed it. That we never gained one battle but at Bannockburn; and as we did so ill even in rude feudal times, we could not have made any defence long in the present state of the art of war. That our great improvements are much owing to the Union. That for these several years there must have been a famine in Scotland if we had not had the liberty of importing corn, which the English could have prevented. I felt strongly my own ignorance, but said I should think of it. Sir Alexander Dick has more than once recommended to me this very plan. Mr Hume said he had heard the Balcarres family had some papers which would throw light on the Union.

I wandered in the streets at night, out as far as the Meadow by the Chapel of Ease;[164] an unlucky practice.[165] My brother John had been a week in town without letting me know. I heard of it by chance, and sent him a note asking him to sup with us tonight. I found him when I came home. He was in the same formal silent state as usual. It was vexing to see my *heir male*. But I hoped for a son, and considered that at any rate he was but an individual.[166]

The following day, Boswell, who had been chosen to be the delegate from the burgh of Culross to vote at the election of the Member of Parliament for the group of burghs in the Stirling district,[167] crossed the Forth and travelled to Valleyfield, the home of the Preston family. The election took place on 31 October at Dunfermline and the candidate supported by Boswell was Colonel Archibald Campbell (later Gen. Sir Archibald Campbell), of whom Boswell said that he found him to be "a man of admirable parts, a good deal like General Paoli". Boswell was afraid that at the election he would be required to take "the Formula", a statutory declaration which was normally required to be taken by each person voting at an election. The purpose of the Formula was to establish that the person wishing to vote was not a Roman Catholic by requiring him to declare that he "abhorred" certain papal doctrines. Boswell's anxiety arose from the fact that he still had sympathies towards Roman Catholicism and could thus not give the declaration in honesty; and yet if he did not do so he was afraid that he would never be able to vote again or stand for Parliament, and if the fact of his "having once embraced the Romish faith" were to be brought out this could irreparably harm his career.[168] However, to his great relief, the delegates were not required to take the Formula after all, and so Boswell, who was specially dressed for the occasion in his crimson and silver suit, proceeded to give his vote and felt "like a man relieved from hanging over a precipice by a slight rope". The outcome of the election was that Colonel Campbell secured control of three of the five burghs of the Stirling district, namely Culross, Dunfermline and Inverkeithing. At Dunfermline, a mob started to celebrate, and at night they broke windows which were not illuminated. As on the occasion in Edinburgh

164 Erected in 1757, "a plain genteel building" (Arnot, p. 161).
165 Boswell here adds a private symbol, "*bs*", which is used nowhere else in the Journals (*Ominous Years*, p. 30, n. 8). The meaning of the symbol is not known.
166 That is, he did not have any children who would inherit from him.
167 The constituency being the Stirling Burghs.
168 For Boswell's interest in Roman Catholicism, see Introduction, pp. 19-20.

when Boswell joined the mob in breaking unilluminated windows after the result of the appeal to the House of Lords in the Douglas Cause, Boswell indulged in some window-breaking himself. "I threw my glass at one [window]," he wrote, "and made it crash one pane of it."

Boswell departed for Edinburgh on 4 November, together with Colonel Campbell.

FRIDAY 4 NOVEMBER. Colonel Campbell and I set out in his chaise about eight. I was not much indisposed. We breakfasted at the North Ferry, stopped at Queensferry, and drank a glass at Bailie Buncle's; drove to town, and came out of our chaise at the Exchange, that all who were at the Cross might see us after our victory. I went home and saw my wife and Veronica, then dined with the Colonel at his lodgings, and, as he was to be busy, just drank half a bottle of port; then sallied forth between four and five with an avidity for drinking from the habit of some days before. I went to Fortune's; found nobody in the house but Captain James Gordon of Ellon. He and I drank five bottles of claret and were most profound politicians. He pressed me to take another; but my stomach was against it. I walked off very gravely though much intoxicated. Ranged through the streets till, having run hard down the Advocate's Close, which is very steep, I found myself on a sudden bouncing down an almost perpendicular stone stair.[169] I could not stop, but when I came to the bottom of it, fell with a good deal of violence, which sobered me much. It was amazing that I was not killed or very much hurt; I only bruised my right heel severely. I supped at Sir George's. My wife was there, and George Webster.

SATURDAY 5 NOVEMBER. Fortune's wine was excellent, for I was neither sick nor uneasy. The sacrament was to be administered next day in this city. I had some doubt whether I should go to it, as I had been so riotous of late. But, considering that it was truly no more than a public declaration of my faith in the Christian religion, and that there was no opportunity for solemn devotion in a Presbyterian kirk, I resolved to go. Charles Hay called, and I kept him to an early dinner. At three my wife and I went to the New Church. I drank tea at Sir George's.

SUNDAY 6 NOVEMBER. Was at New Church forenoon and afternoon. Was much displeased with the Presbyterian method. My attendance was just a piece of decent attention to Christianity in the form established in my native country. I however thought that perhaps I was to blame in not regularly attending public worship in a form of which I approved, especially as there was now a fine Episcopal chapel in Edinburgh. But then I reflected that my doing so would offend my father. Mr Wellwood drank tea with us. *[170]

MONDAY 7 NOVEMBER. Not thinking it necessary to attend sermon today, I stayed at home and wrote an opinion on a case before the Synod of Lothian and Tweeddale on which James Gilkie[171] consulted me. It was Helen Amos against

169 Advocate's Close takes its name from Sir James Stewart of Goodtrees, who was Lord Advocate from 1692 to 1709 and again from 1711 to 1713 (Harris, p. 53).
170 A symbol probably indicating conjugal relations between Boswell and his wife (*Ominous Years*, p. 5, n. 2).
171 A "writer" with a somewhat dubious reputation.

Robert Hope; and the question was in what circumstances the oath of purgation could be put.[172]

TUESDAY 8 NOVEMBER. Mr Lawrie was now with me, having come to town above a week before. I this day studied with great attention Sir John Hall's cause. I dined with my wife at Dr Grant's. In the evening I attended the Synod [of Lothian and Tweeddale] and heard Gilkie plead the cause of Hope, as I would not appear in an inferior kirk court. I was asked to sup at Walker's with the Synod, which I did. There were ten ministers and George Webster and I. Dr Webster took the lead. I was disgusted with their coarse merriment, which frequently seemed to me to be profane, as it turned on absurd passages in sermons. Webster kept so many sitting till towards two in the morning. I was against sitting, but could not refuse Webster.

WEDNESDAY 9 NOVEMBER. I was very ill after my Synod riot, and could not get up till about two. I really suffered severely. I was easier in the afternoon. My wife very justly said that it was inexcusable to be riotous in such low company. I have often determined to be strictly sober, and have often fixed an era for the commencement of my proper conduct. I have a curious inclination to have an era for almost everything. The period of my being strictly sober has been advanced from one time to another. I this day thought I should have it to say that I had not been drunk since I supped with the Synod of Lothian and Tweeddale in November 1774.

THURSDAY 10 NOVEMBER. I was very indolent, and my heel was painful; so I sent Mr Lawrie to make my apology at St John's Lodge, and completed my study of Sir John Hall's cause, to whom I had written making an apology for delay and telling him that when he pleased I should be ready to deliver him my opinion.

FRIDAY 11 NOVEMBER. I breakfasted at Lady Colville's. My father arrived in the afternoon. My wife and I called in the evening. He was cold as usual, but I liked to contemplate his uniform steady character in general, though in politics he had been misled by the President. He talked much of his politics. I thought it was to divert a consciousness that he was wrong.

SATURDAY 12 NOVEMBER. I called at my father's before he went to the Parliament House, and took Veronica to see him. There was no quorum of the Lords today. The session did not promise well. The crop appeared thin. I called on my brother John yesterday, and engaged him to dine with me today. He had never called of his own accord. I had Dr Boswell with him. The contrast between them was striking, yet both had the same constitution differently modified. Sir John Hall supped with us, and I gave him my opinion in writing on his cause.

172 The "oath of purgation" was "the affirmation on oath of his innocence by the accused in a spiritual court, confirmed by the oaths of several of his peers. The General Assembly had enacted in 1707 that the oath was to be administered only in cases where there was a strong presumption of guilt" (*Ominous Years*, p. 371).

SUNDAY 13 NOVEMBER. Having taken a dose of lenitive electuary to cool me after my riotous engagements, I was at home all day.

TUESDAY 15 NOVEMBER. After being in the Parliament House, Maclaurin and I went and attended awhile at the election of the peers of Scotland.[173] I drank tea at Balmuto's.

WEDNESDAY 16 NOVEMBER. The Earl of Loudoun,[174] John Hunter, Writer to the Signet (his agent),[175] Lady Dundonald and Lady Betty Cochrane, the Hon. A. Gordon and Lady Dumfries,[176] Colonel Stopford and Captain Skeffington of the 66th supped with us. This was the first time that Lord Loudoun was in my house. I liked to be well with one of the nobles of the county of Ayr. But I must own that I was somewhat cooled towards the peers when, upon talking to Lord Loudoun of the sheriffship of our county yesterday, he told me that he was not at liberty to speak on the subject, as he believed measures were already taken about it, and from his conversation I guessed that he was engaged for one of whom I thought meanly.[177] I also perceived that his Lordship had not that dignity of spirit which I should have wished, but was ready to join with Sir Adam Fergusson if he saw it for his interest, though Sir Adam had been the avowed opposer of the great families of the county. My scheme of taking the sheriffship and letting Mr Duff[178] retain the salary for life, was by no means fixed in my mind. It would secure me an office somewhat respectable, and be a step to the bench. But then it would be very laborious, and engage me too intimately in my own county, which I would not like; and besides Mr Duff might live many years, during which my having all the trouble for nothing would be irksome. And after all, my warm wish was to be employed in London. And I pleased myself with keeping loose from all engagements in Scotland, that I might more easily take the great English road. I drank rather too much tonight.

THURSDAY 17 NOVEMBER. On Tuesday last I sent a card to Lord Justice-Clerk begging to know when I might have the honour of waiting on him. He fixed

173 At an election the Scottish Peers were required to elect sixteen of their number to sit as representatives of the Scottish peerage in the House of Lords. The elections of the representatives took place at the Palace of Holyroodhouse.
174 John Campbell (1705-1782), 4th Earl of Loudoun, served as adjutant-general to Sir John Cope during the Jacobite rebellion of 1745 and was appointed Commander-in-Chief of the British forces in America in 1756, but "owing to popular clamour at home on account of his dilatoriness in taking the field against the enemy, he was recalled, and sent to Portugal as second in command under Lord Tyrawley to assist the Portuguese against Spain. He was promoted to be lieutenant-general 22 May 1758, general and colonel of the Scots Guards 30 April 1770, and Governor of Edinburgh Castle" (*Scots Peerage*, Vol. 5, p. 509).
175 John Hunter (1746-1823), W.S. (admitted 26 June 1769).
176 Alexander Gordon's wife (Anne (née Duff), widow of William, 4th Earl of Dumfries and Stair).
177 This is almost certainly a reference to William Wallace, Professor of Scots Law at Edinburgh University (for whom, see the entry for 23 July 1769 and footnote), who was appointed Sheriff-Depute of Ayrshire on 9 June 1775. Although Boswell had formerly had some respect for Wallace, he had now taken a different view (as is apparent from the entry for 17 January 1775).
178 William Duff of Crombie, advocate (admitted 8 December 1727), Sheriff-Depute of Ayrshire 1747-75, died 8 January 1781.

between six and seven. I went accordingly.[179] He was very polite; that is to say, civil and obliging and even kind. I told him all the matter of my paper in *The London Chronicle* which had occasioned the correspondence between me and his son; that I considered his Lordship as my proper party and hoped he was satisfied with my explanation. He declared he was; that he was glad I was come to put an end to a very disagreeable affair; that he read the paper at Aberdeen, considered it as calculated for the meridian of London and thrown in *valeat quantum valere potest*;[180] that he should have taken no notice of it, and would have prevented his son had he known. But his son never mentioned it to him, supped with him on Sunday evening, when there was a good deal of company, and was quite cheerful. But in the middle of the night carried off horses and a servant, and in the morning my Lord had a letter from him from which it appeared he was gone about some affair of honour, but to what place or against whom no information was given; and my Lord remained above two days in the greatest anxiety. His Lordship, after declaring that he was satisfied that I did not mean what his son had imagined, said that he was conscious he did his duty to the best of his abilities, which satisfied his own mind; but he should be sorry that a prejudice was entertained against him, especially by me; that it [was] unnatural to be attacked by me, as our families had lived in the greatest friendship, he might say, for ages; at least for generations. (Here I had some difficulty to refrain from being at him, knowing that his grandfather, a surgeon in Kilmarnock, was the first of *his* family. However, I let him go on, as he spoke very well in the main.) He said that, after making out his report on the case of John Reid, he could not assemble all the judges, being in the country, but he knew all their opinions. He however rode over to one for whom he had a great respect, Lord Auchinleck, and showed it to him, and he entirely approved of it. He then said he would give me an advice as a father, not to go beyond the line of my profession for any client; that he imputed his success in life much to his adhering to that rule. That he had often wondered that I did not think more of myself. That a young fellow of no solid foundation in learning or connexions might make a splash in life to distinguish himself and perhaps by a kind of chance to get forward. But a man of my rank and fortune and standing as a lawyer had a higher character to support. He said the less I wrote in newspapers the better, as my being known to do it gave people an opportunity of ascribing to me every abusive thing that appeared.

Upon the whole this was a good interview, and I was really pleased with the Justice-Clerk's warmth of heart and the justice of his reasoning. I am sensible that my keenness of temper, and a vanity to be distinguished *for the day*, make me too often *splash* in life, as he well expressed it. I am resolved to restrain myself and attend more to decorum. I thought that I would not court the Justice-Clerk, with whom I had somehow never been well since the decision of the Douglas Cause; but, if it could easily happen, I should be glad to be on a good footing with him.

179 The Lord Justice-Clerk, Thomas Miller of Barskimming, resided in Brown Square.
180 "For whatever value it might have."

This day, though I had not drank to intoxication last night, I had a severe headache. Lieutenant Graham of the Scots Dutch, and Mackenzie of Dolphinton[181] and his brother[182]—with the two latter I was to consult on a cause of poor Monkland's[183]—drank tea, and then we sat a long time on business. I felt a kind of wonder in observing them pay much deference to my opinion. Young Robert Syme came and gave me my first guinea this session.

SATURDAY 26 NOVEMBER. Claud came to me to read over long papers in a cause in which we were engaged together. He dined with us. At six I went to Charles Hay's, where Maclaurin and I had an appointment to play at whist. William Aytoun was the fourth man. I felt all the former symptoms of gaming which have at times fevered me: anxiety, keenness, etc., etc. I lost about two guineas. We supped and drank but a little. When I came home, I of my own accord gave my word of honour to my wife that I would never play at whist for more than a shilling the game and two shillings the rubber.

SUNDAY 27 NOVEMBER. Was at New Church all day. Dr Blair forenoon; Mr Walker afternoon. At my father's between sermons; Dr Webster there. Evening spent at home, not very profitably; a little of the Bible read. The weather, frost and snow. ✱

WEDNESDAY 30 NOVEMBER. Waked in sad disorder. Struggled up between nine and ten. Saw Mr and Mrs Campbell.[184] Dr Monro and Mr Wood agreed that Mr Campbell's lip should be cut a second time to remove a hard swelling which might prove cancerous. The idea of that distemper was gloomy. In the afternoon, having done all that I had to do in the Court of Session in the forenoon very tolerably, I officiated as Master of St John's Lodge at the procession and feast on St Andrew's day. I was calmly cheerful; quite well.

SATURDAY 3 DECEMBER. Dined at Fortune's with the *Stoic Club*, a society begun by Foote.[185] I had promised at Lady Colville's to Matthew Henderson to be there; and though I had not much inclination to go, I did not choose to break an appointment, and I thought it not amiss to see this club for once. It was just a dinner with Lord Kellie and the other frequenters of Fortune's. Nothing particular. I drank one bottle and came home to tea.

SUNDAY 4 DECEMBER. Was at the New Church in the forenoon;—— preached. Between sermons Dr Boswell and Mr Wood came to have Treesbank's lip cut. Poor man, he looked like one under sentence of death. I was much affected with the idea of the painful operation, which made me think drearily

---

181 John Mackenzie of Dolphinton.
182 John Mackenzie's younger brother, Andrew Mackenzie, who was to be admitted W.S. on 3 July 1778 and died on 10 September 1793.
183 This appears to be a reference to David Hamilton of Monkland, one of the macers at the Court of Session, who "had a constant hoarseness, so that he could scarcely be heard when he called the causes and the lawyers, and was indeed as unfit for a crier of court as a man could be" (*Boswelliana* (ed. Rogers), p. 296).
184 James Campbell of Treesbank (Lord Auchinleck's cousin) and his second wife, Mary Montgomerie (sister of Mrs Boswell): *Ominous Years*, p. 11, n. 1.
185 Samuel Foote, the famous actor and dramatist.

of the various terrible distempers to which man is liable. I could not be present at the operation. It was soon over. Dr Boswell dined, and we sat at home in the afternoon.

THURSDAY 8 DECEMBER. Lady Dundonald having lost her cause before both Lord Hailes and Lord Alva on the bills, I wished to dissuade her from carrying it farther. With that view, I went and dined at Belleville and had Mr George Cooper, her agent,[186] to meet me there. But I found her resolved to go on. The Earl set two bottles of port at once upon the table after dinner, and insisted that Cooper and I should drink them. I was mellow with my bottle. I drank tea. At seven I attended a consultation at Macqueen's on Colonel Campbell's politics. There was now a pretty deep snow lying.

FRIDAY 9 DECEMBER. My poor brother John was now seized with a return of delirium so as to be confined in his room at Mr [Alexander] Weir the painter's.[187] I called this day, but did not go into his room.

SUNDAY 11 DECEMBER. Was at New Church forenoon. Dr Blair preached. Dr Boswell and Mr Macredie dined with us, and we sat at home in the afternoon. It was proposed to send my brother John to the house of one Campbell at Inveresk, who takes in disordered people. Mr Wood was against this, as he heard that Campbell was harsh; but he told me that I need not try to oppose it, for my father was resolved, his wife being clear for it. Wood seemed to think the plan by no means consistent with a proper concern for a relation.

Between five and six I went to Mr Weir's. John was somewhat calmer. The maid told him his brother was there and wanted to see him. He said he would be glad to see me. Upon which I went up to his room, accompanied by Mr Weir, an apprentice of Mr Weir's, and Alexander Macduff, a Guard soldier who was there as a keeper. John had on his nightgown and nightcap with a hat above it, and he waved a poker in his hand, singing some strange articulate sounds like Portuguese or some foreign language to the tune of *Nancy Dawson*, and ending always with "Damn my heart!" He cried, "Come on", and uttered wild sounds. I was at first seized with a kind of tremor. But Macduff and the apprentice having taken the poker from him, and removed the shovel and tongs, I ventured to go near him. He had then taken up his cane, but Macduff and I got it from him with little difficulty. He had taken a liking for Mr Lawrie, who had been with him several times. I got him set down by the fireside, and, when I asked him if Mr Lawrie had been with him, he answered very distinctly that he had been with him yesterday. He had sent for him. Poor man! he was much extenuated, and being now calm, and holding my hand cordially, I felt a tender affection for him. Indeed he was more agreeable than when better in his judgement but sour in his temper. We carried him downstairs to a room more convenient for him. I then took all his keys and locked up everything that belonged to him. It was remarkable to see the great exactness in which he had all his things. I

186 George Cooper (d. 28 March 1777), W.S. (admitted 25 June 1770).
187 Alexander Weir resided at the head of Todrick's Wynd (off the south side of the High Street).

continued with him awhile in his new apartment, but he would not or could not speak to me. It was a curious sensation when I saw my brother, with whom I had been brought up, in such a state. Madness of every degree is inexplicable. I could not conceive *how* he did not talk as usual. I reflected with deep seriousness on the melancholy in our family, and how I myself had been afflicted with it.

I came to my father's, and being much affected spoke against sending John to Musselburgh. My father seemed to have no other concern than to be free of trouble by him, and of a kind of *reproach*, as he called it, from having a relation in such a state. It was resolved that Commissioner Cochrane's opinion should be taken next morning.

MONDAY 12 DECEMBER. The Commissioner agreed with me that it was better to keep John at Mr Weir's till we should see how he was, and if he did not grow soon well, the best thing to be done was to send him to Newcastle, where he was formerly well taken care of in a regular house kept by Dr Hall. And so it was fixed. I had a load of papers to write, yet was listless. I however was obliged to move on, though uneasily. In the evening I went to the Justiciary Court and heard Lord Advocate and Mr Wight[188] charge the jury in the trial of Downie for murder. I could not help feeling a great superiority when I reflected on my own appearances in that court; and it was painful to one who wishes to think highly of human nature to see Lord Advocate on this occasion making every allowance, nay every supposition, in favour of the panel, because he had been impressed with a notion that what he had done was not murder—when in the case of a poor thief, I have seen him so desirous to urge every circumstance against him.

WEDNESDAY 14 DECEMBER. Amidst my throng of business, I could not resist an invitation to dine with Colonel Stopford at the mess kept by him, Captain Skeffington, and Lieutenant Vowel. The other guests were Sir William Erskine of Torrie, Captain Schaw, and Captain Gunning, brother to the Duchess of Argyll. We were very jolly. But I observed they talked mostly of military matters and I of law cases. The mess was at Mrs Brown's in the Exchange. At seven I came home to tea and found Claud, and then went to a ball for young ladies at Madame Marcoucci's given by Miss Schaw, the Captain's daughter. There was a great deal of company at it. I felt myself quite easy, and was very pleasingly amused.

THURSDAY 15 DECEMBER. This day Crosbie told me that he and Maclaurin, etc., had dined the day before at Lord Monboddo's along with Mr Bruce, the great traveller. I was somewhat hurt that Monboddo had not asked me, too; and I was also somewhat hurt at being told that Bruce was displeased with my mentioning in *The London Magazine* that it had been said he was "Nec visu facilis nec dictu affabilis ulli."[189] I had made an apology for his appearing in that style, so he had no reason to be displeased with me. But I could see plainly that he did not like me; probably because I had given the public a good dish of his travels,

188 Alexander Wight, advocate (admitted 6 March 1754), Solicitor-General 1783-4, died 1793.
189 "'Forbidding in appearance, in speech to be accosted by no one' (*Aeneid*, III. 621, describing Polyphemus, the Cyclops)" (*Ominous Years*, p. 45, n. 6).

better dressed than he could give himself. I took[190] myself, and considered it was below me to mind whether I was agreeable to him or not. No man can be agreeable to all kinds of people. And surely I am agreeable to as many as I could well expect. Bruce is a rough-minded man, and has not such principles as that one would court him. I had seen him as a curiosity and extracted from him a good essay for *The London Magazine*; and there was enough.

Sir William and Lady Forbes, Mr Nairne, and Colonel Webster dined with us. After the ladies went away, we got into a conversation on human liberty and GOD's prescience. Sir William and Mr Nairne would not give up the latter, yet maintained the former; which I cannot help thinking an absolute contradiction; for if it is *certainly foreknown* that I am to be at the play tomorrow, then it is certain I am to be there; and if it is *certain* I am to be there, then I cannot have a liberty either to be there or not. This is the subject which most of all has perplexed and distressed me at different periods of my life. Montesquieu in one of his *Lettres Persanes* made it clear to me in 1769, when I was with my friend Temple at Mamhead. But to meditate on it makes me melancholy. Lady Colville and Lady Anne Erskine drank tea with us. I was quite sober today. But the abstruse question saddened me.

FRIDAY 16 DECEMBER. Continued dull, but was obliged to write a representation,[191] which did me good, as it kept me from thinking on myself.

MONDAY 19 DECEMBER. Was roused at night by seeing Mr Johnson's *Journey to the Hebrides* advertised.

TUESDAY 20 DECEMBER. I drank tea with Crosbie and talked over the case of McGraugh, for whom he had undertaken to write answers to a reclaiming petition for the Procurator-Fiscal, and had now almost finished it. I have always the same ideas when I drink tea with Crosbie: learning, antiquities of our courts, etc. While I sat with him, I could not believe that he was a mere *fatal* or *foreknown* machine. Yet I was uneasy because it *might* be so.

WEDNESDAY 21 DECEMBER. The ordinary course of business went on. I made a resolution that I would not dine abroad, except on some particular occasion, while Treesbank was with me. He was recovering pretty well; and I entertained him with accounts of the causes determined in the Court of Session. This forenoon I met with D. Boswell at Leith in P. Williamson's Coffee-house, lent him three guineas, and drank a dram.[192]

---

190 That is, checked.

191 A court writ craving a Lord Ordinary to review his own interlocutor (i.e., judgment).

192 "David Boswell, whom Boswell sometimes calls 'Craigston', though his grandfather had sold that property, was [an] impoverished dancing-master at Leith whom Lord Auchinleck was determined to exclude from his entail. Boswell was forced to meet him at public houses because Mrs Boswell refused to have him in her home" (*Ominous Years*, p. 47, n. 6). The editors of *Ominous Years* indicate, at p. 427, that the coffee-house at which Boswell met David Boswell on this occasion was in Leith; but it may in fact be that this was the famous coffee-house kept by Peter Williamson in the Parliament Close next to the New Tolbooth. This establishment, in which "a great deal of small legal business" was transacted, "served also as a sort of vestry to the Tolbooth Church" (Chambers, pp. 126-7). The words "D. Boswell at Leith" may simply be a reference to David Boswell's name and place of residence, for Boswell regularly referred to David Boswell as "David Boswell at Leith" (see *Ominous Years*, p. 363, and Journal, 8 April 1780). Peter Williamson established a penny-post in Edinburgh and printed the first Edinburgh street directory.

FRIDAY 23 DECEMBER. I was late in the Court of Session hearing the Lords give judgement in a cause, Shaw against Bean, interesting in some degree, as character was concerned, and as it respected a charge of defamation for expressions thrown out in a paper before the sheriff; so that it respected the *liberty of the bar*, as some of the Lords said, practitioners in inferior courts being entitled to the same liberty with practitioners in the Court of Session. While the Lords were giving their opinions, and a crowd attended with much curiosity, I was wondering if all the particulars of this cause and its determination were predetermined.

SATURDAY 24 DECEMBER. Was, after the House rose for the Christmas recess, at the burial of old Drummond the bookseller. Being specially invited to eat venison at Colonel Stopford's mess, I found him, Captain Skeffington, and Mr Vowel and nobody else. I don't know how it was, but the Colonel got into the humour of drinking, which was very extraordinary for him; and we drank a great quantity of port. We sat till near ten. I was very drunk, roved in the street, and went and stayed above an hour with two whores at their lodging in a narrow dirty stair in the Bow. Luckily I had seen enough to prevent me from running any risk with them. But I might certainly by a little degree more of intoxication have done what might have got me a distemper which might have been very fatal. I found my way home about twelve. I had fallen and rubbed some of the skin and flesh off the knuckle of the middle finger of my left hand.

SUNDAY 25 DECEMBER. Lay in bed all forenoon, very ill and very much vexed at reflecting on my depraved wandering last night. I most firmly resolved for the future to be sober and never to come home at night but in a chair. Grange dined with us according to annual custom on Christmas-day, and in the afternoon he and I went to the New English Chapel.[193] It was striking to see so grand a place of worship in Edinburgh. But I cannot say that I was in so good a frame as I could have wished to be in on Christmas-day.

MONDAY 26 DECEMBER. It was now fixed that my brother John should set out next morning for Newcastle under the care of Macduff, the Guard soldier, and Thomas Edmondson, my old servant. I had called for him since I last mentioned it in my journal. This evening I went down and had Mr Lawrie with me, and put up and inventoried what things were to go with him and put the rest in his trunks, which were to be brought up to stand in my house. Poor man!

193 The New English Chapel, also known as the "Cowgate chapel" and the "Episcopal chapel", was situated in the Cowgate and had been constructed between 1771-4 to replace the earlier episcopal chapels (those in Skinner's Close and Carrubber's Close and Baron Smith's chapel in Blackfriars Wynd) which were "mean, inconvenient apartments, too small for their congregations" (Arnot, p. 164). The chapel was "a plain handsome building, neatly fitted up in the inside, somewhat in the form of the church of St Martin's in the Fields, London,... and ornamented with a neat spire of tolerable height" (*ibid.*, p. 165). The service at the chapel was celebrated according to all the rites of the Church of England. As Arnot commented in 1779, "This deserves to be considered as a mark of increasing moderation and liberality among the generality of the people. Not many years ago, that form of worship, in all its ceremonies, would not have been tolerated. The organ and the paintings would have been downright idolatry, and the chapel would have fallen a sacrifice to the fury of the mob" (*ibid.*, p. 166). The chapel, after being acquired by the Roman Catholics in 1856, became St Patrick's Church and was subsequently much altered.

He was quite calm tonight and in a sort of gentle stupor, for he could not speak to me.

TUESDAY 27 DECEMBER. John set out in the morning early. Mr Lawrie saw him into the chaise. I this day bought *Lettres Persanes*, and the letter on presci-ence made me as clear as ever. But indeed I am sensible that this difficult sub-ject affects me rather according to a kind of sentiment at the time than by rea-soning; for the very same arguments have quite different effects on different occasions. My father and Lady Auchinleck, Colonel Webster, Balbarton, and Lieutenant Graham dined with us, and drank tea. Treesbank for the first time came to the table. In the evening, it being St John the [Evangelist's] day, I was at St John's Lodge.

SATURDAY 31 DECEMBER. Having resolved to pay off every account that I owed, and begin with the year 1775 to deal in ready money, I had been busy in that way for some days. George Webster accompanied me this forenoon to Peter Ramsay's, where I paid Peter's account, and George and I got a dram of cherry brandy. I really love drams like a savage. I then called on Mr Isaac Grant[194] to talk of a paper that I was to draw for a client of his and mine, and he gave me a dram of most excellent gin. I said that of all human arts I valued distilling the most.

---

194 Isaac Grant, W.S. (admitted 1 July 1763), died 27 December 1794. "His tombstone in Greyfriars bears that 'in him the poor lost a friend, the rich, a cheerful facetious companion, and the world an honest man'" (*Register of the Society of Writers to Her Majesty's Signet*, p. 128).

1775

SUNDAY 1 JANUARY. Was at New Church in the forenoon; Mr Walker preached. Afternoon, heard Dr Webster preach on the awful cry of the angel in the Revelation that *Time shall be no more*. I drank tea by special appointment with worthy Sir William Forbes, to let him read my Hebrides journal to prepare him for Mr Johnson's book. He was much entertained, and I left him my three volumes, after reading him a great deal.

MONDAY 2 JANUARY. I was with Sir William Forbes at his counting-house in the forenoon, as he had obligingly agreed to show me his account-book, and put me on an accurate plan of management. I gave him a state of my affairs, and reckoning £300 a year from my father, and as much by the practice of the law, my income was £600. For the interest of my debts and other burthens we allowed £100. And the remaining £500 was regulated thus:

My wife to have £20 a month for the expense of the family, exclusive of wine but including servants' wages and children's clothes	240
My wife's clothes	60
House-rent £50 and wine £30	80
My own clothes and pocket-money	50
	£430

So that I should have £70 for contingencies, such as a London jaunt, and smaller expenses and charities. It was admirable to see what a proportion of Sir William's money went in charity, the last year upwards of £70. He said that he had been so much more prosperous than he had reason to expect that he thought giving about a tenth of his income in charity was a proper acknowledgement of gratitude to Providence. It gave me great satisfaction to see myself in prospect an accurate man, and my dear wife cheerfully resolved to help me.

TUESDAY 3 JANUARY. Miss Cuninghame, niece to Mr Trotter the confectioner, supped with us. She entertained me with that kind of intelligence and wit which goes on in an Edinburgh *sweetie-shop*. It was a variety to me. Life and light and cheerfulness are found in all places in different modes.

WEDNESDAY 4 JANUARY. Treesbank and Mrs Campbell left us. Mr Lawrie had gone home on Monday to his father's for a few days. I had therefore this day to write with my own hand answers for Mr Anderson of Inverness to be boxed next day.[1]

---

1 "That [the Lords] may have Time to consider weighty Cases maturely, they get them reduc'd into Writ by the Lawyers: And every Lord hath a Box standing upon a Table in the waiting Room of the Inner-house from Two till Four in the Afternoon, wherein all who have Papers to offer may put them by a Slit in the Cover. This, tho' a mighty Advantage to the Lieges, is… an incredible Fatigue to the Lords: Who, after toiling all Day in hearing Causes, are obliged to shut themselves up to peruse and consider a Multiplicity of Papers at Night; and thereby often to want the necessary Relaxation due to Nature, which visibly shortens their Days" (Forbes, p. x).

The agent's memorial[2] served for the greatest part of the paper. But I wrote eleven pages.[3]

MONDAY 9 JANUARY. Commissioner Cochrane carried me out with him in his chaise. He had called on me a few days before, and talked strongly about the differences between my father and me as to settling the estate. He said my father had entailed the old estate on heirs male as far as Claud, but there he stopped;[4] and that he had vested his own purchases in trustees, to be entailed upon the same series of heirs; but that if any of his heirs should call in question his entail, it should be a forfeiture of his own purchases, which should go past the heir challenging the entail, and his descendants. I was vexed to think that the family acquisitions should be separated, but I remained firm for the support of the male succession, as I considered that to be the only true representation of an ancient barony. I was under great temptations to quit my feudal resolution, for my father would make no immediate settlement on my wife and children, and my wife, who could not understand my feudal principles, upbraided me with want of affection. I was conscious that I had as warm an affection as any husband or father whatever, but I had the resolution of a Roman for the support of my family; and indeed I considered myself bound in honour and fidelity to our ancestor, who, though he had four daughters, gave the estate to his nephew and made it a male fief, that Thomas Boswell, who fell at Flodden Field, might be represented by one of his sons to the latest posterity.[5] At the same time, I suffered great anxiety of mind from the thought that *perhaps* I might die before my father, and leave my wife and children in a very poor situation. Mr Johnson had said that I should not be uneasy, for my wife and children had for them the probabilities of human life, and that was enough. I hoped that my father would not settle his own acquisitions past the family. But suppose he should, it was better to reject a considerable bribe to cut off so many of the sons of the family from a succession which might open to them. That, if they were excluded, the real family might come to an end, while many of its sons existed; and that, as the acquisitions of one man might be equalled by the acquisitions of another at some future period, it would be wrong to sacrifice so many men for a present addition of land. That the family had increased and diminished its possessions during the lives of different lairds, according as they were prudent or lavish; and that, while the old barony remained, the family was still preserved. All these considerations and the recollection of solemn oaths, one

2 That is, an agent's brief.
3 This was an action by Robert Anderson (a goldsmith in Inverness) against Miss Grizel Fraser in connection with a dispute over the ownership of, and the enjoyment of revenue from, a tenement (*Session Papers*, 74 08 06).
4 So as to avoid David Boswell, the dancing-master in Leith. As Boswell explained to Sir John Pringle on 24 March 1772, "my father had in the main the same notions with me and wished to entail his estate on the male line for many generations; but stopped at one of the branches of our family, who is a dancing-master, because his pride cannot bear it: without considering that it is a family's fault when their connexions fall low, and besides, that by the time the succession may open to them, the dancing-master's descendants may be greater than any of us."
5 For Thomas Boswell, see Introduction, p. 4.

in spring 1767, when I swore to my father that if the estate was fixed on heirs whatsoever I would cut my throat, and one in winter 1769, when, with a piece of the Old Castle in my hand, I knelt upon the ruins and swore that if any man had the estate in exclusion of the rightful heir this stone should swim in his heart's blood (I keep the stone)—these kept me as firm as the old rock itself.

TUESDAY 10 JANUARY. I called at my father's, willing to talk with him, but as usual felt myself chilled. I was restless today and went and dined at Dr Webster's because I could not sit at home. He and I and the Colonel, George, and Annie were very social. There is to me a double satisfaction in sociality with near relations. It is like knowing that wine is wholesome while we drink it.

WEDNESDAY 11 JANUARY. This was a very wet day. I went in the forenoon to the Advocates' Library, and in returning felt myself seized with a cold. Grange drank tea with us.

THURSDAY 12 JANUARY. My cold was heavy. I kept the house all day. I wrote a long letter to my brother David, told him my difficulties and my heroism for the family, and said that I trusted any heir male who should get the estate through my firmness would behave handsomely to my wife and children.

FRIDAY 13 JANUARY. I was engaged to dine with Mr George Wallace.[6] My cold was so ill that I sent him an apology. He wrote to me in such terms that I saw he would be much disappointed if I did not come. He is a worthy fellow, and I made a stretch for him. Old Professor Stevenson and Craig of Riccarton[7] and his brother were the men. They revived some particular ideas. There were two Miss Gunnings there. One of them was as fine a seraglio figure as I could wish to see. I passed my time cheerfully and came home early.

SUNDAY 15 JANUARY. Lay in bed almost the whole day; read the first volume of *Histoire des Révolutions de Corse, par l'Abbé de Germanes*, a new book. It entertained me to see a subject on which I myself had written well treated by a Frenchman. I read a little in Walton's *Lives*, and felt the same *unction* as formerly.

TUESDAY 17 JANUARY. At the anniversary meeting of the Faculty of Advocates I intended to make a motion that if the Collector of Decisions did not publish annually he should forfeit his office. I yesterday sent notice of my intention to Mr Wallace, the Collector.[8] He was very much offended, and told me he did not expect [it] from *me*. He spoke to some of our brethren, and they, from friendship to him, begged that it might be delayed. At the meeting I rose and said there seemed to be a necessity for some effectual proviso, and wished that some of my senior brethren would suggest one. The Dean said it well deserved consideration;

6 George Wallace resided in Scott's Close, off the south side of the Cowgate.
7 Robert Craig of Riccarton (1730-1823), advocate (admitted 12 February 1754), second son of James Craig of Riccarton (Professor of Civil Law at Edinburgh University), Judge of the Commissary Court 1775-91. His brother was Thomas, who was usually styled "the Laird". "The Laird and his brother were men of primitive habits. From some unaccountable aversion to matrimony, neither of them married; and they both resided in the same house" (Kay, Vol. II, p. 205).
8 William Wallace, the advocate and Professor of Scots Law at Edinburgh University.

but some of Wallace's friends got the matter slurred over at this time.[9] However, the alarm would, as I thought, probably produce dispatch, and, if it did not, I resolved to have a party prepared for a determined regulation next year. I did not go to Fortune's to the entertainment given by the Dean, as he was not able to attend himself. My wife and I supped at Sir George's.

WEDNESDAY 18 JANUARY. Sandy Murray spoke to me in a very friendly way in the House, and told me that I should check expressing my disapprobation of characters, as people were getting a notion that I was an ill-natured man, which he knew was not my character. That it was of consequence to me to have a general good-will, with the view of representing Ayrshire in Parliament. I took his admonition kind, and considered that I really did express myself against many people in strong terms; that I had made several enemies, and might add to the number till I should be thought by the *world* a malevolent being. That men must be taken as they are, and their faults must be overlooked. At least not keenly detected. Sir George and Lady and Miss and Mr Preston and Colonel Stopford dined with us, and drank tea. Then Mr Burnett, younger of Kemnay, called. He who had been in Prussian campaigns was an excellent companion for Mr Preston. While we were in the drawing-room, Mr Johnson's *Journey to the Western Islands of Scotland* came to me in thirteen franks.[10] I have still a kind of childish satisfaction in seeing many packets come to me, and thinking that I appear important at the post-office. I opened the franks with impatience, read a short letter from Mr Johnson and a part of the book; and, as I had received it the very day on which it was published at London, I was pleased at my being so privileged. I was engaged to sup with Mr Burnett at Mr Andrew Stewart, Junior's,[11] where we had Messrs A. Keith[12] and W. Dunbar,[13] Writers to the Signet. I was lively though ill of a cold, being inspirited by Mr Johnson. I came home as early as I could, sat down by the drawing-room fire, and read on till I had reached the end of the *Journey*. It was then about three in the morning, and the fire was very low and the night very cold. I on this occasion felt cold and pain in my head, but much noble imagery and reflection in my mind; though I must own that the hurry in which I read, and my bodily uneasiness, made me not relish the book so highly as I *knew* I should afterwards do.

THURSDAY 19 JANUARY. I could not but mention that I had a hidden treasure. But as I had written to Mr Johnson that I would not let a soul see it till Mr Strahan's cargo was arrived, I kept it close, though I had many solicitations. I

9 The outcome was that the Faculty recommended that Boswell and two colleagues (Alexander Elphinston and George Fergusson) "revise the list of Cases from 1765 to 1769 inclusive [and] make up therefrom a list of such Cases as may be worth collecting in order that the Faculty may consider of proper measures for having such cases collected" (Stewart, p. 258).

10 That is, thirteen envelopes bearing the signature of a person entitled to send letters post free. "Johnson sent the book in sheets, two sheets in each packet, because a franked packet could not exceed two ounces in weight if it was to go free" (*Ominous Years*, p. 56, n. 7).

11 Andrew Stewart resided in Gosford's Close, off the south side of the Lawnmarket.

12 Alexander Keith, W.S. (admitted 15 July 1763), died 26 February 1819.

13 William Dunbar, W.S. (admitted 4 July 1769), died 18 February 1807.

felt a secret pride in knowing that Mr Johnson had spoken so handsomely of me, and that the public would soon read what he had said. Matthew Dickie and Lawrence Hill[14] dined. I wrote to Mr Johnson at night. I this day read passages of the *Journey* with more pleasure than last night.

SATURDAY 21 JANUARY. Dined at Walker's Tavern—the anniversary meeting of Mundell's Scholars, a good institution.[15] We have always a kind of curious merriment, the same jokes every time, and all are willing to be pleased. Came home quite sober.

WEDNESDAY 25 JANUARY. It was a very rigid frost. I sat long in Parliament House hearing Solicitor plead Elliot against Hewit, etc. His forcible manner gave me satisfaction. My cold grew worse. As I walked home, I felt the frost sensibly dart into my head. My head ached violently. I could scarcely sit till dinner was over. I then went to bed, and was in a violent fever all the afternoon. Mr Wood gave me some mixture to make me sweat. I was ill all night.

THURSDAY 26 JANUARY. Was little better. Mr Wood would not let me attempt going out. Mr Lawrie got anything I had to do in the Court done for me by some of my brethren. We are very kind to one another in that respect; and the Court put off Lady Dundonald's cause, which was to have come on. I was comforted by a cordial letter from Mr Johnson which had come last night. My wife was most tenderly careful of me. In the afternoon I was pretty easy. I never knew before that one could have a fever for a short while. I thought if once it begun it took at least a week to exhaust its force.

FRIDAY 27 JANUARY. Ventured to the Court in a chair at ten, but felt myself weak and feeble. I had gone out to attend the moving of a violent complaint drawn by me against Mr Gordon, minister at Keith. There was a curious contrast, at the time when it was moved, between *its* force and *my* weakness. I came home immediately.

SUNDAY 29 JANUARY. Lay in bed, read Mr Johnson's *Journey* with much relish. Enjoyed the excellence of passages at leisure, as one does fine paintings. Read in the Old and New Testament, and some of the Apocrypha. The oriental style always gives me a kind of Asiatic tranquillity. Read also some of the second volume of Burnet's *History of His Own Times*. ✶

FRIDAY 3 FEBRUARY. After the Court rose, Lord Monboddo desired to have some conversation with me. We walked in the large new room of the Advocates' Library, and he told me that my father had been talking to him of his family settlements, and that he was to disinherit me of his own acquisitions since I would not agree to the limitations of succession which he wished. I repeated to him part of the same arguments mentioned [in the entry for 9 January]. He paid no regard to them, and said that my being so mad upon male succession was in his opinion a sufficient cause for not entrusting me with the estate. I was calm and determined, and told him that Mr Johnson approved of my resolution. "But",

14 A "writer".
15 For Boswell's old school, the academy of James Mundell in the West Bow, see Introduction, pp. 12-13.

said he, "if Mr Johnson knew that you would submit to be disinherited yourself of a great proportion of your inheritance rather than take the chance of cutting out a ninth cousin, he would not approve; and then you would not persist." "Nay," said I, "even Mr Johnson could not change me *there*." I changed the subject, and then he and I were very social. I supped with him at night; Messieurs Bannatyne MacLeod[16] and Charles Hay there. He told us that he was of opinion numbers of spirits besides mankind were in the universe; that they might have communications with our minds; and that he had been told such facts concerning the second sight that *he believed it*. He mentioned Duncan Forbes as giving faith to it, which I have often heard. I was in fine cheerful spirits tonight, spoke a good deal, fancied myself like Burke, and drank moderately of claret.

SATURDAY 4 FEBRUARY. This forenoon came on before Lord Gardenstone two actions of defamation, one at the instance of Robert Scotland in Dunfermline against the printer of *The Caledonian Mercury*. The other at the instance of the same Robert, John his father, and David his brother, against Mr Thomson, minister at Dunfermline, for having attacked them from the pulpit on the 30 of October.[17] Colonel Campbell's lawyers were consulted on these causes last night at Macqueen's. We all gave our advice, but some of us were to plead the one, some the other. Ilay Campbell and Maclaurin put me in good spirits by their defence of the *Mercury*; and I pleaded Thomson's cause really as well as I could wish to plead. I had full command of myself and a fluency that was pleasant to feel, and at proper intervals I threw out sallies of vivacity and humour which had an instantaneous effect on Lord Gardenstone himself and on the most numerous audience that I ever saw at a Lord Ordinary's hearing. Mr Rae, who spoke after me, began with saying, "I have heard Mr Boswell with great pleasure." "And I dare say, so has everybody that heard him", said Lord Gardenstone.[18] Macqueen said to me, "I would give a great deal to make such a speech as you have done just now." I can believe that he was in earnest. I went far against Robert Scotland for having betrayed Colonel Campbell. I said, "He is an *infamous fellow*, and I will prove it." I knew he was standing at my back. When I retired from the bar, bad as he was, I could not help relenting a little. I have really a compassionate heart. I could have given him a little balsam to his bruises. I thought no man is so bad but if we see him much hurt we will help him. Suppose one of the most worthless—nay, the most mischievous—of men were shipwrecked and terribly cut upon the rocks, and exhausted with famine,

16 Bannatyne William Macleod (1744-1833), advocate (admitted 22 January 1765), *later* Sir William Macleod Bannatyne (1823). He was to be appointed Sheriff-Depute of Bute in 1776 and a Lord of Session (as Lord Bannatyne) on 16 May 1799. A keen student of literature, it was said of him that he was "of a gay and easy disposition" and always had "the bearing and manners of the old Scottish gentleman" (Kay, Vol. 2, pp. 234-5).
17 Robert Scotland was one of Colonel Campbell's political agents and had been accused of having been unfaithful to him and having deserted to the opposite party for a pecuniary reward (*Ominous Years*, p. 60, n. 9).
18 On 28 February Lord Gardenstone pronounced an interlocutor finding in favour of Thomson.

we should put him into a warm bed, and be most tenderly careful of him, at least very soft and attentive about him. I comforted myself by thinking that Robert Scotland was not too severely hurt. I felt some uneasiness from imagining that perhaps my peculiar violence of declamation against him might make him attempt to take revenge. I have a timidity in my temper which it requires an exertion to counteract.

TUESDAY 7 FEBRUARY. Dined Sandy Gordon's, a company for David Moncrieffe: Lord Gardenstone, Peter Murray, and several more. Quite an Edinburgh dinner. Local talk, and noise, and wine. I drank rather too much, and lost the afternoon. Played awhile at brag. Was cautious and would not venture so as to risk more than a trifle. Won half a guinea.

THURSDAY 9 FEBRUARY. At six I was at the examination of Mr [James Paterson], younger of [Carpow], upon civil law.[19] Sandy Murray was our *praeses*[20] and acquitted himself so well that I was humbled tonight, and roused to prepare myself better for another occasion.

SATURDAY 11 FEBRUARY. This was a busy and a gainful week to me. I received twenty-seven guineas in fees, two more than I had ever received in one week before. Charles Hay walked with me to Sir Alexander Dick's. The Knight was amiable and classical as usual. He was very fond of Mr Johnson's *Journey*, which I had lent to him, and was writing notes on it. I supped at Mr John Swinton's, in whose house I had not been for many years.[21] There were just Maclaurin and his wife, David Stuart and his wife, a Miss Rose, and a Miss Mercer. We had a single rubber at shilling whist, and a genteel easy supper. I cannot account for it, but it so happened that it was a better evening than I imagined could have been passed in Edinburgh. No rioting—no private stories— no loud laughing. A company is like a chemical composition. Materials may come together and form a *whole* that is better than perhaps more valuable ones united.

SUNDAY 12 FEBRUARY. Last night before I went to Mr Swinton's I called on my father, and had a little serious conversation. I had the better of him, for I told him that I was now doing all that could be wished. I was sober. I was diligent in business. I was successful in business; and if he would tell me anything with which he found fault, I would amend it. He owned he had nothing particular to mention. But still he was cold and dry and indifferent. I could not help it. I was at the New Church today, forenoon and afternoon. Called on Crosbie between sermons, and talked with him of Mr Johnson's *Journey*. He promised me many remarks. Dined at home. My father's dinner between sermons is an unpleasant scene, and I attend only as a piece of duty, and when in finer frame I avoid it. I

19 Boswell was one of the private examinators on Civil Law for the examination of intrants to the Faculty of Advocates (see p. 66, n. 39). James Paterson of Carpow (d. 1824) was to be admitted advocate on 8 March 1776.
20 President (Latin).
21 Boswell's last visit to Swinton's house, which was in Teviot Row, may have been the visit referred to in the entry for 1 August 1769.

was at New Church in the afternoon. Went home with young Donaldson and got the *Monthly* and *Critical Reviews* on Mr Johnson's *Journey*, which were a feast. Drank tea at Sir George's. Found Mr Nairne when I came home, and read the reviews on Mr Johnson to him.

MONDAY 13 FEBRUARY. I went in the evening in a hackney-coach with so many of my brethren of Canongate Kilwinning, or St John's, Lodge and visited Leith Lodge. My spirits were vigorous, and I sung my nonsensical Scotch song, "Twa wheels", etc.[22]

WEDNESDAY 15 FEBRUARY. Drank tea first at home, then at Captain Schaw's; went with him and Mrs Schaw to *The Beggar's Opera*, performed by desire of several ladies of quality. There was an elegant audience. Digges looked and sung as well as ever.[23] I was quite in London. A girl from Ireland who played Polly, by the name of Mistress Ramsay, pleased me very well. Only her notes were sometimes not sweet enough, but like the cry of a peacock. I sat between Lady Betty Cochrane and Mrs Schaw in one of the rows of the pit taken by Lady Dundonald. I was cheerful and happy, having no pretensions, being very well established as an agreeable companion, and being a married man. Life is like a road, the first part of which is a hill. A man must for a while be constantly pulling that he may get forward, and not run back. When he has got beyond the steep, and on smooth ground—that is, when his character is fixed—he goes on smoothly upon level ground. I could not help indulging Asiatic ideas as I viewed such a number of pretty women, some of them young gay creatures with their hair dressed with flowers. But thoughts of mortality and change came upon me, and then I was glad to feel indifference.

After the play and the farce of *The Miller of Mansfield*,[24] I went to Princes Street Coffee-house, joined Sinclair the advocate, Grant the advocate,[25] and three other Highlanders, eat roasted cheese and drank strong rum punch.

SUNDAY 19 FEBRUARY. Was at New Church forenoon and afternoon and at my father's between sermons. I drank tea at Lord Kames's, not having been to see him this long time. He was in moderate spirits, so that he was really very good company, as he gave me rational conversation; but there was nothing important enough or ingenious enough to be put down except his denial that taxation depended on representation. "For", said he, "not only are all artificers and a great proportion of those who pay taxes not represented, but *women*, who have a large share of the property of the kingdom and pay land-tax, and who in other situations pay other taxes, are not represented." He thought taxation depended on

---

22 "Not known to have been preserved; probably indecent. The full title was 'Twa wheels and an axletree'" (*Ominous Years*, p. 65, n. 5).

23 West Digges (1720-1786), the actor, who was renowned for his performances as Macheath in *The Beggar's Opera*. It was said of him that he was a "well-formed and handsome man... with much natural grace. He was, however, rather formal in style, and his voice was imperfectly under control" (DNB). Boswell wrote that Digges "has more or as much of the deportment of a man of fashion as anybody I ever saw" (Journal, 1 December 1762). See also Introduction, p. 25.

24 By Robert Dodsley.

25 James Grant of Corrimony, advocate (admitted 15 February 1775).

protection. An artificer or farmer is guarded by government, so that he can labour in security and gain much more than he could do if interrupted by defending himself, and therefore it is reasonable he should contribute to the support of government. Mrs Drummond, his lady,[26] always revives youthful ideas in my mind, as in my most dissipated days I was much in their house. I ought to be oftener there now. She was fond of Mr Johnson's *Journey*, and my Lord spoke of it more favourably than I had any notion his prepossessions against Mr Johnson would have allowed him. But he was firm to Ossian, was satisfied of its antiquity from *internal evidence*, and wanted to have a splendid edition of it with plates published by subscription. Mr Nairne and Mr Stewart Moncrieffe were here. Nairne supped with me. I spoke to Lord Kames to give me notes of his life. He said he would if I would write it before his death. But like Cicero he would ask to have it done in a flattering manner. I told him I would do it fairly. I know not if he has eminence enough to merit that his life should be written. Perhaps I may do it.

MONDAY 20 FEBRUARY. Busy at home. Miss Annie Dick[27] dined with us. At night read an account in the newspapers of Lord Strichen's death,[28] being the first vacancy on our bench after *eight* years, and the opening for Mr Lockhart, our Dean of Faculty, to be a judge at last, after having been fifty-two years at the bar. What a thought! Had sentence been pronounced on him to do this—to stand fifty-two years at the bar, and to write such a number of long papers—it would have been shocking. His being made a judge would give him comparative ease and a security of above £600 a year; and he would have the pleasing delusion that he had a new life to live. At the bar he had the notion of ending. As a judge he would think of beginning. Lord Strichen had been a judge forty-three years. Mr Lockhart might stretch his imagination very far. I had not of a long time been so much roused as by this event, which was to produce a change which I considered in so many lights. I had resolved to write Mr Lockhart's life, as he had been the first barrister that ever practised in the Court of Session;[29] and the first man in my own line of life was a proper subject for my biographical exertion.

TUESDAY 21 FEBRUARY. Lord Strichen's death was in everybody's mouth in the Court. I said to Crosbie that I felt today that death was necessary, for that we should be very dull were there no changes. Worthy Lord Strichen could not be regretted, as he had lived to a good old age. In the evening I was at St David's Lodge, the Grand Master being there;[30] and then I supped at Crosbie's with Charles Hay and Fergusson of Craigdarroch, concerting measures to be taken in case Crosbie should stand candidate to be Dean, I having promised to be for

26 Lord Kames' wife was styled "Mrs Drummond" because she had inherited her family's estate at Blair Drummond in Perthshire in 1766.
27 Daughter of Sir Alexander Dick.
28 Lord Strichen had died on 15 February.
29 "That is, first in general reputation and practice" (*Ominous Years*, p. 69, n. 1).
30 This lodge met in Hyndford's Close (*Ominous Years*, p. 69, n. 3).

him long ago. Lord Advocate appeared to have a considerable majority on reading the list of advocates. I was against having a King's Counsel for our Dean,[31] but was for a man quite independent. Mr Johnson, I remember, thought this foolish. I argued today in the Court with some of my brethren on the subject. I said we should have no man's servant at our head. Said Sandy Gordon: "You would have a practising lawyer, who is every man's servant." "Yes", said I; "he is every man's servant, but he is his own master." We did not drink to excess at Crosbie's, which was wonderful.

THURSDAY 23 FEBRUARY. I opened the cause of the reduction of the Council of Stirling in the Inner House,[32] and was quite easy and master of myself. I imagined myself pleading at the English bar. The President said, "Mr Boswell, you have pleaded your cause very neatly and very well." It is pleasant to receive praise in public from a man with whom one is not on speaking terms in private. Nothing gives me such spirits as making a good speech in public.

FRIDAY 24 FEBRUARY. In the evening attended at Walker's the taking of a proof, *Hope* against Tweedie, about a foot-race for a pipe of port.[33] Hope, who had won it, was carried on horseback through a river in the way. I was not sure but this might, in strict *race-law*, forfeit the bet. I did not intend to go to Moncrieffe's, but this night I went in the way of my *business*, as we have several members skilled in all kinds of gaming who could inform me as to this *point*. But I got no clear light. I came to think it a quibble, as Hope had run wherever he could, and rode only where it was hardly practicable to go on foot. I marked the conversation tonight at this club, and it was local jocularity and bawdy, and nothing else. I came home a little after twelve.

SATURDAY 25 FEBRUARY. My wife and I were at the play in the evening—

31 By "King's Counsel", Boswell was referring to the Lord Advocate's position as His Majesty's Advocate. The Scottish bar did not in those days recognise a formal distinction between senior counsel and junior counsel, the status of King's (or Queen's) Counsel not being recognised in Scotland until 1892.

32 "Three leading men of Stirling had entered into a bond to unite their interests in all matters relating to the election and government of the burgh, and to divide all profits and emoluments which any of them should procure from Members of Parliament. [Colonel] Campbell's friends presented a cause of reduction, an action to render void the election of magistrates in Stirling. The Court so decided on 1 March and severely censured the signatories; on an appeal in November 1775, the House of Lords affirmed the decree" (*Ominous Years*, p. 70, n. 5).

33 "An amusing altercation between [Robert] Hope, a farmer, and Thomas Tweedie, a country gentleman. In December 1772 Tweedie, a large, apparently athletic man, boasted that he could walk from Tweedsmuir to Edinburgh (some 36 miles distant!) before Hope could—Hope being a much smaller, undersized person. The walk duly started, and although Tweedie had a better start, going off before Hope was ready, he lasted less than five miles; Hope carried on and eventually reached Edinburgh, with witnesses to prove that he had gone the full course. Thereafter Tweedie refused to fulfil the wager, which had been agreed as 'one pipe of port', on the grounds that he had been jesting; but Hope would not have this, and brought the matter to court. N.B. a 'pipe' is equal to 105 gallons, or £40 worth of port in those days. A proof, giving the evidence of Hope's witnesses, occupies nine separately numbered pages" (Ballantyne, 76 06 14). "The cause occupied the Court at least until December 1776... Eventually the Court dismissed the cause, finding 'expenses due to neither party'" (*Ominous Years*, p. 71, n. 8). The reference to "Walker's" in this entry is a reference to Walker's Tavern. In those days, the venue for the taking of a proof (that is, the taking of the evidence of witnesses) was commonly an inn, tavern or coffee-house.

Hamlet—with Lady Anne Erskine, etc. After the play I went behind the scenes and saw Mr Digges, whom I had not seen this winter before. Engaged him to dine with me on Tuesday sennight.

SUNDAY 26 FEBRUARY. I called on Mr Lockhart, and sat above an hour with him alone, and asked him a variety of questions about his life and the history of practice at our bar. I have put down in notes of his life what he told me. He was engaged to dine with me on Tuesday, but was indisposed and hesitated. I insisted on his coming. "Then", said he, "I shall be with you if I am alive. If not, my ghost shall attend you."

MONDAY 27 FEBRUARY. Busy writing law as usual on Mondays, when there is no Court and I stay at home.

SATURDAY 4 MARCH. Dined at Mr Lockhart's; Macqueen, Wattie Campbell, and four more advocates there. We drank hard for a little and were inflamed, at least I was, and then fell to whist. I had a rage for gaming and had once lost *eight pounds* and the loss did not move me. I won it all back but five-and-twenty shillings. Macqueen and Maclaurin and I supped and played after supper. It was humiliating to see the Dean, the eminent barrister whose life I was writing, peevish because he lost. It lessened him. His conversation indeed is very barren. You can see little more of *him* by being in company with him than you see of an eminent engraver or musician. We were impatient for his commission as a judge. He said he was more indifferent about it than any of us. After I came home I promised or rather vowed to my wife that I would never play higher than shilling whist.

SUNDAY 5 MARCH. Stayed at home in the forenoon. My wife with great justice complained that my conversation with her was never rational, but merely childish nonsense. It is not easy to give a distinct specimen of that puerile jocularity in which alone I exert myself at home. The reason of it may be partly indolence, to avoid thought; partly because my wife, though she has excellent sense and a cheerful temper, has not sentiments congenial with mine. She has no superstition, no enthusiasm, no vanity; so that to be free of a disagreeable contrariety, I may be glad to keep good humour in my mind by foolish sport. Was at New Church afternoon. Drank tea at Lord Alva's very cordially. Mr Nairne, Lady Wallace,[34] and Miss Dunlop[35] supped with us.

MONDAY 6 MARCH. Drank tea with David Hume, having half a year's rent of his house to pay him. He spoke of Mr Johnson's *Journey* in terms so slighting that it could have no effect but to show his resentment. He however agreed with him perfectly as to Ossian. But then he disbelieved not so much for want of testimony, as from the nature of the thing, according to his apprehension. He said if fifty barea—d Highlanders should say that *Fingal* was an ancient poem, he would not believe them. He said it was not to be believed that a people who were

34 Antonia Dunlop, second wife of Sir Thomas Wallace of Craigie, Bt (*Ominous Years*, p. 426).
35 Miss Susan Dunlop, Lady Wallace's niece (*Ominous Years*, p. 63, n. 7).

continually concerned to keep themselves from starving or from being hanged should preserve in their memories a poem in six books. He said that Homer had once been written, which made a great difference. He said that the extensive fame of Ossian was owing to the notion that the poems were so ancient; that if Macpherson had given them as his own, nobody would have read them to an end. He acknowledged that there were some good passages in them, and perhaps there might be some small parts ancient. He said the Highlanders, who had been famed as a warlike people, were so much flattered to have it thought that they had a great poet among them that they all tried to support the fact, and their wish to have it so made them even ready to persuade themselves into it. I told him Mr Johnson's saying that he could undertake to write an epic poem on the story of Robin Hood which the half of the people of England should say they had heard in their youth. Mr Hume said the people of England would not be so ready to support such a story. They had not the same temptation with the Highlanders, there being many excellent English poets.

This night the newspapers informed me that Mr Lockhart's commission as a judge was come. It gave me a fresh agitation. Lockhart having been so long a fixed planet at the bar, his being metamorphosed to a judge was an event which my mind did not easily follow. Ordinary men may change their situations and appearances without surprising us. We never dwell long enough upon the contemplation of them to mind them much. But a great man who has for years been in a particular sphere strikes us with a kind of wonder when he moves.

TUESDAY 7 MARCH. I went between nine and ten to congratulate Mr Lockhart. He was gone out to the President's, but his daughter, Miss Annie, spoke to me from a window, seemed sensible of my attention, and promised to tell him. This forenoon he sat within the bar and in the Outer House as Lord *Probationer*. A crowd followed with a strange curiosity wherever he went. Mr Digges and Colonel Stopford and Miss MacLeod of Raasay dined with us. It was quite an easy, genteel dinner. We had two kinds of Greek wine, port, Madeira, mountain,[35a] claret. Digges was to play Macheath at night. So went away early.

WEDNESDAY 8 MARCH. My wife and I drank tea at Mr Samuel Mitchelson, Junior's.[36] I then came home and laboured, and then she and I supped cordially at Sir George's. I was quite in love with her tonight. She was sensible, amiable, and all that I could wish, except being averse to hymeneal rites.[37] I told her I must have a concubine. She said I might go to whom I pleased. She has often said so. I have not insisted on my conjugal privilege since this month began, and were I sure that she was in earnest to allow me to go to other women without risk either of hurting my health or diminishing my affection for her, I would go. Thus I thought; but I was not clear, for though our Saviour did not prohibit

---

35a A sweet white Malaga wine made from mountain grapes.
36 Samuel Mitchelson (d. 1793), W.S. (admitted 16 December 1760), served his apprenticeship with Samuel Mitchelson, Senior, and was appointed Principal Clerk of Session in 1789. He resided at "Riddle's Land" in the Lawnmarket near the head of the West Bow.
37 She had now been pregnant for about two months.

concubinage, yet the strain of the New Testament seems to be against it, and the Church has understood it so. My passion, or appetite rather, was so strong that I was inclined to a laxity of interpretation, and as the Christian religion was not express upon the subject, thought that I might be like a patriarch; or rather, I thought that I might enjoy some of my former female acquaintances in London. I was not satisfied while in this loose state of speculation. I thought this was not like Izaak Walton or Dr Donne. But then the patriarchs, and even the Old Testament men who went to *harlots*, were devout. I considered indulgence with women to be like any other indulgence of nature. I was unsettled.

THURSDAY 9 MARCH. Another day of seeing Mr Lockhart. Yesterday and today both, he *reported* causes with a distinctness which humbled me. I got my table so well cleared that I was not groaning as I had done some of the former days of this week. At night was at Mr Alexander Murray's,[38] determining a case in which he and I were arbiters between Simpson of the Bank and William Taylor. I perceived that each of us leaned to the side of the party who chose us, he to Simpson, I to Taylor. This I suppose almost always is the case. We struck a kind of medium.

FRIDAY 10 MARCH. It was a fine day. Mr Lockhart finished his trials. When he took the oaths Harry Erskine said that was the hardest part of his trials.[39] I said no; for I supposed he did not think any king had a *right*. There was a complacency in his countenance. He was like an old post-horse turned into a clover field. To see him in his gown struck me with a boyish impression of novelty. He made a fine appearance. Crosbie said he only looked too much like a gentleman for a Lord of Session. I said he was like a Lord of Parliament in his robes, and now that he had his gown, he was upon the whole a fortunate man. He had a full crop of fame and money by continuing so long at the bar; and now he was to enjoy, comparatively speaking, *otium*, as he would have vacations, which he had not known for many years, and he would have *otium cum dignitate*.[40] To see him so much pleased with his promotion raised my notion of being a Lord of Session, which had for some time appeared little to me. When he took his seat there was a joyous agitation in the crowd. I began a clap slyly with my foot. The galleries catched it at once. The President was very angry, as he did not like Lockhart's Toryism. They tried a second time to clap.

On 15 March Boswell set off for another jaunt to London, hoping that, in addition to spending a pleasant vacation there, he might obtain some office through the influence of his friend Lord Mountstuart. On the way, Boswell called at the mental asylum at Newcastle where his brother John was an inmate. "He seemed to be affectionate," wrote Boswell, "and was so feeble and dejected in his appearance that I shed tears. He asked if I was really alive, for he thought it was my ghost... He said, 'I am confined and have lost

38 Alexander Murray's house was in Argyle Square.
39 This is an allusion to Lockhart's reputation for having Jacobite sympathies.
40 "'Leisure with honour', a phrase common in Cicero" (*Ominous Years*, p. 75, n. 1).

my senses, and I am surely dying.' Poor man, my heart melted for him... I gave him three [shillings]. He seemed to like some oranges which I gave him... I was much softened by this interview."

At London, Boswell once again settled happily into the company of the usual glittering array of interesting and exciting characters, such as Johnson, Paoli, Topham Beauclerk, Bennet Langton, Garrick, Sir John Pringle, John Wilkes (now Lord Mayor of London), Lord Mountstuart, Lord Loudon, Lord Pembroke, Lord Mansfield, Edmund Burke, Sir Joshua Reynolds, Charles James Fox, Mr and Mrs Thrale, Adam Smith (who had nearly finished The Wealth of Nations) and Thomas Sheridan. Lord Mountstuart was most cordial and assured Boswell that he would use his interest for him. Boswell suggested that an appointment such as that of Keeper of the Register of Sasines[40a] would be desirable if it were to become available. But at the same time Boswell continued to entertain ideas of trying his fortune at the English bar, and he persuaded Sir John Pringle that it would be advisable for him to do this if only Lord Auchinleck would give Boswell sufficient to maintain his family decently in London. As a preliminary to this possible scheme, Boswell began his terms at the Inner Temple (his admission to which had been arranged by Sheridan in 1761) and "ate enough meals at commons to fulfil the requirements of one term's residence".[41]

On 6 April Boswell attended a committee hearing at the House of Commons with regard to a petition in connection with the Clackmannanshire election. Here he heard David Rae, of whose performance Boswell wrote that Rae's "barbarous Bath-metal English [was] shocking to my ear".[41a] Boswell's friend Andrew Crosbie was another of the counsel who spoke. He was "manly and clear, though his pronunciation was pretty much Scots". "I felt a great keenness to speak," adds Boswell, "but could only sit by in my ordinary dress."

In addition to leading a hectic social life, Boswell had a few "dalliances" with a "beautiful Devonshire wench" who was "like a marble statue of antiquity". He also found time to visit Lord Pembroke at Wilton and to spend a week with his old friend the Reverend William Temple at Mamhead.

Boswell left London on 22 May to be in Edinburgh in time for the meeting of the General Assembly of the Church of Scotland. On arrival in Edinburgh he found his wife and children to be well, but, he says, "it required some philosophy to bear the change from England to Scotland. The unpleasing tone, the rude familiarity, the barren conversation of those whom I found here, in comparison with what I had left, really hurt my feelings."

Boswell wrote a review of his life for the summer session from 12 June to 12 August:

I do not remember any portion of my existence flatter than these two months. I was indolent in body and in mind... My father's coldness to me, the unsettled state of our family affairs, and the poor opinion which I had of the profession of a lawyer in Scotland, which consumed my life in the meantime, sunk my spirits woefully; and for some of the last weeks of the session I was depressed with black melancholy. Gloomy doubts of a future existence harassed me. I thought myself disordered in mind. Yet I was able to discharge my duty as a lawyer, wrote sixty papers, though none of them were very long indeed, and got one hundred and eighteen guineas and one pound in fees...

40a The Register of Sasines being the public register of deeds relating to land in Scotland.
41 *Ominous Years*, p. 157.
41a "Bath-metal was a kind of brass used in cheap, flashy jewelry" (*Ominous Years*, p. 124, n. 9). In other words, a sham.

There was some stir about a competition for the office of Dean of the Faculty of Advocates. I was clear for Crosbie as a man of learning and independency. But there was so great a majority for Harry Dundas, the young Lord Advocate,[42] that Crosbie declined standing, and he and his friends voted for Dundas that there might be no division. I was hurt to find no spirit in our society.

On 22 August Boswell set off for Auchinleck, stopping for a few days at Treesbank, in Ayrshire, where he found James Campbell of Treesbank to be seemingly quite well. He arrived at Auchinleck on 28 August and was pleased with the appearance of the house. "The dry gravel roads and new-whitened pavilions gave a fine air to the place, which really looked grand", he wrote.

Back in Edinburgh, Boswell resumed his journal on 9 October on the auspicious occasion of the birth of his son Alexander.

MONDAY 9 OCTOBER. My wife having been seized with her pains in the night, I got up about three o'clock, and between four and five Dr Young came. He and I sat upstairs mostly till between three and four, when, after we had dined, her labour became violent. I was full of expectation, and meditated curiously on the thought that it was already certain of what sex the child was, but that I could not have the least guess on which side the probability was. Miss Preston attended my wife close, Lady Preston came several times to inquire, but did not go into the room. I did not feel so much anxiety about my wife now as on former occasions, being better used to an inlying. Yet the danger was as great now as ever. I was easier from the same deception which affects a soldier who has escaped in several battles. She was very ill. Between seven and eight I went into the room. She was just delivered. I heard her say, "God be thanked for whatever he sends." I supposed then the child was a daughter. But she herself had not then seen it. Miss Preston said, "Is it a daughter?" "No", said Mrs Forrest, the nurse-keeper, "It's a son." When I had seen the little man I said that I should now be so anxious that probably I should never again have an easy hour. I said to Dr Young with great seriousness, "Doctor, Doctor, let no man set his heart upon anything in this world but land or heritable bonds; for he has no security that anything else will last as long as himself." My anxiety subdued a flutter of joy which was in my breast. I wrote several letters to announce my son's birth. I indulged some imaginations that he might perhaps be a great man. Worthy Grange came and cordially congratulated me. He and Dr Young and Lady Preston and Miss Preston supped with me.

I have resolved to keep a journal of my life every day from this important era in my family, and I shall never omit putting down something of each day's history. To record fully and minutely how every hour was employed would be an intolerable labour, or would prevent action in a great measure. If I can look

---

42 Henry Dundas had been appointed Lord Advocate on 24 May 1775, much to Boswell's disgust. "Only think," he wrote to Temple on 22 May, "Harry Dundas is going to be made King's Advocate—Lord Advocate at thirty-three. I cannot help being angry and somewhat fretful at this. He has, to be sure, strong parts. But he is a coarse, unlettered, unfanciful dog. Why is he so lucky?" (quoted in *Ominous Years*, p. 160, n. 7).

back and see how my life has been passed, by having so many marks of each day preserved, it is enough. I shall try to register the state of my mind, and I am resolved for the future to put down the marks of each day before I sleep, or at latest the day after. I may at times make a review of a period and try to form something general out of a number of various ideas, and I think it would be agreeable to have my life drawn out in tables: by months or years, by my progress in knowledge, or by any other plans. I was this night most devoutly grateful to GOD.

TUESDAY 10 OCTOBER. This morning my little son's nurse, Nellie Anderson, wife to William Colville, a tailor in the suburbs of Edinburgh at a place called Goosedub,[43] came. She was a pretty little woman, but a mere simpleton, which we thought no disadvantage. I dined at Sir George Preston's, who was warmly happy upon the joyful occasion. I drank tea in my wife's room and then went down to worthy Grange's,[44] and he and I and Mr James Loch drank a couple of bottles of Malaga, except a few glasses which Mr Lawrie drank. At night Mrs Montgomerie, dowager of Lainshaw, came. She and I supped by ourselves.

WEDNESDAY 11 OCTOBER. Dr Webster was not returned from a jaunt into England. I engaged Dr Erskine[45] to be with me in the afternoon, when I intended to have my son baptized. Commissioner Cochrane dined at Sir George's with Mrs Montgomerie and me, in order to be at the baptism. But as we did not keep precisely to the hour of four, and he was afraid of travelling in the night air, he left my house before the ceremony. There were present Sir George and Lady Preston and Miss Preston, Mrs Montgomerie, Grange, and my cousin Bruce Boswell,[46] who was just returned from an East India voyage. Veronica and Effie, and all the servants too but one, were in the room. It was pretty to see the two little sisters well dressed and quiet. I was serenely happy. Robert Boswell came in after the ceremony, which, as an Independent, he did not like to attend. After drinking some wine and tea, I took Dr Erskine down to my wife's room, and he said a prayer with much fervency. He then said to me, "Allow me to express a wish for your infant son. May he have all the genius and spirit of one connexion, all the sense, knowledge, and application of another, and all the unaffected piety of a third; and then he will not only be an useful member of society but a happy man. And may his parents live to see him such." I understood this to mean myself, my father, and my mother. Dr Erskine, I firmly believe, was sincere. This was a most comfortable afternoon.

THURSDAY 12 OCTOBER. Dr Boswell breakfasted with me, and expressed much joy. I dined at Sir George Preston's, where I had a general pressing invitation while my wife was confined to bed, that no jack might disturb her.[47]

43 On the east side of what is now Buccleuch Street.
44 Grange had by now moved from Roxburgh's Close to a flat below Boswell's at James's Court.
45 The Rev. John Erskine, D.D. (c. 1721-1803), minister at Old Greyfriars, Edinburgh. He produced many literary works and was a leading member of the "Evangelical" party in the Church of Scotland.
46 Son of Dr Boswell and younger brother of Robert Boswell.
47 A jack was a noisy mechanical device for turning a roasting-spit.

FRIDAY 13 OCTOBER. Dined at Maclaurin's,[48] where were Wight, David Erskine,[49] etc. Played at whist. Was seized with the rage of gaming which is in my blood, and played till three in the morning. Lost.

SATURDAY 14 OCTOBER. Having heard that the Royal Highland Regiment[50] was to march in today to the Castle, I was eager to meet them. Grange went with me, and Mr Lawrie also went. We overtook Dr Boswell near the West Port,[51] who harangued what fine fellows the Highlanders were in 1745. He was going but a little way. We walked to the other side of the Coltbridge.[52] I had wrought myself into a kind of enthusiasm about *The Highland Watch*, recollected their not having been in Scotland since the year 1744, and never in Edinburgh Castle, and I said to Grange that he and I would talk of their entry into *Auld Reekie* many years hence. We were disappointed, for there were no more of the Regiment came in than fifty-five men, which were all they had for four companies. There was a great number of people meeting them. The windows in Portsburgh and Edinburgh were crowded. I liked to see them enter the West Port. We saw them fairly enter the Castle.

I then met with Mr Spence, Treasurer to the Bank of Scotland, at his lodging in the Bank,[53] consulted on his cause against Lawrence Spens[54] *as a friend*, and was treated with Malaga and biscuits. I dined at Sir George Preston's, and was in such lively spirits and cordial frame that I drank about a bottle of port quickly, which intoxicated me somewhat. And away I went to the Castle, and viewed it in possession of the Highlanders; and as I saw the tartan in the sentry-boxes and the square swarming with filibegs, I felt as if in the days of one of the ancient kings of Scotland. The officers were engaged in different parties. But I got the sergeant upon guard, Monro, a fine black fellow who had been twenty years in the Regiment, and a sergeant of the Invalids, who turned out to be John Taylor, a Kilmarnock man (who when in the Royal Scots was tried for murder at Guildford, and got off), as also Shearer, the head gunner—and with these three I drank strong beer for two hours. I wanted to have had a number of the men with us. But Monro said they got as much this night from their friends as would do them good. But I made him promise to have all the men then upon guard to meet me next day at four o'clock in the afternoon in the place where we were then drinking; to wit, the little room in which Queen Mary was delivered of King James VI.[55] This was a strange satisfaction to me. I was quite military and Highland. Monro was a true specimen of the Scotch Highlanders: robust and intrepid. It is curious how

---

48 Maclaurin's town house was in Brown Square.
49 David Erskine, W.S. (admitted 18 June 1764), died 1791.
50 The Black Watch.
51 The West Port gateway (to the west of the Grassmarket) remained in place until 1786 (Harris, p. 633).
52 Coltbridge, to the west of the city by the Water of Leith, was in those days no more than "a little secluded hamlet" (Grant, Vol. III, p. 102).
53 The Bank of Scotland was situated in Old Bank Close, off the south side of the Lawnmarket.
54 A "writer".
55 The room was long used as a canteen for the soldiers (Grant, Vol. I, p. 78).

the character is continued through generations. I came home and Mr Wood supped with me.

SUNDAY 15 OCTOBER. Was a little vexed at last night's adventure, and not a little uneasy to think of my engagement for today, which, as it was with soldiers, I resolved to keep. I went down to Grange and prevailed with him to promise to accompany me. I was at the New Church both forenoon and afternoon, and at home between sermons; so that I had a good counterbalance of decency. At four Grange and I repaired to the *cantine*.[56] But luckily for me, Mr Monro had either thought that I was joking or in liquor, or would not remember my appointment, and he was not there. I had resolved to drink only a single glass and leave them. But it is hard to say what might have happened if the Highlanders had been quite to my mind. I gave Sergeant Taylor money to buy beer for them, and came off. I meditated on the Highland character, which I really believe is truly Scythian and does not know the weaknesses which occasion distress to most men. There is a hardiness of body and a firmness of spirit quite peculiar. Grange and I walked to the Abbey calmly, and then he came home and drank tea with me, and I read to him from the manuscript history of our family,[57] and we were most comfortable.

TUESDAY 17 OCTOBER. I was vexed that I was making no progress in any kind of knowledge. I could not read. I however was easier than I have been sometimes, as I had no instant call upon me to labour. I this day received a letter from my brother David, enclosing a genteel settlement on my wife and daughters in the event of his becoming proprietor of Auchinleck. I had asked it of him, to make my mind easy, and was very happy to find that a mercantile life had not made him selfish and evasive. I could have wished that he had not asked of me to make a settlement on him to the extent of from £1,000 to £1,500 in case of his getting no more than he already had from his father. For I should have spontaneously done as much for him. However, I thought that his behaviour to me deserved a good return, and I resolved that he should have it. Though he recommended secrecy, I could not but tell my wife and Grange to comfort them. I was still very indolent notwithstanding this cordial from David. I dined today tête-à-tête with my wife in her bedchamber.

WEDNESDAY 18 OCTOBER. Went out with Commissioner Cochrane in his chaise to Pinkie. The Commissioner and I played off rough jokes as usual. As a specimen, when I told that the hangman of Edinburgh had two guineas apiece for all that he hanged, he said, "James, you would hang all the folk in Edinburgh at the same rate." I answered, "Indeed would I, Commissioner; and I would begin with the Boards of Custom and Excise." When I went to my room after supper, I read some of Lord Kames's *Sketches*; thought them very inferior compilations.[58]

---

56 That is, the canteen in the Castle (see the preceding entry and the relevant footnote).
57 Drawn by Boswell's grandfather (see the entry for 31 December 1775).
58 *Sketches of the History of Man*, 1774. Boswell's view of this work was later to change somewhat: "I looked into Kames's *Sketches*: better than I thought. But rather notes of ideas and facts collected. His own reflections not very valuable, and his style like a coach running on uneven ground on three wheels, bouncing and away a little, and so on" (Journal, 7 April 1778).

THURSDAY 19 OCTOBER. I cannot portray Commissioner Cochrane as he exists in my mind. It pleased me today to see a man of seventy-four without any wretched effect of age, neat in his person, pleasant in his temper.

This forenoon I had a letter from my father wishing me joy on the birth of my son. As the weather had been bad, he had not sent for some time to Ayr for letters, so had not received mine. Knockroon had informed him of it, from the newspapers. His writing to me thus, before he got a letter from me, showed plainly that he was very happy, though he said little. My wife dined upstairs today.

FRIDAY 20 OCTOBER. Dempster had written to me that he was to lodge under my roof on Friday evening in his way to the meeting of Parliament. He came before dinner and sent me a note from Peter Ramsay's Inn. I went to him immediately, and found him as agreeable as ever. But I suppose a little more time and a little more application to business as a lawyer had given a greater degree of solidity and rigidness to my mind; for he appeared to me not so strong in sense as a man and a politician should be. He had with him a Mr Heming, his brother-in-law, for whom I secured a room in the same stair with my house.

SATURDAY 21 OCTOBER. It was rather unlucky that Dempster came at this time, for as my wife could not yet dress to appear before company, it obliged her to be again confined to her room. Maclaurin breakfasted with us today. Then we went to the Advocates' Library, where Sir Adam Fergusson, Dempster's companion to London, came, and got Dempster away with him. George Webster dined with my wife and me. Heming dined at Mr Samuel Mitchelson's, Junior, along with Maclaurin. I went there in the afternoon to play at whist. We had two parties, and played from six in the evening till three next morning, taking only a bit of supper cold, and drinking a little wine and punch by the by. I lost several pounds, and my rage for game made me sit at it on Sunday morning, which I disapproved of as an offence against the notions of decency in Scotland; and I was vexed at having kept my wife awake so long, especially before she was well recovered. Her anxiety prevents her from sleeping till I come home.

WEDNESDAY 25 OCTOBER. Passed a part of the forenoon in the Advocates' Library with Maclaurin and Mr Andrew Lumisden.[59] Talked of foreign literature, while I had a humbling consciousness that I could at present study none, and could seldom study much. We then walked in the Meadow with Dr Boswell, and continued the same kind of conversation. In the afternoon I had Maclaurin and young Honyman[60] to play at whist with me and Mrs Montgomerie. I grew keen, and would go on after supper, and betted sometimes half a guinea, sometimes a guinea extraordinary on the rubber. Lost several pounds, and sat till between two and three. Gave a promise of my own accord to my wife that I would never again play higher than half-crown whist, and never bet on the rubber.

59 For Andrew Lumisden, see Introduction, p. 33.
60 William Honyman, admitted advocate 15 February 1777, appointed Lord of Session as Lord Armadale 7 February 1797, appointed Lord Commissioner of Justiciary 29 June 1799, died 5 June 1825.

THURSDAY 26 OCTOBER. I paid my house-rent to John Buchan, Writer to the Signet,[61] at whose house I saw some old boxes full of manuscript books and papers and printed pieces belonging to the family of Napier, which he allowed me to tumble and examine. There were several little pieces in manuscript, mostly in figures, which had been the operations of the celebrated Napier of Merchiston.[62] There were also some journals by different persons; in particular, notes by this Lord Napier's grandfather, of what his Lordship saw when travelling. It was melancholy to see what had been written with care, and preserved as valuable, treated as lumber; and I could not but moralize on what might become of my own journals. However, they serve to entertain and instruct myself; and though the importance of a man to himself has been the subject of ridicule, it is clear to me that nothing is equally important to a man with himself. A man is called selfish in a bad sense who prefers a small good to himself to the happiness of others; or whose enjoyments are without reference to others. But surely happiness of every kind must ultimately centre in a man's own breast. I dined at Sir George Preston's with my Lady and Miss Preston.

FRIDAY 27 OCTOBER. Wrote to my brother David, and sent him a settlement of £1,500 in case the sum £4,000 was not made up to him by our father. Though it occurred to me that it might possibly happen that my circumstances might be embarrassed, and David and I disagree, and then I might repent this settlement and appear very foolish, I *trampled on such ideas* (to use a phrase of his after suggesting difficulties which he *might* have had of making a settlement on my wife and daughters), and I felt a nobleness of mind.

SATURDAY 28 OCTOBER. Mr Preston, Dr Webster, and Mrs Mitchelson dined with us. I really enjoyed the luxury of a black-cock and claret. We did not drink to excess. I supped at Maclaurin's along with Mr Lumisden, Mr John Fyfe, etc. We played at whist before supper. I won fifteen shillings, and was moderate in every respect this night, and home in good time.

SUNDAY 29 OCTOBER. This was my birthday, when I completed thirty-five years. I did not keep it, nor was I sensible of any remarkable reflections upon it. I stayed at home in the forenoon. Was at the New Church in the afternoon and heard Mr Walker preach very well on the duty incumbent on every man professing the Christian religion to act according to its precepts. That some people excused themselves by saying that they made no great professions of holiness, but that professing Christianity included holiness.

TUESDAY 31 OCTOBER. I dined at Dr Webster's, where were his son George, Colonel Preston,[63] and Mr Preston. We had a truly social meeting. After tea George went with me, along with some others of Canongate Kilwinning Lodge, to visit St Giles's Lodge. Webster's claret had enlivened me pretty well, and some strong

---

61 John Buchan (1742-1822), W.S. (admitted 10 July 1770). He resided in James's Court.
62 John Napier (1550-1617), the inventor of logarithms.
63 Lieutenant-Colonel Robert Preston, brother of Sir George Preston.

negus which I drank at the lodge put me in such a frame that I could not finish the evening but in merry company. George Webster had received a card to come to Wares',[64] formerly Macduffie's, to young Kincaid[65] and Andrew Balfour[66] to sup and play at whist and bring a fourth hand. As there is an appetite for meat, a *fames canina*[67] which will make a man devour anything, there is an appetite of the same kind for company. Away I sallied with George, and we carried with us young Hay, the surgeon. I was directly in such a fit as often seized me in the days of the Soaping Club,[68] and supped and drank and roared and played with vast keenness. Balfour went away soon. Kincaid sat till about five. Webster and Hay and I sat till between six and seven. We were in a low room known by the name of "Hell". I had sent home to tell that I was upon business; and the rage of play so heated me that I abandoned myself to it, and half-persuaded myself that my wife would be fallen asleep. I had once lost about six pounds, but when we rose my loss was only £2.16. It might have amounted to a great sum, for I was quite in the humour of venturing. When I got home there was really a dismal scene. My wife had been up all night in anxiety and terror what I could be about, and poor Veronica had been again taken ill with a hoarseness worse than last time. To reflect on all this, and at the same time on my having passed a whole night in such company, and so employed, vexed me sadly; and my wife's upbraidings galled me. I was miserably humbled.

WEDNESDAY 1 NOVEMBER. Got up about ten. Was somewhat consoled, as Veronica was better. Called at Sir George Preston's. Mr Preston said he wished I could be set in a pillory for my conduct last night. That the ordinary pillory in presence of the rabble would not do. But he wished there were some genteel pillory where I might be made ashamed before creditable people. [After tea] Mr Preston called for a little, and by his advice I bathed my feet in warm water, went early to bed, and took a potation of sack whey.[68a] The recollection that this was All Saints' day calmed my mind.

THURSDAY 2 NOVEMBER. Veronica was hoarse again, and appeared to have a bad cold. It is amazing how little I can do at present in the way of study, and how indolently my time is spent. Dr Cairnie sat with me a little, and we talked of the family of Stuart. I observed there is now an end of the party for them.

FRIDAY 3 NOVEMBER. My little son's nurse had not milk enough, and my wife was very uneasy. I called on Mr Wood a little after three. He had dined, so I eat a bit with him and drank some glasses of wine, and then he went with me to see another nurse, whom we engaged. Her name was ——, wife to —— Ross, a sawer in Nicolson Street. I thought that my son would perhaps read this journal and be grateful to me for my attention about him, for I was twice out speaking to his nurse. My wife, who does not like journalizing, said it was leaving myself

---

64 Francis Wares' tavern in Anchor Close, off the north side of the High Street.
65 Alexander Kincaid, printer, son of Alexander Kincaid the future Lord Provost.
66 Andrew Balfour, advocate (admitted 1763).
67 "Dog's hunger".
68 For the Soaping Club, see Introduction, p. 21.
68a A medicinal drink made of sack (dry white wine from Spain or the Canary Islands) and skimmed milk.

embowelled to posterity—a good strong figure. But I think it is rather leaving myself embalmed. It is certainly preserving myself. It was a kind of distressful scene to remove the first nurse, who was anxious to stay. Mrs Ross came to him tonight. Veronica's cold was worse. Mr Wood thought it might be the measles; I was tortured with apprehension for her. I was ill of a cold.

SATURDAY 4 NOVEMBER. Veronica was easier. I lay long in bed with my cold, stayed at home all day.

SUNDAY 5 NOVEMBER. Having taken physic for my cold, lay in bed till the afternoon, drank tea and took onion soup, and was relaxed and quiet. My son had a rush[69] which alarmed my wife's anxiety. Veronica was still indisposed, and Effie had a severe cold. The house was quite an hospital. I considered that I could do no good, and lay still. Read *The Monthly Review* for September last. Found in it an account of a virtuous religious family by Mrs Chapone, and how they passed their time. It seemed to me a very dull life. But I believe no life will appear happy from a particular description. I thought how insipid, and to many how disagreeable, would the greatest part of my own life appear if exactly put down in writing. I could have written my journal at night, but thought it better to write each day's history the day after, having then the day complete. This I now do, and it shall be my regular practice. I shall mention when it is otherwise.

MONDAY 6 NOVEMBER. It was very wet. Time passed away in the forenoon idly enough. In the afternoon I had a consultation, and relished a new cause as a little particular history. I finished today the reading of a very pretty French piece which I had in a present from Mr Lumisden: *Consultation sur la Discipline des Avocats*.[70] It puts the office of a lawyer in a high point of view, and is beautifully expressed. I really felt myself elevated by it. If I execute my plan of writing an essay on my profession, it will aid me much.

TUESDAY 7 NOVEMBER. Sir Walter[71] dined with us. The children were all pretty well again. My son's second nurse was an excellent one, and he was visibly fuller in flesh and healthier in looks. I really had practical philosophy enough not to set my heart anxiously upon him. Though I was indolent and did nothing this day, I felt no uneasiness. I was only hurt somewhat to perceive that when Sir Walter talked with me about his affairs, I could not give him a decisive sensible opinion. I am sensible that I am deficient in judgement, in good common sense. I ought therefore to be diffident and cautious. For some time past I have indulged coarse raillery and abuse by far too much. I am resolved to be on my guard for the future against evil speaking of every kind, and to cultivate a benevolent disposition, at least an external mildness.

WEDNESDAY 8 NOVEMBER. I had one gold consultation, and one gratis. Went and sat awhile with worthy Sir George. At night was in a sullen frame at

69 A rash or skin eruption.
70 By a M. Duvergier, published in Paris in 1775 (*Ominous Years*, p. 175, n. 3).
71 Sir Walter Montgomerie-Cuninghame, Bt, Mrs Boswell's nephew.

supper with my wife and Mrs Montgomerie. I indulged bad temper in silence, disregarding politeness. Grew better.

THURSDAY 9 NOVEMBER. Lieutenant Graham[72] and Robert Boswell breakfasted with me. I had engaged Robert to be here, that we might consider if any relief could be obtained at law from the hard terms of Colonel Graham's will.[73] Robert spoke with knowledge and accuracy. I was sensible of a sad want of promptness of memory or attention in business. I am better for being a barrister than a counsellor.

FRIDAY 10 NOVEMBER. After breakfast my father and Lady Auchinleck paid us a visit. He was very guarded last night against expressing joy on the birth of my son, and today when he saw him he said very little. I however flattered myself that I detected symptoms of satisfaction in his behaviour. He tasted a little liqueur. It is strange to see such a niggardliness of fondness. Excess of it is no doubt weakness; and to be secure from this, which my uncle the Doctor shows, my father is in the other extreme.

I dined with Mr Alexander Mackenzie, Writer to the Signet,[74] with Barrock, a Caithness laird, and his lady and two daughters, my client Ardross and his lady, and my cousin Lieutenant Graham. I got into a Highland humour and drank first plentifully of port and then of claret, which cost only £16 a hogshead; and, as intoxication rose, I disregarded my solemn engagement of sobriety to my friend Temple, and pushed the bottle about with an improper keenness, as I was not the entertainer. About nine Graham and I drank tea with Mr and Mrs Mackenzie. I was able to be decent then. But when I got into the street I grew very drunk and miserably sick, so that I had to stop in many closes in my way home, and when I got home I was shockingly affected, being so furious that I took up the chairs in the dining-room and threw them about and broke some of them, and beat about my walking-stick till I had it in pieces, and then put it into the fire and burnt it. I have scarcely any recollection of this horrid scene, but my wife informed me of it. She was in great danger, for it seems I had aimed at her both with chairs and stick. What a monstrous account of a man! She got me to bed, where I was excessively sick.

SATURDAY 11 NOVEMBER. My intemperance was severely punished, for I suffered violent distress of body and vexation of mind. I lay till near two o'clock, when I grew easier, and comforted myself by resolving vigorously to be attentively sober for the future. There is something agreeably delusive in fresh resolution. Reason tells me that I cannot expect to be better restrained now than by former vows; and yet, like a man who has had several blanks in the lottery and fancies that another ticket will certainly be a prize, I flatter myself that I shall have it to say that from the 11 of November 1775 I maintained an uninterrupted moderation in drinking. Indeed the horrid consequences with which

---

72 Lieutenant William Graham of the Royal Highlanders.
73 That is, the will of Lieutenant-Colonel Gordon Graham (d. 1772), late cousin of Boswell and father of Lieutenant William Graham.
74 Alexander Mackenzie resided in Carrubber's Close, off the north side of the High Street.

my last night's debauch might have been attended may probably awe my mind.

Sir Walter dined with us. I went to the New Church and heard Mr John Gibson preach very well on "Glory to God in the highest". I drank coffee comfortably at home, and my wife seemed to have quite forgotten my bad conduct. Her unhappy sister, Sir Walter's mother,[75] was still in Edinburgh, ill of a consumption, and preparing to go to France. I allowed my wife to go and see her, as the feelings of natural affection may be indulged towards an unworthy object when dying. Her debasing herself by a mean marriage ought, from a just regard to preserve the honourable distinctions of civilized society, to prevent her from enjoying the countenance of her relations in cheerful intercourse.[76] But sickness and the approach of death may be indulged with a humane attention. I have been rigidly firm in giving no countenance to my wife's unhappy sister. Dr Johnson, in a conversation at Mr Thrale's, judiciously settled the manner in which women who make low marriages should be treated by their relations. It is proper to supply them with necessaries if they are in want, but it is improper to keep them on a footing with those who have not acted unsuitably.

SUNDAY 12 NOVEMBER. There had been a fall of snow in the night. When I looked out from my bed in the morning and saw everything white, I felt a kind of agreeable wintry sensation which the sight of snow always gives me. I was at the New Church forenoon and afternoon, and took the sacrament as a commemoration of Christ's death and a testimony of my belief in His religion. But the Presbyterian communion has nothing of solemn devotion in it. I felt a kind of reluctance at giving my countenance to it, especially as the clergy of that profession appear to me to have no good authority to celebrate the Holy Sacrament, not having ordination flowing from the Apostles. But then I considered that there could be no harm in joining a number of people of my own country in a Christian duty according to the established mode; and that my doing so was essential to my having my father's good opinion. Mrs Montgomerie and I dined with him between sermons. I made my wife stay at home all day, as she was not quite recovered yet. The tediousness of the service in the New Church was really tiresome. I drank tea at home, then sat awhile with Sir George. Supped at home with my wife, just by ourselves.

MONDAY 13 NOVEMBER. Was at the New Church in the forenoon, and heard Sir Harry Moncreiff[77] preach on "O death, where is thy sting",[78] etc. He represented

---

75 Elizabeth Beaumont (née Montgomerie).

76 Her first husband, Captain Alexander Montgomerie-Cuninghame of Kirktonholm, had died in 1770. "When she contracted with John Beaumont a second marriage which [Boswell] considered 'low', he disowned her and forbade Mrs Boswell to have any intercourse with her" (*Ominous Years*, p. 40, n. 1).

77 Sir Henry Moncreiff-Wellwood (1750-1827), Bt, minister at the West Kirk, "a very eloquent and vigorous preacher" who became the highly influential leader of the "evangelical" (or "popular") party in the Church of Scotland. He was to be elected moderator of the General Assembly in 1785, and in 1793 he was to be appointed chaplain to George III (DNB). Cockburn said of him that he was a "most admirable, and somewhat old-fashioned, gentleman" who would walk to church "with his bands, his little cocked hat, his tall cane, and his cardinal air" and after preaching "a sensible practical sermon" would walk home "in the same style" (Cockburn, p. 38).

78 I Corinthians 15. 55.

death under its various dreary views, and then suggested the consolations of Christianity. A strange thought struck me that I would apply to David Hume, telling him that at present I was happy in having pious faith. But in case of its failing me by some unexpected revolution in my mind, it would be humane in him to furnish me with reflections by which a man of sense and feeling could support his spirit as an infidel. I was really serious in this thought. I wonder what David can suggest. I was struck with thinking that the preacher and all who heard him were certainly to undergo death in one way or other.

My father and Lady Auchinleck, Messieurs Kincaid, senior and junior, and Sir Walter dined with us. My father was observed to be visibly duller or failed. Mr Kincaid said, with an air that he thought the contrary, "Is he as *vif*[79] as he used to be?" He indeed had an old look, and a sort of indifference in his manner. He has never been cordial in my house, but today there was something about him like one worn out. I was affected by it tenderly in my own mind, for all his coldness of late to me. My wife very prudently said that I should by no means appear to be sensible of any failure about him. He and Lady Auchinleck went away early, and, as he was going down the stair, he took my wife kindly by the hand, as if by stealth, and said, "God bless you all." This pleased me much. The Kincaids and Sir Walter and I were very cordial as relations,[80] and the old gentleman talked from experience of the advantage of relations keeping up their connexion. I guarded against any excess in drinking, though such a meeting justified a little more than usual. I found that my constitution was quite unfit for the least excess in wine, for although I had but the smallest share of three bottles of claret among four, I was feverish and even sick. Messieurs Kincaids drank tea.

I wrote to Lord Mountstuart and his brother James to ask for me the place of one of the commissaries of Edinburgh, vacant by the death of Mr Smollett yesterday. I had resolved day after day to write to Lord Mountstuart, that my friendship with him might be kept alive, but amazing indolence had hitherto prevented me. He had promised to assist me in getting something better, but I wrote to him that it would be of great consequence to me to show my father that I had his Lordship's patronage, and therefore a smaller office speedily obtained would serve me much. I was in the frame of an old baron, and hoped that my application would have effect, were it only to make him write a letter to my father expressing his friendship for me, which he had promised to do. I am curious to see how he will act. I went to bed early.

TUESDAY 14 NOVEMBER. The weather was fine and clear, but frosty. The Court of Session met, but there was not a quorum of the Lords. The advocates went through the customary form of dissimulation, or rather unmeaning expression, wishing one another a good session, when in reality if the meaning of most of them were known, it would be wishing a bad session, or little business,

---

79 Lively, animated.
80 "Kincaid's wife, the Hon. Caroline Ker, was, like Boswell, a great-grandchild of the second Earl of Kincardine" (*Defence*, p. 286, n. 7).

to every rival; for the profits of our bar do not afford many good shares. Nothing particular struck my mind at the opening of this session. I walked out to the Abbey Hill and met the first division of the 31 Regiment, and walked along and was cheered by their drums and fifes and martial air. Got before them into the Castle, and saw them enter the square. They were to relieve the Highlanders, who were to go to the Forts and other parts of Scotland. I had several session papers to write, having let them lie over instead of writing in the vacation. I was very averse to labour. However, I did tolerably.

THURSDAY 16 NOVEMBER. This forenoon I was glad to find myself able to speak freely and distinctly before the Lords in a cause, Mrs Rickson against some officers of the 19th Regiment of Foot.[81] But I was sensible at one moment of a sort of confusion of mind which sometimes affects me, either from having too many ideas, or not vigour enough to arrange them and keep back all but those immediately necessary. I know not if the ideas can be said with propriety to obey the memory at any time. But I am sure that mine are at times turbulent. They either secrete themselves, so that they cannot be found when I want them, or are disorderly when they appear.

FRIDAY 17 NOVEMBER. My father was ill of a cold, a most frequent complaint this winter. He had kept the house yesterday, and he continued to do so today. I was with him a little yesterday. But today I sat with him a good while, and he entered on the subject of my debt. I had bought Dalblair in 1767, and borrowed £2,000 upon heritable security on it, as also £500 from Lord Marischal[81a] on my personal bond. Full of the idea of being the heir of a great estate, I had been very extravagant; and I was so the more freely that I had laid down a resolution to marry no woman but one with a fortune of £10,000, so that any debt I should contract might be cleared off at once. Dalblair cost me £2,435. The price belonged to a number of creditors, who had various perplexed claims, so their trustees were in no hurry for payment. This was unlucky for me, for it left me the command of the money which I had borrowed. I indeed soon paid up £1,400. But the remainder I dissipated, and was in debt a great deal more when I married. I hoped that my father would then have made me clear. But he let things hang on, and I was unwilling to disturb him. I found now that, after applying in payment of debt and in expense of living my wife's portion of £1,000, I was in debt between twelve and thirteen hundred pounds to Dalblair's trustees, and upon a state of debit and credit in other particulars was owing about £200 more. My father was bound along with me for the price of Dalblair, and he spoke of it today with dissatisfaction. I calmly reasoned that I had formerly been foolish, but was now acting a proper part, and that I hoped he would

---

81 This was an action by Mrs Euphemia Rickson, widow of the deceased Lieutenant-Colonel William Rickson, which was concerned with "a dispute over the perquisites of a company officer in a British line regiment of foot" (*Session Papers*, 75 02 24b). Colonel Rickson had served in Scotland rather than in Gibraltar with his company and "although entitled to his perquisites despite his absence, he was adversely affected by the decision of officers in Gibraltar, with the regiment, to divide the perquisites of absent officers among themselves" (*ibid.*, 75 07 03).
81a For whom, see Introduction, p. 32, and the entry for 7 July 1776.

make me easy. I suggested that the money might be wanted soon. He seemed to acquiesce pretty quietly in his being obliged to pay it. When I got home I considered that he had given me only £200 this year, though my allowance was £300, and therefore I had a claim for £100, which would reduce what he had to pay to £1,175; and I thought it would be better to take £1,000 neat from him rather than have reflections why I had allowed the interest to run on, and that I might in no long time be able to make myself quite clear, and then begin to pay off part of the value of Dalblair. As the interest of the price at five per cent exceeded the present rent (£26 a year), it was an immediate burthen to me. My father was willing to take it off my hands, and my wife pressed me to part with it. But as I hoped good things of myself, and wished to appear in the family archives as having added Dalblair to our territories, and had pleased myself with thinking that at least that estate in the parish of Auchinleck should be entailed on the heirs male of Thomas Boswell, the founder of our family, I determined to keep it. It pains me that my wife has not a spark of feudal enthusiasm, but is always opposing me upon the subject of family.

Sir Walter dined with us. I was very busy with a paper in the afternoon. Donaldson, the painter, came and drank tea.[82] I would have dismissed most visitors sooner. But knowing his temper, and wishing not to hurt him, I bestowed a good portion of time upon him. He was, as usual, constantly aiming at extensive thought and general reflections, such as: "We admire extension. One who kills a single man is abhorred; but a man-killer, a hero who has destroyed numbers, is a high character." He made one remark which seemed just: that the common observation that heroes are the most merciful is not true. For we imagine so because mercy is more conspicuous in such a ferocious being. After he went away I said his conversation was a kind of whale fishing. He always launched into the wide ocean and pursued vast objects. But he catched nothing.

After finishing my paper, I went to David Stewart Moncrieffe's, the first evening of his club, or tavern as he calls it, for this session. I played pretty well at whist, and won a little. We were sixteen at supper. The conversation was flashy and vociferous. I resolved to be at this club every Friday, as a place where I can play whist, see the best company of this country, hear intelligence from various sources, and be exhilarated with sociality once a week. I came away before twelve. My purpose is to do so always, and to speculate without paying the tax of drinking much and sitting up late.

SATURDAY 18 NOVEMBER. After being in the Court of Session, called on my father, who still kept the house, and informed him of my having had a letter from Mr Miller, writer in Ayr, factor for Dalblair's creditors, giving me notice that the remainder of the price should now be paid. It was lucky that my father had happened to talk of it to me yesterday before the letter came, as I got him

82 John Donaldson, an esteemed painter of miniatures. "Donaldson painted a miniature of Boswell in 1769, and of Mrs Boswell in December 1775 and again in 1784. None of them has so far been located" (*Ominous Years*, p. 161, n. 5).

prepared for letting me have the money. Mr Stobie was present when he and I talked together today. I was obliged to hear an unpleasing recapitulation of my extravagance. But after a good deal of dialogue, and Mr Stobie throwing in a word sometimes in my favour, it was agreed that my father should have £1,000 ready at Candlemas, and with this, and what I had to advance, the bond should be cleared. Stobie said he might take an obligation from me for repayment. "No, no", said I. "Let me once be clear, so that no man can look me in the face as a debtor." I was touched with parental affection when I found my father agree to make me easy.

He found fault with me for being against him in the last Ayrshire election. My apology was that he had told me he was to take no side; otherwise I should not have interfered in the least. He said that he had connected himself with his father's friends, and that they were the surest. I had fallen out with the President, though I knew that there had been an intimacy between his father and himself with my father. I said nothing to this. But allowed Stobie to say it was wrong. I was conscious that I connected myself with Sir John Pringle, who was my father's friend, and also with Lord Monboddo, and that my quarrel with the President was for a very sufficient reason: because after I had taken a warm side in the Ayrshire election, in the faith that my father was to take none, the President, without consulting me, beset my father and persuaded him to take the opposite side with great keenness, by which *I* appeared quite insignificant, and to split the superiorities of his estate[83] and make fictitious votes, by which *he* appeared acting contrary to his professions both in public and private. This was a most ungentlemanly conduct. I think it was rascally. I therefore have not seen the President for about two years. Yet I wished today that I could accidentally fall in again to a kind of decent intercourse with him to please my father; and I could be aware, and keep myself out of his power in any degree.

My father mentioned his having made an entail of the family estate, and that, to insure it, he had made a proviso that if a reduction of it was so much as attempted, all his own purchases should be forfeited by me and the heirs of my body. I asked him on what series of heirs he had settled the estate. He said on the heirs whatsoever of his own body. This confounded me, and I calmly spoke a little for the male line. I knew he had not power without my consent to disappoint the male succession. But to lose his own acquisitions was a great hardship. I said with an easy good humour, "You should let the heir male have Tenshillingside and the lime quarry at Stonebriggs as essential; the first as a part of the policy, the other for the improvement of the estate." In my own mind, I quietly thought that I would give up both, with all that he had bought, rather than let a female and her race by a stranger cut out the *sons of the Family*. My father had the money to borrow with which he was to pay off my debt. Stobie said it should be borrowed in small sums, and he could clear it off at his convenience. I was not certain whether Stobie was much my friend or not. I thought he might really be so. If that is the case, I shall not forget it. My father seemed to be failed today. He was gentler than usual, and I was sincerely grateful

83 That is, the superiorities under the feudal system of landholding.

to him. He is an excellent man upon the whole, though he has, as I have, appearances of narrowness and harshness.

Sir Walter dined with us. I drank a little strong ale with him, which, though less than half a bottle, confused me somewhat. My drinking vigour is either quite gone or in abeyance. I was busy writing session papers. In the forenoon I had been to see a little creature shown as a curiosity under the name of a *Corsican Fairy*. It was a very well-made woman not above three feet high. It was said she was born in Ireland, but *Corsican* was a good show title. A man who spoke Italian, and said he was her brother, showed her, and the rogue, having been told who I was, pretended that he had seen me in Corsica. General Paoli will tell me about this. I had also called for one Carmichael, a shopkeeper in Morpeth, confined for debt in the Canongate prison,[84] for whom I was to draw a paper.

I told my wife of the conversation between my father and me, and she was violent to a degree that hurt me, complaining that I would not only disinherit my own daughters, but deprive my own son of a part of his inheritance. I told her that it was a principle in honour and justice with me that the heirs male of Auchinleck should not be deprived of their succession; that a settlement depriving them could not be effectual unless I approved of it, and that my father's acquisitions were no doubt a considerable bribe to act contrary to my principle, but that I could resist it, and might make an equivalent for my son. I was made really uneasy by my wife's violence tonight, though it was natural and excusable. She said I would be looked upon as a madman if I acted as I intended to do; and when I insisted on our title to the estate from the worthy old laird who gave it to his nephew though he had four daughters, she answered with a very good metaphor: that the estate was so much burthened, it was more proper for a man than a woman. It was an old coat which he gave to his nephew, because it would not fit his daughter. The fact however was that, although there was a load of debt, my great-grandfather got a substantial fund.

SUNDAY 19 NOVEMBER. In the early part of last night my mind had been so much agitated with thinking of the entail which my father told me he had made, and with momentary apprehensions of my approving of it, from the temptation of my father's purchases, that I was actually for a little in a state of insanity. The idea of the Old Castle of Auchinleck going to a female in exclusion of *Boswells* was horrid. I composed myself by resolving firmly. I was at the New Church all day, but did not profit by it. The cold was intense. Coughs were so frequent that it would have required the voice of an old field-preacher to be heard. I dined at my father's between sermons, with Mrs Montgomerie and George Webster. I used to drink as much at this weekly meeting as to bring on a degree of comfortable stupefaction. I resolved today not to allow myself this gross kind of indulgence, and I kept my resolution.

84 The old Canongate Tolbooth, with its "sombre tower and spire, Scoto-French corbelled turrets, [and] dark-mouthed archway" (Grant, Vol. II, p. 30) and large clock (a "knock" or "orlache") projecting over the street, resting on "curiously-carved oaken beams" (Wilson, Vol. II, p. 98), was used as a magistrates' courtroom and as a prison. Arnot, writing in 1779, said, "Debtors of the better sort are commonly taken to this prison, which is well aired, has some decent rooms, and is kept tolerably clean" (Arnot, p. 175).

THURSDAY 23 NOVEMBER. At eight I went to an oratorical society in Mary's Chapel,[85] called the "Pantheon", as a militia for Scotland was to be debated; and, as I thought it of consequence to rouse a general spirit for it, I made a vigorous harangue and introduced an eulogium on Lord Mountstuart as the tutelary patron of this country. I believe I did very well. I got applause enough from the company, about one hundred writers, wrights, etc., etc., and the question carried *for a militia* upon the votes of all present being taken.[86] I suppose the visitors bore a great proportion above the members. There were a number of officers of the 31 Regiment there who all voted *against a militia*. They were not fair judges. I was made an honorary member. I supped with my wife quietly. Found two fees lying for me, but was not clear for business.

FRIDAY 24 NOVEMBER. This forenoon I resumed what I had neglected for above two years: reading the records of the Privy Council of Scotland and copying any curious passage. My father has four volumes of abstracts from them by old Robert Mylne. Some books have been found since his death, and these I examine. Mr Robertson, one of the keepers of the records, has been always very obliging to me. I was glad today to find that I could read the old hand pretty easily after a long interruption. I have a kind of calm, comfortable satisfaction in being thus employed in the Laigh Parliament House. I think that I may make a good publication of these abstracts. Sir Walter dined with us. The first week of the session produced me but three guineas. This produced six, and I had but little labour. Lord Eglinton was in town, and had called on me.[87] I called on him yesterday, and this night I met him at Moncrieffe's. I had not an opening for a party at cards. We were eleven at supper. There was nothing to remark. I kept quiet and sober, and came home soon after twelve.

SATURDAY 25 NOVEMBER. My father sent for me this morning into the robing room to engage me and my wife and Mrs Montgomerie to dine with him today, along with the Countess Dowager of Galloway. He and I had a quiet, comfortable chat together, and were very well. The dinner took place and we also drank tea. I supped at Sir George Preston's. He himself was asleep. It was the night before Captain George was to set out for his Marine Corps. George Webster was there. He told that George Fergusson was appointed one of the commissaries of Edinburgh.

---

85 St Mary's Chapel in Niddry's Wynd.

86 The question as to whether or not there should be a Scottish militia was fiercely controversial, for many people feared that while the Young Pretender was still alive a Scottish militia might lend its support to a further Jacobite rebellion. On 2 November, "in a very spirited manner", Mountstuart had spoken in the House of Commons in favour of a bill for the militia, and on 8 December he presented a bill; but, in spite of Mountstuart's "able defence of his bill", the bill was ultimately defeated at a debate on 20 March 1776 (Namier and Brooke, Vol. III, pp. 502-3).

87 This was Archibald Montgomerie (1726-96), the 11th Earl of Eglinton, brother of the deceased Alexander Montgomerie, the 10th Earl. Montgomerie was M.P. for Ayrshire from 1761 to 1768. "A good companion, hard drinking, genial but hot tempered, Montgomerie had few intellectual interests. A 'violent Scotsman', with a contempt for Englishmen equal to Dr Johnson's for Scots, he strongly opposed ministerial dictation in the election of Scottish representative peers" (Namier and Brooke, Vol. III, p. 158).

This was a small disappointment to me. I was remarkably placid tonight. I had not a single paper upon my hands. I had therefore no immediate labour to oppress me.

SUNDAY 26 NOVEMBER. Was at the New Church forenoon and afternoon, and at my father's between sermons, where were George Webster and his sister and Mr Claud Boswell. My father was not very well, and stayed at home in the afternoon. While at church I was very impatient as = had promised to be at home at V.[88] I drank tea at my father's, and was solid with him and Lady Auchinleck. Last night there came a present of silk caps from her to my daughters, and of a silk hat and cloak from my father to my son. This was an agreeable attention. My father seemed to be really kinder of late. I had real happiness in being well with him, and I wished him long life, feeling also a sort of discouraging apprehension that the Family of Auchinleck would not be properly supported by me. Without reserve there cannot be dignity, and my warmth and gaiety, which procure immediate small applause, counteract the wish which my pride forms for respect in general. I may restrain them as I grow older. If not, why should there not be a diversity of characters in the succession of lairds?

A little after five I stole gently to ='s room, which I found to be neat and cosy. I sat about an hour. She indulged me in amorous dalliances of much familiarity, but though I preached from the Old Testament, could not think of allowing me ingress. I was much pleased with her unaffected goodness, and being for the time calmed, I thought we might do more afterwards. There was nothing of art or feverishness on either side. I was clear that I was doing no ill. Such was my sensation or immediate impression.

MONDAY 27 NOVEMBER. Supped quietly at home. Fell into a fit of bad humour because my wife did not pay me respect enough.

TUESDAY 28 NOVEMBER. I had kept my bad humour all night with a strange obstinacy, persisting in a principle or passion never to change till my wife solicits me. When I came home from the House this forenoon, she tried to soothe me; but my sullenness had been allowed to continue too long, and I could not get free from it quickly. I verily believe that I could persist in it for years. I sat awhile with worthy Grange, who had hurt his leg and was a little feverish. I laboured pretty well today. I was calm and placid and easy tonight, though still not reconciled to my wife.

Annie Mill, Effie's nurse, went away yesterday, after having been about eighteen months with her; the separation was a distress to both. We got a fine comely girl to take care of Effie: Jeanie Hardie, a Dunbar girl, who had served at Dumfries House. To divert Effie was a study to me. These little domestic incidents engage me much. After I went to bed, my wife got the better of my bad humour by asking me to be friends before I fell asleep; "For", said she, "the consequence of

---

88 "The lady's name is represented in the manuscript by some initial or symbol which we have been unable to make out. (She may have been Mrs Ross, Sandy's nurse.) The reading 'V' (that is, 'five') is not certain, but is confirmed by what follows" (*Ominous Years*, p. 188, n. 2).

sleep is uncertain." I was struck with the awful reflection that I might not awake again in life, and that it would be shocking to die in such a frame; and I was softened by her tender anxiety. Much do I value and love her.

THURSDAY 30 NOVEMBER. This being St Andrew's day, I walked as Master of the Canongate Kilwinning Lodge in the procession of the Free Masons from the Parliament House to the Theatre Royal.[89] It had an excellent effect upon the New Bridge,[90] while the flambeaux blazed in a luminous train. The Theatre was our place of meeting this year, as the Assembly Hall[91] was newly painted. I was in perfect good spirits, and harangued and sung with ease and vigour. When I observed in a speech that this was "*our first appearance on this stage*", it had a cheerful influence like one of Burke's sallies.

FRIDAY 1 DECEMBER. I make it a general rule neither to dine abroad nor have company with me on Friday, as Moncrieffe's supper is enough for one day. This day, however, we were asked to dine at my father's, and I did not like to refuse. Mrs Montgomerie and Sir Walter were there. It was but a dull day somehow. When I came home I found a letter acquainting me that my lottery ticket was drawn a blank; but to balance that I also found a most friendly letter from Lord Mountstuart telling me that the Commissary's place had been engaged, but that he had no doubt that the Duke of Queensberry and he would be able to obtain something for me. This comforted me. I went to Moncrieffe's, played at cards and lost a little, supped well, and was pretty joyous, and as Lord Monboddo was there, sat till one.

SATURDAY 2 DECEMBER. I sat a little with Crosbie, who was confined with the epidemical cold, and talked with him of the cause, Carmichael against Scott, on which the Lords had ordered a hearing in presence to be on Tuesday.[92] I had made Mr Crosbie be taken in to assist me in it. I dined with Nairne. He had Lord Kellie's brothers, young Pitfour, and Captain Turnbull, etc., with him. We had a deal of profane licentious jocularity and Edinburgh ill-bred raillery. I disliked the company much. Captain Erskine said little. Captain Andrew was seized with the humour of the place. The only satisfaction I had was from Captain Turnbull's relating some of the military operations last war. I drank rather more than I should have done. I was now rather loaded with business to be done, and

89 For the Theatre Royal, see p. 120, n. 48.
90 The North Bridge, leading from the Old Town to the New Town. The bridge had become passable in 1772.
91 For the Assembly Hall, see Introduction, p. 9; see also p. 87, n. 61.
92 This case is reported as *William Scot v John Carmichael* in *Faculty Decisions*, Vol. VII, 1775-77, p. 143. Scott, a merchant in Newcastle, had obtained a warrant from the sheriff for the incarceration of Carmichael, a shopkeeper from Morpeth in Northumberland, on the ground that Carmichael was about to leave Britain to avoid his creditors and to defraud them of their just debts. Carmichael, who claimed that he intended to return to his home and that he was not avoiding his creditors, applied by way of Bill of Suspension and Liberation to be released in return for finding sufficient caution *judicio sisti* (that is, security for his appearance at future diets of court). After a hearing on 5 December at which Boswell represented Carmichael (see the entry for that date), the court held that there was insufficient evidence of fraud on Carmichael's part and that accordingly, being a stranger in Scotland, he was not subject to the jurisdiction of the Scottish courts. He was then released without even having to find caution.

intended to have gone home and laboured; but I received a note from Sandy Gordon to come and play at whist at his house, and I could not resist it. Maclaurin and I played against Lady Dumfries and him, and lost. Maclaurin then went to sup with Lord Monboddo, and Sandy and I and the Countess fell to brag. We grew keen, supped, drank a bottle of claret slowly, having resumed our cards, and so much bewitched were we that we played on till past four in the morning. I was sensible that this was very indecent; I was ill from such rakishness and knew that my dear wife would suffer. Yet I could not quit gaming. I had once won a good deal. When we parted, I had won only seventeen shillings.

SUNDAY 3 DECEMBER. In the afternoon paid another visit to ——.

MONDAY 4 DECEMBER. At nine went to Crosbie's to talk over the cause of Carmichael on arrestment of an Englishman _judicio sisti_, on which he and I were to plead before the Lords next day. John MacGowan and I supped with him, drank moderately, and talked of the history of painting and engraving in Scotland. I talked of a design which I had to collect all the engraved portraits of Scotsmen. Lord Mountstuart has a great collection of British heads. My plan is confined and such as I can afford.

When I came home, I found that my wife had been reading this journal, and, though I had used Greek letters, had understood my visits to ——. She spoke to me of it with so much reason and spirit that, as I candidly owned my folly, so I was impressed with proper feelings; and, without more argument than that it was disagreeable to so excellent a spouse, resolved firmly to keep clear. And when I reflected calmly, I thought it lucky that my journal had been read, as it gave an opportunity to check in the beginning what might have produced much mischief. I wondered at my temporary dissipation of thought when I saw the effects of my conduct. I valued and loved my wife with renewed fervour.

TUESDAY 5 DECEMBER. Pleaded Carmichael's cause with composure and ease, and, the Solicitor told me, very well.[93] Heard Ilay Campbell, Crosbie, and Maclaurin plead it, and was interested. I had dictated any notes that I had for it this morning. Was idly inclined after dinner. Called for Mr Digges at the Theatre, and drank a glass of wine with him. He was as laborious in his profession as I in mine, but he observed that there was more entertainment in his. "Yes," said I, "you are a silversmith. I am a blacksmith. You make fine, glittering, ornamental pieces of work. I make coarse black grates and shovels, and chains sometimes." It was curious to look back fifteen or sixteen years ago, when I viewed him as a being of high dignity and a kind of mysterious refinement, as if he were as superior to most other men as a page of Shakespeare's most exquisite poetry to ordinary prose. However, I must own that he appeared very well in my imagination still.

WEDNESDAY 6 DECEMBER. After the Court of Session rose, walked in the Meadow with Ilay Campbell and Charles Hay, the only time that I have walked for above two months. Was quite an idler in the afternoon, and did nothing. Sat awhile with Grange, and was comfortably social.

93 The Solicitor-General was Alexander Murray, who had replaced Henry Dundas in May.

FRIDAY 8 DECEMBER. After my business in the Court of Session was over, I called on Mr Donaldson, the painter, for a little.[94] He offered to assist me in making my collection of Scottish engraved portraits. He put into my hands some extracts which he had taken from Hawthornden's poems, some of which were very fine. He wished to see a selection of that poet's pieces published. He also showed me some fancy drawings of his own, very well imagined. He said he did not like painters choosing always subjects from books. It made painting a secondary art. Let it supply itself with ideas. I find myself always led into a curious train of thinking by Donaldson, and as he is really a man of genius, and seems sensible of my kindness for him, I wish to befriend him.

I then called on Mr Robert Syme, Writer to the Signet,[95] who was sitting in his chamber in a green night-gown, confined with the cold, and surrounded with processes; a very different scene from Donaldson's, but a very proper one for me, as Mr Syme employs me much as a lawyer. George Webster observed one day lately that the world is just a succession of scenes as on the stage. The thought was the same as Shakespeare's, "All the world's a stage."[96] But George rendered it more applicable to immediate observation. "Shakespeare", said he, "wrote plays in five acts. But we see innumerable acts"; and then he rapidly gave a number of different instances of what we see even in this town of Edinburgh.

Business was now going on with me very well, though I did not rise early. But still I read nothing but law cases or authorities. When I compared myself to a blacksmith when talking with Digges, I should have added that studying dull causes before pleading them or writing on them is the worst part of our profession. If the iron is once heated and laid on the anvil, it is not very disagreeable to wield the hammer or instruments for shaping it into various forms. But it is irksome to have a mass of a *process* laid cold on one's table, and to be obliged to blow the bellows of application in the heat of attention till I can mould it.

Mr Claud Boswell drank tea with us. There is little congenial sympathy between him and me, so that, though I regard him as a worthy cousin, we meet seldom. I however wish to be more with him, and shall be so for the future. Between six and seven I met at John's Coffee-house[97] a detachment of my Lodge of Canongate Kilwinning, and we went and visited St Andrew's Lodge held in Niddry's Wynd. This evening for the first time I saw a kind of quarrel like to fall out in a Mason lodge. The junior warden, ——, an Irish student, was drunk and spoke a little impertinently. Captain Hamilton of the 31st, one of my attendants, took him up; and if there had not been a prudent interposition, they might have fought.

94 John Donaldson, who resided at the Nether Bow at the east end of the High Street.
95 Robert Syme (d. 1780), W.S. (admitted 4 August 1735), uncle of "young" Robert Syme, W.S., who had been admitted W.S. eight days earlier, on 30 November. He resided at the head of Forrester's Wynd, off the south side of the Lawnmarket.
96 *As You Like It*, II. vii. 139.
97 For John's Coffee House, see Introduction, p. 12.

SATURDAY 9 DECEMBER. I took a walk in the Meadow with Nairne. We talked of my notion of an obligation in moral honesty, at least in honour, to continue the male line of succession of an estate, if a predecessor has devised it so, and a man has received it merely because he is an heir male. Nairne did not agree with me. Said he: "If my predecessor gives me an estate because I am an heir male, I am obliged to him; but I am under no obligation in conscience to follow the same line of succession. If he had been resolved on that, he might have entailed the estate under a prohibitory irritancy. But if he has not done so, but has left me the power of choosing what line of succession I like, I will without scruple choose what I think best at the time. If my predecessor, who leaves me an estate or a large sum of money, signifies an inclination that a house on a certain plan should be built, and I think it a bad plan, I will not build it." My answer was that it is not right to counteract the destination of a predecessor, who, instead of fettering you by an entail, trusts to your honour; and the heirs male of an estate so destined have in equity and in good faith, a *right* which it would be robbery in a moral sense, though not in a legal, to disappoint. Nairne was obstinate in his opinion, and his coldness upon my great principle of feudal honour disgusted me. I recollected Dr Johnson's noble sentiments on the subject, and felt a superiority.

Mrs Mitchelson and Mr Stobie dined with us. I had something of a headache from last night's wine, though I had not drank to intoxication. Stobie had told me some days ago that my father did not seem inclined to pay my debt for Dalblair. This vexed me, after having pleased myself with the belief that he was to do it, as I have related on Saturday the 18 of November last. His going back was a sign to me of failure, and I was really perplexed. Stobie said that my father talked now of having an assignation to the debt to keep it up against me, as he thought I would call in question his settlement. I composed myself with thinking that I might, by gentle and prudent methods, get him to do as I could wish; and as an alteration of his settlements in my favour as his heir was in his power to the last hour of his life, I might perhaps in a *beau moment*, as the French say, persuade him to leave me at full liberty. Mrs Mitchelson drank tea. I finished a long paper.

At supper my wife and I had a dispute about some trifle. She did not yield readily enough, and my passion rose to a pitch that I could not quite command. I started up and threw an egg in the fire and some beer after it. My inclination was to break and destroy everything. But I checked it. How curious is it that the thinking principle can speculate in the very instant of anger. My wife soon made up our difference. But I begged of her to be more attentive again.

SUNDAY 10 DECEMBER. Mr Nairne supped with us and drank mulled port, according to a kind of Sunday's private party which he has had occasionally with us since ever we took up house. We were calmly social.

MONDAY 11 DECEMBER. My wife, after much entreaty, went with me to Donaldson's, and sat for a miniature picture for the first time. I did not do much in business today. In the evening I went with a number of my lodge to

The Recruiting Officer with *Love à la Mode*[98] played by desire of the Free Masons. I went from the Theatre with Charles Hay to Princes Street Coffee-house to eat a bit of supper and drink a little brandy punch. George Webster joined us, and we drank pretty freely till my spirits rose and I proposed a rubber at whist. A Mr Esdaile, a young Londoner, made a fourth hand. About one in the morning I sent a note to my wife by Joseph,[99] who had found me out, told her I was sober, and hoped she would go to bed; and then I indulged my love of gaming, and insensibly resolved to make a night of it.

TUESDAY 12 DECEMBER. About seven in the morning my clerk, Mr Lawrie, came and found us sitting like wizards. He told me that my wife had been up all night and was quite miserable. This shocked me. I thought, however, that it was in vain to go home now, but that I would play on till within a little of nine, when I was obliged to be in the Parliament House, having fifteen causes in the rolls, as Mr Lawrie mentioned with much earnestness. He had the dismal look of a faithful servant who saw his master doing what was quite wrong. We retired from the coffee-room into a private room, and played on till near nine. I lost £2. 7. 6 upon the whole. If the Court had not been sitting, I believe we should have played on all day, for I was not at all saturated with gaming. I came home, washed, shifted, and put on my bar wig, and after being severely hurt, by seeing my wife in sad uneasiness, I hastened to the House and struggled through my causes wonderfully. I could not help mentioning to several of my brethren the adventure of last night, but I mentioned it as a very extraordinary debauch for me *now*. I was very ill, and luckily had nothing absolutely necessary to be done this forenoon, so went home and went to bed immediately, Joseph bringing me onion soup. I lay till between seven and eight in the evening, and then got up and dictated a short paper. My wife, who had not been in bed since yesterday morning, was much indisposed, and very justly complained of my behaviour. I pacified her by sincere promises of future attention. Indeed she is wonderfully easy in forgetting my bad conduct. It is curious how differently bad conduct appears to a man when he himself is guilty of it from what it does in the abstract. What would I have thought had I been told of a counsellor-at-law and the father of a family doing what I did last night! I felt a kind of desponding impression that I was unfit for being a married man. I hope I shall be more firm in time coming. My good practice is never of sufficiently long continuance to have a stable consistency. It is shaken loose by occasional repetitions of licentiousness. The wounds of vice break out afresh.

WEDNESDAY 13 DECEMBER. I had a letter from Dr Hall with accounts of my poor brother John, whose mind the Doctor described as in a twilight, but said he was insensible of his misfortune. He enclosed me an affidavit by him that he had no other place from Government than his lieutenancy on half pay. When I saw his subscription, and recollected his situation, it affected me so that I almost cried.

98 By George Farquhar and Charles Macklin respectively.
99 Boswell's Bohemian servant, Joseph Ritter (*Ominous Years*, p. 196, n. 5).

Miss Dick called on us this forenoon, and I wrote a note to worthy Sir Alexander promising to dine with him on Saturday, wondering how I had been so long from Prestonfield, and telling him that I cherished a design of writing his life and hoped for his aid.

THURSDAY 14 DECEMBER. My late scenes of dissipation have hurt my mind. I have been quite a sensualist, quite a being for the immediate time, without thought of future existence. I am sensible that by habit a man may obliterate the traces of moral and religious duty. My thoughts at this period went only to gain and pleasure *de jour en journée*,[100] as the French say. I was abased in my own eyes when I turned them inwards for a moment. Lady Colville, Lady Anne Erskine, Captain Erskine, and Mr Andrew drank tea with us. I played a rubber at sixpence whist.

FRIDAY 15 DECEMBER. This morning between nine and ten Lord Kennet, who had a long roll of causes, and was in a hurry to get through it, expressed himself to me (when I was pleading before him) in a manner that I thought rude. I checked my passion for a little, and spoke of his improper behaviour with some of my brethren, who seemed to think it nothing extraordinary. I however did not like to put up with it; and therefore, after he was gone to the Inner House, I followed and got a word of him, and very calmly and seriously let him know that I thought he had used me ill. He declared he had no such intention, and that I had mistaken him. This was enough. I was put into a flutter with this incident. A judge is certainly obliged to treat counsel at the bar civilly, and if he is impertinent, may be called to account for it. But it is difficult and nice to determine when a judge has exceeded judicial propriety, as he no doubt has a right to proceed with due authority.

Mr Donaldson, the painter, had been here either yesterday or the day before at another sitting for my wife's miniature. He was here again today. I was busy dictating a long paper. It refreshed me to go into the drawing-room now and then and see him painting.

SATURDAY 16 DECEMBER. After the Court of Session rose, Mr Donaldson, the painter, Dr Boswell, and I walked out to Sir Alexander Dick's. This was reviving such a scene as I recollect sixteen years ago when Donaldson was here and the Doctor was in high glee as a virtuoso. He was in brisk spirits today, and Donaldson and he disputed on many topics, especially on religion; Donaldson being a sort of infidel, and the Doctor a vigorous believer. We found Sir Alexander in the same gay, friendly temper as ever. He rejoiced with me on the birth of my Ascanius,[101] as he called my son. We walked a little before dinner, and in a summer-house which he has raised in a corner chosen by old Allan Ramsay, we saw upon the wall a sketch of that poet's head, very like, done by Sir Alexander from memory, in black lead. Donaldson said it was a bold outline, and at my suggestion agreed to copy it. I said that there might be good drawings made for our old

100 "From day to day."
101 The son of Aeneas.

Scotch songs: *The Auld Wife ayont the Fire, Muirland Willie*, etc. Donaldson thought so too. I spoke to Sir Alexander of writing his life. I had a pleasing card from him yesterday saying that it was only for private friends, and he today again modestly declined his being recorded. I however did not doubt that I should get from him the progressive circumstances of his life.

Esdaile, who sat up with me at Princes Street Coffee-house, dined here today. He put me in mind of a curious expression which I used when Mr Lawrie wanted me to come home to my wife: "Tell her I'm doing harm neither to man nor beast." In the evening I called a little at home and then went to the Hon. A. Gordon's and played at whist and brag. A good many people were there. I was a gainer before supper, which was at twelve o'clock; but after it, when the rage of gaming came upon me, and I forgot or disregarded my resolution or promise never to play above half-crown whist and never to bet, I lost, besides my winning, £4. 14. We did not part till near three. I came home in great vexation of spirit. Luckily my wife was in a most gentle frame and soothed me, and I again resolved to be moderate, or give up play altogether. I considered that I might gradually become a deep gamester, and I shuddered at the thought.

SUNDAY 17 DECEMBER. After church I called on David Hume and found him sitting after dinner with his sister[102] and youngest nephew. He had on a white nightcap and a hat above it. He called for a fresh bottle of port, which he and I drank, all but a single glass that his nephew took. I indeed took the largest share. Then we drank tea. Mr Hume said that he had not met with the encouragement which he deserved as a man of genius, for Mr Hume had known several men of letters who never had heard of him.

Mr Hume told me he went to France in the year 1734, being ill, and stayed there three years. David said his first publication was his *Treatise on Human Nature*. He said he had never written any verses. I had really a good chat with him this afternoon. I thought also of writing his life.

It was curious to see David such a civil, sensible, comfortable looking man, and to recollect, "This is the Great Infidel." Belief or want of belief is not absolutely connected with practice. How many surly men are teachers of the gospel of peace!

TUESDAY 19 DECEMBER. The Court of Session by a great majority altered Lord Gardenstone's interlocutor in the cause, Scotlands against the Reverend Mr Thomson, and were very severe on the latter.[103] This was very unexpected to me, and I was a good deal hurt by it, having taken a fixed interest in the question, I suppose from its being connected with Colonel Campbell's success, and believing that Thomson thought himself right.

THURSDAY 21 DECEMBER. After dinner Mr George Laing[104] called on me to talk over a process in which he was agent and I was lawyer. He talked most

---

102 Catherine Home of Ninewells. Hume changed the spelling of his surname from Home to Hume in or about 1734.
103 He was ordered to pay damages of £30 and the sum of 50 guineas in respect of expenses (*Ominous Years*, p. 202, n. 9).
104 A "writer" (admitted by the Court of Session in 1772).

sensibly, and as he has given me a good deal of business, and I never could perceive anything bad in his conduct, I felt a sort of humane warmth for him as one who has suffered from prejudice, his character in the Court being unfavourable, I know not for what. I called for wine and drank some glasses with him. Mr Lawrie joined us after we had drank one or two. My constitution is now such, I suppose from habit, that I can hardly bear any wine at all. Though I drank but about a third of a bottle, my head was for a little disturbed. I however dictated some law and wrote a letter to Mr Garrick, chiefly to recommend to him one Young, a Scotsman, who had gone upon the stage. I enclosed to him a letter to me from Lord Kames, asking me to recommend Young, who had been his clerk. I suggested to my Lord, when he spoke to me, to write such a letter as would be agreeable to Mr Garrick. In writing to Garrick, I felt particles of vivacity rise by a sort of contagion of fancy. At nine o'clock I went to the Pantheon, of which I had been made an honorary member, and heard a debate whether or not lotteries are beneficial to Great Britain.

FRIDAY 22 DECEMBER. This being the day before the session rose for the Christmas recess, and as I was to dine at Lord Alemoor's and sup at Moncrieffe's, I wished to have nothing to do in the afternoon, and therefore finished the only paper necessary to be done directly, and so did not go to hear the last lecture of Dr Black's course of chemistry.[105] Indeed I have missed several of them. It is a certain fact that I have a mind incapable, or at least ill disposed, for science of any kind. I always remember Sir John Pringle's saying to me some years ago in London, "You know nothing." And now the remark is as just as then. There is an imperfection, a superficialness, in all my notions. I understand nothing clearly, nothing to the bottom. I pick up fragments, but never have in my memory a mass of any size. I wonder really if it be possible for me to acquire any one part of knowledge fully. I am a lawyer. I have no system of law. I write verses. I know nothing of the art of poetry. In short I could go through everything in the same way.

Mr David Dalrymple,[106] Mr Nairne, Mr John Davidson, and I went in a coach to Lord Alemoor's.[107] Ilay Campbell, Lord Coalston, and John Mackenzie were there. We dined luxuriously, and my Lord kept us drinking claret till past nine, all but Lord Coalston. I have nothing worthy of registration at this meeting. Ilay Campbell took John Davidson's place up to town. I went directly to Moncrieffe's. I was heated and elevated pretty much; played at whist and lost a trifle, and then supped; but growing uneasy I came off soon after supper, and was ill after I came home, but not drunk. Strange are the manners of this country.

105 In the summer, Boswell had started a course of chemistry with Dr Joseph Black (1728-1799), Professor of Chemistry and Medicine at Edinburgh University, in a class consisting mostly of lawyers.
106 David Dalrymple of Westhall, advocate (admitted 8 January 1743). He was appointed Sheriff-Depute of Aberdeenshire in 1748 and was to be appointed a Lord of Session (as Lord Westhall) on 10 July 1777. He was Grand Master of St John's Lodge.
107 Lord Alemoor's estate was at Hawkhill, Restalrig, near Edinburgh, where he built a beautiful villa and liked to entertain small numbers of select friends. It was said that he erected the first grape-house in Scotland (Ramsay, p. 326, n. 1).

SATURDAY 23 DECEMBER. The Session rose for the Christmas recess. I found business doing well this session, better even than last winter session. M. Dupont drank tea with us. This evening was the meeting of the examinators on civil and Scotch law, of whom I was one.[108] We supped at Fortune's. Before supper I played a rubber at whist and won. Harry Dundas, Lord Advocate, our Dean, was with us, and he gave us so many parliamentary speeches, and talked so seriously on the decline of learning in Scotland, that I saw tonight what I never saw before: a company of advocates free from drunkenness, though we sat till past two in the morning. I was really pleased with Dundas tonight, and half resolved to be well with him, though his interference in the Ayrshire politics had exasperated me. I was in a good, rational, calm frame.

MONDAY 25 DECEMBER. Worthy Grange, who has never failed to dine with me on Christmas-day, was brought up in a chair,[109] and we were as comfortable as usual, and drank my brother David's health in rich Malaga. I went to the chapel[110] in the afternoon, but the music was unpleasing, and my devotion was not aided. Grange drank tea with us. In the evening my wife and I took a fancy to play at brag, and my rage for gaming was such that we played till one in the morning.

WEDNESDAY 27 DECEMBER. In the forenoon sat with Robert Boswell a good while in the Advocates' Library consulting on a difficult cause. Then went to my father's with a view of talking to him of paying my debt, if I saw a proper opening. He came upon the subject himself, but was in quite a different frame from what he was on Saturday the 18 November as mentioned in this journal. He said he had made an entail and settled that if I should even call it in question, I should forfeit all his own purchases; but that he saw this would not restrain me, and therefore he was now determined to allow me no more than £100 a year, which he had formally settled upon me, instead of £300, which he had hitherto allowed me since my marriage; and instead of relieving me of my debt to Dalblair's creditors, he would get a trustee to pay it upon an assignation, and then do diligence against me,[111] and lay me in gaol. He was in a shocking humour today. I was quite calm; told him that I had pursued the very plan of life which he was anxious I should follow, though it was disagreeable to me; that I was doing very well, and that I did not expect such usage from him. That if he would entail the estate on heirs male without stopping short and cutting off the descendants of Craigston,[112] I would join with him; but that as he told me that he went no farther than the heirs male descending from my grandfather, and then went to heirs female, I thought the entail unjust, and could not agree to it. I unluckily mentioned something that Maclaurin had said. This made my father worse. He said, "I see you have been consulting lawyers. I will guard against you." And then

108 At this time, Boswell was one of the private examinators on Civil Law (see p. 66, n. 39).
109 He had hurt his leg (see the entry for 28 November).
110 The New English Chapel (for which, see the entry for 25 December 1774 and relevant footnote).
111 That is, enforce payment by legal means.
112 David Boswell of Craigston (c. 1660-1728).

he said, in a diabolical-like passion, "I shall put an end to it at once. I shall sell it off and do with the money what I please." He also threw out some morose, contemptuous reflections: as if I thought myself a very wise man, and was the reverse, and how I went to London among the *geniuses*, who despised me. He abused Dr Johnson, and when I mentioned keeping up a connexion with Lord Mountstuart, treated him with contempt. In short he was as bad as possible. I told him he no doubt had it in his power to do as he threatened; but I wished he would think seriously if he could do so with a good conscience, and that there was a Father in Heaven to whom both of us were answerable. He said that he himself would have settled the estate on my daughters, failing my sons, but that he had taken a race of heirs male to please me; that he believed I was the only man in Edinburgh who would insist to have his own children disinherited, but that I had not natural affection. I was a good deal agitated inwardly. He appeared truly odious as an unjust and tyrannical man. I recollected Dr Johnson's saying that he would as soon hang himself as sell his estate, but yet I could not be sure what he might do. I however considered that I ought not to be accessory to injustice, to cutting off any of my brethren, and that if he should even sell the estate, I could reflect that I had been firm in what I thought honest and honourable. I pleased myself too with thinking that I might purchase the estate by the intervention of a friend, and so disappoint him totally. It was an abominable altercation.

Balbarton came to dine with him, and he asked me to stay, which I did. Lady Auchinleck was ill and did not dine with us. I appeared quite unconcerned, but was miserably vexed, and drank beer and porter in abundance and a good deal of white wine till I was somewhat intoxicated. I then went down to Peter Ramsay's, where Sir Walter was to take his chaise. He introduced me to his travelling companion, young Maxwell of Calderwood. The rattling conversation of the youths amused my mind and I drank freely of port and claret till they set out. I was very drunk and wandered in the streets about three hours, following girls but luckily retaining rationality enough to keep clear of them. I fell once or twice and came home all dirty and bruised and very ill of a cold immediately catched. My wife, to whom I told what had passed at my father's, which occasioned my drunkenness, was good enough not to upbraid me.

SATURDAY 30 DECEMBER. I went to Sir George's and, feeling myself in a most comfortable social humour, frankly offered to stay dinner if my wife would come. Miss Preston went immediately and secured her. We were made most heartily welcome, and so much kindness was shown that I observed tears in my wife's eyes. Sir George and Lady Preston have been really like parents to us for these several years, and I am happy to think that we have made an affectionate return. This day I was as warm-hearted with the worthy people and as much at my ease, relishing the comforts of life, as I could wish, and they were so much the same that I had no melancholy ideas of their being old. Sir George went to sleep between dinner and tea.

SUNDAY 31 DECEMBER. My cold and sprained ankle were worse. I lay in bed but did not enjoy that tranquillity which I have formerly done in that state of indolence. I read in *The Critical Review* an account of Priestley's edition of Hartley's *Observations on Man* with some essays of his own relative to the subject of that book.[113] While I was carried into metaphysical abstraction, and felt that *perhaps* all our thinking of every kind was only a variety of modification upon matter, I was in a sort of amaze; but I must observe that it did not affect me with "that secret dread and inward horror"[114] which it has occasioned at other times. There is no accounting for our feelings, but certain it is that what strikes us strongly at one time will have little influence at another. Speculation of this kind relieved me from the vexation of family differences, by changing objects and by making me consider, "If all thought and all volition and all that we denominate spirit be only properties of matter, why should I distress myself at present, while in full consciousness, about eventual successions of machines?" I however thought that philosophical theories were transient, whereas feudal principles remained for ages. In truth the mortality or immortality of the soul can make no difference on the enthusiasm for supporting a family, for, in either case, the matter must be of no moment to those who have departed this life. If they have ceased to exist, they know nothing of it. If they exist in another state, they perhaps even then know not what passes here, and, if they do, it is perhaps as trifling in their eyes as our childish concerns are in ours when we have arrived at manhood. How strange is it, then, that a man will toil all his life and deny himself satisfactions in order to aggrandize his posterity after he is dead. It is, I fancy, from a kind of delusion in the imagination, which makes us figure ourselves contemplating for ages our own magnificence in a succession of descendants. So strong is this delusion with me that I would suffer death rather than let the estate of Auchinleck be sold; and this must be from an enthusiasm for an *idea* for *the Family*. The founder of it I never saw, so how can I be zealous for his race? and were I to be a martyr, I should only be reckoned a madman. But an *idea* will produce the highest enthusiasm. Witness the ardour which the individuals at the time have for the glory of their regiment, though they have no line of connexion with it, being picked out from all parts of the kingdom. The officers and soldiers of the Scots Greys boast that "*We* were never known to fly."—"*We* gained distinguished honour at such a battle." Yet the officers and soldiers under that *name* at former periods were as different from its officers and soldiers now as the Romans were. I don't mean that they were different in body or in mind, in any remarkable degree, but that there is not a trace of identity, unless that there is always a remain of a regiment to communicate the same discipline and gallantry of sentiment to those who come into it, so that *l'esprit du corps*, like the fire of Vesta, is kept incessantly burning, though the materials are different. I thought for a little that a man should place his pride and

113 "Hartley... explained thought by an ingenious mechanistic theory of minute vibrations in the nerves and brain. Though a sincere Christian, he denied free will in the philosophical sense. His book was published in 1749, but did not attract much attention until Priestley popularised it" (*Ominous Years*, p. 207, n. 9).
114 Addison's *Cato*, V. i. 4-5.

his happiness in his own individuality, and endeavour to be as rich and as renowned and as happy as he can.

My wife went to church in the afternoon. I got up to tea, and afterwards I took from my drawers the account of our family drawn up by my grandfather, and read it with more attention than I had ever done, and I discovered that in fact my great-grandfather had got little better than a bankrupt estate from his uncle, and that it was so burthened with debt that it appeared to me a question if, at that period, when money was scarce in Scotland and interest high, it was prudent to take it. This at once, like a blaze of light, showed me that I had been in an error as to an obligation in *justice* to give the succession all along to heirs male, seeing that we had not received it as a sacred trust with that view; and if *principle* was removed, I could yield my *inclination* and agree with my father. I was apprehensive that this sudden light would not be steady, and was only struck out by my father's threatenings; at least that my mind was much biased by them. I therefore resolved to wait for some time and to consult Dr Johnson. My wife, who was pleased not a little, cherished the discovery and suggested that if I had any scruple remaining, I might settle my estate of Dalblair on heirs male for ever. I was wonderfully relieved tonight. My feudal enthusiasm for the heirs male of our founder, Thomas Boswell, remained. But this I could yield or modify.

1776

MONDAY 1 JANUARY. Nothing very remarkable filled my mind on this day, the beginning of a new year. Lord Hailes's *Annals of Scotland* came out and I read a little of them, wondering at his extreme assiduity.[1] Upon a review of my expense during the year, I found that, instead of £500 at which Sir William Forbes and I had calculated it on the 2 of January 1775, it amounted to upwards of £650. There were, however, a few extraordinary articles. My wife and I resolved for this year to endeavour to spend less. I must indeed do her the justice to observe that, instead of exceeding what was allowed to her by the calculation, she was about £40 within it. I was in an indolent frame, with my legs resting on a stool to ease my sprained ankle. Young resolutions are sprightly. I pleased myself with hopes that I should be more economical in time coming. I made out a state of my debts and funds, and, abstracting from my debt to Dalblair's creditors, for which my father is bound, I had £100 clear. The Dalblair debt, principal and interest, came to £1,300, so that with the £100 retained of my last year's allowance, my father would have £1,200 to pay.

In the forenoon a curious incident happened to me in the course of my profession. ——, a mason in Dundee, came and consulted me on a process which he had before the sheriff of Forfar. After I had read several papers, heard him patiently, and written a note of my opinion, he asked me how much he should give me. I said whatever he pleased. Upon which he took out three shillings and said, "Will that do?" I smiled and bid him give it to "that young man" (Mr Lawrie). The man appeared to me to have acted with honest simplicity. From his process I saw that he had by his business 1. 6 a day, and I suppose he thought two days' wages very good payment to me for less than two hours' work.

TUESDAY 2 JANUARY. During this recess I have indulged myself in lying long in bed. I had a consultation in the forenoon, but felt an unwillingness to the labour of the law. In the afternoon I wrote a long, serious, and earnest letter to Dr Johnson upon the subject of the settlement of our estate, laid before him my discovery, and entreated a full opinion from him. He had formerly confirmed me in my resolution to be steadfast to heirs male for ever. But I stated to him that I had been in an error as to the *justice* of the case, seeing that my great-grandfather had got very little. My letter was too late for the post, so was to lie till Thursday. I made another discovery this night, which was that three

1 The full title of the work was *Annals of Scotland, from the Accession of Malcolm III, surnamed Canmore, to the Accession of Robert I*. The second part of the work—entitled *Annals of Scotland, from the Accession of Robert I, surnamed Bruce, to the Accession of the House of Stuart*—was published later. In these volumes "early sources of Scottish history were examined and sifted with admirable acuteness and impartiality, and a connected narration was woven out of disputed documents. Many a venerable story and cherished tradition were demolished or banished to mythland... The *Annals* are dry, deplorably dry; but invaluable still for facts—a quarry in which later writers have dug for material out of which to build more artistic works" (Graham, p. 201).

sons of the family who went to Sweden to Gustavus Adolphus's wars were the next heirs after Balmuto, having come off a generation later than the Craigston branch, so that the dancing-master was placed at a much greater distance than we had been supposing, and gallant soldiers came forth. This other discovery showed me how very imperfectly either my father or I had studied the genealogy of our family. I this night made out a sort of tree or table of descent of our males to send to Dr Johnson. I resolved to write a postscript still stronger than my letter to him, in favour of my liberty in point of *justice*, though my *inclination* for the male line of our founder was warm. There was an additional circumstance occurred to me tonight, which was that my great-great-grand-uncle did not give the estate to his brother James, but to his nephew David, which was a proof that he did not think of the strict male succession, and that he gave it to his nephew as a young man who might perhaps make something of it, when his brother could not. My wife suggested that the old laird was ashamed to let his indolence and extravagance be known, and was glad to get his nephew to undertake to pay his debts, instead of letting the estate be torn in pieces and his bad management exposed; and if his nephew could have a reversion, it was but factor fee or commission for his trouble and risk, for at that time it was difficult to get land sold.

WEDNESDAY 3 JANUARY. My wife and I were asked to dine this day at my father's. I was glad the invitation came, as it showed that notwithstanding our last disagreeable interview, we were not at war; but we sent our excuse on account of my lameness. Young Robert Syme drank tea with us. I was consulted today on a mercantile contract at Danzig. I have as yet little power of decision. I am uneasy when I have to give an opinion upon a case. I was at first view dubious as to this case, and rather against my client, but was to think of it more. My state of mind today was still affected by Hartley and Priestley's metaphysics, and was continually trying to perceive my faculties operating as machinery. My animal spirits were so light now that such sort of thinking did not distress me as it has done when I was more atrabilious.[2] I felt an easy indifference as to what was my mental system. I liked present consciousness. Man's continuation of existence is a flux of ideas in the same body, like the flux of a river in the same channel. Even our bodies are perpetually changing. What then is the subject of praise or blame upon the whole? what of love or hatred when we are to contemplate a character? There *must* be *something*, which we understand by a *spirit* or a *soul*, which is permanent. And yet I must own that except the sense or perception of identity, I cannot say that there is any sameness in my soul now and my soul twenty years ago, or surely none thirty years ago. Though souls may be in a flux, each may have a distinct character as rivers have: one rapid, one smooth, etc. I read a little of Lord Hailes's *Annals*.

THURSDAY 4 JANUARY. In the afternoon I was quite charmed with Veronica. She could now sing a number of tunes: *Carrickfergus, O'er the Water to Charlie, Johnnie*

2 Melancholy.

McGill, Wee Willy Gray, Nancy Dawson, Paddy Wake, Ploughman Laddie, Brose and Butter, O'er the Hills and Far Away. It was really extraordinary that a child not three years old should have such a musical memory, and she sung with a sweet voice and fine ear (if that expression be just). She could speak a great many words, but in an imperfect manner: "Etti me see u picture." (Let me see your picture.) She could not pronounce "f." "I heēd." (I'm feared. English, I'm afraid.) She rubbed my sprained ankle this afternoon with rum, with care and tenderness. With eager affection I cried, "GOD bless you, my dearest little creature." She answered, "Od bess u, Papa." Yet she loved her mother more than me, I suppose because her behaviour to her was more uniform. Effie was a stout, cheerful child and very fond of me, but spoke almost none. She aimed at singing ——. I this afternoon felt so much tenderness for Veronica that after hearing my wife say that I might live to have a severe regret for disinheriting her, I for a little had a kind of inclination to let her perhaps be lady of the domains of Auchinleck, and I wrote a postscript to my letter to Dr Johnson. I in a *copy* of it desired the author of *Rasselas*, as a man of tender feelings, to furnish me with philosophy in case Veronica should one day seem to upbraid me for disinheriting her. But I omitted it in the *principal*, having immediately resumed my feudal principle, and considered that a *family* must not be sunk for occasional fondness. That I could do much for Veronica without letting her have what males alone ought to get.

Last night Mr Adam Neill, the printer, called and sat awhile. I asked him many questions on the present operations of the press in Edinburgh, and the profits of publication in different ways; and he gave me such accounts as stimulated my appetite for money, and I wondered that I did not deal more in publication, as by that I might have a good additional income. He spoke of a new almanac and a new newspaper being proposed. He told me that Fleming sold in one year when he was with him nine thousand of the *Edinburgh Almanac*. I found, however, that the clear profit came only to about ninety pounds. I have often thought of engaging in a new newspaper here. I was at present thinking to write a pamphlet in favour of Lord Mountstuart's militia for Scotland; but I doubted of having enough to say, though I warmly wished it success. I still thought in a visionary way of engaging in a newspaper.

This afternoon Grange and young Donaldson drank tea with us. I had some papers to write, some to be printed by Thursday next (one of them a very long one), but I was very unwilling to begin. I put them off today. I was now in a calm frame by keeping the house. Read some of Lord Hailes's *Annals*. My letter and postscript to Dr Johnson made three gilt sheets.[3] As I keep copies of all my letters to him, I copied one sheet, my wife another, and Mr Lawrie another, that the letter might go by the post; yet it was too late tonight again. My wife very judiciously cautioned me against too much openness with Mr Lawrie in letting him read and copy important letters, because though he was an honest, good lad, it was better not to be in his power, as it might happen that I would not like

3 Three pieces of folded gilt-edged paper, making twelve pages in all (*Ominous Years*, p. 214, n. 2).

to keep him longer. I shall profit by this counsel to a certain degree. But really I have a kind of strange feeling as if I wished nothing to be secret that concerns myself. This is a weakness to be corrected. My wife wrote also to Dr Johnson a very sensible, clear letter on the subject of my male succession, entreating his interest with me, that I might agree to my father's settlement; and she did not try to have heirs whatsoever brought in directly. I was much pleased with her letter.

FRIDAY 5 JANUARY. Maclaurin, to whom I had sent a note, came and sat a little with me. He gave me some light on my Danzig case. I read papers by the late Arniston,[4] Craigie,[5] and James Graham, Junior,[6] on a similar case, Carmichael and Stalker, 1735. I mentioned to him Hartley and Priestley. He said he was *sure* he had a soul. He mentioned Whytt on the nerves and Porterfield on the eye as curious books, both ingenious on the hypothesis of an immaterial principle in man. Then Sir William Forbes, to whom I had sent as a merchant, came and assisted me likewise on my Danzig case. In the afternoon, after consulting books enough, I dictated an opinion on it. Dr Young drank tea with us. Lord Hailes's *Annals* engaged me more and more.

SATURDAY 6 JANUARY. Time now pressed me for session papers. I was obliged to begin to a perplexed one: answers, Sandeman and Company to the petition of Doig, a mercantile cause involved in circumstances which had perplexed me much before my father as Lord Ordinary, and even perplexed him.[7] It was still difficult. Robert Boswell and I had met on it in the Advocates' Library. While Mr Lawrie copied passages, I refreshed myself with Lord Hailes's *Annals*. Mr William Wilson, Writer to the Signet, drank tea with us. His knowledge in business, and courteousness somewhat of the last age, pleased me. We talked of Sir Walter's[8] affairs, and he consulted me on two causes. I wrote some letters in the evening. I still possessed much tranquillity.

SUNDAY 7 JANUARY. There had been a fall of snow in the night. The whiteness and wintry appearance gave me a kind of lively sensation. It snowed all day. I read some of the Bible in English, and of the New Testament in French, which put me in mind of the French church at Utrecht. I read a great deal of Lord Hailes's *Annals*. My wife went to church in the afternoon. Young Donaldson, for whom I had sent, drank tea with us, gave me news, and showed me some strange pieces sent for his newspaper.

4 Robert Dundas of Arniston (Lord Arniston), the "first Lord President Dundas", father of the then Lord President Dundas.
5 Robert Craigie of Glendoick, appointed Lord President on 2 February 1754 on the death of Robert Dundas of Arniston, the first Lord President Dundas.
6 James Graham, advocate, who had been admitted advocate on 21 November 1721 and appointed Commissary of Edinburgh in 1761, but had died on 18 November 1771.
7 This was the case of William Sandeman and Company, merchants in Perth, against Robert Doig, manufacturer in Dundee, which was concerned with "a dispute over the alleged non-payment in 1769 of £113. 3. 3d by Robert Doig for a large quantity of yarn bought by him from Robert Lyon, a merchant in Dundee, acting on behalf of W. Sandeman & Co" (Ballantyne, 76 01 11b). William Sandeman was Robert Boswell's father-in-law.
8 Sir Walter Montgomerie-Cuninghame.

MONDAY 8 JANUARY. Got up early for the first time this winter and drudged at Sandeman and Company. Having my account with the Bank of Scotland up to the beginning of this year to settle, I took a chair in the forenoon and was carried thither. It still snowed, and after ten days' keeping the house, the appearance of the High Street struck me strongly. I have great satisfaction in seeing the steady application and regularity of business at the Bank. There is a good paper in *The Spectator* on the Bank of England. I have here an inferior species of the same contemplation. In the afternoon my old master for the violoncello,[9] Mr John Thomson, consulted me on a claim which he had. It was agreeable to me to have it in my power to help him. In the intervals of my drudgery I finished my reading of Lord Hailes's *Annals*, all but the dissertations. I wrote short remarks as I went along, to lay before him, for more information or to suggest doubts; and I put in marks at such passages as I wished to put into a commonplace-book as valuable fragments or quotations.

In the evening my wife had a letter from Dr Cairnie informing her that her eldest sister[10] died at London on the 3rd current. She was a good deal moved. Though I could not regret that a woman who had disgraced herself by a low marriage, and was by that estranged from us, was removed, the recollection of former days made me be a little affected with some sort of tenderness on hearing she was no longer in life. But stern reason soon resumed its influence. When death is brought close to the mind by any particular event, a gloom must in general take place. I this night had something of the same kind of feeling as the night after seeing an execution. This page is worse expressed than usual. I wrote some letters.

TUESDAY 9 JANUARY. In the intervals while Mr Lawrie copied passages, I read *The Monthly Review* on Priestley's edition of Hartley, and found his *material* system refuted with ability and spirit. I was much pleased, and wished to be acquainted with the writer of the article. I could not but think what a strange life a man would lead who should fairly act according to metaphysical conviction or impression at the time. What inconsistency and extravagance should we find! Sometimes he would be rigidly virtuous, at other times abandoned to extreme licentiousness; and at both times acting from *principle*. I have thought of writing a kind of novel to show this: "Memoirs of a Practical Metaphysician". I remember I mentioned this to Dr Reid, who writes on the mind according to common sense.[11] He told me the same thought had occurred to him. Maclaurin observed very well, when he was last with me, that thinking metaphysically destroys the principles of morality; and indeed when a man analyses virtues and vices as a chemist does material substances, they lose their value as well as their odiousness. I was quite fatigued today with Sandeman and Company. Dr

---

9 Boswell had a very good ear for music, and as a young man had regularly played the flute and also attempted the violin and 'cello. He was particularly fond of playing old Scots tunes.
10 Elizabeth Beaumont (for whom, see the entry for 11 November 1775 and relevant footnotes).
11 Thomas Reid (1710-96), author of *An Inquiry into the Human Mind on the Principles of Common Sense*, 1764.

Webster and Grange drank tea with us, which enlivened me somewhat. I sent for Grange. He does not visit me so often as he should. Dr Grant sat awhile with me at night. Mr Wood was with me before dinner, about my sprain.

WEDNESDAY 10 JANUARY. Drudged on at Sandeman and Company, and got it finished to my satisfaction. Drew also a short paper to be in the boxes next day. Finished the dissertations at the end of Lord Hailes's *Annals*. In the evening Mr Burnett, younger of Kemnay, who was secretary to Sir Andrew Mitchell,[12] sat a little with me and revived somewhat my foreign ideas, as I had seen him at Berlin. After supper Robert Boswell came and we read over the proof-sheets of Sandeman and Company. It has been a harassing operation. We sat at it till near two in the morning.

THURSDAY 11 JANUARY. Began to read Macquer's *Chemistry* while I was at stool, and thought that by getting a habit of reading it while at that operation, I would get through it by degrees, and each portion of it would be keenly seized. Mrs Grant, our neighbour, drank tea with us. Grange called in the evening and we prevailed with him to come back and sup. Maclaurin came and sat awhile. He was pleasanter than usual from having drank cheerfully. I was in good spirits though still lame.

I was full of metaphor. I said the Lords of Session were just sponges. They absorbed matter from the papers which we give in to them, and pressed it out again. Some absorbed more; some less. I said the President squeezed them like lemons: "Come, Covington."[13] Some were very juicy; others yielded very little. Alemoor was like a great melon. Alva, a little lime.

I had a letter tonight from Sir John Pringle, which should have come the night before, but the post was kept back by the deep snow. He argued against my quitting a certainty here and settling in London, and put his arguments so well together that I was really convinced. Indeed it is better for me to take London as a high enjoyment in the spring, unless I were sure of being settled there very advantageously. By being there only two months in the year, I feel myself welcomed by all my friends, and relish it more than if I lived always there. But is it not so extensive a place, such a world, that a man may always find novelty and vivid relish in it? And a man may as well think that it is better for him not to be in existence above two months in the year, that he may enjoy it more. My love for London is very strong. It is associated with a vast number of agreeable and grand ideas.

After I went to bed I had a curious fancy as to dreams. In sleep the doors of the mind are shut, and thoughts come jumping in at the windows. They tumble headlong, and therefore are so disorderly and strange. Sometimes they are stout and light on their feet, and then they are rational dreams.

FRIDAY 12 JANUARY. Wrote two papers for Campbell of Blythswood really as well as I would wish to write. I was sensible of having a knowledge of law as

---

12 For Sir Andrew Mitchell, see Introduction, p. 32.
13 Alexander Lockhart, Lord Covington.

well as a faculty of expression. It was indeed but a limited knowledge, but it was quite sufficient for the present occasion. Maclaurin made an observation last night which pleased me. He said that speaking ill of people was a youthful thing and cured by age. I fancy he is right. As we grow old we either become convinced that mankind must not be tried by too strict a standard of virtue, or we grow prudent, or come to think with a sort of indifference. Miss Webster and Grange drank tea with us. The snow still continued.

SATURDAY 13 JANUARY. I had set apart this day for sorting a large parcel of my father's session papers, to select what were worth binding. I like such an operation wonderfully. The succession of different subjects and different lawyers passing quickly before me was amusing, and I had the pleasure of bringing order out of confusion as I arranged. Mr Stobie called for a little in the forenoon. I said nothing to him on my father's difference with me, as I waited for Dr Johnson's oracular response. I had now been a fortnight without tasting wine or having anybody to dine or sup.

SUNDAY 14 JANUARY. Had taken physic the night before and was relieved by it today. It snowed a great deal today. My wife went to church both forenoon and afternoon. I had the children much with me.

MONDAY 15 JANUARY. Mr Lawrie came in the morning with accounts that Lord Alemoor had died yesterday. It gave me much satisfaction that I had dined with him cordially on Friday 22 December last, since we had lost him so soon. On the same day poor John Robertson, the writer, commonly called Black John or Rosebery John, had died.[14] This struck me too, for I was preparing to write a memorial for him in a case where Lord Rosebery accused him of gross malver-sation.[15] It was curious to think that he had escaped. I laid by a copy of the memorial against him with his notes on it, in which he said that while the house of Strowan remained, the sword should not depart from the Earl's house; so it seems he was of Strowan's family, though in low circumstances and of an unfavourable character.[16] How vain did his retaliation now seem! Lord Alemoor's death, though he was a judge of distinguished abilities, did not strike me so much as Lord Strichen's, because there had not been such a period since a death, and because there was no Lockhart to be promoted. I finished today the only paper which I had upon my hands, except some that were chiefly to be done by Matthew Dickie. I was in good steady spirits.

TUESDAY 16 JANUARY. I was carried in a chair to the Court of Session and had a degree of pleasure in observing how many of my brethren inquired with seeming kindness how I was lame. Lord Alemoor's death was universally regretted. It still snowed some. Donaldson, the painter, did something more to-day to my wife's picture. I kept him to dinner. I had received by the post this

14 It seems that the name "Rosebery John" was derived from Robertson's acting for Lord Rosebery.
15 Corruption.
16 "Strowan in Perthshire was the estate of a line of Robertsons who had been forfeited in 1752 because of the participation of the Laird (Duncan Robertson) in the rising of 1745. It was restored to Duncan's son, Col. Alexander Robertson, in 1784" (*Ominous Years*, p. 220, n. 6).

forenoon a most pleasant letter from Dempster and a friendly one from Dr Johnson, but dated before my important one had reached him. I was put into high spirits, felt ambition in my breast, and thought that if properly supported, and indeed if not checked by my father, I would show the Dundases and the people in Scotland what I could do.

WEDNESDAY 17 JANUARY. On Sunday evening I read some of *The Rambler* to my wife, and I wondered to think how long it was since I had read any of Dr Johnson's works, though they are the food of my soul. I hope his excellent principles are firmly rooted in my mind. But to leave metaphor, as I am a loss to carry it on longer, it is of great advantage to me to renew from time to time the impressions of *The Rambler*. Here I am still metaphorical, though in a more common style. This day has passed in the usual manner of a session day, without anything particular. After I went to bed, the absolute certainty of death and what either my wife or I *must* suffer by separation distressed me.

FRIDAY 19 JANUARY. Was at Moncrieffe's in the evening. Played at whist calmly without feeling the gaming rage. There were only eight of us at supper, so that I could not get away so soon as I hoped to do. It was past two in the morning before I rose. I left six sitting. I never choose to stay till the company breaks up, for then there is a kind of dreary feeling of *dissolution*. Whereas while the company is sitting, social jollity remains. I did not drink to great excess.

SATURDAY 20 JANUARY. My father had all this week been so indifferent about me that he had never once inquired how my sprain was. Today however he asked me; and I was a little with him and Lord Monboddo in the robing room, where we talked of Lord Hailes's *Annals* and Scotch antiquities. Monboddo and I stayed awhile by ourselves. He had a curious thought that *attraction*, which philosophers cannot explain, may be *mind*. He pleases me by an enthusiasm for *spirit* against the *materialists*. Dr Boswell and Mr Donaldson, painter, were with me this forenoon. I dined at the anniversary meeting of Mundell's Scholars, and getting into more than common spirits, was exceedingly jovial and flashed a good deal. I do not recollect my sayings, which had an excellent effect at the time. I drank rather too much, and did not rise till near nine. When I came home I found a letter from Dr Johnson in answer to my important one concerning the settlement of the estate. He said he was much impressed by my letter, but he could not yet form a satisfactory resolution. He suggested that Lord Hailes should be consulted, and he said, "I really think Lord Hailes could help us." I wondered that Dr Johnson had not decided upon the full state of the case which I had laid before him.

SUNDAY 21 JANUARY. Though I had not drank to intoxication last night and had left many of the Scholars sitting, I was somewhat uneasy with a headache. My lameness still continuing, I stayed at home and read some of the Bible and some of *Histoire philosophique et politique, etc.*,[17] which elevated me, but I was often

---

17 "By the Abbé Raynal—a history of European conquests in the East and West Indies; a powerful contribution to democratic propaganda. It had first appeared in 1770" (*Ominous Years*, p. 222, n. 1).

interrupted by the children. In the evening I wrote a serious letter to Lord Hailes on the subject of my father's scheme of an entail and my difficulties. I had some doubt as to consulting him, as he was a Whig and a defender of female succession, and had not sentiments congenial with mine. But as Dr Johnson had recommended applying to him as a Christian and a lawyer, I begged in confidence to have his lights, which I should transmit to Dr Johnson.

MONDAY 22 JANUARY. A number of papers to be written were now accumulated upon my table, none of them indeed very difficult or long, but it gave me uneasiness to perceive that I had so much to do. At one o'clock Captain Flint of the 26 Regiment,[18] an old Mundell's scholar whom I had seen for the first time on Saturday, called on me, as I had promised to give him my best advice in making good a privilege to recruit in the High Street of this city. I engaged to draw up for him a proper letter to the Lord Provost,[19] wishing to have a licence for the Edinburgh Regiment; but if that was refused, insisting on it as a *right*. I have a wonderful fondness for everything military, and I wrote the letter in the evening and sent it to Flint. At night the account of the execution of the two Perreaus affected me very much.[20] I could not fall asleep for a long time after going to bed; and the thoughts of my own death or that of my wife or of my children or of my father or brothers or friends made me very gloomy. My spirits were weak. I had this day dictated only a paper of three pages.

TUESDAY 23 JANUARY. I was somewhat better. The return of light and business removed gloom. I delivered into Lord Hailes's hands my letter to him on our family settlements. Balbarton dined with us today, which kept me idle till tea-time; but I could [not] think my time ill employed in entertaining a sensible kinsman aged seventy-five. I dictated none today at all, but studied a cause and made out a note of what the agent should do. Between seven and eight I and Adam Bell, writer, on one side, and David Armstrong, William Hay, Senior, and John Bushby at Dumfries on the other, met at Mrs Dunbar's tavern and settled a cause, Barrow against Drew. It was a meeting not agreeable to me. But it helped a client. I was moderate in drinking and came home to supper.

WEDNESDAY 24 JANUARY. Lord Hailes returned me an excellent answer, which made the point of *justice* as to remote heirs male so clear against my former notion that I was enlivened to a high degree of cheerfulness, and felt myself quite at freedom. But I had still to get Dr Johnson's full response, after he had seen what Lord Hailes wrote. I this day dictated a paper much to my satisfaction.

THURSDAY 25 JANUARY. Matthew Dickie dined with me and entertained me

---

18 Actually 25 Regiment (*Ominous Years*, p. 222, n. 2).
19 The Lord Provost at that time was James Stoddart, an Edinburgh merchant who first became a member of the Town Council in 1764 and was Lord Provost from 1774 to 1776. In 1774 he stood as candidate for Edinburgh in the General Election, but only obtained three votes. In April 1776 he laid the foundation stone of the Observatory on Calton Hill.
20 Twin brothers, Daniel and Robert Perreau, hanged at Tyburn, London, on 17 January 1776 having been convicted of forgery.

with his account of what a clever fellow Wedderburn was when at our bar, and how he was superior to others even in common law business. He said that he believed his last pleading before the Lords was in a cause in which he was agent, Pillans against Clarke, a moving story of unjust imprisonment, and that he made the Lords weep.[21] Perhaps Matthew exaggerated. But I felt a sort of comfortable acquiescence in Wedderburn's great superiority of parts, instead of that struggle which I have felt when ambitiously supposing it possible to vie with such a man.[22] I consulted with Mr Dickie after dinner on some causes, and at seven I was carried out in a chair to Macqueen's to a consultation. The soundness and vigour of his abilities humbled me. I had also consulted with Mr Rae at John's Coffee-house in the forenoon, and been humbled by his quickness and knowledge of law business. I had a poor opinion of my own qualifications as an advocate, but reproached myself inwardly with want of application to the study of the law. Indeed I should recollect that I did not apply to it at any period as other students have done. I got eight guineas today. In the evening Annie Cuninghame arrived from London and lodged with us.[23] We had Grange at supper and were comfortable.

FRIDAY 26 JANUARY. Annie Cuninghame went over to Fife on a visit. David Ross, who was to succeed Lord Alemoor, appeared today with a wig at the clerks' table.[24] "We see", said I, "the gradual progress of making a judge. It is like seeing bees work in a glass hive." Said George Clerk:[25] "The bees make the comb first and then fill it with honey; so Ross gets the wig first." The Solicitor[26] said Ross was preparing to change his state; getting his wig was like getting wings with which he was to fly from the clerks' table to the bench. He alluded to an insect getting wings from being a worm. Such ready metaphorical vivacity is pleasant for the moment, and I like to recollect it. The Solicitor made a very prudent observation to me today when I was speaking strongly against the Dundases, and asking him if they were not bad people: "They never did me any harm. A bad man is one who is bad to me." I laboured hardly any today. I was at Moncrieffe's at night, and though I loved to sit long, came away about one. Perhaps I check myself too much.

SUNDAY 28 JANUARY. My lameness and the severe weather still continued. It was comfortable sitting by my dining-room fire. I read the history of

---

21 As the editors of *Ominous Years* observe (at p. 224, n. 4), Matthew Dickie's account is strangely at variance with that of Wedderburn's biographers (as to which, see p. 171, n. 163).

22 Boswell's view of Wedderburn was somewhat altered after hearing him plead in the House of Lords on 18 March 1776. "I was disgusted with his priggish affectation," wrote Boswell, "and vexed that such a fellow as I thought him should get so high."

23 Daughter of Captain Alexander Montgomerie-Cuninghame and Mrs Boswell's sister Elizabeth (for whom, see the entries for 11 November 1775 and 8 January 1776 and relevant footnotes). Annie Cuninghame was therefore Mrs Boswell's niece. She was about eighteen years old.

24 David Ross (1727-1805), advocate (admitted 30 July 1751), appointed Sheriff-Depute of Kirkcudbrightshire in 1756 and one of the Principal Clerks of Session on 3 September 1763.

25 George Clerk, advocate (admitted 24 November 1767), who was to die later that year on 5 November.

26 That is, the Solicitor-General, Alexander Murray.

Nebuchadnezzar in Daniel and was struck with its circumstances. My worthy uncle, the Doctor, dined with us between sermons. He said he believed Nebuchadnezzar was in heaven, and he thought him the greatest man that ever lived. The Doctor was rather too flashy in his spirits, and showed symptoms of that unquiet temperament which is in our blood. But he and I were warmly affectionate. He said with sincerity that he would not change situations with my father. He would not give up the comfort which he had in his sons Robert and Bruce for four times my father's fortune.[27] He and I joined in regretting my father's coldness, which deprived him of the great happiness of social intercourse and having his sons easy with him. We however agreed that he was at pains to make himself worse than he really was by checking every appearance of kindness of temper. The Doctor said my father had from his youth been set on wealth and on his own personal consequence. I observed that he had not liberal, extensive views of fame—to be known in other countries, to be respected by posterity—otherwise he would have published his researches into Scottish antiquities. He desired only the immediate and confined consequence of a Lord of Session.

Annie Cuninghame returned tonight. Mr Wood was with me in the forenoon, as I had sent for him. He said that there might be something of a rheumatism in my ankle and foot. He ordered me some camphorated spirits of wine.

MONDAY 29 JANUARY. As I wished to read with my own eyes in the records any charters of the estate of Auchinleck which I could find, before writing again to Dr Johnson, I was carried in a chair to the Laigh Parliament House, and read Thomas Boswell's charters *heredibus*, which was clearly heirs general. But then I found my great-grandfather's charter to the heirs male of his own body, whom failing, *propinquioribus suis heredibus masculis*.[28] This for a moment made me return to heirs male *for ever*; but I considered that my grandfather's property was but a small share, and that it was enough to take in the heirs male descending from him.

TUESDAY 30 JANUARY. Captain Flint called on me and gave me copies of letters which he had received from the Lord Provost and Sir Adolphus Oughton[29] with regard to his requisition to beat up in the High Street. The matter was settled in favour of the military; for the Lord Provost could not point out any privilege that the town had to restrain them, and therefore got the Commander-in-Chief to interpose. Balmuto called and was full of the Fife election. I spoke to him of the difference between my father and me as to the entail, and how my difficulties were much cleared up. He had not the least

---

27 It appears that Dr Boswell had by now ceased to practise as a physician and that this was occasioned by "his whimsical change of religion [which] had made people distrustful of him as a physician". He had also evidently taken to "going to bawdy-houses and talking as if the Christian religion had not prescribed any fixed rule for intercourse between the sexes" (Journal, 23 March 1776). Indeed, he was later excommunicated by his church after contritely confessing to whoring (Journal, 10 April 1777).
28 "To his nearest male heirs."
29 Lieutenant-General Sir James Adolphus Oughton was now acting commander of the Forces in Scotland (*Ominous Years*, p. 9, n. 2).

hesitation upon the subject and advised me to agree with my father, and to do it soon. He said he would freely resign his claim as heir male. I told him jocularly that he was a pagan and that I would take care of the right of his sons. My lameness still confined me, otherwise I should have gone to church, I mean the Episcopal meeting, to commemorate with regret the martyrdom of Charles I, since that fast is still kept.[30] I remember Dr Johnson seemed to think that it might cease after a certain term, I think he said a century. I wrote to him today with Lord Hailes's opinion, which however I neglected to enclose, so that it could not go till Thursday. I was busy today with a long paper for the Earl of Eglinton. At eight at night I was at a consultation at Lord Advocate's on Ross against Mackenzie, which was to come on next day. George's Square looked very bleak to me. It was covered with snow and the frost was intense. I felt tonight again my own deficiencies as a lawyer, but was consoled with my superiority to Buchan of Kelloe, who was with us tonight as being the President's son-in-law.[31]

WEDNESDAY 31 JANUARY. The cause, Ross against Mackenzie, came on, and as an instance of the instability of the Court of Session, Ross, who had formerly six of the Lords for him, and only four and the President against him, had today only one (Lord Covington) for him, and eleven against him. Lord Alemoor was dead and Lord Coalston was absent, by which he lost two votes, and perhaps many more, as Lord Alemoor had great weight and kept in awe the President, who was very keen for Mackenzie. It is very unpleasing when the inclination of a counsel is against his client. This was my situation today. My heart was touched with concern for the old family of Ross of Auchnacloich, which had for several generations struggled to recover its inheritance; and I felt a melancholy impression when the cause went against him, and hoped that the House of Lords would reverse the decree. I was conscious of having discharged my duty as *counsel* for Mackenzie, and I concealed my private thoughts as a *gentleman*. Perhaps it would be better for an advocate not to engage in a cause when his wishes are for the other side.

The Earl of Caithness, for whom I had been counsel and of whose family my ancestor Thomas Boswell's mother was a daughter, was now in town.[32] My lameness was an apology for my not visiting him. He and his second son (a lieutenant in Fraser's Highlanders), Commissioner Lockhart[33] and his lady, Miss MacLeod of Raasay, Dr Boswell, Mr and Mrs Mitchelson, and Mr Wood, the surgeon, supped with us. Commissioner Lockhart had been very obliging to me in granting solicitations for offices in the Excise, yet by most unaccountable negligence I had never once waited on him. My wife had been lately introduced to Mrs Lockhart, and we sent them a card to sup, after my wife had called and my lameness had been mentioned. It was very kind in them to come. I was in excellent spirits. Nothing

30 30 January was the anniversary of the execution of Charles I.
31 George Buchan of Kelloe married Anne Dundas in April 1773.
32 William Sinclair (1727-1779), 10th Earl of Caithness.
33 Thomas Lockhart, Commissioner of Excise.

disturbed me but the consideration of my knowing from undoubted authority that Mitchelson, whom I had asked because he was Lord Caithness's agent, disliked me much, I know not for what, and took every opportunity that he could to speak ill of me. His amiable wife being a great friend of my wife's, and as much prejudiced for me as her husband was against me, corrected his acidity, and he did very well tonight, as indeed he always does when we are together. I thought it not worth while to undeceive him, as he was a sordid fellow, and I was diverted with the contrast between *appearance* and *reality*, which I believe is too often to be found in the intercourse of men. Lord Caithness looked so jolly that after his son and Mr Lockhart and the Doctor went away, I from a kind of benevolence joined him and Mitchelson and Wood in drinking strong rum punch, though I hate it and it disagrees with me. We sat till three. I was not drunk.

THURSDAY 1 FEBRUARY. I was very ill but was obliged to go to the Court of Session. I attended the determination of Hope against Wallace in the Inner House, and won it.[34] The severe cold of the air pierced my frame. I had a violent headache, had been very sick before I went out, and was terrified that I should do as Antony did in the Senate House, which Cicero has so strongly arraigned.[35] The awe of disgrace had restrained my squeamishness while I was in the Court, but as soon as the cause was over, I was obliged to go to a corner of the Outer Hall. I got the Hon. Mr Gordon to appear in my place for two small pieces of form which I had this forenoon, and went home, went to bed, and after some hours of severe uneasiness grew better, got up, and dictated some law. I sent off Lord Hailes's letter to me on the entail to Dr Johnson.

FRIDAY 2 FEBRUARY. Matthew Dickie dined with me. I was very well today but for my lameness. I had attended a pleading in the Inner House all the forenoon by Dickson[36] and Wight maintaining that the Act ———[37] is not to be applied to the wages of day labourers, because each day's wages cannot make a term, and there is none other fixed, as in the case of servants who are engaged yearly or half yearly; and by Armstrong and Maclaurin maintaining the contrary. It was well argued on both sides, but so little attention is paid to pleading in the Court of Session that I was the only lawyer who attended today from beginning to end; and for long intervals there was an absolute void in the benches. Ours is a court of *papers*. We are never seriously engaged but when we write. We may be compared to the Highlanders in 1745. Our pleading is like their firing their musketry, which did little execution. We do not fall heartily to work till we take to our pens, as they to their broadswords.

34 This appears to be the case of *Robert Hope v Thomas Wallace and James Duncan* (N.A.S. CS 238H.4/37). Wallace was a mason in Leith and Duncan had formerly been a wright there. "Wallace had tried to extract payment of a bill given [to] Duncan by Hope as part-payment for a tenement in Leith, subject to Hope's finding no incumbrances upon it, a condition not fulfilled" (*Session Papers*, 75 10 14).
35 That is, Boswell was afraid that he would vomit while in the court.
36 James Dickson (1745-1825), advocate (admitted 31 January 1764).
37 It seems that Boswell either did not ascertain, or (when later writing his journal) was unable to recall, the precise Act in question.

I began today a curious bargain which I made with the Hon. Henry Erskine in order to acquire correctness in writing. We were to give to each other a copy of every one of our printed papers, and each was to be censor on the other. For every ungrammatical expression and every Scotticism except technical phrases, a shilling was to be incurred; and for every error in punctuation which hurt the sense of a passage and every error of the press, sixpence was to be incurred. Each was to keep an account of debit and credit, and nothing was to be charged but what was acknowledged by the writer of the paper to be just. Erskine had many objections to a paper of mine today. Lord Hailes was once appealed to and gave it for me. Erskine was too nice; for it was not inelegance but incorrectness that was liable to a fine. The former was very arbitrary. The latter, Johnson and Lowth[38] could determine. He had three shillings against me today. I am persuaded that this will do me much good. In the afternoon I had before me ten papers to draw. So much work awaiting me appeared mountainous. One I did immediately and then went to Moncrieffe's, played moderately at whist and brag, heard Monboddo talk of savage nations, drank little, and came home before one. This day a fine thaw came on.

SATURDAY 3 FEBRUARY. I had time after being in the Court today to dictate a paper. Then I went to dine at Lord Monboddo's. It seems he had asked a great many people of the law today, but not one was disengaged but Mr David Rae and myself. I was at first disappointed, as I had come with my mind tuned for a large company and gay conversation; but I soon let it down to a good social key, and had a very agreeable meeting. My Lord's clerk[39] dined with us, and his daughter[40] came and sat a little after dinner; but the time was mostly spent in a *trio*. My Lord said that he never asked company to his house but those for whom he had a regard, and he looked on this as the great privilege of his office as a judge. That a gentleman at the bar has not this in his power. Clients of any decent rank expect to be asked to dine. Rae observed that merchants entertain their customers. I said that an advocate is obliged to entertain many people whose company he does not like, both clients and agents. I wished to hear Lord Monboddo and Rae on the propriety or expediency of entertaining agents, but the conversation took another turn. My Lord told me that Wedderburn was an excellent Greek and Latin scholar, that he had talked with him on Greek learning; that his parts were always remarkable, and his rising so high, though he was neither loved nor esteemed, was a proof certain both of his parts and education. We had various subjects started: Shakespeare, Pope, Dr Johnson. My Lord's manliness of mind and store of knowledge humbled me. He and I drank each a bottle of claret slowly. Rae took wine and water. We all drank tea. In the evening I dictated another paper.

SUNDAY 4 FEBRUARY. Read the Bible and some of *Histoire philosophique, etc*. Had young Donaldson at tea. Got from him Kenrick's review of Steele's scheme of

38 Robert Lowth's *Short Introduction to English Grammar*, 1762.
39 Kirkpatrick Williamson.
40 Helen Burnett.

recording the measure and melody of speech like music. It struck me a good deal.[41] Also *The Edinburgh Review* of Lord Hailes's *Annals*. Dr Grant sat a little with us in the evening. My wife made a very ingenious remark on the advantage of getting the English language early to have the power of expressing our thoughts. She said that one bred in Scotland has a poverty of language, so that his ideas fade for want of expression as plants do in a poor soil. Mr Wood had been with me in the forenoon and ordered me to pour cold water on my sprained ankle. My mind at present was in a sort of indifferent state.

MONDAY 5 FEBRUARY. Was at home all day; finished one long paper and one of moderate size; had some consolation in seeing my mass of *work to be done* a little lessened. I was agreeably fatigued. I mean that the sensation which I felt at night after my labour was over was pleasing.

TUESDAY 6 FEBRUARY. I had dreamt in the night that my father was dead. All the natural affection and tenderness of my younger years was revived in sleep. I was much distressed and I awaked crying. My mind was much softened. I was anxious to make my father easy and to have nothing in my conduct towards him of later years to regret after he was gone. My instantaneous thought was to go to him and agree to his entail directly. But I waited to hear from Dr Johnson. I recollected with some uneasiness my wild speech at Grange's on the 29 of December last,[42] of which he said I would repent. When I actually saw my father in the Court, his indifference froze my fine feelings. In the evening I was at a consultation at Mr Macqueen's on Blythswood's cause, on which I had written so well; and being quite master of it, I did not feel a disagreeable inferiority at the consultation. It indeed vexed me a little that Macqueen as senior counsel was to draw the printed paper, as it deprived me of an opportunity of having a good paper of mine laid before all the judges. It is a common error that the senior counsel will always write best.

WEDNESDAY 7 FEBRUARY. I intended to have gone this evening to *The Beggar's Opera*, which always inspires me with London sensations. But there was a consultation at Lord Advocate's on the great cause of Maclean against the Duke of Argyll.[43] We sat about two hours, and I had great pleasure in being instructed in law by Macqueen, Rae, and Lord Advocate. Formerly a young lawyer was educated by attending consultations.

There was tonight a ball in James's Court given by the inhabitants. I dislike such corporation meetings, and neither my wife nor I went to it. Worthy Grange came and supped with us, he being also a nonconformist. He said very well that if James's Court were in the middle of a wild moor, its inhabitants must from necessity associate together; but as we are in the middle of a large

---

41 "Joshua Steele's *Essay towards Establishing the Melody and Measure of Speech* was reviewed in *The London Review* (edited by William Kenrick) for December 1775 and January 1776" (*Ominous Years*, p. 230, n. 8).
42 The page containing the entry for 29 December 1776 is missing from the journal, having been removed with three other pages (*Ominous Years*, p. 206, n. 7).
43 This was in connection with Sir Allan Maclean's claim for recovering part of the Maclean estate from the Duke of Argyll (see the entry for 3 August 1774).

city, where we can choose our company, it is absurd to be like the inhabitants of a village. I believe we were ill thought of by the inhabitants who joined in this ball. But it was better to keep clear of a connexion which was not desirable.

I this night received an admirable letter from Dr Johnson with a full opinion on our family settlements so far as *justice* was concerned. He had not received Lord Hailes's opinion on the subject when this was written, so that I got his own original thoughts, and he convinced me by masterly arguments that I was under no moral obligation to preserve strictly the male succession. I shall not attempt to abridge his letter. My wife shed tears. I had now a kind of wavering if I should not agree to heirs whatsoever, as *justice* did not interpose and *Veronica* was so engaging. But my brother David and feudal notions as to barons soon returned. I was struck with wonder at Dr Johnson's abilities.

THURSDAY 8 FEBRUARY. I opened Sir Allan Maclean's cause before Lord Elliock. It was so full of Highland history and facts starting up on all hands that I was much interested. Mr Rae supported me. Mr Crosbie opened on the other side, but did not get his pleading finished; so we were to resume this cause at another time. I had to dine with us Mr Daniel Wardrop, mason in Glasgow and lately one of the bailies of that town, a client of mine; Adam Bell, his agent; Balbarton, Matthew Dickie, and Mr Donaldson, the painter, who had been today doing something more to my wife's miniature picture. I drank moderately. Balbarton and Matthew Dickie stayed to tea. Dr Young came to tea. I dictated well in the evening.

FRIDAY 9 FEBRUARY. The day went on as usual during the session. In the evening I was at Moncrieffe's. My old circuit companion, David Kennedy, was there for the first time as Earl of Cassillis, and Crosbie took his seat for the first time. We were eighteen at table. I played rather too keenly at whist and brag, and lost a little. There was much noise. I sat till near three and drank too much, but did not expose myself by speaking.

SATURDAY 10 FEBRUARY. The wine which I had drank last night, though it had not intoxicated me exceedingly, had fevered me a good deal. I was however able to go to the Court and appear in several causes between nine and ten. I then grew very uneasy, went home, and was obliged to go to bed. My wife was exceedingly attentive to me. I got up to dinner. I received a letter from the factor for Dalblair's creditors proposing that the remainder of the price should be paid immediately. I was thrown into great uneasiness how to act. Sometimes I thought of going directly to my father and telling him that he might now make an entail such as he should think best, and I would agree to it, and so he and I might be on the best footing. But then I considered that he would be offended at my going to London in the spring, and I had better delay agreeing to the entail till that should be over. Then it hurt me to think of being absent from my wife and children, and yet I could not lose an opportunity of being with Dr Johnson since he had been in France. My wife soothed me, for my mind was harassed. She advised me to write to Craigengillan,[44] the trustee for the creditors, and beg of him either to pay the money himself on getting a right to my father's security or mine; or agree to assign the right to some person whom I should find, and this to be done privately without my father's knowledge; or to put off the payment for some time. I accordingly wrote in these terms. I got last night a letter from my friend Temple, in great anxiety about a loan of £1,000 from Mrs Compton as to which some obstacle had occurred. This added to my uneasiness, and my melancholy recurred. I was fretful and horridly passionate to my dear wife, and once swore, which is a sign of my mind being much disturbed. I have much reason for gratitude to GOD that my hypochondria comes upon me now so seldom. I prayed earnestly for a few minutes. It vexed me to think that my promise under the venerable yew at Mamhead, not to drink more than six glasses at a time, had been so ill observed.[45]

I wrote a little law with my own hand, Mr Lawrie having an acquaintance from Glasgow in town who took him out. It shocked me to think of a long paper which I had to write for the boxes of next Thursday. I was, in short, in a woeful state. My wife was a little jocular while I was on the rack, which occasioned my being passionate. I did however perceive inwardly, at the very time, that I had a kind of pride in being melancholy and fretful like my grandfather, and perhaps I exacted more attention than I had a right to expect. But she was in the wrong not to study my humour, for, though I might perhaps have governed it more than I did, I could not subdue it entirely.

SUNDAY 11 FEBRUARY. Was low-spirited beyond what I have been for a considerable time. Veronica was with me in the dining-room all the forenoon, and I read none, but just whiled away the time with the little sweet creature, who was a very pleasing companion to me. In the afternoon I hesitated whether to stay at home or go to the New Church or go to Bell's English Chapel.[46] I was weak and fretful, and it vexed me to find a return of that distemper of mind which formerly afflicted me so much. I should rather have been grateful to GOD for the wonderful good spirits which I have enjoyed of later years. Indeed upon reflection I was so. My wife comforted me by tracing my uneasiness from Friday's riot. I went to Bell's Chapel, as a quiet place of public worship, and was at prayers. I was somewhat pious, but there was a coldness and darkness in my mind. George Webster drank tea with us. His conversation on active life and his fancy amused me. I was also relieved by writing the journal of Saturday. We had George at supper too, and I drank a little claret and became tolerably social. But when the mind has been hurt by hypochondria, it is not soon quite easy again. I had resolved to go very early to bed and get up betimes next morning, as I had a long paper to write; but I yielded to the present inclination and sat till near twelve.

44 John McAdam of Craigengillan, Ayrshire.
45 This pledge had been made to Temple during Boswell's visit to Mamhead in April of that year.
46 This was formerly Baron Smith's English Chapel, which, when the New English Chapel was built, was taken over by the incumbent, the Rev. Dr Robert Bell, and was sometimes referred to as the "Old English Chapel" to distinguish it from the new.

MONDAY 12 FEBRUARY. I awaked relaxed and indolent, and though I recollected the task which I had to perform, I indulged myself in lying in bed till between eight and nine. After breakfast Sir Alexander Dick called and sat awhile with me. His amiable and classical manners pleased me; but my mind was still hurt, and I perceived his good qualities as a man who has a headache views the beauties of a fine prospect. He seemed more willing today than formerly that I should write his life. I had three different consultations this forenoon, one gratis. I was quite harassed with business, and thought of giving up practice. Captain Archibald Erskine then sat awhile with me. In short it was past one o'clock before I could get my long paper begun. Sir Walter and Miss Annie Boswell[47] dined. I hurried away from table and drudged doggedly, as Dr Johnson says, so that at night I had about two-thirds of my task done. This gave me some relief. I received a letter from Dr Johnson on our family settlements, after he had read Lord Hailes's opinion. It was excellently written, and my scruples as to excluding remote heirs male were quite removed. Dr Johnson even showed the justice of the claims of females in the present state of manners. This however I could not yet receive. My mind was so clouded and shattered that I could not think even of Dr Johnson as I used to do when in sound vigour of understanding. But I consoled myself with recollecting that even he has been afflicted with hypochondria. My wife was so kind and engaging tonight, by exerting herself to relieve me from the foul fiend, that I was all love and gratitude.

WEDNESDAY 14 FEBRUARY. I walked to the Parliament House, but with difficulty, I believe chiefly from long disuse. Sir Walter dined with us. Mr Donaldson, the painter, drank tea. I dictated tolerably. My spirits were better, but I felt much of the "stale, flat, and unprofitable".[48]

THURSDAY 15 FEBRUARY. Mr Donaldson finished the miniature picture of my wife. It pleased me to have her resemblance thus secured. He dined with us, as did Surgeon Wood. Either last night or the night before I had again dreamt that my father was dead. It affected me not so tenderly as last time, but with gloom. I called at the Custom House for Commissioner Cochrane. He had been ill, and had an aged, failed appearance very different from what he appeared when I last saw him. This damped my spirits somewhat. After dinner I called on worthy Grange at his kind request, and drank a glass or two of sweet wine with him and Abercrombie[49] and Currie. This, with the little which I had drank at dinner, made me restless and quite incapable of dictating, at least I fancied so; and though papers had come upon me as others were done I resigned myself to absolute indolence.

FRIDAY 16 FEBRUARY. I was well entertained this forenoon with Maclaurin's pleading in favour of the freedom of Negroes in Britain in the case of Joseph

---

47 Presumably, Anne Boswell, daughter of Dr John Boswell.
48 *Hamlet*, I. ii. 133.
49 Alexander Abercromby, W.S.

Knight, one of that race.[50] An extensive subject enlarges the mind, as small subjects contract it. I drank tea at my father's, not having been under his roof since the 27th of last December. He was indifferent as usual. Robert Boswell and his father-in-law, Sandeman, were there. In the evening I was at Moncrieffe's, played whist ill, but won. I had ever since last Friday been in bad spirits. I this night felt a momentary sensation of gay pleasure while drinking a glass of white Cape wine. I came home between twelve and one, quite cool.

SATURDAY 17 FEBRUARY. My head was clearer than it had been for ten days before, and I made several little morning appearances at the bar with more ease than during that time. But still I was depressed with a general indifference and despondency. I went down awhile to the Advocates' Library to consult some English law books on a subject on which I had a petition to write. A large library always comforts me somehow. I cannot at present tell distinctly how.

I then went and called on Mrs Compton; found her inclined to assist Temple, but tedious and timorous. I used my best endeavours to persuade her to be friendly to him. I know not clearly how it happens, but I feel myself a man of more address when with English people than when with those of my own country. It pleased me today to be sensible that the faculty of address returned when I was with Mrs Compton. I then went to the Exchange Coffee-house[51] and was present at settling Sir Walter's purchase of a cornetcy in the Greys. I dined at Walker's as one of the *Parliament* of James's Court, as it is called, being a society of its inhabitants for police, which has subsisted since 1727. I was in bad spirits, but kept a decent social appearance; came home to tea. Then went to the Hon. A. Gordon's and played at brag and won. Worthy Grange had drank too much at the Parliament, and he would needs call for me and bring me home before supper. I complied. It was then twelve.

MONDAY 19 FEBRUARY. I called for a little at my father's. He talked of the extravagance of the age, and of the necessity of entailing; but, what was wonderful, he did not resume the subject of compelling my consent to his entail, so that I did not communicate to him my change of opinion. He talked of

---

50 This is the celebrated case of *Joseph Knight v John Wedderburn* reported in *Faculty Decisions*, Vol. VII, 1778-81, p. 5. Knight was an African, who, when a boy, had been sold as a slave in Jamaica to John Wedderburn, who later came to Scotland and brought Knight with him. Knight subsequently asserted his freedom and left Wedderburn's service, and when Wedderburn had him apprehended he appealed to the Sheriff-Depute of Perthshire who held that slavery was not recognised by, and was inconsistent with the principles of, the law of Scotland. Wedderburn then appealed to the Court of Session where a decision was ultimately to be given on 15 January 1778 upholding the sheriff's judgment. The court, by a majority (the dissenting judges being the Lord President and Lords Elliock, Monboddo and Covington), held that the dominium assumed over Knight under the law of Jamaica was unjust and could not be supported in Scotland to any extent. One of the counsel for Knight was Henry Dundas, whose speech on behalf of "the sooty stranger" was highly praised by Boswell. "I do declare that upon this memorable question he impressed me, and I believe all his audience, with such feelings as were produced by some of the most eminent orations of antiquity" (*Life*, Vol. II, pp. 740-1). Boswell's sympathies, however, may have been on the other side of the case, for he was to become an outspoken opponent of the movement to abolish the slave trade (see Epilogue, p. 545).
51 Situated between Craig's Close and Old Post Office Close (Stuart, p. 169), off the north side of the High Street near the Royal Exchange.

withholding my £300 a year in order to clear the debt for which he was bound with me. I said, "Then I cannot live." He spoke in an indifferent manner, as if he had never thought of the matter before. I just let things remain as they were till I should return from London. I was harassed today with dictating. Law business consumes my time, and indolence wastes it. My mind was upon the whole quiet.

TUESDAY 20 FEBRUARY. Heard the Solicitor and Advocate plead against and for the Negro. David Ross began his trials today to succeed Lord Alemoor. His promotion did not strike the mind as Lockhart's did.

WEDNESDAY 21 FEBRUARY. Was in gay happy spirits at breakfast; was quite charmed with Veronica, who was a pleasing child and wiser than is usual at her age. Effie was bustling and not so attentive or affectionate as her sister. It is impossible not to have a preference for one child over another. But a parent should not show it; and perhaps Effie may yet gain upon my heart. The day was passed in the ordinary course during a session. My son was now a stout infant, and appeared to be of a sweet disposition.

THURSDAY 22 FEBRUARY. The perplexed cause of Sandeman and Company against Doig, which had tormented me, was this forenoon determined. The Lords seemed to know nothing of it, which hurt me though I won.

FRIDAY 23 FEBRUARY. I went at night to Moncrieffe's, it being the last meeting of his club for this session. Played at cards ill, and lost. Was overpowered at supper with Macqueen's noise. Came home quite cool before one.

SATURDAY 24 FEBRUARY. My papers to be written were grown numerous again. I finished one this forenoon; dined at the Hon. A. Gordon's. Monboddo was there and the claret had a fine flavour, so I drank too freely. I was then seized with the fever of gaming, and played at brag and whist till about three in the morning with different people who were there. Lost £3. 12; was vexed and ashamed of my disorderly conduct, and when I came home, was hurt to find my dear wife sitting up for me.

SUNDAY 25 FEBRUARY. Got up with a headache, but went to the New Church. Dr Blair preached on this text: "A wounded spirit—who can bear it?"[52] He said the spirit of man might be wounded by folly, by passion, or by guilt. He pointed out in a striking manner a man who has ruined himself in life by foolish conduct, and the pain which he must feel in looking up to those once his equals but now his superiors, and how miserable he must be to consider how he has degraded himself. I was in bad spirits today and applied this to myself. But I corrected the uneasy apprehension by considering, as Dr Johnson once bid me do, how many had done worse than I had done, or rather to how many I was superior. It occurred to me that the true meaning of the text was the misery of melancholy or a distempered mind, and I felt it in some degree at the time. I felt a regret that I had not asked Dr Blair to dine or sup with me nor been to see him

52 Proverbs 18. 14.

since I came last from London, and I resolved to invite him soon.

My ankle was now surprisingly well.

MONDAY 26 FEBRUARY. Was at a consultation for a Justiciary trial of Gibson and others for an alleged attack of an excise officer, which was to come on next Monday.[53] Felt my mind pretty able, but had no pleasant sensations of vigour or gaiety. Dictated pretty well in the afternoon; but from the trifling circumstance of not being able to find a passage which I had read in Hawkins's *Pleas of the Crown*, I was quite fretted. At last I perceived that I had the second volume before me instead of the first.

TUESDAY 27 FEBRUARY. For some time past my mind has been in a troubled, fretful state. I had a fit of gloomy passion this morning at breakfast, and threw a guinea note in the fire because my wife objected to my subscribing three shillings for a miscellany by a Miss Edwards. I however rescued the note with the tongs before it was consumed, and, though a good part of it was burnt, I got its value from the Royal Bank. This incident shocked me, because it made me dread that I might in some sudden rage do much worse. I attended to business tolerably in the forenoon, and dictated tolerably in the afternoon. Grange drank tea with us. At night I was in an inanimate, sullen frame, and sat poring over the fire in heavy uneasiness. My dear wife was at pains to console me, and relieved me somewhat; but I had a dismal apprehension of becoming as melancholy as my poor brother John, and the weakness of mind which is thought to occasion that distemper made me miserably vexed from the consideration of being despised. I wondered when I recollected how much of my life since my marriage had been free from hypochondria; and it galled me that at present I was so afflicted with it that I had no just ideas or sensations of any kind. I was anxious to be with Dr Johnson; but the confused state of my affairs, and my tender concern at being absent from my wife and children, distressed me. I was exceedingly unhappy. I could fix my mind upon no object whatever that could engage it. Futurity was dark, and my soul had no vigour of piety. I know not if it be right thus to preserve my weakness and woe. Lord Monboddo said on Saturday that writing down hurts the memory. Could I extract the hypochondria from my mind, and deposit it in my journal, writing down would be very valuable. However, as Dr Johnson said to me that it was right to keep a history of my mind, I write exactly the state of it. Probably it will not be long till my present unhappiness will be recollected as a dream.

WEDNESDAY 28 FEBRUARY. At five I went to Mr Solicitor's and compared his notes with mine in the cause, Ross against Mackenzie. I drank tea with him socially. He and I were well together, having been schoolfellows, and there having been a friendship between our fathers. When the Solicitor talked of rising in life, I was in such a sickly frame of mind that I could not relish any scheme whatever. When I came home I found a letter from Dr Johnson, being an answer in course of post to mine of the 20th current. He discouraged me from coming

---

53 For details of this case, see the entry for 4 March 1776 and relevant footnote.

to London. This hurt me somewhat. I could not bear the thought of not seeing him this spring. I resolved to write to him more pressingly on the subject. My dear wife wished that I would not go; but, when she saw me desirous of going, indulged my inclination. It pained me to think of being absent from her. Yet I could not resolve to come to a final agreement with my father till I had heard Dr Johnson upon particulars.

THURSDAY 29 FEBRUARY. Grange dined with us. Sir Walter came in from the hunting with a hare in his hand as we were finishing dinner, quite as if we had been in the country. His animal spirits shocked my nervous sensibility. Worthy Grange and I shook hands cordially, and talked of low spirits with which he has been afflicted, though not so severely as I have been. Talking with him, and hearing his calm reflections, did me good. I dictated pretty well, and wrote an earnest letter to Dr Johnson; but was sensible that I might appear weak and troublesome to him. I trusted to his kindness for me, and his knowledge from experience of dejection of mind.

FRIDAY 1 MARCH. I drank tea at Maclaurin's along with Crosbie, consulting for the trial of Gibson and others. I was humbled by Crosbie's great knowledge of the British statutes, but played my part very well in argument. There was something in the west-country tone of the men that were to be tried that touched me with particular compassion, I believe from some association of it in my youth with distress, while I lived at Auchinleck, as that of a poor tenant unable to pay his rent, or of some one who had lost a father or brother. Their shabby clothes too made the scene piteous. I took no money from them; but Maclaurin and Crosbie did. Perhaps it is from my not having enough of knowledge of the real condition of men in their state of life that I am pained when I think of some guineas being taken from them. What a sum is a guinea to one of them! is my reflection when I see that all that he has on is hardly worth so much. But they were all smugglers that I saw tonight; and I remember Lord Hailes telling me that I should not think a man less able to give a fee because he had a bad coat; for he probably has the money which another lays out upon dress. My imagination melted down the fees into small money, and I thought how many bottles of small beer or such necessaries would two guineas buy, and I really was uneasy when I thought that the men were not guilty of the offence with which they were charged; yet could only be acquitted, and would not be indemnified of their costs. This is a severe circumstance in criminal law. I was a good deal better today. I dictated well in the evening.

SATURDAY 2 MARCH. Melancholy had almost quite left me, it is impossible to explain how. The Solicitor had some friendly conversation with me in the House this morning upon my having good pretensions to something from Government on account of my father's merit.

I called at my father's, but found that a good many people who had dined with him were sitting in the drawing-room. So I did not go in. It gave me a momentary uneasiness to think that he had many entertainments, and did not ask me to them; so that I had not the advantage of being countenanced by him as a son should be; but I instantly checked any swelling on that account by considering that I did not endeavour to be intimate with him since his second marriage.

MONDAY 4 MARCH. This day came on the trial of Gibson and others.[54] I had not appeared in the criminal court since John Reid's trial. I spoke a little on the relevancy, not much to my own satisfaction, knowing that it could have no effect. The trial was over and the panels acquitted by three. Crosbie, Maclaurin, and I, with Mr James Hunter,[55] chancellor of the jury, and David Steuart and Peter Kerr,[56] agents for the panels, went to eat a beefsteak at Princes Street Coffee-house. We grew exceedingly merry; and who begun it, I cannot say. But we three advocates made a number of sketches of songs, by way of a *Criminal Opera*.[57] As for instance, "We're not guilty yet", to the tune of, "We're gaily yet." Such ludicrous extravagance diverted us extremely. We laughed and sung and drank claret till past eleven at night. Though I drank above two bottles I was not at all intoxicated, which was strange. During this scene I often looked back with wonder on my late melancholy. But I disapproved of such intemperance.

WEDNESDAY 6 MARCH. I was all forenoon, almost, attending the decision of the Lords upon Captain Dalrymple's vote in Fifeshire, upon which the election turned.[58] There was a most crowded audience, and all seemed to be much interested, as at any warm contest. It came at last to a casting-vote. My father was in

54 Andrew Gibson, a merchant in Beith, and his son Gavin Gibson, and three other merchants in Beith, were charged with assaulting and wounding James Lawson, an Excise officer, at Hamilton. Counsel for the prosecution were Henry Dundas (the Lord Advocate), Alexander Murray (the Solicitor-General), William Nairne, Robert Blair and John Pringle (for whom, see p. 302, n. 42). Counsel for the defence were John Maclaurin, Andrew Crosbie and Boswell. Notwithstanding Boswell's submissions, the Lord Justice-Clerk and the Lords Commissioners of Justiciary found the libel "relevant to infer the pains of law" and ordered that the trial proceed. The prosecution produced twelve witnesses, including the alleged victim, James Lawson. The defence, however, called no witnesses. The evidence was then summed up for the prosecution by Henry Dundas and for the defence by John Maclaurin. The Lord Justice-Clerk having then "charged" the jury, the court sat until the verdict was reached. In due course, the jury returned and announced that they had unanimously found the libel "not proven". The accused were then discharged and allowed to go free (N.A.S. JC7/39).

55 James Hunter (1741-1787), Sir William Forbes' partner in the banking firm of Sir William Forbes, James Hunter & Co. He later assumed the name of Hunter-Blair when his wife, Jane Blair of Dunskey in Wigtownshire, succeeded to her family's estate. In 1781 he was elected M.P. for Edinburgh, and on 29 September 1784, shortly after vacating his seat as M.P., he was elected Lord Provost. He played a major role in the building of the magnificent new College (now known as Old College) in place of the old, ramshackle buildings. He was also the promoter of the construction of the much-needed South Bridge over the Cowgate, work on which started in 1785. He was created a Baronet of Great Britain in 1786. "In private life, Sir James was affable and cheerful, warmly attached to his friends, and anxious for their interests... His talents were of the highest order—to an unwearied application, he united great knowledge of the world, sagacity in business, and soundness of understanding; and he died unusually respected" (Kay, Vol. I, p. 54).

56 Patrick ("Peter") Kerr, W.S. (admitted 6 July 1768), died 1791.

57 "This amusing skit was published, with considerable interpolations, by Sir Alexander Boswell [Boswell's eldest son] in *Songs in the Justiciary Opera*, 1816" (*Ominous Years*, p. 244, n. 5).

58 The case was concerned with Captain Hew Dalrymple's entitlement to vote at the election of the M.P. for the county of Fife (*Ominous Years*, p. 245, n. 6). For Captain Hew Dalrymple, see the entry for 14 June 1782 and footnote.

the chair, and as he had expressed himself in a sort of dubious, figurative manner, calling the Captain's qualification "only a picture and a very ill-drawn picture", Lord Advocate and some other partisans of Henderson, the candidate against whom the Captain voted, sanguinely concluded that his opinion was to set aside the qualification. But when he gave his vote it was to support it. This made a prodigious hubbub. The Advocate was indecently extravagant in his gestures, and, when I came to the bar, he said to me under cover of great friendship for my father, "I would rather lose all the elections in Scotland than have to represent his conduct at the bar of the House of Commons as I must do. Speak one way, and vote another." I could only say to the Advocate that his Lordship was wrong. I was indeed confounded and uneasy. For I myself had apprehended that my father's opinion was for setting aside the vote. I was impatient to talk with my father of this strange affair. I went and called on him, and told him what Lord Advocate had said, not the whole, but that he had spoken one way and voted another. He said it was not true; that he had been much difficulted; but that as the Court had allowed qualifications as bad to pass, he could not set aside this. He was quite calm, and satisfied my mind that there was not any contradiction between his speech and his vote. Lady Auchinleck was very clear upon it. I told him that I had now freed myself of my scruple concerning remote heirs male. This seemed to please him. He asked me to stay and dine. Dr Boswell dined, and we were pretty cordial, though my father would never let the Doctor enter upon conversation of what he had been reading, or rather would not let him expatiate, but broke the discourse into small talk. I dictated tolerably tonight. Grange supped with us very comfortably.

THURSDAY 7 MARCH. I was made uneasy by hearing murmurs and insinuations from people in the Court that there had not been a consistency between my father's speech and his vote. I avoided the subject, not being cool or firm enough upon it. After the House rose, I was easier. I had been at my father's before it sat down, and had a conversation with him, in presence of Mr Stobie, upon a settlement of our affairs. He was in a placid, kind frame and put his entail into my hands. I read the clauses of it at home, and found them to be very rational.

SATURDAY 9 MARCH. A petition in the Fife politics came in signed by Lord Advocate, who was set out for London. It contained a paragraph which seemed to say that my father had *voted* in *opposition* to his *opinion*. I had been with Grange in the morning, who had told me that many impartial people had a notion that what he said was different from the import of his vote. He very properly advised me not to make a stir about the matter; but laugh it off with indifference. The petition however roused my spirit, and I meditated challenging the Advocate if he did not make an apology, or explain away the paragraph. This was the last day of the session; so the Court was all confusion. I was affected with a kind of confusion and uneasiness that there should be even a hint against the integrity of a man of so established a character as my father. I called on Claud, who was angry and anxious about it. I went to my father and found him quite calm.

He said the Advocate could mean nothing against him. He was too much his friend. I wondered at his coolness, and blindness to these Dundases. I had a letter this evening from Dr Johnson, very kind, and informing me that he was to set out for Italy next month. This put me in a flutter of spirits. I wrote to him begging that he might not be from London when I arrived. My mind was agitated about my father's character.

SUNDAY 10 MARCH. My wife was a little indisposed. I was at the New Church in the forenoon. Between sermons I went up to my father's. I had not resolution to tell him that I was to set out for London next day. I took Lady Auchinleck into another room, acquainted her of it, and asked her "friendly advice" how to proceed; told her that it distressed me to give any uneasiness to my father, but that I was convinced my going to London was for my interest. She said that my father looked on it as idle and expensive, and that I had formerly given him reason to think in that manner; but upon my giving her my reasons she seemed to be convinced that I was right, and she engaged to communicate the matter to him first, and then I might call on him in the evening. I was for the first time on a confidential footing with her, and I was sincere; but I saw she doubted my sincerity. I told her so. She owned it; but said that it never made any odds on her conduct. I assured her that she was wrong. That indeed I had once hated her; but that I now thought very differently, and she *must* have no longer any suspicion of me; that I had great faults, but was upon the whole one of the best men that ever lived; that it gave me uneasiness to be at enmity with anybody. She said, "You cannot be a better man than I wish you, on many accounts." She said that she had for some time been pressing my father to give up his Justiciary gown if something could be got for me; and that he was willing, but doubted of my prudence to negotiate the affair. It was a new and comfortable kind of feeling which I had now. I went and sat a little with Claud,[59] and we talked together of an answer to a false account of my father's opinion which had appeared in last night's *Mercury*. Lady Auchinleck had yesterday and today also talked of the reflection against my father with such a serene contempt that I envied her strength of mind.

I dined at my father's along with Dr Webster. I had called at home and found Dr Boswell, who was to dine at our house. My mind was so much troubled about my father's character being even questioned that I could not bear the Doctor's flashiness. I called on Nairne. He was gone to Sir William Forbes's to dinner. I had said I would perhaps call on Sir William today, as he and my Lady were to set out for London next day. Dinner was over. I had drank a good deal of white wine at my father's. I drank more here. Instead of going to church, we three sat and drank till I declare I was intoxicated. It was a strange thought that I was drinking hard on Sunday, along with Sir W. Forbes and Nairne, two worthy, distinguished Christians. I mentioned its being wrong. They severally declared they did not think so, and they certainly did not at the time. I said I did; but could not resist. Our conversation was of religion, Dr Johnson, and other good topics. I

59 Claud Boswell resided in Old Assembly Close.

suppose neither of them was intoxicated, not having drank so much as I did before we met. But they had above a bottle of wine apiece after I joined them. I shall not forget this scene. I went home with Nairne to his house, and drank tea. I spoke of the insinuation against my father, and hinted that I would call Lord Advocate to account for it. Nairne said I would be wrong; for why cut a man's throat for a mistake into which he might naturally be led from what my father said, and his own warmth upon one side? Nairne declared that *before* my father gave his vote he imagined that he was of opinion against the qualification. But *after* the vote he saw nothing in what he had said inconsistent with it.

Went home, and, instead of going to my father, wrote a letter telling him my reasons for going to London, and mentioning that I had had a return of melancholy and required relaxation. That I would be with him at Auchinleck this vacation, join in his entail, and do everything agreeable to him. I enclosed this in a short note to Lady Auchinleck, made an apology for not calling, and begged she would "soothe my worthy father". Indeed I was unfit to see him tonight.

I had called a little at Claud's as I came home. He seemed to think that my father was a little uneasy, though he did not say much. I was very ill with the wine after I came home, but grew better. It was very unlucky that I had fallen into a debauch the night before my journey. But how could I fear Sir William Forbes and Nairne? Grange was with me a little, and told me that Henderson's friends spoke strongly against my father, as if he had given his opinion with candour *against* the qualification when he thought it was lost; but, finding it come to his casting voice, had voted *for* it, as being for the side which he espoused. I was miserably vexed. I wrote to Sir John Pringle as my father's friend and my friend, stated the matter to him, and sent a sketch of a letter to Lord Advocate insisting that he should say if he meant to *impeach my father's integrity*; and, if he did not give it me under his hand that he did not, I told Sir John I would write to Lord Advocate that he was a *liar* and a *scoundrel*. That in my conscience and before GOD I should be justified in having a *duel*; that his nephew, Colonel Pringle,[60] would perhaps be kind enough to be my second. That Sir John used to think I had bad nerves. It might be so; but that I hoped I was now determined. That I should be with him on Friday night or Saturday morning; but that this letter would come before me, to prepare him.

My excellent wife did not suspect what was in my mind. But comforted me as well as she could when she saw me vexed about my father. Said it would not hurt his established reputation to have such a reflection thrown out, as that he had been biased upon one political occasion, and that this was the worst that could be said; that it was unlucky that our judges talked jocularly and of private anecdotes like old women; and that if he had said nothing, but given his vote with firmness, nobody could have had anything to say as if he had been inconsistent; though no doubt, as he had declared for Mr Oswald, the friends of Mr Henderson would at any rate have called him partial. Her good sense and

60 James Pringle (1726-1809), Lt-Col. of the 59th Foot and, subsequently, of the Buccleuch Fencibles; M.P. for Berwickshire 1761-1779; succeeded as 4th baronet of Stichell 1779.

liveliness relieved me somewhat. But my heart was torn with anxiety. After we were in bed, I could not sleep for agitation, and I was in anguish to think that I was probably to expose my life in a few days and perhaps leave her and my children in a disconsolate situation. It was hard upon me that I could not communicate my distress to her. When I shut my eyes I saw a death's-head. I was quite gloomy and disturbed; but resolved to endure. At last I fell asleep, I think about four; but my rest was broken.

MONDAY 11 MARCH. I got up a little after five. My dear wife gave me tea. Mr Lawrie was ready and serviceable, as was Joseph. But I was both gloomy and in pain. I took leave of my valuable spouse with an earnest embrace, and said, "GOD grant we may meet in a better world!" I had still a duel in view. I went in a chair to the fly. We were four passengers. I read some of Lord Monboddo's third volume on language. I was perpetually thinking of my challenge to Lord Advocate. I dreaded that my nerves might fail me; yet I was conscious of being determined. I travelled like a criminal, or rather a condemned man not a criminal, in a coach to the place of execution. I was ever and anon figuring Lord Advocate and me upon the field. I hoped that Sir John Pringle and Dr Johnson would invigorate my mind. I fancied that I might just think, think of a duel till I should overcome the fear of it by deadening my mind. That timorousness was a fault in my constitution; but that I had a noble principle of fortitude; and that I should have the advantage of Lord Advocate by being better prepared for it by the discipline of meditation. I slumbered a great deal in the coach. I read a little in the Bible which I got from Lord Mountstuart, and which I carry always with me.

As he proceeded south, Boswell became bolder. This was partly on account of Lord Monboddo's views on the superiority of mind in the ancient Greeks and Romans, which, says Boswell, "revived me, and a duel seemed quite easy to me". "It is the imagination which torments us", he reflected. "This duel of mine, now, has alarmed and distressed me… But, when I have an extensive view of it, I consider thus: If I am killed, the shock is momentary; and death comes as well at one time as another. My wife and children will be consoled in a short time. At any rate I shall not feel their uneasiness; but shall look on it as trifling, and expect them soon to join me in the world of spirits. If I am wounded, my spirits will be raised by a sense of honour and a sort of gallant vanity which a duel justly fought inspires. My greatest uneasiness was the fear of fear; an apprehension that my nerves, or whatever else it is, should yield to impressions of danger, though my soul was brave."

On his way past Newcastle, Boswell visited the mental asylum where his brother John was still an inmate. "He looked better than when I saw him in May; but seemed to be quite in a stupor. I sat with him about ten minutes, I suppose, before he spoke a single word, though I said many different things to him, and shook him cordially by the hand." As Boswell was about to leave, John put out his hand and said, "Take me with you." Boswell then stayed a little longer, and when John complained that he was kept a prisoner there, Boswell was very moved. "I covered my face for a little," he wrote, "and shed tears… But it was comfortable to see that he was not in pain of body or anguish of mind."

On arrival at London on 15 March, Boswell hastened to see Sir John Pringle. "I instantly started the subject of which I was so full", says Boswell. But "Sir John instantly made it vanish, by telling me that it would be quixotism to call a man out for abusing my father in a court of justice. That was no private affront to me; and I should let the matter take its course. 'Everybody here', said he, 'is abused in public and it is never thought there should be a duel on that account.' He showed me from the reflection of his mind that I was confined and rash in my view. I was relieved as if he had cured me at once of some painful disorder." The following day, when Dr Johnson confirmed Sir John's opinion, Boswell's mind was put completely at rest on the mattter.

As to the other matter close to Boswell's heart, namely his father's proposed entail of Auchinleck, Johnson stated that, although he believed Boswell was right to resist the exclusion of remote male heirs who had a claim in justice, he thought that Boswell should now do as Lord Auchinleck thought best.

Boswell accepted an invitation from Johnson to accompany him on a jaunt to Oxford, Birmingham, and Lichfield (where Johnson was born and brought up). During the days before this trip, Boswell called on old friends such as Paoli, Garrick and Sir Joshua Reynolds. In addition, in the hope of furthering his ambitions, he visited four Scotsmen of consequence: Lord Mounstuart, who received Boswell "with a more earnest affection than ever" and continued to assert that he would do what he could to assist Boswell; the Duke of Queensberry, who was "cold and indifferent and unmeaning"; Lord Mansfield, who exhibited "stiff formality without dignity"; and Archibald Douglas, who appeared "void both of parts and of gratitude" and disappointed Boswell by making no suggestion of engaging Boswell as one of his counsel in an appeal of his which was due to come before the House of Lords.

At the same time, Boswell did his prospects no good at all by slighting his erstwhile duelling opponent, Henry Dundas, who was in London, by omitting to call on him, even though Dundas evidently expected such a visit. When the offended Dundas gently up-braided Boswell for the omission, Boswell feigned nonchalance.

During this period, Boswell's faithfulness to his wife lapsed significantly, for he twice had "sensual connexions" with a lady (unnamed in the journal) with whom he had formerly been in love. He justified this by reflecting that "these are Asiatic satisfactions, quite consistent with devotion and with a fervent attachment to my valuable spouse".[61]

Boswell's enjoyable jaunt with Johnson took place from 19 to 29 March. On his return to London, Boswell was pleasantly surprised to find papers relating to the Douglas appeal with instructions to appear as one of Douglas's counsel. This put Boswell in a "kind of brutal fever", resulting in three "dalliances" on the same day. Over the following days there were to be further lapses, ultimately resulting in another attack of a venereal disease. After one such incident, Boswell records that he was "dreary and vexed, with remorse rising like a black cloud without any distinct form; for in truth my moral principle as to chastity was absolutely eclipsed for a time... I thought of my valuable spouse with the highest regard and warmest affection, but had a confused notion that my corporeal connexion with whores did not interfere with my love for her. Yet I considered that I might injure my health, which there could be no doubt was an injury to her."[62]

During Boswell's stay in London, he twice had dinner in the company of Captain James Cook, the circumnavigator, who was about to sail on his final, and fatal, voyage. Boswell

61 Journal, 24 March 1776.
62 Journal, 31 March 1776.

talked with Cook a great deal and found him to be "a plain, sensible man with an uncommon attention to veracity" and "very obliging and communicative". The outcome of these discussions was that Boswell felt an inclination to join Cook on his voyage; but nothing came of the idea.

The House of Lords hearing in the Douglas case, which was concerned with a dispute with Lord Selkirk, took place on 3 April, when Boswell appeared with Allan Maconochie, advocate,[63] who was "very cordial" and introduced Boswell to Douglas's English counsel, Edward Thurlow, the future Lord Chancellor. The outcome of the hearing, however, was that, after counsel for the Duke of Hamilton had spoken persuasively in favour of a delay to allow the Duke to bring forward his claim, it was agreed by Douglas's counsel that the hearing should be adjourned, and Lord Mansfield ruled accordingly.

Later that day, the Scottish Solicitor-General, Alexander Murray, at Boswell's invitation, joined Boswell and Johnson for dinner at the Mitre. One subject of conversation which was raised was whether a man should be able to claim damages when one of his deceased relations has been defamed in a publication. Murray was of the view that reparation should be allowed unless the author could justify himself by proving the fact, or at least showing some sort of evidence even if not meeting the requirements of strict legal proof. Johnson, however, was firmly of the view that no such claim should be allowed, on the basis that, if a man could say nothing against a dead person but what can be proved, history could not be written. "The Solicitor", wrote Boswell, "made a very tolerable figure [and] was very complaisant."

The remainder of Boswell's stay in London was full of the usual social whirl. Particularly notable events were Boswell's interviews with the notorious Mrs Margaret Caroline Rudd, who, although the mistress and suspected accomplice of Daniel Perreau, one of the two Perreau brothers hanged at Tyburn on 17 January 1776 for forgery, gave evidence against them for the Crown and then stood trial herself, conducting her own defence with great skill and securing a verdict of "Not Guilty". Another notable event was Boswell's bringing together of Johnson and Wilkes at a special dinner at the house of Dilly the publisher on 15 May—"justly the most celebrated portion of the Life [of Johnson]".[64]

Boswell was back in Edinburgh by 22 May, but only stayed a few days and then travelled west to Auchinleck, where, on 30 May, he wrote, "I am calmly refreshing myself in the country." But his pastoral relaxation did not last long, for he had to return to Edinburgh for the beginning of the summer session.

WEDNESDAY 12 JUNE. The Session sat down. I was not at all well. Everything was indifferent, or rather irksome, to me. I was at my father's a little.

THURSDAY 13 JUNE. I continued to be ill and very averse to labour.

FRIDAY 14 JUNE. The same. Surgeon Wood supped with us, and owned to me that he also was affected with low spirits. This consoled me somewhat, as I knew he did so well in his profession.

SATURDAY 15 JUNE. The same. Walked to Heriot's Garden with Veronica, which relieved me a little.

63 Allan Maconochie (1748-1816), advocate (admitted 11 December 1773), Professor of Public Law at Edinburgh University 1779, Sheriff-Depute of Renfrewshire 1787, appointed Lord of Session as Lord Meadowbank 1796.
64 *Ominous Years*, p. 345.

SUNDAY 16 JUNE. The same. Was at the New Church in the forenoon, and heard Mr Walker and his nephew. Was at my father's at dinner between sermons, my wife, Annie Webster, Dr Boswell, and Veronica there. Was at the Tolbooth Church in the afternoon, and heard Dr Webster. Charles Hay called and would have me out to walk. I went with him to the top of Arthur Seat. I was in a listless frame.

MONDAY 17 JUNE. Lay long in bed, and fancied that the gloomy vapours exuded by insensible perspiration. Was somewhat easier. Veronica lay a good while beside me, and I engaged her attention with telling her how pretty angels would come and carry her from *the kirk hole* (the grave) to Heaven, where she would be with GOD and see fine things. I thought it best to please her imagination. But she seemed to dread death, and would have Bell[65] to carry her to Heaven. A short gleam of light came upon my mind this day.

TUESDAY 18 JUNE. Not well again. In the evening I sat an hour with my father; told him I wished earnestly to make him easy. He seemed more cordial than usual. I shook him by the hand affectionately at parting. My mind was consoled by this interview.

WEDNESDAY 19 JUNE. Grange had come last night. Saw him today, and was cordial with him. Never had greater need of being comforted by him. Dined with my wife at Sir George's. Drank tea at Mr Alexander Donaldson's. Was restless and gloomy.

FRIDAY 21 JUNE. Drank tea with Mr David Rae, and consulted with him on the cause of our client, Mrs Finlayson.[66] Felt myself sadly incapable. Evening Moncrieffe's. Lost at brag. Had no relish of the company.

MONDAY 24 JUNE. The trial of —— was to come on, and Crosbie and I were to plead upon the Act 1701, that a trial must be brought in a limited time. I was not prepared, as I knew he was master of the subject. He was ill. I moved to put off the debate. The Court would not. So I was obliged to speak and did it surprisingly well.[67] Was at St John's Lodge in the evening, having to resign my place as Master. Was in sad spirits. Grange supped with us.

65 Isobel Bruce, Veronica's nurse.
66 "Widow or wife of John Finlayson, miniaturist and engraver, and herself a painter. The nature of her cause is not known, but it was probably somehow related to the cause mentioned below, 8 January 1777" (*Extremes*, p. 7, n. 2).
67 This was a case against Alexander McEwan, dyer, and Isobel Butcher, his wife, who had been imprisoned in Perth on a charge of receiving stolen goods. The Act to which Boswell refers was the Act of the Parliament of Scotland 1701, c. 6 (in *The Acts of the Parliaments of Scotland*, Vol. X, p. 272), which provided that where a prisoner on a non-capital charge petitioned for a trial the prosecutor was required to fix a date for the trial within sixty days after the intimation, and the trial had to be completed within forty days if before the Court of Justiciary. "The question at issue was whether the prosecutor was allowed just one hundred consecutive days from the prisoners' intimation to begin and conclude a trial, or was merely required to fix the date of the trial within sixty days of the intimation, the date to be set at his discretion" (*Extremes*, p. 7, n. 5). Counsel for the prosecution were the Lord Advocate (Henry Dundas) and the Solicitor-General (Alexander Murray). The court asked that written informations be submitted by counsel and the case was adjourned on several occasions. The ultimate outcome was that "when the prisoners had spent about as much time in gaol as they would have if they had been found guilty, the Lord Advocate deserted the charge against them, leaving the question of law still unresolved" (*Extremes*, p. 8, n. 6).

THURSDAY 27 JUNE. My wife and I dined at Sir George's. Dr Webster and his daughter were there. Tea at home. Was better. Walked in the Parliament Close cordially with Grange.

FRIDAY 28 JUNE. Being obliged to have a paper written by nine o'clock today, I for the first time this Session rose a little after six, and dictated very well.

MONDAY 1 JULY. At home all day dictating, but was indolent and gloomy. Grange dined with us. In the evening consulted at Crosbie's. Walked with him on the Calton Hill. Relished nothing.

SATURDAY 6 JULY. Drank tea at Lady Colville's with Lady Anne Erskine and the Captain. Was relieved by their conversation. Lady Colville came home before I went away. It is curious how conversation actually produces a good effect, though beforehand one imagines that it can have none. I had been very idle all this week. I indeed apprehended that I was not able to do better.

SUNDAY 7 JULY.[68] Went in the morning and called on Sir William Forbes after his return from London. Found him and his lady at breakfast. Sat till it was rather too late for church. Thought I would go and see Mr David Hume, who was returned from London and Bath, just a-dying. I found him alone, in a reclining posture in his drawing-room. He was lean, ghastly, and quite of an earthy appearance. He was dressed in a suit of grey cloth with white metal buttons, and a kind of scratch wig. He was quite different from the plump figure which he used to present. He had before him Dr Campbell's *Philosophy of Rhetoric*. He seemed to be placid and even cheerful. He said he was just approaching to his end. I think these were his words. I know not how I contrived to get the subject of immortality introduced. He said he never had entertained any belief in religion since he began to read Locke and Clarke. I asked him if he was not religious when he was young. He said he was, and he used to read *The Whole Duty of Man*; that he made an abstract from the catalogue of vices at the end of it, and examined himself by this, leaving out murder and theft and such vices as he had no chance of committing, having no inclination to commit them. This, he said, was strange work; for instance, to try if, notwithstanding his excelling his schoolfellows, he had no pride or vanity. He smiled in ridicule of this as absurd and contrary to fixed principles and necessary consequences, not adverting that religious discipline does not mean to extinguish, but to moderate, the passions; and certainly an excess of pride or vanity is dangerous and generally hurtful. He then said flatly that the morality of every religion was bad, and, I really thought, was not jocular when he said that when he heard a man was religious, he concluded he was a rascal, though he had known some instances of very good men being religious. This was just an extravagant reverse of the common remark as to infidels.

68 This entry is based partly on Boswell's journal entry for this date and partly on a document dated 5 March 1777 entitled "An Account of My Last Interview with David Hume, Esq." The contents of the latter document have been rearranged somewhat to give them a more cohesive structure.

Speaking of his singular notion that men of religion were generally bad men, he said, "One of the men" (or "The man"—I am not sure which) "of the greatest honour that I ever knew is my Lord Marischal,[69] who is a downright atheist. I remember I once hinted something as if I believed in the being of a God, and he would not speak to me for a week." He said this with his usual grunting pleasantry, with that thick breath which fatness had rendered habitual to him, and that smile of simplicity which his good humour constantly produced.

I had a strong curiosity to be satisfied if he persisted in disbelieving a future state even when he had death before his eyes. I was persuaded from what he now said, and from his manner of saying it, that he did persist. I asked him if it was not possible that there might be a future state. He answered it was possible that a piece of coal put upon the fire would not burn; and he added that it was a most unreasonable fancy that we should exist for ever. That immortality, if it were at all, must be general; that a great proportion of the human race has hardly any intellectual qualities; that a great proportion dies in infancy before being possessed of reason; yet all these must be immortal; that a porter who gets drunk by ten o'clock with gin must be immortal; that the trash of every age must be preserved, and that new universes must be created to contain such infinite numbers. This appeared to me an unphilosophical objection, and I said, "Mr Hume, you know spirit does not take up space."

I asked him if the thought of annihilation never gave him any uneasiness. He said not the least; no more than the thought that he had not been. "Well," said I, "Mr Hume, I hope to triumph over you when I meet you in a future state; and remember you are not to pretend that you was joking with all this infidelity." "No, no", said he. "But I shall have been so long there before you come that it will be nothing new." In this style of good humour and levity did I conduct the conversation. Perhaps it was wrong on so awful a subject. But as nobody was present, I thought it could have no bad effect. I however felt a degree of horror, mixed with a sort of wild, strange, hurrying recollection of my excellent mother's pious instructions, of Dr Johnson's noble lessons, and of my religious sentiments and affections during the course of my life. I was like a man in sudden danger eagerly seeking his defensive arms; and I could not but be assailed by momentary doubts while I had actually before me a man of such strong abilities and extensive inquiry dying in the persuasion of being annihilated. But I maintained my faith. I told him that I believed the Christian religion as I believed history. Said he: "You do not believe it as you believe the Revolution." "Yes", said I; "but the difference is that I am not so much interested in the truth of the Revolution; otherwise I should have anxious doubts concerning it. A man who is in love has doubts of the affection of his mistress, without cause."

He had once said to me, on a forenoon while the sun was shining bright, that he did not wish to be immortal. This was a most wonderful thought. The reason he gave was that he was very well in this state of being, and that the chances

69 George Keith, 10th Earl Marischal, with whom Boswell travelled to Berlin in 1764 (see Introduction, p. 32).

were very much against his being so well in another state; and he would rather not be more than be worse. I answered that it was reasonable to hope he would be better; that there would be a progressive improvement. I tried him at this interview with that topic, saying that a future state was surely a pleasing idea. He said no, for that it was always seen through a gloomy medium; there was always a Phlegethon or a hell. "But", said I, "would it not be agreeable to have hopes of seeing our friends again?" and I mentioned three men lately deceased, for whom I knew he had a high value: Ambassador Keith,[70] Lord Alemoor, and Baron Mure. He owned it would be agreeable, but added that none of them entertained such a notion. I believe he said, such a foolish, or such an absurd, notion; for he was indecently and impolitely positive in incredulity. "Yes," said I, "Lord Alemoor was a believer." David acknowledged that *he* had *some* belief.

I somehow or other brought Dr Johnson's name into our conversation. I had often heard him speak of that great man in a very illiberal manner. He said upon this occasion, "Johnson should be pleased with my *History*." Nettled by Hume's frequent attacks upon my revered friend in former conversations, I told him now that Dr Johnson did not allow him much credit; for he said, "Sir, the fellow is a Tory by chance." I am sorry that I mentioned this at such a time. I was off my guard; for the truth is that Mr Hume's pleasantry was such that there was no solemnity in the scene; and death for the time did not seem dismal. It surprised me to find him talking of different matters with a tranquillity of mind and a clearness of head which few men possess at any time. Two particulars I remember: Smith's *Wealth of Nations*, which he commended much, and Monboddo's *Origin of Language*, which he treated contemptuously. When he spoke against Monboddo, I told him that Monboddo said to me that he believed the abusive criticism upon his book in *The Edinburgh Magazine and Review* was written by Mr Hume's direction. David seemed irritated, and said, "Does the *scoundrel*" (I am sure either *that* or "*rascal*") "say so?" I said, "If I were you, I should regret annihilation. Had I written such an admirable history, I should be sorry to leave it." He said, "I shall leave that history, of which you are pleased to speak so favourably, as perfect as I can." He said, too, that all the great abilities with which men had ever been endowed were relative to this world. He said he became a greater friend to the Stuart family as he advanced in studying for his history; and he hoped he had vindicated the two first of them so effectually that they would never again be attacked.

Mr Lauder, his surgeon, came in for a little, and Mr Mure, the Baron's son, for another small interval. He was, as far as I could judge, quite easy with both. He said he had no pain, but was wasting away. I left him with impressions which disturbed me for some time.

It was amazing to find him so keen in such a state. I must add [a] circumstance which is material, as it shows that he perhaps was not without some hope of a future state, and that his spirits were supported by a consciousness

---

70 "Robert Keith, British Ambassador at Vienna and at St Petersburg, had died on 21 September 1774" (*Extremes*, p. 13, n. 9).

(or at least a notion) that his conduct had been virtuous. He said, "If there were a future state, Mr Boswell, I think I could give as good an account of my life as most people."

SATURDAY 13 JULY. A party of bowls being fixed to be at Craighouse, Charles Hay and I walked out. Rosslyn,[71] Hon. Captain John Gordon, and Maclaurin were there. We played at bowls and whist, and Lord Covington was in wonderful spirits. I was very well.

SUNDAY 14 JULY. Count Mannucci, a Florentine count and an officer of cavalry in the Imperial service, whom I had seen at Mr Thrale's, breakfasted with us. He was a great traveller, and had just come from Ireland. He was a very well-looked man and very knowing and affable. I was burthened with his company (such was my hypochondria), though he revived agreeable ideas. I was at the New Church in the forenoon, and at my father's between sermons. I do not recollect how I spent the afternoon. The Count, Mr Nairne, Lady Elizabeth Heron, and Miss Preston supped with us.

TUESDAY 16 JULY. Lady Colville, Lady Anne, Captain Erskine, Sir William and Lady Forbes, Mr Nairne, and the Count dined with us. The Count had been much hurt by his horse falling under him.

WEDNESDAY 17 JULY. Dined quietly with Mr Nairne on cold mutton and a bottle of claret.

WEDNESDAY 24 JULY. Supped at the British Coffee-house in Bristo Street, at a consultation, Douglas against the Duke of Hamilton. We were a numerous noisy band, and drank rather too freely.

TUESDAY 30 JULY. Went with Nairne to the Edinburgh Ranelagh, and saw fireworks.[72] Was much taken with a Miss Coutts from Montrose. Met there Captain Boscawen,[73] son to the Admiral, recommended to me by Mrs Thrale. The Count set out for London today. I went to the College to see an eclipse of the moon through Short's telescope, but there was such a crowd, I could not get a sight.[74] Came home hungry and supped heartily.

THURSDAY 1 AUGUST. I was very busy with a paper for Lord Eglinton. However, I went for an hour to Canongate-Kilwinning Lodge. Came home and dictated late.

---

71 William St Clair of Rosslyn, last Hereditary Grand Master of Freemasons in Scotland (*Extremes*, p. 15, n. 5).
72 "On Tuesday evening, May 22, was opened... at Kirkbraehead, near the West Church, Edinburgh, Ranelagh Garden, a new kind of entertainment, prepared by Signor Corri, consisting of musical entertainments, transparent machinery illuminated with upwards of four hundred lamps of various kinds, *jets d'eau*, a cascade, fireworks, and a ball-room illuminated with spermacetti candles; the tickets to ladies 1*s.* and to gentlemen 2*s.* each" (*The Scots Magazine*, June 1776, xxxviii. 339, quoted in *Extremes*, p. 17, n. 3).
73 "'Captain' (actually Ensign) George Evelyn Boscawen was later Viscount Falmouth... He was in Edinburgh on a recruiting-party" (*Extremes*, p. 18, n. 5).
74 "Mr Short acquaints the public that he is now fitting up a reflecting telescope of six feet focus and another of four feet for observing the lunar eclipse on Tuesday next. These telescopes, with others, will be placed in the new Library-room of the university" (*Caledonian Mercury*, 23 July 1776, quoted in *Extremes*, p. 18, n. 6).

SATURDAY 3 AUGUST. This being the last Saturday of the Session, resolved to labour. After dinner first Matthew Dickie and then James Gilkie called. I drank some wine with each. I laboured heavily.

MONDAY 5 AUGUST. My father had for some time past been very anxious to have an entail signed by himself and me. I had suggested some additions, to which he consented. I now became uneasy at the thought of absolutely excluding my daughters, and was anxious to have a power reserved to me to call them to the succession in case I should see it to be proper, failing heirs male of my father's body. I wrote an earnest letter upon this to Mr David Erskine, who framed the entail, that he might speak to my father. I dined with Mr Erskine today for the first time.[75] Mr Bruce[76] and Mr Peter Murray, advocates, and Mr Chalmer, now solicitor in London, were there. To be warm and cordial with Mr Erskine upon the great subject of the settlement of Auchinleck, I drank plentifully. He and I sat a little by ourselves, and were both very drunk. I ranged the streets and followed whores, but luckily Joseph was attending and took care of me, and got me home after twelve.

TUESDAY 6 AUGUST. My riot had distressed me terribly. I had fallen and bruised my left knee, and I was so ill today that I could not rise. The Hon. Henry Erskine did all my business for me in the Parliament House, and I lay in bed all forenoon. I was vexed at what had happened, but had an apology, and felt a kind of indolent satisfaction in recovering from a debauch, and a pleasing, kindly comfort in finding a brother lawyer ready to assist me. Mr Stobie called about three and told me that my father said if I did not now sign the entail, he never again would ask me, and would withhold from me my allowance. I told him I should call in the evening. I first went to David Erskine, who told me my father would by no means consent to my having a discretionary power to call my daughters, as he saw that I might make a bargain to get money by such a power; and that my father was fretted. I then came home for a little, and after some conversation with my wife, the workings of natural affection prevailed, and I resolved to ask my father to call my daughters in the entail after heirs male of his own body. My old Gothic Salic male enthusiasm abated. I hoped that I and my brother David might have many male descendants, and having no great opinion of the Doctor's sons or of Claud as representatives, I was overcome by affection. Much uneasiness did I suffer this evening. I would fain have had the discretionary power, and my yielding to natural affection was, I feared, temporary. However, I went to my father, and fairly told him that I was now willing that the succession should be as he had always said he wished it to be. But he was in a very bad frame; said there was not time to write over the alteration. The entail should just stand as now written out, and he would not alter an iota. I told him that I should consent to

75 David Erskine, W.S., resided in Argyle Square.
76 Either John Bruce (1735-88), advocate (admitted 24 February 1761), or Alexander Bruce (d. 1780), advocate (admitted 27 July 1762).

whatever he chose, and I engaged to come down to him next morning and sign the entail. Worthy Grange supped with me, he having consulted with my wife and me. We now saw plainly that my wife was right in what she said all along: that my father was himself set upon the male succession, and only wanted to lay the odium of disinheriting daughters upon me. I was hurt by his uncandid behaviour. My wife said she was now easy, and I should be easy, since I could not upbraid myself with want of affection to my children. It had been rewarded by the gratification of my family pride. In order that I might have a permanent voucher in my own justification, I wrote a letter to my father and kept a copy, earnestly begging to have my daughters called, but submitting with full confidence to him. This I sent to him tonight. My wife and I dined today at Dr Grant's with Sir Alexander and Lady Dick and many more company.

WEDNESDAY 7 AUGUST. Mr Stobie called about seven in the morning. I got up more brisk than usual, dressed, and went in a chair to my father's, as it rained a good deal. He said, "James, you must just take care to make provisions for your daughters by frugality"; so I saw he was not for giving them a place in the entail. He and I signed it in presence of Mr Stobie, and we afterwards acknowledged our subscriptions before Mr Adam Bruce, writer, who was to be the other witness. To confess the truth, my male principle had by this time recovered itself, and it was a comfort to me to think that the estate was now secured to *the sons of Auchinleck*, which I could not regret unless in the very improbable event of my seeing my own daughters next in succession, and excluded.[77]

FRIDAY 9 AUGUST. My father was to have set out for Auchinleck today, when the House rose. But he had been taken ill last night with his old complaint, and was confined today. I went twice in the forenoon and visited him. He was easier, but not well. The members of Moncrieffe's club were to entertain him this day at Fortune's. I felt much reluctance to be there, but thought it would be shabby to stay away, so went. I drank old hock, so was not drunk, but the noise and drinking and obscenity disgusted me. Cosmo Gordon, who sat next me, told me that it was universally agreed that I was malevolent. There is certainly such an opinion entertained of me, I suppose from my indulging myself too freely in a sort of abusive licentiousness of characterizing. This is wrong; and though I am perfectly certain that I am the reverse of malevolent, it hurts me in some degree to be thought so.[78] Cosmo himself was at

---

77 The Disposition and Deed of Entail signed by Boswell settled the estate on heirs male of Boswell's great-grandfather (calling in the first place the heirs male of Lord Auchinleck's body) followed by "heirs whatsoever" of Lord Auchinleck (*Register of Tailzies*, N.A.S. RT. 1/19, Folio 233). As Boswell later discovered, Lord Auchinleck had never had the power to leave the estate which he had inherited from his father on any other basis, for that estate had come to him already entailed on heirs male of Lord Auchinleck's grandfather (*Laird*, p. 37, n. 5). However, Lord Auchinleck was entitled to bequeath as he saw fit those lands which he himself had purchased.

78 See also the entries for 19 September 1774 and 18 January 1775. The true position was perhaps as set out by D B Wyndham Lewis in *The Hooded Hawk*, p. 10: "Alas, tact and discretion Boswell... never knew. His candour is appalling. There is no spark of malice in his nature, but, unlike the rest of us, he simply cannot keep his artless mouth shut... The malign disapproval of censors who can overlook any sin but sincerity follows him round perpetually like a cold white spotlight."

this very time wondering to me if Lord Ankerville minded his business as a judge at all, which was a severe reflection.[79] We went to cards. I played at brag, and betted at whist, and lost £6. 19. 6. I lost six guineas at one stroke. I was vexed. I did not call at my father's, lest I should offend him by appearing at all in liquor, but I sent to know how he was, and heard he was no worse. Indeed I could not easily have quitted the gaming-table. I stayed supper, but came away at the third glass after it.

SATURDAY 10 AUGUST. Moncrieffe's meeting had done me no harm. The Session rose today. I was humbled to think that I had, comparatively speaking, laboured little in the course of this summer, and had got only a hundred guineas in fees, twenty less than last summer. But I consoled myself that I had done so well, considering the relaxed nerves and gloomy mind with which I had been afflicted, and that my fees were in reality of a very handsome amount. My father was much better, but agreed to stay till Monday. Dr Gillespie[80] and I went in a post-chaise and dined with Commissioner Cochrane and drank tea with him. I wished to be well with Gillespie, as he had much influence with my father, and would probably be with him when dying. I was pleased to find Gillespie a Christian, though not quite orthodox. My shock from having been with David Hume was now almost cured. I liked much to hear David Erskine say, while we were drinking, that he was perfectly sure of being immortal. While uneasy from David Hume's conversation, I read part of his worst essays in the Advocates' Library, from a kind of curiosity and self-tormenting inclination which we feel on many occasions. I was roused to noble hope again by an accidental conversation in the Library with Lord Monboddo, who talked of *spirit* like Plato himself, and said, "Show me anything destroyed, and then maintain the annihilation of mind." He urged that we are all sensible that besides organs there is within us a *mover*, a power of producing motion intentionally. My great argument for *soul* is our *consciousness* of all sensations and reflections and passions; something different from all and each of our perceptions, of whatever kind and however compounded.

SUNDAY 11 AUGUST. My father continued to be better. But my wife was ill of a cold which she had catched on Thursday evening. I was at the New Church in the forenoon; dined at my father's between sermons, Dr Webster, Mr Stobie, and Veronica there. Was at home in the afternoon. Passed a part of the evening with my father pretty comfortably. In the forenoon when in church, I was struck with a sort of wondrous feeling when the prospect of my being actually *master of the estate of Auchinleck* moved in my mind.

MONDAY 12 AUGUST. Went and saw my father set out for Auchinleck about nine in the morning. He had said that he would make settlements on my wife and younger children before he set out, but had not done it; and when I put him in mind of what he had said, and suggested that there was a possibility that he and I might both die before anything was settled on them, in which case they would be destitute, it did not seem to strike him much. We parted in very

---

79 David Ross had taken his seat as Lord Ankerville on 22 February 1776.
80 Thomas Gillespie, M.D., a physician in Ayr.

tolerable terms, but it hurt me to find him so cold. I called this forenoon at Mr David Hume's. His housekeeper, who I have reason to believe was his concubine, appeared to be crying, and told me he had seen nobody for two days, and had said he would never be downstairs again to meals.[81] I dined at Sir George's with Colonel Reid, late of the Old Highland Regiment and the composer of their march, to which Sir Harry Erskine made the words, "In the garb of old Gaul", etc. He played to us very finely on the German flute, particularly that march at my desire, that I might say I had heard it played by the composer.[82] I engaged him and Sir George, my Lady, and Miss Preston to dine with us on Wednesday. I came home and drank tea with my wife.

WEDNESDAY 14 AUGUST. Sir George and Lady and Miss Preston, Colonel Reid, Mr Robert Boswell, and the son of Mr Anderson, merchant in London, with whom I had dined at Hampstead, and Mr Robertson, one of the Keepers of the Records, dined with us. Sir George's family and Colonel Reid stayed to tea, and the Colonel played on his flute, particularly his march. In the evening I was at Mr Ilay Campbell's on a Submission between Mr Craufurd of Auchenames and Adam Bell, formerly his overseer. John Tait[83] and Adam Bell, the agents, were with us, and we settled our Decreet Arbitral,[84] and then supped and drank a moderate glass.

SATURDAY 17 AUGUST. Dr Boswell breakfasted with us. I complained to him of hypochondria. He advised me to take a jaunt. He revived Auchinleck ideas. I was truly an epicure this day at dinner. I sat down with my wife and two little daughters, and I eat roasted moor-fowl with a deal of toast and plenty of butter, and had a bottle of claret, which I drank every drop except three glasses. I enjoyed this scene much. I then went and played at bowls at Heriot's Work Green,[85] and was really in very good spirits.

MONDAY 19 AUGUST. Grange breakfasted with us. I had several consultations at Matthew Dickie's, who was confined with lameness.[86] I this day finished

---

81 The housekeeper, Peggy Irvine, was said to have been "much more like a man than a woman" (Carlyle, p. 288).

82 This was John Reid (1721–1807), the founder of the chair of music at Edinburgh University, who was particularly renowned for his playing of the flute. He composed several marches, of which "In the Garb of Old Gaul" is perhaps the best known. Reid joined the army in 1745 and was to rise to the rank of general. The Reid School of Music was built with funds bequeathed by him to the University (Keay and Keay, p. 809). Boswell was well qualified to appreciate Reid's playing of the German flute (that is, the modern, transverse form of the instrument) in view of the fact that he himself had a degree of proficiency in playing that instrument.

83 John Tait (1727–1802), W.S. (admitted 8 March 1763).

84 Ilay Campbell and Boswell had been appointed arbiters and the "Decreet Arbitral" was their written ruling on the matter in dispute. The fact that Boswell was appointed arbiter along with a man of such a high reputation as Ilay Campbell suggests that he was quite highly regarded in legal circles. For another occasion on which Boswell and Campbell were appointed arbiters, see the entry for 12 August 1780.

85 "Work" (or "wark") was a general term for a large building (Harris, p. 332).

86 Matthew Dickie resided in Milne's Court off the north side of the Lawnmarket. This court was built some time between 1690 and 1700 and was "the first attempt to substitute an open square of some space for the narrow closes which had so long contained the town residences of the Scottish noblesse" (Grant, Vol. I, p. 96).

Granger's *Biographical History*. This and Gray's *Life* or *Memoirs* by Mason are all the books I have read since June.

WEDNESDAY 21 AUGUST. My wife and I dined at Sir George's. Dr Webster was there, and accounts having come of the arrival of Captain Robert Preston,[87] a bottle extraordinary was the consequence. I was a good deal intoxicated. After tea my dear wife walked home with me, and when I insisted to go out, she accompanied me, but I insisted on her going home, and walked to the New Town, called at Mr David Hume's, wishing to converse with him while I was elevated with liquor, but was told he was very ill. I then ranged awhile in the Old Town after strumpets, but luckily met with none that took my fancy. Came home and got up worthy Grange to supper. I was noisy and had a voracious appetite. I was shocked by the consciousness of my own situation.

THURSDAY 22 AUGUST. Was very ill; was vexed that I had disturbed my dear wife in the night, who was still distressed with a cough and pain in her breast, and ashamed that I had now thrice broken through my engagement to General Paoli to be sober. Sir Alexander Dick had asked me out to dine with him today. My wife and Veronica went with me part of the way. I grew pretty well. My youthful ideas of Prestonfield revived. I was soothed by the amiable Knight. I eat apricots off the tree, and the sun was cheering. To my surprise after dinner I found Veronica in the garden. Bell had brought her out. I held her up to a tree and let her pull apricots herself, and she and I went home in good time. I did not stay tea.

FRIDAY 23 AUGUST. Was at home all day dictating a paper for Dr Alexander Johnson, which I did very freely.[88] I dictated about thirty-seven pages. I was in tolerable spirits, but alarmed about my dear wife, who apprehended danger of a consumption.[89]

My Consultation Book, in which I engross all my fees from loose leaves in which they are marked at first, is many, many sessions behind.[90] I wonder if I shall ever be able to bring up the several things which *ought to be done*, so as to have only to upbraid myself with the neglect of what *it were better to do*, such as writing every year some book, or at least publishing some selection, arranging my letters to and from different persons, and several other things. But my fear is that I shall continue to be in a confused state, with nothing clear and finished and distinct, but all my affairs in a sort of hurried irregularity, all my exertions being occasional and forced.

87 He was captain of a large ship in the service of the East India Company (see the entry for 10 September 1777) and had been away from Scotland since October 1774.
88 This is the case of *Dr Alexander Johnson v Patrick Crawford of Auchinames and Gilbert Mason* reported in *Faculty Decisions*, Vol. VII, 1775-77, p.327. The court's decision in this case, which was an action for payment of money held on deposit, was pronounced on 13 December 1776 and was in favour of Boswell's client. Counsel for the defenders was the Solicitor-General, Alexander Murray.
89 Her family was particularly prone to this disease.
90 For Boswell's "Consultation Book", see Introduction, p. 37. The last entry in the Consultation Book is dated 11 August 1772. The "loose leaves" referred to by Boswell have not been found (*Extremes*, p. 26, n. 5).

SUNDAY 25 AUGUST. My intention was to walk out to Duddingston and hear worthy Mr Bennet. Grange agreed to give me a convoy. In our way we met Sir Alexander Dick's coachman, who told us that the Knight was quite by himself. It was a delightful day. We went to Prestonfield, and walked with Sir Alexander, and eat fruit in the garden, and were placid and happy. We were too late for the forenoon service, and as the family was to dine at three, we could not conveniently be at church in the afternoon; so we were easily persuaded not to go to church at all today. We dined just with the family, and drank very little; then Mr Johnston and I walked again with Sir Alexander, who gave us a short history of his life. I could not wish to be better than I was today. When I mentioned my low spirits, Sir Alexander said I had very fine sensations, and must fortify my nerves. He advised me whenever I was melancholy to sail to Kinghorn and back again, which would cure me. After tea Grange and I returned in a serene frame. I only felt some disapprobation of our not having been at public worship.

MONDAY 26 AUGUST. I was to have gone to Balmuto,[90a] accompanied by Balbarton. But my wife had been ill during the night with a cough, pain in her breast, and sweatings; and as she was apprehensive of a consumption, she was much distressed. The jaunt was therefore put off, and I took her out an airing in a post-chaise with Veronica, and went to a garden at Restalrig, and pulled gooseberries. This did her good. Balbarton and Betty Montgomerie[91] dined with us. Balbarton informed us that David Hume died yesterday. This struck me a good deal. I went and called at his door, and was told by his servant that he died very easily. Betty Montgomerie drank tea with us. In the evening my wife and I played at brag.

WEDNESDAY 28 AUGUST. The Hon. Henry Erskine and I drove out to Dreghorn, where we had a party at bowls. Lord Covington and Lord Gardenstone, Charles Hay, and Wauchope of Niddrie and his lady and a daughter dined. Maclaurin was in a quiet frame. I drank too much. We had whist after dinner. When I returned to town, I was a good deal intoxicated, ranged the streets, and having met with a comely, fresh-looking girl, madly ventured to lie with her on the north brae of the Castle Hill. I told my dear wife immediately.

THURSDAY 29 AUGUST. Was vexed at my rashness last night, but was somehow in a very composed, steady frame. It was a very wet day. After breakfast Grange and I went and saw David Hume's burial. We first looked at his grave in the burying-ground on the Calton Hill, and then stood concealed behind a wall till we saw the procession of carriages come down from the New Town, and thereafter the procession of the corpse carried to the grave. We then went to the Advocates' Library and read some parts of his *Essays*: of his "Epicurean", his "Stoic", his "Sceptic"; and "On Natural Religion." I was somewhat dejected in mind. The day was passed to little purpose.

MONDAY 2 SEPTEMBER. [T]hough my dear wife was now better, I resolved to stay another week in town and finish what papers were necessary, and then

90a Near Auchtertool, in Fife.
91 Natural daughter of Archibald Montgomerie, 11th Earl of Eglinton.

let Mr Lawrie go home. I sauntered, however, this forenoon. Balbarton and Donaldson, the painter, dined with us. I was afraid that my adventure of Wednesday last might have bad effects, and wished to find out the girl. I employed Cameron, a chairman, formerly a soldier in Montgomerie's Highlanders, and told him how, when in liquor, I had met with a girl who called herself Peggie Dundas, and made him inquire at the house of a woman whom she called her aunt. He discovered her to be a practised strumpet. I had only to wait with patience till time should show how I was in health. It vexed me to be separated from my connubial partner in bliss, which was absolutely requisite.

TUESDAY 3 SEPTEMBER. It was a wet day. Grange dined with us. My wife had given it as her opinion that I might mention my last Wednesday's adventure to him, that he might inquire about the girl. I did so in the warmth of my heart, but did not ask him to make inquiry. He and I joined in extolling the uncommon good sense and good temper of my valuable spouse. We drank a bottle of port apiece, and were most cordial. I was somewhat intoxicated. I however had resolved to charge my blood pretty well with wine, to force out any *virus* speedily, in case it was lurking. I dictated easily today, both before and after drinking.

THURSDAY 5 SEPTEMBER. Sandy, my son, was inoculated.[92] I was somewhat uneasy with apprehension.

FRIDAY 6 SEPTEMBER. Laboured some. In the evening was seized with a restless rage for tavern company. Complained very absurdly to my wife that no care was taken to study my humour and make me happy, when in reality I do not believe that any woman on earth could have indulged me so much and made me so happy as she does. I sent to inquire after Dr Webster, but could not find him. I was ridiculously fretful. I proposed to call at different taverns, and, if I could find a good company, to join it. But I thought this would expose me. My wife, with a ready cheerfulness, offered to go and sup with me at a tavern, where I might take a hearty glass. I grew quiet at last, played at brag, supped well, drank strong negus, and recovered my spirits. What strange weaknesses will come upon one at times!

SUNDAY 8 SEPTEMBER. Grange walked out with me to Duddingston. We were too late for church, even for the afternoon, which I regretted. We took a long walk by Restalrig and the seashore to Leith, went in to Mrs Ritchie's on the shore between four and five, and took some bread and cheese and cold meat, porter, and a dram of brandy, and then walked calmly home. Grange and Surgeon Wood supped with us. I was disgusted with Wood's roughness of manners.

MONDAY 9 SEPTEMBER. Got all the law-papers necessary to be done before October finished. Dined at Lord Dundonald's. My wife came there to tea. I was somewhat uneasy at the thoughts of going away next day.[93]

---

92 Against smallpox. "By the eighteenth century,... smallpox was by far the worst epidemic killer. So common and repeated were its visitations that, as with the relatively innocuous mumps or measles today, it was overwhelmingly a disease of small children. For them, it was often fatal" (Smout, *A History of the Scottish People 1560-1830*, p. 253).

93 Boswell was about to go on his postponed jaunt to Balmuto.

TUESDAY 10 SEPTEMBER. My wife, Veronica, and Effie, and Grange accompanied me in a hackney-coach to Leith, from whence I sailed to Kinghorn. I was in good spirits, and was able to part with my dear wife pretty easily, as I considered that I could return at any time. I got to Balmuto to dinner, and found my father, Lady Auchinleck, and Miss Boswell[94] arrived from Perth. I found little cordiality in my father towards me.

On 12 September, Boswell and his father set off for Auchinleck, where Boswell passed the time serenely by pruning trees with his father, gathering nuts, walking around the grounds with the estate overseer, and paying country visits, including a call on his "old classical friend", Lord Hailes. Later, Lord Hailes came to stay for a night at Auchinleck and he, Boswell and Lord Auchinleck had "a classical evening… looking at books in the library, and talking of editions and of learned men". Throughout his stay, Boswell was on the best of terms with his father and even got on well with Lady Auchinleck ("I really had a satisfaction in talking with her, and my prejudice against her was almost clean gone"). Boswell departed from Auchinleck on 21 October and, after spending several days at Douglas Castle as a guest of the "exceedingly obliging" Archibald Douglas, travelled back to Edinburgh on the 25th.

FRIDAY 25 OCTOBER. [G]ot to Edinburgh about eight o'clock. Found my children all in good health. My little son did not know me, but Veronica and Effie were quite in riotous joy at seeing me again. My wife was at Sir George's, and came home immediately on being informed of my arrival. She was very big with child, and plump and healthful. Our meeting was truly comfortable; nothing of melancholy in it, which is sometimes the effect of tenderness. Sir George and Lady Preston insisted on our supping there. We did so, and were happy in mutual kindness.

SATURDAY 26 OCTOBER. Went and waited on Mr Alexander Boswall from the East Indies; found him to be a sensible, lively man.[95] At twelve o'clock I got a letter from Bruce Campbell that Treesbank had died on Wednesday, and was to be buried on Monday the 28th, so I determined to go west again next day.[96] My wife had a full suit of mournings made for me between two o'clock and ten. I was surprised at this.

SUNDAY 27 OCTOBER. My dear wife had breakfast ready for me between six and seven. Worthy Grange was called up and drank a dish of tea with us. My wife had an alarm of her pains on Tuesday last, so I resolved to be home again very speedily.

After "a very creditable burial", Boswell returned to Edinburgh with his cousin Robert Boswell.

94 Margaret Boswell, sister of Lady Auchinleck.
95 "'The Nabob', as Boswell often called him, was a surgeon who had gone out to India, had there become medical adviser to the Nabob of Arcot, and had returned home with a fortune… He appears to have been a descendant of Thomas Boswell, first of Auchinleck" (*Extremes*, p. 49, n. 3). The term "East Indies" formerly included India.
96 The operation performed on him by Dr Boswell and Surgeon Wood on 4 December 1774 had not cured him.

TUESDAY 29 OCTOBER. We came to Edinburgh in the fly. I was flattered to find Robert highly entertained with an account of my travels in Germany. Found my wife and children as well as I could wish.

WEDNESDAY 30 OCTOBER. Mr Lawrie was come to town. But I could not yet begin to business. Veronica now slept in a little bed in the room with her mamma and me.

FRIDAY 1 NOVEMBER. A wet day. Walked in the outer part of the Parliament House, where the shops are, with Mr Saunders, Writer to the Signet,[97] and was entertained with an account of an additional proof in the cause, Wilson against Maclean, taken lately in Ireland, at which he had attended for Maclean.[98] Sat a good while in Donaldson's back shop,[99] and heard much in favour of the Americans. Called on Mr Alexander Boswall. He asked me to dine with him. I did so. There was a pretty large company. Lady Colville, Lady Anne, and Captain Erskine drank tea, played at whist, and supped with us.

MONDAY 4 NOVEMBER. Began to dictate a law-paper, having ten upon my hands. Did very well. Mr George Wallace came and sat awhile with me, and gave me some anecdotes of David Hume. I found him to be rather sceptical, though a worthy man. My belief at present was pretty firm. My wife and I and Annie[100] dined at Sir George's, along with Mr Alexander Boswall and Dr Webster. There was a hard drink, all in bumpers. I was not drunk, but after I came home was very sick. I was willing to see my East Indian cousin in spirits after a hearty glass. He rose to high briskness, but was much intoxicated with two bottles.

TUESDAY 5 NOVEMBER. Was uneasy after yesterday's riot, and dreaded another today, as Mr Boswall was to dine with me. However, I finished the paper which I began yesterday. Mr Boswall and his sister Miss Peggie, Lieutenant Balfour (Fernie) of the Royals, introduced by them, Dr Boswell and his son Robert, Balbarton, Captain George Preston, and Dr Webster dined with us. Sir George was ill, so we had no more of the Preston family. Things went on much better than I expected. We drank a cheerful quantity, but Mr Boswall was positive not to go to excess. I found him to be pretty opinionative, and hasty in his temper. But as I was sensible of his friendly behaviour to my uncle the Doctor's sons, and he was one of the *clan* who had come home after twenty-seven years' absence with fourscore or one hundred thousand pounds and an excellent character, I resolved to pay him much attention. At the same time I was aware of carrying this to such a degree as could not be kept up; I knew that in Scotland a stranger is at first prodigiously feasted and complimented, and afterwards there is a sad indifference. I thought I should show him an uniform civility.

97 James Saunders, W.S. (admitted 10 August 1775), died 1795.
98 This was an action for payment in respect of goods supplied by Wilson to Maclean in 1771, and the main issue was whether a Captain White, who had allegedly signed a receipt for the goods, had drowned in 1770 or in 1771 (*Extremes*, p. 16, n. 6). If he had drowned in 1770 then the receipt must have been a forgery, as alleged by Wilson.
99 Alexander Donaldson's shop was by the Cross in the High Street.
100 Annie Cuninghame, who has come to stay with the Boswells for some time.

WEDNESDAY 6 NOVEMBER. This day I dictated a law-paper very easily. Called on Miss Wallace at Mr Baron Maule's,[101] and delivered a letter from Lady Betty Cuninghame to her. Had not visited the Baron for many years, I cannot tell how; for he was always very civil to me, and is exceedingly entertaining, being full of anecdotes, and having the true old Scotch gentleman's manners, with a picturesque peculiarity of humour. He was in the country today, but I promised to Miss Wallace to renew my acquaintance.

THURSDAY 7 NOVEMBER. This being the fast-day before the sacrament at Edinburgh, I stayed at home all day, purposing to write to my brother David, and to make out some essays for *The London Magazine*. But I was indolent and did little. Notwithstanding my uncommon activity last autumn, I felt myself almost as much as ever in a state of bodily laziness and mental barrenness. I had received some days ago an agreeable letter from Temple, and answered it well. Part of today passed amiably enough in entertaining Veronica, and teaching her some of the letters of the alphabet. On Tuesday last, the 5 of November, she for the first time got the way of opening the dining-room door, a remarkable acquisition to her. She was very proud of it, opened it very often, and said, "O papa, is it not fine?" For some days past I had been too fond of Annie Cuninghame. It made my wife uneasy, and I was sensible it was *not proper* at least. I drank tea at Sir George's. My father came to town tonight. Sat awhile with him. Was glad to have good sedate conversation again.

FRIDAY 8 NOVEMBER. Mr Alexander Boswall and I dined at Prestonfield. Worthy Sir Alexander was most hospitable. My Indian cousin, who had seen him a little before he left Scotland, was delighted with him. On our return to town, I introduced Mr Boswall to my father, who received him very cordially, and I was glad to observe that Mr Boswall listened with satisfaction to his stories. I had this day read an extraordinary *Gazette* with accounts of the King's troops having taken New York. I regretted it.[102] But as there were not many British killed or wounded, there was not an interesting scene. I finished what I thought a good essay for consolation or cure to a man who complains of impotence of mind, in answer to my essay in *The London Magazine* of [November] last.[103]

SUNDAY 10 NOVEMBER. My wife went to the New Church with me, and we took the sacrament together. An odd accident happened to me. By the awkwardness of a woman who *sat* next me, and my own, the communion cup had almost been let fall. In catching it, a good deal of the wine was dashed upon the table and it had a strange appearance on the white cloth. I was weak enough to

101 John Maule of Inverkeilor (1706-1781), admitted advocate 29 June 1725, Keeper of the Register of Sasines 1737, M.P. for the Aberdeen Burghs 1739-48, appointed Baron of Exchequer 12 August 1748, died unmarried. Boswell always admired Baron Maule's show of elegance. The Baron's house was at the foot of a close—known as Baron Maule's Close—off the north side of the Nether Bow at the east end of the High Street.
102 Boswell's sympathies during the War of Independence were with the Americans.
103 Boswell's essay "A Cure Requested for Occasional Impotence of Mind" had appeared in the *London Magazine*, November 1775, pp. 570-1 (*Ominous Years*, p. 167, n. 2).

meditate if there could be anything *ominous* in this. Luckily I sat in a darkish place under one of the lofts, so that the accident was little observed. I was in a sort of dull, indifferent frame, disliked the Presbyterian mode, and attended from a regard to decency. I went home with my wife, eat a couple of eggs, and drank a bottle of cider, all but one glass. My wife came into the room and said I had drank too much. Veronica said I should drink no more, for I "would be fou (drunk) and ta'en to the Guard". Her observations are wonderfully sagacious. I returned to the church, my wife agreeing to stay in the rest of the day. Dined at my father's with Miss Cuninghame. Heard Dr Blair preach in the afternoon; or rather did not hear him, though I was present. I very foolishly indulged such a fondness for Annie Cuninghame as was truly a kind of love, which made me uneasy; and I cherished licentious schemes, and was fretted, forsooth, when she made any opposition. I was truly Asiatic. Love is an uneasiness which, like sickness, may be produced over and over again by different causes, with much the same sensations. My pride was hurt by this fondness going so deep, and it pained me that anything should at all interrupt my affection for my wife and children. After tea sat awhile at Sir George's. Was restless; came home and read a little in the Bible. Had Captain George Preston to sup with us. Was the better of some social chat. ✱

MONDAY 11 NOVEMBER. Was at church and heard Sir Harry Moncrieff preach against spiritual pride. In the afternoon dictated a law-paper. Was still in love with Miss, which vexed me, and I was exasperated because she was not subservient to my desires. Began an *irregular ode* entitled "The Long Island Prisoners" for *The London Chronicle*, to agitate my mind a little. I intended it for a sort of popular unmeaning American rhapsody, but lines rose as I worked which I thought pretty good, and excellent considering the subject.[104] My heart was more indifferent than ordinary towards my valuable wife. This shocked me. Called today at Sir George's.

TUESDAY 12 NOVEMBER. The Session sat down. Felt myself in a good, healthy, steady state. Dined at my father's; Mr Campbell of Newfield and his two eldest daughters and Claud there. Drank not a bottle altogether, but was somewhat inflamed, so as to saunter a little in the street. Soon checked myself and went home and dictated a law-paper. I need not mention dictating law-papers, more than eating my ordinary meals. Now and then I may *review* myself as an advocate, or mark any remarkable occurrence in my practice. Today my foolish love was almost gone, which was a very agreeable circumstance, and I fully loved my valuable spouse. I had finished before dinner "The Long Island Prisoners". As to the state of my mind, I felt an acquiescence even in annihilation, but hoped as a Christian.

WEDNESDAY 13 NOVEMBER. My father was ill of a cold, and kept the house. I sat with him awhile. My wife, who had before felt threatenings of the pains of

---

104 "This ode, which was printed in *The London Chronicle* for 19-21 November, does attain to a kind of specious eloquence" (*Extremes*, p. 54, n. 7).

childbirth, grew pretty ill this evening. I took my bed in the dining-room. Change of my bedroom gives me a new temporary existence. I had several papers to prepare in a hurry, and Mr Lawrie had gone today to bury an uncle, which was an inconvenience to me. I had one of Matthew Dickie's lads to write to me. This afternoon I for the first time forgot an appointment for a consultation. But I recollected it before the hour was quite run, and got to it. The cause was the curious one of Dr Memis.[105] I did not feel myself anxious at this inlying. Dr Young was in the house all night. I sat up with him too late.

THURSDAY 14 NOVEMBER. My wife's labour went on all day, with intermissions; but about eleven at night it turned pretty hard. Veronica's bed was brought up to the dining-room, and she slept beside me. I lay down, thinking that the delivery would not be till well on in the morning. I was fatigued somehow, and I had some broken sleep.

FRIDAY 15 NOVEMBER. Between two and three in the morning Annie Cuninghame waked me with the good news that my wife was delivered of a son. I received the news with little agitation, got up, put on my clothes, and went down and saw my dear wife, who was in a very good way; but the poor child was sickly. I went to bed again, and rose at the usual time and went to the Parliament House. I had now the four seasons: Veronica born in spring, Euphame in summer, Alexander in autumn, and David in winter. These three forenoons, was entertained with examinations in presence in the cause, Wilson against Maclean. The young child continued to be ill in the evening. He sucked little. His nurse was Annie Mill, Effie's nurse.

SATURDAY 16 NOVEMBER. Mr Lawrie had returned last night. I was glad to have him again to write to me today. I laboured hard. Dr Young was apprehensive about the young child, and Mr Wood was of opinion that his situation was so precarious that he should be christened without delay. So I had Dr Webster at four o'clock, who, after praying admirably at my wife's bedside, christened little David in the nursery in the most private manner, Annie Cuninghame and Mr Lawrie witnesses. I mentioned this before dinner to my father and Lady Auchinleck, and settled that if David should live, we should have a good

---

105 This is the case of *Dr John Memis v Provost James Jop and Others (Managers of the Infirmary of Aberdeen)* which is reported in *Faculty Decisions*, Vol. VII, 1775-77, p. 253. The defenders had authorised a translation of the Aberdeen Infirmary's charter from Latin into English, and in the translation the pursuer (who in the Latin version was designated as *Medicinae Doctor in Aberdonia*) had been styled "Doctor of Medicine", whereas others in a similar position had been styled "physician". Dr Memis considered this to have caused harm to his reputation and his practice and so he brought an action for damages. The case had initially come before Lord Auchinleck (*Life*, Vol. I, p. 485), who, having held that the title of Doctor of Medicine was "in strict propriety superior to, and more to be depended on by strangers than that of Physician, which every dealer in physic may assume", had dismissed the action as groundless; but Dr Memis had then appealed to the Inner House. The report states that in their written answers the defenders "mentioned that they were at a loss how to treat so very singular and ludicrous a case" and "utterly disclaimed all intention to give offence". Nevertheless, the court allowed the case to proceed to a proof. We are told that "a voluminous proof followed,... in which an uncommon degree of ingenuity was displayed on both sides". However, the court ultimately held that Dr Memis had failed to make out his case. Counsel for Dr Memis included David Rae and Henry Erskine. Boswell and Alexander Murray were counsel for the defenders.

merry-making as Mr Alexander Boswall schemed, he having eat seed-cake on occasion of my christening. The two witnesses drank a little with the Doctor and me. He and I took a bottle of claret apiece quite calmly. Then he went home. Surgeon Wood drank tea. I was to go with him to the opening of the Theatre for the winter, Miss Catley's first appearance here, whom I had never seen.[106] He drank tea with Miss Cuninghame and me, and I went with him. But as I had a great deal to do, I resolved that if I was too late for her first appearance, to see the impression on the audience, I would return. I said, "I want to see the thunder break—to see the sun rise. If he be risen, I can see him as well at any time of the day as soon after his rise. I shall see Miss Catley some other night." I *was* too late, came home, wrote letters to different friends on my wife's delivery, and dictated a law-paper. Yesterday I had snatched a little romping pleasure from Annie. Tonight snatched still more. This was an effect very different from gentle fondness. I was quite easy. Poor David was better; did not moan piteously as he had done, and sucked well. I had not been very much affected by the apprehension of losing him. But I was piously grateful to heaven for hopes of his living, and as he had fairly begun to advance into a growing state, I flattered myself he would live.

SUNDAY 17 NOVEMBER. In the forenoon heard Dr Webster in the Tolbooth Church with much satisfaction. Dined along with him at my father's. In the afternoon was at the New Church. Mr Johnston at Leith preached. I had shunned Dr Blair in the forenoon, as he prayed against the Americans. I thought Mr Walker was to preach in the afternoon. Johnston prayed more violently than Blair. Drank tea at Mr Donaldson the bookseller's,[107] who was soon going to London. Buckram Brown[108] was there. Strange conversation.

MONDAY 18 NOVEMBER. Got up early, laboured all day at law-papers and did excellently. At seven at night attended a consultation at Macqueen's about Sir Walter's affairs.

WEDNESDAY 20 NOVEMBER. Little David was now in a fine way. Veronica waked in the night between Saturday and Sunday, and cried so that she was carried to her mother's room again, her bed being taken with her. My father still kept the house with the cold.

THURSDAY 21 NOVEMBER. In the forenoon a cause came on at the instance of General Scott's daughters. The President, as he could not judge in it, being their grandfather, quitted the bench and walked to that part of the bar where I was sitting. I did not look towards him, having had no sort of intercourse with him for above two years, since he, in a most ungentlemanly manner (to use no worse word) persuaded my father, under pretence of being his *friend*, to make

---

106 Ann Catley (1745-1789), vocalist. She was "remarkable for beauty of face and voice", but "her beauty and her manners quickly made her notorious" (DNB). "This lady's peculiar charm of vocalisation at once won the admiration of the Edinburgh public and during her continuance here, which ended December 20th, she drew crowded houses... Before leaving town [she] very kindly gave a special benefit for the Charity Workhouse" (Dibdin, *The Annals of the Edinburgh Stage*, p. 168).

107 Alexander Donaldson's house was at the foot of Donaldson's Close by the West Bow.

108 "Brown, a china-merchant and magistrate of Edinburgh, had received his sobriquet because of the stiffness of his temper and manners" (*Extremes*, p. 56, n. 3).

fictitious votes in Ayrshire contrary to his declared principle in public and private, and that, too, in opposition to the party which I had declared I wished to prevail; my father having first told me that he would take no part in the election. The fellow, from his strong animal spirits, can at times do almost anything. He, with all the familiarity imaginable, accosted me, though I looked another way, "How's your father the day, Jamie?" I was struck with his assurance. I own I somehow admired it. I thought him a clever fellow. I had presence of mind enough to answer him quite easily that I had not seen my father yet today, but that he was better yesterday. I confess I felt a kind of warm regret that I had no social communication with the President, who had, through the general *rotten rock* of his character, *veins* of good *metals*: *hospitality—quickness of apprehension—glowing keenness*. But I could not visit him unless he should make acknowledgements of having been in the wrong to me, or at least a plausible apology. I resolved to be evens with him *in ease*, and some day soon to go round and *whisper* him as in great confidence in open court, telling him something very inconsiderable.

Having been applied to to accept of being Deputy Grand Master of the Freemasons in Scotland, I wished to avoid it. But as worthy Sir William Forbes was to be Grand Master and thought my accepting of the office would be an obligation conferred on him, I agreed. I supped at his house this night with ten more of *the brethren* to concert measures. We talked with most serious importance, and I looked round the company and could not perceive the least ray of jocularity in any of their countenances. I however wondered how men could be so much in earnest about parade which is attended neither with *gain* nor with *power*; but I considered that it was really *honourable* to be highly distinguished in a society of very universal extent over the globe, and of which the *principles* are excellent. I sat till near one in the morning.

FRIDAY 22 NOVEMBER. Though I had not drank very much last night, I awaked very ill, so that I was unable to get up till noon. I suffered much from sickness and a violent headache; and to add to my distress, poor little David, who had been very uneasy yesterday, was worse today. I could not give the least comfort to my wife in her anxiety. All I could do was to lie still and try to procure ease to myself. I rose between twelve and one, and just as I entered the Court of Session, it broke up. The news came that Lord Coalston's vacant gown was offered to Mr Macqueen, and he could not refuse it.[109] This made a great stir amongst us at the bar. Sandy Gordon said a day or two ago, "Take care of yourself, Macqueen. I hear there's a press-gang going about for able-bodied judges." I said Ilay Campbell would cut off his thumbs rather than be pressed up to the bench. I spoke to Macqueen himself today of his promotion, and he said it was cursedly hard. (I think that, or "a damned hardship", was his expression.)

109 Lord Coalston had died on 6 November. Macqueen was to be appointed Lord of Session on 13 December, taking the judicial title of Lord Braxfield.

It was giving him at the most, with a double gown, £900 a year,[110] and his practice as a lawyer brought him near £2,000 a year. It was indeed an honour to have such an office given him without solicitation. But, as Falstaff liked no such grinning honour as that of a dead warrior, Macqueen liked not honour which took so much money from him. But if he should refuse it, he could not expect to have it afterwards. Ilay Campbell said to me that he would not take a judge's place though his income were as much as he gets at the bar, for he thought he had an easier life than he should have as a judge. He now did his duty to his clients and had no anxiety about the event; but, were he a judge, he would have much anxiety in forming his opinions on causes. I imagined this to be somewhat affected, and I observed that a judge should just do *his* duty in forming opinions to the best of his abilities, and not be uneasy. Lord Monboddo, who joined us in the library, said that a judge must have a stock of law. For if he has the law to seek when he is determining causes, he will not judge well, and will have very great labour. Luckily I had only one small piece of form to do this morning in court, and Mr Henry Erskine did it for me. Macqueen's promotion from merit roused my ambition. I called on my father as I have done every day since he was confined. I was vexed to be ill from intemperance. Mr Donaldson, the painter, drank tea with me. I was able to dictate some.

SATURDAY 23 NOVEMBER. After a good sleep I was very well. The promotion of Macqueen was the universal topic in our Court. Maclaurin assured me that Lord Covington was to have my father's Justiciary gown upon his resignation. His resignation was believed by everybody, and when I said I did not know of it, they thought I was prudent or in jest. It is strange that my father never almost confides any of his schemes to me. But I confess I am too open. Captain Erskine invited me to dine today at Lady Colville's, which I did very agreeably. Only a Miss Sharp of Houston there. The Captain read to me a note of genealogy which showed clearly that he and I, as descended of the Mar family, were descended of Edward III of England, the Captain in the fifteenth degree. It was really agreeable to think of having royal blood in our veins. We drank a bumper to the memory of our ancestor, Edward III. There is something generous in the consciousness of noble descent, let philosophers reason and plebeians scoff as they will. We were quite sober, and, Miss Sharp having gone away, we had a most comfortable party at tea with the ladies. I spoke rather too much of myself. However, I had an opportunity of letting Lady Colville have the compliment of knowing certainly that I had once serious thoughts of proposing marriage to her.[111] She said if I had searched all the world over I could not have found a wife that would have done so well with me as my cousin whom I had married. Both the ladies agreed that I was an excellent husband, and they thought I would be a good father. I threw the conversation into too lax a state on the connexion between parents and children. It is wrong to speculate on the great practical duties of life, for I do think it weakens principles.

Davie was better today.

110 For details of judicial salaries in those days, see Introduction, p. 24.
111 See Introduction, p. 25.

SUNDAY 24 NOVEMBER. Was at the New Church in the forenoon and edified by Dr Erskine. Dined at my father's. In the afternoon walked to the top of Arthur's Seat. It was a clear frost, and I was the better of a vigorous exertion.

MONDAY 25 NOVEMBER. I went out a little fretted with some trifling dispute with my wife, saying I would not dine at home. I took myself just as I got into the street, but could not yield. I thought I would punish myself by walking in the fields and fasting; but I had not resolution, so dined at my father's. Claud was there. I drank little, and cannot say I was intoxicated; but my fretfulness worked me, and as I was coming home at five, I met a young slender slut with a red cloak in the street and went with her to Barefoots Parks[112] and madly ventured coition. It was a short and almost insensible gratification of lewdness. I was vexed to think of it.

WEDNESDAY 27 NOVEMBER. Went out with Commissioner Cochrane in his chaise and dined with him. Nobody there. Somehow it happened that I drank enough to be somewhat intoxicated. I returned in the fly. Quitted it in the Canongate, and in the High Street met a plump hussy who called herself Peggy Grant. It was one of the coldest nights I ever remember. I went with her to a field behind the Register Office, and boldly lay with her. This was desperate risking. I read books at night on the subject of Dr Memis's cause.

THURSDAY 28 NOVEMBER. I know not how, my mind was not uneasy at what had happened last night. I pleaded in the Inner House against Dr Memis with much gravity and dull attention for about an hour and three quarters. I spoke as long as I decently could, to make the Lords sensible of what I thought an impropriety—making a serious cause of it. My speech was not finished today. I dined at Lord Monboddo's; a dull party; drank very little. Called on Mr Alexander Boswall, who was ill with a fall from his horse, and sat with him near two hours. The girl with whom I was last night had told me she lodged in Stevenlaw's Close,[112a] and at my desire engaged to be at the head of it generally at eight in the evening, in case I should be coming past. I thought I could not be in more danger of disease by one more enjoyment the very next evening, so went tonight; but she was not there. Had a consultation at home between eight and nine. Little Davie was now in a fine way. I was shocked that the father of a family should go amongst strumpets; but there was rather an insensibility about me to virtue, I was so sensual. Perhaps I should not write all this. I soothed myself with Old Testament manners.

FRIDAY 29 NOVEMBER. Grange breakfasted with me. I finished my pleading against Dr Memis, and heard those of Mr Rae and Mr Solicitor. Grange dined with me. Mr James Currie and Mr Irving, his clerk, drank tea and consulted me. Currie and I went to the play. I was enchanted with Miss Catley in Polly. I am remarkably fond of *The Beggar's Opera*. I thought tonight of publishing an

---

112 Bearford's Parks (corrupted into "Barefoot's Parks") were a range of grass fields lying immediately to the north of the North Loch and extending very approximately to the line of what is now Rose Street. In 1776 Bearford's Parks extended to the east almost as far as St David Street (William Cowan, "Bearford's Parks", *B.O.E.C.*, Vol. 13, pp. 79-91).
112a Off the south side of the High Street by the City Guard-house.

edition of it with notes, for which I would get good materials from the Duke of Queensberry; and then there would be in libraries and shops and catalogues *Boswell's Beggar's Opera.* I supped at Moncrieffe's, won a little at brag, and was in good gay spirits. Did not drink to excess.

SATURDAY 30 NOVEMBER. Was sorry for poor Dr Memis when his cause was given against him with costs. I thought him injured. In the evening walked in the procession of Freemasons, and sat till near twelve in the Assembly Hall. My wife dined today upstairs. At night I slept with her. It was very comfortable to get back to my good bed, and I told her what was true: that I really felt an indifference come upon me by living in a sort of separation from her, and that affectionate endearments were required to remove it.

SUNDAY 1 DECEMBER. I must *confess* that I planned, even when sober, that I would in the evening try to find Peggy Grant, and, as I had risked with her, take a full enjoyment. After sermon I went to Mr Boswall's.[113] I drank a great deal. My mind was agitated by hearing General Howe's aide-de-camp[114] talk of all the various incidents of war, and, seeing my keenness, tell me I should have been a soldier. I was much intoxicated. I drank tea with Mrs Boswall. About eight I got into the street and made Cameron, the chairman, inquire for Peggy Grant at a house in Stevenlaw's Close where she had told me she lived. He brought her out, and I took her to the New Town, and in a mason's shade[114a] in St Andrew's Square lay with her twice. I grew pretty sober by the time I got home, but was in a confused, feverish frame. My dear wife asked me if I had not been about mischief. I at once confessed it. She was very uneasy, and I was ashamed and vexed at my licentiousness. Yet my conscience was not alarmed; so much had I accustomed my mind to think such indulgence permitted.

MONDAY 2 DECEMBER. After a night not very easy I got up surprisingly well and dictated a good deal in the course of the day. But the fear of disease and a consciousness of my acting unsuitably to the character of a paterfamilias distressed me. In the evening I received a letter from Lord Mountstuart enclosing a bill of lading for his picture by Mr Hoare, which I had seen and admired much. This was a circumstance which pleased me elegantly. As I dictated law, I wondered how one so dissolute could treat so gravely of decent concerns. My excellent spouse behaved in an admirable manner to me. I resolved to restrain my appetite for sensual enjoyment rather than hurt her, as it was ungenerous not to pay her all the attention due to any woman of fortune, considering with what nobleness she had acted all along.

TUESDAY 3 DECEMBER. Mr Charles Hay walked with me to Leith, where I inquired for Lord Mountstuart's picture, and found it lodged in Factor Wood's cellar. He gave us a dram of gin, and I had that kind of bustle of spirits which I have usually at Leith. I have a very local mind. I had the picture brought home,

---

113 That is, the house of Thomas Boswall, the accountant (brother of Alexander Boswall), who lived in the Old Custom House Stairs in Parliament Close.
114 Major Nisbet Balfour.
114a Shed (a Scotticism).

and Grange to dine with me to drink Lord Mountstuart's health. I had sent for the Hon. A. Gordon to come and take a glass on the occasion, but he could not come. I went and drank tea with him, and he accompanied me home and saw the picture, and drank a few glasses of claret.

WEDNESDAY 4 DECEMBER. Dined at Princes Street Coffee-house at an entertainment given by Mr Alexander Boswall to Major Nisbet Balfour and a company of his friends. I was hearty and drank well while I sat, but was obliged to go to a consultation at six. At seven I went to Canongate-Kilwinning Lodge, the Grand Lodge being there this evening.

THURSDAY 5 DECEMBER. George and Andrew Cochrane, Lord Dundonald's sons, dined with us. At four two agents came to consult me. I drank some with them, over and above the glasses which I took with the young gentlemen. Lord Covington was ill and confined to the house. His better health was a toast of mine every day. I drank freely to make me sooner know if I had catched infection. I went at night to *Cymon* and *The Apprentice*,[115] acted by desire of the Freemasons. Sir William Forbes was attended by no less than five former Grand Masters, amongst whom was Rosslyn. I liked to see respect paid to his worth. After I came home, drank heartily of brandy punch.

FRIDAY 6 DECEMBER. Dined at Mr Ilay Campbell's with a company to take leave of Mr Macqueen before he went to the bench.[116] Baron Maule kept us all merry with his forcible humour and variety of anecdotes. I drank largely. Then went to Moncrieffe's, played at whist, and lost. Macqueen was here too, and much noisy, coarse jocularity went round. I drank largely again, went home between one and two, gorged but not drunk.

SATURDAY 7 DECEMBER. Was exceedingly ill after yesterday's double dose, suffered severe sickness, and at the same time mortifying abasement of character in my own mind. Had faint hopes of some time or other attaining to sobriety. Was obliged to go out and plead a cause. Was vexed to think how ill I acted in the view of getting an increase of practice by Macqueen's promotion, for I had done almost nothing this week, and papers *to write* were multiplying on my table. Grange accompanied me in a walk to Craighouse. I asked for Lord Covington, and left my compliments, as he did not admit visitors.

SUNDAY 8 DECEMBER. In the evening my wife insisted to read this journal, and finding in it such explicit instances of licentiousness, she was much affected and told me that she had come to a resolution never again to consider herself as my *wife*; though for the sake of her children and mine, as a *friend*, she would preserve appearances. When I saw her in great uneasiness, and dreaded somewhat—though not with much apprehension—her resolution, I was awaked from my dream of licentiousness, and saw my bad conduct in a shocking light.

---

115 By Garrick and Arthur Murphy respectively.
116 Directories for this period state that Ilay Campbell's house was in the area known as the Society (by Brown Square). This either means that he had moved from his house in Brown Square or that his house there had been reclassified as forming part of the Society.

I was really agitated, and in a degree of despair. She comforted me with hopes of my amendment. I went and sat awhile with Sir George. At night I calmly meditated to reform.

MONDAY 9 DECEMBER. The last week I had been very idle. This day I laboured pretty well. My dear wife was uneasy at the folly concerning her niece recorded in this journal. I could only confess, and resolve to be on my guard.

TUESDAY 10 DECEMBER. At seven I attended with the Grand Master the meeting of Mary's Chapel Lodge. It was a most numerous and excellent meeting, and we sat till eleven.

WEDNESDAY 11 DECEMBER. Was vexed at losing the cause, Lord Dumfries against his tenant Hugh Mitchell, late in Craigman, my client; for though I knew that he had deceived on a judicial examination as to his rents, as I have marked on a letter from him, so that he was culpable, yet I was persuaded he owed nothing to the Earl. I hoped that on a review of the case the Interlocutor would be altered.[117] I dined at Claud Boswell's, along with our namesake from India, Sandy Tait, the clerk, and some others. I was disgusted with the coarseness of Edinburgh manners, and being loaded with papers to write, drank little, and came home soon.

THURSDAY 12 DECEMBER. This was the fast appointed by the King to pray for success to his arms against the Americans. I paid no regard to it, but studied a confused cause and dictated part of a paper upon it. At five I went by appointment to tea and cards at the Hon. Alexander Gordon's. Maclaurin was there. I maintained that it was shocking in a nation to pray to GOD for success in destroying another nation; and that it was equally allowable for an individual to pray for destruction to his enemy, like the old Laird of Gilmillscroft, who prayed in his family worship: "Pour down, O Lord, of thy choicest curses on Hugh, Earl of Loudoun, and Mr James Boswell of Auchinleck, Advocate." Maclaurin agreed with me. He lost at whist, grew peevish, and went soon away. Charles Hay and Sandy Mackenzie, the Writer to the Signet, were the other men. We and the Countess, one being out alternately (except myself, who would be out but once), played whist long. Then Charles sat by, and brag was played till half an hour past two. Then she went to bed, and we went to supper, after which we again fell to whist, and then Gordon, Mackenzie, and I (Charles looking on) played brag. We broke up just ten minutes before six. I lost £1. 5 on the whole. I was shocked to find that my dear wife had sat up all night waiting for me. I did not go to bed, but sent for Mr Lawrie, finished a petition, and went to the Court of Session directly.

FRIDAY 13 DECEMBER. Was vexed at my sad dissipation. But was still so fevered with the rage of play that I called at Gordon's a quarter before two, and he

117 This case was concerned with a dispute over an alleged non-payment of rent of £40 for a farm in Ayrshire leased by Mitchell from the Earl of Dumfries. The case was subsequently brought before the Inner House for review, but on 11 February 1778 the court adhered to the interlocutor of the Lord Ordinary (*Extremes*, p. 202, n. 1).

having proposed brag, as I guessed he would, I engaged again keenly, and lost before three £2. 11. I came home miserably ashamed of my weakness of resolution; had worthy Grange at dinner to console me. I had been uneasy for fear of disease, and fancied symptoms of it. Was satisfied today that I was well. Dictated till I fell asleep several times.

SATURDAY 14 DECEMBER. Met at Princes Street Coffee-house as one of Douglas's counsel to consult on his cause with Duke Hamilton. We dined, but did not drink very much. I however could not resist cards. Charles Brown, the advocate,[118] and Charles Brown, the writer,[119] and Sandy Maconochie and I played at brag till near twelve. Mr Lawrie came for me, it being the last night for representing in a cause.[120] I actually dictated a paper of four pages as I played at brag. We supped quietly and I got home before one. Was in vigorous spirits, and my valuable spouse was quite reconciled to me.

MONDAY 16 DECEMBER. Laboured very well. Matthew Dickie and young Robert Syme dined with us. I was elevated somewhat by drinking little more than a pint of port. Consulted with Mr Syme about a road claimed by Crossbasket through a moss, and looked with much attention at a plan. Thought how money will operate in fixing attention; for if I had been looking at a plan in the country, without being fee'd for it, I should not have understood it at all, but have indolently run my eye over it. In the evening was uneasy with a sore throat for a little.

TUESDAY 17 DECEMBER. Was too late of getting up, and fretted by being hurried; and when my wife joked, was exasperated, threw my tea in the fire, and went out without breakfast. It was a frosty morning. I found that I had supposed it later than it was, so went and breakfasted at my father's.

FRIDAY 20 DECEMBER. Drank tea comfortably with Grange, and then he and I went to the pit, snug, and saw *Love in a Village*.[121] I was delighted with the music, and pleased to think that I had seen the first night of this piece at Covent Garden.[122] Supped at Moncrieffe's. Drank much too freely.

SATURDAY 21 DECEMBER. Was very ill in the morning, but went to the Court and pleaded well enough. Had dictated more law this week than any during this Session, which comforted me. This day a petition from my father and me for recording our entail was moved to the Court, and the registration authorized. I felt a slight twinge at being fettered, but instantly acquiesced in the family settlement being rendered stable and my father's mind being made quiet. I was a little melancholy this day on finding him failed when I sat awhile with him. It distressed me to apprehend that if he were gone, the dignity of the Family of Auchinleck would not be properly maintained. I had strange romantic projects

118 For whom, see p. 81, n. 37.
119 Charles Brown, W.S. (admitted 26 February 1753), died 1781.
120 That is, for preparing written representations.
121 By Isaac Bickerstaffe with music by Thomas Arne.
122 On 8 December 1762.

of keeping myself in the most retired state, that my weaknesses might not appear. But then I considered that my vivacity and love of immediate personal distinction would hurry me at times into all kinds of social meetings, and make me exhibit all my powers of jocularity, so that there would be an absurd inconsistency of conduct. I hoped however that I might by habits of restraint form a decent settled character enlivened with moderate pleasantry. And, when I compare myself at present with what I was some years ago, I have good reason to be well satisfied. My present fault is having no elevated views, no great ambition. I see no dignity in the Court of Session, my present sphere. I think that if I were one of the judges, I should feel myself but a little man in a narrow sphere; and I fear it is too late for me to try a more enlarged sphere in England. Yet why not try, if I can contrive to live there on as little or not much more than in Scotland? and though I should fail myself, I may get my heir forward, taking care, however, to keep him sufficiently fond of Auchinleck. Such speculations please me.

The Session rose today for the Christmas recess. I hoped to read something instructive during that interval, and to arrange my books and papers. I had now neither foolish love for A. nor gross rage for strumpets. In short I was very well; only that I drank too much when wine was in my way, and had no warmth of piety, but in effect a cold indifference as to the important objects of futurity. I was sensible how inferior my mind was in this state to what I have felt it. Yet I ignobly acquiesced, without endeavouring to rouse better affections.

MONDAY 23 DECEMBER. Breakfasted with Mr Nairne, there being a meeting at his house on some law business. After it was over, and we were alone, he put me in good humour by stating clearly and calmly the advantages of my situation in life. My father and Lady Auchinleck, Mr Alexander Boswall and his sister Miss Betty, Dr Boswell and his son Robert, Dr Webster and his son Sandy dined with us and drank little David's health. He was better, but still in a sickly state. Dr Webster and the Nabob and his sister drank tea. Alexander appeared to me now not so agreeable as at first. He appeared opinionative and noisy and consequential and snarling and dissatisfied with Scotland. I did not drink too much today; at least was not intoxicated.

TUESDAY 24 DECEMBER. Laboured pretty well in the forenoon. Dined at Crosbie's; a numerous company of lawyers there, and Mr Digges, who said we were like a parcel of schoolboys broke loose. Indeed we were noisy and merry without much subject. I drank too much, and was in bad humour when I came home.

WEDNESDAY 25 DECEMBER. This being Christmas Day, I laboured none; but I was dissatisfied that I was not in a placid pious frame suitable to this most agreeable holy festival. The forenoon passed away indolently. My worthy friend Grange dined with me according to annual custom, and we had a comfortable repast and fine old Malaga, and drank my brother David's health. I indulged myself today in a fancy which pleased me more than anybody would believe. I had a new green cloth waistcoat with silver lace, because my friend Temple had such a one when I first got acquainted with him at Edinburgh College and went with him to Porter's Chapel in Carrubber's Close.[123] Dress affects my feelings as irresistibly as music. Grange and I went to the English Chapel in the afternoon. The singing was bad, and I was not elevated as I wished to be. But to make up for this, I received a friendly letter from Dr Johnson on my coming home. It was peculiarly valuable as a Christmas gift.

THURSDAY 26 DECEMBER. The weather had been snowy for some days. I laboured all this day at a long paper. I was not in good spirits.

FRIDAY 27 DECEMBER. [F]or these two days little Sandy was ill from having eaten something that hurt his stomach and drank a little Malaga on Christmas Day, which I gave him. He was now better. His mother's affectionate anxiety made her appear to me very valuable, though I had nothing of it. She sat up with him last night till near six in the morning; and I complained that my being awaked by her coming to bed broke my natural rest. His fondness for her was very strong. He was now as fine a child as I ever saw; quite a bud of sagacity and complacency. But I dreaded that he would be spoilt by indulgence, and had poor hopes of my own authority as a father. I laboured again today at the long paper for Cutlar against Rae.[124] Mrs Mitchelson supped with us.

SATURDAY 28 DECEMBER. By Dr Johnson's recommendation, I had been reading Cheyne *On Health*, and as he recommends frequent purges, I took one last night, which did me much good today. My wife, with too much keenness but with a good deal of justice, gave me this morning literally a *curtain lecture* upon the coarse, ill-bred, and abusive style of conversation which I now habitually practised. She said that it was so disagreeable and provoking that my company could not be liked, and that I had not the tenth part of the invitations now that I had before I was married. I was very sensible of my fault, but my invitations being less frequent was owing to my having refused many, and by degrees dropped many of my dining visitors. The roughness of manners amongst the Scotch lawyers made me assume that style in self-defence, and I have carried it to excess, as I do everything. I resolved to amend. Grange dined with us today, and he and I drank a very little wine. It was agreeable to be thus temperate. I laboured very well today and finished Cutlar's paper of sixty-nine pages, on which I took uncommon pains, as Mr John Syme, the agent,[125] had made many accurate preparations for it, and it had been given to me to draw in place of Mr Macqueen.

MONDAY 30 DECEMBER. A very snowy day. Laboured some. Took a sudden thought to go down and dine with Grange. My wife came down, and would have us up. We were to have drank just one bottle of white port together comfortably.

123 St Paul's Chapel (for which, see Introduction, p. 15). Porter was presumably the name of the priest.
124 This was the long-running action of John Cutlar of Argrennan and his trustees against Fergus Rae, a flesher (butcher) in Dumfries, for reduction of a heritable bond. The case was not finally determined until 19 March 1779. Boswell's clients (the pursuers) won with an award of expenses (*Extremes*, p. 69, n. 7).
125 John Syme, W.S. (admitted 31 January 1750), Depute Writer to the Privy Seal 1754, died 1790.

We agreed thus: to come up and dine, and return and take our port. We did so, and were calmly social. Veronica came and played beside us awhile. I felt a painful struggle between my resolution to be sober and a craving for more wine. Such a constitution should be a warning against venturing to any depth at all in intoxication. Grange and I came up to tea. I received a card from Mr Syme that he had read my Answers for Cutlar with great satisfaction. This pleased me. I was however dissatisfied with the general unmanly, inactive course of my life. I had not an habitual vigour of action. I read a good deal of the cause, Sir Allan Maclean against the Duke of Argyll.

TUESDAY 31 DECEMBER. Little Sandy was very ill with pains in his bowels. Mr Wood gave him some medicine, which relieved him. I went in the chaise with Mr A. Boswall to Prestonfield in the forenoon. He was only to make a call. I was engaged to dine there. After he left it, Sir Alexander and I went up into the study, and I this day began to execute what I had long schemed: the writing of the worthy classical Baronet's life. He very readily agreed to give me materials. I sat down and wrote from what he said upon questions put by me from his infancy. I left the pages which I wrote in his cabinet. We dined comfortably. No company but Mr Mercer, wine-merchant, and Mr Macpherson, musician. I walked home in the afternoon, and found Sandy pretty well.

1777

WEDNESDAY 1 JANUARY. Employed the morning in summing up my different accounts for the last year, and found that I had spent about £740, which was £140 more than my income; and yet I could not trace any great article of extravagance. I saw indeed a number of trifling expenses which might be spared, and I resolved to try to be more economical this year. I wondered how many people, whose income is not better than mine, contrive to live in a much more showy manner. I reckoned my income to be £600 a year: £300 from my father and £300 of fees; and I settled my annual expense thus:

Interests over and above what are paid by Dalblair rent	£53	
House-rent	54	
Nurses' pensions	5	12
Wine	30	
Clothes	30	
Jaunts to Auchinleck	18	
Paper, magazines, etc.	10	
Certain expenses therefore	£200	
My wife, for family expense, servants' wages, and clothes to herself and the children.	300	
	500	

By this computation I should have £100 a year for pocket-money and incidental expenses, and if my fees should increase, I might begin to save a little.

I called at my father's before dinner, and was kept to dine. Veronica came. Mrs Boswell of Balmuto and Miss Boswell[1] were there. My father today bid me take home with me, to look at in the vacation, his Skene *De verborum significatione* with his many curious manuscript notes.[2] I was pleased with this mark of trust, for he used to keep it from me with a sort of jealousy. I drank tea with Annie Webster and her brother George, and could not help being diverted with their sort of descriptive vivacity.

SUNDAY 5 JANUARY. Heard Dr Webster at the Tolbooth Church in the forenoon, and Warden of the Canongate in the afternoon, imagining Mr Walker was to preach. Was shocked with his praying against the Americans.

TUESDAY 7 JANUARY. Miss Cuninghame and I went in the chaise with Mr A. Boswall and dined at Prestonfield, it being young William's birthday. I was not at all intoxicated. We had a good merry dance after tea. Mrs Young was my partner, and I was in excellent spirits. It was admirable to see Sir Alexander dance a

---

1 Claud Boswell's mother and sister.
2 The *De verborum significatione* of Sir John Skene (who was appointed a judge in the Court of Session in 1594 with the title of Lord Curriehill) was first published as an appendage to his *Laws and Actes of Parliament* in 1597. It was this first edition to which Boswell refers (*Extremes*, p. 73, n. 4). The work was the first Scottish legal dictionary and is even now regarded as a valuable work of reference.

minuet with the foreign air of a man of fashion. Mr A. Boswall came home with us to supper, and was more agreeable than I ever saw him.

WEDNESDAY 8 JANUARY. My wife and I and Miss Cuninghame and Veronica dined at my father's. Claud was there. I drank tea with Mr David Rae, consulting a gratis cause for the children of Mr Finlayson, miniature painter and engraver.[3] I wondered at Mr Rae's fluency of law, but considered that there were people who would wonder at mine. At night my wife and I had some good conversation as to my settling in London.

THURSDAY 9 JANUARY. Began a Reclaiming Petition for the Finlaysons while my conversation with Mr Rae was in my head. Went with my wife and looked at one of Allan Ramsay's new houses on the north side of the Castle Hill.[4] I was much taken with it, as I could there have a good consulting-room quite sacred to myself, and more rooms than in my present house, with the advantage of having no neighbour above me, and a little garden. Veronica, Effie, and Mr Lawrie were with us. Effie could form no opinion, but Veronica was charmed with the new house. Balbarton and Grange dined with us, and after dinner came Mr Cuninghame of the Sheriff-Clerk's chamber, who had the charge of Mr Ramsay's houses. I had sent for him to talk of terms. Balbarton and he drank tea. I did not conclude a bargain, but was to think of it. I had been a good while with Maclaurin before dinner.

MONDAY 13 JANUARY. Sat a little with my father. He had just sold his house in Blair's Land, Parliament Close, for 900 guineas; a great price, as he had paid only £800 and laid out £200 in repairing it; so that he got but £55 less than he paid fifteen years ago, though old-fashioned houses were now much fallen in their value. I was a little sorry that our family had now no longer a property in that land, which it had for more than half a century. But a town property is not the subject of family attachment. I thought that if I pleased, I could afterwards buy back the house, or our still older house on the fourth storey. My father had taken a country-house near the Cage in the Meadow.[5] Mr A. Boswall was to set out next day for London. He pressed me to dine with him, but I refused, as there were ladies and I was not dressed (why am I so circumstantial?), but promised to come after dinner and drink a glass. I came too soon and was ushered into the full company. The ladies soon went away, and Colonel Skene, Colonel Donald Campbell, and some more of us drank freely with my namesake. I was not the worse of it. I drank tea with Mrs Boswall,[6] along with Mr A. Boswall, between ten and eleven; took leave of him, came home, and supped.

TUESDAY 14 JANUARY. This day the Session recommenced. I began to take notes in every cause where there was any point of law, by which I hoped to

---

3 This action by the children of the deceased miniature painter John Finlayson was "a struggle between two sets of heirs for the revenue of a group of shops in Edinburgh" (*Session Papers*, 77 01 14).

4 The houses of Allan Ramsay (1713-84), the painter, in Ramsay Garden.

5 "The Cage" was "a species of ornamental arbour" which stood long at the south end of the central walk in the Meadows (Grant, Vol. II, p. 348).

6 The Nabob's sister-in-law, wife of Thomas Boswall the accountant. The Nabob was a bachelor (*Extremes*, p. 77, n. 5).

improve much, and perhaps at the end of the year to publish an *Abbreviate* of decisions. At eight was at a consultation at the Advocate's for Sir Allan Maclean. The Advocate was very drunk. It was shameful; at least it would be so in any country in the world but this, I believe.

WEDNESDAY 15 JANUARY. I was, and have been for some time, in a morbid state of mind; that is to say, a state of wonderful indifference as to almost anything. I must explain this more fully when I have more leisure.

FRIDAY 17 JANUARY. A sudden inclination seized me to dine with Lord Dundonald, who had come to town a few days ago. I did so; nobody there but Mrs Binning. Drank some fine cowslip wine made of cowslips which grew on Arthur's Seat. Did not at all intoxicate myself. Drank tea at Lord Kames's. Have not for a long time before been at a true Edinburgh tea-drinking, where lady comes in after lady, and all the little news are told. Came and sat a good while most comfortably with worthy Grange, who said he thought it very probable that I would one day live in London, as it might happen that if I had a good estate, people here would not employ me as a lawyer, from a notion that I would think business beneath me; for so they thought as to Sir Gilbert Elliot[7] and Sir Adam Fergusson, both of whom wished to have practice at the bar here. In that case he thought I would weary of being here, and would go to London. We were in a calm, mild, friendly frame, and talked of human life very justly. He readily agreed to go to London if I went, supposing a decent place could be procured for him. It pleased me to find that my going to live at London, except when at Auchinleck, would not be a wild scheme. Yet I felt a sort of piteous concern at being estranged from Scotland, without adverting that the permanent connexion with Auchinleck would ever attach me and mine to North Britain. It was very agreeable both to Grange and me to perceive that our mutual friendship was not weakened. He came up and supped with us. I comforted myself in being absent from the anniversary drunken meeting of the advocates which was held this evening.

SATURDAY 18 JANUARY. Dined at Fortune's at the annual meeting of Mundell's scholars, Mr Solicitor Murray in the chair. There was a numerous company, much noise, and even less pleasantry than usual. I got shockingly drunk.

MONDAY 20 JANUARY. I had yesterday finished Dr Cheyne *On Health*, which Dr Johnson recommended to me. I was disappointed, for I could not help thinking the Doctor whimsical and somewhat of an old woman; at the same time, I found good precepts of temperance and a comfortable strain of religion. I felt some of his counsels fixed in my mind, and hoped to practise them. Captain Erskine called on me a little. I dictated some, and had a consultation at

---

7 Sir Gilbert Elliot (1722-77) of Minto, in Roxburghshire, Bt, was admitted advocate in 1743 and served as Sheriff-Depute of Roxburghshire from 1747 to 1754. He was M.P. for Selkirkshire from 1753 to 1765 and then M.P. for Roxburghshire until his death on 11 February 1777. Appointed Lord of Admiralty in 1756 and Keeper of the Signet in 1767, he was ultimately Treasurer of the Navy from 1770 to 1777. He succeeded to the baronetcy in 1766. In addition to being a statesman, he was a philosopher and a poet, and he associated much with the principal literary figures of the day both in Edinburgh and in London.

Crosbie's, and I dined at Mr Alexander Maconochie's, with Douglas (who came to town today for a little time during this week), Lord Monboddo, Shawfield, and other company for the Laird. Drank too much; had a consultation at home at seven with Colquhoun Grant[8] after which grew very much the worse of liquor, and was shockingly harsh to Miss Cuninghame, which gave me much distress afterwards when I considered that she was an orphan who had no proper refuge but with my wife.

TUESDAY 21 JANUARY. Was justly vexed at my conduct last night, and relaxed and sick. Had twenty causes in the rolls between nine and ten. Got through them badly. Was not right all day. Grange supped with us. Walked in the Meadow before dinner with Maclaurin.

WEDNESDAY 22 JANUARY. Before breakfast was informed that the Lord Provost, Mr Kincaid, died suddenly last night. Was shocked with so striking a memento of the uncertainty of life. Was uneasy this morning because a Petition was to be moved in which there was a violent complaint by Ilay Campbell of an account of the determination of the cause, Jack against Cramond, etc., in *The Edinburgh Advertiser*, which I had sent.[9] It was quite true, and I thought very proper; but I feared that the President, who hates newspapers because he dreads them, might take it up hot and instigate the Lords to harass Donaldson, the printer, on whom I called this morning, and found him disposed to act with spirit. Worthy Grange comforted me and said that my bad spirits made me too apprehensive. Accordingly he was right, for the President said, "The Petition complains of the newspapers, and I think justly. I should be glad to see the printer of a newspaper prosecuted, but we have nothing to do with this." My wife and I called a little at Sir George's this forenoon. I went up to Donaldson's shop and looked to the Cross to see if the death of the chief magistrate of the place made any impression upon the inhabitants. I could perceive none; and was struck with the most humbling impression of the unimportance of any individual considered *per se*. A man must acquiesce in this, and be sensible that the notions which he has formed of the *world* being saddened at his death are the mere chimeras of unexperienced pride. At night I was at a consultation at Lord Advocate's on the cause, Duke Hamilton against Douglas. My feeling was

8 Colquhoun Grant (1721-1792), W.S. (admitted 29 June 1759). He was a large, handsome man who had served in Prince Charles' Life Guards during the 1745 rebellion and was present at the battle of Culloden. He prospered in his business as a lawyer and amassed a considerable fortune (Kay, Vol. II, p. 57).

9 "David Jack, linen-manufacturer in Longforgan, had on 17 December 1776 obtained, by appeal to the full bench of judges, reduction of a Decreet Arbitral between himself and George Cramond, maltman in Dundee, and others, with [an award of expenses], on the ground that the arbiters had decreed certain fees for themselves, to be paid by Jack. Boswell's account, which appeared in *The Edinburgh Advertiser*, 27 December 1776, proclaimed the importance of the determination as setting a precedent: 'The Lord President said from the chair that he hoped the decision would not remain a secret, but... would be attended with a salutary influence all over the country... There was a great deal of excellent doctrine delivered from the bench on this occasion... against everything that could be at all construed as greedy or self-interested in arbiters... The counsel for Mr Jack were Mr Andrew Crosbie and Mr James Boswell... For Mr Cramond and others, Mr Ilay Campbell and Mr Bannatyne MacLeod'"(*Extremes*, p. 79, n. 2).

that property was of no great consequence, as life is so very fleeting. The question is, "Whether are the feelings of this dejected indifference or those of practical life the justest?"

THURSDAY 23 JANUARY. Grew remiss in attending to the decisions, and was satisfied to have the papers with the interlocutors, unless when I was particularly curious as to a cause. Indeed it might seem invidious towards Mr Wallace, the regular collector, to publish decisions unless where I was counsel. I dictated tolerably today.

FRIDAY 24 JANUARY. Had been for some time much afflicted with what I find it is difficult to express so as to give the idea with any force at all like the original feeling. It is truly as difficult as to express any particular sensation of pain by words. My affliction was a kind of *faintness of mind*, a total indifference as to all objects of whatever kind, united with a melancholy dejection. I saw death so staringly waiting for all the human race, and had such a cloudy and dark prospect beyond it, that I was miserable as far as I had animation. Either this morning or yesterday I awaked in terrible melancholy. I found however immediate relief by instantaneously praying to GOD with earnestness; and I felt the comfort of piety. I absolutely was reduced to so wretched a state by my mental disease that I had right and wrong and every distinction confounded in my view. I loved my wife with extraordinary affection, but I had distinctly before me the time which must come when we shall be separated by death. I was fond of my children. But I unhappily saw beyond them; saw the time when they too shall be dead, and seeing that, I could not value them properly at present.

Lord and Lady Alva and my Lord's son and daughters, Major Hunter of Brownhill and his brother James with his wife, Mr Nairne, and Grange dined with us. I was quite flat in sensation, but was able to do sufficiently well as landlord by drinking chiefly weak negus. I was hurt a little in the morning by a rough saying of Bruce[10] the advocate's of me: "He has no law, and he comes here to pick it up occasionally." I *knew* there was too much truth in this, but I despaired of being able to incorporate much law with my mind. It is wonderful how well I do, all things considered.

SATURDAY 25 JANUARY. After the House, went with Lord Braxfield in his coach, Charles Hay also with him, to dine at Craighouse with Lord Covington. I was sensible of the influence of company upon my mind, I could not tell how, any more than how wine has an influence on the animal spirits. Lord Covington— Mr Alexander Lockhart—at seventy-six was a curious object of contemplation to me. Maclaurin and Walter Campbell were here. We had no good conversation, and did not drink much; but we had a great deal of whist. I betted a guinea a rubber, and played very ill, and lost £5. 13. 6. I was vexed at losing and appearing to such disadvantage as I do at whist. Lord Braxfield and Hay and I stayed to supper, and walked in after it in moonlight. I was disgusted with the vulgarity

10 Either Alexander Bruce (d. 1780), advocate (admitted 27 July 1762), or John Bruce (d. 1788), advocate (admitted 24 February 1761).

of Braxfield and with Hay's fulsome flattery of him. I had a low opinion of the Court of Session, and thought of going to England to a higher sphere.

MONDAY 27 JANUARY. Was counsel in a Justiciary trial of John Philip for an outrage at the house of Mrs Brodie of Lethen. He was found to be insane. My Justiciary collection will show the particulars of the case.[11]

TUESDAY 28 JANUARY. Attended the funeral procession of the Lord Provost from the Tron Church to the Greyfriars Churchyard. The idea of the *last day and resurrection* struck me when I saw the churchyard thick-crowded with people. I love show and solemnity so much that my spirits were quite elevated today. Death actually appeared to my mind without any horror. I was comforted to find in my own experience that this *may* be. Lord Kames and his lady and Miss Gascoigne, who was living at their house, Miss MacLeod of Raasay, Lord Monboddo, Mr Nairne, and Grange dined with us. It was a good meeting. Kames and Monboddo were not very fond of each other, but I contrived to unite them by the subject of Banks's circumnavigation.[12] Mrs Drummond never eat and drank in our house before. She very frankly spoke to me, when I drank tea with her lately, to have a day fixed for my Lord and her to dine with us. I was happy to have Lord Kames, aged about eighty yet in lively frame, at my table; and it was comfortable that he and his lady, who had been very good to me in my dissipated days, as appears from my journal in 1762 and is gratefully remembered by me, should now be in my house, when I am a settled advocate in good practice, with a wife and four children. Monboddo likes few of his brethren, and had not visited Kames for a long time. I said I thought a man of eighty should be an exception, and that he should go again and visit him, and I would be of the party. He paid me the compliment of saying, "Well, if you think it right, I'll go with you." He sat very cordially with Grange and Nairne and me, talking in a manly strain as to this world, and with firmness as to a future state. He seemed happy today, and he did my mind much good. He drank tea, and then I read to him passages from Dr Johnson's *Journey*, which he applauded greatly.

THURSDAY 30 JANUARY. Laboured well. Was prevented from going to church, but fasted to a certain degree, and performed some private devotion suitable to the day;[12a] felt something of solemn loyalty.

FRIDAY 31 JANUARY. Pleaded before the Lords a cause for Craigengillan against

11 John Philip was a young "writer" who was infatuated with Miss Anne Brodie of Lethen, "an heiress much his social superior", to whom he had sent two "extravagant and incoherent love-letters". Miss Brodie's mother had enlisted the help of Colquhoun Grant, W.S., to try to put a stop to these unwanted advances. Having been severely warned by Grant to stop his activities, Philip was seen outside Mrs Brodie's house armed with pistols. When two members of the City Guard attempted to arrest him, he fired a pistol at them, but it failed to go off. After being arrested, he was taken to the Tolbooth, where "he behaved in a frantic manner, breaking the windows and tearing off all his clothes in spite of the intense cold" (*Extremes*, p. 81, n. 4).
12 "Joseph Banks, naturalist, had accompanied Captain James Cook in the famous voyage of the *Endeavour* around the world, 1768-1771. When he and Dr Daniel Solander had visited Edinburgh in 1772, Monboddo had eagerly questioned Solander to discover whether the aborigines of Australia had tails" (*Extremes*, p. 82, n. 7).
12a The anniversary of the execution of Charles I.

Shaw of Dunaskin. It was a dull division of a moor. I felt myself not clear-headed. I supped at Moncrieffe's.

SATURDAY 1 FEBRUARY. Dined at Mr George Wallace's with Colonel Fletcher, son to the late Lord Milton,[13] Professor Ferguson,[14] and several more. There was some tolerable conversation, but it was not forcible and lively enough. London conversation has made me very difficult to be pleased. I am in good humour enough when I indulge the common, idle, trifling talk. But when something better is attempted, I am dissatisfied with the imperfection. I drank very little today.

SUNDAY 2 FEBRUARY. Got up about seven, having resolved to pass the day at Prestonfield. Worthy Grange convoyed me to the head of the avenue. I found the family at breakfast. Sir Alexander and I were all forenoon in his library, continuing his life. I was quite calm and placid.

MONDAY 3 FEBRUARY. Laboured well. Found dictating law-papers much easier to me, as Mr Lawrie observed. Little David was now in a very good way, but Sandy ill with teething. I had lately a thought that appeared new to me: that by burning all my journal and all my written traces of former life, I should be like a new being; and how soon may this be done; nay, how soon might all the libraries in Britain be destroyed! Were I just now to go and take up house in any country town in England, it would be just a different existence. Might it not be proper to change one's residence very frequently, so as to be literally a pilgrim upon earth? for death would not be such a violent circumstance, as one would not be strongly fixed.

TUESDAY 4 FEBRUARY. Dined at Lord Monboddo's with a good deal of company; drank rather too much. Called in my way home at Mr John Syme's[15] to consult the cause, Cutlar against Rae. He followed the old method, and read over my paper from beginning to end. I was intoxicated to a certain degree. Met in the street with a coarse strumpet, went to the Castle Hill, was lascivious with her, but had prudence enough to prevent me from embarking. Was vexed that I had begun bad practices in 1777. Home and finished a paper.

WEDNESDAY 5 FEBRUARY. Dined with my wife and Miss Cuninghame at Mr Claud Boswell's. Drank a good deal too much. Tea there. At night was in a certain degree of intoxication; made Cameron, the chairman, send Peggie Dundas to me to the Castle Hill, where I lay with her without fear because I had been once safe; and such was my state of mind that at the time I felt no check of conscience but enjoyed her with appetite. No sooner was I at home than I was sadly vexed at what I had done, and my dearest wife saw from my countenance what had happened. I at once confessed. She was more seriously affected than I ever saw her.

13 Andrew Fletcher, Lord Milton (1692-1766), appointed Lord of Session in 1724 and Lord Commissioner of Justiciary in 1726; Lord Justice-Clerk 1735-48.
14 Adam Ferguson, Professor of Moral Philosophy at Edinburgh University (for whom, see also the entry for 16 August 1773 and relevant footnote).
15 John Syme, W.S., resided in New Street, off the north side of the Canongate.

THURSDAY 6 FEBRUARY. Was vexed at the recollection of last night, and despaired almost of acting properly. We dined at Sir George Preston's. Captain Brisbane, who was wounded at Bunker's Hill, was there, and gave such an account of wounds and death as shocked me. Annie came home and made tea to me. Was busy. Had long consultation, Tait against Lawson[16] at Mr Ilay Campbell's; stayed supper with him and his wife; quiet and pretty well.

MONDAY 10 FEBRUARY. Mr Claud Boswell, his sister Miss Menie, Lady Wallace, and Miss Susie Dunlop dined with us. I drank a bottle and a half of claret, which was too much. But I considered that I had a branch of our ancient family with me, and I would be cordial with him. I however found that he had nothing of *family spirit* in him, so that even wine could not unite him and me. I was not the worse of drinking so much. Matthew Dickie was with me on business at night, and supped.

TUESDAY 11 FEBRUARY. For these several days my dear wife had been distant to me, and no wonder. This day she abated of her displeasure. I was in remarkable vigour of health and spirits, as I have sometimes been after drinking freely. I was early out of the Court, and walked with my wife in the New Town, and looked at a house which was to sell.

WEDNESDAY 12 FEBRUARY. Surgeon Wood and his wife and daughter and brother in partnership with him, whom I had not seen before, and Grange supped. I was in a flow of spirits, and though I was to open Sir Allan Maclean's cause against the Duke of Argyll next day, and had not made out notes for it, I most improperly pushed about the port wine, and drank till between two and three in the morning. I deluded myself by imagining that I was thinking of the cause and brightening my ideas. I was much intoxicated.

THURSDAY 13 FEBRUARY. Could not get up till it was almost nine, and was very sick and confused and had a violent headache. I was truly miserable, and shocked at my inexcusable ill-timed excess. I was for two hours in a wretched state; could get no rest for sickness and pain. The hearing did not come on till between twelve and one. I said to Mr Lawrie, "This is terrible. It is like going into a battle." I had, however, a wonderful indifference as to the appearance which I was to make. I thought Macqueen's Information had stated the cause ably. I could not therefore go wrong if I kept to it; and indeed it might save me the exertion of finding out arguments of my own. As I had a ship, why should I quit it and swim? At any rate, I need not be afraid while swimming, as I could always take refuge in the ship. I would have asked to have the cause put off by pleading *indisposition*; but I thought the real fact would come out, and my character as a practitioner would be hurt. I spoke about an hour and a half, and though I had

16 This was the action of *John Tait, W.S. v James Lawson* for recovery of some £3,000 which had been advanced to purchase a share in a copartnery in an ironworks in Virginia. The action had started in 1774 and went all the way to the House of Lords. The cause was not finally determined until 4 August 1779, when Tait succeeded in obtaining decree. Tait's counsel were Alexander Murray, William Baillie, Ilay Campbell and Boswell (*Extremes*, p. 84, n. 2).

not a single note, I really went tolerably through the cause; indeed to my own astonishment, though I visibly did worse than usual; and Lord Monboddo told me next day that I was not sufficiently prepared. To get through at all decently was a great deal. This must be a warning to me for the future. Balbarton dined with us, and he and I drank negus, which did me good. Matthew Dickie drank tea, and I dictated a Condescendence[17] for the Magistrates of Kilmarnock while he was by and suggested hints.[18]

SATURDAY 15 FEBRUARY. Lady Colville, Lady Anne, and Captain Erskine dined with us. Mr Andrew was engaged. It was a calm, agreeable party. Lady Colville insisted on my attending her to the play. It was *The Clandestine Marriage*.[19] I had company to sup with me, so came out at eight. I was a little elevated with wine, and picked up a girl in the street, with whom I went to the Meadow and had some lascivious sport, but did not embark. I was ashamed of my low appetite immediately.

SUNDAY 16 FEBRUARY. Heard Dr Webster in the forenoon. Dined with him at my father's. He mentioned the success of His Majesty's arms today in his prayer in such a manner as hurt me, and I thought I should not hear him again while the war in America continued. Heard Mr Walker in the afternoon. Was foolish enough to indulge a desire to see Peggie Dundas, the girl whom I had twice enjoyed on the Castle Hill when I could not distinctly see her face, and ordered Cameron to bid her be on the Hill at seven. I drank tea at Sir George's. At seven I walked on the Hill. I was resolved not to venture, had she come; but luckily she could not be found, so a foolish indulgence was prevented. I came home in a calm, sleepy state, and went to bed early.

TUESDAY 18 FEBRUARY. Was pleased with Mr Solicitor Murray's pleading for the Duke of Argyll against my friend, Sir Allan. It was ornate eloquence. But I told him afterwards that it was lost upon our judges. It was like playing fine Italian *allegros* to a parcel of strong ploughmen dancing in a barn, who would call out, "Pooh! Play 'Greig's Pipes'." He said he pleaded to please himself. From that motive I have written law-papers with elegance. In the evening I attended Sir William Forbes on a visit to St David's Lodge. It was most agreeable to witness the mutual happiness of him and his brethren on meeting after his recovery. Never were compliments more sincerely exchanged. Yet I was sensible of a sad, cold indifference as to good and evil of every sort in this transient, dubious state of being.

WEDNESDAY 19 FEBRUARY. My uncle the Doctor's wife died this morning. It affected me only as another instance of mortality. I attended a long consultation

17 A condescendence is a statement of the facts on which a party's claim is based.
18 "The Magistrates of Kilmarnock were opposed by the inhabitants in their claim to be able to lease for building a portion of the town's green which had long been used for washing, bleaching, drying wool, etc. On 19 December the Lords of Session had pronounced an Interlocutor in favour of the inhabitants. The Magistrates had appealed from this decision. Dickie was their agent, Andrew Crosbie and Boswell their counsel" (*Extremes*, p. 86, n. 5).
19 By George Colman the Elder and David Garrick.

at Mr Rae's on Sir Allan Maclean's cause. Was sensible of improving in knowledge of law by discoursing with my senior brethren.

THURSDAY 20 FEBRUARY. Mr Rae pleaded admirably for Sir Allan Maclean. I was roused more to the desire of excellence than I had been for a long time.

FRIDAY 21 FEBRUARY. Before dinner called on my uncle the Doctor. Found him pretty well. He had given up his house and garden in the Meadow. There could not be a finer little place for my children. I went and secured it immediately for a year, at £15 of rent.[20] I had agreed to continue in my house in James's Court another year. This evening my table was clear, all but two papers, part of one of which I wrote. I called on Maclaurin. He said he was now come to think that nothing was so good as a man's own fireside and his own bed, and that he would not be with General Howe for all America. I made him go with me to Moncrieffe's. I played a little at brag. Drank moderately.

MONDAY 24 FEBRUARY. Wrote to Dr Johnson, as also a letter of candid expostulation to Dr Blair on his praying against the Americans. Supped the Hon. A. Gordon's with Grange and several others, very cheerfully.

TUESDAY 25 FEBRUARY. Ilay Campbell pleaded excellently for his Chief, Argyll. I was well in practice.

WEDNESDAY 26 FEBRUARY. Grange and I went with my two little daughters and saw a small museum of automaton figures of different sorts.[21] Had a consultation of three hours on Sir Allan's cause. Learnt much from it. Received a very pretty answer from Dr Blair, though his opinion differed from mine. I preserve both the letters. I had not been in company with him since last spring. Dr Gregory had made me suspect him of infidelity, but the publication of his beautiful sermons reconciled me to him; and this letter from *the Professor of Rhetoric* justly flattered me.

THURSDAY 27 FEBRUARY. The Miss Duns, Mr Stobie, Grange, Clerk Matthew[22] (to settle our annual account), and Maclean of Cornaig, whom I had seen in Coll, dined with us. I got into an uncommonly cordial frame, and drank greatly too much. I unhappily went to the street, picked up a big fat whore, and lay with her upon a stone hewing in a mason's shade just by David Hume's house. My dear wife had gone and walked on the Castle Hill thinking to find me. I confessed when I came home. I never saw her so uneasy. She was really distressed, and no wonder. I could only resolve to be on my guard, and to make up to her by most affectionate attention.

20 The house still stands and is at 15a Meadow Place (*Extremes*, p. 88, n. 2). The building was "greatly altered and extended in 1881 to form two separate houses" (Cant, *Marchmont in Edinburgh*, p. 126).
21 "This 'Grand Museum' exhibited in a room in World's End Close, Netherbow, included an elephant the mechanism of which was 'finely contrived… to animate the trunk, eyes, and tail to perform the various motions of life, as if in actual existence'; a girl at a spinning-wheel, a Chinese, a moving chariot with horses ('the coachman whipping them, to the surprise of the spectators'), and a 'self-moving machine, that goes without horses' (*The Caledonian Mercury*, 22 February 1777)" (*Extremes*, p. 89, n. 4).
22 Matthew Dickie.

FRIDAY 28 FEBRUARY. My wife and I dined at Sir George's, as did Miss Cuninghame. Veronica came after dinner. I walked in the Castle with her. It was consoling after the dissolute scenes of yesterday to feel myself a calm, fond father.

SATURDAY 1 MARCH. Mr Solicitor, Ilay Campbell, Maclaurin, Wight (for the first time), and Samuel Mitchelson, Junior, and his wife dined with us. Ilay Campbell went away before tea. The rest stayed and played cards. The Hon. A. Gordon joined. He and Mr and Mrs Mitchelson supped. I was rakish enough to propose cards after supper, and the three gentlemen played till two. Very wrong.

MONDAY 3 MARCH. That the effects of Thursday might be the sooner known, I plied my blood pretty freely with wine ever since. I laboured today, but took a sufficiency of cider and port at dinner.

WEDNESDAY 5 MARCH. I was exceedingly hurried writing law-papers for the press.[22a] My dearest wife permitted me to enjoy that pleasure which I did not deserve. How grateful am I to her.

THURSDAY 6 MARCH. Captain George Preston breakfasted with us. I received accounts in the Parliament House that Mrs Campbell of Treesbank had died on Tuesday (the 4). I hastened home to communicate the affecting news to my dear wife in the most tender and soothing manner; but she was gone out, and unluckily she met the postman and took from him a letter for me sealed with black, which she opened, and received a sudden shock. Grange, my worthy friend, was with her, and told me that she burst into tears. When I met her at home, I comforted her as well as I could. It was gloomy to her to be now the last of her father's children, and to dread that she would be carried off by the lingering distemper, a consumption, as the rest had been. She blamed herself too for neglect of her poor sister, because she had not gone to see her. I took that upon me; for I had prevented her from going, as it might have hurt her much. She and Miss Cuninghame dined alone. The Laird of Fairlie,[23] Commissioner Cochrane, Matthew Dickie, and the Hon. Bute Lindsay, who had been engaged before the accounts came, dined with me. I was a good deal affected, and talked of the striking circumstance of both Treesbanks and his wife being carried off in so short a space. The *Commissionaire*, who is truly unfeeling, said, "Pooh! James. This is just what has been going on for hundreds of years." His kind of liveliness, which is owing to his want of feeling, instead of hurting me, relieved a little the dreary scene within me. I was very busy in the afternoon. Miss Susie Dunlop supped with us.

SATURDAY 8 MARCH. So tender is my heart still that I was last night affected with anxious concern at leaving my dear wife and children, and did not rest in tranquillity. Veronica ran to me this morning with eager affection, crying, "O papa!" and would scarcely be prevailed with to let me go. Such charming fondness is the sweetest luxury! It is an immediate felicity which I enjoy; and

22a All law papers in proceedings in the Inner House were printed.
23 Alexander Fairlie, of Fairlie, in Ayrshire (*Extremes*, p. 396).

let me not unreasonably allow it to embitter my life should I afterwards be deprived of it. Let it rather balance what woes I may feel, and its own privation if I should have that to suffer. Certainly much may be done by philosophical calculation and chemistry. Worthy Grange came up; and after breakfasting comfortably and bidding adieu to my kind spouse, who by this time had forgotten my faults, I went in the fly to Glasgow, a humdrum journey enough, with a Whitby shipmaster, a Paisley manufacturer, and Joseph my servant.

Boswell's account of the "very creditable interment of worthy Mrs Campbell" on 10 March shows that the event was remarkable for the somewhat macabre fact that in the digging of her grave the skull of the first Mrs Campbell was thrown out and had to be hastily "tumbled into the earth again". Ten days later, Boswell arrived at Auchinleck, where he was well received by his father and Lady Auchinleck. "My mind was quite sweet and pure", wrote Boswell, "without fretfulness, and without trouble of any kind. I loved the country after the labour of a Winter Session, and I had solid notions as a country gentleman." To his pleasant surprise, his father consented to Boswell's going to London in the spring; but at the same time Lord Auchinleck expressed the view that the idea was nonsense and he clearly had no faith in Boswell's getting Lord Mountstuart to keep his promise to find him a position. "James," he said, "for all your promises you have got nae siller but from mysel'." In response to this, Boswell was compelled to acknowledge that his father was his best patron, but he was delighted that the way was now clear for another jaunt to London. "I now felt myself not only relieved, but fluttering with joy", he wrote. "Auchinleck and London were now amicably connected. When I went to my room at night I thanked GOD for my happiness with animated devotion. I was to have the rose without the thorn." Boswell was even pleased with Lady Auchinleck. "I must observe", he wrote, "that Lady Auchinleck, though her mind is narrow, has discernment and sound judgment in many instances, which I have really esteemed much."

When Boswell left Auchinleck on 24 March, his father embraced him with a "cordiality" which, wrote Boswell, "I valued more than the fond embrace of the finest woman".

Boswell got back to Edinburgh on 25 March.

WEDNESDAY 26 MARCH. *Immediate enjoyment* I considered as the great object, whether consisting of *sensation* or *reflection* or *hope.* I saw that in the universe, as in one great picture perpetually changing, some parts of it slower and some quicker, everything served the purpose either of light or shade, and no individual part was shade long. If a man is wounded, he soon is in a way of recovery, and he gradually dawns from shade into light again. If he is killed, he is either deprived of feeling, or he feels himself in a new state of being probably better than this, or in another modification of this—*as good as new.* I endeavoured to exalt my mind to that text: "And GOD saw everything that he had made, and behold it was very good." These however are but the speculations of a vigorous fancy playing in "a mind at ease", as Marcus in *Cato* says. I "held fast"[24] my faith in the Gospel, trusting that the charter itself would appear most precious when the seals should be opened in a future world. The writings of

24 Probably an allusion to I Thessalonians 5. 21 (*Extremes*, p. 102, n. 1).

the New Testament are but labels to give us a faint notion of its contents. We indeed see *divine characters*. There is a *star* in the east sufficiently bright for us to follow till we arrive at the glorious *sun* of righteousness, the fountain of light and beneficence.

THURSDAY 27 MARCH. Sir William Forbes came and sat awhile in the evening. I relished much his worthy and amiable society. He praised my "Journey to the Hebrides" very much, and said we had no travels like it.[25] He was clear for my going to London.

SATURDAY 29 MARCH. Grange dined with us. Poor little David had been very ill for some days of a teething fever which was very severe on his delicate frame. Grange and I went and brought Mr Wood after dinner. He said he could do nothing for the child. I drank tea with Grange, but was called home before it was finished, the child having grown worse. I found him in sad distress, and his anxious mother in much affliction. I had not before been seriously alarmed for him, as he had struggled on wonderfully. But I was now affected to the heart, and to make my wife easy, I sent for Dr Young. He bathed his limbs in warm water, which relieved him a little. But he was pale and feeble, though in as much pain as he apparently could suffer. The Doctor then put a blister on his back. But it had no effect, and he expired a little before nine. I was calm as I could wish, and resigned to the dispensations of GOD. My wife was in real grief, but composed her mind better than I could have expected. His nurse was sincerely sorry. Grief appeared strongly in her countenance, though her behaviour was quiet. I carried the little corpse on my arms up to the drawing-room and laid it on a table covered with a table-cloth, parts of which again I spread over my child. There was something of dreariness in the blank in our nursery. Yet the gentle death of the sweet innocent, and his appearance like waxwork and at peace after his sufferings, affected us pleasingly. I wrote a few lines to my father on this event.

SUNDAY 30 MARCH. I had almost resolved not to go [to London]. Little David's death determined me finally. For it would have been very unkind to leave my wife, unless I had been called away on important business. I must observe that while I was undetermined my valuable spouse behaved charmingly. "Do not", said she, "disturb yourself. I shall have your linens in readiness, and as you have your father's consent, you can go or not as you find yourself inclined." Having leave to go made me not so keen for it as I used to be.

This morning Veronica and Effie would see their little brother. Veronica calmly kissed him. But Effie was violently affected, kissed him over and over again, cried bitterly, "O my poor billy[26] Davie", and run to his nurse, who had also been hers, and clung about her, blubbering and calling to her, "O come and take him off the table. Waken him, waken him, and put him in his cradle." With much difficulty we got her pacified. I shall regard her all my life for the strength

25 The journal had not yet been published. Sir William had read the manuscript (see the entry for 1 January 1775).
26 "Billy" is Scots for brother.

of her affection. She will take the greatest care of me in my old age, though Veronica may be the most pleasing companion when I am well. Veronica is of my temper. Euphame of her mother's. Yet I was tenderer today than I imagined, for I cried over my little son and shed many tears. At the same time I had really a pious delight in praying with the room locked, and leaning my hands on his alabaster frame as I knelt. I prayed *for* his spirit, but chiefly *to* it as in the region of felicity, looking to a beautiful sky. There was not the least horror of death in this scene. My wife was not shocked by seeing him. I wrote to Sir Alexander Dick for leave to bury David in his vault, where my eldest son is laid. My letter, of which I keep a copy, is a fine picture of my mind at the time. His kind answer, which I keep, was very fine. Worthy Grange, who had been up last night and shown friendly concern, dined with us. He and I drank chiefly cider and were very comfortable. I was even in admirable spirits, moderated by the death of my child. I uttered several lively sayings, some of them indeed prompted by him. I had intended to take the sacrament, today being Easter. But went out too late. For when I came to the Chapel in Blackfriars Wynd founded by Chief Baron Smith, which I preferred as a privater assembly than the New Episcopal Chapel, *the doors were shut*. There was a solemnity in this which pleased me. At six Dr Young and Mr Wood and one of his lads opened little David's body, my wife having agreed to it. They said his bowels were not right, some of them being too tight and some too large, and that there were hardnesses in his lungs which would have grown worse, so that he could not have had a good life. I was alarmed at any complaint as to his lungs, the consumption being the disease of his mother's family, with which her other children might be infected. But they assured me (though I did not mention my fear) that there was nothing consumptive about him.

MONDAY 31 MARCH. One of Lamb the upholsterer's men came and, after I had put my little David into his coffin, screwed down the lid of it. I locked myself in the drawing-room with the little *dead*, and read the funeral service over him. I went to Mr Crosbie's to a consultation. Grange dined with us, and after dinner Robert Boswell came. They and I and Joseph had a mourning-coach at five, in which we conveyed David's corpse to Duddingston. Sir Alexander Dick and the Reverend Mr Bennet met us at the churchyard, and accompanied the interment in my excellent friend's vault, where I saw the coffin of my eldest son quite entire, except that the varnishing was a little worn off. We were kindly entertained with tea and wine at the manse, where Lady Dick was waiting. Such obliging attention was truly comforting. I was in the very best frame.

THURSDAY 3 APRIL. Grange employed me to draw a Bill of Advocation.[27] He acted as my clerk, Mr Lawrie having been for some time in the country, from whence I did not expect him to return for a fortnight. It was a delightful day. The sun shone bright. I dictated easily and admirably. Grange breakfasted with

27 A Bill of Advocation was the name given to the court writ whereby a party could appeal from the decision of an "inferior judge" (such as a sheriff) to the Court of Session.

us. I met Dr Blair in the street after dinner. He asked me to drink tea with him, which I did.[28] He shocked me by an expression which he used concerning my father: that he was beginning to *vegetate*. It conveyed a disagreeable idea as if man grew by age into a *material* substance. I must make him explain this. I was rather too lively and fluent, and gained little improvement by this interview.

SUNDAY 6 APRIL. Kept the house in the forenoon. Went with Mr Nairne to the English Chapel in the afternoon, and drank tea with him. He came to call and see my wife. We met Mr Solicitor on the street, and took him with us. He drank tea. I was in such spirits that I could not restrain myself from talking a great deal; I imagine with too much gaiety for the character of a lawyer. The Solicitor was prudent and formal, which I believe procures a kind of respect. Yet why lose the pleasure of gaiety? There should however be *some* restraint. Much of the beauty of which we are agreeably sensible is formed by restraint, by *shapes*, and by *sounds limited by time*. My wife and I supped at Sir George's. I was exceedingly cordial.

MONDAY 7 APRIL. My wonderful spirits continued. Betty Montgomerie, Lord Eglinton's natural daughter, young Donaldson the printer, and Matthew Dickie dined. My fancy was pleased with Miss Montgomerie having noble blood in her veins. She was not sixteen, and was fresh, plump, and comely. Before dinner she allowed me luscious liberties with kindly frankness. I repeated them so often in my eagerness that my wife saw me and was offended. She agreed to meet me some evening in the Meadow. I at present had free notions as to plurality of women, though without a fixed plan. I drank rather too much after dinner. In the evening I met an old dallying companion, now married. She willingly followed me to a field behind the Register Office. She seemed to wish to have me to press her to let me enjoy her fully, for she was big with child. But I thought it wrong, so only indulged a lesser lascivious sport; struck, however, with the insensibility to the moral doctrines of their country which some women have. I could not help indeed being somewhat flattered with the fondness which this woman showed for me, as there never was the smallest hint of anything interested.

I had agreed to set off next morning with Robert Boswell to visit the school at Witton on the Ware, a few miles from Bishop Auckland, to see if it would be proper for the young Campbells of Treesbank.[29] The fly was to go off at two in the morning, so I thought it best not to let myself sink into sleep, as I should only suffer the shock of being roused from it, without having enough of it for refreshment. I however lay down in naked bed for a while and enjoyed my dear wife excellently. I then rose and wrote letters and had some good soup and was in a frame so firm and happy that I cannot describe it.

TUESDAY 8 APRIL. My dear valuable spouse, notwithstanding my entreaties

28 The Rev. Dr Hugh Blair's house was at the centre of the north side of Argyle Square.
29 Boswell, being one of the trustees of the young sons of the deceased James Campbell of Treesbank, had undertaken to make enquiries as to a suitable school at which the boys could be educated.

that she should not stir, got up to see that I had everything right before I set out. My heart felt for her all that human nature can feel of affection and gratitude. I made Joseph run before with my *sac de nuit* or *de voyage* which I bought in Paris eleven years ago, and I got to the fly in good time.

Boswell and his cousin Robert reached Witton on 9 April, but they were not impressed with the school, finding it to be "not... sufficiently liberal for the education of gentlemen". On their way back to Edinburgh, the two travellers called on Boswell's brother John, who, although still confined at the mental asylum near Newcastle, "talked quite sensibly of many little matters".

THURSDAY 10 APRIL. My arrival at home was unexpected. Dr Webster had supped once in my absence; Miss Susie Dunlop tonight. It was truly comfortable to be again with my valuable spouse; and after a journey of more than a hundred and fifty miles without being in bed, I relished my conjugal blessings very keenly.

FRIDAY 11 APRIL. Mr Lawrie had returned on Monday, and was ready to attend me today. I was in excellent spirits, master of everything, somehow, in imagination. My wife and I and Veronica and Effie drank tea at Dr Boswell's.[30] It was very agreeable to see my little daughters fond of what was to be my garden. I had sat awhile with Sir William Forbes in the forenoon, and mentioned to him my dilemma as to a school for the Campbells. He advised me not to be in a hurry but to make full inquiry; and he recommended it to me to talk with Mr Walter Scott, Writer to the Signet, who had been at great pains to look out for a good school, and had found one near Dumfries, where he had placed his eldest son.[31] I called on Mr Scott this evening at his house in George's Square, and as he is much of a gentleman, I had a very agreeable conversation with him. His notions and mine just coincided as to the North of England schools, and I was pleased to find that the school of which he had approved after the most particular and attentive inquiry was that of Closeburn, of which Mr Alexander Mundell is Master.[32] There was a comfortable feeling when I thought that the boys would not be sent out of Scotland. Mr Scott went and introduced me to the Hon. Captain Charles Napier, captain on the impress service, as John McBurnie, an Auchinleck man, had been taken aboard, and I was much solicited to get him off. The Captain had heard of his father and mine being intimate. He showed me his warrant: that he was ordered to press all seamen and men who had worked in ships or boats, and he was informed that McBurnie, who was a notorious smuggler, had worked in boats. But if it was not so, he should be discharged.

SUNDAY 13 APRIL. I saw the 70th Regiment mustered on the Castle Hill by their Major (Hicks), who was just come from London, and then walked with Captain Irving near to the Nether Bow[33] and up again, reviving former ideas of

30 That is, at Dr Boswell's house in the Meadows.
31 This was not the future Sir Walter Scott, but his eldest brother, Robert.
32 Alexander Mundell was the brother of Boswell's old schoolmaster, James Mundell (*Extremes*, p. 409).
33 That is, the area at the eastern end of the High Street by the site where the old Nether Bow Port stood until demolished by order of the city magistrates in 1764. For the Nether Bow Port, see Introduction, p. 5.

Edinburgh while walking on a Sunday evening in animated humour. I engaged to go down with the Captain to Leith Links next morning and see the Regiment exercised. I was all briskness and gaiety. Lady Wallace and Miss Susie Dunlop supped with us.

MONDAY 14 APRIL. Rose with agility and went to the Castle between seven and eight. Thought of Captain Irving as a good Border gentleman, the nephew of my father's old friend, Mr Robert Irving.[34] Drank a little brandy and eat a bit of ammunition bread[35] with him. Then walked down and joined the Regiment near the Tron Church, and walked with him to Leith Links. Was much enlivened by seeing the evolutions, and was pleased to perceive that a man may be made anything by habit. I walked up near to Edinburgh with the Regiment, cheered by the martial music, joined my friend on the Castle Hill, and marched into the garrison with him. I was in the admirable philosophical frame which I have recorded on Wednesday the 26 of March last. I was engaged to breakfast with the Captain. He introduced me to Major Hicks and Captain Skinner. My breakfast was good cold corned beef and a couple of eggs, small beer and porter. The Major and I would not taste tea, though the two captains and Sharpe of Hoddom, who was of the party, drank it. I was in joyous health. Bless me! how sound and vigorous am I now in comparison with what I was once. It is wonderful. I thank GOD, and I hope to be as much more happy in a future state of existence. How strange would this meditation appear to men of uncultivated or cold minds. I was somewhat elevated by the exercise and fermented beverage.

My wife was displeased in the morning at my juvenile fondness for military company. She was unreasonably displeased. I begged of her not to be so on such an occasion, for it lessened the effect of her judicious and lively admonitions when I was really wrong. To unite the spirit and vivacity of a soldier with the reasoning and application of a lawyer was surely desirable. The more good in various ways which a man possesses, he is the more agreeable. She reminded me of the maxim, *Jack of all trades, master of none.* But I would be pretty much master of my own profession, as the capital object, and at the same time have ideas and accomplishments borrowed from an acquaintance with other modes of life. I know my own meaning here very well. I may perhaps have failed in my explanation of it.

TUESDAY 15 APRIL. Found myself at a loss as to the law concerning impressed men. Called on Maclaurin, who is always communicative. He said his way was first to look at statutes, then at writers on law, then at decisions. I am not sure but he put decisions after statutes. He directed me to the famous case of Captain Fergusson.[36] I found him inclining to belief in a future state, which pleased me. But he found great difficulty to imagine how we can be employed in a future

---

34 Robert Irving (1704-1772), W.S. (admitted 28 July 1751), who hailed from Dumfriesshire.
35 That is, the bread supplied to soldiers as rations.
36 This case has not been positively identified (*Extremes*, p. 112, n. 4).

state. He said Plato is stopped short by this difficulty. He had been reading him lately. I could not solve it. But I think *now* that, *a priori*, it would be difficult to make us perceive how *this life* can be spent even tolerably; and yet in general we get through it very well. I walked with him in the Meadow, and was very lively. After dinner Gilkie came to me on a consultation, about a trial for murder, or rather, as I advised, a culpable assault on which death ensued, for which I was to be counsel for the prosecutor at the next circuit at Jedburgh.[37] I drank rather too heartily of port. But I was eloquent in dictating my opinion. Consulted at Ilay Campbell's on Tait against Lawson.

WEDNESDAY 16 APRIL. Walked to Leith to talk to Captain Napier about John McBurnie, and found that the oaths of two men that he never worked on salt water would set him free. Mr Simon Fraser, the advocate,[38] whom I met on Leith Walk, was so good as turn and accompany me down and up again. He said I would make an excellent Highland chief, which flattered me, and he convinced me he was a believer in a future state, which pleased me. His brisk opinion that, upon the whole, a man could not be happier than as a soldier, taking all the good and evil of the profession, I could not refute. Yet there is a fallacious notion as to *security* in other professions, as if *life* were not quite *uncertain*. I sat awhile with Crosbie. He said he had little or no faith *himself* in testimony, though courts of law must be guided by it. In short he was a sceptic. He said Maclaurin was a good subject to make a fanatic. No *reasoning* can change notions. They can only be cured by impressions from experience, or irradiations from above.

THURSDAY 17 APRIL. It was a snowy day. I dictated easily, having papers to prepare to be put into the Lords' boxes on the 26 current.

SATURDAY 19 APRIL. The weather was a little better. Signora Marcoucci, the Italian dancing-mistress, who lives on the same flat with me, was asked to dine at Prestonfield. I was asked also. The coach was sent in for us to come together. This was quite a regale to me. We went and returned tête-à-tête and I was enlivened to Italian pitch, though La Signora seemed so strict a religionist that I saw no prospect of gallantry.[39] We had a dance at Prestonfield. Lady Dick said they were much obliged to me. I was the life of every company. I was somewhat hurt to find that I was still too combustible by women.

SUNDAY 20 APRIL. (Writing from notes on Sunday 4 May.) On the forenoon of this day, or a former forenoon, I had a most pleasing conversation with my dear Veronica, sitting with her on the floor of my dining-room while the sun shone bright. I talked to her of the beauties and charms of Heaven, of gilded houses, trees with richest fruits, finest flowers, and most delightful music. I filled her imagination with gay ideas of futurity instead of gloomy ones, and she

37 This was the case of *Rule v Smith and Others* which was to come before the Circuit Court at Jedburgh on 16 and 17 May.
38 Simon Fraser (1734-1810), advocate (admitted 28 July 1767), Sheriff-Depute of Invernessshire 1781-1811.
39 For Boswell's exploits in Italy, see Introduction, pp. 32-3.

seemed to lift her eyes upwards with complacency. Yet when I put it to her if she would not like to die and go to Heaven, the *natural* instinctive aversion to death, or perhaps the *acquired*, by hearing it mentioned dismally, made her say, "I hope I'll be spared to you." I for the first time mentioned *Christ* to her; told her that he came down to this world for our good; that ill men put him to death; that then he flew up with silver wings and opened the great iron gates of Heaven, which had long been shut, and now we could get in. He would take us in. She was delighted with the idea, and cried, "O I'll kiss him." One cannot give rational or doctrinal notions of Christianity to a child. But it is a great blessing to a child to have its affections early engaged by divine thoughts. "Suppose," said I, "Veronica, when you come to Heaven, you do not find me there. What would you do?" Said she: "I would cry, 'Angels! where's my papa?'" She said this with such an enchanting earnest vivacity, as if she had really been addressing herself to the *celestial ministers*, that I was quite happy. "But", said I, "suppose they should let you see me walking upon wild mountains and shut out because I had not been good enough?" Said she: "I would speak to GOD to let you come in." I kissed her with the finest fondness. The brilliant light shone into my very soul. I was all hope and joy. I trusted that I should yet have supreme felicity with Veronica in a better world. I looked at her sweet little mild countenance with steadfast speculation. And may not her prayers to GOD avail much for me yet? Much good is gained to us in this state of being by others; and why not in the next?

MONDAY 21 APRIL. Being to set out next day with Annie Cuninghame for Lainshaw, where she was ordered to go for country air and exercise, as she had been ill for two months with a pain in her breast and a spitting of blood, I had all my law-papers done.

TUESDAY 22 APRIL. It was so bad a day with rain and snow that it would have been improper to take out Miss Cuninghame. We waited in uncertainty till one. Having a day longer in Edinburgh at this time, I thought I might certainly have all the letters written which I wished, and everything in calm order. But I was disappointed. And thus it is that death comes upon us before we have all our affairs arranged. The truth is that each additional day brings along with it something additional to be done; else there would be the abhorred *vacuum*. Yet a man should certainly have essential matters all in order. I pleased myself that before the Session in June, I might shut myself up for some days and arrange all my papers in complete accuracy. I kept the house all this day. Lady Wallace and Miss Dunlop supped.

WEDNESDAY 23 APRIL. I parted more easily than last journey west, with my wife and children. Annie Cuninghame and I set out about eleven.

After leaving Annie Cuninghame at Lainshaw (where the house was "the image of desolation" and where Boswell was "too fond" of Annie "but observed decorum"), Boswell proceeded to Auchinleck, where he found his father "more failed" than when he had last left him; and this time Boswell was not on such good terms with Lady Auchinleck, objecting to her "peevish temper" and "narrow-mindedness" and finding her "studying to estrange" him from his father. Later, Annie Cuninghame came to join them, and Boswell records that he was "too amorous" with her, which, he says, "was a sickly state of feverishness".

Lord Auchinleck set off on 9 May to preside over the circuit at Glasgow and Boswell followed him there; but Boswell disgraced himself at Glasgow by getting inebriated after the court, thus making his father "justly angry". Boswell then took the Campbell boys to Lanark Grammar School, it having been decided that this was where they should be educated, and from there he proceeded to Edinburgh. The following day he had to set off for the circuit at Jedburgh where he was due to appear as counsel for the prosecution in the case of Rule v Smith and Others, *in which he was instructed by the mischievous, unpredictable and somewhat disreputable James Gilkie. It was only very rarely that Boswell appeared as counsel for the prosecution. Whether this was to any extent a matter of choice or not is not clear, but there is no doubt that by nature Boswell was much more inclined to favour appearing for the defence. In the present case, however, as has been observed,*[40] *"the side of generous feeling... happened to be the prosecution". In any event, this was not a Crown prosecution, but was an example of the much rarer private form of prosecution. Archibald Rule, a tenant of a farm at Graystonelees, Berwickshire, had tried for years to persuade the officers of the Crown to bring this prosecution, but to no avail, and so he had been compelled to raise proceedings himself (the necessary concurrence of the Lord Advocate having been given). The charge was to the effect that the three panels (that is, the three accused), who were George Smith, a merchant in Greenlaw, Robert Hamilton, a sheriff officer in Duns, and Alexander Christie, a "writer" in Duns, had murdered Archibald Rule's son, Alexander, or had beaten him in an unmerciful manner so that death followed shortly afterwards. The alleged offence had occurred while the panels were executing a sequestration of Archibald Rule's effects at the farm of which he was tenant. Henry Dundas, who had considered the case when he was Solicitor-General, had taken the view (with which the then Lord Advocate, James Montgomery, had concurred) that the affair was "merely a scuffle without any premeditation or malice, and in which Rule himself seems to have been the unprovoked aggressor"*[41] *and that there was therefore no ground for any proceedings against any of the persons involved in the scuffle. The judge at the circuit at Jedburgh was Lord Gardenstone, and counsel for the defence were Patrick Murray and John Pringle.*[42] *The defence argued that Archibald Rule had by certain actions disclaimed the prosecution; but Rule stood behind Boswell in court "authorizing the prosecution with tears in his eyes".*[43] *Lord Gardenstone ordered that the trial should proceed, but instead of hearing the trial himself, he reported the case to the Court of Justiciary at Edinburgh to be heard by a full bench of that court.*

---

40 *Extremes*, p. 122.

41 Quoted in Roughead, "The Wandering Jurist; or Boswell's Queer Client", in *In Queer Street*, p. 104 ff (where a full account of this case may be found), at p. 158.

42 John Pringle (1741-1811), advocate (admitted 25 January 1763), was appointed Professor of Civil History at Edinburgh University 1765, Sheriff-Depute of Stirlingshire 1780, Sheriff-Depute of Edinburghshire 1790 and one of the Principal Clerks of Session 1794. Died unmarried.

43 From the Information prepared by Boswell for the Court of Justiciary on 16 December 1777 (reproduced in *Extremes*, p. 361 ff, at p. 365).

MONDAY 26 MAY. In General Assembly for Gillies, to oblige Lord Gardenstone.[44] Found *that vulgar and rascally* court too much for me. Spoke [a] few words. Pres[iden]t signified aversion.[45] Was weak enough to be hurt. Grange comforted me, evening. Supped Sir George's. Drank too much rum punch as medicine for cold.

WEDNESDAY 28 MAY. Family hurried with flitting.[46] Erse-grammar Shaw[46a] and Grange dined. Dull. Took Grange and young Donaldson to tea at my country-house. Supped Surgeon Wood's. Too much claret. No ambition or anything rousing.

SATURDAY 31 MAY. In General Assembly. Dined with Commissioner. Evening a little with Bailie Walker, etc. In liquor and walked out [to Meadow house] slow, though in rain, like perverse madman.

MONDAY 2 JUNE. Dined Sir Alexander Dick's; drank too much. Curious proposal of marriage in morning. Good opportunity. Sent for Miss ——.[47] Much freedom. Home terribly wild with rage and swore, etc. πλεασυρε.[48]

TUESDAY 3 JUNE. Awaked pretty well. Prayed for forgiveness for rash and profane utterance. Wife mild.

FRIDAY 6 JUNE. Listless at villa. Dined Sir George's, Dr Webster there. Appointment with Miss M. Intoxicated a little. Tea Sir George's. Walked two hours, but she came not. Home quiet enough. Letter from father consoled, yet abashed by his permanency.

THURSDAY 12 JUNE. Up six. Father's, morning a little.[49] Session sat down. Was quite indisposed for business. Dined Meadow house... In after dinner, two fees.

FRIDAY 13 JUNE. Up six. Father's, morning a little. Did not like Session. Yesterday or today felt as if I'd give up business altogether from low spirits. Wife and I dined father's. Cold. Children there after dinner and at tea, tolerable. Town, evening; two consultations. Wrote a short Representation. Drank gin punch.

---

44 "James Gillies, who had less formal education than the Assembly required, had been licensed by a class of dissenting ministers at Newcastle, and his licence was sustained by the Presbytery of Brechin. The Synod (Angus and Mearns) condemned the conduct of the Presbytery. The Assembly, on appeal, reversed the action of the Synod because of irregularities of procedure" (*Extremes*, p. 128, n. 4).

45 Probably Lord President Dundas (*Extremes*, p. 128, n. 5).

46 The family were moving to their new house—referred to later in this entry as "my country-house"—on the south side of the Meadows. From this house Boswell wrote to Samuel Johnson on 9 June 1777 as follows: "We have a garden of three quarters of an acre, well stocked with fruit-trees and flowers and gooseberries and currants and peas and beans and cabbages, etc., etc., and my children are quite happy. I now write to you in a little study, from the window of which I see around me a verdant grove, and beyond it the lofty mountain called Arthur's Seat" (quoted in *Extremes*, p.128, n.7). "Boswell slept at the Meadows house, but the house in James's Court was kept open, and during the session he generally went there to dictate to Mr Lawrie and to dine" (*ibid., loc. cit.*). The address given for Boswell's new house in directories for the period is "back of the Meadows".

46a William Shaw (1749-1831), a well-known Gaelic scholar (hence the soubriquet "Erse-grammar Shaw"), whose first work, *An Analysis of the Gaelic Language*, was published in 1778.

47 Betty Montgomerie. See the entries for 6 and 21 June.

48 "Pleasure" (Greek); that is, conjugal relations.

49 Lord Auchinleck's new house, like Boswell's, being in the Meadows, Boswell and his father were living in close proximity to each other.

SATURDAY 21 JUNE. At ten, called Rubra, and dalliance.[50] Breakfasted Lady Eglinton. Then had Betty Montgomerie to talk of her marriage; dallied with her too, and attempted but she would not. Walked with Grange in Meadow. Lord Eglinton joined us. Walked long with Earl. Got off from dining at Fortune's with him. Dined James's Court with wife and Grange. Earl and Countess, Sir Allan Maclean, Captain Hoggan, James Gordon, Nairne, Annie, and Sir Walter and Grange supped. Noisy. I was not drunk.

MONDAY 23 JUNE. In Justiciary Court about Rule's prosecution.[51] Supped Lord Kames's. Wonderful man, past eighty.

WEDNESDAY 25 JUNE. Had heard from Lord Stonefield that Lord Mountstuart was coming. Was to dine on cold meat at home with Mr Lawrie. Walked out between two and three. Found my Lord at Cross, *nonchalant ut mos est*.[52] Walked with him, Matthew Henderson, etc. Dined Fortune's; tea, whist, supper. Intoxicated. Angry at Joseph for following. Twice up Arthur Seat from perverseness. Shocking folly and badness of humour.

THURSDAY 26 JUNE. Ashamed of myself. Took no notice to Joseph. But wife commended him and gave half-crown. Called Lord Mountstuart at Robert Chalmers's;[53] drank cinnamon water. Spoke to him of getting me something. He said Sir Archibald Grant's place was promised, and seemed indifferent, and said my father would die and then I would have no occasion—it would be a shame.[54] I was displeased at his indifference. Dictated tolerably, but was very sleepy. Dined ——; tea with worthy Grange. Consultation at eight at Lord Advocate's on Sir Allan. Much difficulty to attend. Very comfortable bed at night and slept sound, which perhaps I should not have otherwise done on night before Dr Dodd's execution.[55]

---

50 "'Rubra' (probably a girl in a red dress or cloak) is again mentioned under that name on 2 December 1777. Possibly the same as 'Dolly', below, 11 July 1777" (*Extremes*, p. 130, n. 6).

51 "Counsel for the defence and the prosecution repeated the arguments as to the relevancy advanced at Jedburgh, but the counsel for the defence now also complained strongly of Gilkie's unwarrantable conduct in publishing memorials and other writings tending to give an unfavourable opinion of the accused. George Fergusson was this time listed as senior counsel for the prosecutor, but Boswell appears to have done all the speaking, as before. The judges were unanimously of opinion that as Rule's disclaimer was made after the Criminal Letters were raised, the trial could not proceed; but that if Rule chose to execute a new indictment, he could bring the accused to trial. They then declared Gilkie's conduct highly culpable and very dishonourable to the Court, and sentenced him to a month's imprisonment and until he should find £50 bail for his good behaviour for two years. He was allowed the choice of the Canongate gaol, as being considerably more comfortable than the Tolbooth, and his period of confinement was somewhat shortened because of illness. When he got out, he made direct appeal to the King in Archibald Rule's name requesting that the Lord Advocate be ordered to prosecute, and of course was informed that the usual forms and practices of the law officers of the Crown would be followed. He then obtained new Criminal Letters dated 15 September 1777" (*Extremes*, p. 130, n. 7).

52 "'Nonchalant, as is his wont' (Horace, *Satires*, I. ix. 1, adapted)" (*Extremes*, p. 131, n. 8).

53 Robert Chalmers's house was in Adam Square.

54 Sir Archibald Grant of Monymusk (1696-1778), advocate (admitted 16 November 1714), who had been M.P. for Aberdeenshire from 1722 to 1732, was Principal Clerk to the Register of Hornings (a post he had held since 1749). He was married four times. "Letters of horning enjoined payment or performance on a debtor within a certain number of days under pain of being held in rebellion and outlawry ('being put to the horn')" (*Extremes*, p. 131, n. 9).

55 William Dodd, a popular English preacher and chaplain in ordinary to the King, had been found guilty of forgery and had been sentenced to be hanged. His execution was appointed to take place on 27 June.

FRIDAY 27 JUNE. Did not call Lord Mountstuart, but met him on street, indifferent enough. Sandy Cuninghame had come. Looked watch, thinking always of Dr Dodd. It seemed nothing when over, in comparison of "horrible imagining".[56] Yet I hoped perhaps rescue. Met John Home on street, keen against Dodd, the keenness of a worldly mind against a pious.[57] Wife and I dined father's by invitation. Quite alone; well enough. Tea Sir George's. Consultation Lord Advocate's about Sir Walter. Home calm.

SATURDAY 28 JUNE. Grange had very wisely advised me to take Lord Mountstuart in his own way. Called forenoon and found him at *baps* and butter and tea and strawberries. Invited by Culdares to supper.[58] Cards at my house with Lords Covington and Braxfield and Maclaurin before dinner; Maclaurin went away. Grange, Erskine, David Erskine, John Syme, Lord and Lady Macdonald,[59] George Wallace, Annie, Sir Walter, and Sandy dined. Very well. Impromptu with *sposa*[60] clothed. Whist till I went to Culdares's. Great company there. Cordial with my Lord, but not *manly*. Hard drinking. Home sadly intoxicated, even insane. Vexed most valuable spouse. Was almost unconscious.

SUNDAY 29 JUNE. Awaked miserably vexed and very ill. Saw myself a depraved creature. Lay till four. Wife had kindly made soup and chicken for me. Then beer; then pottage; then coffee. Could neither think nor read. Wet afternoon. Hoped to be better. Hurt that I was not more with father, yet so indolent I was glad of rain for excuse to stay at home.

TUESDAY 1 JULY. The news came of Dr Dodd's execution. Read it calm in Advocates' Library; was shocked and angry against King.[61] Thought I'd take no office from him. Lord Mountstuart sent he could not sup; was vexed a little.

WEDNESDAY 2 JULY. Ill from drinking. Very low and desponding. Sir Allan's cause won in part. *Some* pleasure from this.

FRIDAY 4 JULY. Very wet. Asked Lord Advocate to sup, he me to dine. Took this opening. Drank too much. Lord Mountstuart, etc., supped with us. Drunk. Slept town. Felt Miss Montgomerie.

WEDNESDAY 9 JULY. Night wandered and had handkerchief stolen.

FRIDAY 11 JULY. Marriage of Betty Montgomerie.[62] Supped Moncrieffe's. Was croupier, and drank too much. Wandered. James's Court. Dolly.

SATURDAY 12 JULY. Awaked very ill. Wife had sat up late for me. She the

---

56 *Macbeth*, I. iii. 138.
57 John Home, former minister of Athelstaneford and author of the tragedy of *Douglas* (as to which, see Introduction, p. 10).
58 Archibald Menzies of Culdares, one of the Commissioners of Customs (*Extremes*, p. 132, n. 3).
59 Sir Alexander Macdonald of Sleat, Bt, had become Lord Macdonald in 1776 by virtue of an Irish peerage conferred on him. Boswell, in his *Journal of a Tour to the Hebrides*, was highly critical of Macdonald's lack of hospitality—unbecoming a great Highland Chief—when Boswell and Johnson visited him at Armadale on the Isle of Skye in 1773.
60 Spouse (Italian).
61 The King had refused a pardon.
62 She married Robert Ramsay, a "writer".

worse of it. Lay forenoon. Dined with her at S. Mitchelson's.[63] Charles Hay there. Disgusting meanness. Vexed to recollect intimacy with such. Temporary blindness of discernment occasions sad regrets. Was prudent, *retenu*, and sober. Seward,[64] Lord Monboddo, Dr Gregory, and Nairne supped with me. No drinking. Wife and I slept town. Had been alarmed with her bad health.

SUNDAY 13 JULY. Was made very serious by my wife's bad health. Felt a kind of *amazement* when I viewed the possibility of losing her. At New Church with her; Mr Walker, forenoon. Then to children. Dined Monboddo's with Seward and Nairne. Walked Calton Hill. Seward supped at Meadow with us. Insipid and tiresome, *I* thought him.

TUESDAY 15 JULY. Wandered evening and embarked. Wife waiting at entry. Sad vexation.

WEDNESDAY 16 JULY. Sunk and ill. Wife and I tea father's. Called Nabob. Comely maid. Even *now* dallied. Had Grange to walk with me, evening. Wife justly not reconciled.

MONDAY 21 JULY. Intoxicated. Dalliance with Betty.

WEDNESDAY 23 JULY. Wife much better; indulged me.

THURSDAY 24 JULY. Wife ill with spitting of blood; I sadly alarmed and gone. Dined Jack's[65] and paid bet; intoxicated. Assembly. Wandered, but guarded. Hurt backbone by fall.

FRIDAY 25 JULY. Backbone much pained.

TUESDAY 29 JULY. Wife miscarriage. Very low and ill.

WEDNESDAY 30 JULY. Up at seven and had Mr Lawrie and dictated in Meadow house. Wet morning. Grange dined; only small beer. Wife dined home. I tea with him. Very gloomy. Went out early, having great desire to be with wife and children. Pleased with Veronica.

THURSDAY 31 JULY. Wet, wet. Awaked thinking, "Oh, must I rise and endure another day?" Very ill in Parliament House.

SATURDAY 2 AUGUST. Somewhat better. Went with Lord Covington in his chaise to Craighouse. Proposed to him to mark his life. He said, "We move in a narrow sphere." Walked with him, and he said he had always hated law business, and did yet. Seemed to be an excellent machine, not conscious of his own operations. Braxfield, Maclaurin, etc., dined. Whist, riotous a little. I lost, and played very ill, which puts one in inferior light. Cannot describe it. But life seemed lighter by being agitated, as a porter shakes his burthen. Walked in with Maclaurin.

WEDNESDAY 6 AUGUST. Continued well. Out of house early. Called Lord Kames.

---

63 Samuel Mitchelson, Junior, had now moved from Riddle's Land to a house in Nicolson Street.
64 William Seward (1747-99), "well known to a numerous and valuable acquaintance for his literature, love of the fine arts, and social virtues" (*Life*, Vol. II, p. 682, note). But *cf.* entry for 13 July below.
65 Andrew Jack's tavern in Writers' Court.

Was admitted to his bedside. He was like a vision but quite alive. Said he never had an hour in his life heavy on his hand. Then called Crosbie. Asked him, though gout pained him, how whole man was? "Oh," said he, "fine animal." He was reading Cook's *Voyage*.[66] I spoke of how little our sphere was. A soldier says, "*We* beat the French." Even an Under-Secretary of State is *pars* of something great. "Yes," said he, "*we* have declared war." "But", said I, "[if some one asked you or me, 'As] a lawyer, what have you done?' [what could we say but,] 'Written such a number of long papers'?" CROSBIE. ["But then if he asked,] 'And what have you done with 'em?' [we could say,] 'Wiped my backside.'" I wondered how a man was ever dull or melancholy, so well did all things appear. Grange dined with me. Tasted tarts after. Wife in country. Tea with him. Dictated.

SATURDAY 9 AUGUST. Up early and finished Rep[resentation for] Dr A. Johnson. Very wet morning. In with father in coach. Was so well that the crowd and heat did not disturb. Strange how different we are at different times. Rising of Session rather pleased me today, to have feeling of ease. Solicitor and I went to John's Coffee-house a little. Had not been in coffee-house for long time. Dined father's with wife. Veronica came to tea, as did Solicitor. Went with him in his carriage to Murrayfield.[67] He owned objects at Scotch bar limited, "But what can man do better after he is once there?" Nairne walked out. Was struck with his serene notion. He did not read. No knowledge as well as crime.[68]

Boswell now started to put into practice a scheme which he had considered for some time, namely, to write an anonymous series of essays entitled The Hypochondriack, *one of which would be published each month in the* London Magazine. *It has been explained that "the purpose of the essays was to defeat inertia and depression by a definite task, and in the course of the task to consider the unreasonable fluctuation between good cheer and the dumps, to sort out symptoms and causes, and to collect a variety of crisp ideas and interests which might shake the black dog from any hypochondriac shoulder".[69] The first of these essays ("No. 1"), on the subject of periodical papers, which seems to have been completed in draft form on 11 August, was to be published in October.*

WEDNESDAY 13 AUGUST. Went and saw father set off. He said not a word of seeing me. Felt a sort of lightness that father was gone. Evening, wife and I went with Ve and Effie to Grange Garden.

THURSDAY 14 AUGUST. Still idle but enjoyed it. Saw Lord Kames take carriage, feeble. Grange and Matthew Dickie, dinner and tea. A few glasses of port sickened me.

---

66 Cook's *Voyage towards the South Pole and round the World*.

67 Murray was owner of Murrayfield House, lying to the west of the city. The main part of the house was built by his father in the 1730s and was extended by Murray after he inherited it in 1773. The house still stands.

68 The editors of *Extremes* surmise (at p. 137, n. 8) that this means, "I am content to be a man of no knowledge as well as a man of no crime."

69 Bailey, *Boswell's Column*, pp. xii-xiii.

FRIDAY 22 AUGUST. Visited Lord Kames. Dined Lord Dundonald's. Drank little, but had great desire for it. Strolled in streets to find companion. Luckily escaped. Called Crosbie. Home with wife. Had tea and read *Rasselas* from first to last.[70] Was delighted.

SATURDAY 23 AUGUST. Dined Dr Webster's with George Preston. Was intoxicated. Wandered about three hours but nothing happened. Home at eleven. Valuable spouse had soup for me.

WEDNESDAY 3 SEPTEMBER. Had George Preston's horse and Sandy[71] to ride on it before me for a while. Then breakfast. Prestonfield. Worthy Sir Alexander said to me he would not live long. But this gave him no uneasiness. Immortality. Read over the sketch of his life to him so far as done. It pleased him. Then to Lord Hailes. Found him at *Annals*. Was cordial enough in appearance, but when *two struck*, no invitation to dinner. Dined by engagement with Commissioner Cochrane. Drank too much. Wandered a little. Lapsed. George Preston supped. Punch. Letter from Dr Johnson to meet him, Ashbourne.

WEDNESDAY 10 SEPTEMBER. Got up sound and well and happy in the prospect of my interview with Dr Johnson. But human happiness is seldom pure. Mine was now allayed somewhat by my dear wife's thinking that there was not a sufficient reason for my leaving her and the children and putting myself to as much expense as a journey to London would cost me. Though sensible and lively, she has not so much philosophy (or rather enthusiasm and superstition) as I could wish. She could not feel the warm notions that I was now setting out to meet an exalted instructor whom I loved as well as revered. That I was like one going upon a pilgrimage to some sacred place, and that I should have my soul elevated towards a better world and my understanding improved for this world. She was, however, most obliging in having everything in good order for my setting out, and did not vex me by repining. I was sincerely grateful to her, and the consciousness that I was right calmed my disquietude. I considered that the expense, though something at present, would appear of no moment if I should live to have our family estate. After breakfast I called on my cousin, Captain Robert Preston of the *Hillsborough* East Indiaman, who was returned after three years' absence. It was comfortable to find him the same as when we parted. He had a violent toothache, and Rae came while I was with him and pulled one of his teeth. I was struck with an uneasy sensation of the weakness of man, to see a bold captain of a large ship, who had been often in Asia, shrinking under a surgeon's instrument. But if the most renowned of our species were watched, they would seem little at times. What hurts me is that the *present* state of a man impresses us so that it is not easy to retain his general character. Had I seen Clarendon[72] with the toothache, I could not have reverenced him at the time.

Boswell travelled to Ashbourne via Carlisle, Shap, Kendal, Lancaster and Manchester.

70 By Samuel Johnson, 1759.
71 Boswell's son, Alexander, now almost two years old.
72 Edward Hyde, first Earl of Clarendon (1609-1674).

Between Carlisle and Shap, Boswell rode on horseback and on arrival at Shap discovered that he had lost an "almanac" containing "a number of memorandums and private writings", which, if found, he feared might lead to his being "exposed". After a restless night, he rode back towards Carlisle; but, to his immense relief, he came across a boy who had found the book and he promptly rewarded him with payment of half a crown. At Lancaster, Boswell took a fancy to the pretty maid. In the morning, as she was taking the sheets off the bed, "she looked so inviting, and my desire was so strong, that after being allowed liberties enough I attempted to lie with her, but to this she would not consent." At Leek, near Macclesfield, two more maids were to receive his attentions, but he did not get beyond fondling them.

Boswell arrived at Ashbourne on 14 September and was cordially welcomed by Dr Johnson and their host, the Rev. Dr John Taylor. Apart from a jaunt to Derby for a day, Boswell was to stay at Ashbourne until 24 September. Throughout this period, he relished the company of Dr Johnson, and for much of the time was serene and happy. One of the many topics of conversation which arose was Boswell's scheme of becoming an English barrister. "[Dr Johnson] said that if my father lived ten years longer, it would not be worth while for me to try the English bar; but I might try it if I should be master of the family estate in a few years. He said that although I should fail, I could not reproach myself with folly for having given up a small certainty for a chance of something great. He however was of opinion that I have such a mind that I must have my father's employment, or one as busy, to preserve me from melancholy. I must therefore be pretty sure of occupation in London before I venture to settle there."

None of Dr Taylor's maids was handsome, and so, wrote Boswell, "I had no incitements to amorous desires, and all the time that I was at Ashbourne I had not the least wish for women. I thought that Dr Johnson's company would afford me so much of a higher kind of pleasure—intellectual delight—that I could live quite well without the pleasure of enjoying women."

On 23 September, the Duke and Duchess of Argyll, while on their way to London, stopped at Ashbourne to change horses. As at Inveraray, the Duchess, while "courteous" to Dr Johnson, took "hardly any notice" of Boswell. Later that day, Boswell consulted Johnson on the case of Joseph Knight, the African who had asserted his freedom from slavery, for whom Boswell was now acting as one of his counsel (the other counsel being John Maclaurin, Allan Maconochie and Henry Dundas).[73] Johnson dictated to Boswell a pleading in support of Knight's case.

Boswell travelled back to Edinburgh by post-chaise and fly via Doncaster and Newcastle. At Newcastle, Boswell visited his brother John, whom he found to be "in a much worse state" than when he had seen him in April, "being now quite insane and raving incoherently". "I prayed for him", wrote Boswell, "and came away in sadness."

On his arrival at Edinburgh on 27 September, Boswell found his wife and children well, and was comfortable to be once again at his house at "the back of the Meadow".

WEDNESDAY 1 OCTOBER. In town revising *Hypochondriack* No. 1 and bringing up journal. And gave opinion easily. Doctor and his sons Robert and Bruce, Mr and Mrs Lindsay and two misses, dinner and tea.

---

73 See the entry for 16 February 1776 and footnote.

FRIDAY 3 OCTOBER. Sposa read my journal and was justly displeased with my fondling of maids at inns. Children convoyed me towards Sir Alexander Dick's. Was a little with him, fine as usual. Then home; to town with wife in good humour. Milliner's and fish-market with her. Home, dinner. Sandy Webster tea.

MONDAY 6 OCTOBER. Called Dr Boswell a little, two Septuagints[74] and English Bible before him. Christ left morals of law of Moses. Thought, then, plurality of women. Grange at dinner. Walked in with him. Wife bed except a little. *Gil Blas*.[75] Read Johnson's life of Pearce in Donaldson's shop.

MONDAY 13 OCTOBER. Exceedingly ill; as dreary and horrible as ever. Called Grange; groaned and could hardly speak. Wretched, wretched. Afternoon, coffee and fell to *Hypochondriack* on fear.[76] Did better than expectation, but quite sunk. Bad cold appeared.

TUESDAY 14 OCTOBER. Sunk with the cold. Vexed and fretful. Lay long. Dr Boswell and Bruce called. Did not ask them to dinner. Was quite inhospitable. Did more of *Hypochondriack* on fear. Grange dined. Home all day. At night, dictated Answers for Fullarton's commissioners, the only paper I had to write. It did me good.

WEDNESDAY 15 OCTOBER. Veronica went to town with me and saw her curiosities. Sandy came. Was harsh to him. Had check of conscience. Thought I deserved to be miserable if I made another so. Invited by Dr Grant to dine. Called on him with Ve. Grange dined with us. Was ill. Invited Mr Lindsay's.[77] Cruel kindness, as cold bad. But went. Displeased with Mrs Lindsay. Said, "Was saying your company just a comedy or a farce." Was well enough. Resolved not [to] set out [for] Auchinleck till Friday.

THURSDAY 16 OCTOBER. In town house, removing presses to low room, etc. Had cold still. Miss Preston, tea. Sandy too much afraid of me. Dubious a little as to going, as wife not well. Bad weather. Meadow house dreary.

The following day, Boswell set off for Auchinleck, where he had a "tolerable reception" and found his father "better than for two years". Boswell spent some time pruning trees with his father and going for country walks with him. Lady Auchinleck, however, was disagreeable; and Lord Auchinleck's "coldness" was "shocking". Boswell was particularly appalled when his father asked: "And how ca' they your youngest son?", forgetting not only the name of young David, but also that he had died.

On hearing news that his wife had a cough and was anxious to see him, Boswell departed for Edinburgh on 28 October and he got home the following day. The family had now returned to James's Court, presumably on account of Mrs Boswell's condition.

WEDNESDAY 29 OCTOBER. Wife in bed, like vision. Had been very ill

---

74 Septuagint: the Greek version of the Old Testament.
75 By Alain René Le Sage.
76 No. 2 in the series.
77 The Lindsays were neighbours of Boswell at "the back of the Meadow".

indeed. Children quite fond of me. Worthy Grange with me a little. Resolved after thirty-seven, *retenu*, etc.[77a] Thoughts of second marriage should be checked and concealed.

THURSDAY 30 OCTOBER. Wife better. Just attended on her and wrote letters. Grange with me a little.

FRIDAY 31 OCTOBER. Wife still rather better. Grange bid farewell in boots, going to Annandale. Was hypochondriacked, but only to insipidity. Walked out to Sir A. Dick's. *Amenity* refreshed me. But was still too *rattling*. One glass strong beer and a few currant [wine] intoxicated a little. Restless and frettish, evening. Studied a little Smith against Brown.[78] Fallacy of metaphor: polite man cannot be known, because varnished. Wish to see plain wood. Yet coarse outside conceals pebble. We must polish to see flaws, etc.

MONDAY 3 NOVEMBER. Mr Lawrie had come. Called Mr A. Boswall. Was too *rattling* as to wishing to go to East Indies, etc. Was in Advocates' Library. Miss Lindsay dined. Ve angry *she* had not head of table. Was gloomy and listless. Began to read *Gil Blas* to wife in English. Was insensibly entertained. Received first number of *Hypochondriack*. Wife very ill, night-time. I wretched; thought seat of reason would break.

TUESDAY 4 NOVEMBER. *Gil Blas*. Wife better. I got bed separate in room with her. Counted bottles in cellar.

WEDNESDAY 5 NOVEMBER. Walked to Castle Hill with Surgeon Wood and heard Castle fire.[79] Was quite in easy frame. Poor little Sandy said, "Papa no like me." I had frightened him too much by hiding myself, etc. Resolved against this.

FRIDAY 7 NOVEMBER. Walked out and breakfasted Lady Colville. Was too lively. Saw not respected. Home. Robert and Bruce Boswell called. Called Donaldson's shop. News of Burgoyne's battle with Arnold; agitated.[80] *Gil Blas*, evening. Wife bad fit after emetic. Slept with her.

WEDNESDAY 12 NOVEMBER. Father had come last night. Walked out. Commissioner came. Called Hon. Alexander Gordon. Asked to dine, Robert Boswell, with Nabob. Captain Sands there. Drank too much port and too rattling. With girl in street moment, but soon flew off. Nought done. Intoxicated. Soup.

SATURDAY 22 NOVEMBER. Maclaurin censured my accepting of business from Gilkie. As he said parody was making a seeming resemblance between a low thing and a high, where there was no proportion, he said Gilkie was a parody

---

77a This day was Boswell's thirty-seventh birthday.
78 Concerning a boundary dispute between two proprietors of adjacent estates in Ayrshire (*Extremes*, p. 192, n. 9).
79 "This day, being the anniversary of the Popish Conspiracy ['Gunpowder Plot', 1605], the same was observed as a holiday at the banks and other public offices. In the morning the flag was displayed from the Castle; at noon, a round of the great guns was fired; and, at the same time, the music bells were set a-ringing" (*The Caledonian Mercury*, 5 November 1777, quoted in *Extremes*, p. 192, n. 1). For the music bells, see Introduction, p. 12.
80 "False reports had reached Edinburgh that Burgoyne had defeated the American forces under Benedict Arnold. Actually, on 17 October, Burgoyne had surrendered to Gates at Saratoga" (*Extremes*, p.193, n.3).

of Boswell. Tea father's. Labouring hard Brown against Smith. Finished Replies. Wife moderate. Sir William Forbes kindly came and insisted, his house.[81]

MONDAY 24 NOVEMBER. Justiciary Court, relevancy of Indictment, Rule against Hamilton, etc. Was not warm as I have been, but well enough.[82]

TUESDAY 25 NOVEMBER. Wife had been worse in the night. Was sadly alarmed. Called Mr Wood at nine; dish of tea with him. He comforted me that it was good honest common cold. Was not as yet much employed. Yet did slowly what I had to do. [B]egan *Hypochondriack* No. 3.[83] Wife grew better today.

MONDAY 1 DECEMBER. Up dictating speech. At Justiciary Court. Heart sore for poor Bell, whose face I had so often seen in Stewarton kirk. Hurt that I was against him, though his offence very criminal if true.[84] Spoke tolerably. Was too tender-hearted. Called father. Balbarton dined with us. Was a little after four in Parliament House to take chair as Depute Grand Master. Bad spirits. Procession. Pretty well in Assembly Hall.[85] Home before nine.

TUESDAY 2 DECEMBER. Father in court. Bad spirits. Harassed with business delayed. No pleasure in life. Justiciary Court. Hurt again with seeing poor Bell. Court's prejudice against him bad. Did not speak to him.[86] Laboured diligently night. Negus, dinner. Had appointment at four, *Rubra*. But could not go.

THURSDAY 4 DECEMBER. Flat and unprofitable. Had quiet walk in Outer House among shops with Grange, who said he and I, when in good frame (notwithstanding our doubts at times), had more satisfaction in thinking of future state than such as Lady Auchinleck, who were *crusty* about it if any doubt was hinted. Volupt.[87]

SUNDAY 7 DECEMBER. Walked to New Town with Monboddo, who, on hearing Washington was fop, said, "So was Julius Caesar", and repeated Suetonius on this. I said Duke Hamilton's, etc., drinking port not strength but *trick*, like fire-eater. Roused by Monboddo's strength of mind. Lord Macdonald a little;

81 "Sir William probably pressed them to come to the Forbes's house in the New Town, where [Mrs Boswell] could have all the conveniences, and the air would be better. The generous offer was not accepted" (*Extremes*, p. 195, n. 6).
82 "The Court, after a debate which lasted two days, ordered the parties to lodge printed Informations, those for the prosecutor to be submitted by 16 December" (*Extremes*, p. 195, n. 7).
83 On war.
84 Boswell had reluctantly agreed to be counsel for the prosecution at the trial of John Bell, schoolmaster at Stewarton, who was charged "with seducing and debauching the minds of young girls to lewd, indecent, and vicious practices and behaviour, by using them in an indecent manner while under his charge as their schoolmaster" (*The Caledonian Mercury*, 3 December 1777, quoted in *Extremes*, p. 197, n. 5).
85 "The annual election meeting of the Grand Lodge of Freemasons was held on this day in the Parliament House. Sir William Forbes was re-elected Grand Master, and Boswell Depute Grand Master. After the election, the members 'walked in procession to the Assembly Hall, where a genteel collation was provided' (*The Caledonian Mercury*, 1 December 1777)" (*Extremes*, p. 197, n. 8).
86 "The Court found the libel too vague in certain respects, and dismissed the cause. But it availed 'poor Bell' nothing. He was re-indicted and tried with shut doors at Ayr in the following May, found guilty by unanimous verdict, and sentenced to be whipped through the town of Ayr and then to be banished from Scotland for life" (*Extremes*, p. 197, n. 9).
87 Short for *Voluptas*, i.e., "Pleasure"; in other words, conjugal relations.

weary. Robert Boswell a little. Afternoon home. Tea father; comfortable with *him*, but *her* cold uncouthness disagreeable.

MONDAY 8 DECEMBER. Laboured pretty well, having had paper for Lord Eglinton to write over again to be fuller. Called Dr Blair. Vain but mild. Said David Hume had said to him too much fanaticism in this country, so give rod full stretch other way, and 'twould come right. Then Lord Alva; lively, though to be cut for stone. Was restless. Grange dined. *Stoops to Conquer*, Masons' play.[88]

TUESDAY 9 DECEMBER. Laboured tolerably. Wife spit a little blood at night from pears disagreeing with her. She and I both sadly alarmed.

WEDNESDAY 10 DECEMBER. Wife still afraid. But grew better. Mrs Mitchelson, tea. Laboured tolerably. But was in bad spirits.

THURSDAY 11 DECEMBER. [At] Justiciary Office for Cases in trial Rule against Smith, etc. Dined Monboddo's. Pretty well. But was indifferent self and wondered at his vigour. A little intoxicated and wandered, but no harm.

SATURDAY 13 DECEMBER. Quite averse to labour. But was *obliged* to prepare Justiciary Information. Sent apology to Bailie Hunter[89] not dine with him, and dictated all the afternoon so as to finish the *Introduction* about ten at night.

SUNDAY 14 DECEMBER. I called Crosbie about Rule's trial. Chapel afternoon. Dined Baron Gordon's.[90] Lady Wallace, Monboddo, Maclaurin, Alexander Gordon, etc. Noise and drinking, and bad humour with Maclaurin. Sat till near twelve. Wandered, but *incapax*.[91] Home about one. Harm done to wife. Vexed.

MONDAY 15 DECEMBER. Sadly ill. Was to have been up at five. Lay till ten. Up. Vexed to think there had been bad words with Maclaurin, and that perhaps I had to resent. *Obliged* to write Justiciary Information. Got Mr Robertson of Records to read Justiciary books for me. Worthy Grange comforted me. Major Preston called. Dictated wonderfully, though quite indifferent as to everything. Dictated hard.

THURSDAY 18 DECEMBER. Heard some Lords on Maclean and Wilson. Was roused a little by their abilities, though blushed for my country at the high tide of prejudice which overflowed all bars. Dined Nairne's with Sir John Ogilvy, etc. Sober and well. Home at six. Wife said father saw a thing sooner than I, as my mind wavering, his steady. One sees quicker in a calm pool than in agitated waves.

FRIDAY 19 DECEMBER. Maclean and Wilson decided. Was pleased with President's warm humanity.[92]

---

88 "*She Stoops to Conquer* was performed at the Theatre Royal by desire of the Freemasons. Such requests were traditional in Edinburgh" (*Extremes*, p. 199, n. 2).
89 Probably James Hunter, the future Sir James Hunter-Blair (see also the entry for 29 January 1768).
90 Cosmo Gordon, who had been appointed Baron of Exchequer on 27 March of that year. He resided in the area known as the Society, by Brown Square.
91 Incapable (Latin).
92 "The Court decided in favour of Wilson, that is, that Captain White had been drowned in 1770, and that the many testimonies to his being alive later were either false or mistaken" (*Extremes*, p. 200, n. 8).

SATURDAY 20 DECEMBER. Well enough. Session rose. Evening, Faculty meeting. Well with Maclaurin. Excess of hock.

TUESDAY 23 DECEMBER. Uneasy about wife. Called Wood.[93] Breakfasted Lady Colville. Saw not respected, as she said would not wish to see me very rich, as 'twould put me in a situation not fit for. Spoke to me of wife so as to alarm me. Poor Dash sad.[94] Called Wood, who cheered me about wife.

WEDNESDAY 24 DECEMBER. Mr Lawrie went to country. Was at a loss for want of him. *Idled* all day, sorting Session papers. Was fretful. Dissatisfied with life, yet not miserable.

THURSDAY 25 DECEMBER. Awaked with thinking I should *sweep* my mind. Walked with Grange to the Abbey. Then had good dinner. Temple's cider and David's Malaga. Then Chapel.[95] Grange also tea.

SUNDAY 28 DECEMBER. Sunk, yet wrote *Hypochondriack* [No.4] pretty well.[96]

93 Surgeon Wood now resided at the Exchange in the High Street.
94 "Dash" was Andrew Erskine's nickname.
95 This had become an annual ritual. See the entries for 25 December 1776, 25 December 1779 and 25 December 1783.
96 On excess.

1778

MONDAY 5 JANUARY. Wife better, so that Wood between eight and nine said if weather was good and we had her in motion, would be as well as ever. And I tried *volupt.*, which brought on spitting of blood about midnight. O direful! thought herself gone. Prospects gloomy and dark. *I* miserable. Went to Wood. Brought him. He was calm and mild, but alarmed. I followed to door and cried bitterly, and loved him for his friendship. He said, "You'll have a great charge." But he hoped there might be only blood from throat. We had a sad night. I regretted that I had not been so good to her as she deserved, and that she had not been mistress of Auchinleck. She slept none and I very little. Prayed earnestly. Was in state of wildness.

TUESDAY 6 JANUARY. Was to have gone out to father's and expostulated on his coldness to my wife now that I was in grief. But he and Lady Auchinleck came. She was better somewhat, as no more blood had come. Worthy Grange sympathized with me.

WEDNESDAY 7 JANUARY. After good sleep, my wife was better. I attended her close.

SATURDAY 10 JANUARY. Was very low. Went to call on Lord Eglinton. Walked with him at Cross, and thought same thing being earl or caddie. He came with me and took dram. He and Hugh Montgomerie[1] and Surgeon Wood supped. Wife cheered. I was frightened by Wood's saying, "She's not well."

WEDNESDAY 14 JANUARY. In forenoon shocked that wife spit blood again.

THURSDAY 15 JANUARY. Wife had taken opium, which had eased the cough but not made her sleep. I called Wood at nine. He said he was *afraid* of her. But travelling might do good, at least prolong life. He was for calling Dr Young. I was *less* affected than by the first shock. In Parliament House I spoke with apprehension to Hon. A. Gordon. He said if such a misfortune as my losing her should happen, I should marry again immediately, or I'd go to the devil. "No, no", said I. "I'm done with the Devil." "But", said he, "the Devil's not done with you." *Wit.* Negro cause interested a little.[2] Went out in coach with father, cold wet day, and he cold as to poor John. Dined. Altercation with *her* as to *feeling.* Evening was amazingly easy in mind. Wife better.

FRIDAY 16 JANUARY. Nothing particular. Wife much sunk. Lady Auchinleck with her, and said nothing should be grudged.

1 Major Hugh Montgomerie of Skelmorlie and Coilsfield (1739-1819), cousin of Archibald Montgomerie, 11th Earl of Eglinton, whom he was to succeed in 1796. He entered the army in 1756 and served as Captain in America during most of the Seven Years' War, acquiring a reputation as a martinet, and was promoted to Major in 1774. In 1778 he was appointed Major in the West Fencibles.
2 Joseph Knight's cause was determined on this day. For details of this case, see the entry for 16 February 1776 and footnote.

SATURDAY 17 JANUARY. Was wonderfully easy. Existence, instead of being a load, was a gentle pleasing state. Wife better. Was uneasy that I was preses[3] of Mundell's meeting. But no help for it. Dressed and went and performed my part very well. Hon. James Stuart on one hand, Solicitor Murray on other. Was not disagreeably drunk. Home between nine and ten. Supped.

WEDNESDAY 21 JANUARY. In forenoon Solicitor Murray said of me to Nairne in my hearing how Swinton and he had been regretting that a man who could tell a story in so interesting a manner as *Corsica* and in most elegant language should make himself a common newspaper-writer. Very well said. Also how pleasant I was some years ago, and now very different. I said I meant that; I was too old to *divert* every company. Was a little intoxicated after dinner. Evening did very little.

THURSDAY 22 JANUARY. My wife better. She went out in a chair.

FRIDAY 23 JANUARY. Wife out again in chair. With much difficulty I agreed to dine with W. Wilson,[4] having resolved to dine always at home. Had lost relish of *business* as formerly. Tea by appointment with Sir William Forbes. Showed him last interview with David Hume.

SATURDAY 24 JANUARY. Faculty meeting and dinner at Fortune's. George Wallace and I agreed to sit together and drink negus. Was sent ambassador with Old Erskine,[5] so drank some claret. A little intoxicated. About nine went out to street. Met fine wench; with her to room in Blackfriars Wynd and twice. Back and coffee and whist. Home near twelve. Felt no disapprobation. Wife still well.

MONDAY 26 JANUARY. Wife had bad night and was ill again. Had been quite negligent last week, and had six papers on hand. Rule's trial in Justiciary Court.[6] Was quite indifferent. Weather vastly cold. After dinner took warm port negus just to comfort me. Felt universal indifference. This made my wife's death, my own death, anybody's appear of little consequence.

THURSDAY 29 JANUARY. Was overloaded with law-papers to write. I went out in chaise with wife and Ve. Stopped Petrie's.[7] Pleasing jaunt. Intoxicated a little with drams.

SUNDAY 15 FEBRUARY. Had been slightly feverish all week. Waked exceedingly

---

3 Preses = *praeses*; that is, chairman or president.
4 William Wilson, W.S., resided in New Bank Close.
5 It is assumed that this means that Boswell and Erskine were sent round with the drinks (*Extremes*, p. 206, n. 8). "Old Erskine" was James Erskine (1713-1785), advocate (admitted 2 July 1734), third son of the Hon. James Erskine, Lord Grange (Lord of Session 1707-1734). In October 1740 Erskine married Lady Frances Erskine, only daughter of the 6th (or 11th) Earl of Mar. Erskine was a rather remote blood relation of Boswell's and was also connected with him by marriage (*Ominous Years*, p. 26, n. 3). Boswell described him as being consistently lively and good-spirited (Journal, 20 October 1774, 1 November 1774).
6 The judges found that Gilkie's signing the list of witnesses (issued with the Criminal Letters), which should have been signed by the prosecutor in accordance with the usual practice, rendered the execution of the Criminal Letters and the citation of the witnesses null and void, and therefore deserted the diet against the panels, dismissed them from the bar, and found them entitled to expenses (*Extremes*, p. 207, n. 2).
7 A tavern. A James Petrie had a tavern in Anchor Close, off the north side of the High Street, but Boswell's jaunt in the chaise may have taken him to another tavern of the same name farther afield.

ill. Severe headache and sickness. Ill all day. Was really alarmed that I was in danger, but not uneasy on that account. Wood with me three times. Wife's attention angelic. Better, evening. Grange with me a little.

TUESDAY 17 FEBRUARY. Little to do in Court, so kept house. Cullen and W. Wilson at consultation at tea.

WEDNESDAY 18 FEBRUARY. In coach with wife to see father. Continuing better. Pleaded ably as I could wish.

THURSDAY 26 FEBRUARY. The Fast by proclamation.[8] Took physic. Intense frost, so that Mr Wood could not give me mineral. Dictated well. Evening began *Hypochondriack*.[9] Could not see how I should end it. Yet wrote well what I did write. Wrote several letters.

FRIDAY 27 FEBRUARY. Short while in Court. Home and got forward in *Hypochondriack* wonderfully.

SUNDAY 1 MARCH. As Lord North had now brought in bills for conciliation with the Americans, our clergy who were for the violent measures could no longer pray in a hostile strain. So I went to hear Dr Blair, from whose ministry I had absented myself for more than a year. I heard him again with much relish. He gave an excellent lecture on the Lord's prayer, and had the resolution to make it serve *alone* as his prayer between the lecture and sermon. To introduce it at all into Presbyterian prayers was once thought almost popish. But I believe this was the first time that it was the whole of a Presbyterian minister's public prayer. Stayed at home all the afternoon. Had much satisfaction in hearing Veronica repeat a psalm and the Lord's prayer.

MONDAY 2 MARCH. My wife was now a good deal better. My mind was sound and easy. I found Lord Monboddo at home. He told me that during his late dangerous illness he felt no uneasiness at the thought of going into the world of spirits, and that a man's life must be very miserable who is afraid of death. He said he believed that according to the state of a man's mind so would be his happiness in the world of spirits; that a man habituated to spiritual employments would be happy. He talked with such confidence as communicated it to me for the time. I thought I could die easily in company with him. I was like a weak-sighted passenger at sea who acquiesces in the assurance of a steady, strong-eyed pilot that he sees land. He said Adam Smith was educated at Oxford and came down a good Greek and Latin scholar. But that he quitted those studies, wrote a foolish book upon morals, and has now published a book upon trade,[10] from the style of which one would think that he had never read any of the writers of Greece or Rome.

FRIDAY 6 MARCH. I should have mentioned that either on Tuesday or Wednesday

8 "February 26 in Scotland and February 27 in England had been proclaimed by the King as days of fasting and prayers for success against the Americans" (*Extremes*, p. 209, n. 1).
9 No. 6, on a subject particularly close to Boswell's heart—hypochondria.
10 *The Theory of Moral Sentiments* (1759) and *An Inquiry into the Nature and Causes of the Wealth of Nations* (1776).

last, I sat half an hour with Sir William Forbes at his counting-house, and was told by him that he was never indolent. For that the business of his house kept him active the greatest part of his time, and his leisure from it for other things was so little that he was stimulated to activity by his inclination for study and society. I envied his situation in this respect. He is never quiescent long enough to collect a large portion of the *vis inertiae*, as a room which is frequently swept never gathers much dust. But he must have a good constitution. There are rooms which, dust them as often as you please, will not be quite clear. Old buildings, the materials of which are mouldering, are very dusty. The minds of old men are generally most clouded with cares. A young mind is like a new, sound, fresh building. Sir William made me a little uneasy by mentioning a report in the newspapers that Dr Johnson was very ill. I say a little, because newspaper reports are often without much foundation; and I thought that if he had been really ill, I should have had a letter. *The London Chronicle*, which arrived on Wednesday afternoon, removed any apprehension by assuring the public that Dr Johnson had only a slight cold. Mrs Young drank tea with us. The Doctor (her husband), Sir William and Lady Forbes, her sister Miss Hay, Mr Solicitor Murray, Mr Nairne, and young Cuninghame of Caddell passed the evening and supped. We played whist and *vingt-un* before supper. I was so much out of the habit of genteel company that I was not easy. I had this party chiefly on my wife's account. She was cheerful and pleased. I had a letter this afternoon (by return of post) from Sir John Pringle, giving it as his opinion that, as my wife was with child, she should not accompany me to London. His attention and kindness flattered and pleased me.

SATURDAY 7 MARCH. I was in admirable spirits in the Court of Session today. I liked the business, and I thought the supreme civil court of Scotland or North Britain a scene important enough for me. A man cannot be happy if he thinks his occupation beneath him. I think too closely. I am too concave a being. My thoughts go inwards too much instead of being carried out to external objects. I wish I had a more convex mind. And yet the happiness of a rational being is reflection. But I am too minute. I am continually putting the Roman praetor's question, "*Cui bono?*"[11] to every incident of life, to each part of a whole.

I had not been at Sir Alexander Dick's for a very long time. He sent to me that he was in John's Coffee-house, and begged I would go out in his coach with him to dinner. I got Grange to be of the party. Sir Alexander's amiable temper was unclouded as ever. But from disuse for four weeks of being from home, I was not happy. I had been in a train of thinking that I could do very well without going into company to dine or sup—nay, better; and that the rotation of mutual entertainments was unnecessary and burthensome. Harry Erskine had a pretty good thought upon this. He said, "If you refuse to lend a friend a little money, you are disliked as a churl. Is it not as bad to refuse him your company?" My wife tells me that to keep up an intercourse with genteel society is a duty which

---

11 "For whose good?"; "Who benefits from it?" (Cicero's *Pro Milone*, xii. xxxii).

I owe to my family, that my children may see good company. From a foolish complaisance and a no less foolish desire to let myself feel that I had the resolution to stop short, I drank one glass of wine at dinner. It was a match to the particles of inflammation in my blood and brain, and altered me sensibly. I was vexed that I took it. Grange and I had Sir Alexander's coach into town. I had not time to take down more materials for writing the worthy Baronet's life.

I went to Lord Kames's and found him at eighty and upwards as entire—nay, as lively—as I ever remember him. I drank tea with him and his lady, and my spirits were agreeably agitated by their cheerful conversation. There was nothing of the gloom of old age here. I entertained him with an account of Lord Monboddo, who told me that during his late fever he had been some hours in Elysium, having conversed with superior intelligences. Monboddo said to me the other day that a man who is afraid of death must be very miserable. Lord Kames, to whom I quoted the remark, said nothing. But he talks of making his exit from life with so much ease that makes me believe he is not afraid of death. Lord Kames told me this evening that a Mr Bayne of Logie, known by the name of Logie Bayne, was the first regular Professor of Scots Law here. He was first an advocate at this bar, but did not succeed. He then went to London and resided some years, thinking to try the English bar. But that would not do either. He returned to Scotland in low circumstances and knew very little law. But such was the effect of a grave countenance and a slow, formal manner, a neatness of expression and the English accent, that the advocates sent a deputation to ask him to accept of being professor, which he did most readily. Stirling of Keir was once invited to dine with him. One o'clock was then the hour. When he went in to Mr Bayne's study, Mr Bayne took no notice of him at first, but kept his eye intent looking through a telescope to the clock of the Tron Church. Then suddenly rising, said, "You're welcome, Sir. It is precisely one o'clock." He was a sort of musical composer but of no taste in music, for he was quite inattentive to the finest pieces at the concert till his own performances were played, and then he fell to the harpsichord and was all alive. He was a kind of mechanic too, and tried to boil snuff in place of toasting it. I found Lord Kames held Bayne very cheap. I got from Lord Kames tonight some more materials for his own life. I left him about nine, though he asked me to sup. I was afraid of the night air and did not like to be too long absent from my wife, though she was now in wonderful health, considering her late dreary apprehensions.

SUNDAY 8 MARCH. Went to the New Church in the forenoon and heard Mr Paul, Lord Leven's chaplain; liked him very well. Had not been at my father's for several weeks, my indisposition having kept me at home. Went out in the coach with him and his lady today and dined and drank tea, and although there was not that close cordiality which I wish, we were very well. I was calmly entertained with his stories, and was pleased to observe his steady, uniform temper. He repeated the motto which he put upon the front of his house at Auchinleck:

Quod petis, hic est,
Est Ulubris, animus si te non deficit aequus.[12]

"But", said I, "the *animus aequus* is a rare gift." He seemed to think a man *faber sui animi*,[13] as an ancient says every one is of his fortune.

He told me a very pretty story which I have heard him tell often without any variation. Lord Dun, his predecessor in the office of judge in the Court of Session, resigned very honourably when he found himself aged and infirm.[14] When my father received his commission, he went next morning to pay his respects to Lord Dun, and told him of his appointment, saying, "My Lord, as I have the honour to be appointed your Lordship's unworthy successor, I am come to ask your blessing." "Sir," said Lord Dun, "I held that office too long. For I was become but half a judge. But what do I say? I was not even half a judge. For I gave corporal presence but one half of the year, and then I am conscious that I could not give that accurate attention which is necessary to every man who judges of the property of others. However, I held the office, being apprehensive that they might put in even worse than half a judge. But, Sir" (taking my father by the hand), "since you are to be my successor" (here he paid some compliments; then, in answer to my father's asking his blessing, as he was a High-Churchman, he said) "I have no title to give a blessing. But if my prayers can be of any use to you while I live, they shall not be wanting."

I talked to my father of my intended jaunt to London this spring. He did not oppose it. But seemed to hold my expectations of any good from it very cheap. He however advised me to keep close to Lord Mountstuart. I regretted that he remained in a state of ill-informed prejudice as to my great friend and instructor, Dr Johnson. For in the general notions of life I knew they were agreed, though their ecclesiastical and political systems were widely different. There are things which cannot be helped. This is one; and the want of cordiality between my father and me is another. My father was better now than he had been for two years. I came home calmly in a chair. My wife was now in a fair way of recovery, and being with child she looked comfortably. Veronica repeated a psalm and the Lord's prayer.

WEDNESDAY 11 MARCH. Was but in indifferent spirits. Wondered how the business of the Court of Session was carried on with such constancy. Had no satisfaction in anything, not even in the Advocates' Library, which generally pleases me substantially. I went and sat a good while with Sir William Forbes. He told me he never had experienced one moment of vapours or melancholy, so could not conceive another afflicted in that way. He never was uneasy but from some cause which he could distinctly tell. Grange dined and drank tea with us. The Session rose today. I felt a sort of uneasiness from being free from immediate business.

12 "'What you are seeking is here, here at Ulubrae, if steadiness of mind does not desert you' (Horace, *Epistles*, I. xi. 29-30). Ulubrae, a decaying town in the Pomptine marshes, is used as a type of the remote and unfashionable" (*Extremes*, p. 214, n. 9).
13 "Maker of his own mind."
14 David Erskine (1670-1758), appointed Lord of Session as Lord Dun in 1710 (resigned 1753).

THURSDAY 12 MARCH. I sent to Mr Crosbie, who was going to London, and he came and settled with me that we should set out next day, afternoon. I expected good conversation with him, as he has much knowledge. I made my agreement that I should have my natural rest in bed every night during the journey. I revised my notes of the opinions of the Lords of Session in Douglas's causes which were to come on by appeal this spring in the House of Lords, and had them copied by Mr Lawrie. This was a pretty agreeable occupation. I found that my mind was not firm enough yet. For the prospect of going to London agitated me much more than I wished it should. Grange dined and drank tea with us. So worthy and prudent a friend is very valuable. My wife having had reason to be offended with me, we were at present in a state of coolness. I could not hope for better till I had deserved it by a course of more prudent behaviour. I therefore rested in hope, and I considered that I was a gainer at present, as I should suffer less in parting with her.

FRIDAY 13 MARCH. Found myself in a more composed and steady frame than I expected. Wrote some letters, and was in no hurry or confusion. Wished that I might be in as good a state of mind when death should come upon me. Veronica cried enchantingly when I spoke of my going to London. She walked out with me to my father's, and being soon cheerful again, when I resumed the story of my leaving her, she bid me not speak of it again, for it made her cry. I was delighted with her. It was agreeable to have her with me when I took leave of my father, for he never cordially approves of my going to London; and by the influence of habit since ever I remember him, I am depressed in his presence and cannot get free of the imagination that I am still a boy, or at least a youth, and that, too, pretty much "void of understanding".[15] Having a child of my own before me elevates me to the rank of a father and counteracts the depressing imagination to a certain degree. It is like having a little footstool to raise one. He upon this occasion recalled, as he does often and often, my former extravagance, and found fault with me for not cultivating the friendship of the Arniston family, insisting that a man's father's friends are the surest that he can have. I dislike that overbearing, selfish, Whig family, and I cannot think they are my father's friends. He advised me today, since I was going to London, to keep close to those who could be of real service in advancing me. We parted in very tolerable terms.

I dined quietly at home. At four I left home to go to Mr Crosbie's, where the post-chaise was waiting for us. My parting from my wife was more tender than I had presupposed. Veronica cried much and clasped her little arms round my neck, calling out, "O Pap-ā!" Sandy cried too, which pleased me exceedingly, for I wished there should be affection between me and my son. Effie, though in general the most affectionate of the three, was upon this occasion singularly indifferent. Worthy Grange and Mr Lawrie accompanied me to the chaise.

At Greenlaw, Boswell and Crosbie were joined in the chaise by Ilay Campbell and Charles

15 Proverbs 10. 13.

Brown, Writer to the Signet. Boswell, as usual, called on his brother John at Newcastle and found that John had recovered his sanity and had taken lodgings. "He had indeed that reserved, proud, and morose behaviour which I scarcely ever saw him without", records Boswell. "He had, however, less moroseness than I have observed when he was going about as an officer in the Army; and it gave me some degree of tender uneasiness to think that his father was unwilling that he should return home."

During the journey, Boswell and Crosbie had wide-ranging discussions on such subjects as law and religion. And, says Boswell, "Crosbie and I amused ourselves at times… with making more of The Justiciary Opera, *adapting the proceedings of the Criminal Court to tunes and putting them in rhyme, with much merriment produced by parody and ludicrous contrasts of various kinds. Our associated travellers, Campbell and Brown, were humdrum, and ineffectual in doing us any good." On arrival at London, Crosbie told Boswell that this had been the pleasantest journey he had ever made, which remark gave Boswell much pleasure as he considered it to be a compliment to him as a travelling companion.*

The day after his arrival in London, and having lodged at General Paoli's house, Boswell was pleasantly surprised to be informed by John Spottiswoode, the London-based solicitor for Archibald Douglas, that Boswell was to be counsel at the bar of the House of Commons for John Francis Erskine of Mar (grandson of John Erskine, 6th Earl of Mar, leader of the Jacobite rebellion of 1715) and others, being a number of small proprietors of land in Stirlingshire, in connection with their petition opposing the Strirlingshire Highways Bill, which would, in Boswell's words, deprive them of "the right of assessing themselves for making high roads". Spottiswoode gave Boswell a brief and a handsome fee of ten guineas and told Boswell to attend a consultation on the case that evening. The case was heard on 24 March and Boswell considered that he spoke "well", having presumably not followed John Wilkes' advice, which was that the best way to plead at the bar of the House of Commons was to be "as impudent as you can, as merry, and say whatever comes uppermost". However, the Bill, in an amended form, was passed in the House of Commons on 14 April and was then sent to the House of Lords.

On 6 April, Boswell attended a hearing at the House of Lords in connection with the Duke of Hamilton's continuing litigation against Archibald Douglas, but the case was merely remitted to the Court of Session and it seems that Boswell did not speak.

The following day, Boswell called on the elderly Duke of Queensberry, the Lord Justice-General, from whom Boswell solicited the post of Lord Treasurer's Remembrancer in the Scottish Court of Exchequer. This post, which carried a salary of £200 a year, was held by one of the Commissioners of Customs, George Clerk-Maxwell (1715-1784), to whom the Duke promised to write to see if he would resign his place so that Boswell could take it.

Boswell revelled in his customarily wide social circle in London; and during this period he was almost invariably happy, which he attributed in no small measure to the fact that he was at that time an almost total abstainer from alcohol. Boswell's consistent amiability drew praise from Dr Johnson, who said, "You make yourself agreeable wherever you go. Whoever has seen you once wishes to see you again."

Boswell made a number of calls on a lady cryptically referred to in his journal as "No. 36" and it seems that this may have been the house number of Mrs Love, widow of Boswell's friend James Love, the actor (it also seems that this may have been the lady so mysteriously referred to in Boswell's journal in the spring of 1776 as the "lady with whom I had once been amorously connected").[16] *Boswell's first few visits to this lady were unfruitful as he had reason to think that he was not yet fully cured of his latest venereal disease. However, his visit on 25 April resulted in felicity: "Away and met 36, vastly snug. I said, 'What harm, in your situation?' 36 said, 'To be sure. Or in yours, provided it does not weaken affection at home.' (What a slut! To be thus merely corporeal!) Twice... Refreshed." And again on 26 April: "Went to 36. Refreshed, and 36 said I was better than formerly."*

On 30 April, Boswell received an urgent request from Spottiswoode, the solicitor, to speak before the committee of the House of Lords on the Stirlingshire Highways Bill. He hastily borrowed a gown at Lincoln's Inn and rushed to the House of Lords, where, after a meeting at a coffee-house in the same building, he appeared before the committee. "Just talked a little", he records, adding: "Went against us smoothly". The outcome was that the Bill was passed by the Lords on 1 May and received the Royal Assent on 15 May. However, for this appearance Boswell was to receive a further fee of ten guineas.

Boswell once again took the opportunity afforded by his presence in London to plead with Lord Mounstuart for his assistance in finding him a suitable position. It was becoming increasingly apparent that Mounstuart was quite indifferent to Boswell's requests, but he nevertheless assured Boswell that he would do what he could.

On the day of his departure, 18 May, Boswell finished a further "term" at the Inner Temple by dining there on the last dining day of the term. To be admitted to the bar, he would have to finish twelve "terms", of which he had now finished three.

As he was about to leave, Boswell told Johnson, "This is the best London I ever had, owing to no wine." He then enquired, "Shall I keep to the letter of the law and not taste, though 'twere the most curious wine?" To this Johnson replied, "Keep to the letter of the law." "But", asked Boswell, "if a physician prescribes it, I may take it?" On receiving Johnson's assurance that he could, Boswell said, "So I'm not to bind myself strictly down?" "What!" exclaimed Johnson, "a vow? Oh no, Sir. A vow is a horrible thing. 'Tis a snare for sin."

Having visited his brother John at Newcastle and found him to be "wonderfully easy and even social", Boswell reached Edinburgh on 28 May at about eleven at night. "Valuable spouse quite well", he records. "Veronica, in our bed, embraced me and hung about my neck with the keenest affection. Saw the other two asleep. Delighted with M.M."[17]

At this point, Boswell's journal lapses and we know little about his life during the summer. However, the journal resumes in August when Boswell went for a jaunt to the Carlisle Assizes, where he enjoyed the processions and ceremonies and the hustle and bustle of the crowd. He took great interest in the court procedures; observed and socialised with the judges and barristers; and considered that he "could do very well" as a barrister in England.

Boswell set off back to Edinburgh on or about 26 August, fearing that his wife, who

---

16 See *Extremes*, p. 234, n. 2. When Mrs Love was Boswell's mistress in Edinburgh in 1761-62 (see Introduction, p. 23), he referred to her, rather dismissively, as "old Canongate" (Pottle, p. 477). In his journal entry for 18 September 1769 Boswell said that she was then "verging on fifty", and so by 1778 she was presumably close to sixty.

17 "M.M." stood for Margaret Montgomerie, Mrs Boswell's maiden name.

was in an advanced state of pregnancy, might be suffering from labour pains. However, the child—a further son, James—was not born until 15 September.

TUESDAY 15 SEPTEMBER. The birth of another son is a new era in my life; and I flatter myself that I may continue my journal from this day on which my son *James* was born, with more constancy than I have done for some time past. I had rested ill all night, having been disturbed by being raised from bed with my wife, and having more than ordinary anxiety about her, as she had been very ill and apprehensive of being in a consumption at the time she fell with child. I rose between nine and ten. She was in great distress all the forenoon. I prayed earnestly for her to GOD and to Jesus Christ, and I addressed myself (if I could be heard by them) to the Virgin Mary, to my dear mother, to my grandfather and hers, and to her father and mother for their intercession. About ten minutes after two she was safely delivered of a fine, big, stout boy, and she herself was better than ever she had been on such an occasion. She however had suffered so severely that she told me she had now for the first time expressed a wish that she might have no more. I was satisfied to think she should not. Dr Young and Grange dined with Miss Cuninghame and me. In the evening arrived little James's nurse, ——, wife of ——, a day-labourer at Gilmerton, a strong, brown-coloured woman. I wrote letters to my father and several friends, with the good news. Grange supped.

WEDNESDAY 16 SEPTEMBER. I had pleased myself with thinking that I should drink no wine since the birth of my son James. But I dined today with Mr Donaldson, the bookseller, and tasted some whisky; and then being pained with the toothache, took two half glasses of port, which excited in me the desire of drinking, and I resolved to indulge myself in liberal moderation this evening with my friends after the christening, for which purpose I brought up a bottle of old Malaga for myself. I drank tea at my wife's bedside, and between six and seven little James was baptized by Dr Webster in presence of Miss Cuninghame, Balbarton, Mr Alexander Boswall, who had arrived from England the night before, Grange, George Campbell and David,[18] and my other three children. I was more impressed with religious faith by the ceremony tonight than I had felt myself for some time. The gentlemen and I passed a couple of hours most agreeably. I drank all the Malaga but one glass which Grange took, and which I supplied with a glass of Madeira. I was sedate; yet my heart was very warm, and as the child was named for my worthy grandfather, Mr James Boswell, I had peculiar satisfaction.[19] It was curious to compare the ages of the oldest and youngest James Boswell: Balbarton, seventy-eight years; my James, two days. I had good steady views of real life while I drank. But I felt the inflammation rise too high.

THURSDAY 17 SEPTEMBER. I had been restless and uneasy all night, and in

18 George and David Campbell, the two sons of the deceased James Campbell of Treesbank.
19 In accordance with Scottish tradition at that time, Boswell's first son had been named after Boswell's father, and his second son had been named after Boswell's grandfather.

the morning I was very sick and had a violent headache. I lay till past one o'clock and should have lain longer. But this was the last day on which I could send *The Hypochondriack* No. 12 to be in time for this month's *London Magazine*, and only three pages of it were as yet done. I set myself steadily to it, and by taking some good onion soup I made it out wonderfully well.[20] My wife continued to recover well.

FRIDAY 18 SEPTEMBER. I was very ill with a colic and looseness all the forenoon. However, I was amused by taking care of myself, drinking a great deal of beef tea, which cured me. My mind was in a state of unpleasing indifference, and I was fretted to think that I had neither solid science nor steady conduct, and that my two daughters were under no awe of me. I read some of the *Biographia Britannica*. How insignificant is my present existence!

SATURDAY 19 SEPTEMBER. I engaged to dine with [Sir Alexander Dick], which I did. I was in a tolerable state of spirits; drank some cider and three glasses of port. Nobody there but Mr Bennet[21] and Alison of the Excise,[22] who walked in with me part of the way and told me that he remembered to have seen my grandfather, a big, strong, Gothic-looking man; and that he was present in the General Assembly when patronages began first to have a party for them, and some of the young clergy spoke very slightingly of the common people as unfit to judge of their teachers, there being a cause under consideration in which the people were concerned. That my grandfather got up and said, "Moderator, I am an old man; and I remember the time when the Gospel was not so easy as it is now. But those who wished to hear it according to their conscience were subject to persecution. Several of those I myself have seen. But amongst them were not many rich, not many noble. They were mostly common people, whom we have heard treated with much contempt this day." Mr Alison said "*a vote*" was immediately called, and it was carried for the people by a great majority. He said what my grandfather spoke had a great effect. He was a man of weight. I was pleased thus accidentally to hear another good anecdote in addition to many which I have heard of my grandfather. I came home and drank coffee in my wife's bedroom. It is wonderful how uneasy sleeping in solitude has been to me upon this occasion. Though the dining-room where I lie is agreeably spacious, I have an unwillingness to go to bed.

SUNDAY 20 SEPTEMBER. Was too late for church in the forenoon. Read the *Critical* and *Monthly Reviews* for August. Between sermons walked down to Belleville. Lady Dundonald talked keenly of planting, and said she would plant on the very day that she was sure to die.[23] "Yes", said I. "With my very last grasp I would put an acorn into the ground." Grange was kind enough to walk down with me and wait in the King's Park till I came from my visit. I was languid, but pretty well. I heard Dr Blair preach on rejoicing in the Lord in the New Church

20 The subject of the essay was love (as was the subject of Nos 11 and 13).
21 The Rev. William Bennet, minister of Duddingston parish.
22 Alexander Alison, cashier at the Excise Office.
23 Lady Dundonald was now a widow, Lord Dundonald having died on 27 June 1778.

in the afternoon. Both my own children and Sir George Campbell[24] and David did very well in little religious exercises. I read Mr Carr's —— sermon twice: once to my wife and once to Grange, who supped with me.[25] I drank cider both at dinner and supper. I read at night in the *Biographia Britannica*.

MONDAY 21 SEPTEMBER. This day I indulged my two daughters and Sandy and the two Campbells with a visit to Prestonfield in the forenoon. Grange accompanied us. Everything appeared pleasing. The day was beautiful. They got fruit (the children, I mean), and my daughters and son rode up and down the garden on a sheltie. Grange dined with me, and in the afternoon he and I walked down to the country-house of M. Dupont and Miss Scott at the foot of Leith Walk and drank tea. I never felt a more delightful day. The sun shone so bright and benignant that existence was a pleasure. It was a calm and comfortable scene at tea. M. Dupont, who was seventy-nine last March, was quite entire and even lively. At night I read part of Young *On Opium*.[26] I have not had so agreeable a day of a long time.

TUESDAY 22 SEPTEMBER. This day being the anniversary of His Majesty's coronation, there was a good deal of bustle in the town, the Duke of Buccleuch's Fencibles having marched into the Castle and Lord Seaforth's Highlanders being to march out. A large body of the private Highlanders with a few sergeants were dissatisfied to such a degree that they resolved not to allow themselves to be embarked at Leith as ordered. They complained of being cruelly treated, of having large arrears both of levy-money and pay owing to them, and they had a notion that they were to be sold to the East India Company. Above a hundred of them were on the Castle Hill with loaded muskets when I walked there about twelve. It was as fine weather as yesterday. The mutineers marched down to the Canongate, and when the regiment marched down the street, seemingly in good humour, they met it at the entry to the New Bridge, and a strange tumultous struggle took place. The mutineers carried several more of the regiment back to the Canongate with them.

I dined with Dr Young[27] (his lady in the country), with several physicians, and Mr Cruickshanks, a popish priest. There was no valuable conversation, though we were cheerful enough. I drank only cider. When we went to coffee, we were informed that the mutinous Highlanders were on Arthur's Seat. Dr Monro, Dr Home, and I walked down to the King's Park, where crowds were gathered. It was truly picturesque to see the Highlanders in arms upon that lofty mountain. Several people had been up amongst them, and bread and beer had been carried to them. They were quite irregular, and they fired many shot. It was supposed they would march off for the Highlands by Stirling in the night.

---

24 Boswell erroneously thought that George Campbell was heir to a baronetcy.

25 A two-volume edition of the sermons of the Rev. George Carr, senior clergyman at the New English Chapel, was brought out by Sir William Forbes in 1778. "Moderate and charitable, though they preached regulation of all the appetites, they went into eight editions by 1796" (*Applause*, p. 54, n. 5).

26 *A Treatise on Opium, Founded upon Practical Observations*, by George Young, M.D. (1753).

27 Dr Young resided in New Street, off the north side of the Canongate.

I was wonderfully animated by this extraordinary scene, and came home and wrote some account of it in a great hurry for the *Public Advertiser*. But was too late for the post.

WEDNESDAY 23 SEPTEMBER. The weather had been very fine all night, and continued to be so. The mutineers kept possession of their hill. I walked up to the Castle Hill after breakfast and found Lord Loudoun entering the Castle.[28] I attended his Lordship. He told me he would have gone into it last night, but thought it might give an alarm. He would give no opinion what should be done with the mutineers, which I imputed to his being dissatisfied that he was not Commander-in-Chief. He said, "If I defend this castle, I do my duty." Plomer of the Southern Fencibles told me that it was thought the mutineers could not be reached with any kind of artillery from the Castle while they remained on the top of Arthur's Seat, but that one of the engineers had talked of throwing a shell amongst them while they were upon a lower part of the hill. I walked down to the King's Park with young Robert Syme, and walked a part of the way up the hill. Then Grange and I walked out to Sir Alexander Dick's, where we dined upon invitation of last Monday. Mr Bennet and Mr Mercer were there, and we had much conversation about the men on the hill. I was much too violent for them. Worthy Grange did his best to moderate me. I drank cider and a little port.

THURSDAY 24 SEPTEMBER. Carried Sir George Campbell and David to wait on Lord Loudoun. Waited on Lord Eglinton and engaged him to sup with me tonight. There was a wonderful animation in the town from there being a Highland camp on Arthur's Seat. I was in admirable spirits. Loch of Drylaw and I walked to the top of the hill. I do not insert particulars in my journal, as I write a separate account of all that I observed or heard about the singular event of the mutiny. I read, I think, nothing at present but newspapers. I wrote a little yesterday and more today about the mutiny for the *Public Advertiser*, and sent it off tonight. Lord Eglinton came very cordially and visited my wife before supper, and then Miss Cuninghame and he and I supped. I drank one glass of Sitges with him, and after supper we had a bowl of brandy punch and I drank fair with him, as he was now upon a sober regimen.

FRIDAY 25 SEPTEMBER. This morning the Highlanders marched down from Arthur's Seat. Luckily Grange and I just reached the King's Park in time to see the singular scene. He dined with me, and I drank a little; I forget whether wine or cider. I had my pocket-book stolen in the crowd, which vexed me. Dr Young drank tea with us. I supped at the French tavern[29] with Lord Eglinton, Lord Cassillis,[30] Sir Patrick Warrender, and Commissioner Brown.[31] I was in

28 Lord Loudoun was the Governor of the Castle (see p. 175, n. 174).
29 This was presumably John Bayle's tavern. Bayle was a Frenchman who had come to Edinburgh in 1777 and ran a tavern in Bridge Street. In 1793 he was to open a tavern (again known as the "French tavern") where various clubs, including the New Club, held their meetings (Stuart, pp. 81-2).
30 David Kennedy, tenth Earl of Cassilis.
31 George Brown, Commissioner of Excise.

excellent health and spirits, eat heartily, drank cider, two glasses of wine, and some brandy punch. We were exceedingly merry. I was quite sober, but sat till two. I had now for (I think) two nights slept in my wife's room.

SATURDAY 26 SEPTEMBER. Passed the forenoon at the Court of Inquiry in the Canongate court-house to hear the complaints of the mutineers against their officers.[32] Dined at Prestonfield. Nothing to remark.

SUNDAY 27 SEPTEMBER. Was at the New Church in the forenoon and heard Dr Blair. In the afternoon took the young Campbells to the English Chapel. At night walked down to the Abbey Close with Lieutenant Farquharson of Gordon's Highlanders to hear what particulars he could tell about the mutineers. But I could not trust to his authenticity. After I parted with him, a wanton-looking wench catched my eye in the street. I accosted her, but without intention to transgress. She endeavoured to hold me, and named me, "*Mr Boswell.*" This was a proof to me that I must not suppose I am not known by such creatures in Edinburgh, so that if other motives fail, a regard to my reputation as a man of some decency may restrain me. Grange supped in my wife's room. I now slept with her.

MONDAY 28 SEPTEMBER. Called on General Skene and wished him joy on having settled the mutiny so agreeably. My spirits were now as good as when I am in London, such is the effect of agitation upon me. I called on Maclaurin and talked over the mutiny with him.[33] He took a sufficient interest in it. He and I went and called on Mr Robertson, minister of the Erse congregation, and got him to engage to have Sergeant Robertson and some of the most sensible of the mutineers to drink a bowl of punch with us at a tavern at six this evening. I called a little at home, Maclaurin waiting for me; and then I went and dined with him on a leg of his own mutton, and drank half a bottle of old hock. We were really social. At six we went to the Cross, where Mr Robertson was to meet us. We drank tea in the Exchange Coffee-house. But our curious interview did not hold, the Highlanders having been prevented from coming, either by suspicion or some other reason.

TUESDAY 29 SEPTEMBER. [Grange] and I drank tea at Lord Macdonald's, where was Young Lady Wallace (Eglinton Maxwell) with whom I went home, being asked by her.[34] She was charming. I twice tasted her delicious lips, and did not mind the reproof which she gave or affected to give me. I was quite free of *love* in the *tender* sense. I was a *hearty* admirer.

WEDNESDAY 30 SEPTEMBER. My time passed away at present, I cannot tell how. But I was easy and cheerful. Grange dined with me; I drank cider. After dinner we walked to Leith. He returned with me and drank tea. I ought not to be satisfied with living thus ingloriously.

---

32 For the Canongate court-house, see p. 211, n. 84.
33 John Maclaurin was at this time residing in George Square.
34 The beautiful and eccentric sister of the Duchess of Gordon (for whom, see p. 58 and relevant footnote). Earlier this year she had divorced her husband, Thomas Dunlop-Wallace, for adultery. Her house was in St Andrew Street.

FRIDAY 2 OCTOBER. My wife, for the first time since her last in-lying, dined upstairs. Grange was with us at dinner. I drank cider and wine, but in fine moderation.

SUNDAY 4 OCTOBER. Was at home all day, I know not how, and did very little good except reading one of Mr Carr's sermons and hearing my children say psalms. Veronica could say two: the 23 and ——; and part of the first, and the Lord's prayer quite well. Poor Effie could say only a little of the 23 imperfectly. But what was wonderful, Sandy could say the Lord's prayer down to "daily bread" very distinctly, and could say more of it imperfectly.

TUESDAY 6 OCTOBER. I intended this day to begin to write an Information for Marshall against Crosse.[35] But I was idly lively and sauntering all the morning. Before two, Lady Rothes and her three eldest children paid us a visit with Miss Wauchope of Niddrie, her Ladyship being on a visit to that family. Then came Maclaurin, whom I asked to take a dinner with me today as I had done with him last week, and we should drink just one bottle of my old hock. He agreed. We first drank cider and Sitges, and then the hock. I did not feel myself comfortable, as he has no congenial religious dispositions; and what I had drank made me unfit to write my Information, I was so fretted with a sort of irritability of blood which wine sometimes produces in me.

WEDNESDAY 7 OCTOBER. This morning I had a message from Mr William Wilson begging that I would send him by the bearer the Information, Marshall against Crosse. This roused me. I sent for answer it should come in the evening. I fell to work after breakfast, but was volatile. Walked out as far as Portsburgh. Called on Mr Wilson and talked a little on the cause; came home, and went on very well. Charles Preston and Mr Wellwood dined with us. I drank a little wine. I laboured assiduously and had fifteen pages finished before I went to bed.

THURSDAY 8 OCTOBER. Finished my Information this forenoon, and was pleased with my work.

SUNDAY 11 OCTOBER. In the morning before breakfast I walked out as far as Portsburgh. Heard Dr Blair in the forenoon and Mr Walker in the afternoon. Between sermons sat awhile with Maclaurin, whom I found reading the Sixth Book of the *Aeneid* with Warburton's commentary upon it in his *Divine Legation of Moses*. In the evening made my children repeat psalms and the Lord's prayer. Lady Colville and Lady Anne Erskine called and sat some time. Sir Thomas Wallace called and stayed supper. I drank two bumpers of raspberry brandy which had been set down by mistake for Madeira, and half a bottle of Madeira. I was so much intoxicated as to be fiery and passionate. V.[36]

---

35 Lord Gardenstone had reported the question of expenses in this action to the full court and had appointed counsel to lodge Informations in the Lords' boxes by 10 October. The action was an action for damages in respect of alleged damage to a water-colour miniature of a lady with whom the pursuer (William Crosse, a retired merchant in Glasgow) had had an affair (see *Laird*, pp. 488-9).
36 An abbreviation of "Voluptas" (as to which, see p. 312, n. 87).

MONDAY 12 OCTOBER. Got up not at all well. Sat a while in the forenoon with Grange. Walked a little in the street. Grew worse; went to bed at three and lay all the rest of the day in great distress with a headache and sickness. My mind just acquiesced.

TUESDAY 13 OCTOBER. Nothing particular to remark, but that at night I had a severe toothache after I was in bed. My wife took the most affectionate care of me by rising and getting me tincture of myrrh, etc. V. At last I fell asleep.

TUESDAY 20 OCTOBER. I intended to have set out for Auchinleck next day, but was detained till a new frock-suit should be made for me. I was in good spirits. I received an excellent letter from my friend Temple, which made me think favourably of myself, without which I never am happy. In the forenoon I called on Dr Blair at his country-house between Edinburgh and Leith,[37] and, at Mr Charles Dilly's desire, made him an offer of £300 for a second volume of his sermons. The Doctor said Strahan had behaved so handsomely to him that he could not but give him the first offer, but he would let me know before a bargain was concluded, that Messieurs Dilly might treat either with himself or with Strahan. I was disgusted with the Doctor's vanity, burring pronunciation, and drawling manner with the Lothian tone. It is in vain to attempt to break associations of ideas. Let a man, instead of losing time in the attempt, choose companions who present to his mind pleasing ideas, unless it be his duty to reconcile himself to those who disgust him, or other companions cannot be had. I dined quietly at home and drank small beer. Lord Advocate's lady's intrigue with Captain Fawkener was now the great topic of discourse.[38] I went and sat an hour with Maclaurin, who had been with her, and heard all the particulars. I then drank tea with Mr George Wallace, knowing that he would relish with me this first rub in the prosperous career of the overbearing Dundases. He read to me part of an essay on the ancient Scottish peerage which he was preparing for the press. I liked it well. (Perhaps I have written too strongly of my dissatisfaction with Dr Blair. But the truth is that the conversation which I enjoy in London has made me very difficult to be pleased.)

WEDNESDAY 21 OCTOBER. Breakfasted at Lady Colville's, and was more upon my guard than usual, being more swift to hear and more slow to speak. Grange dined with us. I drank some cider. I was uneasy from a very trifling cause: want of power of mind to decide whether I should ride or take post-chaise to Auchinleck. I was quite fretted to find myself so weak. Worthy Grange bid me consider how unhappy I was this time twelvemonth when my valuable wife was so ill. This did me good. V.

THURSDAY 22 OCTOBER. It would be ridiculous to mark down the waverings of my mind between riding and taking a chaise. My wife and Grange determined for the latter. I breakfasted early and set out at nine. Poor little Sandy cried to go to

37 Dr Blair had a house at Restalrig (Grant, Vol. III, p. 136).
38 Henry Dundas divorced his wife the following month. She had left him, complaining of neglect. "Doubtless not the first Parliament House widow, she was assuredly not the last... The law of the age was merciless to such women. She forfeited the entire property she had brought into the family, and never saw her children again" (Fry, p. 60).

Auchinleck with me. It was painful to think that he would not be welcome. But I did resolve to take him next year. I was somewhat uneasy at going from home, because my wife and Veronica and little James had all the cold, and I feared they might grow worse. However, I thought it was a duty to pay a visit to my father, and I had to inquire about setting[39] Dalblair and several other things.

Boswell arrived at Auchinleck on 23 October. "My father gave me a pretty good reception", says Boswell. "But his indifference about my wife and children hurt me." Three days later he writes that "my mind was now so very sound that I was constantly serene", and he found himself taking pleasure in rural affairs: planting trees and seeing those which he had planted earlier advancing well; conversing with tenants and contemplating possible improvements to their estates; walking in the grounds of Auchinleck and gathering nuts and pears in the garden to take back to Edinburgh for his children.

On 30 October, the Lord Justice-Clerk, Thomas Miller of Barskimming, arrived and "was in such good spirits and talked so heartily", says Boswell, "that I liked to contemplate him… I regretted that there was an unhappy coolness between him and me. I hoped to bring about better terms in time, though I own I did not wish for an intimacy with so near a neighbour."[40]

Boswell left Auchinleck on 6 November and after a visit to Lord Eglinton's estate—a "den of drunkenness" where, to "humour" the Earl, Boswell drank "small beer, strong beer, old hock, port, and claret till the Earl dissolved the company"—Boswell got back to Edinburgh on 11 November and was "comfortable and happy" to be re-united with his "dear wife and children".

Boswell says that "the winter passed upon the whole pretty well till the close of 1778. I had not much labour as a lawyer, but a competent crop of fees. I renewed my intercourse with Lord Advocate, and had him to dine at my house… I once or twice drank more than was right, and strayed into three different strange countries." The reference to the visits to "strange countries" was evidently an allusion to a number of assignations at Writers' Court and Portsburgh.[41]

---

39 "Letting" or "leasing".
40 The Lord Justice-Clerk's Ayrshire estate of Barskimming was not far from Auchinleck.
41 *Laird*, p. 44, n. 2. An indication of the nature of such assignations is given by Boswell's note of a later visit to Portsburgh (on 30 January 1779): "Having risked yesterday, out between seven and eight to Portsburgh. Tedious to open. Man in closet. Wonderful presence of mind; *to it*. Man off. Going. But allured back: *twice*. Found I was known."

1779

SATURDAY 2 JANUARY. Poor Veronica had this day slipped upon the ice in the Grassmarket, fallen and hit her head against a stair, so that all around one of her eyes was bruised. She had said, "What will my papa say?" I was very affectionately concerned. It pleased me to find honest Effie sitting beside her and diverting her. π.[1]

SUNDAY 3 JANUARY. At home in the forenoon. Between sermons went to my father's; found him not well, with his old complaint. His lady and I dined tête-à-tête disagreeably enough. To make some variety in my feelings, I drank too much bad port, came home inflamed, and after tea got into a shocking bad state of temper. As the only relief, got into bed about seven. Veronica prevailed with me to rise again before nine, by asking "to be allowed to help me on with my clothes, that she might learn to do it when I was old". Grange was sent for. My good spirits returned. We supped agreeably, and drank a bottle of mountain.[2] π.

MONDAY 1 FEBRUARY. I lay long today, did little in the forenoon, went to the burial of the wife of Mr Alexander Gray, Writer to the Signet,[3] from her father a Mr Stewart's house at Sciennes to the Greyfriars churchyard. I was perhaps somehow related to her, for I was one of the pallbearers, as was Hamilton of Wishaw, who is my relation. I make it a kind of pious rule to go to every funeral to which I am invited, both as I wish to pay a proper respect to the dead, unless their characters have been bad, and as I would wish to have the funeral of my own near relations or of myself well attended. I did not feel the least symptom of melancholy or gloom today, so strong was my mind. How it was so, I cannot account. The Reverend Bishop Falconer,[4] Mr Brown, Librarian to the Faculty of Advocates (who had been reader to Mr Thomas Ruddiman,[5] and talked much of him with the Bishop), and Grange dined with us. It was quite a cordial and venerable day, as in the last age. They drank coffee and tea. I suppose the Bishop laid his hands on Veronica's and Effie's heads. I saw him do it to Sandy and Jamie, which pleased me. Grange supped with us. I was warmed with wine at dinner.

TUESDAY 2 FEBRUARY. Lord Monboddo, Maclaurin, Balmuto, Hon. A.

1 An abbreviation of πλεασυρε (as to which, see the entry for 2 June 1777 and relevant footnote).
2 For "mountain", see p. 194, n. 35a.
3 The wife of Alexander Gray (who was admitted W.S. on 30 June 1760) was Ellen Stewart, daughter of Archibald Stewart, a merchant in Edinburgh. Gray had married her in 1773. He himself was to die in January 1780.
4 The Right Rev. William Falconer (or Falconar) was Bishop of Edinburgh in the Episcopal Church of Scotland from 1766 to 1784.
5 Thomas Ruddiman (1674-1757), philologist. He was Keeper of the Advocates' Library from 1730 to 1752 and was succeeded by David Hume.

Gordon, and Mr Dalzell, the advocate,[6] dined with us. It was agreeable to think that two hundred and sixteen years ago there was an alliance between the family of Auchinleck and Mr Dalzell's (afterwards Earl of Carnwath). I drank above a bottle of claret, and was the better of it. Lord Monboddo, Mr Gordon, and Mr Christian[7] drank tea. On my return home from a consultation at Mr Rae's between nine and ten, I found Signora Marcucci, the Italian dancing-mistress who lives in our stair, had taken refuge with my wife, there being an outrageous mob against the papists.[8] It was strange that I heard nothing of it at Mr Rae's, though just at the Cross. I got Grange and walked down the High Street and found so many of the South Fencibles drawn up before the head of Blackfriars Wynd, in which Bishop Hay has his mass-house.[9] But the mob had been for some hours employed in burning a house at the foot of Trunk Close[9a] which formerly belonged to Lord Edgefield[10] and had been lately purchased and fitted up as a Romish chapel. I went close to the scene of action and found so many both of the Town Guard and the Fencibles standing with their arms, which made me suppose that the people whom I heard knocking in the house in flames were extinguishing the fire. But to my astonishment I soon perceived that they were throwing in fuel, and the Lord Provost[11] did not think it prudent to attack them. I was really shocked, and having called silence, I harangued to them a little very keenly; said I loved a mob, but was ashamed of them now, for what could the papists do worse than this? That if the bill should pass, let them march to London and hang Lord North, but as they were assured it was not to pass, why go on in this way?[12] A fellow who did not know me said, "You had better not speak so among the mob." I said, "I'm not afraid of the mob." One who knew me called out with a significant look and manner, "Mr Boswell, you know we're in the right", and then was great huzzaing and no more could be said. It hurt me to see a large book, perhaps some venerable manuscript, come flaming out at one of the windows. One of the mob cried, "They" (i.e., the papists) "burnt us. We'll burn them." Another cried, "Think what they did to our worthy forefathers." It was striking to see what one has read of religious fury realized. I lost Grange in the crowd, and I went with Mr John Pringle, the advocate, to the Calton Hill,

6 Robert Dalzell (1755-1808), advocate (admitted 23 July 1776), second son of Alexander Dalzell, Earl of Carnwath. Appointed Advocate-Depute in 1783.

7 "John Christian, a young man with estates at Milntown in the Isle of Man and Ewanrigg in Cumberland... Lord Ellenborough was his first cousin, as was Fletcher Christian, the *Bounty* mutineer" (*Laird*, p. 2).

8 The riots were the result of popular resentment against proposals to relax the penal laws against Roman Catholics in Scotland.

9 George Hay (1729-1811), Roman Catholic Bishop. "The greatest of the vicars apostolic, Hay succeeded in rehabilitating [Roman Catholicism] after the setbacks of 1745. An able administrator, he was also a prolific devotional writer and controversialist" (*Dictionary of Scottish Church History and Theology*).

9a Off the north side of the east end of the High Street.

10 Robert Pringle, Lord Edgefield, appointed Lord of Session 1754, died 1764.

11 Walter Hamilton (Lord Provost 1778-1780).

12 Henry Dundas, the Lord Advocate, who was M.P. for Edinburghshire from 1774 to 1782 (and again from 1783 to 1790), is said to have indicated during the course of that evening that the bill to allow relief for Catholics in Scotland would be dropped (Fry, p. 74).

where crowds were gathered, and there we saw the conflagration very fully. I came home about ten. Signora Marcucci and Grange supped with us.

I should have mentioned that I received a strange shock this morning. When I came to the Court I saw Mr George Fergusson and several people around him looking surprised and concerned. I asked him what it meant. I shall not forget the affectionate appearance which he had when he said to me, "I am told your father's dead."[13] I was stunned, and knew not what to think or do till Mr Goodwillie[14] was brought to me and told me that he was in a tavern last night when a card came in to Matthew Dickie: "Lord Auchinleck died this evening at eight o'clock." I was then morally certain it was a brutal lie by way of a joke, as I must have heard of it. I sent immediately to Mr Dickie and got the card, which was a palpable forgery, if that term can be properly applied in such a case. Yet I was not quite easy till Mr Lawrie, whom I sent out to my father's to ask *if he was to be out today*, returned and brought me word that he was very well, and was to call his roll of causes at eleven. He accordingly came, looked very well, and gave as far as I could observe a cordial satisfaction to everybody. I got him by the hand with great affection, and was truly comforted after the alarm I had felt, which for a time made me quite giddy. I took no notice to him of the gross trick, and both Balmuto and Grange thought it best not to make any anxious inquiry to find out the wretch who had written the card.

WEDNESDAY 3 FEBRUARY. The mob pillaged Bishop Hay's library in the forenoon with impunity. I went and sat awhile with my father before dinner. Commissioner Cochrane, Charles Preston, and John Webster[15] dined with us. I drank too much port, and was inflamed. Grange walked down with me with intention to go to Canongate-Kilwinning lodge, but there was no meeting, the mob was so violent again tonight. A troop of the 11 Dragoons, commanded by my school-fellow Captain Hart, were placed at the head of the Canongate to protect the corner shop possessed by Daniel Macdonald, grocer, a papist. The mob had broke his windows. I was quite keen to disperse them, and had it not been for worthy Grange I should probably have been hurt. He and I then went to Crosbie's, whom the mob had threatened, as he had drawn up the bill. Twenty dragoons guarded his house for a while, and he had loaded guns and pistols in abundance, and friends about him. As we returned we saw the mob attacking the house of Bayll, the French cook upon the bridge.[16] Grange and Miss Susie Dunlop supped with us. Robert Boswell and Barlay sat awhile, they having been employed in getting some Catholics into the Castle for safety.

FRIDAY 5 FEBRUARY. Laboured well at a law paper in the forenoon. Dined with Mr Gordon, Keeper of the Minute-Book.[17] His brother (a Madeira-merchant), the Hon.

13 Cockburn was later to describe Fergusson (when Lord Hermand) as "tall and thin, with grey lively eyes, and a long face, strongly expressive of whatever emotion he was under" (Cockburn, p. 120).
14 John Goodwillie (or Goodwille)), "writer", the Luckenbooths.
15 Captain John Webster, son of Dr Alexander Webster.
16 For Bayll (or Bayle), see p. 327, n. 29.
17 Alexander Gordon, the Keeper of the Minute-Book in the Court of Session.

A. Gordon, Grange, etc., were there. We drank plentifully both of Madeira and claret, and I was a good deal intoxicated. But our noisy merriment and cordiality were great. I had Answers to write for Sir Walter M.-C.[18] to a complaint against him for cutting trees at Lainshaw, and it was necessary that paper should be done this night so as to be printed next forenoon. It was wonderful how well I dictated seven pages, though there were some flashes of intoxication in it. My dear wife then made me bathe my feet in warm water and clear my stomach by drinking warm water, which made me pretty well, only that I talked grossly.

SATURDAY 6 FEBRUARY. Was wonderfully well, though not firm and steady. The paper which I had dictated last night required a good deal of correction. I dined at my father's. He appeared to be weary with failure.

SUNDAY 7 FEBRUARY. In the evening Veronica said psalms and catechism, and Effie answered a few questions. Miss Cuninghame was threatened with consumptive complaints. I was somewhat drearily affected with thinking of her danger. I was not quite satisfied with the state of my own life at present. But was not very uneasy. π.

TUESDAY 9 FEBRUARY. This was the fast ordered by the King.[19] I did not think myself bound in conscience to keep it; and having a very long Memorial for Mackilston to write, I dictated busily all day.[20] My father was in church for the first time after his indisposition.

SUNDAY 14 FEBRUARY. Went to the New Church with my wife in the afternoon and had some comfort in hearing Mr Walker preach, but was woefully deficient in steady principles. Grange had gone to the country for a day or two. Paid a visit to my father, whom I had not visited since Sunday last. My two daughters and Sandy followed me, and though it came on a pretty heavy rain, they were sent away without the coach. Such cold and unfeeling treatment shocked me. I went home with them. I was feeble and sunk. My father was failed, and his appearance affected me gloomily. Yet I envied the steady, regular, prudent conduct he had maintained through life, and did not think with any

18 Sir Walter Montgomerie-Cuninghame, Bt (died 1814), the impoverished laird of Lainshaw (and nephew of Boswell's wife).

19 The fast had been called as a day of prayer for victory against the French and against the rebels in North America.

20 Although the editors of *Laird* state that when that volume was prepared no copy of this Memorial had been found, a copy has now been found in the Advocates' Library (SPAL, 131:3). The action was by John Alexander-Shaw of McKilston, executor of the deceased John Alexander of McKilston, against Mary Kerr. "A tale worthy of some novel. A week before his death, an aged miser apparently gave his young housekeeper a bill [due to him by a banker in Ayr] for [over] £1000, practically his whole [moveable estate]. She, unable to leave the house, in turn passed the bill to a local squire, who cashed it with speed, not bothering to tell the banker that the old man was at death's door. He then refused to hand over the money to her. Later the miser's executor uncovered the whole affair, leading to the cause to which this paper relates" (*Session Papers*, 79 02 16). Boswell alleged that the endorsement on the back of the bill, although perhaps in the miser's handwriting, was not his usual signature and that the miser had perhaps been persuaded to write his name on it in the belief (induced by the housekeeper) that it was the back of a letter to another person of the same name or that it was to be used as a direction for some parcel which was to be sent to the miser's house. The final outcome of the action is not known.

pleasure of the superior warmth of enjoyment in various ways which had been my lot. I drank coffee and grew a little better at night. Was affectionate to my wife and children.

Sir George Preston died at Valleyfield on 2 March and Boswell attended the funeral. On 10 March Boswell set off for another jaunt to London, stopping off on the way to visit his brother John at Newcastle, where Boswell found John to be "remarkably well", talking "quite sensibly", and in such a state as to enable Boswell to "indulge brotherly affection".

At London, Boswell was embraced with "cordial complacency" by Dr Johnson. "He looked better than ever I saw him do," says Boswell, "and I was in better health and spirits than I ever experienced, so all was gladness." As on his previous visit, Boswell lodged at Paoli's house and, once again, proceeded to lead a hectic social life.

Boswell attended (as an observer) the celebrated trial of the Rev. James Hackman, who had shot Lord Sandwich's mistress, Martha Ray, with whom he was infatuated and who had rejected his proposal of marriage, and had then attempted to kill himself. Hackman was found guilty and sentenced to be hanged. Boswell, who had a morbid fascination for such scenes, attended Hackman's execution at Tyburn on 19 April, but felt himself "little affected in comparison of what might [have] been expected".

Having sat for another dinner at the Inner Temple to complete another "term", Boswell departed for Edinburgh on 4 May, worried by news from his wife that his father, although "in no immediate danger", was "so much indisposed" that she thought Boswell should not be absent. Boswell reached Edinburgh on 10 May and was greeted enthusiastically by his family, but ascertained that his father was in fact sufficiently well as to be departing for a trip to Auchinleck.

Later that month, Boswell appeared in two cases before the General Assembly. The second of these cases—in which Boswell represented a Peter Lumisden, who had appealed against a finding of adultery by the synod of Perth and Stirling—was due to be heard by the General Assembly on 27 May, and Boswell planned to depart for Auchinleck the following day.

THURSDAY 27 MAY. In General Assembly getting time fixed for Lumisden; committee appointed at eight. Dined at the Golf House[21] with the West Fencibles. Vastly jovial, but drank greatly too much. Capt. James Campbell came up with me. I was not able to speak. But at any rate, committee had resolved not to hear us. Home very ill.

FRIDAY 28 MAY. Awaked ill and vexed at excess. Thought it very wrong that I had not been able to speak. No tickets to be had in flies. So stayed another day. Lucky this, as the cause came on in the Assembly and I spoke a little; so won my fee.[22] Was assured by the committee that they would not have let me speak at any rate. But as I was conscious I was not able, it was a nice casuistical case whether I could take my fee. Harry Erskine said I should. For it was my *luck* that they would not let me speak. But as I spoke this forenoon in the Assembly, the

---

21 At Leith Links.
22 Boswell may have won his fee, but he lost his case.

thing was made clear. I had first seen the Highland mutineers pardoned on the Castle Hill, the West Fencibles being all drawn up.[23]

Boswell then set off that afternoon for Auchinleck, travelling initially on horseback. He found the riding not at all easy, and that night, at Holytown, he went to bed directly— "[with] all my bones sore", he records. The following morning, Boswell had a lift in a chaise to Glasgow, but there he remounted and rode to Auchinleck, arriving there in the evening. He found his father "better and rather more kind".

A few days later, Boswell visited Annie Cuninghame, who was very unwell. "Found Miss Cuninghame quite pale and emaciated and solitary", wrote Boswell. "It was very affecting. But I put on cheerfulness... Poor girl! She said she sometimes thought it was better for her not to recover, as she had already suffered a great part, and she would have to suffer it all over again. She spoke really with resentment (just indeed) of Lady Auchinleck, and said she wished only she could live to see her obliged to quit Auchinleck, which, though she might have pride enough to conceal it from me, would vex or gall her (or some such word). She said how could she set herself up in the corner of the seat at church, and pretend to be religious, when nothing could be more wicked than to estrange a father from his children? She might well be said to make religion a cloak for maliciousness[24]... I got home in good time, and was so shocked with thinking of Lady Auchinleck's barbarous indifference that I was very silent. At night alone, I was tenderly sad for the amiable, distressed young creature, Miss Cuninghame."

On 7 June, Boswell was alarmed by news from his wife that she had been ill again with a spitting of blood and that she was very anxious for his return. He duly set off the following day, passing on the way his moorland estate of Dalblair, which, he says, "I surveyed with unskilful satisfaction at its extent and regret at its small rent."

Boswell reached Edinburgh on 9 June and found his wife to be better and his children "quite overjoyed" to see him again. "Effie and Sandy actually cried", he records.

SATURDAY 12 JUNE. The Session sat down. But there were only six lords present, so nothing could be done. It was indecent to see no quorum. Old Thomas Belsches[25] said to me that if such a thing were to happen in Westminster Hall, the King would be addressed with a complaint. I was in good steady health and spirits. Sir Alexander Dick came in his chaise and carried me and Sandy out to dine with him. He was amiable and pleasing as ever as we drove along. But after dinner he seemed failed and took a nap. It hurt me to see his decline. It was agreeable to think that his daughter, Miss Dick, was staying with my wife at present. After tea Sir Alexander's coach carried me home, as it rained hard. Mr and Miss Macredie and young Macredie supped with us. π.

MONDAY 14 JUNE. I had yesterday received a letter from my father, enclosing his excuse to Lord President for not coming to the Session. I had asked him to

---

23 The Highlanders had mutinied at Leith on 20 April on account of a rumour that they were to be drafted into a Lowland regiment. Three of the mutineers were condemned to death after a trial by court-martial, but they were subsequently pardoned by the King, and the pardon was read to them on the Castle Hill.
24 I Peter 2. 16.
25 A "writer".

send it to me, as it was decent and proper for his son to deliver it, and as I knew that my waiting on the President, which I had not done for several years, would be agreeable to my father; and this was a good opportunity. I called this morning.[26] But he was confined to bed with a flying gout, so I did not see him, but left the letter. In the evening, however, I wrote a few lines to him, mentioning that I had called and begging he would write to my father not to come in to this Summer Session. He sent me for answer that he was not able to write, but I should hear from him. This forenoon I was consulted by the Earl of Dundonald on a troublesome cause between him and Captain William Roberton.[27] His Lordship, Commissioner Cochrane, and Mr Ramsay of the Excise dined and drank tea with us. A little wine and rum punch disturbed me. I was unable, at least quite unwilling, to labour.

TUESDAY 15 JUNE. Should have written and sent off *The Hypochondriack* No. 21.[28] But delayed it from mere aversion to any kind of application. There were judges enough in the Court today. Business in the Court of Session appeared to me more dull and inconsiderable than ever, except when my mind has been sick with low spirits, which was not the case now. Walked half round the Meadow with Lord Monboddo. Felt a deficiency of knowledge and of vigour of mind.

THURSDAY 17 JUNE. Was at the review of the West Fencibles on Leith Links. Was much pleased and animated. But was put out of conceit with the drudgery of the profession of the law. Major Montgomerie[29] and Captain Kennedy of that regiment went home with me before dinner and refreshed themselves with cider and Madeira and rum and water. I drank some cider and Madeira, which warmed my animal spirits and made me think for the time of good social intercourse as the most valuable employment of time. I began to my *Hypochondriack* No. 21 and laboured close at it all the afternoon, hoping to have it ready for the post. But could not accomplish it. So wrote to Mr Dilly that it should come by next post. Wrote with a fluency of ideas and expression which surprised me. But was uneasy to feel myself much averse to labour as a lawyer, and at the same time uneasy that my practice seemed to be scanty this Session, only two consultations having come. I dwelt with comfort on the estate of Auchinleck. But I resolved to be assiduous this first session of my father's absence, as that was to be considered as a trying era for me, because people might imagine that I would not apply to business when he was not present.

FRIDAY 18 JUNE. Lord President had sent me yesterday a letter to my father. I called on him again this morning. But he was gone to Arniston. Worthy Grange

26 The Lord President's house was in Adam's Court (see the entry for 28 January 1768 and footnote).
27 The Earl of Dundonald was Archibald Cochrane, the 9th Earl (son of Thomas Cochrane, the 8th Earl, who had died on 27 June 1778). He was a gifted inventor and superintended the family's coal mines and salt works at Culross, Kincardine and Valleyfield. The action in which Boswell was involved was concerned with a claim by the manager of the coal and salt works, Captain William Roberton, for sums allegedly due under the contract entered into between him and the Earl. The claim was in the sum of £2,000, but on 15 July Lord Alva was to grant decree for only £979 (*Laird*, p. 111, n. 9).
28 The subject of the essay was quotations.
29 Major Hugh Montgomerie of Skelmorlie and Coilsfield (as to whom, see p. 315, n. 1).

had returned last night. I sat awhile with him in the forenoon. He dined and drank tea with me, and we went and heard Wesley[30] preach in the evening, and afterwards were at the roll-calling of the West Fencibles with my wife and the children. Was uneasy that I could not consistently with my business upon hand ask a number of the officers to sup with me. Felt a kindly sort of pity for them, as if they did not know well where to spend the evening. This was foolish, I dare say, as they probably were most of them agreeably engaged, and perhaps pitied me as a dull drudge. I finished No. 21 and sent it off. But a long Memorial for Lord Dundonald hung over me. π.

SATURDAY 19 JUNE. I drank tea at Grange's and conversed rationally on the value of land and such solid topics with him and Mr Gordon, Keeper of the Minute-Book. My wife and I played cards and supped at Mr Sinclair of Freswick's. John Fordyce was there, the first time of my being in company with him since his bankruptcy.[31] I took no manner of notice of him, as I have all along thought that his living in plenty while numbers have been reduced to indigence by him, is (without going deeper) such dishonesty that he ought not to receive any countenance. Besides, his manners are forward and assuming, and he is a fellow of low extraction. It was unpleasant to sit in his company. It kept me from being gay and convivial.

SUNDAY 20 JUNE. Heard Mr Walker lecture and preach in the New Church in the forenoon. Dined with Lord Monboddo, to whose card of invitation I had answered that I seldom dined abroad on Sunday; but I considered him as a *sacerdos*,[32] by whose conversation my mind was improved. Maclaurin and Runciman, the painter,[33] were his other guests. Maclaurin told my Lord that he liked his book better than anything he had read upon metaphysics.[34] But that the great defect in all the systems as to a future state (that of Mahomet excepted) was that they did not represent the next world as agreeable, so that we would much rather choose to remain in this. Monboddo said if a man had a proper taste for intellectual pleasure, which was the highest of any, he would think a future state very agreeable. Maclaurin owned that his father had great satisfaction in mathematics.[35] "Well," said Monboddo, "if there is so much satisfaction in the contemplation of lines and figures, which is but an inferior species of intellectual enjoyment, how much more must there be in the contemplation of higher subjects, of GOD and providence and all his operations?" But to have this high relish, our minds must be cultivated and spiritualized.

30 John Wesley, the famous Methodist preacher, who was visiting Edinburgh for a few days.
31 John Fordyce, from Ayton in Berwickshire, had been head of an Edinburgh banking house which had collapsed in 1772.
32 A priest (Latin).
33 Alexander Runciman (1736-85).
34 The first volume of Monboddo's 6-volume *Antient Metaphysics* had been published earlier this year. "Here ancient philosophy is maintained against David Hume... and against the physical theories of Sir Isaac Newton. To ancient Greece we are told to look for all truth and for all physical and intellectual perfection" (Graham, p. 192).
35 His father was the celebrated Colin Maclaurin (1698-1746), Professor of Mathematics at the University of Edinburgh.

Monboddo would not allow a philosopher to indulge in women as a pleasure, but only as an evacuation; for he said that a man who used their embraces as a pleasure would soon have that enjoyment as a business, than which nothing could make one more despicable.

MONDAY 21 JUNE. My wife was seized again with a little spitting of blood. I did very little. Grange dined with us.

WEDNESDAY 23 JUNE. Attended with some satisfaction to the reasonings of the Lords upon causes before them. Miss Macredie dined and drank tea. Commissioner Cochrane and Mr James Baillie[36] drank tea. I again called at Lord President's. His servant said he was gone out a little. I left a card with my name, and resolved not to call again till he either called on me or made some advance. I was not in good humour at present, though not very bad either. I was dissatisfied at not making a better figure in life; at not having more business as a lawyer, nor any office under Government. I thought myself insignificant. This was not reasonable. But who is long content in this state of being?

FRIDAY 25 JUNE. Was happy at finishing a troublesome Memorial for Lord Dundonald. Drank tea at Mr Samuel Mitchelson's, Junior, the Earl's agent, and talked of the cause. This week, and particularly this day, fees came in so well that I got up again in spirits as to my practice at the bar.

I was now in very good spirits. But what was I doing? I was engaged in no sort of study. I was not improving my mind. I had a fine letter this week from my friend Temple which humbled me. For it showed me that he continued constant to literature, so that *in himself* he was much my superior. But then as a social being I had the advantage of him. I was doing pretty well as an advocate. I was bringing up my children. I had good hopes of obtaining some preferment by Lord Mountstuart's interest, and if I lived, I was to succeed to an estate of £1,500 a year. It however hurt me to be sensible that I was deficient in vigour of mind, was not enough a *man*. But then I could not tell but others, who appeared to me sufficiently manly, might feel as I did. Upon the whole, I had no just reason to complain. π.

SATURDAY 26 JUNE. Grange dined with us. He and I walked to Leith, drank a bottle of porter, eat speldings[37] and bread, and walked up again.

SUNDAY 27 JUNE. Heard Dr Blair in the forenoon and Mr Walker in the afternoon. Dr Webster dined with us between sermons. He drank to poor Miss Cuninghame in a mode truly remarkable, as perhaps the last time: "All happiness to her here and hereafter." We were both warmed a little with wine, though we drank but little. I heard the children say the Lord's prayer, etc. I read a good part of Goldsmith's first volume of the *History of the Earth* with pleasing wonder.

MONDAY 28 JUNE. Sat awhile with Maclaurin and got instruction from

36 A "writer".
37 Small salted fish, dried in the sun.

him on the law concerning adjudications.[38] Dined early and hastily, that I might attend the judicial sale of Crawfordston, which I was informed would go cheap. Matthew Dickie engaged to be my cautioner[39] to the extent of £1,200. I have really a rage for buying land in the shire of Ayr, and I had a kind of curious inclination to purchase this small estate because my grandfather had written in old Crawfordston's chamber. But it went £200 above my price.

SATURDAY 3 JULY. Sir James Campbell (Lieut.-Colonel), Captains Earl of Glencairn,[40] Craigends, and Dunure, and Lieutenants Sir William Cuninghame and McDowall of the West Fencibles, Lord Monboddo, Mr Crosbie, Lady Colville and Lady Anne Erskine and Miss Susie Dunlop dined with us. I was steady though jovial, and passed an excellent day, though without much other conversation than social dialogue; and although I drank freely, I was not drunk. In the evening my wife was in uncommon good humour, just as during courtship. It was very fine.

SUNDAY 4 JULY. Was somewhat uneasy with the excess of yesterday. Lay long and breakfasted in bed. Then Grange and I walked out to Prestonfield and found worthy Sir Alexander very well, and had a pleasing walk and social seat in the garden, we three alone, the sun shining warmly upon us. We dined with him. Had his chaise into town, and drank tea at my house, where we found Old Lady Wallace. In the evening I heard the children say psalms, etc., and read some of Goldsmith's *History of the Earth.*

MONDAY 5 JULY. It was an exceeding wet day. Grange dined with us. I took a chair and went to the judicial sale of Lainshaw, which was to have come on this afternoon. It hurt me much that Lainshaw, where I had been so happy and which had been a very permanent idea in my mind, should be disconnected. There was but one offerer, and we got the sale adjourned till next day.

TUESDAY 6 JULY. I gave in a Petition to the Lords for the postponed creditors on Lainshaw,[41] and had a warm debate at the bar with the counsel for Douglas, Heron, and Company, who wanted the sale to proceed. But I got it adjourned to Thursday the 15. This was a sort of reprieve.

THURSDAY 8 JULY. I was to dine with Major Montgomerie at the mess at Fortune's. I went up to him in the Castle before dinner; drank some excellent porter, which set me a-going. Walked down with him to the mess and drank so heartily there that I was quite intoxicated. It was a very hot day. I went to the roll-calling at night on the Castle Hill, and talked a great deal to many people.

---

38 The law of adjudication, which has changed little since 1672, enables a creditor, by obtaining a decree of adjudication, to acquire a judicial security over the land or other heritable property of his debtor. The decree entitles the creditor to have the debtor removed from the property and to collect any rents of the property towards his debt. Should the debt remain outstanding after ten years, the creditor can obtain a title to the property, thus becoming the owner (Gretton, *The Law of Inhibition and Adjudication*, 2nd edn, pp. 208-9 and 220).
39 That is, to be guarantor.
40 James Cunningham (1749-1791), 13th Earl of Glencairn, appointed Captain of the West Fencible Regiment in 1778.
41 All that remains of the process in this case is the inventory, which discloses that the petition was against William Brown (the factor on the estate of Lainshaw) and Sir Walter Montgomerie (N.A.S. CS.237 L1/115).

I did not recollect one word that I said. But Mr Lawrie told me that Lord Dunmore and I took off our hats to one another and bowed very often. So we had been very complimentary. His Lordship had dined at the mess, but was sober. I asked him and Sir James Campbell and Sir John Paterson of Eccles to sup with me, and I went home to give notice. They all came, but by that time I was so ill that I was obliged to go to bed. My valuable spouse behaved admirably, had supper prepared, and pressed them to stay. But they did not.

FRIDAY 9 JULY. I awaked in sad distress and in great vexation at what had happened last night. I was very grateful to my wife and said she was worth a million. I had some enjoyment during this day (which was also very warm) in cooling my blood with lemonade. My father had desired me in his letter to wait on the Lord President and tell him he was better. As I had left my name at his house and had never heard from him, I did not choose to appear to court him; and therefore I just showed him the letter as he sat today in his chair in the Court of Session.

SATURDAY 10 JULY. It was very agreeable to be calm and easy after yesterday's fever. I spoke very well before the Lords for a *cessio bonorum* to young Carruthers of Hardriggs.[42] Grange and I walked slowly out to Prestonfield. It was a very warm day. We sat down in the garden and eat raw turnips. There was no company at dinner but Mr Mercer, the wine-merchant, and Mr Robert Gillespie. The worthy Knight was remarkably well. But had little conversation in comparison of what I have heard him have. I was indolent myself and satisfied with little. Grange and I walked in to tea and drank it agreeably with my wife. Painter Donaldson also was with us. I went up to the Castle and sat awhile with Duntroon. He and Sir William Cuninghame and Grange and Captain Graham of the Scots Dutch, Mrs Dr Grant, and Miss Grant supped with us cheerfully. I drank only cider, one glass of wine, and negus. I was existing easily, my sore toe excepted. But I was neither advancing in knowledge, nor rising in life, nor, in short, doing anything of which I could boast. Yet I was very well satisfied. Even my practice as a lawyer was very scanty. What a state of mind is this? Not a bad one. π.

MONDAY 12 JULY. Mr Alexander Wood looked at my sore toe, which was very painful. He advised me to wait till it was better, and then he would cut the nail. Either yesterday or today my dearest wife found out from me that my visit to [a woman at] the Pleasance [on 1 July] had been in the day and when sober, which hurt her.[43]

TUESDAY 13 JULY. Little done. My practice was sadly deficient, and my toe very troublesome.

42 Boswell was instructed in this case by John Johnston of Grange, who borrowed most of the writs in the process on 8 July 1779 and never returned them (N.A.S. CS.228 C10/30). A *cessio bonorum* was "an equitable relief from the severity of the law of imprisonment for debt". The action was by way of summons in the Court of Session at the instance of the insolvent debtor, who had to call all his creditors. The debtor was required to produce a full statement of his affairs and to "satisfy the court that his inability to pay his debts had arisen from innocent misfortunes" (*Bell's Dictionary of the Law of Scotland*, 7th edn, p. 157).
43 The Pleasance, a suburb to the east of the city, was described at this time as consisting of "one mean street: through it lies the principal road to London. There is nothing remarkable in this suburb except a large brewery, with spacious vaults, belonging to Mr Bell, where the best strong beer is made of any brewed for sale in Scotland" (Arnot, p. 190).

WEDNESDAY 14 JULY. I never passed a more insignificant summer than I am now doing.

THURSDAY 15 JULY. I had tolerable practice this week, though but little money. The sale of Lainshaw came on before Lord Elliock. It sold for about £2,000 more than it would have done on the 5th, which was so much that I gained to the younger children by obtaining an adjournment. All my endeavours by writing to different people to try if they would bid for Lainshaw proved ineffectual. While the macer was calling out, "The lands and estate of Lainshaw", I felt as if I were stunned by some dismal, wonderful casualty. I was glad that Mr Cuninghame,[44] who had a gentleman's name, got it rather than Mr Speirs. My dearest wife was much affected. When I came out from the sale, I met her walking from a shop in the Parliament Close. Grange and I accompanied her home. She went into her own room a little and shed tears. I could almost have done the same. Grange drank tea with us. At eight o'clock he went with me to the Pantheon, to which I had been particularly invited this night, as it was to be debated "Whether the British Legislature could alter the Articles of the Union?" I had no mind to go. But as they had made me an honorary member, I thought it would be uncivil to resist a pressing invitation. I was pretty well entertained. But what was strange, I was so bashful inwardly that I delayed to speak till I had only time to give a short flourish seconding a motion to adjourn the debate till this day sennight, that it might be maturely considered. Grange came home with me and we supped on cold meat and drank negus. My valuable spouse had recovered her cheerfulness, and we were comfortable. She was so very good as to be disposed in two nights' time to forgive what I feared would have remained long against me. I vowed fidelity, and it was my sincere resolution to devote my utmost attention to make her easy and as happy as possible, and now that her own family was quite extinguished, to make up to her for the want to the utmost of my power. It is amazing how callous one may grow as to what is wrong by the practice of it. I trust this night's resolutions will by GOD'S grace make me act as a good husband and father of a family. My father's absence this summer, I suppose, lessened my practice. But it gradually habituated me to be without that respectable protection. π.

SATURDAY 17 JULY. My toe was very uneasy; but what was worse, I for the first time since I last left London felt myself in low spirits. A *cessio bonorum* for young Hardriggs, in which Grange was agent and very anxious came on. I spoke well enough. But the Lords were not in good humour, and delayed it till we should *condescend* more specially.[45] This disconcerted us a good deal. I should have dined at Prestonfield by invitation with Andrew Frazer[46] and his lady and some more company. But was so sickly in mind that I could not bear the thoughts of cheerful company, and so contracted by disease that I grudged coach hire. So I sent an apology. I was vexed afterwards. I roused myself and wrote a very good

---

44 William Cuninghame of Bridgehouse, a wealthy tobacco merchant (*Laird*, p. 120, n. 2).
45 That is, provide fuller written particulars.
46 Captain Andrew Frazer, son of George Frazer, excise officer (*Laird*, p. 537).

additional Condescendence for young Hardriggs. Grange and Mr James Baillie drank tea with us. π.

SUNDAY 18 JULY. I had resolved to try what rest would do for my sore toe; and as I had also a pretty heavy cold, I lay in bed all forenoon, drank tea and eat bread and butter and honey plentifully, and read *Rasselas* from beginning to end. I resolve to read it once every year. I rose before two and dined on soup maigre[47] and bread and water. Lay all afternoon upon a sofa and read in Goldsmith's *History of the Earth, etc.*, and in Burke's *Sublime and Beautiful*, which it is strange to think I never read before. I fell into a slumber some part of the time, and awaked disturbed, thinking of death, of Lainshaw being sold, and of other dreary subjects. I was gloomy and dejected. I heard the children say little today. It lessened me sadly in my own estimation to be conscious of such a *break* in my existence. But I should conceal it.

MONDAY 19 JULY. My spirits were very bad. I dictated a law paper with difficulty. Lord Eglinton called for a little before dinner. I was awkward and indifferent, and had no satisfaction in anything. My toe was painful, and I had an excoriation which alarmed me lest it might be a taint from my Pleasance adventure. But I hoped it might be only a little heat from the very warm weather. Grange dined with us. I finished today Burke's *Sublime and Beautiful*. Wrote to Dr Johnson upon various topics.

TUESDAY 20 JULY. Was still in worse spirits than yesterday. But dictated law very well. My dear wife insisted on my going in a coach with her and Veronica and Effie and Sandy to the sands of Leith to see part of one of the races.[48] There was no sport.[49] But the variety of company did me good insensibly. I was much obliged to her. She also persuaded me to go to the Assembly at night, which did me more good. Before I went to it, we had a visit from Lord Chief Baron.[50] I came home before twelve and drank negus cheerfully.

WEDNESDAY 21 JULY. This day I insensibly recovered good spirits. Grange dined with us, and he and I drank cider with relish. I dictated law well.

THURSDAY 22 JULY. I had in the course of this session resumed my old seat in the *Laigh Parliament House*[51] and copied some more of the Privy Council records. Nothing composes my mind more than that kind of occupation. I associate it with being like my father, a laborious antiquarian. Miss Dick was with us at present. I went this evening to the Pantheon, and in order to oblige the Society who had made me an honorary member and to get some reputation among people of various ranks and professions who would spread it, I had studied the question, and I spoke really well to show that such Articles of the Union as

---

47 Without meat.
48 "The Leith race week was a species of carnival to the citizens of Edinburgh, and in many instances caused a partial suspension of work and business" (Grant, Vol. III, p. 269).
49 This probably means that there was no race while the Boswells were there.
50 James Montgomery of Stanhope, former Lord Advocate and now Lord Chief Baron of Exchequer.
51 The lower Parliament House, i.e., the basement below Parliament House. See also the entry for 16 August 1773.

are not plainly temporary, or when no reservations are made, cannot be altered by the British Legislature, which *sits under those Articles*. The debate becoming rather too grave and serious, I rose again and made a reply which produced high entertainment and applause, expressing my anxiety lest the fair part of the audience should go from the Pantheon with a decision which would alarm them. For of what were we debating—Whether a *contract* is to be kept? Whether Articles of *Union* are to be kept? I assimilated the Union between England and Scotland—the stronger and the weaker country—to a contract of marriage. I had great pleasure tonight in speaking, and the question carried by a great majority for my opinion.

FRIDAY 23 JULY. I dictated very easily. My wife and I dined at Lord Chief Baron's;[52] Lord Eglinton, Lord Haddington,[53] etc., there. It was half an hour after six before we sat down to table, the race was so late. My toe was painful. Mr Wood told me today I had a corn which he would cut, and the thought of an *operation* frightened me. I also still feared some taint, so was not at ease. However, I took claret plentifully, though it was not of flavour to my relish. Sir Patrick Warrender (with those I have mentioned) and I sat till half an hour past twelve very socially, drinking slowly. I walked home. By the way from bad habit stopped a little with a girl on the street, but soon took myself and had no sort of connexion with her. Was not drunk, but took warm water and cleared my stomach.

SATURDAY 24 JULY. Was exceedingly ill and obliged to lie all forenoon in bed. It vexed me that I had several causes to attend. But Mr Lawrie got them well managed for me, and it is wonderful how the mind acquiesces in necessity. Was better after getting up and taking soup, and my wife and I walked out and saw my father, who had come in last night. I fairly told what had detained me. He was much better.

TUESDAY 27 JULY. My father came to the Court and called two causes. I dined with him. Wished to have somebody to divert me at night. Matthew Dickie supped with me.

WEDNESDAY 28 JULY. Practice was very scanty and I was sadly discouraged. Commissioner Cochrane called on me in the morning and told me that my father was anxious to have Dr Gillespie[54] to attend him constantly and intended to settle upon him £200 a year during his own life and £50 a year after his death, during the Doctor's life; and the Commissioner said that he had said to my father that his son should be informed of all his transactions now; that my father answered, "Might he not dispose of his own money?" but added, "You may do as you please." The Commissioner therefore desired that I would meet him at my father's in the evening and tell my father that I approved of the plan. I suggested that I should now have an additional £100 a year from my father, as my family was

---

52 Lord Chief Baron Montgomery's residence was at Queensberry House in the Canongate. For Queensberry House, see the entry for 19 July 1769 and relevant footnote.
53 For Lord Haddington, see p. 132, n. 89a.
54 Thomas Gillespie, M.D.

increased. The Commissioner said it had occurred to himself. But that it should not be mentioned at present when my father was giving away £200 a year. I had some difficulty as to the propriety of this bargain with Gillespie, when it was first mentioned. But I considered that as my father had done a great deal for his family, he had a good right to make himself comfortable; that what he paid in his own time would probably not have been saved for me; and that £50 a year was not a heavy burthen upon me. I made no objection to the Commissioner, and agreed to meet him. Lady Wallace, Miss Susie Dunlop, and Miss Dick dined with us. I went to my father's after dinner, and when I had him alone, told him that I thought he was quite right to secure Dr Gillespie. It shocked me when he pronounced the words, "He is to have £50 a year *after I'm dead*." My father's death is to me a dreary idea. He seemed pleased with what I said as to his fixing Gillespie. But he showed himself still shrewd and sagacious, for he suggested that it should be inserted in the agreement with Gillespie that he should have his £200 a year only while he was able to officiate, as he might perhaps become incapable. I drank tea at my father's. His lady was as disagreeable as ever. But I was wonderfully guarded. I never thought I could have been so much so. It is, however, disagreeable to me to be obliged to practise any dissimulation.

SATURDAY 31 JULY. Dined at my father's, my two daughters and Sandy with me. Nobody at table but himself and Lady Auchinleck and her sister and Robert Boswell. He seemed to be indifferent about the children. As there were no strangers there before whom I could be ashamed of the coldness to my children, I was pretty easy. Stayed to tea. This was a very poor week. I got but two guineas. I was vexed too at Grange's uneasiness that Christopher Carruthers's *cessio bonorum* was put off again, and that he did not think me keen enough about it. In the evening I read so much of a journal kept by the deceased Mr Bogle of Hamilton Farm, which had been produced in a process of reduction of a bond for £5,000 obtained from him by fraud. He had absolutely died of intemperance and dissolute conduct of every kind. Yet he had for some time kept a regular diary of his life and account of his expenses; and in that diary his acts of profligacy were recorded in plain terms, and his folly and vanity set down, while at the same time there were several reflections on his own insignificancy and on the unhappiness of life, which I excerpted. Reading this journal made me uneasy to think of my own. It is preserving evidence against oneself; it is filling a mine which may be sprung by accident or intention. Were my journal to be discovered and made public in my own lifetime, how shocking would it be to me! And after my death, would it not hurt my children? I must not be so plain.

MONDAY 2 AUGUST. It was a wet day. I wrote an additional Condescendence for young Hardriggs. Grange and I went and saw *Macbeth* acted. He supped with me.

THURSDAY 5 AUGUST. Balbarton dined with us. My wife and I drank tea at Lady Dundonald's, all the children with us. I supped at Lord Kames's with Mr Nairne and Lady Wallace. Passed a very cheerful evening.

FRIDAY 6 AUGUST. Was applied to by the Honourable Andrew Erskine for a loan of £50 by a letter yesterday. Wrote to him today that I was vexed I could not supply him, as my credit with the bank was almost exhausted. But I desired he would call on me in the Parliament House this forenoon. He did so, and talked in such a manner that I resolved to try what could be done. I spoke to my dear wife, who, with her usual generosity of disposition, was for my advancing the sum, as I had found honest James Baillie ready to let me have it in case I should want it before the first of February, on which day Erskine had engaged to repay it. Grange dined with us. In the evening I lent Erskine the money, telling him it was really a favour. I hope I shall one day be easy in my circumstances, for I have friendship in a high degree. I sauntered in the New Town with Erskine. I said it was a misfortune to have too lively an imagination—to see the end of our pursuits—for that prevented us from being keen. Erskine said, "Seeing their end often prevents their beginning."

SATURDAY 7 AUGUST. Spoke pretty well in the Inner House on a short reduction on death-bed.[55]

SUNDAY 8 AUGUST. Surgeon Wood called, poor Effie having been ill. He was violent against my father's settlement on Dr Gillespie, which he said Gillespie told him was £200 a year for five years certain, besides £50 a year for his life afterwards. This stunned me. But I resolved to keep myself quiet, and thought it might be set aside as an imposition upon an old man in a state of failure.

TUESDAY 10 AUGUST. Accounts came of poor Miss Cuninghame's death. My wife bore the news of her niece's death pretty well. But it affected us both in a tender manner.

WEDNESDAY 11 AUGUST. This day the Summer Session rose. It vexed me that I had received not one half so much money in fees as I had done in other summer sessions of late years. Yet it was some comfort to me that my practice was apparently not less; nay, that I had written more than last Summer Session.

THURSDAY 12 AUGUST. Was uneasy about the settlement on Dr Gillespie. Called on Lord Advocate and talked to him confidentially of my father's failure, and of that settlement. His Lordship, though he and I have not been on good terms for years, was very obliging, seemed to think the settlement might be reduced on incapacity and imposition, but was of opinion that it could not affect me as heir of entail. I thought being thus confidential might pave the way to Lord Advocate and me being better together.

SUNDAY 22 AUGUST. By appointment when in good spirits last night, worthy Grange and I walked out to Duddingston church and heard the apostolic Mr William Bennet (as I call him), and saw the Earl of Abercorn sitting with stately decency in his loft. After which we walked into the manse and tasted Mr

---

55 That is, a judicial setting aside of a deed or will made by a person on his death-bed.

Bennet's whisky, then accompanied Lady Dick to Prestonfield, and found the excellent Sir Alexander pleasingly well. It was a charming day, and he walked with us in the garden as amiable as ever. There was nobody at dinner but ourselves. We walked home quietly. My wife and Miss Dick had walked out to Prestonfield thinking to find us there. Effie made tea to us, Veronica being in the garden. I did not hear Veronica say anything divine tonight. Effie and Sandy did what they could. Grange supped with us.

MONDAY 23 AUGUST. The alarm of the French and Spanish fleets being in the Channel kept up an agitation. I really felt little. My toe was now very easy.

WEDNESDAY 25 AUGUST. I dined at Commissioner Cochrane's.[56] General Stewart was there. I drank a bottle of claret. Was heated. Called at a house in Portsburgh and had some porter. P.D.[57]

THURSDAY 26 AUGUST. Grange dined with us. I took a desire for rum punch, which I generally dislike, and drank heartily of it. He and I drank tea with M. Dupont and Miss Scott at their country-house near Broughton.

SUNDAY 29 AUGUST. My father was in his own seat in the New Church. But he looked to be much decayed. My wife and I were there too. I went out in the coach with him and the ladies and dined with him. Lady Auchinleck read aloud a sermon of Dr Blair's after dinner. My wife and children came to tea. It was sad work. I heard the children say divine lessons at night. Dr Webster and his daughter dined with my wife today.

MONDAY 30 AUGUST. Went with Maclaurin, Crosbie, and Sinclair of Freswick and saw the observatory.[58]

TUESDAY 31 AUGUST. Matthew Dickie had been frequently asking me to make an appointment with him to dine at my father's. My father had said to me he would be very glad to see him when I said he talked of coming out; but as dinner had not been specified, I was uneasy this morning to think that I had engaged Matthew for today. So out I went, and mentioned before my father and Lady Auchinleck that he was talking of dining there today. Upon which she flew into a very violent passion and abused Matthew most terribly, alleging that it was he himself who had written, by way of wit, the false card on the 2 February last pretending to announce my father's death. I declared upon my honour I never

56 Commissioner Cochrane was no longer residing at Pinkie but had moved to Dalry House, a seventeenth-century mansion house in Dalry, then a suburb to the west of the city. This fine house, which still stands (in Orwell Place), was acquired by Cochrane in 1778 and was to be his home until his death on 2 October 1788 (Cant, *Edinburgh: Gorgie and Dalry*, p. 8; *B.O.E.C.*, Vol. 20, pp. 42-3).
57 The editors of *Laird* surmise (at p. 131, n. 9) that these initials may have stood for Peggie Dundas.
58 The observatory, situated on Calton Hill, was at this time still under construction, not being completed until 1792. The project had started in 1776 when the Town Council acquired a large reflecting telescope of James Short (1710-68), the celebrated maker of scientific instruments, but progress on the building was very slow through lack of funds. Writing in 1779, Arnot observed: "Thus an optical instrument, perhaps the finest in the world, is lost for want of a proper place to keep it in; and the observatory stands a half-finished work upon the highest hill of Edinburgh, speaking this emphatick language to the eye of every beholder: 'Here is a building, which the folly of its contrivers led them to begin, without considering, that, by their poverty, they were unable to finish it'" (Arnot, p. 246).

suspected him, and I was surprised how she had heard of such a shocking thing. She in rage answered, "I hear much more than that", seeming to signify that she heard bad things of me. I was quite calm, and said it was hard to entertain such a suspicion against a poor man unless she could give a reason. She said my father had never heard of it before. He insisted to know what it was, and I told him. He acquitted poor Matthew of any suspicion; and with more spirit than I thought he now could show, insisted that I should bring him out to dinner. I did so; and my father was very cordial with him, and was really entertained by having an old Ayrshire acquaintance to talk to. He even snubbed the old sister before him.[59] Dr Gillespie was not there today. Matthew went away, and I stayed and drank tea. Lady Auchinleck appeared as smooth to him as if he had been her intimate friend.

WEDNESDAY 1 SEPTEMBER. [D]ined at my father's. I drank just as much as to give me a relish for more; so when I returned to town (after being passionate at home from hasty pride) I got Matthew Dickie to go with me to Dalrymple's tavern[60] and drink punch. We first tried if we could find any of my acquaintance sitting at Walker's. But there were only some of the Town Council. Neither could I find anybody at the Cross. I was at this time conscious of what is the state of a man who has a craving for strong drink; and I dreaded being perhaps at some future period of my life a wretched sot. However, I persisted. At Dalrymple's I found Mr Elliot, the bookseller, and Mr Smiton, the bookbinder, just rising from their bowl. I ordered a fresh one. I did not rise till between eleven and twelve, indeed *about* midnight. I came home after this strange debauch and eat eggs and drank negus alone; and then, after having gone to bed with my dear wife, I started up in shocking gloomy intoxication and raved in solemn rage about my being miserable. It was a horrid night.

THURSDAY 2 SEPTEMBER. Was in deep melancholy. Life was quite black to me.

FRIDAY 3 SEPTEMBER. I called at Robert Boswell's,[61] and was carried in to see his father,[62] who was now wonderfully restored to his senses. He was reading aloud to one of his daughters some poetry (I know not what) when I entered his room. He was sitting in an easy chair with a tartan night-gown and white nightcap, and was so thin that he looked just like a spectre. I was struck with a kind of confused trepidation on first seeing him. But except that he was a little fretful, and his saying that it was several years since he saw me, he was really pretty much in his former usual way. It was very comfortable to have him thus revived, as it were.

59 This was Margaret Boswell, the elder of Lady Auchinleck's two spinster sisters. Margaret Boswell lived with Lord and Lady Auchinleck.
60 George Dalrymple's tavern in the President's Stairs, off the south side of the Parliament Close.
61 Perhaps by this time, and certainly by 1780, Robert Boswell resided at 13 St Andrew Square.
62 Boswell's uncle, Dr John Boswell, whose mind was evidently beginning to wander. He was now living in St Andrew Square.

SATURDAY 4 SEPTEMBER. I supped at Middlemist's oyster-cellar[63] with Lord Glencairn, Sir James Campbell, Major Montgomerie, Duntroon, etc., and got into excellent glee. Had resolution to quit them at one in the morning. Lord Glencairn, who was very much in liquor, went with me. He had made me many professions of regard, which from so honest a man were valuable. I supported him to the head of Writers' Court, where he lodged.

SATURDAY 11 SEPTEMBER. Was in exceeding bad spirits. Met Mr Alexander Boswall, who had come to town for a little with General Smith. He and I and my wife and two daughters and Sandy were entertained by him with sweetmeats at Elder's.[64] I went with him and visited General Smith. I was quite listless and disconsolate all day, and could do nothing.

SUNDAY 12 SEPTEMBER. Was puzzled with a letter from Miss Sibthorpe[65] desiring information for her father and mother as to the education at Glasgow and the expense of it. Could not get a distinct account. Felt myself very impotent in business. Talked of it with Dr Blair, whom I visited today between sermons. My wife and I and the three eldest children drank tea at my father's very disagreeably. My dejection of mind could ill bear his shockingly cold behaviour. In the evening the three children went through sacred exercises admirably. This was a real pleasure to me amidst my hypochondria.

TUESDAY 14 SEPTEMBER. Asked Adam Smith's opinion at the custom-house as to education at Glasgow.[66] He preferred it to Edinburgh. He said, "We never meet, though we live now in the same town." "Very true", said I. "What can be the meaning of it?" "I don't know", said he in his awkward, mumbling manner. I fairly told him that I did not like his having praised David Hume so much.[67] He went off to the board huffed, yet affecting to treat my censure as foolish. I did

---

63 "In Edinburgh there is a species of taverns of lower denomination, which, however, are sometimes resorted to by good company, when disposed to enjoy a frolic. These are the oyster cellars, a sort of ale houses, where the proper entertainment of the house is oysters, punch and porter; but where a supper may be had, upon warning, equal to any in the taverns. Most of these oyster cellars have a sort of long-room, where a small party may enjoy the exercise of a country dance, to the music of a fiddle, harp, or bag-pipe. But the equivocal character of these houses of resort prevents them from being visited by any of the fair sex who seek the praise of delicacy, or pique themselves on propriety of conduct" (Arnot, 1816 edn [based on the text of the 1788 edition], pp. 271-2). Chambers described these oyster cellars as "abysses of darkness and comfort" where the oysters and porter were "arranged in huge dishes upon a coarse table, in a dingy room, lighted by tallow candles" (Chambers, p.160). The cellar which Boswell mentions—that of "Lucky" Middlemist (or Middlemass), celebrated by Robert Fergusson in "Caller Oysters"—was in the Cowgate (Stuart, p. 94). The title "Lucky" signified "a guidwife" (*ibid.*, p. 90).
64 Perhaps the shop of Robert Elder, the grocer, in the Grassmarket.
65 "Boswell's second cousin, daughter of Robert Sibthorpe of County Down. Her grandfather, General Cochrane, was Boswell's great-uncle. Her parents were planning to send a son, Stephen James, to a university" (*Laird*, p. 135, n. 7).
66 Adam Smith had been appointed Commissioner of Customs in 1777 and he had taken up residence at Panmure House, in Panmure Close, off the north side of the Canongate. For the Custom House, see p. 171, n. 162.
67 Hume's *Autobiography*, published by William Strahan in 1777, contained a letter from Smith in which he declared that he had always considered Hume "as approaching as nearly to the idea of a perfectly wise and virtuous man as perhaps the nature of human frailty will permit" (quoted in *Laird*, p. 135, n. 9).

not care how he took it. Since his absurd eulogium on Hume and his ignorant, ungrateful attack on the English university education, I have had no desire to be much with him. Yet I do not forget that he was very civil to me at Glasgow.[68]

WEDNESDAY 15 SEPTEMBER. Dined out at the Coates with Mr Ilay Campbell, who had taken the house there as summer quarters.[69] Had no satisfaction in existence; did not drink too much.

THURSDAY 16 SEPTEMBER. Some French ships had come up the Firth of Forth, as far as Inchkeith almost, last night. This gave an alarm which animated me a little.[70]

FRIDAY 17 SEPTEMBER. Walked up to the Castle and saw the West Fencibles alive for action, should they have an opportunity, and cannon put upon carriages to be taken to Leith; in short, the appearance of war. But I was quite indifferent about everything. Nothing gave me any satisfaction at present but eating and drinking and lying in bed.

SATURDAY 18 SEPTEMBER. Though in sad low spirits, got the 24 number of *The Hypochondriack* finished;[71] and what was a curious experiment, except the first page, I read none of it over before sending it off, that I might be agreeably surprised with it in print. Maclaurin called on me in the afternoon and he and I drove in a hackney-coach to Leith and Newhaven and saw the batteries which were erected to guard the coast. It was a dreary damp afternoon; I was sunk and dejected, and viewed the batteries as I have done potato beds at Auchinleck.

SUNDAY 19 SEPTEMBER. Heard Dr Blair in the forenoon and Mr Walker in the afternoon. Drank tea at my father's. Heard the children say sacred lessons agreeably. They were particularly fond of the Creed. Was somewhat better. Grange supped with us.

MONDAY 20 SEPTEMBER. Had for some time inclined to give warning to my servant, James Clark, as he did not give sufficient attendance. But was so weak-nerved that I could not bring myself to do it till this morning, and then I did it very awkwardly. The poor fellow received his warning, though sudden, with much steadiness; yet I could not help pitying him. I was in great pain all day about it. For warning a servant from a good place is in my apprehension a distressing thing to him; so that there really should, as I think, be very good cause for it. This however is not the common opinion; and, as Grange observed,

68 Smith had been one of Boswell's professors at Glasgow University (see Introduction, p. 19).
69 This was presumably either the house of Easter Coates (now in the close of St Mary's Cathedral), lying to the west of the city and built in about 1611, which was (and remains) "a picturesque old mansion, with turrets, dormer windows, and crowstepped gables in the Scoto-French style" (Grant, Vol. II, p. 116) or the nearby house of Wester Coates, which was removed in 1869 to make way for the gardens of Lansdowne Crescent immediately north of Grosvenor Street (Harris, p. 178).
70 John Paul Jones, the Scots-born American naval commander, who was on a voyage around Ireland and Scotland with French and American vessels in search of prizes and was soon to achieve great fame on account of his celebrated naval engagement off Scarborough on 23 September, had planned to attack the port of Leith, but was prevented by contrary winds.
71 The subject of the essay was censure.

I probably suffered more upon this occasion than James did. I was for engaging no other servant till he got a place, and if he got none, was for keeping him.[72] This was not the firmness of a master of a family. Grange supped with us.

TUESDAY 21 SEPTEMBER. Had a hogshead of Malaga bottled. Grange dined with us, and he and I drank a bottle of my old Malaga and a bottle of cider. When at dinner, I received a message from Colonel Stuart[73] that he would be glad to see me at Fortune's as soon as I could come. This was kind. Therefore I resolved to go. Went about five. What I had already taken had intoxicated me to a certain degree. I drank a good quantity of claret with him, Matthew Henderson, etc.; and growing uneasy, took to strong gin punch, which soon quite knocked me up, and I was brought home in a chair, I know not how. The Colonel in a very friendly manner asked me to go up with him, see his regiment at Leeds in Yorkshire, and then go on to London: "and", said he, "you have a very good excuse to your father: that you are going to see my brother before he goes abroad,[74] which I think you should, and the journey up shall not cost you a farthing." I agreed to go.

WEDNESDAY 22 SEPTEMBER. Awaked excessively ill. Lay in bed till between five and six. Told my wife of the Colonel's proposal to carry me up. She readily agreed, thinking it might be for my advantage, in getting me the Colonel's interest joined to his brother's. Only she trusted that I would not drink hard. Grange supped with us.

THURSDAY 23 SEPTEMBER. Called on Commissioner Cochrane and talked with him of Colonel Stuart's proposal to me. He approved much of my accepting it, and said my father would be much in the wrong if he did not approve of it. I went to my father's and with some hesitation mentioned it. To my agreeable surprise he did not oppose it. Worthy Grange was much for it. So that I had many opinions to confirm my own.

FRIDAY 24 SEPTEMBER. Was in somewhat an awkward state of uneasiness lest Colonel Stuart's proposal might have been only the momentary sally of a drinking fit, and that I might appear ridiculous for having thought him in earnest. He returned this day between two and three. I saw him for a few minutes at his hotel, and we talked of our journey as a fixed thing. My wife, who has more discernment than I have, undertook to find out from Colonel Stuart if he really wished I should go with him. He came early tonight; and I left them awhile together. Maclaurin was my only other guest; and though at first I was a little uneasy that I had not more company, it was better as it was. For Maclaurin was very good company till two; and then the Colonel and I had an admirable cordial seat by ourselves till about seven. We drank a good deal of my own importation claret (by means of Wight), which he liked much. We drank slow, and

---

72 "Clark had been with Boswell since some time in May 1778. Boswell kept him eight months longer" (*Laird*, p. 137, n. 3).
73 The Hon. Col. James Stuart, second son of the Earl of Bute and brother of Boswell's friend Lord Mountstuart.
74 Lord Mountstuart had been appointed British envoy to Turin.

were both merry and rational. It pleased me very much to hear him declare that he loved his wife now as much as he had ever done. I never before drank for hours without a toast. But he convinced me that it was very easy and pleasant. I was much taken with his manly good sense and knowledge of the world. My jaunt with him was now clearly fixed. I was not at all drunk.

SUNDAY 26 SEPTEMBER. Was at the New Church in the forenoon. My father was in the seat. I went out to his house in the coach with him and Lady Auchinleck. By the road he talked a little of my setting out with Colonel Stuart next day, and seemed pretty indifferent. His being so was in my opinion a sign of his being failed. For had he been quite himself, he would have been violent against it. I then called on Maclaurin and told him I was to set out next day. He said I would drink half a hogshead of claret before I returned. I dined comfortably at home; heard Dr Blair in the New Church in the afternoon, and my wife and I (and some of the children, I think) drank tea at my father's. I did not take leave of him tonight, as I expected I should be out to wait on him next day before setting out.

Boswell's journal of his jaunt with Colonel Stuart—which journal Boswell described (in a letter to Samuel Johnson dated 7 November 1779) as "truly a log-book of felicity"—is unaccountably missing; but it is known that Boswell was in London by 4 October, where he was greeted by Johnson "with as much vivacity as if he had been in the gaiety of youth",[74a] *then went to Chester (via Lichfield), where he stayed for at least two weeks and was entertained by Colonel Stuart and his fellow officers, and then returned to Edinburgh, getting back there on 9 November.*

[Extract from a letter from Boswell to Bennet Langton dated 23 December 1779.] "[T]he Session rose [on Saturday 18 December] for the Christmas vacation. No period of my life has been more sound and cheerful than this [i.e., since 9 November]. The stock of fine spirits which I laid in upon the jaunt kept me in all this former part of the Session quite as I could wish. I wrote twice the number of pages of law papers that I did in the same space last winter. I went through business with ability and ease. I had not the least hypochondria. I relished life much. I was several times out at dinners and suppers, and had several companies with me; and I was very little intoxicated at any time. I was one week confined to the house with a cold, which was very general this winter in Edinburgh, but it did not sink my spirits. I had been troubled for some time with a scurvy on my thighs and legs, for which I drank a decoction of guaiac[75] and sassafras.[76] My left great toe troubled me a good deal. Mr Wood cut out the nail which fretted the flesh, and made me apply vitriol to burn and dry the fungous substance, but it was not yet well when the Session broke up. On Monday 6 December I began to rise early, and ever since that day got up with ease. I was only once with a coarse Dulcinea, who was perfectly safe. I however must own that amongst many good circumstances of this period of my life, I omitted to write to many eminent friends in England, which was so much

74a *Life*, Vol. II, p. 858.
75 The resin of the guaiacum tree—also known as the lignum vitae ("wood of life") tree—was thought to be a cure for many illnesses.
76 Dried bark of the root of the North American sassafras tree, used medicinally to induce sweating.

loss to my elegant improvement. Young Arniston[77] seemed to take much to me, which was agreeable, as there had been a friendship between his grandfather and mine and my father and his father; in short, an hereditary kindness, which, though interrupted by his father's bad conduct to our family at last Ayrshire election, was not to be lost. He supped with me very cheerfully one night. My wife was in as good health this winter as I ever saw her, till a week before the Session broke up, she also was seized with the cold, and had a pretty severe cough. As she was with child, I was afraid she might be much the worse of coughing. My brother John was in Edinburgh all this period, but never would call upon me, having an unhappy prejudice against me.[78] Yet when I called on him he was civil enough. My children had all what we thought the chin-cough[79] in a mild degree. My father was seized (18 November) with the cold, and it rose to a high fever, his pulse being at ninety-five. He had at the same time an obstinate cough, and his bladder was in a bad state. He was for several days really in danger, and Dr Gillespie said to me that he feared it would stand hard with him this winter. I was out every day calling on him for some time, but saw him little. However, I found that his illness made him more kindly. One night he said to me, "I am much obliged to you for this visit." He grew better, and though much shaken, was pretty well again before the Session broke up. I must record a curious dialogue which I witnessed between him and John Stobie when he was lying in bed one forenoon, better, but weak. "Come awa', John. Are aw the Lords of Session living yet?" "Ay, my Lord. But mony a ane's wishing them dead. Ony body that has a post has folk to wish them dead." "Wha are expectants now?" "Plenty of expectants, my Lord." My father was not in the least discomposed by this odd suggestion. He had been remarkably well the few days of this Session that he attended the House. The study shown by his lady to prevent my being with him alone was offensive. I was a little uneasy to think that I had neglected to get him to sign an addition to the entail of Auchinleck allowing of liferent leases to any tenant and of nine hundred and ninety-nine years' leases in our village. But it would have been indelicate to have troubled him with it while really ill. I did not see my uncle the Doctor during this period. I regret this. But lameness and bad weather were against going to the New Town. Having been for so many weeks

77 Robert Dundas (1758-1819), advocate (admitted 6 July 1779), eldest son of the Lord President. He was M.P. for Edinburghshire from 1790 to 1801, and was appointed Solicitor-General in 1784, Lord Advocate in 1789, Dean of the Faculty of Advocates in 1796, and Chief Baron of Exchequer in 1801. He was renowned for his amiability. Cockburn, who in his youth knew Dundas well, described him as "a little, alert, handsome, gentleman-like man, with a countenance and air beaming with sprightliness and gaiety; and distinguished by considerable fire, altogether inexpressibly pleasing. It was impossible not to like the owner of that look." However, Cockburn, who also says that Dundas was "curiously bad" at speaking, lacked "intellectual depth and force" and had only "moderate" abilities and acquirements, suggests that had it not been for "the accident of his birth" he would never have risen so high (Cockburn, pp. 150-1).
78 John, who had taken lodgings in Edinburgh, was offended because he had discovered that Boswell had taken, and worn, some of his old gloves and shirts which had been stored in Boswell's house. Although Boswell had offered to pay for them (see the entry for 11 January 1780), John refused to forgive him.
79 Whooping cough.

the intimate companion of Colonel Stuart, I had insensibly become so far as-similated to him as to have high manly notions; for mental qualities are communi-cated by contagion as certainly as material qualities. I cannot analyse the effects of my last autumn jaunt, but I felt them very animating. Indeed, I have a wonderful enthusi-astic fondness for military scenes. My wife however observed that my temper was grown more violent since being with Colonel Stuart. I perceived this to be true. But I did not think it a disadvantage to me."

SUNDAY 19 DECEMBER. It was a very wet day. So I stayed at home and made the children say divine lessons. In the afternoon I read one of Mr Carr's sermons aloud, and my wife another. At night after we were in bed, Veronica spoke out from her little bed and said, "I do not believe there is a GOD." "Preserve me," said I, "my dear, what do you mean?" She answered, "I have *thinket* it many a time, but did not like to speak of it." I was confounded and uneasy, and tried her with the simple argument that without GOD there would not be all the things we see. "It is HE who makes the sun shine." Said she: "It shines only on good days." Said I: "GOD made you." Said she: "My mother bore me." It was a strange and alarming thing to her mother and me to hear our little angel talk thus. But I thought it better just to let the subject drop insensibly tonight. I asked her if she had said her prayers tonight. She said yes, and asked me to put her in mind to say them in the morning. I prayed to GOD to prevent such thoughts from entering into her mind. π.

MONDAY 20 DECEMBER. By talking calmly with Veronica, I discovered what had made her think there was not a GOD. She told me, she "did not like to die". I suppose as she has been told that GOD takes us to himself when we die, she had fancied that if there were no GOD, there would be no death; so "her wish was father to the thought". I impressed upon her that we must die at any rate; and how terrible would it be if we had not a Father in Heaven to take care of us. I looked into Cambrai's *Education of a Daughter*,[80] hoping to have found some simple argument for the being of GOD in that piece of instruction. But it is taken for granted. I was somewhat fretful today from finding myself without fixed occupation; and my toe seeming not to heal. But my mind had a firm bottom.

TUESDAY 21 DECEMBER. My father was remarkably well. But with his health his harshness was returned. I had thought it would be proper for me to go to Auchinleck for some days this vacation and see how things were going on. But when I spoke of it to him, he said, "Ye hae nae skill." I afterwards said, "So you don't think it would be of use that I should go west this vacation? If that is the case, I shall not go, for it would cost me some trouble and some bank notes." Said he: "Ye had as good keep them in your pouch." I therefore laid aside thoughts of going. Claud, Robert Boswell, and Stobie were at dinner. It was a disagreeable scene. After dinner my father, recollecting no doubt my aversion

80 By Fénelon, Archbishop of Cambrai.

to the Lord President and the too good cause of it, drank his health, "—and may all that don't like him be despised and contemned." This was really shocking. Yet his memory was wretchedly bad as to other things. He asked me if I ever visited Old Erskine's wife (who died several years ago), and if they had "ony bairns".[81] After Claud and Robert were gone, I was a little with Mr Stobie privately, and I suggested to him that tacks[82] should not be set on the estate of Auchinleck at present, for if I was to get an entailed estate and tacks on it, I would have no power. The little wretch answered, "Sae muckle the better. It 'ill keep ye frae playing the fool." As Grange well observed, he ought to have been kicked; and nothing but hearing me treated as I am, daily and hourly, at my father's could have made him dare to be so impertinent. I must have patience in my present state. Dr Gillespie drank tea there. I had a chair to take me home.

WEDNESDAY 22 DECEMBER. Wrote several letters to friends in London. Kept the house all day to let my toe heal if it would. Grange dined. Drank strong ale and cider and eat pickles, all which produced an uneasiness in my stomach. Took a good deal of pains this and former days to settle a dispute between Mr James Craig, baker, Deacon Convener of the Trades of Edinburgh, and William Watson, poulterer. Mr Craig was much satisfied. Watson was unreasonable. Time must finally adjust it. Grange drank tea. It was very cold.

THURSDAY 23 DECEMBER. Attended the funeral of the Earl of Caithness. His Lordship had died here above three weeks or a month ago. But the corpse had been kept till instructions should come from his family in Caithness where to inter him. It was fixed to be in Roslyn Chapel.[83] I was solemnly pleased with this funeral. I thought of the grandmother of Thomas Boswell, the first laird of Auchinleck, having been a daughter of the family of Caithness.[84] I went and came with Mr Gilbert Mason in his post-chaise. I was the only man who kept off his hat in the venerable chapel, so rare is pious reverence in Scotland. Bailie Macqueen came up to me in the street after I returned, to consult me about something. I took him home with me to dinner. Grange joined us after dinner. My wife and I supped and played whist at Dr Young's; Sir William and Lady Forbes, Sir Philip and Lady Ainslie, etc., etc., there. A very cheerful evening.

FRIDAY 24 DECEMBER. Did little. Time just glided on. Dined at Mr Solicitor Murray's with Major Flint of the 25th Foot, commanding four companies of it in the Castle, Mr George Wallace, and several more. A motley company. Was happy to meet worthy Flint after an interval of about four years, and felt myself pleased with military ideas when I looked at his regimentals and heard him talk of his regiment. I eat and drank too much for my scurvy and sore toe. But could not resist salmon, goose, or brandy. Drank claret moderately. Would have sat longer. But could not

81 Old James Erskine's wife, Lady Frances Erskine, had died on 20 June 1776. They had two children, John Francis Erskine and James Francis Erskine, for the former of whom, and possibly also the latter, Boswell had acted in connection with the Stirlingshire Highways Bill in the spring of 1778.
82 Leases.
83 Usually spelt either Rosslyn or Roslin, this is the famous fifteenth-century chapel between Lasswade and Penicuik.
84 She was actually the mother, not the grandmother, of Thomas Boswell (*Laird*, p. 152, n. 3).

bear a forward priggish fool, Stewart Macarthur,[85] and would not warm in his company. Was at a consultation at Mr Rae's. Felt his superiority as a knowing lawyer. Uneasy a little from excess, at night I was in danger of peevishness. But escaped it. The Hon. Major Erskine,[86] who had just come over from Dublin, sat with me part of the forenoon, as did Major Montgomerie. My wife was exceedingly good to me tonight, and said, "Will you ever say again that I don't love you?" I answered that I never would.

SATURDAY 25 DECEMBER. Lay longer in bed than usual. The forenoon slipped away, I knew not how, so that I did not get out to see my father as I intended. Grange dined with us comfortably, as he always does on Christmas Day; and he and I and my two daughters went to the English Chapel in the afternoon. Effie was there for the first time, I having made a rule to begin to take each child to it in the sixth year of its age. It was very cold, and the congregation was thin. I had not such warmth of devotion as I have sometimes experienced. Yet I was very well. The children were impressed with good thoughts of Christ. The town was illuminated on account of the news of a victory in Georgia over Count d'Estaing and the Americans. It gave me no pleasure, for I considered that it would only encourage a longer continuance of the ruinous war. Grange and Signora Marcucci drank tea with us. While we were at it, my brother John came in. He had called before this. He was silent and sulky, and soon asked me to go into another room with him. I did so. But found he only wanted to shun the company. He sat a short while. I engaged him to dine with us on Tuesday. It was painful to find him so unsocial. Though he took no notice of the children, Veronica gave a pleasing and curious proof of natural affection. She had never seen him before that she could recollect. But she said, "I like him." Signora Marcucci supped with us. I was easy and really as I could wish to be. π.

SUNDAY 26 DECEMBER. Heard Dr Blair lecture and preach in the forenoon. He preached on "All is vanity",[87] but smoothed it over prettily. He said no man who would calculate fairly would find that he had more hours of unhappiness than of happiness or ease. In short, he tried to *modify* the general infelicity of life too much. I shook my head as he preached. I sat awhile with Mr David Erskine between sermons. I dined at my father's with him and his lady. He was in pretty good health, but not in the least cordial. I was obliged to be constantly upon my guard while the *noverca*[88] lay in wait to catch at every word. I read aloud after dinner at her desire one of Fordyce's *Sermons to Young Women*. I was quite disgusted with the affected, theatrical style. I left out many superfluous words in many sentences. Yet they were still florid. My father very judiciously said they were not

---

85 Archibald McArthur Stewart (1749-1815), advocate (admitted 27 January 1773). He was "notorious for such eccentricities as dressing in white and keeping a litter of pigs in his bedroom" (*Laird*, p. 153, n. 5). The first eccentricity was at one time also associated with Lord Monboddo (see Appendix, p. 557) and the second brings to mind Lord Gardenstone (see Appendix, p. 559).
86 Andrew Erskine's brother Archibald, who had now been promoted to Major.
87 Ecclesiastes 1. 2.
88 Stepmother (Latin).

for Sunday. I then read in Duncan's commentary on the first chapter of the Hebrews, the learned cast and correct language of which pleased me much. Indeed the chapter itself is noble. I stayed to tea. Dr Gillespie came in after it. I walked both out and back again; and my toe was sore and inflamed and mysterious, so that I was really uneasy about it. I had mentioned our having half a seat in the New Church along with my father while I was at his house today. *She* opposed it in so shameless a manner, showing that she would not have *any* connexion between him and my family, that I was quite fretted and vexed. I was in a sad frame after I came home. For although, as Grange observed t'other day, my father's life was now not desirable even by his friends (and I added he now lived only for his second wife), I had still such an affection for him as affected me tenderly. Yet I suffered much. My daughters said divine lessons. π.

MONDAY 27 DECEMBER. Mr Lawrie went this day to the country, which made me put off several letters till he should return to copy them, I having some time ago sworn him to secrecy upon the Bible. Old Erskine, who had drank tea with my wife on Friday and missed me, had sent me a card desiring to see me this forenoon. I had accepted of being one of his trustees, being mindful of his kindness to me when I was raw and fiery and on bad terms with my father.[89] I walked down to him to his present habitation, Lord Napier's house in the Abbey Close, and breakfasted with him. He was in bed, and complained of a sprained *ankle*, but probably this was to save his *heels* from being laid fast. For his creditors were pressing, and his house was in the Sanctuary.[90] He talked very plausibly. I then went to Mr John Syme's, and was shown his very accurate books of all the lands in the Stewartry of Kirkcudbright: their extent, valuation, proprietors, etc., with alphabetical indexes of lands and persons. They pleased me much. I had not seen Lady Colville since my last English expedition. I had made my peace by means of my wife and an epistle; and this day Major Erskine carried me out in the coach and I dined with her. No company there. Just she and Lady Anne, the Major, and Andrew. Their sneering and censoriousness, and their narrow preference of Edinburgh to London for happy living, disgusted me. But I kept my temper well, and drank more than a bottle of claret. I was firm in my own opinion as to England, which I have now tried sufficiently and find it more and more confirmed. My dear wife had some good soup for me at night. My toe was very sore, and Wood allowed me to put a poultice to it.

TUESDAY 28 DECEMBER. I must remark a curious incident. I dreamt that I saw the cause of my toe being so painful: viz., a piece of the nail sticking in the flesh. When I took off the poultice this morning, I observed a piece of nail appearing through the ball of my toe. Dr Gillespie called. He desired to see it. He said it

---

89 "Old Erskine", who was heavily in debt, was arranging to sign a trust deed whereby his estate would be conveyed to a trustee for the benefit of his creditors.

90 The grounds of Holyrood Abbey and a large part of the grounds around the Palace of Holyroodhouse, including the royal park, were recognised as a sanctuary for impecunious debtors. "This peculiarity brought many far from respectable visitors to a cluster of houses round the palace—a cluster nearly entirely swept away about 1857—as varied in their appearance as the chequered fortunes of their bankrupt inmates" (Grant, Vol. II, p. 60).

should be pulled out with a forceps. I took hold of it with my finger and thumb, and out it came. I was then at once easy, except that the wounded flesh smarted a little. Wood called, and I showed him how I was relieved. I had now only to let the wound heal. My brother John dined with us. He was silent and sour at dinner. But grew better after it, and he and I drank port negus really comfortably. The children paid him great attention, and he seemed kindly somewhat to them. But was strangely shy to my wife. Did not even drink to her. She was angry with him, which vexed me; for she should have considered it was disease. He drank tea with us. My wife was again exceedingly good to me tonight.

THURSDAY 30 DECEMBER. Again idled away the forenoon. Called at the custom-house and talked a little with Commissioner Cochrane about my father's giving me another £100 a year, which the Commissioner had proposed. He seemed to think I would get it. I then visited my father. He had on his wig for the first time and looked greatly better. I had been a little with my brother in his room this forenoon, and found him quite social. Robert Boswell, his wife and sisters, Dr Grant, his wife and eldest daughter, Dr Gillespie, and Grange dined with us, and all but Grange drank tea. Dr Grant and I went to the playhouse and saw the first part of *Henry IV* and a harlequin dialogue entertainment called *The Touchstone of Truth*.[91] Wilkinson's Falstaff did not please me. He spoke too fast.

FRIDAY 31 DECEMBER. Yesterday and today laboured *invita Minerva*[92] at a New Year's Day address for the *Caledonian Mercury*; and though it was but short, got it done only at night, and sent it careless whether it should be inserted or not. My wife and I dined at Prestonfield. It was hard frost. My toe was uneasy. I was fretful.

---

91 By Charles Dibdin.
92 "'Doggedly, without inspiration', a phrase from Horace (*Ars Poetica*)" (*Laird*, p. 156, n. 5).

1780

SATURDAY 1 JANUARY. As usual at the beginning of a new year, made up a state of my affairs, and found with uneasiness that I was really in a disagreeable situation, having debts which I was obliged to pay, while my funds could not be commanded for some time, as I had advanced a good deal for my wife's nephews, whose patrimonies could not be touched but by a circuit at law. Upon the whole, I had as much as I owed, reckoning my books and furniture; and I had spent £100 less than last year. Worthy Grange sat with me while I made my calculations, and comforted me. I had said the day before yesterday that I would dine at my father's today. My wife was *invited* this morning for the first time this winter. There was nobody but my father and Lady Auchinleck and my wife and I at dinner. My father was quite callous. It was very galling. I began tonight again to write ten lines each day, hoping to do one full year.

SUNDAY 2 JANUARY. I intended to have gone to Bothwell Castle on Monday. But as my toe was still sore, I resolved to nurse it, and stay in the house one whole week to give it ease and let it heal. And as the weather was very cold, I thought it would be more agreeable to visit Mr Douglas in the spring vacation. Found my *Mercury* address inserted. Liked it. I lay in bed till the afternoon, and read in Sir David Hamilton's *Private Christian's Witness for Christianity*. I was pleased with the mystical piety of his mind, but could not acquiesce in all his instances of particular experience of Providence in the course of his life. Abating the objections which occurred to me, and a weakness at times observed by my wife, the book is full of religious unction and amiable practice. Nor would I take upon me to deny that he may sometimes have had answers to his prayers by extraordinary effects. I no doubt read his book with much partiality from having heard all my life of his excellent character and great friendship for my grandfather. The style is not good, being all long, long sentences and often incorrect. The children said divine lessons very well. I talked to them of the fall of man, the curse of death, and the restoration by Christ. Sandy was very angry with Adam, and said he should have been put in the guard.[1] I was in a dull, easy frame. I wondered to find death and immortality affect me very little. I was however very well, upon the whole. But it is amazing in what diversity of states a thinking man will perceive himself to exist, and how unlike the impressions of the very same objects will be at various periods. This evening I have no ardent desire for anything, nor have I on the other hand any lively fear. My wife, to whom I read but a little of Sir David Hamilton's book, thought very meanly of him. Commissioner Cochrane told me that Dr ——, who was very angry that he was knighted for his eminence as a man-midwife, made these lines upon it:

1 That is, the City Guard-house (for which, see Introduction, p. 6).

"Rise, Sir David", said the Queen:[2]
The first c—t knight that e'er was seen.

MONDAY 3 JANUARY. Had dreamt again of my toe, and that a piece of nail was deep in it. Felt it very uneasy when I rose after breakfasting in bed. Resolved to have Mr Wood to cut it effectually. Sent a note to him to come this forenoon or tomorrow forenoon, so as to have daylight. He did not come today. I had a strange *desire* to *taste* of *pain*, as one will *long* for what is bitter. I sat with my nightcap on all day, and did nothing but bring up so far my Register of Letters sent and received, of which I had only loose notes from April last. Grange drank tea with us. My mind, though listless, was not unquiet. I had indeed neither elevation nor gaiety. But I was content with mere tranquillity. I was fretful only when the children made noise. π.

TUESDAY 4 JANUARY. Breakfasted in bed. After I got up, continued my Register of Letters. Mr Wood came. Would not cut my toe, but said he would separate the flesh from the nail by stuffing in lint, and would dress it every day, and cure it, be it what it would. I had no appetite for pain today. My brother John called for a little. He was in a strange humour, and talked of returning to Dr Hall's St Luke's House.[3] I asked him to dine, but he would not. Grange dined and drank tea. I wrote to Temple.

WEDNESDAY 5 JANUARY. Mr Lawrie had returned last night, so that I had him to pay accounts and do many things for me. His services are very convenient. Perhaps they accustom me to be too helpless. I brought up my Register of Letters to the end of this year. Dr Gillespie sat awhile with me. Grange drank tea. My brother John came and drank a dish of coffee. He was grievously sulky. I was very passionate at night.

THURSDAY 6 JANUARY. My passion on Wednesday night was occasioned by a very trifling cause, which is not worth mentioning. Yet it was shockingly violent, and was directed against my dear wife, who, though now in good health, was with child, and required tender treatment. I was much vexed with myself both last night and this morning. Yet I was this morning in an obstinate fit, and would take no breakfast till my wife came and solicited me after hers was over, though I had a headache. I insisted with her that she ought in duty as a wife to be ever attentive, ever ready to soothe my temper and be complaisant. She said very sensibly that she had been educated without that timorous restraint in which I had been kept, and that it was much easier for me not to insist on subjection than on her to submit to it. But she was certainly wrong in contradicting my favourite notions and partialities. In particular, she was much to blame in endeavouring to counteract the principle of *family* which has prevailed in the family of Auchinleck from generation to generation. She said, and perhaps with some truth, that our pride and high estimation of ourselves as if German princes (my phrase) was ridiculous in the eyes of other people, who looked

2 Queen Anne. Sir David Hamilton was her physician (*Laird*, p. 159, n. 9).
3 The asylum at Newcastle.

upon us not only as no better than any other gentleman's family, but as a stiff and inhospitable family. But as I have great enjoyment in our fancied dignity, and cannot be persuaded but that we do appear of more consequence in the country than others, from a certain reserve which has always been maintained, and am also of opinion that this pride makes us act in a nobler manner, I wish to encourage it; and my wife therefore should at least not oppose it. My son Sandy seems to imbibe it as I could desire. I catechize him thus: "What is your first duty?" "My duty to GOD." "What is your second duty?" "My duty to the family of Auchinleck." "Who was the first laird of Auchinleck?" "Thomas Boswell." "From whom did he get the estate?" "From his king." "Who was his king?" "King James the IV of Scotland." "What became of Thomas Boswell?" "He was killed at Flodden Field fighting with his king against the English, for Scotland and England were then two kingdoms." "Who was Thomas Boswell's son?" "David." "What became of him?" "He fought for his sovereign, Queen Mary, at the Battle of Langside, lived a worthy gentleman, and died at Auchinleck."[4] He seems much pleased with this genealogical instruction. I shall go on with it and habituate him to think with sacred reverence and attachment of his ancestors and to hope to aggrandize the family.

It occurred to me on reading over the entail lately that the clause which was at my desire inserted giving power to the last heir male called to choose any of the descendants of Thomas Boswell, was truly giving it to that heir's daughter or nearest heir female in prejudice of an heir female descending from my father, unless that heir should have an enthusiasm like mine for male succession. I considered that if such a power were to take place soon—for instance, if Claud were to be last heir male while Veronica is alive—it would be very hard that his daughter should cut her out. I wished to guard against this. But I was afraid to touch upon the clause for fear my father should insist to have it annulled altogether. I considered that I might perhaps save such a fund as to purchase myself a power of settling our estate on heirs male forever, by so far altering the entail, and fixing that any heir who should call that alteration in question should forfeit all right to my fund. I felt already some uneasiness at the thought of being fettered by an entail. Yet it does no more than prevent me from selling or loading my estate with debt, which I would be very sorry to do.

My brother John dined with us. But was sour and sneering while my wife sat. I recollected having some years ago injured him by turning him away abruptly when he called, I suppose to dine with me, on a day when I had a good deal of company; and it was agreeable to think that I now made up for it by attention to him. My large Consultation Book had been neglected by me for about nine years. As it is a very accurate and well-written register of my practice, it would have

4 "It was not David, the second laird, but David's son John, the third laird, who fought at Langside (1568). David did not even fight for Queen Mary: he followed his step-father, Cuninghame of Caprington, to the Battle of the Butts (1544), fighting in the English interest against his brother-in-law, the Earl of Arran, Governor of the Kingdom in the infancy of Queen Mary. Boswell's enthusiasm for Scots history and the genealogy of the family of Auchinleck was genuine but was based on very little accurate information" (*Laird*, p. 160, n. 2).

been a pity not to carry it on. I therefore resolved to transcribe into it two pages of the leaves which I have kept, every day, which I calculated would bring it up to this Session in thirty days. I did my task today.[5] In the night between the 3d and 4th current, I thought with sudden anxiety of my having as yet neglected to make a nomination of tutors and curators to my children, which was all I could at present leave them. I next evening wrote it, appointing *one* friend in whom I had full confidence, as suggested to me by Dr Johnson in autumn last. That friend was Sir William Forbes, banker, whom when I mentioned to Dr Johnson, he said he was just thinking of. And with him I joined my dear wife, of whose disinterested affection I have had so many proofs. This was the first deed that I ever wrote *in contemplation* (to use our law phrase) of my death; and what is strange, I felt a sort of tremor while I wrote. I must write to Sir William and beg he will accept of the trust. I hope he will not refuse. Mr Wood dressed my toe tonight. There was a little matter issued from the flesh, and he said he was not sure but there might be some nail under it. Veronica had this winter played on the harpsichord so wonderfully well by the ear that we got a music-master for her, Mr Cooper. He began to teach her on Monday 3d current. She now read pretty well, and was fond of reading.

FRIDAY 7 JANUARY. During this recess or vacation I have ceased to rise early, and have had great enjoyment of lying in bed. I was in a good deal of uneasiness today, from looking at a copy of the wretched deed which my father prevailed with me to copy over and sign, under melancholy fear of his selling the estate, soon after I came of age.[6] I dreaded that perhaps he might leave me under trustees. Yet I thought that the entail put an end to all settlements of the estate before it, and any made after it would be set aside on incapacity. I pleased myself too with imagining that, in the worst event, I might by Lord Mountstuart's interest obtain relief by an Act of Parliament. The state of my debts too gave me uneasiness, as I had risked too much to support my wife's nephews, but upon honour unasked by her. π.

SATURDAY 8 JANUARY. I this morning beat Sandy for telling a lie. I must beat him very severely if I catch him again in falsehood.[7] I do not recollect having had any other valuable principle impressed upon me by my father except a strict regard to truth, which he impressed upon my mind by a hearty beating at an early age, when I lied, and then talking of the *dishonour* of lying. I recollect distinctly having truth and honour thus indelibly inculcated upon me by him one evening in our house, fourth storey of Blair's Land, Parliament Close. Mr Wood dressed my toe this forenoon. It was a little more painful, but he said it was doing well. I trusted to him, having defied him to cure it, by way of piquing him as a chirurgeon.[8] I idled away much time today in clearing the drawer of my writing-table, etc., and did not write letters as I intended. My brother John

5 For Boswell's Consultation Book, see Introduction, p. 37. Boswell only took the Consultation Book up to 11 August 1772. What came of the loose leaves is not known (see also the entry for 23 August 1776 and relevant footnote).
6 See Introduction, pp. 23-4.
7 This seems to be the only recorded occasion on which Boswell beat any of his children.
8 Surgeon.

drank tea with us. He was quite sensible, but very cross. I pitied him and was angry at the same time. Grange also drank tea.

SUNDAY 9 JANUARY. Had taken physic the night before; so was in a state of "*valetudinarian indulgence*" (to use an expression of Dr Johnson's in conversation with me). Balmuto visited me between sermons, and Mr James Donaldson, bookseller and printer, drank tea with us. I kept the house all day, and heard the children say divine lessons. I told them in the evening so much about *black angels* or *devils* seizing bad people when they die and dragging them down to hell, a *dark* place (for I had not yet said anything of *fire* to them, and perhaps never will), that they were all three suddenly seized with such terror that they cried and roared out and ran to me for protection (they and I being in the drawing-room), and alarmed their mother, who came upstairs in a fright, and she and Bell Bruce took them downstairs. This vexed me. Yet without mixing early some *fear* in the mind, I apprehend religion will not be lasting. Besides, however mildly we may interpret the divine law, there *is* reason for *some* fear. I this day finished the reading of Sir David Hamilton's book. He recommends such confidence in *experience upon the soul* without *argumentative conviction* as I am afraid might be dangerous. For if one's soul, for instance, should glow with licentious love, there will be an *irrational experience* that "this must be right". Yet Sir David's system is, it must be owned, somewhat similar to the *axiomatic* and *common-sense* doctrines of Reid, Oswald, and Beattie.[9] Mr Donaldson sent me some *Critical Reviews*, which entertained me a good deal at night, sitting by the fire in my wife's bedroom, where for some time past we have supped comfortably. All last week I did not taste any fermented liquor, nor shall I till I find some call upon me. My wife read to me tonight the *Critical Review* on Dr Johnson's *Prefaces to the Poets* (No. 1st of that critique) and considerable extracts. I was happy at this, for I regret that one of such good sense reads so little.

MONDAY 10 JANUARY. Mr Wood, who had not called yesterday, dressed my toe today. It was more painful. In the afternoon, while Grange was with me, my brother John came in, and was so sulky that I grew rather too warm and spoke strongly to him of his behaviour. He drank tea in the drawing-room and then came and sat in the room by me, in obstinate perverse silence, till about eight, and then went away. I was hurt by having such an object before me. My wife observed that he was so disagreeable that one suffered less for him than if he were dejected; and that his shocking manner would make one shun the least appearance of insanity, for that it excited disgust. This was a good memento to me, who sometimes have fancied something dignified and amiable in madness. I idled away this day and did none of my Consultation Book.

TUESDAY 11 JANUARY. The Session sat down again. I went to the Court in a chair. After a long quiet confinement, the bustle of the Court seemed harsh, and it was unpleasant to perceive how little one cared for another. I should have mentioned that I yesterday did what I had long meditated but had been

9 The Scottish philosophers Thomas Reid, James Oswald and James Beattie.

restrained by magnifying the scheme too much. Biography is my favourite study; and amongst other lives I had wished much to write that of *Mr Alexander Lockhart—Lord Covington*. I had put down a few notes from what conversations I had held with him occasionally. But I thought the best method was to try if a man of his distinguished abilities would himself furnish me with materials. Yesterday I took resolution and wrote out a series of queries, and addressed a letter to him begging that he would favour me by answering them. I had the packet delivered to him today just as he was leaving the House, that he might read it calmly, and that some time might intervene between that and my seeing him. My mind was less firm today than for some time past, and I felt a kind of timid uneasiness lest Lord Covington should think that I took too much liberty with him, and should disregard my request, and perhaps be offended.

I found Dr Gillespie when I came home. Mr Wood came and dressed my toe while he was with me; and today they both saw a corner of the nail in the flesh, pretty deep; but Mr Wood could not get at it to cut it out till the fungous flesh at the side was more separated from the nail. I heard today that Lord Eglinton had come to town on Sunday; and before my toe was dressed, he came and paid us a visit. I had a desire to dine with him at Fortune's today just to enjoy social eating and drinking. But as he had engaged to sup with me next day, my wife wisely persuaded me to dine at home, especially as I had company tonight at supper.

My brother John came in the afternoon, and was still more sulky and perverse than on any day this winter. I told him in plain terms that I could not admit him to my house if he behaved in such a manner. He did not mind me, but went to tea, and sat all the time with his hat on, and frowned horribly. He then followed me into the dining-room and placed himself on the opposite side of the fire to me; and when I spoke to him and he did not choose to answer, made a noise as if going to spit. He showed a good deal of shrewdness and even a sort of wit amidst his gloomy, horrid ill-nature; for, as he had railed against me for having used some linen of his, the value of which I was always ready to pay him, when he abused Scotland compared with England, and I asked him why then he had come to Scotland, he said, "Don't you know? What do you hold in your hand?" "A paper", said I. "Of what is it made?" said he. "Of rags", said I. "And of what are rags made?" said he. "Of linen", said I. I had perceived his drift. He now thought he had hit me full. Upon which, "What is a man's face made of?" said he. "Of skin and bone", said I. "Of *brass*", said he. A little after, when I wanted to talk with him, he called out, "I've given you the parole: *brass*." Once he called me a scoundrel; and as he held a staff in his hand, and even lifted the tongs, I was in some apprehension of his doing violence. It was a sad trial. As company were to sup with me, I had to leave him, saying I was going down to Mr Johnston's, and I really did go. He still sat. But upon my wife's coming into the room and sitting down, or appearing to stay, he went off; and then she came to Mr Johnston's and informed me. I was much affected by him tonight, and thought of writing to his father, or going out to him in a chair next day, that he might have proper measures taken to prevent him from harassing my family and exposing himself and his relations. Grange well observed that my father and Lady Auchinleck should have the weight of so disagreeable a business, for that, as I was not allowed to interfere in other things, I should *not* in *this*. For ten days I had drank no fermented liquor. Tonight I drank small beer and Madeira and water. I felt my mind feeble, and company rather a trouble to me. I was idle today, though I should have written some law. I did nothing to my Consultation Book. There was a pretty deep snow and very hard frost. π.

WEDNESDAY 12 JANUARY. After a night's sleep since venturing to address Lord Covington for memoirs of his life, I was still uneasy till I should know how he would receive my application. This day at ten, while the Lords were going to the bench and his Lordship was passing through to take his seat in the Outer House, I met him, and having said, "My Lord, did you get a letter from me?", he answered in a very courteous manner, "Yes; and I'll give you an answer. But—" here he shook his hand as if he had said, "But I'm so old I cannot answer distinctly enough." I was very happy and said, "Your Lordship's very good. I hope you're very well." "Far from it", said he mildly.

I was a short while in court; and then went to Dunn's Hotel[10] and waited upon Lord Eglinton, with whom I sat more than an hour, somebody or other being with him all the time till he was just going out, when I sounded him if he would lend me any money, but found he would not. He said it was foolish in him to pay his brother's debts. I said no. For he could have done nothing that would have given him more satisfaction and been more to his honour. He said it was foolish except as to his own satisfaction. For if he had bought land with the money, would he not have had more influence in the county than by paying these debts? This was a shrewd remark. I am never very happy in his company, for he has no high opinion of me; and as we are not of congenial tempers, I am under restraint. Balbarton came and dined with us. We had also worthy Grange; and we three drank warm port negus moderately and comfortably. Balbarton said he had seen eighty New Year's Days. My brother John called. Was told I was not in. But he walked up-stairs. Hearing voices in the dining-room, he went away and did not return this night, which was lucky. Lord Eglinton, Lord Glencairn, Colonel Macdonell, and Mr John Wauchope[11] supped with us. Mr Wood promised to come, but did not, nor did he call today. I very foolishly drank first Madeira, and then two bottles of port, Lord Glencairn and I taking that liquor; and after his Lordship and Wauchope were gone, I joined Lord Eglinton and Colonel Macdonell in strong rum punch, so that altogether I was quite destroyed.

THURSDAY 13 JANUARY. The inflammation and sickness from riot, and the violent frost had given me a terrible headache. I got up about nine, but was obliged to go to bed again. I lay all day in great pain till the evening. My brother John drank tea with my wife, and was shockingly sulky. I rose at nine and was sadly vexed. Mr Wood did not call today.

10 A fashionable hotel in St Andrew Square in the New Town.
11 John Wauchope (1751-1828), W.S. (admitted 24 June 1774).

FRIDAY 14 JANUARY. I rose pretty well. It was the most intense frost that I ever felt. But I went to the Parliament House, though I really suffered severe pain from the cold. My brother John being in a state either of great insanity or terrible perverseness, I was quite at a loss what should be done with him. My spirits were sadly sunk. Worthy Grange joined me in opinion that my father and his lady should take the direction of so disagreeable an affair. I walked out to my father's and sat a little while with him by ourselves, and found him in good calm temper. When his lady came into the room, I mentioned my dilemma as to poor John. She treated my concern with abominable unfeeling ill-nature, as if I had only an affectation of humanity, and said she had borne more from John than I had, or would have done; but that I felt much more for myself than for my neighbours; and that it was very easy for me to keep him out of my house if I chose to do it, by speaking to him in a determined manner that I would send to him when it was convenient for me. I told her she was fit to be captain of a man-of-war. My father sat by quite unconcerned. I was hurt at her infernal harshness, but governed my temper. Dr Boswell's two daughters dined there today, as I did. When I was going away, my father showed a little extraordinary kindness, for he said to me, "Now that you can walk, let us see you often." When I came home, I found that my brother John had called and tried to get into the dining-room, but, as my wife and I had concerted, the door was bolted. Mr Wood called when I was out. I dictated law pretty well, but was by no means in a state of enjoyment. Only at night I loved my wife warmly, though I was affected with thinking of the deplorable situation I and my children would be in if she should die, which a pretty severe cough which she now had made me fear. π.

SATURDAY 15 JANUARY. It was painfully cold. I was a little while in the Parliament House, and in very bad spirits. I had a return of hypochondria in that way as to see nothing worth while. Sat a little with worthy Grange. Then went home and wrote *The Hypochondriack* No. 28,[12] having only two or three notes beforehand. Wrote wonderfully well, considering my state of mind. Dined at Fortune's at the annual meeting of Mundell's scholars, a very thin company and nothing joyous in it. Slipped away quietly about seven, very sober; revised Mr Lawrie's copy of my *Hypochondriack* and wrote to Mr Dilly calmly, having drank some green tea. Also studied part of a long cause on which I had a Memorial to write. Was somewhat uneasy that my practice since this year began was very scanty. Was much affected with reading tonight in the *London Chronicle* that the celebrated Captain Cook was killed.[13] Mr Wood did not call today. My brother John called this afternoon again, but the dining-room door was again bolted. So he went away.

MONDAY 17 JANUARY. I had set apart this day for writing a dull paper. But Lord Eglinton called and asked me so cordially to dine along with him at Leith, just he and I and Colonel Macdonell and Willie Haggart,[14] that I could not refuse. So I

12 On criticism.
13 Cook had been killed by natives in Hawaii on 14 February 1779.
14 Willie Haggart was a wine merchant in North Leith.

went down with him in a hackney-coach to Lawson's,[15] where Mr Haggart only joined us; and we three took a good Scots dinner, and drank bumpers till near twelve o'clock at night. Our conversation was not lively but cordial. I should have been comfortable had not the Earl been quite despotic in making me drink hard. He sang "*Row me owr the lea-rig, my ain kind dearieo*"[16] with so much taste that I could almost pay a headache to hear it again. He and I drove up in a post-chaise. I came out at the north end of the New Bridge and walked home. I was excessively sick and in violent uneasiness, though not so much intoxicated as I have been on some occasions. I this day omitted my ten lines, which broke a year's series.[17]

TUESDAY 18 JANUARY. Awaked in terrible distress. Thought I would lie all day. But upon my wife's suggesting that being frequently out of the House would hurt my practice, I resolved to show myself in court if it were but for a few minutes. So I went about eleven, when I was surprisingly better. I took a hackney-coach and went to Leith with my wife and daughters and Sandy, and saw a part of the West Fencibles that had come over from Fife. We met with Lord Eglinton, who was just setting out for London. We eat raw oysters at Mrs Thomson's. I was quite feeble and dejected. By the way home we found Grange walking, and as it snowed, carried him home, and he dined with us. Mr Wood was not with me either yesterday or today.

THURSDAY 20 JANUARY. Was now pretty well, but my spirits were still shattered. Was uneasy at my practice being diminished. Mr Lawrie was of opinion with me that my father's absence from the House did me hurt. I never before this winter felt real uneasiness from embarrassed circumstances. For I knew not how to raise £200. I had written both to Temple and Dilly on the subject; and I trusted most to English friends. Sir William Forbes and Mr Hunter, with whom I sat awhile this forenoon, said they could let me have a little money only for a few months. I called on my father today and found him placidly insensible. My brother John came and dined with us today, without invitation, though he would not come the two preceding days when invited. He was sulky. I was weakly humane enough to ask him to tea. He came and was very disagreeable. I dictated well.

FRIDAY 21 JANUARY. My wife and I dined at Balmuto's.[18] I just kept myself quiet in a coarse company. I mean where conversation was Scottishly rough. I did not drink much, but when I came home was not inclined to do any business; and luckily I had none that required immediate dispatch. I found a letter from Lord Covington, in very obliging terms, but waiving particular answers to my queries. This was a disappointment to me. But I thought I would get answers

---

15 The "Old Ship" tavern in Leith. "A courteous host and excellent food attracted numerous patrons thither, especially the Edinburgh lawyers who came down to the Shore on Saturdays to do justice to [the fare] and to linger over the chestnuts and prawns which always accompanied the wine at Lawson's" (Stuart, pp. 152-3).

16 "Row = roll; lea-rig = the unploughed ridge between two cultivated fields. The song is now known in the purified revision of Robert Fergusson, 'Will ye gang o'er the lea-rig?'" (*Laird*, p. 170, n. 5).

17 It seems that Boswell did not write any further ten-line verses this year.

18 Claud Boswell of Balmuto was now residing in Argyle Square.

from him in conversation. I eat a couple of eggs, drank tea, and went to bed. Lay long awake. π.

SATURDAY 22 JANUARY. The cold was really painful. At a meeting of the Faculty of Advocates I spoke with spirit for our behaving liberally to the good town of Edinburgh in agreeing to pay our share of the contribution to repair the damages of the Roman Catholics. Mr Andrew Balfour was against our paying, and asked where was the difference between this and subscribing to the Edinburgh Regiment, which was treated with contempt by a majority? I answered warmly that every man would speak from his own feelings. But I saw a great difference between subscribing to a regiment raised to *commit* injuries upon our fellow-subjects, and contributing to *repair* injuries which had been committed. I sent a note of this to the *Caledonian Mercury*, but did not mention *who* had made the answer.[19] I walked out to my father's, who had catched a fresh cold. Lord Advocate called on him for a little to talk about his Justiciary gown. I did not join them till they were done with it; and then I convoyed Lord Advocate to the gate into the Meadow from my father's field. He told me that the King had given it in command to Lord Stormont[20] to lay before him the pretensions of the several candidates for being judges, being resolved to prefer those who will be most for the advantage of this part of the country. He and I talked quite easily. I dined at my father's. He was in a bad frame, talking of the evil of contracting debt, and recalling my bad management. I got home about four o'clock. Mr James Baillie drank tea with us, and in a very friendly manner engaged to supply me with money for some time. I dictated well and finished a long Petition. But I had no vivid enjoyment of life.

SUNDAY 23 JANUARY. The frost was so intense, and my body so susceptible of cold by not getting any exercise taken by reason of my sore toe, that after being dressed to go to church, I resolved to stay at home. The children said divine lessons in the most agreeable manner. Indeed I find them quiet and good on Sunday much more than on other days. Little Jamie was now a fine child as ever I saw. On Thursday last he first began to speak by uttering one word, *here*, which he continues to cry briskly. Mr Wood called between sermons and began to cut the nail out of my toe. But it was so painful with the cold that I could not bear it, and he desisted very humanely. Dr Webster dined with us. I was so cold in the afternoon that I went to bed before seven, just for warmth and quiet repose. Read some of *Ancient Metaphysics*.[21]

19 At a meeting on 12 January 1778, the Faculty had declined a request from the Lord Provost to subscribe to a regiment of foot to be called "The Edinburgh Volunteers", the ostensible reasons being that the Faculty was a national body rather than an Edinburgh corporation and that its funds were to be used only for the Faculty's own purposes (but the real reason being perhaps more to do with the political ambitions of the Dean (Henry Dundas), who, in an effort to acquire influence in Edinburgh, was determined not to co-operate with the town council (Stewart, p. 289, n. 452)). On this occasion, however, the Faculty unanimously voted to pay their proportion of the levy (*ibid.*, p. 310). Boswell's note appeared in the *Caledonian Mercury* for 25 January 1780.
20 David Murray (1727-1796), 7th Viscount Stormont (*later* 2nd Earl of Mansfield), an eminent diplomat and, from 1778-94, Lord Justice-General of Scotland (i.e., titular head of the Court of Justiciary).
21 By Lord Monboddo (see the entry for 20 June 1779 and relevant footnote).

MONDAY 24 JANUARY. I received tonight a most friendly letter from Mr C. Dilly agreeing to lend me £200 for two years. This was truly pleasing.

TUESDAY 25 JANUARY. Lady Dowager Colville had called on me on Saturday and asked me to dine with her today with Lords Glencairn and Balcarres.[22] But I kept to my engagement with Lord Monboddo, who had Sir David Carnegie, a very pretty young man, his mother and sisters, Mr Baron Gordon, etc., to dine with him. I was in a state of *indifference*, so that I really cared for nothing. I drank rather too much claret, as I always do at Monboddo's. I went at eight to Lord Kames's, where I had not been all this winter, which hurt my feelings, as he has really been at all times exceedingly obliging to me. I found Mrs Drummond by herself and in very good humour. She and I talked cheerfully. My Lord came home between eight and nine from dining at Lord Braxfield's. He had taken so much wine as to be visibly intoxicated a little. He shook hands with me in the most cordial manner, and both he and his lady readily accepted of my apology of indisposition that I had been so long of seeing them. He said that he would not live long. I forget his exact words. But that was the meaning. She said to him he was very well. He answered keenly that he knew or felt that he would not live long. He fell asleep on a chair. Before this Mr David Hume, advocate,[23] had come in. Though I was offended by his publishing his uncle's posthumous poison, I liked the sedateness of his manner. Lord Kames was waked when supper was on the table, and he recovered wonderfully. But we had no interesting conversation. I resolved to see him oftener. Worthy Grange said to me this forenoon, when I acknowledged to him Lord Kames's kindness to me, that I should not allow myself to speak, or if possible even to think, ill of him.

THURSDAY 27 JANUARY. Before dinner Mr Wood came, and I felt myself resolved to bear the pain, so he cut a good deal of the nail of my great toe out of the flesh. The operation hurt me much. But as soon as it was over I perceived that I was much relieved, for I felt only the pain of a green wound instead of the pain of my toe irritated by the nail in it. Grange drank tea with us. At eight o'clock I had a party which I had long projected—a social meeting in the public house under the pillars in the Parliament Close, where Dr Pitcairne used to take his bottle every evening. It was called the *graping* office, from groping in the dark. It was lately advertised ignorantly by the name of the *Grapewine* Office. Grange had engaged for us the very room where the Doctor sat. It was underground from the pillars, very low-roofed, and had

---

22 Alexander Lindsay (1752-1825), 6th Earl of Balcarres, entered the army in 1767 and was promoted to Major in 1775. "He served in the unfortunate expedition of General Burgoyne in North America and was wounded at Ticonderoga, 7 July 1777" (*Scots Peerage*, Vol. 3, p. 42). He rose to the rank of General and was appointed Civil Governor and Commander-in-Chief of the Island of Jersey in 1793, and of Jamaica in 1794.
23 David Hume (1757-1838), advocate (admitted 13 July 1779), nephew of David Hume, the philosopher. Sheriff-Depute of Berwickshire (1783-93) and then of Linlithgowshire (1793-1811), Professor of Scots Law at Edinburgh University (1786-1822), Principal Clerk of Session (1811), Baron of Exchequer (1822-34). In 1779 he published his uncle's *Dialogues Concerning Natural Religion*.

no window.[24] The party was Grange, Mr James Baillie, Mr John Graeme,[25] and myself. Sir Walter[26] was admitted as an additional man. We had oysters and minced pies, and drank whisky punch and were heartily merry. I did not drink too much. Miss Preston, who was come to town for a while, called in the forenoon. π.

FRIDAY 28 JANUARY. My wife was ill with a cold which made her dull of hearing and alarmed her. I had a load of papers lying on my table, and felt a dread of the labour of dictating which hung over me. But I could evade it for a while, so was pretty easy in the mean time.

SATURDAY 29 JANUARY. It is unpleasing to observe how imperfect a picture of my life this journal presents. Yet I have certainly much more of *myself* thus preserved than most people have. I was hurt by a furious decision of the Lords this forenoon against a client of mine, Grigor Grant, a sheriff officer in Edinburgh, proceeding as I thought upon the narrow ground of what they *supposed* he knew, though there was no *legal document* of it. The weather was now much milder. My toe was very easy. At one o'clock there was a meeting of several of Sir Walter Montgomerie-Cuninghame's creditors in the Exchange Coffee-house. But it was found that he could not give a state of his affairs sufficiently distinct as yet. He resolved to go home and return with an accurate state. He and I dined with his agent, Mr Andrew Blane,[27] and also drank tea. Mr Blane's sister and Miss Grissie Wallace made the rest of the company. I know not when I have been more comfortable than I was here. We had a good dinner neatly served up in a clean new house in St David's Street, New Town, and I had full liberty to drink negus as I chose, without being asked to take more than I liked. Sir Walter followed me home, as I took a chair. He complained with some justice that I treated him as if he were still a boy. I should guard against this, which I find so disagreeable in my father. I went down to Grange and brought up him and Mr James Loch to supper. π.

SUNDAY 30 JANUARY. Awaked placid and cheerful. The change from hard frost to milder weather was benignant to me. I was dressed in good time and walked out with intention to go to the New Church. But in the street it occurred

---

24 Archibald Pitcairne (1652-1713) was a physician in Edinburgh and a poet. "The tavern celebrated by... Pitcairne in his Latin lyric on the Edinburgh inns under the name of *Greppa* was more colloquially dubbed the 'Greping-office' by the wits who felt their way down its dark stairs and through its underground passages." Situated beneath the piazza (the arcade) at the northeast corner of the Parliament Close, it was "a much-frequented and fashionable resort in the early eighteenth century and there, too, of all places, doctors were wont to hold consulting hours for their patients, Pitcairne himself usually being found there at six o'clock in the morning for this purpose... The convivial doctor was a notable man of his time who laid the foundations on which future anatomists built up Edinburgh's medical renown. Notorious for his unorthodox views and 'twice drunk every day'..., Pitcairne was nevertheless popular in society and it was probably due to his well-known generosity that he died poor, though he had possessed a large practice" (Stuart, pp. 40-1).
25 John Graeme, W.S. (admitted 10 July 1770), died 1814.
26 Sir Walter Montgomerie-Cuninghame.
27 Andrew Blane (1744-1839), W.S. (admitted 24 November 1774), Sheriff-Clerk Ayrshire 1815-21, died unmarried.

to me that I would not go and join with Presbyterians on the 30th of January.[28] So I returned and sat awhile with worthy Grange, and then came home and found Sir Walter. Mr Wood called and took a part of our dinner. He had not called since Thursday. As my toe was easy, he would not open it down yet. The children said less of their divine lessons than usual today. After dinner, I was in a guzzling humour and eat a great deal of roasted cheese; and Sir Walter and I drank each two bottles of strong beer. He set off between four and five on his way home. I was very drowsy, and consoled myself with the intention of going snug to bed after tea. But Sir Charles Preston came to tea; and as my wife saw that he meant to stay supper, she asked him and he agreed. This was right in her, but it was very hard on me. I could hardly talk at all. I suffered as one must do with company in the country. After he went away I unloaded my stomach.

MONDAY 31 JANUARY. Rose much better than I could have expected to be. Dictated a good deal with pretty good ease. My wife kept her room with the cold and deafness. Lady Auchinleck called on her. Sandy insisted to go out and dine with his grandfather, whom he had not seen for a long time. Lady Auchinleck carried him out in the chariot with her. I was in very reasonable spirits today. My brother John, whom I had asked to dine but who sent me word that he could not wait on me, had desired Mr Lawrie to see if I could be at leisure at seven to settle accounts with him. I was at leisure; and he came and was as clear-headed as a man could be. He was even cheerful in his appearance, but I found that he had a pleasure in keeping up his charge that I had not accounted fairly for his effects; so we came to no settlement. I regretted tonight his unhappy disease, as he was so well that I could look on him as a comfortable brother till he came upon the accounting. Andrew Erskine called before dinner and paid me £50 which he owed me, with interest. It is strange how he and I, who once were so much together, live now quite apart. I told him I had not felt poverty till this winter. But that it was nothing in comparison with what he and I had felt (meaning hypochondria). He said it was next to that. I agreed. Poor fellow, he has not such a prospect as I have of relief from poverty. But then he has no wife or children.

TUESDAY 1 FEBRUARY. Was in very good spirits. My practice was brisker, which enlivened me. Between two and three there was a meeting of Mr Erskine of Mar's trustees:[29] the Earl of Buchan,[30] his brother Mr Henry Erskine, Lord Gardenstone, myself, and Mr Lawrence Inglis.[31] We met in Bain's Tavern, President's Stairs, and had soup, accepted of the trust deed, and appointed an accurate state of Mr Erskine's debts, funds, and claims to be prepared. There was a

---

28 The anniversary of the execution of Charles I.
29 "Old Erskine's" style of Mar was purely one of courtesy (*Laird*, p. 154, n. 9).
30 David Steuart Erskine (1742-1829), 11th Earl of Buchan, founder of the Society of Antiquaries of Scotland (as to the formation of which, see the entry for 18 November 1780). Although a patron of the literati, he was widely considered to be unduly ostentatious. Indeed, Sir Walter Scott said of him that his "immense vanity bordering upon insanity obscured or rather eclipsed very considerable talents" (Scott, 20 April 1829).
31 A "writer".

manliness and a fashion about Erskine amidst his embarrassed affairs that, though I knew he at that moment might be apprehended for debt, I could not but hold him in consideration. My having looked upon him in my early years as a grand English-bred man ("*Old Erskine*") no doubt aided my imagination in respecting him.[32] I dictated well today, and in short had a comfortable existence. π.

WEDNESDAY 2 FEBRUARY. Was in excellent spirits, so as to feel myself pleasant even in the Court of Session. Came home soon from the House. My two daughters and Sandy walked out with me to my father's, where I had not been since Saturday sennight, nor my daughters all this winter. We were received well enough. My father was in good temper, but seemed to be much failed today. His lady, I found, was set upon making him buy a house in the New Town. I thought it most prudent not to interfere, though it vexed me to observe her selfish views.

THURSDAY 3 FEBRUARY. This was a fast by Proclamation.[33] As I was now dubious whether the Americans were not in the right to insist on independence, I did not go to church. I sat in all the forenoon. I had resolved to employ it in making notes of a dull proof for drawing a Memorial which I had delayed too long. But I thought I would look into my journal in London in 1762, that I might console myself in Edinburgh by being reminded that I had been as weary and melancholy in London as here. And I was so engaged by my own life that I read on all the time that I had appropriated to the Memorial. This was wrong. I was sickened in mind by reviewing my own sickly weakness. Yet I thought that it was not fair to judge of London now to me by what it was when I had a narrow acquaintance in it. For *now* how delightful is it to me! And I can scarcely imagine that it would not continue to be so were I constantly there. Dr Webster called and sat some time with me, and I was waited on by Mr William Tait, son to Mr Alexander Tait, who was to be examined next day on the Scots Law.[34] Mr Wood called, as I had sent for him. But as my toe was quite easy, he would not open it down yet. Miss Susie Dunlop dined with my wife. I dined with Mr Erskine of Mar at his house in the Abbey Court, Lord Napier's. I knew that he was liable to be apprehended for debt, and I wondered to observe his high spirits. Lord Gardenstone and Dr Heron were the rest of the company till Harry Erskine, who could not get in time to dinner, joined us. We drank very moderately. There was not much good conversation. Harry Erskine and I drank tea after the rest were gone. I liked to be with my Erskine kindred. After I came home, I went and sat awhile with Grange. I could do nothing, not even write my journal. I could not help a gloomy imagination of this day like an old Edinburgh Sunday.

32 "Old Erskine" had studied at Oxford (*Laird*, p. 176, n. 9).
33 See also the entry for 9 February 1779.
34 Boswell was one of the private examiners on Scots law (see p. 66, n. 39). William Tait was admitted advocate on 12 February 1780 and, after serving as Advocate-Depute from 1787 to 1790, was appointed Sheriff-Depute of Stirlingshire on 29 May 1790. He was elected M.P. for the Stirling Burghs in 1797 and died unmarried in 1800.

SATURDAY 5 FEBRUARY. After the Court, Grange went with me for a little into Signora Marcucci's school and saw Veronica dance a minuet very well. Then he and I walked out to Sir Alexander Dick's, as I was resolved that the first long walk I took with my whole toe should be to Prestonfield. Sir Alexander was remarkably well. Mr John Macpherson and Mr Robert Gillespie and Mr Andrew Bennet were at dinner. After they were gone the worthy Baronet grew exceedingly cordial and social, called for a bottle of his best claret and a toasted biscuit, and was quite lively and classical. Mr Gillespie returned and we had another bottle, the conversation then taking a more rustic turn. We were excellently happy. We drank coffee and tea, and had his chariot to town. He said the only inconvenience he felt from old age was that he could not go about and see his friends so much as he would wish to do. Grange was supremely pleased. I was a little heated and fretful after I came home, having taken rather too much wine.

SUNDAY 6 FEBRUARY. In the evening Veronica and I sat a good while on the settee in the drawing-room by ourselves. I was dotingly fond of her, and talked with earnest, anxious, tender apprehension of her death; how it would distress me, but that I must submit to GOD's will and hope to meet her in Heaven. She was quite enchanting. I prayed extempore while we knelt together. I supped at Lord Kames's by particular invitation; three Miss Baillies of Jerviswood, Lords Braxfield and Kennet, Young Mar,[35] etc., there. There was no relish tonight either instructive or lively. π.

TUESDAY 8 FEBRUARY. Grange dined with us, and he and I drank cider joyfully to the success of our trial for expenses in the cause, Brown against Smith, as to which a long Representation by me was appointed to be answered.[36] At night my wife was very good to me.

THURSDAY 10 FEBRUARY. Drank tea with Mr Nairne and saw him firmly persuaded that living quietly and out of the bustle of life was the most agreeable way.

SATURDAY 12 FEBRUARY. That unhappy being, James Gilkie, had a question before the Lords as to his being admitted a procurator. I had drawn a very conciliating paper for him, which really had a good effect. The cause was delayed. But the Court seemed to be humane towards him. I was engaged to dine at Craighouse with Lord Covington. Grange and Mr Lawrie walked with me to the avenue foot. Mr Murray of Broughton and Charles Boyd and I were all the company. It was a very good day, upon the whole. Mr Murray carried me to town in a chaise which he had. I went to the Hon. A. Gordon's, not intending to stay; but got to whist and brag, and grew keen (as I always do) in an uneasy manner. Lost only three and sixpence, yet was vexed, so ill does gaming agree with my temper. I supped there. Mr Walter Scott, Writer to the Signet, played at *that*,[37]

35 "Young Mar" was "Old Erskine's" eldest son, John Francis Erskine.
36 See also the entry for 31 October 1777.
37 "Boswell's italics. It is not clear just what he means, but a satiric reference to Mr Scott's strictness is probably intended" (*Laird*, p. 179, n. 5).

and Lord Haddo came in after supper.[38] I was feeble-spirited and indifferent, and felt myself like a child, or a sick old man. When I came home I was vexed that my wife had been uneasy from uncertainty where I was. I found a letter lying for me from my brother David that he was preparing to return to Britain. It gave me most comfortable joy. It was quite romantic to think of seeing him again. My wife was very good to me.

SUNDAY 13 FEBRUARY. Heard Dr Blair in the forenoon and Mr Walker in the afternoon. Called for a little at my father's between sermons. David's return was full in my mind, and cheered me affectionately. It was strange to observe how cold his father was. I said to him that it was very comfortable that David was coming home. That when David set out he had said, "Poor man, I'll never see him again." But it had turned out more agreeably. He said nothing, I think. Miss Susie Dunlop dined with us. Lord Macdonald and Mr James Baillie drank tea with us. After which the children said divine lessons, and I prayed extempore with my two daughters kneeling by me. They were pleasingly affected. I went to Lord Kames's and got more materials for his life. Young Mar supped with him, which he took very kindly. I drank to my shaking hands with him at a hundred.

MONDAY 14 FEBRUARY. Washed my feet for the first time this winter, my toe being now well. Was in a fretful frame, there being some scurvy breaking out again slightly upon my legs and thighs.

TUESDAY 15 FEBRUARY. Was not at all right. The Court of Session disgusted me in the forenoon, and in the afternoon I grew so low-spirited and languid and fretful that I could do nothing, but sat moping by my fire. I should have written *The Hypochondriack* No. 29. But had not a single thought. I was not ashamed of showing my wretched disease before Grange and Mr Lawrie. I once thought of getting into bed and being quiescent at once. But was persuaded to sit up and have Grange to eat a bit of supper and drink some negus with us, which relieved me a little. How sad is it that I am subject to such dreary fits, which absolutely deprive me, while they last, not only of happiness but even of the very imagination of happiness! It hurt me that I made my valuable wife uneasy, especially when she was with child.

WEDNESDAY 16 FEBRUARY. Rose a good deal better. Began my *Hypochondriack* No. 29[39] and wrote with tolerable ease. I had on Tuesday forenoon sat awhile with Sir William Forbes at the counting-house, but was so languid that it was a pain to me to keep up conversation even with him. He advised me not to think of settling in London, and argued very justly that I should correct the error of my imagination which made me look upon Edinburgh as so narrow and inconsiderable. But still, as Sir John Pringle said to me, I was born for England; and I am so much happier in London—nay, anywhere in England—than in Edinburgh that it is hard I should be confined to this place. However, I must prudently

---

38 George Gordon (1764-1791), Lord Haddo, eldest son of George Gordon, 3rd Earl of Aberdeen.
39 On pity.

wait till I see if my circumstances shall ever be such as to enable me to live in London. I went out and dined at my father's. Just he and his lady and I at table. He was in a dull, cold humour and seemed quite indifferent about me. This was very hard. But I could not help it.

THURSDAY 17 FEBRUARY. Finished my *Hypochondriack* No. 29 with satisfaction, and dictated easily in law too. π.

FRIDAY 18 FEBRUARY. Had not much relish of life, neither was I very uneasy. Balmuto and his sister Miss Menie, Mr Nairne, Mr George Wallace, Mr David Erskine, and Mr John Hunter dined with us. I was steady and rational in appearance. But though I did not drink much more than a bottle of wine, I was disturbed by it. My wife was at Signora Marcucci's Public[40] with my daughters, who she told me danced well; and indeed I regretted that I did not go and see them. I walked in the street some time to sober myself. Was disgusted with seeing the coarse Edinburgh whores, so much more refined am I now. Then Hon. A. Gordon met me in the street. I went to his house and eat oysters and cold beef and drank small beer with him. When I came home, was sick and threw up.

SATURDAY 19 FEBRUARY. Was in languid spirits from having drank rather too much yesterday. Felt the practice of the law a burthen. Hesitated between labouring hard all day on law papers or taking a walk to rouse me. Preferred the latter. Took Veronica with me to Lady Colville's. Frost had returned, and the cold was intense. Veronica behaved exceedingly well. I insensibly agreed to dine with her Ladyship, though at first resolved against it. So took Veronica home, and went out again. Dined well, nobody there but Lady Anne, the Major, and Mr Andrew. Came to town in the coach with the Miss Elphinstones. Mr James Baillie, who had drank tea with my wife last night, drank tea with us again tonight. My spirits were so sunk that I was just going to steal into bed. My wife wisely prevented me. I studied Lord Eglinton's political causes.

SUNDAY 20 FEBRUARY. I heard a Mr Henderson lecture twice on the Good Samaritan in the forenoon, or rather was present without hearing; and I heard with pretty good attention a fine discourse by Dr Blair on the house of mourning in the afternoon. My wife and Phemie were with me. I drank tea at my father's, who was failed but not at all morose today. But his lady was very disagreeable. I went by special invitation and supped at Lord Kames's; Sir John Stewart and his lady, etc., there. I was cold and unhappy and got very little for my life of him.

MONDAY 21 FEBRUARY. Dictated well, though my spirits were dull. Between eight and nine went to Fortune's on a consultation on Lord Eglinton's political causes, which were to come on before the Lords on Wednesday. Mr Wight, the laird of Fairlie, and Messieurs John Wauchope and George Cumming,[41] the joint agents, made the company. After business was over, we supped, and drank claret

---

40 "Signora Marcucci's 'Public' was an exhibition of dancing by her pupils to which their parents were invited" (*Laird*, p. 181, n. 1).
41 George Cumming (1746-1804), W.S. (admitted 3 July 1778).

till about three in the morning. I was riotously inclined and thought that a hearty dose of wine might produce a change upon my spirits for the better. When I got home, I was shockingly rude (as I was informed, for I soon was insensible).

TUESDAY 22 FEBRUARY. Rose very ill. But went to the Parliament House and appeared in eight causes, that I might do my duty and afterwards get to bed. In one of the causes there was an oath to be read by me. With much difficulty I made it out, for my eyes wavered grievously. I took care not to get into conversation with anybody; and as the crowd was offensive to me, I went between causes and walked in the space where the shops are. Much did I long for this difficult warfare being over. At last it *was* over, and home I went. The cold was intense and my sickness and headache severe. I got into bed and fell asleep. Awaked before three, still in pain. But soup and small beer and toasted bake[42] did me good. My dearest wife's kindness when I did not deserve it was very great. I rose about six. Worthy Grange drank tea with us. I was shattered. Yet I declared that the state in which I now was seemed to be ease compared with my hypochondriac uneasiness for some time past. I eat a comfortable supper. π.

WEDNESDAY 23 FEBRUARY. Was somewhat better. The Court of Session was so much engaged with trying one Reid, accused of forgery, that for a good part of the Session for some time past most of the lawyers have had nothing to do in the Inner House. This day however the Lords determined a parcel of Ayrshire votes, after which I went to my father's and sat awhile with him, negatively well. Walked half round the Meadow.

THURSDAY 24 FEBRUARY. Either yesterday or today, sitting by Mr John Swinton at the bar, I told him that I must make a bargain with him as Dr Pitcairne did with his friend: that he should come back and tell him what the other world was. And he should tell me what it was to be a Lord of Session after he was on the bench, which he would be among the first.[43] I said I was afraid it was a dull life. He said he was afraid so too. But then he added that one never tires sitting reading or writing in one's study, and he supposed it might be like that: a kind of negative enjoyment. At two there was a meeting of Old Erskine's trustees at Mr Inglis's on Heriot's Bridge.[44] I attended bodily. But my mind was quite feeble. I thought everybody had more force of mind than I had. I could have cried from weak, painful dejection.

SATURDAY 26 FEBRUARY. I dined at Mr Baron Gordon's;[45] Lord Monboddo, Crosbie, etc., there. I was in excellent spirits. But there was little good conversation. London and Dr Johnson have made me unhappy in ordinary company. But it was much to be easy, in place of saying within myself as I did some days ago, "*I exist in misery*", so weary and fretful was I. Lord Monboddo and I stayed tea. Both he and the Baron were violent against Lord Kames. They both said they knew him to be a worthless scoundrel. Monboddo said he was malevolent

---

42 A small biscuit.
43 Swinton became a Lord of Session (as Lord Swinton) on 21 December 1782.
44 Heriot's Bridge was the main entrance to Heriot's Hospital from the Grassmarket.
45 Baron Gordon's house was in St Andrew Square in the New Town.

against people, not only for censuring his writings, but for not admiring him. He said he was excessively dull as well as wrongheaded, and that he was suitably employed only when he compiled the *Dictionary of Decisions*, which just required drudgery. The Baron said he was avaricious and envious, and would cut your throat if he could do it safely. I was somewhat confounded to hear him attacked in terms so very strong. I said he had always been very good to me. When I got home, I found that though I had taken care to be quite sober, I was in a restless state which was still more uneasy than my general drowsiness at night, for I could not have the immediate relief of sleep. I went to bed without supper. But for the first time these many nights, tossed in a wakeful state for perhaps an hour.

MONDAY 28 FEBRUARY. Did nothing but settle two bills which I owed Grange, by paying him out of my cash account with the bank and money lodged with Sir William Forbes and Company. Drank tea with him and eat milk bakes and honey comfortably. Miss Preston supped with us. π.

WEDNESDAY 1 MARCH. The Hon. Alexander Gordon and I dined at Lady Colville's; Mr Erskine of Cardross and his lady, etc., there. We drank liberally of good claret; then went to coffee and tea and played at whist. I never grow better at the game, yet play and bet very foolishly. I lost about two pounds, which vexed me in my present state of want of money; and Lady Anne Erskine observed justly that I should not play, because I then appeared inferior to others. I shall scarcely ever do it, as I have not attention enough. Gordon and I stayed supper, and as it was a wet night, had my Lady's coach to town. Yesterday I was uneasy to think of Lord Covington's disappointment by Lord Braxfield's getting my father's Justiciary gown, which, by the influence of the Dundases and his own prejudice against Lord Covington, he would not resign unless Lord Braxfield should get it, though Lord Covington had Lord Mansfield's promise. I admired the spirit with which Lord Covington bore his disappointment. He was as attentive and acute upon the bench as ever. I had spoken to Lord Advocate for him, pressing the hardship of disappointing him. My Lord gave me a very solid answer: that it would be wrong to give the gown resigned by one old man to a man still older, especially as Lord Kames, a very old man, had one of them. He added he would agree to Lord Covington's getting it if Lord Kames were out of the way. He said the Chancellor[46] was firm against giving it to Lord Covington, which he said would be a job.[47] But Lord Stormont desired Lord Advocate to think of some mark of the royal favour to Lord Covington. I still could not help thinking, or at least feeling, that Lord Covington might have been gratified with being a Justiciary Lord, which I suppose the narrowness of his views makes him look upon to be as great a dignity as it appeared to me when a boy at school.

FRIDAY 3 MARCH. I sent a note at night to Maclaurin sincerely sympathizing

46 The (English) Lord Chancellor, Lord Thurlow.
47 As the editors of *Laird* point out (at p. 186, n. 7), the words "a job" are used here in the sense of a "transaction in which duty is sacrificed to private advantage" (*Concise Oxford Dictionary*).

with him on the death of one of his sons and anxious to hear how his wife was. I got an answer from him that she was dead.[48] Burke in his *Sublime and Beautiful* says we have some pleasure from the distress of others. There was an agitation in my mind tonight which was better than melancholy. Yet I felt for Maclaurin and his children, thinking of my own situation, should such an event happen in my family. My wife was much affected. π.

SATURDAY 4 MARCH. Dined at Lady Colville's. Was not joyous, but well enough. Being a little intoxicated, I called at Portsburgh in my way home with a gross appetite. But luckily had not an opportunity.

SUNDAY 5 MARCH. Heard Mr Walker in the forenoon and Dr Blair in the afternoon. Was at Mrs Maclaurin's burial between sermons. It did not shock me so much as I supposed it would do. My apprehension of my dear wife's death was not so lively as it has been sometimes. Called on Lord Braxfield by appointment at five and walked out with him to my father's and drank tea. Lord Braxfield announced to him his pension of £200 a year being fixed, to begin just where his salary ended.[49] He affected indifference about it, which I did not like, and he was in bad humour with me. After I came home my children said divine lessons very agreeably. π.

TUESDAY 7 MARCH. Called on Maclaurin before dinner.[50] He appeared to be wonderfully easy. In the evening my wife and I were at Signora Marcucci's ball and saw our daughters dance very well. I could not quite divest myself of a strange dejected bashfulness. Sandy was with us for a little.

FRIDAY 10 MARCH. Craigengillan and Mrs McAdam, Commissioner Cochrane, and Grange dined with us. I had been shut up for two hours in the Court of Session attending as counsel for Macredie, a Stranraer merchant accused of fraudulent bankruptcy, whom the Lords were examining.[51] My spirits were bad.

48 Maclaurin's young son had died of a fever following on an attack of whooping cough, and his wife had died a few hours later.

49 Lord Auchinleck's salary as a Lord Commissioner of Justiciary was £200 a year, and so his pension on retiring from the Justiciary bench was the same as his salary had been.

50 Maclaurin was now residing in Adam Square.

51 This case (N.A.S. 1779/12/30 CS 222/491) is an example of the harshness with which debtors could be treated in those days. Alexander McCredie, a young merchant in Stranraer, had been declared bankrupt by order of the Court of Session in December 1779. Subsequently his shop in Stranraer was broken into and goods of some value were uplifted. His creditors suspected that he was an accessory to this act and that he had thus committed a gross fraud. They lodged a petition setting forth their suspicions and craving the court to grant a warrant for his apprehension with a view to having him examined before the court. A warrant was granted on 12 January 1780 and McCredie was duly arrested later that month. He was incarcerated in the Tolbooth at Edinburgh on 1 March and was brought before the Inner House for examination on the 10th. McCredie declared that at the time his shop was broken into he was in the Sanctuary at Holyrood Abbey and that he knew nothing about the affair until some time later when he was on the road from Glasgow to Stranraer near Ayr and was informed of the matter by a Stranraer bookseller. On 11 March Boswell presented a petition to the court seeking McCredie's release from prison in the hope that the answers given at the judicial examination were such as to have removed any suspicion of fraud on McCredie's part. Their Lordships ordered that McCredie be set at liberty, but only on producing caution (security) to the extent of £100 to attend all further diets of the court on the matter. At the same time, the court allowed McCredie's creditors to prove all relevant facts and circumstances with regard to the alleged fraudulent bankruptcy. However, as Boswell ex-

I drank some rum punch today, which never agrees with me. Grange and I walked down to the Canongate, and strolled looking at some curious old houses on the south side which had once been the lodgings of people of rank. This amused us, and we returned to tea. I was not in a happy state. π.

SATURDAY 11 MARCH. Was somewhat uneasy that my fees this Session amounted to less than they had formerly done. Apprehended a failure of my practice now that my father did not attend the Court, and thought I should be unhappy for want of business. Yet I was sensible that a great deal of the coarse labour of law in Scotland would hurt my mind; and I should have considered that one of my fortune should be satisfied with little practice. I however dreaded insignificance, while at the same time I had all this year as yet been so averse to the business of the Court of Session that I had no keenness for it, as I once had, and wished always to have anything I had to do decently over. I saw no opportunity for ambition in this narrow sphere. What practice I had, I had with the dignity of a gentleman; not having used the artifices which many advocates have done, and not debasing myself by familiarity with vulgar agents. Fain would I have indulged gay, animating hopes of exerting myself in London. But I felt indolence and gloom too heavy upon me, and I was conscious that I could not persist in uniform application. Then I considered that the expense of living in London would impoverish me, and that I might perhaps in my hypochondriac discontent wish for the *home* of Edinburgh. I was sick-minded today. The Session rose, which was rather dispiriting to me, as I was not to go to London and would mould in inactivity.

I dined at my father's. Lady Auchinleck had a headache and did not dine with us. But she with venom talked to me of people being quick to see others failed, which was not a sign of a good disposition. She plainly meant my being

---

plained in a later petition lodged in December 1780, the bond of caution which McCredie subsequently produced was rejected by the Clerk of Court as he was unacquainted with any of the cautioners (guarantors) and could only accept the bond if the factor appointed to McCredie's sequestrated estates would consent, which he did not. Boswell stated in this later petition that McCredie's case had now become "truly piteous" as he had been confined in jail for twelve months, with the consequence that his health had been "very much impaired". "And", declared Boswell, "the horror of his imprisonment is aggravated by the consideration that his subsistence depends upon the compassion of accidental acquaintances by whose kind assistance alone he has been prevented from starving." Boswell added that the creditors had done nothing in consequence of the interlocutor allowing them a proof and he suggested that the court would surely not permit them to keep McCredie "in perpetual imprisonment". "Severity", pled Boswell hopefully, "is not the character of this court and [the petitioner] trusts that humanity can be expected so far as is consistent with law." In these circumstances, Boswell craved the court to order McCredie's immediate release. However, after a hearing on the matter on 23 December, the court refused the petition on account of the delay in presenting it. A few days later McCredie evidently received a letter from one of his principal creditors stating that everything should be done for his immediate liberation; but he heard no more on the matter, and so on 13 February 1781 Boswell presented another petition explaining the latest developments and once again entreating the attention of the court to McCredie's "unhappy situation". The outcome was that the court ordered written answers to the petition to be lodged, and when no answers were made an interlocutor was pronounced on 1 March authorising the Clerk of Court to receive the bond of caution and authorising the magistrates of Edinburgh and the keepers of the Tolbooth to set McCredie at liberty. McCredie was thus finally released after having been confined in squalor for two years without any evidence having been led against him.

sensible of my father's failure, which it is possible she does not perceive clearly, and wishes not to see, as her consequence depends on his life. I kept my temper. My father was very ungracious. I came home today quite sunk, as I often do from my father's, which is really sad. I was engaged to sup tonight with Mr John Swinton.[52] But having had a hint in the morning from Mr Ilay Campbell, who was to be there, that they were to have a dance, and when I came to the door having heard a fiddle and the noise of dancing, I considered that such merriment was very unsuitable to my present gloomy, fretful state of mind, and that it was probably a hearty meeting of people all intimate with one another, while I was not intimate with any of them. I therefore returned home, and sent a card that something had happened which prevented me from being there. Had it been a company where I would have been missed, my benevolence would have made me go, though disagreeable. But with some of my friend Colonel Stuart's judicious firmness, I avoided what I disliked. I passed the evening quietly with my wife.

SUNDAY 12 MARCH. Having gone to bed last night ruminating on my melancholy, I awaked this morning with this text full in my mind: "Howbeit this kind goeth not out but by prayer and fasting."[53] This seemed to be a supernatural suggestion that piety alone could relieve me from the evil spirit. I was much impressed with it, and my devotion was fervent today. Heard Dr Blair in the forenoon and I think Mr Walker in the afternoon. Was a little at my father's between sermons. Dined at Lord Monboddo's with Mr David Rae, Lady Duffus and one of her grand-daughters, a Miss Sinclair, and Mrs Hamilton and some of her boarders. The invitation was to see the rising generation of females. We were very cheerful. But my Lord and I drank too much claret. I stayed tea. Walked home a good deal inflamed; met an old acquaintance in the street, and was in danger of being licentious with her, so soon had wine overpowered my morning seriousness, which was indeed "like the morning cloud".[54] However, I got off. My wife was hurt by my being again on the confines of low debauchery. I was very uneasy.

MONDAY 13 MARCH. It was quite a tempest. Old Erskine breakfasted with me. My wife did not appear. While his straitened circumstances were humiliating, his spirit and anecdotes amused me. Grange had received an express that his mother was just dying, and the man who came had heard she was dead; so he was to go south next day. She was very old and had not been a kind mother to him, so he was not grieved. He dined with us today. I was not at all right. Yet I wrote letters wonderfully well.

THURSDAY 16 MARCH. Yesterday and today wrote *The Hypochondriack* No. 30.[55] Wondered how I could write so well.

FRIDAY 17 MARCH. Attended Lords Gardenstone and Stonefield at the

---

52 John Swinton's house was in Brown Square.
53 Matthew 17. 21.
54 Hosea 6. 4, paraphrased.
55 On drinking, as were Nos 31 to 33.

visitation of some disputed property near the Calton. My wife and I drank tea, played cards, and supped at Dr Monro's. Our two daughters were there at tea, music, and dancing. It was a very good scene. But I wearied a little, and saw how the fondness of parents may trouble other people with the performances of their children. At present the stagnation of my spirits for want of objects to rouse them is, I suppose, my malady. I was excellent company tonight.

SUNDAY 19 MARCH. Was at the New Church during the whole service, forenoon and afternoon. Received the Holy Sacrament as a memorial of Christ's death and a public evidence of my faith. But was offended by the irreverent form of the Presbyterians. My father was there in the forenoon, and communicated. He looked very old and very unkindly. The children said divine lessons in the evening. But some bad fit had seized Veronica, for she said to me in a kind of plaintive, upbraiding tone, "I am not to go up to Heaven. I am just to rot." I quieted her, but was hurt to think of the darkness which covers our hopes of futurity unless when Christian faith bears us up.

MONDAY 20 MARCH. My father grew very uneasy with his old and now constant complaint.

TUESDAY 21 MARCH. My mind was now in a better state, though at intervals I was exceedingly gloomy. I this day dictated a law paper with more vigour than I have done of late. In the forenoon I visited my father and found him pretty well again. Sandy was with me. π.

THURSDAY 23 MARCH. Was at a consultation at Mr Ilay Campbell's, and found myself pretty clear.

The following day, Boswell and Alexander Murray, the Solicitor-General, went to Bothwell Castle to pay a sympathetic call on Archibald Douglas, whose wife, Lady Lucy, had died. They stayed with Douglas until the morning of the 27th and then returned to Edinburgh.

MONDAY 27 MARCH. The Solicitor and I drove to his country-house at Murrayfield, where I agreed to set him down. But finding Mrs Murray at dinner, I agreed to stay, so dismissed the chaise and sent my servant home before me. We dined quietly and drank a bottle of claret apiece, and the Solicitor walked with me very near to the town. It was agreeable to be thus social with the son of an old friend of my father's. I was welcomed by my dear wife and children, and happy to be at home again. π.

WEDNESDAY 29 MARCH. I dined and drank tea at my father's, Dr Gillespie there. He and I took a walk after dinner, and he said my father would be the better of going to Auchinleck and seeing his trees and improvements. I told the Doctor I was glad to hear him talk so, for that people had said he would keep my father in Edinburgh for the convenience of his own practice. I thought I would observe the Doctor's conduct as to this, and treat him accordingly.

THURSDAY 30 MARCH. Dictated a law paper. Met at Mr H. Erskine's with him and Lord Alva about Old Erskine's affairs.[56] Was nervous and not well.

MONDAY 3 APRIL. While in bed yesterday, I thought with concern how I had both a brother and an uncle in the same town with me whom I had not seen for a long time. My affection warmed, and I resolved to see them. Their being both victims to our family disorder, while it was a melancholy consideration, was also a tender one. I called on my brother John a little in the evening. But he was very silent and sour, and refused to sup with me along with John and Alexander Webster. They and Captain Mingay[57] and Mr James Donaldson supped. I drank negus and was calm.

TUESDAY 4 APRIL. Saw my poor uncle, whom I had not seen since 3 September last. He was now very weak, and his legs were shrunk so that he could not walk. He was in bed, and was quite emaciated, and spoke indistinctly. But what he said was sensible enough, though his memory was decayed. I do not think I should have known him had I seen him without being told who it was. He seemed very glad to see me, held my hand, and brought my face down to salute me. He spoke with relish of old hock; and I told him I was lucky enough to have seven bottles of it, very good, and I would send him first two, and if he liked it, he should have the whole. He expressed his usual impatience for it. So I went home and sent him two bottles; and Robert told me that he took three or four bumpers of it, and next morning when he awaked, the first thing he said was to let him have some negus of it.

WEDNESDAY 5 APRIL. Hallglenmuir and Old John Boswell[58] called on me. Hallglenmuir brought me very discouraging accounts of the setting of Dalblair, in so much that he was for my lowering the rent eight or ten pounds. I walked with them to Leith and called at Mr David Boswell's, and engaged him and his son James, now a midshipman, to dine with me today. My wife never would agree to my having poor David at dinner, because of his being a dancing-master; but I lately prevailed with her upon his son's coming home a midshipman. I had a good clannish dinner: Balbarton, John Boswell, David Boswell, James Boswell, Robert Boswell, myself, and my two sons; making eight Boswells (seven at table, as Sandy sat), and my two daughters nine, and my wife and Hallglenmuir, both Boswells' bairns. I got into a most comfortable frame. We had abundance of solid dishes, and we drank heartily. Robert left us early. But we drank three bottles port, one Mataró, and about one and a half rum in punch. I drank punch, and what was a *curiosa felicitas*,[59] I was not disturbed by it in any way, either in mind or body, so well can cordiality preserve a man. Balbarton stayed tea. I went out a little to my father's in the evening; found him at cards with his women (as Dr Johnson said) and his physician. Drinking did not at all appear upon me. I sat about an hour. This week I have been dutiful to relations.

THURSDAY 6 APRIL. I wrote letters to my tenants of Dalblair offering them

56 Henry Erskine's house was at 27 George Square (*B.O.E.C.*, Vol. 26, p. 149).
57 Captain Eyre Robert Mingay, husband of Dr Webster's daughter Anne.
58 Father of John Boswell of Knockroon.
59 "An extraordinary blessing."

their possessions with deduction of £8 upon the whole each year for four years. I was engaged to dine at Commissioner Cochrane's. Dr Gillespie and I walked out. Dr Webster was the only other guest. We had a good rational day. I was in excellent spirits. Dr Webster and I had the Commissioner's chaise into town. By the way, Webster and I talked of my not having visited the Lord President for several years. I explained the President's bad behaviour in taking advantage of my father's failure, to make him act so foolishly in the Ayrshire election. But that as this was politics, I forgave him now, and would go out with him to Arniston and see his Lordship. But I doubted whether it would be best to talk over what was past. Webster with his admirable good sense and experience of mankind was clear that there should not be a word said. But I should just go see him, and drinking a glass of wine would be understood as putting an end to all differences; and he added the President would be very happy to see me. So it was agreed.

FRIDAY 7 APRIL. I was very well. Yet gross desire hurried me to a coarse paramour. I did not however risk with her. π.

SATURDAY 8 APRIL. Read some of the second volume of the *Biographia Britannica*. My agreeable ideas and wishes for distinction and relishes of life revived. I dined at my father's, Robert Boswell there. Lady Auchinleck was confined to her room. My father was somewhat more kindly than usual. When I went away, he said, "Good-night, my dear Jamie." I went home with Robert and drank tea. His father was very low tonight and could not see me. He soon lost his fondness for the old hock.

MONDAY 10 APRIL. Dined at Dr Gillespie's[60] with Commissioner Cochrane, Dr Webster, and John. Was in sound spirits, but drank so as to be intoxicated a good deal, so that I ranged an hour in the street and dallied with ten strumpets. I had however caution enough left not to run a risk with them. Told my valuable spouse when I came home. She was good-humoured and gave me excellent beef soup, which lubricated me and made me well.

WEDNESDAY 12 APRIL. Breakfasted with Lady Colville. Lady Anne was ill and did not appear. I always feel a kind of constraint in the company of the ladies of Kellie, knowing their satirical turn and having been with them in my early life while I was awkward and timid. But we have all along been on a good footing, and what is rare, they have been as well with me since my marriage as before, and have kept up a good intercourse with my wife. It was, I recollect, a remark of one of themselves many years ago that a man's female friends before marriage are seldom his friends when he has changed his state. I began today to amuse myself with reading the Register of Baptisms for the City of Edinburgh, beginning with the year 1700, and taking notes of all the persons now alive whom I knew. Miss Susie Dunlop and Mr Robert Syme, Junior, dined with us. I drank a very little wine. Miss Dunlop and my wife and I played at *vingt-et-un*. Why should I be vexed that I am not superior to the generality of men, who really do not pass their time

60 Dr Thomas Gillespie resided in Hanover Street.

more rationally than I did this day? After a long silence, I received a letter today from Dr Johnson [who] rebuked me for complaining of my melancholy, and charged me for the future not to talk of it, and then it would not trouble me. His advice may perhaps be good. I shall try to follow it. π.

FRIDAY 14 APRIL. Was awhile in the Advocates' Library looking for a motto for a *Hypochondriack*. Found one in Aulus Gellius. Read a little in the Register of Baptisms. Dined at my father's, Dr and Mrs Gillespie there. Lady Auchinleck confined to her room.

SATURDAY 15 APRIL. My dear wife has for some months been troubled with a cough, sometimes better, sometimes worse. This morning she had a severe fit, so that she spit some blood. This frightened her and made me uneasy. But I hoped that the blood came only from her throat. Sandy has had a deafness from a cold for more than a month. Mr Wood says it will go off. All this winter from a weakness in his eyes he has squinted at times. I have often washed his eyes with cold water. He grows fast and is stout-made, like a true son of Auchinleck. I set myself to write *The Hypochondriack* No. 31, and found that a chapter in Aulus Gellius with a translation into English saved me almost all the labour of composition at this time.[61] I went at night to the play (to *The Beggar's Opera*), to have London ideas revived and to meet Miss Susie Dunlop, who had asked me to be there. Finding that she was in a box with a very disagreeable woman, I did not go near her, but sat in the pit. I was rather callous to the songs, which used to affect me in a lively manner, and came away when two acts were done. Played whist and supped at Maclaurin's. There was singing too. It hurt me to see all appearance of regret for a wife so lately dead effaced. Yet is it not good sense to get free of grief as soon as one can? However, there is something in doing so which shocks my feelings.

I should have mentioned that last night I had a very lively dream that I was at Constantinople. That it was the season of a great religious ceremony, and that I was admitted into a mosque, where I saw a company of Turks sitting round a table with the cloth laid and plates and other preparations for a repast. I remember a good deal of gilding upon what appeared to be china-ware on the table. I suppose my dreaming imagination has given a Turkish cast to the Christian sacrament of the Lord's Supper. I remember I was very devout in this dream, and it left a pleasing impression on my mind. I have long thought that Mahomet had a divine commission, and so, I am pretty certain, Sir John Pringle once owned to me he thought.

TUESDAY 18 APRIL. Dictated well a good deal of a law paper. Went out with Commissioner Cochrane and dined at my father's. Poor Hallglenmuir was in much distress, as the Douglas and Heron Bank threatened to bring his estate to sale to get payment of £1,000 for which they had a preferable security on his estate.

---

61 In his essay, Boswell states that the "excellent passage" from Aulus Gellius "proves that the divine Plato was sensible that drinking wine is a great pleasure, and that it requires being trained to resist excess in it. It also shows in the plainest manner the advantages which the wise may derive from Drinking."

To get the sale delayed was a matter of great consequence to him and this could not be done unless some friend would advance the £1,000, come in place of the Ayr bank, and have patience. I had mentioned to Commissioner Cochrane that I wished my father would do it, and the Commissioner seemed to acquiesce, and be inclined to forward the scheme. But when I proposed it today in his presence, he sat quite silent, while my father refused strongly to interfere. He treated my humane application with contempt. I was obliged to desist. Sandy came after dinner. I played whist with my father and his lady and the Commissioner. My two daughters came to tea. My father's indifference about all of them was sad. In the evening I continued to dictate as I could wish to do.

WEDNESDAY 19 APRIL. Finished my law paper quite to my satisfaction. Dined with Commissioner Cochrane at Commissioner Lockhart's, a hearty good dinner.[62] No other company there but a Miss Christie and Mr Ross, Secretary of the Post-Office. I drank porter and port and Madeira and a bottle of claret, and wished for more. I stayed tea. After which, having still a desire for more social drinking, I went to the Cross and sent a caddie to find out where Dr Webster was. He was at Mr Samuel Mitchelson, Junior's. I called there and found them tête-à-tête upon Lord Dundonald's affairs. They however drank one bottle of claret with me. And then I drank tea with Mrs Mitchelson and talked a great deal of nonsense which vexed me afterwards. I then wandered an hour in the streets and followed girls, but happily did not go with any of them or run any kind of risk. It was however very disagreeable to think that I had from intoxication been so foolish as to debase myself by intruding at Mitchelson's, and so gross as to follow after low Edinburgh whores. I had been cutting my great toenails this week and had hurt the flesh, and by walking a good deal today they were both inflamed. The toe which troubled me before was much swelled and very painful. I put a poultice to it and went to bed. My dear wife had soup ready for me, which I took comfortably amidst my contrition.

THURSDAY 20 APRIL. Was in great pain and much dispirited. Lay in bed all forenoon. Read ten of Dr Blair's second volume of sermons. Did not relish them so much as I expected to do. Found too much uniformity of flourish and not enough of philosophy. After dinner I read one of Dr Ogden's *Sermons on the Articles of the Christian Faith*, which I had got from London lately, that I might compare his manner of preaching with Blair's, and I found it much superior. Blair in his sermon on GOD's unchangeableness showed his opinion that prayer *doth not avail* with our Heavenly Father, and that man is indeed fatally carried on. Such a system is dreary and dispiriting, and I am convinced is not true. I read the rest of Blair's second volume this night.

FRIDAY 21 APRIL. Had cried much in my sleep, having dreamt that Veronica was shot dead. Mr Wood, for whom I had sent yesterday, called this morning and said

62 Commissioner Lockhart's house was at 23 George Square (*B.O.E.C.*, Vol. 26, p. 146).

my toe looked worse than he had ever seen it; but all that could be done was giving it rest and poulticing it till the swelling was gone. I read some of Palmer on Human Liberty against Priestley for Necessity, and was refreshed by it. This I did after dinner. But in the forenoon I was wretchedly relaxed, and humbled to find that I could be reduced to low spirits in so short a time by so slight a complaint. Major Montgomerie sat awhile with me. Lady Auchinleck paid us a visit. I talked to her of Hallglenmuir and wished she would persuade my father to lend him the £1,000. She said he had it not, and if he were to begin to embarrass himself by borrowing money to lend to other people, he would get into the same confusion which was so ruinous to other people. That he had let a farm of £36 a year to Hallglenmuir for which he did not expect to get rent, which was pretty well. That it would be impossible to extricate Hallglenmuir, and it was better to bring his circumstances to a crisis, and afterwards, if one could afford it, give his family £50 a year. She talked with so much rational sense and showed such strength of mind that I could not but be pleased with her. I was convinced. I tried to dictate a *Letter to Lord Braxfield on His Promotion To Be a Lord of Justiciary*, which I had meditated for some time and wished to publish before he began his first circuit.[63] But I had no vigour of mind at all. So let it alone.

---

63 Lord Braxfield had been appointed a Lord Commissioner of Justiciary in place of Lord Auchinleck on 1 March, and his first circuit was to commence on 27 April. Boswell's motives in writing his presumptuous letter—which was to be published, anonymously, on 8 May under the title *A Letter to Robert Macqueen, Lord Braxfield, on his Promotion to be one of the Judges of the High Court of Justiciary*—are not entirely clear. The *Letter* starts ominously with the words: "It is not the intention of this letter to pay your Lordship compliments on your promotion to a seat in the Supreme Criminal Court of Scotland. These you may have from other quarters"; and then proceeds to give his Lordship a lecture on how he should conduct himself in carrying out his judicial duties. The "most essential requisite", says Boswell, is "solemnity in the administration of judicial proceedings concerning life and death", and, above all, "a constant attention to piety"; for "without piety there can be no true solemnity, none of that awful reverence which makes a deep impression upon the human mind, and contributes so much to the principal purpose of a Criminal Court, the prevention of crimes". Boswell goes on to hint darkly at the reputation of Lord Kames for crude and insensitive behaviour by emphasising the importance of the avoidance by criminal judges of "that *'foolish jesting'* which is so incompatible with the solemn business of the Court, and would be so offensive in any of its Judges". Furthermore, remarks Boswell, in an allusion to the High Court's tendency in those days to lean in favour of the prosecution, criminal judges "should, upon all occasions, appear humane, not eager to seize upon victims for punishment, but rather desirous that unhappy prisoners who stand before them in dread suspense should be found innocent; and if they are found guilty by the verdict of a jury, should with regret denounce the necessary vengeance of the law, consoling them at the same time with hopes of obtaining mercy at a higher Tribunal." Boswell then proceeds to express views on the importance of maintaining a due impression of the High Court's dignity when on circuit, and bemoans the fact that some of the judges (of whom he had Lord Kames particularly in mind) had a reputation for parsimony when it came to spending the official allowances conferred on them to cover the expenses of a circuit. Boswell points out, by way of example, that "the abolishing of a covered waggon for the baggage of the Circuit, though a paultry [*sic*] saving, is a great grievance. Without it, how shall the mace; how shall the official clothes of the trumpeters; nay, how shall the record of Court, and the essential papers be carried? Not to mention the gowns and clothes of others who ought to be decently drest [*sic*]. Without it, there must be such shifts and such pinching as is to be found only in a company of strolling players. Shall the mace, the badge of authority, be crammed into the boot of a coach amongst black-ball, shoe-brushes and curry-combs? The trumpeters be forced to ride in their official clothes, and look shabby? The embroidered G.R. upon the breast of their coats, be turned out to the rain and the tempest, by the King's own Judges, as poor King Lear was turned out by his own daughters?" Boswell also took the opportunity to assert the right of juries to be independent and free from judicial dictation as to how they should decide: "[I]s there not... too often", he asks, "an intention discovered by

SATURDAY 22 APRIL. Wrote a good deal of my *Letter to Lord Braxfield*, and was as animated as I could wish to be.

SUNDAY 23 APRIL. My toe was a good deal better. But I kept the house all day, and read one of Dr Ogden's sermons and heard the children say divine lessons. Veronica read some aloud in my large quarto Oxford prayer-book with cuts, bound in red morocco and gilt. She and Phemie and Sandy are taught to have a reverence for this book. They repeat the Creed along with me, and then kiss the prayer-book. I did some more of the *Letter to Lord Braxfield*. It was solemn writing. Phemie said today, "Christ is just like GOD." Said Veronica: "He's a part of GOD." Very well. π.

MONDAY 24 APRIL. Was awaked with a card from Dr Webster that Lord President had fixed this day for us to dine with him at Arniston; that we must not disappoint him, and that the Doctor would call on me with a post-chaise at half past eleven. I was somewhat muddy from having drank strong port negus overnight, but I shook off indolence and prepared myself for a scene which I had for a considerable time wished to realize. I prayed to GOD to bless a reconciliation this day with an old friend of our family. Luckily my toe had healed so much as to be very easy. I dressed myself in my Chester coat and waistcoat, and got into as good a frame as I could wish. At twelve Dr Webster was at the head of our court, and away we drove most comfortably. It was a pleasing, clear, mild day, and my mind was gentle. As this was a scene of some importance, I shall be at pains to write it down minutely and well.

I had not been at Arniston for seven years. I observed a change to the better whenever we approached it. We got there about half an hour after two. I entered the threshold with some agitation, wishing that the first meeting between the President and me were over. He was out an airing. Dr Webster and I sat for some time in the old dining-room by ourselves, looking into Arnot's *History of Edinburgh*. Then came Mr Goldie, the Minister of Temple, who did not say much. Then came Sheriff Cockburn, and then old Sheriff Dundas,[64] who was staying at Arniston. Dempster once observed to me with approbation that the Arniston family all stick together and support one another. At length entered the President, swaggering in a suit of light grey cloth with mother-of-pearl buttons. He took me by the hand and asked me how all was at home, and the awkwardness was nothing like what I apprehended. Then came his amiable son, who had been out with him, and he and I met very agreeably. The President went and put on clean linen, and then returned to us. He talked away with his

---

the Bench, to direct and control the jury?... [O]ught the judges to discover to the jury the opinion which they have formed as to the fact? And after the jury have returned a verdict upon their great oath, have the judges any right to censure that verdict because the jury have not entertained the same notions of the nature of evidence in general, or of the evidence upon that trial in particular, that the judges have done?... All encroachments of one department of administration upon another, whether in the state or in courts of judicature, should be steadily resisted."

64 Thomas Dundas (1706-1784), advocate (admitted 5 February 1730), sixth son of Robert Dundas, Lord Arniston (grandfather of the second Lord President Dundas). He was appointed Professor of Civil Law at Edinburgh University in 1732 and Sheriff-Depute of Wigtownshire in 1750.

usual flow of animal spirits; arraigned the judgement of the Court of Session finding themselves not competent to review a sentence of the justices and commissioners adjudging a man to be a recruit. "And why?" said he. "Because Sir Michael Malcolm, one of the justices, was Kennet's friend (Kennet acknowledged to me afterwards he believed they were in the wrong); and because the man came from the Mearns, where Monboddo was connected." In this last reason he was mistaken. For Monboddo had no connexion with the parties. It proved to me that he is in the habit of abusing Monboddo for partiality, as Monboddo does him; nay, that he does not spare better friends among his brethren when they differ from his opinion even in his absence.

We waited dinner till past four o'clock for Sir Archibald Hope, who then came from the hunting. At dinner the President sat at the head of his table, I on his right hand, and Dr Webster on his left. The dinner as usual was substantially good. I eat heartily as his Lordship did; and he soon called for a glass of white wine and had Dr Webster and me to join him. Many a hearty hob and nob there was. I was cheerful but guarded. My wife cautioned me not to drink. For she said that would spoil all. However, the claret was admirable; and as the grave yet pleasing satisfaction of reconciliation so engaged my mind that wine did not affect me quickly, I drank freely of it but not to excess. The President drank port and water, only tasting the claret to be sensible that it was good. He addressed a great deal of his discourse to me, and from time to time as he chuckled, shook hands with me. He repeated a lively thought of mine in a paper for Sir Alexander Dick about Lord Abercorn's horse being in quest of prescription in Duddingston Loch, a thought which must have been told him, for my paper was never before the Inner House.[65] He told how, when Charles Erskine[66] said in

65 This is a reference to the case of *Sir Alexander Dick v The Earl of Abercorn* (N.A.S. CS.226/2729), in which Boswell had acted for his friend Sir Alexander. For the factual background to this case, see Introduction, p. 39. The "paper" which Boswell mentions was the memorial which he drafted for Sir Alexander in February 1767. In this memorial, Boswell had stated that the Earl of Abercorn had attempted to establish a right of ownership of the soil of Duddingston Loch by seeking to acquire a right of prescription over it (such a right being one which arises by virtue of the possession of land founded on an *ex facie* valid recorded title over a period of time). Boswell, having narrated that the Earl, in his efforts to found his right, had been "at pains to drive his cattle as far into the Loch as he could thinking that by paddling in [Sir Alexander's] water and leaving the footsteps of his beasts at the bottom he might by degrees found a kind of possession", went on to state: "A whimsical enough story happened to the noble Lord, for one day having made a large heavy black horse advance a good way into the Loch in quest of prescription [the] soil which... is nothing else than a loam or slimy substance could not support the weight of this black horse so down he went and was never more heard of." The editors of *Laird* state (at p. 205, n. 8) that when that volume was published no copy of Boswell's paper had been found, but it is clear that the memorial traced by the present editor is the paper in question. Although the memorial is not in Boswell's hand, this is not surprising given that he had a clerk to assist him in the preparation of legal documents; and although the signature on the memorial is partially obliterated, what remains appears to be "... well". In any event, the process relating to this action contains an account of expenses prepared by Sir Alexander's agents, and the account includes an entry dated 11 February 1767 referring to a payment of two guineas "to Mr Boswell to draw the memorial for the pursuer". Boswell's Consultation Book makes no mention of the fee, which suggests that he may have waived it in view of his friendship with Sir Alexander.
66 Charles Erskine (1680-1763), advocate, who was elevated to the bench as Lord Tinwald in 1744 and was Lord Justice-Clerk from 1748 to 1763.

the General Assembly that he was a Presbyterian, but according to law, my grandfather said, "Moderator, I was a Presbyterian when it was against law"; applauded my grandfather's spirit, and cried, "Eh, Old James!" But his address was complete in one instance. He cried, "Come, I'll fill a bumper to my worthy old friend, Affleck.[67] Here's to him, honest man. Long may he keep you, James, from being laird." A bumper went round. Here was a compliment paid to my father, to *the present* representative of our family, after having done honour to *the past*. But that *the future* might, as he supposed, be pleased with the prospect of succession and see that his Lordship would be equally friendly with him, he jogged me and whispered, "It won't do long." He said to me, "I shall be happy to see you here whenever you are at leisure." There was much merriment, and everybody seemed pleased. I was lucky enough, without forwardness but from the neglect of everyone else, to beg leave that his right-hand neighbour might be allowed an extraordinary toast: a bumper to Mrs Dundas. She was at London and Miss Dundas, her daughter, with her. After he had said, "I'll give you but one bottle more", and in that bottle we had drank to the roof-tree of Arniston, he cried, "Come, I'll have one other bottle more to all your roof-trees"; and we had it. Dr Webster told me we had two bottles each. I was gladdened, not intoxicated. When going away, the President shook hands with me and said, "My dear James, nobody wishes you better than I do." And Dr Webster told me he said to him, "I'm very happy with this meeting."

Thus was a reconciliation at length brought about between the President of the Court of Session, the hereditary friend of our family, and me. It was sincere on my part. For I had forgiven him for some time. What a blessed precept is that of our SAVIOUR to forgive those who have injured us! Dr Webster and I chatted quietly in the chaise, and got to town about ten. I insisted that he should come home with me. He stipulated that he should have first a dish of tea, and that we should drink only one *chopin*[68] bottle of claret after supper. We had tea and then prayers, and then excellent soup and some good dishes. I had no chopin bottles of claret out of the cellar, so set down a Scotch pint. He was resolute, and made one half of it be bottled, and we drank only the other half. I felt myself a little uneasy at the *stomach*. But my *heart* was happy. I thought myself obliged to Dr Webster's friendly interposition on this occasion. I should have liked to have seen the cards or letters which passed between him and the President about it, as his memory is not accurate; but he had burnt the President's. He told me he had written to the President that Mr Boswell wished to wait on his Lordship and draw a veil over misunderstandings, and he and I would dine at Arniston any day he pleased next week except Wednesday; that the President had answered he would be exceedingly happy to see us, but that nothing must be mentioned either of past or future. I doubt[69]

---

67 Lord Auchinleck's title was often pronounced "Affleck" (in accordance with the local pronunciation of the name of his estate) and was sometimes even recorded as such in court writs.
68 A chopin was half a Scots pint, or about one and a half imperial pints (*CSD*, p. 818).
69 That is, "I suspect".

he did not report it right. However, the President certainly behaved very well in the matter.

TUESDAY 25 APRIL. Rose in good health and spirits. Was one of the jury on the service of John Francis Erskine, Esq., as heir of entail in the estate of Alloa, etc.[70] There was a hearty dinner at Walker's. Dr Webster and I were next one another. It was a joyous afternoon. Old Mar and Mr William Wemyss, Writer to the Signet,[71] and I had some supper at a side-table. Dr Webster and Mr David Erskine took none. We five were left sitting long after everybody else. I was strong this afternoon, and imagined that the claret did not make an impression on me. But I grew intoxicated all at once, and was obliged to go home.

THURSDAY 27 APRIL. I have no distinct recollection of this day. I finished my *Letter to Lord Braxfield* either yesterday or today, and read it to Mr Nairne, who was much pleased with it in general, but suggested some judicious hints which made me leave out parts of it. Mr David Erskine, seeing me from his window this afternoon, would have me to come in, and he and I and another gentleman drank two bottles of claret. I was in excellent spirits. I said to Nairne that if I had a pamphlet to write every day, I should be happy. I had been at my father's today and told him of my having been at Arniston, which pleased him much.

FRIDAY 28 APRIL. My *Letter to Lord Braxfield* went to the press today. I employed Mr Adam Neill to print it, as I might be suspected for the author had Mr Donaldson been the printer.

SATURDAY 29 APRIL. Worthy Grange had returned last night. He breakfasted with us today. I got twenty-four pages of my *Letter to Lord Braxfield* in print, and was much pleased with the spirit and expression, as was Grange. I had felt a little uneasiness from thinking that it would perhaps give pain to Lord Kames, whose improprieties and parsimony on the circuits it pointed out keenly; and this morning I had a letter from good Mr William Nairne suggesting the same humane scruple. Grange however thought that Lord Kames would not feel the censure; and I thought that if he should, he deserved it. So I resolved to go on.

SUNDAY 30 APRIL. Was at the New Church in the forenoon and heard a Mr Macaulay (I think), a preacher. Dr Webster dined with us, and I gave him the half of the pint bottle of claret which we left on Monday night. It rained hard in the afternoon, so I stayed at home. Read one of Ogden's sermons, and heard the children say divine lessons very agreeably. My mind was full of my *Letter to Lord Braxfield*, the whole of which I had now in print. π.

MONDAY 1 MAY. Poor little Jamie was taken ill yesterday afternoon with a severe vomiting and purging during his teething, and continued to be ill all this day. His mother and I were in great uneasiness about him.

TUESDAY 2 MAY. Last night (I think) my father made me such a family speech

---

70 John Francis Erskine (1741-1825), "Young Mar", had succeeded to the entailed estate which had been held by his mother, daughter of the 6th (or 11th) Earl of Mar, whose estates had been forfeited. John Francis Erskine was restored to the earldom of Mar in 1824, thus becoming the 13th Earl.
71 William Wemyss, W.S. (admitted 8 March 1763), died 1802.

as he has not done since his second marriage. He said, "You know all my study (or scheme) is to leave a good estate to you." He talked of the necessity of good management, and when I told him that I was now convinced of that and acted accordingly, he said, "I wish you could get your wife to think in that way." I saw that means had been used to prejudice him against her. And I assured him upon my honour that nobody was more economical than she was. I spoke strongly to him on this head. For it vexed me to find that he entertained a suspicion against her which she so little deserved. I sent Dr Johnson my *Letter to Lord Braxfield*, to show him my mind was not languid; and I begged he would review it for my private satisfaction.

WEDNESDAY 3 MAY. Little Jamie was pretty well again this morning, thank GOD. I had worthy Grange to accompany me to the Quakers' Meeting in Peebles Wynd,[71a] that I might revive agreeable mild religious impressions which I had here in company with my dear mother, I believe twenty years ago. Two women from London preached, and one man from Newcastle preached and prayed. But none of them had a pleasing manner.

FRIDAY 5 MAY. Drank tea at my father's. He was dull. Messieurs Maclaurin, David Erskine, Charles Brown, Mr and Mrs Mitchelson, and Miss Cuninghame of Bonnington supped with us. We had whist and brag before supper. I lost a little, but it did not disturb me. I was in a good firm frame. We (the men) sat till three in the morning drinking claret. I was not a bit the worse for it.

SATURDAY 6 MAY. Little Jamie pronounced *papa* on Wednesday last, and continues to do it. My toe is never well yet, but pretty easy. This morning my son Sandy was made very happy with the present of a little Shetland sheltie from Mrs Mitchelson, which she got from Mr Honeyman of Graemsay. He rode on it today, forenoon and afternoon.

MONDAY 8 MAY. My *Letter to Lord Braxfield* was published. I kept out of the way. Went with the children to Lauriston, where they all three rode on Sandy's sheltie. Sandy himself rode boldly. My daughters and I were invited by the Reverend Dr Bell into his garden, which was very pleasant. We then walked to Lady Colville's, where they were happy. Balbarton, Grange, and Mr Lawrie dined with us. I am from this day to mark Mr Lawrie's dining or supping with us, because he is no longer like one of my family since having a wife and house of his own. My wife and I played cards and supped at Mr S. Mitchelson's, Junior, with Mr David Erskine, etc. Mr Charles Brown had read part of the *Letter to Lord Braxfield*, and quoted parts of it. The company agreed that the author was in the right. I was not charged with it.

TUESDAY 9 MAY. Yesterday the weather was delightful. It was also so today. Sandy rode all the way to Prestonfield, James Clark, my servant, leading his sheltie and walking by him. I walked all the way, happy to see him so; and Grange went almost to the avenue to give us a convoy. Sir Alexander and I had a pleasing walk in the garden, and he obligingly asked me to send the sheltie to run on his grass. I accepted of the kind offer. It rained hard in the afternoon and Sandy and I had the chaise to town, and the sheltie was left.

71a Off the south side of the High Street near the Tron Church.

WEDNESDAY 10 MAY. Two men were to be hanged in the Grassmarket today: Dalgleish for robbery, Donaldson for shop-breaking. I felt a strange inclination to go and see the execution as usual. But I resolved to avoid it, as it always makes me gloomy for some time after.

THURSDAY 11 MAY. I had gone last night to the Justiciary Office by way of looking the record for the authenticity of a trial at Glasgow mentioned in my *Letter to Lord Braxfield*. I knew it to be authentic, as Mr Nairne was my author- ity, but I wished to see the particulars and hear what the clerks said of the pamphlet. I was mentioned as one of the authors or persons supposed to be the writer. I denied it, as a man is entitled to do, as to deny his being at home, because denying is the only mode of concealing what a man has a right to conceal. Mr Crosbie, Mr Hugo Arnot,[72] and the Hon. Henry Erskine were also mentioned. The author was allowed to be well-informed. This forenoon I called on Crosbie and introduced the *Letter*. I was surprised to find he had not seen it, but he said he heard it was very severe. I paid a visit to the Miss Ords, and then to Young Lady Wallace, whose indelicate effrontery made her beauty affect me little.[73]

FRIDAY 12 MAY. Called on Sir William Forbes at his counting-house. Had a little social tête-à-tête with him. He spoke of the *Letter to Lord Braxfield*, and asked me if I was not the author. I denied it even to him, though I scrupled a little, considering my confidential regard for him. But I wished to be con- cealed, at least for some time, as much as possible. He seemed to like the *Letter* much. Mr Daniel[74] gave a dinner today at Princes Street Coffee-house to Grange and me and Messieurs Butler and Norris, M. Derosey, a Swede,[75] and a Mr Cooke. We were exceedingly jovial. Lady Maxwell of Pollok, her brother-in-law Mr Cathcart, and Mr David Steuart, her husband's cousin, and Grange supped with us. I was heated with my drinking at dinner, but con- ducted myself very well. Only played too keenly at brag. Lost a little, which always vexes me more or less. Did not drink to excess after supper. This was an entertainment truly of duty, from respect to the Pollok family and par- ticularly Mrs Montgomerie of Lainshaw.[76] David Steuart praised the *Letter to Lord Braxfield* very much. Grange was afraid I would discover myself, I was so warm. He, Mr Nairne, Mr Lawrie, and Mr Neill, the printer, only knew it in Scotland.

SUNDAY 14 MAY. My wife and I were at the New Church in the forenoon and heard Mr Finlayson, a minister from Shetland, who preached very well. My father was there. Dr Webster dined with us. I was at the New Church in the

---

72 Hugo Arnot (1749-1786), advocate (admitted 8 December 1772). In 1779 he published his cel- ebrated *History of Edinburgh*. Tall, thin and suffering from severe asthma, he died at the age of only thirty-six.
73 *Cf.* the entry for 29 September 1778. Lady Wallace was now residing in St David Street.
74 A medical student at Edinburgh (*Laird*, p. 528).
75 Actually Gideon Herman de Rogier, a Swedish physician (*Laird*, p. 211, n. 8a).
76 She was Lady Maxwell's sister-in-law (*Laird*, p. 212, n. 9).

afternoon and heard Mr Walker. My wife took my daughters and Sandy to a low seat, as they are not welcome to my father's seat. They said divine lessons well in the evening. My wife and I and they walked out and paid a visit to Lady Colville. It was a sweet evening.

MONDAY 15 MAY. Received a card that my affectionate uncle, Dr Boswell, died this morning. Though he had been almost dead for more than a year, I was struck with the actual event. Though Death over him "his dart shook but delayed to strike",[77] the stroke was affecting when it really happened. One day before this, I had walked along the New Bridge with Principal Robertson, who told me he had read the *Letter to Lord Braxfield*, and that it would do good, for it would show the judges they are not above censure. He thought it must be written by a man of business, well acquainted with the Court. I mentioned Gilbert Stuart.[78] He said it had not the *bounce* of his style. I suppose Robertson has felt it like a boxer's head thump the pit of his stomach.[79] "It is a plain style", said he. "But very well written", said I. He agreed. I then met Crosbie, and wondered to find he had not yet seen it. But from what he had heard of it he said, "I take it to be written by one of the old Clerks of Justiciary." Robert Auld was then mentioned, either by him or me. Grange dined with us; and then I went and called on Mr Robert Boswell, whom I found in submissive tranquillity. Mr George Wallace had in a very friendly manner offered me a loan of fifty pounds. He had called some time ago (I know not if I have marked it) to put me in mind of it, and to ask when I would have it. I said at Whitsunday. I called on him this forenoon, before I heard of the Doctor's death. But he had first called on me. I sent to him to beg he would drink tea with me. He came with the money in his pocket, and I gave him my bill. His conversation, full both of facts in common life and learning, did me good. In the forenoon I had been at Sir W. F. & Co.'s counting-house, where was Dr Blair. Hunter, I thought to induce me to own it, said the *Letter to Lord Braxfield* was well spoken of. I said nothing; for Sir William Forbes had before that again asked me if I was the author, and I had again denied it. I went in the evening to the Meadow with intention to visit my father. But it was too late. Mr George Wallace accompanied me. We met Harry Erskine, who asked me if I had seen the *Letter to Lord Braxfield*. I told him I had, and asked him his opinion of it. He said, "Very well." "Very well!" said I. "It is capital." I had before this denied it to George Wallace. He asked Harry *who* was the author? He said he did not know. I looked him steadily in the face and said, "Do you *really* not know?" He denied again, but looked embarrassed, and said, "I know Lord Kames will believe I wrote it, and I must go and assure him I did not; for some of the things mentioned in it happened when I was with him." "Oho!" said I. Said he: "John Swinton's penetration has found out that Lord Hailes wrote it." "Well," said I, "do you know, I was going to mention Lord Hailes. It is very like him. There is

---

77 Milton, *Paradise Lost*, xi. 491-3.
78 A historian and reviewer (1743-1786), founder of the short-lived *Edinburgh Magazine and Review*.
79 Gilbert Stuart, in his *Observations Concerning the Public Law and the Constitutional History of Scotland* (1779), had referred, at p. 175, to Robertson as "an author of elegant talents, and of great industry, but who is nowhere profound" (quoted in *Laird*, p. 213, n. 3).

a seriousness and an anxiety about the dignity of the Court which he has." "Yes," said Harry, "and he has not the faults pointed out in it." Said I: "The only passage not like him is that where the independency of juries is asserted. But he may have written that to disguise himself." Said George: "Lord Hailes can write in a lively style." "Do you know," said I, "Mr Erskine, they say that it is written by Robert Auld and seasoned by you"; and when we parted I said, "Good-night; Auld and Erskine, Beaumont and Fletcher."[80] I had some scruple as to all this disguise. Yet I thought it allowable, and it was very entertaining.

TUESDAY 16 MAY. Called at my father's in the forenoon. He did not seem to be much affected with his brother's death. I wrote a good deal of *The Hypochondriack* No. 32,[81] but could not be ready for the post. Grange and Mr Lawrie dined with us.

WEDNESDAY 17 MAY. My father and Lady Auchinleck paid us a short visit in the forenoon and heard Veronica play on the harpsichord. They had called some forenoons ago when my wife and children were out. Though my father was not at all cordial, I was glad to see him again under my roof. He did not take much notice of Veronica. I went out and dined with him today. Mr Stobie, who was in town in his way to Auchinleck, was there. My father was little moved with his brother's death. Indeed it was a circumstance rather to be wished. Yet natural affection, and its being so near a *memento mori*[82] to himself, might, I should have thought, have made it more affecting to him. I thought at dinner how different it would have been had his brother *Johnnie* died when they were both boys at Auchinleck. ——.[83]

SATURDAY 20 MAY. [Dined at Prestonfield.] We were social after dinner; Robert Gillespie, Samuel Mitchelson, Junior, there, as Captain Butler and little Norris were to set out on Monday. Mitchelson carried Sandy and me to town in his chaise, and sent it home with us. I have always found him very obliging, so that I regret the petulance of his manner and there being no cordiality between him and me. He commended the *Letter to Lord Braxfield* after dinner, and said, "I hear it was written by Mr James Boswell." "He denies it", said George Wallace, and told how Harry Erskine had been embarrassed when charged with it. Old Erskine of Mar had been with me in the forenoon and talked of it, though he had not seen it. He controverted the doctrine which he was told was in it as to the independency of juries. He and Grange and Mr George Wallace supped with us. We were exceedingly cheerful. Mar told a great many stories. Grange doubted of their perfect authenticity.

SUNDAY 21 MAY. I had long intended to go to the Glassite Meeting-house and

80 "Beaumont and Fletcher" is an allusion to the playwrights Francis Beaumont and John Fletcher.
81 One of the series of essays (Nos 30-33) on drinking.
82 A reminder of death.
83 "This dash at the end of an entry, which now begins to appear occasionally in the MS., is clearly a private symbol, probably of the same nature as the asterisk, π, and V, which Boswell had previously employed" (*Laird*, p. 214, n. 6).

hear Robert Boswell preach.[84] I chose this day, as I fancied there might perhaps be something of a funeral sermon on Dr Boswell. Grange went with me. Mr Lawrie showed us to the gallery. He sat in view. Grange and I were concealed. It is, I believe, more than twenty years since I was in this meeting-house, when my mind was tender and sore with religious terrors. I was pleased to find that they were not in the slightest degree renewed today. We were disappointed, for Robert did not preach. A man whom I did not know and John Young, a writer, preached. The latter harangued with a clear, strong voice and a fluency of words. But he uttered strange doctrine. He in explicit terms asserted predestination and election, and inculcated that his hearers should not only not imagine that anything they could do to distinguish them from the most profligate had the least influence in obtaining their salvation, but if they had even a wish to be better, that they might recommend themselves to GOD, they were departing from the Christian faith. What a wretched system is this which makes us absolute machines, and destroys the connexion between morality and religion, taking away from us the hopes and fears of a future state, where we are to be judged according to our conduct in this life, under the benign influence of the propitiation offered up by Jesus Christ. The Glassites indeed require morality as an *evidence* of faith. But if a man is persuaded that it is to have no *effect*, he will act foolishly if he does not gratify every passion so far as he can do it with safety. I thought that such *teaching* as I heard today should not be allowed. The only circumstance in this meeting not of a piece with their dreary creed was very fine singing in parts. It reminded me of a choir of monks or nuns. I could not but reflect with some uneasiness on the state of uncertainty which all men of all religions must be in as to their happiness after death; since, whether it depends on *election* or on *pious merit*, we cannot *know* with *confidence* that *we* are of the blessed number. I comfort myself with the notion that in progress of time there will be universal felicity. Grange dined with us between sermons, and he went to the New Church and heard Dr Blair preach beautifully and rationally. My wife and Sandy and I were in my father's seat. He had not been in church today. Miss McAdam of Craigengillan and Miss Ellie Ritchie and Grange drank tea with us. The children said divine lessons in presence of Grange. He and I walked down to the Abbey of Holyrood House, and in the garden near it, which was once Dr Alston's botanical garden. I was in excellent health and spirits. ———.

MONDAY 22 MAY. Dr Gillespie and his brother George, surgeon to the Fourth or King's Own, Commissioner Cochrane, and Robert Syme, Junior, dined with us. I communicated to Syme my being the author of the *Letter to Lord Braxfield*, in order to employ him in advertising a meeting of jurymen on the 1 of August next, to take it under their serious consideration and assert their rights and privileges. This

84 Robert Boswell was of the Glassite sect, one of the essential doctrines of which was set out on the tombstone of Glas's son-in-law, Robert Sandeman, as follows: "The bare death of Jesus Christ, without a thought or deed on the part of a man, is sufficient to present the chief of sinners spotless before God" (quoted in *Laird*, p. 215, n. 7). Robert Boswell had married Sandeman's niece.

advertisement I thought would promote the sale much, and perhaps a meeting might really be held. Letters (post-paid) addressed *To the Secretary of the Jury Association at Edinburgh* were to have due attention paid them. Clerk Matthew was to be told to deliver any that should come, to Mr Syme; and I thought there was a chance of good amusement.[85] The Commissioner did not stay tea. After tea Dr Gillespie and I walked out to my father's. I sat awhile. But he said little tonight, and when both his women and Doctor are present, I am very guarded. The Doctor tonight hinted to me, as he had done once before, that he wished my father would give up Auchinleck to me altogether. I protested against it, and declared upon my honour I never would go to it upon these terms. I was aware of his interested views, and I disliked the taking possession of another man's place in his own time. Dr Gillespie spoke much in favour of Lady Auchinleck's great care of my father. I was prudent.

WEDNESDAY 24 MAY. Robert Syme, Junior, dined with us. I drank some brandy and port, and was restless. Walked out to Portsburgh and drank some whisky, and indulged with a coarse but safe companion. Felt myself debased, and was cured. Called on Grange, who had been drinking after dinner and was in joyous spirits. Went with him to a tavern in the Old Post House Stairs,[86] and supped and was merry with John Graeme, James Baillie, George Kirkpatrick,[87] and Johnston, a wine-merchant.

MONDAY 29 MAY. I had an application today to appear as counsel for certain feuars in the Gorbals of Glasgow against the Rev. Mr Anderson, their minister, a General Assembly cause. My difficulty was that he was John Stobie's brother-in-law. My wife wisely suggested I should consult my father. So I went to him, he having this day come to his house in Adams's Square.[88] As Anderson had not employed me, he was, according to his old sagacity, for my taking the other side; so I agreed.

TUESDAY 30 MAY. Pleaded in the General Assembly for the people of Biggar against the patron very well.[89] Did not get out till seven. Came home; could not dine, but drank tea and eat bread and butter. Was happy with my dear wife. Supped at Lord Traquair's; Commissioner Clerk,[90] etc., there. Played a rubber

---

85 However, no letters were sent, nor was any meeting held (*Laird*, p. 216, n. 8).
86 The lower part of the steps which had formerly led from the Cowgate to the High Street immediately east of St Giles' (Harris, p. 375).
87 Deputy Clerk of Session.
88 Lord Auchinleck had now moved to a house in Adam Square and had thus become a neighbour of the Lord President.
89 "A typical case of the struggle of the 'Moderate' party in the Church to uphold lay patronage [the right of landowners with churches on their land to select the ministers] and of the 'Popular' party to resist it. Lady Elphinstone, the patroness, had presented Robert Pearson, a probationer, to the church at Biggar. In order for the settlement to be legal, the people, through the elders and heads of families, had to subscribe to a 'call', which in this case they quietly declined to do. Later the patroness was able to secure the 'concurrence' of some of the non-resident land-holders of the parish and of several heads of families. By a close vote (85 to 77) the Assembly upheld the settlement. Henry Erskine was counsel for the patroness" (*Laird*, p. 218, n. 4).
90 George Clerk-Maxwell, Commissioner of Customs.

at whist. Had resolved never again to play deeper than a shilling a game. Won a trifle. Was gay and satisfied.

FRIDAY 2 JUNE. Made an admirable appearance for the people of Fenwick against the patron. John Home[91] told me afterwards it was the best he had ever heard (or seen) at that bar.[92] I dined after it with the Lord Commissioner[93] after seven. Was warmed with wine. Dr Andrew Hunter[94] carried me to sup at his house, the first time I had been in it. His lady was ill and could not appear. Her sister, the Hon. Miss Napier, was at table, and there were several ministers; psalms and prayers and formal conversation. I was much upon my good behaviour.

SATURDAY 3 JUNE. Pleaded the cause of the feuars of Gorbals against the Rev. Mr Anderson. Was mild and decent. It turned out a wicked cause on the part of my clients. But *the fact* was concealed from me.[95] I came out and dined cordially with my dear wife, and returned and heard the decision in favour of Mr Anderson.

SUNDAY 4 JUNE. Waited on the Lord Commissioner, being earnest to sit in my father's seat in the New Church the last day of its existence, as this week the church was to be demolished in the inside in order to be put into a new form. I fulfilled my purpose, and just seated myself at the foot of it, next to Maclaurin. I meditated curiously on my remembering this seat almost as far back as my memory reaches—of my pious mother sitting at the head of it—of my dreary terrors of hell in it—of my having an *impression* of its being so connected with the other world as to be as permanent. Yet now it was to be removed, and not a vestige of it to be left. A multitude of ideas went through my mind. But my spirits were so gay and my mind so sound that I had no uneasiness, and even wondered that there should ever be such a thing. Maclaurin joined in singing psalms. Religion seemed light and easy and universal. A Dr Cramond at Yarrow, who had been minister of a dissenting congregation in England and was like an Englishman, preached agreeably enough. I dined with the Lord Commissioner, who has all along shown me an attention which I felt with pleasing gratitude, at least in proportion to the favour.

MONDAY 5 JUNE. Dined quietly at home. Before dinner shook hands with the Rev. Mr Anderson at the Cross and assured him that if I had known how bad a cause

---

91 The author of the tragedy of *Douglas*, which had caused great scandal when first performed in 1756.
92 "The same sort of case as that of the people of Biggar, with the same result" (*Laird*, p. 219, n. 6).
93 "George Ramsay, eighth Earl of Dalhousie, was Lord High Commissioner to the General Assembly of the Church of Scotland, 1777-1782" (*Laird*, p. 219, n. 7).
94 The Rev. Andrew Hunter, D.D., Professor of Divinity at the University of Edinburgh. He resided in St Andrew Street.
95 "Mr Anderson was accused of adultery with one Helen Simpson. The defence maintained that the prosecutors had bribed her with money and drink to sign a paper declaring Anderson to be the father of her children, and that, among the witnesses for the prosecution, one had been transported for life after a capital conviction and had returned illegally, one was a common prostitute, and one (Helen Simpson's mother) had been heard to declare that if swearing a lie would hang the defender, she would do it. The Assembly dismissed the whole process and 'seemed unanimous in expressing in strong terms their disapprobation of the prosecution' (*Scots Magazine*, May 1780, xlii. 278-279)" (*Laird*, p. 219, n. 8).

my clients had against him, I would not have appeared in it. He was satisfied with my candour. Attended the magistrates and drank the King's health.[96] Called on my father. Heard Sir John Pringle was come. Waited on him. He seemed to be somewhat failed. It was *comfortable* to see him in Edinburgh. But he did not impress me with equal *greatness* as when in Pall Mall. The Rev. Dr Andrew Hunter, Dr Findlay at Glasgow, Messrs James Thomson, Andrew Mitchell, Moody at Perth, and Professor Anderson at Glasgow supped with us. We had prayers before supper. All was decent and well.

MONDAY 12 JUNE. About seven in the evening they told me that a gentleman in a chaise at the head of the court wanted to know if I was at home. I said yes, being persuaded it was [my brother David]. In a little he appeared walking from the eastmost entry in a light grey frock. There was a *little* of the air of John. I received him in the drawing-room. He embraced me with warm agitation and said, "You see me the same affectionate brother as ever"; and he shed some tears. My wife soon came to us, and she was agitated as he was. I was duller. The children came, and he was curiously happy to see them and they him. After a few minutes of desultory conversation, we went to our father's. When we entered the dining-room, he ran to his father, embraced him, much agitated and with tears, and kissed his hand; and then saluted Lady Auchinleck respectfully. He talked with great composure and accuracy, but I thought with formality and what appeared to me affectation. At first I thought his countenance such that I should not have known him. Twelve years and eight months must no doubt make a considerable alteration on a face from nineteen to about thirty-two. But by degrees his likeness appeared again to me. He said he should not have known me. Miss Boswell and Dr Gillespie came in, and we stayed supper. Our father was placid, and more cheerful than ordinary. We left him a little after ten and walked home. Sat awhile with my wife, and then he went to bed in my little north room. On his arrival we told him that my father's people, not having room for him, had a lodging ready, for which my father was to pay; and we asked him whether he would have that or accept of our small room. He said, "I'll do anything that's agreeable. I want to see you all live in harmony together." At our father's he said, "I think it is more natural for me to live either with my father or my brother, and if you please" (to Lady A.) "I will take the room which my brother offers me." She seemed not quite fond of this. But it was so settled. I felt myself under some restraint with him, his manners were so mild and grave and correct, contrasted with the familiarity of Edinburgh.

TUESDAY 13 JUNE. David was polite and orderly at breakfast. The Session sat down today. I was in the House for a little, and had the satisfaction to see my father again on the bench and looking really well. I soon came home. Robert Boswell visited David. Then David and I visited Dr Webster, Commissioner Cochrane at the custom-house, who did not know David at first, and Robert Boswell's family.

---

96 The magistrates gave a collation in the Parliament House in honour of the King's birthday, which was on 4 June.

[In the evening] came home and found the Hon. Alexander Gordon sitting with my wife and David. I insisted on his supping, which he did. But David was disgusted at his manner, and showed it with some heat.

On 15 June, Mrs Boswell gave birth to another daughter, Elizabeth, who was to be her last child.

SUNDAY 18 JUNE. David and I went to the English Chapel in the forenoon. I was happy in a considerable degree. Then called on Lord Monboddo (not at home), then on Lord Kames, whom we found wonderfully well. I was not uneasy to think of the keen reflections pointed at his conduct in my *Letter to Lord Braxfield*, for I thought he deserved them. We saw his lady a little. Then David and I dined calmly at home, Veronica, Phemie, and Sandy with us. Till this day David's manner, which seemed affected, had hurt me somewhat, and I was shocked to a certain degree to find him, as I thought, grown strange. But tonight we sat up and talked with a confidential freedom which pleased me.

As usual after his wife's confinement, Boswell went wandering.

FRIDAY 14 JULY. In a wild desperation, for last time, Pleasance.

SATURDAY 15 JULY. I came home to tea and had an affecting conversation with wife, having confessed wandering.

Boswell's transgressions had the almost inevitable consequence: he fell victim to yet another attack of venereal disease, thus requiring him to summon the assistance of Mr Wood.

SUNDAY 30 JULY. Took salts. Read part of Dr Clark to renew belief of Supreme Being. Sir J. Pringle and Mr Nairne sat awhile between sermons. Read a good deal of my London journal in 1762 and 3, and was humbled by my weakness. David and Miss Tait dined. Read Dr Blair's sermon on GOD'S unchangeableness. Took after it as a cure one of Ogden's on prayer. Then children said divine lessons. Grange with me at night.

WEDNESDAY 2 AUGUST. [C]alled on John a little. Had affectionate concern about him. But found him not at all inclined to be well with me. He would not agree to dine with me.

THURSDAY 3 AUGUST. Had headache. Dined with David at Maclaurin's. Sir John Pringle, Lord Monboddo, etc., there. Was quite feeble in spirit. Heard conversation on happiness. Monboddo alone spoke with relish of old age and prospect of futurity. Sir John said the prospect was faint. Was so ill in the evening that I could not sup at the Hon. A. Gordon's with David. Was obliged to go to bed. Mr Wood came and made me take sack whey.[97] Got a sweat.

SATURDAY 5 AUGUST. Sat a little with Sir J. Pringle in the forenoon.[98] My father, Lady Auchinleck, and Miss Boswell dined. Dull. But it was decent and a compliment to us. They went away at four. Then Grange, David, and I went and

97 For "sack whey", see p. 203, n. 68a.
98 Williamson's *Edinburgh Directory* for 1780/81 gives Sir John Pringle's address as St Andrew Square. However, at some time in 1780 he acquired number 32 George Square (*B.O.E.C.*, Vol. 26, p. 150).

saw Watson's Hospital[99] for the first time. I was fatigued. Sir John Pringle came and sat in the evening till near ten. My spirits were better. He pleased me by reviving London ideas, and by impressing me (while I considered him) that a man should do what he finds agreeable, without too much consideration or attention to what others think.

SUNDAY 6 AUGUST. Commissioner Cochrane came in the morning and he and I went to the Tron Church.[100] Dr Drysdale lectured. I was pretty easy. Mr Wood had called and told me I was doing as well as could be wished. Walked on Castle Hill with Commissioner Cochrane and Sir J. Pringle. The Commissioner and Dr Webster dined with us. Commissioner and I sat *in* the afternoon.[100a] He drank tea. I just felt with him as twenty years ago, but firmer. The children said divine lessons. Lady Colville called between sermons.

WEDNESDAY 9 AUGUST. I called on my father, and he was confidential with me about John. I respected his calm solid sense, though I could not but regret his feeling so little. We were well together for a little by ourselves, he having called me into his room with him. I said I hoped he was now pleased with me. He said "*Yes*", but not with warmth. I said if he would tell me anything, it should be done. He said the great point was to be frugal and sober. I spoke of how much he had done. He said he had been lucky in having a good wife—two good wives, he might say. I said he was better now than he had been five years ago. He repeated, "Threescore and ten years do sum up", down to "*remove*".[101] I wished to hear him talk on religion, but saw no fair opening. When we returned to the drawing-room, I proposed to Lady Auchinleck to take Sandy with them. She said she had care enough without him, and said (I think) she had no wish to live but to take care of my father, and in a whimpering tone talked of his being the worse of being at Auchinleck. She said that perhaps, being overjoyed at my brother's return, I might think it was to be a merry meeting at Auchinleck. But it was quite different. My father went there to be quiet and retired. That company disturbed him, especially at night; and why have people who wanted to drink and be merry and would go away and say he was useless? It was hard, when people were willing to give up the world, that they could not be allowed to live in their own way. She said she was glad she had spoken to me. I said, "Well then, I give you my word of honour I shall not invite anybody. If you will be so kind as mention anything, it shall be done." I wanted to know if my father's bonds to my children did not leave them independent of me. She said she had never read them. But she should look them out. But I would not, she said, have my father to write them over again now. She was for people making settlements when in good health, but not to be troubled when indisposed. I said it was proper to alter what was wrong in settlements. She said she never had been so anxious. In short she talked absurdly. I kept my temper finely, and I was really disposed for peace. I was in good spirits tonight.

---

99 For Watson's Hospital, see p. 153, n. 140.
100 The Tron Church, in the High Street, was so named on account of its former proximity to a public weighbeam known as the Tron (or "Salt Tron") which had stood in front of the church.
100a "By emphasising *in*, Boswell means that they stayed at home and did not go back to church for the second sermon" (*Laird*, p. 225, n. 9).
101 Psalm 90, verse 10.

FRIDAY 11 AUGUST. Had my table clear, and was pleased that I had written more than double and received more than one half more fees than last Summer Session.

SATURDAY 12 AUGUST. Was a little in Justiciary Court at trial of David Reid, a forger.[102] Met with Mr Ilay Campbell on a Submission [to us as arbiters] where he thought an eldest son, to whom a tenement in Edinburgh was disponed by his father, failing himself, was not obliged to serve heir.[103] The Court of Session had determined the point differently. I wished to consult Lord Braxfield. Mr Campbell said Lord B. would determine him. My Lord was so good as to go to Mr Campbell's with me when he came out of Court, and was clear against his opinion. But struck out a new point quite clear which had not occurred either to parties or to us Arbiters. My wife and I dined alone today.

MONDAY 14 AUGUST. Mr Wood called and gave me directions about my health while in the country. My wife and I dined at Sir John Pringle's, a company of his old friends' sons: Solicitor, George Wallace, Maclaurin, Dr Young, myself. He talked of religion. Maclaurin said he was *bona fide*, and started his doubts. Sir John appeared to me to have very *small* Christianity, as was said of Shakespeare's Latin. Yet he believed *immortality* to be revealed. He seemed more happy than usual with this company. Maclaurin had read the most part of Luke in Greek the day before. Declared he spoke *bona fide*. I had my *Hypochondriack* No. 36 to write.[104] Went home and wrote some pages of it. Was hurried as usual before a journey. Went to bed about twelve.

TUESDAY 15 AUGUST. Got up about six. Finished No. 36 and was pleased. Mr Lawrie attended faithfully. My valuable spouse had breakfast ready in good time. I was foolishly agitated with hurry about trifles. Grange came. My dearest wife and he and Mr Lawrie went with me to the fly at the Corn Market.[105] I was most grateful to her. Mr Ross, the Under-Clerk of Session, and Mr Robertson, a mercantile man of Glasgow, were my companions.

Boswell joined his brother David in Glasgow and they reached Auchinleck on 16 August, where, says Boswell, "we were comforted and elated by seeing the seat of our ancestors... It was truly a feast to my mind to see all the scenes of my youth, and David here again after so long an absence." Their reception, however, remarks Boswell, was "indifferent". And a few days later, when Boswell and Lady Auchinleck went to church together, Boswell brought up the subject of Sandy: "I said I wished I had brought out Sandy notwithstanding she was not for it. She said it would have been very impertinent. And she talked of the heavy charge she had already (meaning my father), and that she did perhaps more than was her duty. I abhorred her. Saw her pride in keeping him like a child, and her unfeeling selfishness in keeping his grandson at a distance. But I was silent."

102 See entry for 23 February 1780. Reid was found guilty and hanged.
103 Serve heir: carry out the legal procedure whereby an heir acquired a right to the estate of his ancestor.
104 Actually No. 35 (on imitation).
105 At the eastern end of the Grassmarket.

A welcome guest at Auchinleck was Lord Braxfield, who arrived (with his lady and daughter) on 2 September and was joined two days later by Lord Kames (with his lady and son). Boswell had a long discussion with Braxfield as to how he had acquired such great knowledge of law. "[H]e said he had learnt law chiefly by thinking", *records Boswell.* "The rudiments, to be sure, must be had from books, but he had acquired his knowledge by considering points by himself. He regretted as I did that the Civil Law was gone into disuse so much, as it was from thence that the great principles of reason and sound sense were to be drawn; and he said that it was true, what I observed, that it was the glory of our law to proceed on principles and be more of a system than the law in England. As to decisions, he said one should not learn law by reading them, but after studying a point should then see what the decisions have been upon it."[106] *That evening, Boswell* "felt that company disturbed the calmness of Auchinleck. Lord Kames raved and Lord Braxfield roared—both bawdy."

In spite of the coldness of his father and Lady Auchinleck, Boswell found that he was as happy at Auchinleck as he had ever been. One day, he records, "I was... happy with a thought which never occurred to me before: that I might pass all the rest of my life in independent tranquillity at this place and have no reproach either from my own mind or the world as if I were acting improperly. For I would be at* Auchinleck, *which comprehends so many romantic, pious, and worthy ideas in my imagination—at the seat of my family—at home. This was quite a new way of thinking. I indulged the novelty with curious pleasure. I have from my earliest years been so habituated by my father to suppose it necessary to be of some profession, and to view a country gentleman who lives constantly upon his estate as an idle man, that it is not easy for me to think otherwise. But I am sensible that it is better—nay, necessary—for me to have more occupation, at least for some years; and it is consolatory to consider that I have always the respectable resource of Auchinleck." Later that day, Boswell and David rode over to Barskimming to visit the Lord Justice-Clerk, who received them "with great kindness", walked with them and took them sailing in his boat on the river Ayr.*

On 13 September, Boswell and David set off in a chaise for Edinburgh. "David and I", *says Boswell,* "disputed too warmly upon the road in the forenoon. I said he would be on a larger scale when he had been a winter in London; and I said his behaviour to the* noverca *was* butler-like. *He seemed hurt. I asked his forgiveness for hasty expressions. At night his precision and self-conceit fretted me. He said we should not travel together. I said I would not travel with him for five guineas a day."*

THURSDAY 14 SEPTEMBER. David and I got to my house to breakfast. Had the comfort and joy to find my wife and children all well. Little Jamie was now walking finely. He had lost his word *papa*, and could only cry *Bell*.[107] Jeanie Campbell from Liverpool and her brothers from Lanark were all in my house. I was happy to have worthy Treesbank's children about me.

FRIDAY 15 SEPTEMBER. Colonel Mure Campbell,[108] Lady Raasay, Miss Jeanie

106 From a "paper apart", quoted in *Laird*, p. 239, n. 3.
107 "Bell" being the name by which the nanny (Isobel Bruce) was known.
108 Colonel James Mure Campbell (1726-1786), *later* Major-General (1781) and 5th Earl of Loudoun (1782).

MacLeod, Mrs Vernon, and the Rev. Dr Erskine[109] dined with us. It was a dinner of comfort to the Colonel and his connexions.[110] I managed very well, so as to drink but one glass in the time of dinner and one after, and yet to be fully social. If I can once get free of a notion that my company is dissatisfied when I do not drink with them, I shall do well.

SATURDAY 16 SEPTEMBER. David and I had an agreeable walk to Belleville, where we paid a visit to Lady Dundonald. I had all my old ideas at this place, where I have enjoyed much happiness, as fresh today as ever. David dined with his old master, Hunter-Blair.[111] Mr Fraser, one of the masters of the High School, drank tea with us and examined the young Campbells excellently well, to settle what classes they should enter.[112]

SUNDAY 17 SEPTEMBER. Heard and joined devoutly in the first division of the forenoon service in the Old English Chapel,[113] as I felt that I could not be easy without being at public worship. Was in the gallery concealed, and came off quietly, Grange and David waiting for me at Grange's. We walked out to Sir Alexander Dick's. Mr Charles Hay walked out with us, and waited till David had bid adieu to the worthy Baronet, and then accompanied him to Edinburgh, David being to dine with Bailie David Steuart.[114] I was in perfect serenity, and saw everything in a comfortable light. Worthy Grange was also quite happy, and we walked in the garden and eat fruit joyously. I drank one glass of currant wine. A heavy rain came on. We had the coach to town. My children and the three Campbells said divine lessons. I was pleased to have them all about me. My health was almost fully restored. At least I had little uneasiness, and my mind was unclouded.

TUESDAY 19 SEPTEMBER. Rose early and saw David into the Berwick fly. His sense and accuracy and sobriety made me esteem him. But his rigid uncomplying manners, except by force of studied complaisance, and his want of generosity in every respect (a strong instance of which was his not feeling with the least indignation what I, his kind brother, am obliged to suffer from the incessant ill-will of a *noverca* who governs my father as if he were a child), made me not love

---

109 The Rev. John Erskine, D.D. (for whom, see p. 198, n. 45).
110 The Colonel's wife, Flora (née MacLeod), had died on 2 September shortly after giving birth to a daughter (*Laird*, p. 248, n. 4).
111 James Hunter-Blair had been David's master during his apprenticeship.
112 The High School had recently moved from its ancient, incommodious building at what is now Infirmary Street to new premises situated nearby. A list of subscribers for the new building had been set up in 1775 by several prominent figures, including Sir William Forbes and Alexander Wood, the surgeon. The foundation stone was laid by Sir William Forbes, in his capacity as Grand Master Mason of Scotland, on 24 June 1777. One of the young boys at the new school was the future Sir Walter Scott who was sent there in 1779 and was taught by Luke Fraser (the same Mr Fraser as is mentioned by Boswell), for whom Scott had a high regard. However, the only subject taught at the school was Latin, and even by the time Cockburn was sent there in 1787 the only extra subject was Greek (Cockburn, p. 4).
113 For the "Old English Chapel", see the entry for 11 February 1776 and relevant footnote.
114 "Bailie" David Steuart, an Edinburgh merchant and banker, had formerly been a bailie, but was now in fact the Lord Provost, having been elected earlier that year. He remained Lord Provost until 1782.

him. I went with George Campbell and breakfasted at his master Mr Fraser's, where was Mr French, David [Campbell]'s master. But David, being a little indisposed, could not be with us. I was soundly happy conversing with these schoolmasters. I walked with them to the school, and was present at Mr Fraser's opening his class with a decent prayer, after which I heard him examine some of the boys on a passage of Caesar. I was much pleased with his perfect investigation of the elements of the Latin and with his instruction in the sense, particularly the geography. David had grown better and gone to Mr French's class, but I did not see him. I felt much satisfaction in my present superiority of understanding, while my vivacity recalled the state of a school-boy, and I thought I would yet advance in literature. I dined at Maclaurin's, and was introduced to Sir Lawrence Dundas. He said he hoped he and I would be better acquainted, and was very courteous.[115]

WEDNESDAY 20 SEPTEMBER. Went to Lady Colville's and found her and Lady Anne and Mr Andrew sitting after dinner. I was in excellent spirits. After the ladies had left us, he and I had some excellent conversation upon hypochondria. He said I was right in not struggling against it while it is strong. A man should just follow his inclination at the time. He said when one is in good spirits, everything, even the most indifferent, gives him pleasure. But we agreed that there was an essential difference between him and me. For he never had at any time the least anxiety as to a future state, as he was persuaded that it was in vain to think of it, as nothing could be known. He thought it might be; and that virtue and vice might be rewarded and punished. He said he had given over poetry, being convinced that he never could be better than a minor poet, and of these he had observed a succession all forgotten. I however think that to have moderate fame even for a short period is desirable. It is a pleasure. It is so much enjoyment. I had a good deal of satisfaction in conversing with

---

115 So enters on the scene the immensely rich and gout-ridden Sir Lawrence Dundas (c. 1710-81), now about seventy years old, who was to live for only one more year, but during that time was to see much of Boswell. Although a remote relation of the mighty Dundases of Arniston, he came from a much humbler branch of the family; indeed, his father had been the proprietor of an Edinburgh drapery business in the Luckenbooths. However, Dundas amassed a fortune during the Seven Years' War by virtue of lucrative contracts for the provision of supplies to the troops in Germany, thus acquiring the soubriquet of "the Nabob of the North". He was created a baronet in 1762, and a few years later he began to build up considerable political power in Scotland, starting with the purchase of Orkney and Shetland in 1766. In 1768 he and several of his political adherents were elected to Parliament, Sir Lawrence being elected as representative for Edinburgh (which seat he was to hold until 1780). Although never appointed a Minister, it was said of him that he had at that time "the diposal of almost everything in Scotland" (Ramsay, p. 154). From 1764 to 1777 he was the highly successful governor of the Royal Bank of Scotland and in that role is chiefly remembered for financing the Forth and Clyde Canal. However, not being one to be averse to adopting unscrupulous political methods, "he was neither liked nor trusted, the Scottish nobility in particular resenting the extension of the 'upstart's' influence" (Namier and Brooke, Vol. II, p. 360). He was never on good terms with the Dundases of Arniston, and, indeed, it soon became apparent that his principal opponent was the rising Henry Dundas. Sir Lawrence's house, built on land lying to the east of St Andrew Square in a line with George Street, now a branch (and for long the head office) of the Royal Bank of Scotland, has been described as "the finest house in the New Town, a three-storey building of splendid dignity and fine detail, built to the plans of Sir William Chambers" (Youngson, *The Making of Classical Edinburgh*, p. 84).

him this afternoon. But I felt my advantage in believing a benignant revelation of immortality. We drank tea with the ladies. He walked with me to town.

My interview yesterday at Maclaurin's with Sir Lawrence Dundas gave me a good deal of satisfaction. It was adding a new distinguished character to my collection. He appeared to me not a cunning, shrewd man of the world, as I had imagined, but a comely, jovial Scotch gentleman of good address but not bright parts. Lady Wallace was there, and entertained us exceedingly. I told her today that she was happy in saying a multiplicity of good things and none that were bad. There was nothing in flashing away sometimes well, often ill. She had fired above forty shot without missing. I had paid her a visit some days ago and also this forenoon; was amused and charmed with her, without being feverishly amorous. Several of the Town Council dined at Maclaurin's.[116] We drank success to him.[117] I resolved not to be warm in the Town politics. I played at whist tonight and lost a little without fretting. Went home at nine. Had drank at dinner four glasses, and felt that quantity heat me. Wrote yesterday *The Hypochondriack* No. 36, I think all of it.[118] Sir Lawrence said, "I am old and lame and cannot visit my friends, but I shall be very glad to see you at my house." I waited on him this morning, and was well received by him, his lady, and son. I liked him much. I even felt for him as a man ungratefully used in his old age.

THURSDAY 21 SEPTEMBER. Went with Commissioner Cochrane and visited Sir L. and Lady Dundas. The Rev. Mr Nicholls and Grange dined with us. My spirits were so excellent at present that I was a full match for Nicholls in vivacity, so that I relished him better than when he was last here. After tea I went with him to his lodgings and heard him read his journal of his travels in Scotland. His landscape was very well done. But it wanted figures.[119] I again in my journals have little else but character, not having as yet attended much to inanimate objects. We read a little of *J.-J. Rousseau jugé par lui-même*,[120] a new publication which we thought genuine. I was roused by his eloquence, but saw with a sound look that he was mad. I stayed with Nicholls and supped. I eat apple pie and drank water, and had a deal of animated talk.

FRIDAY 22 SEPTEMBER. Dined at Commissioner Cochrane's; young Craigengillan[121] and his governor, Dr Adams, Rector of the High School,[122] etc., there. I drank only water, and was quite as I could wish to be. Found my association of ideas in my boyish days as to the High School dissolved. Saw it as a good

---

116 That is, on the 19th.

117 The editors of *Laird* surmise, at p. 251, n. 1, that Maclaurin may have been managing Sir Lawrence's politics.

118 The essay was on living in the country.

119 The Rev. Norton Nicholls (*c.* 1742-1809) was a close friend of Temple's and had visited Boswell in Edinburgh in August 1774. The journal of his travels in Scotland was never published and the manuscript has not been traced (*Laird*, p. 252, n. 3).

120 The actual title was *Rousseau jugé de Jean-Jacques*.

121 Quintin McAdam, son of John McAdam of Craigengillan (*Laird*, p. 550).

122 Dr Alexander Adam (1741-1809), LL.D., Rector of the High School, "had most of the usual peculiarities of a schoolmaster; but was so amiable and so artless, that no sensible friend would have wished one of them to be even softened" (Cockburn, p. 252, n. 3).

place for education.[123] What a world of chimeras had I when young! It is impossible to give a notion of this to others. Both Berkeley and Hume have a good deal of truth in their systems. Their fault is excess, by which, while they augment the dominion of perceptions, they annihilate the substance and power both of body and mind.

SATURDAY 23 SEPTEMBER. Carried Nicholls to visit Lady Wallace, after which we visited Maclaurin. I was as lively as when in London. Commissioner Cochrane, his son Willie, young Craigengillan and his governor, the young Campbells, and the laird of Logan dined with us. I went in the evening to a concert for the benefit of H. Reinagle,[124] and enjoyed it much. Nicholls and Maclaurin supped with us. We laughed a great deal, but Nicholls gave a ridiculous, profane account of his ordination, which offended me much.[125] I could not check him before Maclaurin, who would have taken his part, and he would have grown worse. I was quite disgusted, and bore him only as my friend Temple's friend, in the common loose acceptation.

SUNDAY 24 SEPTEMBER. Stayed at home in the forenoon. Called on Nicholls to have talked to him of his indecent behaviour last night, but did not find him. Dined calm at home, and went in the afternoon with my wife to the Tolbooth Kirk and heard Dr Webster preach. In the evening the children said divine lessons well.

MONDAY 25 SEPTEMBER. Nicholls was to set out this morning. I sent to see if he was gone, that I might have called if he was not. He was just stepping into the chaise. Perhaps it was as well I did not see him. I might have been too warm and have exasperated him. I shall write to Temple about him; and I believe shall have no more to say to him. For a profane clergyman is contemptible as a fool and detestable as a cheat.

TUESDAY 26 SEPTEMBER. I had Mr James Cummyng to dine with me, and was amused and interested with genealogy and antiquities of various kinds. He stayed till pretty late in the evening. This was a little feast. I should have mentioned some days ago a scene equal to any one in Sterne. I went to one McGrigor, a lapidary in the Potterrow, to get some pebbles cut.[126] The poor industrious lad had a room which served for kitchen and bed-chamber, and a closet off it which served for working in. He had a wife and a young child. His wife was busy washing plates in the room; and that the child might be kept without wearying, he had it set down on a board at a little distance from his wheel, the

123 Boswell was never a pupil at the High School.
124 Hugh Reinagle, a talented 'cellist, younger son of the composer Joseph Reinagle.
125 Nicholls said that, when he applied to the Archbishop of York for ordination, he confessed to the Archbishop that he had not read any books on divinity, and that when he was later examined by a clergyman in London he scarcely knew what to say in response to a question on "the necessity of a Mediator", and that he had never read the Greek New Testament (letter from Boswell to Temple dated 3-4 September, 3 November 1780, quoted in *Laird*, p. 253, n. 8).
126 Grange had suggested to Boswell a few days before that he should have the Boswell crest (a hooded hawk) cut on one of the pebbles Boswell had found at Auchinleck during his recent stay there (*Laird*, p. 254, n. 2).

quick motion and noise of which amused it as well as if it had been dandled and sung to by its mother. A better picture of industry and contrivance in miniature cannot be imagined.

THURSDAY 28 SEPTEMBER. Dined at Sir Lawrence Dundas's. Lady Wallace was there, as were Commissioner Cochrane and Dr Webster, who had never seen her before. Even the Commissioner was amused, though a little afraid. Webster was delighted. Maclaurin was there too. The dinner was excellent, the dessert of fruits elegantly luxurious. I drank a few glasses of wine. I was good company. I liked Sir Lawrence more and more. There was a kindliness and even a simplicity in his manner that put me in mind of Lord Strichen. He talked a great deal of his *adventures*, as I may call them, with the Duke of Cumberland's army in 1745-6.[127] I thought I might get materials from him for my intended history of that period. We went to coffee and tea, so many of us. I felt some of that cloudy dreariness which has so often come upon me. I suppose I had loaded my stomach too much, and dress and good behaviour cramped me somewhat. On coming home I got a card from young Mr Sibthorpe,[128] with a letter from his father. The young man was arrived at Macfarlane's inn,[129] and weary after his journey. So I wrote back I would wait on him in the morning and conduct him to my house to breakfast. Dr Webster and Grange supped with us. We had prayers. I grew clear again.

FRIDAY 29 SEPTEMBER. Called on young Mr Sibthorpe and brought him and Mr Irwin, scholar of Trinity College, Dublin, with me to breakfast. Dr Webster came by appointment. It was agreeable to have an Irish cousin, a grandson of General Cochrane's, with us. But as Mr Irwin, who had been his tutor, had no instructions as to settling him, I was anxious; and though I had written to his father on Thursday stating the different schemes, I wrote again tonight. I had yesterday talked again on the subject with Adam Smith at the custom-house, and had agreed to breakfast with him today. Sibthorpe's arrival made me break this engagement, but I went to Smith before breakfast and made my apology. As he had been very obliging to me when at Glasgow, I thought it not right to keep altogether at a distance from him, though I disapproved of his praise of David Hume and attack upon Oxford. I walked about with Mess. Sibthorpe and Irwin in the forenoon. They dined with me along with old Lady Grant, etc., and they stayed the evening and supped.

SATURDAY 30 SEPTEMBER. Mr Irwin went off for Ireland. Dr Webster, Mr Sibthorpe, and I went to Valleyfield, the Doctor and I having intended to go this day.

The following day, the party went from Valleyfield to Culross Church for the Sunday service. "I never was sounder or more cheerful in my life", remarks Boswell. And two days

---

127 Details of these adventures are not known, but Sir Lawrence was Commissary for the supply of bread and forage to the Hanoverian army in Scotland from 1746 to 1748.
128 Stephen James Sibthorpe (as to whom, see the entry for 12 September 1779 and relevant footnote).
129 The "White Hart" at the foot of the Pleasance, owned by Duncan Macfarlane (Stuart, p. 117).

later, Boswell records: "I was as fond of Culross, and had my mind as serenely filled with such sentiments and affections as my dear mother gave me, as at the best periods of my youngest life." Boswell's short, but "most agreeable", stay at Valleyfield (during which, says Boswell proudly, "I never drank above four glasses of wine any day") ended on 5 October when the party returned to Edinburgh. Here, Boswell and his wife invited Mr Sibthorpe to stay at their house until he was settled with a professor.

FRIDAY 6 OCTOBER. Mr Sibthorpe appeared both to my wife and me to be a most amiable young man; just seventeen, very little, somewhat dull of hearing, quiet, modest, of good principles, and of decent good sense. We had already an affection for him as if he had been our own child. He seemed happy living with us. He and I visited Lady Dundonald this forenoon and afterwards Commissioner Cochrane. Baron Maule was with him. He and I had a good deal of lively conversation while the Commissioner and Sibthorpe sat silent by us. As I expressed myself somewhat warmly on my friend Major Montgomerie's side,[130] the Commissioner admonished me with a kind of heat which I did not like at the time. He said, "You are cutting your own throat. It will be told to your father that you speak at the Cross against his side, and he will be offended." Perhaps the old, cool, prudent Commissioner was right. Yet it is hard not to have the liberty of speaking when I have not a vote as I ought to have. My father has not treated me as a man should be treated, but has looked on me as a mere dependant on him. This has, I dare say, prevented me from making a greater figure in the world than I do. Though it may be it has secured me from splendid ruin.

SATURDAY 7 OCTOBER. My wife and three eldest children and Mr Sibthorpe and I dined at Sir Alexander Dick's. I was in choice spirits, in so much that I was entertained even with Anthony Barclay.[131] Sir Alexander was all life. I had visited Lady Colville in the forenoon.

SUNDAY 8 OCTOBER. Mr Sibthorpe and I were at the New English Chapel forenoon and afternoon, in Lady Colville's seat. I enjoyed devotion delightfully.

MONDAY 9 OCTOBER. Mr Sibthorpe was quite easy in our family, and not in the least troublesome. He generally goes up every evening to Dr Grant's to a card party.

TUESDAY 10 OCTOBER. This day alone I left Mr Sibthorpe and dined with Mr Hunter-Blair,[132] where were Sir Lawrence and Lady Dundas, Maclaurin, Mr Watts from New York, and Captain Kennedy, heir male of the Earl of Cassillis, who was married to Watts's daughter, etc. Kennedy and I took to one another sympathetically. There was a long drink of claret. I tired of the noise, though I drank a few glasses and sung with jovial humour. Between nine and ten as I passed by Lady Wallace's, I saw her at the window, and having beckoned her, she threw up the sash. I asked if she was in; she said yes. So I paid her a visit,

---

130 Major Montgomerie was standing for election as M.P. for Ayrshire against Sir Adam Fergusson.
131 Anthony Barclay, W.S. (admitted 20 June 1769), died 1811. It seems that Boswell normally found Barclay's company to be somewhat dull.
132 James Hunter-Blair's house was in George Street.

heard her read several pieces of poetry of her own composition, made fine speeches to her, and also talked to her freely as to her conduct, as she was going to Bath. Her indelicacy disgusted me. I was not in such good spirits tonight as for some time past, being jaded.

THURSDAY 12 OCTOBER. One of these days I had a walk in the High Street with Andrew Erskine, who was then in bad spirits. I stipulated that we should say nothing of the Ayrshire election, but talk of ourselves and our own feelings. He said that bad spirits distressed one more than any real evil; and as an instance he mentioned that Miss Clemie Elphinstone had found the pain of a broken leg and the apprehension of lameness much easier than the uneasy weariness and discontent of hypochondria. I told Erskine I was to write Dr Johnson's life in scenes.[133] He approved. This forenoon I visited Colonel Mure Campbell, and was much pleased with his conversation. We walked a long time in the Meadow, after having talked two hours in the house. I mentioned to the Colonel my intention of offering myself a candidate at our next election, and that I had spoke of it to Lord Loudoun, who seemed to approve. The Colonel said he durst say Lord Loudoun would be very well pleased I should be the man. I said I did not desire any answer from the Colonel now. But I hoped he would keep in mind what I had proposed, and I mentioned Thomas Boswell of Auchinleck having been married to a daughter of the family of Loudoun. Mr Sibthorpe and I dined at Sir Lawrence Dundas's, whom I had visited again yesterday forenoon and found alone and talked with cordially of the President's conduct to my father at the last election, adding, "He is a hollow dog." Sir Lawrence said, "Do you think I don't know him?" The dinner today was as good as when I dined here before. Sir John Whitefoord, Maclaurin, etc., were there. We drank coffee and tea. Sir John and I grew a little warm upon my relating Colonel Campbell's conversation and mine on both the candidates for Ayrshire being Ministerial tools, and in his fretfulness maintained that Sir Adam Fergusson was not uniformly Ministerial, and said he would be at Colonel Campbell for this. After he went away, Sir Lawrence said Sir Adam was as hackney a Ministerial Member as ever went from Scotland. I played whist and lost, but was in fine spirits. Mr Sibthorpe and I stayed supper quite easily. I eat an egg and drank water.

FRIDAY 13 OCTOBER. I called at Harry Erskine's, where came Old Erskine, whom I was really glad to meet again. My mind was so sound and clear, I fully relished ancient family—high spirit—vivacity, etc., etc. I breakfasted with Colonel Mure Campbell, having first taken him out and put him on his guard in case Sir John Whitefoord should come and talk with him of what I had told. I was somewhat hurt to think that I was yet so apt to repeat what passed in conversation, though I am much cured of the bad habit. The Colonel took it so easily, I was made easy. I felt a slight fear of a duel ensuing, as I had heard of one at

---

133 "That is, was to build his book around his dramatic recordings of Johnson's conversation. It must be remembered that this method, which now seems so obvious, was highly original and daring. Such intimate treatment of a biographical subject was a violation of an unwritten law of biographical dignity" (*Laird*, p. 260, n. 4).

the Kirkcudbright election. I thought I could go on with it pretty well. Lady Raasay and Miss MacLeod breakfasted with us. The Colonel is one of those who animate and call forth my faculties. We were very happy this morning. I found that, as Captain James Erskine said I was a Tory with Whig principles, the Colonel was a Whig with Tory principles. So we did not differ in effect. Nay, though a professed Presbyterian, he had no objection to some livings of £500 a year to encourage merit, nor to a form of prayer, nor to a crucifix. Grange dined with us today and was introduced to Mr Sibthorpe. I called a little on Maclaurin this forenoon.

SUNDAY 15 OCTOBER. Commissioner Cochrane came in the morning and went with Mr Sibthorpe and me to the New English Chapel. It was curious and pleasing to see him there. It gave me the agreeable view that in time "all may be saved and come to the knowledge of the truth".[134] As yet indeed he knew but little of religion. He dined with us, sat the afternoon, and drank tea. It was perhaps wrong to stay from worship on his account. But as I am not quite regular in town, it may be pardoned. The children said divine lessons agreeably at night. Mr and Mrs Erskine of Alloa[135] and Dr Webster supped with us. The Doctor prayed.

MONDAY 16 OCTOBER. Lords Eglinton and Kellie paid us a visit before dinner. I had by desire visited Lord Buchan this forenoon and heard him read a speech intended for the peers' election.[136]

TUESDAY 17 OCTOBER. Visited the Earls of Eglinton, Cassillis, and Dunmore. Was in high spirits. Was introduced to Lady Dunmore and the two young ladies, beautiful young creatures with Parisian vivacity, air, and ease. Went with Mr Sibthorpe to the election of the peers. Stayed a very short while. Sir Charles Preston, Major Preston, Mr Wellwood, and the Rev. Dr Cooper dined with us. I was disgusted by Cooper's coarse manners and unlettered conversation. This day at intervals of leisure I wrote No. 37 of *The Hypochondriack*.[137] I went with Mr Sibthorpe to the Assembly. Was wonderfully easy and gay.

WEDNESDAY 18 OCTOBER. Visited the Earl of Loudoun. No news as yet of the Ayrshire election. Was anxious to uneasiness. Lords Eglinton and Kellie had gone this morning to the Hunters' meeting at Kelso.[138] I was much pleased to see Lord Kellie improved after an absence of about six years. He was more sedate and well

134 I Timothy 2. 4.
135 John Francis Erskine ("Young Mar") and his wife.
136 That is, the election of the sixteen Scottish Representative Peers.
137 Like Nos 36 and 38, the subject of this essay was living in the country.
138 The meeting at Kelso was a meeting of the Honourable Company of Scottish Hunters. Arnot, writing in 1779, states: "This club has its headquarters (if we may be allowed the expression) at Edinburgh; and meets occcasionally in different parts of the country as the inclination of the members dictates. The club is composed of nobility and gentry of the first distinction. They wear an uniform at their meetings; and they give annually a magnificent ball at the palace at Holyroodhouse. Among other rules of this company, they have established proper regulations to prevent gaming... Their uniform is scarlet, turned up with green, and a silver button" (Arnot, pp. 211-2).

behaved, and not like Mount Vesuvius, as my uncle, the Doctor, described him formerly. I met Harry Erskine and went with him to Maclaurin's for a little, and got some difficulties in law cleared. Prevailed on Maclaurin to join Sir Charles Preston, Dr Webster, and so many more of us at a dinner at Jack's. We were hearty. I drank very little, as I now constantly do, not six glasses at any time, but was excellent company. Maclaurin, Major George Preston, and I played at heads or tails for shillings, Dr Webster exclaiming, "Dreadful! Gaming in miniature!" I had breakfasted today with Ulbster and revised some of his letters on the Scotch language addressed to me.[139] Maclaurin and I went from Jack's to Sir Lawrence Dundas's. Went into the drawing-room quite easy and sat with Lady Dundas and her company till the gentlemen came from the dining-room. Lady Dundas had called on my wife yesterday, and my wife on her today, so that an acquaintance was forming. Sir Lawrence very kindly said he had a quarrel with me (or a phrase to that purpose) because I had not dined with him on Monday when Lord Kellie proposed it to me. I said I did not think I could take that liberty. He spoke so warmly in the affirmative that I said, "Well, I shall never do so again." "Then", said he, "I forgive you." I played whist and won. It was quite comfortable tonight. We stayed supper. Sir Lawrence said he had been engaged in politics since the year 1747, and had named beforehand the Lords of Session on each question he had. This charge of partiality, which is very general and that too amongst our most sensible observers (for David Erskine told me a few days ago that, tell him the county and he would tell the votes of all—or perhaps he said *most*—of the judges in political questions), shocked me and made me dread being a Lord of Session. As Maclaurin and I walked home, he said he wished Major Montgomerie success, for he liked him, and he hated George Fergusson[140] and "would crack him like a louse". He maintained that a man who was not vindictive had no warmth of friendship. He "would not ride the water on him".[141] For his part he never forgave. "Curse your enemies", said he with keenness. I said to him he was encouraging a diabolical principle. I hope it was the spleen of the moment. I went home resolved to be distrustful of so unchristian a being.

THURSDAY 19 OCTOBER. Called on Lord Loudoun pretty early. He had no final account of the Ayrshire election, but that the previous votes were ten of majority on Major Montgomerie's side. After leaving him I got a letter from Sundrum[142] with the joyful news, franked *Hu. Montgomerie*. I run to Lord Loudoun and wished him joy. Then to Sir Lawrence Dundas, then to Lord Cassillis, who

---

139 Sir John Sinclair of Ulbster's *Observations on the Scottish Dialect* was published in 1782. Sinclair (1754-1835) is now primarily remembered as editor of the first *Statistical Account of Scotland* (1791-1799).

140 George Fergusson, the advocate (*later* Lord Hermand), was assisting his brother Sir Adam Fergusson in his election campaign (*Laird*, p. 237, n. 2).

141 "Would not trust him in an emergency; literally, would not ford a river on his back" (*Laird*, p. 264, n. 8).

142 John Hamilton of Sundrum.

was rather *cool*. He did not much rejoice that the family of Eglinton had succeeded. I was in capital spirits. Grange rejoiced with me. I dined at Dr Blair's at North Merchiston; Commissioners Cochrane and Smith[143] and Mr Morehead there. It was a very tolerable party. In the evening Mr Sibthorpe and I walked to the New Town in a storm of wind and rain and supped at Mr Wellwood's with Sir Charles Preston, etc.[144] I was cheerful, and more calm than I could have supposed after the Ayrshire victory. But there was danger from a petition.[145]

SATURDAY 21 OCTOBER. Maclaurin and I went in his chaise to Craighouse and took up Lord Covington, and then we drove to Arniston, where we arrived between three and four. Nobody at home. The butler said he could only give us a bit of bread and a glass of wine; but when we seemed inclined to take it, he said he could not give us a fire. This was cold indeed. So we turned and jogged on to Melville,[146] where we had intended to dine next day. Lord Advocate had Lord Glencairn and Sir William Murray sitting with him after dinner. We had some good things at a table by ourselves and excellent champagne. Then we joined and drank claret. I was allowed to be moderate. I felt myself quite comfortable here. I was satisfied that my prejudices against Lord Advocate were imaginary. Lord Glencairn went away. The rest of us went to tea and coffee with Lady Augusta Murray and old Lady Arniston,[147] and played whist. I drank only water at night. I had a warm bedchamber, and was quite as I could wish.

SUNDAY 22 OCTOBER. Breakfast was as good a meal as ever I saw it. Lady Arniston was wonderfully well. Lord Covington went away after breakfast. Lord Advocate expressed his wonder that I had never before been at Melville; and though it had rained a good deal and the ground was wet, he very obligingly walked with me over the best part of his place, which I found to be truly a treasure so near Edinburgh. The River of Esk and well-planted banks and well-dressed fields formed a goodly scene. He seemed to me the frankest and best-humoured politician that could be. I joked with him on the strange forgetfulness as to my father's votes.[148] Told him I was trembling for some days for fear they should be recollected, and that he would have set them a-going. He said he certainly would if he had thought of them, and laughed with me. Maclaurin walked with us and led him to speak of the differences between Sir Lawrence Dundas and him till he really made me view his conduct with no violent disapprobation. I was quite easy with him, and felt with some pleasure the old connexions of my father with both his father, and grandfather by the mother's side. I asked him if he never went to church; he said he generally did, and if we had not been with him, would have been there today. I was

143 Adam Smith.
144 Robert Wellwood resided in St Andrew Street.
145 That is, a petition challenging the validity of some of the votes.
146 Henry Dundas's estate near Dalkeith.
147 Henry Dundas's mother, Anne Gordon, second wife of Lord Arniston, the first Lord President Dundas.
148 That is, the fictitious votes which Lord Auchinleck had created in connection with Sir Adam Fergusson's election campaign in Ayrshire in 1774.

a little uneasy at my not being today at any place of worship. He said Sir Alexander Dick was the happiest man alive. This was a proof that he could think with some just delicacy of sentiment. Many people waited on him today. Several stayed and dined. I should have been very happy had not the assuming villain John Fordyce been there. I wondered how Lord Advocate could receive him. I took no manner of notice of him, but was pleasant without looking towards him. I should have mentioned that there are at Melville five remaining trees which tradition says were planted by David Rizzio.[149] I saw four of them. Maclaurin and I returned to town at night. He was better tonight than when I last mentioned him. Dr Webster and Grange supped with us. My spirits were fine.

MONDAY 23 OCTOBER. I dined by the Earl of Glencairn's invitation with the Countess, his mother, at the Coates.[150] I wished to pay him all attention now that his affairs were embarrassed. Harry Erskine was there. We were well enough. I drank more claret than I have done for some months. I stayed tea and heard Lady Betty Cunningham play wonderfully well on the pianoforte. There was a circumstance which was unlucky. I did not recollect having once been in company with the Countess at the late Earl's, though she recollected having talked with me of Paoli. This was, I fear, a sad forgetfulness of a proud woman. I played a rubber at whist, lost a shilling, and walked home before supper.

THURSDAY 26 OCTOBER. I breakfasted with Lord Eglinton, who was returned from the Hunters' Meeting at Kelso. He was not as warm as I was in his joy on Major Montgomerie's success; at least he was not so much so in appearance. I walked with him to Leith. He there joined Sir John Whiteford, Andrew Erskine, and the bankrupt John Fordyce. I had at breakfast expressed my indigation at the countenance shown to that fellow; and when I saw that Lord Eglinton chose his company, I walked off. I dined at Lady Colville's with the Earls of Eglinton, Kellie, Matthew Henderson, etc. There is nothing to be recorded but that there was a good deal of animal spirits and much drinking. I was obliged to drink about two bottles. I walked home and was pretty well.

FRIDAY 27 OCTOBER. Got up with a very slight headache, but was somewhat uneasy to think that any company whatever could make me exceed in wine and depart from my general plan of sobriety. However, I thought that at times a little indulgence was not wrong. I was displeased that my drinking so much yesterday was from a kind of compulsion. I supped at Sir Lawrence Dundas's. Nobody at table but he and Lady Dundas and her niece, Miss Bruce. How curious is it that I am so easy in the house of a man whom I have known so short while, and to whom I was in keen opposition six years ago.[151]

---

149 "Unauthenticated tradition states that the ancient castle of Melville was a residence of David Rizzio, and as such, was, of course, visited occasionally by Queen Mary" (Grant, Vol. III, p. 361).
150 The house at the Coates which is referred to in this entry is perhaps Wester Coates house (as to which see the entry for 15 September 1779 and relevant footnote), for that house was feued to the Countess of Glencairn in the early 1790s (Harris, p. 179).
151 At the election for the Stirling Burghs in the autumn of 1774, Sir Alexander Gilmour was Sir Lawrence Dundas's nominee (*Laird*, p. 339, n. 6).

SATURDAY 28 OCTOBER. Our little daughter Betty was under inoculation and had many smallpox. My wife's anxiety made it difficult for me to persuade her to dine abroad. But by entreaty I prevailed with her to dine today at Sir Lawrence Dundas's. Mr Sibthorpe was with us. She was well dressed and looked as well, perhaps better, than ever she did in her life, and she was quite easy. I was vain of her and very happy. Dr Webster and Surgeon Wood were there. It was a luxurious dinner. I enjoyed it much, and drank hock and claret with pleasure, but not to excess. My wife went away after tea. I played whist, lost a little money, and stayed supper.

SUNDAY 29 OCTOBER. Went with my wife to the Tolbooth Church in the forenoon and heard Dr Webster, who dined with us. Went with her again in the afternoon and heard Mr Kemp. Mr Sibthorpe and our three eldest children were there too. In the evening the children said divine lessons very agreeably. I hoped to live better from this day, being now forty years of age.

MONDAY 30 OCTOBER. I dined at Lady Dundonald's; Mr Sibthorpe, Dr Webster, and Commissioner Cochrane there. It was very comfortable. Mr Sibthorpe and I stayed tea. In the evening I toyed with a young lady, which had an effect that I have not experienced for some time but in a dream. Mr Sibthorpe went to lodgings tonight.

TUESDAY 31 OCTOBER. Sir Lawrence and Lady Dundas and Miss Bruce, the Lord Provost[152] (on whom I called yesterday), Dr Webster, Commissioner Cochrane, Mr Hunter-Blair, Mr Maclaurin, Surgeon Wood, and Mr Sibthorpe dined with us. Veronica sat at table. Phemie and Sandy dined at Dr Grant's and came to us after dinner. It was as good a party of the kind as could be. My wife had an excellent plain dinner, and my wines were very good. The conversation was mostly on Sir Lawrence's political contests. I drank too much, so as to be in some degree intoxicated.

TUESDAY 7 NOVEMBER. Maclaurin said to me lately that a man might be very happy without being of consequence if he did not consider being of consequence as essential to him. I may come to think in that cool way as Maclaurin does. But at present I would rather be Burke than Lord Hopetoun.[153]

WEDNESDAY 8 NOVEMBER. Went out with Commissioner Cochrane in his chaise and dined with him. Lord Gardenstone was there. He entertained us with lists of the ages of eighteen kings, eighteen philosophers, and eighteen poets. The philosophers were by much the longest lived. The kings the shortest.

THURSDAY 9 NOVEMBER. The New Kirk was opened in its new form, this being the Fast Day. I was there forenoon and afternoon, and was pleased to find the old association of gloomy ideas with its former appearance dissolved.

SUNDAY 12 NOVEMBER. Received the Sacrament in the New Church. Was in a good calm frame. Regretted that we had not the decency of the Church of England established in this country.

152 David Steuart (as to whom, see the entry for 17 September 1780 and relevant footnote).
153 John Hope (1704-1781), the immensely wealthy second Earl of Hopetoun.

MONDAY 13 NOVEMBER. I was at the New Church and heard a most excellent sermon by Sir Harry Moncreiff on "He that provideth not for his own household",[154] etc. He inculcated the duties of good economy on the one hand and kindly connexion with our kindred on the other. My father was in church. I thought the second branch of the discourse might touch him.

TUESDAY 14 NOVEMBER. This was the first day of the Winter Session. I visited my father first. Then went to Lord President's, where most of the judges and Lord Advocate were.

FRIDAY 17 NOVEMBER. I was very unwilling to rise this morning, but was obliged to be in the Court of Session. Last night the street was covered with snow. This morning there was a thaw and all was black and wet. My spirits were low as upon many former occasions. I had a poor opinion of myself. I however was not deeply miserable. I had begun *The Hypochondriack* No. 38[155] yesterday, but had done very little to it. This afternoon I finished it very well. This gave me some satisfaction. I also wrote to worthy Langton. How insignificant is my life at present! How little do I read! I am making no considerable figure in any way, and I am now forty years of age. But let me not despond. I am a man better known in the world than most of my countrymen. I am very well at the bar for my standing. I lead a regular, sober life. I have a variety of knowledge and excellent talents for conversation. I have a good wife and promising children. Sandy, upon being told some days ago that the Devil was once an angel in Heaven and thrown down for disobedience, asked me, "Who was Devil before him?" I said there was none. But I thought the existence of an evil principle a curious investigation. Mr Sibthorpe continues to be with us generally at every meal but breakfast.

SATURDAY 18 NOVEMBER. My father had been seized with a cold on Thursday, which confined him to the house, after having walked home that day very imprudently. I did not miss him in court yesterday. This forenoon I did, and called on him. He was asleep. So I did not see him. I sat awhile with Lady Auchinleck. I had for a day or two had a cold myself. It grew worse today; and I took too much balsam of cappivi[156] at night, which loaded my stomach so that I was so ill that I could not call again at my father's. On Tuesday last there was a meeting at the Earl of Buchan's for the purpose of forming an Antiquarian Society in Scotland. I had a card from his Lordship inviting me to it. But as I think him a silly, affected being, I did not go; and I was pleased next day when I heard a ridiculous account of the meeting from Wight and Crosbie, who were there; as also that he proposed a house should be purchased for the Society. So there was expense for folly. I wrote next day a card to him evading the Society.[157] I sat today three hours reading the Register of Baptisms and making notes from it of people whom I knew.

154 I Timothy 5. 8.
155 The third in the trilogy on living in the country.
156 "Properly spelled *copaiba*, a resinous juice obtained from various South American trees and shrubs [which] was recommended for many... maladies, including bronchitis" (*Laird*, p. 271, n. 2).
157 Boswell's opinion of the Earl of Buchan was to be shared by Sir Walter Scott (see p. 372, n. 30).

MONDAY 20 NOVEMBER. Dictated a Petition very well. There was a poor appearance of practice for me this Session, which hurt me somewhat; yet I was sensible that I could not go through a great deal of that coarse labour. So that it was unreasonable to repine. It was a dreary day of snow and cold.

TUESDAY 21 NOVEMBER. It was hard frost. I went to the Court of Session. Had no relish of it. Was vexed to think that I was now forty and had no office from Government. Called on my father and sat with him a little. He was still loaded with the cold, and he was dull and without any kindliness. I was sadly hurt. Lady Auchinleck was confined to bed with a severe cold. I dictated pretty well in the afternoon. At night Mr Muir, an agent, brought me a poor-looking Highland client with an involved series of claims to plead. I found out that Mr George Fergusson had been his lawyer before. So I refused his fee, and, after thanking Mr Muir, desired they might go to Mr Fergusson. Perhaps I was wrong. But aversion to study perplexity, and uneasiness at seeing the wretched anxiety of the man, prevailed. Professor Robison[158] came and I introduced Mr Sibthorpe to him, and they went together to his house. In the forenoon I sat above two hours making extracts from the Register of Baptisms. That kind of research amused me. But I was humbled to think how little I read, and what inconsiderable objects occupied my mind. I am depressed by the state of dependence in which I am kept by my father, and by being actually in straitened circumstances. I felt with some warmth Lord Mountstuart's neglect of my interest.

SATURDAY 2 DECEMBER. Was in very bad spirits, but just resolved to bear my distress. Thought I had no spirit, no manly firmness. Went with Mr Nairne and called on Lord Kames, who, though confined with a cold, was clear and lively. I wondered while he talked, and thought my dreary despondency foolish, since here was a man past eighty-four quite cheerful. We visited Mrs Drummond also. I walked awhile in the New Town with Mr George Wallace, who has a never-failing fund of conversation. Then walked on the Castle Hill with Grange, and groaned from low spirits. He and Mr Lawrie and the three Campbells dined with us. Miss Susie Wellwood drank tea. At night π.

SUNDAY 3 DECEMBER. The children said divine lessons at night. Phemie and Sandy said theirs at their grandfather's, who was more kindly to them than usual. While quite sunk, and in the state of everything seeming "stale, flat, and unprofitable",[159] I tried to read some of Dr Johnson's *Preface* to Milton, and was at once animated and ennobled. But it shocked me to think that Dr Johnson must die. I hoped to meet him in immortality.

MONDAY 4 DECEMBER. Called on Lord Alva, whom I had not visited for some years.[160] His chattering and minute insignificance disgusted me.

TUESDAY 5 DECEMBER. Was still in sad low spirits. While in the Court of Session was uneasy and restless. Was vexed on account of a charge of fraudulent intention

---

158 John Robison (1739-1805), M.A., Professor of Natural Philosophy at Edinburgh University.
159 *Hamlet*, I, ii, 133.
160 Lord Alva was now residing at Drumsheugh.

against Matthew Dickie, who had charged fees to me which had not been paid and had at first alleged to me they *were* paid, or counterbalanced by claims on me, and afterwards said that he *meant* to pay them if allowed.[161] In my honest indignation against what I suspected to be dishonest, I had suspected him strongly, and had communicated my suspicion to Mr Blane, the agent on the other side, who was his inveterate foe. Blane had accused him before Lord Hailes. I was apprehensive that poor Matthew, whom I had known from my earliest years, might be severely punished. I tried to soften Blane, but in vain. Mr Alexander Tait also tried. I talked of the matter with Mr Ilay Campbell, who was an old acquaintance of Matthew's. He said his *age* should protect him, but the bad practice should be checked; and he promised to try what he could do to put an end to the accusation. I am dwelling too long on this. But in my fretted, sore state of mind, it hurt me exceedingly. I was vexed to be the evidence against a *poor body* whom I looked upon as a kind of diminutive Falstaff, a droll knave but without ill nature.

WEDNESDAY 6 DECEMBER. Was still uneasy in mind. The Lords determined some of the Ayrshire votes and showed such a partiality as really sickened me.[162] I went to Lord Kames's and supped. Nobody there but just Mrs Drummond and he and I. I said I came to get a supply of good spirits; and indeed his animation had a very happy effect on me for the time. I supped with appetite and drank near a bottle of sherry. He would not rise till past twelve.

THURSDAY 7 DECEMBER. Was still uneasy in mind. Dictated pretty well. But concern about Matthew Dickie's danger hurt me. My dear wife suggested that it was very possible I had blamed him without good reason, and imputed to dishonesty what was only forgetfulness and confusion. This suggestion relieved me much. I sent for Sandy Walker, his clerk, to worthy Grange's, where we talked of this and drank some strong ale. It was after supper. How much obliged am I to my valuable spouse upon many, many occasions!

FRIDAY 8 DECEMBER. I dined at the Lord President's. Lord Monboddo was there, I believe the first time for many years. I was not at all in spirits, and the President's uncultivated manners displeased me. I took care not to drink much wine. I called a little at my father's, and then went to a consultation on Lord Eglinton's politics.

SATURDAY 9 DECEMBER. Was somewhat better. My wife and I and our three eldest children dined at my father's. The two Campbells were with us. It was pretty comfortable. Sandy went through the family catechism, which I really thought gave satisfaction to his grandfather. I played whist and supped at Maclaurin's; Lord Maitland,[163] David Erskine, and Cullen there. Cullen was so entertaining with his mimicry that (except D. Erskine, who went at two) we sat till four.

161 Matthew Dickie, who had been admitted and enrolled as an agent by the Court of Session in 1772, had engaged Boswell as counsel in several cases.
162 Sir Adam Fergusson had presented a petition for review of the validity of the votes controlled by the Earl of Eglinton.
163 James Maitland (1759-1839), styled Lord Maitland (*later* 8th Earl of Lauderdale). He had been admitted advocate on 1 August, and in the general election of 1780 was elected M.P. for Newport.

SUNDAY 10 DECEMBER. Awaked with a severe headache. Lay all forenoon. Had drank but about a bottle and a half, but was hurt by sitting up. Major Montgomerie, who had called the day before, came and sat awhile by my bedside when I was better. I liked to see him as Member for Ayrshire, and hoped he would keep his seat. I would not have risen all day had I not been engaged to dine with Lord Monboddo for the first time since the misfortune of his daughter's marrying his clerk.[164] I went; and as I walked downstreet felt myself in better spirits than for some time past. There was too numerous and mixed a company at Lord Monboddo's. But I enjoyed life pretty well. I met here Mr Dalzel, our Greek professor.[165] Somebody mentioned Othello's speech in the Venetian Senate. Lord Monboddo himself repeated,

> That I have ta'en away this old man's daughter, etc.

His firm philosophy struck me. I drank moderately, stayed tea, and came home in a pretty good frame.

WEDNESDAY 13 DECEMBER. Was not at all well. Business was a burthen to me. I was fretted by it. I dined at my father's; just he and his lady and I at table. Was quite sunk at night. Worthy Grange tried to console me. I got a sudden invitation to sup at Dr James Hunter's with Major Montgomerie, and after declining was so pressed that I went.[166] This was a wonderful transition. I did better than I could have imagined. But was inwardly dark and cold.

THURSDAY 14 DECEMBER. In the evening I dictated pretty well, but had no satisfaction. I asked Mr Blane by a note to call on me this evening, as I was hopeful I might prevail with him to desist from prosecuting Matthew Dickie. He came, though I had not spoken to him for a week, being angry at his *obstinate justice*, to say the best of it. But we came to no agreement. He seemed to require too much from Matthew. In the mean time, Lord Hailes had refused to report the accusation to the Lords, which was favourable. I was too anxious about the creature.[167]

FRIDAY 15 DECEMBER. Got up in sad hypochondria. Had several law papers and a *Hypochondriack* to be written without delay.[168] Was quite in despair. Could not see any good purpose in human life.

WEDNESDAY 27 DECEMBER. Dined and drank tea at Mr David Erskine's with Lord Braxfield, the Solicitor, Harry Erskine, Maclaurin, and several more. I had been near an hour with Maclaurin last night in a dejected, uneasy state. His conversation can afford no relief to one in such a state. He said he would go mad if he were to study metaphysics, that his head turned when he thought of a Supreme Being, and that he imagined we were machines moved by motives.

---

164 Monboddo's eldest daughter, Helen Burnett, had married his clerk, Kirkpatrick Williamson; but, so Boswell informed Bennet Langton in the letter he wrote to him on 17 November, Monboddo did not seem to mind it (*Laird*, p. 270, n. 9).
165 Andrew Dalzel (or Dalziel), M.A., Professor of Greek at the University of Edinburgh.
166 Dr James Hunter resided in Old Bank Close, off the south side of the Lawnmarket.
167 It seems that nothing further came of the matter.
168 This essay, No. 39, like Nos 5 and 6, was on hypochondria and is considered to be one of the finest in the series.

Such was his meaning. I have put his fatality into concise expression. I continued to be gloomy and had no relish of society. I sat by and saw whist played, and I betted against the Solicitor. Lord Braxfield, exultingly pleased that the Solicitor and Maclaurin, against whom he played, were losing, called out that Maclaurin, whom he had named "Captain", played like a colonel. I in the same humour called out, "And I'm sure his partner plays like a colonel." The Solicitor, who was fretted by losing, lost his temper and said he would not be insulted. I grew warm and asked him what he meant. He said, "I shall let you know afterwards."[169] Maclaurin and I were to play cards and sup at Cullen's. When the Solicitor went away, I said I would go to Cullen's and we should send for Maclaurin. I wished to give the Solicitor an opportunity of explaining himself. When we got into the street, he said I had behaved to him in a way that no gentleman could put up with, and he desired to have satisfaction. "With all my heart", said I. "Then," said he, "what day is this?" "Wednesday", said I. "On Friday morning," said he, "at five o'clock in the King's Park." "Very well", said I. "Name your second", said he. "I shall," said I, "good-night"; and went and rung at Cullen's door.[170] I had no fear; and what was curious, I was speculating all the time whether this could be a piece of fatalism, though there was a feeling of liberty. Cullen's servant luckily was long in coming; and in that space I thought that I should pass the evening disagreeably with such a duel hanging over me. I was conscious the Solicitor had no just cause of offence, and perhaps was not in earnest. So I took a sudden resolution, and run after him and overtook him. I asked him if he was in earnest. He said yes. But we got into conversation, and he said if I did not mean any offence, he was satisfied. I said, "How could I possibly mean it?" and I would refer it to the company. He said if I would tell them or tell Maclaurin that I meant none, that was enough. I said I would if he would go back with me, but he declined this. In short, there was to be no more of it. I then went to Cullen's, and he and I had a very good chat by ourselves for half an hour. Then came Counsellor Charles Dundas and his friend Counsellor Steele, an Englishman, and we played whist. Lord Maitland came, and then we played brag. Maclaurin came and sat by. I lost, but did not grudge it. We had a very good comfortable supper. It was the first time of my being at Cullen's. I was pleased to see all his furniture new, and his table well served, and an air of orderly ease. I drank some glasses of wine, and Maclaurin having mentioned the difference between the Solicitor and me, I related what had passed, which entertained the company much. Maclaurin told me that he and all the company thought the Solicitor in the wrong, which comforted me. Our conversation was neither brilliant nor learned, but did very well at the time. I was in better spirits than I had been for many days. I saw the intercourse of social life with some degree of satisfaction, though life be uncertain and indeed, to an expanding imagination, very short. We sat rather too late, which hurts me now.

169 As the editors of *Laird* observe (at p. 279, n. 7), Boswell's jest was obscure and Murray's being offended by it is equally hard to explain.
170 Robert Cullen's house was in Argyle Square.

THURSDAY 28 DECEMBER. This morning I sent a note to the Solicitor that all the company thought him in the wrong; that I was surprised and uneasy he had supposed what I was sure I did not mean. That a misunderstanding between him and me must not be made up by halves, and that I hoped he would call this forenoon and shake hands cordially with his old friend. He wrote to me that he would see me before dinner. He came and owned he was sorry, and we were quite reconciled. Thus a sad quarrel between two men whose fathers were friends, and who had all along lived on good terms, was prevented. At night when in bed with my dear wife, I was wonderfully free from gloom, and trusting to Mr Wood's opinion that I had no infection, I prevailed with her to allow me to enjoy her.[171]

SATURDAY 30 DECEMBER. My son Sandy is really a fine boy. I should keep a register of his progress. I put him to Mr Stalker's reading-school last autumn, but he did not like it, and as I think six an early age enough, I did not force him. But he is honest and kind, and has quite the air and manner of a gentleman. On Christmas a glass of the chair in which Phemie and he came from chapel was broke. Mr Johnston was positive the chairmen were wrong in alleging that any of the children had broke it, and my wife scolded them for attempting imposition. When Sandy saw the poor chairmen in danger of losing the price of the glass, he gently told his mother that he had broke it. There was in this confession both honesty and humanity. His mother praised him warmly and paid the glass cheerfully. Last time that he and I breakfasted at Lady Colville's, as we walked down the Bow, he was going to attack a boy who happened to jostle him. I said, was he not afraid, as the boy was much bigger than him? "What's the matter," said he, "when I'm stronger than him?" A spirited thought, to think one's self stronger than superior appearance. Courage is one of the most valuable qualities that can be possessed. I feel sad uneasiness from timidity. Talking of the fall of man and that it occasioned death, Sandy said one day some months ago with real indignation that "Adam should be put in the Guard."[172] If Sandy turns out an eminent man, or is ever the representative of the family of Auchinleck, these anecdotes will be valuable to him. He is now quite easy with me. He is very fond of his brother Jamie, and treats him with tender care. My wife and Veronica, Phemie and Sandy and I went to Prestonfield today in Sir Alexander Dick's coach, dined and drank tea comfortably. Sir Alexander was quite well. He said to me, "*C'est la grâce de Dieu.* I wonder at myself." At night enjoyed.

SUNDAY 31 DECEMBER. I supped at Sir William Forbes's, and was in good spirits. Came home between eleven and twelve, that I might enjoy again this year, and did it.

---

171 The editors of *Laird* explain, at p. 281, n. 9, that this "probably means that, having risked an infection on or soon after 15 December, [Boswell] had gone to Wood, and that Wood, finding no symptoms after an interval of ten days or so, had told him he could stop worrying."
172 See the entry for 2 January 1780 and relevant footnote.

1781

Boswell did not keep a regular journal in 1781 until 16 February, but he left a note of a visit to Bothwell Castle from 5 to 10 January. Here he had what for him was an unfortunate experience. "[T]he very day after my arrival there", he wrote, "I read in Lord Monboddo's Ancient Metaphysics *that there* could be no such thing as contingency, *and that every action of man was absolutely fixed and comprehended in a series of causes and effects from all eternity; so that there was an universal Necessity. I then looked into Lord Kames's* Sketches, *where, though he retracts his foolish notion as to there being an intended delusive feeling of Liberty, he maintains the necessity of human resolutions and actions in the most positive manner. I was shocked by such a notion and sunk into dreadful melancholy, so that I went out to the wood and groaned... I saw a dreary nature of things, an unconscious, uncontrollable power by which all things are driven on, and I could not get rid of the irresistible influence of motives."*

FRIDAY 16 FEBRUARY. Mr Hunter-Blair paid me a bet of a rump and a dozen,[1] laid above ten years ago, that I should be first married to a widow. I named the company. We dined at Fortune's, nine in number nine:[2] he and I, Colonel Mure Campbell, Hon. A. Gordon, Sir W. Forbes, Mr David Erskine, Grange, Maclaurin, Surgeon Wood. It was a most jovial day.

SATURDAY 17 FEBRUARY. I was ill after my indulgence, but went and did what I had to do in the Court of Session. Grange and Mr Sibthorpe and Don Martino, an unfortunate Spaniard who was at the dancing-school with my daughters, dined with us.

TUESDAY 20 FEBRUARY. My wife was alarmed by spitting some blood.

WEDNESDAY 21 FEBRUARY. Dictated well. Went to the play of *Henry IV, First Part*, and saw all the High School in the Theatre. It was a fine scene of boyish amusement and tumult. The profits of the play went to pay for the new school. So all the masters and all the boys were there. My wife kept her bed all day.

THURSDAY 22 FEBRUARY. This was a General Fast by Proclamation.[3] Lady Dowager Colville came to my seat and heard Dr Blair. I then drove awhile about in her coach with her. She told me she knew by my face whether I was well or ill. I was at present excellently well. Liberty and Necessity was quite a *distant* speculation, which did not affect me. I walked round the Meadow with Mr David Erskine and got some useful instruction from him as to our Ayrshire political cases. I dined at my father's. He was in very bad humour; and though I had engaged to be counsel on Lord Eglinton's side with his consent and approbation, he seemed to be quite angry at my zeal. I regretted inwardly that he had so little knowledge of or value for his son. I could not help it.

---

1 A rump of beef and twelve bottles of claret (*Laird*, p. 284, n. 6).
2 "Boswell probably means 'nine persons in room No. 9'" (*Laird*, p. 284, n. 7).
3 See also the entries for 3 February 1780 and 9 February 1779.

FRIDAY 23 FEBRUARY. Was in keen agitation about our Ayrshire election. Had seen in the newspapers that three counsel on each side were admitted before the Committee on the Orkney election. Mentioned this to Mr Cumming, who said, "Then there will be Lee[4] and Wight and you." He told me that even if Crosbie had gone to London, I was to have been preferred. This was very agreeable. It gave me a good reason to state to my father for my going to London

TUESDAY 27 FEBRUARY. Was busy with the Ayrshire election business. I was now kept quite in a fever with it, I was so keen. The agitation kept off all melancholy.

THURSDAY 1 MARCH. Dined at Lady Colville's; Hon. A. Gordon and his Countess and Lord Justice Clerk there. Andrew[5] was very good company. My spirits were just as I could wish. In the evening after a consultation at Mr Rae's, went home with Mr John Wauchope and had a very merry conference, he and I and his partner Cumming, on our Ayrshire politics.[6] Mrs Wauchope sung and played to us, and we drank *plotty*.[7]

SATURDAY 3 MARCH. It is amazing how the warmth of my anxiety for Major Montgomerie's election cleared my mind of all gloomy vapours. Harry Erskine gave me some good hints upon it today. He walked to Leith with me, and came and took a share of my family dinner. At night I was in an excellent social frame. Called on Maclaurin; asked if he was busy. Found he was not. Told him I was come to eat cold meat and drink one bottle of wine with him. We talked over several questions in the Ayrshire politics, supped and drank a bottle apiece of good claret. We were quite social and comfortable. I only regretted that he had not religion. He said, however, it was a great happiness to believe in immortality, and as Sir John Pringle, who was once an infidel, was now a believer, so might he.

MONDAY 5 MARCH. I had devoted all this week to Major Montgomerie's election business, and resolved not to dine or sup abroad but at my father's. I dined there today. I laboured excellently.

TUESDAY 6 MARCH. We had a great many of our political cases decided this day. I was very warm. I avowed it. I said, "Major Montgomerie is my friend, my social friend. I love him as a brother. I only wish your Lordships knew him as well as I do." The President somehow or other got into an absurd passion today, and said there was much said of independency. There was not an independent gentleman in Ayrshire. I fired and called out, "No, my Lord?" "No," said he, "nor yourself neither." I replied warmly, "I beg your Lordship's pardon", and I think I added, "Not so!"—and then said, "I crave the protection of the Court." Some of the Lords shook their heads to make me quiet, and some about me also composed me; and so it rested. I dictated excellently today.

4 John Lee, an English barrister.
5 Andrew Erskine.
6 John Wauchope's house was in Horse Wynd.
7 "A rich and pleasant hot drink, made with spices, wine, and sugar, mulled" (*Chambers's Scots Dictionary*).

WEDNESDAY 7 MARCH. We had another series of political cases. The President was much calmer today. I was very angry at what he had said, and wrote a determined letter to him, which I showed to my friend Sandy Gordon.[8] He advised me not to send it, but he would carry it to Lord Braxfield and let *him* talk to the President. Grange dined with us today. I dictated with vigour.

FRIDAY 9 MARCH. Called in the morning on Sandy Gordon, who told me Lord Braxfield had been with the President and would himself tell me what passed. Accordingly, I went to the robing-room, and Lord Braxfield told me the President desired him to say to me that he did not mean to say anything against the gentlemen of Ayrshire or any one of them; that he only meant to say they were not independent of party. This was pretty well. The President came up and we shook hands, but he said nothing. I dictated well. Sandy Gordon and Painter Donaldson drank tea with us.

SATURDAY 10 MARCH. I was not yet satisfied with the President's conduct. Sandy Gordon thought he should say something in public. I resolved to wait on his Lordship this morning. I called about nine. He was not got up. I went to Maclaurin's and talked to him, and he also thought the President should say something in public. I went again before ten, and was shown into his own study, where he was at breakfast by himself. He asked me if I would have some tea. I said I had breakfasted. His clerk was present. I said to him I wanted to speak a single word to Lord President. He left the room. I then in a calm tone told his Lordship that what he had said of the gentlemen of Ayrshire had hurt them. He seemed a little fluttered, and said he had said something to somebody of it (trying to evade it), and that he certainly did not mean to offend the gentlemen of Ayrshire or any one of their number, which I might tell them from him. "I am very well convinced of it," said I, "and I am sure I should be the last man in the world to lay hold of expressions hastily uttered in heat. But, my Lord, you said in public that there was not an independent gentleman in Ayrshire. Should not your Lordship take an opportunity of mentioning publicly that you did not mean what has been supposed? I think it would become your dignity." He shrugged his shoulders at first, and did not seem to like a public declaration. But seeing me firm he said, "If I can find an opportunity easily of bringing it in, I will do it. I meant no more than what I said of Roxburghshire, and will say of every county where there is a contested election: that both parties go on doing everything they can, and that none of the gentlemen vote sometimes one way, sometimes another. But I certainly did not mean any reflection against the gentlemen of Ayrshire or any one of them. There is not", said he, "a more honourable man than Mr Montgomerie of Coilsfield or than Mr Hamilton of Sundrum." This was very well. He then said, "Will you tell me, James, how does it stand? For I

8 "... Your Lordship, the head of civil justice in Scotland, certainly cannot wish to hurt and offend the gentlemen of Ayrshire, unprovoked. What suddenly burst from your Lordship yesterday has that effect on such of them as have yet heard of it; and it undoubtedly will have a still stronger effect if nothing shall be said by way of apology or explanation" (quoted in *Laird* at p. 287, n. 4).

really don't know." "Why, my Lord," said I, "I'll tell you in general that if your Lordships' opinions hold good, we are sure of the election." "Ay?" said he. "Why," said I, "they have but two of majority against us in the Court of Session; and, my Lord, all the votes we have got there are gold tried in the fire.[9] They have passed the ordeal. For the Court was much against us." "James," said he, "it is true." He added, "I declare to GOD that in these political questions I have been at the utmost pains to keep my mind free from bias to one side or another." "My Lord," said I, "we give you credit for it." "Now," said he, "you'll perhaps be angry if I give you an advice." "By no means", said I. "I have often been obliged to your Lordship for good advice." "Then," said he, "keep your temper before the Committee. You have done very well in this business. Only you have now and then been heated." "My Lord," said I, "your Lordship certainly does not dislike a man for having a little heat of temper. I am obliged to you for your advice, and shall be upon my guard." He said, "I am sorry I shall not see you before you set out. You will come to me when you return?" "I certainly shall, my Lord." "You will perhaps be a little crestfallen then." "I hope not, my Lord." I really liked him this morning.

Mrs Dundas desired to see me. I drank a dish of tea with her tête-à-tête, and was gay. Then went to the Court. The President took an excellent opportunity of making an apology. Talked of heat on both sides, and said, "By the by, I am sorry an expression of mine has been misunderstood. I did say there was not an independent man in this county. I will say so of every county where there is a warm contested election. But I certainly meant no disrespect to the gentlemen of the county or any one of them. I certainly did not mean that Lord Justice Clerk is not independent, or that Lord Auchinleck is not independent, or that Mr Montgomerie of Coilsfield or Mr Hamilton of Sundrum are not independent. I mention these gentlemen because I have a special regard for them." Somebody at the bar invidiously said, "A palinode!"[10] I warmly bore down any such reflections, and said, "Very well. Very handsome. '*Un gentilhomme est toujours gentilhomme.*'" Thus this affair was settled in the most agreeable manner. I was much obliged to my friend Sandy Gordon for keeping me in the lines of prudence as well as spirit. I dictated, or rather corrected, the notes of the Lords' opinions. I had pushed on a case to a hearing in presence, and fixed one of Sir Adam's votes not to be reckoned before the Committee. In short, I was active and animated and full of hope. How very different from the dreary metaphysical wretch that I had been! I supped at my father's.

SUNDAY 11 MARCH. I was damped a little by a letter from Wight which Wauchope read to me today, saying that the Committee would lay great weight on the decisions of the Court of Session. I was really uneasy. I supped at Old Lady Wallace's, where was Colonel Mure Campbell, and I was quite gay and

9 "The count as originally returned was sixty-five votes for Montgomerie and fifty-five for Sir Adam Fergusson. The Court of Session had thrown out enough of Montgomerie's votes to give Fergusson a majority of two" (*Laird*, p. 289, n. 6).
10 A recantation.

entertaining.[11] When I came home, being a little flustered, I took a proud pet because my wife, who had not been well and was half asleep, was not in unison with my joyousness; and for the first time I angrily went to bed in another room. She rose and asked me to come to her. I sulkily would not. This was a very bad effect of intoxication.

MONDAY 12 MARCH. Was agitated with the prospect of London. Had a good consultation at Mr Wauchope's. Announced to my father (what I believe he knew well enough before) that I was to set out next day, being engaged as counsel. He affected surprise, and said *I* was an *independent man* who did not consult him as to my going. *She* said, "At a certain time of life a son is independent of parental authority." "No", said he; "I never was independent of my father's authority." She wickedly said, "I am of your opinion. But that is just as people think." I said, "A man at a certain age is entitled to judge for himself. A man is a fool or a physician at forty."[12] I dined at my father's; Commissioner Cochrane, Balbarton, Mr Stobie, and Dr Gillespie there. In the evening my wife and I were at Marcucci's ball, and had the pleasure of seeing Veronica and Phemie dance very well. I was quite pleasant and happy.

TUESDAY 13 MARCH. Busy going about in forenoon. Was not light-headed. Took leave of father; cold but not so ill as I supposed he might. Grange dined with us. Adieu calm to wife and children. At six went to Cameron's; Wauchope, Cumming, Anderson,[13] Lieutenant Cameron all there. Glass of white wine and set off. Grange went with me as far as Liberton.

Boswell's route to London was by way of Hawick, Carlisle, Ripon, Leeds, Biggleswade, and Southill. During the journey he found himself in high spirits, which he attributed to his thoughts all being directed to the forthcoming hearing before the Select Committee of the House of Commons on the Ayrshire election. He reached London on 19 March, and the following day he called on John Spottiswoode, the solicitor, and "dictated some of the election brief", which he finished the following day. On the evening of 23 March he attended a consultation with Thomas Erskine, the barrister who had been appointed instead of John Lee. Erskine, who was a younger brother of the Earl of Buchan and Henry Erskine and was a distant cousin of Boswell's, was later to rise to be Lord Chancellor; but Sir Walter Scott was to say of him that he was "positively mad".[14]

The Committee met on 24 March. "I was a little fluttered", records Boswell, "but spoke well. I suffered sad torment while the Committee was locked up, and I dreaded that they might find the judgements of the Court of Session conclusive. But I was relieved from this fear." On the 26th the Committee met again. Boswell considered that this time he spoke "with ease and fluency, and was well heard." "But", he adds, "we lost a point which we thought ourselves sure of gaining. I was cast down." A further point was lost at the next day's hearing, but on this occasion Boswell "began to be a little habituated to such misfortunes and to bear them more easily." The following day, says Boswell, "Erskine spoke on our side... inimitably. I really

11 Old Lady Wallace resided in Hanover Street.
12 "A Scottish proverb, based on a saying attributed to the Emperor Tiberius" (*Laird*, p. 290, n. 8).
13 William Anderson (d. 1785), W.S. (admitted 24 June 1774).
14 Scott, 20 April 1829.

trusted that we could not possibly lose the question. The honest Major [Montgomerie] and I walked about in sad anxiety while the Committee were locked up, and when they determined against us, we were grievously hurt." However, the proceedings were not yet concluded. On the 29th Boswell reports that "the Committee went on sadly against us. I began now to grow callous"; but the following day he felt that he "really spoke well", and on the 31st there was a "keen battle". The election then turned on one vote, and on Sunday 1 April Boswell attended at Spottiswoode's and prepared for the next day's hearing. "[A]ll the charters, etc., being laid before me, I had a room to myself and wrote out a clear, strong state of the case. I had no scruple at doing this on Sunday when time was so short." That evening Dr Johnson "dictated… a good argument upon the effect of a deed being [registered]". "This", said he, "you must enlarge in speaking to the Committee. You must not argue in a popular assembly as if you were arguing in the schools. Close reasoning will not fix their attention. You must say the same thing over and over again in different words. If you say it but once, they may miss it while not attending." However, the eventual outcome was that on 2 April, after the Committee had held that a certain number of votes cast in favour of Major Montgomerie at the election were invalid, Sir Adam Fergusson was declared to have been elected.[15]

In the meantime, Boswell, who had been put up at the house of his friend and publisher Charles Dilly, was, as usual, relishing London society. Dr Johnson had greeted him with the words, "I love you better than ever I did", and Boswell not only spent many happy hours with Johnson but also took delight in the company of Sir Joshua Reynolds, Burke, Wilkes, Paoli, Henry and Hester Thrale[16] *and many others (including several Scots, such as Sir Lawrence Dundas, the Earl of Eglinton and the Earl of Kellie). "My spirits", he wrote on 28 March, "were gay and I indulged them; and [I] compared my then gaiety with my dreariness in Scotland." "I must", he reflected, "allow my temper an easy play." After the Committee hearings came to a conclusion, Boswell, relieved of the stress of preparing for and attending hearings, became positively carefree and joyful. While travelling in a coach to London after a "hearty" visit to Woodford, it started to rain, whereupon, says Boswell, "A well-looked, stately woman who sat on the coach-box begged as a favour we would make room for her in the coach. I told her all the seats were filled. But if she chose to sit on my knee, and the company had no objection, she was heartily welcome. This being agreed, in she came, and I had a very desirable armful… I grew very fond of her, cherished her in the coach, and when she went from us, kissed her repeatedly and warmly, and wished to be better acquainted with her." "Such incidents", reflects Boswell, "are marrow to my bones."*

On 5 May, Boswell realised a long-held ambition to be received at the house of the Earl of Bute, the former Prime Minister (father of Boswell's friend Lord Mountstuart). During their wide-ranging conversation, Bute asked Boswell if he was at the Scottish bar. "Yes, my Lord," answered Boswell, "to get beef for my wife and milk for my children. It is hard work. Sometimes a guinea, sometimes two, for a great deal of writing." Later that month,

15 Major Montgomerie was, however, to be elected in 1784; but he gave up his seat when he was appointed Inspector of Military Roads in Scotland in 1789. About five years later, he was appointed Lieutenant-Governor of Edinburgh Castle. In 1806 he was created Baron Ardrossan of Ardrossan.

16 Henry Thrale, however, was very unwell and died on 4 April, causing much grief to his great friend Dr Johnson.

on the 16th, Boswell attended the Court of St James and was presented to the King, with whom he had not conversed since being introduced to him fifteen years earlier. However, all that the King said was, "You are come to make some stay?", to which Boswell made the mortifying mistake of absent-mindedly replying, "Yes, my Lord" instead of addressing the King as "Sir".[17] *Another person present on this occasion was Lord Loughborough (Alexander Wedderburn, the former Scottish advocate),*[18] *who treated Boswell with "cold stiffness". Boswell gently provoked him by saying, "I remember your Lordship on the top of the Cross at Edinburgh, drinking." To this, Loughborough responded: "You have a memory for bad things." Later that day, Boswell finished another term at the Inner Temple, merely by breaking bread in Temple Hall.*

On 2 June, Boswell went with Dr Johnson to Dilly's house at Southill for a few days, and Boswell was back in Edinburgh by the 9th. While he had been away, his family had moved from the house in the Meadows to a house at Drumsheugh, and had thus become neighbours of Lady Colville and her brother Andrew Erskine. Boswell was often to refer to the new family home as their "country-house", which seems rather amusing nowadays given that the area which was known as Drumsheugh is now a fairly central part of the city .

On his arrival at Edinburgh, Boswell was informed of the dismal news that Dr Webster's second son, Lieutenant-Colonel James Webster, who had been serving in America as commander of a brigade, had died from wounds received at the battle of Guildford Court House on 15 March.

SUNDAY 10 JUNE. Visited Dr Webster. Was agitated when again in the house where I had seen the poor Colonel so often, but behaved decently. The Doctor supported himself by GOD's grace wonderfully well. I went to his seat forenoon and afternoon, and he to the elder's seat.[19] Mr Peckwell preached in the forenoon. Mr Kemp in the afternoon, an affecting funeral conclusion. I cried much, and most of the congregation shed tears. I shook hands with Mr Kemp after church, thanked him, and desired to be better acquainted with him. My wife and I dined with Dr Webster between sermons.

TUESDAY 12 JUNE. Went to the Lord President's and paid my respects. Was free and easy among the judges. Felt luckily a kind of avidity for practice in the Court of Session. Dr Webster and Commissioner Cochrane dined and drank tea with us at our country-house.

One of Mrs Boswell's Irish cousins, Captain (later Admiral) John Macbride, commander of the frigate Artois, *one of the vessels in the squadron convoying the Baltic merchant fleet which had arrived at Leith, invited Boswell and his family to visit him on board his ship; and Boswell, who found the captain to be a "pleasant, clever, fine fellow", arranged a visit to take place on 15 June.*

FRIDAY 15 JUNE. Got what little business I had in the Court of Session managed for me, and my wife and I and Miss Grant (Dr Grant's daughter), Veronica, Phemie, and Sandy got into a hackney-coach, which came for us about six in the morning, and drove to Leith, taking with us the Lord Provost, Hon. A. Gordon and

17 Boswell was to have longer conversations with the King on 27 and 30 May.
18 For Lord Loughborough, see p. 171, n. 163.
19 At the Tolbooth Church.

his Countess, and other ladies; or rather being joined by them. Evory[20] and Sibthorpe also joined; and away we sailed in two boats sent by Captain Macbride to his ship, the *Artois*. I was pleased to see my children sail for the first time. It was a charming day. We had a good breakfast, saw all parts of the ship, then sailed to a three-decked ship, the *Princess Amelia* (Captain Macartney), Sir Hyde Parker[21] being with us all the time, and saw her well. Then sailed back again through the numerous fleet of merchantmen bound for the Baltic, back again to Leith. My wife and children were sick returning. I was entertained with this naval sight, but was also shocked to see such a number of men shut up in a state little better than dogs in a kennel, with the addition of horrible dangers. I did not like to think of the *system of things*. My spirits were not as when in London. Edinburgh operates like the *Grotta del Cane*[22] on my vivacity. I dined at the Lord Provost's with Admiral Parker[23] and all the navy captains, Hon. A. Gordon, Sir W. Forbes, Sir P. Ainslie, etc.[24] Lived freely, but not to excess.

TUESDAY 19 JUNE. [I]n Captain Macbride's cutter, which was manned for me, and thus did I sail to the *Latona* and visit Sir Hyde Parker and the company on board of him. Sir Hyde came with me to the *Artois*. After an uneasy sail back to Leith, I went home with Lady Colville to dinner. The Scottish vulgarity of manners and censorious cast of her and Lady Anne and Andrew disgusted me. I drank tea at home; then went to town and dictated some. Was uneasy at night that my indisposition did not seem abating.[25]

WEDNESDAY 20 JUNE. Was still languid and without relish of life. However, I said nothing, but attended the Court of Session, dictated wonderfully well, dined in town by myself on a broiled chicken, and in the evening sat a long time with Sir John Pringle, whom I found quite alone.[26]

FRIDAY 22 JUNE. Drank a dish of tea at Lord President's in the morning. Such a day as this may be simply recorded *ditto*. George Wallace's observation is very just: that one is quite a different animal in Edinburgh and in London. Was at the concert.

SATURDAY 23 JUNE. When I got to my town house, Captain Macbride called on me to make an apology that he could not go to Drumsheugh this morning to see my wife. I know not well how the forenoon loitered away. I dined at Dunn's Hotel in St Andrew's Square with the Admiral and several officers both of the Baltic and Jamaica squadrons. Had no *gaieté de cœur*. Was very sober; drank tea with them. Went home quiet.

20 Thomas Evory, "a student of physic" (Journal, 27 October 1780); that is, a medical student.
21 Sir Hyde Parker was commander of the frigate *Latona*.
22 A grotto near Pozzuoli in Italy which contained a suffocating vapour comprised of carbon dioxide (*Laird*, p. 379, n. 8).
23 Vice-Admiral Hyde Parker, commander of the squadron. Father of Sir Hyde Parker.
24 The Lord Provost (David Steuart) resided in Queen Street.
25 While in London, Boswell had "ranged" and he suffered the usual consequence: another bout of venereal disease.
26 Sir John Pringle was now residing at 32 George Square (see p. 400, n. 98).

SUNDAY 24 JUNE. My wife and I and three eldest children walked decently from our country-house to the New Church and heard Dr Blair. Lord Kames stumbled at the foot of the stair which leads up to the lords' loft, and fell on the pavement, by which he cut his forehead and three of his fingers a little. I visited him afterwards, and found him not a bit disconcerted. I dined by special invitation with the Admiral and the captains of the squadron—a turtle feast, eighteen in company. I drank more today than I had done for some time, and was a little disturbed. Drank tea, and at ten visited Sir John Pringle.

MONDAY 25 JUNE. Was somewhat uneasy from the small excess of yesterday. Sir Hyde Parker and Captain Macbride called on me, and I went with them to Dr Grant's and heard Miss Grant play. My wife dined with me in our town house. Worthy Grange arrived today. I drank tea with him, and was consoled and revived by his sensible, cheerful, friendly conversation.

TUESDAY 26 JUNE. Admiral Parker, Sir Hyde, and Captain Macbride, Sir W. and Lady Forbes, Mrs Dundas of Arniston[27] and Miss,[28] and Miss Grant passed the evening with us and supped. My wife and I lay in town.

WEDNESDAY 27 JUNE. This day I dined on board the *Latona*; Sir Hyde Parker, the Admiral, Captain Macbride, Lord Balcarres, and several ladies and gentlemen there. It was now a fair wind for the Baltic fleet. So they were all afloat while we were on board, as was the *Latona*. It was a fine animating scene, and I really liked the sea today. Captain Napier had two boats which took us to Leith. I drank more today than was good for my health. But it strengthened my spirits. I was glad to be again in my garden at night.

SATURDAY 30 JUNE. This was a very poor week of practice as a lawyer. I got only one guinea. I thought that my having little practice would make my removing to London more rational. Sir John Pringle and Miss Gray and Surgeon Wood dined and drank tea with us at our country-house. Sir John sauntered with me in my garden pretty placidly, and I liked it. He pressed me to go home with him, saying it would do him more good than anything else. So I went from sincere gratitude; and we talked a long time tête-à-tête. I was near growing too violent against his Arian notions. His despondency and weariness hurt my spirits. I had no vivid enjoyment.

TUESDAY 3 JULY. Lost two causes: one before Lord Braxfield and one before the Lords. I was quite clear I was in the right in both, and was really hurt to find justice so ill administrated. Worthy Grange walked out with me to Sir Alexander Dick's, who had been ill of his annual asthmatic complaint and really in danger, but was now better. I was uneasy to think I had not visited him since my return from London. But my apology was soon accepted. I had little relish of

27 Jean Dundas (née Grant), second wife of Lord President Dundas.
28 The editors of *Laird*, at p. 381, identify this as Lord President Dundas's daughter Grizel (the elder of his two daughters by his second wife, whom he had married in 1756). However, she married in September 1778 (*Arniston*, p. 189) and so the Miss Dundas referred to in this entry may in fact be her younger sister, Ann.

existence, and was perpetually thinking of this, and wearying. Baron Maule had died last night. As he had been a man whom in my early years I had viewed in a grand style, I was saddened by such a memento of the *end* of human consequence. Visited Sir John Pringle at night. Mr George Wallace with him.

WEDNESDAY 4 JULY. Was not at all in good spirits. My dear wife persuaded me to go out with her to dinner. I was so much pleased with my garden and children that I grew pretty easy and indulged tranquillity instead of going into town to labour.

FRIDAY 6 JULY. My father did not come to the Court. I dined with him. But was fretted to find him show me no affection. I dictated pretty well. Drank tea with Grange. Visited Sir J. Pringle.

TUESDAY 10 JULY. Nothing to remark but that life was dull. I had a little satisfaction this session in resuming my occupation of copying from the records of the Privy Council. I was now troubled with a kind of inflammation in my eyes. I dined at my father's. He was quite indifferent.

THURSDAY 12 JULY. My wife and I and our three eldest children dined and drank tea at my father's. He was, I fear intentionally and perversely, neglectful of us.

FRIDAY 13 JULY. Dined at Mr Maclaurin's with Sir John Pringle, Lord and Lady Macdonald, Mr George Wallace, Dr Adam Smith, Mr Baron Gordon, etc. Was now, on account of my inflamed eye, on a vegetable and water regimen. Had no relish of life. Maclaurin and I walked with Sir John in the Meadow and went home with him. Maclaurin confessed his doubt, or rather belief, that there would be no future state. He expressed himself curiously: "I might flatter you, Sir John" (as if he himself had no concern in the matter). "But I really think we have no reason to expect a future state. It is a beautiful fancy. But what right has man to it?" and said that thinking on the subject made men mad or whimsical like Lord Kames or Lord Monboddo. Sir John said he should talk with men like his father, who was a rational Christian. It was unpleasing to hear Maclaurin express his infidelity. But he had not studied the subject.

SATURDAY 14 JULY. My wife and I and our three eldest children dined at Prestonfield by special invitation. I was soothed by worthy Sir Alexander's placid old age, but my inflamed eye hurt my spirits.

SUNDAY 15 JULY. Took salts for my eye. The children said divine lessons. I stayed at home all day and read reviews, and was tolerably easy, though dejected.

MONDAY 16 JULY. My eye continued painful. I had to dictate a good deal. Was in town all day, and had the room much darkened. Dictated none, but wrote *The Hypochondriack* No. 46.[29] At night had a *happy* reconciliation.[30]

---

29 On parents, children and education.
30 "With his wife, who had been cool to him because of his rakish behaviour in London" (*Laird*, p. 384, n. 5).

THURSDAY 19 JULY. My eyes became wonderfully better today. I had washed them with a water sent me by Mr Wood, the composition of which I know not, and with vitriol water sent me by Mr George Wallace; and every night I had bread steeped in water and put between the folds of a cambric handkerchief laid upon them. They had both been uneasy. I dined at my father's either today or yesterday. My spirits were better as my eyes grew well.

SUNDAY 22 JULY. Was in pretty good spirits; free from fretfulness, though not vividly happy. Heard Dr Blair in the forenoon. Dined at my father's between sermons. In the afternoon it was exceedingly warm, and I was quite languid. I resolved to go home to my country-house and be calm with my children, and perhaps find my wife, who for some days was troubled with a cold, which gave me some apprehension. When I got home I found that she and Veronica and Phemie were gone to church in town. I had my two sons to walk with me and eat gooseberries in the garden, and go half-way to town to meet their mother and sisters; but we did not meet them. I was in a quiet, placid frame. When all the family was assembled, we had tea most agreeably. Old John Boswell, who had arrived the night before from London, came to tea. After which he and I walked in the garden, and I got into a comfortable Auchinleck frame. It is in vain to investigate ideas and feelings of this kind. They are as immediate as the tastes of different substances. I went to Sir John Pringle's in the evening. Nobody there but Dr Adam Smith. I had read today some of Lord Kames's book on education, and I talked slightingly of it. Smith said, "Every man fails soonest in his weak part. Lord Kames's weak part is writing. Some write above their parts, some under them. Lord Kames writes much worse than one should expect from his conversation." David Hume, he told us, observed, "When one says of another man he is the most arrogant man in the world, it is meant only to say that he is very arrogant. But when one says it of Lord Kames, it is an absolute truth." Smith said *The Elements of Criticism* was Lord Kames's worst work. "They are all bad", said he. "But it is the worst." He said *taedium vitae*[31] was a particular disease. I fear it is general. His conversation was *flabby*, as Garrick said of it.

MONDAY 23 JULY. News came to me this forenoon that Sir Adam Fergusson was arrived, having been appointed a Lord of Trade, so that there was to be a new election for Ayrshire. It fluttered and vexed me that a man whom I disliked so much should be so lucky, and that by the sudden vacancy the roll of electors would just be in his favour as before. Craufurdland,[32] Fairlie, Grange, Old John Boswell, Mr Matthew Dickie, and Mr Walker his clerk, dined with us in the country. I drank port and water, and was pretty comfortable. After tea I walked in with such of the company as stayed. I had nothing to dictate. Grange and I supped at Mr John Gordon's, Writer to the Signet,[33] with Dr Beattie.[34]

TUESDAY 24 JULY. We were asked to dine at my father's. My wife, Veronica,

---

31 "Weariness of life" (Latin).
32 Lieutenant-Colonel John Walkinshaw of Craufurdland in Ayrshire (*Laird*, p. 527).
33 John Gordon's house was in St Andrew Square.
34 James Beattie, the poet and moral philosopher.

Phemie, and Sandy went. I sent word that I was engaged, for I could not bear the triumph which I supposed he and his women would express on Sir Adam Fergusson's success. I went to the race at Leith in Old Erskine's chaise, little Sandy, my son, with us. I was really entertained. I called on Sir John Pringle, intending to have dined with him, but he was engaged out. I came to the Cross and sauntered. Followed Lord Eglinton and Fairlie to the Earl's lodgings, where was Mr Wauchope, and there we talked of the election. I adjourned with Fairlie to Wauchope's, where we dined; and having considered the state of the roll, a very sensible letter from Lord Loudoun, and a very well-written one from Lord North asking of Lord Eglinton as a great favour to suspend his political operations and permit Sir Adam Fergusson to be rechosen at this time without opposition, we sent a joint letter to Major Montgomerie giving it as our opinion that it would be best to make a virtue of necessity. We were quite sober today.

WEDNESDAY 25 JULY. Went to the race in Lady Colville's coach with her three nieces and my three eldest children. Sat on the coach box while the horses ran, and was pretty well amused. Dined at home. It rained pretty heavily about dinner-time, and I felt such uneasy sensations as I have had in wet weather in the country. Dictated some in town in the afternoon.

THURSDAY 26 JULY. My left eye was a little sore this week. Sir Charles Preston dined and drank tea with us. I was in a most listless state; felt no pleasure in life, nor could imagine any. My fancy roved on London and the English bar, yet I had faint hopes of happiness even in the metropolis, which I dreaded would pall upon me; and I thought it would be wrong to desert Scotland. In short I did not know what to do. I had more business as a lawyer these three weeks than the Session at first seemed to promise. But the embarrassed state of my affairs and my father's indifference distressed me. I came to our town house a little; was indolent. Went out again.

FRIDAY 27 JULY. Went to the race with Maclaurin in his coach. Was sadly dispirited; thought myself insignificant and subjected to a wretched destiny. Had no clear thoughts of anything, no consoling pious feelings. Had been with Lord Eglinton once since Tuesday. Went to him today near three and had a consultation on the election with his Lordship and Mr Wauchope, an express having brought letters from Major Montgomerie and Mr Hamilton of Sundrum. Had some pleasure in observing the Earl's sense and spirit, but was saddened by speculative clouds composed of the uncertainty of life, the forgetfulness of things years after their happening, and such dreary truths. Wondered how I had ever been active and keen in anything. Went and dined with Mr Wauchope to concert again what should be written to Major Montgomerie. I myself wrote him a friendly letter recommending a cessation of arms at this time, when he could not succeed, and might obtain from Administration what he wished by not opposing. I was grievously hypochondriac in the evening. Went early to bed and fell soon asleep.

SATURDAY 28 JULY. Got up so well that I eat an egg and two rolls and butter to breakfast. Was pretty well in the Court of Session; called on Lord Eglinton, visited Dr James Hunter with him, and saw him take his chaise and set out. I felt a warm kindness for him and a sort of pity that he had lost the election. Grange dined with us in the country. It rained a good deal in the afternoon. When it faired, I walked into town, was shaved and dressed, and went to sup with Lord Kames; but finding company was to be there, I did not go in, but walked quietly home. I borrowed today out of the Advocates' Library, David Hume's *Treatise of Human Nature*, but found it so abstruse, so contrary to sound sense and reason, and so dreary in its effects on the mind, if it had any, that I resolved to return it without reading it.

SUNDAY 29 JULY. Grange and I walked out to Duddingston and heard the apostolic Mr William Bennet lecture on the miracle of Cana in Galilee, and in good plain terms inculcate the truth of our Saviour's divine mission. We were calmly happy. Lord Abercorn and his brother Dr Hamilton, prebendary of Salisbury, and Mr Burgess, Lord Somerville's brother-in-law, being all decently in church, confirmed the good frame. We were afterwards quite pleasant, eating gooseberries with the young folks in the garden at Prestonfield in warm sunshine. We dined comfortably with worthy Sir Alexander, who was remarkably well and walked agreeably with us. I then paid a visit to my father, whom I had not visited since the Ayrshire election was again in agitation. Not a word was said of it, and he was very well with me. I had a satisfaction in observing his steadiness even in old age. Went home and heard the children say divine lessons very well.

TUESDAY 31 JULY. In the evening DOUGLAS, Lord and Lady Macdonald, etc., played cards and supped with us in town. I drank moderately. My wife and I lay in town.

WEDNESDAY 1 AUGUST. In the evening was at St John's Lodge at the entering of the Hon. George Cochrane.[35]

FRIDAY 3 AUGUST. I supped at Lord Kames's, but was very dull and unhappy.

SATURDAY 4 AUGUST. Why keep a journal of so "weary a life"? I yesterday spoke to Lord Advocate of Major Montgomerie, and his Lordship frankly agreed to assist him in getting a battalion to go to the East Indies. This pleased me; and as he asked me to come and take mutton and claret with him, reminding me that I had said in London that was the best way to keep up old friendship (which however I had not exactly said), I resolved to be well with him. The young Campbells dined with us today, as usual on Saturday. I was in the humour of drinking wine with pleasure, and took more than half a bottle of white wine. I then went over to Lady Colville's, and her brother Andrew and I drank a bottle of port. His sensible, firm manner of talking of low spirits, which he had sadly experienced, did me some good. I drank tea there too. Took Grange and Mr James Loch to sup with me in the country. I took only buttermilk.

35 Son of the 8th Earl of Dundonald.

MONDAY 6 AUGUST. Went to hear the examination of the High School, which pleased me. Had met Major Montgomerie returned from Ayrshire, and informed him of Lord Advocate's good intentions. Appointed to meet the Major at the Cross at one and inform him when we could see the Advocate together. His Lordship was at the High School examination, and appointed two o'clock. I went with the Major. But my spirits were so woefully sunk, I could hardly open my lips. We walked a little in the Meadow. I was somewhat shocked with the idea of the honest Major's going to such a distance from his wife and children, and into the dangers of war. But he was keen for it. So I was satisfied. Lord Advocate engaged to write that very night both to the Secretary at War and to Lord North's secretary, and said it was a shame the Major had not got a battalion before. I dined at my father's; Commissioner Cochrane, Balbarton, etc., there. I was dull, but, I cannot tell how, am easier there when in wretched hypochondria. I drank tea with Grange. I was quite feeble and sunk at night, and could not sleep for some time from thinking drearily of Hugh Montgomerie's going to the East Indies.

WEDNESDAY 8 AUGUST. Dined at Mr Maclaurin's; Lady Wallace, Lord Monboddo, Lord Ankerville, etc., there. Drank pretty liberally and was cheered. Stayed tea. At night, just as Maclaurin and I were preparing to go to Sir John Pringle's, Lady Wallace returned and brought Lord Maitland. We sat down to cards, and played till near one. I lost and was vexed. I would not stay supper, but walked home in a disagreeable feverishness. But this occasional sally into the agitation of fashionable life made me view with satisfaction that domestic tranquillity which had appeared insignificant and wearisome.

THURSDAY 9 AUGUST. Cultivated the feeling which last night's excess had given me. Dined at my father's; Balmuto and Robert Boswell there; an unpleasing scene. Supped at Sir John Pringle's. Felt going out at night, now that it was dark, disagreeable. Met Lord Braxfield in the Meadow as I was going to Sir John's. He said, "It's a cursed business, ours." I was mischievous enough to join with him, and say, "You labour hard and get no thanks." I had now lost all relish for the Court of Session, and could not think of being a judge there but merely with a view to have an annual income to assist my family and an occupation only better than being idle. I languished for London; yet feared I should not be able to rise to any eminence there. Sir John Pringle said to me one day this summer, "I know not if you will be at rest in London. But you will never be at rest out of it." I felt a kind of weak, fallacious attachment to Edinburgh. But I considered, "I hope to be in Heaven, which is quitting Edinburgh. Why then should I not quit it to get to London, which is a high step in the scale of felicity?" I thought I might try the English bar and be sent down a baron of exchequer. In short I was very wavering.

FRIDAY 10 AUGUST. Was rather better. Mr Solicitor-General, Colonel Craufurd of Craufurdland, and Mr Robert Dundas dined with us in the country. I was steady and relished company and good wine. They drank tea.

SATURDAY 11 AUGUST. Rose quite well. I have not been so since my return from London. I relished everything, even the Court of Session. I however was not displeased that it rose today. There was something comfortable in the prospect of being for some time free from any fixed attendance.

SUNDAY 12 AUGUST. Went to the Quakers' Meeting built by Mr Miller; only twelve present. All silent. I had calm meditation. Then dined at Sir John Pringle's. Thought I would try if I *could* be saturated with wine there. Drank six glasses in the time of dinner and three large draughts of port and water, which, with the few glasses after dinner, made me warm and hearty.

MONDAY 13 AUGUST. Grange dined with us in the country and drank tea. I grew weary, walked to town, heard the dreary news of Admiral Parker's engagement with the Dutch.[36]

WEDNESDAY 15 AUGUST. Grange and Sandy and I walked out to Prestonfield. There came on such a rain that we stopped above an hour in Sharp's coachyard in the Pleasance. Mr Bennet was at Prestonfield, so we had a most comfortable day. I shunned the execution of Daniel Mackay for stealing from the post-house, though I felt an inclination to see it. Sandy rode home. I was dreary at night, thinking of the execution.

FRIDAY 17 AUGUST. Sir Alexander and Lady Dick, Miss Dick, Miss Annie, Miss Peggie, and Mr Robert and worthy Mr Bennet dined with us at our country-house. I relished it excellently and was quite well for the time. They drank tea.

TUESDAY 21 AUGUST. Was exceedingly sunk, and could see no comfort. I could not call up my principles of religion. All was darkness and uncertainty. Yet I prayed to GOD as a Christian morning and evening amidst all this gloom. Yesterday and today I dictated so much of a law paper, but with no animation. I dined at my father's very dully, and took leave of him. He expressed no wish to see me at Auchinleck, and was silent when I said I intended to be out soon. I was so melancholy that I saw little difference between age and youth. I called on Dr Gillespie; then sauntered uncertain and uneasy as I used to be when at the College. Drank tea at Sir John Pringle's and walked in the Meadow with him and some ladies, very dully. At night felt the blessing of having a cheerful wife.

WEDNESDAY 22 AUGUST. Last night had a card from Lord Graham[37] inviting

---

36 Parker's squadron had engaged a Dutch squadron on the Dogger Bank on 5 August and there had been heavy casualties on both sides.

37 James Graham (1755-1836), Marquess of Graham (*later* 3rd Duke of Montrose), was elected to Parliament in 1780 as representative for Richmond, Yorkshire. He obtained the repeal of the statutory proscription of the wearing of Highland dress in Scotland. In 1783 he was appointed a Lord of the Treasury, and the following year he was appointed President of the Board of Trade, joint Postmaster-General and joint Paymaster of the Forces. He succeeded to his father as 3rd Duke of Montrose in September 1790, and in 1791 became a Commissioner for Indian Affairs and a Privy Councillor. In 1795 he was appointed Lord Justice General of Scotland (titular head of the High Court of Justiciary) and was the last layman to hold that office (*Scots Peerage*, Vol. VI, p. 268 ff).

me to meet him at Bothwell Castle, but in terms by no means such as I liked, because he put it on being *diverted* with my company. I hesitated however whether or not I should go, and at last resolved not. I was very low-spirited today; and during this late fit, there has come into my mind the horrible thought of suicide. It was most effectually checked by thinking what a triumph it would afford to my enemies, or rather enviers, and how it would hurt my children. I had *some* rationality therefore in store.

THURSDAY 23 AUGUST. It rained all day. I did not go to town, but read some of the *Arabian Nights* to Veronica, and was entertained, though my attention was not seized as it was in my early years by tales. I was upon the whole pretty easy. Lady Colville invited us all today to tea. We went and were comfortable. I know not how it happened, but I had a complete relief from melancholy for an hour or two, and enjoyed some of Dr Johnson's *Lives of the Poets* fully. We played a rubber at whist. My wife, who had been a little hoarse for some time, spit some blood, which alarmed both her and me. I persuaded her to go to bed early. She said my father and I were quite different. My spirits required agitation, no matter by what. His did not. I was brandy kindled, the flames of which, if not stirred, went out. He was a good coal fire, which burnt steady.

FRIDAY 24 AUGUST. Went uninvited to dine with Sir John Pringle. Found it was not *the thing*, as the saying is. Miss Hall[38] went home with me to tea, as Sir John was going out. In the evening I was restless. Walked into town, intending to sup at Princes Street Coffee-house. But luckily changed my mind and came home.

SATURDAY 25 AUGUST. It was a very wet day. But I passed it very easily. My wife was no longer ill, which was a great comfort. Veronica and Phemie read each a chapter in the Bible to me, which they now generally do every morning. Veronica played on the harpsichord, and I read the *Arabian Nights' Entertainments*, which engaged me more the more I read.

TUESDAY 28 AUGUST. Read more of the *Arabian Nights* and some of Erskine's *Principles*,[39] and played at catch-honours and birkie[40] with Veronica and Phemie. Was charmed with Veronica's playing on the harpsichord. At night my dear wife talked seriously of our state in this world; that we ought to be submissive and trust in GOD, and not inquire eagerly into futurity. This seemed sensible, but humbling to an aspiring philosophical curiosity. It however pleased me at the time.

SUNDAY 2 SEPTEMBER. Thought the New Church had been opened again, after having been shut on account of being painted, but it was still locked. Went to Barclay the Berean's meeting and heard him pray and lecture drearily and wildly.[41] It was hearing a sect somewhat new to me. But he differed little from the Glassites. I was shocked that the chapel at the foot of Carrubber's Close,

38 Isabella Hall, Sir John's niece (*Laird*, p. 540).
39 John Erskine, *Principles of the Law of Scotland* (1754).
40 Card games. "Birkie" was the same as "beggar-my-neighbour".
41 John Barclay (1734-1798), minister of the Church of Scotland and founder of the sect of the Bereans (otherwise known as Barclayites or Barclayans). On account of his unorthodox doctrines he was barred from holding any benefice in the Church of Scotland (DNB).

where I first was charmed with the Church-of-England worship, should be debased by such vulgar cant. It was a fine day. I dined at home between sermons. Went in the afternoon to the West Kirk and heard Sir Harry Moncreiff.

MONDAY 3 SEPTEMBER. Went in a post-chaise with Colquhoun Grant and dined at Arniston, to pay a visit to the President after his late illness and before his going to Buxton. It was just an Arniston day. Twenty-two men, women, and children dined, and there was much hearty laughing and drinking. I was in pretty good spirits. It rained much. I came home somewhat intoxicated.

THURSDAY 6 SEPTEMBER. Visited Mr Solicitor at Murrayfield. Sir Walter Montgomerie-Cuninghame and Grange dined with us. I supped at Dunn's Hotel with Lord Graham and Douglas. Was moderate.

FRIDAY 7 SEPTEMBER. Mr Sibthorpe and Grange dined with us. I supped at Mr Ilay Campbell's with Lord Graham and Douglas, etc. Was moderate. Had an alarm that little Jamie might have water in his head, as he used to wake in the night and complain of pain in his head. But I hoped this was only apprehension in his mother and me. He was now a delightful child.

SUNDAY 9 SEPTEMBER. Heard Mr Walker in the New Church in the forenoon; respected his decent manner and seriousness, but had too much philosophy for his orthodoxy. Had not an unpleasing sensation of wonder as to what *may be* the real result of this dubious, changeful state. My wife was at the West Kirk. I dined comfortably at home, and drank some port comfortably. I have relished my wife and children and the comforts of life very much for some days. Should I not be content with such enjoyment? The children said divine lessons in the afternoon. After tea I went to town, visited Lord Macdonald, and walked a good while with Major Montgomerie. Then came to Grange's and put the finishing paragraph to a *Hypochondriack* on dreaming,[42] in which I indulged an agreeable superstition. I had written it during these three days with satisfaction. I was really very well just now, though my existence would not bear an analysis so as to appear to advantage in description. My notions are too high.

Early in the morning of 11 September Boswell set off for Auchinleck in the fly and took a fancy to one of his companions, a "very pretty-looking, pleasing woman" whom, he thought, he "fondled... too much". He reached Auchinleck at tea time and "felt for the first time the agreeable wonder of coming from Edinburgh in a day". However, his stay at Auchinleck was dreary and he was hurt by the "coldness" of his father and the "venom" of Lady Auchinleck and her sister. Attempts at partridge-shooting proved wholly unsuccessful, as did "two short chases of hares" when visiting Eglinton later in the month. Boswell returned to Edinburgh on 5 October, again accomplishing the journey in one day.

FRIDAY 5 OCTOBER. On arriving at my house of Drumsheugh, to which I walked from Bristo Port,[43] found my dear wife ill, she having had a miscarriage.

---

42 No. 48.
43 The site of an arched gateway (possibly removed by this time) in the city wall on the south side of the city.

This gave me uneasiness. The children however were well, and she was better.

TUESDAY 9 OCTOBER. Prepared for the press Answers for Commissioner Cochrane.[44] Dined at his house with Dr Webster and Dr Blair.

THURSDAY 11 OCTOBER. Was amused yesterday by having a hogshead of claret bottled, and today by having it put into a catacomb.[45] Was very listless.

MONDAY 15 OCTOBER. Should have written a *Hypochondriack*. But could not. Resolved to make an old essay serve.[46] But could not find a motto. Was very insignificant. Lady Colville and her sister were very uneasy from a letter mentioning that Lord Kellie was ill at Brussels. I drank a little port with them after dinner. In the evening, as for some nights past, played at commerce[47] with the children.

TUESDAY 16 OCTOBER. Happily found a motto for my old essay in Holyoke's *Dictionary*, and was content. Dined at Dr Blair's with Dr Webster, Commissioner Cochrane, and Mr Blair, the advocate. Drank too much. His Holiness [Dr Webster] was obliged to go away rather early to meet a party at Walker's tavern. Good Dr Hugh proposed that he and I and his cousin should take one bottle. We did so. The claret was excellent. I was pleased to find they could both trace themselves from a fifth son of the laird of Blair. I walked to town a good deal intoxicated. Had worthy Grange with me till I wrote to Dilly and sealed up my *Hypochondriack*. Supped at Dr Webster's. He not in. Nobody but Mrs Mingay and Mr Macpherson. Was not pleased with myself. Was in bad frame at home.

WEDNESDAY 17 OCTOBER. Was very ill in the night and morning, but could not blame myself. Veronica made me a very good answer today, when I asked her in the usual way if her sister's getting more sugar almonds than her made her poorer. "Yes," said she, "it makes me poorer than her." I grew better, walked to town, dressed, and had worthy Grange to accompany me almost to Prestonfield, where Sir Alexander and I and the Rev. Mr Bennet got into the Knight's coach and drove to Lord Somerville's, where we were to dine by appointment.[48] Sir Philip Ainslie was there, and talked with a lofty vivacity which was very entertaining and gained much upon Sir Alexander. Mr Wauchope of

---

44 Although the editors of *Laird* state (at p. 400, n. 9) that when that volume was prepared this cause had not been traced, a copy of the Answers written by Boswell has now been found in the Advocates' Library (SPAL, 143:41). The Answers were in response to a petition by the trustees of the deceased William Kirkpatrick, a Principal Clerk of Session (one of the trustees being James Erskine, Lord Alva). This was "a dispute over the paying off of an incumbrance on lands bought by Cochrane from the petitioners, whom he understood to have undertaken to clear off the incumbrances on his behalf" (*Session Papers*, 81 10 12b). The lands in question were those on which Cochrane's residence, Dalry House, was situated.

45 That is, a wine cellar.

46 *The Hypochondriack* No. 49, on "identification by numbers", had first appeared in the *Public Advertiser* for 22 January 1768 (*Laird*, p. 401, n. 1).

47 A card game in which the principal feature is exchange or barter.

48 James Somerville, 13th Lord Somerville, son of Boswell's first patron, James Somerville, 12th Lord Somerville, resided at the family estate at The Drum (in Gilmerton, near Edinburgh), where the 12th Lord had taken the broken shaft and sculptured capital of the ancient Mercat Cross of Edinburgh after it had been removed from its site in the High Street in 1756. The shaft and capital stood in the grounds of Drum House for over a hundred years.

Niddrie and a young midshipman were there. My heart warmed to be again here, where in the late Lord's time I was so happy. This Lord, though very silent, seemed very well pleased to see us, and all was elegant. He promised to dine with me before he went to London. I hoped to bring about a cordiality between us. Sir Philip carried me to town. We were quite sober, which was agreeable. I sat a little at his house, and then at Lady Macdonald's. Was in better humour than ordinary; something in London spirits. When I got home, heard Lord Kellie was dead. Was somewhat agitated by the news.

THURSDAY 18 OCTOBER. Lord Kellie's death kept my mind from stagnating. Lady Colville did me the honour to send a letter, announcing it, to copy, and to let me know that perhaps she would have more occasion for my assistance. I wrote at her desire to Captain James Francis Erskine and to Lord Eglinton. Had Mr Stobie, in his way to Auchinleck, and Grange to dine with us. In the evening wrote to my father, James Bruce,[49] and Dr Gillespie, with a degree of application and ease which gave me satisfaction. Had talked to Mr Stobie of several things about the estate of Auchinleck. Had been somewhat gloomy since I last came home, contemplating my father's death and my insufficiency for representing our ancient family. I however hoped to do well, and thought that probably hypochondria made me think the duty more difficult, and myself more unfit, than was really just.

SUNDAY 21 OCTOBER. Little Jamie could now answer the first six questions of the *Mother's Catechism.*[50]

MONDAY 22 OCTOBER. Walked to Craighouse and breakfasted with Lord Covington, whom I had not seen for many months. He was grown very dull of hearing, and gave me a discouraging view of life and old age and human existence. He said his memory was failed, and that the mind and body failed together; and he seemed to acquiesce in that dreary notion, without hope of restoration. And he said when one looked back on life, it was just a chaos of nothing. He however was not cast down, and said he would meet Maclaurin and me at a party at cards. I walked to town and found Dr Webster had been in quest of me to go with him to dine with Lord Advocate. I dressed, and we drove to Melville Castle. The Advocate said he was very glad to see me, and all went on cordially. He mentioned after dinner an anecdote of me for which he said he had frequently given me credit: how last spring in London, when he had got the better of me in the Ayrshire election, I came up to him and said that our families had long been friends; that somehow he and I had taken different lines, but that should be no more. In short, he made a very good story of it for me; better, I am sensible, than the reality. And we now agreed that we should henceforth be well together. We had no strangers at table; just his old uncle and brother and Blair the advocate and Dr Grieve of Dalkeith, and we drank liberally. When the Doctor and I were taking our chaise, Lord Advocate came and said to me, "It

49 The overseer at Auchinleck.
50 By John Willison; first published in 1731.

never does to go against old connexions. It never succeeds." "Why, my Lord," said I, "I will not say that. You have been very fortunate. But it never *should* succeed." His making up thus to me showed a generosity of mind in his prosperity; and perhaps he may be of essential service to me yet. He had a good effect upon me after Lord Covington's languor. He appeared all life and activity. I told him Lord Covington's reflection on life. It struck him at first. He seemed to shudder. It was like throwing cold water on hot iron to give Lord Advocate in all the glow of his prosperity a glimpse of the sad indifference of old age, which, if he should live, he himself was to feel. He said, "I shall take care that *my* life shall not be a chaos of nothing" (dashing high-flavoured claret into his glass). Dr Webster and I jogged quietly to town, and I went home to Drumsheugh.

FRIDAY 26 OCTOBER. Had Mr Martin Lindsay to look at my garden at Drumsheugh and advise me what I should get done to it. He and Grange dined and drank tea with us. I was in a comfortable frame.

SUNDAY 28 OCTOBER. Stayed at home in the forenoon. Heard Mr Walker in the afternoon. It was wet and dull. Called on Grange, and he and I drank a couple of bottles of Teneriffe cordially. We enjoyed this much. But it was not right to take it on Sunday, for it disturbed me so much that I was not in condition to hear the children say divine lessons. Poor Phemie had been ill since yesterday with a feverish disorder.

MONDAY 29 OCTOBER. Had been uneasy all night, and awaked ill. Grew better. Went to town, dressed, and attended Hunter-Blair's election dinner in the Assembly Hall.[51] Was not gloomy. But felt a cold indifference. Got next to Maclaurin. He was not jovial and went away early. I joined a jolly set gathered about Colonel Hunter, and grew brisker. After much solicitation I sung *Sir Dilberry Diddle* better than I ever did, having first made a speech that I hoped none of the gentlemen of the Edinburgh Defensive Band would suspect any ridicule upon *them*. (I had seen this band with great satisfaction perform their exercise last week on Heriot's Work bowling-green.) I then was called up to Hunter-Blair's right hand, and by various requests was induced to sing *Twa Wheels and an Axletree*.[52] I had no vivid enjoyment, but just moved along the tide of life. I got up and was pleased with a hunting-song, and wished there had been more tonight, in honour of the great Hunter at my hand; and I gave this toast: "May the Hunter of Edinburgh prove a mighty Nimrod in the House of Commons." This had an admirable effect. The deacons,[53] etc., got up on their feet and drank it. I kept myself quite sober, and got home between ten and eleven.

TUESDAY 30 OCTOBER. I took a ride in the forenoon with Sandy round about

51 James Hunter-Blair had been elected M.P. for Edinburgh in place of Sir Lawrence Dundas, who had died on 21 September.
52 One of Boswell's own compositions (see the entry for 13 February 1775 and footnote). *Sir Dilberry Diddle* may have been one of Boswell's compositions too. Neither song is known to have survived (*Laird*, p. 405, n. 1).
53 The chairmen of incorporated trades who, by virtue of their office, were members of the Town Council.

Dalry, Bells Mills,[54] etc., which made him very happy. Went to town in the evening and saw my father, who arrived about five o'clock. Found him in his ordinary way of late, and rather more kindly.

WEDNESDAY 31 OCTOBER. Poor Phemie had been ill since Saturday of a cold and pretty high feverishness. I went into town, and got a message from my wife to get either Mr Wood or Dr Gillespie for her. I carried out Mr Wood to dinner. Miss Annie Boswell was there.[55] He thought Phemie in no danger. As a message had been also left for Dr Gillespie, I resolved that he should come, but as it was a bad afternoon, I walked in with Mr Wood to stop him from coming till next day. We sat down with him and drank a little port. I was alarmed about poor Phemie, and vexed that I had ever shown more fondness for Veronica, so as to hurt Phemie's spirit at all. I stayed tea at Dr Gillespie's. Commissioner Cochrane was ill of a fever and really in danger. Dr Gillespie had been with him in the forenoon and was to go again at seven. I accompanied him in the Commissioner's chaise and found the old gentleman in bed, quite lean and pale, but retaining his spirit. I really was sorry for him, and uneasy at the thought of one whom I had so long known being carried off and seen no more in his life. I went to my father's with Dr Gillespie and supped. I found it proper to be well with Gillespie.

THURSDAY 1 NOVEMBER. I should have marked that since the accounts came of Lord Kellie's death, my wife was exceedingly attentive to Lady Colville and Lady Anne Erskine, and I called several times on Andrew, whom I found more affectionate than I supposed him to be. He took my visits kind. I dined today at the Rev. Dr Hunter's with Hunter-Blair, etc. Was not vivid, but liked to be at the Professor of Divinity's.

FRIDAY 2 NOVEMBER. We came to our town house. The change was comfortable. I dined at my father's with my two sons. I visited Commissioner Cochrane in the forenoon, who was better.

WEDNESDAY 7 NOVEMBER. Dr Webster insisted I should dine with him, as he had some good claret which would be gone. I did so, and we took a bottle apiece. In the evening I was agreeably surprised with a visit from my brother John, who had returned from Moffat last night. He was well dressed, and behaved wonderfully well. He supped, and he and I drank a little mountain comfortably. I thanked GOD for the happy change.

FRIDAY 9 NOVEMBER. My brother John supped with us, and was really companionable in a grave style. I was however under restraint with him. Mr George Wallace sat an hour with us in the evening.

SUNDAY 11 NOVEMBER. Attended the New Church and took the Sacrament, but without fervour.

---

54 Bell's Mills, on the north bank of the Water of Leith near the site where Belford Bridge now stands, was "a hamlet deep down in a grassy glen, with an old bridge, over which for ages lay the only road to Queensferry" (Grant, Vol. III, p. 63).
55 Daughter of Boswell's late uncle, Dr John Boswell.

TUESDAY 13 NOVEMBER. Had been ill last night from drinking too much port, and was still so much indisposed that I wished to lie in bed; but got up to make my appearance in the Court of Session. Thought it dull and poor.

THURSDAY 15 NOVEMBER. (Writing on Friday the 23.) Nothing to recollect except that either last night or this (last, I am pretty sure) I supped with Lord Kames. Nobody there but Mr Russell, the surgeon,[56] who seemed to be of more pleasing manners than young men about Edinburgh usually are. I found my Lord dictating to his clerk a proposal to give premiums for planting oaks near the banks of the Great Canal.[57] He was as entire in his faculties as ever I knew him, and so was Mrs Drummond. I supped well, as I always do there. We had no conversation to be registered.

SATURDAY 17 NOVEMBER. Had laboured for some days under an impotence of mind, so that I could not write No. 50 of *The Hypochondriack*. This day wrote it all but a little.[58] The Lords altered their interlocutor in the simple question as to a paragraph in the *Edinburgh Gazette* being published *animo injuriandi* against the Edinburgh Procurators, or Solicitors, before the inferior courts. It vexed me that the judges of this country should be so wavering, and I feared too a mixture of partiality.[59] My brother John dined with us today with the young Campbells, the first time of his seeing them. He was really conversable with me, and he and I drank a bottle of mountain. What a comfort was it to have a social afternoon with a brother who had been so long insane! He stayed tea.

WEDNESDAY 21 NOVEMBER. Was so ill that I could not get up till late. Luckily had nothing to do in the Court of Session. However, I grew better, and went down to it a little.

56 James Russell (1754-1836), Fellow of the Royal College of Surgeons of Edinburgh (admitted 1777), later professor of clinical surgery at Edinburgh University.
57 The Forth and Clyde Canal, which was not completed until 1790.
58 The subject of this essay was learning.
59 This is a reference to the case of *The Preses and Society of Solicitors before the Commissary, Sheriff, and City Courts of Edinburgh v Thomas Robertson*, which is reported in *Faculty Decisions*, Vol. IX, 1781-87, p. 4. The Society of Procurators, whose members were entitled to appear only in the inferior courts, had obtained a royal charter establishing them as a corporation under the name of "The Society of Solicitors before the Commissary, Sheriff, and City Courts of Edinburgh". Soon afterwards, *The Edinburgh Gazette* published a satirical paragraph saying that "the Worshipful Society of… *Cadies*, or *Running-Stationers*, of this city, are resolved, in imitation, and encouraged by the singular success of their brethren of an *equally respectable* Society, to apply for a Charter of their Privileges, particularly of the sole privilege of PROCURING, in the most extensive sense of the word." The Solicitors considered themselves injured by the innuendos conveyed by this paragraph and sued Thomas Robertson, the publisher of the *Gazette*, for damages. Robertson was represented by Ilay Campbell, Boswell, and Hugo Arnot. They argued that a body-corporate "is as little susceptible of hurt by defamatory words as by blows" and, in any event, the "raillery" of which the pursuers complained was merely a "harmless and inoffensive… effusion of mirth and pleasantry upon an appearance of vanity in their deportment". However, the Lord Ordinary, Lord Hailes, held that the paragraph was malicious and calculated to injure the pursuers. Nevertheless, taking the view that "no great damages could have ensued from a publication meriting rather scorn than complaint", he modified the damages to £5. The pursuers were also found entitled to expenses, modified to £15. Robertson then appealed to the Inner House, where it was at first held that no sufficient intent to injure had been established and the action was therefore dismissed; but when the Solicitors appealed in turn the Lords changed their view and adhered to the interlocutor of Lord Hailes.

FRIDAY 23 NOVEMBER. Dined at my father's; Phemie and Sandy, Dr Gillespie and Mr Stobie there. Stayed and played whist and drank tea. Felt myself well employed in contributing to divert my father, whose bladder complaint was since autumn last so increased that he required the catheter three times a day, and when he took exercise had bloody urine, so that he kept the house close. I was tenderly affected with his situation, for all his coldness.

SUNDAY 25 NOVEMBER. Was at New Church all day. Drank tea at Commissioner Cochrane's. Visited my father both forenoon and evening. The children said divine lessons. Was happy on this anniversary of my marriage day.

MONDAY 26 NOVEMBER. Dictated part of a Petition for Robertson, the printer,[60] and was pretty well. Sent for my brother John to tea. He came, and was social enough.

TUESDAY 27 NOVEMBER. Dined at my father's; Mrs Boswell of Balmuto[61] and Mr Claud there. Mr and Mrs Macredie drank tea with us. I had today a disagreeable struggle in endeavouring to settle an exchequer process against my father about his carriage duty,[62] while Claud and John Stobie wanted to push it on. They had my father biased for it, so that I could not move him. The Hon. A. Gordon and I supped at Lord Kames's cheerfully.

THURSDAY 29 NOVEMBER. My client, Mr Mercer of Lethendy,[63] insisted on entertaining me in the evening with a glass of claret at Walker's tavern. I went at six. Had heard he was an extraordinary character. Found him naturally and habitually odd, and also somewhat in liquor, so that he was very curious company. He had wild fancies and odd gestures, but was withal a man of sense and a Latin scholar. Mr Mitchell, writer in Perth, his country agent, was with him. We made claret circulate very briskly. Mr Robert Boswell joined us for some time, he being his agent in the process in which I am his lawyer. I grew jovial and somewhat extravagant, and being remarkably strong in head at the time, drank freely and humoured my client, who after every sentence or two sung *The Humours of the Glen*, without words. After Mr Robert Boswell went away, we got in Walker, the landlord, who drank a little with us. It was a very singular scene. I had asked my client to sup with me tonight, but luckily he could not. I engaged him and Mitchell to dinner next day, Mr Robert Boswell being to be with me. About ten my client was carried off in a chair. Mitchell and I sat a few minutes after him, and thought ourselves very sober, though

60 The publisher of the *Edinburgh Gazette*. See the entry for 17 November and relevant footnote. Boswell's petition sought a further review of the case, but the prayer of the petition was refused.
61 Claud Boswell's mother.
62 No papers relating to this case have been located.
63 Charles Mercer of Lethendy, in Perthshire, had had a servant by the name of John Duff, who, in 1778, had attended as a witness in a court case before the Justices of the Peace and Commissioners of Supply for the county of Perth and had been declared by them (without hearing any evidence on the matter) to have been idle and disorderly, thus rendering him liable to be compelled to serve in the army. In February 1779 Duff had been sent to America as a private soldier in a Highland regiment. Proceedings at the instance of Duff and Mercer were then commenced in the Court of Session against the Justices for an award of damages (see *Laird*, Appendix B, pp. 490-502).

eight bottles of claret were drank, besides part of a bottle of Madeira, which Mr Mercer called for. I walked home; and though flustered, did really imagine that I was not much intoxicated.

FRIDAY 30 NOVEMBER. Awaked very ill, but grew better, and was in the Court of Session at nine. At one saw the Edinburgh Defensive Band exercised on Heriot's Green, and Mr Crosbie appear for the first time as their lieutenant-colonel. At dinner Mr Mercer, my client, having been drinking in the forenoon, was much in the same state as when I first saw him last night. Mr Robert Boswell, wife and sisters, and Mr and Mrs Cannan, and Mr Mitchell were with us. I was sorry that I had with too much openness described him to some of my brethren in the forenoon, for a client's oddities should not be exposed. Sandy Gordon came and sat awhile with us after dinner to see him. But he sunk into inarticulate drunkenness very soon, and insisted to be handed to his chair by his counsel. He however kept his old spirit; for on the stair he muttered, "Pro rege et patria".[64] The account of Lord Cornwallis's surrender came today.[65] It pleased me much as I trusted it would at length put an end to the American war. Mr Gordon insisted on my coming to his house to make up a party at whist. When I went, I found a party without me; and as my feelings on public affairs were very different from theirs, I did not stay supper.

SATURDAY 1 DECEMBER. Restrained my joy on Lord Cornwallis's surrender, not to give offence. But it inspirited me, in so much that though for some time I have been quite lazy in the morning, relaxed and unable to rise, I this day sprung up. I supped at my father's. I was a little heated with wine. He had his old republican humour, reading the King's speech: "What a clattering's this— *my* forces! I think he might have said *ours*."[66]

SUNDAY 2 DECEMBER. Stayed at home in the forenoon. Heard Mr Walker in the afternoon. The children said divine lessons. Mr Boswall of Blackadder,[67] whom I had not seen for two years (I think), called and supped with us very agreeably. I was pretty well, though my enjoyment was not vivid.

MONDAY 3 DECEMBER. I am too fat at present. My belly is more swelled than I ever remember it; and perhaps my humours are gross. I have a torpidity of mind that I have not often experienced. I have not "a lively hope of immortality". It occurred to me today that perhaps a man is immortal or not as he happens to die in a dull or a lively frame. I have often been an immortal soul. At present it seems to me that I am not of celestial fire. I am quite sensual, and that, too, not exquisitely but rather swinishly. My wife and I and our three eldest children dined at my father's and drank tea; an ungracious scene. Last week I called on Sir W. Forbes, who had read forty of my *Hypochondriacks* and liked them; said there

---

64 "For King and Country".
65 Cornwallis had surrendered to Washington at Yorktown on 19 October.
66 In a speech on 27 November 1781 the King had said: "It is with great concern that I inform you that the events of war have been very unfortunate to my arms in Virginia, having ended in the loss of my forces in that province" (quoted in *Scots Magazine*, November 1781, xliii. 562, and in *Laird*, p. 411, n. 8).
67 Alexander Boswall, "the Nabob".

were many original thoughts, and always a good tendency. He is to give me remarks on each. I just lounged today. Only studied a long cause. For the first two weeks of this Session got only one guinea. Was desponding, but too dull to feel much. Last week got seven.

WEDNESDAY 5 DECEMBER. This day to my agreeable surprise the Court of Session determined my client Mercer of Lethendy's cause for him.[68] I was clear he should gain it, but had experienced such a procedure upon it before that I had no hope but in an appeal. I was pretty keenly agitated, which I had not been for many weeks. I dined with my client at Mr Robert Boswell's, but kept myself sober. Supped at Lord Kames's with General Gordon of Fyvie, his brother Alexander, Miss Jardine, etc. Lord Kames drank after the ladies were gone, "Good rest to us all with Miss Jardine." "I fancy", said I, "there would not be much rest with her. It would be old Hardyknute's rest:

> Full seventy years he now had seen,
> With scarce sev'n years of rest."[69]

My Lord seemed a little stunned by this, as if a joke upon himself, which was certainly not meant. But he soon plucked up spirit and said for himself, "Old Hardyknute would do as well as any of you."[70]

THURSDAY 6 DECEMBER. Called on my brother John in the morning. Had him at dinner and Mr Lawrie. Was indolent and did no business. Was at a consultation at eight, this week being pretty prosperous. Went and supped at my father's. He was in a quiet state of failure. I was in a state of indifference.

SATURDAY 8 DECEMBER. There was a debate in the Faculty of Advocates whether we should oppose Mr John Wright's petition to come among us, he being of low origin and gaining his livelihood as a teacher of law and mathematics.[71] I was keen for him, being of opinion that our Society has no *dignity*, and must receive every man of good character and knowledge.[72] There was a vote, and the party for him carried it by *ten*.

MONDAY 10 DECEMBER. Dictated well. Dined at Balmuto's, where Lord Monboddo and Dr Gillespie were introduced and took well to each other. Mr

---

68 The court held that the Justices had been arbitrary and oppressive and found them liable to pay damages to Duff in the sum of £40 together with his legal expenses (*Laird*, p. 412, n. 3).

69 "Lines 3-4 of *Hardyknute: A Scottish Fragment*, circulated as an ancient ballad, actually the composition of Elizabeth, Lady Wardlaw (1677-1727)" (*Laird*, p. 413, n. 4).

70 "Rather coarse jesting, considering that Miss Jardine was to become his daughter-in-law in less than a year" (*Laird*, p. 413, n. 5).

71 John Wright, eldest son of John Wright of Kilfinan in Argyll. His first employment was as a shoemaker in Greenock, but he moved to Edinburgh in 1769 and became a private teacher of Civil Law, Municipal Law (i.e., Scots law), Mathematics and various other subjects (Stewart, p. 323). He was to be admitted advocate on 28 January 1783.

72 Dr John W Cairns has pointed out that when suggesting that the Faculty of Advocates had no "dignity" Boswell uses the word "in a relatively technical sense relating to the right to bear a title of honour or have a coat of arms" and that this opinion was contrary to the generally held view that advocates possessed a dignified, noble status (and a right to a coat of arms) by virtue of their learning in Roman law (John W Cairns, *Alfenus Varus and the Faculty of Advocates*, in *Ius Commune: Zeitschrift für Europäische Rechtsgeschichte*, 28 [2001]).

David Erskine too was there. We had really a good afternoon, without drinking too much. I was in such spirits that I chose to end the day socially; so supped at Lord Kames's with Dr Blair and Mr and Mrs Morehead. Walked home in hearty vigour. Was in danger from dalliance in the Luckenbooths, but shunned it.

WEDNESDAY 12 DECEMBER. Dictated well, and was as busy at night as I ever have been as a lawyer. Mr Alexander Walker, who came late to consult me, supped with us, along with Mr Lawrie, whom I now have seldom at meals.

THURSDAY 13 DECEMBER. I was in strong spirits all day, and was sensible that a great deal of my unhappiness is mere cloud which any moment may dissipate. I thought that at any period of time, a man may disencumber himself of all the *accessories* of his identity, of all his books, all his connexions with a particular place, or a particular sphere of life; and retaining only his consciousness and reminiscence, start into a state of existing quite new. That therefore I should be more *myself* and have more of the "*mihi res non me rebus submittere*".[73] Dictated a great deal, and when weary went and supped at my father's.

SATURDAY 15 DECEMBER. There was a debate in the Faculty of Advocates whether we should give our approbation to the scheme of the magistrates for removing the slaughter-houses a mile from the Cross. I alone opposed it, from a principle of *justice* to the fleshers, and, I will own, at the same time from a wish to appear the champion even of *that* corporation. It is wonderful to what keenness I worked myself up. Mr Moodie, Minister of Riccarton,[74] my brother John, Painter Donaldson, etc., dined with us. I was a staid, sensible man today, but drank too much wine. I visited my father in the evening; and then being heated wandered in the street, but did no harm. Called on Matthew Dickie, who had the gout.

SUNDAY 16 DECEMBER. Heard Dr Blair in the forenoon and Mr Walker in the afternoon. This day the custom of having only one discourse in the forenoon was introduced into the New Church. I visited Dr Webster in the afternoon. The children said divine lessons in the evening. Grange supped with us. I drank too much.

SATURDAY 29 DECEMBER. I visited Laird Heron[75] at Clarke's Hotel, my

73 "'[I try] to subdue the world to myself, not myself to the world' (Horace, *Epistles*, I. i. 19)" (*Laird*, p. 415, n. 9).
74 As the editors of *Laird* observe (p. 414, n. 7), Moodie was "pilloried" by Burns in *The Holy Fair*. See, for example, verse 13:

> Hear how he clears the points o' Faith
>   Wi' rattlin and thumpin!
> Now meekly calm, now wild in wrath,
>   He's stampin, an' he's jumpin!
> His lengthen'd chin, his turn'd-up snout,
>   His eldritch squeel an' gestures,
> O how they fire the heart devout –
>   Like cantharidian plaisters
>   On sic a day!

75 Patrick Heron of Kirroughtrie.

former house in Chessel's Buildings.[76] I heard from Mr Hunter-Blair this fore-noon so good an account of the comedians that I resolved to go at night to *The Beggar's Opera*, inhale London cheerfulness, and be of service in dissipating my wife's gloomy apprehensions. There was but a very thin house. I took my place in the pit, got in at the song "'Tis woman that seduces", and really had the same pleasure that I used to have at seeing *The Beggar's Opera* in my youth. Charles Crookshanks appeared unexpectedly to me in the pit, and I sat by him. I came home enlivened.

MONDAY 31 DECEMBER. Commissioner Cochrane called and told me he had seen my father, but that before he came, Lady Auchinleck had settled with him that I should have my £100 of arrear; and he said I should thank her. My wife was still very ill. My brother John and Grange dined with me today. My wife did not come to dinner. John drank tea with us.

76 "On 16 June 1781 James Clark announced the opening of Clark's Hotel 'for the reception of the nobility and gentry' in Chessels Building, with public rooms which were 'perfectly elegant and airy', furniture 'neat and entirely new', and 'every convenience for carrying on that business with propriety'... The hotel, however, was not a success, opening just as rival establishments were beginning to thrive in the New Town" (R Ian McCallum, "Historical Notes on Chessels Court", *B.O.E.C.*, New Series, Vol. 4, p. 12).

1782

TUESDAY 1 JANUARY. I felt nothing particular on the beginning of a new year. My mind was depressed with anxiety about my wife. After breakfast I had a message from my father to come to him. I went; and he and I and John Stobie went into his bedroom, where he told me that he had once resolved not to give me the £100, but he was now to do it. But that he declared upon his honour that if I ever again exceeded my income, he would give me no more. I calmly mentioned that this £100 was a part of my income. Stobie said *my Lady* insisted on it. When we went into the drawing-room, my father mentioned his giving me the £100. I said to *her* I believed I was obliged to her. She answered no. She never interfered. "I'm sorry for it", said I. "Why?" said she. "Because", said I, "I'm glad when there's any good." "That would not have been good", said she. Since she chose to *deny* her influence, I had no more to say. I came home and dined, the young Campbells with us, and returned to my father's and drank tea.

WEDNESDAY 2 JANUARY. Dictated all day Answers for John Duff and his master Lethendy.[1] Was in able spirits for business, though sadly uneasy about my dear wife. Miss Betty Dick came to be some days with us.

THURSDAY 3 JANUARY. Dictated also this day the same paper, having given in a note of apology to the Lord President's box for not being ready on this day as ordered. Mr Lawrie had gone to the country and thoughtlessly stayed too long.

FRIDAY 4 JANUARY. Was amused with correcting the proof-sheets of my paper, and was pleased with my own performance, regretting however that my abilities were confined to so narrow a sphere. My wife's illness confined me to town this vacation. These three days I was not out of my house.

SATURDAY 5 JANUARY. Walked out as far as Bristo Port with Dr Gillespie. It was a damp day. Felt a pain in my bowels. Drank one glass of wine at dinner. Had my brother John at tea.

SUNDAY 6 JANUARY. Stayed at home all day, my bowel complaint continuing. Read Bryant's *Address to Priestley against Philosophical Necessity*. Had this day so clear a head and so stout an understanding that I did not fear this subject which has often distressed me; and I studied it with a firm ease. I liked part of Bryant's treatise, but wondered to see inconsistencies which so able a scholar unconsciously uttered, particularly on prescience.

MONDAY 7 JANUARY. Was still indisposed a little. The young Campbells dined

1 The Justices had lodged a reclaiming petition seeking to persuade the Lords to review their decision pronounced on 5 December 1781. In his answers to the petition Boswell alleged that there was clearly ill will on the part of two of the Justices towards Mercer and an enmity on the part of another Justice against Duff. A copy of extracts from Boswell's answers is to be found in Appendix B to *Laird*, p. 490 ff.

with us. Heard a debate in the Midlothian County meeting about erecting a turnpike on the road to Musselburgh. Lord Advocate was in the chair. After the meeting rose, he shook hands with me cordially, and promised that if he could, he would dine or sup with me before he went to London, and would let me know when. My dear wife desired me to ask him. I had resolved to have no company as long as her illness continued. She had no spitting of blood. But had a severe hollow cough in the night-time, unless when quieted by laudanum, and sweatings every night. Also at times during the day heats all over her body and a quick pulse. Also swellings in her legs; and she was very, very thin, and had pains shooting through her neck and breast. All these symptoms might be nervous. But both she and I dreaded the consumption, the fatal disease of her family. The apprehension of losing her and being left with five young children was frightfully dreary. All my affection for her and gratitude to her, and the consciousness of not having acted as her husband ought to do, overwhelmed me; and several times I cried bitterly, and one night lay long awake in misery, having wild schemes of desperate conduct floating in my imagination upon supposition of her death. The consideration of her cold, unworthy treatment by my father added much to my distress. It hurt me deeply to think that she should have been my wife only during my narrow and dependent state, and not have lived to be lady of Auchinleck. My views of futurity too were dim. In short I was very wretched. Miss Betty Dick left us this forenoon. I prayed to GOD in his mercy to restore my wife to health.

TUESDAY 8 JANUARY. I sat a good while with Sir William Forbes at his counting house, and talked of religion and Fate and Free Will with an easy firmness quite different from the feeble melancholy with which I have conversed with him in that place on those subjects. For distress had given a kind of fever to my mind that produced a temporary strength. I often *wonder* what will be the view which one shall have at last when fairly in another state of being. I visited my father before dinner. But found such indifference that I did not stay. My bowels too were still not right. Grange supped with us and I took a little port negus. My wife was better.

WEDNESDAY 9 JANUARY. At tea my wife said, "What will you give me for a letter?" I guessed it was from Doctor Johnson. A kind letter it was. My heart was comforted and my spirits raised by it.

TUESDAY 22 JANUARY. I omitted to mention on Friday that Baron Sir John Dalrymple,[2] who has several times flippantly told me that "We never meet" (though he published a scurrilous pamphlet against Lord Barrington[3] and then refused a challenge from his Lordship, which I think should exclude him from the company of every gentleman), came up to me again, and with his usual pertness said, "How d'ye do? We never meet. We're wearing out of acquaintance.

2 Sir John Dalrymple (for whom, see the entry for 4 August 1774 and relevant footnote) was a Baron of Exchequer.
3 Lord Barrington was Secretary at War from 1765 to 1778.

What's the meaning of it?" I answered, "I'm afraid Lord Barrington would take it amiss." And left him. This was well done. Yet I know not if anybody shuns him, except Lord Monboddo because he praises David Hume extravagantly. This day Duff and Mercer's cause came on. The Lord President did me the honour to praise my Answers for them from the Chair. "They are drawn with moderation, precision, and firmness. I have not seen a paper that pleased me more." I was very agreeably solaced with this praise. No philosophy can resist such a solace. But such is the discontent of my disposition that I was vexed such a display of my abilities had not been made in London. I gained my cause finally, but by one vote. Lord Monboddo had altered his opinion. I was truly alarmed at the danger the cause was in. It was comfortable to have it made *certain* at last, unless the Justices should appeal. Having been informed by Mr George Wallace that Sir John Pringle was taken very ill, I went out and visited Miss Hall, his niece, and found it to be too true, and that there was no hope of his recovery. Sir Charles and Miss Preston and Surgeon Wood dined with us. Major Brown of Knockmarloch forwardly made his way upstairs after dinner and broke in upon Sir Charles, Mr Wood, and me, sitting comfortably. We soon ended drinking wine and went to tea. Mr Wood had brought accounts of Sir John Pringle's death. I was somewhat struck, but not with near so much sensibility as some years ago would have been the case. I was a very little heated with wine. My wife with much propriety prevented me from going to my father's and announcing to him the death of his old friend, who was just two months younger than himself. I went and sat a little with worthy Grange. At night had again enjoyment.

WEDNESDAY 23 JANUARY. This day I lost Garrallan's cause against Lord Dumfries, about a march-dike.[4] I thought the Lords wrong and was vexed. Grange dined with us. I drank tea at my father's, who seemed little moved by Sir John Pringle's death. He informed me that he had bought a house in the New Town.[5] I found out afterwards that there had been a secret combined exertion to make him do this. Commissioner Cochrane, Claud, and Stobie had all aided the Lady on Monday the 14, and carried the point. I apprehended that the liferent, if not the property, would be settled on her. I was vexed and irritated, but resolved to be quiet.

THURSDAY 24 JANUARY. Visited Sir James Pringle and Miss Hall.[6] Dined at the Lord President's; the Duchess of Buccleuch and Lady Frances Scott, Mr Baron Norton,[7] Dr Hugh Blair, etc., there. The President himself was wonderfully jovial, and he and his company drank a great deal. He talked to me of John Duff's decision. I observed it turned all upon Lord Ankerville. He said, "It did

---

4 This case was concerned with a dispute over the cost of erecting a boundary wall between properties respectively owned by Patrick Douglas of Garrallan and the Earl of Dumfries (*Laird*, p. 421, n. 6).
5 At 20 St Andrew Square. The house stood at the north-west corner of the square adjacent to Thistle Street on the northernmost part of the site now occupied by the Scottish Life office (No. 19).
6 At 32 George Square (*B.O.E.C.*, Vol. 26, p. 150).
7 Fletcher Norton (1740-1820), son of Fletcher Norton, first Baron Grantley. He was an English lawyer and was appointed Baron of Exchequer in Scotland on 27 February 1776.

so. And I don't know if you would have had Ankerville if he had not dined here the day before. I fixed him. I said, 'Ankerville, we have that case of the recruit tomorrow. We'll never alter *that*.' 'No,' said he, 'we'll never alter *that*.'" I was struck with the strange *management* of justice in this country. I came home in a chair a good deal intoxicated. Grange supped with us.

FRIDAY 25 JANUARY. Awaked exceedingly ill. However, I went to the Court of Session, and dined with Dr Gillespie in company with Lieutenant Bligh,[8] who had gone round the world as Master of Captain Cook's ship, the last voyage. Maule of Panmure[9] and Mr Macredie were there. I have not had so good a day since I left Dr Johnson, we had so much good conversation. I drank wine and water, and came home sober and placid.

SATURDAY 26 JANUARY. My dear wife has for some days been a good deal better. She had an excellent night, and awaked well this morning. Miss Dick came in Sir Alexander's coach and conducted me and my three eldest children and Mr George Wallace to Prestonfield, that the worthy Knight and Mr Wallace and I might lament together the loss of Sir John Pringle. Sir Alexander was quite placid and gay, though he regretted his old friend. I felt Sir John's death more gloomily today than at first. It impressed me with the vanity of human life very sadly. Mr George Wallace came home and supped with us soberly. I liked his variety of knowledge, but was uneasy to think of his want of belief; though to do him justice, he does not offensively obtrude it. It hurt me to be conscious that if I were strictly interrogated as to my own precise articles of faith, I should appear very unsettled.

SUNDAY 27 JANUARY. Heard the celebrated orator Mr Cleeve[10] in the New English Chapel in the forenoon. Felt his manner as too theatrical.

TUESDAY 29 JANUARY. Dined at Dr Webster's with Sir Charles and Miss Preston, Mr Seton on Leith Walk's family, etc., an excellent dinner and enough of claret. Being pretty well warmed, I was foolishly amorous, but shall register no more. Went to a concert for the benefit of the music of the Defensive Band. Was noisy. Got General Mure Campbell and Colonel Craufurd to go and sup at Fortune's. I drank negus, and we parted about twelve.

WEDNESDAY 30 JANUARY. Had been restless all night. Was ill in the morning and lay all forenoon, as the Court did not sit today. Rose, and *thought* solemnly of this anniversary,[11] though I did not keep it publicly. Dined at Lord Monboddo's with Mr Bligh, the circumnavigator, Dr Gillespie, etc.; drank port and water, had good conversation, and came home well.

SATURDAY 2 FEBRUARY. Walked out with my brother John and showed him

---

8 William Bligh (1754-1817), who was to achieve particular fame as the captain of the *Bounty* at the time of the mutiny in 1789.
9 "Boswell *hoped* he would be 'of Panmure', but the Court of Session ruled otherwise" (*Laird*, p. 422, n. 8).
10 The Rev. John Cleeve.
11 The anniversary of the execution of Charles I.

our country-house at Drumsheugh. Sandy was with us. They returned to town, while I paid a visit to Lady Colville and Lord Kellie.[12] John and Grange dined and drank tea with us. John drank rather too much. He was more sulky than usual today. I was heated with wine and was foolishly licentious in Liberton's Wynd[13] with the landlady, whom I had never seen before. Would not with P.C.,[14] as now married.

MONDAY 4 FEBRUARY. In the forenoon I waited on the Lord President; found him ill with a cold and depressed, so that he was more mild and kindly than when in high spirits. I went on purpose to have a confidential conversation with him about my situation with my father. He gave me the same advice that Lord Advocate did: just to be quiet and say nothing. I suggested a doubt whether deeds executed by him would stand. The President said, "That is an inquiry which I wish may be prevented", or words to that purpose. He said that many days my father did not know what was going on in the Court. "He had" (said his Lordship) "flashes of understanding. I alwise knew when he understood." In short it appeared to me that the President thought him in a state of incapacity. "James," said he, "the best thing that can happen to him is to die quietly." It shocked me to hear a man whom my father all along considered as his great friend speak thus of him without any tender regret; and the general dreary view of death hung upon my mind. I then visited my father for a little.

THURSDAY 7 FEBRUARY. This was the Fast by Proclamation.[15] Before knowing it was so, I had engaged Lords Eglinton and Kellie, Lady Colville, and Lady Anne Erskine to dine with us. I was very well pleased that we had them on this day, as I cannot join in imploring Heaven's blessing on the arms of the present Administration. We had an excellent dinner, choice wines, and the best company. The two Earls had never met till now, and they took to one another much. My dear wife was now much better, though this forenoon she was alarmed with spitting a little blood. The two Earls and I sat till half an hour after nine. I was a good deal intoxicated.

SATURDAY 9 FEBRUARY. I dined at Lady Colville's; nobody there but her Ladyship, Lady Anne, and Lord Kellie. He and I drank our claret very cordially. When I got to town I was a good deal heated, and went grossly to Liberton's Wynd. Thought meanly of myself.

WEDNESDAY 13 FEBRUARY. A very cold day. Was shocked by seeing the procession of Wilson Potts, late Commander of the *Dreadnought* privateer of Newcastle, going to Leith to be executed.[16] Fell into a wretched melancholy and was hopelessly gloomy. Called in Forrester's Wynd and sat with a strange woman, I dare say half an hour, but without any folly.

12 Archibald Erskine, who had succeeded his brother as 7th Earl of Kellie.
13 Off the south side of the Lawnmarket.
14 Unidentified.
15 See also the entries for 9 February 1779, 3 February 1780 and 22 February 1781.
16 He had been found guilty of piracy, having robbed a Danish vessel of 20,000 crowns. "The sentence directed that, as a pirate, he be hanged at Leith, within the flood-mark" (*Laird*, p. 425, n. 5).

FRIDAY 15 FEBRUARY. Did very little. I was indolent, yet uneasy that I had no distinguished occupation. Supped at my father's. He appeared somewhat kindly to me tonight, which warmed my heart.

SATURDAY 16 FEBRUARY. Was in exceeding good spirits, just from some better state of my blood. Dined at Lady Colville's, the last day of Lord Kellie's being in Scotland, or rather at his sister's, before his return to his regiment in Ireland. Just he and I and the ladies as last Saturday. I insisted on a peremptory bottle of claret and was quite as I could wish, pleasing myself that the Earl of Kellie and the laird of Auchinleck would pass many good days together. Returned to town a good deal intoxicated. Was foolishly licentious with landlady. Was sulky and violent at home.

MONDAY 18 FEBRUARY. Dined at my father's with Sir Charles Preston, Dr Gillespie, Mr Stobie. Drank a bottle of claret and some port and white wine. Was cautious and grave, but warmed and intoxicated. Had heard today that Old Balbarton had been ill for some time and had delayed too long to call Dr Gillespie, who told me he had no hopes of his recovery. This agitated me. I went from my father's and called on Balbarton; found him in bed, distressed with strangury, dropsy, and asthma. He had the same countenance of tranquillity that he used to have, and shook hands with me cordially. I told him I did not hear till today of his being ill, and found fault with him for not sending for me. He was all his life modestly shy as well as indolent. He said to me, "It 'ill no do wi' me now"—plainly letting me know he was sensible he was dying. I immediately started the subject of a future state. He said Ovid gave a beautiful description of transmigration. He did not know but it might be true.

TUESDAY 19 FEBRUARY. I walked with Grange to Duddingston Loch and saw a number of people skating. Went to Prestonfield and dined cordially. Grange and I returned to town to tea. Colonel Craufurd came in again from Ayrshire tonight, and we had a consultation at Crosbie's on Gemmill's cause against him, which was to come on next day.[17] I went to take Hunter of Thurston's house in St Andrew's Square, my wife having liked it. I looked at it with her in the forenoon. But I found it was already taken. I had brought my mind to remove to the New Town, as better for the health of my wife and children, and as I should be near to my father in his new house.

WEDNESDAY 20 FEBRUARY. Colonel Craufurd won his cause unanimously, which animated me. I called on Balbarton in the forenoon, but was told he died last night. Was struck much. Dr Gillespie told me Balbarton gave his dying testimony that I

17 Colonel John Walkinshaw Craufurd of Craufurdland had had Thomas Gemmill and Peter Gemmill, his father, prosecuted for writing and sending an anonymous threatening or "incendiary" letter. Boswell served with Maclaurin and Crosbie for the prosecution and presented the evidence of handwriting experts that Thomas Gemmill had written the letter. The jury, however, returned a verdict of "not proven". Gemmill then sued Craufurd in the Court of Session for damages. Craufurd's defence was that he had been justified in suspecting that Gemmill had written the letter. The court held that the claim could not be dealt with by them as it could only competently be brought before the High Court of Justiciary. The action was therefore dismissed. The case is reported as *Thomas Gemmill v Colonel John Walkinshaw-Craufurd* in *Faculty Decisions*, Vol. IX, 1781-87, p. 56.

was the best man of the name. The Doctor mentioned my father. Balbarton said he was a good man for himself. Sir Walter M.C. and his man of business, Mr Andrew Blane, dined with us, and we talked of his affairs. But he was too wise in his own conceit.[18] I drank rather too freely with them for my weak head. Grange supped with us, and he and I drank three bottles of strong ale. I insisted on it. I loved it at the time. But it intoxicated me. In the forenoon Grange and I visited M. Dupont and Miss Scott, and I was at the opening of Balbarton's repositories.

THURSDAY 21 FEBRUARY. Awaked exceedingly sick. Rose; was obliged to go to bed again. Grew better and drank smoked milk.[19] Resolved not to be one day absent from the Court this Session. So got up and went to it. The Lords were up. But Lord Hailes was still sitting in the Outer House, so I had an opportunity of appearing in wig and gown. Had a cold and hoarseness.

FRIDAY 22 FEBRUARY. At two I attended Balbarton's funeral. It made a dreary impression upon me. The day was very cold, and my mind relaxed and gloomy.

SUNDAY 24 FEBRUARY. Was at the New Church forenoon and afternoon. In the afternoon Dr Blair preached very well on the last verse of the 17 Psalm, displaying the agreeable hopes of a blessed future state. He reserved till another opportunity the time when it was to take place; viz., "when I awake". I shall be curious to hear him on this. I doubt[20] he is not divine enough to enter into the disquisition whether the soul at death passeth immediately into a new state of existence, or if it sleepeth till the General Judgement. My family was now quite an hospital; Sandy and Veronica were not recovered from the measles, and our other three children were taking them. Some divine lessons however were said. Lord Kames had been in the Court of Session for a little yesterday. I went to him this evening and had I fancy about an hour's conversation by ourselves. I found his principles very lax, and was convinced he was not a Christian. Was dissatisfied with him. Supped there; Miss Carre of Nisbet and Miss Grizzy and nobody else.[21] He was feeble and silent, and coughed hardly.

TUESDAY 26 FEBRUARY. I am really in a state of constant, at least of daily, excess just now. I *must* pull the reins. But I feel my dull insignificance in this provincial situation. I have even little employment as a lawyer, and my mind is vacant and listless till quickened by drinking. I called at Liberton's Wynd, but was not licentious. Sat awhile with the Hon. A. Gordon. Came home restless. Sir Walter supped with us. I have been so lazy all this Session that I believe I have not been out of bed any one morning before eight. But I have not had that relish of bed which I have sometimes experienced, my mind not being at ease but fretted by my situation, so ill-suited to my aspiring views.

WEDNESDAY 27 FEBRUARY. (Writing 4 March.) [E]ither yesterday or today I

---

18 Proverbs 26. 5,12.
19 "Several popular medicinal recipes of the eighteenth century call for milk darkened over a fire" (*Laird*, p. 427, n. 2).
20 That is, "I suspect".
21 Margaret Carre of Nisbet and her sister Grizel (*Laird*, p. 524). For the Carre sisters, see the entry for 29 November 1782 and relevant footnote.

left this my journal lying open in the dining-room while I went downstairs to look for some book or paper, and my dear wife having taken it up, read the account of my life on Monday the 18,[22] with which she was shocked, and declared that all connexion between her and me was now at an end, and that she would continue to live with me only for decency and the sake of her children. I was miserably vexed and in a sort of stupor. But could say nothing for myself. I indulged some glimmering of hope, and just acquiesced in my fate for the present. I was still heated with wine.

THURSDAY 28 FEBRUARY. Called at Liberton's Wynd, being anxious lest conception might have taken place. Could not learn as yet. Was not licentious.

FRIDAY 1 MARCH. I dined at my father's, this being his birthday, on which he entered on his seventy-sixth year. Old Mrs Boswell,[23] Miss Menie,[24] and Mr Stobie were there, but no notice was taken of *the day*.

TUESDAY 5 MARCH. Supped Lord Kames's with Charteris. Heard him against Beattie for attacking D. Hume, which I contradicted. He told of Hume resolving never to write against religion.

SATURDAY 9 MARCH. Early at father's, then Lady Crawford's tea. Then Parliament House a little, very well. It rose. Dined home with Grange. At *Recruiting Officer*[25] with Duchess.[26] At Princes Street Coffee-house with Sir Charles.

TUESDAY 19 MARCH. Uneasy with last night's cups.[27] Was to have dined at father's with wife. Had not nerves on hearing number there. Lady Crawford went. Home calm. Charity Assembly at Dunn's at night. Whist and lost.

WEDNESDAY 20 MARCH. Dined at father's, only he and Lady A. Played whist ill. He said in his old style, "James, d'ye work at this for siller?" Horatius Cannan at tea and consultation. Supped at Baron Gordon's with Maclaurin.[28] Whist.

THURSDAY 21 MARCH. Breakfasted with President tête-à-tête. He spoke of father's being duller, but said, "He may live a long time." Had seen him that morning.

FRIDAY 29 MARCH. Blackfriar Wynd Chapel, devout. Grove preached. Then father's. Wife and two sons there. He pleased more than ordinary. Said of Jamie, "That's a dear creature." Back to prayers. Then walked in King's Park and Piazza.[29] Home. Coffee. Calm, supped.

SUNDAY 7 APRIL. New Church all day. Father's between sermons. Divine

---

22 The relevant part of the entry for 18 February was subsequently removed from the journal (*Laird*, p. 426, n. 9).
23 Claud Boswell's mother, Margaret Boswell (*Laird*, p. 518).
24 Marion Boswell, the younger of Lady Auchinleck's two spinster sisters (*Laird*, p. 519).
25 By George Farquhar.
26 The duchess has not been identified. The editors of *Laird* speculate, at p. 431, n. 2, that she may have been the Duchess of Buccleuch.
27 In other words, he had drunk too much the previous evening.
28 Baron Cosmo Gordon was now residing in St Andrew Square.
29 The piazza of the Palace of Holyroodhouse (i.e., the arcade around the central court).

lessons. With Dempster evening. Saw him weak and indifferent, was vexed a little. π.

TUESDAY 9 APRIL. Still idle. Dined father's. Drank too much. Was heated. Dr Gillespie told me of his filing[30] breeches.

WEDNESDAY 10 APRIL. Very ill. Public at Dunn's. Quite sunk. Afraid of virus. Miserable. Wife had heard neighbour in Liberton Wynd.

SUNDAY 14 APRIL. Took physic. Lay in bed all day and read Priestley's second volume of *Institutions on Truth of Christian Religion*. Less in it than I expected. But had my degree of faith somewhat confirmed. Still afraid of virus. Was in miserable hypochondria. Saw my ambitious views in London all madness. Vexed at being neglected by Burke. Thought I'd indulge a proud distance and just be an old Scottish baron and Tory. A slumber in the afternoon produced shocking melancholy. Up to tea. A *little* better. Thought myself unworthy of valuable spouse. Was quite sunk. To bed without supper. Divine lessons.

MONDAY 15 APRIL. Still uneasy. Wrote *Hypochondriack* No. 55 agreeably.[31]

TUESDAY 16 APRIL. Found Sandy Cuninghame returned from America far gone in a consumption. Melancholy sight.[32]

WEDNESDAY 17 APRIL. Yesterday and today read Priestley's third volume. Thought it flimsy.

THURSDAY 18 APRIL. Was in sauntering humour, applying my mind strongly to nothing. Got into good spirits, imagining not *virus* but only gleet from hard drinking of punch on Tuesday the 9th. Was told by Maclaurin of the death of Sir James Dunbar, Judge Advocate.[33] He advised me to write up soliciting the office. I wrote to Lord Pembroke, Burke, and Dempster.

FRIDAY 26 APRIL. Letters from Lord Pembroke and Dempster: nothing to be done about Judge Advocate's place. Was fretted at this, and no answer from Mr Burke.

SATURDAY 27 APRIL. Wife and three eldest children and I dined father's. First time wife dined there since illness. Virus gone. Supposed only gleet.

MONDAY 29 APRIL. [L]etter from Mr Burke enclosing one from General Conway. Burke as friendly as I could wish. Wife pleased. She said [it showed what] interest [I had]. Maclaurin said I'd get *this* office or an equivalent. Went to father's. Saw no opportunity to mention letter; read it after to Dr Gillespie. In fine frame. So well now that ventured π. Wife wonderfully good.

TUESDAY 30 APRIL. Dined at father's and played cards. Communicated letters from London showing what interest I had. Father was pleased.

---

30 Soiling.
31 On religion (as was No. 54).
32 "Mrs Boswell's nephew, the third of the Cuninghame boys. He was captain in the 76th Foot" (*Laird*, p. 437, n. 7).
33 The Judge Advocate's principal responsibility was to provide advice on law and procedure at courts-martial. His salary was £180 a year (*Laird*, p. 437, n. 8).

THURSDAY 2 MAY. Breakfasted Lady Colville's in fine spirits. Visited Dr Blair, confined with gout. Supped father's. He was in shocking humour. Said, "Have you seen your wife the day?" As if I rarely saw her. Mentioned my intention to go west on Tuesday. Miss Boswell asked if I was to be at Auchinleck. I said yes. Lady Auchinleck said, "Ye'll get cold quarters there." Dr Gillespie, when we came away, talked with wonder of their conduct, and advised me to stay away a day and just to leave them to themselves and see if they would have the civility to write out and order things to be comfortable for me.

SATURDAY 4 MAY. Was told in street by Dr Gillespie that Mark Pringle had got Judge Advocate's office.[34] Was a little disappointed, but soon recovered. Called on Mr George Wallace, and wondered at his knowledge. Carried him home to dine with me in a friendly way; Dr Gillespie and my brother John with us. We were very social. After tea, walked with Mr Wallace in Abbey and St Anne's Yards, and on Castle Hill. Did not like his violent resentment against the Arniston family.

SUNDAY 5 MAY. Little James was in kirk for first time; in New Kirk. When the minister spoke of "the Father", he spoke out, "He should not say 'Father'. He should say 'God'."

MONDAY 6 MAY. Called at father's. Was told by her I should have bad quarters at Auchinleck, etc. Told it to Maclaurin and to Mr Lawrie. Was quite hurt. Resolved not go till Friday.

TUESDAY 7 MAY. Up in good calm spirits. Called. Found *noverca* alone. SHE. "What, not gone?" I. "No. I think I could not well go after what you told me yesterday." (Repeated what she had said.) "I thought my father's son might have been at least as well taken care of as Mr Stobie." She was fluttered, and I think for the first time I saw her blush. SHE. "What was I to do? What was I to order?" I. "You know that best." SHE. "You might have ordered what you pleased." I. "I should not have presumed. I should have expected common civility." SHE. "You seem not to think it necessary to acknowledge my Lord or me. If you had asked if there would be proper accommodation for you—" I. "I mentioned my going. I resolved to say nothing about my accommodation, but leave that to you." SHE. "I only meant to put you on your guard in case you had taken people there." I. "I certainly should not have done that. So far from inviting, I have begged people not to come, even when the family was there; and far less would I invite when the family is not there." SHE. "There is a way of asking company not to come which may make people ridiculous." I. "One does not know what to do." SHE. "It is plain enough what to do when there's kindness." Father came to door. She went and told him. He came in. She said with a sneer, "I've been telling him you're angry I did not make preparations." I. "I am not angry now. I was angry. I thought my father's son might have been as well taken care of as Mr Stobie." Father stood by fire and said nothing. Before he came in, she said, "What's all this now? You said nothing yesterday." I. "I was angry yesterday. I don't like being angry, and I went away till I should cool."

34 Mark Pringle (1754-1812), advocate (admitted 5 August 1777), M.P. for Selkirkshire 1786-1802.

She was so plausible and my feelings are so tender that I declare I was sorry for her, and thought she *might* not intend any ill. But on recollection I saw her devilish insolence.

THURSDAY 9 MAY. I drank tea at father's. His *women* never said a word about my accommodation at Auchinleck, or indeed my being to see it. He was mild and even kindly, and bid me see how many larches were cut, and seemed willing to purchase Haugh multures. When I went away, he took me by the hand, *like* a father, and said, "Fare you well, my dear James." My heart was warmed. I was in the evening hurried as usual before a journey.

At Auchinleck, Boswell met a number of the tenants at the funeral of the woman who had been nurse to Boswell's brother David and was glad to observe their "cordial attachment" to his family. "Was confirmed in my opinion", he writes, "that an affectionate tenantry is better than a high rental." And he beheld "with solemn emotion" the family vault beside the church where his body would one day be laid to rest. "Was not shocked at the thought of death", he records. "Had the comfortable hope of future happiness. My mind was sound and piously calm."

Boswell, increasingly aware of his father's frailty, began to look around the family estate with a proprietorial eye: "I felt", he says, "a kind of exultation in the consciousness of a line of ancestors, and in the prospect of being laird *myself, and ruling over such a fine Place and such an extent of country."*

On 15 May, having abstained from any alcoholic beverages for over a month, Boswell had a headache. "I imagined it might be owing to my having lived too low for a month, and that there might be vapours in my stomach. So drank a little both of whisky and of strong ale. Felt a cordial glow."

Boswell returned to Edinburgh on 21 May and appeared in several cases before the General Assembly. From 6 to 11 June he was at Valleyfield, where he left his daughter Veronica. The evening before his departure for Edinburgh Boswell was uneasy at the thought of leaving her. "Poor little thing, though wishing to stay, she came once back at night and said 'Good night' (second time), and another time, 'Papa, write to me.'" However, Boswell returned to Edinburgh "in excellent spirits"; and his good humour continued so that at the Lord President's levee on the first day of the summer session (12 June) he felt himself to be "really superior to the mere men of this narrow country".

THURSDAY 13 JUNE. I continued to enjoy wonderful spirits. In the Parliament House, Old Erskine, Sandy Gordon, and I found ourselves in glee together. Said I, "We three are well. Are we engaged to dinner?" They said, "No". "Why then," said I, "will you two take a leg of roast mutton with me?" Erskine answered, "Accursed be he by whom it is denied." I sent to my wife that two gentlemen were to dine, and I sent for MacGuarie, who was now in town, and I asked David Cuninghame. I went home with Gordon and visited Lady Aberdeen and her young ladies, and there I asked Lord Haddo and Sir John Scott. Gordon and I then visited my father for a little. Bringing such a company suddenly was not fair to my wife. But she acquitted herself wonderfully. There was an excellent dinner and plenty of good claret, and every man at the table was blood. I liked Sir John as the representative of Balweary. Old Erskine rashly said that he had heard that there was a custom among the lairds in the Western Isles to keep a dunkerer, a teaser, for their ladies.[35] MacGuarie denied it. "What, Sir," said Erskine, "did you never hear this before?" "No, Sir," said the old chieftain pretty sternly, "I think I hear it soon enough now." "Are not the women cold?" said Erskine. "No, Sir", said MacGuarie; "and if you have a curiosity to try, I think you have no time to lose." This was pretty well. I got them kept in good humour. I was in as high roaring spirits as ever the late Dundonald was, with more genius. I went with Lord Haddo, Gordon, and Sir John Scott to Dunn's Hotel to sup with Bargany,[36] whom I had visited in the morning. Met there Lord Cassillis, for whom I had called, Countess of Dumfries and Stair,[37] etc. Played at brag. Lost a pound and was vexed. Rarely does one both dine and sup happily the same day. But I did not get drunk.

FRIDAY 14 JUNE. Awaked sick and uneasy. However, Sandy Gordon prevailed with me to dine with him, and we called on MacGuarie and had him with us. I resolved to be home soon and not to play cards. However, I was warmed while MacGuarie stayed. And after he went away, I played whist and brag and supped and played again, Bargany and Hew Dalrymple of North Berwick[38] having come, and I lost £2. 14. I came home at two in the morning, really miserable, but manfully determining to bear my game misfortunes, and never again to play but for trifles, and not at all at brag.

SATURDAY 15 JUNE. There was no meeting of the Court of Session today, the Lords having adjourned till Tuesday.[39]

SUNDAY 16 JUNE. Imagined I was taking the influenza. Lay in bed till about one. Had excellent spirits. Sandy was very attentive to me. William Lennox[40] brought inquiries about us from my father's. I took him into a room and examined him as to my father's state of memory and other particulars. Found him very distinct; desired he might not leave my father, and bid him be careful to observe and remember, as he might be perhaps called upon.

MONDAY 17 JUNE. Was better. Had still wonderful spirits. Finished my *Hypochondriack* No. 57.[41] The Earl of Kellie called. I asked if he would eat a part of

---

35 That is, a man employed to stir the passions of his master's lady, but not to have sexual intercourse with her himself.

36 John Hamilton (born Dalrymple) (1715-1796) of Bargany, Ayr, advocate (admitted 19 February 1735), M.P. Wigtown Burghs 1754-61, Wigtownshire 1761-2, Wigtown Burghs 1762-8. His second wife (whom he married in 1769) was the sister of Colonel Hugh Montgomerie of Coilsfield (later 12th Earl of Eglinton). He is said to have been "a man of vigorous personality and pawky humour" (Namier and Brooke, Vol. II, p. 569).

37 The Hon. Alexander Gordon's wife.

38 Hew Dalrymple of North Berwick (1746-1800), Capt. 1st Foot 1768, 92nd Foot 1779, M.P. Haddingtonshire 1780-86, Auditor of the Excise in Scotland 1786, baronet 1790. He was considered to be particularly amiable.

39 On account of so many of the judges being ill with influenza.

40 Lord Auchinleck's coachman.

41 On penuriousness and wealth.

a fine roasted hare without ceremony. He agreed, and we were really cordial. I walked with his Lordship to the New Town, visited my father, and took bread and butter and port and water. Lady Auchinleck and some of the servants having the influenza, it seems there was no meat supper of any kind. There was a wonderful importance about the sickness in *their* house. My father was very unsocial. He had the influenza a day or two when it first began in Edinburgh. I came home and eat my egg cordially.

TUESDAY 18 JUNE. Still in wonderful spirits. Felt myself easy and *above* the Court of Session. Why cannot such spirits always last? For I now have as full satisfaction in my own existence as Mr Burke has, only that I wish for greater objects. But I am quiet when I consider that during my father's life, I *cannot* have them. I sat an hour with Sir William Forbes in high happiness and read to him my 56 *Hypochondriack*,[42] with which he was much pleased.

WEDNESDAY 19 JUNE. Dined at my father's; Lady Auchinleck not at table. He said very little. I drank seven or eight bumpers of port, which intoxicated me somewhat. My head was stuffed, and I had a little of a headache. In short, I apprehended I was taking the influenza, which was now raging. I sat a little with Maclaurin, who was ill.

THURSDAY 20 JUNE. Awaked hot and profusely sweating, with a violent head-ache; in short with the influenza. Lay all day in great pain.

FRIDAY 21 JUNE. Continued just as ill as yesterday. If I but raised my head from the pillow, it grew quite giddy. But I resigned myself to my fate, Mr Wood assuring me I had only to sweat. I drank a deal of tea and water gruel and bitter-orange and water.

SATURDAY 22 JUNE. Had a miserable night of pain and sickness and distress of mind; for my dear wife, who had taken too much exercise during the late hot days, had a violent coughing between three and four, and spit up a great quantity of blood. She was much alarmed. I was so too. But without emotion; for I was so overcome by the effects of the influenza that if she had been carried dead from my side, I could not have stirred. Mr Wood was called about seven. He made her remove to the drawing-room and have her bed there for better air. I lay all day. Sandy Gordon paid me a short visit. I was in a sad state, but not hipped.[43]

SUNDAY 23 JUNE. Was somewhat better. Rose about noon, I think, and sat awhile by my wife. The children said divine lessons. I missed my sweet Veronica.

MONDAY 24 JUNE. I was now free from influenza, but it had flown out on my lips all up to my nose, and made me a fright.

TUESDAY 25 JUNE. I dictated a law paper.

WEDNESDAY 26 JUNE. I dictated another law paper; a good part of one. My

---

42 Like No. 57, this was on penuriousness and wealth.
43 "Hipped" was Boswell's word for suffering from hypochondria, i.e., depression.

time passed not unhappily. Hypochondria never assaulted me. I was less frightened for my wife than upon former occasions, except in solitude when night and darkness came.

THURSDAY 27 JUNE. I was awaked early yesterday morning, my wife having been worse. This last night she had also been much distressed. She was ordered by Mr Wood to be kept very quiet. She had read *Rasselas* this week. She now wished to have *Tom Jones*, which she had never read. I read to her. Finished my law paper.

SATURDAY 29 JUNE. My confinement was unlucky in session time. But there was no help for it, and I did not fret. Yesterday and today the Court of Session did not sit for want of a quorum. This pleased me. I should have liked a surcease of justice till I was well again. I did not think of its being of any hurt. And indeed I doubt if it would have been of much hurt. The day passed much as yesterday. *Tom Jones* entertained both my wife and me. I was more entertained than her, having a warmer fancy. But I did not admire the work so highly as when I heard it read in the year 1761 by Mr Love, the player.

MONDAY 1 JULY. I had nothing to trouble me about myself but the remains of a scurf on my lips, which was wearing away. My wife was a good deal better.

TUESDAY 2 JULY. My wife continued to be a good deal better, which cheered me finely. During the course of last week my spirits had been wonderfully good, owing, I suppose, to my light diet and tasting no fermented liquor. I had even flights of fancy in the view of my being a widower. These shocked me afterwards.

WEDNESDAY 3 JULY. My dear wife was worse. I finished *Tom Jones*. My wife disliked Fielding's turn for low life, and did not think even his Sophia quite refined. She suspected Miss Bridget to be Jones's mother from the time that the account of her death is told. That was truly penetrating, or rather sagacious.

THURSDAY 4 JULY. This day also my dear wife was worse. Worthy Grange visited me twice today. In the forenoon I was visited by Lord Kellie, Commissioner Cochrane, Mr Lumisden, Major Preston, and Matthew Dickie upon business, and in the afternoon by Horatius Cannan. I had been visited since I was ill by Mr John Young and by Mr McNab, clerk to Mr David Erskine, upon business. Mr Maclaurin did for me what I have done for him by appearing for me at the bar. I dictated law papers with satisfaction. I made a good many excerpts from *Tom Jones*. My wife disliked Fielding's turn for low life, as I have observed yesterday. But it is human nature. She has nothing of that English juiciness of mind of which I have a great deal, which makes me delight in humour. But what hurts me more, she has nothing of that warmth of imagination which produces the pleasures of vanity and many others, and which is even a considerable cause of religious fervour. *Family*, which is a high *principle* in my mind, and genealogy, which is to me an interesting amusement, have no effect upon her. It is impossible not to be both uneasy and a little angry at such defects (or call them differences); and at times they make me think that I have been unlucky in uniting myself with one, who, instead of cherishing my genius, is perpetually checking it. But on the other hand, I consider her excellent sense, her penetration, her knowledge of real life, her activity, her genuine affection, her generous conduct to me during my distracted love for her and when she married me, and her total disinterestedness and freedom from every species of selfishness during all the time she has been my wife. And then I value her and am fond of her, and am pained to the heart for having ever behaved in a manner unworthy of her merit. I also consider that a woman of the same imagination with myself might have encouraged me in whim and adventure, and hurried me to ridicule and perhaps ruin, whereas my excellent spouse's prudence has kept me out of many follies, and made my life much more decent and creditable than it would have been without her. She was very apprehensive today and sadly dejected. She said yesterday it was desirable to live long for one reason: because old people come to be as little afraid of death as children are. Balmuto visited me this evening. The prospect of going out again was not pleasing to me. I find the life which I now lead, upon the whole, the most agreeable to me. I am calm, I am heavenly-minded. Shall I end my days in a convent? This often seems probable to me. My dear wife's illness was more distressing to me that I reflected she had never had the advantages to which the match she had made entitled her, my father having kept me upon a small allowance, and he and his women having treated her with shameful coldness. When I thought she might perhaps die before my coming to the estate of Auchinleck, which would place her in a situation which she so well deserves, I was grievously vexed; and as a wife is to be preferred to a father, especially when he lives only to continue the harsh and unjust power of a stepmother, I could not help viewing his death as a desirable event. I know not what to think of this. Certainly the death of a father *may* be a desirable event. It is nice to determine in what cases. A son should be able to give strong reasons. I have given mine; and I do not see as yet that I am in the wrong. It is not on my own account that the wish rises. It is a wish formed upon the principle of choosing the least of two evils. In my devotions during this alarming illness of my dear wife, I earnestly beseech GOD to restore her to health; and I vow that with the aid of His grace, which I earnestly implore, I shall maintain a conduct becoming a Christian. *That* I am bound to do at any rate. I know it, yet there is something natural in vowing upon an occasion of deep concern; and this vow may do me good.

SATURDAY 6 JULY. My lips, which had been quite crusted with eruption, were now almost quite clean, the scurf having gradually come off.

SUNDAY 7 JULY. I had omitted to make the children say divine lessons till they were in bed. Recollecting this, I hurried to the nursery, and to keep up the good custom uniformly, made them say shortly. Grange visited me, as did Mr John Hunter, who asked me to be judge of Lord Loudoun's roup.[44]

44 A sale by way of auction. Major-General James Mure Campbell, 5th Earl of Loudoun (who had succeeded his cousin, the 4th Earl, on the latter's death, unmarried, on 27 April 1782), was seeking to sell some farms.

MONDAY 8 JULY. Got myself fully shaved and dressed, and my coat on for the first time since my illness. My brother John visited me in the forenoon. In the afternoon I ventured out. The town had a strange appearance to me. My head was giddy, and I walked feebly. I went by the timber bridge for shortness and privacy,[45] and reached my father's. Found him and his lady and Commissioner Cochrane at whist, and Dr Gillespie reading the *London Chronicle*. The unfeeling reception (at least it seemed so) after my illness and such anxious distress in my family, quite shocked me. My father had never visited us all the time, though he had been once at Commissioner Cochrane's, and this very day at the Countess of Sutherland's. I went up to my father and offered him my hand, which was accepted awkwardly. He never asked me about my illness, nor did he open his mouth about my wife, till after a long time he said, "Is your wife bravely the day, James?" I calmly answered, "She is rather better." I tried to get him to buy the farm of Willockshill next day at Lord Loudoun's roup. But he avoided it, and said he had no money, nor he believed would have money. "What," said I, "will you not have £400 in a year or two years?" "What if I die?" said he, with a kind of angry tone. "Any of us may die", said I. "Hoot!" said he, as if despising an attempt to seem insensible of his being near death or in danger of it soon, at least much more than most of us.

TUESDAY 9 JULY. I went to the Court of Session. I felt a languor which was not unpleasing; perceived a kindness of inquiry in some, which was a cordial, and a total inattention in others, which gave me a just view of how little consequence an individual is. My wife was better. I was judge this afternoon of Lord Loudoun's roup.

WEDNESDAY 10 JULY. My dear wife was so much better today that she went out and took an airing in a chaise. While she was out, my father and Lady Auchinleck called, for a wonder. I got them upstairs with me for a short and cold visit. Yesterday and today I dictated a paper in the cause, Walker against Young, in which the Lords and Mr Russell, the accountant, were all egregiously wrong; and I thought I demonstrated they were so.[46]

THURSDAY 11 JULY. I had a degree of vertigo and weakness about me. But I took special care of myself. Grange and I and Phemie went out in Sir Alexander Dick's coach and dined at Prestonfield; nobody there but Mr Andrew Lumisden, who was very entertaining. We walked in the garden, and sat down; and Grange and I agreed we were now as happy as we had ever been in our lives, and looked up to the skies with hope of permanent felicity.

45 This bridge may have been the temporary stone and plank structure known as "Geordie Boyd's Mud Brig" which extended over the North Loch (for which, see Introduction, p. 8) to the New Town on or near the site later occupied by the Mound (see Grant, Vol. II, p. 82).

46 In this case Boswell was counsel for John Walker, a tenant in Acquhirrie, who had commenced proceedings against William Young, Sheriff-clerk of Kincardine, trustee on the estate of an insolvent tenant of a mill in Stonehaven. Walker was seeking an accounting and payment, and the action turned on the question of the proper times of year for collecting the rents of a miller, "whose income, unlike that of most tenants of an estate, came not from a crop planted by himself but from multures (shares of all the grain he ground at his mill)" (*Laird*, p. 457, n. 4).

FRIDAY 12 JULY. Time went on placidly. I had little business in the Court of Session this summer. But I did not fret. My wife was this evening so well that she thanked GOD she was quite a different woman from what she had been lately.

SUNDAY 14 JULY. My wife was more uneasy today. I went to the New Church in the forenoon, Grange in my seat. Dr Andrew Hunter preached. I was in firm spirits. Dined at my father's, where I had not been since Tuesday, as I was yet so tender in my feelings that I could not bear the coldness and harshness. The Commissioner dined today. He and I sat the afternoon chiefly with my father, who said almost nothing today. I came home to tea. These two Sunday mornings I have made Sandy repeat to me the history of the lairds of Auchinleck, that he may hold the family in some degree sacred. I was pleased today when I told him the story of an old man warning James IV not to go to Flodden, and how some thought it a man in a venerable dress and some an angel or a ghost, he took the superstitious alternative. He and Phemie and Jamie said divine lessons in the evening. At night my wife was hoarse and feverish and dejected. I thought that my sleeping with her might soothe her, and lay down by her. But she felt herself too much heated, and coughed much; so I rose and went to my own bed downstairs. I was alarmed about her.

TUESDAY 16 JULY. My words to the Quick March by Mr Muschet for the Edinburgh Defensive Band was this morning published by George Reid *for the small price of one penny*, and sold at the Parliament House. I felt a little awkward at this, though I really liked the *War Song*, as I entitled it; for though too high perhaps in panegyric, it pleased Crosbie and many of the band, and I did mean it as an exaggerated eulogium, a caricatura compliment.[47] It was *omnia magna loquens*,[48] and there were good verses in it. It is curious how one may be in some measure hurt by the censure of the lowest creature, though one knows it to have no kind of judgement in the matter which it censures. I experienced this today when Robert Jamieson, the Writer to the Signet,[49] told me the song was "too severe", and when I contradicted him, maintained the composition was bad. An insect's sting will be felt. One has only to avoid insects. Lord Advocate, to whom a King's Messenger had come from Lord Shelburne on Sunday with an offer of the Signet for life and being Treasurer of the Navy, was in the Court of Session today in a coloured coat and bob-wig. I asked him if I could have ten minutes conversation with him before he set out for London, which he was to do in a day or two. He said he would speak with me now, upon the benches. So he walked up, I following him; and there we sat in the sight of the crowd in the Outer House, who wondered and

---

47 The only copy of this song known to exist is reproduced in *Laird* following p. 250. The song opens with the words:

> Colonel Crosbie takes the field,
> To France and Spain he will not yield,
> But still maintain his high command
> At the head of the noble Defensive Band.

48 "'Putting everything in grand style' (Horace, *Satires*, I. iii. 13)" (*Laird*, p. 460, n. 4).
49 Robert Jamieson, W.S. (admitted 2 January 1759), son of a merchant in Aberdeen, died 1808.

conjectured while we talked seriously and confidentially. I told him I was doing very well here, but I wished for something better. "You would have something in the other end of the island", said he. I said yes. But I consulted him if my wish was irrational and ought to be checked. He said no. I told him that I had been so often amongst the people there, I felt myself so much at home there, I had such a desire for something upon a larger scale and being connected with matters of consequence, that I was very desirous of being employed in London. I said I had no right to ask him but old hereditary friendship and our early friendship; but would he have his thoughts (or think) of me, and see if something could be procured for me? He said he would. He added that it would require time to consider deliberately and give his advice. He would be down again in September. I said I intended being in London when the Session was up. He said, very well, we could talk there. He told me that he *knew* Burke wished to assist me. I had mentioned this; and I concluded from what he said that Burke had expressed himself warmly to him. I was pleased in thinking I had now another string, and that a strong string, to my bow.

THURSDAY 18 JULY. My wife went in a chair to my father's. I met her there, and afterwards walked with her on the pavement in the New Town. The coldness at my father's was shocking. The chariot was at the door, yet there was no offer of it to her. It was a bright, sunny forenoon.

SUNDAY 21 JULY. Having long wished to read calmly with Mr Andrew Lumisden his accurate and classical account of Rome and its environs, I had appointed this forenoon for it at his suggestion. I in general wish to keep Sunday with a good degree of strictness; not from express obligation, but from an opinion of its being expedient and advantageous to do so. But I thought the study of Rome might be indulged on that day. So I went to his lodgings in the back part of Miln's Square, and we sat about three hours. I was quite cheerful and manly, and relished what I read as much as I did the specimen of the work which I had read at Rome seventeen years ago.[50] This was very agreeable. In the evening I walked with my wife in Lord Chief Baron Ord's garden.[51] She was much worse today and thought herself gone, so that she cried when Mr Wood was with her. I met him in the New Town and talked with him about her. He could not conceal his apprehension of her being in danger, so that I was woefully alarmed. He said the best thing for her was change of air and exercise, and if she could be persuaded to it, a southern climate. Even England, he thought, might be of benefit to her if her mind would give her to it. I regretted her having nothing of my roving disposition. There was in the midst of my anxiety and shooting pains of grief a sort of agitation that rather gave a kind of pleasure.

MONDAY 22 JULY. Dined at my father's; the Commissioner, Lieutenant,[52] etc.,

50 Boswell had been friendly with Lumisden while staying in Rome in 1765 (see Introduction, p. 33). Lumisden's work was published in 1797 as *Remarks on the Antiquities of Rome and its Environs.*
51 Lord Chief Baron Ord had died in 1778.
52 Boswell's brother John.

there. My father was in bad frame. I had visited the Commissioner at the Custom House in the forenoon, and he found fault plainly with the treatment which I suffer. My dear wife was wonderfully better today. She walked on the Castle Hill and in the Castle with me and Jeanie Campbell, and was refreshed and amused, and looked like herself again, like Miss Peggie Montgomerie. She received a visit from Lord Kellie after she came home. I walked with his Lordship to the end of the bridge. I slept with my wife tonight. π. It was a renovation of felicity.

TUESDAY 23 JULY. (Writing the 29.) This morning (I believe) visited Lord President at breakfast. Grange dined with us. One evening last week I visited Lord Kames and read to him two of my *Hypochondriacks*: Nos 45 and 46.[53] He was much pleased with them and agreed to revise some more numbers. So I sent him yesterday the first forty. So long ago as 1762, as appears from my journal at the time, he recommended to me to write essays of that kind.[54] I put him in mind of this; and as I had never since my return from abroad communicated any of my writings to him, I thought I would pay him a compliment now. His criticisms might do me some good. After dinner today Grange and I walked down to Leith sands in our usual way to see a race. Surgeon Wood joined us. I was in strong spirits, which I never recollect to have been at the time of the races, hypochondria being by some curious periodical influence always with me at that time. I got up to the magistrates' scaffold at the distance post and saw the whole round very well. There was an excellent match between a horse of Duke Hamilton's and a mare of a Squire Wetherell's for the King's Purse. I was entertained much, though a little disturbed by the thought that the poor animals suffered. I again slept with my wife. π.

WEDNESDAY 24 JULY. I went with Mr Maclaurin in his coach and paid a visit to Lord Covington in the forenoon.[55] We found him walking in his garden, and he stated a plea he had against Mr Baron Gordon, holding Mr Maclaurin by the neck of his waistcoat, with all the recollection and keenness he had ever shown at the *fore bar*. It was about dung and furniture bought from him at Craighouse. He grew so warm he once swore by his Maker (pronouncing the awful name). He took himself, and said "Beg pardon for swearing." My wife went in a chair to Lady Colville's; drank tea. I met her there. The ladies only at home. Grange supped with us. I was very well. π.

THURSDAY 25 JULY. I supped at my father's. He was in a pretty good frame, though dull. One evening this summer he observed to me that I was sadly fallen out of business, for he seldom saw my name at printed papers. As my *noverca* was present, I waived the subject. But it hurt me. I however observed that a man could not solicit business. π.

FRIDAY 26 JULY. I was in a roving frame and wished to dine at Lady Colville's with Lord Kellie. Lady Anne happened to call. Phemie and I walked out with her. I had a good day of it. No company there. But, for the first time since I had

---

53 No. 45 was on parents and children; No. 46 was on parents and children and education.
54 Journal, 14 October 1762.
55 Lord Covington was at this time residing in Restalrig, to the east of the city.

the influenza, I drank a good many glasses of wine: two or three of port, and a third share of two bottles of claret. This disturbed me considerably. The Earl and the ladies went to town. I took a long walk in the garden and round the place with my old friend Andrew, who told me that all he wished was to pass his time agreeably, but it was hard he should be miserable from some disorder in his stomach, or some other unknown cause. That he had been quite well for some time last winter in London. But, he knew not how, had grown dreary again. On comparing notes, I found he differed from me in this: that he at no time had any ambition or the least inclination to distinguish himself in active life, having a perpetual consciousness or imagination that he could not go through with it.[56] Whereas I have a restless wish for distinction in England, in short on a great scale. When I came home I found a letter from Temple after a long silence. I would not open it while disturbed by wine.

SATURDAY 27 JULY. Read my old and most intimate friend's letter with calm satisfaction at breakfast over tea, and was comforted to find myself extended into Cornwall.

MONDAY 29 JULY. I was engaged as sole counsel in an Advocation before the Court of Justiciary to try whether two young men could be tried before the Sheriff of Midlothian on a libel concluding for corporal punishment, without a jury. It was an important question, and there was to be a hearing upon it next day.[57] I shall never forget the obliging behaviour of Mr Morthland, my brother advocate,[58] who had been on the same side of the same question at the Glasgow Circuit last autumn. I had asked his assistance. He called himself this forenoon and put all his authorities that he had collected into my hands. There was a liberality and obliging attention in this which gave me much pleasure. I drank tea with Lord Kames. I had sent him the first forty of my *Hypochondriacks*, hoping to have some criticisms from him. He had read them. But he was much offended that in my essay on war[59] I had taken no notice of what he says on that subject in his *Sketches*. He said he thought it supercilious; and he returned my essays without giving me any remarks. He talked a little with me on the question concerning a jury trial. When he went out in his carriage with Mrs Drummond, I sat awhile with his clerk, who frankly expressed a very bad opinion of him, and promised me anecdotes of him. I asked Mrs Drummond with

56 Erskine did at one time have *some* ambition, for in 1763 he had written a farce entitled *She's Not Him, and He's Not Her*. The work was produced by West Digges at the Edinburgh Theatre, but was short-lived.
57 There were actually three Bills of Advocation—one for each of William Brown, William Ballantyne and Henry Young—and the only Bill drafted by Boswell was the one for Brown. Brown was charged with being guilty art and part of assault. The charge against him sought various punishments, such as whipping, imprisonment or being placed in the pillory, and also sought to have him banished from the shire. The hearing duly proceeded before the Court of Justiciary on 30 July, when the Court announced that its decision would be given on 18 November (N.A.S. JC3/41). The outcome is not known.
58 John Morthland, advocate (admitted 9 February 1773), appointed Advocate-Depute in August 1783, died 1807.
59 No. 3.

wonder how she married him. She said if she had known she was to be heiress of Blair Drummond, she probably would not have married him. But she had but £1,000 fortune, no better offer appeared, and he was a rising man. Lord Graham, on whom I had not called, sent me an invitation to sup with him tonight. I hesitated, as he had not called on me. But I resolved to go. At Lord Graham's there was a choice company: Douglas, Campbell of Calder,[60] Sir Gilbert Elliot,[61] young Scott of Harden,[62] Lord Haddington—not a man except myself who was not a Member of Parliament or a peer; and *I* was an old baron, *moi*. I had one good image: that Burke's indignation when the Members were leaving the House while he was relating the reasons of his resignation was like that of a man at the fatal tree whom the crowd should leave just as he is making his last speech and dying words: "What! Will you not stay and see my execution?" But upon the whole, I was not well, though not near so ill as I have been on many occasions, my spirits having been better this summer than I almost ever remember them. But the *tone* of my speaking amongst so many English accents seemed uncouth. I thought I should not make a good figure in Parliament or at the English bar. We were sober. I got home before one. Slept alone, as my wife was quiet.

WEDNESDAY 31 JULY. Maclaurin, Cullen, and I dined at Lord Covington's and found him wonderfully well. He had on his wig, and was absolutely better company than I ever saw him. It was really striking to observe Mr Alexander Lockhart when past fourscore. We soon went to whist. My Lord was as keen as ever he was in his life. I lost fourteen shillings, which vexed me. I am determined never to play for more than a shilling, and very seldom.

THURSDAY 1 AUGUST. I went to my father's at night. He spoke of poor John with contemptuous disgust. I was shocked and said, "He's your son, and GOD made him." He answered very harshly, "If my sons are idiots, can I help it?" I supped with him, and was patient.

SATURDAY 3 AUGUST. Dined with Mr David Steuart, Writer to the Signet, at Newington, the very house where our family lived in 1745.[63] I went early, that I might walk about the place, where I had not been for thirty-seven years. I was in a calm, pleasing frame, and though I had a very imperfect reminiscence of the particulars, I had much satisfaction in surveying the spot. I went into a park which I clearly recollected, and lay upon a little green rising ground where I had lain when a child; and for a few moments I was as calm and gentle as at that time.

---

60 John Campbell (1755-1821) of Calder (Cawdor), Nairn; M.P. Nairnshire 1771-1780; M.P. Cardigan Boroughs 1780-1796; created Baron Cawdor 21 June 1796.

61 Sir Gilbert Elliot (1751-1814), Bt, *later* first Earl of Minto, eldest son of Sir Gilbert Elliot of Minto, Bt, was called to the English bar in 1774. He was M.P. for Morpeth 1776-77, Roxburghshire 1777-1784, Berwick-upon-Tweed 1786-90 and Helston 1790-95. In 1806 he was to be appointed Governor-General of India.

62 Hugh Scott of Harden (1758-1841), M.P. for Berwickshire 1780-84, *later* 6th Baron Polwarth. Sir Walter Scott was to refer to him as "my dear chief whom I love very much" (Scott, 3 April 1826).

63 "This was probably during the Highland occupation of the City. The house appears to have been the one known in the nineteenth century as West Mayfield House" (*Laird*, p. 467, n. 8). This house was situated in what is now Mayfield Loan but was removed in the latter part of the nineteenth century (Grant, Vol. III, p. 51).

MONDAY 5 AUGUST. I called at my father's, and fortunately the ladies were engaged with a Miss in the parlour; so I had my father for about a quarter of an hour by himself, and found him calm and even somewhat kindly. Dr Gillespie had told me in the strongest terms that exercise hurt him. I mentioned this when I asked if he was going to Auchinleck. He said it was not true; and he said he intended to go to Auchinleck. Therefore the Doctor was deceiving me in order to keep my father in Edinburgh, or my father was so much failed as to forget what recently affected him. I suspected the first. I took this opportunity of telling him that I was now upon good terms with Lord Advocate, and that he had promised to assist me. I found my father's notions of me unhappily very poor. The ladies came. I sat a little and went home. I was a little heated. π.

SATURDAY 10 AUGUST. The Session rose. I felt nothing particular. Mrs Mitchelson and Grange dined with us, as did the young Campbells. Lady Colville came in her coach and took my wife and me and Sandy and Jamie out to tea. The boys were delighted, running about in the garden and fields. It vexed me that they were banished from Auchinleck. I was very well this evening. Supped at my father's. π.

SUNDAY 11 AUGUST. Went to the New English Chapel in the forenoon. Felt an unpleasing indifference, and thought that if I were to become a constant attendant there, I should experience insipidity and perhaps disgust. Mr Nairne and I were engaged to dine with the Solicitor at Murrayfield. [W]ent to Murrayfield by a very pretty walk along the Water of Leith, and over walls, so as to have a straight road. The Solicitor first entertained us by giving us full freedom to pull cherries off six trees richly loaded. Then there was old brandy, then a good hearty dinner, and then abundance of wine. Mr Menzies of the Customs,[64] Mr Andrew Stewart, Junior,[65] Mr Carnegie the advocate,[66] and a Mr Anderson from London were there. We were exceedingly jovial. The two last went away earlier than the rest of us. We drank till between nine and ten. I was much intoxicated, and having insisted to walk to town, fell and hurt my hands; after which Mr Menzies took me into his chaise, in which he had Mr Nairne. I came out at the foot of the West Bow. Mr Nairne walked with me to the head of James's Court. I then wandered about an hour in the street, but most fortunately met with no strong temptation, so got home clear. Mr Kentish obligingly endeavoured to see me home. But I cunningly evaded. I was quite unhappy to find myself again in such a brutal state, after a full Session of sobriety. I was vexed that I had employed Sunday so ill, and that my children had not said divine lessons. I resolved to be more strictly upon my guard. I was very sick. I went to my own bed.

MONDAY 12 AUGUST. Mr James Baillie had been anxious last night to have me to write a paper for him this forenoon. He called this morning between eight and

---

64 A customs officer.
65 Andrew Stewart (or Steuart), W.S. (for whom, see p. 119, n. 44).
66 George Carnegie (1759-1786), advocate. He had been admitted advocate only five days before, on 6 August, but was to die less than four years later, on 19 May 1786.

nine. I begged to be allowed to repose till ten. I then rose. Was curious to think that I was instantly to write upon a case of which I then knew nothing. I soon understood it, and had the paper done to my satisfaction before dinner, though I had made my appearance at the High School examination and the review of the Defensive Band. I was however sadly uneasy. Worthy Grange consoled me. He dined with us, and the young Campbells came in after. I was quite dislocated in mind. This forenoon I had a note from Lord Hailes, to whom I had sent [*The Hypochondriack*] No. 40, "that it was a good essay, and gave an air of novelty to a threadbare subject".[67] This encouraged me.

SUNDAY 18 AUGUST. I dined by special invitation with Commissioner Cochrane, who had returned yesterday from his jaunt to see Craigengillan with Dr Webster. Dr Gillespie was there, and we were social over old rum punch sweetened with marmalade of oranges. We stayed tea. As Dr Gillespie and I walked together into town, he assured me that my father had not recollected when he said exercise [did not] hurt him; for that any motion, even walking round St Andrew's Square, occasioned bloody urine. He said my father showed no more signs of religion than a stock or a stone, and that I must not expect his temper to soften as he grew older and more afflicted with his disorder, but on the contrary. He told me Lord Justice Clerk spoke to him warmly of me and my family not going to Auchinleck, saying, "How different is my situation with my son. His happiness is my happiness. We have no divided interests. What an appearance has it to the world that Mr Boswell and his family do not go to Auchinleck. I have a great regard for Lord Auchinleck's family. I wish I could do anything to make things better." There was a benevolent effusion in all this which pleased me much, and I resolved to be cordial with the worthy Justice.[68] Dr Gillespie called with me and visited my wife. After he went away, I found myself in a good frame, and went to see my father. But was at once damped by his coldness and the devilishness of his women. The children said divine lessons. I had worthy Grange to sup with me on moorfowl and Malaga. I was comfortable. π.

MONDAY 19 AUGUST. A very disagreeable scene of ill humour in my father happened after dinner. For all the money that is spent by his women, there is a meanness at his table in grudging claret, which very seldom appears. When Dr Webster is there a bottle is set down to him; and as it is a great chance no more will be allowed, I generally never take any of it. Today I chose a glass of it, and said easily, "Doctor, will you give me a glass of your wine?" He made me welcome, to be sure. As I was taking the bottle to me, my father said with a snarl, "That's Dr Webster's bottle, man." "I know", said I. "But the Doctor makes me welcome, and I like to take a glass of claret when I'm with a man who can afford it. But if it is disagreeable to you, I shall not take any of it." He was ashamed

---

67 The subject of the essay was pleasure.
68 The Lord Justice Clerk's judicial title had now changed from Lord Barskimming to Lord Glenlee. This change (which was necessitated by the directions contained in his father's deed of entail) had been authorised by an Act of Sederunt of the Court of Session dated 13 December 1780.

when I thus spoke out. But he looked displeased. I repeated, "If it is disagreeable to you that I should drink claret, I shall let it alone." He wished to have the meanness concealed, and said, "Never fash your head." So I drank claret. Lady Auchinleck called for another bottle of claret. This roused him, and with a vengeance he filled my glass with sherry. I was stunned, and hesitated for a little what to do. I once thought of instantly leaving the company. But I luckily restrained myself; said, "It's all one"; and then putting some claret into my glass, said, "I'll make burgundy of it." After this the other bottle of claret was decanted; I partook of it as if nothing had happened, and he was quiet. It was really wretched treatment. [When] I went home [my] dear wife was hurt by my father's treatment of me and thought I should have instantly resented it, because submitting to it seemed mean. She said, "If a father slaps his son in the face, when he is a man, the son ought not to bear it peaceably." I was much disturbed reflecting on it. But her temper is keen; and the Commissioner convinced me next morning that I did well not to take notice of it. In the forenoon I met Andrew Erskine on the Bridge, who told me it was impossible to be happy upon a system. I am not sure if he is right. He said if he could have been a very eminent man, he would have liked it. But he was sure he never could. So he desired only ease. I insisted he should have cultivated his poetical talents. He said he never could have been great, and he did not care for being like Pomfret or others whom I told him I would like to be. But surely the higher a man is in point of eminence, the better, though he should not be among the most eminent. I was restless this night.

TUESDAY 20 AUGUST. I sat awhile with Sir William Forbes at his counting-house, where I find a never-failing source of good conversation, mixed with some local and personal prejudices, but all good-natured.

Later that day, Boswell and his wife set off for a visit to Valleyfield in the hope that the country air would be good for Mrs Boswell's health. Their first attempt to cross the Forth was in stormy weather, causing Mrs Boswell to be "sadly frightened", and they had to turn back. "I never shall forget this scene", writes Boswell. "She was quite gone, and I was in a kind of despair." However, it turned fair and they got safely over. At Valleyfield they were reunited with Veronica, who "was grown a good deal bigger, but had a coarse appearance and the Fife accent".

The following day, Boswell took his wife for a walk. "I was charmed with her looks; quite the lady", he records. And one morning, when she went riding for a good many miles and got into good spirits, Boswell says that she "looked so genteel that I was as much in love with her as a man could be". "But", adds Boswell, "in the afternoon she grew uneasy and spit some blood mixed with matter, coughed severely, and felt the pain between her shoulders very painful. She was sadly cast down, and I was sadly alarmed." There was a recurrence of these distressing symptoms two days later.

On 29 August Boswell set off with Sir Charles Preston to visit Dunfermline and on their way Boswell received news of his father.

THURSDAY 29 AUGUST. Just before roads parted, [came] caddie on horse with letter express. Knew at once father ill. Was not shaken. Into chaise; agitated curiously. Over with Calder, and to town. Rather wished it over, yet tender.

Dressed at home. Then over. Was told by R. Boswell of illness particularly. Went upstairs. Miss Peggie:[69] "Don't go in hastily; not an agreeable sight." Went in. He took no notice as I passed, curtains open. Went round; she sitting by curtains. Shook hands. I asked if in pain. "Has the pains" (or "struggles" or some such word) "of dissolution on him." Her hardness was amazing. I wished to go near. She said, "It will confuse his head. Don't torture him in his last moments." I was benumbed and stood off. Wept; for, alas! there was not affection between us. Went backwards and forwards. Commissioner came; was affected, but with spirit. I went home and took coffee. Quite confused. Over again; just as before. Claud came. [Father] did not know *him*. Commissioner to tea [with] Miss Hogg. Dr Cullen came: "All we can do is make [him] easy." Wife came. Went to her. Stayed home while she went and paid visit, but to no avail. When she returned, I went. Lady Auchinleck, [when I asked to] see if he could speak, [said,] "There's all that remains of him." Wished to stay all night. Miss Peggie like a devil. Went home to bed.

Raised. Went back. Women servants gathered. Miss Peggie: "Come and see." [He was] very low. Stayed in room. She[70] carried off, Robert Boswell attending. Miss Peggie's flutter shocking. Strange thought: "Still alive, still here! Cannot he be stopped?" Breathing [grew] high, gradually ceased. Doctor closed eyes. Miss Peggie's exclamations. Up all night. Young sent for. Breakfasted next morning. Sent for Commissioner; consultation about burial. Over to wife: had spit blood. Grange, I think, dined. [Some time] writing letters in giddy state. At night looking at his Skene,[71] [from] affection and nervousness cried and sobbed.

SATURDAY 31 AUGUST. After a sleep was better. Saw the irrationality of grieving. At home all day writing. Evening went over. Lady Auchinleck had said she would see me. I said too late.[72] Supped with Balmuto, Miss Boswell, Mr Stobie. Was calm and *retenu*. Inventory of presses at Auchinleck read to me. I was hurt to think how easy all might have been made without death. Had visit of Sir W. Forbes today. Told R. Boswell [I] did not take kind his concealment.[73]

SUNDAY 1 SEPTEMBER. Was really well. Sir Alexander and Lady Dick came. Went over. Was taken up to Lady Auchinleck. Doleful-like, really. Told her all should be decent. I could say little. She spoke of three generations being sober, etc.; hoped would continue. Wished me to take W. Lennox.[74] [I said] I thought she had wished Sandy.[75] SHE. "*Me*? I've thought of nothing. My mind just a vacancy." I said I wished she would mention everything she chose. I would endeavour—mumbled. She said she believed me; and the more so that I would

69 Margaret Boswell, Lady Auchinleck's sister.
70 Lady Auchinleck.
71 Sir John Skene's *Laws and Actes of Parliament*, 1597, which included the *De verborum significatione* (for which, see the entry for 1 January 1777 and relevant footnote).
72 That is, "too late in the evening for an interview that was bound to be difficult" (*Laird*, p. 477, n. 2).
73 "Robert Boswell had drawn and witnessed the Trust Disposition which gave Lady Auchinleck liferent of the new house. Boswell had expected this (in fact, he had feared she might be given the house outright), but perhaps felt that Robert Boswell should have told him about the disposition as soon as it was made" (*Laird*, p. 477, n. 3).
74 That is, take him on as a coachman.
75 This is presumably a reference to another servant.

find all right, or some such phrase. She grew moved, and we went away. Had asked Mr Ilay Campbell to come to me. He came kindly, and talked accurately of all particulars. Drank tea with Commissioner. Sorry for him. Told him what [my] debt was.[76] He surprised; wished he had known, to tell father. Told him of wife's good conduct. Evening a little at father's after visit from Nairne and Dr Gillespie. Tried π, [but thought,] "What! when he who gave you being is lying a corpse?" Checked.

On 2 September Lord Auchinleck's hearse, accompanied by Boswell, his brother John (who was in a sound state of mind), Claud Boswell and probably Robert Boswell, set off for Auchinleck. Lady Auchinleck remained in Edinburgh, leaving Boswell responsible for all the funeral arrangements.

The funeral cortège arrived at Auchinleck the following day at about noon. "From that time on till late afternoon of the next day Boswell would have been almost constantly engaged in receiving the gentry of Ayrshire, most of whom would have called to pay their respects and some of whom would have remained overnight."[77] Boswell records that the following day he was "in agitation all the forenoon, and rather awkward with the company", being "confused in mind and somewhat dreary". But he fulfilled his duty of drinking a toast to the health of the tenants (for whom a cask of rum had been provided) and he "felt manly all the way to church, and acquiesced in the course of things". The funeral itself was "very decent". However, as he helped to carry his father's coffin to the family vault beside the church, Boswell felt like a man going to his execution, "being", he says, "hardly sensible of what was around me". Later, in the loft of the church, Boswell was overcome with emotion and cried. It is clear that no costs were spared in paying respects to the dead laird, for the total funeral expenses amounted to almost £300, which by today's standards amounts to about £18,000.

Boswell then returned to Edinburgh, but by 18 September he was back at Auchinleck, this time with his wife and children. It was Boswell's intention, however, to leave his family there while he went off for another jaunt to London. He set out on 24 September, even though, as he reported to Dr Johnson, "my dear wife had the night before a disagreeable return of her spitting of blood and was very uneasy to think of my going away". "I imagined", Boswell tells Johnson, "I could neither act nor think in my new situation till I had talked with you."[78] But while he was staying at an inn waiting to catch the Glasgow to London fly, he received word from William Lennox, the coachman, that Mrs Boswell had had a more violent attack of spitting blood than ever before and was anxious that he return, whereupon he hastened back to Auchinleck on horseback. Boswell still intended to make his way to London, but while at Auchinleck he received a letter from Johnson dissuading him from "deserting" his "station". This at once settled Boswell and he resolved to stay at his new estate; indeed, he soon found that his presence was necessary, for several farms required to be let.

---

76 Boswell had calculated that his indebtedness amounted to £443, but this did not include interest which he was liable to pay on borrowings of nearly £4,000 (*Laird*, p. 478, n. 5).

77 *Laird*, p. 478, n. 7.

78 Letter from Boswell to Johnson dated 1 October 1782, reproduced in *Laird*, pp. 480-3, at p. 481.

Mrs Boswell's health improved greatly and Boswell started to enjoy his role as the new laird of Auchinleck. "I felt myself so comfortable and of such consequence at Auchinleck", he writes on 18 October, "that I doubted if London could, upon the whole, make me enjoy life more." In addition to occupying himself contentedly with the affairs of his estate, Boswell entertained guests and visited country neighbours, paying several calls on the Lord Justice Clerk at Barskimming; and on 29 October Boswell was joined by his friend John Johnston of Grange. However, in spite of his pastoral pleasures, Boswell resolved to return to Edinburgh in time for the beginning of the winter session.

MONDAY 11 NOVEMBER.[79] (Writing on Friday the 29.) Came to Edinburgh from Auchinleck in a day; my wife and Veronica in the chaise with me, the rest of our children to follow. Found myself in steady vigour of mind, which I experienced next morning when I waited on the Lord President and saw him and his brethren at the beginning of a session. Lord Covington's death, of which I had notice by a burial-letter, made an impression upon my mind not deep but pensively grave. I attended his funeral on Wednesday from the Coates where he died. He was buried in the floor of the Greyfriars Church. There was a wonderful indifference in the appearance of all who did him the last honours, except Lord Justice Clerk, whom I observed saying twice with an agitation which pleased me, "There lies all his eloquence." I felt myself quite reconciled to the course of nature, without any gloom; but by looking forward was sensible that Mr Alexander Lockhart was in his progress of being, and had only made a great move. I felt myself quite as I could wish in the Court of Session. I applied to business with independent avidity, from love of occupation rather than love of money, and I with pleasure found that I was still employed, though Laird of Auchinleck. I did what I should not have done when I was in a dependent state: I challenged an attempt of Lord Eglinton's agents to give Wight my place as Counsel in Ordinary to his Lordship. I spoke to Cumming, whom I in my own mind blamed less than Wauchope. I told him both the Earl and Fairlie had told me I was to be Counsel in Ordinary. The pecuniary consideration was nothing to me. But there was a credit in it to which I thought myself entitled, unless there had been different instructions given. But I had observed Mr Wight was oftener enrolled for the Earl than I was, though I understood he was only to be an occasional counsel. Cumming admitted a wrong; and the consequence was, a cause was in a day or two brought to me which had been enrolled with Mr Wight's name. I thought it wrong that the Earl's obliging intention should be defeated by his agents in favour of one of their cronies; and I had spoke of it to Fairlie. They now saw that I was not so simple or so weakly delicate as to permit it.

MONDAY 18 NOVEMBER. [Lord Kames] had been so ill, was said to be dead; had come to town night before. Went to him at night. His clerk was reading *Cecilia*[80] to him. "My Lord, I am happy to see you. How do ye do? Are you here?"

79 This is really a review of the period from 11 to 29 November.
80 By Fanny Burney.

"Yes, I am here. I know I am here, as Descartes that he existed." BOSWELL. "*Cogito, ergo sum.*[80a] I am sure you are here, for I've shaken hands with you. Well, what news from the other world?" KAMES. "They told me it was not time for me yet." BOSWELL. "We're much obliged to them. We shall take as good care of you as we can." I talked of my father's easy death. He said, "Some men die very easily." The thought did not seem to strike him deep, nor did he seem to be affected when I spoke of Lord Covington's death. I asked him if he was writing anything for us. KAMES. "No, I shall write no more. I shall leave that to men who have more vigour of mind." BOSWELL. "Pray, how long time did the *Dictionary* cost you?" KAMES. "I don't like to recollect." BOSWELL. "I have heard your Lordship tell that the scheme of it was thought of by MacEwan the bookseller, and he employed poor Bruce, who blocked it out."[81] KAMES. "Yes. And after he had advanced a great deal of money from time to time, it was like to stop, by which he would have lost much. So he applied to the Faculty to see if they would authorize its being published. Some of us were appointed to consider it, and really from compassion I undertook to smooth it over so as it might pass. But when I came to set about it attentively, I found it was like taking down an old ruin: I should bring it about my ears. So I had to begin it anew. I employed Peter Haldane,[82] Archie Murray,[83] and William Grant[84] to abridge Durie's *Decisions*[85] for me, as I could not trust to Bruce there. But what they did was so short, I was obliged to do it all over again. Pitfour did some which were well done. The difficulty was to trace the steps which led to each decision, find out a *ratio decidendi*,[86] and place it under a head." BOSWELL. "Ay, there was the genius." KAMES. "I have been ten hours studying one decision to fix its proper principle and place." "But, my Lord, there is some difficulty in finding out the head under which a decision is placed unless one is acquainted with the *Dictionary*. A man must be a good lawyer to be able to consult it." KAMES. "No doubt it is of no use but to one acquainted with it."

I told him that I had experienced a wonderful change upon myself this autumn. I had felt a high relish of the country, of actual farming; had looked with eagerness on ploughed land, and upon a dunghill with as much pleasure as upon Lady Wallace. "I am glad of it", said he. "But take care lest, like a fit of enthusiasm in religion, it go off and leave you as you were." I said I hoped not. But I was

80a "I think, therefore I am" (Descartes, *Discourse on the Method*, Part IV).
81 James MacEwan had succeeded to Allan Ramsay's bookshop and library in the Luckenbooths in 1752. Alexander Bruce was an advocate (admitted in 1702) who in 1720 published the abridged *Decisions of the Lords of Council and Session* for the latter part of 1714 and the early part of 1715.
82 Patrick ("Peter") Haldane (1683-1769), advocate (admitted 1715), M.P. for the Perth Burghs from 1715 to 1722, Solicitor-General from 1746 to 1755.
83 Archibald Murray of Murrayfield, advocate (admitted 1718), appointed Sheriff-Depute of Peeblesshire in 1760, died 28 October 1773. Father of Boswell's friend, Alexander Murray, the Solicitor-General (*later* Lord Henderland).
84 William Grant (1701-1764) was admitted advocate in 1722, appointed Lord Advocate in 1746 and elevated to the bench as Lord Prestongrange (both as a Lord of Session and Lord Commissioner of Justiciary) in 1754.
85 The *Decisions of the Lords of Council and Session* (from 1621 to 1642), reported by Alexander Gibson of Durie (who was elevated to the bench as Lord Durie in 1621), were published in 1690.
86 The underlying principle of a judicial decision, that is, the ground on which a judgment is based.

only mentioning it as an extraordinary metamorphosis. I had acquired a new sense.

Lord Monboddo was spoken of by one of us. I said he was not well. He had a bad cough notwithstanding all his exercise. And I had told him it brought to my mind a passage in our translation of the Psalms:

An horse for preservation
is a deceitful thing.[87]

KAMES. "I met him at Gordon Castle lately. I never argue with him except now and then throwing out a sly joke" (or some such expression to denote his playing with him). "He took it into his head to praise Milton's prose. I could not agree with him. 'Who writes better?' said he. 'I'll tell you who writes better', said I; 'Lord Monboddo.' He was down in the mouth. He found fault with Tacitus. Now I admire the concise and beautiful expression of Tacitus. I think there is as much pleasure in reading Tacitus as Horace." BOSWELL. "Lord Monboddo says it is not history, but notes for history." KAMES. "But are they not fine notes?"

Speaking of the sale of books, I told him it was very limited in Scotland, for a London bookseller told me he sold more to York than to all Scotland. My Lord controverted this, and said there were more readers in Scotland in proportion than in England, and more books sold in proportion to the two countries, London not excepted. "Well," said I, "you should know something of this." He said he was obliged to me for a reading of Dr Johnson's *Lives of the Poets*, which had given him some hours of entertainment. He was pleased with Miss Burney's *Evelina*, in particular with the characters of a disagreeable City family, well diversified; equal, he thought, to *Tom Jones*.

He approved of Sibbald's circulating library,[88] as it gave him a sight of books and let him judge if he should buy them. In talking of the sale of books, I told him John Balfour[89] said very few Greek and Latin books were now sold. "Because", said my Lord, "people are stocked with them. I have not bought a classic for many years, except a particular fine edition which has come out, such as the Glasgow Homer or the Edinburgh Horace.[90] There is another kind of books which do not sell at all: the commentators on Civil Law, of which I have a great number purchased by my father-in-law while he studied in Holland. Nobody reads them now." BOSWELL. "The study of Civil Law is much gone out. In the Session papers when your Lordship first began to collect decisions, there is a

87 Psalm 33, ll. 53-56. Boswell is presumably alluding here to Lord Monboddo's action against the farrier in whose care Monboddo's horse had died (as to which, see Appendix, pp. 557-8).
88 James Sibbald, bookseller and literary antiquarian, had acquired in 1781 the old circulating library which had once belonged to Allan Ramsay (that is, the same library to which James MacEwan had succeeded in 1752).
89 A bookseller and printer in Edinburgh.
90 "Kames clearly alludes to the folio edition of Homer's works edited by James Moor and George Muirhead, Professors of Greek and Latin respectively at the University of Glasgow, published in two volumes by the Foulis Press, 1756 and 1758, and to the works of Horace published at Edinburgh by Robert Freebairn, 1731" (*Applause*, p. 20, n. 3).

great deal of Civil Law. Every case is illustrated by it. Whereas now we seldom see it." KAMES. "Because then there were many points to settle. But a man would be laughed at were he to quote Civil Law now that they are settled." BOSWELL. "One should think, then, that as many points are settled, the papers should now be shorter. Yet they are much longer." KAMES. "Because there are more points to settle. At first there is a very gross view of a subject. Refinement sees with a more piercing eye, and a variety of questions appear."

He asked me to stay and sup. I said I was afraid it would be inconvenient for him. He said, "If it were so, I would not ask you." Mrs Drummond came into the room and introduced ludicrous mirth, describing Lord Monboddo dancing the Groningen Minuet at Gordon Castle,[91] Baron Stuart's awkward, stammering vanity,[92] Lord Braxfield's getting himself drunk on the Circuit with the Laird of Udny[93] and kissing her in the coach, etc., etc., etc. Before supper he called for a glass of port and asked me to pledge him, which I did. I declare his judgement, memory, and vivacity were the same as ever, except that there was some failure of animal spirits, as he had for some time been weakened by a looseness. It was truly a pleasant scene, and as I was in sound cheerfulness, I relished it egregiously. It was agreeable to see a man who had been tortured by Liberty and Necessity and other metaphysical difficulties sitting at his ease by the fireside.

Lord Kames supped well tonight on oatmeal porridge and cream and rice and milk, and drank a glass of water. He said the President had no conversation and very little reading.

FRIDAY 29 NOVEMBER. Went to [Lord Kames] in the evening. His clerk was with him. He had been dictating I know not what. His clerk went away. He put me in mind of finishing the reading of my *Hypochondriack* No. 61,[94] in which I had been interrupted one forenoon. "But", said he, "begin it." I read it all to him, and he was much pleased with it. I then read him my paper on this age being better than former ones, to which he listened with seeming satisfaction and said I was right.[95]

I said my never having been at Blair Drummond was really incredible.

I said this was a comfortable night when I had him just alone. He said I was very kind to him. We were truly easy and cordial tonight. He seemed to be a good deal better. I was struck with wonder while I thought of his great age, and at the same time perceived he was so clear in his judgement and memory.

We supped with Mrs Drummond. He took sowans[96] and cream. Both he and she were pleased with my attention in waiting upon them so often. She said of me tonight at supper, "This is a good man. He's very good to us." He went to bed about eleven. She insisted on my sitting longer.

91 "The Groningen Minuet" was either a piece of music or a Dutch form of dancing.
92 Andrew Stuart, W.S. "The title 'Baron' is jocular" (*Applause*, p. 21, n. 6).
93 Alexander Udny of that Ilk, advocate (admitted 4 February 1729), Commissioner of Excise 1742-87, proprietor of Udny Castle, near Oldmeldrum in Aberdeenshire. Died 1789.
94 On dedications.
95 *The Hypochondriack* No. 52, on "past and present".
96 A kind of porridge made by steeping and fermenting the husks of oats in water, and then boiling.

She told me she was sixty-nine last May. I mentioned that it was now two-and-twenty years since I was introduced to Lord Kames. "Ay," said she, "since you and my poor daughter were first acquainted." This was a strange subject.[97] I kept myself steady, and expatiated on that unfortunate lady's many engaging qualities. Mrs Drummond said Mr Heron was a most unfit husband for her, a good-natured, weak man. She should have had a man who would have held her in with bit and bridle. She was not seventeen when she married him. Everybody about her paid her such compliments on her superiority she despised him. She told me how Lord Kames and she were first informed of their daughter's ruin. He had gone in to the Winter Session leaving his wife and son and Mrs Heron at Blair Drummond. Mr J. R. Mackye[98] put into his hands in the lobby of the Parliament House a letter from Heron to this purpose: "My Lord, I have discovered such circumstances in your daughter's conduct that I shall not be two nights in the same place for some months. I am resolved to take legal measures to be separated from her for ever. Make no opposition, for I am confident of success." He put the letter in his pocket, went upon the bench, and did his duty. She complained of this letter as cruel. Said it was like shooting him with a pistol. He went home and wrote to her that he wished to see them all in town, the sooner the better. Before this the affair had become public.

They arrived at Edinburgh to tea. Miss Carres of Nisbet[99] were with my Lord and them that evening. Mrs Heron laid her hand on her father's knee and said, "Papa, for all the faults that follow me I believe you was right sorry for me when I was ill." "Yes", said he. Nothing transpired that night. Next morning Mrs Drummond herself received a letter from Mr Heron. One of the Miss Carres was with her. "Oh," said she, "what is this?" Was in great distress. My Lord came into the room. "There is something wrong", said he. "Yes", said she. "My dear, can you explain it?" Said he, "Mr Heron is jealous." Said she, "I shall never again see my daughter's face." He flew into a passion. "What!" said he, "would you abandon your daughter because a man is suspicious?" Said she, "She must be guilty since he condemns her." He stood petrified, then said, "It is very hard, but there's no help for it. Inquire for somebody to go abroad with her." Drummond the French teacher was going to France with a daughter. He agreed to take her. Mrs Drummond saw her. Was not minute upon the subject. She did not deny it. But said she despised him. Was not much affected.

[Mrs Drummond] gets no money but by asking it of [Lord Kames]. He thinks a small sum will last for ever. He likes to see a genteel table, but were he told the

97 The "poor daughter" was Jean Home, Boswell's lover in 1761-2 when only recently married to Patrick Heron of Kirroughtrie. Heron divorced her in 1772 on account of her adultery with a young army officer.
98 John Ross Mackye (1707-1797), advocate (admitted 6 January 1731), M.P. for Lanarkshire 1741-47, M.P. for Kirkcudbrightshire 1747-68, private secretary to Lord Bute, Treasurer of the Ordnance 1763-1780, Receiver General of Stamp Duties 1780.
99 "George Carre, Lord Nisbet, judge in the Court of Session 1755-1766, had three unmarried daughters: Margaret, Grizel and Anne. They were Mrs Drummond's cousins, her mother having been half-sister to Lord Nisbet" (*Applause*, p. 27, n. 9).

cost, he would sit down to a withered cabbage. She attempted to maintain he was not fond of money. "Why, Madam," said I, "he is unwilling to part with it. He lends it out and he's very rich." She said he had really enriched himself considerably by farming. She never hears from Mrs Heron, but sends her every year £10 in addition to £80 from her father, also linens, etc. She shed some tears tonight as she talked of this distressing history. I sat with her till half an hour after twelve, amazed at my present vigour of mind.

SUNDAY 1 DECEMBER. I walked in the Meadow with Grange. Met Lord Monboddo, who told me he was sunning himself like a fly, which, when laid in the sun, will revive. I was in such spirits that everything gave me agreeable feelings.

MONDAY 2 DECEMBER. Got up early. Was *robust*. Wrote notes for Sir John Pringle's life, which I sent to Dr Kippis by this evening's post.[100] Attended for a little in the forenoon a committee of the presbytery of Edinburgh taking evidence against Affleck, the preacher. Dined with them at Walker's Tavern, John Tait, Junior,[101] entertaining there for the heritors of Carsphairn.[102] Was quite sober and as I could wish to be. I never before experienced constitutional sobriety. What a happy change to be free of the rage of drinking!

TUESDAY 3 DECEMBER. Was in full health and spirits. Pleaded with force, ease, and pleasure. Delighted in the practice of the law. Drank tea at Lady Auchinleck's, whom I had not visited since Sunday sennight. Only she and her sister. Both in most complaisant frame. Curious to observe such a difference in their behaviour to me now from what it was when they had influence and I was dependent. Not in favour of human nature. Sat a long time, and talked much—perhaps with too little reserve. My father's picture, which hung in the room, affected me with an awful tenderness. I came home and sent Dr Kippis some additional notes for Sir John Pringle's life. Then went in cheerful spirits to Lord Kames's. Found him weaker and somewhat fretful. Found Mr Craig the architect showing him plans of the New Town, which he looked at with a keen eye.[103] Miss Home of Ninewells,[104] Craig, and I supped. My Lord was so weak it not only was difficult for him to rise but to sit down. Yet he had his old spirit to a surprising degree. As his length went suddenly down on the settee he said to Miss Home, "I just fall like a sack of dross" (grains). Mrs Drummond said he would not take any help in rising or sitting down should she be ever so earnest, and she was afraid

100 Andrew Kippis (1725-1795), D.D., biographer and nonconformist Presbyterian minister, was preparing his *Life of Sir John Pringle*, which was prefixed to his edition of Pringle's *Six Discourses*, published in 1783.
101 John Tait (1748-1817), W.S. (admitted 16 November 1781).
102 "Boswell was counsel for the heritors of Carsphairn in their cause against Robert Affleck, their probationary minister, who was accused of ante-nuptial fornication, fraud, and simony. The General Assembly revoked his licence as a probationer in 1783" (*Applause*, p. 29, n. 7).
103 James Craig (1744-95), the architect, whose plan for the first phase of the New Town was adopted by the Town Council in 1767.
104 David Hume's elderly sister, Catherine Home (see also the entry for 17 December 1775 and relevant footnote).

he would hurt himself. Most old people were hurt from their feebleness. When I came home, found my wife uneasy with a cold. She coughed severely.

WEDNESDAY 4 DECEMBER. Whether a sort of damp from seeing Lord Kames last night as a dying man, as I thought, or something in my stomach had hurt my spirits, I know not. But I felt myself somewhat fretted this morning, and spoke angrily to my clerk for being late and looking sulky when I found fault with him. I was vexed to feel any return of bad spirits.

In the forenoon I visited Lord Kames, whom I found weak and not in good humour. But he talked tolerably well, and I grew better. My Lord said [David Hume] had no settled character—I think that was the phrase. He said it was unaccountable how he should be easy when he knew he had laboured in vain. He had laboured to free mankind from the fear of futurity. He had convinced nobody but his brother and his nephew David.[105] My Lord said to him, "You and I may differ as to the question of a future state. No help for it. But why will you endeavour to take the belief of it from people to whom it is a comfort?" David said he wished to relieve them from false terror, which made them miserable. My Lord said, "David's atheism was owing to his want of sensibility. He did not perceive the benevolence of the Deity in His works. He had no taste, and therefore did not relish Shakespeare. His criticism was in the lump, all general. He could not see the beauties. He could see the want of order in Shakespeare's dramas because that is obvious. But could not see the fine poetry in his works."

I kept Mr Lawrie to dinner today, that I might not seem to "keep my anger".[106] I dictated a good deal of law after dinner. Grange drank tea with us. I was much better in the evening, though troubled with a slight cold, which I suppose had fretted me. Got my feet washed.[107]

THURSDAY 5 DECEMBER. Was well again this morning. Sat awhile with Lord Kames in the forenoon. Found Mr Baron Norton sitting with him. He was violent against the people at large having the choice of their representatives in Parliament because they in his opinion were not proper judges, and much riot is occasioned by popular elections. I spoke keenly on the other side. Put him in a passion by not agreeing that his running off from Inveraray the third day of a circuit was proper. I mark the debate. After the Baron went away I spoke of narrowness, which I owned I often felt but said he would not own it, mentioning as a proof of his having it his savings at circuits. He grew really angry and asked how I could believe infamous falsehoods of him? I said a very good man might have the disease of narrowness, but "I see, my Lord, you think it a very bad thing." He said such reports of him might be raised because when he first came to be a Lord of Justiciary he found the judges were grossly imposed upon at the

---

105 David Hume, the advocate (and later Baron of Exchequer); as to whom, see the entry for 25 January 1780 and relevant footnote.
106 "A paraphrase of Jeremiah 3: 12: 'For I am merciful, saith the Lord, and I will not keep anger for ever" (*Applause*, p. 31, n. 6).
107 That is, bathed his feet in warm water to alleviate the symptoms of his cold.

circuits, there being no regularity or order in their expense; and it had cost him much exertion to get the better of this. "There was", said he, "an innkeeper at Inveraray who would not agree to my terms of three shillings a head for dinner. Very well. I called for his bill the first day and paid it. I did the same the second day. The third day I ordered my horses and left the town. The innkeeper had provided provisions for five days, so he suffered from his attempt to impose upon me." "So" (said I with a sarcastical smile), "you put the expense of three days in your pocket." Growing serious, "My Lord, I'm glad you have mentioned this. It made a great deal of noise, and I shall be glad to have it explained. Did not the man prosecute you and get damages?" "No, Sir", said he. "The consequence was, he was ever after most reasonable and obliging." "But", said I, "was it not too severe a punishment? The poor man had provided provisions for five days upon the faith of an Act of Parliament, by which your Lordship was obliged to stay so long in the place." Said Lord Kames, "Everybody thought me in the right." "My Lord," said I, "I cannot help being of a different opinion." "What would you have done?" said he, angrily. BOSWELL. "I would have said, 'Very well, Sir. You won't furnish dinner on my terms. Go on, and let me have your bill at the end.'" KAMES. "What, Sir, and pay what he pleased? Since he refused to agree for three shillings a head he might have charged three pounds, and I am clear in law I would have been obliged to pay it." BOSWELL. "No, my Lord, you would have been obliged to pay only what was reasonable; and if he would not take that let him prosecute you for his bill, and a court of justice would settle it." KAMES. "But he would have arrested me and my horses." BOSWELL. "Your Lordship would have found bail." KAMES. "What, Sir, a supreme judge find bail!" BOSWELL. "Better find bail than go away, and, as I am informed, have the bellman going through the town calling a sale of the judge's provisions. But, my Lord," said I, "I'll tell you what I would have done, had I been to go away. I would have sent for the minister of the parish and said, 'Sir, this fellow wanted to impose upon me. I am going to punish him by leaving his house. If I had been three days more with him and he had charged me reasonably, I should have spent so much. Here is the money for the poor of the parish.' People could not then have said your motive was saving money. And, my Lord, if I was a Lord of Justiciary I would give to the poor of each of the three towns what of the King's money remained after entertaining. It is the King's money. My father always said so." I insisted on the genteel behaviour of the English judges at the circuit. He was quite enraged and hurt and said, "Are you come to distress me?" I asked his pardon and said there was no help for difference of opinion. He grew calm. It was really amazing how he could be so blindly partial to himself or imagine I could be so blind as to think he was in the right in this shabby piece of injustice. I made a happy transition to the first volume of my Hebrides journal, which I had in my pocket, and read him passages of it concerning Lord Monboddo, etc. He was much pleased and said it would sell better than Dr Johnson's *Journey*.

SATURDAY 7 DECEMBER. At night called on Lord Kames. He was so ill he could not see me. Supped with Mrs Drummond, Dr Roebuck,[108] his wife and daughter. π.

SUNDAY 8 DECEMBER. Had Grange with me at the Old English Chapel, the first day of an organ playing there. Dr Bell preached. We were very comfortable.

MONDAY 9 DECEMBER. In the evening had a message from my friend the Hon. A. Gordon to come and read the King's Speech.[109] Went, and was truly hurt that my sovereign should be so humiliated. Supped and was sober. No company there. No card-playing. This day, after much consulting about it, Veronica went a day-boarder to Mrs Billingsley.[110]

TUESDAY 10 DECEMBER. Was well in the Court of Session. Only was angry to observe the Lord President attempt to hurry a Petition of mine to inconsiderate refusal, trusting to the chance of the Lords not having read it, or not having spirits at the time to oppose him. A trick he plays too often. Lords Justice Clerk, Gardenstone, Eskgrove[111] spoke for the Petition (Isobel Bruce's), and it was appointed to be answered. Mr Donaldson, the painter, came at two and helped his miniature picture of my wife.[112] He dined with us. I was firm in spirit, so that his infidel nibbling only made me smile. He stayed tea, and made the children happy by drawing little things to them. I went to Lord Kames and had, I think, the most agreeable interview of any. Had not seen him since Friday forenoon. He was so ill on Saturday night he could not see me. I had sent every day to inquire for him. His clerk told me today in the forenoon, when I was on my way to call on him, that he was out taking an airing in his carriage, and I might see him. I called about five. He was then taking a nap. I told his servant I would probably call again. I did so about eight. He was sitting on the settee in the parlour. He seemed to be very low at first. I sat down on the settee by him. I said I was afraid of disturbing him. I would stay only six minutes. Said he: "If you'll let me draw my breath sometimes, you may stay the evening." He asked me how the President was. I said, very well. I mentioned a curious question in law which occurred in a cause of mine before the Court in a Petition this day.[113]

He said there was an impenetrable veil between us and our future state, and being sensible of this, he never attempted to think on the subject, knowing it to be in vain. And he applied his mind to things which he could know. "But", said I, "we may conjecture about it." Said he with that spring of thought, that kind of

108 John Roebuck, a physician.
109 In this speech (delivered before Parliament on 5 December) the King acknowledged the American colonies to be "free and independent states".
110 "Of St James's Square [to the east of the New Town]. Her name suggests that she was English or had been married to an Englishman, and that Veronica, and later Euphemia, were placed with her to correct the Scotch accent" (*Applause*, p. 34, n. 9).
111 David Rae had been appointed Lord of Session in place of Lord Auchinleck and had taken his seat as Lord Eskgrove on 14 November.
112 "Boswell may mean that Donaldson mended or repaired the miniature, which was painted on tile or porcelain. It seems more likely, however, that he now asked Donaldson to improve the portrait, which had been completed in 1776" (*Applause*, p. 35, n. 1).
113 A man pursued by a woman as the father of her illegitimate child had sworn on oath that he was not the father. However, when dying, he had acknowledged in writing before witnesses that the child was his. The "curious question" was whether this acknowledgement would make the man's representatives liable to pay aliment (maintenance) for the child. The Lord Justice Clerk had said that he thought it would. But Lord Kames told Boswell that he disagreed, on the basis that, the man having denied on oath that the child was his, the claim had come to an end and could not be revived. Boswell responded that it had just occurred to him that the acknowledgement might be considered as a new obligation. To this suggestion Lord Kames said, "Yes, that will do."

sally for which he was ever remarkable, "You'll not go to hell for conjecturing."

I told him how Maclaurin had pushed Sir John Pringle at Lord Monboddo's upon the subject, and had asked him what we were to have that could make us wish for a future state: "Shall we have claret, Sir John?" "I don't know but you may, Mr Maclaurin." "Well," said my Lord, "it is true this body is put into the grave. But may we not have another film, another body, more refined? The ancients", said he, "all describe a future state as having enjoyments similar to what we have here. Let us lay aside the prejudices which we have been taught. Suppose we have other bodies. Why may we not have all the pleasures of which we are capable here? For instance, the pleasure of eating. Why not that, in a more delicate manner?" I mentioned, before he spoke of eating, our being told we are to have music. "And", said he (raising himself with an earnestness while I was all attention, and coming closer to me), "and there is another pleasure"; (I thought, though I divined what he meant clearly enough, that he should speak it out plainly, so waited in silence till he proceeded) "why not have the pleasure of women?" "Why not", cried I, with animation. "There is nothing in reason or revelation against our having all enjoyments sensual and intellectual." I mentioned advances in knowledge, and seeing our friends again and eminent men. He was calm and kindly tonight and seemed to acquiesce quietly in the course of Providence.

I told him my father's death had relieved me of the horror I used to have at the act of dying, yet there was something discouraging that one could see no appearance of transition in death. "None to our senses", said he. He seemed to be firm in his belief of future existence. I said to him, "It is curious what a propensity there is in the mind of man to listen to anything like information as to the particulars of a future state. I was all attention to your Lordship just now, as if you had been there and had returned again. And yet you can tell no more about it than I can." I laughed a little at this.

There was in his appearance tonight something that put me in mind of my father when in a calm, serious frame. He quieted me somehow. I told him I frequently could not help thinking my father was alive and that I might go and consult him; and when I was taking care of his improvements at Auchinleck I thought I was doing what he approved; and I wished always to preserve the notion of his seeing what I was about. My grandfather was introduced into the conversation. He repeated to me the pretty story of asking his assistance and how my grandfather came to him and said, "I helped you when you was young. You must help me now when I am old." "And this", said he, "without a blush, quite frank." He also told me again how my grandfather thought it heroism to restore his family, and how he travelled home for sevenpence.[114]

114 That is, from Edinburgh to Auchinleck. During a previous discussion between Lord Kames and Boswell, Kames had explained how Boswell's grandfather had accomplished the journey at such little cost: "In the middle of the day he just let his horse eat a little grass upon the roadside. At night he came to an inn; the keeping of the horse cost fourpence and his own supper threepence. Next morning he set out very early and got home without more expense" (*Private Papers*, Vol. 15, p. 283). When Boswell's grandfather inherited the estate at Auchinleck it was heavily encumbered with debt, from which he gradually freed it as he built up his practice as an advocate.

I was so intent on his conversation tonight I let the candles be long without snuffing. So there was a dim, solemn light, which increased my feelings as sitting with a dying man. Yet he was as much Mr Henry Home, as much Lord Kames as ever. Sometimes death is like a fire going out gradually. Sometimes like a gun going off, when the moment before the explosion all is as entire as ever.

He put to me this curious question, "It is said in the Bible 'GOD created man in His own image, in the image of GOD created He him.'[115] What's the meaning of that?" "I really do not know", said I. "It has often puzzled me. I never read any of the commentators upon it which I might have done. I have no notion what it means. I wish to know your Lordship's interpretation of it." "Why," said he, "you'll think it very simple when you hear it." "What is it?" said I. "It is", said he, "that He has a head, two arms, and two legs." "Do you mean that the Deity has the human form and figure?" "Yes, I do. Plato and Aristotle and the ancient philosophers represented Him so, and we find this in many places of the Bible. For instance, when He appears to Moses He says, 'You may behold my back parts, but nobody ever saw my face but he died.'"[116] "Why," said I, "I like the notion and I have frequently wished it were true, for an aggregate of abstract qualities of extension and light and power and so on cannot be the object of regard and affection. There must be a person. But I am afraid it is not a philosophical idea, for we are told GOD is a spirit extending over all." "He does not extend as space does, and therefore GOD is not space." "But", said I, "if He be of a form and figure, how is He omnipresent?" "He is not omnipresent", said my Lord. "In what manner, and with what rapidity He darts from one part of the universe to another, I cannot tell." This was curious and new to me. I have since learnt that there was a sect of Christian heretics called Anthropomorphites who held this notion.

My Lord took sowans and milk. Mrs Drummond and I supped. I paid him a fine compliment tonight on his variety of writing, from sublime metaphysics to practical farming.

THURSDAY 12 DECEMBER. My practice at the bar this session seemed much better than expectation. I talked a little insolently. "Now that I don't want money," said I, "I'm determined to have it." I meant that I could more easily refute any attempts of agents to make me labour gratis in causes where it was not charity. I paid a visit to Lady Auchinleck this forenoon, and was rather pleased with her conversation; perhaps by contrasting my present independent state with my former uneasy one. I also sat some time with Sir Philip Ainslie.[117] DOUGLAS was in town for a day or two. He and I, Sir Alexander Don, and Sir John Scott dined at Bayle's elegantly.[118] I drank a glass or two and then

115 Genesis 1: 27.
116 "And I will take away mine hand, and thou shalt see my back parts: but my face shall not be seen" (Exodus 33: 23).
117 Sir Philip Ainslie's house was at 38 St Andrew Square.
118 For Bayle's tavern, see the entry for 25 September 1778 and relevant footnote.

port and water. It was genteel company. But I felt it insipid for want of stronger talk. The Hon. A. Gordon made a very good remark to me next day, that "sitting in such company is pleasing for a while; but as when one is sitting with whores, there comes a thought, 'What have I to do here?'" We went and drank tea with Douglas at Walker's Hotel.[119] I then came home and read law papers.

FRIDAY 13 DECEMBER. In the evening I met Young Tytler[120] by appointment at Lord Kames's, and supped there. We talked of second sight. [Lord Kames] was very dull and fretful tonight. He told a story of Sir H. Campbell's son being seen before his birth to be drowned, and that he *was* drowned.[121] I asked him what we were to infer from this. He gave the common answer of the incredulous, that it was by *chance* the *seer* was right; for that a hundred prophecies which do not come to pass are forgotten; one that does is remembered. I said that where one simple fact happens when foretold, it may be imputed to chance. But when there is a group of circumstances, there *must* be something more. I did not push the argument, as he was quite languid tonight. We supped. He was almost quite silent, and dozed away by us.

SATURDAY 14 DECEMBER. Though it was a cold, frosty morning, he was in the Outer House and called a roll of seven causes, not judging, I believe, but only going through little forms. He looked miserably. I mentioned to him his not being very well last night. He did not like the observation, and I think said he was wearied in the evening.

THURSDAY 19 DECEMBER. [L]ast night I sat with Mrs Drummond a good while in her own room. Russell, the surgeon, had told her [Lord Kames] was losing ground daily, and she was satisfied there was no hope. She cried, and talked much of his good qualities.

Pleaded with extempore vivacity for the College of Physicians against Dr Hunter before Lord Justice Clerk and Mr Swinton, Lord Probationer.[122] Was pleased to find my *Burkeish* talents in vigour. Finished [*The Hypochondriack*] No.

---

119 The hotel of Alexander Walker in Princes Street.
120 Alexander Fraser Tytler (1747-1813), advocate (admitted 23 January 1770). In 1778 he published a supplementary volume to Lord Kames' *Dictionary of the Decisions of the Court of Session* and in 1780 he was appointed joint Professor of Universal History at Edinburgh University. He was to be elevated to the bench as Lord Woodhouselee in 1802. Five years later, he published his *Memoirs of the Life and Writings of the Hon. Henry Home, Lord Kames*. Boswell refers to him as "Young Tytler" to distinguish him from his father, William Tytler of Woodhouselee, W.S.
121 "There can be little doubt that the person actually meant was Sir *James* Campbell of Ardkinglass. He had nine children but only one son, who was drowned when a boy" (*Applause*, p. 40, n. 2).
122 "The Royal College of Physicians of Edinburgh claimed payment of ten guineas which Dr James Hunter had promised towards the building of a library and museum, and £20 of expenses. Decreet was given against Hunter by interlocutor of the Lord Justice Clerk on 24 February 1783" (*Applause*, p. 42, n. 8). John Swinton, advocate, had been selected to take the seat of Lord Covington as Lord of Session and was at this time serving his probationary period. He took his seat two days later as Lord Swinton.

63.[123] Little Jamie's rush pained him much. My practice was better this winter than the last at this time.

FRIDAY 20 DECEMBER. Supped at Lord Kames's. Was shown into his room. He was sitting in his armchair. His clerk was with him, but soon went away. He seemed very spiritless from bodily weakness. I wished much to hear him say something as a dying man. It was unsatisfactory to be with a very old man, and a judge, and perceive nothing venerable, nothing edifying, nothing solemnly pious at the close of life. I mentioned how comfortable my father had been in never having an anxious fear of death, as also how Sir Alexander Dick was perfectly easy, and how Sir John Pringle had been quite different in that respect. I hoped this would have led him to speak of his own way of thinking. He sat silent. I then fairly said, "I believe, my Lord, you have been lucky enough to have always an amiable view of the Deity, and no doubt of a future state." He said nothing. I said the doctrine of the eternity of hell's torments did harm. "No", said he. "Nobody believes it." I could make nothing out of him tonight. I rose to go away. He asked me to stay supper. I said I was afraid of intruding (or being troublesome, or some such expression). He cried with keenness, "O GOD!" I went into the parlour and was a little with Mrs Drummond. When he came, he said to her with his usual vivacity, "My dear, Mr Boswell was going away because you did not come to him." He spoke, I think, nothing, till, after trying some sago[124] at a little table set by the settee, he said, "Tell Hannah to make me a little porridge." He had that, and took as small a tasting as of the sago. He then called for rusks and put some into milk and eat a very little. He said, "I have made out a supper *put* and *row*."[125] It was a dreary novelty to see Lord Kames sitting silent.

SATURDAY 21 DECEMBER. Just saw him in the Court of Session like a ghost, shaking hands with Lord Kennet in the chair, and Lords Alva and Eskgrove patting him kindly on the back as if for the last time.[126] The session rose for the Christmas recess. I called [on Lord Kames] in the evening. Mrs Drummond told me he had been very weak since he came in from his airing and had been in bed. She desired I would go in and see him. I first sent in the servant to tell I was there. He desired I would wait half a minute and he would come into the parlour. Mrs Drummond came there and was with me till he was supported by his servant, Samuel, while he moved along like a spectre and was set down on

---

123 On hypochondria.
124 "A pudding made of a starch by that name and commonly fed to the sick" (*Applause*, p. 43, n. 1).
125 "With difficulty, with much ado" (*Applause*, p. 43, n. 2).
126 According to Chambers, Lord Kames retired from the bench in memorable style. "When his lordship found his end approaching very near, he took a public farewell of his brethren. I was informed by an ear-and-eye witness, who is certain that he could not be mistaken, that, after addressing them in a solemn speech, and shaking their hands all round, in going out at the door of the court-room he turned about, and casting them a last look, cried, in his usual familiar tone: 'Fare ye a' weel, ye bitches!'" (Chambers, p. 145). However, Boswell's account of Lord Kames' farewells to his fellow judges suggests that Chambers' version may be apocryphal.

the settee. He looked miserably ill. I sat down by him. He sat silent. I felt no power to speak. At last I said, "My Lord, you show a remarkable instance of philosophy, as it is called; practical philosophy—patience." "Oh," said he, with a fretful tone, "I cannot bear you; flattering me when I'm ——." I did not hear what followed, he spoke so indistinctly. I told him I was very sincere. I went to the opposite settee and sat by Mrs Drummond. He seemed to be very uneasy. He bid the bell be rung, and when his servant came, had his legs laid up on the settee and remained in a listless state till I went away, which I did in a few minutes, after shaking hands with him and saying, "Good night, my Lord. GOD bless you." His servant told me Dr Cullen said tonight he should not be surprised if he was dead in the morning.

SUNDAY 22 DECEMBER. Passed the forenoon with Mr Blane and Mr Alexander Mackenzie about Sir Walter, who was in danger of being apprehended for debt. In the afternoon heard Dr Blair preach to Lady Derby.[127] Dined and drank tea at Lady Dundonald's. I called [on Lord Kames] between three and four. Mrs Drummond said he was weak as yesterday, and in bed, and she desired I would go in and inquire for him. He liked it. I went to his bedside and said, "As I was passing by, I just called to inquire for you, my Lord. I am going to dine with your old friend Lady Dundonald." "Not at that time of day!" said he. "Yes," said I, "it is after three o'clock.[128] How are you, my Lord?" "Oh, dinna' ask foolish questions. I hope to be better in the evening." "Then in the evening I will have the honour to attend you." I then went and dined and drank tea at Lady Dundonald's, with whom I talked of him, and begged she would give me something to tell that would divert him. She did so. I called again on him and was shown to his bedside. "How are you now, my Lord?" He recollected clearly his having desired I would not ask him, and catching me at it again, he said, "Have you been debauching with Lady Dundonald?" "No", said I, and immediately gave him *un précis*, as the French say, of what had passed. "She says she used to get suppers from Mr Harry Home when you and Succoth lived together in James's Court.[129] Does your Lordship remember giving any present to Lady Dundonald?" He said no. "But she tells me she has two presents which she got from you: Dryden's *Fables*, which she will keep as long as she lives, and a set buckle[130] for a girdle. I said to her, 'It

127 "Boswell is being playful. See below in this paragraph, 'I told him that I had heard Dr Blair preach this afternoon to a very crowded audience, Lady Derby being in the church.' 'Lady Betty Hamilton' of the *Tour to the Hebrides* (Journal, 24, 25 October 1773) married the Earl of Derby in 1774, but he had turned her out because of an intrigue with the Duke of Dorset. The prominence of the families concerned and the notoriety of the separation made her a marked figure in any audience" (*Applause*, p. 44, n. 7).

128 Ramsay of Ochtertyre tells us that before the elevation of Robert Dundas of Arniston as Lord President "the dinner-hour of the people of fashion was three o'clock, and that of writers, shopkeepers, etc, two, when the bell rung", but Dundas's making the court sit "late and irregular hours" to get through the backlog of cases "made the ladies agree to postpone their meal till four" (Ramsay, p. 337, n. 1).

129 "Kames and his cousin John Campbell, younger of Succoth, another aspiring advocate [admitted advocate in 1725, died in 1749], were among the earliest if not the original inhabitants [of James's Court]. Kames withdrew from the 'pretty riotous and expensive' fellowship of the Court when he was faced with debts of £300 [*Private Papers*, Vol. 15, p. 272], but he continued to live there privately, probably until his marriage" (*Applause*, p. 45, n. 8).

130 A buckle set with stones (*Applause*, p. 45, n. 2).

seems there has been more courtship between you and him than the world knows. It was coming close to come to the girdle.'" (This tickled his fancy. He put out his cold right hand and chucked me under the chin, as if he had said, "You're a wag.") He did not speak to me any more. He lay with the same countenance which he has had for several years, though somewhat emaciated; and while I looked at him, I could not help wondering why he did not answer me as usual. To perceive Lord Kames, who used to be all alive, now quite quiescent, was a change to which my mind could not easily agree. I told him that I had heard Dr Blair preach this afternoon to a very crowded audience, Lady Derby being in church, and that he gave us an excellent sermon on our years being as a tale that is told. I sat a little longer by him. He twice put out his hand and took mine cordially. I regretted that he did not say one word as a dying man. Nothing edifying, nothing pious. His lady told me he had not said a word to her of what he thought of himself at present. I sat a long time with her. Mr Sandilands, his agent,[131] came. And soon after, my Lord to my surprise was supported into the room and sat down on a settee. But he did not speak and seemed to be very uneasy, so in a few moments he made a sign to his servant and was led away. I came home.

WEDNESDAY 25 DECEMBER. Breakfasted doubly after lying comfortably in bed, quite in Christmas frame, as with Temple in youth. Had a message from Mr Drummond,[132] who had come last night. Went to him. Was pleased to see him in tears for his dying father. Was confidentially consulted as to his funeral.

Lord Kames, who was in his eighty-seventh year, died two days later, the same day on which Boswell set out (without his family) for Auchinleck. Boswell did not attend the funeral, which was at the parish church of Blair Drummond.

Boswell's visit to Auchinleck coincided with severe food shortages across the country as a consequence of crop failures. Boswell adopted an admirable concern for the welfare of his tenants. Indeed, as Irma Lustig observes, "the concern that Boswell showed for the people of Auchinleck is the noblest feature of his performance as laird. Abundant entries in his journal, expense accounts, and other papers document his kindness, deliberate and spontaneous. The cost to him was not always trifling. He reserved grain for his tenants when it was in short supply and other landowners were selling it for malt at high prices; he did not raise rents though his calculations showed increased costs; and he withheld eviction indefinitely when payments were long overdue."[133]

---

131 Matthew Sandilands, W.S. (admitted 2 December 1779), one of whose masters as an apprentice was Walter Scott, W.S., the father of Sir Walter Scott. Sandilands' father was the Rev. Matthew Sandilands, minister of Eccles in Berwickshire, in which parish Lord Kames' estate was situated.
132 Lord Kames' only son, George Home Drummond, of whom Boswell had said in 1763, "he is a good honest fellow and applies himself well to his business as a merchant" (Journal, 2 January 1763).
133 *Applause*, pp. xii-xiii.

1783

After paying calls on the Earl of Eglinton (3 January) and the Earl of Loudoun (4 January), Boswell rode out on 7 January to see John McAdam of Craigengillan, whose beautiful young daughter Margaret was to accompany Boswell to Auchinleck and from there to Edinburgh, where she was to be lodged with the Boswell household. Boswell found himself becoming very fond of the attractive young girl, recording that at Auchinleck on 9 January, "my beautiful charge and I passed the afternoon and evening very agreeably. I was vain of such a trust. I recollect this as one of the most pleasing days of my life: the certainty of being undisturbed by company; looking at books, medals, etc., with a sweet creature; in short a group of good ideas."

Boswell and Miss McAdam set off for Edinburgh the following morning.

FRIDAY 10 JANUARY. [A]fter a very good journey got to my house in Edinburgh about eleven at night. It was comfortable to me to be with my wife and children again.

TUESDAY 14 JANUARY. Dr Webster and I dined at Commissioner Cochrane's. The Commissioner's gentlemanly good sense pleased me. But I was sorry to think he was so old, and when he shivered a little, he said it was a coldness before death.

THURSDAY 16 JANUARY. After making my appearance in the Court of Session, where I had nothing to do today, I went to Lady Colville's and took a second breakfast, Lord Kellie, who was come from Fife, having called on me. My spirits were pretty good. But the enamel of my sound mind was a little broken. Wrote a part of *The Hypochondriack* No. 64.[1]

FRIDAY 17 JANUARY. The Court of Session was irksome to me. Old Mar[2] came to me in the afternoon and absurdly opposed my writing Dr Johnson's life, against whom he had the most ignorant Scotch prejudice. He and the Rev. James Cochrane[3] drank tea with us. I waited by invitation on Mrs Drummond, who was anxious about my scheme of writing her husband's life, which I however resolved should not be done in a hurry. I could not sup with her, as I was busy with law. There was a dreariness in the thought that Lord Kames was gone, while I sat in his house. Miss McAdam is so sweet and amiable a part of our family that I cannot sufficiently express my happiness at having her with us. My wife is now in as good health and looks as I ever saw her. Poor little James is miserably distressed with a scorbutic disorder, but Mr Wood declares it not dangerous. Veronica is a day-boarder with Mrs Billingsley. I am pleased in assisting her to learn French.

1 On change.
2 James Erskine of Mar (also known as "Old Erskine").
3 The Rev. and Hon. James Atholl Cochrane, vicar of Mansfield, nephew of Commissioner Cochrane (*Applause*, p. 29, n. 6).

SATURDAY 18 JANUARY. To what purpose waste time in writing a journal of so insipid a life? I had a cold and hoarseness, but would not be absent from the annual dinner of Mundell's scholars, at which I got into better spirits than I could have imagined. I sat by Mr Ilay Campbell, who had in the most obliging manner given me his opinion in writing upon my father's settlements. I half resolved to drink pretty freely on so merry an occasion, but found my constitution so altered in that respect, I really could not. Ilay Campbell said this meeting grew better every year. I came home about nine.

SUNDAY 19 JANUARY. Had a hoarseness and sore throat, having been troubled with a cold some days. Lay in bed all forenoon. Was not in a good frame, but kept myself quiet. Rose at dinner-time. Miss Preston and Sir William Augustus Cunynghame sat awhile with us. I read today two of Mr Carr's sermons and the first volume of Miss Burney's *Cecilia*. In the evening the children said divine lessons. Sir Charles and Colonel Preston and Sir W. A. Cunynghame supped with us.

MONDAY 20 JANUARY. Dictated some law tolerably, but with no relish. Supped by earnest invitation with Mrs Drummond; read her a part of my notes for her husband's life, and was shown his and her settlements. Had visited the Hon. A. Gordon before I went to her. Was sadly impressed with a conviction of the transient nature of human life with all its concerns and occupations.

SATURDAY 25 JANUARY. Could not refuse an invitation to dine with poor Crosbie, with whom I had passed many a jovial and instructive hour in his better days, but who was now ruined in his circumstances and married to a strumpet.[4] We had with us a Major Poynton who could tell us about the North American Indians,[5] Mr John Donaldson, the painter, and Mr Anderson, Remembrancer of Exchequer.[6] It was awkward and humiliating to see Crosbie in this state.

MONDAY 27 JANUARY. Breakfasted with Baron Gordon. Heard him read my first *Hypochondriack* on saving money, of which he highly approved. I left him it and the next, and the three on death, to read.[7] [V]isited Commissioner Cochrane,

4 Crosbie had suffered financial misfortunes as a result of the collapse of the Ayr bank of Douglas, Heron & Co in 1773 (which had ruined many an estate). This calamitous blow had occurred shortly after he had completed the building of his splendid new house—adorned with majestic Ionic columns—at 35 St Andrew Square, immediately to the north of Sir Lawrence Dundas's house. "For a while he bore this sad reverse apparently with Roman fortitude, applying himself closer than ever to business. But ere long pressing demands were made upon him for money, which could not be paid by the sale of his estate, of which he was passionately fond. These things, and the being continually exposed to duns, soured his temper and made him seek relief from the bottle, to which he had always been sufficiently addicted... By degrees he estranged himself from most of his old friends, who were by no means disposed to give him up on his reverse of fortune; but he was too proud and of too independent a spirit to court sympathy... These things, joined to his allowing a woman of more than dubious character to assume his name and sit at the head of his table, made the latter part of this poor gentleman's life less pleasant and respectable... [F]or two or three of the last years of his life his faculties were visibly impaired, which lost him his practice, now the only thing he had to depend on" (Ramsay, pp. 457-9). He died in 1784.
5 "He served with General Wolfe at the Battle of Quebec and was now a major in the army and a captain in the 21st Regiment of Foot" (*Applause*, p. 55, n. 9).
6 William Anderson, W.S. (for whom, see p. 426, n. 13).
7 The two essays on saving money were Nos 46 and 47 ("On Penuriousness & Wealth"); the three on death were Nos 14-16.

who had been ill, but was better. Felt that the exercise of walking and variety of visiting cleared my mind of the gloom and languor which had for some time distressed me. My table was now clear. I had not one paper to write.

TUESDAY 28 JANUARY. My mind was again cloudy and listless. I looked back with wonder and wishfulness on my healthful state of mind last autumn and this winter till after my return from Ayrshire, which I had flattered myself was to be permanent. Sir Walter, Grange, and Mr James Loch dined with us. Sir Walter stayed tea and then came the Hon. and Rev. James Cochrane, whom I kept to supper, though I was in such want of spirits that I not only had difficulty to speak a little, and affect attention, but was obliged to go for a little and lie down on my bed, just for a kind of relief from teasing pain.

WEDNESDAY 29 JANUARY. My wife and I and Miss McAdam and Sir Walter dined at Lady Auchinleck's; Miss Preston, etc., there. I was dull, but conducted myself sufficiently well. I was tenderly affected while I viewed the furniture which I had used to see in my honoured father's time; and when I passed the door of the room where he died, my heart was touched with a tremulous awe. My client Killantringan[8] supped with us. Sir Walter and his brother David came in late and also supped, and assisted in entertaining him, for which I was not very fit. During this hypochondria *Cecilia* entertained me.

THURSDAY 30 JANUARY. Called on Lord Eglinton, who had been two nights in town. He walked to my house with me and saw my wife. I then called with him at Lord Chief Baron's; not at home. My wife and I, Miss McAdam, and Colonel Montgomerie dined at Lord Justice Clerk's;[9] Lord Kellie, Lady Colville, etc., there. A great feast, and his conversation hearty and animated. Sir Walter supped with us. Had some regret at not keeping the day. But thought it rather long.[10]

FRIDAY 31 JANUARY. My wife and I and Miss McAdam dined and drank tea at Lady Colville's. Her Ladyship was ill and did not appear. Sir William and Lady Forbes were there. I drank more than was necessary. I supped at Maclaurin's with Baron Gordon, Cullen, Drimnin,[11] and Corrimony. Cullen's mimicry entertained us so much that we did not part till near three in the morning. I had a bad cold and drank a good deal of Madeira to keep out the night air, so that I was heated.

SATURDAY 1 FEBRUARY. Awaked so ill that I could not rise, but was obliged

---

8 John MacMikin, Laird of Killantringan (*Applause*, p. 56, n. 8).

9 The Lord Justice Clerk's residence was an ancient mansion known as Dean House lying to the west of the now unremembered Village of Dean (not to be confused with Dean Village) at the top of the hill on the north side of the Water of Leith on the site now occupied by Dean Cemetery. The house was pulled down in 1845. Although it is stated in Grant, Vol. III, p. 67, that the house was the Lord Justice Clerk's residence in 1784, it is clear that he occupied the house earlier than that, for the house is given as his residence in Williamson's *Edinburgh Directory* for 1782-3. "This handsome building displayed every conceivable example of Scottish vernacular architecture, with a variety of turrets, corbels and crowstepped gables" (Cant, *Villages of Edinburgh*, Vol. 1, p. 84).

10 That is, too long since the event to continue to observe the anniversary of the execution of Charles I.

11 Charles Maclean of Drimnin.

to lie in bed till near three. Was somewhat vexed that I had allowed myself such an indulgence last night. But it could not well have been avoided. Rose and entertained Killantringan, his wife and daughter and son, and Matthew Dickie at dinner and tea. Was quite sober.

SUNDAY 2 FEBRUARY. My cold continued. I kept the house in the forenoon. Heard Dr Blair in the afternoon. The children said divine lessons. I was in a dull state of mind.

MONDAY 3 FEBRUARY. I breakfasted at Lady Colville's. Lord Kellie had gone for London on Saturday. The Hon. Andrew walked with me to town. It was curious to hear from him that he had not at any time even a wish to distinguish himself.[12] He just acquiesced in a consciousness of want of spirits and activity. The Earls of Crawford, Eglinton, and Cassillis, and Colonel Hugh Montgomerie supped with us. I drank negus, and was quite calm.

TUESDAY 4 FEBRUARY. Sir Charles and Miss Preston, Baron Gordon, Miss Leslie, Dr Webster, Mr George Wallace, Mr Maclaurin, Mr Robert Dundas dined with us; a good creditable day. Dr Webster, the Baron, and Mr Wallace drank tea with me, my wife having gone out, after the ladies had drank tea, to Corri's concert[13] with Miss McAdam. Sir Walter and Grange supped with us.

FRIDAY 7 FEBRUARY. Felt myself restless and uneasy after dinner. Went down to my worthy friend Grange, and he and I drank one bottle of good old mountain and eat some toasted hard biscuit, and were cordial, and I soon grew well. I experienced clearly that *mental* distress may be removed by *material* applications.

SATURDAY 8 FEBRUARY. Awaked with a rheumatism in my right shoulder. Attended a Faculty meeting of my brethren, where we had a debate for two hours whether we should oppose the granting of a royal charter to the Society of Scottish Antiquaries. Only eleven of us were against opposing. Thirty-seven were for opposing. I was vexed that there was such a majority on the illiberal side.[14] I was very uneasy with the rheumatism all day. My good friend the Hon. A. Gordon came and took a share of our family dinner and a bottle of claret cordially. I took very little wine, not to inflame my blood. He drank tea with us. In the evening I received a letter from Dr Johnson so rigorous against my drinking wine at all, and so discouraging to my settling in London, that I was a good deal hurt.

SUNDAY 9 FEBRUARY. My rheumatism pained me much. I kept at home and

---

12 But see p. 468, n. 56.
13 Domenico Corri (1746-1825), an Italian composer who lived in Edinburgh from 1771 to 1787, was conductor of the concerts of the Musical Society of Edinburgh.
14 According to the minutes of the meeting, the votes cast were actually twelve against opposing the charter and thirty-eight for opposing. The concern of the members, as set out in a letter from the Curators of the Advocates' Library to the Lord Advocate, was that the Advocates' Library had for a century been "the general Repository of the Ancient Manuscripts and monuments illustrating the History and Antiquities of Scotland" and that the Society of Antiquaries might "form a separate and rival repository" (Stewart, pp. 344-5). "Though the Society of Antiquaries did not obtain a royal charter, its museum soon became the depository of choice for antiquarian artefacts of national importance... The Advocates Library continued as the depository of choice for literary materials of national importance until the foundation of the National Library of Scotland in 1925" (*ibid.*, pp. 345-6, n. 539).

heard the children say divine lessons till after church hours (except being at Dr Young's funeral), and then went in a chair and dined (for the first time) with the Hon. Henry Erskine; the Hon. Alexander Gordon, Mr David Erskine, and his brother Archibald there. I drank Teneriffe negus and was comfortably warmed in body, but my mind roved on London, and was discontent, though we had good social talk.

WEDNESDAY 12 FEBRUARY. It was a very long time since I had paid a visit to Sir Alexander Dick. There is no accounting for such eclipses. It vexed me to think of them. I at once resolved to go out to him. Worthy Grange accompanied me, and we found him as happy as ever. But I had not such a relish of anything as I could wish. Grange both drank tea and supped with me.

THURSDAY 13 FEBRUARY. Was weary and fretful. Sir Walter dined with us. His thoughtless conduct and wretched circumstances hurt me. In the evening I felt all at once a flow of good spirits, and with great ease wrote several letters for next night's post, one of which was to the Bishop of Killaloe, a correspondence which I had delayed to begin for almost two years after we had cordially settled it in London. I *must* believe that man is in many respects subject to influence quite unknown to him. I have day after day resolved to write to the Bishop, yet it has been deferred, though I was vexed at the delay and loss of real pleasure from his correspondence. On a sudden I have written to him, and now cannot imagine *how* it was put off or *where* was the difficulty. Father of Spirits! I implore thy benignant influence!

FRIDAY 14 FEBRUARY. Paid a visit to Mr Crosbie, and found with him a son of Paul Sandby's, a young officer in the army, whom I asked to dine with me, that I might show some civility to the son of so fine an artist.[15] The rest of the company were Capt. William Dick,[16] the Rev. Mr William Bennet, and Grange. I was not at my ease. I viewed all things with a sad indifference. Phemie had been tried as a complete boarder at Mrs Billingsley's. But she was so unhappy at not coming home at night that she was made only a day-boarder as well as Veronica. Little James and Betty were still distressed with a scorbutic eruption.

SATURDAY 15 FEBRUARY. Was very feeble-minded. Looked into books in the Advocates' Library for a motto to *The Hypochondriack* No. 65. Found one on time[17] in Josephus. Put down some hints, but was indifferent whether I should write well or ill. Went with the Hon. Alexander Gordon and Grange to Hall's Cellar, near Nicolson Street, and tasted some claret. Was in a dissipated frame. Grange dined with me. In the evening I was quite in the humour of London life, and wished to go to Princes Street Coffee-house and sup. But was persuaded to stay at home, and indulged myself with a broiled bone and some rum punch, which I seldom choose. I was hearty at home.

15 Paul Sandby (1725-1809), painter, engraver, and caricaturist, was born in Nottingham and while employed in Scotland on a military survey after the 1745 rebellion made a large number of sketches of Edinburgh scenes and public figures. He greatly advanced the technique of watercolour painting and was one of the original members of the Royal Academy.
16 Son of Sir Alexander Dick.
17 The subject of the essay.

SUNDAY 16 FEBRUARY. At Gordon's pressing request I went to him in the afternoon, after hearing my children say divine lessons, and tasted different kinds of claret, and then drank tea with him. Tasting heated me a little and made me wish if possible to be a pure water-drinker. Sir Charles and Colonel Preston, Mr William Nairne, Hon. Alexander Gordon, and Hon. Andrew Cochrane supped with us; a good cheerful evening.

MONDAY 17 FEBRUARY. Was in poor spirits, but wrote an *Hypochondriack* with curious ingenuity of thinking. I wrote chiefly to please myself, and with a view to make out a couple of proper volumes of that periodical paper; for my partners of the *London Magazine* did not relish it much. I was not in the least affected by this, because I had no opinion of their taste in writing, for they wished rather for a *merry essay*. I wrote to Dilly that I wished to continue it to No. 70, the years of man's life.[18] But if the partners really thought they could find a variety of materials all better, I should close it next month. It is wonderful how the spur of engagement makes me write.

TUESDAY 18 FEBRUARY. Was rather better, but quite dissatisfied with the narrow sphere here, and perpetually languishing for London eminence. Dined at Commissioner Cochrane's; Dr Webster there. They both approved much of my continuing to apply to business as a lawyer. My mind however was so clouded and so broken that I could not feel with clearness and strength the distinction between doing well and doing ill in this uncertain and short life. Strange that one should think so differently at different times. For upon some occasions I am quite animated with good ambition. I however this day wrote an able Petition for Garallan in support of a Decreet Arbitral which a majority of the Lords had very erroneously reduced.[19] I was pleased with my own powers, while I at the same time did not *feel* that it was of much consequence to have talents. Such was the state of my mind.

WEDNESDAY 19 FEBRUARY. Felt all at once in the Court of Session a happy state of mind which made me view it with complacency instead of disgust. I wondered, while I experienced how little reality there is in external things. I went and visited Lord Gardenstone, who was confined to the house, this forenoon.[20] I had not visited him for many years, I know not why. I found his conversation both substantial and animated; and as we are prone to look at objects

18 The series duly ended with the essay No. 70, published in August 1783.
19 "The late Robert and William Alexander in 1778 had exercised their privilege of mining coal at Dalmelling, that portion of the estate of Blackhouse, Ayr, which Patrick Douglas of Garallan held on a long lease. Eight of the ten enclosures were so affected that the subtenants would not pay rent to Douglas. Compensation for damages went to arbitration, but the Alexanders appealed the award to the Lords of Session. They decided for the appellants 7 February 1783. Boswell asserted in his Petition for Douglas that only the arbiters were empowered to set damages, and that their settlement was just because waste from the mines had damaged farms and crops on which the mines did not actually sit" (*Applause*, p. 61, n. 5).
20 Williamson's *Edinburgh Directory* for 1782-83 gives Lord Gardenstone's address as Fountainbridge, which in those days was "a long and straggling suburb... among fields and gardens" containing "several old-fashioned villas with pleasure grounds, and... bordered on its northern side by a wooded residence, the Grove" (Grant, Vol. II, p. 218).

with the eyes of those with whom we are at the time, if we have any respect for their faculties, I was the better for hearing him give an account of his views of life. He told me he never had higher views than to be a judge in Scotland, and he was made a judge in his forty-second year. I asked him if he never had high ambitious views, which make me unhappy. He said never. Nay, he had his mind prepared for being disappointed of a judge's place, and was to have retired to the country. He said he never had five minutes' uneasiness at a time except from a bad hand at whist or a bad partner. All this (if true) was sound philosophy, and I thought I might have it. But it was being contented with a lower state than what my keen and constant wishes for years have prompted, and which I have an impression I ought not to despair of obtaining. The great difficulty is to settle between foolish fancy and spirited ambition; and probably I shall dream and balance till it is too late to exert.

THURSDAY 20 FEBRUARY. I called a little on Maclaurin after dinner. Went to the Pantheon in the evening to hear a debate on this curious question: whether it was most culpable for a young woman to marry an old man or for an old woman to marry a young man. But it was so crowded and blackguard, I soon left it in disgust. Grange supped with us. I was now happy in the consciousness that I had written every letter which I had any call to write, and in short that I was upon very even terms with my duty in life in small or in great things. I had not much practice in the Court of Session. But I did well what was entrusted to me. I had a regular weekly return of work and weather from Mr James Bruce, my faithful overseer at Auchinleck, and I wrote to him as regularly.

SATURDAY 22 FEBRUARY. I took a walk to Leith and paid a visit to David Boswell and his wife. Poor man, though he be a dancing-master, he is a branch of the family of Auchinleck, and gets his bread honestly. I regret that my wife will not receive him and his wife to dine with us privately. She is wrong. I am however to have him to dine with me soon. I met Colonel Montgomerie a little before dinner in Princes Street, and engaged him to dine with us without ceremony. We had also the Laird of Fairlie, Mr Thomas Smith, Craigengillan's agent (first time), young Craigengillan and his tutor, and the young Campbells. I was quite sober, and was truly happy to find that the rage for strong liquor, which used to vex me, had ceased. Such is the agreeable change which I have experienced in my constitution within these seven or eight months. In the evening I accompanied Colonel Montgomerie to Fortune's, where he was engaged with a party, all of my acquaintance but one, to sup and hear MacLauchlan, the excellent fiddler, play Highland tunes. I drank a little weak gin punch without souring, and relished the fiddler's music and the company so well that I did not get home till about two in the morning. But I was not in the least inflamed. I thought in my chair coming home of Dr Johnson's observation that no society is so agreeable as that in a tavern. My rheumatism was now gone. But a large pimple on one of my hands had turned to a sore which was painful and troubled me. I am too easily troubled.

MONDAY 24 FEBRUARY. [D]ictated law papers pretty well. Was at a meeting of proprietors of land to consider of an application to Parliament to improve the rights of voting in our counties; was in such low spirits that it seemed to me a matter of indifference. There was a fire in the close next to our court just before dinner, which gave some alarm but was extinguished. Grange dined with us. Mr George Wallace and the Hon. Alexander Gordon, who came to inquire how we were, drank some wine.

TUESDAY 25 FEBRUARY. Had a large company at dinner: Lord Gardenstone, who had never before been with me, Lord Eskgrove, the successor of my father on the bench, Commissioner Cochrane, etc. Had no vivid enjoyment, but in a discontented frame speculated on every man's situation who was at table compared with my own, but relished none of them. Languished for London, Parliament, or any state of animated exertion. Was vexed this forenoon by hearing the Lord President and several others of the judges give what I thought most erroneous opinions against my client Garallan, though Lords Braxfield, Monboddo, Hailes, and others were for him.[21] Perhaps it is a weakness to be hurt like Heraclitus at observing the faults of human nature. But I cannot help it.

WEDNESDAY 26 FEBRUARY. Mr R. Mackintosh, who after an absence of many years appeared at our bar today to support the Earl of Crawford against Lady Mary Campbell's claim for the family estate, interested me as an able unfortunate man. His stately appearance too had influence upon me. I had been very keen against him in his contest with my friend Dempster, and knew not how he might think of me. Yet I wished to show him attention. He addressed himself to me very politely, and I sat down by him and had some good talk. There was something curious in seeing him in the Court again after so long an absence, and something humbling to think that it was much diminished in dignity and abilities since he left it.[22] I dictated a great deal today, having several law papers to write. I was sensible that I was not fit to go through a great deal of business.

21 "On 29 July 1783 the Lords of Session adhered to their decision reducing the award for damages made in the Decreet Arbitral" (*Applause*, p. 64, n. 6).

22 Robert Mackintosh (or MacIntosh) (1727-1805), advocate (admitted 30 July 1751). Although a "sober, serious" man who built up a good practice, he was "filled with self-conceit and an overweening fondness for his own opinions" and "his overbearing turn in conversation as well as in business, created an unspeakable prejudice to him, and proved a great obstruction to his success", so that "in an evil hour he resolved to quit the Scottish bar, at a time when it was evidently his interest to have persevered" (Ramsay, pp. 416-420). In or about 1761 he moved to London, where he came successively under the patronage of the Duke of Queensberry, Earl Temple and the first Lord Clive. In the General Election of 1768 Mackintosh stood against Boswell's friend George Dempster for the Perth Burghs, but without success. Before the election took place Mackintosh commenced a private prosecution against Dempster in the Court of Justiciary for bribery and corruption and at the last moment Dempster withdrew his candidacy, thus allowing his substitute (his friend William Pulteney) to win the seat; but after protracted debates the court held that Mackintosh's case be dismissed, and Dempster ultimately regained the seat at the by-election in 1769 (Namier and Brooke, Vol. I, p. 509). Mackintosh then became involved with the York Building Company, which had acquired a number of Scottish estates forfeited as a consequence of the Jacobite Rebellion of 1715. Having become the principal shareholder in the company, and subsequently Governor of the company, he set about trying to dispose of some of the company's valuable estates, resulting in acrimonious, expensive and seemingly endless litigation. It was with a view to pursuing these cases that Mackintosh returned to the Scottish bar, at which he had last appeared almost twenty-two years earlier.

Yet I repined that I had too little; though I considered that a gentleman of good fortune never gets much practice at our bar, and that I had more than anyone in that situation ever had. Grange and Mr Lawrie dined with us. Formerly Mr Lawrie used to eat almost constantly at my table, but it being disagreeable to my wife and indeed to myself to have him constantly since he had a family of his own, I invite him rarely.

THURSDAY 27 FEBRUARY. I went in the forenoon and paid a visit to Mr R. Mackintosh at Paterson the stabler's in the Pleasance; I found him surrounded with law books and papers and quite like a man immersed in business. He talked in a style much above common, with a force and a command of expression and a manly manner which I admired, while I felt for him on account of the state of his affairs, which I was told was bad. I paid him much attention, partly from benevolence, partly from my never-failing wish to know distinguished men. Clerk Matthew[23] and some more secondary company dined with us. In the evening I was sadly shocked by a visit of Mr Crosbie's clerk, Mr Maule, who with tears in his eyes showed me a letter to his master telling him that if he did not pay fifteen guineas, he should be apprehended next day. I had been put upon my guard against applications for money from that quarter, and told what was true: that I had at present no money but what I borrowed; and so waived the demand at the time, but said I should endeavour to get the affair settled next morning, which indeed I hoped to do with the assistance of others at the bar. How wretched a change was it for a man of uncommon knowledge, abilities, and spirit to be thus in danger of imprisonment for a small sum!

FRIDAY 28 FEBRUARY. Maclaurin accosted me in the Court of Session thus: "You would do nothing last night for an old friend", and told me that Mr Ilay Campbell had paid ten and he five guineas to relieve Crosbie. I was uneasy a little to think that my benevolence might be suspected. Yet I was conscious how sincerely I felt for Crosbie, and that in case of necessity, I should have advanced the fifteen guineas for him, though I doubted if it would be right to contract more debt while in reality I as yet owed more than my funds could discharge. And Maclaurin observed that it was wrong in Crosbie to take money from one of us and give to any other person. It would be better for him to clear himself by a *cessio bonorum*, and then take aids from his friends. I had this evening Mr R. Mackintosh, Mr Ilay Campbell (appointed Solicitor-General), Mr George Wallace, the Laird of Fairlie, and Grange at supper. I drank almost a bottle of claret, as we sat till near three in the morning. Mackintosh harangued fluently but with too much vanity. Mr Campbell was as usual silent and indifferent. But he gave a wonderful testimony of his confined Scottish views. He said Sir Gilbert Elliot and Lord Advocate, he thought, would have done better to have continued at the bar here. I exclaimed, "I would rather have vital motion in the House of Commons than be Lord President of the Court of Session." Mackintosh seemed to think of returning to the practice of the law here, as there was

23 Matthew Dickie.

now a great opening for one of his seniority and abilities. The Solicitor encouraged him to return. I secretly dreaded that he might be mortified by neglect.[24]

SUNDAY 2 MARCH. I have for some time been in a state of mind not so bad as miserable, but insipid and uneasy, having no pursuits that animate me, and viewing life as hardly worth being in earnest. I am lamentably indifferent to religion. It is amazing how very different I am at different times.

MONDAY 3 MARCH. Had Mr James Donaldson at dinner. His petulance was displeasing. But I take notice of him on his father's account.[25] Was at Barnard's ball at night and saw my daughters dance. First time of my being at a public place since my father's death, and this was a kind of duty. My wife got a fright with a carriage coming near a chair in which were two of our children, which made her spit blood.

THURSDAY 6 MARCH. Dictated a paper of forty pages for the proprietors of the Edinburgh and Dumfries Fly against a judgement obtained against them by Dalziel, one of their number.[26] Was pleased with my abilities.

SATURDAY 8 MARCH. I dined at Lord Eskgrove's with Lord Alva and son, Maclaurin, etc. Drank so much as to be a little heated. But our conversation was pretty good. Lord Eskgrove made a pretty just remark which was new to me: that decisions of the courts in England are not found fault with as in Scotland, because *there* a number of lawyers who are not in a cause attend to it and form an impartial opinion. Whereas here, except in a very few instances, no lawyers attend to a cause except those interested in it, so that in every case there is one side to rail from prejudice or bias.

SUNDAY 9 MARCH. Little James, who had been very ill from the effects of mercury given him for his scorbutic complaint, was now a good deal better. His mother and I had a sad alarm about him. She had no return of the spitting of blood.

TUESDAY 11 MARCH. The Lords of Session disregarded my paper for the fly proprietors. I was so much hurt by what I thought gross injustice that I really inclined never to enter the Court again. I thought of setting out for London next morning, but resolved to stay two days quietly and write *The Hypochondriack* No. 66.

24 The outcome was as Boswell feared, for although Mackintosh appeared in some notable causes he failed to attract much business, being largely unknown to the legal agents of the day except as a person with a reputation for being unpopular. He retired from public life, seldom if ever venturing from his house in Argyle Square, and he died unmarried.

25 James Donaldson (died 1830), son of the publisher Alexander Donaldson, succeeded to his father's business and made a fortune, the bulk of which he bequeathed for the foundation of a hospital for the maintenance and education of poor children. The hospital, erected between 1842 and 1851 on ground near Murrayfield and built to the magnificent designs of William Playfair, became known as Donaldson's Hospital (now Donaldson's School for the Deaf).

26 Nothing is known about this cause other than the identity of the litigants. "Boswell's clients were Hugh Cameron, innkeeper and stabler at the Cowgate Head [the west end of the Cowgate by the Grassmarket], from which the fly to London by way of Dumfries and Carlisle set out, and John McVities, innkeeper of the George, at Dumfries. George Dalziel kept a famous posting establishment and inn at Noblehouse, Peeblesshire, seventy miles south-west of Edinburgh" (*Applause*, p. 68, n. 1).

WEDNESDAY 12 MARCH. After much search among books in the Advocates' Library, found a good motto for keeping a diary, the subject of No. 66.

On 14 March Boswell set off for another visit to London, stopping off on the way at Moffat to see his brother John who was living there and was in a sound state of mind. Boswell reached London on the evening of the 20th and immediately went to Charles Dilly's house. The following day, he says, "[I] felt a steadiness as Laird of Auchinleck which I never before experienced in London."

On calling on Dr Johnson, Boswell found his old friend to be unwell, looking very pale and suffering from a breathing difficulty. However, Johnson later recovered somewhat, enabling Boswell to have many conversations with him and to record another good crop of memorable sayings.

Boswell's brother David had now become settled in London as a banker, but Boswell found his brother's "cold formality" displeasing. On the other hand, the members of Boswell's usual circle of London friends, such as Burke, Sir Joshua Reynolds and General Paoli, were most welcoming. Indeed, Boswell discovered that his room at Paoli's house was in readiness for him, and he was soon comfortably at home there.

Boswell was still hoping, through the influence of Lord Mounstuart, to obtain some good office, preferably in London. "I am clearly persuaded", he reflected, "that a man of my family, talents, and connexions may reasonably endeavour to be employed in a more elevated sphere than in Scotland, now that is in reality only a province. But if I find after some time that there is little hope of being so employed, I shall set my mind to be satisfied with a judge's place in Scotland."[27] However, Lord Mountstuart (who had returned to London, his envoyship at Turin having come to an end) was "strangely cold and distant".[28]

On 3 April Boswell called on the Lord Advocate, who was "open, frank, and hearty" and held out the prospect of a judicial appointment for Boswell if he were to continue "assiduously" at his profession.

On Sunday 18 May Boswell was in a particularly fine frame of mind. "Went to high mass in Portuguese Chapel", he records. "Was as devout as I could wish; heavenly and happy. Vowed before the altar no more filles *while in London. A memorable moment."*

Later that week, on Thursday 22 and Friday 23 May, Boswell, together with the Lord Advocate and George Fergusson, appeared in the House of Lords as counsel for Mrs Jane Fergusson, the respondent in an appeal concerning a former Glasgow partnership by the name of John McDowall and Company. The appeal was against a decision of the Court of Session finding in favour of Mrs Fergusson in an action raised by her as residuary legatee of her deceased son, who had been a partner in the firm, for payment of the sum owing to him by the firm at the time of his death. Counsel for the appellants were John Morthland and Ilay Campbell, the newly appointed Solicitor-General.[28a] The hearing went smoothly and Boswell felt no uneasiness. On the second day he considered that he "spoke distinctly" and just as he could have wished. "And", he says, "when Lord Advocate perceived by a question that Lord Mansfield was satisfied, and whispered to me, 'Finish', I did so in a very little, which was being perfectly master of myself." The outcome was that

27 Journal, 23 March 1783.
28 Journal, 25 March 1783.
28a *Applause*, p. 147, n. 5.

the Court of Session's decision was affirmed and the appellants were found liable for the expenses of the appeal. This put Boswell in such high spirits that he ended up "shockingly drunk" and took a prostitute to St James's Park, "but happily had sense enough left not to run risk". However, he subsequently discovered that his watch was missing.

During most of May, Boswell's old friend Temple, whom Boswell had not seen since 1775, was in London and they spent much time together. However, this was a far from happy reunion on Temple's part, for he found Boswell's behaviour selfish, insensitive and coarse. Moreover, Temple was anxious to travel to Berwick-upon-Tweed and Boswell, who had undertaken to accompany him, kept delaying their departure. "Sorry I came to town to meet him", Temple wrote in his diary. "Detaining me here to no purpose. Seems often absurd and almost mad, I think. No composure or rational view of things. Years do not improve him. Why should I mortify myself to stay for him?"[29]

On 29 May, the day before his departure, Boswell was given some friendly advice by Dr Johnson. "He advised me to set my mind on practice as a lawyer in Scotland. Every new cause would teach me more law, and the more causes I had, the less surprising it would be that I was made a judge. I should court employment by all honest and liberal means, be still more civil to agents than before, as they naturally suspect a rich man to be proud. 'Have them to dine and show them you are desirous of practice.' I was animated by his manly conversation."

Boswell and Temple reached Berwick-upon-Tweed on 5 June, and after staying there for several days Boswell returned to Edinburgh, arriving in time for the opening of the summer session on 12 June. He then went for a brief visit to Auchinleck, where the children were staying, and was back in Edinburgh by 27 June.

Boswell's journal, which had lapsed after 29 May, was resumed on 1 August.

FRIDAY 1 AUGUST. I was in very bad spirits. Yet I went and supped at Lord Justice Clerk's with Mr Ross Mackye and a large company.

SATURDAY 2 AUGUST. I just appeared in the Court of Session, and then drove in my chaise with Grange, by special invitation, to the Hon. A. Gordon's at Rockville.[30] My spirits were bad. But viewing the ruins of Seton[31] and particularly the chapel did me some good.

TUESDAY 5 AUGUST. Lord Mountstuart and his lady had come to town last night in their way to Bute. I waited on them this morning and found a numerous levee and not a warm reception. My wife called afterwards, but Lady Mountstuart was not at home. I called on my Lord for a little before dinner and asked them to supper. But they were to set out next morning, and would not sup abroad. I dined at Bayle's, a party made for Mr Ross Mackye; Hon. A. Gordon at the head, I at the foot. Sir William Erskine was very good company. I drank very liberally, just to dissipate dreary dulness. I came home somewhat intoxicated.

WEDNESDAY 6 AUGUST. My wife and I dined at Lady Colville's; the Hon. A. Gordon and Lady Dumfries, Sir William and Lady Forbes the company. I was in such miserable spirits that I resolved to drink a great deal of wine. I did so, and

29 Quoted in *Applause*, p. 149.
30 Gordon's estate in Haddingtonshire.
31 Seton Palace, in Haddingtonshire.

afterwards played ill at cards. In short, it was a day not to be remembered with satisfaction. I went to bed immediately on my getting home.

THURSDAY 7 AUGUST. Was still in bad spirits. I indeed was sensible that drinking was a bad remedy. Yesterday the dismission of Mr Dundas from the office of Lord Advocate was announced. It did not agitate me much, as it was expected, and as my spirits were so wretched.[32] I felt a woeful difference upon myself from what I was in London. I was quite discontented. Worthy Grange endeavoured to soothe me, and to persuade me that I should reconcile my mind to living in Scotland. At night I felt some relief from gloom.

TUESDAY 12 AUGUST. I was kept in Edinburgh till [today], though the Session rose on the 9th, because I was engaged to plead a cause before the Commissaries, my first appearance in that Court. I liked it very well.[33]

Boswell then set off for Auchinleck, where he was initially "pretty well". "But", he says, "a fit of low spirits came upon me, which distressed me much for some time." This was followed by "a kind of dull indifference, a sort of callous stupor. The promotion of Harry Erskine to be King's Advocate while I thought myself more deserving of that office, vexed me, especially as a kind and candid letter from Mr Burke gave me faint hopes of any promotion by his influence. All my lively ambition was mortified. I had no object, and indolence seemed to overwhelm me." However, he was not short of pleasant company. On 1 September he was joined for a few days by Commissioner Cochrane and Dr Webster; on the 3rd he had to dinner the Lord Justice Clerk, his lady and Dr Hugh Blair; and on the 12th Sir Alexander Dick paid a visit "most cordially". The following month Boswell's guests were the Prestons and George Wallace and this company made Boswell as "sound and happy" as he could wish. But he started to despair of ever acquiring much knowledge of rural affairs. "My ignorance in the management of ground vexed me," he wrote, "and I was fretted at the cunning of the country people and the little regard which appeared to me to be felt for my prosperity."

A pleasing mark of respect to Boswell as the new Laird of Auchinleck was his appointment on 28 October as a Justice of the Peace at Ayr. He was chosen preses of the Quarter

---

32 Dundas had been dismissed as Treasurer of the Navy on the formation of the Fox-North Coalition in April 1783, but was initially able to retain his position as Lord Advocate, for he was on good terms with North. "He was reckoning, however, without the enmity of Fox, into whose hands he cavalierly played by boasting that 'no man in Scotland will venture to take my place'. Such insolence could not be long tolerated, and a terse letter of dismissal arrived in August" (Fry, p. 94). Ilay Campbell was likewise dismissed as Solicitor-General. "Though Boswell was too dull to be very hopeful, he wrote to Burke the next day complaining that he languished 'in provincial obscurity' and stating his pretentions for preferment as Lord Advocate or even joint Solicitor-General" (*Applause*, p. 160, n. 4). However, Dundas and Ilay Campbell were respectively replaced by Henry Erskine and Alexander Wight.

33 Edward Topham, writing in 1775, described the Commissary Court (which was in the Parliament Close) in the following terms: "It is a little room of about ten feet square, and, from the darkness and dirtiness of it, you would rather imagine that those who were brought into it, were confined there. To this Chamber of Justice you ascend by a narrow, dismal, winding stair-case, and where you are in danger of falling every step you take" (from letter dated 5 May 1775 in Topham, pp. 299-300). The chief functions of the Commissary Court were "to confirm testaments, to ascertain debts contracted by persons deceased, and give decree for payment of them: ... and [to take] cognizance of all actions to prove a marriage, to procure a divorce, &c." (Arnot, p. 289).

Sessions and considered that he "did very well in the chair".[34] *Two days later, however, there was a disagreeable scene when his wife made some careless remark which hurt his pride, causing him to "burst into a paroxysm of horrible passion". But his pride was fully restored on 7 November when he was chosen to preside over a meeting of county landholders held to press for the abolition of nominal and fictitious votes.*

On Monday, 10 November, Boswell and his wife, with Veronica and Euphemia and their governess, set out for Edinburgh. The other three children remained behind. "Sandy seemed sorry at parting," says Boswell, "though he liked to stay. I was afraid little James would have been very sorry, and perhaps have made a noise. But he looked bold and steady; and when I asked him if he was not going to cry, he said briskly, 'I'm too good a bairn.'" During the course of their journey to Edinburgh, Mrs Boswell began to fret about the children they had left behind as the dairymaid had come down with an illness. There was a fever prevalent in the country which had caused a number of deaths and Mrs Boswell feared that it might transpire that the dairymaid had become another victim. She therefore wrote to Isobel ("Bell") Bruce, the children's nurse, telling her to come to Edinburgh with the children if the surgeon thought it dangerous for them to stay at Auchinleck. The Boswells got to Edinburgh on the evening of Tuesday the 11th.

WEDNESDAY 12 NOVEMBER. The Court of Session sat down. The Hon. Henry Erskine and Mr Wight were received as Lord Advocate and Solicitor-General. I was sadly vexed that I had not been promoted to either of these offices. I paid a visit to Mr George Wallace, who was sitting quietly at home. I was in bad spirits. The weather was cold.

THURSDAY 13 NOVEMBER. The weather was exceedingly cold, and I much upon the fret. While I sat dull by the fire before dinner, the Hon. A. Gordon came and cordially asked if I would give him a dinner. I made him heartily welcome, and by drinking some wine with him I was cheered.

FRIDAY 14 NOVEMBER. Worthy Sir Alexander Dick paid me a visit in the forenoon. But I was insipid. The vulgarity and bustle of the Court of Session was very disgusting after my consequence at Auchinleck. I drank tea at Lady Auchinleck's.

SATURDAY 15 NOVEMBER. Waited on Lord President while at breakfast. Found him as hearty as ever, though parted from his lady. But I was shocked at such an instance of the instability of human connexions. Dined at Prestonfield rather dully. We had an alarm today that the dairymaid at Auchinleck had really a fever. By Mr Wood's advice, we ordered our three younger children to come to us directly.

MONDAY 17 NOVEMBER. Breakfasted at Lady Colville's. The conversation of her Ladyship, Lady Anne, and the Hon. Andrew had much the same effect on me it has had for some years. My views of life were dim. I drank tea at Mr George Wallace's.

---

34 "The justices for each county were required by statute to meet quarterly... Those statutory meetings of justices... constituted the court of quarter sessions. The quarter sessions had miscellaneous administrative functions as well as power to review the judgments of individual justices in [certain] offences" (*Stair Memorial Encyclopaedia of the Laws of Scotland*, Vol. 6, para. 1159).

TUESDAY 18 NOVEMBER. Nothing to be marked except that the children arrived at night, Mr Millar with them.[35]

WEDNESDAY 19 NOVEMBER. It was a great comfort to their mother to have the children again with her. She had yesterday a slight return of spitting of blood, owing, I believe, to anxiety about them. She had a little more today. It was a thick, wet day as I ever remember. I had a dreary struggle against it. I was helped somewhat by Mr Millar's company, and by the children. Mr Millar and I drank tea at Dr Webster's. Col. George Preston and Captain Trotter supped with us.

FRIDAY 21 NOVEMBER. (Writing the 25.) One of these days I had a serious conversation with the new Lord Advocate. He could make but awkward excuses for my not being appointed Solicitor-General; and I plainly saw that Scotland was in the hands of understrapping managers, of which I wrote to Mr Burke in strong terms. Erskine however professed much willingness to serve me. I did not trust too much to what he said. I was impatient and fretful, and revolved various schemes for having some better share of wealth and distinction.

TUESDAY 25 NOVEMBER. Balmuto and his young wife[36] and Miss Menie and Mr Nairne dined with us. My wife and I had paid our visit of compliment duly. This being my wedding-day, I most sincerely renewed my most affectionate vows to my valuable spouse. I had warmed myself rather too much with wine at dinner. But I believe it was necessary.[37]

SATURDAY 13 DECEMBER. This day I had ten processes upon my table, so that my practice as a lawyer made a goodly appearance. I had a bad cold, which added to my uneasiness. I have it to remark that during my wretchedness on this occasion, I have given my son Sandy pretty regular lessons in Latin and Miss Young[38] in Italian, and have dictated several law papers very well. But I at present thought of keeping clear of society as disgusting, or at least insipid. I *felt* how easily I could do with very little of it, and I wondered how people could be animated to so much exertion in carrying it on.

SUNDAY 14 DECEMBER. Lay in bed all day and took a sweat for my cold. Was quite indifferent to everything. Had a kind of false *pride* in this. But surely I had

---

35 The Rev. Alexander Millar (or Miller), the assistant minister at Auchinleck, who, as the editors of *Applause* observe (p. 6, n. 7), was "later immortalized (not, however, as he would have wished)" by Burns in *The Holy Fair*. See verse 17, where Burns tells of Millar gabbling orthodox doctrines hypocritically:

> ...in his heart he weel believes,
> An' thinks it auld wives' fables:
> But faith! The birkie wants a manse:
> So, cannilie he hums them;
> Altho' his carnal wit an' sense
> Like hafflins-wise o'ercomes him
> At times that day.

36 Claud Boswell, who had remained a bachelor for over forty years, had married Anne Irvine of Kingcausie, Kincardineshire, on or about 28 April 1783.
37 "Boswell's renewal of his vows was followed with ironical swiftness by a relapse" (*Applause*, p. 171). See the entry for 14 February 1784.
38 Governess of Boswell's daughters.

not *pleasure*. Rose at night. The children said divine lessons. Sandy read the Bible to me while I was in bed.

SATURDAY 20 DECEMBER. News had come by express that the House of Lords had made a noble stand against Fox's East India Bill,[39] which would have overwhelmed the Crown. This rejoiced my Tory soul; and in the forenoon I went down to the library and drew up an Address to His Majesty from the Dean and Faculty of Advocates to congratulate him on it, and I moved for our addressing at our anniversary meeting this day. The dastardly fellows, afraid to take an open part, were all against it. I despised them, and felt myself an ancient constitutionalist.[40] My best amusement at present is playing at draughts. My health is much as it was. But starving has calmed my spirits.

MONDAY 22 DECEMBER. I went to a puppet-show with my children.

THURSDAY 25 DECEMBER. There was snow on the ground, and the weather was very cold. I and my three eldest children read devoutly in the prayer-book. The comfortable family dinner on this holy festival was held as usual. I did not take the children to the New English Chapel, but Grange and I went. The rigour of the season chilled my good feelings, and the consciousness of disease vexed me.[41] I began tonight to write again to my friend Temple, which I had not done for many months.

FRIDAY 26 DECEMBER. I had resolved to write and publish a *Letter to the People of Scotland on the State of the Nation*, to endeavour to rouse a spirit for *property* and the *Constitution* in opposition to the East India Bill, and I read in the Parliamentary journals and debates with attention, which amused me. The present fluctuation of Councils in the kingdom agitated my mind, while I at the same time had a wonderful philosophical power of indifference. I could view objects with as much light as others do, and at once let down a curtain and shade them.

SATURDAY 27 DECEMBER. I dictated my *Letter to the People* with animation, and advanced a good way in it. Time passed better than one would imagine in my situation.[42]

SUNDAY 28 DECEMBER. The weather continued inclement. I stayed at home all day. Sir William Forbes called for a little while. I wrote some more of my *Letter to the People*, which I did not scruple to do on Sunday, considering it as labouring for sacred monarchy. I read two of Carr's sermons to my wife and children and Miss Young. The children said divine lessons.

39 The Bill, which was rejected by the House of Lords on 17 December, had been designed to give control of the East India Company to a board of commissioners.
40 The minute of the Faculty meeting makes no mention of Boswell's motion.
41 That is, a further bout of venereal disease (see the entry for 25 November and relevant footnote).
42 "The pamphlet, a brief, and on the whole temperate, document, begins with characteristic references to the American war, General Oglethorpe, and Dr Johnson, proceeds to attack the East India Bill as undermining property rights and the Constitution in general, continues with a historical account of the influence and prerogative of the Crown, and concludes with an exhortation to the Scottish people to address the King on this occasion" (*Applause*, p. 174, n. 8).

MONDAY 29 DECEMBER. Finished my pamphlet, and had my calm friend Nairne to revise it. Sir William Forbes, who drank coffee with us in the evening, also heard a good part of it read. Both of them approved of it. I had this evening a delicate hint from Sir William that my credit with his house was exhausted. This gave me a kind of sensation which I had never before experienced. My valuable spouse and I talked together and resolved on strict frugality till I should be easier.

TUESDAY 30 DECEMBER. The printing of my pamphlet entertained me, and I was really animated about public affairs, but still was conscious of indifference when I chose it.

WEDNESDAY 31 DECEMBER. (Writing 7 January 1784.) Was kept busy about my pamphlet, and had it advertised as published *this day*. But it could not be in the shops till next morning. I sent the first copy tonight to Sir Charles Preston for the ancient burgh of Culross. I had yesterday or today (the post coming very irregularly by reason of the frost) an excellent letter from Dr Johnson. I flattered myself he might live some time yet.

1784

THURSDAY 1 JANUARY. Began the new year with no peculiar emotion. I found that keeping the house and tasting no fermented liquor kept me calm to a great degree. Yet I had spirited sentiments of monarchy. I thought my pamphlet might, at least ought, to do me good with a Tory administration, and surely with the King himself. And if it did not, I had the satisfaction of standing forth as a loyal gentleman, which would all my life give me better feelings than any preferment could do without the consciousness of that character. I went out in a chair and visited poor Sandy Cuninghame.[1] The severe weather affected me so that I resolved not to go abroad soon again. Grange dined with us. In the evening I wrote letters with copies of my pamphlet to several eminent persons.

MONDAY 5 JANUARY. No diversity to mark except that Lady Colville and the Hon. Andrew Erskine drank tea with us and praised my pamphlet most agreeably.

TUESDAY 6 JANUARY. I awaked in horror, having dreamt that I saw a poor wretch lying naked on a dunghill in London, and a blackguard ruffian taking his skin off with a knife in the way that an ox is flayed; and that the poor wretch was alive and complained woefully. How so shocking a vision was produced I cannot imagine. But its impression was such that I was dismal the whole day. Worthy Grange dined with us. His sensible, friendly talk did me good.

WEDNESDAY 7 JANUARY. During this confinement I declare my life has been happier than in many portions of it when I was going abroad. I have shunned all the inconveniencies of a most severe season. I have had visits of Sir William Forbes, Mr Hunter-Blair, Sir John Henderson, Sir James Pringle, Sir Charles Preston, Col. George Preston, Col. Christopher Maxwell, Major Andrew Frazer. I have felt the comfort of doing well and at my leisure all that I had to do. So that my mind has had, as it were, ease and elbow-room. It hurt me a little that I did not get out to Auchinleck to receive my rents myself and have my tenants about me, and, as Dr Johnson advised me in an excellent letter, "wrap myself up in my hereditary possessions", which I should have done in my good house, with a wood fire. But I gave a commission to James Bruce to receive money from the tenants *to account of rents*, and remit it to me. The consciousness of being Laird of Auchinleck was a *constant* support. The applause my pamphlet got pleased me for a time.

FRIDAY 9 JANUARY. This day was kept in Edinburgh as a thanksgiving day for peace and plenty by the last good harvest.

SATURDAY 10 JANUARY. (Writing the 13.) Awaked after a very agreeable dream that I had found a diary kept by David Hume, from which it appeared that though

1 For Alexander Cuninghame, see the entry for 16 April 1782 and footnote.

his vanity made him publish treatises of scepticism and infidelity, he was in reality a Christian and a very pious man. He had, I imagined, quieted his mind by thinking that whatever he might appear to the world to show his talents, his religion was between GOD and his own conscience. (I cannot be sure if this thought was in sleep.) I thought I read some beautiful passages in his diary. I am not certain whether I had this dream on Thursday night or Friday night. But after I awaked, it dwelt so upon my mind that I could not for some time perceive that it was only a fiction. I read nothing regularly just now. Revising my *Hypochondriack* pleased me.[2] I had a little agitation as to the effect which my *Letter* on the East India Bill might have on my future fortune in life. I thought it might perhaps seriously offend my friend Burke.[3] And yet I trusted that he was of too liberal a mind to be angry because I, who had always avowed my Tory principles, should stand forth for the King when an attempt was making to create a power greater than that of His Majesty. I also thought it might offend Lord Mountstuart, as it with a generous warmth supported the cause of royalty, from which, to my astonishment, he had retired, and associated himself with Opposition. I had written a letter of congratulation to him in the full belief of his being *against* the East India Bill; and after my letter was sent off, I received the newspaper mentioning him in the list of Lords *for* it. I next night wrote to him again, anxious to have this explained to me as an old Tory friend. I have as yet had no answer from him, and probably will have none, he is so indifferent.[4] I made up my mind as to both his Lordship and Burke being offended, as I was fully conscious I was in the right, and had even reason to glory in my zeal. I at the same time, without allowing myself to indulge sanguine hopes, pleased myself with fancying that perhaps the Sovereign or Lord Temple or some other of the great men to whom my congenial sentiments and good talents might recommend me, would call me into a respectable employment, and not improbably bring me into Parliament. I brought to my recollection such things having sometimes happened; and why might not I have the same success which others had experienced without deserving it better? At any rate, by proper economy I could certainly never fail to be an independent baron.

SUNDAY 11 JANUARY. My health was now so much better that I might have gone abroad. But I was afraid, kept the house, and took physic.

TUESDAY 13 JANUARY. The Session sat down again. Felt a reluctance to renew the bustle of life. Went out in a chair and had two causes before the Lords. Had some weak uneasiness lest I might meet with some coarse jokes from my brethren upon my *Letter* on the East India Bill. But I soon was firm, and indeed got such compliments as pleased me.

WEDNESDAY 14 JANUARY. Got six guineas in fees, which animated me. My mind was at present in a good tranquil state, for which there is no accounting.

2 Boswell was working on a collection of his *Hypochondriack* essays, but he never published the work.
3 Burke, who had absorbed himself in Indian affairs and was convinced that the East India Company was managed corruptly, was a fervent supporter of Fox's bill and had influenced some of its terms.
4 There is no record of a reply (*Applause*, p. 177, n. 7).

My children delight me. I tell my valuable spouse that we should be sensible of the immediate happiness which we enjoy from them. Sandy has for some days had sore eyes, which prevents him from reading and attending Mr Morton's writing-school. I make him say a little of his Latin lessons from memory.

FRIDAY 16 JANUARY. Walked to the Court of Session, the first time of my being upon the street (I should have said in good English *in* the street, I believe) since the 20 of December last.

SATURDAY 17 JANUARY. I had last night an excellent letter from the Marquess of Graham upon my pamphlet, and upon the present political contest. It gave me fresh spirit. I had this forenoon a visit of Mr Hamilton of Bargany, who as an old, sly politician sounded me as to my engagement in the Ayrshire election. I with per-haps too much frankness told him that I rather thought I was engaged to support Lord Eglinton's interest, independent of my friend Hugh Montgomerie being the candidate; and therefore I must vote for the Devil if his Lordship should set him up. But I was very sorry I was engaged, and would take care again. He put on an air of friendly regard and bid me say nothing till Lord Eglinton applied to me; and that as I had been one of his Lordship's steadiest friends, I or my friends should insist with him that the Administration he supported should promote me in the law. Bargany himself would insist. I told him I did not like the Coalition party, and that I thought the Constitution in danger. He kept himself very quiet upon that subject. Little did I suspect that he was a keen partisan of the *late* Administration. He asked me if I would accept of being Sheriff of Ayrshire; for that the present Sheriff[5] had behaved so that it would not do long with him (or words to that purpose). I said it was an office I did not desire, but I believed I should not refuse it if it were offered to me. "Very well", said he with an air of significancy. I said too much to Bargany as to my thinking myself engaged to Lord Eglinton. I dined today with Mundell's scholars, and was allowed to drink only water. I was the merriest man there, such command of spirits had I. Dr Webster, as the father of several scholars, was entertained by us today, and invited to be with us at every meeting.

SUNDAY 18 JANUARY. My health was now almost quite restored. But with Mr Wood's approbation I resolved to take medicine twelve days more to be quite secure. I was at home all day. The children said divine lessons. I read two of Mr Carr's sermons to my wife, etc.

TUESDAY 20 JANUARY. In the evening the Earl of Dundonald unexpectedly paid me a visit. His Lordship had not done me that honour for some years. My heart warmed to him from remembrance of his father and other relations. Blood is blood. He wished I would hear him read over something which he had drawn up for preventing smuggling and improving the revenue in Scotland. I fixed next day, and he promised to dine with me.

WEDNESDAY 21 JANUARY. My spirits had now been for some time calm and

5 William Wallace (who remained Sheriff until his death in 1786).

steady, owing, I really believe, to my living abstemiously. My life, I am certain, was happier upon the whole than when in a state of more fermentation. Lord Dundonald read his paper to me, which was very well done. He dined and drank tea with us. I must here remark a curious circumstance in my own character at present, which is a consciousness of having, if I choose to indulge it, a total insensibility to what others may think of me in point of decorum. I am indifferent as to all censure of my mode of living. To feel thus gives one a wonderful feeling of independence. But too much of it is not right. The late Lord Eglinton regretted to my father my want of the sense of shame. It has been owing partly to a vain idea of my own talents; partly to a kind of philosophical impression of the nothingness of all things in human life. I was at present much pleased with my fame on account of my late pamphlet, which Mr Dundas had quoted in the House of Commons. I thought I might have much reputation as a writer were I but more concealed in a large society; and therefore wished to settle in London, at least to be a good deal there. But indeed I keep myself wonderfully abstracted here.

SATURDAY 24 JANUARY. I was in admirable spirits today. But in the evening was suddenly informed that Dr Webster was dying.

SUNDAY 25 JANUARY. Grange, who went up to inquire how Dr Webster was, informed me about ten o'clock that *it was all over*. Both he and I were struck with the removal of so eminent a man, and regretted that we had not been more with him of late. Commissioner Cochrane paid us a visit. In the evening, divine lessons and two of Mr Carr's sermons.

MONDAY 26 JANUARY. I visited the Lord President, who was confined by the gout.

THURSDAY 29 JANUARY. The weather had all this time been very severe. This day was uncommonly so. Yet a most numerous company attended the funeral of Dr Webster. I was affected with a dreary impression of mortality, but not with tenderness. For Webster was a man more to be admired for his talents and address than to touch the heart with affection. Grange dined with us. After the funeral I visited poor Sandy Cuninghame, who was in bed, and so ill that it distressed me to see him. It was the last time. My present indisposition was an excuse for my having been but little with him. I was somewhat uneasy that I had not been more.

FRIDAY 30 JANUARY. My practice went on very well at present, though I did not get much money. But I had a creditable appearance, was useful to many people, and hoped I might be better in time. This forenoon Dr Webster's repositories were opened, and it appeared he had appointed six trustees, of whom I was one, and had settled all his property on his daughter and her children, except a mother-of-pearl cabinet and silver tureen given to his son John, who was miserably vexed to find himself unjustly used, as he thought. I resolved to think a little before accepting of the trust.[6] I should have mentioned that I

6 "Boswell did accept appointment as one of Dr Webster's trustees" (*Applause*, p. 182, n. 5).

found there was no service performed in the chapel in Blackfriars Wynd today,[7] where I have a seat. So I went down to my worthy friend Grange and read the best part of it from my Oxford Prayer-Book, and he said amen. In the evening John Webster was with me, quite disturbed. He and Sir Walter and Lady Frances Montgomerie[8] supped.

SATURDAY 31 JANUARY. Mr Stalker, my son Sandy's English-master, Grange, and Mr Donaldson, the painter, who had not been with me for a long time, dined.

SUNDAY 1 FEBRUARY. About ten o'clock in the morning, I got a note from Henry Cuninghame that poor Sandy, his brother, was just dead. I went to him and saw the dead body. I was not much shocked. I paid a visit to Mrs Jefferies, an officer's widow who lodged in the house with the Cuninghames (Zeigler's in Alison's Square[9]), and had been humanely attentive to them. Sir Walter and Henry dined and supped with us; and their presence prevented the usual divine lessons in my presence. But Veronica and Phemie said some to their governess. In the forenoon I paid a visit to Mr R. Mackintosh and heard him harangue consequentially.

WEDNESDAY 4 FEBRUARY. My health was now almost quite restored. My wife sat to Painter Donaldson for a better miniature, for his own credit, than one he had done for her.[10] While she sat, Lord Chief Baron and Mrs Montgomery paid us a visit. Miss Young described my wife's agreeable countenance when she is in good humour exceedingly well. She said, "Mrs Boswell has at times the pleasantest look I ever saw. Her eye glistens." Mr Donaldson dined with us. I would give a great deal could I have but the look described by Miss Young preserved by painting. I have neglected to mention that Grange and I and Sir Walter M.-C. and his brother Henry searched poor Sandy Cuninghame's papers one forenoon, and saw him put into his coffin one evening. The corpse was by his earnest desire to be carried to the family vault.

FRIDAY 6 FEBRUARY. Lady Colville, her sister and brothers, Sir William Forbes and Lady, and Lady Frances Montgomerie dined and drank tea with us. I was in good spirits, but (for the first time this fit of sobriety) felt my not drinking wine somewhat awkward.

SUNDAY 8 FEBRUARY. I awaked with a severe nervous headache. Rose and called on Grange. But was so ill I was obliged to go to bed again. Lay all day in great distress. Sent for Mr Wood. He bid me just lie still. Mr Boswall of Blackadder came and sat by me as a kindly medical friend. He returned in the evening. Mr Nairne also sat by my bedside awhile. I grew better, and they both supped. I was able to sup with them. This day's illness gave me a striking impression of my own frailty.

7 That is, no service to commemorate the execution of Charles I.
8 Sister of Archibald Montgomerie, 11th Earl of Eglinton (*Applause*, p. 408).
9 Alison's Square was later demolished to make way for what is now Marshall Street (Harris, p. 422).
10 This miniature has not been traced.

MONDAY 9 FEBRUARY. Walked out and breakfasted at Lady Colville's. I was free from the headache. I attended some part of the Justiciary trial, the Rev. Dr Bryden against Murray of Murraythwaite. I was vexed by the partiality of *some*, at least, of the judges against Dr Bryden.[11] I received tonight a letter from the Prime Minister[12] applauding my East India *Letter*. This raised my mind.

TUESDAY 10 FEBRUARY. My practice as a lawyer made a decent show. My domestic happiness was more relished than usual.

SATURDAY 14 FEBRUARY. (Writing the 18.) I recollect nothing remarkable except feeling myself perplexed with a cause, Malcolm against Malcolm, in which I had a paper to write.[13] My health was now clear. ——.

SUNDAY 15 FEBRUARY. Intended to have gone to church. But there was such a fall of snow I stayed at home. Went down and sat part of the forenoon with my worthy friend Grange, whose faithful friendship and mild manners are my never-failing consolation. I have observed with satisfaction that his religious principles have of late grown stronger, and it pleases me that by having a seat for myself by the year in the Old English Chapel I accommodate him, so that his attendance upon public worship is more frequent. The children said divine lessons, and I read two of Carr's sermons to my family, by which is to be understood my wife and children and Miss Young. Sir Charles Preston, etc., supped with us. ——.

TUESDAY 17 FEBRUARY. My wife had been troubled for two days with a bad cold, Veronica with a sore throat, and little James with a complaint which we supposed might be worms. My mind was at this time so healthful that I could think with philosophic serenity of the evils which *might* befall me, and imagined I could counterbalance them by recollecting the good I had actually enjoyed. I thought of my happiness from my dear wife and children, and that if I should lose them, still that happiness might soothe me. "O gracious GOD, be pleased to preserve them to me!" was my constant prayer; and I also prayed often for Dr Johnson, that his health might be restored, and that at least he and I might still have a comfortable meeting in this world.[14] Since Dr Webster's death, Dr Erskine paid me a visit. I started a curious thought: that we wish much that we may know one another in a future state. But alas! how seldom are people who have a sincere regard for each other in company in this life, where we are sure of personal knowledge, and have it certainly in our power to meet. How seldom do he and I meet. He did not see the force of the remark. For he said, "Ay, but when they have an eternity!" Indeed we may consider that everything in a future state will be amazingly different from what we experience in

---

11 This was a private prosecution by the Rev. Dr William Bryden, minister of the parish of Dalton in Dumfriesshire, against John Murray of Murraythwaite, a heritor of the parish and a Justice of the Peace, for allegedly assaulting Bryden while in church. The jury found Murray not guilty (*Applause*, p. 184, n. 9).
12 William Pitt the younger.
13 No court papers or process relating to this case have been traced.
14 In the summer of 1783 Johnson had suffered a paralytic stroke and had temporarily lost his speech.

the imperfection of this. Sir Walter M.-C. and his brothers David and Henry, and Mr Cummyng, the painter, etc., dined. Cummyng's curious variety of knowledge entertained me. The state of the nation was now wavering. I feared that Mr Pitt might yield to at least a coalition with the factious opposers of the Crown. Several of my brethren at the bar were of the factious party. I endeavoured to maintain a composed elevation as a royalist, and to rest upon my pamphlet. ——.

THURSDAY 19 FEBRUARY. Sir Walter M.-C. was apprehended for a debt of £20. I thought a *cessio bonorum* the best thing to keep him easy, and was against relieving him. But his brother David, with tears in his eyes, was so earnest, I yielded to his request and paid the money. This affair agitated me sadly, as I hesitated between humanity and prudence—I may add, strict honesty, as my own affairs are as yet embarrassed.

FRIDAY 20 FEBRUARY. Sir Walter was apprehended for another debt of £30. I was quite determined not to interfere again. He was all day detained in a private house. In the evening poor David and Thomas Baillie, his agent,[15] became bound to present him on the 6 of March. He went to the Abbey.[16] I dined at Mr Nairne's, where I had not dined for two years, so that he insisted on my coming.[17] I still drank only water, and [as] there was no conversation to my mind I wearied and came home soon. There was this night a disagreeable domestic affair, of which I forbear to record the particulars.[18]

SATURDAY 21 FEBRUARY. I awaked in vexation on account of what I allude to last night, and I had a severe nervous headache and sickness. I took a little cognac brandy, which did me some good, so that I was able to do my duty in the Court of Session. I starved myself all day, and was in a sort of desperation. It is enough that my mind may recall why. It ought not to be registered. Lord and Lady Eglinton, Lord Chief Baron, his lady and daughter, and Colonel Macdonell supped with us. I grew better and got through the evening easily, and the domestic affair was wonderfully quieted. ——.

SUNDAY 22 FEBRUARY. Awaked in fine spirits. ——. Stayed at home in the forenoon and had all my five children sitting round a table with me in the drawing-room most agreeably, while I read the first chapter of the *Revelations*, which I do every Sunday, and heard them say divine lessons. It was a mild thaw. I called on Lord Eglinton, who was gone abroad, but I sat a little with the Countess. I went to the New Church in the afternoon, the first time for many Sundays, and heard a Mr Singer; poor entertainment. Sir Walter had come out of the Abbey[19] and was to go

15 A "writer", admitted and enrolled in the Court of Session in 1774.
16 That is, to the sanctuary in the precincts of Holyrood Abbey.
17 William Nairne's house was in Argyle Square.
18 For recurrences of the "disagreeable domestic affair" see the entries for 12 and 21 March. The editors of *Applause* speculate, at p. 256, that these disturbances may either have had something to do with Miss Young, the governess, who, according to Boswell, was "well looked" and "elegant in dress", used "many perfumes" and was "fond of admiration", or with the fact that Boswell had a "pretty maid" who "[opened] the window shutters every morning".
19 It was safe to come out of the sanctuary that day as debtors could not be apprehended on a Sunday.

home next day, as he trusted no messenger could seize him there, and he believed he could raise money to clear the debt for which he was last apprehended. I visited him at Wallaces's Inn.[20] I then drank tea with Mrs Drummond of Blair Drummond tête-à-tête, and had so much conversation that I sat almost three hours and thought the time much shorter. I was not melancholy when I reflected on her husband, Lord Kames, being gone. My spirits were so good I took everything well. In the evening I was happy to be sure that the domestic *trouble* was over. ——.

MONDAY 23 FEBRUARY. Breakfasted with Baron Gordon and had a good flow of conversation. I mentioned how Lord Monboddo denied to me that there was any contradiction between any action of mine being *certain from all eternity*, and *human liberty*. The Baron said he also thought there was none. "For", said he, "it is certain from all eternity that everything is to be either one way or another. Yet there is liberty of determination." I was now for the first time again after a long interval brought into the distressing perplexity of fate and free will. I suffered for laughing at what I thought, and still think, an absurd obstinacy in Lord Monboddo not to perceive that previous *certainty* is a contradiction to *liberty*. I was disturbed by the vile metaphysical perplexity during the day. ——.

WEDNESDAY 25 FEBRUARY. I drank tea with Lord Eskgrove. His daughter and her governess were with us. I had inquired of his clerk and been informed that I could be with my Lord at that time. I wished to pay him respect as my father's successor on the bench, and I found his conversation instructive and entertaining.[21] He stated to me some causes which he had lately decided. We joined in regretting that the custom of a drawing-room and tea-table was gone out, and we thought that kind of society much better than what we now have at laborious dinners and suppers.

THURSDAY 26 FEBRUARY. (Writing 2 March.) William Lennox came to town last night with my chaise to carry out our three youngest children. This had a curious effect upon my *metaphysicized* mind. I recollect nothing particular today except being at Corri's concert with my wife and daughters.

FRIDAY 27 FEBRUARY. My wife and I went in our own chaise and dined at Lady Auchinleck's; Balmuto and his wife, Commissioner Cochrane, and the Rev. Dr Andrew Hunter there. I was inwardly thoughtful; and as I passed the door of the room where my father died, I prayed for his soul. We drank tea. It was really a decent and pretty comfortable day. ——.

SATURDAY 28 FEBRUARY. My practice in the Court of Session, though not very profitable (yet more so than last winter) was pretty extensive at present, and I did it easily and well. I was still disturbed by *poring* with *my mind's eye* on the *machinery* of *Necessity*, which I was not *sure* was not the true condition of man. ——.

20 "The George" in that part of Bristo Street called the Bristo Port. The inn was run by William Wallace, a stabler.
21 Boswell's high opinion of Lord Esgrove as an individual was diametrically opposed to that of Lord Cockburn (see Appendix, p. 561).

SUNDAY 29 FEBRUARY. Heard Dr Blair preach on "Take no thought for the morrow",[22] etc. He gave us some plausible declamation, but one part of his discourse contradicted another; for he talked of everything being ordered by GOD, and yet that our fanciful discontents were against his designs. This was the import of what he said in fine language. I went to him to his *vestry*[23] afterwards, and he owned to me that too much *acquiescence* would make us poor members of society. Visited Old Mar between sermons.[24] I sat at home in the afternoon and looked at some old letters and other papers. The children said divine lessons. The three youngest seemed dearer to us that they were to leave us next morning.

MONDAY 1 MARCH. We rose early and saw our three youngest children set out for Auchinleck. I had an abhorrence at metaphysical speculation, while I perceived that it sickened my perceptions of real life. I paid a visit to Mr Boswall of Blackadder, who talked to me in a kind, friendly manner about my health, as I was now thin, and advised me to ride. He said bad spirits was as real a disease as any; and that the mind and body mutually affected each other. I asked him if the Asiatics of better rank were serious in religion, or only appeared to be so from a regard to decency. He said they were serious, as the people of this country were formerly. He said it was the fashion in India to be religious, and that the Nabob of Arcot was really so. He said that a plurality of women did not hurt men there. But that in every country there is a difference of constitutions, upon which more or less communication with women being hurtful or not depended. I sounded him on predestination, which is a Mahometan doctrine. He did not enter far into the subject. My spirits were raised by moving about, and talking with one who had been long in Asia, for which I have a warm fondness in my imagination. I dined by pressing invitation at Lady Colville's; a good deal of company there. Sir John Whiteefoord and I talked to one another pleasantly as opposing candidates against the next election for Ayrshire. While conversation and wine circulated, I sat calm on my water regimen, and while I *half apprehended* that all was *irresistible fate*, I *half hoped* that there was *free volition and agency*, though I could not understand it. I was not well here. I was not animated. It was a labour to me to do my part tolerably. When I came home, I felt myself exhausted. But I bathed my feet in warm water and grew easier both in body and mind. ——.

TUESDAY 2 MARCH. Was rather better in mind. Lady Dundonald and her son Andrew, Old Mar, and Captain John Webster dined with us. Mar was so insolent after the ladies were gone that I was obliged to give him a pretty strong check. I commended Tod's pamphlet on hospitals,[25] and said Dr Webster had

---

22 Matthew 6: 34.
23 "Boswell underlined the word to indicate that Blair, or perhaps he himself, was using Anglican terminology for one of the lesser apartments in St Giles's" (*Applause*, p. 189, n. 3).
24 James Erskine of Mar's house was in the Cowgate.
25 "Thomas Tod, a merchant, treasurer to the Orphan Hospital, had defended the Edinburgh system of hospitals and poor-houses in *Observations on Dr McFarlan's Inquiries Concerning the State of the Poor*, published 1783" (*Applause*, p. 190, n. 4).

commended it. Said he: "I shall read it on his opinion; I would not read it on yours." This was really impertinent. I said calmly, "You pay me a great compliment", with an ironical look, and thought of saying no more. "I do not pay you a great compliment", said he. It then instantly occurred to me to reply, "Yes, you pay me a great compliment in supposing my understanding to be so different from yours." This had some effect upon him, and no more passed. I was sorry to have said such a thing to an old gentleman of his blood, and who in my younger days had shown me kindness. But there was no bearing his rudeness. Metaphysical clouds were broken by variety of conversation.

WEDNESDAY 3 MARCH. Lady Auchinleck dined with us today for the first time since my father's death. We had Balmuto and his wife, etc., a creditable company, and all was decent and indeed comfortable. ——.

SATURDAY 6 MARCH. Drank tea and eat *whigs*[26] with old Mr James Spence, Treasurer of the Bank of Scotland, who had been at the same class in the College with my father. Got from him many anecdotes for a life of Dr Webster. Wrote them down afterwards.[27]

SUNDAY 7 MARCH. I went out to my worthy friend Sir Alexander Dick, and having made out a requisition to the Sheriff of Edinburghshire for a meeting to address His Majesty, I got him with great zeal to sign it, having informed him that the Arniston family had a delicacy as to beginning the matter, as it might look like supporting their relation. But they would promote it. I dined with him. Found Miss Semple at tea at my house. The children said divine lessons.

MONDAY 8 MARCH. Had Mr Lawrie running about all day among the Edinburghshire freeholders to get the requisition for an Address signed; and after getting a sufficient number, sent it to the Lord President. An advertisement for it appeared in tonight's papers. It was curious how *I* managed all this. Not one freeholder knew of another, or from whence the application came, except Sir Alexander Dick and Young Arniston.

THURSDAY 11 MARCH. The Session rose. I was in excellent spirits. I attended the meeting for the Edinburghshire Address, and had the satisfaction to see it carried by a great majority.[28] I in the very time of the meeting indulged a metaphysical speculation on cause and effect, Liberty and Necessity, being *sure* that *I* was the *secret cause* of all that was now doing; and that though the honest freeholders did not know it, they were in reality moved by *me*. [After tea] I was for the first time at Corri's concert or academy for his scholars, and heard Veronica sing —— admirably. I was delighted. She had played before I came in.

FRIDAY 12 MARCH. Was to go to Auchinleck next day and from thence to London, which kept me in a state of some agitation. There was an unhappy

26 Currant buns.
27 These anecdotes have not been recovered (*Applause*, p. 191, n. 6).
28 "Alexander Fraser Tytler, later Lord Woodhouselee, wrote the Address, which is in a strain of conventional eulogy" (*Applause*, p. 192, n. 8).

renewal of the domestic disturbance, which vexed me exceedingly. My wife and I were at Barnard's ball, where our daughters are scholars.

Boswell duly departed the following day, leaving his wife behind in Edinburgh, and he got to Auchinleck that night, where he was pleased to be reunited with his three youngest children. His purpose in coming west was to support a loyal Address to the King from the county of Ayr denouncing the East India Bill and he had been busy preparing such an Address; but when he got to Ayr on 17 March he discovered that there was a "considerable opposition". Nevertheless, Boswell was more than a match for his antagonists and acquitted himself with complete success. "I never in my life felt myself better than I was today", he writes. "I recalled to my mind all the ideas of the consequence at county meetings and of the credit of the family of Auchinleck which I had acquired from my father in my early years, and I superadded the monarchical principles which I had acquired from Dr Johnson." Boswell was evidently the most prominent speaker, and all of his proposals were accepted. He also announced that he was prepared to stand as candidate for the county in the next election if Colonel Hugh Montgomerie were to decide not to do so.

As he set off for Edinburgh in his own chaise on 19 March, Boswell was accompanied up the avenue by his son Sandy. "I spoke of the beauty of Auchinleck", says Boswell, "and at the same time calmly reminded him how inconsiderable everything upon this earth was compared with heaven. The sun shone bright, and I thought the rays of religion beamed on his young mind."

Boswell reached Edinburgh the following morning.

SATURDAY 20 MARCH. It was the preparation day before the Sacrament. I went to the New Church in the afternoon. Was busy with several things in the evening, as I was resolved to set out for London on Monday, that I might at any rate be present at the general meeting of the County of York to address His Majesty. I was quite happy to be again with my dear wife.

SUNDAY 21 MARCH. I received the Sacrament in the New Church with a decent devotion. Dr Hope sent me a most refreshing letter from Dr Brocklesby that Dr Johnson was wonderfully relieved. I was a good deal agitated tonight. There had unfortunately been another fit of the domestic disturbance. I had delayed fixing as long as I could in hopes of getting a partner in a post-chaise. At eleven I engaged a seat in the diligence by Berwick. My wife's accuracy in having all my things ready was admirable.

Boswell set off on 22 March with the intention of travelling to London and stopping on the way at York to attend the meeting held for the Address to the King by the freeholders of that county. The Address was approved by a majority of the meeting, and Boswell gave a full report to the Edinburgh Evening Courant, *declaring, "I would willingly have gone a thousand miles to have been present at the Yorkshire meeting, and witnessed such an union of loyalty and freedom, to both of which I am warmly attached." However, he then returned to Edinburgh, having heard that Parliament had been dissolved on the 24th and thinking that he might be about to stand as candidate for Ayr. He arrived at Edinburgh on the 29th, finding his house unoccupied as Mrs Boswell, with Veronica and Euphemia, had gone to Auchinleck. Boswell now learned that Colonel Montgomerie, with the backing of Henry Dundas (who had been restored as Treasurer of the Navy), had declared his candidature for Ayr. Boswell evidently thereupon asked Dundas to get him a judge's place.*

TUESDAY 30 MARCH. Breakfasted well. Then Mr Dundas, a levee. Taken in to him. Found him very agreeable. Breakfasted with him, Hunter-Blair, etc. Ayrshire election all uncertain.[29] Ran about forenoon as in London. Dined on beefsteaks home. Evening Col. James Stuart arrived and sent he was to sup at Fortune's. I went to bed.

WEDNESDAY 31 MARCH. Called Mr Dundas. People with him. Went to call Colonel James, met him on bridge. Were lively and well.

THURSDAY 1 APRIL. Found Mr Dundas, excellent conversation with him. Not gown yet, first *waste* of Opposition, etc.[30] Settled burgess of Edinburgh.[31] Lord Provost asked to dine with Lord Provost, etc. Very lucky. Freedom of City proposed. Very jovial.[32] Asked to Sir W. Forbes. But did not go as intoxicated a little and to go off early. Saw Lady Auchinleck, well.

Boswell went to Auchinleck on 2 April. Eight days later, having heard that his friend Edmund Burke (who had been elected Lord Rector of Glasgow University) was staying at the Saracen's Head Inn in Glasgow, Boswell hastened to see him there, and on the way had a very narrow escape when he was thrown from his horse and was very nearly run over by a heavily laden cart. Boswell was concerned that Burke might have been upset by Boswell's recent political antics, but Burke embraced him with good humour and, says Boswell, "conveyed a compliment that my pleasantry was such that one would be a loser by quarrelling with me."

For a few days in mid-April Boswell was back in Edinburgh, but he returned to Auchinleck on the 18th. At the end of the month he set off for London to complete the Easter term at the Inner Temple, and on his arrival he was pleased to find Dr Johnson greatly recovered. As usual, Boswell was put up at General Paoli's house and he plunged into the swirl of London social life. On 3 June he accompanied Johnson to Oxford, but returned to London that night to be at court the next day for the King's birthday; and on 5 June Boswell attended the Handel Celebration performance of The Messiah *at Westminster Abbey, the impression of which was such that he resolved that he "never would go again lest it should be effaced". Boswell returned to Oxford on 9 June and stayed there until the 16th, during which period he collected a record of some memorable conversations with Dr Johnson. On their return to London, Johnson was clearly failing, and Boswell, who knew that*

29 The outcome was that Montgomerie was elected unopposed.

30 "'First waste of Opposition' is cryptic but presumably bears the same general sense as the advice Dundas gave Boswell later, 12 December 1784: 'He said... I should first get something that I might carry to the bench with me.' Perhaps: 'First, pick up some office that will become vacant as the Opposition is plundered of its spoils'" (*Applause*, p. 201, n. 3).

31 "A consolation for patience, apparently. Boswell was enrolled a burgess of Edinburgh on 15 September 1784" (*Applause*, p. 201, n. 4).

32 "The Lord Provost (John Grieve) invited him to attend the dinner at Walker's where the Magistrates and Town Council of Edinburgh honoured their Member of Parliament, Hunter Blair. He was returned again three days later. Other invited guests included Henry Dundas, Robert Dundas the Solicitor-General (son of the Lord President), Sir William Forbes, and Dr Hugh Blair. Boswell sang a ballad of his own composition, *The Midlothian Address*, which made flattering reference to all three Dundases. He also put an account of the dinner, with one stanza of his song, into the *Edinburgh Advertiser* for 2 April" (*Applause*, p. 201, n. 5).

Johnson had expressed a desire to spend the winter in Italy, wrote to the Lord Chancellor, Lord Thurlow, entreating that the King be persuaded to provide the necessary addition to Johnson's pension so as to meet the expense of such a trip. Boswell felt that it was appropriate that Johnson should be able to defray the expense "in a manner becoming the first literary character of a great nation and, independent of all his other merits, the author of the DICTIONARY OF THE ENGLISH LANGUAGE". Lord Thurlow was much in favour of Boswell's proposal and confirmed that he would press it as far as he could, taking the view that "it would be a reflection on us all, if such a man should perish for want of the means to take care of his health". When Boswell broke the news to Dr Johnson (who had hitherto been completely ignorant of the scheme), he was overcome with emotion, saying, "This is taking prodigious pains about a man." "O Sir," said Boswell, "your friends would do everything", to which Johnson exclaimed with tears in his eyes, "GOD bless you all." However, Boswell had to depart for Scotland on 2 July before the matter could be settled. His last meeting with Johnson was on 30 June when they dined with Sir Joshua Reynolds. When they were taken back to Johnson's house in Sir Joshua's coach, there were emotional farewells. "We bade adieu to each other affectionately in the carriage", writes Boswell. "When [Johnson] had got down upon the foot-pavement, he called out, 'Fare you well!' and without looking back sprung away with a kind of pathetic briskness (if I may use that expression), which seemed to indicate a struggle to conceal uneasiness, and was to me a foreboding of our long, long separation."

Boswell had now resolved that he would move to the English bar. "Let us see", he wrote to Temple on 6 July 1784, "if my resolution (which after years of wavering came at once upon me with wonderful power) will make me an eminent barrister." In the meantime, he had embarked on a private study of those aspects of English law which he needed to get started at the bar, and he told Temple that "it is amazing with what avidity I read to fit me for trying what I wish for so much". But two days later in another letter to Temple (written in Carlisle) he observed, "I must… have a philosophical resolution not to be cast down though I should have no practice. Of this I am aware as a thing possible. My retreat to the bench in Scotland will, I trust, be secured." Nevertheless, he felt that he had reason to be confident of success: "I think my pretensions to employment as a lawyer of fifteen years' good practice in Scotland in all questions of the law of that country should be strong." But he was apprehensive of the possible reaction to his resolution among his Scottish colleagues. "It is unpleasant to me", he told Temple, "to go to Edinburgh for the remainder of this Summer Session and be stared at and talked to with Scottish familiarity concerning my change of situation."

After spending three nights with his family at Auchinleck, Boswell set off for Edinburgh accompanied by his wife. Here he started to have serious second thoughts about the scheme to move to England. As he explained in a letter to Temple dated 20 July 1784: "All is sadly changed…I was no sooner arrived than at once, as if plunged into a dreary vapour, my fine spirits were extinguished and I became as low and as miserable as ever. There certainly never was a mind so local as mine. How strange, how weak, how unfortunate is it that this my native city and my countrymen should affect me with such wretchedness. I have been harassed by the arguments of relations and friends against my animated scheme of going to the English bar. I have lost all heart for it…[W]hen I go [to London] at present as a gentleman of fortune I am on a footing with the first people, easy, independent, gay. But were I settled as a man of business, labouring uphill and anxious for practice, my situation would be quite different. Add to all this, the weakness of [my wife's] lungs renders her very unfit to live in the smoke of London…But alas! What is to become of my ambition? What of my love of England, where I am absolutely certain *that I* enjoy life, *whereas* here *it is* insipid, *nay*, disgusting… *The coarse vulgarity all around me is as shocking to me as it used to be to Sir John Pringle. Dr Blair accosted me with a vile tone,* 'Hoo did you leave Sawmuel?'[33] What right *have I to be so nicely delicate?"*

Boswell returned to Auchinleck on 13 August and was to stay there until 10 November when he came back to Edinburgh. Throughout this period he remained in a state of miserable indecision.

FRIDAY 12 NOVEMBER. Awaked with the first *image* my mind has produced for a long time. "My spirits", thought I, "are worse now than ever. Formerly I could appear gay, though inwardly sad. Now I cannot. The garrison is now so weak that not only is there not a sufficient complement of men within it, but it cannot even furnish as many as to make a show upon the walls." I visited Lord Rockville.[34] Then attended the Court of Session. Was quite hypochondriac. Called on my brother John. He drank tea with us, which added to my sadness.

SATURDAY 13 NOVEMBER. Was exceedingly ill. Visited, after the Court of Session rose, Mr George Wallace, Lord Advocate,[35] Lord Henderland.[36] My brother John dined and drank tea drearily.

SUNDAY 14 NOVEMBER. A wet day. Heard Dr Blair forenoon. Afternoon read a good part of *Hamlet*, to interest me in a melancholy character. Mr Sibthorpe supped with us. I was quite low.

MONDAY 15 NOVEMBER. Visited Lord Provost (Hunter-Blair),[37] Lady Auchinleck, and Commissioner Cochrane. Was very unhappy. I drank tea at Lord Rockville's; grew a little better. He seemed reconciled to my attempting the English bar. But I shrunk from it now with the horror of timid indolence. I read his session papers in the evening, which engaged my attention; and insensibly I was relieved and felt myself so as I had not been for four months. I was convinced that occupation is absolutely necessary for me.

TUESDAY 16 NOVEMBER. Visited Lord President and drank some tea with him at breakfast. Was displeased with his vulgar jocularity amidst a number of young advocates. My mind continued better. James Donaldson the bookseller drank tea with us. Law papers again amused me.

THURSDAY 18 NOVEMBER. I walked to Leith with Mr Allan Maconochie. His uncouth communication of various knowledge was wearisome to me. But I

33 That is, Samuel Johnson.
34 The Hon. A. Gordon had been appointed a Lord of Session as Lord Rockville on 1 July 1784.
35 Ilay Campbell, who had replaced Henry Erskine earlier that year and had been elected M.P. for the Glasgow Burghs.
36 Alexander Murray had been appointed a Lord of Session as Lord Henderland on 6 March 1783.
37 He had been elected Lord Provost on 29 September 1784 (see p. 248, n. 55). His house was in George Street.

envied him for the knowledge. Miss Susie Dunlop drank tea with us. Her gaiety pleased me. Captain Wemyss of Unthank came after tea and was introduced by her. I went over to Lord Rockville by invitation a little before nine and had a friendly conversation, in which he seemed not averse to my trying the English bar, though he rather wished I should be soon a judge with him. I eat some cold meat and took a little *eau de noyau*[38] and was wonderfully cheerful.

FRIDAY 19 NOVEMBER. After the Court of Session rose, met the Hon. Andrew Erskine on the street and walked with him to St Anne's Yards discoursing of the wretchedness of hypochondria. I was animated by hearing him talk rationally of it, as of a *fact* inexplicable like many others.

SATURDAY 20 NOVEMBER. I fairly sat out the Court of Session every day this week, and having read all the papers, was amused, but did not find myself strong enough to launch into society. Visited Mr John Spottiswoode, now in Edinburgh. Mr Sibthorpe and the young Campbells dined with us. —— ——.

SUNDAY 21 NOVEMBER. Was at New Church forenoon and afternoon, with little edification. In the evening read some of Heylyn's *Lectures*[39] and *The Rambler* to my wife, and was wonderfully well.

MONDAY 22 NOVEMBER. My wife was so good as to walk out to Lady Colville's with me to breakfast. I was greatly better, and had some good talk with the Hon. Andrew. He and I walked into town together, my wife having gone with Lady Colville in her coach. In the evening Veronica and Phemie and their governess[40] and Miss Jeanie Campbell came.

TUESDAY 23 NOVEMBER. I was not quite so well. Mr Spottiswoode, solicitor in London, etc., supped with us. I drank a glass or two of wine and some punch, which I had not done for some time.

WEDNESDAY 24 NOVEMBER. Went to the Grassmarket after dinner and looked at horses with Lord Rockville.[41] Then went home with him and drank some wine cordially. Thought I had a cold, so bathed my feet and went to bed early.

THURSDAY 25 NOVEMBER. Dictated two law papers wonderfully well. This was the anniversary of my marriage. I sincerely approved of my choice after fifteen years.

SATURDAY 27 NOVEMBER. Lord Lyle,[42] etc., dined with us. I eat and drank more than usual, and was a little disturbed. Played a great deal at draughts, my only amusement at present.

MONDAY 29 NOVEMBER. Walked out and visited worthy Sir Alexander Dick,

38 "A liqueur made of brandy flavoured with the stones of fruits" (*Applause*, p. 264, n. 1).
39 John Heylyn's *Theological Lectures at Westminster Abbey*, first published in 1749.
40 Miss Young (as to whom, see the entry for 20 February 1784 and the footnote with regard to the "disagreeable domestic affair").
41 The Grassmarket was the site of the principal horse and cattle market of the county.
42 Sir Walter Montgomerie-Cuninghame, who had claimed the peerage, which had been dormant for over 200 years.

and was revived somewhat. Lord Lyle gave me some concern at present, his manners were so agreeable and his affairs so perplexed. My brother John dined and drank tea with us. I conversed a good deal with him pretty cheerfully.

TUESDAY 30 NOVEMBER. Afternoon with my daughters saw procession of Freemasons. It did not strike me as usual.

WEDNESDAY 1 DECEMBER. One afternoon lately Surgeon Wood drank tea with us, and as I was troubled with scorbutic complaints, especially on my head, he advised me to take flour of brimstone and honey, and have my head shaved. I have taken his advice, and this night I again submitted to the razor, which was a kind of change to my existence. I was still by no means well. Lord Rockville called and supped with us, which cheered me somewhat.

FRIDAY 3 DECEMBER. My wife had asked Sir Andrew Cathcart to spend the evening with us, which luckily obliged me to rouse myself to a capacity of entertaining company. We had Lord Rockville and Lady Dumfries, etc., etc., and I played cards and was a lively companion, though by no means *content*, as the French say. Lady Colville and Lady Anne Erskine had drank tea with us, which did me good. As it was the first time the Knight of Carleton, the ancient Mair of Carrick,[43] had been in my house, my heart warmed and I drank a good deal too much.

SATURDAY 4 DECEMBER. Awaked very ill and continued so all day in bed. Luckily had no causes in the Court of Session. Rose at night. Was alarmed somewhat on account of Lord Lyle and his brother David having been apprehended by a Justiciary warrant, David having beat a Glasgow merchant and he and Lord Lyle and Henry having deforced a messenger and party.[44] David made his escape. Lord Lyle found bail.

THURSDAY 9 DECEMBER. These three days I have regularly visited my brother John, who was ill of a cold. He was calmly social. I had been sketching a letter to Mr Henry Dundas, entreating his counsel what to do in the present situation of my affairs and ambitious restlessness. But I could not please myself. Lord Rockville called before dinner and told me he had dined in his company the day before, and they had some conversation about me. Mr Dundas said my pamphlet on Fox's East India Bill was excellent. That the Ministry felt it. And that if anything of two or three hundred a year had fallen then, he believed I would have got it. Lord Rockville kindly said, "Has he not the same

43 "Sir Andrew Cathcart, Bt, of Killochan Castle, had inherited the estate and the title upon the death of his brother in March of this year. A 'mair (mayor) of fee' was an officer having delegated judicial or executive functions who held his office as a heritable possession. Sir Andrew's ancestor, the first of the Cathcarts of Carleton, became mair of fee of Carrick (the southernmost of the three districts of Ayrshire) by charter in 1485" (*Applause*, p. 267, n. 5).

44 "That is, they forcibly prevented a messenger-at-arms (his name was Govan) from performing his official duty, perhaps the execution of an attachment for a debt due to the 'Glasgow merchant'. Boswell wrote to [David] Boswell to get Henry Cuninghame, who had fled to London, to join his brothers in posting security of £100 to answer Govan's claim for damages and expenses. Henry sailed soon after for the East Indies with some money which Boswell advanced him on assignment of his allowance. He died there in 1790" (*Applause*, p. 267, n. 6).

merit yet?" Lord Rockville told my wife privately that my jocularity was against me in my claim for a judge's place, as also my openly declaring my antipathies to many people. He was very desirous I should have a more sedate behaviour. This was very friendly. He told her Mr Dundas told him he had received a letter from her on the subject of my settling in London. That he did not like to write, because it was a very delicate matter, for if he dissuaded me from my project, I might afterwards reproach him and say he had prevented me from rising in life. He said he would call and speak with her on the subject. This did not satisfy her. She thought he ought at least to have acknowledged receipt of her letter. I was discouraged to think that my merits were so coldly considered; and I indulged a kind of satisfaction in discontent, and earnestly wished for an opportunity to treat the world with disdain. In short, I was not at all as I could wish, but yet better than if sunk in listless melancholy. My wife rationally said I would be the better to have an agreeable company at my house one evening every week, and that it was a duty I owed to my family to keep up an intercourse with genteel people who might be friends to my children. She said that by keeping myself abstracted, I saw people's faults; whereas if I would mix with them, I would find they were better than I now thought them. All this was very proper. But my indolence, joined with the sadness of disappointed eagerness for distinction, made me live almost entirely without society at Edinburgh. I had today at dinner Mr French of the High School, to converse as to the course my son Sandy should follow to keep equal with his class.[45] I was tolerably tranquil. In the evening I revised the accounts of my father's trust, with the vouchers. His death was a gloomy, dejecting thought. How vain is human life!

SUNDAY 12 DECEMBER. Mr Henry Dundas had appointed with me to breakfast with him this morning to have a confidential conversation. I considered that taking measures to establish myself in life was a work of necessity for myself and mercy for my family, and therefore might be done on Sunday. After breakfasting with his sister and daughters, we retired to his room, where we talked, I think more than an hour. The import of what he said was this: that when he approved of my going directly to settle in London and try the English bar, he took it for granted I had £1,000 or £1,200 a year to spend, so that I could maintain my family in London. But as I had now informed him I had not above £500 a year to spend, his opinion was different. That he would not give me a rash advice, but would think seriously, and talk with Mr Pitt, with the Attorney-General,[46] and with the Chancellor,[47] and see whether I could get an office of some hundreds a year, or could be assured of immediate practice; either of which was indispensably necessary to make my settling in London rational. He said no man ever got good by pleading poverty; but I should give out that though a man of fortune, I had not a fortune that

45 "Sandy had been left at Auchinleck, probably because of the inguinal hernia from which he suffered" (*Applause*, p. 268, n. 8).
46 Richard Pepper Arden.
47 Lord Thurlow, the Lord Chancellor.

could afford a large expense. He said he could not find fault with my wishing to be in a wider sphere than in Scotland, for if an office of £10,000 a year should be created for him on condition of his being quiet here, he would not accept of it. (My imagination suggested this idea, and he eagerly adopted it.) He owned that the bar here was not what it has been; and he said he would not have me go to the bench for some time, at any rate, for that there would be an end of me (or some such phrase). He said I could then get no additional office; and I should first get something that I might carry to the bench with me. He gave me his hand and promised he would be in earnest to assist me; told me he had read my East India *Letter* at a Cabinet dinner; and if any office of some hundreds a year had then fallen, I should have had it. He told me he had a note of mine concerning my friend Johnston, and if an opportunity offered, would do for him.[48] He also said he had been active to get my brother David an office, as he had pledged himself to my father. He told Lord Carmarthen, "It was a deathbed promise and I must fulfil it."[49] I left him quite animated and full of manly hope, and saw no desponding objections. My wife thought all this might be artful, to keep me off from interfering with his numerous claimants of a seat on the bench. But I thought him sincere. We shall see. He promised to write me fully from London. I shall send him a memorial.[50] I was in such agitation I could not settle. Wished to dine and drink wine with Sir W. Forbes. But having met Lord Lyle, walked with him to the Abbey and King's Park, and then dined at a tavern with him and his brother David, who was in hiding from a caption.[51] I was to give good advice. Drank rather too much. Not a well-spent Sunday.

MONDAY 13 DECEMBER. The father of William Spence, a matross[52] indicted for destroying a distillery at Ford, had solicited me so anxiously to appear for his son this day in the Court of Justiciary that though my mind was not as it should be, I could not resist. I acquitted myself very well; boldly opposed the sanguinary keenness of the Court, and gave a good charge to the jury. I had the satisfaction to be informed in the evening by a note from Mr Jollie, one of their number, that the verdict was *not guilty*.[53] This gave me an agreeable agitation. ——.

48 "[Boswell] had been soliciting Dundas since 1782 for some office for Grange, whose legal practice was limited and whose small estate was encumbered by family debts" (*Applause*, p. 269, n. 1).
49 "He did, at last, in 1791, when David was appointed a clerk in the Navy Pay Office" (*Applause*, p. 269, n. 2). See Epilogue, p. 550.
50 "There is no record of such a memorial, or of the promised letter from Dundas. Boswell wrote to him 1 March 1785 soliciting the vacant office of Knight Mareschal of Scotland; Dundas replied on 30 March that he had not forgotten the conversation recorded above, but he declined to make the appointment, and firmly discouraged Boswell from leaving his home 'to embark on other pursuits here equally precarious and uninviting'" (*Applause*, p. 270, n. 3).
51 A judicial warrant for the apprehension of a debtor.
52 An artilleryman.
53 "Spence was accused of having been an active member of a riotous mob which on 7 June 1784 burned to the ground the distillery of Alexander Reid at Ford, a village about ten miles south-east of Edinburgh. This was one of several violent outbursts occurring about the same time. The rioters believed that in a time of great scarcity (in August and September the *Public Advertiser* was reporting famine in Scotland) the distillers were using huge quantities of all kinds of grain and even of potatoes, turnips, and carrots, thus inflating prices. The Lord Advocate (Ilay Campbell) prosecuted the case in person, and the Lord Justice Clerk gave a charge to find Spence guilty" (*Applause*, p. 270, n. 6).

TUESDAY 14 DECEMBER. When Spence was acquitted, I made him come home with me. The mob huzzaed and accompanied us to the head of James's Court. I had told him in the morning that he was safe. I gave him a glass of wine, and a good admonition to keep out of mobs again. Lord Rockville came and joined. I insisted that his Lordship and I should dine together, either at my house or his, as I was in high spirits. He made me dine with him. We were cordial.

WEDNESDAY 15 DECEMBER. I enjoyed the credit of bringing off Spence,[54] and continued to attend the Court of Session assiduously.

FRIDAY 17 DECEMBER. This must be ever remembered as a melancholy day, for it brought me the dismal news of my great and good friend, Dr Samuel Johnson. His physician, Dr Brocklesby, favoured me with a very full letter dated on Monday the 13, the night of his death. I was stunned, and in a kind of amaze. I had company engaged to sup with us; and as it might have appeared vain affectation to forbid their coming, I received them and behaved with much ease, and said nothing of the dismal news but to worthy Sir William Forbes, just as he was going away. I did not shed tears. I was not tenderly affected. My feeling was just one large expanse of stupor. I knew that I should afterwards have sorer sensations. ——.

SATURDAY 18 DECEMBER. I mentioned Dr Johnson's death to Mr George Wallace, Mr Nairne, Mr Maclaurin, and Lord Hailes. He said, "I wish every-one were as well prepared for the great change as he was." I sat again some time with Sir William Forbes and talked of this sad event. My mind had for some days been unexpectedly vigorous, so that I could bear more than when relaxed by melancholy. My resolution was to honour his memory by doing as much as I could to fulfil his noble precepts of religion and morality. I prayed to GOD that now my much respected friend was gone, I might be a follower of him who I trusted was now by faith and patience inheriting the promises. But it gave me concern that I was conscious of a deadness of spiritual feeling, and indeed a cold indifference as to the awful subject of religion, having just a sort of superficial speculation that I might take my chance with a careless hope of mercy. This, I believe, is the state of most people, even of those who have had the ordinary religious education. I was desirous to be better. In the evening I read two accounts of Dr Johnson's death in the *Public Advertiser* and *London Chronicle*. And I had a letter from Mr Dilly mentioning it, and in the true spirit of *the trade* wanting to know if I could have an octavo volume of 400 pages of his conversations ready by February. I had had a letter from him lately suggesting that I might be the editor of all his works and write his life. I answered him that I had a large collection of materials for his life, but would write it deliberately. I was now uneasy to think that there would be

---

54 "He deserved it: the newspapers report a long list of rioters who were imprisoned, and to the end of the summer many others were still being prosecuted successfully" (*Applause*, p. 271, n. 7).

considerable expectations from me of memoirs of my illustrious friend, but that habits of indolence and dejection of spirit would probably hinder me from laudable exertion. I wished I could write now as when I wrote my *Account of Corsica*. But I hoped I should do better than I at first apprehended.

MONDAY 20 DECEMBER. (Writing 28) I recollect nothing except making a motion in Exchequer for the first time.[55] It was for the Laird of Logan. Also attended a meeting of the Faculty of Advocates.

THURSDAY 23 DECEMBER. My worthy friend Lord Rockville asked me to his family dinner with Lady Colville. I was in such sad spirits I could not go, but did not dine at all, and walked in the Greyfriars churchyard. The weather was severe.

FRIDAY 24 DECEMBER. The Court of Session rose for the Christmas vacation. I was quite dull.

SATURDAY 25 DECEMBER. The holy festival of Christmas could not dissipate the dreary clouds which hung upon my mind. It vexed me much that my old and confidential friend John Johnston of Grange, who had dined cordially with me every Christmas since ever I had a house, was not come to town. He had been ill, and the weather was rigid. But I was really angry that he had now failed to be with me. It seemed that this was an extraordinary year. Dr Johnson was gone. Grange was absent. My chief satisfaction was a kind of obstinate firmness which despair makes us feel. I went to Mr Wight's[56] in the forenoon to consider a Submission to him and me by Craigengillan and his brother David concerning the extent of heirship movables, a question never decided by the Court of Session.[57] I was sufficiently clear-headed. But my heart and imagination were dreary. I took my two daughters Veronica and Phemie to the New English Chapel. They were charmed with the evening service. I was cold and unhappy. Our three youngest children being in the country was a great want of pleasing variety.

SUNDAY 26 DECEMBER. Heard Dr Blair in the forenoon and Mr Hardy in the afternoon, with little profit. Drank tea at Lady Auchinleck's, and then paid a visit to Old Lady Wallace.[58] Grew somewhat better. Was convinced that I require a succession of different company. Mr Nairne supped with us.

MONDAY 27 DECEMBER. I had been supinely lazy in the morning for a long time. Today for the first time I made Sandy Walker, my clerk, come at seven,

---

55 That is, in the Court of Exchequer (for which, see Introduction, p. 10).
56 Alexander Wight resided at 16 Princes Street.
57 "Boswell and Wight were the arbiters in a dispute between David McAdam, heir to the landed estate of his brother Quintin, and his younger brothers, John and James, who had inherited the movable effects (furnishings, livestock, and equipment). John and James challenged some of the movable articles that David had claimed on the legal principle that protected an heir from succeeding to a dismantled property. In a Decreet filed 28 December 1784 the arbiters rejected some of David's claims…, but they also allowed him items he had not requested" (*Applause*, p. 273, n. 4).
58 Old Lady Wallace now resided in Thistle Court, between St David Street and Hanover Street.

when I rose and fell to dictating a Memorial for Dr Hall of Newcastle in an action for the freight of a ship.[59] I laboured all day and finished the paper to my mind.

TUESDAY 28 DECEMBER. Revised a long Memorial, altered it a little, and made several additions so as to form Answers for my friend Dempster to a Petition against him in the Court of Session by Watson of Turin.[60] Went to drink tea with Mr George Wallace. But he had company at dinner. Drank tea with Mr James Donaldson, bookseller. Mr Mercer, wine-merchant, was there. I was somewhat cheered by conversation. Here I read Dr Johnson's will in an English newspaper. His death still made an impression of amazement upon my mind. I could not fully believe it. My *imagination* was not convinced. I was a little uneasy that I was not mentioned in his will amongst other friends who had books left them "as a token of remembrance". But I considered that I had several books in a present from him, and many more valuable tokens. I resolved however to make the most of my connexion with him in an honourable way.

Boswell went to Auchinleck by himself on 30 December. "I ... found my three youngest children well," he writes, "was attracted by country affairs, and instantaneously was relieved of that wretchedness which had depressed me." And Boswell expressed himself "highly satisfied with Sandy's progress in Latin".

59 This was John Hall, M.D., the physician in charge of the asylum at Newcastle in which Boswell's brother John had formerly been an inmate. Dr Hall was also the owner of a commercial ship, the *Morning Star*. "Two Dunbar merchants, Charles and Robert Fall, had chartered the 'Morning Star'... to carry merchandise between Newcastle and the Baltic. They refused to pay the full sum for the hire which had been agreed because the ship had not completed the journey in the time stipulated" (Ballantyne, 85 06 22). For the outcome of the action, see the entry for 14 March 1785 and relevant footnote.
60 "A renewed attempt to enjoin George Dempster to restore a dam on Restennet, a small loch entirely on Dempster's property but the chief source of water for an ancient mill of which Watson was proprietor. Watson argued traditional usage, Dempster that Watson had been granted only an indulgence. The real point at issue seems to have been that Dempster wished to prevent the washing away of a marl (a valuable soil-conditioner) from his lake, whereas Watson, by continuing the overflow, wished to reduce competition with marl-dragging on a loch of his own. The Lords reaffirmed their interlocutor favouring Dempster" (*Applause*, p. 273, n. 5).

1785

13 JANUARY – 27 FEBRUARY.[1] I returned to Edinburgh on the 13 January. My good spirits continued. I found Grange returned from the country, by no means in good health and spirits. I did him good by my company. During this month and February (till the 23 of that month, on which I am now writing), I had upon the whole a pretty good life, though not quite as I could wish; for I could not apply to the writing out of my *Tour to the Hebrides in Company with Samuel Johnson, LL.D.*, as I hoped I might do. Fortunately for me, Mr Baron Gordon and Dr Blair, to the first of whom I read a good deal of my original MS. in the forenoon of Monday the 21 and to the latter in the afternoon, confirmed me in thinking that it might be printed with little variation; so (writing 27 February) I resolved that I would set myself down quietly in London and get the work executed easily.

I had been several times at Lady Colville's, and often at Lord Rockville's; had dined at Lord Stonefield's,[2] Lady Auchinleck's, Balmuto's, and some other houses, and on 23 February took an occasional family dinner with Mrs McAdam, where I drank wine enough to be heated;[3] then drank tea with Dr Blair and sat with him till nine o'clock upon literary discourse and a little upon religion. He freely owned he did not believe the eternity of punishment. I dined one day with Commissioner Cochrane cordially. My practice in the Court of Session, though not very lucrative, made a creditable appearance. But my wish for "being a spoke in the great wheel", as Jack Lee expressed it to me,[4] made me restless. I had not many company to dine and sup with us. But had some. The state of my affairs disturbed me a good deal. But Sir William Forbes obligingly proposed I should give him and Company security on my house in St Andrew's Square[5] for my debt to them, making £1,400; and if I paid the interest regularly, I might clear off the principal at my leisure. This was a relief to me. On Tuesday [22 February] Sir Philip and Lady Ainslie and Baron Gordon supped with us. There had been a coldness between Maclaurin and me, as I had disapproved of his deserting Mr Dundas when he was turned out of office. I expostulated with him, and we got into tolerable terms again. I dined with him one day at Mr Mackintosh the advocate's,[6] a

1 This entry and the entries for 5 and 7-14 March are taken from Boswell's "review" of the period 30 December 1784 to 24 March 1785 set out in *Applause*, pp. 275-284.
2 Lord Stonefield's house was at 11 George Square (*B.O.E.C.*, Vol. 26, p. 141).
3 As the editors of *Applause* observe, at p. 277, n. 7, there is some confusion here, for Boswell later says that on this day he dined with Walter Campbell of Shawfield and supped at Hamilton of Grange's.
4 John Lee, who had been Attorney-General under the Fox-North Coalition, had given advice to Boswell with regard to his proposed move to the English bar.
5 That is, the house at 20 St Andrew Square which Boswell inherited from his father and of which Lady Auchinleck had the liferent.
6 Robert Mackintosh had by now acquired the house in Argyle Square which he was to occupy for the rest of his life (see the entry for 28 February 1783 and footnote).

good rational social day; more like a London day than any I have had for a long time. On Wednesday [23 February] I dined jovially at Shawfield's and supped at Hamilton of Grange's.[7] Was so ill on Thursday morning that I was obliged to return home from the Court of Session in the forenoon and go to bed again for some time. On Friday was still a little uneasy from having taken too much wine on Wednesday. I dined once with Grange at Sir Alexander Dick's [and] we had [a] hearty day, which pleased both Grange and me at the time, though I felt it a little incongruous with the classical temperance of Prestonfield. Drinking may be had in a thousand places. Classical elegance is rare. [This winter] I had upon the whole tolerable spirits. But I did not perceive myself improving, and no wonder, for I read almost nothing but law papers.

Colonel Montgomerie was one night in Edinburgh in his way to London. We drank only a bottle of old Madeira in negus. He had at the time of last election said to Sir John Whitefoord he could not be for him, for he would be for me were he not to be Member himself. I sounded him to discover what return I might expect for my most generous friendly keenness for him. My wife had with her usual penetration assured me that he would not be for me, but would be for one of his own brothers. I expressed to him my wish to be in Parliament. He said he wished I was. I asked if he could get a good office, would he go out of Parliament? He said he would not choose to do it. "But", said I, "supposing you to become Earl of Eglinton, would you support me as a candidate for the county?" He said he could not say. In short, I perceived that I had indulged a fallacious notion of his having a reciprocal wish for my obtaining what I was so happy he had at last obtained. It hurt me a good deal. I resolved to stand upon my own legs and exert myself to secure if possible a respectable share of the independent interest of the county, by which in the midst of contending parties I might perhaps be successful. My wife observed very justly that Colonel Montgomerie would be much more inclined to oblige people who lived in his own style than me who avoided much visiting and entertaining.

SATURDAY 5 MARCH. The Laird of Fairlie supped with us, together with Matthew Dickie. I was at this time hurried with a variety of business in the Court of Session, though it was observed by many of my brethren at the bar that there was much less business in the Court this winter than had been formerly. I had one evening played at whist and brag at Lord Rockville's, and sat late, and felt the feverish fretfulness of gaming, though I did not lose much. I had attended regularly Signor Corri's concerts for his scholars, at which my two daughters sung and played wonderfully well; and I had been at Dunn's assemblies twice,[8] once with my wife, who dressed better this winter and went more into company than she used to do. My faith and piety were quiet and constant, though not vigorous. I suppose I am too nicely anxious for a dignified course of existence.

7 Alexander Hamilton of Grange (d. 1837), advocate (admitted 6 March 1781). He resided in James's Court.
8 At Dunn's hotel in St Andrew Square.

529

Mine is, I dare say, better than that of most of those of my rank. Yet I am sadly dissatisfied.

MONDAY 7 MARCH. I laboured hard all day dictating a long Petition for Janet Buchanan for marriage or damages against the Laird of Macnab.[9]

TUESDAY 8 MARCH. Clerk Matthew and Grange dined with me, and Grange and I went to Schetky's concert and heard the music in *Macbeth* well performed.[10]

WEDENESDAY 9 MARCH. I dined at Mr Matthew Dickie's with the Laird of Fairlie, and my wife and I supped at Dr Blair's very agreeably.

THURSDAY 10 MARCH. [T]he Hon. Andrew Erskine, Grange, and I dined at Fortune's to revive old acquaintance. We were very cordial, but I pushed the bottle too much. We drank two bottles of port apiece. But I was not much the worse for it.

FRIDAY 11 MARCH. I dined at Lord Rockville's (a party made about three weeks ago to be very merry) with Harry Erskine, Maclaurin, Cullen, Baron Gordon, Lord Eskgrove, Lord Swinton, Mr John Anstruther;[11] and Lord Haddo was added to the party by his coming to town accidentally. The party did not do so well as we expected till Cullen's mimicry made us laugh immoderately. There was too much law topics and not enough of variety and wit. I was checked too by thinking that it was the night of Barnard's ball, where both Lord Rockville and I had children dancing, yet we did not go to it. There was a great deal of wine drank. I in particular indulged in it, and challenged Lord Haddo to cordial bumpers, and when the company broke up about twelve, he and I sat by ourselves, had a little table in a corner by the fire, and took an additional dose. Then we joined the ladies and several of the gentlemen who stayed, and we played brag till about two in the morning. I was so much intoxicated that I knew very little of what went on, and after I came home was exceedingly ill.

SATURDAY 12 MARCH. [D]id not get up till past four in the afternoon. I was really vexed, and in a horrid state of relaxation. It shocked me too that I did not recollect what had passed, so that I might have perhaps behaved absurdly; and as I had borrowed of Lord Haddo to play at brag, I could not be sure how much I had lost. I thought I recollected owing Lord Haddo just a guinea. But as my wife well observed, I was in his power for whatever sum he might name. I grew a little better at night.

9 Janet Buchanan claimed that she was married to the Laird by virtue of a mutual declaration, which in those days was one of the modes by which a marriage could be constituted in Scotland. She lost her action in 1786, after Boswell had moved to London (*Applause*, p. 281, n. 1).

10 "Johann Schetky, a well-known composer and cellist descended from an ancient Transylvanian family, settled in Edinburgh in 1772. He was a friend of Robert Burns, at whose request he set to music his song, 'Clarinda, mistress of my soul'. The instrumental and vocal music to *Macbeth*, which was popular since the beginning of the century and was once attributed to Purcell, is now believed to have been composed by the singer Richard Leveridge" (*Applause*, p. 281, n. 2).

11 John Anstruther (1753-1811), *later* Sir John Anstruther, Bt, admitted advocate 2 August 1774, called to the English bar 1779, M.P. Anstruther Easter Burghs 1783-90, Cockermouth 1790-96, Anstruther Easter Burghs 1796-97, 1806-11, Chief-Justice Bengal 1798-1806, Receiver General of Bishops Rents in Scotland 1780.

SUNDAY 13 MARCH. I visited Lord Rockville, and found my loss at play did not exceed a guinea and a half. I drank tea with Lord Eskgrove by appointment.

MONDAY 14 MARCH. Instead of going to Auchinleck as I intended, I stayed and dictated a law paper for April boxes,[12] which I saw in print; as also the greatest part of the Case for Mercer of Lethendy in his appeal to the House of Lords for more damages on account of John Duff, his servant, having been adjudged as a recruit;[13] as also the greatest part of a Reclaiming Petition for Dr Hall, most of which was copied verbatim from my Memorial for him.[14] I had a satisfaction in getting business thus dispatched.

On 16 March Boswell and his wife went to Auchinleck, where their three youngest children were "well and lively by having been all winter in the country". Five days later Boswell set off for London, arriving there on the 30th and availing himself as usual of the room reserved for him at Paoli's. Less than a month later, Ilay Campbell introduced a bill in the House of Commons to reduce the number of the Lords of Session from fifteen to ten and to increase the salaries of the remaining judges.[15] Boswell resolved to write a pamphlet expressing his opposition to the proposal, and he set to work almost straight away. However, as Lustig and Pottle point out, "The bill was actually Henry Dundas's, whom Boswell should have conciliated in every way if he was really serious in his suit for political preferment. But he was outraged by all innovation, particularly as regarded English guarantees to Scotland, and the sense of having truckled to Dundas rankled. He threw prudence to the winds and wrote the most extravagant of all his publications, calling Dundas 'Harry the Ninth' and airing his grievance over the Ayrshire election. But he also argued to the point that the law would be delayed by reducing a court already overburdened with cases, and that increasing the salaries of fewer judges would make their appointments altogether an object of political preferment. Written in the first person and with great fervour, the Letter to the People of Scotland *(1785) is both a patriotic document and a calculated effort to win the independent interest [see the entry for 13 January – 27 February 1785] for the seat in Parliament that Boswell announced he would seek at the next election."[16] The pamphlet was to be published on 26 May and within two days the fifty copies which Boswell sent to Edinburgh were all sold.*

Boswell also kept himself busy preparing the first edition of his Journal of a Tour to the Hebrides *(much of the revisal of which was done with his friend and literary collaborator,*

---

12 That is, the judges' boxes in which papers requiring to be submitted in April could be lodged.
13 See the entries for 29 November 1781, 5 December 1781 and 2 January 1782 and relevant footnotes.
14 See the entry for 27 December 1784. "Boswell had argued that the charter-party (a contract between ship-owners and merchants for safe delivery of a cargo) did not specify a time-limit but called only for 'expeditious' delivery, and that despite repairs, problems in loading, bad weather, and ill winds, the *Morning Star* got back faster than other ships. But on 19 February 1785 Lord Kennet reduced the charges more than £1 sterling per last (eighty bushels) of grain to the rate generally effective when the *Morning Star* actually sailed from Newcastle for the Baltic... Three months later the Court adhered to the Lord Ordinary's decision. Boswell advised Dr Hall that the sum at issue did not warrant an appeal to the House of Lords, but offered to assist him without fee if he was determined to try it" (*Applause*, p. 283, n. 7).
15 The bill was known as the "Diminishing Bill".
16 *Applause*, p. 288, n. 4. The full title of the pamphlet is *A Letter to the People of Scotland, on the Alarming Attempt to Infringe the Articles of Union, and Introduce a Most Pernicious Innovation, by Diminishing the Number of the Lords of Session.*

Edmond Malone), obtaining materials for his proposed biography of Johnson, and revising Mercer of Lethendy's Case in connection with his appeal to the House of Lords. In addition to all of this, Boswell immersed himself as usual in the bustling London social scene, feeling himself "quite at home *in* England".[17]

By 12 May Boswell had started to have regular assignations with a prostitute by the name of Betsy Smith, of whom he seems to have been genuinely fond; but later that month she became ill (perhaps suffering from a sexually transmitted infection) and reluctantly allowed herself to be admitted to St Thomas's Hospital. Boswell visited her on a number of occasions and met the hospital's initial charges. When she came out of hospital on 6 July Boswell offered to find her a place as a lady's maid, but she indicated that she would prefer to return to her former ways.

On 20 May Boswell attended the King's levee and was delighted to see the King approaching "with a truly benevolent, smiling countenance", and was even more pleased to find the King enquiring as to how Boswell was progressing with his life of Johnson. "This was really a valuable conversation," writes Boswell, "and the King's gracious benignity refreshed the loyal flame in my bosom." Boswell followed this up by writing to the King (on 6 June) to consult him "on a point of delicacy" with regard to Boswell's forthcoming edition of the Journal of a Tour to the Hebrides, *namely, would the King permit Boswell when referring to Prince Charles Edward Stewart to call him "Prince Charles" rather than "*Pretender*"? Boswell assured the King that he was clear that the right of the House of Stewart was "extinguished", but added that he could not help feeling that the expression "Pretender" would be "an insult to an unfortunate man who must think very differently, and who is still alive". At the King's levee on 15 June, Boswell was able to speak to His Majesty on the matter and the result was that Boswell received permission to refer to the Prince as "the grandson of King James the Second".*

The House of Lords' hearing in the appeal of Mercer of Lethendy took place on 8 June, when Boswell and an English barrister argued against Ilay Campbell and Thomas Erskine. The outcome was that the Lords refused the appeal, taking the view that the level of damages awarded by the Court of Session was quite sufficient.

On 5 July Boswell started to sit for the famous portrait of him by Sir Joshua Reynolds, the fee for which Boswell promised to pay out of the first fees which he hoped to receive as an English barrister. (The painting, however, was ultimately given to Boswell as a gift.)

Boswell took the opportunity afforded by this visit to London to indulge his morbid fascination with public executions and to renew his acquaintance with the notorious Mrs Rudd, with whom he had several flirtatious meetings leading finally to sexual relations (referred to by Boswell as a "gross folly"[18]).

The Journal of a Tour to the Hebrides *was published on 1 October and was an immediate success, the first edition of 1,500 copies being sold out in less than three weeks. A second and third edition appeared within a year. "Yet", as Lustig and Pottle explain, "the general character of the reception was vigorous applause alternating with strident disapproval of the same subject matter. Reviewers, while they were entertained, were disquieted and baffled by Boswell's lack of reticence and his method of characterization by*

17 Journal, 6 May 1785.
18 Journal, 24 November 1785.

minute detail—what he later called his giving of a 'Flemish picture'. To such critics the Tour *had on principle to be condemned as a farrago, a torrent of indiscriminate minutiae. Contemporaries of a great innovative work, they recoiled from its revolutionary feature: familiar and ignoble detail controlled by a presiding impression of magnanimity, goodness, and compassion."*[19]

Boswell left London on 24 September and reached Auchinleck on 3 October. After staying for a month at Auchinleck, Boswell went to Edinburgh for a week prior to setting off for London once again, this time to complete the required number of meals at the Inner Temple to gain admission to the English bar. He reached London on 17 November, arriving in bad spirits on account of indecision as to whether or not to settle in London. In his journal entry for 1 December he writes, "I was in dejected perplexity... The idea of making my children aliens *from Scotland was dismal... I shrunk from the English bar... Was very sad."*

Another matter that was depressing Boswell was a "most shocking, abusive letter" which he had received from Lord Macdonald on 27 November complaining about Boswell's pejorative comments on him in the Tour *with regard to the poor hospitality shown to Boswell and Johnson in September 1773 during their stay with Macdonald at Armadale on the Isle of Skye. Boswell thought it might be imperative for him to challenge Lord Macdonald to a duel; and he went so far as to get his new-found friend John Courtenay (an Irish-born M.P.) to show him how to stand and fire a pistol. However, after several days of acute anxiety, the whole matter was patched up to Boswell's satisfaction by persuading Lord Macdonald to withdraw the offensive remarks from his letter. Nevertheless, Boswell was soon once again in a state of acute depression as a consequence of his other worries; and on 20 December, having completed the revisal of the second edition of the* Tour, *he decided to return to Scotland to be reunited with his family and to leave it to his wife to decide on the proposed move to London. He departed on the 22nd and arrived in Edinburgh six days later.*

WEDNESDAY 28 DECEMBER. I felt a little strange but not so much so as I expected. Had the highest consolation in seeing my dear wife and children, and the cloud of melancholy was quite dissipated by *experiencing* that I could so soon be at home from London.

THURSDAY 29 DECEMBER. Cold weather. At home all day except seeing Grange, who had been very gloomy, but was better.

FRIDAY 30 DECEMBER. Had visits of Sir W. Forbes, Captain A. Cochrane, Balmuto, and Mr Stobie. At home all day. Enjoyed my tranquillity, but dreaded a relapse.

SATURDAY 31 DECEMBER. Walked out with Captain A. Cochrane and dined with Commissioner Cochrane, who was very glad to see me. Mr Stobie there. It was a great comfort to me after my dreary suffering to find old ideas of Sir John Cochrane of Ochiltree,[20] and of Culross, etc., revived. I just enjoyed the *present,*

19 *Applause*, p. 345.
20 "Sir John Cochrane, second son of the first Earl of Dundonald, had founded the line at Ochiltree" (*Experiment*, p. 22, n. 6).

seeing the Commissioner easy and cheerful. Heated myself somewhat with wine, which made me a little violent in my temper when I came home. Visited my brother John. ——.

1786

SUNDAY 1 JANUARY. Heard Dr Blair preach an admirable sermon on "Peace be with thee, peace be with thy household",[1] etc. Visited him between sermons and found him wonderfully pleased with my *Tour* and Court of Session letter.[2] Heard a Mr Finlayson preach in the afternoon. My brother John drank tea with us. In the evening, heard my children say divine lessons. The result of being abroad this day convinced me that my *imaginations* as to *conjectures* about my settling in London, and *difficulties* of various sorts, were only in my own mind. Grange supped with us, and grew quite comfortable. ——.

TUESDAY 3 JANUARY. Having drank wine the day before both at dinner and supper, and the frost being intense, I had a headache, and breakfasted calmly in bed. I had done some good since I came home in assisting Sandy in Latin and Veronica and Phemie in French. Mr G. Wallace paid me a visit. [He expressed the] opinion that I should make a fair trial of the English bar (though he did not imagine I could have great success); and he suggested that there are a great many places in the gift of the Lord Chancellor, who might give me one. He was clear that if the trial should not succeed, I need be under no difficulty of return-ing to the Court of Session. In short, I was much the better for hearing his thoughts. Lunardi (at the earnest desire of my children I invited him)[3] and Corri and Miss Mary Grant supped with us. We had a cheerful gay evening, and I thought with pleasure of having a house in London. ——.

WEDNESDAY 4 JANUARY. George Campbell dined with us. He and I drank tea with Lady Auchinleck, nobody with her but her old mother. I was quieted and had my loose fancy consolidated by her steady sense and firmness of spirit, and by the recollection of my worthy respectable father. What a blessing it is to have a strong mind! In the evening helped my children with their lessons, but still I was so sickly in mind that I could not *feel* the advantage of good educa-tion. Mr Wood had been with me one morning. He was of opinion that if I had not come down to see my family, my disease might have pressed upon me to such a degree that I might not have recovered for some time. The frost was intense. ——.

THURSDAY 5 JANUARY. Very bad weather. At home all day. Helped my chil-dren with their lessons. Played at whist with my wife and some of them. Sir Archibald Grant[4] visited us in the forenoon, Robert Boswell in the evening.

FRIDAY 6 JANUARY. Went with my wife and two eldest daughters to see the

1 I Samuel 25: 6.
2 That is, the *Letter to the People of Scotland*, 1785.
3 "Vincenzo Lunardi, a celebrated balloonist, had made his most recent ascent in Edinburgh on 20 December 1785, when he fell into the sea and narrowly escaped drowning" (*Experiment*, p. 24, n. 4).
4 Sir Archibald Grant of Monymusk (1731-1796), 3rd Bt.

model of a balloon in the Outer Parliament House. Walked in it and in the Inner House with curious sensations. Went a little into the Advocates' Library. Felt how easily I could return to my place as an advocate. But it seemed a narrow sphere. Sat a good while with Maclaurin, who was of opinion I would succeed in Westminster Hall, and if not, that there was not the least objection to my returning to the Court of Session. It relieved me to find that what I had dreaded as alarming, dangerous, and ruinous was a simple and easy experiment. After dinner even three glasses of port heated me and made me restless and weary and fretful. Tea did me good. Knockroon, who had come to town today, was with us and did me good. My wife was not well tonight.

SATURDAY 7 JANUARY. Visited Grange, as I have done many times which are not mentioned. Bad day. Life was passed much in the same way as it has been on several days since I came last down. My brother John and Mr Lawrie dined with us. ———.

SUNDAY 8 JANUARY. I set out, intending to walk to Prestonfield, being uneasy that I had delayed so long to pay my respects to the family of my valuable departed friend.[5] But as I passed by Mr Gib's seceding meeting-house, I asked if he was to preach, and being informed he was, I thought I would gratify my curiosity in experiencing in some degree the vulgar and dreary fanaticism of the last century in Scotland. So in I went and heard him preach with great fluency, in their way, though now very old.[6] A probationer also preached, so I was too late for Prestonfield. They did not preach long, and there was nothing wild, but just the common old-fashioned Presbyterian way of haranguing.

MONDAY 9 JANUARY. My wife and I went in a coach and paid a visit at Prestonfield. I was much affected to think that Sir Alexander was gone. Grange dined with us. In the afternoon I received a long letter from the Lord Chancellor which I thought seemed to decide against my venturing in Westminster Hall. It sunk me a good deal. But my excellent wife suggested that I could not take it as a *decision*, but only as an able evasion of taking any charge of me.

TUESDAY 10 JANUARY. It pleased me that I was every day of *some* use to my children in assisting them in their lessons. Mr George Wallace came and stayed dinner. I had a bowel complaint from cold, and drank rather too much warm punch. He made my staying here, going and returning—in short, doing as I should find agreeable—to be not at all embarrassing. But I had no keen and high impulses.

WEDNESDAY 11 JANUARY. Very bad weather. I was somewhat uneasy from having taken punch yesterday. It always disagrees with me. My wife talked to

5 Sir Alexander Dick had died on 10 November 1785.
6 The Rev. Adam Gib (1714-88), who in 1741 had been appointed minister of the secession congregation in Bristo Street, Edinburgh, had been forced to give up the church there in 1753 on account of a legal dispute over the building; but his congregation then "built a large meeting-place for him in Nicolson Street [now the South Side Community Centre (Harris, p. 288)], where till near his death... he ministered to an immense congregation". A strict Presbyterian, an "active controversialist", and by nature "rude, scornful, and despotic", he was given the soubriquet of "Pope Gib" (DNB).

me most rationally of taking care of my estate and living within my income, and thus (whatever trials I should make) being independent.

THURSDAY 12 JANUARY. Was at a meeting of the curators of the Advocates' Library.[7] Felt myself very easy. Lord Monboddo came into the Library. I bowed to him, but he did not speak to me. I understood afterwards that he was violent against me.[8] I did not care. I considered that it would make him *fair game* in Dr Johnson's *Life*. I sat some time in the room behind Creech's shop,[9] and had an impression of Edinburgh being a very good place.

FRIDAY 13 JANUARY. Breakfasted at Lady Colville's; was very well received and asked to dine. Walked into town with the Hon. A. E.,[10] and compared notes on hypochondria. He had felt its making one imagine oneself inferior to every mortal. I went out and dined. He and the ladies all thought that my making a trial of the English bar was rational, since I had such a desire for it, and I might afterwards be quiet. He and I drank claret cordially till near ten at night and had a great deal of good conversation.

SATURDAY 14 JANUARY. Not being in the habit of drinking much wine, I awaked uneasy. I walked out to Lady Colville's and made my apology to the ladies, who told me they were happy I had done so well. My spirits, however, were a good deal sunk. The Hon. A. E. and I walked into town, and for a large portion of the way had the company of Sir John Whitefoord, who met us. He wished I were returned from my trial of London, for that "our lots were not cast there". I had at dinner Mr French, Mr Cauvin, Mr Stalker, my children's masters, and Mr Legat, who engraved the print from my picture of Mary, Queen of Scots.[11] I had one of these days walked with Principal Robertson, who was much pleased with the print, and in good humour with my *Tour*.

SUNDAY 15 JANUARY. Went to the New Church in the forenoon. Lord Rockville paid me a visit, and was clear that I should appear in court in my wig and gown as usual. The children said divine lessons. Went with Sir Charles and Colonel George Preston and dined soberly at Commissioner Cochrane's, supposing that we should not all meet again. Sir Charles drank tea at our house, and he and George and Grange supped. It was comfortable to feel myself as much *at home* as ever.

---

7 He had been appointed a curator on 24 December 1784 (*Experiment*, p. 27, n. 2).

8 In his *Letter to the People of Scotland*, 1785, Boswell had referred to Lord Monboddo as a "grotesque philosopher, whom ludicrous *fable* represents as going about avowing his hunger, and wagging his tail, fain to become cannibal, and eat his deceased brethren". Monboddo must also have been offended by some of the references to him in Boswell's *Journal of a Tour to the Hebrides*.

9 "Creech's shop", at the east end of the Luckenbooths facing down the High Street, was where Allan Ramsay's old bookselling and publishing business (which had been run by him in the flat above) was carried on by his successors. The business had now been taken over by the celebrated William Creech (1745-1815), who was Lord Provost of Edinburgh from 1811-1813.

10 Andrew Erskine.

11 Boswell's picture of Mary, Queen of Scots (depicting her abdication), was a large painting commissioned by him from the Scottish artist Gavin Hamilton in Rome in 1765. Boswell saw the completed picture for the first time in London eleven years later, when both he and Sir Joshua Reynolds were disappointed with it. The Queen, thought Boswell, "had neither beauty in a high degree nor grace in any degree" (Journal, 18 March 1776).

TUESDAY 17 JANUARY. Went to the Court of Session, and first walked in with my hat and stick as a gentleman. My spirits were good, so that though I felt a little awkwardly, I was not uneasy. My brethren stared a good deal at me in the Inner House. Upon which I said, "I must go and put on my wig and gown, not to be particular." Having done so, I walked about and shook hands with numbers, and talked quite easily of having two strings to my bow, and not ceasing to be an *advocate* by taking my degree as a *barrister*; and I was most agreeably surprised to find that I might go and come as [I] found most agreeable.

WEDNESDAY 18 JANUARY. Again attended the Court of Session, and had this day a Petition for Fairlie, which I had drawn with great care, put in as a proof that I might practise when I chose to do it.[12]

THURSDAY 19 JANUARY. This morning my Petition for Fairlie was moved in court, and I took care to support it by a few words from the bar, that my voice might again be heard. I was listened to with attention, and my Petition had the effect of showing the judges that their former interlocutor, which had been pronounced in my absence, *nem. con.*,[13] was not just; so it was ordered to be answered. The Lord President then said, "My Lords, I yesterday found fault with papers I have much more pleasure in commending. And I must say that this petition by my friend Mr Boswell (whom I am happy to see here) is very well drawn, both as to matter and manner. And let me tell him, as we know he can do so well, we will not take worse off his hand." I bowed respectfully and said, "I am always happy when I am honoured with the approbation of your Lordships."[14] He then sent one of the clerks of court to invite me to dine with him next day. I went round to the back of his chair and told him I was very sorry I was engaged next day to the christening of Balmuto's son. "But", said I, "I won't be without my dinner with your Lordship. I'll wait upon you any day you please." "Come today at four", said he. This public praise and this invitation (which I took care to make known) had a wonderful effect. The narrow-minded and timid were confounded at my being so received after my *Letter* upon diminishing the number of the judges, etc. I had a very hearty day with the President, and it would have been more so had not Balmuto been there, for he was a check on my gaiety. There was nobody else but Mr Liston, minister of Aberdour, Newbigging his clerk, and a young man who seemed to be a reader to him or one in some such capacity. We drank till near nine. His Lordship and I took a better share than the rest. He was now almost deprived of sight, but his animal spirits were as good as ever. His coarseness was not pleasing. But upon the whole we did admirably.

FRIDAY 20 JANUARY. Appeared in the Court of Session, and talked of my jovial

---

12 "Alexander Fairlie, a noted agricultural improver, was being sued for non-payment by Thomas Clayton, a plasterer, who had worked on Fairlie's new house. Boswell, a good friend of Fairlie's, having offered to submit a petition on his behalf, drew one up on very short notice" (*Experiment*, p. 29, n. 3).
13 Abbreviation of *nemine contradicente*, meaning unanimously.
14 "The Court nevertheless upheld its earlier decision in favour of Clayton by one vote" (*Experiment*, p. 29, n. 4).

interview of yesterday. I felt with disgust the vulgar familiarity of some of my brethren, and contrasted it with the manners of my London friends. It provoked me a little that my literary superiority seemed to have no effect here. I went to Prestonfield and attended a meeting of the guardians of Sir Alexander Dick's younger children. I then was present at the baptism of Balmuto's son and heir, and dined with Balmuto; Dr Blair, etc., there. Not London, yet I *judged* it *unreasonable* to be dissatisfied in Edinburgh.

SATURDAY 21 JANUARY. I appeared today in the Court of Session and attended a meeting of the Faculty of Advocates, where the Judges' Bill was *certainly* to be considered. But upon Lord Advocate's saying that he *believed* it would be given up so far as concerned diminishing the number, they agreed to *adjourn* the consideration of it, and though I moved that as our opinion might have some influence we should now consider it, not one would second me. I heartily despised their servility.[15] I dined at the annual meeting of Mundell's scholars. Did not get drunk.

SUNDAY 22 JANUARY. New Church forenoon; sat awhile with Lord Rockville, also with Grange, who dined with us after sermons and drank tea, as did Mr Nairne. I stayed at home all the afternoon and evening, read the Bible, and heard the children say divine lessons. Was not by any means well as I could wish to be, nor have I been so for some days. Veronica alarmed us by spitting a little blood; we hoped it was a stress in throwing up from a disordered stomach.

MONDAY 23 JANUARY. The forenoon was wasted at home in idleness. I walked in the street a little before dinner. I was melancholy from thinking that I was so soon to leave my wife and children, and was uncertain what plan of life to pursue; sat awhile with Grange, who was himself much hipped. Lady Colville and Lady Anne Erskine drank tea with us and played whist. My views were dim and dreary. Yet I thought I might yet enjoy existence.

TUESDAY 24 JANUARY. Little done. My brother John drank a glass with me after dinner. I drank tea at Dr Grant's.

WEDNESDAY 25 JANUARY [V]isited Lord Eskgrove, who was very kind.

THURSDAY 26 JANUARY. Having resolved to set out for London next day, I put some books, etc., in order. Went and heard Mr French's class. Visited Lord Dumfries and Lady Dundonald (if not a day before), and saw no difficulty in trying London. Grange supped with us. It was animating to find my children desirous of going to London. I thought they would be improved by it.

FRIDAY 27 JANUARY. My son Alexander kindly accompanied me to the inn from whence the Newcastle fly set out at six in the morning. Mr John Wilson, son of my old friend Mr William Wilson who gave me my first fee,[16] went with

---

15 The members of the Faculty did not want to alienate Henry Dundas, who had been the principal promoter of the Bill. The eventual outcome was that the Bill was withdrawn; but another, restricted to increasing the salaries of the judges, was enacted as the Salaries of Judges (Scotland) Act 1786 (26 Geo. 3, c. 46).

16 For Boswell's first fee, see Intoduction, p. 37.

me, and as he had been for some years in the profession of an attorney and solicitor in London, he entertained me usefully with information upon points of practice, and made me feel solidly as to London. The truth is that *imaginary* London, gilded with all the brilliancy of warm fancy as I have viewed it, and London as a scene of real business, are quite different; and as the *changes* of fanciful sensation are very painful, it is more comfortable to have the duller sensation of reality.

EPILOGUE

Boswell was called to the English bar on 9 February 1786 and celebrated the occasion in style four days later at a lavish inauguration dinner in the Inner Temple Hall. "A more jovial, pleasant day never was passed", remarks Boswell. "And the lustre was lighted, which had not been the case for thirty years." However, in spite of assiduously attending the Northern and Home Circuits and making a point of being periodically seen year after year in Westminster Hall, where the law courts sat, Boswell never acquired a practice at the English bar. Although he did pick up the occasional case, the fees that he received were trifling; and, indeed, any fees earned on a circuit were invariably exceeded by Boswell's expenses. Boswell must have seemed an increasingly lonely figure as he haunted the courts in the forlorn hope of receiving instructions. After only a few months, he wrote to his wife that "it is shocking to me, who have been used to have a competent share of practice, to be altogether without it, and I am impatient and fretful".[1] But when work *did* come his way, he did not always display the necessary commitment. In May 1787 he received a brief in respect of a client procured by General Paoli's servant, but Boswell failed to ascertain in time when the case was to be heard, with the consequence that he arrived at court only to be told that the case was over. "It occurred to me", wrote Boswell with good reason, "that this visible neglect might hurt me much in my chance of getting practice."[2] Indeed, Boswell eventually came to accept that he "never applied seriously to English law, and could not bear the confinement and formal course of life which practice at the bar required".[3]

However, in November 1786 Boswell came under the patronage of the immensely rich and influential James Lowther, 1st Earl of Lonsdale, who employed Boswell as counsel for the Mayor of Carlisle in connection with the by-election there at which Lonsdale was putting forward a candidate. Boswell thus found himself a "counsellor-at-law on [the] bench with [the] mayor, deciding on English election law"; and he felt "a real elevation on being a kind of ally of the great Lowther of Westmorland".[4] But Boswell soon discovered that Lonsdale was a mean, selfish and tyrannical man who could brook no opposition and who liked all around him to be subservient and dependent on him. After experiencing Lonsdale's overbearing company for several days, Boswell wrote: "I was kept in a kind of fever of agitation, and also in that kind of awe which I had not experienced but in my father's company—seeing all round *kept down*."[5] The outcome of the election was that Lonsdale's candidate obtained more votes than his opponent, but most of the votes were from "honorary freemen" (brought in by Lonsdale) whose entitlement to vote had been upheld by Boswell—notwithstanding his usual strong antipathy to nominal and fictitious votes (the legal position being "at least technically opaque enough to justify Boswell's decision"[6])—thus prompting the opponent to petition against the return. Boswell then had to attend meetings of the Carlisle Committee of the House of Commons in February 1787, the result of which was that Lonsdale's candidate was unseated and his opponent declared elected. Nevertheless, for his services as counsel to the Mayor, Boswell was paid a handsome fee of £157. 10s.[7]

At the end of 1787 Boswell was to be employed by Lord Lonsdale again, this time as Recorder (chief legal officer) of Carlisle. On 21 December Boswell set out with Lonsdale for Lowther Castle, near Penrith, so that Boswell could be duly elected to his new post. The castle was very cold and Lonsdale's behaviour, being as obnoxious as usual, prompted Boswell seriously to regret being associated with him. "I felt", records Boswell, "how unworthy it was of the Laird of Auchinleck to hang on thus upon a savage."[8] In desperation, Boswell resolved to resign the Recordership and he made an abortive escape bid in deep snow, but turned back after reaching Penrith. "I feared that [my wife] would despise my impatience and flight," he explains, "and that I should be made ridiculous on account of thus forfeiting my expectations from the Great Lowther."[9] On his return to Lowther Castle, Boswell informed Lord Lonsdale that he no longer desired the Recordership; but Lonsdale put the matter "in the most favourable light", referring to Boswell as "a man of great sense, of talents, who when a thing is properly prepared can judge of it with ability". These flattering remarks made Boswell ambitious to have the Recordership after all. However, he was kept hanging on for two weeks waiting for the arrival of the alderman of Carlisle before his election as Recorder could take place. After being finally elected on 11 January 1788, Boswell, feeling "really elated", was able to return to London (his duties as Recorder—for which he was paid a modest salary of £20 a year—only occasionally requiring him to be in attendance at Carlisle). But in mid-1790 Boswell's relations with Lonsdale came to an unfortunate head when Boswell was required to be in Carlisle for a by-election. Boswell, whose enthusiasm for the Recordership had waned considerably on being informed that Lonsdale evidently had no intention of trying to bring him into Parliament, was reluctant to leave London; and he told Lonsdale that, although he would on this occasion do the necessary business as Recorder, he would then resign. "I was as proud as Lucifer," wrote Boswell, "and… would have no connection with Lord Lonsdale farther than paying my respects to him as an independent gentleman."[10] Boswell and Lonsdale set out together in Lonsdale's coach on 17 June and as they were about to depart Lonsdale confirmed that it had never been his intention to try to bring Boswell into Parliament, explaining that in his opinion it would do Boswell harm to be in Parliament in that he "would get drunk and make a foolish speech". In response to this Boswell indicated that his "liberal and independent views" were inconsistent with being brought in by Lonsdale "unless special terms were granted". This provoked Lonsdale, and his passion having been raised "almost to madness", he offered to give Boswell satisfaction. However, Boswell, wishing as ever to avoid a duel if at all possible, was able later to smooth it all over by apologising for using expressions which Lonsdale had imagined had attacked his honour. At Carlisle, Boswell pleased Lonsdale by delivering a "firm and decided opinion" in favour of the honorary freemen, which, says Boswell, "I inwardly wondered at my being able to do, my mind being so weak and depressed."[11] And a few days later Boswell had to deal with quelling a violent mob intent on chairing one of the anti-Lonsdale candidates through the streets before the poll had been declared, an action which Boswell considered to be verging on a breach of the peace. The poll was at last concluded on 14 July and Lonsdale's candidates were returned (but were later unseated on petition to the House of Commons[12]). Boswell was thus finally able to return to London in great relief that he had faithfully discharged his burdensome and unrewarding duties.

In the summer of 1792 Boswell became involved in the remarkable cause of a group of prisoners—four men and one woman (Mary Bryant, née Broad)—the survivors of a group of convicts who had made a perilous escape from Botany Bay, Australia (the colonial destination for criminals sentenced to transportation), but had been captured in Timor and shipped back to Britain. Boswell, like the public at large, had great sympathy for the poor convicts and earnestly sought an interview with Henry Dundas, who was then the Home Secretary, to plead for them to be dealt with compassionately. Eventually, on 14 November 1792, Boswell saw the Under Secretary of State for the Home Department, who assured Boswell that the Government would not treat the convicts with harshness, "but at the same time would not do a kind thing to them, as that might give encouragement to others to escape". Mary Bryant (whose offence was that of street-robbery and stealing a cloak[13]) was released in early May 1793 and Boswell set about trying to secure a royal pardon for her. At the same time, he sent a petition entreating the Home Department to release the male prisoners and to give them "a second chance". Boswell went to see the four men at Newgate Prison to assure them that he was doing all in his power for them, and on 2 November he found to his surprise that all four had been set at liberty. Boswell took a special interest in Mary Bryant, who was informed in August 1793 that her aged father in Cornwall had inherited a fortune. She resolved to go to him and her other relations to establish the truth of the story. Boswell paid her passage and saw her off from Southwark on 12 October, promising to send her £10 a year in case the inheritance was a delusion, as indeed it proved to be. Boswell adhered to his word.

Notwithstanding his move to the English bar, Boswell continued to be engaged occasionally as counsel in Scottish appeals to the House of Lords. Indeed, this is an indication of the esteem in which he was still held in certain legal circles in his native country. The first of these appeals was in the case of *Henry Drumlanrig Cuninghame, and others, postponed creditors on the estate of Lainshaw*, which was concerned with the profits from a lease of certain land at Lainshaw in Ayrshire. Boswell and Ilay Campbell (the Lord Advocate) were counsel for the respondents, Henry Drumlanrig Cuninghame (Mrs Boswell's nephew) and the other creditors. The appeal was heard on 24 and 25 April 1786. On the first day, Boswell records, "the Lord Chancellor [Lord Thurlow] started a crotchet which [the] Lord Advocate was afraid might be fatal to us, though quite wrong. I was in sad fear." However, Boswell's fears were unfounded, for the outcome was that the appeal was dismissed and the interlocutors of the Court of Session upheld.[14]

Boswell's next appeal to the House of Lords was the appeal of Miss Jean Whitefoord against a decision of the Court of Session finding against her in a dispute concerning the inheritance of her late father's estate.[15] The hearing took place on 14 and 15 March 1788, and although Boswell was initially "frightened a good deal from not being used of late to speak in public", his speech (on 15 March) was well received. "When counsel were called in," records Boswell, "I had no uneasy apprehension and stated the case to my own satisfaction. I soon was satisfied that the Lord Chancellor saw through my reasoning, and it is very unpleasant to talk what one is conscious is mere plausibility when it is addressed to a man of sense. His Lordship said, 'Mr Boswell, you state your case very ingeniously. But—' and then he put a question which showed he knew the fallacy, and smiled. However, it was my business to do justice to my client, and I spoke about an hour. He affirmed the Decree without hearing the respondent's counsel." Although the appeal was unsuccessful, Miss Whitefoord was evidently very pleased with Boswell's efforts on her behalf.[16]

Five years later, in April 1793, Boswell appeared in the appeal in the case of *William Gillespie and Matthew Reid v. Adeliza Hussey or Bogle, and Husband*. Boswell's clients, Gillespie and Reid, the appellants, had successively held certain land, but the creditors of the original owner claimed a right to the land and sought to have Gillespie and Reid found liable for arrears of rent going back many years. The Court of Session had granted decree in favour of the creditors. After making what he considered "a very good speech", Boswell was delighted to find Lord Thurlow coming down to him from the bench, shaking him by the hand, and "very courteously" asking how he did.[17] However, the court's decision, dated 3 May 1793, was against Boswell's clients.*

It seems that the last case in which Boswell appeared in the House of Lords was the case of *David Stewart v. Newnham, Everett & Co.* Boswell's client, David Stewart, as trustee on the estate of a James Stein, had sued Newnham,

---

* This case is reported in Paton, Vol. III, p. 305.

Everett & Co. (a London banking firm) in connection with a bond. The Court of Session had found in Stewart's favour, and Newnham, Everett & Co. had thereupon appealed to the House of Lords. When drawing the case for Stewart to be lodged in the House of Lords, Boswell imagined himself "ill-qualified for such kind of labour", yet considered that he "did it well enough".[18] The appeal was heard on 6 and 10 March 1794 and Boswell's speech was on the 10th. "Want of use made me feel awkward and not clear", records Boswell. "But I got on sufficiently well." In any event, the court found in favour of Boswell's client and upheld the decision of the Court of Session.*

Significant though Boswell's House of Lords appearances were, by far the greatest of his achievements after moving to London was the composition and publication of his *magnum opus*, the monumental *Life of Samuel Johnson*. He started work on this immense project on or about 5 June 1786 and he did not finish it until April 1791. It is clear that the book would never have been written if Boswell had not settled in London, for if it had not been for the selfless encouragement, tireless support and valuable advice of Boswell's friend Edmond Malone (the great Shakespeare scholar)—with whom Boswell spent innumerable evenings in Malone's "elegant study"[19] revising the manuscript—Boswell would not have found the necessary energy and commitment to go on with what often seemed an interminable task. The work was published on 16 May 1791 and was immediately a great success, bringing Boswell the "fame and profit"[20] for which he yearned. His profit from the first edition alone was £1,550, which was, he remarked, "very flattering to me as an author".[21] A further mark of respect accorded to Boswell was his election in July 1791 as Secretary for Foreign Correspondence of the Royal Academy.

One of Boswell's works which was somewhat less to his credit than the *Life*, but was certainly consistent with his inherently conservative principles, was his verse pamphlet *No Abolition of Slavery* which came out one month before the *Life*. This pamphlet was written in opposition to Wilberforce's bill to abolish the slave-trade, which was considered by Boswell to be an unwarrantable threat to the property rights of the slave owners and a "wild and dangerous" attempt to terminate a "very important and necessary... branch of commercial interest".[22]

It might have been thought that the publication of the *Life* would have brought Boswell the sense of fulfilment that he so earnestly sought. However, literary renown was not enough for Boswell: his principal ambition continued to be the attainment of some legal or political position of real consequence. The constant failure to achieve this objective was the source of much unhappiness for him; indeed, for this among other reasons, there were many lengthy periods during his residence in London when he lived in a state of deep depression. During one such period, his friend John Courtenay, M.P., wrote to Malone:[23] "Poor Boswell is very low and dispirited and almost melancholy mad... He complains like Solomon that 'all is vanity'[24]."

* This case is reported in Paton, Vol. III, p. 345.

§II

Two of Boswell's greatest Scottish friends died while he was in London. The first of these was John Johnston of Grange, who died only a few months after Boswell had moved there in 1786. "The death of my oldest friend Grange, who was steady to me upon all occasions, is a melancholy event", Boswell wrote. "It is a loss that never can be made up to me. My comfort is that he was a benevolent and pious man; so that I trust he is gone to a better place, where it may please GOD that we may meet, never to undergo the distress of being separated."[25] The second of these friends to die was Andrew Erskine, who took his own life in October 1793. He had evidently run up considerable gambling debts, and being also depressed and in poor health, had filled his pockets with stones and walked into the Firth of Forth. His body was discovered opposite Caroline Park. When Boswell read of his friend's death in a newspaper article (which, however, did not disclose the circumstances), he wrote that the dismal news of his "old friend and correspondent and confidant in hypochondria" affected him "with a kind of stupor, mixed with regret".[26]

§III

Boswell's family did not immediately follow him to London when he made his move there in 1786. During his first few unsettled months there he indulged in a passionate relationship with his old acquaintance, the notorious Margaret Caroline Rudd, who, wrote Boswell, "made the greatest pleasure of human life new to me".[27] However, he broke off their relationship after a few months, having decided that he "disliked this *low* association".[28] On 16 May he moved into a house at 56 Great Queen Street, "the solitude of which", he wrote to his wife, "is very dreary and gives room for very uneasy thought".[29] His wife in the meantime had had recurrences of spitting of blood and Boswell earnestly sought the advice of Sandy Wood, the Edinburgh surgeon, suggesting that she would not be hurt by living in his house in London, which, he said, was in "a wide, well-aired street".[30] However, Mrs Boswell was very uneasy at the thought of moving the family to London and leaving Auchinleck desolate; and Boswell for his part was initially very undecided as to whether he should stay in London given his woeful lack of practice at the bar. Nevertheless, Boswell eventually resolved to give London a fair trial, and he brought his entire family there in September. Mrs Boswell soon "found herself quite easy in London, going about to markets and all manner of shops with perfect freedom";[31] but by March the following year she had had a return of her "alarming complaints" and did not think that she could be fully restored "but by the air and comforts of Auchinleck".[32] Although there were periods when she seemed to get better, she had recurrences of her distressing symptoms, and, finally, on 13 August Boswell resolved to take her with him to Auchinleck. "She might die," he reflected, "and I should upbraid myself for not having given her the benefit of travelling, change of air, and rural amusement. Besides, her good sense and activity would be of essential service to me."

Boswell and his wife, together with Veronica and Sandy, arrived at Auchinleck on 20 August and they stayed there for over a month, but were back in London on 29 September. Mrs Boswell became very dissatisfied with her life there, complaining that it was expensive, injurious to the health of herself and her sons, and resulted in her daughters being kept in a state of obscurity, whereas if the family was back at home in Scotland they might all live "comfortably and creditably".[33] On 17 March she had such a bad attack of fever that she said, "Oh, Mr Boswell, I fear I'm dying." But Boswell, although he constantly upbraided himself for this, did not have the same concern for her as he had formerly; he was wrapped up in his own thoughts and was engrossed in the writing of the *Life*, which he felt he had to complete before he could contemplate leaving London. Meanwhile, Mrs Boswell continued to deteriorate. She became emaciated and had feverish fits at night, when she sometimes "wandered and roved strangely"[34] and had to take laudanum. Eventually, Boswell consented to taking her back to Auchinleck. They set off on 15 May with all the children other than Veronica, who had now come to love London and was placed in a boarding school there.

The country air and the comfort of being at home had a very beneficial effect on Mrs Boswell's health. And Boswell took the opportunity afforded by this visit to become active in local politics, canvassing as declared candidate for Ayrshire. On 25 September he obtained the support of what seems to have been a sparsely attended meeting of the "real freeholders" (that is, the freeholders with a genuine entitlement to vote, as opposed to those on the roll with only nominal and fictitious votes). Less than a month later, however, he set out for London with Sandy and Jamie, leaving Euphemia and Betsy at Auchinleck with their mother.

On his return to London, Boswell found Veronica to be "quite a lady"[35] and acquiring some accomplishment in music and French. And Boswell started to entertain high hopes in respect of young James who was doing well at school and had become head of his class. Meanwhile, Sandy, who had a private tutor as his hernia prevented him from attending school, was regarded by Boswell as being likely to make "an excellent worthy gentleman".[36]

In January 1789 Boswell sub-let a "very small but neat"[37] house at 38 Queen Anne Street West, Cavendish Square, not far from Malone's house. But his wife's health continued to deteriorate and so in April he returned to Auchinleck, taking Veronica with him. His wife was worse than ever: unable to digest her food; "emaciated and dejected"; and "very weak".[38] Boswell found her situation so distressing that he spent much time away from home canvassing.* The following month he was summoned to London by Lord Lonsdale to appear as Recorder of Carlisle in an action against the Corporation in the King's Bench. Boswell had been in London only a week when he received word from Euphemia

---

* Boswell's political exertions came to nothing, for at the by-election held on 3 August 1789 to replace Hugh Montgomerie (who had been appointed Inspector of Military Roads in Scotland) the seat was won by Henry Dundas's candidate, William McDowall of Garthland.

and the Ayrshire family doctor that Mrs Boswell was sinking. He immediately set off with his two boys, travelling by day and night without stopping. But, as he informed Temple, "Alas! Our haste was all in vain. The fatal stroke had taken place before we set out. It was very strange that we had no intelligence whatever upon the road, not even in our own parish, nor till my second daughter came running out from our house and announced to us the dismal event in a burst of tears." Boswell cried bitterly and upbraided himself for not being with his wife at the end. "This reflection", Boswell told Temple with prescience, "will I fear pursue me to my grave."[39]

Boswell was now a lonely, middle-aged widower with sole responsibility for five children. The first matters that were decided were that Euphemia, at her own request, would pass the winter at Edinburgh "in order to finish her education",[40] while Veronica was to live as a boarder in the house of a friend of hers in London. However, it was not until October that Boswell, together with Veronica, Sandy, Jamie, and Betsy made the journey south.

Sandy was now enrolled as a student at Eton; little Betsy was sent to a boarding school in Chelsea; and the following year young James, Boswell's favourite, was enrolled as a boarder at Westminster School. Unfortunately, Euphemia was miserable at the boarding school in Edinburgh and so Boswell arranged for her to come home. Veronica also came back to live with him. Betsy occasionally came to visit, delighting Boswell with her English accent and her "sense and vivacity".[41]

At or about the beginning of 1791 Boswell and his family moved house again, this time to 47 Great Portland Street, which was to be Boswell's home for the rest of his life. Here Boswell found it difficult being responsible for Veronica and Euphemia, who had become unruly and disrespectful and assumed that they could come and go as they pleased and bring home company whenever they wished. In August 1791 Boswell went to Auchinleck for a few weeks, but he was unhappy and lonely there and was "haunted by memories of his wife".[42] After his return to London he had additional cause to feel in low spirits, for in February 1792 his great friend Sir Joshua Reynolds died. Although Boswell continued to lead an active social life he was now resorting more and more to the bottle to keep his spirits up.

Boswell made further visits to Auchinleck in the spring of 1793 and the summer of 1794. During the latter visit, which was to be his last time at Auchinleck, Boswell was accompanied by Veronica and Euphemia and he was initially in very good spirits. On their arrival, Boswell and the girls were greeted joyfully by Sandy, who had been studying law at Edinburgh University. However, Boswell was much displeased with Sandy's "loud familiarity of manner" and "very broad pronunciation", which, Boswell considered, Sandy had acquired "by being so long in Scotland and so much of late among his inferiors".[43] As for Boswell's daughters, they were at first dissatisfied with Auchinleck, but soon came to appreciate the joys of a country life. Boswell wrote to Jamie informing him that his sisters seemed to be "fully as well entertained as in London, and that in a manner which does not dissipate their minds and fret me, so that there is scarcely any degree of that feverish altercation which was so painful to me".[44]

Boswell's only visit to Edinburgh after his move to London in 1786 was a brief stay of ten days in the spring of 1793 (during which time, he told Sir William Forbes in a letter dated 11 May 1793, "my wonder and cordial gladness were at once excited in an extraordinary degree"[45*]); but, notwithstanding his long absence, he often thought of his native city and he continually wondered whether he had done the right thing in leaving it. If he had remained as an advocate in Scotland and (contrary to what had happened) had avoided alienating the all-powerful Henry Dundas, it is not impossible that he would eventually have had at least some prospect of being elevated to the bench as a Lord of Session.[†] However, as Boswell appreciated only too well, his character was such that the thrill of being appointed a judge would in due course have evaporated and all his "former dreary sensations"[46] would have recurred. In any event, he felt that returning to the Scottish bar would soon be "intolerably dull and contracted"[47] and, by indicating the failure of his English ambitions, would be "a wretched sinking", making him appear "a disappointed, depressed man".[48] But when he read on 3 January 1788 that his friend John Maclaurin had been elevated to the bench as Lord Dreghorn he experienced a momentary pang of regret. "I felt *somewhat* uneasy", he wrote, "to think that had I steadily remained at the Scotch bar I might have had the judge's place"; but he consoled himself by thinking "how much more enjoyment have I had than if I had been in Scotland!"

Any lingering doubts Boswell had about the wisdom of his decision to move to London were dispelled after the publication of his *Life of Samuel Johnson*. Temple and he both agreed that he was "better as the distinguished biographer than as a Lord of Session".[49] He even looked down on the idea of being Lord President (although he reflected that "surely in *solid reason* I was wrong"[50]). And as to his failure to obtain preferment in London, young James reassuringly told him that "they who have obtained places and pensions etc. have not the fame of having been the biographer of Johnson or the conscious exultation of a man of genius...[W]ould you rather... have been a rich, though dull, plodding lawyer?"[51]

Boswell returned to London from Auchinleck with Veronica and Euphemia in January 1795. Here he resumed his usual hectic social life, and on 18 March he wrote to Sandy: "I am wonderfully happy at present. What a varied life do I lead!"[52] However, Boswell was drinking excessively, and on 14 April he suddenly came down with a severe illness. "He was overcome with fever and chills,

---

* Unfortunately, Boswell's letter to Sir William Forbes contains no details of any significance with regard to Boswell's activities during his stay in Edinburgh.

† As it was, when Boswell applied to Dundas on 10 July 1786 for appointment as a Lord of Session, Dundas did not reply until 26 November 1786 (by which time he had received a reminder from Boswell), when he said that "while he had 'not the least disposition to depreciate' Boswell's political services, he could not admit—turning Boswell's argument in the [*Letter to the People of Scotland* (1785)] against him—'that political merit of any kind is the proper road to judicial preferment'. And he added that though he did not regret that *Letter* on his own account, he certainly did on Boswell's" (Brady, p. 344).

headache, and nausea, and had to be taken home and put to bed. He remained in great pain for three weeks, suffering from progressive kidney failure and uraemia, perhaps as a result of his recurring bouts of gonorrhoea."[53] Although the pain went away, Boswell had become very weak; and, despite the anxious care and attention of Veronica and Jamie, he passed away at two o'clock in the morning of 19 May.

On 8 June Boswell's body was laid to rest in the family vault adjacent to the parish kirk at Auchinleck.

§IV

Boswell was survived by his two brothers, John and David. However, John died only a few years later, in or about 1798. David, on the other hand, who had adopted the name Thomas David Boswell and had settled in London in 1780, lived until 1826. He married in 1783 and worked in London first as a banker and then as a "free-lance business agent".[54] His situation changed in 1791 when Henry Dundas, in implement of his promise given to Lord Auchinleck to find him a place, appointed him a clerk in the Naval Pay Office. "A toehold was all this worthy, industrious, punctilious, and stingy man needed; he worked his way up until he was affluent enough to buy Crawley Grange, an extensive estate in Buckinghamshire."[55]

Apart from Euphemia, who led a long but tragic life, none of Boswell's children lived beyond middle age. The first to suffer was Veronica, who fell victim to consumption very shortly after her father's demise and died only a few months later, on 26 September 1795, aged 22.

Elizabeth ("Betsy") left school in 1797 and went to live at Auchinleck with Euphemia. "In the summer of 1798 she fell violently in love with her second cousin, William Boswell,* Robert Boswell's eldest son, and the pair of them, she eighteen and he a year and a half older, importuned Alexander for instant marriage. Alexander... thought [his sister] was marrying beneath her station and condemning herself to a life of squalid penury. He finally gave in with a completely bad grace, and was not mollified when Robert Boswell gave his son a marriage settlement guaranteeing him an income of £500 a year—a very considerable commitment, for William was still a student and did not pass advocate till the following July." It seems that after Elizabeth married in 1799, Alexander and James "never visited, spoke to, or wrote to her again".[56] Elizabeth was to die young, on 1 January 1814, leaving three sons and a daughter.[57]

Young James studied at Brasenose College, Oxford, from 1797 to 1806 and was called to the English bar on 24 May 1805. Renowned for his charm and the depth of his learning, he had strong literary inclinations. "While a student at Brasenose he contributed notes signed 'J.B.O.' to the third edition of his father's life of Johnson, and afterwards carefully revised and corrected the text for the sixth edition... He was intimate from an early age with his father's friend Malone, whom he assisted in collecting and arranging the materials

* William Boswell (1779-1841), advocate (admitted 8 July 1800), Sheriff of Berwick 1815-41.

for a second edition of his Shakespeare, and was requested by him in his last illness to complete it, a task which he duly performed... He died suddenly at his chambers in the Temple, unmarried and apparently in embarrassed circumstances, on 24 February 1822."[58]

Alexander was dead only a few weeks later. After completing his studies at Edinburgh University he had studied law at Leipzig in 1795. That same year he succeeded to the estate of Auchinleck on the death of his father; and in 1799 he married Grisel Cuming (the daughter of an Edinburgh banker), by whom he had one son and three daughters. He never became a lawyer, but instead "made a mark for himself as a poet, antiquary and bibliophile. He established a private printing press at Auchinleck in 1815, mixed with Walter Scott and his circle [and had] an active interest in agricultural improvement... In July 1816 [he] secured the seat at Westminster which had eluded his father by buying his return for Plympton." He gave his support to the Tory administration and evidently regarded the Whigs as "dangerous and irresponsible maniacs".[59] He was created a baronet on 16 August 1821. "Handsome, spirited, likeable, eminently sane, he was also imperious, impatient of opposition, and unforgiving";[60] and he had a tendency to extravagance, which he funded by greatly increasing the rental from his estate. Although Cockburn said of him that "in general he was boisterous and overbearing, and addicted to coarse personal ridicule",[61] he was also "cultured, brave, magnanimous [and] was a lover of scholarship and of literature—indeed, was an author himself."[62] He was a great admirer of Burns' poetry and composed several songs in the Scottish dialect which were published anonymously in 1803; and in 1817 he contributed twelve songs to George Thomson's "Select Collection of Original Scottish Airs". In 1822 he was the author of a series of anonymous newspaper lampoons against James Stuart of Dunearn (1775-1849), W.S. (admitted 1798), a political opponent, in which Stuart was accused of cowardice. When Sir Alexander returned to Scotland after his brother James' funeral he found a card waiting for him from Stuart, who had obtained evidence of Sir Alexander's authorship. Headstrong as usual, Sir Alexander refused to apologise or to offer any explanation and duly met his opponent in the field. The duel took place near Auchtertool in Fife. Sir Alexander, who was an experienced shot, either fired in the air, or was about to do so, when he received a mortal wound from his opponent, who had very rarely used firearms and was evidently astonished to hit his opponent. Sir Alexander was carried to the nearby home of the Boswells of Balmuto, where he died. Stuart was subsequently tried for murder, but was acquitted. Sir Alexander's only son, Sir James, who succeeded his father as Laird of Auchinleck at the age of fifteen, lived until 1857 and was "the last of Boswell's descendants to hold the estate under the entail".[63]

Euphemia, who never married, "lived at Auchinleck from 1796 to 1801, in Edinburgh from 1801 to 1805, and then went to London, where she hung loose upon society, making efforts to support herself as a writer and musical composer. She was most of her time in desperate straits because of her debts, and wrote urgent begging letters to her father's friends and to various great personages of the day, representing herself as cruelly neglected and repressed by her family... She solicited a pension on the Scots and presumably also on the Civil List, and did actually get from Government a pension of £50 a year."[64] The pension supplemented the annuity of £140 payable to her under her father's will. However, that was not the end of her troubles, for she continued to be extravagant and became ever deeper in debt, and in 1805 she signed a trust deed for creditors, who allowed her to retain only £50 from her annuity for her own use. Furthermore, "some time in... 1816, probably because of physical prostration or some particularly outrageous act of self-advertisement, she was declared insane and put by her brothers in Fisher House, Islington, a private asylum for lunatics... She remained there for the next twenty years."[65] When she was eventually discharged from the asylum in 1836 she lived at various addresses in London and finally settled at 48 Great Portland Street, adjacent to or across the street from number 47 "where she had spent the happiest years of her life".[66] It seems that her release from the asylum was arranged by a benefactor and protector in the shape of the Accountant General in Chancery, who took a great interest in her affairs. However, she did not have long to enjoy her new-found freedom, for she died on 7 September 1837. In accordance with her request, she was buried in St Paul's Cathedral.

§NOTES

1 Letter from Boswell to Margaret Boswell dated 3 July 1786, reproduced in *Experiment*, p. 77.
2 Journal, 26 May 1787.
3 Journal, 24-26 September 1793.
4 Journal, 30 November and 1 December 1786.
5 Journal, 10 December 1786.
6 Brady, pp. 347-8.
7 *Experiment*, p. 119.
8 Journal, 26 December 1787.
9 Journal, 28 December 1787.
10 Journal, 15 June 1790.
11 Journal, 6 July 1790.
12 *Great Biographer*, p. 92, n. 8.
13 *Great Biographer*, p. 157.
14 *Experiment*, p. 61, n. 5.
15 *Experiment*, p. 189, n. 2.
16 *Experiment*, p. 199, n. 2.
17 Journal, 24 December 1793.
18 Journal, 24 December 1793.
19 Letter from Boswell to Temple dated 13 February 1790, quoted in *Great Biographer*, p. 40.
20 *Ibid.*, *loc. cit.*
21 Journal, 24 November 1792.
22 *Life*, Vol. II, p. 735 (23 September 1777).
23 Letter dated 22 February 1791, quoted in *Great Biographer*, p. 125.
24 Ecclesiastes 1:2.
25 Letter from Boswell to Alexander Boswell dated 4 August 1786, reproduced in *Experiment*, pp. 92-3, at p. 92.
26 Journal, 13 October 1793.
27 From an undated memorandum, quoted in *Experiment*, p. 51, n. 6.
28 Journal, 23 April 1786.
29 Letter from Boswell to Margaret Boswell dated 18 May 1786, reproduced in *Experiment*, pp. 63-65, at p. 63.

30 From letter dated 9 May 1786 from Boswell to Sandy Wood quoted in *Experiment*, p. 63, n. 7.

31 Journal, 18 October 1786.

32 From letter dated 8 March 1787 from Boswell to Robert Boswell quoted in *Experiment*, p. 120, n. 3.

33 Journal, 20 February 1788.

34 Journal, 29 April 1788.

35 Letter from Boswell to Margaret Boswell dated 9 November 1788, reproduced in *Experiment*, pp. 252-5, at p. 255.

36 Letter from Boswell to Margaret Boswell dated 11 February 1789, reproduced in *Experiment*, pp. 272-3, at p. 273.

37 Quoted in *Experiment*, p. 265.

38 Quoted in *Experiment*, p. 280.

39 Letter from Boswell to Temple dated 3 July 1789, reproduced in *Experiment*, pp. 285-7, at p. 285.

40 *Ibid., loc. cit.*

41 Journal, 10 December 1792.

42 *Great Biographer*, p. 153.

43 Letter from Boswell to James Boswell, Jr, dated 14 July 1794, reproduced in *Great Biographer*, p. 301.

44 Letter from Boswell to James Boswell, Jr, dated 21 July 1794, reproduced in *Great Biographer*, pp. 301-2, at p. 302.

45 Letter from Boswell to Sir William Forbes dated 11 May 1793 (in the Fettercairn Papers deposited by Mrs Peter Somervell in the National Library of Scotland (Acc. 4796/87) and now owned by Miss Katherine Somervell), quoted in Brady, p. 472.

46 Journal, 2 August 1786.

47 Journal, 20 March 1787.

48 Journal, 20 February 1788.

49 Journal, 9 September 1792.

50 Journal, 16 September 1793.

51 From letter dated 18 October 1794 from James Boswell, Jr, to Boswell, quoted in *Great Biographer*, p. 305.

52 Quoted in *Great Biographer*, p. 312.

53 *Great Biographer*, p. 314.

54 *Great Biographer*, p. 17, n. 3.

55 Brady, p. 464.

56 *Pride and Negligence*, pp. 17-18.

57 *Pride and Negligence*, p. 32.

58 DNB.

59 Thorne, *The House of Commons 1790-1820*, Vol. III, p. 230.

60 *Pride and Negligence*, p. 18.

61 Cockburn, p. 373.

62 *Pride and Negligence*, p. 30.

63 *Pride and Negligence*, p. 40.

64 *Pride and Negligence*, p. 32.

65 *Pride and Negligence*, pp. 32-3.

66 *Pride and Negligence*, p. 45.

APPENDIX

Certain Notable Judges and Advocates at the Time of Boswell's Admission to the Faculty of Advocates in 1766

JUDGES

ROBERT DUNDAS OF ARNISTON, LORD PRESIDENT OF THE COURT OF SESSION

Robert Dundas of Arniston (1713-1787), the second Lord President Dundas, was admitted advocate on 28 February 1738 and was highly regarded on account of his quick apprehension and natural abilities; but he was no scholar, and "was never known to read through a book, except, perhaps (and that but seldom), to look at parts out of curiosity, if he happened to know the author".[1] As an advocate, he was not inclined to devote great amounts of time to the drudgery required for a large practice, preferring instead to restrict himself to cases of the greatest significance, thereby obtaining a suitable reputation for himself while at the same time ensuring that he was able to indulge his fondness for convivial society. In August 1742 he was appointed Solicitor-General for Scotland, and on 25 November 1746 he was elected to the honourable and prestigious office of Dean of the Faculty of Advocates—the highest accolade which can be conferred on an advocate by his brethren.

Dundas's fortunes went from strength to strength. On 25 April 1754 he was elected Member of Parliament for Edinburghshire (Midlothian), giving his support to the Whigs; on 16 August of the same year he was appointed Lord Advocate; and on 14 June 1760 he reached the zenith of his career when he was appointed Lord President of the Court of Session. Inevitably, there were some who thought that Dundas's fondness for pleasure and society would prevent him from applying himself to his high judicial office as much as he should. Such doubts, however, were dispelled immediately, for Dundas set about his duties with such determination and dispatch as to surprise even his warmest supporters. He was to preside over the court for twenty-seven years, and it was said of him that during that time "he devoted himself to the duties of his office with an ardour and zeal only equalled by the ablest of his predecessors. With an active and penetrating genius, he immediately applied himself to dispose of the long arrear of law-suits, which had hung upon the rolls of the Court for five years previous; and while the current business was disposed of, he cleared away in less than three months a load that had been accumulating for two years and a half. Thus was the long roll cleared almost at once, which had been constantly in a state of arrear from a very early period; nor was it ever revived while he sat in the President's chair. Stimulated by his example, the other judges exerted all their powers, and the business of the country was thus carried on with a degree of regularity and dispatch hitherto without parallel in the annals of that Court."[2]

The method used by Dundas to get rid of the arrear of cases was to impose a firm discipline on counsel and judges alike, keeping them always strictly to the point; and to ensure that his judicial colleagues did not speak for too long when delivering opinions, he is said to have used a sand-glass to set the maximum time permitted for each speech. Nevertheless, he always listened with great patience and politeness to the submissions of counsel, only interrupting when absolutely necessary. Indeed, it seems that Dundas—whose nickname, incidentally, was the most unjudicial appellation of "Bumbo"—was peculiarly suited to the judicial tasks which he took upon himself, and he is rightly regarded as being one of the great Lord Presidents, albeit noted more for his efficient dispatch of business than for any remarkable profundity as a lawyer.

On several occasions, Boswell was a guest of Dundas at his estate at Arniston, near Temple, Midlothian. The first reference which Boswell makes in his journals to being there is in the entry for 28 October 1762.

THOMAS MILLER OF BARSKIMMING, THE LORD JUSTICE-CLERK

The Lord Justice-Clerk, Thomas Miller of Barskimming (1717-1789), was admitted advocate on 21 February 1742, appointed Sheriff-Depute of Kirkcudbrightshire in 1748, and succeeded Andrew Pringle (later Lord Alemoor) as Solicitor-General on 17 March 1759. On 30 April 1760, he was appointed Lord Advocate in place of Robert Dundas and in 1761 he was elected Member of Parliament for the Dumfries Burghs. When at the bar, Miller acquired a good practice and was much respected by his colleagues, not only for his legal abilities, but also for his candid and courteous manner.

On Miller's elevation to the bench on 14 June 1766 he was simultaneously appointed Lord Justice-Clerk, and it is in this capacity that he is particularly remembered. "When presiding in the Court of Justiciary the Justice-Clerk appeared to be in his proper element... Without appearing to anticipate the facts of the culprit, he listened with deep attention to every argument which ingenuity could urge in their favour... Though well aware that offended justice required satisfaction, he knew that the vilest criminal was entitled to a fair and dispassionate trial... [I]n the discharge of this unpleasant duty, he never uttered a harsh or taunting word, an indecency which some of his brethren were apt to fall into. By that time, however, a new style of defending prisoners was coming in, which in times of greater strictness would not have been tolerated. Besides using great freedoms with law and fact (a practice very ancient among lawyers), they were sometimes deficient in respect to the Court. As the law then stood, the prisoner's counsel spoke immediately before the jury was enclosed, nor were the judges understood to have title to interfere. What wonder, then, that bold asseverations and perverse ingenuity should sometimes induce half-learned, pragmatical jurymen to acquit culprits of whose guilt nobody entertained any doubt? Nor was the benefit of this abuse of eloquence confined, as formerly, to the rich and well connected, for these gentlemen went sometimes most improper lengths for murderers and sheep-stealers, who had neither money nor friends. The Justice-Clerk, with all his gentleness and command of temper, felt often indignant at the bad spirit that began to appear among the lawyers."[3]

During the period when Miller was Lord Advocate, Boswell considered that he and Miller were always on easy terms, and on several occasions in 1763 they socialised together in London.

HENRY HOME, LORD KAMES

When he became friendly with Boswell in 1761,* Lord Kames (1696-1782) had recently published the first edition of his highly influential *Principles of Equity*. An earlier work, the *Historical Law-Tracts*, first published in 1758, was also highly regarded. And in 1751, before his elevation to the bench, Kames had published the first edition of his *Essays on the Principles of Morality and Natural Religion*, which originally aroused much controversy. Indeed, the "impious and infidel principles" of both Kames and David Hume were severely censured by the General Assembly of the Church of Scotland in 1755. This, and a further hostile campaign by the Evangelical (or "Highflying") Party at the General Assembly the following year—designed primarily (but unsuccessfully) to achieve the excommunication of David Hume—so shook Kames that in subsequent editions of the *Essays* he largely withdrew the most offending theories. However, the work for which Kames perhaps deserves most to be remembered, and to which he probably devoted more time than to the preparation of any other work, is his *Dictionary of the Decisions of the Court of Session*, which was published in 1741.

By the time Boswell was called to the bar Kames had published his most important non-legal work, the *Elements of Criticism* (which was brought out in 1762), and on 15 April 1763 he had finally achieved his long-thwarted ambition of becoming a Lord Commissioner of Justiciary. Kames quickly made a reputation for himself as being a harsh and

---

* For an account of Boswell's friendship with Lord Kames in 1761 and 1762 and for details of Lord Kames' character, see Introduction, pp. 23-25 and 35.

sarcastic judge in criminal matters. It was said of him that "in trials of life and death he sometimes lowered the majesty of justice by the levity or harshness of his expressions... To gravity and appearances he paid perhaps too little attention, and therefore did not check those petty ebullitions of spleen or impatience as he ought to have done. Neither had he much reverence for forms and modes of procedure sanctioned by a train of precedents. Thinking himself superior to rules which he considered either as nugatory and cumbersome, or else hurtful to the interests of justice, he sometimes set at nought the maxims and practice of his predecessors... The chief effect of these peculiarities was to render Lord Kames less popular than he ought to have been as a criminal judge."[4] At the close of a celebrated criminal trial in 1765, in which the accused were Katharine Nairn and Patrick Ogilvie, who were charged with incest and murder, he made what was then considered the astonishing and reprehensible innovation of addressing the jury on the evidence after the counsel for the defence had concluded their speeches. This, however, soon became standard practice, and, indeed, was made a requirement by Act of Parliament within a year of Lord Kames' death.*

On the death of Lord Milton on 13 December 1766, Lord Kames became the eldest (albeit not the most senior) judge on the bench, being then about seventy years old. That same year a major change occurred in Lord Kames' life in that his wife unexpectedly inherited her family's estate of Blair Drummond in Perthshire. Kames enthusiastically set about developing the estate, which was said to bring in an income of almost £2,000 a year. And in about 1767, as if not content with the acquisition of his new country estate, Kames purchased a new house in Edinburgh: a grand, recently built house near the top of the east side of New Street, off the north side of the Canongate. This street, as its name implies, was "a modern offshoot of the ancient city"; and it was said of Lord Kames' house that the edifice was "thought so fine, that people used to bring their country cousins to see it".[5]

JAMES BURNETT, LORD MONBODDO

The judicial title of Lord Monboddo which James Burnett (1714-1799) adopted when elevated to the bench on 12 February 1767 was derived from the name of the ancestral estate in Kincardineshire which he inherited from his father, a staunch Episcopalian and Jacobite who fought at Sheriffmuir in 1715. At an early age Burnett acquired that love of the philosophy and literature of ancient Greece and Rome which was to be of paramount importance to him throughout his life, matched only by a corresponding aversion to the philosophies of the "moderns", such as Locke, Hume and Newton. After attending a three-year course on Civil Law at Groningen in Holland, he returned to Scotland on 6 September 1735, the day before the Porteous riot, and took lodgings in Edinburgh near the West Bow. The following night, while getting ready to go to bed in his temporary accommodation, he heard a disturbance in the street and went down, wearing his nightcap and holding a candle, to find out what was going on. He was soon carried along by the surge of the crowd into the West Bow and down to the Grassmarket, where to his horror he beheld the sight of Captain Porteous being hanged. This dismal scene had such an effect on the young man that it not only gave him a sleepless night but also made him think of leaving Edinburgh as an unsuitable place in which to live.[6] However, he stayed in Edinburgh, and on 17 February 1737 he was admitted advocate. He gradually built up a practice at the bar, joined the Freemasons, regularly attended the fashionable dancing sessions (or "assemblies") at the Assembly Hall, and was a founder member of the Select Society. Furthermore, he took a great interest in the Canongate Theatre and was a warm admirer of John Home's tragedy of *Douglas*, hailing it as greater than anything by Shakespeare.

---

* Justiciary and Circuit Courts (Scotland) Act 1783 (23 Geo. 3, c. 45).

Burnett's legal career progressed on 5 August 1760 when he was appointed Sheriff-Depute of Kincardineshire sitting at Stonehaven, where he received a judicial salary of £150 a year. He did not find this post excessively time-consuming and was able to carry on his practice in Edinburgh; indeed, he had time to become extensively involved in the great Douglas Cause as one of the counsel for Archibald Douglas. His first assignment was to go to France to help collect evidence there, and he had to make two subsequent visits there for the same purpose. He acquitted himself so well on these occasions that he obtained a very high reputation for himself. After one of his visits to France, he appeared at a dancing session at the Assembly Hall dressed in a white velvet suit of which he was especially proud.

Shortly after Burnett's elevation to the bench, he moved from his old residence in Advocate's Close to a fashionable new house at 13 St John's Street, off the south side of the Canongate, where he was to be renowned for his Roman-style suppers at which it is said that his table was bedecked with garlands of roses and flagons of wine and that he served food and drink prepared in accordance with ancient recipes, such as "Spartan broth" and *mulsum* (mead). Boswell was to be a frequent guest at these suppers.

Monboddo was a great believer in the virtues of exercise and a controlled diet. "It was his custom, summer and winter, to take a cold bath on rising, usually at a very early hour. When staying at his Kincardineshire seat, he enjoyed this luxury in a structure erected for the purpose at some distance from the mansion, and near a running stream which supplied the water. He took a light dinner about noon, but considerably neutralised his excellent system of hygiene by making his supper the heartiest meal of the day. Before retiring to rest he indulged in an air-bath [that is, walked in his room naked, with the window open], and then did homage to the Ancients (for whom he considered no sacrifice too great), by applying to his body a lotion composed of rose-water, olive oil, saline, aromatic spirit, and Venetian soap. Besmeared with this formidable concoction, he slept the sleep of the just."[7] Monboddo's love of manly exercise included a fondness for hunting, and he made all his long journeys on horseback, including regular journeys to and from London, deeming it undignified, unhealthy and effeminate to travel in a carriage.

By virtue of his eccentricities and oddities of thought, some of which were only to manifest themselves after his elevation to the bench, Monboddo was to bring on himself much ridicule and derision. Nevertheless, in his capacity as a Lord of Session he was always regarded as being "not only a master of legal principle, but a wise, independent, impartial, and learned judge", even though "he often differed from his brethren, and found himself in a minority of one".[8] But it was said that his appearance on the bench was far from prepossessing, at any rate in later life. "He looked", claims Chambers, "rather like an old stuffed monkey, dressed in a judge's robes, than anything else." However, Chambers adds that "his face,… 'sicklied o'er' with the pale cast of thought, bore traces of high intellect".[9]

One of Monboddo's well-known peculiarities as a judge was his insistence that, rather than sitting on the bench with his judicial colleagues, he should sit in the well of the court at the clerk's table. It was said that he adopted this practice after his fellow Lords of Session found against him in an action at his instance which came before the Inner House in December 1771. The action arose out of a dispute between Monboddo and an Edinburgh farrier who had been engaged by Monboddo to look after one of his horses which was unwell, and Monboddo had given strict instructions that the horse should be given no medicine of any kind except nitre. The farrier accordingly gave the horse nitre, but in order to make the medicine more palatable mixed it with some treacle. The unfortunate horse died the next day, which prompted the indignant judge to sue the farrier for the price or value of the horse. At the hearing before the Inner House, Monboddo was evidently represented by Boswell and other counsel, who, in support of the first ground of action referred to several Roman law authorities. However, it was all to no avail, for the court found in favour of the farrier.* Although it was said that it was on account of this rebuff that Monboddo henceforth refused to sit with his judicial brethren, it has also been suggested that there was in fact a far more mundane reason for Monboddo to choose to sit at the clerk's table, namely, that he was hard of hearing and would thus have found it easier to hear counsel if sitting in the well of the court rather than on the bench.

Another of Monboddo's characteristics which was considered by his contemporaries to be an eccentricity (indeed, in this case, a risible folly) was his belief in the existence of men with tails. In the first volume of his 6-volume book *Of the Origin and Progress of Language*, which volume was published in 1773, Monboddo, having referred to a report that a tribe of men with tails like those of cats had been discovered on the Nicobar Islands in the Bay of Bengal by a Swedish sailor in 1647,[†] went on, somewhat incautiously, to say (at page 238): "[T]hat there are men with tails... is a fact so well attested that I think it cannot be doubted." This belief was mocked by many, including Monboddo's judicial colleague Lord Kames, who, on meeting Monboddo in the street and being invited by him to take precedence, is reported as saying: "By no means, my lord; you must walk first, that I may *see your tail*."[10] Other views of Monboddo's which came in for a fair amount of derision included the notion that man is related to the orang-outang, the belief that it was surprising that the orang-outangs which had been brought to Europe had never learned to speak, and the conviction that all nations were at one time or another cannibals. The truth was, however, that Monboddo's views deserved more respect than they were given, for he was really to a certain degree a pre-Darwinian evolutionist (taking the view, as explained by Cloyd, that "man and the ape must have had some common ancestor similar in form, structure, and appearance to the great apes"[11]) and, to that extent, was ahead of his time.

SIR DAVID DALRYMPLE, LORD HAILES

The youngest judge on the bench when Boswell was called to the bar was Boswell's "worthy Maecenas", Sir David Dalrymple, Lord Hailes (1726-1792), who was elevated to the bench on 6 March 1766, at the age of thirty-nine.[‡] His early rise to the bench reflected the high regard in which he was held for his legal acumen. It was said of him that "his skill and assiduity in sifting dark matters to the bottom were well known", but at the same time he was perceived as paying unwarranted attention to minutiae; indeed, "his plaguing the lawyers and agents with needless scruples and inquiries made them sometimes regard him as a trifler".[12] His chief pleasure continued to be that of spending as much time as possible at his country retreat at New Hailes, where he indulged his passion for antiquarian research.

FRANCIS GARDEN, LORD GARDENSTONE

Francis Garden, Lord Gardenstone (1721-1793), was admitted advocate on 14 July 1744 and was appointed Sheriff-Depute of Kincardineshire in 1748. On 30 April 1760 he was appointed conjunct Solicitor-General with James Montgomery (afterwards Lord Advocate and then Lord Chief Baron of the Court of Exchequer) and was elevated to the bench on 3 July 1764, taking his judicial title from the name of the fishing village of Gardenstown in Gamrie parish, Banffshire, founded by his father in 1720. It was said of him that while he was "more remarkable for his propensity to pleasure than for application to study or regard to appearances", he was a very popular and well-respected advocate and developed a substantial practice, and "notwithstanding the awkwardness of his person, the harshness of his features, and tremulous voice, he spoke with a grace and fire

---

* The case is reported as *James Burnett of Monboddo v. James Clark* in *Faculty Decisions*, Vol. V, 1769-1771, pp. 347-8. The lengthy memorial which Boswell submitted on behalf of Lord Monboddo was "remarkable for its Latin tags and quotations" (*Session Papers*, 71 04 25b).

† It seems that the truth of the matter is that men on the Nicobar Islands wore a perineal band made of cloth with a tail behind.

‡ For an account of Lord Hailes' earlier life, see Introduction, pp. 17-18 and 30.

which made every word tell".[13] Furthermore, he was evidently "one of those ancient heroes of the Bar, who, after a night of hard drinking, would, without having been in bed, or studying a case, plead with great eloquence upon what they had picked up from the opposite counsel".[14] He was appointed one of the counsel in the great Douglas Cause and, like James Burnett, was sent to France to take part in the proceedings there.

As to Lord Gardenstone's social hours, he always seemed to manage to make himself popular with everyone. "His talents for convivial intercourse were confessed on all hands to be truly fascinating; for whatever turn the conversation took—whether grave or gay, serious or frolicsome—he displayed the same strength, openness and ardour of mind which distinguished him as a pleader."[15] He never married, but he devoted a great deal of his time, energy and money to his country estate which he purchased in 1762 at Johnston, adjoining Laurencekirk in Kincardineshire. Here he revelled in the role of country gentleman and began improving and enclosing the estate with great enthusiasm and energy; but his main desire was to convert Laurencekirk, then a small village with few inhabitants, into a manufacturing town. In 1765, the year after his elevation, he took the first step towards realising this ambition, for he then started to build a new village at Laurencekirk and injected large amounts of his personal funds into the venture, to such an extent that he ended up severely in debt.

Lord Gardenstone was noted for two particular eccentricities: a predilection for pigs and an excessive fondness for snuff. He evidently took snuff "in enormous quantities, and used to say that if he had a dozen noses he would feed them all". As to his affection for pigs, we are told that "he took a young pig as a pet, and it became quite tame and followed him about like a dog. At first the animal shared his bed, but when, growing up to advanced swinehood, it became unfit for such companionship, he had it to sleep in his room, in which he made a comfortable couch for it of his own clothes."[16]

ADVOCATES

ALEXANDER LOCKHART

Alexander Lockhart (1700-1782), the future Lord Covington, was admitted advocate on 6 November 1723. Before then he had been regarded as being unduly fond of recreation and amusements, but he applied himself seriously to business and built up an extensive practice. His profits were said to have been about £1,000 a year, which is equivalent by today's standards to about £60,000 tax-free. He was described as handsome and eloquent; and although no legal metaphysician, it was said that he had "a plentiful fund of common-sense to direct him" and "few men had a quicker conception or a clearer head". He was renowned for the passion of his speeches, which often attracted a numerous audience. "He not only spoke with more fire than most of his brother advocates, but frequently accompanied his perorations with tears, and that sometimes in cases where there seemed little room for the pathetic. But though he had vast business in the Court of Session, it was in addressing juries in the Courts of Justiciary and Exchequer that his eloquence was most powerful and formidable."[17] As a consequence of the extremely high regard in which he was held by his colleagues, he was elected to the prestigious office of Dean of the Faculty of Advocates on 15 June 1764, which office he was to hold until his long-delayed elevation to the bench in 1775 at the advanced age of about seventy-five.

JAMES MONTGOMERY

When Boswell was called to the bar, the Lord Advocate was James Montgomery (1721-1803), who had been appointed in April 1766. He was admitted advocate on 23 February 1743, appointed Sheriff-Depute of Peeblesshire in 1748, selected as conjunct Solicitor-General with Francis Garden (later Lord Gardenstone) in 1761 (becoming sole Solicitor-General on Francis Garden's elevation to the bench on 3 July 1764), and elected Member of Parliament for the Dumfries Burghs in 1766 (which seat he was to retain until returned for his native county of Peeblesshire in 1768). He was, however, more interested in agriculture than the law, and in 1763 he purchased a large area of waste ground in Peeblesshire known as "The Whim" (on account of the absurdity and whimsicality of the idea of reclaiming the land). He set about improving the land with great enthusiasm and he later added to his property by acquiring the estates of Stanhope and Stobo, thus becoming known as James Montgomery of Stanhope.

It was said of Montgomery that "his talents were by no means of the highest order; yet, by judicious mental cultivation—by throwing aside all ingenious subtleties, and boldly grasping at the solid practical view of every question, he in time acquired the character of a sound lawyer."[18] Kind, accessible and universally esteemed, he was evidently of a remarkably slender build and it was said that "his air, though not undignified, had more in it of winning grace than of overawing command".[19]

Although Montgomery was to remain a member of the House of Commons until 1775, the only Parliamentary business with which he is associated is the Entail Improvement Act of 1770* (known as the "Montgomery Act"), the improvement of entailed estates being a matter of particular interest to him. In 1775 he was to resign his place as Lord Advocate "to the eager grasp of Henry Dundas" and was to retire into "the dignified position of the Lord Chief Baron of Exchequer".[20]

ROBERT MACQUEEN

Robert Macqueen (1722-1799), who was the eldest son of a writer (that is, a solicitor) with a small estate at Braxfield, near Lanark, was admitted advocate on 14 February 1744. After he was called to the bar, people gradually began to appreciate his merit, which, it was said, "was not inaptly compared to a rough diamond";[21] and on 1 March 1745 he was appointed joint sheriff-substitute for the Ward of Lanarkshire along with his father. What really started Macqueen's career in earnest, however, was the litigation which arose in respect of the forfeited estates of the Jacobite leaders after the supression of the 1745 Rebellion. In these law suits he was retained as counsel for the Crown on account of his well-known skill as a feudal lawyer.

On 15 January 1759, the then Lord Advocate, Robert Dundas of Arniston, appointed Macqueen and Andrew Pringle (the future Lord Alemoor) conjunctly and severally as Advocates-Depute, and Macqueen continued to serve as an Advocate-Depute until August 1760. Consequently, during that period he was regularly engaged to appear for the Crown in criminal prosecutions. And in time he came to acquire what was considered to be the largest, and hence the most remunerative, practice at the bar, regularly pleading from 15 to 20 causes a day in the Outer House. His earnings in one year alone were reported to have been as much as £1,900, which was considerably above a Lord of Session's salary of £700 per annum.

While Macqueen was without doubt a legal giant of his time, his conduct and expressions were undeniably crude and he was considered by persons of a more sensitive disposition, such as Cockburn, to be "illiterate and without any taste for refined enjoyment".[22] Moreover, he was a furious imbiber and never hesitated to speak his mind in the most forthright terms. Cockburn gives us a vivid impression of him: "Strong built and dark, with rough eyebrows, powerful eyes, threatening lips, and a low growling voice, he was like a formidable blacksmith. His accent and his dialect were exaggerated Scotch; his language, like his thoughts, short, strong, and conclusive."[23] He was to acquire particular notoriety for insensitive conduct after being elevated to the bench on 13 December 1776 with the infamous judicial title of Lord Braxfield. However, it seems that within his immediate circle of friends, family and colleagues he was always much liked.

DAVID RAE

David Rae (1724-1804) was admitted advocate on 11 December 1751 and soon acquired a considerable practice. He was one of the Commissioners appointed by the court to take evidence in the Douglas Cause, and in that capacity went with James Burnett (later

* 10 Geo. 3, c. 51.

Lord Monboddo) to France. He is said to have been for many years the foremost advocate in the Court of Exchequer in Scotland, and he was generally held in high esteem. He was to be elevated to the bench, with the judicial title of Lord Eskgrove, on 14 November 1782 following the death of Lord Auchinleck, and was to be appointed a Lord Commissioner of Justiciary on 20 April 1785, and Lord Justice-Clerk on 1 June 1799. However, his reputation after becoming a judge was not good: Cockburn said of him that although he was "a very considerable lawyer" and "cunning in old Scotch law", the fact was that "a more ludicrous personage could not exist" and "never once did he do or say anything which had the slightest claim to be remembered for any intrinsic merit. The value of all his words and actions consisted in their absurdity."[24]

JOHN MACLAURIN

John Maclaurin (1734-1796), eldest son of Colin Maclaurin, professor of mathematics at the University of Edinburgh, was admitted advocate on 3 August 1756. "A more singular young man, or one less prepossessing in his appearance to a stranger, could hardly be seen. The affected gravity of his dress and demeanour formed a strange contrast to the brilliant sallies of wit, with which he never failed to enliven his discourse, in season and out of season... Though regarded as a pleasant good-natured fellow, the exuberance of his fancy, which was ever too strong to be controlled by discretion, made him perpetually deal in poetical squibs or burlesque pieces on some of his companions, who were seldom offended at them, because they knew them to be the ebullitions of a playful humour which meant no harm."[25] However, perhaps as a consequence of being snubbed by the Select Society, he published some serious, but misguided, shots against that Society and "the three Homes"—David Hume, Henry Home (Lord Kames) and John Home (the author of the tragedy of *Douglas*). As to Maclaurin's career as an advocate, "his early appearances at the bar did not recommend him to people of business— his speeches and papers being for some time strings of epigrams, more calculated to entertain than to inform the judges. The oddity of his figure, and a grotesque mixture of solemnity and pleasantry in his expressions, made him be considered as a singular man, whose real character it was difficult to fathom. Meanwhile they that knew him best believed that years and experience would in time make him drop most of his crotchets, which neither impaired his knowledge nor trenched upon his good qualities. By degrees he became more sparing of his wit and humour, giving close attention to business, in which he displayed much acuteness and ingenuity, which by degrees reconciled the agents of a graver cast to him. But when five-and-twenty years of age, or a little more, it was matter of merriment to his companions to see him assume the state of a barrister of sixty, arrayed in stiff clothes and stiffer wigs, parading the streets, with a servant carrying a lantern before him, before supper, more for form than use. His companions tried sometimes to run away first with the lantern and then with the cloak from his old domestic, and then get him to adjourn with them to the tavern, which he did not bear with his usual good-humour. He was, however, one of those who were more the worse of wine than the better for it, for it rather damped than exhilarated his spirits."[26] During Maclaurin's later years at the bar, he was "admired both as a speaker and a writer, especially in causes where it was necessary to touch the passions". However, "the old practitioners complained that with all his gravity and solemnity, his fancy was still too strong for his judgment, which was occasionally warped by whim or caprice. And it was likewise alleged that his law papers in common cases were slight and superficial, which might proceed from spleen or distaste, to which he was much too prone in his riper years. But when engaged in a cause which attracted the attention of the public, or was connected with liberty, he displayed great eloquence and compass of thought, both in his speeches and papers."[27] His practice was evidently never extensive, for it is said that even as late as 1789, when Maclaurin was elevated to the bench with the judicial title of Lord Dreghorn, his earnings at the bar were only £200 a year.

ILAY CAMPBELL

Ilay Campbell (1734-1823) was admitted advocate on 11 January 1757 and was in due course to be appointed Vice-Dean of Faculty (1783), Solicitor-General (1783), Lord Advocate (1784) and Lord President (12 November 1789). He established a very large practice at the bar, and it was said that there was "scarcely any cause of importance in which he was not engaged or consulted; and many of his written pleadings [were] held as perfect models of brevity, force and elegance".[28] Cockburn, writing of the position after Campbell had been appointed Lord President, remarks that "his speaking, always admirable in matter, was the reverse of attractive. He could only be severely argumentative, and the painfulness of this was increased by the minuteness of his elaboration, and the dryness of his manner. His voice was low and dull, his face sedate and hard. Even when heaving internally with strong passion, externally he was like a knot of wood."[29]

ANDREW CROSBIE

Andrew Crosbie (1736-1785) was admitted advocate on 9 August 1757 and was to be elected Vice-Dean of Faculty on 24 December 1784. It was observed that "of him it may be said with truth and deep regret, 'Great were his faults, but glorious was his flame'... His heavy look and clumsy figure, which seemed to bespeak a degree of clownishness, did not promise that compass and energy of thought for which he was distinguished in the afterpart of life... As no man had a more generous, manly way of thinking, or a heart more capable of friendship, he was exceedingly liked by his companions, who knew they should learn from his conversation things which it imported them to know. Of one thing they were assured—namely, that they should never meet him with a new face. Even at that early period he had a number of singularities which he had better have wanted; but they did not affect his better qualities, or make him appear mean or ridiculous. It was a great misfortune to him that he did not, when approaching to manhood, find admittance into the circles of the gay and polite of both sexes, from whom he would have learned their graces of behaviour and that knowledge of the *petites morales* of life which adorn and heighten genius. The want of these external accomplishments made him sheepish and uneasy in the company of ladies of rank and fashion. He had, indeed, neither that ease nor small-talk which enables every flippant coxcomb to make a figure in their company. Being very fond of the sex, it made him associate with a set of inferior females who were most unworthy of his favour."[30] He soon established a reputation as a brilliant and talented young advocate, particularly at first in the Court of Justiciary. "His original genius, which delighted in striking into untrodden paths, made him devise arguments that either did not occur to other barristers, or were considered as untenable. The last circumstance only disposed him to press them with redoubled ardour, regardless of censure or of prudential considerations."[31] In criminal cases he was so successful in persuading juries of the innocence of his clients, even in cases where he himself was convinced of their guilt, that some judges accused him of going to improper lengths. Although in later life financial misfortunes were to make him drink heavily and lose his practice at the bar, at the time Boswell was admitted advocate Crosbie's practice was substantial.

ALEXANDER MURRAY

Alexander Murray (1736-1795), son of Archibald Murray of Murrayfield, advocate, was called to the bar on 7 March 1758. He succeeded his father as Sheriff-Depute of Peeblesshire in 1761 and was appointed one of the Commissaries in Edinburgh in 1765. He was in due course to be appointed Solicitor-General (24 May 1775) and from 1780 to 1783 he was Member of Parliament for Peeblesshire. On 6 March 1783 he was appointed Lord of Session and Lord Commissioner of Justiciary, with the judicial title of Lord Henderland.

HENRY DUNDAS

Of all the advocates at the bar when Boswell commenced practice, the one destined to rise the highest in public life was Henry Dundas (1742-1811), who was then

Solicitor-General, having been appointed in 1766 at the age of only twenty-four. In October 1774 he was to be elected Member of Parliament for Edinburghshire (Midlothian) and his future offices were to include Lord Advocate (1775-83 and December 1783-1800), Dean of the Faculty of Advocates (1775-85), Treasurer of the Navy (1782-April 1783 and December 1783-1800), Home Secretary (1791-4), Secretary of State for War (1794-1801) and First Lord of the Admiralty (1804-5). In 1802 he was created Viscount Melville. With such power and influence, he became, in Cockburn's words, the "absolute dictator of Scotland".[32] He was the fourth son of Lord Arniston (the first Lord President Dundas) by his second wife, Anne Gordon. The second Lord President Dundas (whose mother was Lord Arniston's first wife, Elizabeth Watson of Muirhouse) was thus his half-brother, albeit his senior by twenty-eight years. Lord Arniston died on 26 August 1753 when Henry Dundas was only eleven years old, with the consequence that Dundas became deeply attached to his mother, "and for the rest of his life he was more attracted by dames and crones, by termagants and even amazons than by the demurer ladies whom conventional taste extolled".[33] He was called to the bar on 1 March 1763 and it was said of him as an advocate that he entered "so warmly into the interests of his client as totally to forget himself and to adopt all the feelings, sentiments, and interests of his employer".[34] As a consequence of these attributes and his natural abilities, he was soon employed in major cases.

On 16 August 1765, Dundas significantly improved his financial position by marrying Elizabeth Rannie, eldest daughter of David Rannie of Melville, who had died in 1764 leaving her a large fortune, including Melville Castle, near Dalkeith, with "an estate of 600 acres valued at over £1500 a year".[35] Dundas's appointment as Solicitor-General in 1766 was the next step in his inexorable rise to power. Notwithstanding his general acclaim, however, he was not without his detractors, of whom Boswell, who had been at university with him, was one. Boswell greeted the news of Dundas's appointment with some incredulity. Writing to Temple on 17 May 1766, Boswell said: "Do you remember what you and I used to think of Dundas? He has been making £700 a year as an advocate, has married a very genteel girl with £10,000 fortune, and is now appointed His Majesty's Solicitor General for Scotland." However, a contrary and more prevalent view was that held by Boswell's other friend, George Dempster, who wrote to William Carlyle on 7th June 1766 saying: "Harry Dundas is a great acquisition as things now stand. You may judge... of the high opinion entertained of his talents, and upon my word, I think it well founded... He appears to me to have an exceeding good capacity and a very good heart."[36]

§NOTES

1 *The Scots Magazine*, quoted in *Arniston*, p. 111.
2 Brunton and Haig, pp. 524-5.
3 Ramsay, pp. 347-8.
4 *Ibid.*, pp. 189-190.
5 Chambers, p. 322.
6 The details of this scene are taken from Cloyd, p. 10; Kay, Vol. I, p. 31; and Chambers, p. 148.
7 Gray, *Some Old Scots Judges*, p. 51.
8 *Ibid.*, p. 49.
9 Chambers, p. 148.
10 *Reminiscences*, p. 176.
11 Cloyd, p. 163.
12 Ramsay, pp. 397-8.
13 *Ibid.*, pp. 369, 371.
14 Grant, Vol. I, pp. 171-2.
15 Ramsay, p. 373.
16 *Reminiscences*, p. 175.
17 Ramsay, pp. 132-3.
18 Kay, Vol. I, p. 136.

19 *Ibid.*, p. 138.
20 Omond, p. 76.
21 Ramsay, p. 381.
22 Cockburn, p. 105.
23 *Ibid.*, p. 104.
24 *Ibid.*, p. 109.
25 Ramsay, pp. 441-2.
26 *Ibid.*, pp. 442-3.
27 *Ibid.*, p. 446.
28 Brunton and Haig, p. 539
29 Cockburn, p. 116.
30 Ramsay, pp. 449-451.
31 *Ibid.*, p. 451.
32 Cockburn, p. 79.
33 Fry, p. 20.
34 *Ibid.*, p. 22
35 Carlyle, p. 468.
36 *Letters of George Dempster to Sir Adam Fergusson 1756-1813* (ed. James Fergusson), p. 221, n. 1.

SOURCES

MANUSCRIPT SOURCES

National Library of Scotland:
James Boswell's *Consultation Book*, 1766-1772
Fettercairn Papers, deposited by Mrs Peter Somervell and now owned by Miss Katherine Somervell
Minutes of the Select Society (Adv. MS. 23. 1.1)

National Archives of Scotland:
West Register House, Edinburgh, papers relating to the following cases:
James Johnston & Company v. Quintin Hamilton and John McAulay CS 228/I&J/1/83
Sir Alexander Dick v. The Earl of Abercorn CS 226/2729
John Kincaid v. William Black CS 238 K1/41
Hugh Ker v. Margaret and Lilias Thomson CS 228/K2/19
Margaret Clark v. Adam Bell and Others CS 238/C3/49
Alexander Donaldson v. John Reid CS 238/D2/15
Alexander Lockhart v. The Earl of Eglinton CS 235/L/2/10
His Majesty's Advocate v. John Reid JC 3/34, p. 489 ff
Jean Robertson v. James Storrie CS21/1767/2/7
Bills of Advocation for William Brown, William Ballantyne and Henry Young JC3/41
His Majesty's Advocate v. Robert Hay JC7/34, p. 292 ff
His Majesty's Advocate v. John Raybould JC7/35
His Majesty's Advocate v. James Archibald JC7/35
His Majesty's Advocate v. John Reid JC7/38
Robert Hope v. Thomas Wallace and James Duncan CS 238H.4/37
His Majesty's Advocate v. Andrew Gibson and others JC7/39
Petition for the Postponed Creditors on Lainshaw v. William Brown and Sir Walter Montgomerie CS 237 L1/115
Christopher Carruthers v. Archibald Douglas CS 228 C10/30
James Yule v. Creditors on estate of Alexander MacCredie 1779/12/30 CS 222/491
Major Thomas Weir and Jean Weir JC7/38

H.M. General Register House, Edinburgh:
Register of Tailzies, RT. 1/19 Folio 233

PRINTED SOURCES
(Items marked with an * are volumes of the Yale Editions of the Private Papers of James Boswell)
Acts of the Town Council of Edinburgh (SL12/64 – Collection of Printed Acts of Council, 1678-1786: Edinburgh City Archives, City of Edinburgh Council)
Acts of the Parliaments of Scotland, The (1124-1707), 11 Vols, 1814-1844
Acts of the Parliaments of Great Britain, 1707+
Acts of Sederunt of the Lords of Council and Session from 15 January 1553 to 11 June 1790 (Advocates' Library)
Alison, Archibald, *Principles of the Criminal Law of Scotland*, Edinburgh, 1832, reprinted 1989
Alison, Archibald, *Practice of the Criminal Law of Scotland*, Edinburgh, 1833, reprinted 1989
Anderson, W E K (ed.), *The Journal of Sir Walter Scott*, Edinburgh, 1998
Armet, Helen (ed.), *Extracts from the Records of the Burgh of Edinburgh 1689-1701*, Edinburgh and London, 1962
Armet, Helen (ed.), *Extracts from the Records of the Burgh of Edinburgh 1701-1718*, Edinburgh and London, 1967
Arnot, Hugo, *The History of Edinburgh*, Edinburgh, 1779 (reprinted 1998) and 1816
Bailey, Margery (ed.), *Boswell's Column*, London, 1951
Balderston, Katharine C (ed.), *The Collected Letters of Oliver Goldsmith*, Cambridge, 1928
Ballantyne, G H, *Session Papers of James Boswell in the Signet Library, Edinburgh*, 1969/1971 (National Library of Scotland)

Bell's Dictionary and Digest of the Law of Scotland, 7th edn, Edinburgh, 1890

Book of the Old Edinburgh Club, Vols 1-35, and New Series, Vols 1-4

Boswell, James, *An Evening Walk in the Abbey Church of Holyroodhouse*, in *The Scots Magazine*, August 1758

Boswell, James, *Disputatio Juridica, Ad Tit. X. Lib. XXXIII. Pand. De Supellectile Legata*, Edinburgh, 1766 (Advocates' Library)

Boswell, James, *Dorando, A Spanish Tale*, 1767

Boswell, James, *The Life of Samuel Johnson* (ed. Roger Ingpen), 2 Vols, London, 1907

Boswell, James, *A Letter to Robert Macqueen, Lord Braxfield, on his Promotion to be one of the Judges of the High Court of Justiciary*, 1780

Boswell, James, *A Letter to the People of Scotland, on the Alarming Attempt to Infringe the Articles of Union, and Introduce a Most Pernicious Innovation, by Diminishing the Number of the Lords of Session*, 1785

Boswell, James, *Memoirs of James Boswell, Esq.*, in *The European Magazine*, 19 (1791), 323-6

Boswell, James, *Petition of Hugh Cairncross* (National Library of Scotland)

*Brady, Frank, and Pottle, Frederick A (eds), *Boswell on the Grand Tour: Italy, Corsica, and France, 1765-1766*, London, 1955

*Brady, Frank, and Pottle, Frederick A (eds), *Boswell in Search of a Wife, 1766-1769*, London, 1957

Brady, Frank, *Boswell's Political Career*, New Haven and London, 1965

Brady, Frank, *James Boswell: The Later Years, 1769-1795*, London, 1984

Brunton, George, and Haig, David, *An Historical Account of the Senators of the College of Justice*, Edinburgh, 1836

Burnett, James, Lord Monboddo, *Of the Origin and Progress of Language*, 6 Vols, Edinburgh and London, 1773-1792

Burnett, James, Lord Monboddo, *Antient Metaphysics*, 6 Vols, Edinburgh and London, 1779-1799

Burt, Edward, *Letters from a Gentleman in the North of Scotland to his Friend in London*, 5th edn, 2 Vols, London, 1818

Burton, John Hill (ed.), *The Autobiography of Dr Alexander Carlyle of Inveresk 1722-1805*, London and Edinburgh, 1860, 1910

Burton, John Hill, *Life and Correspondence of David Hume*, 2 Vols, Edinburgh, 1846

Cairns, John W, *Alfenus Varus and the Faculty of Advocates*, in *Ius Commune: Zeitschrift für Europäische Rechtsgeschichte*, 28 (2001)

Cant, Malcolm, *Marchmont in Edinburgh*, Edinburgh, 1984

Cant, Malcolm, *Villages of Edinburgh*, Vol. 1, Edinburgh, 1986

Cant, Malcolm, *Villages of Edinburgh*, Vol. 2, Edinburgh, 1987

Cant, Malcolm, *Edinburgh: Gorgie and Dalry*, Edinburgh, 1995

Chambers, Robert, *Scottish Biographical Dictionary*, Glasgow and Edinburgh, 1832-5

Chambers, Robert, *Traditions of Edinburgh*, "New Edition", Edinburgh and London, 1868

Chambers, Robert (ed.), *A Biographical Dictionary of Eminent Scotsmen* (revised and continued by the Rev. Thomas Thomson), 3 vols, London, Glasgow and Edinburgh, 1875

Chambers's Scots Dictionary, Edinburgh and London, 1911, 1968

Clive, Eric M, *Husband and Wife*, 4th edn, Edinburgh, 1997

Cloyd, E L, *James Burnett, Lord Monboddo*, Oxford, 1972

Cockburn, Henry, *Circuit Journeys*, Edinburgh, 1888, 1975

Cockburn, Henry, *Life of Lord Jeffrey*, Vol. I, Edinburgh, 1852

Cockburn, Henry, *Memorials of His Time*, Edinburgh and London, 1856, 1910

Cokayne, G E, *Complete Baronetage*, 6 Vols, Exeter, 1900-1909

Cokayne, G E, *The Complete Peerage* (New Edition, by various editors), 12 Vols, London, 1910-1959

*Cole, R C (ed.), *The General Correspondence of James Boswell, 1766-1769*, Vol. 1, 1766-1767, Edinburgh, 1993

Colston, James, *The Edinburgh and District Water Supply*, Edinburgh, 1890

Concise Scots Dictionary (Editor-in-Chief: Mairi Robinson), Edinburgh, 1999

Cooper, The Rt Hon. Lord, "The Central Courts after 1532", in *An Introduction to Scottish Legal History* (q. v.), chap. 24

Craig, W S, *History of the Royal College of Physicians of Edinburgh*, Edinburgh, 1976

Craik, Roger, *James Boswell (1740-1795), The Scottish Perspective*, Edinburgh, 1994

Cullen, The Hon. Lord, *Parliament House, A Short History and Guide*, Scottish Courts Administation, 1992

Daiches, David, *James Boswell and His World*, London, 1976

*Danziger, Marliesk, and Brady, Frank (eds), *Boswell: The Great Biographer, 1789-1795*, London, 1989

Davis, Michael C, *The Castles and Mansions of Ayrshire*, Ardrishaig (privately published), 1991

Deane, Phyllis, and Cole, W A, *British Economic Growth 1688-1959*, 2nd edn, Cambridge, 1967

Devine, T M, *The Scottish Nation 1700-2000*, London, 2000

Devine, T M, and Mitchison, Rosalind (eds), *People and Society in Scotland*, Vol. I, 1760-1830, Edinburgh, 1988

Dibdin, J C, *The Annals of the Edinburgh Stage*, Edinburgh, 1888

Dictionary of National Biography from the Earliest Times to 1900 (ed. Sir Leslie Stephen and Sir Sidney Lee), various printings

Dictionary of Scottish Church History and Theology (organizing editor: Nigel M de S Cameron), Edinburgh, 1993

Donaldson's Collection of Original Poems by Scotch Gentlemen, Edinburgh, 1762

Douglas, Sir Robert, *Baronage of Scotland*, Edinburgh, 1798

Douglas, Sir Robert, *The Peerage of Scotland*, 2 Vols, 2nd edn, Edinburgh, 1813

Dunbar, John G (ed.), *Sir William Burrell's Northern Tour, 1758*, East Linton, 1997

Duke, Winifred, *Boswell Among the Lawyers*, (1926) 38 Juridical Review 341

Edinburgh Almanack, The, 1765+

Encyclopaedia Britannica, Chicago, London, *et. al.*, various editions

Faculty Decisions, Old Series, Vols IV (1765-69)-IX (1781-87)

Ferguson, William, *Scotland: 1689 to the Present*, The Edinburgh History of Scotland, Vol. 4, Edinburgh and London, 1968

Fergusson, James (ed), *Letters of George Dempster to Sir Adam Fergusson 1756-1813*, London, 1934

Findlay, Bill (ed.), *A History of the Scottish Theatre*, Edinburgh, 1998

Forbes, William, *A Journal of the Session*, Edinburgh, 1714

Fraser, G S (ed.), *Selected Poems of Robert Burns*, London, 1960

Fry, Michael, *The Dundas Despotism*, Edinburgh, 1992

Gifford, John, McWilliam, Colin, and Walker, David, *Edinburgh*, in *The Buildings of Scotland* series, Harmondsworth, 1984, 1991

Gordon, William M, *Scottish Land Law*, Edinburgh, 1989

Graham, Henry Grey, *Scottish Men of Letters in the Eighteenth Century*, London, 1901, 1908

Graham, Henry Grey, *The Social Life of Scotland in the Eighteenth Century*, 2nd edn, London, 1909

Grant, Sir F J, *The Faculty of Advocates in Scotland 1532-1943*, Scottish Record Society, Edinburgh, 1944

Grant, James, *Old and New Edinburgh*, 3 Vols, London, c.1882

Gray, W Forbes, *Some Old Scots Judges*, London, 1914

Green's Encyclopaedia of the Laws of Scotland, Vol. 8, Edinburgh, 1929

Gretton, George, *The Law of Inhibition and Adjudication*, 2nd edn, Edinburgh, 1996

Groome, Francis H (ed.), *Ordnance Gazetteer of Scotland*, "New Edition", Edinburgh, 1901

Guide to the National Archives of Scotland, Scottish Record Office, Edinburgh, 1996

Hannan, Thomas, *Famous Scottish Houses, The Lowlands*, London, 1928

Harris, Stuart, *The Place Names of Edinburgh*, Edinburgh, 1996

Harrison, John, *The History of the Monastery of the Holy-Rood and of the Palace of Holyrood House*, Edinburgh and London, 1919

Henderson, James S, *James Boswell and His Practice at the Bar*, (1905) 17 Juridical Review 105

Hutchinson, Roger, *All the Sweets of Being: A Life of James Boswell*, Edinburgh and London, 1995

Introduction to Scottish Legal History, The Stair Society, Edinburgh, 1958

Jay, Douglas, *Sterling*, Oxford, 1986

Keay, John, and Keay, Julia (eds), *Collins Encyclopaedia of Scotland*, London, 1994

Kinnaird, Alexander, *The History of Edinburgh from the Earliest Accounts to the Present Time*, Edinburgh, 1784

Law, Alexander, *Education in Edinburgh in the Eighteenth Century*, London, 1965

Lawson, John Parker, *History of the Scottish Episcopal Church from the Revolution to the Present Time*, Edinburgh, 1843

Leask, W Keith, *James Boswell*, Edinburgh and London, 1896

Lees, J Cameron, *St Giles', Edinburgh, Church, College, and Cathedral, from the Earliest Times to the Present Day*, Edinburgh and London, 1889

Letters between the Honourable Andrew Erskine and James Boswell, Esq., London, 1763

Letters of an English Medical Officer in 1745-46, reproduced in *The Contrast: or Scotland as it was in the Year 1745, and Scotland in the Year 1819*, London, 1825

Lewis, D B Wyndham, *The Hooded Hawk*, London, 1946

Lindsay, Maurice, *The Burns Encyclopaedia*, 3rd edn, New York, 1980

Lockhart, J G, *Life of Sir Walter Scott*, Edinburgh, 1838

London Chronicle, The, 1769

Lord Provosts of Edinburgh, The, 1296-1932, Edinburgh, 1932

*Lustig, Irma S, and Pottle, Frederick A (eds), *Boswell: The Applause of the Jury, 1782-1785*, London, 1981

*Lustig, Irma S, and Pottle, Frederick A (eds), *Boswell: The English Experiment, 1785-1789*, London, 1986

Lynch, Michael, *Scotland: A New History*, London, 1991

Macaulay, Lord, *Samuel Johnson*, 1831, in *The Works of Lord Macaulay*, Vol. I (Literary Essays from "The Edinburgh Review"), London, 1906

McElroy, Davis D, *A Century of Scottish Clubs, 1700-1800*, Vol. 1, Edinburgh, 1969 (National Library of Scotland)

Maitland, William, *The History of Edinburgh from its Foundation to the Present Time*, Edinburgh, 1753

Malcolm, C A, "The Parliament House and its Antecedents", in *An Introduction to Scottish Legal History* (q. v.), chap. 34

Martin, Peter, *A Life of James Boswell*, London, 1999

Miller, R, *The Municipal Buildings of Edinburgh, 1145-1895*, Edinburgh, 1895

Morison's *Dictionary of Decisions of the Court of Session* (1540-1808), 21 Vols

Mossner, E C, *The Life of David Hume*, 2nd edn, Oxford, 1980

Murray, John, *Some Civil Cases of James Boswell, 1772-74*, (1940) 52 Juridical Review 222

Namier, Sir Lewis, and Brooke, John, *The House of Commons, 1754-1790*, 3 Vols, London, 1964

Notes and Queries, 3rd series, Vol. 7, London, 1865

Omond, G W T, *The Lord Advocates of Scotland*, 2 Vols, Edinburgh, 1883

Omond, G W T, *The Arniston Memoirs*, Edinburgh, 1887

Osborne, Brian D, *Braxfield the Hanging Judge?*, Argyll, 1997

Paterson, James, and Maidment, James, *Kay's Edinburgh Portraits*, 2 Vols, London and Glasgow, 1885

Paton's Reports of Cases decided in the House of Lords, upon Appeal from Scotland, from 1753 to 1813, Vols II (1757-84) and III (1784-97)

Paul, Sir James Balfour, *The Scots Peerage*, 9 Vols, 1904-1914

Pinkerton, J M (ed.), *The Minute Book of the Faculty of Advocates*, Vol. 2, 1713-1750, The Stair Society, Edinburgh, 1980

Plant, Marjorie, *The Domestic Life of Scotland in the Eighteenth Century*, Edinburgh, 1952

Pottle, Frederick A, *The Literary Career of James Boswell*, Oxford, 1929

Pottle, Frederick A, *Boswell and the Girl from Botany Bay*, London, 1938

*Pottle, Frederick A (ed.), *Boswell's London Journal, 1762-1763*, London, 1950

*Pottle, Frederick A (ed.), *Boswell's London Journal, 1762-1763, together with Journal of My Jaunt, Harvest 1762*, London, 1951

*Pottle, Frederick A (ed.), *Boswell in Holland, 1763-1764*, London, 1952

*Pottle, Frederick A (ed.), *Boswell on the Grand Tour: Germany and Switzerland, 1764*, London, 1953

*Pottle, Frederick A, and Bennett, Charles H (eds), *Boswell's Journal of a Tour to the Hebrides with Samuel Johnson, LL.D.*, 1773, London, 1961

Pottle, Frederick A, *Boswell's University Education*, from *Johnson, Boswell and their Circle*, Oxford, 1965

Pottle, Frederick A, *James Boswell, The Earlier Years, 1740-1769*, London, 1966

*Pottle, Frederick A, *Pride and Negligence: The History of the Boswell Papers*, London, 1982

Proceedings of the Society of Antiquaries of Scotland, Vols II (1854-57), IV (1860-62), XLV (1910-11) and LXXIV (1939-40)

Ramsay, Edward B, *Reminiscences of Scottish Life and Character*, "New Edition", Edinburgh and London, 1924

Ramsay, James, *Boswell's First Criminal Case*, (1938) 59 Juridical Review, p. 315

Ramsay, John, of Ochtertyre, *Scotland and Scotsmen in the Eighteenth Century* (ed. Alexander Allardyce), 2 Vols, Edinburgh and London, 1888

*Reed, Joseph W, and Pottle, Frederick A (eds), *Boswell, Laird of Auchinleck, 1778-1782*, London, 1977

Register of the Society of Writers to Her Majesty's Signet, Edinburgh, 1983

Rogers, Rev. Charles (ed.), *Boswelliana, The Commonplace Book of James Boswell, with a Memoir and Annotations*, 1874

Ross, I S, *Lord Kames and the Scotland of His Day*, Oxford, 1972

Roughead, William (ed.), *Trial of Katharine Nairn*, Edinburgh and London, 1926

Roughead, William, *In Queer Street*, Edinburgh, 1932

Royal Commission on the Ancient and Historical Monuments of Scotland, *An Inventory of the Ancient and Historical Monuments of the City of Edinburgh*, HMSO, Edinburgh, 1951

*Ryskamp, Charles, and Pottle, Frederick A (eds), *Boswell: The Ominous Years, 1774-1776*, London, 1963

Scots Magazine, The, 1758+

Scott, Geoffrey, and Pottle, Frederick A (eds), *Private Papers of James Boswell from Malahide Castle, in the Collection of Lt-Colonel Ralph Heyward Isham*, 18 Vols, privately printed, 1928-34

Scott, Sir Walter, *The Heart of Midlothian* (ed. Claire Lamont), Oxford, 1982

Session Papers, Arniston Collection, Advocates' Library, Edinburgh

Session Papers, Signet Library, Edinburgh

Session Papers by Boswell in the Advocates Library (Volume (a): Arniston and Campbell Collections), searched by Dr C J M MacLachlan, Edinburgh, 1975 (National Library of Scotland)

Simpson, T B, *Boswell as an Advocate*, (1922) 34 Juridical Review, p. 201

Sinclair, Sir John (ed.), *The Statistical Account of Scotland 1791-1799*, Vol. II, The Lothians, reprinted 1975

Skinner, Robert T, *The Royal Mile*, 3rd edn, Edinburgh, 1947

Smith, Charles J, *Historic South Edinburgh*, Vol. 2, Edinburgh and London, 1979

Smout, T C, *A History of the Scottish People, 1560-1830*, 2nd edn, London and Glasgow, 1970

Somerville, Thomas, *My Own Life and Times, 1741-1814*, Edinburgh, 1861

Spottiswood, John, *The Form of Process before the Lords of Council and Session*, Edinburgh, 1718

Stair Memorial Encyclopaedia of the Laws of Scotland, Vol. 6, and "Glossary", Edinburgh, 1988

Stapleton, Michael, *The Cambridge Guide to English Literature*, 1983

Steuart, A F (ed.), *The Douglas Cause*, Glasgow and Edinburgh, 1909

Stewart, Angus (ed.), *The Minute Book of the Faculty of Advocates*, Vol. 3, 1751-1783, The Stair Society, Edinburgh, 1999

Stuart, Marie W, *Old Edinburgh Taverns*, London, 1952

Thorne, R G, *The House of Commons 1790-1820*, 5 Vols, London, 1986

Tinker, C B (ed.), *Letters of James Boswell*, 2 Vols, Oxford, 1924

Topham, Edward, *Letters from Edinburgh 1774-1775*, Edinburgh, 1971

Turnbull, Gordon, "Boswell and Sympathy: The Trial and Execution of John Reid", in *New Light on Boswell* (ed. Greg Clingham), Cambridge, 1991

Turnbull, Gordon, *'Generous Attachment': Filiation and Rogue Biography in the Journals of James Boswell*, unpublished Ph. D. dissertation, Yale University, 1986 (microfiche in the National Library of Scotland)

Turner, A Logan, *Story of a Great Hospital: The Royal Infirmary of Edinburgh 1729-1929*, Edinburgh, 1937

Tytler, A F (Lord Woodhouselee), *An Account of the Right Honourable Robert Dundas of Arniston, Lord President of the Court of Session in Scotland*, in *Transactions of the Royal Society of Edinburgh*, Vol. II, Edinburgh

Tytler, A F (Lord Woodhouselee), *Memoirs of the Life and Writings of the Honourable Henry Home of Kames*, 2 vols, Edinburgh, 1807

Universal Scots Almanack, The, 1774+

Walker, David M, *The Scottish Jurists*, Edinburgh, 1985

Walker, David M, *A Legal History of Scotland, The Eighteenth Century*, Edinburgh, 1998

Walker, David M, *The Scottish Legal System*, 5th edn, 1981

*Walker, Ralph S (ed.), *The Correspondence of James Boswell and John Johnston of Grange*, London, 1966

Watson, J Steven, *The Reign of George III, 1760-1815*, Oxford, 1964

*Weis, Charles McC, and Pottle, Frederick A, *Boswell in Extremes, 1776-1778*, London, 1971

Williamson's *Edinburgh Directory*, 1773/74 – 1786/88 (various volumes)

Wilson, Daniel, *Memorials of Edinburgh in the Olden Time*, 2nd edn, 2 Vols, Edinburgh and London, 1891

*Wimsatt, William, Jr, and Pottle, Frederick A (eds), *Boswell for the Defence, 1769-1774*, London, 1960

Youngson, A J, *The Making of Classical Edinburgh, 1750-1840*, Edinburgh, 1966

INDEX

Where appropriate, entries in this index give the position of a person either by stating his or her position at the time of the reference or by stating the position ultimately attained during the period covered by the journal entries (i.e., January 1767-1786). The word *later* as used in this index signifies changes to a person's status occurring not only after the period covered by the journal entries but also during that period. Maiden names of married women are given in parentheses. Places which are now parts of Edinburgh but lay outwith the city in Boswell's day (such as Corstorphine and Craighouse) are treated, for convenience, as being within the environs of Edinburgh at that time (and hence appear under the heading "Edinburgh (and environs)". The names of Edinburgh streets, squares, courts, wynds and closes which still exist appear with the modern spelling although in the text the spelling may be an old form (such as "George's Square" rather than the modern "George Square"). Abbreviations used are D. (Duke), E. (Earl), V. (Viscount), B. (Baron), Bt (Baronet), Kt (Knight), W.S. (Writer to the Signet), JB (James Boswell).

n.22; I Peter, 337 and n.24; Philippians, 86 and n.58; Proverbs, 245 and n.52, 321 and n.15, 455 and n.18; Psalms, 401 and n.101, 455, 477 and n.87; Revelation, 183, 513; Romans, 48 and n.37; I Samuel, 115n.20a, 535 and n.1; Thessalonians, 294n.24; I Timothy, 411 and n.134, 416 and n.154

Bickerstaffe, Isaac: *Love in a Village*, 279 and n.121

Biggar, people of, cause against patron, 397 and n.89

Biggleswade, 426

Billingsley, Mrs, schoolmistress, 483 and n.110, 490, 494

Binning, Mrs, in Edinburgh, 285

Biographia Britannica, 325, 326, 384

Birmingham, 253

Bishop Auckland, 297

Black, Joseph, Professor of Chemistry and Medicine at Edinburgh University, 221 and n.105

Black, William, Procurator-Fiscal of the Lyon Court, 134 and n.96

Blair, Capt. Alexander, 122

Blair, Anne (Blair), of Adamton, mother of Catherine Blair, 52, 56, 58, 60

Blair, Catherine, of Adamton, 49 and n.50, 52, 56, 57, 58 and n.97, 59, 61, 63-67, 69, 70, 72

Blair, Hugh, The Rev. Dr, 28, 29, 53, 78, 106, 113 and n.10, 121, 123, 126, 130, 147, 177, 178, 245, 246, 270, 272, 292, 297 and n.28, 313, 317, 325, 328, 329, 330 and n.37, 340, 348, 350, 351, 353, 357, 375, 376, 379, 381, 386, 394, 396, 413, 422, 430, 432, 439, 447, 451, 455, 458, 488 and n.127, 489, 493, 502, 515 and n.23, 518n.32, 520, 526, 528, 530, 535, 539; *Sermons*, 330, 386, 400

Blair, Jane, of Dunskey. *See* Hunter-Blair, Jane (Blair), wife of James Hunter-Blair

Blair, Margaret (*or* Janet), Catherine Blair's Glasgow cousin, 58

Blair, Robert, advocate, *later* Lord President, 82 and n.45, 248n.54, 439, 440

Blair Drummond (place), 191n.26, 469, 478, 489, 556

Blane, Miss, sister of Andrew Blane, 371

Blane, Andrew, W.S., 371 and n.27, 418, 419

Bligh, Lieut. William, R.N., 452 and n.8

Blythswood. *See* Campbell, John, of Blythswood

Bogle, John, of Hamilton Farm, 346

Boscawen, "Capt." (Ensign) George Evelyn, *later* V. Falmouth, 259 and n.73

Bosville, Elizabeth Diana. *See* Macdonald (Elizabeth Diana Bosville), Lady

Boswall, Alexander, of Blackadder ("the Nabob"), 267 and n.95, 268, 269, 272, 275, 277, 278, 280, 282, 283, 284 and n.6, 306, 311, 324, 350, 445 and n.67, 511, 515

Boswall, Elizabeth, sister of Alexander Boswall, 280

Boswall, Margaret, sister of Alexander Boswall, 268

Boswall, Thomas, accountant, 82 and n.38, 276 and n.113

Boswall, Mrs Thomas, née Balfour, 276, 284n.6

Boswell, Alexander. *See* Auchinleck (Alexander Boswell), Lord

Boswell, Alexander, *later* Bt, son of JB, 168n.156, 197, 198, 201, 203-205, 211, 213, 232, 234, 245, 266-268, 271, 281, 282, 287, 289, 308 and n.71, 310, 311, 321, 324 and n.19, 326, 329, 330, 332, 335, 337, 344, 346, 348, 350, 360, 362, 363, 368, 372, 373, 379, 382, 383, 385, 386, 388, 392, 394, 395, 396, 400-402, 409, 415-418, 421, 428, 429-433, 436, 441, 442, 444, 445, 452, 453, 455-457, 460, 465, 470, 503-505, 509, 511, 513-515, 517, 523 and n.45, 526, 527, 531, 535, 539, 547, 548, 550, 551; letter from JB quoted, 549 and n.52; *Songs in the Justiciary Opera*, 248n.57

Boswell, Anne (Cramond), wife of Dr John Boswell, 291

Boswell, Anne (Irvine), wife of Claud Boswell of Balmuto, 504 and n.36, 514, 516

Boswell, Anne, dau. of Dr John Boswell, 243 and n.47, 359, 367, 442 and n.55

Boswell, Bruce, son of Dr John Boswell, 198 and n.46, 236, 309-311

Boswell, Charles, JB's illegitimate son, 23, 31, 79n.22

Boswell, Claud Irvine, advocate, *later* Lord Balmuto, 35, 67 and n.52, 70 and n.67, 77 and n.8, 79, 80 and n.27, 82, 84, 111, 120, 168, 175, 177, 179, 184, 213, 216, 227, 236, 237, 249, 250 and n.59, 251, 260, 270, 275, 278, 284, 289, 290, 332, 334, 355, 356, 362, 364, 368 and n.18, 376, 435, 444 and n.61, 446, 451, 463, 473, 474, 504 and n.36, 514, 516, 528, 533, 538, 539

Boswell, David, brother of JB, 4, 34, 54 and n.73, 57, 61, 100, 114, 141, 185, 200, 202, 222, 241, 260, 269, 280, 314, 375, 399, 400, 402-405, 459, 500, 524 and n.49, 550

Boswell, David, dancing-master, 180 and n.192, 184n.4, 383, 496

Boswell, David, of Craigston, 222 and n.112

Boswell, David, son of JB, 271-275, 280, 287, 289, 295, 296, 310

Boswell, Elizabeth, dau. of Dr John Boswell, 359, 367

Boswell, Elizabeth, dau. of JB, 400, 415, 455, 494, 503, 504, 513-515, 517, 526, 527, 531, 547, 548, 550

Boswell, Euphemia, dau. of JB, 111, 148, 168, 171, 196, 198, 200, 202, 204, 211, 213, 228, 232, 234, 245, 263, 267, 268, 271, 284, 287, 292, 295, 296, 298, 307, 321, 324-326, 329, 332, 335, 337, 344, 346-348, 350, 357, 358, 368, 373, 375, 376, 379, 382, 383, 386, 388, 392, 394, 400, 409, 415, 417, 418, 421, 422, 426,

Hart, Capt. Alexander, 334
Hartley, David, 224 and n.113, 227, 229;
  Observations on Man, 224 and n.113, 230
Harwich, 31
Hastie, John, schoolmaster, 98
Hawick, 426
Hawkins, William: *Pleas of the Crown*, 246
Hawthornden. *See* Drummond, William of
  Hawthornden
Hay, ?Grace, sister of Lady Forbes, 318
Hay, Charles, advocate, *later* Lord Newton, 104
  and n.13, 118, 121, 122, 132, 134 and n.101,
  135, 136 and n.103, 138-140, 142-147, 149,
  150-156, 162, 165-168, 171, 173, 177, 188,
  189, 191, 215, 218, 255, 259, 265, 276, 278,
  287, 288, 306, 404
Hay, George, Roman Catholic Bishop of Daulis,
  333 and n.9, 334
Hay, James, brother of Charles Hay, 150
Hay, James, of Cocklaw, W.S., 66 and n.38, 71,
  104n.13, 118n.38
Hay, Lady Mary, dau. of 15th E. of Erroll, 90
Hay, Robert, soldier, JB's client, 47 and n.23,
  48, 72
Hay, Thomas, surgeon, 203
Hay, William, W.S., 69 and n.61, 234
Hebrides, the, 108
Heming, George, of Caldecote Hall, 201
Henderland (Alexander Murray), Lord, 36, 65
  and n.33, 108 and n.31, 117, 130, 186, 189,
  195 and n.38, 215 and n.93, 235 and n.26,
  245-247, 248n.54, 254, 255n.67, 264n.88,
  271n.105, 275, 285, 290n.16, 291, 293, 297,
  307 and n.67, 316, 318, 356, 382, 402, 419,
  420 and n.169, 421, 435, 438, 470, 520 and
  n.36; biographical details, 562
Henderson, John, *later* Bt, son of Sir Robert
  Henderson, 130; in Fifeshire election, 249,
  251
Henderson, Capt. Matthew, antiquary, 64 and
  n.28, 65, 177, 304, 352, 414
Henderson, Rev. ?John, 376
Henderson, Sir John, Bt, 507
Heraclitus, 111
Herbert, John, of Auchencross, 136
Heriot, George, jeweller and philanthropist,
  125n.64
Heron, Andrew, M.D., 373
Heron, Jean (Home), dau. of Lord Kames, first wife
  of Patrick Heron, 23, 24, 479 and n.97, 480
Heron, Lady. *See* Cochrane, Lady Elizabeth
Heron, Patrick, of Kirroughtrie, 23, 24, 117 and
  n.33, 447 and n.75, 479 and n.97
Heylyn, John: *Theological Lectures at Westminster
  Abbey*, 521 and n.39
Hicks, Maj. Edward, 298, 299
High Court of Justiciary. *See* Court of Justiciary
Highlanders, mutiny of, 326-328, 337 and n.23
Hill, Lawrence, writer, 187 and n.14

Hillsborough, East Indiaman, 308
Hoadly, Benjamin: *The Suspicious Husband*, 63 and
  n.11
Hoare, William, painter, 276
Hogg, Miss, at Edinburgh, 473
Hoggan, Capt. James, 304
Holmains. *See* Carruthers, John
Holytown, 337
Home, Catherine, sister of David Hume, 220 and
  n.102, 480 and n.104
Home, Francis, physician, 326
Home, Henry. *See* Kames, Lord
Home, Jean. *See* Heron, Jean (Home)
Home, Rev. John, 10, 305 and n.57, 398 and n.91,
  561; *Douglas*, tragedy of, 10, 163, 305n.57,
  398n.91, 556, 561
Home, Patrick, of Billy, 82
Homer, 194; *Works*, Glasgow edn, 477 and n.90
Honeyman, Patrick, of Graemsay, 392
Honyman, William, *later* Lord Armadale, 201 and
  n.60
Hope, Sir Archibald, Bt, 389
Hope, John, M.D., 517
Hope, Robert, cause of, 238 and n.34
Hope, Robert, farmer, 192 and n.33
Hopetoun, John Hope, 2nd E. of, 415 and n.153
Horace, 477; *Ars Poetica*, 359n.92; *Epistles*, 52n.62,
  320 and n.12, 447 and n.73; *Satires*, 304n.52,
  465 and n.48; *Works*, Edinburgh edn, 477 and
  n.90
House of Commons, 212n.86, 322, 498, 510, 543,
  560; bill to abolish slave-trade, 545; bill to
  diminish the number of Lords of Session
  ("Diminishing Bill"), 531 and n.15, 539 and
  n.15; cause of John Francis Erskine of Mar, 322;
  Committee on Carlisle election, 542;
  Committee on Clackmannanshire election,
  196; Committee on Ayrshire election, 426, 427;
  "the Formula", 172; General Election of 1768,
  61n.1, 497n.22; General Election of 1774,
  123n.55
House of Lords, 41, 74, 76, 98, 173, 192n.32,
  235n.22, 254, 290n.16, 321-323, 500, 505n.39,
  531n.14, 532, 544-545; election of
  representatives of Scottish Peerage, 175 and
  n.173
Howe, Gen. Sir William, *later* 5th V. Howe, 276,
  292
Howgate, 145
Hume, David, 2, 16, 23, 25, 30, 34, 48 and n.29,
  74, 94, 97, 100, 103n.11, 104, 115, 133 and
  n.91, 171 and n.162a, 193, 194, 207, 220 and
  n.102, 256-259, 262-265, 268, 292, 313, 316,
  339n.34, 350 and n.67, 351, 407, 408, 432, 451,
  456, 481, 507, 555, 556, 561; *A Treatise of Human
  Nature*, 220, 434; *Autobiography*, 350n.67;
  Dialogues Concerning Natural Religion, 370n.23;
  Essays, 265; *History of England*, 28, 258

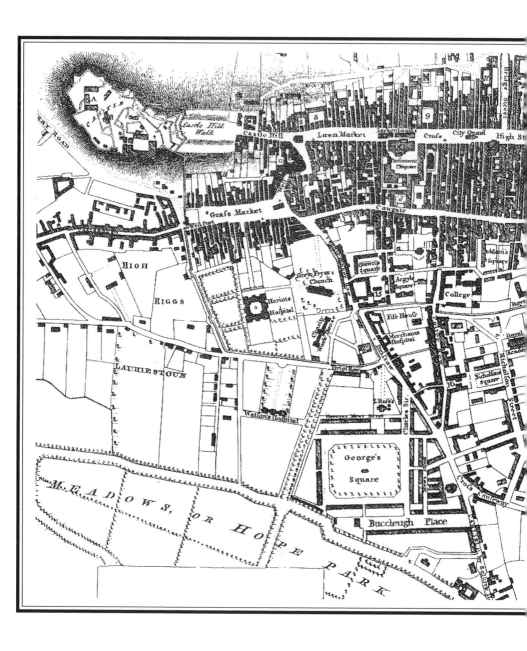

Plan of the CITY, CASTLE and Suburbs of Edinburgh.

(Detail of a map included in Arnot's *History of Edinburgh*, 1779)